ON BEST BEHAVIOR
The Clinton Administration
and Ethics in Government

ON BEST BEHAVIOR
The Clinton Administration and Ethics in Government

Gregory S. Walden

Hudson Institute
Indianapolis, Indiana

Dedicated to my parents

Hudson Institute
Indianapolis, Indiana

ISBN 1-55813-056-X
Copyright © 1996 Hudson Institute, Inc.

Printed in the United States of America
This book may be ordered from:
Hudson Institute
Herman Kahn Center
P.O. Box 26-919
Indianapolis, Indiana 46226
(317) 545-1000

Contents

Part Four
Allegations Against Members of the Clinton Cabinet

Part Five
Other Ethics Issues

Foreword

It is difficult these days to find sensible and useful discussions of ethics in government. Part of the reason is that the current preoccupation of this country's political class with issues of personal ethics has tainted origins.

In the mid-to-late 1960s, as the opposition to the Vietnam War grew, antiwar activities increasingly focused their criticism on the corruption of the politicians prosecuting the war, the alleged corruption consisting of hunger for power or indebtedness to special interests. The aim of the critics was to dramatize the immorality of the Vietnam involvement. In the same way, the pursuit of President Richard Nixon during Watergate was not driven exclusively by a thirst for justice; it was also an attempt to reverse the growing conservative sentiment of the American electorate. Today's attention to the private doings of politicians, especially their sexual conduct, has its roots in women's-movement writings that strove to delegitimatize political figures who, by their personal actions, perpetuated women's powerlessness.

Because of these partisan elements, recent ethics campaigns have sometimes done as much harm as good. The media have exposed plenty of politicians' private peccadilloes and have probably reduced the incidence of certain kinds of sexual misconduct. Yet the same media have perpetuated such vast invasions of privacy that we often can hardly bear to talk about their revelations. Similarly, tighter campaign finance and lobbying laws have almost surely made the system cleaner in a technical sense; but, perversely, they have in some ways increased elected officials' preoccupation with raising money. More rigorous enforcement of post-government employment lobbying restrictions has also tidied up the ethical parlor, but has done so at the cost of keeping a number of outstanding qualified individuals out of government jobs where their skills are urgently needed.

It is sometimes said that in the "olden days" standards of decency and integrity in government were bred into the bone and enforced without the modern panoply of rules and publicity. To the extent that this was once true, it is not so any more, and will not be the case for the foreseeable future. Heightened sensitivity to ethics problems will persist. Officials will remain subject to detailed scrutiny. We must find an area of public sanity, and of relative nonpartisanship, within these constraints.

Greg Walden has begun the job. He subjects the Clinton Administration to criticism, but he does so on the basis of general standards that are clearly articulated and open for readers' inspection. He follows with a series of prudential rules and recommendations that are clearly universal rather than skewed by someone's particular political agenda. Not everyone will agree with his particulars, of course, but his laying out of the problem will enable us to discuss it without constantly worrying about whose ox is being gored.

It remains to been seen whether officials and administrations will be capable of using Walden's principles to keep themselves out of trouble. Some of the rules of conduct—"Don't play cute with financial disclosure reports,"—for instance, or, "When a financial scandal looms, do not circle the wagons,"—are well enough known; yet political figures persist in violating them over and over in the same stupid ways. The pressure of politics and the psychology of politicians will keep the scandal pipeline well enough supplied.

Suzanne Garment
December 1995

Preface

The purpose of this study is to analyze the current system of ethics laws and regulations governing the Executive Branch, and, specifically, the various ethics matters that have beset the Clinton Administration, from the inauguration through the fall of 1995. This study contains both a legal and policy analysis. I evaluate conduct and statements under current ethics laws and standards, as well as in terms of what I consider to be the optimum public policy. I look at what is as well as what ought to be.

I began this study in January 1994, after receiving a research grant from the Federalist Society for Law and Public Policy Studies. The idea to study the current system of ethics laws and regulations governing the Executive Branch, and, specifically, the ethics of the Clinton Administration, occurred to me in early 1993. The idea stemmed, in part, from my previous experience in the Government, and in part from my observation of the Clinton Administration's handling of ethics issues in its first few months in office.

I had recently concluded two years of service in the White House Counsel's office under President Bush, where I provided day-to-day ethics advice for the White House staff, reviewed the financial disclosure reports of White House officials, and participated in the clearance process for Presidential Executive Branch appointees. Like other agency ethics officials, I conducted damage control; like other agency ethics officials, my efforts met with mixed results. Much time and energy were devoted to the development of the first set of uniform, comprehensive standards of ethical conduct for Executive Branch employees, which was published by the Office of Government Ethics in July 1992.

While at the White House, I became aware of a growing sentiment within the Government, held even by some ethics officials, that our scheme of ethics regulation somehow had gone awry. In addition to the frequently expressed complaint that the financial disclosure requirements were burdensome and only partially related to genuine ethics concerns, the very standards of conduct I championed were criticized, as much for their length and complexity as for their substance. In particular, some of my colleagues worried that the standards of conduct, including a codification of an appearance standard governing nonfinancial conflicts, would serve only to facilitate unfounded and exaggerated charges of unethical conduct from political opponents.

This was not a concern to treat lightly. As a political appointee in the Justice Department from 1983 to 1988, I witnessed the repeated use of ethics allegations and investigations to frustrate the Reagan Administration's legal and justice agenda. In the Bush White House, I saw firsthand how adept some Democrats had become in using ethics allegations to distract and preoccupy, if not defeat, their policy opponents. Ethics scandals, major, minor, and would-be, in the Executive Branch as well as in Congress, in business as well as in government, were regular fare during the years I served in the Executive Branch from 1982-1993.

Nevertheless, the Bush Administration's ethics record was, on the whole, good: Bush issued Executive Order 12674, charging OGE with issuing a single set of standards for the entire Executive Branch workforce, and banning completely all outside earned income for noncareer fulltime presidential appointees. President Bush argued for and pushed through a major piece of ethics legislation, the Ethics Reform Act of 1989, which was for the most part a balanced bill.

And the Bush Administration, including the White House, was relatively free from major scandals. Perhaps the most celebrated ethics controversy—Chief of Staff John Sununu's frequent use of military aircraft—was also perhaps the only one involving a high-level official in the Bush Administration. (And Governor Sununu's abuse of government property and privileges did not even trigger an independent counsel.) The Iran-Contra and HUD independent counsel investigations continued throughout the entire Bush Administration, but involved conduct that occurred during the Reagan Administration. October Surprise and INSLAW, two putative scandals that were fodder for conspiracy enthusiasts, also dated to the Reagan Administration. The so-called Iraqgate scandal was not really about ethics, but part of a protracted blame game following the Gulf War. At the tail end of the Administration, an independent counsel was appointed to investigate the search of Bill Clinton's passport file by State Department officials during the election campaign. Reports of the search in the last month of the campaign caused considerable embarrassment to the White House and to President Bush, although the President had no involvement with the matter whatsoever. Indeed, Independent Counsel Joe diGenova, after a lengthy investigation, charged no one with any violation of law, and noted that the matter should not even have been referred to the Justice Department in the first place. In the Administration's last week, outgoing Attorney General Bill Barr forwarded to our office a scathing report of FBI Director William Sessions' ethics transgressions. (Sessions vigorously contested the report) The Attorney General's report would have to wait for the new Clinton team.

On January 19, 1993, as I left the first floor of the Old Executive Office Building and walked up West Executive Avenue for the last time, I wondered how the new administration, and especially the new White House Counsel's office, would fare. Just a week earlier, after discussing how our ethics program had been run with two transition attorneys who were likely to join the White House Counsel's office, I briefly met Bernard Nussbaum and Vince Foster. I wondered whether they had any idea that their White House job would be unlike any other. Would they feel the quotidian stress we felt? Would they not shy from telling senior White House officials, including the President, "no" when required by law or ethics standards to do so? Would they lose sleep over the many times they said "yes," fearful of not having all the facts or, just as bad, not accurately gauging the reaction of the White House press corps? And how eager would they be to continue raising appearance problems within the White House after colleagues began regarding them as a hindrance to the President's agenda or their colleagues' own actions? Would most of their time be consumed by damage control efforts?

My interest was piqued in large part by statements made during the 1992 campaign attacking the "sleaze" of the Reagan-Bush years. The Clinton/Gore campaign not only refused to acknowledge the relative success of the Bush Administration in keeping free of ethics scandals, which was understandable, it also decried existing ethics standards as inadequate, which was not. Hence, the promise to impose an even higher standard of ethical behavior on Executive Branch employees. During the transition, tougher "revolving door" restrictions were showcased as an example of a new day in government, free of the stranglehold of special interest lobbyists. I wondered if anyone in the Clinton team, which was largely being assembled from the campaign and from Arkansas, appreciated the extensive scheme of post-employment restrictions currently in place in statute and regulation.

I expected the new administration, like any new administration, to hit some bumps in the ethics road. Given that both Houses of Congress remained under Democratic control, however, any mistakes or misconduct would likely be easily contained without an embarrassing investigation, and thus prevented from being a distraction, much less from interfering with the President's program and message. I also was unsure of how the White House press corps would operate, given the general sympathy I suspected many had with candidate Clinton's policy prescriptions and pronouncements.

I did not anticipate what would soon occur. Who did? In just the first six months of the Clinton Administration, three events of some notoriety occurred that cried out for stronger, yet more refined, criticism than the White House was receiving from the media or the Democratic Congress. First, President Clinton issued an ill-considered, politically driven executive order toughening the post-employment restrictions, as was promised during the transition. Second, the First Lady was given the official responsibility to come up with the Administration's health care reform proposal, while nothing was done to rid her of her investments in health care-related firms. Third, the White House Travel Office employees were summarily fired under questionable circumstances, suggesting the improper influence of persons with a personal or financial interest in taking over the Travel Office, as well as the White House's misuse of the FBI.

My first thought was to write an op-ed piece or two, but subsequently considered conducting a lengthier, more involved study. Such a study would examine the current state of ethics regulation as well as the ethics controversies involving the Clinton Administration under current law, policy, and practice. It would not be satisfied with making charges or accusations, but would attempt objectively and thoughtfully to analyze the ethics issues that were confronting the Clinton Administration, and make recommendations for changes in law and policy.

I did not decide to conduct this study until the end of my brief tenure at the Interstate Commerce Commission. In December 1993, as a private citizen for the first time since 1982, I reviewed the Clinton Administration's first year, envisioning a study covering just a handful of issues. Thus, I initially thought I could conduct this study in a space of a few months. But this estimate proved way off, once the number of ethics issues began to proliferate in 1994 and some of the existing ethics matters matured into full-fledged scandals. Indeed, there is no entirely satisfactory cut-off point short of the end of the Administration **and** the end of the investigations into the Administration's conduct, which, given the track record of independent counsel, could take us close to the millennium.

However, my major purpose in writing this study is not historical. Although this study can serve as a historical reference work, my purpose in writing this study is prescriptive, in three ways. First, I wish to provide a guide to the next administration on how to avoid the ethical mistakes of the Clinton Administration (and other previous administrations), most of which were avoidable. The sidebar to Chapter One contains a list of fourteen principles, which, if followed (a big "if"), would keep an administration out of a lot of the trouble the Clinton White House has been in for three years. Second, I wish to recommend several changes or revisions to current ethics laws and standards. Most of the individual chapters contain recommendations at the end; all these recommendations have been collected in Appendix One. Third, my audience is the ethics community, broadly considered. I hope that agency ethics officials, congressional oversight staff, self-appointed public interest ethics gadflies, reporters on the ethics beat, and lawyers who represent public officials accused of unethical conduct all will find the analyses and recommendations useful in their work.

The scope of this study is defined by the parameters of the Clinton Administration and the system of ethics statutes, regulations, and policies in place during this time. In examining the performance of the Clinton Administration, this study is confined for the most part to what has occurred since January 20, 1993. For instance, this study does not analyze what may have occurred in Arkansas with respect to Madison Guaranty and Whitewater Development Corporation, or with respect to Bill Clinton's campaigns for, or service as, Governor. Specifically, it does not include an analysis of the allegations that Governor Clinton misused Arkansas State resources while engaging in sexual indiscretions. It also does not include an analysis of Mrs. Clinton's commodities trades in 1978-79. It does include an analysis of the response of the President, First Lady, the White House, and the Administration to some of these matters, because, as the Watergate scandal illustrated, how an administration handles an ethics controversy is an important measure of its own integrity.

Chapter One is intended as an overview and synthesis of the analysis and conclusions of the remaining chapters. Thus, certain summary passages of the individual chapters are included, in slightly modified form, in the overview.

Except in a few instances, I have relied exclusively on public record materials and have not conducted an independent factual investigation of these matters. For news sources, I have relied primarily on the *Washington Post*, the *Washington Times*, the *New York Times*, and the *Wall Street Journal*, for these four daily publications, along with the *Los Angeles Times*, consistently devoted the most attention to ethics matters, in reporting as well as analysis and comment.

I wish to thank the many friends, colleagues, and others who provided assistance to me on this project, in reviewing drafts, providing me with source documents, and exchanging ideas. In particular, I wish to thank Michael Horowitz, who was instrumental in getting me to consider a project more substantial than an op-ed or two. I am also grateful to the Hudson Institute for agreeing to publish this study in its entirety, and for the editorial and publishing assistance Mike and the Hudson staff in Indianapolis provided. Sincere thanks go to the Federalist Society, and its Executive Director Gene Meyer in particular, for accepting my project in the first place, for affording me complete independence and freedom to perform the kind of study I wanted, and for the patience in allowing sufficient time to complete this study. At Mayer, Brown & Platt, I wish to single out Barbara Fisher and MBP's library staff, who provided me with expeditious and reliable research assistance. Others who deserve my thanks for their insight, perspective and support include Professor Kathleen Clark, Barbara Comstock, Boyden Gray, Lisa Odle Kaufman, Phil Larsen, Jane Ley, Mark Paoletta, John Schmitz, Rob Swanson, Glenn Tait, and Genevieve Young.

In the end, I alone am responsible for the analysis and conclusions contained in this study.

Gregory S. Walden
December 1995

Part One

Overview

Chapter One

Ethics
in the
Clinton
Administration

On his first day in office, President Bill Clinton issued an executive order placing "revolving door" restrictions on his appointees in addition to the statutory restrictions in place.[1] Within his first month, he also clamped down on perks.[2] Despite statements made during the campaign and presidential transition, pledging an administration that would be subject to and comply with tougher rules, those are the only standards that this Administration has racheted up in three years in office (aside from several minor policy changes made in response to ethics mishaps concerning travel and contacts with law enforcement agencies). The President did not tighten or strengthen any of the basic standards of conduct that apply to the Executive Branch workforce in the performance of their duties, a fact largely unrecognized, either then or now.[3] Indeed, the basic ethics standards have been in place, without significant change, for thirty years.

Because it has not been challenged, the accuracy of the President's assertion that his Administration is subject to the highest ethical standards, which he has repeated several times during his presidency, has been implicitly accepted. In March 1994, at his initial news conference to answer questions on Whitewater, the President cited his executive order in support of his assertion that his Administration is subject to the highest ethics standards of any administration:

But since you raised the issue, let me also ask you to report to the American people that **we have and we have enforced higher standards against ethical conflicts than any previous administration.** When people leave the White House, they can't lobby the White House. If they're in certain positions, they can't lobby the White House for a long time. If they're in certain positions now, they can never lobby on behalf of a foreign government.[4]

A year later, the President was asked, in light of the several pending independent counsel investigations of Administration officials, "how can you explain what's happened to your administration after you came into office promising the most ethical administration in history?" In the middle of an extended response, the President asserted, **"Everybody knows that I have tougher ethics rules than any previous President."**[5]

From these statements it is plain that the President has focused all his attention on ethics rules that operate **after** an official leaves the Government; he made no change in, nor did he devote any apparent attention to, the standards of conduct which Executive Branch employees must observe **during** their government service. And it is these latter standards that have given the Clinton Administration so much trouble. To employ a metaphor, the Clinton Administration has suffered from an acute case of ethics far-sightedness: its vision concerning the restrictions that apply at the conclusion of government service is focused (even, if, as argued in this book, it is also wrong), but its vision is blurred when dealing with the standards that directly apply to its conduct in office.

My overall conclusion about the ethics performance of the Clinton Administration is that it has regularly failed to live up to the maxim that public service is a public trust. In a myriad of situations, the White House has taken actions, failed to take actions, and made statements that justifiably would cause one to question the basic integrity of the Administration. In addition, several Clinton appointees in the Cabinet Departments have failed to comport themselves with basic ethical standards.

It is not the purpose of this study to portray the Clinton Administration's ethics as the worst in history or even in recent times; comparisons between administrations spanning different eras and political climates are difficult, if not impossible, to make fairly. It is true, as defenders of the President and ethics commentators alike point out, that alleged ethics transgressions are today more publicized, that there are now more institutions to discover and investigate scandal, and that ethics has been increasingly employed as a weapon by political or policy opponents.[6] Furthermore, the media are no longer as tolerant of ethical lapses as they were a few years ago, but instead compete vigorously to uncover scandal and to pursue allegations. But none of these external factors should excuse the misconduct and mistakes recounted in this study. These factors were facts of political life for the Reagan and Bush Administrations, and they are likely to remain with us for many more.

The fundamental question is whether the Clinton Administration has fostered the public's confidence in the integrity of the Federal Government or has instead caused further erosion of the public's trust. I believe that, on the whole, it has done the latter. Its failures can be organized into three general observations:

First, the White House has conducted itself often as if it were oblivious to ethics concerns, taking action without regard to whether ethical restrictions exist or whether the action would give rise to improper appearances.

Second, the White House has compiled a consistently poor record of responding to ethics controversies, exacerbating rather than mollifying the public's suspicion of wrongdoing.

Third, in these and other matters, the President and White House have displayed a fundamental lack of candor—a repeated unwillingness or inability to tell it straight.

How to Judge the Ethics of an Administration

Before explaining these conclusions, it is instructive to consider how the ethics performance of an administration has been and should be judged. To answer this question, it is useful to consider the **quantitative** approach Congress and the media have used in the recent past. Both were extremely critical of the ethics of the Reagan Administration and (to a lesser degree) the Bush Administration. In making their case, they gathered together all reports of ethical lapses, and drew general conclusions about the ethics of an administration based on these reports. Three-quarters through the Reagan Administration, *Time* magazine pronounced judgment on its ethics, noting that 100 Reagan appointees "have had ethical or legal charges leveled against them," a number that it called "unprecedented."[7] *Time* concluded that the "accumulation of cases produces a portrait of impropriety on a grand scale."

During both the Reagan and Bush Administrations, a central objective of the Democratic Party was to paint the Republican administrations as corrupt, dishonest, and insensitive to the ethics of public service. (Likewise, the Republican minority in the House of Representatives used the lax ethics of certain Democratic leaders as a major weapon against the entrenched Democratic majority.)

An excellent discussion of this phenomenon is contained in *Politics By Other Means*, by Benjamin Ginsberg and Martin Shefter.[8] The authors conclude that the revelation, investigation, and prosecution of ethical misconduct has emerged as "a central vehicle of political competition in the United States. . . . Democrats and Republicans have learned to use allegations of impropriety to discredit and weaken one another."[9]

Democrats were partial to assembling lists of Executive Branch officials tarred by allegations of unethical conduct. On October 4, 1988, one month before the elections, Representative Pat Schroeder released an "Index To Clippings Of Alleged Ethics Violations And Other Improprieties By Reagan Administration Appointees."[10] In September 1991, the Democratic National Committee circulated a "working draft" of "Welcome to the Bush Hall of Shame; Republican Ethics and Sleaze in the Bush Administration."[11]

But in their zeal to produce the lengthiest possible list, these Democrats stretched the concept of ethics well beyond reason—to include allegations that an official failed to comply with a statutory duty or acted contrary to the agency's authority—and abandoned any notion of fairness, by including allegations without any attempt to determine their credibility.

Similarly, the ethics of the Clinton Administration could be evaluated quantitatively, using any of several criteria. For example, the **number of independent counsel appointed** (in just three years) is unprecedented for any administration.[12] As of this writing, several current or former Administration officials are the subject of four separate independent counsel investigations.

Since January 1994, the conduct of the **President and First Lady**, and subsequently that of **Webster Hubbell, Bruce Lindsey, Roger Altman**, and other White House and Treasury officials, has been under investigation by the independent counsel (first Robert Fiske, then Kenneth Starr) in the Madison and Whitewater matter.

Since September 1994, independent counsel Donald Smaltz has been investigating whether Agriculture Secretary **Mike Espy** improperly accepted gifts from, and took official action in favor of, companies regulated by the Department.

Since May 1995, independent counsel David Barrett has been investigating whether Housing Secretary **Henry Cisneros** made materially false statements to the FBI and other Federal officials during the nomination and appointment process, by not being truthful about his payments to a former intimate.

Since July 1995, independent counsel Daniel Pearson has been investigating Commerce Secretary **Ron Brown** and his business partner Nolanda Hill on allegations that Brown falsified his financial disclosure statements and illegally accepted payments from his former business.[13]

Or the list could include **the number of high-level officials who have resigned** while under an ethical cloud: Bernard Nussbaum, David Watkins, and William Kennedy from the White House alone, and Webster Hubbell, Roger Altman, Jean Hanson, and Mike Espy from the Cabinet Departments.

Still another quantitative measure of the degree to which this Administration has been beset by ethics scandals is to consider the **number of days a story on the ethics of the Administration was featured on the front page** of major daily newspapers. This figure would reflect the fact that many ethics stories have "legs," because of new revelations or the involvement of other actors (Congress, Inspectors General, courts).

The **number of congressional investigations**, another possible criterion, has been relatively small. There are two explanations for this. First, the Congress and the presidency were controlled by the same party in 1993-94, and the Democratic Congress lost nearly all of its appetite for investigating the Executive Branch once President Clinton was sworn in. Second, on several occasions, the 103d Congress (and 104th, to date) postponed or did not convene hearings in deference to pending criminal investigations into the same conduct.

Ultimately, all quantitative measures are unsatisfactory. There is no consensus about what allegations should be considered a matter of ethics, and most lists link the serious with the trivial, the proven with the unproven, without distinguishing among them. Therefore, only a qualitative approach should be used in determining the ethics performance of an administration.

Despite *Time*'s penchant for the quantitative approach in evaluating the ethics of the Reagan Administration, *Time* also attempted somewhat of a qualitative one. Its analysis of the types of ethical trouble in which the Reagan Administration found itself is instructive. *Time* categorized the "fallen" officials into four groups:

> **Foxes in the Chicken Coop**: those appointed to enforce regulations they chafed under while in the private sector and who, once in office, seemed eager to undermine them. There are the **Public-Service Privateers**: appointees from the business world who carried their Wall Street ethos into the public sector. The **True Believers**: officials whose loyalty and ambition overcame their judgment and principles. And **People with a Past**: officials undone by acts committed before entering government.[14]

Time's categories may fit the nature of the sins of the Reagan Administration, but while they would serve to portray the Clinton Administration also in a bad light, they are not the best means of evaluating it.[15]

The ethics of the Clinton Administration and others that follow should be judged by reference to the ethics laws and standards of conduct. In addition to specific restrictions concerning conflicts of interest, gifts, and outside income and activities, the major focus should be on how well the Administration, as a whole, comports with certain cardinal principles that have guided the Executive Branch since the presidency of John F. Kennedy.

Particular attention should be paid to three general principles that flesh out the basic obligations of public service:

> • Employees shall not use public office for private gain.

> • Employees shall act impartially and not give preferential treatment to any private organization or individual.

> • Employees shall endeavor to avoid any actions creating the appearance that they are violating the law or the ethical standards[.][16]

In addition, an administration's conduct should be evaluated in terms of whether, on the whole, it fostered the public's confidence in the integrity of government, or whether it contributed to the loss of public confidence in government.

A Brief Survey of Ethical Mishaps

The Clinton Administration has been relatively free of actions taken by officials to line their own pockets, whether by kickbacks, bribes, or taking actions to benefit their financial interests. There are some, but few, reports of Administration officials using their office to enrich themselves or their friends. But two of the most serious scandals of the Clinton Administration, the firing of the Travel Office employees and the White House's response to the Madison-Whitewater investigations, demonstrate a failure of the White House to observe these three cardinal principles. In the White-water matter, Clinton appointees repeatedly used the authority of their office to fur-ther the personal interests of the President and the First Lady. In the Travel Office affair, White House officials misused their public office for the private and personal gain of friends and former colleagues, giving them preferential treatment.

In these two matters, and in other ethics controversies, the White House has engaged in acts creating the appearance of impropriety. On the whole, the Clinton Administration has failed to foster the public's confidence in the integrity of govern-ment, in three major respects:[17] first, in taking action without regard to whether eth-ical restrictions restrained or limited their conduct or whether the action would give rise to improper appearances; second, in responding poorly to ethics controversies; and third, in displaying a basic lack of candor. These three themes emerge from a quick survey of the most celebrated ethics-related controversies.

The White House's handling of the First Lady's health care interests featured a series of ethical mishaps:

First, the White House failed to recognize the presence of at least a "lay" con-flict of interest posed by her partnership interest in Valuepartners when the President appointed her to chair the Task Force on National Health Care Reform on January 25, 1993. At the very outset of the Administration, the White House Counsel's office should have reviewed the financial disclosure report the President filed as a candi-date, which included a list of the Valuepartners' holdings. Regardless of whether the First Lady's holding of an interest in health care companies would constitute a crim-inal conflict of interest under 18 U.S.C. 208, it should have been obvious that it would appear to the public and the media as a classic conflict.

Second, the White House Counsel's office should have promptly recommended that she sell her interest in Valuepartners; apparently it did not do so.

Third, a blind trust was not set up until six months into the Administration; although a blind trust could not cure a conflict as a legal matter, the delay suggests a nonchalance concerning the Clintons' financial interests.

Fourth, the White House Counsel's analysis of the application of the conflict-of-interest statute to the First Lady's financial interests was flawed.

Fifth, the White House Counsel failed to secure the views of the Justice Depart-ment on the question of whether the ethics laws applied to the First Lady in her Health Care Task Force role, relying instead on a clearly distinguishable Justice De-partment precedent involving Mrs. Reagan.

Sixth, the White House ignored the Justice Department's long-standing counsel that the First Lady consider herself subject to the conflict-of-interest laws as a matter of policy.

Seventh, the White House Counsel improperly asserted that the First Lady was not an official or employee subject to the ethics laws while, at the same time, the White House took the position in court that she be considered the functional equiv-alent of a full-time Federal employee for the purposes of the Federal Advisory Com-mittee Act.

The White House also committed a series of ethical missteps in setting up the Health Care Task Force to develop a comprehensive health care legislative proposal.

The White House designed a process that included outside health care interests in White House deliberations, many of whom possessed their own agenda for reform, yet kept these deliberations and their records from the public's view. This not only violated the spirit of the Federal Advisory Committee Act, but also gave the appearance that special interests were "calling the shots" behind the scenes. Many outsiders who should have been considered special Government employees (and therefore subject to the conflict-of-interest and financial disclosure laws) were not. Outsiders participated freely in discussions relating to their profession and employment, with no regard to potential ethics concerns. Ira Magaziner's initial declaration in support of the Justice Department's defense of litigation involving the Task Force was inexcusably misleading in two significant respects.

Essentially, the White House appeared unaware of the ethics concerns posed by turning over the development of health care legislation to an assemblage of health care professionals. Whether this resulted from inattention, neglect, or a legal judgment that no legal conflict could arise as a matter of law, it gave birth to the notion that this White House would not let the ethics rules and principles stand in the way of what the White House wanted to do.

The White House Travel Office affair is perhaps the best example of this notion. Ethics alarm bells should have been ringing loudly when Harry Thomason, Darnell Martens, and Catherine Cornelius, all of whom had a financial or personal interest in the Travel Office operations, began their efforts to oust the Travel Office staff. Perhaps the reason no alarm went off is because David Watkins, who knew these basic facts, seemed ethically tone deaf. (His later use of a military helicopter to take in a round of golf supports this characterization.)

Perhaps the reason no alarm bells rang is that all of the major players, both inside and outside the White House, knew each other and had worked together or assisted in the 1992 campaign; the Travel Office affair is the prime example of the Arkansas cronyism that the Clinton Administration has featured..[18] Perhaps the reason is that the First Lady let it be known that she wanted the Travel Office staff replaced, so that concerns someone might register about the precipitousness—as well as the appropriateness—of getting rid of entire the Travel Office staff were not welcomed.

Whatever the reason that ethics concerns were not identified at the outset, the objective within the White House was to build a case to fire the Travel Office employees, and replace them with persons the White House officials knew from the campaign and from Arkansas. In doing so, several White House officials abused their office, pressuring the FBI to find a predicate to conduct a criminal investigation and then interfering with the timing and public explanation of the investigation. White House officials often misstated the facts in attempting to cover for its misconduct and mismanagement of the matter. They publicly accused the Travel Office employees of misconduct (the White House disclosure that the facts warranted an FBI investigation implied criminal behavior) and falsely characterized the basis for the firings. When it conducted a review of its actions, the White House's candor was selective and its assessment inadequate. Ethics standards were clearly implicated (and violated), yet the White House Management Review did not address the ethics rules.

Congressional hearings held during the fall of 1995 demonstrated the extent to which the White House still has not leveled with the public about the magnitude of the misconduct that occurred and the degree of involvement of certain White House officials in that misconduct. If one ethics scandal serves as a paradigm for the ethics performance of the Clinton Administration, it is the Travel Office affair.

The White House's sloppy attitude toward potential conflicts of interest and the appearance that outsiders have special access and influence in the White House, initially displayed in its handling of the Health Care Task Force, was reinforced by the President's unprecedented reliance on informal advisers, particularly Paul Begala, James Carville, Stanley Greenberg, and Mandy Grunwald at the beginning of the Administration, and Dick Morris, more recently. The White House was slow even to recognize the possibility of an ethics problem; when ultimately it was forced to acknowledge a potential problem, the several steps it took failed to convince anyone that it regarded the regular presence of outside consultants in the White House as a serious issue.

The controversy over the role of the consultants did lead to the discovery of a lax process for issuing White House passes, resulting in further criticism of the White House Counsel's office. When the four main political consultants finally disclosed their financial interests and affiliations, some of them reduced their West Wing profiles. Not long after the controversy abated, and the pass and clearance backlog was addressed, the President resumed his heavy reliance on outsiders. He first brought Tony Coelho and then Richard Morris into White House deliberations, treating them as de facto White House staff. Thus continued the President's apparent insensitivity to ethics concerns presented by the role of outsiders.

Perhaps the most egregious misconduct by the White House occurred in efforts at damage control. As shown earlier, the White House abused its authority in its effort, at several stages of the Travel Office affair, to explain its prior actions. In another case, the President himself improperly attempted to kill or affect publication of news stories containing allegations of sexual indiscretions and misuse of Arkansas State resources, by calling one State trooper and discussing Federal job opportunities for a fellow trooper in that conversation. Others both inside and outside the White House, including Bruce Lindsey and Betsey Wright, also worked toward this end, although it has not been alleged that they offered anything to any of the troopers. But the President did offer to assist a trooper get a Federal position. Even assuming that he did not intend this as a *quid pro quo*—which would constitute a Federal crime—the President was grossly insensitive to the appearance that he was misusing his office for his own personal benefit.

The White House also frustrated the legitimate law enforcement interests in investigating the death of Vince Foster. It is not known for certain whether one or more White House officials intentionally sought to keep investigators from discovering some evidence of illegality, misconduct, or embarrassment in Foster's office or files. But one could reasonably draw such a conclusion from the actions of several White House officials, including the White House Counsel, in the hours and days following his death. Notwithstanding the grief that understandably beset the West Wing upon hearing of Foster's death, the White House should have accorded the Park Police and Justice Department the leeway to do their jobs, and should not have thrust itself into playing the role of sleuth or guardian of the office.

The most prominent example of the Clinton Administration's abuse of authority and insensitivity to appearances of impropriety, however, was the White House's response to allegations concerning Madison Guaranty and Whitewater Development.

The White House would have been better off had it refrained from getting involved in the matter in the first place. As the President and First Lady have said repeatedly, Whitewater relates to events that occurred in Arkansas years ago. So, why then did the White House insist on monitoring the investigations, obtaining inside information from the Treasury Department and the SBA? Why did it respond officially to media inquiries rather than the Clintons' personal attorneys? Was it a desire to protect the President from criticism, whether or not the criticism concerned actions taken before he became President? Or, as the White House explained, was it just a desire to give the President a "heads up" about developments that might concern him? Why did the President need any "heads up" in the first place? It matters not what motivated the White House to engage in a damage control exercise on such a grand scale. None of these motives justified using the offices of the Government to inquire about (even if not to affect) the deliberative process in pending criminal and administrative proceedings relating to the Clintons in their personal capacity. The White House was not acting in furtherance of any legitimate governmental interest in meeting with and calling Treasury and SBA officials.

To date, there does not seem to be any solid evidence that White House officials attempted to affect the two sets of Resolution Trust Corporation (RTC) referrals to the Justice Department. But the entire story of Paula Casey's appointment as U.S. Attorney in Little Rock, her involvement in the matter, and her belated recusal from the case, is not known. Other questions that are not resolved at this point are why Kansas City RTC investigator Jean Lewis was removed from the investigation, why one of the referrals was subject to an unusual RTC headquarters legal analysis before being referred to Justice, why Jean Lewis and her two superiors in the Kansas City office were placed on administrative leave, and, in light of the series of indictments secured by the independent counsel in recent months, why the Justice Department (specifically, Paula Casey) found the first referral insufficient even to investigate.

The White House also mishandled the disposition of the Clintons' Whitewater files. These documents are not government documents, and thus should have been handled strictly by the Clintons' personal attorney after they had been assembled from various offices inside and outside the White House. The White House resisted public disclosure of these documents from the start. The Clintons could legally withhold these documents from the public (at their political risk), but it was improper for the White House to explain that it could not release these documents to the public because they were the subject of a grand jury subpoena. At least some White House officials knew that a grand jury subpoena does not legally shield preexisting documents from public disclosure, and yet the media largely accepted the line that the White House could no longer provide these documents. More than a year later, when these documents were provided to congressional committees—and some of them were publicly disclosed in connection with committee hearings—there was no mention of the grand jury secrecy excuse the White House had wrongly cited.

Moreover, questions remain whether some Whitewater files, as well as some files on Madison Guaranty generated by the Rose Law Firm and removed from the law firm in 1992 by Vince Foster, were improperly destroyed or tampered with.

Acting With Seeming Disregard of Ethics Parameters

When all these reports are considered together, the first theme emerges: the

White House conducted itself as if the ethics laws and principles did not govern their actions:

• The First Lady was assigned responsibility to come up with a health care legislative proposal, with no apparent attention given by the White House to the conflict-of-interest laws and policies.

• The White House established a Health Care Task Force for the First Lady to chair, assisted by an interdepartmental working group headed by Ira Magaziner and staffed with hundreds of outsiders, without apparent regard for the legal implications, under either the Federal Advisory Committee Act (FACA) or the ethics laws.[19]

• The President brought several outside consultants into the White House, fully integrating them into the White House staff, yet seemingly insensitive to the ethics consequences of doing so.

• The White House decided to replace the Travel Office staff with their Arkansas friends and campaign workers. The Travel Office employees were fired, based on the allegations made by persons with an interest in getting the travel business, and the FBI and Peat Marwick were used to justify this decision. When the White House reviewed its own conduct, it did so without any reference to the letter of the ethics laws and standards. The entire Travel Office episode unfolded with no attention to the ethics principles that would have signaled "yellow" if not "red lights" at several intersections.

• Even something as minor as the attendance of White House staff at dinners sponsored by media organizations illustrates this theme.[20] The White House Counsel determined that White House staff could attend these events, notwithstanding an inconvenient ethics provision that requires invitations to such events to come from the event sponsor. The White House Counsel simply declared the ethics rule inoperative! (Eventually, the White House asked the OGE to amend the rule.)

Through its first three years, the single picture of the Clinton White House is one that did not take seriously the need to conduct its business free of improper appearances.[21]

This theme is also found, to some extent, in the ethics problems of the Clinton Cabinet. In accepting gifts from companies he regulated (and even soliciting at least one gift), Agriculture Secretary Mike Espy violated a simple principle of ethics that is well-known and easy to follow. It remains to be determined by the independent counsel whether Secretary Espy and his appointees were so oblivious to ethics concerns in the conduct of their office as to risk criminal exposure.

Elsewhere in the Clinton Administration, these three years witnessed a variety of misconduct and abuses that occurs in any administration. Travel privileges were abused, most notably by Veterans Secretary Jesse Brown and General Services Administrator Roger Johnson, but also by senior military officials, despite the President's early and earnest effort to reduce the abuse of perks. Several political appointees awaiting confirmation (and some even awaiting nomination) went to work at their new posts as "consultants," thereby overstepping the legal limits of their roles.

Midlevel State Department political appointees were found rummaging through the personnel files of Bush Administration political appointees. The abuse was quickly contained within the State Department, without serious damage to the Administration, but was nonetheless inconvenient given the President's impatience with the same sort of conduct when he was the victim of it in 1992.

The ethics problems of Secretaries Ron Brown and Henry Cisneros are different, however. Both are still plagued by conduct and associations that began well before they were sworn in. Secretary Cisneros, who years ago weathered the controversy of an adulterous relationship, has been tarred by the residuum of the same relationship, which (at least on a conversational level) had not ended at the time of his appointment. Whether the amount or timing of his payments to Linda Medlar would have, in fact, doomed his nomination with the White House is not known, but Cisneros certainly feared this. So, wanting the HUD appointment, he did not level with the White House or the FBI—Attorney General Reno determined, in fact, that Cisneros made false statements—and was exposed when Medlar went public with the fact of the payments and alleging a promise to continue making them, suing Cisneros, and granting a television interview.

Secretary Ron Brown's most serious ethics problem stems from his association with Nolanda Hill (although his involvement with Lillian Madsen on a real estate matter has also placed him in trouble). Secretary Brown's murky role and participation in a Hill company named First International has assumed real importance because of the several links to another Hill company, Corridor Broadcasting. The Secretary rebuffed Representative Bill Clinger's legitimate questions about whether he had taken sufficient steps to avoid potential conflicts of interest involving First International and a few other closely held companies. Considered with the Secretary's sloppy financial disclosure reports, and media reports of Nolanda Hill's business problems, Secretary Brown was unable to keep his business relationships from developing into a serious ethics controversy during his tenure as Secretary. The unusual manner in which he sold his interest back to First International only piqued interest in the propriety of his relationships with Hill and his compliance with financial disclosure and other laws. An independent counsel may take years before determining whether Secretary Brown violated any law, but his own failure to provide a satisfactory account of his financial arrangements ensures that a heavy ethics cloud will hover over him throughout his tenure as Secretary.

A Consistently Poor Record of Responding To Ethics Controversies

A second, recurring theme runs through the responses of the President, the White House, and the Administration to reports of ethics allegations and requests for documents or investigations. Almost without exception, their responses have exacerbated rather than mollified the public's suspicion of wrongdoing, as nearly all observers from right to left have concluded.[22] The Clinton Administration's *modus operandi* has featured a circle-the-wagons attitude, categorical denials made by persons without personal knowledge of the facts, the withholding of relevant documents, and impugning the motives of those raising ethics concerns. It may not be fair to conclude that the Clinton Administration always assumes this posture because it has something to hide from the public, but this is the impression such conduct has given the public.[23] It may be that the Clinton White House bridles at the ethics inquisitors in the media and the Republican Party because it does not wish to be distracted from its substantive agenda, or because, in their hearts, they know they are good people incapable of the graft or abuse of the public trust they routinely witnessed in previous Republican administrations—or at least thought they did.[24] It may even be that there are legitimate privilege and privacy concerns to be respected.

But these reasons do not justify or excuse the White House's mismanagement of the Travel Office and Whitewater affairs. **Appearances matter**. The public no longer trusts government officials (if it ever did). It is repeatedly told of the corruption of public officials, not just by ethics gadflies in the media and public interest groups, but also by other public officials, and not only during campaigns. And the public knows two other things: Lord Acton's maxim that power tends to corrupt, and a basic element of the human condition, the corruptibility of man.

Ethics transgressions are more widely publicized now, and thus it takes only occasional reports of actual misconduct to cement the public's impression that the Federal Government is staffed with officials who are prone to abuse their power and privilege. A public official and an administration can try to improve this image by defending conduct based on the facts and law. However, more often than not, such a defense, even if true, has no appreciable effect on the general public's view of the ethics of an administration. Thus, it is imperative that public officials conduct themselves in a manner that avoids even the appearance that they are abusing the public trust.

This imperative is more urgent when it comes to responding to a developing ethics scandal. In such situations, the specific reported allegations of wrongdoing mix with the presumption of rascality to produce a higher level of public suspicion and mistrust. At such times, when the White House is in a damage control mode, it must decide whether to hunker down, to open up and let the chips fall where they may, or to adopt a midway course. There is a continuum of responses, from complete candor and cooperation to complete obstruction and obfuscation. Too often the Clinton White House's response to an ethics controversy has fallen nearer the obstruction and obfuscation end of the continuum. Even where the President and White House have pledged to cooperate fully with investigators, such as in Whitewater matter, their candor has been spotty.[25]

A Fundamental Lack of Candor

The lack of candor is the third broad ethics failure of this White House—nothing short of a consistent failure to tell it straight. This is a White House failure, and the President has been a primary offender. The credibility gap that he alone has created has cost his presidency greatly in terms of the public's trust. More than anything, the President's inability or unwillingness to give straight answers has injured his Administration's standing with the media and the public.[26]

But the problem extends to the White House staff as well. In an unusually direct, critical column, Ruth Marcus lambasted the White House for its "pattern of knowing or reckless disregard for the truth." Marcus wrote from her personal difficulty in getting the straight story out of the White House:

> In Washington, White House special counsel Lloyd N. Cutler likes to say, trust is the coin of the realm. By that measure, the Clinton White House is flat broke when it comes to its dealings with the reporters who cover it.

... Apparently putting its short-term political interests ahead of accuracy, it regularly fails to provide trustworthy information—whether out of inability, unwillingness or both. . . .

Nineteen months of repeated falsehoods and half-truths have corroded the relationship between this White House and the reporters who cover it. The corrosion breeds cynicism among reporters, which in turn contributes to a siege mentality inside the White House. . .[27]

Perhaps the best examples of the Clinton Administration's lack of candor are the House and Senate Whitewater hearings held in the summer of 1994, when a parade of White House and Treasury officials testified. (The 1995 Senate hearings provide a further example.) The testimony of Administration witnesses was variously described by observers of all political persuasions as evasive, inconsistent, contradictory, conveniently forgetful, and worse. But it was the Majority Report of the Senate Banking Committee, released on the last day of the 103d Congress, that brought the Administration's lack of candor into such sharp relief. The Report actually recommended that President Clinton issue an executive order "reinforcing that executive branch witnesses testifying before Congress should be fully candid and forthcoming and that they must testify truthfully, accurately and completely."[28] An Administration that—according to officials of its own party—must be reminded to tell the truth has a serious credibility problem.

The public's trust in an administration suffers when it regularly doubts the truth or accuracy of statements from the President or White House. In some respects, it is more important to have the truth of your words and statements respected and believed by the public than it is to be seen as wholly avoiding ethics violations, because the public cannot easily separate lies and misstatements about a government decision from the decision itself.

No doubt there will be some who find the conclusions in this chapter too harsh or unwarranted. The Clinton Administration has not lacked defenders. One explanation of the President's (and the White House's) susceptibility to controversy refers to the significant change from the politics in Arkansas to the politics in Washington.[29] In this formulation, the White House is a fishbowl, in which every little peccadillo is noticed and capable of magnification into a scandal. Arkansas, by contrast, is portrayed as a one-party state less likely to fight ethics battles in the open, and even less likely to wage such battles in the first place because of a closeknit Democratic apparatus. But this "naivete" defense, even if true, goes to the White House's purity of intent, not to its compliance with ethics statutes and regulations.

To other defenders, the spate of ethics charges are Republican-inspired, a payback for the Democratic Congress's treatment of the past two Republican administrations, or designed to distract and disrupt the President from putting out his message or getting his program adopted. This is, in fact, the fervently expressed view of the President and First Lady. Commenting specifically on Whitewater, the President lashed out at Republicans at a March 1994 news conference:

I think that it is clear that the Republicans have behaved in a fairly blatant, bald, and totally political way in this regard. And since there is no evidence of abuse of authority on my part as President, or any of the kinds of things for which their parties [sic] and administrations were accused, and since they have often complained in the past of political motivation, I think that they would show a little more restraint and judgment in this case.[30]

Still others, including the President, see little wrong in what has occurred. These persons can list Secretary Ron Brown's exoneration from the Vietnam allegations; the indictment of Travel Office Director Billy Dale as justification for the Travel Office firings (although Dale's quick acquittal significantly, if not completely, under-cuts any reliance on the indictment); OGE's report on Treasury-White House White-water contacts (ignoring its many qualifications); and OGE's finding of no basis to support the charge that the First Lady violated the conflict-of-interest law in holding onto health care interests. They point out that much of the to-do about the Clintons, both financial and personal, antedated Mr. Clinton's inauguration, and thus should not be counted in the ethics scorecard of this Administration. They argue the gist of the allegations against Secretary Cisneros (and Secretary Brown, to a lesser extent) concern alleged conduct that occurred before they entered office.

At a news conference in March 1995, the President claimed:

> [I]f you look at the work that people [under investigation by independent coun-sel] have done in their public capacity since I have been President, you would be hard-pressed to cite examples that constitute abuse of authority.[31]

He added, "no one has accused me of abusing my authority here as President."[32]

The individual chapters that follow this overview examine several areas in which the ethics of the Clinton Administration has been on trial. The more extended treat-ment of the individual ethics mishaps provides the best basis of evaluating the asser-tions of the President and his supporters. Below are summaries of the analysis and conclusions contained in those chapters.

The President and the Revolving Door

The single area in which it can be accurately stated that the President raised ethical standards is the "revolving door." On his first day in office, he signed Execu-tive Order 12834, putting in place additional post-employment restrictions for his appointees, as promised during the campaign and previewed during the transition. The President has repeatedly cited his revolving door executive order in support of the broader claim that he has subjected his administration to the highest standards of any administration. In fact, other than a modest effort to reduce the abuse of perks, the only action he has taken to tighten or raise ethics standards has been this execu-tive order, which does not apply until officials leave office. Moreover, and ironically, the revolving door may be the one area most in need of relaxation and rationality.

When he came into office, the President faced a scheme of over-inclusive, ex-cessive, and unduly complicated statutory post-employment restrictions. It is all these things largely because of Congress's recent proclivity to legislate myopically follow-ing each ethics scandal involving a perceived abuse of the revolving door. Even so, the President and many others have regarded amendments of the post-employment restrictions regime as inadequate.

In fact, the revolving door is not as large a problem as portrayed by politicians. While it is certainly capable of abuse, evidence is slight to show that abuse is serious or widespread. Moreover, the revolving door can foster a higher caliber of talent in government and can assist private interests in making responsible and constructive requests of government. The Clinton Administration belatedly recognized these benefits only after the President had issued his executive order and only when put on the defensive by the departures of Howard Paster and Roy Neel before the end of the Administration's first year.

Two motivations that have nothing to do with ethics appear behind the push for even greater revolving door restrictions. First, there is a hostility to high-level Executive and Legislative Branch officials who leave government, after a brief tour of a year or two, and "cash in" by accepting a large salary increase. Second, and more important, some advocates of increased revolving door restrictions wish to establish and maintain a permanent separate and adversarial relationship between the public and private sectors. These advocates believe that the public interest is not advanced by the regular exchange between the regulators and the regulated. Thus, professors and public interest advocates are encouraged to enter government service, but corporate officials are discouraged from doing so.

The President's executive order falls far short of the rhetoric he employed against the revolving door in the campaign and during the transition; it is replete with loopholes and qualifications. It does not "stop" the revolving door, as the public realistically could have expected the President to do, based on his campaign and transition rhetoric. Indeed, it turns out that the Executive Order actually covers only ten to twenty White House officials. Here again, the President has failed to deliver as he promised.

Despite its loopholes, the executive order is simply excessive in several key respects, such as its five-year "cooling-off" period for senior appointees. In other respects, like current 18 U.S.C. 207, the order is discriminatory or without ethical foundation. The fundamental problem with the executive order, however, is neither its limited application nor its differential treatment of subject matters and clients, although there is plenty of both. Rather, the fault lies in the President's initial failure to grasp that every racheting up of post-employment restrictions carries a real public policy cost. Although the notion is always difficult to establish empirically, White House officials have nonetheless freely admitted that good people have stayed away from accepting positions in the Clinton .*.dministration because of the order's five-year ban.

The President is unlikely either to rescind the executive order or to push for reform of the criminal statute. Under frequent criticism for his Administration's perceived ethical missteps, the President is understandably reluctant to take any action that would be seen as a loosening of ethical standards for his Administration—and, unfortunately, any relaxation of revolving door restrictions would be so perceived. But the next President should do so soon upon assuming office.

Congress regrettably appears determined to up the ante across the board (although relief from the onerous and duplicative procurement integrity post-employment restrictions may be provided in this Congress). Congress is seriously considering an even tighter post-employment restrictions regime, featuring provisions lacking a rational basis. That is also unfortunate, because there is a broad-based coalition that supports a rational rewriting of the post-employment laws: OGE, the American

Bar Association (ABA) Committee on Government Standards, the Council for Excellence In Government, the Senior Executives Association, the Government employee unions, the American Civil Liberties Union, and, most recently, Judge Abner Mikva, who spoke out against the current scheme of revolving door restrictions (including the executive order) in his last days as the President's third White House Counsel.

The excessive and irrational nature of the current post-employment restrictions regime is demonstrated by the case of George Stephanopoulos, who may have violated the criminal post-employment restrictions to which he was subject as a former Capitol Hill staffer, when he met with House leaders in the summer of 1992 on behalf of candidate Bill Clinton. As a former assistant to House Majority Leader Richard Gephardt, Stephanopoulos was probably subject to a one-year cooling-off period when he left the Hill in the fall of 1991. The Ethics Reform Act of 1989 extended post-employment restrictions for the first time to former Members of Congress and certain senior congressional staff.

The cooling-off period prohibited Stephanopoulos, for one year after he left the Hill, from making any communication to or appearance before any House leader or leadership staff member in connection with any matter on which he was seeking official action on behalf of another person. "Another person" includes political candidates and parties. From the latter part of 1991 through the 1992 election, Stephanopoulos served on Bill Clinton's paid campaign staff as deputy campaign manager and communications director. In that capacity, it is clear that he personally met with the House leadership on issues of legislation of importance to the campaign at least on one occasion; undoubtedly he met or spoke with the leadership at other times.

There is a legitimate question whether Stephanopoulos was covered by the law because of the unusual nature of his compensation (he was paid from two accounts, with his pay varying from month-to-month), but the better statutory analysis is that he was covered by the law. If he was exempt, the law contains a potentially large loophole that should be closed, because Stephanopoulos was precisely the sort of senior Hill aide who should be subject to a cooling-off period. But should Stephanopoulos and other former government officials be restricted in their representation of political candidates or parties? Is this what the post-employment restrictions are designed to prevent? As a matter of policy, the law should not restrict purely political communications by recently departed high-level officials, made on behalf of political parties or candidates, even if some official action is sought as part of such communications.

Other than a couple of stories, Stephanopoulos avoided press scrutiny and apparently was not the subject of any congressional or criminal ethics investigation. But others may not be so fortunate in 1996. Section 207, if it is complied with, imposes a substantial burden on campaigns. The Bush Administration took the law very seriously. Even as it tried to get the statute amended to permit political communications (an amendment passed the House but died in the Senate), Clayton Yeutter, Robert Mosbacher, and Sam Skinner all had to circumscribe their political activity significantly after they left the Administration to work for the Republican Party and the President's reelection. Absent from reports that Ron Brown, Mac McLarty, or Harold Ickes may leave the Clinton Administration to work for the President's reelection has been any recognition of the potential exposure to criminal liability should they contact the White House and Executive Branch on behalf of the campaign. Accordingly, Congress should amend the post-employment restrictions law now, as originally proposed by the Bush Administration and passed by the House in 1991, and as proposed in H.R. 1639, introduced in the 104th Congress, explicitly to permit political communications that otherwise would be barred by the cooling-off periods.

The First Lady's Health Care Stocks

An early illustration of the White House's insensitivity to ethical concerns is the failure of the First Lady to rid herself of financial interests in health care related companies upon her designation by the President in January 1993 as Chairman of the Task Force on National Health Care Reform. This was not a ceremonial title; in the discharge of her Federal responsibilities, the First Lady was indistinguishable from the Secretary of Health and Human Services or an Assistant to the President. Indeed, most observers believe she was and remains as influential in the development of health care (and other) policies as any other White House or Administration official.

It is inconceivable that Secretary Donna Shalala or Ira Magaziner would have been permitted to retain an interest in health care companies while engaging in discussions about health care legislation. As a matter of common sense, or lay understanding, the conflict of interest in holding interests in health care companies is patent. But the First Lady was permitted to retain her interest in Valuepartners, a non-publicly traded fund that invests in a number of stocks, including many in the health care industry that likely would be directly affected by any comprehensive health care reform legislation. Reports that Valuepartners engaged in short selling of health care stocks, and that remarks by the President and First Lady, both before and after coming to the White House, contributed to a dramatic decline in certain pharmaceutical stocks, led to allegations, by Republicans and some in the media, of a conflict of interest. Most observers, however, refrained from accusing the First Lady of taking official action for the purpose of financial profit.

For reasons that remain unknown, the First Lady did not sell her interest in Valuepartners. Thus, the White House Counsel's office and the Office of Government Ethics were forced to take legal positions—some unprecedented, others untenable—to defend her from allegations that she violated the criminal conflict-of-interest statute. A brief summary of these legal conclusions demonstrates the interpretative gymnastics often required when performing damage control after the fact.

The White House Counsel said that the First Lady was not a Federal employee subject to the ethics laws. The White House Counsel did not secure a Justice Department opinion in support of this claim, but relied instead on the easily distinguishable Justice Department precedent involving Nancy Reagan's participation in charitable fund-raising. Moreover, this claim was contemporaneously inconsistent with the White House's claim, in litigation involving the Health Care Task Force, that for purposes of the open meeting requirements of the Federal Advisory Committee Act, she was the "functional equivalent of a Federal employee."

Unlike the President, who enjoys an express exemption from the conflict-of-interest statute, the status of the First Lady under the conflict-of-interest laws is uncertain, and is in need of legislative clarification. But in the absence of an express exemption for the First Lady, the White House should have treated her as a Federal employee as a matter of policy, given the nature of her Federal responsibilities as well as the long-standing Justice Department policy recommendation to the White House that the First Lady and President should conduct themselves as if they were bound by the ethics laws.

The White House pointed out that she exercised no control or direction of Valuepartners' investments, and the fund's manager indicated that, from some point in 1992 on, he kept information about the fund's investments from the First Lady, suggesting that she was ignorant of Valuepartners' health care holdings. The first defense is irrelevant under the conflict-of-interest law, as the White House should have known; all that is required is knowledge of the underlying investments of the fund. Under section 208, a passive investor is as subject to its reach as is an active investor. Evidence of the second defense—that she lacked knowledge of Valuepartner's health care holdings—is weak; notably, neither the White House nor OGE claimed specifically that the First Lady was unaware of the fund's investments.

The White House Counsel's office, backed by a May 3, 1994 letter from OGE to Congress, stated that health care legislation was so broad and comprehensive that it was not a "particular matter," thus rendering the conflict-of-interest statute inapplicable. The OGE analysis looked at the universal entitlement element in the health care proposal, which would affect every American, and concluded that the entire package of health care legislative reforms "cannot be seen as focusing on the interests of specific persons or a discrete and identifiable class of persons," which is how the term "particular matter" has been defined by OGE and the Justice Department.

The fundamental flaw in OGE's analysis was to treat health care legislation in its entirety, as an indivisible whole. Clearly, the Administration's health care proposal, as a whole, would affect all Americans and all American businesses. But certain individual parts of the proposal were limited in focus and effect: for example, provisions affecting primarily hospitals, pharmaceutical companies, surgeons, or Health Maintenance Organizations (HMOs). In any comprehensive legislative package, there will be provisions with a broad focus and others with a narrower focus. The Administration's health care proposal, like most comprehensive proposals, was not offered on a take-it-or-leave-it basis. A number of provisions were subject to amendment or removal. Ira Magaziner himself referred to the Administration's health care legislative package, the Health Security Act, introduced as H.R. 3600, as "800 moving parts." One of those parts was a provision that would have regulated the price of prescription drugs for Medicare and Medicaid patients. Even the interdepartmental working group included a separate Pharmaceutical Price Control Working Group. The health care debate between the Administration and Congress necessarily moved from the general (Is there a health care crisis? Should we adopt a managed care or single-payer approach?) to the specific (should the price of new prescription drugs be controlled?); from the proposal as a whole to discrete provisions.

Moreover, a thorough analysis would not have been limited to a review of the Administration's health care proposal, because the First Lady undoubtedly participated also in discussions concerning the many rival health care bills introduced in the 103d Congress.

Would OGE conclude that Reconciliation bills, such as the one fashioned in the 104th Congress, is not a particular matter? Reconciliation contains many discrete provisions of great interest to a small industry or sector of the economy, and yet it undoubtedly affects all Americans, given its breadth. If not, why not? OGE's interpretation of the term "particular matter" essentially removed many legislative proposals from the definition. As a result, many situations that would appear to a reasonable person to pose a conflict of interest would not be subject to the protection of the ethics laws.

Finally, White House Counsel Nussbaum determined that the First Lady's activities did not have a "direct and predictable effect" on any of Valuepartners' interests or investments. Thus, under OGE and Justice Department precedent, she did not have a financial interest in health care legislation. OGE examined only the claim, made by some Republicans, that her speeches had a direct and predictable effect on the value of pharmaceutical stocks, and concluded that there was no showing that the value of any specific company's stock was affected by her speeches. Even if OGE's analysis is correct, that does not mean that the First Lady lacked a financial interest in health care legislation. This factor was not thoroughly examined by either the White House or OGE, in light of their other legal conclusions. But to several observers of the health care debate, there was no doubt that her activities—her speeches, testimony, and Task Force deliberations—significantly affected the value of health care stocks, including those she held through her Valuepartners investment.

In sum, a proper application of the conflict-of-interest statute to the First Lady and her Valuepartners' investment does not support the categorical conclusions reached by the White House and OGE. That is not to say the opposite, that the proper application of the law would reveal her commission of a crime. That is something that cannot be known without a full investigation of the facts and a fair construction of the law. **For any regular Executive Branch official, such as Secretary Donna Shalala or Ira Magaziner, these facts would have triggered an immediate, serious criminal investigation by the Justice Department**. Because of the uncertain legal status of the First Lady, however, a criminal investigation of her would not be appropriate. But that does not mean there should not be any investigation of this matter. Notwithstanding OGE's incorrect construction of the term "particular matter," it would be appropriate for Congress to determine what the First Lady knew of her investments, what advice (if any) she or the President received from the White House Counsel's office regarding her investment, and whether any of her activities—not just her speeches—had a direct and predictable effect on her investment.

What is clear is that the White House failed to remedy this apparent conflict, both in January 1993 and thereafter. Regardless of the potential availability of defenses and interpretations, the White House should have strongly recommended that the First Lady get rid of her Valuepartners interest at the time of her appointment. Further, the blind trust belatedly established in July 1993 did not give her any legal protection. It is blackletter law—although generally not understood by the media—that assets placed into a blind trust are attributed to an official as if she held the assets outright, unless and until the trustee informs the official that the asset has been sold. In short, the blind trust did not remedy the First Lady's conflict, even if it made the story go away.

The Health Care Task Force

Another matter in which the White House engaged in a series of inappropriate acts was in the conduct of the President's Task Force on National Health Care Reform. The legal question, which involved the White House in a protracted and messy lawsuit from the very outset of the Administration, was whether the Task Force or the Task Force's interdepartmental working group was a Federal advisory committee under the Federal Advisory Committee Act (FACA), requiring its meetings to be open to the public. The Task Force was properly held by the court of appeals not to be an advisory committee under FACA, because all of its members, save the First Lady, were full-time government employees and the First Lady was the "functional equivalent" of one. The working group, on the other hand, acting through subgroups, was such an advisory committee, although judicial resolution of this legal issue was obviated by the eventual release of working group records.

The interdepartmental working group set up to provide policy options to the Task Force resembled a typical Federal advisory committee in nearly all respects—excepting its failure to comply with the requirements of FACA. FACA is indeed a restraint on the President's constitutional authority, and it is probably true that the interdepartmental working group, **as it was created and intended to operate**, could not have accomplished its mission in the time it was given had it complied with FACA. Yet, FACA is not entirely, not even largely, to blame for the Administration's predicament. The White House must shoulder the bulk of the blame. The White House, namely, Ira Magaziner, designed a health care process that intentionally (and quite reasonably) sought the views of outside experts, employers, professionals, and state and local government officials. Of course, most of these outside persons had a personal, professional, and/or financial interest in any Federal health care legislation. Magaziner brought these persons into the White House, and gave them Federal responsibilities to draft options papers for the Task Force's, and later the President's, consideration. The White House did attempt to deputize some of these outsiders, cloaking them with the mantle of the Federal Government, thereby subjecting them to a strict ethical regime. But many others were not so deputized.

The White House failed to determine precisely who in the working group was subject to the ethics laws, and failed to ensure that all those it deemed to be special Government employees filed a financial disclosure report and steered clear of conflicts of interest. Many others were not checked for financial conflicts. Indeed, the White House scoffed at the idea of a conflict, relying on the questionable defense that health care reform—whatever its content or contours—is not a "particular matter."

The better approach would have been to use outside persons as representatives of their employer or profession, rather than as government employees. This would have more readily triggered application of FACA, opening up meetings and records. It also would have avoided the widespread suspicion that the Administration's proposed Health Care Security Act was developed in secret by persons with a direct financial or professional stake in the fate of health care legislation. It further would have avoided conflict-of-interest allegations that beset the working group.

The way in which the White House wanted to use such outsiders is precisely why there is a law requiring (semi-) organized meetings to be open to the public. Unlike Federal employees, outsiders are not required to resign from their outside affiliations or dispose of any of their financial holdings. Thus, the public does not have any assurance that these individuals are pursuing the public interest, free of particular private interests in the matter. The sunshine of open meetings and availability of advisory committee records are the public's primary protections against the improper or inordinate influence of special interests. Here, the White House wanted it both ways. Bring in outsiders, but keep the process from public view (and, in the process, ignore the law).

Thus, the White House deserves criticism for creating such a Byzantine structure for such an important undertaking, and for keeping the working group's efforts out of the public's view for over a year until confronted by the realities of litigation.

The White House (Magaziner and the Counsel's office) made matters worse by asserting first, that the outside persons who were not made part of the Federal workforce (either regular employees or special Government employees) would not perform any supervision or decisionmaking, when the district court found that some of them indeed did. Second, it asserted that all of these outsiders would adhere to the same ethical standards to which regular Federal employees are subject. The White House did not, and could not, live up to this latter assertion. It fell to the Justice Department to explain, unconvincingly, that the comprehensive nature of health care reform and the preliminary stage of its development made the conflict-of-interest statute inapplicable. This position, even assuming that it is a correct statement of law, did nothing to dispel concerns that certain special interests were playing prominent roles behind the scenes in shaping the Administration's plan to their liking.

In two respects, Ira Magaziner's March 1993 declaration in the lawsuit challenging the Health Care Task Force was misleading. The district court's identical conclusion led to calls for the appointment of an independent counsel. Attorney General Janet Reno correctly determined that Magaziner's conduct could be investigated fairly within the Justice Department, although it would have been better to assign the matter to the Public Integrity Section of the Criminal Division, rather than to the presidentially appointed U.S. Attorney Eric Holder.

The decision of the U.S. Attorney's office not to prosecute Magaziner appears correct because the apparent lack of evidence that Magaziner intentionally misled the court. Although the U.S. Attorney's office charitably refrained from expressly finding Magaziner's declaration misleading, the facts as revealed in its own analysis show that the declaration was indeed materially misleading in several respects. And it also appears that the White House Counsel's office (and perhaps the Justice Department attorneys) knew of its misleading nature, if not on March 3, 1993, then soon thereafter, but did nothing to apprise the plaintiffs or court of its misstatements.

The U.S. Attorney's office correctly identified the negligence and mistakes made by the White House Counsel's office, in drafting the Magaziner declaration and in failing to correct or amend the declaration to comport with the evolutionary nature of the working group, and (to a lesser extent) those made by Justice Department attorneys in their conduct of the litigation. Leaving aside the question of whether anyone in the White House acted in bad faith, it is clear that the White House Counsel's office acquitted itself very poorly in the conduct and defense of the lawsuit, and may be more responsible for Ira Magaziner's legal travails than Magaziner himself. We know that Magaziner relied on the White House Counsel's office to draft the declaration; however, we do not know the extent to which the Counsel's office relied on Magaziner, the architect of the multilayered process, for knowledge about how the working group was expected to operate. Thus, Magaziner may not be blameless, either.

The one large piece of the puzzle that remains missing, even after the U.S. Attorney's office's analysis, is the relationship between the Justice Department's Civil Division and the White House Counsel's office. Why did the White House draft Magaziner's declaration instead of a Justice lawyer? What advice did the White House receive from Justice on FACA before drafting the declaration? Did the Civil Division lawyers assume, or did they assure themselves, that Magaziner's declaration was truthful and accurate? If so, how did they assure themselves? What understanding did the Civil Division lawyers have of the meaning of the terms used in Magaziner's declaration? Did they rely on representations from the White House Counsel's office that were false or incorrect? Answers may result from an Office of Professional Responsibility (OPR) investigation of the conduct of the Civil Division lawyers, if one is conducted. If not, a congressional investigation is in order, because the roles both the White House and Justice Department played in this matter, including how they dealt with each other, represent appropriate lines for further inquiry.

The White House Travel Office Firings

A third major ethics problem for the White House in 1993 resulted from the abrupt dismissal in May of all seven White House Travel Office employees. No other matter raising concerns about the ethics of the Clinton Administration was as heavily reported or investigated. Editorials and op-ed pieces were especially harsh on the President and the White House, and justifiably so. White House officials made a series of missteps and engaged in many improper activities in the Travel Office matter. Several officials with a personal and some with a financial stake in the matter inappropriately participated in the internal review of the Travel Office, the virtually simultaneous decision to fire the entire Travel Office staff, and the contemporaneous efforts to manipulate the process so as to justify the firings by reference to findings of misconduct and the predicate for a Federal criminal investigation.

In particular, Catherine Cornelius, a distant cousin of the President, was interested in taking over the reins of the Travel Office. Cornelius had served as Director of Travel Services for the Clinton-Gore campaign and for the transition, where she used the services of World Wide Travel. Even before the Inauguration, Cornelius began pushing to restructure the Travel Office and become its director. David Watkins hired Cornelius, after which she authored memoranda to Watkins recommending changes in the Travel Office. In one of them, she and her colleague and coauthor, Clarissa Cerda, proposed that each would serve as "co-directors of travel," and that World Wide Travel would serve as outside travel agent. Watkins tasked Cornelius to study the Travel Office's operations and report back on whether the Office should be restructured. Cornelius took this assignment as license to take documents home and overhear intra-office conversations.

On a second front, Harry Thomason, a Hollywood producer and close friend of the Clintons, who had worked on the Inaugural and now had an office in the White House, along with his business partner Darnell Martens began lodging complaints about the Travel Office with the White House, alleging misconduct and a refusal to permit competition for charter business. Thomason and Martens were two of three owners of TRM, an aviation consulting business that represents and advises air charter companies, such as Air Advantage, which served as the charter airline for the Clinton-Gore campaign. Thomason and Martens made several appeals to the White House to open up the press charter business to competitive bidding so that TRM might serve as the broker and Air Advantage might get some or all of the White House press corps business.

The White House improperly replaced the Travel Office staff with officials from World Wide and Air Advantage whom White House officials knew from the presidential campaign. This step was taken without engaging in competitive bidding, although the general press outcry cut short the time these friends worked in the Travel

Office, and the White House thereafter began to bid press charters competitively.

The participation of White House officials with a personal or financial stake in the matter did not just present a problem of appearances; it also constituted violations of the standards of conduct in that they used their public office for private gain and gave preferential treatment to their Arkansan friends and former business or campaign associates. Another person with a financial stake in the Travel Office, Harry Thomason, should have been regarded as a special Government employee subject to the same ethics standards for regular White House officials, considering his role and activities in the White House. As a government employee, Thomason's conduct arguably violated the criminal conflict-of-interest law, because he participated personally and substantially in a particular matter in which, to his knowledge, he had a financial interest.

White House officials, including but not limited to Vince Foster and William Kennedy, put pressure on the FBI to initiate a criminal investigation of the Travel Office employees and then interfered with both the Bureau's timing and public explanation of the investigation. White House officials clearly influenced the FBI's decision to initiate an investigation, nothwithstanding the denials from the FBI. It strains credulity to believe that the FBI would have decided that a criminal investigation was warranted in the absence of the pressures brought to bear at the White House. Although it was not improper for the White House to seek the assistance of the FBI in the first place (assuming the improper motives of Thomason, Martens, and Cornelius were not known to Foster and Kennedy), the White House clearly overstepped in how it presented to the FBI the need to come to a quick decision. Worse was the White House's rewriting and then release of an FBI press statement. Even worse was Foster's insistence that the FBI investigation, for which the White House initially pushed so vigorously, should take a back seat to the Peat Marwick review and that the FBI was not welcome to observe the Peat Marwick review.

The White House's public statements on May 19, 1993 and thereafter were lacking in candor. The White House had ample authority to dismiss the Travel Office employees without cause, but chose instead to attempt to justify the firings based on findings of misconduct. In doing so, the White House misled the public as to what prompted the internal review of the Travel Office in the first place as well as the reason for the dismissal of the Travel Office employees.

As in other episodes, the White House appeared to have reached internal agreement on how to explain the firings, but that explanation—or more accurately, those explanations—did not comport with the facts. Even the President misspoke on more than one occasion, although it is not clear whether he did so intentionally, negligently, or that he simply was given bad information from a compromised staff. Foremost among these misstatements was the repeated insistence that the firings came about as a result of mismanagement uncovered by a review conducted by Peat Marwick as part of the Vice President's National Performance Review. In fact, the decision to fire the employees was probably made on May 13, **before** the Peat Marwick team even began its three-day review, and was based solely on allegations made by Thomason, Martens, and Cornelius, all of whom had at least a personal stake in replacing the Travel Office staff.

The White House did "reprimand" four White House officials (Watkins, Cornelius, Kennedy, and Jeff Eller), although the reprimands consisted only in the (incorrect) public statement at the July 2, 1993 press conference that they each **had been** reprimanded. The opprobrium that resulted from being criticized by name in the White House Management Review and at a White House press conference should not be underestimated. Yet, Foster and George Stephanopoulos at a minimum (and perhaps Dee Dee Myers) should also have been given reprimands for their role in the Travel Office matter.

The FBI deserves a measure of criticism for allowing itself to be put in a position where, **in a single afternoon** on May 13, 1993, it concluded (1) there was not sufficient evidence to warrant a criminal investigation; (2) there was sufficient evidence to warrant a criminal investigation; (3) the criminal investigation could wait for the conduct of a Peat Marwick review. Even if the FBI agents truly believe they were not pressured into changing their assessment of the facts, the FBI acted precipitously in finding that a sufficient criminal predicate existed, based solely on the allegations of Cornelius and the documents she presented to them.

Once the FBI agreed with the White House that there was sufficient evidence to conduct a criminal investigation—assuming that conclusion was made in good faith and was correct—the FBI should not have allowed the Peat Marwick review to take place. Moreover, the FBI did not safeguard the integrity of the Travel Office documents during the Peat Marwick review (from which it was shut out) and thereafter.

Within a week of their firing, five of the seven Travel Office employees were reinstated; within a couple of months, the Justice Department informed them that they were neither targets nor subjects of the investigation. The head of the Office, Billy Dale, remained under investigation and was eventually indicted on one count of embezzlement and one count of conversion. Notably, the indictment did not include the kickback allegation made by Thomason (he called it a rumor) and Cornelius. Dale's indictment was cited by the White House as justification for its initial decision to remove Dale and the other Travel Office employees and to conduct an audit of the Travel Office. Dale was acquitted, however, despite being precluded from putting on evidence to show the improper motivations for the firings and the destruction of exculpatory logs and other papers by one or more improperly motivated persons. Dale's acquittal raises a serious question whether the White House, Attorney General, or FBI improperly encouraged the Department of Justice to prosecute a weak case in which the evidence fell short of the standard generally used by Federal prosecutors.

The White House Management Review of the Travel Office matter, although candidly acknowledging a series of inappropriate and improper actions, was faulty in several significant respects. First, the Management Review did not analyze the conduct of White House officials under the standards of ethical conduct; indeed, it is not apparent that anyone in the White House Counsel's office participated in the review (other than Foster and Kennedy, who were interviewed). Second, the Management Review failed to appreciate that several persons (namely, Cornelius, Thomason, and Martens) not only had a personal stake, but a financial stake in the matter. Third, the Management Review failed to acknowledge that White House officials engaged in improper conduct, not simply that they were insufficiently attentive to appearances of impropriety. Most notable in this respect was the Management Review's failure to appreciate the egregiousness of Foster's request to the FBI to desist from any action while the Peat Marwick review was conducted.

Another significant failure of the Management Review was in downplaying, if not ignoring, the substantial participation of the First Lady in monitoring developments and essentially providing the go-ahead (if not the direct order) to conduct a pretextual internal investigation and subsequently fire the Travel Office staff. The Management Review also ignored the responsibility of Vince Foster for much of the conduct of William Kennedy, for which Kennedy, not Foster, was criticized. Kennedy, although deserving of a reprimand based on his conversations and meeting with the FBI post-May 12, was clearly following Foster's direction. Kennedy's initial call to the FBI on May 12 and his expressions of urgency came from Foster. Indeed, it was Foster, not Kennedy, who prevailed on the FBI to postpone its investigation. Reportedly, both Foster and Bernard Nussbaum believed that Kennedy was made to shoulder a disproportionate share of the blame in the Travel Office matter.

The completeness and accuracy of the Management Review's investigation was also called into question by the review subsequently conducted by the General Accounting Office (GAO), although GAO failed to include in its report many important details it obtained through its interviews. Nonetheless, the GAO Report provided more information than did the White House Management Review to support the criticism of White House officials. But its analysis of the conduct of White House officials suffered from the similar failure of seeing the ethical problems only in terms of appearances or as an already-fixed management problem. GAO's analysis of the applicability of the conflict-of-interest statute to Harry Thomason was plainly inadequate. And GAO chose to omit many clarifying (as well as damning) details of what occurred, with the effect of shielding the First Lady and others from criticism.

A study conducted by House Republicans brought to light the facts uncovered (but not revealed) by GAO. In so doing, it raised several questions about what had occurred as well as the adequacy of the previous White House and GAO investigations. These outstanding questions warranted an additional congressional investigation, which the House Committee on Government Reform and Oversight began in the fall of 1995 with an initial hearing in October. The hearing shed more light on the involvement of Harry Thomason and the First Lady, as well as highlighted the White House's resistance to the investigations conducted by GAO and the Justice Department's Office of Professional Responsibility. Additional hearings should be held to explore the remaining questions, including whether Dale's prosecution was conducted in accordance with Justice Department guidelines and free of involvement by the White House, FBI, or political officials at the Justice Department.

The President's Use of Consultants
A fourth area in which the White House has shown its insensitivity to ethics concerns is the President's heavy use of informal advisers whom the White House does not consider Federal employees. While every President has relied in varying degrees on the advice of persons outside of the Government, and while every President has maintained a regular line of communication with his party's key officials, this President's reliance on the advice and counsel of advisers and consultants who are not Federal employees appears unprecedented. The manner in which these advisers have functioned in the White House, as much as the scope and extent of their involvement in official government decisionmaking, renders them largely indistinguishable from senior White House staff. Informal advisers appear to have played a

critical role in virtually every significant action President Clinton has taken in office.

The presence of these advisers raises a host of ethical concerns, because the advisers have jobs, interests, clients and affiliations outside of Government. And yet, because they are not considered Federal employees, they are not subject to the conflict-of-interest laws or required by law to submit a financial disclosure report.

When an informal adviser performs functions that ordinarily would be performed by a government employee, the adviser risks being considered a "special Government employee" (SGE). An SGE is not necessarily required to sever any outside financial interest or affiliation, but is subject to the criminal conflict-of-interest statute, which prohibits the adviser from providing counsel or otherwise participating in any particular matter in which he has a financial interest. In order to remedy an identified conflict or potential conflict, SGEs must either rid themselves of the conflicting interest or association or recuse themselves from the matter which gives rise to the conflict. Also, most SGEs must file a confidential financial disclosure report (some must file public reports) within thirty days of assuming their duties. These reports are intended to assist agency ethics officials in identifying potential conflicts of interest.

The meaning of the term "special Government employee" remains elusive; yet whether an adviser is subject to certain criminal laws turns on this meaning. The line between an SGE subject to the criminal conflict-of-interest laws and a non-government person not subject to any ethics standards is unclear. A continuum exists, from the onetime visit with the President, to the periodic one-on-one visits by the President's pollster, to regular participation in White House meetings, to the adviser with a White House pass, office, and phone. Harry Thomason and Paul Begala were far enough along this continuum to be considered SGEs (although the White House did not so conclude), and Dick Morris should be regarded as one now. It is not clear whether the law covered any of the other regular advisers, but the matter needed and needs examination and findings.

An ethics concern exists regardless of whether or not an adviser is technically considered a SGE. Because the adviser is often given access to the White House that is not otherwise given to persons outside of the Government, the suspicion may arise that the adviser may be acting on behalf of a client or in furtherance of a financial or fiduciary interest in addition to, or instead of, providing advice based on the adviser's general experience, expertise, or political perspective. Thus, the public may conclude that the adviser (and the interests he represents) are being given special access and preferential treatment, in violation of the standards of conduct.

The White House was very slow to acknowledge the potential for any ethical problems. It took a major scandal (the Travel Office firings, in which Harry Thomason played a central role) and a minor one (the inordinate delays in processing White House passes and conducting security checks of many of the advisers), the dogged persistence of Representative Frank Wolf, and several detailed, published reports of the advisers' prominence inside the White House, before the Clinton Administration took steps to address the problem. To their credit, the four main political consultants (James Carville, Paul Begala, Mandy Grunwald, and Stanley Greenberg) at the outset took some measures on their own initiative. Yet it was disingenuous for the four to state that they "stick to political consulting," if by that statement they mean to suggest they do not get involved with official government policy. Bob Woodward's

Agenda and Elizabeth Drew's *On The Edge* completely refute that explanation. Similarly, Dick Morris may be called a political adviser, but he clearly has been identified as involved centrally in official White House policy deliberations.

The steps the White House subsequently took were partly constructive and helpful, partly symbolic, and in the end highly inadequate. First, in September 1993, in satisfaction of a recommendation of the White House Management Review of the Travel Office firings, the White House announced a new policy limiting access to the White House. Second, also as a result of the Management Review, the White House Counsel's office gave one or more ethics briefings to the political consultants. Third, in March 1994, the four political consultants were directed to submit the necessary paperwork to undergo the full field FBI background investigation. This action was taken in response to media and congressional criticism. Fourth, in June 1994, also in response to media and congressional criticism, the four political consultants were required to file financial disclosure statements, both initially and on an annual basis. All of these steps, while they were reactive and late in coming, were nonetheless steps in the right direction. On closer examination, however, they are far from adequate.

The access policy was, in the end, merely a limit on the number of persons able to may obtain "blue" White House passes. As the White House's experience with Dick Morris shows, this policy does not limit any outside adviser's access to the White House, provided an appointment is made beforehand with a member of the White House staff. Other than the cachet a White House pass signifies, it only reduces the time and hassle involved in entry to and exit from the White House complex. The access policy also expressly permits White House passes to be issued to persons "retained" by the Democratic National Committee (DNC) "whose duties require regular consultation with the President and his staff," and permits the Chief of Staff to provide a White House pass to other non-government persons upon a showing of exceptional circumstances. Thus, the access policy is more a symbolic limitation than a real one.

Requiring the four political consultants to undergo a full field FBI background investigation made sense because of their regular presence in the White House. The White House's initiation of ethics briefings for informal advisers was a positive step and should be institutionalized for all informal advisers on whom the President and White House staff depends, not just the four political consultants who received ethics briefings in the fall of 1993. What the advisers were told is not known, but, at a minimum, they should have been told what actions and conduct they must refrain from to avoid becoming an SGE. They also should have been told that so long as they are being called upon as individuals and not as representatives of special or specified interests, the advisers will be treated as if they are subject to the conflict-of-interest laws.

If, as is likely, the White House did not institute a recusal policy, whereby an adviser may not participate in any particular matter in which he has a financial interest, it was imperative for the President and senior White House staff to be aware of an adviser's financial interests, so that any advice given could be put in the proper context. Either way, the advisers should have been required to disclose their financial interests to the White House.

The White House's policy requiring the four political consultants to file a financial disclosure is clearly inadequate. No financial disclosure is required of informal advisers who neither hold nor seek to hold a White House pass. Moreover, if Carville and others surrendered their blue White House passes, as reported, they are no longer required to file an annual report, yet they are just as free to continue to provide advice within the White House. And Dick Morris was not required to submit a report until *USA Today* reported Morris' non-filing as an "ethics loophole." The financial disclosure directive also is confined to "political advisers or political consultants." Thus, informal advisers without a formal relationship with the DNC, such as Vernon Jordan, Betsey Wright, and Susan Thomases, do not appear to be covered—yet another loophole in the directive.

In sum, the White House's policies on informal consultants appear largely to be responses to media and congressional criticism, rather than institutionalized policies to guard against conflicts of interest.

The Response of The President and White House to Allegations of Misconduct Concerning Events before Bill Clinton became President

Although this study does not examine the allegations of misconduct before the President was sworn in, it does look at how the President and White House have responded to the allegations concerning Bill Clinton's past that have surfaced and resurfaced since his Inauguration. How the President and White House respond to a scandal is an important factor in evaluating the integrity of a President and his Administration, because of the risk that a President may improperly enlist the powers of his office to contain the adverse reports or prevent them from surfacing in the first place. This is an area where the Clinton White House has, for the most part, performed very poorly.

Three matters remain prominent: the response of the White House to the Whitewater and Madison Guaranty stories and investigations; the President's response to allegations of sexual indiscretions and improper use of state resources made by several Arkansas State troopers; and the Clintons' establishment of a legal defense fund to cover legal fees incurred in connection with the Whitewater investigations and the Paula Jones lawsuit alleging sexual harassment.[33]

Whitewater in Washington

As of this writing, the full story of the White House's response to Vince Foster's death and the Madison and Whitewater investigations is not known. Further Senate hearings may shed light on what happened, and months (if not years) from now, the independent counsel's report may also provide additional information or perspective. But it is most likely that the public will never know for certain the answers to many of the large questions involving Whitewater in Washington. It will be up to the public to weigh the conflicting testimony, the plethora of "I don't recalls" from White House officials versus the mostly solid recollections of career investigators, agents, and attorneys, and come to a judgment. But a few conclusions can be made.

First, White House officials engaged in many activities in furtherance of the Clintons' personal interests. By failing to observe the basic distinction between what is personal and what is official, White House officials violated the standards of conduct. They used their public office for the Clintons' personal benefit; they allowed the use of nonpublic information for unauthorized purposes; and, overall, they gave the appearance of attempting to interfere in law enforcement investigations in order to attend to the personal interests of the Clintons.

Second, the White House consistently failed to level with the media and the public as to what happened in Washington and why. The testimony of White House and Treasury officials, in both 1994 and 1995 hearings, constitute clear evidence of malfeasance on this score. The Whitewater documents initially were withheld from the public on a questionable legal basis; even their release two years later was piecemeal, raising further questions. The White House was not forthright with the public as to the July 20, 1993, search of Foster's office, the discovery of Whitewater files in Foster's office, the transmission of the Whitewater files to the Executive Residence, and the transmission of the files to Justice. Roger Altman, Deputy Treasury Secretary, was not forthright with Congress about his meetings and conversations with the White House. The testimony of Treasury and White House officials concerning conversations between and among them often conflicted; memories regularly failed at opportune moments. The White House assumed a damage control posture from the very beginning (perhaps as early as Foster's death, if not the 1992 campaign), keeping the public from a full and timely accounting of the Clintons' conduct concerning Whitewater and Madison, as well as the White House's conduct with respect to the investigations.

Third, Administration officials in the White House, Treasury and Justice Department, and RTC headquarters acted in many ways that **appear** as attempts to affect the conduct of the RTC's and Justice Department's investigation of Madison. These included attempting to dissuade Altman from recusing himself; protesting the hiring of Jay Stephens and asking whether the decision was final; relaying nonpublic information about the investigation to persons whose conduct is at issue in that investigation; declining the RTC's first referral and refusing to negotiate with David Hale (decisions taken by the U.S. Attorney Paula Casey); removing Jean Lewis from the investigation; visiting the Kansas City office (by April Breslaw) to express headquarters' views about the outcome of the investigation; and suspending Lewis and her supervisors for several days pending an investigation into their conduct. Any one of these might be discounted as minor or innocuous. When all these are considered together, however, there is, at a minimum, a clear appearance that the Administration attempted to ensure that the Madison investigation did the least amount of political (as well as legal) damage to the Clintons—and that it did so in violation of the Standards of Conduct.

Of course, all these clumsy efforts thus far have produced exactly the opposite of the White House's intentions. The White House, more than any other person or entity, has succeeded in transforming Whitewater from an arcane and stale Arkansas financial and real estate scandal into a present-day Washington scandal, felling the political careers of four Presidential appointees (Altman, Hanson, Nussbaum, Hubbell), keeping regular occupancy of page one of the national press, subjecting the White House staff to legal bills and adverse publicity unprecedented since Watergate, and failing utterly to dissipate the ethical cloud over the Clintons.

The Aftermath of Vince Foster's Death

The special Senate Committee established in May 1995 held thirteen days of hearings in July and August 1995, focusing almost exclusively on the conduct of the White House following Foster's death. Additional hearings, some of which concerned the aftermath of Foster's death, were held in November and December. Yet, a clear picture of what occurred still has not emerged, and given the conflicting testimony and failures of memory, we may never know for certain what actually happened. But some observations can be made at this point.

The July 20, 1993 visit to Foster's office. White House officials should not have entered Foster's office the night of his death without at least notifying the Park Police, since the Park Police had expressed an interest in searching the office and sealing it pending the search. It is not clear whether Patsy Thomasson, Bernard Nussbaum, or Maggie Williams knew of the Park Police's request that the office be sealed at the time they went through Foster's office, but others in the White House were aware of this that night. **If** these three officials were not aware of the Park Police's investigative interests, and **if,** as they have testified, they did not remove any documents (Williams' testimony has been rebutted by a Secret Service agent), then they committed no wrongdoings. It is natural for friends and colleagues of someone who is suspected of committing suicide to look for a note. Still, the presence of Williams **and** Thomasson **and** Nussbaum suggests another motive in looking for a note other than to discern Foster's reason for taking his life.

The procedure employed for the July 22 search. On July 21, the Justice Department reached an agreement with Nussbaum on a procedure to search Foster's office. By the next day, however, Nussbaum had changed his mind. Why? There is evidence that Nussbaum's change of mind was prompted by what he took from a conversation with Susan Thomases that the First Lady wished that investigators not get "unfettered access" to Foster's office.

Given the privileged nature of many of Foster's documents, it was proper for Nussbaum to attend to those privileges. All official White House documents are privileged to some extent, because the Freedom of Information Act does not apply to the White House Office. However, White House Counsel Nussbaum was not shielding documents from the press, or the public, or even from Congress. **He was shielding documents from investigators of Executive Branch agencies**. Governmental privileges are not lost or waived by sharing documents with law enforcement agencies, especially if the documents remain physically in the White House. The media could not obtain these documents had they been reviewed by the Park Police or Justice Department. In any event, Nussbaum could have sufficiently protected the privileged nature of the documents by conducting the search pursuant to the understanding reached with Justice the day before. Essentially, White House Counsel Nussbaum conducted the search of Foster's office, not the investigators, and the investigators were at his mercy in terms of what they saw of the documents or knew of their contents.

The Whitewater documents in Foster's office were not government records. As such, no governmental privilege attached to them. The documents may have been protected by the attorney-client privilege, although this is far from certain, given Foster's dual role in the White House, as well as the content of the files. By allowing a government official (Foster) to be privy to the documents, the Clintons may have waived the privilege. In any event, Nussbaum was not the person to assert or protect that privilege. Nussbaum should have called for the Clintons' personal attorney to participate in the search; he should have realized from the start that Foster's office would contain some personal records of the Clintons, given the internal notoriety of Foster's personal work for the Clintons. Park Police and Justice investigators could have dealt with the Clintons' personal attorney separately.

Transferring the Clintons' Whitewater file to the Clintons or their attorney. Nussbaum was likely correct in determining that Foster's Whitewater file was the property of the Clintons. At this point, the documents could have been sent to the Clintons' personal attorney, or to the Clintons. If the documents were in fact the Clintons' property, it was entirely appropriate for the Clintons to review them, at their discretion. The handling of the Clintons' Whitewater file was controversial mainly because of (1) conflicting statements and testimony as to where the documents would go and whether they would be reviewed by the Clintons; (2) the belated revelation that Foster's office contained the Clinton's personal Whitewater files; and (3) the even more belated admission that the documents remained in the Residence for several days before being picked up by the Clintons' personal attorney.

The July 26 discovery and subsequent handling of the torn-up handwritten note. The official White House account of the discovery of the note (the testimony of Neuwirth, Nussbaum, and Sloan) is suspect, because of the testimony of nearly everyone else who observed the July 22 search or worked in the West Wing Counsel's office. The torn-up note should have been discovered then; a Foster family lawyer testified that it may have been discovered immediately thereafter. The mystery surrounding its discovery, as well as the inordinate delay in providing the note to investigators, fuels suspicion that the note was tampered with. In October 1995, three handwriting experts announced that the note was a forgery. The reasons for the delay in alerting law enforcement—notifying Mrs. Foster and the President—are legitimate, but should not have required twenty-seven hours to satisfy. (It is also curious that Susan Thomases was apparently told of the note before the President.) The delay suggests that the White House contemplated not turning over the note, but there was no testimony to this effect.

The White House's Response to the Requests for Whitewater Documents

The White House initially rebuffed media requests for the Clintons' Whitewater files found in Foster's office. The documents were eventually turned over to the Justice Department, pursuant to a subpoena. Once the subpoena was issued, the Clintons were for the most part off the hook. Most observers in the media and some Republicans accepted uncritically the explanation that the subpoena operated to keep the Whitewater documents from public view, but did criticize the discussions between the Clintons' attorney, David Kendall, and the Justice Department. They were wrong on both counts. Lawyers, on the other hand, for the most part found nothing improper or unusual in David Kendall's discussions with Justice or his request for a subpoena.

Because the Clintons' involvement in Whitewater and Madison does not relate to the actions of the President or First Lady in their Federal roles, it was correct to use David Kendall, instead of White House lawyers, to handle the requests for the Clintons' Whitewater documents. Moreover, as of December 1993, the Whitewater files physically were not in the White House (unless they were kept in the Executive

Residence). Many press reports refer—incorrectly as far as is known—to the White House as the (or at least an) active player in discussions with the Justice Department concerning the documents. The White House alas contributed to this misperception: senior White House aides repeatedly answered reporters' questions as if the matters involved official government documents. Even public statements made by White House officials about the documents should have been avoided, because such statements could be seen as indirect, but not-so-subtle, White House directions to Justice Department political appointees.

Contrary to what was widely reported, neither the grand jury subpoena nor the transmission of the Whitewater documents to the Justice Department prevented them from being released to the public. Criticism of the President for not releasing the Whitewater files largely subsided when the President agreed to turn over the documents to the Justice Department and a subpoena was served soon thereafter. The media accepted the explanation that the subpoena prevented the public from obtaining the Whitewater documents. But this explanation is not true; no law stood in the way of a public release of the Clintons' Whitewater documents.

The entirety of Whitewater documents were created outside the grand jury—indeed, all the documents were created before the grand jury was convened—and were created and maintained for other purposes. Pre-existing documents are not covered by grand jury secrecy rules. Thus, if the Clintons desired to turn over their Whitewater files to the public, they could have done so. **Indeed, the Clintons and White House did provide at least some of these documents to Congress and to the media, on a selective basis, two years later**.

The White House's Failure to Separate the Personal from the Official

The Clinton White House has repeatedly demonstrated its failure to observe the fundamental distinction between matters of interest to the Government and matters that are personal to the Clintons. At the margins, the distinction between what is official and what is personal may not be clear, but the distinction is critical nonetheless. There are occasions when the interests of the presidency may diverge from the personal interests of the President, requiring Federal officials, such as the White House Counsel, to give allegiance to the President only in his official capacity. Most of the time the White House staff has shown little regard for this distinction; White House officials have played various roles assisting the President and First Lady with personal affairs.

The two most celebrated examples come from the White House Counsel's office, Bernard Nussbaum and Vince Foster. White House Counsel Nussbaum probably lost his job because, after vigorously asserting the Clintons' personal interests during the search of Vince Foster's office, he continued to attend to their personal interests relating to Whitewater. Foster was criticized after his death for having continued to serve, formally or informally, as the Clintons' personal attorney while also serving as Deputy Counsel to the President. In the end, Foster's personal work for the Clintons did not violate any law. However, in doing so, Foster went beyond his official duties, and he was responsible for bringing Whitewater documents into the White House Office (as opposed to the Executive Residence) that would prove to be a sustaining headache for the White House after his death.

But the problem with the White House has been endemic. In 1993 and early

1994, Bruce Lindsey served as the White House official to respond to specific questions reporters posed about the Clintons' financial affairs and about alleged extramarital conduct by Governor Clinton. And the problem has not been confined to responding to media requests. White House officials proactively sought information about the Madison and David Hale investigations and even attempted to affect the conduct (questioning the hiring of Jay Stephens) and supervision (resisting the recusal of Roger Altman) of the Madison investigation.

Later, when a Special Counsel was appointed and Congress contemplated hearings, damage control teams were set up, with John Podesta and then Mark Fabiani serving as spokesmen. At this point, some White House involvement was necessary to respond to requests for official White House documents and the testimony of White House officials. But there would have been no White House documents and no information to elicit from White House staff had the White House not brought the Whitewater affair into the White House in the first place by its insistence on handling media inquiries relating to Whitewater.

When questions arose during the 1992 campaign concerning the Clintons' investment in Whitewater and their relationship to the McDougals and Madison Guaranty, it was natural for the campaign to prepare the candidate to respond. After Foster died on July 20, 1993, the Whitewater files found in his office on July 22 were properly sent to the Clintons in the Executive Residence and eventually given to the Clintons' personal attorney. At this point, Whitewater was neither a matter of public concern nor (apparently) a concern within the White House.

That changed in September 1993, when word came to the White House, via Treasury Department political appointees, that the RTC had prepared a set of referrals to the Justice Department in which the Clintons were named as potential beneficiaries of alleged illegal conduct. Also in September 1993, David Hale's allegation that Governor Clinton pressured him to make a loan to a company owned by fellow-Whitewater owner Susan McDougal surfaced in the Arkansas media. (There are indications that the White House knew of Hale's difficulties—and perhaps his allegations—earlier through communications from the SBA or Hale's attorney.) This was the critical juncture for the White House. Should the White House get involved in preparing for and answering media inquiries concerning the Clintons' personal investment decisions made years before he became President, or should the matter be handled by the Clintons' personal attorney and accountant? There is no indication that anyone in the White House even flagged the issue, much less urged that these matters be handled privately. Instead, White House officials, many of whom had endured the brief Whitewater controversy during the campaign, naturally assumed that they would get involved in order to defend and protect the Clintons. This was an enormous mistake, revealing the political rather than the institutional mode of White House conduct.

Once the Clintons retained a personal attorney to handle their business affairs (Robert Barnett then David Kendall), all questions directed to the White House from the media relating to Whitewater or Madison Guaranty (as well as questions about the trooper allegations) should have been referred to their private attorney. This would have allowed the President and the White House to devote their full attention to official Government matters, and would have avoided the steady tide of conflicting, uninformed, and disingenuous statements from the White House staff on these matters. It also could have kept the White House staff from engaging in various information-gathering activities with Treasury Department and Small Business Administration officials.

Most White House officials have no personal knowledge about what occurred relating to Madison and Whitewater, and thus they were put in a difficult position, risking misstatements and inaccuracies, when called upon to answer Whitewater questions. Even the Clintons' Arkansas friends, such as Mac McLarty, Bruce Lindsey, and Patsy Thomasson, could not be completely aware of the Clintons' financial investments. But even assuming that the Clintons could and did inform the White House staff of their opinions, their recollection of the facts, and supplied them with their Whitewater documents, it would not be appropriate for White House staff to engage in major activities regarding the matter, because they did not concern Bill Clinton as President or Hillary Rodham Clinton as First Lady. Moreover, the involvement of White House staff in information-gathering and "heads ups" served to bring the Whitewater controversy into the West Wing. Without any White House staff involvement, there would be no White House documents of interest to Congress or the independent counsel and no information to elicit from White House staff.

There is some evidence that the White House gradually realized its error, as David Kendall (concerning Whitewater and the First Lady's commodity trades) and Bob Bennett (concerning the Paula Jones lawsuit) assumed the proper role of responding to media inquiries. Media squeamishness may be the reason why the Paula Jones allegations did not stick to the White House, but one major reason why the damage resulting from the stories on Mrs. Clinton's commodity trades was limited is that the controversy was confined to the Clintons, and to a period of time antedating the presidency. By contrast, the White House made Whitewater a White House scandal, directly leading to present allegations of perjury and obstruction of justice.

The Administration received a great deal of criticism for several contacts between Treasury officials and members of the White House staff concerning various aspects of the RTC's investigation of Madison. After the initial crescendo of stories in March 1994 about three White House meetings (additional discussions between Treasury officials and senior White House staff were revealed later that month), Special Counsel Robert Fiske immediately subpoenaed each official present at these meetings, as well as others who were privy to the substance of what was discussed; Republicans in the House and Senate called for these officials to appear before Congress to reveal what was discussed; and Bernard Nussbaum resigned.

Fiske issued a report in June 1994 concluding that "the evidence is insufficient to establish that anyone within the White House or the Department of the Treasury acted with the intent to corruptly influence an RTC investigation."[34] He added that his review did not look into the propriety of the meetings or whether anything unethical occurred at the meetings, noting that this determination was up to the Office of Government Ethics. One month later, OGE issued a report on its examination of the Treasury-White House contacts under the standards of conduct, concluding that no ethics standards were violated by current Treasury officials. Although OGE did not find that any Treasury official violated any standard, its conclusion was phrased quite narrowly: "we believe that **you [Secretary Bentsen] might reasonably conclude** that the conduct detailed in the report . . . did not violate the Standards of Ethical Conduct for Employees of the Executive Branch. However, many of the contacts detailed in the report are troubling."[35]

OGE's conclusion, qualified as it was, was based on two premises, both of which are questionable. First, OGE deferred to the White House's view that "dealing with press inquiries regarding the President's and First Lady's personal lives" (regarding alleged misconduct antedating the presidency) is a proper White House function.[36] The second premise was that the **only** purpose of Treasury officials in contacting the White House was to assist the White House in responding to press inquiries. OGE specifically found no intention of any Treasury official to advance another person's private gain. The same cannot be said of White House officials, however.

This study accepts the Fiske judgment that, based on the present record, no White House official intended to obstruct justice in the contacts with Treasury in the fall of 1993 and winter of 1994. However, OGE's reasoning should not be applied in evaluating the conduct of **White House** officials under the **standards of conduct**, because it is inappropriate to apply OGE's premises to the conduct of White House officials.[37] First, there is, for the White House staff, a proper dichotomy between what is official and what is personal, and White House officials failed to observe it. Second, it is clear that there was more than one purpose behind the activities of White House officials in obtaining information about the RTC's referrals.

The issue for White House officials is whether obtaining nonpublic information from Treasury, about matters of personal interest to the Clintons, in order to relay that information to the Clintons (and others), constitutes using public office for private gain. It would seem it does, thus violating a standard of conduct. Moreover, the Treasury-White House contacts surely created the appearance of improper interference with a law enforcement investigation for no official purpose.

White House officials disagreed, of course. Nussbaum, as well as all other White House aides who participated in the contacts with Treasury officials, all asserted an official interest in apprising the President of matters that are likely to break in the press and require the President's response, regardless of whether those matters concern the President in his official or personal capacity. (This explanation would not appear to cover the efforts made to find out about the SBA's investigation of David Hale and Capital Management Services.) Lloyd Cutler, appointed to replace Nussbaum, was promoted by the White House (and Cutler himself) as one who understood the distinction between matters personal and matters official. Yet he defended the Treasury-White House contacts on the same "heads up" rationale. The press query, or "heads up" defense, soon became all-encompassing. George Stephanopoulos, who called Treasury officials to complain about the RTC's hiring of Jay Stephens, justified his actions on the basis of "anticipated" press inquiries! But the Treasury contacts provided information beyond what would have been necessary to discharge an obligation to respond to a media inquiry.

Alleged Interference With the Madison Investigation

Various allegations have been made that White House or Administration officials engaged in improper activities concerning the RTC's investigation of Madison Guaranty, the subsequent handling of the RTC's referrals by the RTC headquarters, the Treasury Department, and the Justice Department, the internal investigations of the Treasury-White House contacts, and the Administration's preparation for congressional hearings.

There have been reports (all of them denied) that Whitewater and Madison Guaranty documents maintained at the Governor's Mansion in Little Rock and at the Rose Law Firm were destroyed during and after the 1992 campaign and as late as January-February 1995, following the appointment of Robert Fiske as Special counsel. It has also been suspected that Whitewater documents maintained in Vince Foster's office were destroyed or tampered with, following Foster's death. Any person who destroyed or tampered with a document after an investigation was commenced, or perhaps even in anticipation of a request or subpoena from the RTC, the United States Attorney, or the Special Counsel, could beprosecuted for obstruction of justice.

From what is now known, the criminal investigation conducted by the independent counsel and the civil investigation pending with the RTC do not appear to have been prejudiced or otherwise affected by these efforts. But these allegations, including the document destruction allegations, have not yet been resolved, and are properly before the independent counsel and the Congress.

The special Senate Committee hearings heard testimony in the fall of 1995 suggesting that the White House was very interested in the SBA's investigation of Capital Management Services and David Hale. Neil Eggleston requested and obtained confidential information from SBA about its investigation, although he denied sharing the information with anyone else and was forced to return the documents a few days later. The most damaging allegation against the White House concerning the SBA investigation, however, was made on December 5 by Steven Irons, of the FBI's Little Rock office. Irons testified that an SBA lawyer told him of a White House effort to enlist the SBA to discredit Hale. The allegation is hearsay, of course, but must be pursued vigorously by the Senate Committee. If true, White House's contacts with SBA officials could prove to be a even greater scandal than what resulted in 1994 from the disclosure of the contacts with the Treasury Department.

At this point, it is important to point out two things: (1) we do not yet know (and may never know) the true extent of the Administration's actions that may have affected the investigation of Madison and Whitewater (and Capital Management Services), and whether they did in fact hinder the investigation; and (2) the **ethics** of the Administration may be justly criticized, and unambiguously, on the basis of the concerted effort by White House and Administration officials to protect the Clintons by using their Federal positions and by failing to level with the public, the Congress, and official investigators in doing so.

The President's Response to the Arkansas Trooper Allegations

In December 1993, several reports surfaced in which Arkansas State troopers who had served on Governor Clinton's security detail recounted a series of alleged personal and official indiscretions by the Governor, most of them of a sexual nature, including the use of State troopers to facilitate these indiscretions. What gave these reports some currency was the personal involvement of the President and others in a concerted effort to kill the story and discredit the allegations. As it turned out, the President was quite fortunate that the primary focus of these reports was on his personal conduct before he became President rather than the serious issue involving possible presidential misconduct in office.

In his article on the trooper allegations in the *American Spectator*, David Brock wrote of the effort of "Clinton and his surrogates" to attempt to "thwart publication of the [troopers' allegations]."[38] Brock described conversations the President had with one trooper, Danny Ferguson, based on the account of another trooper, Roger Perry, in which the President allegedly offered Ferguson a Federal job "explicitly in exchange for his help in thwarting publication of any stories." On December 21, 1993, the day after the Brock story came out, the *Los Angeles Times*, which had conducted its own investigation of the troopers' allegations, featured a lengthy front page article in which the troopers' allegations were detailed: "Two of the troopers say that Clinton, as President, sought to discourage them from speaking out by offering them federal jobs."[39]

Reports that the President offered Federal jobs to one or more Arkansas troopers in an effort to save himself considerable embarrassment present the most serious single allegation against the President. This is because the allegation directly linked President Clinton with the commission of a Federal crime, and because the allegation was not frivolous, but based on sufficient testimonial evidence to warrant a criminal investigation. Section 211 of Title 18 provides that "whoever solicits or receives . . . any money or thing of value, in consideration of the promise of support or use of influence in obtaining for any person any appointive office or place under the United States" is guilty of a felony. This statute would cover the President if he solicited or received anything of value in consideration of assisting a trooper, or promising to assist the trooper, with obtaining a Federal position. That "thing of value" could constitute (1) silence; (2) a change in the troopers' story; (3) refusal to cooperate further with reporters; (4) assistance in preventing publication of any stories; or (5), information on what the other troopers were saying.

The following facts are unrefuted: After the President learned that some members of his former Arkansas security detail were talking to reporters, the President called one of the troopers, Danny Ferguson, and in the course of inquiring into what the troopers were telling reporters and why they were talking, the President and Ferguson discussed the prospect of Federal employment for at least one of the troopers. The only factual issue that is controverted is also critical: whether the President promised, offered, or suggested a Federal job for one or more troopers in return for something of value. Proving an oral offer of a *quid pro quo* is often elusive, however, as it was in this case.

In addition to the President's personal efforts to kill the stories, Bruce Lindsey from inside the White House and Betsey Wright from outside were substantially involved in an effort to discredit the troopers' credibility, primarily by attempting to Ferguson to recant his account of his conversation with the President. This Ferguson would not do, although Ferguson's attorney signed an unusual affidavit that was widely misunderstood by the media as Ferguson's sworn statement. The White House (and those in the media who wanted the story to go away) pointed to the misnamed "Ferguson affidavit" as proof that the jobs-for-something allegation had been refuted. But all Ferguson was willing to say (he spoke with the *Los Angeles Times* after the release of his lawyer's statement) is that the President had not expressed, in so many words, a *quid pro quo*; otherwise, Ferguson stood by his initial account of his conversation.

Imagine if the same allegation—that an official had offered assistance in obtaining a Federal job for a person in exchange for silence or something else of value from that person—surfaced against a mid-ranking Federal official. Would the allegation simply die on its own, after the official denied it, or would the matter be investigated further? Unless the source of the allegation were inherently incredible, a denial would not alone suffice, and the allegation would be referred to the Justice Department for an appropriate investigation, in which both witnesses and subjects would be put under oath.

This is what should have been done in response to the initial reports that the President had offered a Federal job to one or more troopers. The FBI could have interviewed Ferguson and Perry under oath. Then, if their sworn testimony suggested a *quid pro quo* between the President and a trooper, the Bureau could have interviewed the President (and others such as Bruce Lindsey and Betsey Wright) to elicit a direct and specific response to the allegations. The Attorney General could have appointed a special counsel to conduct an independent investigation, if she were concerned about the appearance of a political conflict. But this was not done. Nonetheless, the issue went away following the President's denial and the sort-of-denial from Danny Ferguson; there was little, if any, clamor for an investigation.

Initially, there was a widespread aversion to reporting on the troopers' allegations, because the allegations concerned Bill Clinton's personal life before he became President, or because they tended to present an unflattering image of the President that could hinder his ability to get things done. Although the media for the most part did not relish covering the troopers' allegations, it was clearly legitimate to pursue the job offer issue, because it involved the alleged abuse of (Federal) public office. Yet, instead of calls for an investigation, the media allowed the issue to fade away, and rather quickly, to the obvious relief of the White House (and the apparent relief of the mainstream media and Congress).

There are several possible explanations why the jobs-for-something allegation, as a news story, died so quickly and completely. But as justifications for why there was no call from any of the so-called public interest groups or ethics gadflies for an investigation of this allegation, they are less than satisfactory. A Justice Department investigation, or one conducted by a special or independent counsel, should have been conducted. Not conducting an investigation suggests that the President (or perhaps just this President) enjoys a de facto immunity from investigation of certain criminal offenses, either because of the nature of the presidency, or the nature of the offense, or both. The scope of such immunity, of course, is unclear, to say the least. In all events, it is not too late to conduct such an investigation, and the Attorney General should do so, or explain why not. Congress should also look into why apparently there was no apparent Justice Department inquiry when the story broke, and whether Justice would respond any differently if the same allegations were made against a Federal official other than the President.

The Clintons' Legal Defense Fund

The President's decision to create a legal defense fund to defray his legal expenses was reasonable, under the circumstances, and given the alternatives. The Clintons face legal fees in excess of one million dollars because of the Paula Jones lawsuit and the Whitewater investigations, fees that the President probably would not incur had he not been elected. Presidents, like other politicians, officials, and citizens, should be permitted to set up a fund to receive help in paying legal bills. But a political official should never assume that because a legal defense fund can help pay the bills, that he may hire the highest priced legal talent. The President's decision to retain attorneys who charge in excess of $400 an hour contributes significantly to the magnitude of his legal fees.

None of the President's options was attractive. Allowing one wealthy individual to underwrite his legal expenses was undesirable. So was the notion of accepting free or discounted services from a Washington law firm that simultaneously represents clients with business before the White House and Executive Branch. Setting up a legal defense fund, as other Federal officials had done, was the best of the available options. The Presidential Legal Expense Trust contains several salutary provisions that reduce, but do not eliminate, the appearance that donors are contributing to further a personal or financial interest in a matter before the Government. In particular, providing for periodic public disclosure of contributions, and limiting both who may contribute and the amount of contributions are positive measures. The key disincentive to improperly motivated contributions is public disclosure of all contributions over $200. This disincentive would be strengthened if contributions were reported monthly or quarterly, instead of bi-annually.

The Trust nonetheless was the subject of criticism, some warranted, and some not. Although roundly criticized, the $1000 (per year) limit is reasonable, because it is the same as the limit on individual contributions to candidates for Federal office, and because there is no other widely accepted figure. The initial decision to receive contributions from lobbyists, since reversed, was inconsistent with the President's rhetoric on the pernicious influence of lobbyists, and to this extent it was rightly criticized. In addition, the Clintons could reduce criticism further by rejecting contributions from persons seeking action from or doing business with the Government, regardless of whether they fit the narrower definition of a lobbyist.

Although the President's authority to accept contributions and to set up a Trust was questioned, his authority to accept gifts from any person has long been established in the law and ethics standards. However, the President may not engage in solicitation, directly or indirectly. Thus, the Trust was justifiably criticized, because its express terms allow the trustees to solicit contributions. (As a donor trust instrument set up by the Clintons, solicitation by a trustee would be tantamount to solicitation by the President.) After belatedly consulting with OGE, the trustees subsequently decided that they would not engage in solicitation, thereby avoiding the regulatory proscription against solicitation by the President. The White House Counsel's failure to obtain a written, detailed opinion from OGE before the Trust was established led to some problems that should have been avoided.

It is likely that some contributions resulted from solicitation by trustees after the Trust was created, but before the discovery that solicitation was prohibited by the standards of conduct (only about a three-week period). Although, as a matter of principle, these contributions should be returned, it would likely be impossible to determine whether a contribution was the product of improper solicitation without someone coming forward to admit to this. The Trust could offer the return of any contribution, the donor of which believes resulted from solicitation from a trustee or a Trust employee. But it is highly unlikely that any donor would come forward to ask for a refund. This recommendation is not really practical, but the Trust should ask OGE whether any remedial action needs to be taken, if it has already done so.

The Trust is now operating under much tighter restrictions than when it was first created. In addition to the prohibition on trustee solicitation, contributions by registered lobbyists are now prohibited. The Trust need not return the contributions received to date from lobbyists; the problem, in my view, has always been more one of hypocrisy than of serious concern that a $1000 contribution from a lobbyist would present an improper appearance. In a year's time, lobbyists and the entities they represent contribute much greater sums in "soft money" campaign contributions and in the total contributions made for the Democratic party candidates. An additional $1000 is not going to make any difference.

Allegations Involving Members of the Cabinet

No administration is immune from having one or more Cabinet members embroiled in an ethics scandal. The Reagan Administration saw Ray Donovan, Ed Meese, and Sam Pierce beset with serious ethics inquiries, although the allegations against Pierce were for the most part raised after Pierce left office. The Bush Administration came closest to a clean record among members of the Cabinet. The Clinton Cabinet, by contrast, has featured several members who have been the subject of serious ethics allegations.

Although only Secretary of Agriculture Mike Espy left office under an ethical cloud, Secretaries Brown and Cisneros are both currently the subject of an independent counsel investigation, and Secretary Pena has also been the subject of some controversy.

Secretary Espy

Secretary Espy's conduct in accepting gifts from Tyson Foods, associating with Tyson Foods, and soliciting a gift from Quaker Oats was patently unethical, and violated the standards of conduct for Executive Branch employees. Both Tyson Foods and Quaker Oats are heavily regulated by the Agriculture Department. The fact that Espy's girlfriend, Patricia Dempsey, also accepted gifts from Tyson may raise problems if he had any control over or knowledge of these gifts. Gifts the Secretary received from his friend Richard Douglas, if they were in fact paid by Douglas's company, Sun-Diamond Growers, also violated the gift restrictions. The value of the gifts may be small, but the nature of them demonstrated the Secretary's gross insensitivity to the appearance that he was partial to the poultry industry in general, and Tyson Foods in particular, and further demonstrated his inattention to the standards of conduct. Secretary Espy also did not comply with procedures in requesting approval to accept lodging and transportation from Tyson during an official trip; had he followed procedures, approval probably would not have been given.

The reason Secretary Espy is the subject of an independent counsel investigation, however, is that in accepting gifts from Tyson Foods, he may have violated a criminal provision of the Federal Meat Inspection Act. The Meat Inspection Act imposes a sort of strict liability on Agriculture Department employees who accept anything of value in connection with their work; Espy has some technical defenses that may allow him to escape indictment, but they do not remove the opprobrium he deserves for taking gifts from Tyson and others. The Meat Inspection Act provisions may be arcane, but the principle that a Secretary should not accept gifts or special favors from a company he regulates is not.

The independent counsel is also looking into whether the Secretary violated the general illegal gratuities statute, although what is publicly known does not suggest that Espy took any action as a result of any gift, or that any gift from Tyson was a reward for action taken, thus seemingly negating any *quid pro quo* for which prosecution would be called for. The precise scope of Independent Counsel Smaltz's investigation is unclear. One line of inquiry, concerning allegations that Governor Clinton received cash payments from Tyson, was apparently precluded by the Attorney General and the courts.[40]

Secretary Espy's closeness to Tyson Foods and his acceptance of gifts from the company raise the question whether of he gave preferential treatment to the company, as suggested by several Department actions favorable to the poultry industry. Most intriguing are allegations that Espy and his political appointees stalled a rulemaking on fecal contamination of poultry at the request of Tyson and other poultry interests. There are other allegations that he took official actions favorable to Sun-Diamond Growers and the EOP Group. A final verdict on whether the Secretary improperly accepted gifts from Sun-Diamond Growers, and whether he gave preferential treatment to any of these firms must await the independent counsel's investigation and report. On the reports to date, it can safely be concluded that Secretary Espy was insensitive to appearances of preferential treatment, and that he failed to use the process provided in the standards of conduct to resolve such appearance issues.

In addition, Secretary Espy was found to have used a government car for personal purposes, in violation of Federal law. Lower-ranking Federal employees have received suspensions for similar conduct. Espy also traveled frequently to his hometown of Jackson, Mississippi, on ostensible official business, repeating the sins of many a former presidential appointee, and giving the strong appearance that Secretary Espy was using his public office for his personal benefit, in violation of the standards of conduct.

For months, Secretary Espy steadfastly defended himself, providing a series of explanations: his missteps were technical; they were caused by his inattention to detail; he had reimbursed entities for the gifts and benefits, and had made the Government whole for any alleged misuse of government property; the allegations of favoritism were false, spread by embittered employees; there would have been no controversy had Tyson Foods not been located in the President's home state; and the outstanding job he was doing as Secretary should trump any minor ethical transgressions. The White House, too, defended Espy up to the end, along the lines of "innocent until proven guilty."

Secretary Espy's resignation (or firing) was appropriate under the circumstances. There are conflicting accounts whether he was forced or was asked to resign; no one seems to believe that he simply did so on his own. Departures of Cabinet members under an ethical cloud often are portrayed as voluntary, made for "personal reasons," with little or no acknowledgment of the public controversy encircling the official. When there is a hint of candor, it is usually to the effect that the official resigned for the sake of appearances, not because the official is contrite, much less admitting of any culpability. In truth, most such resignations are forced and are directly related to the reality and extent of ethical misconduct. It is a measure of how large has been the traditional dissonance between resignation statements and reality that the President's prepared statement released on the day Secretary Espy announced his resignation, which was quite gentle (criticizing Espy only for appearances), was reported by the media—probably based on off-the-record "spin" from the White House—as quite critical.

The President should have publicly stated that he had asked for the Secretary's resignation (assuming he or the White House did), or at least issued a reprimand. Once again, the President was unwilling to acknowledge any violation of the standards of conduct by a member of his Administration, criticizing only the improper appearances. True, a high-level official's resignation amid ethics allegations is widely regarded as sufficient damage to one's reputation, so that publicly firing Espy or issuing a reprimand could be seen as overkill, or at least redundant. In Secretary Espy's case, however, the President should have struck a clearer blow for the ethics of his Administration by decrying his conduct, not just lamenting appearances. A reprimand, containing findings that Secretary Espy violated the standards of conduct, could have been written and delivered in a manner that would not interfere with or prejudice the ongoing independent counsel investigation. Instead, the release of a noncommittal White House Counsel's report on October 11, 1994, a week after Secretary Espy's resignation was announced, undercut the force of the Secretary's resignation in terms of the Clinton Administration's commitment to strict ethical standards.

Given the pending criminal investigation, it was right to insist that Secretary Espy recuse himself from participating in meat and poultry inspection matters for the remainder of his tenure. However, the White House should have insisted on a broader recusal, to cover all particular matters involving Tyson Foods, Sun-Diamond Growers, and the EOP Group. A recusal was necessary only because the Secretary did not resign immediately, but remained on the job for three months. As in the case of the delayed departure of Roger Altman, the delay in Espy's departure received little notice and no apparent criticism. By contrast, recall the chorus of indignation at reports that Senator Robert Packwood might remain in the Senate for three months after he announced his resignation in September 1995 under threat of expulsion; Packwood wound up leaving by the end of the month.

More seriously, the White House Counsel's Report contained no finding that Espy violated any standard of conduct, including even the appearance standard! After a lengthy statement of the applicable standards, the report simply noted Secretary Espy's (and Dempsey's) reimbursements, and concluded that in light of the Secretary's resignation, recusal, and reimbursements, no further action was warranted. If the White House believed it should not make any finding while the criminal investigation is pending, it should have said so. That it did not rely on the pendency of the criminal investigation suggests that the White House Counsel's Report was abbreviated significantly, after Espy agreed to resign, to remove the adverse findings and soften the blow. While such a compromise or accommodation is understandable, it should not have been made. Again, the White House missed the chance to highlight its professed intolerance of ethical misbehavior.

Further, White House Counsel Mikva, interviewed on the "MacNeil/Lehrer Newshour," downplayed the seriousness of Secretary Espy's conduct, explaining it in part by reference to Espy's difficult adjustment from lax congressional ethics standards to the high standards imposed by the President. (Subsequently, the President, too, downplayed the gravity of Espy's misconduct.) Other commenters noted the Secretary's previous service in the House in an effort to understand how someone like Espy could have committed such egregious ethical errors. This is not an adequate explanation, however.

At the time, ethics standards were not as strict for Members of Congress as they were for Executive Branch officials. But this disparity should have come as no surprise to a former Congressman such as Secretary Espy, because of the highly publicized, and successful, effort to enact tighter congressional ethics standards. (In 1995, both Houses of Congress passed tighter gift standards for Senators, Representatives, and their staffs. However, Congress remains free of other ethics restrictions that apply to the Executive Branch, such as 18 U.S.C. 208.) Moreover, Secretary Espy knew he would be subject to different, tougher standards in the Executive Branch, for it is inconceivable that he was not given adequate ethics briefings at the time he joined the Cabinet. Even if Secretary Espy was correct in asserting that he never received notice of the gift provisions of the Meat Inspection Act, the very same conduct is clearly proscribed by the standards of conduct on which he was briefed (the only difference is the sanction). Also, Secretary Espy presumably was aware of the troubles that beset Bush Administration officials, most notably Chief of Staff John Sununu, for abuse of travel privileges. Significantly, many other former Members of Congress have come into the Executive Branch and complied with the more rigorous ethics standards without difficulty. In the Bush Administration alone, Jack Kemp, Lynn Martin, Ed Madigan (Secretary of Agriculture), and Manuel Lujan all entered the Bush Cabinet from the House of Representatives.

Ironically, it was another former Member of Congress, Leon Panetta, who best expressed why the White House determined that Secretary Espy had to resign, saying:

> I think it was pretty clear that we were looking at some fairly clear breaches with regard to ethics rules and it had reached the point where we had to take action. . . . If you begin to ignore or excuse that kind of behavior it sends a terrible signal to others. It becomes acceptable. All of us, particularly myself, and the president, recognized that Mike was an outstanding secretary of agriculture . . . and yet what was clear was that . . . with the information we had received, that ultimately it would impact not only on our standard of ethics but ultimately on his ability to do his job.[41]

Judge Mikva also was wrong to explain Espy's difficulties by reference to the standards of the Clinton Presidency. In fact, the standards of conduct that apply to all Executive Branch employees, including Secretary Espy, were promulgated by OGE during the Bush Administration. The Clinton Administration did not tighten or change these standards. Moreover, the basic ethics principles Espy violated were not invented in the Bush Administration, but have existed in Executive Branch standards for decades.

Secretary Cisneros

The Justice Department's findings that Henry Cisneros lied to the FBI during its background investigation of the Secretary-designate were serious enough to warrant the appointment of an independent counsel. The Justice Department's preliminary investigation determined that Cisneros misrepresented to the FBI the amount of money he had been providing to his former girlfriend, Linda Medlar, significantly understating the maximum individual amount and total annual amount of these payments. The possibility that Cisneros conspired with Medlar to conceal information about the payments from the FBI is also a legitimate avenue of inquiry for an independent counsel. It remains to be determined whether these false statements were "material" to the President's decision to appoint Cisneros or to the Senate's vote to confirm him. Because the Attorney General could not rule out the possibility that these statements could have had a bearing on Secretary Cisneros's appointment, the law required the matter to be referred to an independent counsel.

While the Attorney General was rightfully criticized for taking too long to conduct a preliminary investigation, she did not deserve the criticism she received for deciding to request an independent counsel. Although there is no reason to believe that the Public Integrity Section could not have conducted a fair and objective investigation, that is not the standard for determining whether to request the appointment of an independent counsel. The proper object of criticism should be the independent counsel law itself.

The central question before the independent counsel is whether any one (or more than one, in combination) of these false statements could have affected the President's decision to appoint Cisneros or the Senate's vote to confirm him. The courts have repeatedly held that a false statement will be found to be material if it tended to influence **or was capable of influencing** a government decision or other action. However, the amount of weight to be accorded the views of the persons to whom the false statements were directed is not clear. The Secretary is not likely to be charged if the question of materiality depends on the testimony of the President, White House officials, transition officials, and Senators. It is a virtual certainty that transition officials, White House officials, and, most importantly, the President all will tell the independent counsel that Henry Cisneros would have been nominated even had he told the complete truth concerning the size of individual payments and the total amount of payments. Indeed, the President, through his press secretary, has already weighed in on this question: "Nothing contained in the attorney general's statement today would have changed the president's determination to nominate Henry Cisneros."[42] The unequivocal and immediate nature of the President's public statement sent a clear (and questionable) signal to would-be witnesses from the transition and the White House.

The President's statements aside, it should be noted that had Secretary Cisneros kept the fact of his payments to Medlar from transition and White House officials (as opposed to the amount or timing of the payments), the case against him would be much stronger. But he disclosed to the FBI and the transition the most damning single fact: that he had been making regular payments to Medlar. The other facts, while certainly magnifying the potential scandal, might not have led these officials to pull the nomination. And, given the President's own alleged past indiscretions, it might have even seemed inconsistent to keep Cisneros from the Clinton Cabinet because of a single extramarital affair, even if the payments added a twist. (On the other hand, such statements might have led the White House not to nominate Cisneros for fear of raising issues on which the President may have been vulnerable.)

Whether Secretary Cisneros's false statements materially misled the Senate is a more difficult question, but ultimately is likely to be resolved in his favor. In 1993, the Senate was controlled by the Democrats. It is unlikely, although not impossible, that a Democratic senator would testify that Cisneros's nomination would not have been reported out of committee or that he would not have been confirmed had the full truth about the payments been told. Indeed, the day after the announcement of the Attorney General's request for the appointment of an independent counsel, it was reported that Senators Don Riegle and Alfonse D'Amato previously had written letters to the Secretary's personal lawyer to the effect that Cisneros would have been confirmed, even had he told the full truth with respect to the payments.

A potential wildcard is the conspiracy angle. Did Henry Cisneros and Linda Medlar conspire to keep the truth from the FBI? The FBI did not interview Medlar during the background check. The transcripts of her tapes, while highly relevant to this question, are inconclusive. Medlar's testimony is therefore critical on this question, but it may be unlikely that she would admit to engaging in a criminal conspiracy, even if promised immunity from prosecution.

Secretary Ron Brown

Secretary of Commerce Ron Brown has been under one ethical cloud or another since virtually the start of the Clinton Administration. Brown's problems stem primarily from business relationships that antedate his service in the Cabinet, but his actions as Secretary, especially his response to allegations concerning these business relationships, have also contributed to his ethics problems.

Secretary Brown initially was the subject of an allegation that he received or discussed receiving money from a Vietnamese businessman or the Vietnamese Government as a bribe to get him to push for the lifting of the U.S. trade embargo against Vietnam. The Secretary's innocence was eventually established by the Justice Department, which closed the investigation for lack of credible evidence. However, Secretary Brown exercised poor judgment in meeting with the businessman twice after being chosen to be Secretary and apparently after knowing something of the businessman's interest. Moreover, the Secretary exhibited belated and inadequate candor with the public regarding whether the meetings even occurred.

Looking into the Vietnam allegation led to a series of questions about a Washington town house Secretary Brown and his son purchased for Lillian Madsen, a friend of the Secretary who was present at two of the three meetings between Brown and the Vietnamese businessman. The full story about the financing of the town house has yet to be told. But, based on what is now known, the town house arrangement is suspicious in at least two particulars. First, the terms of the deed of trust originally stated that the Browns would use the property as a second home and did not permit them to rent it out. Second, Madsen provided the down payment (from a loan arranged by a Brazilian business friend of Brown) and "contributed to" the mortgage payments. Her name is not on the deed, and Secretary Brown did not report the down payment as a gift or loan on either of his first two financial reports. The Secretary's third (and most recent) financial disclosure report obliquely stated that he owns the town house "pursuant to an option agreement" with "L. Madsen." The town house arrangement is part of the independent counsel's investigation. It should be investigated fully for compliance with false statement, real estate, banking, and tax laws, in addition to the truthfulness of Secretary Brown's financial disclosure reports.

Secretary Brown's third ethical cloud is the darkest. When he was confirmed, the Secretary took a number of steps to rid himself of potential conflicts of interest, but he held on to several holdings in closely held companies, some of which, upon closer examination, are affiliated in varying degrees. The sloppiness of the Secretary's financial reports, and a *Washington Post* story suggesting that his single largest asset, First International Communications Corporation, was connected somehow to Corridor Broadcasting, an owner of two television stations, led to many questions about the Secretary's finances and his continued business ties. The link is important because of the Secretary's role in communications policy, and because Corridor's default led to a significant loss to the taxpayer. Secretary Brown denied any interest in Corridor and for nearly a year kept Representative Clinger in the dark about First International and several of his other holdings. When Clinger's staff uncovered evidence suggesting that First International and Corridor were linked financially, that Secretary Brown may have filed materially false financial disclosure reports, and that Brown may have participated as Secretary in matters involving his financial interests and partners, investigations were initiated at the FDIC and Justice Department at the request of Clinger and other congressional Republicans. Representative Clinger raised enough serious and substantial questions of legality that the Attorney General's eventual request for the appointment of an independent counsel was inevitable.

Although First International was Ron Brown's largest single asset, valued at between $500,000 and $1,000,000, the Secretary conceded he put no money into First International and was not actively involved in its business. Soon after the publication of the initial *Washington Post* article suggesting First International and Corridor Broadcasting were alter egos of each other, Brown apparently sold his interest back to the company. His financial disclosure report filed in May 1994 stated that he sold his interest in First International on December 15, 1993, for between $250,000 and $500,000, but he reported no capital gains on this transaction, which was curious, given that he had invested no money in the company. Moreover, **all the consideration Secretary Brown reportedly received for the sale was exchanged before and after December 15, 1993**: He received three checks of $35,000 each from First International Communications Limited Partnership (a slightly different name) in April, July, and October 1993; two of the checks bear the notation, "Partnership Distribution." (Secretary Brown did not report these checks as income on his financial disclosure report.) Also, Nolanda Hill, through First International and other companies she controlled, assumed or paid off several of the Secretary's debts, including a $78,000 loan to KNOW, Inc. (which apparently changed its name in 1991 to First International!), and payment of $190,000 in other personal debts by other companies, such as Jasas Corporation. The Secretary thus received benefits of at least $400,000 from First International, yet he invested no money; he did not participate in the company's business deals; and no business venture was successful.

The outcome of the independent counsel's investigation is difficult to predict, although a lengthy investigation is likely, given the complexity of Brown's financial interests and relationship with Nolanda Hill, his partner in First International and the head of Corridor, and the slow start-up pace of the independent counsel, which, alas, is not unusual.

What is clear from the reports that surfaced in the past year and one half is that an independent counsel was warranted to determine whether Secretary Brown (1) made any actionable false statements on his financial disclosure reports in violation of 18 U.S.C. 1001; (2) took any actions as Secretary to benefit his current business partner Nolanda Hill or her partners in violation of 18 U.S.C. 208; (3) improperly accepted or received things of value from Hill or First International in violation of 18 U.S.C. 201 (illegal gratuities) or 209 (supplementation of salary); and (4) committed any violation of Federal criminal law in obtaining financing for and buying the town house in Washington for Lillian Madsen. Attorney General Reno's decision to foreclose an investigation into the conflict-of-interest allegations appears dubious, but it is difficult to attack without knowing the facts and depth of the Justice Department's preliminary investigation.

Congressional hearings held the promise of exposing the shady business relationships Secretary Brown had with Hill and Hill had with others, as well as resolving whether the Secretary misused his office. However, the terms of the independent counsel law required the appointment of an independent counsel.

The FDIC and RTC investigations into Nolanda Hill's business dealings are also proper, but may appropriately be subsumed within the independent counsel's investigation. If so, Attorney General Reno should also give Pearson authority to investigate violations of civil law. Given Pearson's charter, the investigation of Hill can and should move forward regardless of evidence of Secretary Brown's involvement. If the FDIC and RTC are permitted to proceed, the reports prepared by these agencies should be available to the public.

Secretary Brown is entitled to the presumption that he is innocent of any criminal law violations. To date, the allegations that he has compromised his job in giving preferential treatment to his business associates are few in number and peripheral to his stewardship of Commerce. (They are arguably not even within the independent counsel's jurisdiction at this time.) But neither qualification mitigates the gravity of the misconduct that has been alleged. Further, Secretary Brown has only himself to blame for the criticism he received for his stubborn refusal to cooperate with the House Government Reform and Oversight Committee and other congressional requesters who, for over a year, sought information and explanations from the Secretary and the Commerce Department. Moreover, the allegations that Secretary Brown has, to date, failed to refute or even answer, paint at best a very unflattering portrait of his business relationships when he entered public service.

As the negative stories about Secretary Brown's finances accumulated, reaching an initial crescendo with the Justice Department's decision to conduct a preliminary investigation, some called for him to resign, or the President to fire him. Secretary Espy was eased out in October 1994, one month after the appointment of an independent counsel. Would Brown also be eased out before an independent counsel was appointed? The President said no:

> He's the best Commerce Secretary we've ever had. And he's gotten more results. That ought to be the test. He's a good Commerce Secretary. The questions that have been raised about what happened before he became Commerce Secretary are being looked into in an appropriate fashion. And meanwhile, he's on the job, and I'm supporting him in that.
>
> No Commerce Secretary has ever done more than he has to create jobs for Americans and to support the interest of American business. And that is the test. And he should go forward and do his job. That's what I want him to do.[43]

Once again, the President discounted the significance of reports of misconduct by pointing out that they allegedly occurred before the start of his Administration. This was the distinction made between the respective fate of Secretaries Espy and Cisneros. The appointment of an independent counsel would not result in the resignation of Cabinet member so long as the alleged misconduct antedated the official's service in the Clinton Administration. This dichotomy between public and private corruption, which has also been an important part of the President's public defense against allegations relating to Whitewater, the reported misuse of State troopers, and Paula Jones' suit alleging sexual harassment, may have some merit.

However, with respect to the allegations against Ron Brown, the President's account does not comport with the facts. The allegations against the Secretary focus on financial disclosure reports Brown was required to file because of his government position. The allegations include the deal, reportedly made in 1993 (while he was Secretary), to sell his interest in First International. The allegations include reports of Nolanda Hill's access to the Clinton White House, and her effort to get the Commerce Department to arrange a meeting with Jasas owner John Foster.

If the President defended Secretary Brown by relying on the presumption of innocence, he did so only indirectly, by noting the pendency of "appropriate" investigations. However, what the President clearly implied—that a public official's contributions, performance, and worth to the Government may trump serious unethical conduct by that official—is very troubling as a general principle. Although it may fit into the President's own effort to mitigate the damage caused by the pending Whitewater probe, it is dramatically at odds with the principle that government officials, in order both to function effectively and to maintain the trust and confidence of the public, should remain free of ethical scandal, whether it results from conduct on the job or from activities before joining the Government that are publicly disclosed post-confirmation.

After the decision was made to request the appointment of an independent counsel, the President did not budge, calling Ron Brown's success as Secretary "unparalleled" and getting in a dig at the independent counsel law he had recently championed:

> As I have noted in the past, the legal standard for [the appointment of an independent counsel] is low. I am confidant at the conclusion of the process, the independent counsel will find no wrongdoing by Secretary Brown. In the interim, I value his continued service on behalf of this country.[44]

Pressed to defend Ron Brown's continuing presence in the Cabinet, given that much of the alleged misconduct occurred while he was Secretary, the White House conceded that (in the words of the *Washington Post*) "there is no consistent principle about whether officials should continue in their jobs while being investigated[.]" White House Press Secretary Mike McCurry said that the President decided these matters case-by-case, explaining, "[t]here are different facts, different issues involved."[45]

Secretary Pena

The Southern California Rapid Transit District Pension Board awarded a contract to Secretary Pena's former management firm, Pena Investment Adviser's (PIA), just days after Pena was sworn in as Secretary. Together with the Secretary's subsequent approval of more than a billion dollars in funding to the District, these actions raised legitimate questions of propriety. The ethics question is whether Secretary Pena improperly participated in decisions awarding billions in funds to the Southern California Metropolitan Transit Authority (MTA) (the successor entity), with whom

PIA has a management contract. The Justice Department, after a quick investigation, determined there was no specific and credible evidence of a violation of Federal criminal law. Secretary Pena severed all financial ties to his former company, apparently before becoming Secretary. Thus, the criminal conflict-of-interest statute is not implicated. The Justice Department's declination may well have been predicated on this fact alone.

It is clear that both PIA and the Transit District sought to benefit financially from their association with Pena's name, given the Secretary's position as head of DOT. But Secretary Pena apparently was ignorant of these efforts. If he deserves any criticism, it is that he allowed PIA to continue to use his name.

Secretary Pena also recused himself for one year from participating in any particular matter having a direct and predictable effect on PIA. Secretary Pena's recusal is consistent with the long-standing advice the White House Counsel's office and agency ethics officials have given to prospective Presidential appointees. In essence, a reverse "revolving door" restriction, or cooling-off period, is imposed to guard against the appearance that the official is providing preferential treatment to a former employer in violation of ethics principles and standards. In some cases, involving a prior employment or affiliation that is highly visible or that goes back many years, a recusal of longer duration—perhaps for the official's entire tenure—is recommended.

The standards of conduct do not require recusal in so many words. Instead, the standards establish a process whereby potential non-financial conflicts or appearance concerns may be raised with agency ethics officials and resolved before the official may participate in the matter giving rise to the concern. Under section 502 of the standards of conduct, Secretary Pena may not participate in any particular matter where he knows PIA is a party to that matter, where he determines that the circumstances would lead a reasonable person with knowledge of the facts to question his impartiality in the matter, unless Secretary Pena informs the agency ethics official of this appearance problem and receives authorization to participate. The agency ethics official thereupon evaluates a number of factors to determine whether the interest of the Government in the Pena's participation outweighs appearance concerns. Technically, PIA was not a "party" to the grants. But section 502 contains a residual provision to address appearance issues that do not fit squarely within the terms of the section's "appearance" trigger. Thus, assuming that Secretary Pena was aware that PIA was under contract with MTA, he should have used this process before participating in the funding decisions.

Secretary Pena's involvement in approving funding for the Los Angeles subway clearly raised a question of appearances, given that his former firm is under contract with the local government entity that is the recipient of the Federal funding. There is no indication that the Secretary asked for or received advice under section 502, or even under the terms of his recusal commitment, before participating in the decisions relating to funding for the subway construction project. (Had Secretary Pena obtained approval to do so from DOT ethics officials, his office surely would have noted this to the media.) The lack of review by the DOT ethics office suggests that it made no connection between PIA and the Los Angeles subway funding. Indeed, Secretary Pena would likely argue that he did not know his former firm was a possible beneficiary of the Federal funding, the release of which he approved, even though as a PIA official in 1992 he had personally sought a management contract with the

District's pension fund. Without any additional facts, the Secretary's explanation that he was unaware of PIA's renewed push for a contract should be accepted. Furthermore, it is far from clear that his funding decisions would likely have a "direct and predictable effect" on PIA. So, even if Secretary Pena knew of PIA's contract to manage the pension fund, he may not have violated his recusal commitment.

Thus, on the facts that are known, Secretary Pena did not violate any law or ethical standard in connection with decisions regarding the funding for the construction of the Los Angeles subway. The Secretary would have been better served, however, if, following the Justice Department's closure of the investigation, the White House or DOT ethics office had announced such a finding.

However, Secretary Pena's one-year recusal commitment is plainly insufficient, given PIA's retention of Pena's name in its title, and PIA's apparent proclivity to emphasize the Secretary's former association with the company as a selling point.[45] Further, Secretary Pena was not merely associated with PIA, but founded it and has not ruled out returning to the firm after his service as Secretary. Under these circumstances, the Secretary's recusal from matters having a direct and predicable effect on PIA should be permanent.

Moreover, now that Secretary Pena knows of PIA's contract with the Pension Board, and of the controversy that surrounded that contract, he should not participate in future MTA funding decisions without advance approval from the DOT ethics office. In particular, the DOT ethics office should determine if the funds going to MTA may result in some benefit to PIA.

Secretary Pena is still not in the clear concerning the new Denver airport, the development of which he championed as Mayor of Denver. Investigations by the SEC, FBI, DOT Inspector General, Denver City Attorney, and Congress are all currently underway concerning cost overruns, delays, alleged bid-rigging, other alleged corruption in connection with contract awards, and diversion of airport revenue for non-airport purposes. Pena's conduct (as Mayor, not as Secretary) is at issue in some of these investigations, but it cannot be determined at this point whether he is at serious risk. One of the matters under investigation could adversely affect Secretary Ron Brown, who in private practice allegedly received funds from airport revenue to lobby on behalf of the City of Denver on matters unrelated to the airport, which expenditures would violate Federal law. If true, an allegation by a former DOT investigator that he was fired in retaliation for uncovering and revealing diversion of airport revenue for unrelated lobbying activities also could tar Secretary Pena, even if he played no role in the firing.

Secretary Pena appropriately recused himself at the outset from participating in any particular matter involving the new Denver airport.

Other Ethics Issues Involving the Clinton Administration

The State Department's Search and Disclosure of the Bush Administration's Political Appointees' Files

The disclosure to a reporter of contents of State Department White House Liaison Office files on Bush Administration political appointees violated the Privacy Act as well as ethics standards. Various reasons were offered for the initial retrieval of the records, some of them transparently unconvincing (e.g., to learn how the Office of White House Liaison functioned in the Bush Administration; to respond to the Passportgate independent counsel's subpoena) and some of them plausible, if not particularly noble (to see if any negative information could be found; to determine whether any Bush Administration political appointees had "burrowed" into the civil service at State). The statements given to the Inspector General on this point were inconsistent in several material respects. The IG found that the **retrieval** of Bush Administration Liaison Office files, "standing alone," did not violate any standards or policies, whatever its purpose. (The IG concluded that the Liaison Office probably retrieved the records to locate burrowed Bush Administration appointees.)

Regardless of the motive for the retrieval of the files, proper or improper, there could be no legitimate motive in **disclosing** their contents to the *Washington Post*. The purpose of disclosure was most likely to provide some negative information, or at least a smidgen of gossip, about two Bush Administration officials, Elizabeth Tamposi and Jennifer Fitzgerald. The Privacy Act prohibits the disclosure of records, such as White House Liaison Office files, that are contained in an approved Privacy Act system of records, without the written consent of the person whom the records concern. Willful disclosure of records protected by the Privacy Act, knowing that disclosure is prohibited, is a crime. The IG cited several ethics standards that were breached. Most relevant is the prohibition against the knowing unauthorized disclosure of nonpublic official information for the purpose of furthering a private interest.

Given the recent notoriety surrounding efforts of the Bush Administration State Department to locate files on Bill Clinton's passport during the 1992 election (so-called Passportgate), which resulted in the highly publicized dismissal of Tamposi and the appointment of an independent counsel, the Clinton appointees' conduct was also just plain stupid. Clinton Administration appointees at all levels were put on notice also from the statement President-elect Clinton made that such conduct would not be tolerated:

> If I catch anybody using the State Department like that [referring to Tamposi's conduct] when I'm President, you won't have to wait until the election to see them gone. . . . [I]f I catch anybody doing it, I will fire them the next day. There won't be . . . an inquiry, or rigamarole, or anthing else[.][47]

Secretary Christopher properly fired the two mid-level political appointees who participated in the retrieval and disclosure (he also appropriately awaited the report from the IG before doing so, notwithstanding the President's remarks). No evidence was uncovered that any Presidential appointee at the State Department or White House was involved in the retrieval, search, or disclosure, however, and thus this ethics controversy quickly faded from public view.

Was the misconduct by the two State Department officials serious? Yes, of course. From the perspective of the Bush officials whose files were raked over, it makes no difference that only junior politicos leaked contents to the *Washington Post*. The damage was done nonetheless. The *Washington Post* called it "no trivial matter, and it is no less offensive than when Mr. Clinton himself was on the receiving end of such abuse."[48] In some respects, what these State Department officials did was just as bad as, not worse than, what the Bush Administration State Department political appointees were found to have done in Passportgate. The Bush Administration State Department officials, although of higher rank, were responding to several FOIA requests filed by the media and a separate request from a Congressman. The motive of the Bush Administration officials in expediting the search and disclosing it to the media may have been improperly political, but the apparent motives of the Clinton Administration officials in retrieving, searching, and disclosing the files were just as base.

It is not known why the Justice Department declined to prosecute, but in light of the prompt firing of the culpable officials, and the strong public opprobrium attached to their actions, declination was probably appropriate.

Preconfirmation Activities of Presidential Appointees

In the Clinton Administration, like previous administrations, some Presidential appointees were brought into the agency for which they were designated before they were confirmed by the Senate. Some who were brought in were given a title; others were simply designated as a consultant. Some were brought in after they were nominated, or after the President's intention to nominate was announced; others waited until their confirmation hearing was held. It was not clear to the Clinton Administration, as it should have been, that waiting until confirmation is the only safe choice for a nominee, the agency, and the administration.

A prospective appointee who arrives before confirmation may do so for a number of unobjectionable reasons: to receive advice on ethical restrictions to which the appointee will be subject; to receive assistance in completing financial disclosure reports for the Executive Branch and the appropriate Senate committee; and to receive overview briefings of the agency's duties and other briefings to prepare a nominee for the confirmation hearing. Because a nominee generally can receive all this advice and assistance in just a couple of visits to the agency, there usually is another reason why a nominee is formerly retained as a consultant and given office space and a title before confirmation. The reason is that the White House or agency head wants the prospective appointee immediately to begin participating in deliberations about agency policies and programs, either because of a existing policy void in the agency, or perhaps because of the special expertise or perspective the individual is expected to bring to the agency. An administration that wants to hit the ground running, or an agency in need of particular expertise to address time-sensitive priorities, sees the weeks and sometimes months that elapse between nomination and confirmation as a hindrance. This is when agencies and nominees begin to court trouble.

An agency has legal authority to hire prospective appointees as consultants under 5 U.S.C. 3109(b). By regulatory definition, a "consultant" provides views and opinions on problems or questions before the agency, but neither performs nor supervises the performance of any operating function. A clarifying rule issued by the Office of Personnel Management in 1995 provides that consultants may not "perform managerial or supervisory work, . . . make final decisions on substantive policies, or . . . otherwise function in the agency chain of command[, or] . . . do work performed by the agency's regular employees."[49]

The Senate, of course, dislikes the practice of nominees beginning work at an agency prior to confirmation. The Senate's advice and consent responsibilities are expressly grounded in Article II, section 2, clause 2 of the Constitution. Coming on board before confirmation gives the appearance of taking the Senate's consent for granted. *A fortiori*, the Senate likes it even less when a person takes a consultant position in the agency before his nomination, because it gives the appearance of treating the Senate's advice as irrelevant.

In addition to the obvious affront to the Senate, this practice poses even greater dangers for nominees. First, nominees are likely to face a more difficult confirmation process, because they will be charged with knowledge of and responsibility for decisions made by the agency during their tenure as consultant. Their desire to begin their formal appointment without a track record and without an extensive list of commitments to Congress is often dashed. Second, a person who settles into an agency office and begins to participate in agency deliberations becomes a special Government employee, subject to nearly all of the ethics restrictions to which the person would be subject upon being sworn in. Third, while consultants do not have authority to make agency decisions, the line between giving advice and making decisions tends to blur as agency officials naturally tend to defer to the views of a person who will shortly be their superior. An agency decision made by or approved by one who has not yet been sworn in may also be challenged and overturned in court for lack of authority.

Given these risks, an administration should be very wary of bringing on board a prospective appointee before confirmation. In its first year, the Clinton Administration did not exhibit this reluctance, learning these lessons only the hard way. Several Clinton Administration appointees, acting as consultants before they were confirmed, exceeded their authority by taking part in policy or management decisions. Four among them received scrutiny by Senate Committees that took affront at their conduct: Ashton Carter, nominated to be Assistant Secretary of Defense for Nuclear Security and Counter-Proliferation, Graham Allison, nominated to be Assistant Secretary of Defense for Plans and Policy, and George Frampton, nominated as Assistant Secretary of Interior for Fish and Wildlife, all were eventually confirmed. (Two internal reviews found that Frampton did not engage in any improper activity.) Morton Halperin, nominated to be Assistant Secretary of Defense for Democracy and Human Rights, was not as fortunate. His nomination was eventually withdrawn, after substantial opposition arose, for various reasons, including his pre-confirmation participation in Defense Department decisionmaking.

Webster Hubbell, who began service in the Justice Department as the informal liaison to the White House even before an Attorney General was confirmed, served as a consultant until his nomination and confirmation as Associate Attorney General later in 1993. Hubbell's pre-confirmation role at Justice received a great deal of media scrutiny and some criticism, but largely based on what was perceived as inordinate and inappropriate **White House** direction of the Justice Department, and based on Hubbell's close association with the other Rose Law Firm alumni in the White House, rather than **Hubbell's** pre-confirmation decisionmaking and supervisory activities.

These breaches, while avoidable, are not unexpected for a new administration. Part of the problem stems from inadequate guidance from OPM to agencies and from agencies to prospective nominees. Part of the problem stems from inadequate attention to existing guidance by agency managers and by prospective appointees. In the case of the four officials noted above, existing guidance, if properly followed, could have prevented much (but not all) of the mistakes. Clearer guidance, along the lines of what then Defense Department General Counsel Jamie Gorelick issued in May 1993, after the Carter and Allison episodes erupted, should be disseminated throughout the Executive Branch. Further, tighter regulatory and management controls on the use of consultants by Federal agencies should be promulgated. Ultimately, administrations should exercise greater self-restraint in placing prospective appointees at agencies prior to their confirmation, especially before their nomination.

Travel

Abuse of travel privileges, including the use of government aircraft, continues to plague administrations. The Clinton Administration, despite initial efforts by the President to avoid another Sununu controversy, has experienced a comparable number of embarrassing stories, although they have not attracted nearly the same amount of media attention as did the travels of Governor Sununu on board military aircraft. This is one area where the President marginally tightened a standard of conduct (governing the use of government aircraft), although the ethics standards (governing the use of government property) were not changed. The use of a military helicopter to attend a golf outing by the White House Office Director of Administration was the most notorious example of the continuing misuse of Government aircraft by senior Clinton Administration officials. Further, several members of the President's Cabinet and agency heads made a disproportionate amount of official trips to their hometowns; often the official event appeared simply as a pretext to justify the expenditure of official travel funds.

Abuse of travel privileges implicates several ethics provisions in the comprehensive standards of conduct: "[e]mployees shall not use public office for private gain[;]" and "employees shall protect and conserve Federal property and shall not use it for other than authorized activities.[50] Similarly, a separate standard of conduct provides: "An employee has a duty to protect and conserve Government property and shall not use such property, or allow its use, for other than authorized purposes."[51]

Government Aircraft

As part of his campaign against perks and misuse of government resources, President Clinton issued a memorandum dated February 10, 1993, to limit strictly the use of government aircraft by Executive Branch officials.[52] The President did not write on a clean slate, however. The Bush Administration had recently issued two policies on the use of government aircraft: a May 9, 1991 policy on the use of military aircraft by the Chief of Staff and National Security Adviser, and, May 22, 1992 revision of OMB Circular A-126, entitled "Improving the Management and Use of Government Aircraft."

The effect of President Clinton's memorandum was to further restrict who could use government aircraft and under what circumstances. The major difference from the May 1991 policy is that express White House authorization would be required on a trip-by-trip basis for the limited number of Cabinet and other officials authorized to use government aircraft for nongovernmental purposes. For all other senior officials, the President prohibited the use of government aircraft for "[u]ses other than those that constitute the discharge of an agency's official responsibilities[.]"[53]

Thus, the President severely restricted the number of officials who could use government aircraft for personal travel, and it appears that he prohibited senior officials from using government aircraft, unless the travel was also to meet mission requirements. In other words, Presidential appointees and White House staff could not use government aircraft to give speeches or attend conferences, meetings, or site visits.

But old habits die hard, especially among the military services and civilian agencies with their own fleet of aircraft, such as NASA, DOT, and FAA. Notwithstanding OMB Circular A-126 and the President's February 1993 policy statement, there have been regular reports of high-level officials' inappropriate use of Government aircraft in the Clinton Administration. The late Secretary of Defense Les Aspin, Deputy Secretary John Deutsch (now Director of the CIA), and General Joseph Ashy all were singled out for alleged abuse of their Government aircraft privileges. Civilian agencies with aircraft fleets also came under scrutiny and criticism. In the first year of the Clinton Administration, an audit performed by NASA's IG found that travel by NASA officials on NASA aircraft in Fiscal Year 1993 (covering part of the Bush Administration) cost $5.9 million more than the cost of travelling on commercial flights.

The misuse of government aircraft was not limited to fixed-wing aircraft; helicopters, too, were often used where less expensive ground transportation would suffice. The *Washington Post* found that in 1993 Pentagon generals and admirals had taken 238 helicopter trips between Andrews Air Force Base and the Pentagon, costing about $1000 to $3000 per trip, instead of taking a cab which costs about $22 (a 14-mile drive).[54] It is hard to understand how many of these trips could be squared with OMB Circular A-126 and the President's February 10, 1993 policy.

The most infamous use of Government aircraft was a single use of a military helicopter by David Watkins, Assistant to the President for Management and Administration. On May 24, 1994, just three weeks after the page one *Washington Post* report on the abuse of military helicopters by Pentagon officials, Watkins and Alphonso Maldon, the politically appointed Director of the White House Military Office, took a military helicopter for an afternoon golf outing at Holly Hills Country Club in Ijamsville, Maryland, an hour's drive from the White House. The helicopter costs about $2400 per hour to operate; it made two round trips in transporting Watkins. The ignominy of the trip was starkly illustrated by a page one picture of Watkins carrying his golf bag from a golf cart to the waiting "United States of America" helicopter; an Air Force officer stands at attention by the steps, saluting one of Watkins' golf partners. It was not Watkins' first brush with an ethics scandal; he was knee deep in the mishandling of the Travel Office firings. The President wasted no time in asking for Watkins' resignation, announcing that the Government would be reimbursed for the cost of the trip. The White House said that Maldon was reprimanded, removed from his position, and would soon be reassigned.[55]

The White House suffered further embarrassment from the episode because the White House Press Office initially explained the trip on the basis of a statement prepared by the White House Military Office that turned out to be just a cover story. The Military Office attempted to justify the trip as a "'training mission' to familiarize the crew with the layout of the course" in anticipation of a Presidential visit. The round of golf was played "in order to familiarize themselves with all aspects of the course, especially those aspects related to actual time of play and associated impact of security plans." But neither Watkins nor Maldon was responsible or qualified to conduct security or advance for a Presidential visit, and the White House had no plans for any such Presidential visit there.

The day after the golfing trip was revealed, the White House (after initial denials) acknowledged that a second helicopter made the trip, too, as usually occurs with all trips of Marine One.[56] On May 31, the White House Chief of Staff issued by memorandum a new policy regarding the use of military aircraft (not just helicopters) by White House staff and Cabinet officials for "White House Support Missions," requiring trip-by-trip approval by the Chief of Staff or his Deputy (or White House Counsel or his Deputy, in the case of a request involving the Chief of Staff as passenger). Approval previously rested with the Director of White House Administration, the position Watkins held until his dismissal. So, in 1994 the Clinton White House put in place what essentially was the same review and approval process the Bush White House issued three years earlier in response to the publicity of Governor Sununu's travels, the only difference being the official designated to review and approve the use of aircraft. [57]

A GAO report requested by Representative Roscoe Bartlett was not issued until a year later. The skimpy report found that White House and Cabinet officials took fourteen trips without the President or Vice President between January 21, 1993 and May 24, 1994, the date of the golf outing. It found no written procedures for requesting the use of helicopters or criteria governing their use, and thus the report contained no finding that any of the trips was proper or improper. However, GAO failed to note that OMB Circular A-126 and the President's February 10, 1993 memorandum expressly prohibited the use of a Government helicopter (1) for personal travel, or (2) when less expensive ground transportation was available (subject to some limited exceptions). Thus, the GAO report was clearly inadequate.

Travel Home

There is no law, rule or policy that prohibits a Federal official from using government funds to take a trip to one's hometown, provided the trip is made to attend one or more official events. Nor is there any provision discouraging the frequency of official trips taken to one's hometown. Many Federal officials have for years made a disproportionate amount of official trips to their hometowns or to other locations where personal events have been scheduled. Of course, it would be improper to arrange for an official event in one's hometown or other location solely to permit the official to use government funds to attend a personal event (like a child's wedding, birthday, or graduation) or simply to go home. This would be using public office for private gain, in violation of a cardinal principle of ethics. But rare is the government official who will concede that an official trip was scheduled to get the Government to cover the travel expenses in order to attend a personal matter.

Yet, this is exactly what the public sees when it is reported that a certain Federal official travelled a disproportionate amount of time to his hometown, primarily on weekends, with only a light schedule of official events. These officials are contributing to the distrust and disgust in which Americans hold public officials, for it appears that these officials are using taxpayer funds to underwrite personal or political travel.

This is not a new problem. Several Bush Administration officials, most notably Chief of Staff John Sununu and Peace Corps Director Paul Coverdell, made frequent official trips to their home State, with itineraries thin on official events and thick with time with family and friends. And one of the reasons for the President's dismissal of FBI Director William Sessions in July 1993 was a finding by the outgoing Bush Administration Attorney General that Sessions engaged in "a pattern of abuse of travel . . . resulting in the use of government funds for clearly personal travel on a number of occasions."[58]

Given the tremendous notoriety of the travels of both Sununu and Sessions, the

Clinton Administration's appointees should have assiduously avoid this travel trap. On the contrary, the Clinton Administration's record appears no better, perhaps even worse. During his first eighteen months as Agriculture Secretary, Mike Espy took eighteen official trips to his hometown of Jackson, Mississippi. And while in Mississippi, Secretary Espy used a jeep leased by the Government for personal travel. Many of his trips were transparently personal, yet they were paid for by the Government, because the Secretary attended one or more official events. One weekend trip consisted of just one "official" event: a thirty-minute talk to his children's school about pursuing a career with the Department of Agriculture.

Secretary of Veterans Affairs Jesse Brown traveled to his hometown of Chicago on official business twenty times in his first twenty months, amounting to 40% of all his official travel during this time. As the *Los Angeles Times* reported, "[m]any of the visits included weekends or involved lengthy stays with light public schedules."[59] The *Los Angeles Times* noted that "no official events were listed on Brown's schedule for thirty-five of the weekdays he was in his hometown[.]" Secretary Brown even counted as an official visit a five-day stay in Chicago in 1994 where the "only public activity listed . . . was an address at the eighth-grade graduation ceremonies at St. Dorothy's School. Brown's nephew was among the graduates."[60]

Kathy Jurado, Secretary Brown's Assistant Secretary for Public and Intergovernmental Affairs, shared his propensity to make official visits home. Jurado, who is from Tampa, Florida, made eleven official visits to Florida (seven to Tampa) out of twenty-five official trips in sixteen months at the VA. To her credit, Jurado also traveled home nine times at her own expense. But as *Washington Post* columnist Al Kamen noted sardonically in reporting on Jurado's travels, "[t]he first trip she made in her new job, in November 1993, forced her to return to Tampa over Thanksgiving."[61]

Roger Johnson, Administrator of the General Services Administration, also came under fire for his travels. Johnson took five of his first nine official trips to the Los Angeles area, where his wife and home are. Generally, Johnson conducted official business in southern California on Fridays and Mondays. He also visited his other home in Utah on two weekends during official trips. Johnson protested that "I have not ever contrived or structured trips to go through Orange County." But he acknowledged, "Did I take every opportunity to get home? I certainly did."[62]

Johnson reimbursed the Government for certain expenditures, following a review conducted by GSA's Chief Financial Officer, who concluded that Johnson did not violate any Federal travel rules. Johnson also reimbursed the Government for thirty-nine overnight pieces of mail and 184 long distance phone calls that were determined to be personal. The Inspector General's report, released on April 20, 1994, found in addition that Johnson improperly used his government credit card on a few occasions when he received the government air fare rate for personal trips. But the IG exonerated Johnson of the charge that he conducted personal travel at government expense, and concluded that his misuse of government resources was due to his "unfamiliarity with official travel rules and regulations."[63]

Johnson was unable to avoid getting into further trouble. It was reported in October 1994 that the Inspector General had initiated a second investigation of Johnson, this time looking into reports that Johnson used GSA employees for personal errands and other business, such as writing memoranda to Johnson's personal business consultants, going to Johnson's house to wait for furniture deliveries and repairmen, and taking his Mercedes to the car wash. Johnson's tin ethics ear was explained by reference to mistakes made in his transition from thirty-five years as a corporate executive in the private sector. GSA called them "inadvertent actions," most of which occurred during his first months on the job. "As Mr. Johnson became aware of any actions which were inappropriate, he took full responsibility for the infractions and ensured that similar actions did not occur."[64]

These stories are only the reported abuses of travel privileges by the Clinton Administration. Undoubtedly, a comprehensive investigation of the travel of Cabinet and sub-Cabinet officials would reveal others.

Chapter Two

The Current State of Ethics Laws and Regulations

Many have complained that our ethics system has gone awry. A prime exhibit in support of their complaint is the purported inverse variation between the ever increasing degree of ethics regulation and the ever decreasing public confidence in the integrity of government. Assuming both indicators are true, however, does not result in the conclusion that the ethics system is responsible for the decrease in the public's trust in government, or even that it has failed to arrest this decline. There are many reasons, most of them unrelated to the ethics regime, why most Americans no longer have faith in the integrity of the Federal Government.

Our system of ethics also is criticized for keeping good, talented persons from entering public service. And many fault the ethics system for the prominent role it now plays in the political arena, where allegations of ethical impropriety often take center stage in public policy and electoral debate, crowding out a discussion of all issues other than "character."[1]

The steady decrease in the public's confidence in government is undeniable, measured both by public opinion polls and the ballot box. But the other part of the equation, that ethics regulation has steadily increased during this same time, is for the most part wrong. With few exceptions, the Federal ethics **standards** are basically the same as the ones put in place thirty years ago during the Johnson Administration. The general principles enumerated in President Bush's executive order on ethics are borrowed heavily from President Johnson's executive order.[2] And the standards of conduct promulgated by the Office of Government Ethics in 1992, pursuant to President Bush's executive order,[3] are largely derived from the regulations issued by the Civil Service Commission under authority of President Johnson's executive order.[4]

What has changed during this period are the revolving door restrictions, which were stiffened in 1978 and several times since then, and the limitations on outside earned income, which were instituted by law and executive order in 1989. Otherwise, the basic provisions on gifts and conflicts of interest are essentially unchanged, save for refinements and clarifications.

Presidents Bush and Clinton Both Began Their Presidency with Great Emphasis on Government Ethics, Increasing Public Expectations.

Although the basic ethics principles and standards have not changed dramatically over the last thirty years, the emphasis and attention Presidents (and Congress) have given to government ethics in recent years certainly have. This is evident in the dramatic growth in the number of officials with responsibility to provide ethics training and guidance. Nearly all recent Presidents have exhorted their appointees and the civil service at the beginning of their administrations to conduct themselves with utmost regard for the maxim that public service is a public trust. And the public's expectations of improved ethical performance have been raised, largely because of promises personally made by candidates George Bush in 1988 and Bill Clinton in 1992 that their administrations would be subject to and abide by a strict ethical code of conduct (in explicit or implicit contrast to the previous administration).

During the 1988 campaign, Vice President George Bush promised to subject his appointees to an "exacting code of conduct." "The test for appointment to office in the Bush administration . . . will be unquestioned character, integrity, talent, and, yes, dedication to public service."[5] Specifically, Vice President Bush urged the creation of an ethics office in the White House and each agency (things already in existence), annual ethics briefings, and tighter revolving door restrictions (which would require legislation). Yet, to his credit, he did not propose simply to tighten or toughen current standards. He also pledged a set of "clear, concise and simple" ethics rules, as well as sanctions that would be "fair and proportionate," including expanding the range of available sanctions for violations of the conflict-of-interest law to provide a sanction other than criminal prosecution. Vice President Bush even promised to "examine the constant complaint from experts in a variety of fields who are reluctant to enter government" because of revolving door and other ethics rules "to see if there's a way to accommodate these people without compromising ethics."[6]

Once in office, President Bush did not waste time. In January 1989 he created the President's Commission on Federal Ethics Law Reform,[7] which issued its report less than two months later, containing twenty-seven recommendations for legislative and regulatory action.[8] His executive order on ethics, issued in April 1989, prohibited his fulltime appointees from receiving any outside earned income during their Government service, required all employees to receive annual ethics training, and directed OGE to promulgate a single set of ethics standards for the entire Executive

Branch workforce.[9] He also submitted ethics legislation to Congress, which formed the basis for the Ethics Reform Act of 1989 enacted that November.

As a Presidential candidate, Bill Clinton also gave government ethics a feature role in his campaign. In his published blueprint of his agenda, he decried the Washington influence of special interest lobbyists, and vowed to clean up the Capital:

> . . . We must take away power from the entrenched bureaucracies and special interests that dominate Washington. . . .
>
> It's long past time to clean up Washington. The last twelve years were nothing less than an extended hunting season for high-priced lobbyists and Washington influence peddlers. . . .
>
> During the 1980s . . . [h]igh-level executive branch employees traded in their government jobs for the chance to make millions lobbying their former bosses. Experts estimate that nearly one of every two senior American trade officials has signed on to work for nations they once faced across the negotiating table.
>
> This betrayal of democracy must stop.
>
> To break the stalemate in Washington, we have to attack the problem at its source: entrenched power and money. We must cut the   bureau-cracy, limit special interests, stop the revolving door, and cut off the unrestricted flow of campaign funds. The privilege of public service ought to be enough of a perk for people in government.[10]

At a news conference held shortly after his election, President Clinton pledged to issue a:

> code of ethics requirements on the Executive Branch [that] will give people confidence that whatever decisions we make in dealing with economic issues here and beyond our borders will be made by people who cannot in turn profit [from] them for several years after they leave the government. And that will increase the credibility of our decisionmaking.[11]

The President thus signaled that his efforts to improve the ethics in Government, aside from legislation, would be focused primarily, if not exclusively, on the revolving door.[12]

The President also imposed ethics restrictions on his transition staff, which Warren Christopher boasted were "by far the strongest, toughest rules ever put forward for a presidential transition." Transition members were required to sign a pledge committing (1) not to participate in any transition matter in which they had a financial interest, (2) not to use nonpublic information for private gain during or after the transition, and (3) not to lobby for six months any Federal agency for which they had substantial responsibility during the transition.[13]

In office on his first day, the President issued an executive order placing revolving door restrictions on his appointees in addition to the statutory restrictions in place.[14] Within his first month, he also clamped down on perks.[15] These were the only ethics standards he stiffened. The President did not tighten or strengthen **any** of the basic standards of conduct that apply to the Executive Branch workforce in the performance of their duties, a fact hardly any of the media recognized, then or now.[16] Because it has not been challenged, the accuracy of the President's assertion that his administration is subject to the highest ethical standards, which he has repeated several times during his Presidency, has been implicitly accepted.

In March 1994, at his initial news conference to answer questions on Whitewater, Clinton cited his executive order in support of his assertion that his Administration is subject to the highest ethics standards of any administration:

> But since you raised the issue, let me also ask you to report to the American people that **we have and we have enforced higher standards against ethical conflicts than any previous administration**. When people leave the White House, they can't lobby the White House. If they're in certain positions, they can't lobby the White House for a long time. If they're in certain positions now, they can never lobby on behalf of a foreign government.[17]

A year later, the President was asked, in light of the several pending independent counsel investigations of Administration officials, "how can you explain what's happened to your administration after you came into office promising the most ethical administration in history?" In the middle of an extended response, the President asserted, **"Everybody knows that I have tougher ethics rules than any previous President."**[18]

From these statements it is plain that President Clinton placed all his attention on ethics rules that operate after an official leaves the Government; he made no change in, nor did he devote any attention to the standards of conduct which Executive Branch employees must observe during their Government service.

No Major Overhaul of the Ethics Laws Is Necessary.

In order to evaluate the current system of ethics laws and regulations, the promises and boasting must be disregarded, and the rules should be evaluated on their own terms. Examining their substance reveals only one glaring problem: the revolving door rules are completely out of whack. As explained at great length in Chapter Fifteen, the revolving door laws must be relaxed and made rational. The regime of post-employment restrictions, which consists of several criminal provisions and President Clinton's executive order, is as irrational as it is complex. It is contrary to the sound public policy of encouraging and attracting the best qualified persons to come to work for the Government. The current revolving door restrictions function to keep many good, talented, people from entering public service. Moreover, Congress (Democrats and Republicans) and the President each have actually **designed** the restrictions to punish foreign interests, both public and private. This whole scheme needs significant legislative reform. Indeed, a good argument can be made that the overreaching of the post-employment restrictions alone has given the ethics system a bad name. Regretfully, it does not appear that Congress or the President fully understands the problem to which they each have contributed, much less its seriousness.

Aside from the post-employment restrictions, the ethics laws are not in need of a substantial overhaul. A tune-up in several areas would be desirable, however. First, the financial disclosure requirements are far more extensive than necessary to guard against conflicts of interest. Congress's recent amendment of the financial disclosure laws—to require the reporting of additional categories of assets, income, and liabilities over one million dollars—shows that constructive reform of the financial disclosure laws will be an uphill battle in Congress.[19] The recent amendment, tucked inside of the lobbying disclosure bill passed by both Houses with great fanfare, serves only to reveal the extent of a person's wealth. A holding or source of income of one million dollars that poses no ethical concern will under no circumstances pose one if its value is instead five or ten million dollars. (The amendment also promises to be an administrative nightmare for Federal agencies in the short term.)

Second, the application of the basic conflict-of-interest statute to legislative proposals is in need of clarification, and—because of a recent construction by OGE—tightening. Third, also in need of clarification are the laws which govern parttime advisers and consultants. These matters are discussed at greater length in subsequent chapters. Finally, the outside activities and income rules (i.e., restrictions on the receipt of honoraria for speaking and writing) should be more narrowly tailored to prevent conflicts of interest and abuses of Government information and privilege.

The Appearance Standard Is an Essential Component of Any Ethics System.
One frequently expressed complaint about the ethics rules is directed at the appearance of impropriety standard. The criticism is that the appearance standard is too protean and subjective, and thus more susceptible to misunderstanding and misuse. A secondary criticism is that the appearance standard paints Federal officials as unethical in circumstances where no ethics rule has been violated. It is true that the appearance standard is capable of being misused, by ignorance as well as design. All ethics standards are vulnerable to misuse. But this is a necessary price to pay for the benefit an appearance standard provides to a system of ethics.

Before defending the appearance standard, it is necessary to define it. The appearance standard has been in place for decades. In President Kennedy's message to Congress forwarding a comprehensive program of ethics reform, he stated:

> There can be no dissent from the principle that all officials must act with unwavering integrity, absolute impartiality and complete devotion to the public interest. **This principle must be followed not only in reality but in appearance.** For the basis of effective government is public confidence, and that confidence is endangered when ethical standards falter or appear to falter.[20]

President Kennedy's executive order on ethics, issued in May 1961, decreed that it "shall be deemed incompatible with" a discharge of an Executive Branch employee's discharge of responsibilities:

> for any such official to accept any fee, compensation, gift, payment or expenses, or any other thing of monetary value in circumstances in which acceptance may result in, or **create the appearance of**, resulting in:

> (a) Use of public office for private gain;

(b) An undertaking to give preferential treatment to any person;

(c) Impeding government efficiency or economy;

(d) Any loss of complete independence or impartiality;

(e) The making of a government decision outside official channels; or

(f) Any adverse affect on the confidence of the public in the integrity of the Government.[21]

President Johnson's executive order on ethics, which superseded President Kennedy's, broadens this guidance to direct employees to "avoid **any action,** . . . which might result in, **or create the appearance of**" doing the same improper activities enumerated above.[22]

Similarly, President Bush's executive order provides that "[e]mployees shall endeavor to avoid **any actions creating the appearance** that they are violating the law or the ethical standards promulgated pursuant to this order."[23] OGE amplified and refined this provision in the comprehensive standards of conduct:

> Employees shall endeavor to avoid any actions creating the appearance that they are violating the law or the ethical standards set forth in this part. Whether particular circumstances create an appearance that the law or these standards have been violated shall be determined from the perspective of a reasonable person with knowledge of the relevant facts.[24]

OGE intentionally added a "reasonable person" test that was absent from the executive order to provide an "appropriate assurance to an employee that his or her conduct will not be judged from the perspective of the unreasonable, uninformed or overly zealous."[25] However, this sentence assures an employee only that the **standards of conduct** will not be used to judge and criticize his or her conduct on a basis other than an objective one. OGE cannot provide any assurance that others will refrain from judging appearances subjectively, and criticizing conduct on the basis of such a subjective evaluation. Nonetheless, OGE demonstrated a sensitivity to the complaint that an appearance standard, untethered to an objective criterion, is capable of misapplication and abuse.

In the standards of conduct, OGE ventured even further into codification of the appearance principle. Subpart E of the standards concerns "impartiality in performing official duties." It provides a process whereby an employee who believes his conduct in a particular matter involving specific parties may give rise to an appearance problem must consult with an agency ethics official before participating in the matter.[26] The standards set out several factors to consider in determining whether to authorize the employee to participate in the matter, notwithstanding the appearance problem.[27]

This process applies expressly only to certain personal and business relationships, such as relatives, business partners, agents, and former colleagues and clients, and covers conduct only in connection with a particular matter involving specific parties.[28] However, the standard also contains a residual provision, indicating that employees who are concerned about an appearance problem in a context outside the circumstances of the rule should also use the process of prior consultation to determine whether participation is appropriate.[29]

The appearance standard is needed because the public evaluates the integrity of government conduct almost exclusively based on appearances, unless that conduct is the subject of an investigation or is otherwise publicly known. The face of government the public sees is, after all, often only an appearance. In a thoughtful essay, Professor Dennis Thompson states that "[b]ecause appearances are often the only window that citizens have on official conduct, to reject the appearance standard is to reject the possibility of democratic accountability."[30] Perhaps an appearance standard was not necessary when Americans had full confidence in the integrity of the Federal Government and the good faith of its public servants (if there ever was such a day). But today, when Americans repose little trust in the Government, it is incumbent on Government employees more than ever to appear as ethical as they are in fact.

Professor Thompson asserts that "Appearing to do wrong while doing right is really doing wrong." He explains:

> Officials who appear to do wrong actually do several kinds of moral wrong: they erode the confidence in government, they give citizens reason to act as if government cannot be trusted, and most of all, they undermine democratic accountability.[31]

The appearance standard plays a crucial role in any ethics system, because the fundamental objective of any system of Government ethics is to give the public:

> some reason to believe that officials are making decisions based on the merits. It citizens have this assurance, they are less likely to raise questions about the motives of officials, and are themselves more likely to concentrate on the merits of decisions and on the substantive qualifications of the officials who are making the decisions.[32]

This is why it is imperative to include an appearance principle in the ethics standards. It does not mean that a violation of the appearance principle is tantamount to a violation of the underlying ethics rule of conduct, or that an employee should always be disciplined for failing to avoid an appearance of impropriety. But appearances matter.

This is also not to suggest that compliance with the appearance standard renders compliance with the underlying rules of conduct unimportant or even less important. It does not. Federal employees must conduct themselves both to comply with ethics rules and to give the appearance of compliance.[33]

Having an appearance standard also does not mean that judgment of an appearance problem cannot be revised based on new or additional information. An appearance problem may go away once additional facts are brought to light. But the public is not usually privy to the facts needed to prove or disprove compliance with the ethics rules. All the public sees or hears is the outward manifestations of conduct, and if lucky, an explanation of this conduct by the employee or the agency ethics official designed to ease any suspicion.

Our Ethics System Does Affect the Overall Quality of the Federal Workforce, But the Ethics Rules (Apart From the Revolving Door Rules) Are Not A Major Reason For This.

Our system of ethics rules and standards does have an effect on the overall quality of persons who enter public service, especially the ranks of political appointees but also those from science and other technical fields. Ethics rules also limit the freedom of Government employees, although whether ethics rules interfere with an employee's freedom to do one's job (as opposed to pursuing private endeavors), as has been argued, is a different question.

How much of an effect? No empirical data have been assembled, nor is it likely that we could, with any degree of reliability, assemble such data. Determining accurately the number of persons who did not pursue a Federal position because of the ethics rules is an impossible undertaking for three reasons. First, the universe of persons to be queried would include not only those who pulled out after being nominated and those who declined to apply after being invited to do so by the White House or Transition Teams, but all those who never applied in the first place or failed to express an interest because they did not want to be subject to the ethics regime. But this last group of persons could never be determined. Second, a person who decided to back out of a potential appointment might chose to explain the decision by referring to the ethics rules, when in fact, ethics was a substitute for some other reason the person did not wish to disclose. Third, the list of those who kept away from Federal service because of the ethics rules would include some persons who most would agree are not suitable for government service for that very reason.

All of the evidence that good people[34] stay away from government service is, therefore, anecdotal. This is not to discount or denigrate such evidence, but only to note the impossibility of accurately quantifying the scope of the problem.

This chapter assumes that good people are discouraged or dissuaded from entering public service, and asks what is it that keeps them away? How has our system of ethics laws, standards, and enforcement discouraged persons from public service?

To answer this question, it is helpful to examine the complaints frequently lodged against our ethics system. It has been charged with being:

- too onerous
- too intrusive
- too complex, and
- too easily subject to abuse or misuse

However, the ethics rules have not been charged with being too exacting, in the sense that many people are **unable** to meet these standards, as would be a requirement that employees must speak a foreign language fluently, or run a mile in under five minutes. Those who object to our ethics rules do not say, "I cannot comply." The ethics rules also have not been charged with being inconsistent with human nature or common practice, the way Prohibition was perceived and the 55 mile per hour speed limit is still. The only ethics rule that approaches one that would be honored more in the breach than in the observance is the prohibition against receiving anything of value, no matter how inexpensive, from a prohibited source, or if given because of one's official position. The theory is that you cannot stop small gifts of appreciation or good will, so you might as well allow them within certain guidelines. In the comprehensive standards of conduct published in 1992, OGE carved out a $20 *de minimis* exception to take care of this matter.[35]

There are reasons other than ethics why good people refrain from entering public service. There is the financial sacrifice: the highest pay for Executive Branch officials is less than $150,000. Corporate executives, law partners, and other professionals often make three to ten times this amount. At the lower levels of the Government, the disparity in income between the public and private sector is just as acute, especially for lawyers and other professionals, who may have sizeable school loans to repay.

An Executive Branch appointment entails a loss of privacy, initially as a result of the nomination and confirmation process, and subsequently from the nature of a high-profile position. During the vetting process within the White House and later in the Senate, prospective appointees must publicly disclose their finances (and those of their spouse), associations, and arrangements with their former employer, as well as privately disclose to the FBI, the White House, and the Senate committee many details about their personal life and conduct. FBI background investigations consist of interviews of friends, former colleagues, associates, and neighbors, including any former spouse, and are intended to track down adverse or critical reports from any of these persons. Prospective appointees are asked, in writing and orally, at least two times, whether there is "anything in their background, personal or otherwise, which, if revealed in connection with the appointment, could prove embarrassing to either you or the President." As Zoe Baird (and a few other of the President's nominees) discovered, getting by the White House vetting process is not the end of the clearance gauntlet. Persons with a record of provocative or controversial positions and statements are also likely to receive even greater scrutiny, complete with distortions of one's record. The experiences of Robert Bork and Clarence Thomas demonstrate that political or policy opponents of a nominee will not hesitate to resort to investigating a nominee's past with the intent of derailing the appointment over some public or private sin committed, or allegedly committed, in the past.

High-level positions inevitably attract a great amount of scrutiny from the media, too, throughout the official's Government tenure. The media are always on the lookout for scandal, whether it occurred during or before one's Government service, and whether on or off the job, because scandal sells newspapers and helps ratings. Political (Congress, political parties, and candidates) and policy (interest groups) opponents also hunt for any trail of scandal and, whether they feed the media quietly or disseminate a press release, they intend the ensuing controversy to distract the official and frustrate the agency's objectives.

A corollary of this scrutiny is high stress level associated with a top appointment. Some persons who expertly handle the stress in the private sector with which they are familiar shy away from the differently stressful inside-the-beltway environment.

These are real factors that discourage many persons from seeking or accepting a Federal appointment, and the ethics statutes and regulations (i.e, public financial disclosure and conflict-of-interest requirements) have little, if anything, to do with them.

Are the ethics standards **too onerous?** In some respects, yes. The scheme of post-employment restrictions places too great a burden on senior appointees' employment opportunities following Government service. The common vices in section 207 are the foreign entity and trade or treaty negotiation provisions, but the worst feature of the revolving door scheme is the pledge to observe a five-year cooling-off period President Clinton exacts from his appointees.

The longstanding requirement that officials divest themselves of conflicting and potentially conflicting interests (where recusal is impractical and a waiver would be inappropriate) is an inconvenience to many, and results in financial loss to some. But it is unlikely that persons stay away from government service just so they can hold onto one or more financial interests. These persons would just as likely refrain from public service because of the absolute financial sacrifice, which is mainly a function of salary.

Executive order and statute restrict the receipt of outside earned income during the tenure of a fulltime noncareer official. But again, there are few persons who want to serve in the Government but turn down the chance because of the prohibition against outside earned income.

The financial disclosure requirements are probably excessive, in that some bear little, if any, ethics nexus. But it is infrequent, if not rare, for someone to decline Federal service because he or she refuses to disclose publicly a financial interest. Some persons may not want to publicly disclose anything about their finances, but some disclosure is essential to guard against actual conflicts of interest. Public disclosure provides a better check against potential conflicts than would confidential disclosure, in part because agency ethics officials are not always aware of programs and matters handled by their own agency. Would those who favor doing away with public financial disclosure also recommend doing away with public disclosure of contributions to a public official's legal defense fund (trusting the official or agency ethics office with returning inappropriate contributions)? Would they be content with private filings of political contributions with the Federal Election Committee (FEC)?

Are the ethics standards **too intrusive** on the private sphere of activity Federal employees enjoy during their public service? The answer to this question is both yes and no. Certain core ethics provisions, dealing with gifts, outside earned income, and financial conflicts of interest, do not adversely affect the Federal service applicant pool. Current restrictions on the receipt of honoraria and participation in outside professional activities do place greater limitations on the Federal workforce than are necessary. These rules hit the Government scientific community hardest; they are less problematic for high-level positions. In any event, violations of these restrictions are seldom fodder for congressional investigations or media headlines. Indeed, employees who deliberately refuse to abide by these restrictions and challenge them in court are sometimes treated sympathetically by the media.

Are the rules **too complex?** The matrix of post-employment restrictions is needlessly intricate, overlapping, and replete with interpretative questions. Section 207 could be simplified, and the procurement integrity provision repealed, without watering down the main protections.

Section 208 is also fraught with interpretive difficulties, such as the meaning of the terms "particular matter" and "direct and predictable effect." The uncertain terrain of section 208, however, does not keep people out of government for fear of unwittingly committing a crime. The history of the Justice Department's enforcement of section 208 confirms that it has not been abused by prosecutors. The same, unfortunately, cannot be said of Congress. Members have regularly charged an Executive Branch official with a criminal conflict-of-interest without any appreciation for the actual wording of the statute or the interpretative gloss the Justice Department has put on it.[36]

The financial disclosure requirements are technical, perhaps even "hypertechnical" (Reid Weingarten's term used in defending Ron Brown), but all high-level officials receive assistance in completing the forms, so the disclosure requirements are not particularly burdensome. (Those officials with extensive financial portfolios are the very persons who can afford to hire private counsel or accountants to complete their forms.) There is a stronger argument that the financial disclosure requirements go well beyond what is necessary to guard against conflicts of interest. In fact, they do.

The standards of conduct, on the other hand, are not too complex. Any rule, at its margins, may appear arbitrary. The appearance standard, for example, has been criticized as too amorphous and subjective. But, as noted earlier, OGE changed the appearance standard in the standards of conduct to place it on a more objective basis.

Some critics cite the length of the comprehensive standards of conduct as proof that our ethics rules have become too unwieldy. They long for a return to the old days, when they believe—incorrectly—that the ethics rules basically consisted of a set of general principles. Regardless of their appreciation for history, these critics fail to recognize that what resulted in the length and complexity of the standards was the push for greater liberalization and consistency. **Liberalization** results in crafting exceptions and exclusions to the otherwise strict prohibitions.[37] **Consistency** requires a degree of explanation to ensure that agency ethics officials construe the ethics standards similarly in similar situations, and is achieved in part by narrowing the interstices of regulation. Strip the standards of conduct of the examples and its size is cut in half. Take away the many qualifications, exceptions and exclusions and it is halved again.

But an ethics regime that consisted only of basic core principles would not be good for the Federal workforce or the public. Federal employees would be subject to tighter restrictions, uneven application, and greater susceptibility to charges of unethical conduct, because of the protean nature of general ethical principles such as, "employees shall act impartially and not give preferential treatment to any private organization or individual."[38] It would not be good for the public, either, because the well-intentioned and base alike would be less likely to understand that certain conduct would be seen as unethical or improper by others.

One area in which the standards of conduct appear overly complex is section 502, governing non-financial conflicts. During the drafting of the standards, a vocal element within the ethics community did not want any standard concerning appearances of impropriety (apart from a hortatory principle). They did not prevail, of course, except that they were successful in watering down the eventual standard. It now is triggered by a "covered relationship" and applies only to "particular matter involving specific parties." The standard can and should be simplified and broadened at the same time.

Are the ethics standards **too easily subject to misuse and abuse?** Ethics is used as a political weapon by policy opponents, and serves as fodder for the media. But in my view this is more a reflection of our increasingly contentious political climate, the adversarial press, and the public's ever-growing distrust of government and government officials, than because of our system of ethics rules. Imagine an ethics system that consisted only of basic core principles, such as the executive order issued by Presidents Kennedy, Johnson and Bush. Would the media's and political opponents' thirst for scandal and the hunt for ethical transgressions be reduced? It is doubtful.

The independent counsel law, however, stands out as a special problem. Among the many problems of the statute, the threshold for appointment of an independent counsel is too low. Another problem is the fact that an appointment is treated as an indictment, when it is no such thing. Charters are often too broad, allowing independent counsels to engage in fishing expeditions to justify their protracted and expensive investigation. Political opponents (of both parties) know these things, of course, and exploit them in calling for an independent counsel at the first mention of an alleged ethical scandal involving a member of the Cabinet or senior White House official.

More generally, the criminal nature of some of the ethics laws also renders them more susceptible to abuse by political and policy opponents. A charge that an official has committed a crime packs more punch that a charge that the official has violated the standards of conduct.

Many thought the appearance standard in section 502 would lead to unfair charges of unethical behavior, and would exacerbate the problem of subjectivity that is posed by having any appearance standard. In fact, section 502 has largely been ignored by the ethics gadflies.[39]

Conclusions

In sum, the current state of ethics laws and regulations is, on the whole, healthy and not in need of major reform, except with respect to the ever-tightening set of revolving door restrictions. What is often perceived as a problem with our ethics laws is more accurately seen as a product of our current political climate and the evolving nature of competitive, adversarial journalism. The mistakes made by the Clinton Administration officials recounted in the chapters that follow, and by officials of previous administrations, were for the most part not caused by the erection of higher, unrealistic or unfair ethics standards. The core ethics principles from which the standards of conduct are drawn have remained essentially unchanged for thirty years. So the notion of the current ethics system under President Clinton as tougher than any previous administration's is basically a myth.

One of these core principles, the appearance of impropriety standard, has gained a bad reputation primarily from its use as a political weapon. But the appearance standard would still be with us, even if it were eliminated from the standards of conduct, because appearances are often the only basis upon which the public evaluates government action. Thus, the appearance standard must be taken to heart by political appointees if they hope to earn the public's confidence in their integrity.

Postscript to Chapter Two:

Fourteen
Principles
for a
New
Administration

Fourteen
Principles
for a
New
Administration

To assist future administrations in establishing their ethical programs, here are fourteen principles that, if followed, should significantly help keep an administration out of ethical hot water:

1. **Keep ethics rhetoric to a minimum; don't ratchet up an ethics standard unless you are willing to answer for it.** President Clinton's "revolving door" executive order raised expectations that were dashed when the fine print was read and the order's loopholes were noticed. Worse, his rhetorical pledge of an administration subject to the toughest ethics standards and cleaner than its predecessors came back to haunt him each time the White House blundered or an Administration official fell. Considering the immense size and scope of the Executive Branch, and that no vetting process is fail-safe, some ethical transgressions are inevitable in any administration. Presidents should focus on ensuring their appointees's compliance with the basic ethics standards that have been in place, without significant change, for thirty years.

2. **Appearances matter**. The appearance standard is not new, but it is more important in today's climate, given the adversarial press, a contentious opposition party, and the public's skepticism of the Government's good faith and integrity. The reality is that the public evaluates the integrity of government conduct almost exclusively based on appearances and, moreover, as those appearances are presented through

the media. A President should tell his Cabinet and White House staff that it is not good enough that they regard themselves as honorable and well-intentioned. The public's trust is based both on their actions and how those actions appear.

3.   **Keep nominees away from their agencies, or at least out of the deliberative decisionmaking loop, until confirmation.** Improper assumption of authority or responsibility by appointees who have not yet been confirmed is an affront to the Senate's constitutional advice-and-consent authority, seeding distrust of the administration from the beginning. It also sours the new team of political appointees with the career civil service, and subjects agency actions with the prospective appointee's fingerprints on them to challenge in court as *ultra vires*.

4.   **Don't play cute with financial disclosure reports and other background investigations; err on the side of overdisclosure.** This is a lesson learned the hard by Secretaries Ron Brown and Henry Cisneros. This is somewhat outside of the President's and White House's control, but the President can send a clear message at the beginning of the vetting process that he will not tolerate false, misleading, or selective disclosure.

5. **Appoint a White House staff based on a different kind of diversity: limit the number of loyalists and campaign aides.** The White House staff should include a sufficient number of persons with proven experience and judgment, who can be relied on to make the right policy calls, to say "no," and to be able to understand and observe the distinction between the presidency and the person occupying the office. Having a few experienced "old hands" in place may make an important difference. Conversely, the number of persons appointed to the senior White House staff, based solely on campaign experience or a previous close personal or professional relationship with the President, should be limited.

6.   **Keep tight reins on informal advisers to the President.** They are either special Government employees, and accordingly subject to the ethics and financial disclosure laws, or they should not take part in the White House deliberative process. The unprecedented access and influence of informal consultants in the Clinton White House has diffused accountability and raised serious questions about the improper influence of private interests.

7.   **Consult the Office of Government Ethics (OGE) or the Justice Department's Office of Legal Counsel (OLC) before making a sensitive judgment call or reaching a legal conclusion on ethics issues of first impression or novel application.** The wisdom of this advice may seem obvious: it gives the White House much protection from subsequent media and congressional criticism; it obviates putting OGE and OLC in the difficult position of analyzing the propriety of an action already taken; and it makes it more likely that the White House's decision will be correct. Here, the Clinton White House's failures in this regard are many and include: (1) the legal defense fund was set up without fully consulting OGE; (2) the First Lady was allowed to hold on to her financial interests in health care companies and serve as the Chairman of the President's Health Care Task Force without obtaining Justice's views

on her legal status, which had ramifications both for section 208, the conflict-of-interest statute, and the Federal Advisory Committee Act; (3) Harry Thomason was given a White House office and tasks without consulting with Justice or OGE about whether he thereby became a Federal employee subject to the ethics laws; and (4) The President committed during the campaign to issue an unwise policy on the revolving door; whatever consultation with OGE occurred too late and without the possibility of a serious change to the thrust of the policy.

8.   **Don't mix the personal with the official.** Ethics allegations that do not relate to actions taken during Federal service should be answered by the official personally, or by his lawyer or representative, but not by a government official. Government personnel and resources should not be enlisted unless there is an official nexus to the allegations. This is an especially important lesson for the White House Counsel's office to grasp. But the rest of the White House should observe this distinction, even if the White House press corps won't seem to let them. Among the most damning aspects of the Whitewater affair to date has been the specter of White House officials stonewalling (and perhaps worst) to protect the President and the First Lady, much of which could have been avoided had Whitewater questions been referred to the Clintons' private attorneys from the start. The President, of course, would not have been able to duck his personal responsibility to answer such questions, but the White House staff (all save Bruce Lindsey, who has some firsthand knowledge of the facts) would have avoided being seen misusing their office, lying, or covering up. Assembling from the start a Whitewater damage control team within the White House ensured that the White House press corps and public would treat these allegations as involving the presidency. (Also, compare the White House's proper approach to the Paula Jones lawsuit with Bruce Lindsey's assigned responsibility to deal with the reports of the Arkansas State troopers' allegations.)

9.   **When a potential scandal looms, do not circle the wagons, withhold documents, impugn the motives of those making the allegations, or lean on witnesses.** Instead, cooperate by agreeing to an appropriate review or investigation, whether by an Inspector General, the Justice Department, an independent counsel, or Congress. Subject to some limitations, disclose documents freely to Executive agencies, such as the FBI, and relevant Congressional committees, as well as to the public. Candor and truthfulness are musts; their absence is stonewalling. This is easier said than done, of course. The Clinton White House performed poorly in responding to each of the following ethics controversies: Whitewater, the Health Care Task Force, the White House Travel Office firings, and Mrs. Clinton's commodities trades. As a result, the media grew more critical and less trusting and suspicion of wrongdoing increased among the general public.

10.   **Refrain from contacts with law enforcement and investigative agencies except through established channels, and then only for policy matters.** It took several blunders by the Clinton White House (e.g., Travel Office, Whitewater) before it understood the need to refrain from contacting law enforcement agencies except through certain channels and then only when there is an obvious official governmental purpose. The guidance memoranda the White House put out, before and after

the blowup over the White House contacts with Treasury officials relating to the Resolution Trust Corporation's (RTC) Madison Guaranty investigation, should be synthesized into one memorandum given to White House staff on their first day. It will be the rare case when the White House has a proper occasion to contact the Justice Department or other law enforcement agency about a specific pending investigation or case. When it does, it should be done by the White House Counsel's office and only through the Attorney General or Deputy Attorney General (or agency General Counsel), who can independently determine the appropriateness of the inquiry or communication.

Moreover, it should be made clear that it is not appropriate for any person in the White House, including the President, to seek or receive advance notice of any law enforcement action concerning that person in his or her personal capacity, where such advance notice provides any opportunity to affect the merits, timing or publicity of that law enforcement action.

11. **If the President's spouse is to be given responsibilities equivalent to an Executive Branch official, she should be considered a Federal official subject to the ethics standards to the same extent as others**. Presenting the First Lady as an administration official only begged the question whether the ethics laws applied. Administrations avoid criticism and take the high road if they consider such a Federal functionary subject to the ethics laws, even if the law does not expressly cover a President's spouse.

12. **Don't rely on blind trusts to avoid conflicts of interest**. Actual and potential conflicts should be remedied by divestiture, recusal, or, in limited circumstances, a waiver. A blind trust protects an official only from the possibility of conflicts arising from assets acquired after the trust's creation. Blind trusts are useful for officials with substantial financial portfolios, who do not want their entire holdings converted into mutual funds and government securities. In the past, blind trusts have also been successfully employed to satisfy the media that an ethics problem has been cured. But an administration should not assume that reporters will continue to be ignorant or indifferent to the law.

13. **Require presidential appointees who intend to make an official trip back home or to another location where a personal event will take place to obtain clearance by an agency ethics official to ensure there is a *bona fide* purpose that preexisted the personal event**. This may seem the height of presidential micromanagement of the conduct of his appointees and display a lack of trust in their sound judgment. But history proves that such micromanagement is necessary and such distrust is well-founded. Abuse of travel perks and privileges, when revealed, strikes a chord of resentment and anger in most Americans, because the message it sends of an official using public office for private gain is so clear and confirms a stereotype of political appointees abusing their office.

14. **Fire officials who commit serious violations of the ethics laws and regulations.** Perhaps the most difficult principle for Presidents to live up to, it is also one of the most important to observe. The reluctance Presidents historically have

exhibited in dismissing an official who has violated ethics standards hurts an administration's public standing, and causes some to doubt the President's commitment to integrity in government.

Part Two

The White House

Chapter Three

The
First Lady's
Conflict of Interest

Given her Federal responsibilities, the First Lady should be considered a Federal employee subject to the conflict-of-interest restrictions governing Federal employees. Even if, as a legal matter, she is not subject to the ethics laws, she should conduct herself as if she were bound by those laws, consistent with long-standing White House policy. Her financial interest in stocks of health care related companies, although small and not subject to her control, conflicted with the health care legislative responsibilities entrusted to her by the President. Whether (assuming Mrs. Clinton is a Federal official) she violated 18 U.S.C. 208 is open to question, largely because of interpretative difficulties in applying that section, not because the facts are unknown or controverted. The legal conclusion of the Office of Government Ethics (OGE) that Mrs. Clinton was not engaged in a "particular matter" in chairing the President's Task Force on National Health Care Reform is wrong. If allowed to stand, this interpretation creates a loophole in the conflict-of-interest laws for legislative matters.

The First Lady should have divested herself of this conflicting interest upon assuming her Federal responsibilities in January 1993. The blind trust created belatedly in July 1993 did not give her any legal protection.

The First Lady's Government Responsibilities

On January 25, 1993, President Clinton created the Task Force on National Health Care Reform, naming Hillary Rodham Clinton as Chairman.[1] All other members of the Task Force were Cabinet or senior White House officials. The Task Force was charged with preparing comprehensive health care reform legislation to submit to Congress. Although the Task Force terminated on May 30, 1993, as specified in its charter, the First Lady continued to represent the Administration on the health care issue, appearing before Congress and in briefings of reporters.[2]

Although Mrs. Clinton's activities in the health care reform area have been the most visible, she has also served in the White House as an adviser to the President on many other issues.[3] Indeed, from just the published reports of Mrs. Clinton's participation in internal White House meetings, the list of matters in which she has not participated is perhaps shorter than the list of matters in which she has been involved. First Ladies have traditionally provided regular advice to their husbands, but this advice tended to be provided privately and quietly, as well as infrequently. In addition to the advice Mrs. Clinton undoubtedly provides the President privately, she has participated in White House and Cabinet policy deliberations as if she were a full-time Assistant to the President.[4]

The First Lady's Health Care Interests

It is difficult to obtain a complete and accurate understanding of Mrs. Clinton's financial interests in health care related companies during the time she has served as the Administration's point person on health care reform, from January 25, 1993, until the present. Information about Mrs. Clinton's financial interests was obtained from the several public financial disclosure reports (SF-278) Bill Clinton was required to file first as a candidate, and then later as President.[5]

According to the financial disclosure report filed by the President in May 1993, Mrs. Clinton is a limited partner in Valuepartners I, Ltd., an investment partnership managed by Smith Capital Management, Inc. of Little Rock.[6] As of December 31, 1992,[7] Valuepartners had total investments of $8.9 million. Mrs. Clinton owned a 0.975% share, or about $90,000.[8] She received between $5,001 and $15,000 in unspecified income from Valuepartners in 1992.[9]

At the close of 1992, Valuepartners had holdings in the following health care related companies:[10]

Common stock

Columbia Hospital Corporation.[11] (health care facilities/services)
Coventry (health benefits services & HMO operator)
Grancare (long-term health care and rehabilitation facilities)
Lincare (in-home respiratory therapy services)
National Rehabilitation Centers Inc.
Health Care and Retirement Corporation (long-term health provider)
Phycor, Inc. (operator multi-special medical clinics)
REN Corporation (outpatient dialysis centers)
United HealthCare Corporation (HMO operator)

Short stock

Bioplasty, Inc. (plastic surgical devices and implants)
Cryomedical Sciences (developmental stage low temperature medical products)
Health Professionals (health care personnel services)
Royce Labs (generic drug manufacturer)

Rowland Smith, the vice president of Smith Capital, explained that Valuepartners is a "'special growth' fund because it buys shares in small and medium-sized companies and also engages in short-selling of stocks."[12] Smith noted that Mrs. Clinton, as a limited partner, has no control over the investments but is informed of the fund's performance.[13]

Short-selling is:

a technique used by investors who believe a stock's price is about to go down. The short-seller sells stock he does not yet own, but is able to borrow from a broker. He then delivers the borrowed shares to the buyer, collects payment and waits for the price to fall. Once it falls, he buys shares at the lower price and gives them to the broker to replace those he borrowed.[14]

The short-seller pockets the difference. "So the more prices fall, the more you can profit."[15]

Smith, who is reportedly "an old family adviser,"[16] explained to *Money* magazine that:

overall his ValuePartners fund lost money on health stocks in this year's [1993] first quarter. He said losses on the ones he owns for future appreciation more than wiped out gains on those he sold short. Turning to the Clintons, Smith told MONEY: "They have handled themselves with absolute ethical purity." [H]e said, "Not once in 15 years has Hillary or the President tried to influence what I've bought or sold in their portfolios. I'm the only guy in the country that knows that." Moreover, he added: "I haven't talked to Hillary since last August or September [1992], and then individual stocks weren't mentioned.[17]

In July 1993, Mrs. Clinton's limited partnership interest in Valuepartners, along with other assets, was placed in a blind trust.[18]

The financial disclosure report filed by the President in May 1994 covers calendar year 1993. As he was required to do, President Clinton listed, as an attachment to Schedule B, the individual transactions over $1,000 made by Valuepartners for the portion of 1993 before Mrs. Clinton's interest was placed in the blind trust.[19] The report listed over 50 purchases and sales of stock of health-care related companies:[20]

Company (P(Purchase)/S(Sale), date) (asterisk denotes newly acquired stock)

Chiron Technology (therapeutic, diagnostic products) (P, 3/19; S, 3/22)
*Collagen Corp. (biomedical products: human tissue) (S, 1/28, 1/29; P, 3/22)
Columbia Healthcare (S, 2/22)
Coventry (S, 2/17, 2/22, 2/23)
Cryomedical Sciences (P, 6/4)
Grancare (S, 1/5)
*Immune Response (R&D immune system pharmaceuticals) (P, 6/4, 6/9)
Lincare (S, 2/22)
*Medical Action Ind (P, 1/8, 1/11)
*National Medical Enterprises (specialty & general hospitals) (S, 4/23,
    4/26; P, 5/27)
National Rehabilitation Centers (P, 1/5, 1/13, 1/18; S, 2/10, 3/24, 4/12,
    4/13, 4/16)
*Oxford Health Plans (health benefit services in NY) (S, 5/7; P, 5/27)
Phycor, Inc. (S, 2/9)
Physicians Clinical Lab (clinical laboratory services) (P, 1/6; S, 1/22, 1/25)
*Procyte (pharmaceutical products) (P, 5/12, 5/13, 5/17, 5/18)
REN Corp. (S, 1/18, 2/22, 2/23, 2/25)
*Synergen (biological products) (S, 1/5, 2/3, 2/8, 2/18; P, 2/22)
U.S. Healthcare (P, 1/12; S, 2/12)
United HealthCare (P, 1/10; S, 2/12, 5/7; P, 5/10, 6/10)
Vital Signs (mfrs single patient medical products) (S, 4/8)
*Wellpoint (health care services in Cal.) (P, 1/29, 2/2)

Because this report does not indicate whether a particular sale disposed of all of Valuepartners' interest in a company, it cannot be determined from this report whether any of the health care companies was no longer part of Valuepartners' portfolio by the time the blind trust was created in July 1993.[21] It is clear, however, that Valuepartners continued to hold stock in several health care related companies as of June 1993.[22]

The Conflict-of-Interest Statute

The central conflict-of-interest statute is 18 U.S.C. 208. That law prohibits an "officer" or "employee" of the Executive Branch, including a "special Government employee," from participating as a Government officer or employee, personally and substantially, in any particular matter in which, to her knowledge, she has a financial interest.[23] A violation of section 208 is punishable by imprisonment of one year (five years if "willful") and may result in a fine of not more than $50,000.[24]

Applying these terms to the First Lady, her financial interests, and her activities is not without difficulty. Both those who have accused her of a criminal conflict of interest, and those who have defended her against this charge, have failed to recognize the several interpretive difficulties. True, working on health care reform while holding interests in health care related companies fits the lay person's notion of a conflict of interest. That Mrs. Clinton failed to guard against an appearance of impropriety and failed to remedy this conflict, resulting in a spate of criticism from Republicans and the media, is plain. However, whether her conduct was criminal is not.

Allegations of a Conflict and the Administration's Responses

Soon after the release of the President's financial disclosure report in May 1993, a couple of articles appeared suggesting that the First Lady's financial interest in the Valuepartners fund posed a conflict of interest with her Task Force responsibilities.[25]

After the suicide of Deputy White House Counsel Vince Foster in July 1993, columnist William Safire wrote of the First Lady's conflict of interest in the context of attempting to divine what may have prompted Foster to take his life.[26] Safire noted that Foster may have unintentionally provided the basis for concluding that the First Lady was subject to the conflict-of-interest laws, in arguing that Mrs. Clinton was a "functional equivalent of a federal employee" in an effort to keep the Health Care Task Force meetings private.[27]

Safire was referring to a lawsuit filed by the Association of American Physicians and Surgeons, the American Council for Health Care Reform, and the National Legal and Policy Center, seeking access to Task Force meetings under the open meeting requirements of the Federal Advisory Committee Act (FACA).[28] The gist of the plaintiffs' argument was that meetings of the Task Force must be open to the public because Mrs. Clinton is not a "full-time officer or employee of the Federal Government." FACA exempts from the definition of advisory committee "any committee which is composed wholly of full-time officers or employees of the Federal Government."[29] Other than the First Lady, all other Task Force members were Federal officials. In response, the Justice Department, representing the First Lady and the Task Force, argued that Mrs. Clinton was the "functional equivalent of a Federal employee."[30]

U.S. District Judge Royce Lamberth rejected this argument, concluding Mrs. Clinton did not fit the definition of either "officer" or "employee" used in 5 U.S.C. 2104 and 2105, respectively.[31] In addition, Judge Lamberth stated that there was "no evidence or other indicia of employment[,]" such as the oath of office or a Standard Form 50.[32]

On appeal by the Government, the U.S. Court of Appeals for the District of Columbia, in an opinion by Judge Lawrence Silberman, reversed the district court.[33] Seeking to avoid deciding the constitutionality of FACA's application to a committee created to advise the President, the court of appeals held that Mrs. Clinton was a *de facto* full-time Federal officer under FACA:

> The question whether the President's spouse is a "full-time officer or employee" of the government is close enough for us properly to construe FACA not to apply to the Task Force merely because Mrs. Clinton is a member.[34]

However, the court expressly declined to decide Mrs. Clinton's "status under any other statute[,]" including the conflict-of-interest laws.[35]

In January 1994, Representatives Bob Livingston, George Gekas, and Chris Cox, wrote to the White House Counsel and the OGE.[36] In their letter to the White House Counsel, they asked the White House to respond to several articles enclosed with their letter that discussed Mrs. Clinton's "holdings of stock in pharmaceutical companies before and during the Clinton Presidency when a blind trust has not yet been established." They asked OGE whether "the announcement of proposed Administration policy, at a time when the officials responsible for the announcements owned investments whose prices would reasonably be expected to be impacted by these statements, [would] constitute a violation of the Ethics in Government Act by those officials?" They also asked whether OGE was conducting an investigation into possible violations of the Ethics in Government Act.[37]

The White House Counsel responded that "[t]he First Lady, as a limited partner in Value Partners, never had any input, control, communication, review or oversight with respect to any investments made by Value Partners."[38] He also stated that "the First Lady never had any involvement in or sought to profit from any transactions involving health-related stocks, and we are aware of no factual basis for suggesting that she ever attempted to do so."[39] As a legal matter, Nussbaum concluded that "the First Lady's activities did not constitute participation in a 'particular matter' and, in any event, had no 'direct and predictable effect' on any of Value Partners' assets or investments."[40]

In its response, OGE stated that it was not conducting an investigation.[41] "Furthermore, OGE is not aware of any information, including that provided in your letter, that would call for such an investigation." OGE explained the elements of section 208,[42] but in doing so did not refer to the facts involving the First Lady or her financial interests. In particular, OGE neither agreed nor disagreed with whether the announcement of Administration policy constituted participating in a "particular matter."

Because it was devoid of any analysis applying the facts to the law, OGE's nonresponsive letter simply prompted another letter from Congress. In March, eighty-one House Republicans signed a letter to OGE, providing additional materials relating to the Valuepartners partnership and asking OGE to conduct an investigation.[43] The letter charged that:

> At the time that Mrs. Clinton's actions caused the drop in the prices of these stocks, her personal investment in ValuePartners I, of which she had repeated notice, was intentionally structured to profit from price declines in pharmaceutical company stocks.[44]

On May 3, 1994, OGE provided its first detailed, substantive response.[45] For purposes of the letter, OGE assumed that the First Lady was subject to 18 U.S.C. 208—a legal issue OGE noted was "unsettled"—and gave the information available "its most expansive interpretation to see if it could support your allegation."[46] OGE concluded:

> [T]his Office believes that the elements required for a violation of 18 U.S.C. 208 or the standards of conduct can not be established from the circumstances and concerns that are the basis of your allegation. That is most clearly true of "particular matter." Therefore, we see no basis to refer this matter for investigation.[47]

Although OGE analyzed each element of section 208 in light of the facts, its only legal determination was that Mrs. Clinton's involvement in the development of health care reform legislation did not constitute participation in a "particular matter."[48]

This study proceeds to analyze each element of section 208, including the various responses from OGE and the White House.

Does Section 208 Apply to the First Lady?

Because section 208 applies only to Federal officers and employees, a threshold question is whether the First Lady is even subject to the law. That question does not permit a quick or simple answer. OGE is correct that the question is unsettled, in that no court has had occasion to determine whether the ethics laws apply to the First Lady.[49] The issue was not presented in *Association of American Physicians and Surgeons* and therefore there was no need for the D.C. Circuit to decide the question.

Justice Department Precedent

Initially, the White House Counsel asserted: "It is the view of the White House Counsel, consistent with the views of prior administrations, that the First Lady, like the President, is not covered by the conflict-of-interest statutes and regulations."[50] By the "views of prior administrations," Nussbaum meant opinions of the Justice Department's Office of Legal Counsel (OLC).

Since at least 1974, the Justice Department has taken the position that the President and Vice President are not subject to the conflict-of-interest laws.[51] In 1985, OLC determined that the First Lady was not an "officer or employee of the United States" and therefore she also was not subject to the conflict-of-interest laws.[52]

In that instance, OLC was asked whether any ethics law or regulation would be implicated by the establishment of a private charitable fund in Mrs. Reagan's name and by certain activities the First Lady might undertake on behalf of such a fund. The only reason offered in OLC's opinion was its previously expressed view that **the President** was exempt from the conflict-of-interest standards. The First Lady's situation, however, bears no resemblance to the facts in Mrs. Reagan's case. The only active involvement expected of Mrs. Reagan was her participation in fund-raising on behalf of the **private** charitable fund.[53] By contrast, the First Lady was charged to develop the **administration's** health care proposal and to represent the administration's position in testimony, speeches and meetings.

Considering that the OLC opinion is bereft of analysis, and that the factual situation here is vastly different from what OLC considered in 1985, the opinion should not be given any weight. (In fact, an earlier OLC opinion, discussed subsequently, is more relevant.)

The Conflict-of-Interest Statutes

Section 208 applies to "officers or employee of the Executive Branch, including a special Government employee." The definitional section in the conflict-of-interest chapter of Title 18, section 202, does not define the term "officer" or "employee", nor does it incorporate by reference any other statute's definition. However, the term "special Government employee" is defined in section 202(a).

Under section 202(c), the President and Vice President, along with Members of Congress and Federal judges, are not considered "officers" or "employees" for the purpose of the conflict-of-interest provisions. Section 202(c) was enacted as part of the Ethics Reform Act of 1989. It codified, as to the President and Vice President, the Justice Department's long-standing view. However, the First Lady enjoys no such statutory exemption; she is not among the list of exempted persons. It is fair to assume that neither the Bush Administration, which promoted the exemption, nor Congress, which passed it, considered whether the First Lady should also be given statutory protection. Perhaps no one anticipated that a conflict-of-interest issue would arise with the First Lady, given the traditional, limited responsibilities of the First Lady.[54]

The Concept of a Special Government Employee (SGE)

Although section 202 does not define "officer" or "employee," the broad reach of the conflict-of-interest restrictions is made clear by the definition of a "special Government employee" in section 202(a):

> [T]he term "special Government employee" shall mean an officer or employee of the executive . . . branch of the United States Government . . ., who is retained, designated, appointed, or employed to perform, with or without compensation, for not to exceed one hundred and thirty days during any period of three hundred and sixty-five consecutive days, temporary duties either on a full-time or intermittent basis[.][55]

A prominent example of an SGE today is a member of a government board or commission that meets from time to time. The concept of an SGE originated in 1962 with President Kennedy's desire to ensure that informal advisers and consultants to the government were subject to the same conflict-of-interest standard to which regular Federal employees were subject, while not as subject to other ethics laws that might discourage them from providing advice.[56] SGEs serve the public interest and therefore are subject to the conflict-of-interest restriction of section 208 to the same extent as a regular employee.[57]

The difference between an SGE and a regular Federal employee is length of service; special government employees are not expected to serve more than 130 days in any 365-day period.[58]

The criteria generally used to determine whether someone is an SGE, as opposed to someone who is not any type of Federal employee, are whether: the person has sworn or signed an oath of office, is paid a salary or expenses, enjoys agency office space, serves as a spokesperson for the agency, is subject to the supervision of a Federal agency, and serves in a consulting or advisory capacity to the United States.[59] Applying these criteria to the First Lady's participation in health care reform points to the conclusion that she is an SGE.

As Chairman of the Health Care Task Force and subsequently, the First Lady has functioned as a government official. Even though First Ladies traditionally occupy office space in the White House complex, the First Lady's office space in the West Wing is a significant indicator that she has an official role in the development of White House policy.[60] The First Lady has represented the Administration in testimony before Congress, and in interviews and speeches. When the First Lady speaks, she speaks as a White House official.[61] She has held and presided over internal Task Force meetings. All of these functions are Federal functions; they are not tasks to be performed by a private citizen. They are very similar to functions performed by an assistant to the President or a cabinet official.[62] If President Clinton had given these responsibilities to a person outside of government, there would be no question that such person would become a Federal officer or employee by virtue of that assignment.[63]

The considerations used in determining whether someone is an SGE are similar to, **but not the same as**, the criteria in the definition of "officer" and "employee" in the Federal personnel statutes, 5 U.S.C. 2104 and 2105. Recall that Judge Lamberth determined that Mrs. Clinton was not a government employee under FACA because she did not satisfy the criteria in these statutes.

> An "officer" means "an individual who is—
> (1) required by law to be appointed in the civil service . . . ;
> (2) engaged in the performance of a Federal function under authority of law or an Executive act; and
> (3) subject to the supervision of [the President or Federal officer], while engaged in the performance of the duties of his office. . . .[64]

> An "employee" means "an individual who is—
> (1) appointed in the civil service . . .;
> (2) engaged in the performance of a Federal function under authority of law or an Executive act; and
> (3) subject to the supervision of [the President or Federal officer] while engaged in the performance of the duties of his position . . . . [65]

The First Lady satisfies the second and third criteria in both statutes,[66] but probably does not satisfy the first in either one. She is not "required by law to be appointed in the civil service" and she was not "appointed in the civil service" in a formal sense. But these statutes, at best, are illustrative. They should not be used to determine whether the First Lady is subject to ethics laws, for several reasons.

First, both sections 2104 and 2105 begin with the phrase, "For the purposes of this title" (Title 5), so that these laws do not expressly define the words "officer" and "employee" in Title 18.[67]

Second, these provisions in Title 5 concern the civil service; most employees of the White House Office are hired under authority of Title 3.[68] The distinction between Title 5 employees and Title 3 employees is significant. Under 3 U.S.C. 105(a)(1), the President enjoys broad discretion to "appoint and fix the pay of employees in the White House office without regard to any other provision of law regulating the employment or compensation of persons in Government service." In the early weeks of the Clinton Administration, the White House provided retroactive salary payments to many White House staffers, covering work done by them before their appointment papers were signed. The Justice Department determined that the President could legally authorize retroactive pay to certain White House Office employees in view of the President's broad discretion under 3 U.S.C. 105(a)(1).[69] The General Accounting Office (GAO), which was asked to review the propriety of such retroactive appointments and other pay adjustments, noted that the law was not as flexible for Title 5 employees.[70] The Justice Department opinion confirms that employee status in the White House can arise from work actually performed, not simply the formal execution of appointment papers. If White House Office staff can receive pay for work done before a formal appointment is executed, surely the formal appointment requirements in sections 2104 and 2105 have little, if any, bearing on whether someone working in the White House Office is, in fact, an officer or employee.

Third, exempting a Federal employee from the ethics laws merely for lack of a formal appointment would exalt form over substance and create the potential for a gap in coverage.

Fourth, the definition of SGE in 18 U.S.C. 202(a) is broader than the definitions in sections 2104 and 2105. In the latter statutes, the second criterion requires an "appointment." Section 202(a), however, includes all those who are "retained, designated, appointed or employed" to perform government duties.

Both Justice and OGE have employed a functional test for determining the status of an SGE, using the personnel statutes as instructive as a general rule, but not dispositive or applicable to all situations. In 1977, OLC was asked to determine whether frequent informal consultations with the President made an informal Presidential adviser a "special Government employee." OLC held that they did not.[71] OLC examined the criteria noted above in 5 U.S.C. 2104 and 2105, stating that:

> "variants of these same three factors have, in fact, been utilized in one context or another under the conflict-of-interest laws:

>> For example, the first criterion under the civil service test—that the person be appointed in the civil service—is analogous to the definition of the term "special Government employee" for the purposes of the conflict-of interest laws: an officer or employee "who is retained, designated, appointed, or employed" to perform duties .... The quoted phrase connotes a formal relationship between the individual and the government. ... In the usual case, this formal relationship is based on an identifiable act of appointment. ... **However, an identifiable act of appointment may not be absolutely essential for an individual to regarded as an officer or employee in an a particular case ... perhaps where there was a firm mutual understanding that a relatively formal relationship existed.**[72]

OLC determined that even frequent consultations did not make the adviser an SGE, "just as Mrs. Carter would not be regarded as an SGE solely on the ground that she may discuss governmental matters with the President on a daily basis."[73]

However, OLC determined that because the individual in question had gone beyond the role of informal adviser, he had become a special Government employee and should be formally appointed and duly sworn. OLC's reasoning is reprinted in full, because the reasoning applies just as forcefully to the First Lady :

> Mr. A, however, seems to have departed from his usual role of an informal adviser to the President in connection with his recent work on a current social issue. **Mr. A has called and chaired a number of meetings that were attended by employees of various agencies, in relation to this work, and he has assumed considerable responsibility for coordinating the Administration's activities in that particular area. Mr. A is quite clearly engaging in a governmental function when he performs these duties,** and he presumably is working under the direction or supervision of the

President. **For this reason, Mr. A should be designated as a special Government employee for purposes of this work,** assuming that a good faith estimate can be made that he will perform official duties relating to that work for no more than 130 out of the next 365 consecutive days. If he is expected to perform these services for more than 130 days, he should be regarded as a regular employee. In either case, he should be formally appointed and take an oath of office.[74]

In its first extended discussion of the concept of an SGE, the Office of Government Ethics rendered similar advice:

3. Individuals Outside the Government Who Advise an Official Informally
    A Federal official may occasionally receive unsolicited, informal advice from an outside individual . . . regarding a particular matter or issue of policy that is within his official responsibility. . . . An incident of this sort sometimes prompts the inquiry whether the outsiders have become SGE's of the agency. In general, the answer is that they have not, for they are not possessed of appointments as employees nor do they perform a Federal function.
    However, as so often happens in considering the applicability of the conflict-of-interest laws, a generality is insufficient here and a *caveat* is in order. An official should not hold informal meetings more or less regularly with a non-federal individual . . . for the purpose of obtaining information or advice for the conduct of his office. If he does so, he may invite the argument that willy-nilly he has brought them within the range of 18 U.S.C. 202-209.[75]

The 1977 OLC opinion should be read to recognize that the First Lady would be considered an SGE were she to venture beyond the informal advice the First Lady has traditionally provided the President and assume Federal responsibilities other than the ceremonial and representational responsibilities she has traditionally performed.

As a Matter of Policy, the First Lady Should Consider Herself Subject to the Ethics Laws
    Even if the First Lady enjoys an exemption from the conflict-of-interest laws, however, the public's trust in Government nonetheless comes into play when the First Lady engages in significant Government functions. Thus, **as a matter of policy**, the First Lady ought to observe the conflict-of-interest standards in the performance of her health care responsibilities as if she were a Government employee subject to section 208.
    Indeed, this is the advice the Justice Department has consistently given the White House, at least until the start of the Clinton Administration:

[A]s we have advised previously, there are policy reasons for the President and First Lady to be guided in their conduct by the statutes and regulations, ...and we recommend that they do so in their activities related to the Fund.[76]
So, regardless of whether, as a matter of law, the First Lady is exempt from the

conflict-of-interest laws, the White House should have considered her covered as a matter of policy, and expeditiously taken steps to remove the conflict.

Application of Section 208 to the First Lady

Determining whether the First Lady has run afoul of section 208 by participating in health care reform while holding financial interests in health care companies requires an analysis of the following words in the statute: (1) "personal and substantial" participation; (2) "particular matter"; (3) "financial interest in the matter"; and (4) "to her knowledge."[77]

Personal and Substantial Participation. There is no question that Mrs. Clinton's involvement in the health care issue has been "personal and substantial." OGE defines the term as follows:

> To participate personally means to participate directly. . . . To participate substantially means that the employee's involvement is of significance to the matter. Participation may be substantial even though it is not determinative of the outcome of a particular matter. . . . Personal and substantial participation may occur when, for example, an employee participates through decision, approval, recommendation, investigation or the rendering of advice in a particular matter.[78]

Particular Matter. The element of section 208 that has proven most difficult to apply is "particular matter."[79] Both the White House[80] and OGE[81] determined that Mrs. Clinton's participation in health care legislation does not constitute participation in a "particular matter."

I disagree.

Federal ethics laws employ the concepts of "matter," "particular matter," and "particular matter involving a specific party or parties." The first and third terms are easy to comprehend. "Matter," a term used in the one-year cooling-off restrictions in section 207, covers any subject before Government, no matter how broad or general. "Particular matter involving specific party or parties" is the term employed in the lifetime and two-year post-employment restrictions in section 207, and is confined to matters such as a contract, claim, or adjudication. The term "particular matter" used in section 208 is not as broad as "matter," but not as narrow as "particular matter involving a specific party or parties." The principal difficulty arises from applying the term to rulemaking and legislative matters.

According to OGE, a "particular matter:"

> encompasses only matters that involve deliberation, decision, or action that is focused upon the interests of specific persons, or a discrete and identifiable class of persons. Such a matter is covered . . . even if it does not involve formal parties and may include governmental action such as legislation or policymaking that is narrowly focused on the interests of such a discrete and identifiable class of persons. The term particular matter, however, does not extend to the consideration or adoption of broad policy options that are directed to the interests of a large and diverse group of persons. . . .[82]

Thus, although health care legislation and policy-making may constitute "particular matters," only such legislation or policy-making that is "narrowly focused" on the interests of a "discrete and identifiable class of persons" is covered.

OGE's analysis in its letter to House Republicans is presented in full:

> The legislative proposal developed by the Task Force and submitted by the Administration to Congress is directed at every sector of American society; every person in the United States is intended to be affected by its terms. Hence, the health care reform legislation proposed by the Administration is not narrowly focused on the interests of such a discrete and identifiable class of persons and is therefore not a "particular matter" under section 208. If it were a "particular matter," no employee of the executive branch (since all are covered by section 208) could participate personally and substantially in the development or support of this proposal. Each would have a personal financial interest in it through the proposed legislation's universal entitlement element. That element, we must point out, has been an announced cornerstone of this Administration's policy since the beginning. Accordingly, this legislation cannot be seen as focusing on the interests of specific persons or a discrete or identifiable class of persons.[83]

The fundamental flaw in OGE's analysis was to look at health care legislation in its entirety, as an indivisible whole. Clearly, the Administration's health care proposal, as a whole, would affect all Americans, and all American businesses. But certain individual parts of the proposal **were** limited in focus and effect, for example, provisions affecting primarily hospitals, pharmaceutical companies, surgeons, or HMO's. Such specific proposals should be considered "particular matters."

In any comprehensive legislative package such as the Clinton Administration's health care proposal there will be provisions with a broad focus and others with a narrower focus. The error in OGE's analysis is in failing to address the individual constituent elements of the Administration's health care proposal.[84] The Administration's health care proposal, like most comprehensive legislative proposals, was not offered on a take-it-or-leave-it basis. A number of provisions were subject to amendment or removal. Ira Magaziner himself referred to the Administration's health care legislative package, the Health Security Act, introduced as H.R. 3600, as "800 moving parts." One of those parts was a provision that would have regulated the price of prescription drugs for Medicare and Medicaid patients.[85] Even the interdepartmental working group included a separate Pharmaceutical Price Control Working Group. The health care debate between the Administration and Congress necessarily moved from the general (Is there a health care crisis? Should we adopt a managed care or single-payer approach?) to the specific (should the price of new prescription drugs be controlled)—from the proposal as a whole to discrete provisions.

Moreover, a thorough analysis would not have been limited to a review of the Administration's health care proposal, because the First Lady undoubtedly participated also in the discussions concerning the many rival health care bills introduced in the 103d Congress.

There is apparently no Justice Department or OGE precedent for such a narrow interpretation of the phrase "particular matter"; none is cited in OGE's letter. More-over, OGE's interpretation of the term "particular matter" would, as a practical mat-ter, remove many legislative proposals from the definition. As a consequence, many situations that would appear to a reasonable person to pose a conflict of interest would not be subject to the protection of the ethics laws. A couple of examples will show this.

• Campaign finance reform legislation. Most bills to reform the conduct and financing of Federal campaigns are comprehensive. All Americans would be affect-ed by such legislation, because it would likely affect the amount of money we may contribute, to whom, and in what manner. Several campaign finance bills provide for free television time to candidates, or otherwise provide for certain broadcast dis-counts. Under OGE's interpretation, an employee who owns interests in television or radio stations could participate in the development of the Government's position on the media provisions if they were contained in a comprehensive campaign finance package.

• The Corporate Average Fuel Economy (CAFE) standard for automobiles re-quires auto manufacturers to produce a fleet of cars that achieves a certain average fuel efficiency. The law is administered by the National Highway Traffic Safety Ad-ministration. Although the CAFE standard primarily affects the Big Three auto man-ufacturers (General Motors, Ford and Chrysler), tens of millions of Americans are affected by the CAFE standards in the fuel efficiencies and prices of new cars. Under OGE's interpretation, a Federal employee who owns stock in an auto manufacturer could participate in deliberations about CAFE law and policy.

• The so-called Reconciliation bill that is a prominent feature in recent Con-gresses is more than a multi-year budget plan. All Reconciliation bills have included many separate and distinct provisions that focus on one small industry or sector of the economy. Under OGE's interpretation, no conflict-of-interest issue would arise, no matter what the issue and regardless of the employee's financial interests.

These examples demonstrate why OGE's interpretation of "particular matter" is wrong and must be revised.

In September 1995, OGE published a notice of proposed rulemaking proposing several exemptions from the conflict-of-interest law and defining the terms used in section 208.[86] OGE's discussion of the term "particular matter" in both the preamble and text of the proposed rule provides an amplification of its views. OGE notes in the preamble that:

> broad policy matters may later become particular matters **when they are implemented** in a way that the interests of specific persons or groups of persons are distinctly affected.[87]

In the proposed rule, OGE uses health care legislation as one example of something that is not a particular matter:

> *Example 8:* A legislative proposal for broad health care reform is not a particular matter because it is not focused on the interests of specific per-sons, or a discrete and identifiable class of persons. It is intended to affect every person in the United States. **However, the implementation, through**

regulations, of a section of the health care bill limiting the amount that can be charged for prescription drugs is sufficiently focused on the interests of pharmaceutical companies that it would be a particular matter.[88]

The illogic in OGE's limiting construction of the term "particular matter" is apparent in this example. OGE first notes that legislation may constitute a particular matter. OGE next states that "broad" health care legislation is not a particular matter. OGE then states that a regulation implementing **a section of the legislation** may be a particular matter. If so, that section of the legislation should also be considered a particular matter. If it is not, OGE has created a distinction between legislation and regulation that is not reflected in the law. In other words, it would be legal for an Executive Branch employee holding pharmaceutical company stocks to participate in the drafting of a legislative provision focused on pharmaceutical concerns so long as that provision is part of a comprehensive health care bill. But it would be illegal for that same employee to participate in the drafting of regulations implementing that provision. Would OGE's views be any different if the scope of the rulemaking proceeding were coextensive with the health care legislation?

Neither section 208 nor OGE's interpretation of that provision draws any distinction between participation in preliminary or early stages of a decision and participation in the decision itself. Similarly, OGE should not distinguish an Executive Branch employee's participation in legislation from her participation in a rulemaking proceeding to implement that legislation.

Financial Interest in the Matter. OGE has opined that a Government employee:

has a financial interest in a particular matter when there is a real possibility that he might gain or lose as a result of developments in or resolution of the matter. . . . It is not necessary that the potential gain or loss be of any particular magnitude. Nor must the potential gain or loss be probable for the prohibition against official action to apply. All that is required is that there be a real, as opposed to a speculative, possibility of benefit or detriment.[89]

There is no minimum threshold of a holding for the restrictions of section 208 to apply.[90] Thus, the First Lady's limited partnership interest in Valuepartners is a financial interest, notwithstanding the relatively small amount of her interest.[91] The argument of the White House Counsel that only a small percentage of Valuepartners' holdings are in health care stocks, and that the First Lady's "share of any such health-related assets [is] insubstantial," is legally irrelevant.[92]

The Justice Department has long construed the term "particular matter" further to apply to section 208 only "if the particular matter will have a direct and predictable effect on that interest."[93] In the standards of conduct, OGE defines the term "direct and predictable effect" as follows:

A particular matter will have a direct effect on a financial interest if there is a close causal link between any decision or action to be taken in the matter and any expected effect of the matter on the financial interest. . . .

A particular matter will have a predictable effect if there is a real, as opposed to a speculative possibility that the matter will affect the financial interest. It is not necessary, however, that the magnitude of the gain or loss be known, and the dollar amount of the gain or loss is immaterial.[94]

The White House Counsel wrote that "the First Lady's activities . . . had no 'direct and predictable' effect on any of Value Partners' assets or investments."[95] But this conclusion was not supported by any analysis, and runs counter to what several observers of the health care debate seemed to take as a given. For example, William Safire asserted that "Mrs. Clinton's public pronouncements about health and her hints at the need for particular price controls had a direct and predictable effect on stocks in that field."[96] Focusing on the practice of short-selling engaged in by Valuepartners, Tony Snow claimed:

> [I]nvestors could have made bundles betting on the demise of health-care equities, which have plunged dramatically since Bill Clinton surged ahead of George Bush in mid-1992. The total value of stocks in pharmaceuticals, medical hardware, biotechnology and health insurance has fallen $200 billion, and analysts trace almost all of the collapse to statements by the Clintons.[97]

Robert Novak agrees: "[H]er task force's public pronouncements helped run down health stocks held by the fund."[98]

In their March 9, 1994 letter to OGE, the House Republicans attached a study by University of Michigan Professor S. Craig Pirrong in support of their assertion that speeches by the First Lady drove down the stock prices of pharmaceutical companies.[99] OGE found that the study failed to address the effect on the market value of any specific company's stock as a result of speeches by Mrs. Clinton, addressing only the aggregate effect on the pharmaceutical industry:

> Consequently, since the article was not written to support and does not support the conclusion that Mrs. Clinton's speeches on health care reform as Chairman of the Task Force had a direct and predictable effect on the value of any specific company's stock, it does not follow that it will support the conclusion that the speeches had a direct and predictable effect on the market value of the stock of, or profitability of, any company in which she might have owned stock either directly or through the limited partnership or mutual fund.[100]

OGE did not proceed further, noting that it was unnecessary to do so in the absence of a particular matter.

OGE is correct that the information provided by the House Republicans is insufficient to **establish** that the First Lady's **speeches** had a direct and predictable effect on her financial interests. In particular, the Pirrong study was concentrated on the effect Clinton Administration positions and pronouncements had on twenty-three pharmaceutical companies. None of these companies was part of the Valuepartners portfolio from January 1, 1993 to June 30, 1993. However, during this time Valuepartners held interests in several other smaller pharmaceutical firms (Royce Labs,

Immune Response, Procyte), and there is no reason why the performance of their stock would vary from the twenty-three surveyed in the Pirrong study. The study also did not examine the effect Clinton health care pronouncements had on other health care related sectors or companies, such as hospitals, HMO's, and medical equipment and product manufacturers.

Nonetheless, a strong inference may reasonably be drawn from the Pirrong study that the Clinton Administration's health care reform proposal likely had a significant effect on other sectors of the health care industry. Valuepartners has maintained holdings in many health care related companies, not just in pharmaceutical firms. These other companies may have been affected "directly and predictably" by the Administration's actions. Moreover, in discussing the Pirrong study, OGE focused on only the First Lady's health care speeches.[101] Her involvement in health care reform clearly is not confined to her public speeches. Her "personal and substantial participation" has included internal meetings, discussions with members of Congress, and other actions taken in the Administration's deliberative process. Given the preeminent Administration role the First Lady has played on health care, it is fair to attribute to her any Administration proposal, pronouncement or policy position.

Thus, while the information provided by the House Republicans may not have established the "direct and predictable effect" element of section 208, it does not follow that the First Lady's actions have not have a direct and predictable effect on the interests she has held in Valuepartners. This conclusion is implicit in OGE's response.

To Her Knowledge. Section 208 is not violated if an employee did not know that she held a financial interest in the particular matter in which she was involved personally and substantially. Without such knowledge, it would be unfair to visit criminal sanctions on an employee for an unwitting conflict.

While **knowledge** is an essential element, it is irrelevant as a matter of law whether the First Lady exercised or was capable of exercising any **control** over Valuepartners' investments. White House Counsel Bernard Nussbaum stated that, "[t]he First Lady, as a limited partner in Value Partners, never had any input, control, communication, review or oversight with respect to any investments made by Value Partners."[102] He also stated that "the First Lady never had any involvement in or sought to profit from any transactions involving health-related stocks, and we are aware of no factual basis for suggesting that she ever attempted to do so."[103] In a later interview, Bill Smith of Capital Management confirmed that the First Lady did not attempt to influence any particular investment decision.[104]

These statements serve to refute only the implication of the First Lady's **active** investment. As a matter of ethics law, however, all that is required is **knowledge** of the underlying investments of the fund. There is no active-passive investment dichotomy in the ethics laws; under section 208, a passive investor is as subject to its reach as is an active investor.[105]

The First Lady could avoid culpability by showing that she had no knowledge that she held interests in health care stocks through the Valuepartners partnership. Significantly, however, neither Nussbaum nor any other White House official specifically claimed that Mrs. Clinton was unaware of Valuepartners' health care investments. OGE determined that it need not examine the extent of her knowledge because the "particular matter" element was not met.[106]

Ordinarily, as a limited partner, Mrs. Clinton would be expected to receive regular reports of the status of Valuepartners' investments, even if she had no control over them. That is what the House Republicans charged. Columnist Paul Greenberg interviewed Bill Smith to get his response:

> Not true, says Bill Smith. Because, he explains, once Bill Clinton began to rise in the Presidential polls early in '92, probably around March of that year, he took the liberty of cutting off any reports about specific stocks to investors in ValuePartners I. . . .
>
> A Reagan Republican who says he's never voted for a Democratic Presidential candidate, Bill Smith was taking no chances with the Clintons. "I think they've always been a bit careless about the appearance of conflicts of interest," he told me, "and if you're involved with their assets, you have to be sensitive to the Clintons' position. . . ."
>
> In effect, Bill Smith created a blind trust for the Clintons more than a year before they had the sense to do it for themselves.[107]

However, at least two reports of Valuepartners' holdings were subsequently sent to President Clinton to enable him to complete his financial disclosure report. A December 31, 1992, Valuepartners portfolio listing is included as an attachment to Schedule A of President Clinton's financial disclosure report filed in May 1993.[108] Although it is possible that the December 31, 1992 printout was not sent to the Clintons until months later, when it was needed to complete the report filed on May 14, 1993, President Clinton's two previous financial disclosure reports contain a similar Valuepartners portfolio listing. His report dated January 8, 1992, filed as a candidate for President, contains an October 31, 1991 portfolio summary, and his report dated May 16, 1992, contains a May 1, 1992 portfolio listing (**after** the date Smith claims the last report was furnished to the Clintons).

By his certification of his financial reports as "true, complete and accurate," the President is charged with knowledge of their contents. But these reports were the President's alone; the First Lady did not co-sign the report, or file her own report. We do not know for certain who in the White House reviewed the Valuepartners information, other than the signatories on the financial disclosure reports (and probably Vince Foster). However, it strains credulity that the First Lady did not review her husband's financial disclosure reports, at least those portions of his reports that pertained to her own assets and income. Note, again, that the White House has never denied that she was aware of these investment listings.

Even if Smith's effort to blind the Clintons to Valuepartners' holdings and investments after March 1992 was completely successful, Mrs. Clinton was most likely aware of her holdings prior to that time. The May 1, 1992 Valuepartners printout lists a number of health care stocks, including short positions in pharmaceutical companies such as Merck & Co. and Bristol-Myers Squibb. It is fair to assume that these holdings existed as of March 1992. If Mrs. Clinton no longer received monthly reports after March 1992, she would have no basis to conclude that all these health care-related stocks had been sold by January 25, 1993,[109] and therefore should be charged with knowledge of these stocks at the time she entered the White House.

The First Lady Should have Disposed of Her Conflicting Interest

A potential conflict of interest may be resolved one of several different ways: disqualification (recusal), waiver, sale (divestiture), or a blind trust.[110] The Clintons and the White House Counsel's office deserve criticism for not taking **any** step to remove the conflict for months, until the creation of the blind trust in July 1993. Further, as explained below, placing Mrs. Clinton's assets in a blind trust did **nothing** to remedy the conflict.

A Waiver Could Have Been Obtained

Considering the insubstantiality of the First Lady's interest, she could have sought and obtained from the President a waiver from the conflict-of-interest restriction under 18 U.S.C. 208(b(1). President Clinton could have granted the waiver upon a determination that her interest "is not so substantial as to be deemed likely to affect the integrity of the services" which the President expected of her.[111] After all, this has been the consistent explanation of White House officials why the First Lady's interest in health care stocks does not, in their view, pose a problem.[112] Even if the White House adhered to its view that the First Lady is not covered by the ethics laws (or that she has not participated in a "particular matter"), a protective waiver would have been appropriate to show the White House's recognition of the potential concern, and its advance determination that it did not believe any appearance of impropriety should result.

Divestiture Could Have and Should Have Been Made; Divestiture Can and Should Still be Pursued

A waiver does not immunize a person against criticism, for a waiver acknowledges the existence of, or the potential for, a conflict of interest. A better remedy would have been for the First Lady simply to sell her interest in Valuepartners. It is inexplicable why the White House Counsel's office apparently did not urge her to divest herself of her limited partnership interest. Selling her interest in Valuepartners would have immediately removed any potential conflict with her health care responsibilities.

As a general matter, it may not be as easy to dispose of a limited partnership interest as it is to dispose of stock held directly. Limited partnerships are not liquid investments; they are not publicly traded or available, so a buyer must be located. However, given the good performance of Valuepartners in recent years, Mrs. Clinton could have sold her interest without much difficulty. Moreover, given the health care responsibilities the President gave her, it was imperative that she sell her interest to allay any ethics concern, even if she would suffer a financial loss in doing so.[113]

Although the Clintons are generally prohibited from communicating with the trustee of their blind trust, they may, with the approval of the Director of the Office of Government Ethics, instruct the trustee in writing to sell any interest that is deemed to create a real or apparent conflict.[114] Because the blind trust did not remedy this conflict, the First Lady should pursue divestiture of her partnership interest.

The Blind Trust Did Not Cure the Conflict

Instead of divestiture, her assets, along with other assets held by the President and the First Lady, were placed in a blind trust in July 1993. Although blind trusts are recommended for Presidents and other high-level officials with extensive financial portfolios, a blind trust is not effective in precluding preexisting conflicts, as to either future or past actions. The Clintons' blind trust did **nothing** to remove Mrs. Clinton's conflict.

Of course, the establishment of a blind trust in July 1993 could not exculpate Mrs. Clinton for actions taken before that date. So the Clintons deserve criticism for failing to ensure that the blind trust would be established contemporaneously with the Presidential inauguration, or soon thereafter.[115]

What has not been generally recognized in the media, however, is that a blind trust does not protect the First Lady from legal liability for those assets placed in the trust about which she has knowledge, because, as to those assets, the trust is not "blind."[116] OGE explains:

> A trust is considered to be "blind" only with regard to those trust assets about which no interested party has knowledge. When an interested party originally places assets in trust, that party still possesses knowledge about those assets. Those original assets remain financial interests of the Government official for purposes of 18 U.S.C. 208 or for any other Federal conflict of interest statutes or regulations, until the trustee notifies the official either that a particular original asset has been disposed of or that the asset's value is less than $1,000.[117]

Thus, unless and until the Valuepartners interest is disposed of, its health care stocks are imputed to the First Lady as if she held the interest outside the blind trust.[118]

So, although the creation of the blind trust is a commendable (even if expected, and even if belated) step for the Clintons to guard against **prospective** conflicts, the failure of the blind trust to remedy the First Lady's conflict should have been noticed by the White House Counsel's office. Knowing the inefficacy of a blind trust would have buttressed what should have been the Counsel's office recommendation to her in the first place: Sell!

Recommendations and Conclusions

Applicability of Conflict-of-Interest and Other Laws to the President's Spouse

It should be clear from the analysis of the law that the legal status of the First Lady is unclear and that legislation is desirable. If she was not given formal and defined responsibilities over Federal policy—responsibilities both important and different from the those traditionally exercised by the First Lady—it would not have been necessary to determine the First Lady's status. But it certainly is possible, if not likely, that future Presidents will consider giving their spouse similar responsibilities. Congress should provide such clarification for purposes of section 208, the Federal Advisory Committee Act,[119] and the anti-nepotism law.

Should the President's spouse be given the same exemption from the conflict-of-interest laws as the President, Vice President, and Members of Congress enjoy? In my view, the reasons for the exemption for these elected officials do not recommend extending the exemption to include the President's spouse. There are two bases for the exemption. First, the President has authority over the entire Executive Branch;

indeed, he has a constitutional duty to ensure that the laws are faithfully executed.[120] His decisionmaking and policymaking authority covers virtually all of what Americans and American businesses do. Almost any financial interest could pose a conflict; recusal would not be practical or fair to the President. In essence, this argument is akin to the Rule of Necessity, which at common law permitted judges to decide cases that could affect them personally because all judges could be similarly affected.[121] The same argument can be said in support of the exemption for Members of Congress.

A President's spouse is not given any authority as a result of the President's election. It is up to each President to delegate any authority or assign any responsibility to his or her spouse. Even the pillow talk that inevitably goes on regularly between President and spouse need not concern every subject under the sun. Thus, the President's spouse does not need an exemption in order to perform the limited functions she may assume.

Second, as an elected official under the most intense public scrutiny, the President is held accountable to the public for any conflicts of interest or apparent conflicts. This accountability discourages Presidents from holding any interests or outside affiliations that would give rise to an appearance of impropriety.[122] (Members of Congress, on the other hand, historically have not been held accountable to the electorate to the same degree.) The President's spouse, by contrast, is not accountable to the electorate. Because a spouse's financial interests must be disclosed in the President's financial disclosure report, the public is guaranteed to be informed of her interests. However, the public is not likely to know all of the spouse's activities without the visibility of a formal delegation, such as President Clinton's delegation of health care reform, to his wife. Moreover, the electorate is not necessarily going to hold the President accountable for a spousal ethical lapse.

Legislation should provide that the President's spouse shall not be considered an employee of the Government simply by virtue of the informal advice she may directly provide the President from time-to-time, nor by her supervision of her immediate staff (assuming the staff is limited to the traditional ceremonial functions of the First Lady). However, she should be regarded as a Federal official as to any supervisory or line responsibility she is given, as well as to her participation in the White House or government deliberative process.[123]

The Federal Advisory Committee Act should be amended to conform to the holding of the D.C. Circuit in *Association of Amer. Phys. and Surgeons*. A group consisting entirely of Federal officials and the President's spouse should not be considered an advisory committee under FACA.

It is not a satisfactory answer to whether the anti-nepotism law has been violated to say that there is no legal sanction for its violation.[124] Presidents are charged with upholding and complying with all laws to which they are subject, not simply the ones with criminal or civil penalties attached, and the President is subject to the anti-nepotism law. The public policy against nepotism seems less urgent in the White House Office, where it is normal practice for the President to hire persons on the basis of long-standing friendships and other loyalties.[125] Moreover, the President's spouse does not receive a separate salary, so there is no concern that the President is putting his family members on the Federal payroll. Thus, the President should be free to appoint his spouse to a White House Office position.

Application of Conflict-of-Interest Statute to Legislative Proposals

The Office of Government Ethics should consult with the Justice Department and revise its interpretation of "particular matter" as it applies to legislative proposals.[126] OGE's current interpretation weakens section 208, exempting some conduct that fits the classic notion of a conflict of interest. It also creates an untenable distinction between legislation and rulemaking. If OGE is unwilling to revise its current interpretation, Congress should do the job by amending section 208, or directing OGE and the Justice Department to revisit the matter.

Remedying the First Lady's Conflict

The President or the First Lady should obtain permission from OGE to communicate with the trustee of the blind trust for the sole purpose of instructing the trustee to sell the First Lady's partnership interest. After obtaining permission, the trustee should promptly sell the interest.

Chapter Four

The
Health Care
Task Force

The interdepartmental working group set up to provide policy options for the President's Health Care Task Force resembled a typical Federal advisory committee in nearly all respects—excepting its failure to comply with the requirements of the Federal Advisory Committee Act (FACA). The court of appeals properly held the **Task Force** not to be an advisory committee under FACA. But the **working group**, acting through subgroups, was such an advisory committee. Although the resolution of this legal issue was obviated by the eventual release of working group records, the White House deserves criticism for creating such a Byzantine structure for such an important undertaking, and for keeping the working group's efforts out of the public's view for more than a year until confronted by the realities of litigation.

The White House also failed to determine precisely who among the hundreds of working group participants was subject to the ethics laws. It also failed to ensure that all those it deemed to be special Government employees filed a financial disclosure report and steered clear of conflicts of interest. The better approach would have been to use outside persons as representatives of their employer or profession, rather than as government employees. This would have more readily triggered an application of FACA, opening up meetings and records. It also would have avoided the widespread suspicion that the Health Care Security Act was developed in secret by persons with a direct financial or professional stake in the fate of health care legislation.

In two respects material to the lawsuit challenging the Health Care Task Force, White House official Ira Magaziner's March 1993 declaration was misleading. The Attorney General correctly determined that Magaziner's conduct could be investigated fairly within the Justice Department. That said, it would have been preferable to assign the matter to the Public Integrity Section of the Criminal Division, rather than the presidentially appointed U.S. Attorney. The Attorney General's decision may signal a growing realization within the Clinton Administration of the perils of the independent counsel law:

> The decision of the U.S. Attorney's office not to prosecute Magaziner for perjury or criminal contempt appears correct, given the apparent lack of evidence that Magaziner intentionally misled the court. The U.S. Attorney's office also correctly identified the negligence and mistakes made by the White House Counsel's office in drafting Magaziner's declaration and in failing to correct or amend the declaration to comport with the evolutionary nature of the working group. It further identified similar errors—though to a lesser extent—made by Justice Department attorneys in their conduct of the litigation. Although the U.S. Attorney's office charitably refrained from expressly finding Magaziner's declaration misleading, the facts as revealed in the its analysis show that it was indeed so.

On January 25, 1993, President Clinton established the Task Force on National Health Care Reform, naming the First Lady as Chairman.[1] All other members of the Task Force were Cabinet or senior White House officials.[2] The Task Force was charged with preparing comprehensive health care reform legislation to be submitted to Congress. As an adjunct to the Task Force, an interdepartmental working group was established under the leadership of Assistant to the President Ira Magaziner to assemble information and ideas and to provide policy options for the Task Force.

Pursuant to its charter, the Task Force terminated on May 30, 1993. Although the President charged the Task Force with coming up with a health care reform proposal within the first 100 days of his Administration, the Clinton Administration's legislative proposal, the Health Security Act, was not transmitted to Congress until October 27, 1993.[3]

The Federal Advisory Committee Act

Soon after the Task Force was created, Representative Clinger charged in a letter to the President that the Task Force violated the requirements of FACA.[4] FACA was enacted in 1972 to regulate the number and use of committees established to provide advice to the President and Executive Branch agencies.[5] The Act defines "advisory committee" as:

any committee, board, commission, council, conference, panel, task force, or other similar group, or any subcommittee or other subgroup thereof . . ., which is . . . established or utilized by the President, . . . in the interest of obtaining advice or recommendations for the President or one or more agencies of officers of the Federal Government, except that such term excludes . . . (iii) any committee which is composed wholly of full-time officers or employees of the Federal Government.[6]

Clinger asserted that the Task Force was an advisory committee because the First Lady is not a "full-time officer or employee."

Representative Clinger claimed that the Task Force had held a closed meeting on January 25 without notice to the public, in violation of the open meeting requirements of the law.[7] FACA requires that, subject to certain exceptions, advisory committee meetings be open to the public and "detailed minutes" be kept for each meeting, including a record of the persons present.[8] FACA provides that advisory committee records ("records, reports, transcripts, minutes, appendixes, working papers, drafts, studies, agenda, or other documents which were made available to or prepared for or by each advisory committee") are subject to disclosure requirements of the Freedom of Information Act (FOIA).[9]

Timely notice of each meeting and a summary of the agenda must be published in the *Federal Register*,[10] fifteen days in advance, except that in "exceptional circumstances," an advisory committee meeting may be held on less than fifteen days notice.[11]

Clinger also charged that the Task Force had not yet filed a charter with the General Services Administration (GSA), as required. FACA provides that no advisory committee "shall meet or take any action until an advisory committee charter has been filed" with GSA, containing, among other things, a description of the committee's scope of activity and duties, the committee's estimated operating costs, and the estimated number of meetings.[12]

White House Counsel Bernard Nussbaum responded that FACA "does not, and was not intended by Congress to, apply to the health care task force. The participation of the First Lady on the task force does not trigger application of the Act."[13]

History of Health Care Task Force Litigation

The Filing of the Lawsuit

On February 24, 1993, three groups—the Association of American Physicians and Surgeons, the American Council for Health Care Reform, and the National Legal and Policy Center—filed suit in Federal court, seeking access to Task Force meetings and records under FACA.[14] The gist of their argument was that meetings of the Task Force must be open to the public because the First Lady is not a "full-time officer or employee of the Federal Government."[15] The Justice Department's Civil Division, representing the Task Force, responded that the First Lady was the "functional equivalent of a Federal employee."[16] Plaintiffs also charged that the interdepartmental working group, and its various subgroups, also were FACA advisory committees.[17]

The Magaziner Declaration

The Justice Department explained that the interdepartmental working group was "formed by or under the direction of the President on January 25, 1993 for the purpose of documenting the impact of existing health care systems and alternatives for health care reform."[18] In a declaration filed on March 3, 1993, Ira Magaziner drew a sharp distinction between the Task Force and the working group. The working group:

> is gathering information concerning the impact of existing health care policies and delivery services, and possible alternatives to those policies. The information that is gathered and analyzed by the working group will be used, in turn, by the Task Force in formulating its recommendations to the President. Only the Task Force will have authority to forward recommendations to the President, and only the Task Force will provide advice to the President. The interdepartmental working group is not charged with responsibility for making, and will not make, recommendations to the President, and will not otherwise directly advise him.[19]

Magaziner declared that "[o]nly federal government employees serve as members of the interdepartmental working group[,]"[20] a statement that would dog him throughout the course of the lawsuit, and beyond. He explained that (as of March 1) the Federal employees who were "members" of the working group fell into two categories: about 300 full-time, permanent employees of the Executive and Legislative Branches, and about forty "special Government employees" (SGEs). Magaziner correctly noted that both sets of employees were subject to the ethics laws and standards for the period of their Federal service.[21]

Magaziner then noted that "[t]he working group has also retained a wide range of consultants, who attend working group meetings on an intermittent basis, with or without compensation." The consultants consisted of "physicians, nurses, health and political economists, sociologists, human resources management experts, health educators, health administrators, public health experts, health researchers and policy analysts." In another statement that subsequently gave Magaziner much difficulty, he declared that the consultants "have not had any supervisory role or decision-making authority in connection with the consulting services they have provided to the working group, but instead provide information and opinion to working group members." Magaziner explained that these consultants, too, were informed that they were subject to the ethics laws and standards in connection with their working group participation.[22]

For **ethics** purposes, Magaziner did not draw any distinction between SGEs, who were working group "members," and consultants, who implicitly were not. The declaration committed the White House to the position that consultants would be considered covered by 18 U.S.C. 208, the central conflict-of-interest statute, and the standards of conduct for Executive Branch employees to the same extent as regular and special Government employees.[23]

Magaziner concluded the declaration by stating his belief that, given the magnitude of the Task Force's responsibilities and its short lifespan, it was critical "that the Task Force and the interdepartmental working group be able to retain flexibility in their operations and be free from formalistic reporting or mandatory public meeting requirements."[24]

Judge Lamberth's Initial Decision

On March 10, 1993, U.S. District Judge Royce Lamberth concluded that the First Lady is not a full-time officer or employee under FACA.[25] Therefore, Judge Lamberth held that Task Force fact-gathering meetings must be open to the public, and enjoined the Task Force from holding any meetings until it complied with the requirements of FACA.

On the other hand, Judge Lamberth ruled that it would be unconstitutional to apply the open meeting requirements of FACA to the Task Force when it engages in policy deliberations resulting in advice or recommendations to the President. In this latter capacity, FACA's application to the Task Force would be an unconstitutional encroachment on the President's authority to receive advice for the purpose of proposing legislation.[26] He also ruled that the interdepartmental working group was not covered by FACA because it engaged only in fact-gathering and did not provide advice directly to the President.[27]

Pursuant to the court's ruling, and required by FACA, the White House on March 17 filed the Task Force's charter with GSA. The charter explained that Magaziner:

> leads an interdepartmental working group that is gathering information for, and will provide information and policy options to, the Task Force. The working group consists of government employees and is consulting with a wide range of citizens in the public and private sectors. The Task Force, in turn, will review information provided by the working group and make recommendations to the President.[28]

In March and April 1993, the three associations that had filed suit submitted separate requests to the Task Force for documents and information pursuant to FACA and the Freedom of Information Act (FOIA). Because the district court had previously ruled that the Task Force was an advisory committee, and the intergovernmental working group was not, White House Counsel Nussbaum responded that nonexempt Task Force documents would be made available, but that working group documents would not.[29] Responding to a specific request for the names of working group members, Nussbaum added that, "the names of persons on the working group and its consultants have been made public." Nussbaum denied the FOIA requests on the grounds that:

> neither the Task Force nor the interdepartmental working group or its "cluster" groups are agencies for purposes of FOIA because their functions are, respectively, to advise and to assist the President.[30]

In a second declaration filed in June 1993, Magaziner stated that the working group "did not make recommendations to the President, and did not otherwise directly advise him."[31] He stated that the working group disbanded "during" May 1993.

In April and May 1993, the Task Force held twenty meetings.[32] By the end of May, the Task Force:

> had presented to the President a comprehensive set of proposals and options for health care reform legislation. The Task Force thus completed its

mission. The Task Force's charter was not renewed when it expired on May 30, 1993, and the Task Force therefore terminated on that date.[33]

The D.C. Circuit's Decision

Meanwhile, both parties appealed Judge Lamberth's ruling to the U.S. Court of Appeals for the District of Columbia.[34] On June 22, 1993, in an opinion by Judge Lawrence Silberman, the D.C. Circuit reversed the district court.[35] Obviating a decision on the constitutionality of FACA's application to the Task Force, the court of appeals held that the First Lady is a *de facto* full-time Federal officer under FACA. The court stated:

> the question whether the President's spouse is a "full-time officer or employee" of the government is close enough for us properly to construe FACA not to apply to the Task Force merely because Mrs. Clinton is a member.[36]

Therefore, the Task Force could close all of its meetings to the public.[37]

However, the court of appeals also disagreed with the district court's ruling on the interdepartmental working group. The court held that the working group's status as an advisory committee could not be decided upon the present record. In particular, the record was inconclusive as to the form, structure, and membership of the working group:

> The government suggests that the working groups, composed as they are of a crowd of 340 virtually anonymous persons, do not bear the characteristics of the paradigm FACA advisory committee. That may well be so. The working groups, as a whole, seem more like a horde than a committee. On the other hand, the groups have been created ("established") with a good deal of formality and perhaps are better understood as a number of advisory committees. We simply cannot determine how to classify the working groups on the record before us.[38]

The court thus remanded the case to the district court.[39]

Further Proceedings in the District Court

The plaintiffs returned to district court seeking discovery relating to the makeup and composition of the interdepartmental working group, its cluster groups and subgroups, and contending that the working group had failed to comply with financial disclosure and conflict-of-interest requirements.[40] Faced with the Justice Department's failure to respond in a timely manner to the request for documents, the plaintiffs moved to compel discovery in September 1993. At a hearing on this motion before Judge Lamberth on October 20, 1993, the Justice Department conceded that the working group's membership could not be accurately determined, and also acknowledged that the working group had failed to create or keep some payroll records, vouchers, meeting minutes, agendas, and membership rolls. Justice admitted that it could not determine whether all working group members had complied with financial disclosure and ethics requirements.[41]

Responding to press reports of this hearing, the Chairman and Ranking Member of the House Committee on Government Operations wrote the White House Counsel the following day, concerned that complete records of the Task Force's activities, its membership, and other personnel matters, such as expenses and ethics reviews, were not being maintained.[42] They asked whether Justice or the White House could account for the status and location of these records.

White House Counsel Nussbaum responded at length, calling the press report of the October 20 hearing "baseless."[43] Specifically, the White House Counsel stated that all Task Force and working group records were preserved by the White House Office of Records Management, and that a "full listing of more than 500 working group participants and their affiliations" was produced in court. Nussbaum acknowledged only that the Justice Department had conceded that a small number of persons who attended one or more working group meetings were not included on the list.[44]

On November 9, Judge Lamberth granted plaintiffs' motion to compel and threatened the White House with contempt of court unless it produced all records within twenty days.[45] In unusually frank and harsh language, Judge Lamberth castigated the Justice Department's previous responses, describing them variously as "incomplete and inadequate," "preposterous," and "egregious." The court found that Justice had "improperly thwarted plaintiffs' legitimate discovery requests." The court pointedly "condemn[ed] [the] litigation tactic" of incomplete and piecemeal responses and noted that it would not be tolerated in the future.[46]

Judge Lamberth explained that the working group and any subgroup would be considered an advisory committee under FACA if the group "[was] asked to render advice or recommendations as a group." Lamberth permitted discovery on this question, as well as whether all members of the working group were full-time Federal employees (as claimed), whether all working group members and consultants submitted financial disclosure forms and complied with ethics requirements (as claimed), and whether the consultants, by the nature of their participation, were in fact indistinguishable from members of the working group.[47]

The Justice Department obtained a protective order, allowing it to file a small portion of the Task Force records under seal.[48] On November 30, Justice submitted the records to the court and plaintiffs' attorneys.[49]

Motions for Summary Judgment are Filed by Both Sides
In March 1994, plaintiffs moved for summary judgment and an injunction.[50] Plaintiffs charged that "numerous individuals from the private sector . . . were active participants in the Interdepartmental Working Group . . . and were indeed some of the prime architects of the proposed Health Security Act of 1993[.]"[51] They alleged that Ira Magaziner misled the court in his first declaration when he claimed that "[o]nly federal government employees serve as members of the interdepartmental working group."[52] The plaintiffs, citing language from the court of appeals decision and from FACA's legislative history, argued that the working group and its cluster groups and subgroups were advisory committees under FACA.[53] The plaintiffs also alleged that many SGEs and consultants who were required to file a financial disclosure report did not do so, and that several members had serious conflicts of interest.[54]

The Justice Department responded to these arguments in May. First, Justice argued that the working group was not covered by FACA because it lacked a formal structure, limited and fixed membership, a specific purpose, and because it operated informally and performed only a staff support function.[55] Justice noted that the working group and its subgroups held thousands of meetings; meetings were held "spontaneously," "constantly" and "simultaneously." The size of the working group, initially estimated to be ninety-eight, grew to 506.[56] Justice further argued that the working group could not have accomplished its mission within the constraints imposed by FACA.

Justice's response included a third declaration of Ira Magaziner.[57] Attached to the declaration was a January 26, 1993 memorandum from Magaziner to the Cabinet and senior White House officials, asking them to "identify people from within your department who can be assigned full-time to the Task Force for the next 100 days[.]"[58] Attached to the memorandum was a "Preliminary Work Plan for the Interagency Health Care Taskforce," which Magaziner described in this declaration as his "preliminary conceptions of the structure and operation of the interdepartmental working group."[59] The charge of the "interagency taskforce is to prepare comprehensive health care reform legislation in the next 100 days." Thus, at the very start of the Task Force, Magaziner blurred the distinction between the Task Force and working group. From this early date, Magaziner saw the working group as part of the Task Force.

Magaziner declared:

> The interdepartmental working group effectively served as the staff to the Task Force and I served as the working group's staff director. The President vested me with responsibility for ensuring that the working group developed thorough and intelligent health care reform policy options for consideration by the Task Force within 100 days. . . . The working group participants ultimately reported to me and provided me with their principal work products.[60]

Magaziner envisioned that the working groups, by the "clash of views, the testing of assumptions and the process of narrowing a broad array of options" would produce "the best policy options for the Task Force's consideration."[61] He thus charged each working group with presenting a menu of options for consideration.

Magaziner described a "guiding principle of the working group that a wide variety of outside parties be consulted and that members of the public and interested groups and organizations have meaningful opportunities for input."[62] To accomplish the task assigned by the President "required a large and fluid group of participants, a flexible structure . . . as well as an informal mode of operation unburdened by time-consuming administrative procedures imposed on the conduct of meetings."[63] Magaziner noted that, "Ultimately, over 500 different people served on the interdepartmental working group at some point during its existence[,]" including State and local government employees and congressional staff.[64]

In an obvious effort to differentiate the working group from the typical advisory committee—the key legal issue before the district court on remand—Magaziner declared:

> The interdepartmental working group did not provide me written advice as a group. . . . [T]he group did not integrate [separate tollgate papers] into a unified document. Nor did the interdepartmental working group deliberate on policy issues or provide oral advice as a group.

The President's health care reform proposal contains some of the options developed by the working groups. The interdepartmental working group, its cluster and working groups did not, however, create the President's health care reform proposal. . . . The working groups did not decide what options would be recommended to the President by the Task Force or what options would be included in the President's reform proposal.[65]

Magaziner conceded that some working group members attended some Task Force meetings, "to serve as a resource to answer questions[,]" and on other occasions working group members, at his request, provided information to respond to a Task Force inquiry. Also, some working group members attended some preliminary policy discussions with the President and Vice President in March and April 1993.[66]

In its response, Justice also abandoned its reliance on the "full-time employee" exemption from FACA, implicitly recognizing that such an argument could not be sustained.[67] However, contrary to news reports, Justice did not back off of Magaziner's statement that all working group "members" were regular employees or SGEs.[68] Rather, Justice decided that it was unnecessary to determine the status of each participant, given its legal position.

For Justice to stand by Magaziner's statement, **it had to maintain the distinction between "members" of the working group and mere participants**.[69] This distinction was central to Magaziner's defense from charges soon lodged by the plaintiffs that Magaziner lied in his first declaration. Recall that in that declaration, Magaziner divided working group participants into three groups, separating consultants (non-employees) from regular and special Government employees (SGE's). Justice was not able or prepared to claim that all "participants" in working group meetings and deliberations were government employees, so it relied on the narrower (in theory) concept of "member." However, many consultants degree of participation was such that they were functioning as SGE's and should have been treated accordingly.

Justice acknowledged that many SGEs had not filled out financial disclosure forms, but argued that the SGEs retained by the White House Office for the working group were exempt from the financial disclosure filing requirements.[70] The exemption claimed by Justice states:

Any individual or class of individuals, including special Government employees . . . may be excluded from all or a portion of the confidential reporting requirements . . . when the agency head or designee determines that:
(a) The duties of a position make remote the possibility that the incumbent will be involved in a real or apparent conflict of interest[.][71]

Justice further argued that no working group member could be involved in a conflict of interest within the meaning of 18 U.S.C. 208, because the health care reform work they were engaged in was not a "particular matter." Additionally, it argued that the effect on the financial interests of working group members could not be considered "direct and predictable" as required, because "so many contingencies" existed at the time they worked on development of health care options.[72]

In response to the Justice Department's change of defense, plaintiffs on May 16, 1994 moved for sanctions against the Justice Department and contempt against Magaziner, largely because of the enormous time and expense plaintiffs had spent up to that point in order to prove what Justice now would no longer contest.

Judge Lamberth's Decision Denying Summary Judgment, and Further Proceedings

Judge Lamberth was unable to reach a decision on the papers submitted by the parties. So on July 25, 1994, he ordered that a trial be held to determine whether the working group or any subgroup was covered by FACA. He deferred until after trial the issue of whether to hold Magaziner in contempt of court. A trial date was set for September 12, at which time the First Lady and other White House officials were expected to be called to testify.[73]

At a pretrial conference before Judge Lamberth in early August, held pursuant to Federal Rule of Civil Procedure 16, the Justice Department began settlement discussions, and the parties began exploring settlement.[74] The White House was interested in settling the case before health care legislation went to the floor of the Senate and House in August. Also, the White House wanted to avoid the spectacle—as well as the distraction—of the First Lady testifying in Federal court.[75]

However, on August 14, after more than a week of settlement talks held in the Judge's chambers, a settlement offer from the Justice Department was rejected by the Board of Directors of the Association of American Physicians and Surgeons, one of the three plaintiffs. The Association rejected the offer because it would have obviated a ruling on whether Magaziner committed contempt of court.[76] At the request of the Justice Department, and also to accommodate a change in attorneys for the plaintiffs, Judge Lamberth postponed the trial date to December 14.[77]

White House Counsel Cutler announced on August 17 that the Administration, within twenty-one days, "would make public all documents that had been generated or received by" the working group.[78] Accordingly, on September 7, over 230 boxes of documents, each containing over 2,000 pages, were made available at the National Archives office in College Park, Maryland.[79]

With this unilateral move by the White House, the Justice Department argued that the lawsuit was moot. The Task Force was terminated, so there were no more meetings to be held; all of the Task Force records were released (or so it appeared at the time), so the document requests were satisfied. Alternatively, Justice argued that the working group was not covered by FACA, and that Magaziner's first declaration was truthful at the time it was executed.[80]

At an October 13, 1994 hearing, Judge Lamberth again declined to rule on the motions for summary judgment filed by the parties in the spring. The court expressed concern that the working group may have continued to operate after the announced termination of the Task Force at the end of May 1993,[81] and that the plaintiffs' document requests had not been responded to in full.[82] In an order issued the next day, Judge Lamberth ordered Magaziner to submit to a deposition under oath to answer questions concerning the completeness of the Administration's document disclosure, and permitted the plaintiffs to depose other White House employees for this purpose.[83]

The parties returned to court on October 27. Judge Lamberth again postponed a decision on the dispositive motions filed by the parties. An assistant to Magaziner had testified in a deposition that any health care records dated after May 31, 1993 were removed from the set of documents released to the plaintiffs and the public. She also testified that some working group members continued to work on health care legislation after the dissolution of the working group.[84] Justice explained that this health care work constituted a "different phase" of work—drafting legislation following the President's decision on the Task Force's options—and thus was not part or continuation of the working group.[85] Justice argued the documents were not responsive or relevant to the suit. On November 10, Judge Lamberth decided to review *in camera* several boxes of nonpublic White House documents before ruling on the motion to dismiss the suit.[86]

The Justice Department Undertakes Steps to Moot the Lawsuit

After reviewing the records *in camera*, Judge Lamberth announced on December 1 that he would dismiss the suit as moot once the Justice Department provided an index of the withheld working group documents and a satisfactory explanation of why they were withheld.[87] Judge Lamberth determined that the suit would be moot because the working group was defunct and Justice had released records of the working group as if the working group were an advisory committee under FACA. Lamberth noted that Justice used a "database list of 630 individuals who actively participated in the interdepartmental working group process" in conducting a document search, remarking that these persons appeared to fit the FACA definition of a member of an advisory committee: one who "regularly attends and fully participates in working group meetings."[88]

The next day, the Justice Department told Judge Lamberth that it would make available all remaining records at issue in the case, "in the spirit of putting this case behind us."[89] On December 16, Justice informed the court that all of the documents were now available at the Archives for public inspection. On December 21, 1994, Judge Lamberth dismissed the case as moot.[90]

In his December 21 order, Judge Lamberth considered whether Ira Magaziner committed criminal contempt of court (or perjury or a false statement) in his March 3, 1993 declaration.[91] The court stated:

> We now know, from the records produced in this litigation, that numerous individuals who were never federal employees did much more than just attend working group meetings on an intermittent basis, and we now know that some of these individuals even had supervisory or decision-making roles. The extent to which these individuals were subjected to conflict-of-interest scrutiny is also questionable.[92]

Magaziner's culpability, Lamberth continued, would turn on whether he had been "intentionally untruthful at the time he signed the document[.]"[93] Responding to the Justice Department's defense that the structure of the working group was "fluid," the court stated:

> [N]one of that "fluidity" is included in Mr. Magaziner's March 3 declaration. The defendants' later position, that "membership" on the interdepartmental working group is impossible to determine, simply demonstrates how misleading, at best, Mr. Magaziner's March 3 declaration actually was.[94]

Because Lamberth concluded that the "record is simply insufficient as to what Mr. Magaziner knew and when he knew it[,]" he referred the question to the United States Attorney for the District of Columbia "for appropriate consideration."[95]

Attorney General Reno Declines to Appoint or Request the Appointment of an Independent Counsel to Investigate Magaziner; Assigns the Matter to the U.S. Attorney

Following Judge Lamberth's December 21 ruling, Attorney General Reno stated that Magaziner is not a covered official under the reenacted independent counsel provisions of the Ethics in Government Act.[96] Thus, it was within the Attorney General's discretion to seek a court-appointed independent counsel, appoint a special counsel herself, allow the U.S. Attorney to handle the matter himself, or assign the matter to the Department's Public Integrity Section.

In February 1995, in a letter to the Attorney General, all twenty Republican members of the House Judiciary Committee requested the appointment of an independent counsel, citing a "political conflict of interest" in that the U.S. Attorney had represented Magaziner and the White House in the Health Care Task Force litigation, and the Justice Department had a stake in "protecting the President's 'Health Care Czar,' Mr. Magaziner, and other federal officials from further legal and political embarrassment."[97] The letter also noted reports, denied by the White House Counsel, that the U.S. Attorney was under consideration for a judicial appointment.

Under the independent counsel law, the Attorney General may conduct a preliminary investigation of a person that ultimately could result in a request for the appointment of an independent counsel if she "determines that an investigation or prosecution of a person by the Department of Justice may result in a personal, financial, or political conflict of interest[.]"[98]

In March 1995, the Attorney General determined that "there is no basis" to determine that the U.S. Attorney's investigation may result in a "personal, financial or political conflict of interest."[99] In a letter to House Judiciary Committee Chairman Henry Hyde, the Attorney General first corrected the misimpression that the U.S. Attorney had participated in the Health Care Task Force litigation. The name of the U.S. Attorney for the district where the case is pending is routinely included on filings by the Department, without regard to whether the U.S. Attorney or anyone in his office actually participates in the conduct of the litigation. Here, Magaziner and the Task Force were represented by the Department's Civil Division. Indeed, Judge Lamberth had specifically found that neither the U.S. Attorney nor his staff had participated in the litigation.

Second, the Attorney General explained that there is "no basis for disqualifying the entire Department of Justice from the matter simply because of the involvement of one component of the Department." She accurately cited the regular practice of the Criminal Division and U.S. Attorneys' offices to prosecute criminal law violations and other potential offenses by Federal employees who were involved in cases handled by one of the Department's civil litigation divisions.

Third, she attempted to refute the charge of a political conflict in stating: "This matter concerns a narrow allegation of personal misconduct against one administration official[.] . . . I do not overlook the central importance of the health care initiative to this Administration, but this matter is not a challenge to the legitimacy of that initiative." Given that the impetus for comprehensive health care reform as envisioned by the White House died with the election of a Republican Congress in November 1994, the Attorney General's conclusion was correct only in a narrow sense. If the health care initiative were still a vibrant reform proposal pending before Congress, however, a formal investigation of one of the initiative's leaders for perjury would certainly jeopardize the prospects for its passage and enactment.

The U.S. Attorney's Office Declines to Prosecute Magaziner

On August 3, 1995, the Office of U.S. Attorney Eric Holder declined to prosecute Ira Magaziner.[100] In his letter to Judge Lamberth, Marshall Jarrett, Chief of the Office's Criminal Division, explained:

> There is no significant evidence that his declaration was factually false, much less that it was willfully and intentionally so.[101]

Jarrett found "no evidence that Mr. Magaziner intended to mislead the court." Jarrett went on, however, to explain at length why the falsity *vel non* of the declaration could not be **factually** established, because "the challenged statements . . . depend upon characterizations and matters of opinion, both legal and factual."[102] In particular, Jarrett found the terms "special Government employee" and "consultant" and the terms "member" and "participant" incapable of being determined with precision.

While Jarrett declined to prosecute Magaziner, his letter placed much of the blame for Magaziner's predicament on the White House Counsel's office, which drafted Magaziner's declaration, advised him on the meaning of it,[103] and later resisted amendment or supplementation of the declaration when it became clear that the nature of the working group had changed dramatically.

In a rather incredulous statement, a White House spokesman said:

> The bottom line is that the White House counsel's office and the Justice Department attorneys succeeded in vindicating Mr. Magaziner by offering a sound legal defense. The counsel's office has said all along that Mr. Magaziner did not make misleading statements and defended him against inaccurate charges made by politically motivated plaintiffs.[104]

Jarrett's decision was not the final word, however. Representative Bob Barr wrote the Attorney General requesting that she initiate an Office of Professional Responsibility investigation of the role "government counsel played in misleading the Court[.]"[105] There were also hints of a possible congressional investigation or hearing.

Judge Lamberth, too, did not accept Jarrett's letter as the end of the matter. Lamberth held a status conference *sua sponte* on August 11, 1995, to address the remaining question of sanctions.[106] Plaintiffs' counsel sought sanctions for alleged misconduct by government counsel, relying in part of statements made in Jarrett's August 3 letter. Lamberth thereupon asked government counsel for a further clarification of several of the letter's statements. At the same time, the Justice Department informed the court that it would also seek sanctions against the plaintiffs under Federal Rule of Civil Procedure 11, apparently because the plaintiffs persisted with the lawsuit after the Justice Department had offered to settle the suit on terms as favorable as what plaintiffs ultimately achieved, if not more so.

Marshall Jarrett responded to the Judge in a letter of August 30. Jarrett explained:

> What our investigation found concerning the government's conduct
> was that several mistakes or missteps by government counsel, coupled with
> certain aggressive or strained positions taken during discovery, led to the
> problems and concerns surrounding Mr. Magaziner's declaration. As a re-
> sult of that combination of factors, it may well be that in the end the Court
> ended up believing it had been misled concerning the nature of the work-
> ing group. We concluded, however, that this was the result not of any de-
> sign to mislead the Court, but rather of a combination of oversights, tacti-
> cal misjudgments, and aggressive—perhaps, in hind sight, overly so—ad-
> vocacy in the context of a hard-fought civil litigation.[107]

Jarrett also repeated that he found no "significant evidence" that the declaration
was "factually false," adding that terms such as "special Government employee," and
"member" are "not the sort of terms that can be proven 'false' or 'true'."[108] Thus, he
"did not intend to imply that the government, in the drafting of the declaration or in
later interpretations of its terms, intended to misrepresent facts to the Court."

In an August 28, 1995 order, Judge Lamberth established a briefing schedule to
resolve the parties' request for sanctions against each other. Thereafter, the parties
filed briefs in support of their sanctions requests. As of December 1995, Judge Lamberth had not ruled. It appeared that Judge Lamberth would not inquire further into
the Government conduct of the litigation, and that the August 30, 1995 Jarrett letter
would be the last word.

Ethics Issues Arising from The Task Force and Working Group

Was the Intergovernmental Working Group an Advisory Committee?
The central issue in *AAPS* was whether the interdepartmental working group, or
any of its subgroups, was an advisory committee under FACA. This is not an easy
question to answer, more because the working group operated as if it were oblivious
to FACA than because of any lack of clarity in the Act.

The Justice Department is certainly correct that merely because some members
of the working group were not full-time Federal employees (regular or special) does
not mean that the working group was a FACA advisory committee.[109] Rather, the
inquiry turns on the purpose, structure, functions and operation of the working group.
As the D.C. Circuit explained in its decision:

> When we examine a particular group or committee to determine wheth-
> er FACA applies, we must bear in mind that a range of variations exist in
> terms of the purpose, structure, and personnel of the group. Perhaps it is
> best characterized as a continuum. At one end one can visualize a formal
> group of a limited number of private citizens who are brought together to
> give publicized advice as a group. That model would seem covered by the
> statute regardless of other fortuities such as whether the members are called
> "consultants." At the other end of the continuum is an unstructured ar-
> rangement in which the government seeks advice from what is only a col-

lection of individuals who do not significantly interact with each other. That model, we think, does not trigger FACA.[110]

In many respects, the working group, **as designed**, resembled a typical advisory committee. The purpose of the working group was to gather information and develop a set of options for health care reform legislation, to be considered by the Task Force for submission to the President.[111] Both the organization of the working group, and the process by which its work was to be conducted and reviewed, were highly structured, albeit complex and elaborate. Although one of the working group's functions was to assemble information, other, more important functions were to evaluate that information and put forward policy options.[112]

Except in a few areas, the working group functioned fairly closely to Magaziner's initial work plan. Briefing books and tollgate papers were prepared in which the subgroups and clusters submitted policy options as a group. The groups and subgroups may have not reached any consensus as to which options were preferable, but consensus is not a prerequisite for an advisory committee. If a committee submits a set of options as a group, rather than separately, as individuals, the committee functions as a FACA advisory committee.[113]

In other respects, however, the working group differed from the typical advisory committee. The main difference was that the group observed none of the requirements of a FACA advisory committee! Notice for working group meetings was not provided; meetings were held privately; few agendas or minutes of the meetings were prepared; the line between a member of the working group and a mere participant was blurred; the working group *qua* working group did not complete a report (although papers and reports were prepared by subgroups).[114] As this list shows, the working group differed from the standard advisory committee mainly by its noncompliance with FACA procedures. It is clear that the working group operated as if it were not subject to FACA. That does not mean, however, that the working group was not subject to FACA as a matter of law. In gathering information, listening to experts, discussing ideas in group settings, and coming up with sets of health care reform options, the working group and its subgroups functioned collectively, as advisory committees usually function.

In my view, therefore, the working group, acting through its various subgroups, was an advisory committee (or advisory committees) within the meaning of FACA. Judge Lamberth ultimately refrained from deciding this question, because the Justice Department, in a successful effort to moot the case, decided to turn over documents as if the working group were covered by FACA. Thus, the White House was spared a new round of criticism for flouting the law. Much of this criticism would be deserved, however, because it was the White House that created such an elaborate and bizarre structure—one that was as formal on paper as it was loose in operation—and gave the working group its charge. And it was the White House that insisted that the working group's meetings and deliberations were to be conducted out of the public's view, its records unavailable for public review.

Who was Subject to Federal Conflict-of-Interest Restrictions and Who was Required to File a Financial Disclosure Report?

The White House's noncompliance with FACA does not mean that the White

House and working group members violated **ethics** laws and regulations. These laws apply only to regular Federal employees or SGEs, as defined by 18 U.S.C. 202(a).[115] SGEs are not required to sever outside interests or affiliations, but are subject to conflict-of-interest restrictions that prohibit them from participating in any particular matter in which they have a financial interest.[116]

Often advisory committees are composed largely of representatives of private interests, just as the health care working group, cluster groups, and subgroups included hundreds of non-Federal participants (if not "members"). The very *raison d'etre* of most advisory committees is to obtain the views of persons and entities who would be directly affected by the regulation or legislation under consideration. These persons are appointed **because** of their position in the private or non-Federal sector, and are expected to provide their particular perspective and represent their interests on the advisory committee. They are not called upon to shed their background, opinions, and affiliations and represent only the public interest, however that might be defined.

For these reasons, advisory committee members are often considered "representatives," neither regular employees nor SGEs, and they are not subject to the conflict-of-interest laws and standards. The check on the inordinate or improper influence of private interests on government deliberations is to place an advisory committee's deliberations in the sunshine, where the public can monitor the propriety and integrity, as well as the reasonableness, of the Government's decisionmaking. The distinction between SGEs, who are subject to ethics standards, and representatives, who are not, was first drawn by the Kennedy Administration. And subsequent administrations have followed the distinction without material change.[117]

Although this distinction was available to the White House at the time the interdepartmental working group was created, the White House did not use or appreciate it. Recall that in his first declaration, Magaziner described **consultants**, "who attend working group meetings on an intermittent basis, with or without compensation," as a class of persons distinct from SGEs. But consultants who receive compensation for their services (excluding payment of per diem and expenses) **are** SGEs. Conceivably, Magaziner distinguished consultants from SGEs because he envisioned that consultants—"physicians, nurses, health and political economists, . . . health administrators, . . ." —would act as representatives of their employer, profession, or responsibility in the non-Federal sector. Yet, Magaziner announced that these consultants, too, would be informed that they were subject to the ethics laws and standards in connection with their participation on the working group. It is unclear from the declaration whether the White House determined that these consultants were legally subject to the ethics laws, or whether they were simply treated as if they were subject to these laws as a matter of prudence.

If, on the other hand, the working group asked these consultants to provide their independent judgment, without regard to their employer's interests or opinions, these consultants would likely be considered SGEs, regardless of whether they received compensation, and regardless of whether they were ever formally designated as a "member."

Jarrett found that the White House and the Department of Health and Human Services (HHS) both believed, contrary to the March 3, 1993 declaration, that consultants could be and most likely were, SGEs.[118] Indeed, the Magaziner declaration, while putting consultants and SGEs in separate categories, also noted that they would be treated similarly with respect to ethics issues.

The narrower concept of "member" was critical to Ira Magaziner's defense from allegations that he misled the court in his first declaration.[119] According to Magaziner's first declaration, only Federal employees served as "members" of the working group. By definition, then, consultants, who the declaration implies were not Federal employees, were not "members" of the working group. But the D.C. Circuit frowned on Magaziner's, and the Government's, purported distinction between members and consultants:

> We are confident that Congress did not intend FACA to extend to episodic meetings between government officials and a consultant. . . .
> But a consultant may still be properly described as a member of an advisory committee if his involvement and role are functionally indistinguishable from those of other members. Whether they exercise any supervisory or decisionmaking authority is irrelevant. If a "consultant" regularly attends and fully participates in working group meetings as if he were a "member," he should be regarded as a member.[120]

Furthermore, whatever theoretical distinction Magaziner and the White House intended broke down in the day-to-day operation of the working group. The district court found that some consultants had indeed exercised supervisory or decisionmaking authority.

The failure of the working group to maintain meeting records, such as minutes, agendas, membership and attendance lists, made it exceedingly difficult to determine who among the non-regular Federal employees (including consultants) were SGEs. It also makes it difficult to determine how many special Government employees (including potentially some of the consultants) failed to file financial disclosure forms as required. Papers filed by the plaintiffs in *AAPS* showed that many persons who regularly attended working group meetings did not file financial disclosure reports.

Apparently, the SGEs retained by the White House Office (there were other SGEs retained by HHS) were granted an exemption from the requirement to file a confidential financial disclosure report, based on the White House's finding that the prospect of a conflict of interest was remote.[121] In my view, it was wrong for the White House to resort to this exemption. The exemption was intended to cover those persons who, because of the **non-substantive** nature of their duties, are not in a position to affect the Government's decisionmaking process. The example used in the OGE regulation is that of a draftsman who prepares drawings to be used by an agency in soliciting bids for a bridge construction procurement.[122] The health care working group counterpart would be a person who assembled, stapled, collated, or bound the tollgate papers, but otherwise did not provide substantive input in the paper. The exemption was not intended to cover persons who are involved in substantive policy discussions, as were the participants in the working group.

HHS ethics officials, by contrast, did not resort to this exemption from the financial disclosure requirement. At least five special Government employees retained by HHS to work on the working group filed public financial disclosure requirements, and at least another twenty-five filed confidential disclosure requirements.

A bigger ethics problem concerned application of the conflict-of-interest restrictions to those persons from outside the regular Federal workforce who were brought in because of their position in the non-Federal sector. If they were SGEs, "members" or no, they were subject to the conflict-of-interest laws. Apparently, no working group participant sought or obtained a waiver from the conflict-of-interest laws. Given their positions in the health care field, many were in a clear conflict situation. They were being asked to participate in the development of health care legislation, which, if enacted, most certainly would have an effect on their employer, their profession, and themselves.[123]

Under such circumstances, a Federal employee would be required to be free of financial interests in, or outside affiliations with, health care concerns, to recuse himself, or to obtain a waiver. Here, those working group participants who were not regular Federal employees were not required to resign their positions, divest themselves of their financial interests, or terminate their affiliations. And apparently none sought a waiver. Of course, they were also not disqualified from participating in the working group. Indeed, it was their outside positions and affiliations which had **qualified** them for the working group in the first place!

A possible response would be to claim that these members or participants (not just the consultants) were "representatives," not special Government employees. This claim would be hard to sustain, however, given Magaziner's first declaration and Judge Lamberth's findings. So the Justice Department responded by arguing that the conflict-of-interest laws were not triggered because health care legislative reform, given its breadth and its preliminary stage, was not a "particular matter," and because the effect of the health care reform on the financial interests of members "could not be considered 'direct and predictable.'"[124]

Elsewhere in this study I have examined these arguments, and found them wanting.[125] Health care reform, **taken as a whole**, may not be a particular matter. But the same cannot be said for many of the component parts of health care reform, which focus on a discrete problem or segment of the health care sector. The structure of the working group was split first into clusters, and then into subgroups. At some point, a subgroup's focus turned to one or more discrete pieces of the health care reform project. In many of these situations, working group participants were engaged in particular matters.[126]

Did Ira Magaziner Commit Contempt of Court or Perjury in His March 3, 1993 Declaration? Did the U.S. Attorney Properly Decline to Prosecute Magaziner?

These questions essentially turn on the answers to two factual questions: (1) was Magaziner's declaration untrue; and (2), if so, did Magaziner know it was untrue at the time he signed it? Whether the offense is criminal contempt (18 U.S.C. 401) or perjury (18 U.S.C. 1623), the Government has the burden of proving these elements beyond a reasonable doubt. Contempt also involves a finding of intent to obstruct the judicial proceeding.

Judge Lamberth found that Magaziner's declaration was "misleading" in at least two respects. First, some of the working group "members" were not Federal employees, contrary to Magaziner's categorical statement. Second, some of these non-Federal employee members exercised supervisorial or decisionmaking responsibility in the working group, also contrary to a flat statement in the declaration. Because Magaziner's declaration deliberately used a narrow, formalistic concept of "membership," one that is inconsistent with case law (and was also inconsistent with how the working group operated), it would be difficult to establish that Magaziner knew of the falsity of this statement when he made it. Moreover, it is not clear whether Magaziner, even as involved as he was with the structure and operation of the working group, knew all the main players of all the various cluster groups and subgroups as of March 3, 1993, and what they had been doing for the previous five weeks. It seems unlikely that any one person, even Magaziner, could have been aware of the identity and actions of all the consultants whom Magaziner's declaration purported to exclude from the concept of "Federal employee" or "member."

We know from the U.S. Attorney's investigation that the White House Counsel's office drafted Magaziner's declaration. The *Washington Post* identified the drafters as Vince Foster and Steve Neuwirth.[127] It is unclear whether the Justice Department's Civil Division lawyers advised the Counsel's office or made any substantive suggestions or changes to the declaration. It strongly appears that Magaziner's declaration was framed to conform to the legal position Justice initially contemplated asserting in court: that the working group was not subject to FACA because all of its "members" were full-time Federal employees.[128] Magaziner's declaration may have insisted that all working group "members" were Federal employees because he was told that such an assertion would help make the lawsuit go away. Of course, a declaration must conform to the facts, regardless of whether it also supports a party's theory of the case. And it is not known what steps, if any, Magaziner took to determine whether the working group (at the time) in fact conformed to the description contained in his declaration. Jarrett simply states that Magaziner relied on representations and advice from the White House Counsel's office. Jarrett accepted Magaziner's most plausible defense, which is that while he may have been careless or negligent, he did not purposefully deceive the court.[129]

The Conduct of the White House Counsel's Office Deserves Serious Criticism

Until the U.S. Attorney's August 1995 letter to Judge Lamberth declining to prosecute Magaziner, not much was known about the role of the White House Counsel's office and Justice Department in this matter. Jarrett's letter reveals that Magaziner's predicament was the result of confusion largely created by the Counsel office's misuse of several terms with legal significance.

Recall the highlighted words used in the single sentence in Magaziner's March 3, 1993 declaration that gave rise to the criminal investigation:

Only federal government **employees** serve as **members** of the interdepartmental working group.

This statement was misleading in two ways (even if it was not, *pace* Jarrett, "false"). First, read in conjunction with another portion of the declaration that separated "employees" from "consultants," this sentence could be read to mean only that no "consultant" is a "member." In fact, several (if not many) consultants were members of the working group, under any reasonable construction of the term "member," because these consultants chaired a cluster group or subgroup of the working group or otherwise exercised significant responsibility within a subgroup. Jarrett found that the White House, almost from the start, recognized that consultants could be, and were, SGEs, although Magaziner's declaration indicates otherwise.[130]

Jarrett found that the consultants retained by HHS were deemed SGEs by HHS, and completed paperwork and financial disclosure forms as required of SGEs. The White House, however, failed to complete financial disclosure forms for many of the consultants it would later argue were SGEs, relying later on a dubious exemption.[131]

Jarrett added that "[t]he confusion generated by the terms used in the declaration was also exacerbated by positions taken by the government during discovery."[132] After the declaration was filed, the size of the working group grew to a point where it was clear that many participants in the working group did not "fit neatly" into Magaziner's three distinct categories:

> Attorneys in the White House, however, appear to have been reluctant to file a supplemental declaration or anything else that might suggest that the declaration, although accurate when filed, was no longer a complete description of the working group process. Instead, the defense persisted in an attempt to go back after the fact and make everyone who had been involved in the working group "fit" into the original categories of the declaration. This was possible due to the malleability of the language of the declaration, but it led to additional strained interpretations . . . and was ultimately unconvincing.[133]

Second, the White House purposefully employed the term "member" for litigation purposes, suggesting a concept narrower than mere participation in the working group. Yet, it did not employ the term in the actual operation of the working group. In fact, "no generally agreed upon 'membership' criteria were ever written down."[134] As Jarrett noted, "[a]t the time the declaration was filed, [the government] clearly gave the impression that 'membership' was a meaningful concept and that one could determine who was and was not a 'member' of the working group." However, in an August 1993 discovery response signed by Magaziner, in which the Government provided lists of working group "participants," the Government stated that these lists:

> should not be considered "membership" rosters. . . . Given the fluid and dynamic process by which the interdepartmental working group was formed and operated, **"membership" was not a significant or operative concept.**[135]

Jarrett also rejected the plaintiffs' view that "member" and "participant" were interchangeable terms, noting that under plaintiffs' view, there were more than 1,000 members of the working group, whereas Judge Lamberth accepted the Government's participant database of "only" 630 names. So, without any definition of the term "member," the falsity of Magaziner's statement using that term could not be proved or disproved.

The other statement that Judge Lamberth found misleading was Magaziner's assertion that consultants "have not had any supervisory role or decision-making authority in connection with the consulting services they have provided to the working group[.]" Jarrett did not take issue with Judge Lamberth's finding that some consultants performed supervisory roles (*i.e.*, some consultants served as cluster group leaders). Thus, this statement is false. Jarrett demurred. He found that each of these consultants was considered as an SGE "by others and appears as an SGE on different lists." Jarrett concluded that "these disparate positions cannot be factually proven either right or wrong."[136] But confusion over the concepts of consultant and SGE should not have been used to shield this statement from scrutiny. It is true that consultants (some or all) were SGEs. Regardless of whether they were SGEs, however, the fact remains that some of them performed supervisory roles, contrary to Magaziner's declaration. Jarrett seemed to imply that Magaziner's statement could be defended on the theory that a consultant who exercised supervision became an SGE as a result of such supervisory role But this is nothing more than rewriting the declaration after the fact to avoid its falsity.

Jarrett devoted only brief attention to this statement, yet it was as materially misleading as any made in Magaziner's declaration or during the subsequent conduct of the litigation. The declaration intended to assure the plaintiffs, the court, and the public that outsiders brought into the working group would not run the show, but merely provide information and expertise. In fact, many outsiders, whatever legal appellation used, played key roles in developing options for presentation to the Task Force, and subsequently the President.

Did the Attorney General Correctly Determine to Not Seek the Appointment of an Independent Counsel?

Although Ira Magaziner is not a covered official under the independent counsel law, the Attorney General nevertheless had discretion to seek the appointment of an independent counsel, if in her judgment the Justice Department's investigation would result in a personal or political conflict of interest. Attorney General Reno correctly concluded that there was no political conflict of interest with the Department **as a whole**, and thus no independent counsel was warranted. In doing so, the Attorney General struck a blow for the competence and integrity of Justice Department investigations, as opposed to investigations conducted by independent or special counsel. This should not have been an easy decision for her, however, considering her—and the President's—rhetoric, which extols the virtues of, and necessity for, the independent counsel law in order to avoid the inevitable appearance issue, while it ignores the law's heavy costs and consequences.

Given the Justice Department Civil Division's deep involvement in the conduct of the litigation, Magaziner's high profile White House position, and the strong interest of the White House (including the First Lady) in the litigation, the situation clearly presented an issue of appearances. To those who do not know of, or accept, the institutional and historical separation between and among components within the Justice Department, the situation also posed a political conflict of interest. And the Attorney General was wrong to deny that prosecuting Magaziner would tarnish the Clinton Administration's health care efforts.

The Attorney General was headed in the right direction in relying on the institutional separation between the Justice Department litigating divisions and the U.S. Attorney's offices, as well as on the factual separation between the two in the Health Care Task Force litigation. But the Attorney General was inattentive to the appearance issue involving the U.S. Attorney's position as a political appointee with the potential for further advancement. Holder is a Clinton appointee, and reportedly was—and perhaps may still be—a potential candidate for a judicial appointment.[137]

The Attorney General should have referred the matter to the Public Integrity Section of the Criminal Division, to be investigated (and prosecuted if warranted), without direction or supervision by the Attorney General or any other Departmental political appointee, including the U.S. Attorney.[138] The relevant internal departmental separations in this matter were between the Civil and Criminal Divisions, and the career attorneys and political appointees.

Conclusions

The Federal Advisory Committee Act is a restraint on the President's constitutional authority, and it is probably true that the interdepartmental working group, **as it was created and intended to operate**, could not have accomplished its mission on time had it complied with FACA.[139] Yet, FACA is not entirely, not even largely, to blame for the Administration's predicament. The White House must shoulder the bulk of the blame. The White House, namely Ira Magaziner, designed a health care process that intentionally (and quite reasonably) sought the views of outside experts, employers, professionals, and state and local governments. Of course, most of these outside persons had a personal, professional, and/or financial interest in any Federal health care legislation. Magaziner brought these persons into the White House, and gave them Federal responsibilities to draft options papers for the Task Force's, and later the President's, consideration. The White House did attempt to deputize some of these outsiders, cloaking them with the mantle of the Federal Government, thereby subjecting them to a strict ethical regime. But many others were not so deputized. Many others were not checked for financial conflicts.[140]

The way in which the White House wanted to use such outsiders is precisely why there is a Federal Advisory Committee Act requiring (semi-) organized meetings to be open to the public. Unlike Federal employees, outsiders are not required to resign from their outside affiliations or dispose of any of their financial holdings. Thus, the public does not have any assurance that these individuals are pursuing the public interest, free of particular private interests in the matter. The sunshine of open meetings and availability of advisory committee records are the public's primary protections against the improper or inordinate influence of special interests. Here, the White House wanted it both ways. Bring in outsiders, but keep the process from public view (and, in the process, ignore the law).

Even before the *AAPS* suit was dismissed as moot, the first revisionist account of the failure of the Administration's health care reform effort was published. James Fallows, writing in the January 1995 *Atlantic Monthly,*[141] attempted to debunk every bit of "conventional wisdom" of the effort, including the criticism—made in this chapter—that the plan "was hatched in secret." What makes Fallows' article interesting is that he based his conclusions on discussions he had with the First Lady and Ira Magaziner. In my view, Fallows failed to absolve the White House from the primary criticism that it illegally conducted working group meetings in private.

Fallows explained that the Task Force "went out of its way to hear a variety of views." He pointed out that among the "500 task-force members"[142] were "outside scholars and experts, plus several doctors and nurses[,]" and the Task Force engaged in a tremendous outreach effort to solicit the views of all interested groups and individuals. This is beside the point. Outreach efforts cannot cure or remedy the closing of deliberations to the general public.

Fallows also believes that criticism of the Task Force's secrecy resulted from a White House communications office decision to muzzle Magaziner from discussing the Task Force's deliberations before the plan was announced. He quoted the First Lady:

> Even though we had a process unlike any other that has drafted a bill—more open, more inclusive—we got labeled as being secretive because of. . . our failure to understand that we should be more available to the press along the way. That was something we didn't do well. . . . We were not aware of how significant it is to [shape] the inside story in Washington, in order to make the case . . . for whatever your policy is.[143]

This explanation bewilders, given the notoriety of the *AAPS* lawsuit that haunted the White House and especially Ira Magaziner from its filing in February 1993.[144] The process was not open **in any traditional sense of the word**. Although hundreds of outsiders worked on parts of the plan, the **public** was not privy to any meetings or deliberations of the working group, the very purpose behind the public meeting requirements of FACA. The lawsuit challenging the secrecy of the Task Force and working group meetings was not brought by news organizations, but by three associations representing interested members of the public. News organizations did file FOIA requests, and the Reporters' Committee for the Freedom of the Press participated in the litigation as an *amicus curiae*. Even had Magaziner provided daily White House briefings, it still would have been accurate to describe the process as secret.

Moreover, once the working group papers were given to the Task Force, the Task Force met many times, always closed to the press and general public.[145] Thus, the health care plan was indeed "hatched in secret." And, for the reasons stated in this chapter, it was illegal and improper for the working group to participate as it did in the "hatching" of the plan.

The White House (Magaziner and the Counsel's office) made matters worse by asserting first, that the outside persons not made part of the Federal workforce (either regular employees or SGEs) would not perform any supervision or decisionmaking, when the district court found that some of them did. And second, they asserted that all of these outsiders would adhere to the same ethical standards to which regular Federal employees are subject. The White House did not, and could not, live up to this latter assertion. It fell to the Justice Department to explain, unconvincingly, that the comprehensive nature of health care reform and the preliminary stage of its development, made the conflict-of-interest statute inapplicable. This position, even assuming that it is a correct statement of law, did nothing to dispel concerns that certain special interests were playing prominent roles behind the scenes in shaping the Administration's plan to their liking.

The decision of the U.S. Attorney's office not to prosecute Magaziner appears correct, because of the apparent lack of evidence that Magaziner intended to lie to the court. But it is clear from Jarrett's own analysis (even if Jarrett shied away from this conclusion) that Magaziner's declaration was materially misleading in several respects. And it also appears that the White House Counsel's office (and perhaps the Justice Department attorneys) knew of its misleading nature, if not on March 3, 1993, then soon thereafter, but did nothing to apprise the plaintiffs or court of its misstatements. Leaving aside the question of whether anyone in the White House engaged in bad faith, it is clear that the White House Counsel's office acquitted itself very poorly in the conduct and defense of the Health Care Task Force litigation, and may be more responsible for Ira Magaziner's legal travails than Magaziner himself. We know that Magaziner relied on the White House Counsel's office to draft the declaration; however, we do not know the extent to which the Counsel's office relied on Magaziner, the architect of the multilayered process, for knowledge about how the working group was expected to operate. Thus, Magaziner may not be blameless, either.

The White House spin on the U.S. Attorney's decision not to prosecute Magaziner, like so many of its other public explanations involving ethics issues, was way off the mark. Recall the spokesman's statement:

> The bottom line is that the White House counsel's office and the Justice Department attorneys succeeded in vindicating Mr. Magaziner by **offering a sound legal defense**. The counsel's office has said all along that Mr. Magaziner did not make **misleading** statements and defended him against inaccurate charges made by politically motivated plaintiffs.[146]

These statements simply cannot be reconciled with Jarrett's letter, and the decisions of the district court and court of appeals in *AAPS*. Magaziner's defense was one part "I did not intend to lie," one part "My lawyers told me what to say and I went along", and one part "The words I used have no workable meaning." By resorting to this defense, Magaziner successfully avoided indictment, but it is another thing entirely to give credit to the White House Counsel's office and the Justice Department! And although Jarrett steadfastly avoided labeling the declaration misleading, that is exactly what it was, to the plaintiffs, to the court, and to the author.

The one piece of the puzzle that remains missing, even after Jarrett's letter, is the relationship between the Justice Department's Civil Division and the White House Counsel's office. Why did the White House draft the declaration instead of a Justice lawyer? What advice did the White House receive from Justice on FACA before drafting the declaration? Did the Civil Division lawyers assume, or did they assure themselves, that Magaziner's declaration was truthful and accurate? If so, how did they assure themselves? What understanding did the Civil Division lawyers have of the meaning of the terms used in Magaziner's declaration? Did they rely on representations from the White House Counsel's office that were false or incorrect? Representative Barr's request for an OPR investigation of the conduct of Justice Department lawyers in the litigation, if one is conducted, may result in answers to these questions. If it does not, a congressional investigation is in order.

Chapter Five

The
White House
Travel Office
Firings

The White House bungled the Travel Office matter from the very start, by allowing persons with a personal and financial stake in the matter to participate substantially in both an internal review of the Travel Office and the virtually simultaneous decision to fire the entire Travel Office staff. The White House also improperly replaced the Travel Office staff with persons whom White House officials knew from the Presidential campaign, without engaging in competitive bidding. The general press outcry cut short the time these friends spent working in the Travel Office, and the White House thereafter began to competitively bid press charters. White House officials also put pressure on the FBI to initiate an investigation and then interfered with both the timing and public explanation of the investigation. Harry Thomason's role and activities in the White House should have made him a special Government employee (SGE), subject to the ethics laws. The conduct of both Thomason and Catherine Cornelius warranted investigation by the Justice Department to determine whether either violated criminal laws.

White House officials, including the President, made several untruthful, misleading, or wrong statements to the public about the Travel Office on May 19, 1993, when the seven Travel Office employees were fired, and over the next several days. Foremost among these was the repeated insistence that the firings came about as a result of a review conducted by Peat Marwick as part of the Vice President's National Performance Review. In fact, the decision to fire the employees was probably made on May 13, **before** the Peat Marwick team even began its three-day review, and was based solely on allegations made by Harry Thomason, Thomason's business partner Darnell Martens, and Cornelius, all of whom had at least a personal stake in replacing the Travel Office staff.

The White House Management Review of the Travel Office matter, although candidly acknowledging a series of inappropriate and improper actions, failed to recognize that the misconduct went beyond failing to be sufficiently sensitive to the appearance of impropriety. The completeness and accuracy of the Management Review's investigation was also called into question by the review subsequently conducted by the General Accounting Office (GAO), although the GAO Report failed to include many important details it obtained through its interviews. The study of the House Republicans brought these GAO interviews to light and, in so doing, raised several questions about what occurred as well as the adequacy of the previous White House and GAO investigations. These outstanding questions required an additional congressional investigation, which the House Government Reform and Oversight Committee began in the fall of 1995 with an initial hearing in October. The hearing shed more light on the involvement of Harry Thomason and the First Lady, as well as highlighted the White House's resistance to the investigations conducted by GAO and the Justice Department's Office of Professional Responsibility.

The indictment of former White House Travel Director Billy Dale on charges of embezzlement and conversion was cited by the White House as justification for the initial decision to remove Dale and the other Travel Office employees and to conduct an audit of the Travel Office. Dale was acquitted, however, despite being precluded from putting on evidence to show the improper motivations for the firings and the destruction of exculpatory logs and other papers by one or more improperly motivated persons. Dale's acquittal raises a serious question whether the White House, Attorney General, or FBI improperly encouraged the Department of Justice to prosecute a weak case in which the evidence fell short of the standard generally used by Federal prosecutors. Whether Dale's prosecution was conducted in accordance with Justice Department guidelines and free of involvement by the White House, FBI or political officials at the Justice Department deserves to be examined by Congress.

No other matter raising concerns about the ethics of the Clinton Administration was as heavily reported or investigated as the White House's May 1993 firing of seven Travel Office employees. Initially, the White House conducted a White House Travel Office Management Review, releasing a report on July 2, 1993.[1] GAO also conducted a review, as required by law,[2] and issued a report in May 1994.[3] On October 7, 1994, Representative Bill Clinger, Ranking Member of the House Committee on Government Operations, and fifteen other Republicans (most of whom also served on the Committee), issued a staff report, which took issue with both the White House and GAO reports.[4] A year later, Chairman Clinger of the renamed House Committee on Government Reform and Oversight heard testimony from the authors of the White House and GAO reviews, in addition to the author of review of the FBI's actions conducted by the Justice Department's Office of Professional Responsibility. This chapter relies heavily on these reports and analyses for the factual history recounted in this chapter.[5]

Although the Travel Office firings have been thoroughly investigated, recounted, and analyzed, questions concerning the propriety of the conduct of White House officials remain. Moreover, none of these reports contains a satisfactory analysis of this matter under the letter of the ethics statutes and regulations. This chapter provides such an analysis.

A Brief Historical Review

On May 19, 1993, all seven employees of the White House Travel Office were fired, effective immediately.[6] Although as White House Office staff the employees enjoyed no civil service protection, the White House did not base the terminations on the simple turnover of personnel following a change of administration. Rather, the firings ostensibly resulted from the findings of an outside review of the Travel Office conducted in a few days by the accounting firm of Peat Marwick. The audit was requested by the White House after reports surfaced internally of alleged misman-agement and misconduct by Travel Office staff. The White House Counsel's office also contacted the FBI for assistance in this matter. The Bureau did eventually deter-mine that there was cause for an investigation of the Travel Office and that it would conduct an investigation, findings that Dee Dee Myers disseminated to two reporters on the day of the dismissals. Yet, the Bureau held its investigation in abeyance, at the White House's request, pending completion of the Peat Marwick review.

At the time of their dismissal, the White House Travel Office staff handled two primary responsibilities: commercial (non-Air Force One) travel of White House staff, and travel for the media persons who accompany the President on trips. There was no allegation of mismanagement or misconduct with respect to the travel ar-rangements for White House staff. The entire controversy about the White House Travel Office concerned its role in facilitating travel arrangements for the White House press corps. The Travel Office arranges charter airplane flights,[7] lodging, ground transportation, and office space on site for members of the White House press corps. News organizations are billed after the trip and reimburse the Travel Office. The Travel Office does not handle Government funds in this capacity.

The role and personal interest of **Catherine Cornelius**, a staff member of the White House Office of Management and Administration and a distant cousin of the President, **Harry Thomason**, a friend of the Clintons with access to the White House on virtually the same terms as a member of the White House staff, and **Darnell Martens**, Thomason's business partner, soon came to light, calling into ques-tion the *bona fides* of the stated White House reasons for firing the Travel Office staff.[8] In addition, the role of Associate Counsel William Kennedy in contacting the FBI, and of Kennedy and other White House officials in revising and releasing an FBI press statement on May 21, was sharply criticized in the media and by Republi-cans in Congress.[9]

The resulting furor in the media led the White House on May 25, 1993 to announce an internal management review of the Travel Office matter, by then widely dubbed "Travelgate," to be conducted under the supervision of White House Chief of Staff Mac McLarty and OMB Director Leon Panetta.[10]

Beginning on May 24, Senate Minority Leader Bob Dole wrote three letters to FBI Director William Sessions, asking for a complete explanation of the FBI's actions in the Travel Office Matter.[11] Dole also asked the Attorney General to appoint a special counsel to investigate the matter. Senator Orrin Hatch also wrote the FBI, concerned about "political abuse" of the FBI "in order to protect Administration officials from charges of political cronyism."[12]

Republicans began pushing for adoption of a Resolution of Inquiry, which would lead to a congressional investigation of the Travel Office matter. Instead, Congress passed a provision requiring GAO to conduct an investigation.[13] The "White House Travel Office Management Review" was issued on July 2, 1993,[14] the same day the provision requiring a GAO review was signed into law.[15]

The White House Management Review, relying on the findings of the Peat Marwick review, concluded that the firings of Travel Office Director Billy Dale and Deputy Director Gary Wright were justified because of the serious deficiencies in their financial management of the Travel Office. In particular, the White House review cited unaccounted for funds and a lack of financial controls. However, the White House review decided to reinstate the five Travel Office employees "who exercised no financial control over the Office." These employees would not return to the Travel Office, but would be given "an appropriate assignment consistent with their background and experience in the Executive Office of the President or other federal agency, pending completion of the ongoing [criminal] investigation."[16]

The White House Management Review criticized the handling of both the deliberations that led up to the dismissals as well as the dismissals themselves, finding errors in:

• Not treating the Travel Office employees with more sensitivity:

• Not being sufficiently vigilant in guarding against even the appearance of pressure on the FBI;

• Permitting people with personal interests in the outcome to be involved in evaluating the Travel Office;

• By not being sufficiently sensitive to the appearance of favoritism toward friends; [and]

• Not engaging in the kind of deliberate, careful planning that the reorganization of an Office like this warrants and requires.[17]

In making these findings, the White House Management Review made no reference to the standards of ethical conduct to which White House officials are subject.[18]

The White House Management Review announced that the Travel Office would henceforth save money by competitively bidding for press charter services, outsourcing travel arrangements for White House staff, and implementing a new accounting and internal controls system in the Travel Office. The White House Management Review also announced changes in policy and procedures with respect to contacts with the FBI and IRS, disclosure of ongoing criminal investigations, and access to the White House by part-time consultants such as Harry Thomason.[19]

The White House Management Review included no recommendation that any White House official be disciplined. However, at the July 2 press conference, the White House announced that four officials—David Watkins, Catherine Cornelius, Jeff Eller, and William Kennedy—had been "reprimanded."

Soon after the release of the White House Management Review, House Republicans continued to push for a congressional investigation of the Travel Office matter, but were rebuffed by Democrats in the Judiciary Committee, who pointed to the recent law requiring a GAO investigation into the matter.[20]

The GAO report, released on May 2, 1994, confirmed Peat Marwick's conclusion that "significant financial management weaknesses existed in the press travel operations" and further found that the White House had historically provided "little guidance or oversight to Travel Office employees" notwithstanding indications of these weaknesses.[21] Yet, GAO's review of selected trip files "showed that major expenses were documented, travelers were identified, and calculations were made to divide the costs of the trips and bill those costs" appropriately. In its review of financial records, GAO "identified no discrepancies with Travel Office records."[22] GAO noted some improvement in the management of the Travel Office as a result of changes implemented by the White House in 1993, but found that these changes had not yet been fully implemented, and that press organizations had complained of inadequate service.[23]

GAO found that the White House failed to guard against the appearance that "personal interests" played a role in the decisions to dismiss the Travel Office employees, although it concluded that the "facts did not support a conclusion that [Thomason and Martens] were special government employees[.]" GAO also found that Kennedy's contacts with the FBI did not violate any existing policy, but that his actions and the actions of other White House officials "created [an] appearance of pressure on [the] FBI" and that it was improper for the White House to divulge the existence of a criminal investigation.[24] GAO made several recommendations to the White House concerning the management and internal controls of the Travel Office, and one recommendation to "better ensure that White House access is commensurate with accountability":

> [W]e also recommend that the Chief of Staff develop policies governing appropriate activities by nongovernment employees granted unrestricted White House access and establish a mechanism for periodically assessing the implementation of those policies.[25]

Soon after release of the GAO Report, David Brock wrote an extensive and carefully researched piece in the *American Spectator* that took issue with the White House Management Review and what he termed the GAO's "whitewash of the affair."[26] Brock called Travelgate "a story of influence-peddling and sleazy deal-making."

On October 7, 1994, sixteen House Republicans asked House Committee on Government Operations Chairman John Conyers to conduct hearings at the start of the next Congress, to examine the conduct of the GAO's investigation of the Travel Office firings and the truthfulness and cooperation of the White House officials in the GAO probe.[27] In particular, the Republicans concluded that "[s]erious questions regarding the terminations of Travel Office workers and efforts by the White House to justify their actions remain unanswered: "Most seriously, . . . significant efforts were made by senior White House officials to withhold or possibly distort information provided to the GAO and relevant congressional committees."[28]

The House Republicans found that Cornelius did not act independently, as the White House Management Review suggested, but carried out the directions she received from David Watkins. They accused Watkins of not being truthful with GAO in several respects. They took issue with GAO's conclusion that neither Thomason nor Martens was a special Government employee, asserting that GAO's investigation was inadequate.

Concerning the White House and FBI, the House Republicans concluded that the White House interfered with the FBI's investigation, focusing on the timing, scope, and nature of the FBI's investigation rather than on Kennedy's initial prodding of the FBI to advise him on what to do. They also charged the FBI failed to ensure the integrity of Travel Office records, arguably relevant to the FBI's investigation.

Finally, the House Republicans questioned the truthfulness of statements of Chief of Staff McLarty and OMB Director Panetta that they had personally reprimanded several White House officials for their role in the Travel Office matter.[29]

No formal response to the House Republicans' request was provided before the midterm elections, which resulted in a Republican House of Representatives. Soon after the election, Representative Clinger, in line to be the Chairman of the House Committee on Government Operations (later renamed the House Committee on Government Reform and Oversight), indicated that his committee would hold hearings in the 104th Congress.[30]

In December 1994, former Travel Office Director Billy Dale was indicted on two counts, one for embezzlement and one for conversion. His trial began just a few days after the Committee on Government Reform and Oversight held the first congressional hearing on the Travel Office matter.[31] The highlight of this hearing was learning for the first time of Harry Thomason's efforts with the President and other White House officials to obtain a government contract for his business to study the use of aircraft by civilian agencies. Michael Shaheen, Director of the Justice Department's Office of Professional Responsibility (OPR), which conducted a review of the FBI's actions in the Travel Office matter, testified that the White House's lack of cooperation in OPR's probe was "unprecedented." Shaheen was particularly upset that during the conduct of his inquiry, he was not shown or told of a notebook maintained by Deputy White House Counsel Vince Foster on the Travel Office matter.

Chairman Clinger expressed his frustration with the White House's conduct by suggesting the establishment of an Inspector General in the White House:

Too often, administration attorneys responded to investigators like private defense attorneys rather than public servants charges with preserving our trust in the highest office of the land. . . . The highest office in the land cannot be held to a lower level of accountability.[32]

He also suggested that when the Congress and Presidency are held by the same party, the minority party members of House and Senate committees be given subpoena authority now held only by the chairmen and majority party members, because of the lack of meaningful congressional oversight, historically exercised by the majority party.

The existence of the Foster notebook was first reported in July 1995 by the *Washington Times*.[33] But in September, on the eve of congressional hearings, it was reported that Special Counsel Fiske was not told about the notebook until July 1994—after he had concluded his investigation into Foster's death—and the notebook was not given at all to OPR, despite being responsive to documents requests from both investigators.[34]

The notebook contains Foster's reconstruction of the Travel Office events, which he began on May 30, eleven days after the firings.[35] Foster wrote of his concern whether Dale in fact had committed any wrongdoing, and whether evidence relevant to this issue had been removed by Catherine Cornelius. Foster also noted his discussions with the First Lady and his determination to protect her against criticism resulting from the Travel Office scandal. The notebook also contains Foster's reference to the potential criminal exposure of Harry Thomason were he determined to be subject to the ethics laws.

White House Counsel Lloyd Cutler, after reading Fiske's report on the Foster death, asked another White House lawyer whether a Travel Office file existed, and the notebook was found in the Counsel's office files and thereafter turned over to Fiske. It was not, however, given to OPR. When Shaheen learned of the notebook from press reports, he wrote a memorandum to Deputy Associate Attorney General David Margolis dated July 24, 1995 in which he said that he was "stunned" to learn of the notebook, "since it so obviously bears upon the inquiry we were directed to take. . . . Even a minimal level of cooperation by the White House should have resulted in its disclosure to us at the outset of our investigation." He called the failure to turn over the Foster notebook "another example of the lack of cooperation and candor we received from the White House throughout our inquiry."[36]

The White House initially attempted to make former White House Counsel Bernard Nussbaum responsible for this episode.[37] Nussbaum, explained that he discovered the notebook in Foster's briefcase when he conducted the search of Foster's office on July 22, 1993, in the presence of law enforcement officials.[38] Nussbaum said that he "specifically identified" the notebook to investigators, but contemporaneous notes indicate that Nussbaum identified it as the White House Management Review, a document made public on July 2, 1993. In any event, Nussbaum retained the document in the Counsel's office files, because it was properly considered an official White House document. However, Nussbaum was not the White House Counsel when Special Counsel Fiske made the request for documents. When Fiske issued a broad subpoena to the White House, Nussbaum called Neil Eggleston in the White House Counsel's office to alert him to the existence of the notebook and its arguable responsiveness. Eggleston and Jane Sherburne, another lawyer in the Counsel's office, explained that the White House Counsel's office negotiated with Fiske's office to narrow the scope of the subpoena, and that the Counsel's office determined that the notebook was not responsive to Fiske's subpoena, as modified. After Fiske's report was issued on June 30, 1994, Lloyd Cutler asked Eggleston whether any Travel Office files existed. When informed of the notebook, Cutler told Fiske about it in a July 5, 1994 letter.

Among the documents obtained from the White House and released by the Committee at the October 1995 hearing were notes of interviews conducted as part of the White House Management Review. These notes showed a much greater involvement of Harry Thomason in the deliberations leading up to the firing of the Travel Office staff. Other documents released portrayed a larger role for the First Lady, too.

The internal White House documents were obtained after extensive negotiations with the White House Counsel's office over their privileged nature. As of November 1995, several hundred pages, including internal legal analyses, were still being withheld from the Committee on grounds of privilege, and it remained to be seen whether the Committee would subpoena the documents and whether the President would formally invoke a claim of executive privilege.[39]

Billy Dale was acquitted on November 16, 1995, following just two hours of jury deliberations. Chairman Clinger immediately indicated that he would look into whether Dale's prosecution was the product of improper motives or other misconduct. Clinger also indicated that if Harry Thomason failed to provide documents previously requested of him by December 8, he would schedule a December 12 vote for a subpoena to compel production.[40]

Factual History

Events Before the Inauguration

Catherine Cornelius served as Director of Travel Services for the Clinton-Gore campaign and later handled travel arrangements for the Clinton transition staff. She used World Wide Travel, a company located in Little Rock, as travel agent. Both Cornelius and World Wide were interested in performing the same functions for the Clinton White House.[41] During the transition, Cornelius and World Wide officials met with David Watkins, who had served as the campaign's Chief Financial Officer, and who was slated to be Assistant to the President for Management and Administration, "to discuss future possibilities."[42] In a memorandum to Watkins dated December 31, 1992, Cornelius proposed that the White House Travel Office's responsibility for **staff** travel arrangements be privatized and competitively bid, although the memorandum hinted that World Wide Travel should be chosen to perform the travel agency services. Cornelius envisioned savings would result from the reduction in White House staff and from a rebate that World Wide would remit to the White House Travel Account out of its commissions.[43]

Events from January 20, 1993, Through April 1993

In January 1993, Watkins, now in the White House, hired Cornelius and Clarissa Cerda, another transition worker, as "general assistants," with responsibilities to be determined later. Cornelius sent Watkins a second memorandum, dated January 26, 1993, in which she compared the White House's organization of travel and advance responsibilities with the organization used by the Clinton campaign.[44] On February 15, 1993, Cornelius and Cerda co-authored a "Briefing Book and Proposal" on the Travel Office, featuring them as "co-directors of travel," reporting directly to Watkins.[45] The proposed organizational chart included World Wide Travel as the outside travel agent for White House staff and White House press corps travel.[46] Among the putative benefits to the proposed reorganization, the authors cited a reduction in cost, efficiencies in staffing and use of dollars, and centralized coordination of all travel in connection with Presidential travel. Two additional cited benefits related to the proposed assignment of Cornelius and Cerda and selection of World Wide:

8. Incoming Clinton Administration More Comfortable and Familiar with this Proven System

9. Recommended Staff are More Knowledgeable and Familiar with the Personalities Involved as well as the System; thus, allowing for BETTER SERVICE.[47]

Around this time, Harry Thomason called Dee Dee Myers on behalf of his business partner, Darnell Martens, to find out whether "the White House charter business was subject to competitive bidding."[48] Harry Thomason, with his wife Linda Bloodworth-Thomason, are Hollywood producers and good friends of the Clintons. Thomason is also a one-third owner of Thomason, Richland & Martens (TRM), an aviation consulting business that represents and advises air charter companies.[49] One carrier represented by TRM, Air Advantage, served as the charter airline for the Clinton presidential campaign. TRM performed billing and consulting for Air Advantage in connection with the campaign. Sometime after the election, Martens expressed an interest in getting the White House press corps charter business for Air Advantage and other charter companies and in February asked Thomason for help.

At the time of Thomason's call to Myers, Thomason was working out of an office in the East Wing of the White House.[50] Thomason came to Washington after 1992 election to work on the Presidential Inaugural. Soon after the President was sworn in, Thomason was given a White House office and a White House pass allowing him unrestricted access on White House grounds.[51] Thomason was asked to "consult on the staging of presidential events."[52] GAO concluded, somewhat more specifically, that Thomason was "in the White House to provide advice to the President on the use of the White House physical facilities in the staging of public events and improving communications."[53]

Thomason's conversation with Myers ultimately led his business partner Martens to speak with Billy Dale about competing for the White House press charter business. According to an undated memorandum prepared by Martens (but written in the third person), Dale told Martens that "there was no possible combination of price/service under which TRM could earn the White House business and to not waste his time discussing the matter."[54] After Martens attempted to persuade Dale that TRM could provide a better price and service combination, Dale reportedly responded:

I have been here 31 years and no one has seen fit to replace me with a commercial operation yet. So until they do, I will continue to handle this without your help. However, if you are ever in Washington, I would be happy to meet you but do not bother making a special visit because you will not get the business.[55]

Martens told Thomason and Air Advantage owner Penny Sample of his conversation with Dale.[56]

Martens also concluded, on the basis of some "research" conducted after his phone call with Dale,[57] that the two carriers then used by the White House Travel Office for domestic and international travel by the press, UltrAir and American Trans Air, "did everything possible (and then some) to get President Bush re-elected apparently with the full knowledge and cooperation of the White House Travel Services Department[.]"[58]

Thus, at the very start of the Clinton Administration, **Cornelius and Cerda** were interested in personally replacing the White House Travel Office staff; **World Wide Travel** was interested in serving as the Travel Office's outside travel agent for the White House staff; and **TRM** (Martens and Thomason) was interested obtaining the White House press charter business on behalf of Air Advantage and perhaps other carriers, replacing the two carriers primarily used by the White House press corps for domestic and international presidential travel. TRM would presumably receive compensation as a broker, as it did during the campaign.[59] (TRM, as discussed presently, was also interested in a bigger project to study the use of government aircraft by non-military agencies.)

In early March, Martens passed on to Thomason a rumor he said he had heard "suggesting that there was corruption in the Travel Office."[60] The source for this rumor was unidentified and remains so.[61] In late March, Thomason raised the matter with the President, mentioning that "he thought there was trouble in a White House department having to do with travel, but did not give the President any details."[62]

No action was taken on the Cornelius/Cerda proposal of February 15, despite "periodic" inquiries by Cornelius (presumably made to Watkins), until April 1993, when Watkins assigned Cornelius to the Travel Office to handle commercial travel for the White House staff. Watkins also asked her to observe the operations of the office and file a report with him by May 15 on whether the Office should be reorganized.[63] Cornelius began work in the Travel Office in early April, perhaps as early as April 3.[64]

Around this time, Thomason called Watkins, passing on "rumors about the Travel Office staff receiving kickbacks from airlines" and complaining that Billy Dale "had expressed no interest in doing business with Mr. Martens."[65] Watkins relayed the substance of Thomason's call to Cornelius and asked her to "keep her eyes and ears open."[66]

Cornelius conducted her review of the Travel Office by inspecting the office's records, copying some of them, and taking others home with her. She also eavesdropped on office conversations. Cornelius attempted to perform her review surreptitiously.[67] Cornelius told GAO that she discovered several discrepancies in Travel Office records,[68] and that she overheard Travel Office employees talking of outside activities suggesting to her a life-style beyond the means of their Federal salary. Cornelius relayed these observations to Watkins.[69]

Thomason's and Martens' Efforts to Obtain a Government Contract for TRM[70]

During this time, Harry Thomason and Darnell Martens were heavily lobbying White House officials, including the President, to adopt a proposal whereby TRM would receive a government contract, without competitive bidding, to conduct a review of civilian government aircraft to determine their "financial and operational appropriateness." Martens eventually proposed a $499,000 project under the auspices of the extant Interagency Committee on Aircraft Policy (ICAP), $270,000 of which would go to TRM as financial consultant to the project under a contract with the General Services Administration (GSA). This activity was not revealed publicly until late October 1995, when the first congressional hearing was held on the Travel Office matter.

As early as January 29, 1993, Martens wrote Thomason and Dee Dee Myers a memorandum suggesting that TRM be retained as a consultant to conduct this review. The President raised the subject generally at a Cabinet meeting on February 10, the day he directed Federal agencies to take steps to reduce costs in their use of government aircraft. Martens wrote to Thomason again on February 11, asserting: "Harry, I can state without qualification that TRM is uniquely qualified to conduct this study. . . . Put me in front of the right person at the White House and I will prove the value of both the project and Thomason's [TRM's?] capabilities." Thomason gave this memorandum to the President. It was stamped "The President has seen" and forwarded on February 17 to Chief of Staff McLarty, Mark Gearan, and David Watkins for "Action." The President appended a handwritten note saying, "These guys are sharp. Should discuss with Panetta/Lader."

Martens wrote Thomason again on March 12, referring to a previous discussion on the TRM proposal Thomason apparently had with the President. Martens provide a "very conservative" estimate of potential savings from the project: $300 million in the first year, and $150 million each year thereafter. A month later, on April 6, Martens wrote Bruce Lindsey; Lindsey met with Martens the next day to discuss TRM's proposed "operational and financial audit" of civilian government aircraft. Thomason and Martens kept after Lindsey during the month of April, with Martens sending additional memoranda to him on April 12 and 29, and Thomason calling Lindsey to check on the status of the White House's review of the TRM proposal. The April 12 memorandum listed several steps that "the Office of the President" needed to take, including issuance of an executive order to give ICAP authority to conduct the study, and executing a financial consulting contract with TRM which would actually be done by GSA.

From the White House, Martens was directed to OMB. On May 6, Martens sent a copy of his two most recent memoranda to Lindsey to Jack Kelly, a career OMB official with responsibility over policies and procedures governing the use of government aircraft by Federal agencies. Kelly wrote an internal OMB memorandum on May 7 to his superior Frank Reeder, who wrote back that the issue and materials Kelly received from Martens should be given to GSA, which should determine how to proceed, adding "I would hate to prejudice a future procurement." GSA reportedly gave the TRM proposal serious consideration, for a while. The proposal did not move after Thomason's and Martens' role in the Travel Office debacle was revealed. In August 1993, Roy Neel, Deputy White House Staff, sent a memorandum to OMB Director Leon Panetta stating that "no government action should be taken on this proposal."

Events of May 1993

Thomason spoke with Watkins on **May 10**, first on the phone and then in person, asking about the status of the Travel Office. Watkins told Thomason that he had assigned Cornelius to the Travel Office.[71] Watkins asked Cornelius to meet with Thomason, telling her that Thomason could assist her in completing her report. In preparation for the meeting, Thomason asked Martens to fax to Watkins the memorandum Martens wrote following his February phone call with Billy Dale.

Cornelius and Thomason met on **May 12**.[72] They "discussed their respective concerns about the Travel Office and concluded that persons there might be engaged in wrongdoing."[73] The two of them then met with Watkins and Martens (who was in Washington at the time) to discuss their concerns.[74] Thomason then met with the First Lady, who told Thomason to "stay ahead of this" and that ridding the Travel Office of corruption would be "a good story."[75] Thomson and Cornelius met again at lunch, before an afternoon meeting with Deputy White House Counsel Vince Foster and Watkins. Watkins had previously asked to meet with Foster concerning the Travel Office to express the First Lady's interest in the matter. The meeting with Foster, at which Cornelius and Thomason (but apparently not Martens) were present, took place at 2:45 p.m. Cornelius apparently left the meeting to go home to retrieve Travel Office documents she had removed from the White House. At the meeting, Cornelius outlined her concerns about how the Travel Office was being managed.[76]

A discussion about the proper course to investigate these allegations of misconduct ensued, with Associate Counsel William Kennedy joining the meeting in progress. An audit was suggested, but Watkins explained that the White House lacked any audit capability. Kennedy was assigned to come up with a proposal.

After the meeting, Thomason called the First Lady to relay his "concerns," and then told Watkins that he had spoken with the First Lady.[77]

At Watkins' request, Cornelius called up Betta Carney at World Wide Travel and asked that the company "be prepared to come to Washington in the event changes were made in the Travel Office."[78] Carney recalled that she received two calls from Cornelius: on May 11, Cornelius reported to her that the Travel Office staff "would possibly be dismissed in the near future, due to allegations of wrongdoing."[79] On May 12, she asked Carney if World Wide could fill in for the Travel Office staff pending a competitive bidding process.[80]

Following the meeting, Kennedy called the FBI (for the first time) concerning the Travel Office.[81] Kennedy called Jim Bourke, whom Kennedy knew well from their work together in the clearance process for prospective presidential appointees. "Kennedy told Bourke that there was a problem in a White House office, that he was unsure how to proceed and that he sought guidance on handling the matter."[82] Bourke said that he would get back to Kennedy, which he did the next morning, **May 13**. Bourke asked Kennedy for more details to enable him to determine the appropriate Bureau unit to consider the matter. This time, Kennedy impressed upon Bourke the need for expedition, telling Bourke that "he needed to hear from Bourke within the next fifteen minutes and that, if the FBI were unable to provide guidance, Kennedy might have to seek guidance from another agency, such as the IRS."[83]

Howard Apple, Chief of the Interstate Theft and Government Crimes Unit of the FBI, subsequently called Kennedy on the 13th, but obtained little information from him[84] other than the matter was "directed at the highest levels" in the White House.[85] Apple then went to the White House with another agent, meeting with Kennedy only briefly. Kennedy shared some of the allegations against the Travel Office with the agents, and gave them the impression that he was "clearly under pressure." Kennedy again mentioned that he might resort to the IRS if the FBI did not agree to assist.

Apple returned to the FBI, at which point the Bureau determined that the White Collar Crime Division's Government Fraud Unit was the appropriate office to consider the matter. Two senior Unit officials, Richard Wade and Thomas Carl, then went to the White House to meet with Kennedy around 3:30 on the 13th. After listening to Kennedy's concerns (Foster was also present during some of this meeting), Wade told him that "insufficient grounds existed for a criminal investigation."[86] Kennedy then had the FBI officials meet with Cornelius. Cornelius told the FBI agents of "checks made out to cash that were not accounted for, questionable practices in ferrying aircraft by the principal air charter carrier, lack of bidding for air charter services, and kickbacks."[87] Cornelius apparently made a difference, for Wade and Carl concluded that there was at least a possibility of a criminal violation that warranted investigation. They informed Kennedy and Foster of this conclusion, and contacted the FBI's Washington Metropolitan Field Office, which would handle the investigation.[88]

While the Counsel's office was engaged in these discussions with the FBI on May 13, Watkins called Larry Herman of the accounting firm of KPMG Peat Marwick and requested a financial review of the Travel Office to begin the next morning, May 14. Foster, believing the Peat Marwick review to be "a more cautious and low-key approach" than an FBI investigation, asked the FBI to await the completion of the Peat Marwick review before beginning its investigation.[89] Wade requested that FBI agents at least be present during the Peat Marwick review. Foster told the FBI that he needed to check with "higher authority" on the matter. He called Wade later to inform him that the FBI would not be welcome. Wade did not persist.

Foster, Watkins, and Patsy Thomasson brought Chief of Staff McLarty up to speed on these developments in the afternoon of May 13. In this meeting, Foster noted the President's and the First Lady's interest in the matter. Around 6 p.m. several additional meetings and discussions took place in the White House to set up the Peat Marwick review to begin the next morning.[90]

On **May 13 and 14**, Cornelius and Thomason agitated for prompt action.[91] On May 13, they met with Jeff Eller, Deputy Communications Director, ostensibly to provide guidance on how to handle press inquiries.[92] Eller then met with Watkins and Patsy Thomasson later on May 13, a meeting not mentioned in the White House Management Review. According to GAO notes of its interview with Eller:

It was a foregone conclusion that Mr. Watkins and Ms. Thomasson had decided to fire the employees during the May 13 meeting and that they were only asking him how the matter should be handled from a media standpoint.[93]

The next morning, **May 14**, Eller argued "vigorously" to McLarty that the Travel Office employees should be fired by the end of the day.[94] However, McLarty accepted Foster's advice "that no action be taken" until the Peat Marwick review was complete, **which in fact had just started that morning.**[95]

Also on May 14, Watkins spoke on the phone with the First Lady. According to his notes of this conversation, the First Lady said:

"Harry says his people can run things better; save money, etc. And besides we need those people out—We need our people in—We need the slots—[96]

The Peat Marwick team worked throughout the weekend, providing periodic updates to Watkins and Patsy Thomasson, who, in turn, briefed Foster and the First Lady.[97] On the first day of Peat Marwick's review, Watkins informed the First Lady that:

> KPMG had found sloppy management in the Travel Office. He said that she urged that action be taken to get "our people" into the Travel Office to help achieve the 25-percent White House staff cut.[98]

Two members of the White House staff were present during much of the time the Peat Marwick team was at the White House.[99] Peat Marwick finished its "field work" on Sunday, **May 16**, and submitted a draft of its report to Kennedy on **May 17**.

The White House Management Review states that Watkins decided to fire the Travel Office employees on Monday, May 17, and that McLarty "approved."[100] Watkins wrote a memorandum to McLarty (with a copy to the First Lady), describing Peat Marwick's draft findings, and stating his intent to dismiss the Travel Office employees (save Cornelius) the next day, "with pay through June 5."[101] Watkins' memorandum did not seek McLarty's approval or concurrence. Watkins wrote that he would place Cornelius in charge of the reorganized Travel Section, "on an interim basis," and World Wide Travel "temporarily" would "take over travel services[.]"[102] Watkins added that the White House would request bids for this business on a permanent basis.

Watkins stated the Peat Marwick review was part and parcel of the "internal management review" of the Travel Office, which, in turn, was part of the National Performance Review:

> Urged by Harry Thomasson [sic], who had heard rumors of criminal activity in the Travel Office, and Catherine Cornelius, who had been observing the Travel Office for 45 days, we placed the Travel Office at the front end of the review and began an emergency review this past Friday.[103]

Watkins stated that the Peat Marwick team found "abysmal management" and discovered about $18,000 in "unaccounted-for-funds." However, Watkins noted that Peat Marwick's final report would not be completed until May 19. Thus, it appears that Watkins' memorandum was based only on the oral updates Peat Marwick provided Watkins and others "several times a day over the course of the weekend,"[104] and not on the May 17 Peat Marwick letter to William Kennedy.

Peat Marwick's May 17 letter to Kennedy (which appears to be a final report, not a draft) contained a disclaimer made at the outset:

> Our procedures do not constitute an audit, examination, or review in accordance with standards established by the American Institute of Certified Public Accountants and, therefore, **we do not express an opinion or any other form of assurance on the information presented in our report.**[105]

The letter summarized manifold weaknesses and discrepancies in the management and recordkeeping of the Travel Office: lack of accountability, lack of accounting controls and systems, lack of documentation, lack of contractual support, and an inadequate billing process.

Watkins personally met with some of the Travel Office employees at 10 a.m. on **May 19**, summarily dismissing them and requesting that they leave the complex by noon.[106] Collecting their personal belongings, they went through standard checkout procedures for departing employees and were escorted from the building by the Secret Service.[107] Watkins told GAO he referred to the findings of mismanagement discovered by the Peat Marwick review, and his commitment to cut White House staff by 25 percent,[108] but he did not allude to the FBI investigation or allegations of criminal misconduct, nor did he discuss the allegations made by Harry Thomason or Darnell Martens, "since he had no proof of them."[109] Watkins told GAO he decided to fire the entire office because he understood them to work "interchangeably."[110] Five of the seven Travel Office employees, when interviewed by the *American Spectator* in 1995, said that Watkins referred to the Peat Marwick findings of "mismanagement" and "poor" or "sloppy accounting." The first they learned of any FBI involvement or allegations of corruption was from the White House press briefing later that day.[111]

Around 8:30 a.m. on May 19, before Watkins met with the Travel Office employees, he delivered talking points to Dee Dee Myers that explained that the employees were being fired as a result of a "routine review conducted as part of the Vice President's National Performance Review."[112] The talking points also alluded to the White House's **request** to the FBI to investigate the matter.[113] When Foster and Kennedy reviewed the talking points, sometime around 9 a.m., they directed Watkins to delete any reference to the FBI, but Myers was not reached until afternoon, after she had revealed the existence of the FBI investigation to two reporters in separate conversations. Myers first revealed the FBI investigation in a conversation with a reporter during a visit to Capitol Hill that morning. Myers told the reporter (Terry Hunt of the Associated Press) only that an FBI investigation was "likely."[114] The White House Management Review describes the second contact as Myers "tak[ing] a press call and disclos[ing] the FBI inquiry in response to a reporter's question."[115] Note that two reporters were on to the story even before the firings were announced that afternoon.

Watkins met with Myers just before her mid-afternoon press briefing. At that briefing, however, Myers twice denied that an ongoing FBI investigation was pending. She responded with, "There is no investigation at this point. I think it is likely that they will[;]" and "There is no investigation going on right now."[116]

Events After the Firings

On May 19, following the dismissals, World Wide Travel personnel moved into the Travel Office to handle commercial travel arrangements for White House staff, "on an interim basis."[117] Also that day Martens called Air Advantage owner Penny Sample and asked her to work in the Travel Office to handle press charters on a temporary, volunteer basis. Sample began in the Travel Office on May 20.

White House and FBI press statements. On May 19, following Dee Dee Myers' disclosure to two reporters of the (likely) FBI investigation (and her denial of such an investigation to the White House press corps), the Bureau put out a one-sentence press release: "We understand that the results of the audit of the White House Travel Office will be referred to the FBI for our review."[118] The next day, **May 20**, the Bureau prepared two press "responses," to be given out only in the event an appropriate question were asked. Both versions similarly noted that the FBI would review the results of the audit and then conduct whatever investigation would be appropriate, although the second version implied that an investigation had already begun.[119]

On Friday afternoon, May 21, John Collingwood, the FBI's head of Public and Congressional Relations, was summoned to the White House Communications Office to "clarify the facts and indicate what could properly be said about the investigation."[120] In the meeting were Collingwood, Stephanopoulos, Myers, Nussbaum, Foster, Kennedy, and a representative of Peat Marwick.[121] According to the White House Management Review, Collingwood was asked "whether it would be accurate to state that the FBI had determined there to be sufficient evidence to warrant further criminal investigation. Collingwood confirmed that this would be an accurate statement."[122] According to GAO, Collingwood was asked "(1) whether **a White House statement** about the investigation was accurate [he said it was] and (2) whether there was predication for the FBI investigation [he said there was]."[123]

Thereafter, Collingwood revised his press response to include a statement about the sufficiency of the evidence and faxed a revised copy to the White House. According to the GAO Report (not mentioned in the White House Management Review), Dee Dee Myers asked Collingwood "to make it clearer and 'consistent with the facts.'" As further revised, the FBI press response read:

> At the request of the White House, the FBI has had preliminary contact with the White House and the auditors brought in to audit the White House Travel Office. **That contact produced sufficient information for the FBI to determine that additional criminal investigation is warranted.** We anticipate receiving the final report of the auditors soon and will analyze their findings to determine the next steps in the investigation. Beyond that, we are not in a position to comment.[124]

The White House press office, ostensibly mistaking this FBI press response for a press release, released the statement to reporters at the May 21 afternoon White House briefing.[125] Collingwood said that he did not realize the White House would release the response.[126] The Attorney General, who had never been informed of the White House's request to the FBI to investigate, by either the FBI or the White House, also was kept in the dark about this FBI press response until after its White House release.[127]

The brief, two-day tenure of World Wide Travel. At the request of David Watkins, World Wide Travel began work in the White House on May 19, the day the Travel Office employees were let go. World Wide was asked to handle travel arrangements for White House staff. When World Wide could not get the White House to agree to pay the company for its services (World Wide was surprised to find that no commissions were being paid on airline tickets issued to White House employees), and in the face of negative publicity surrounding the Travel Office, World Wide told the White House on Friday, May 21, that it would leave the White House upon the White House's finding of a suitable replacement.[128] The White House staff travel business was awarded to American Express through a competitive bidding process conducted by GSA over the weekend and concluded on Sunday, May 23. American Express began work on May 24 pursuant to an interim, 120-day contract, which was extended several times thereafter.[129] World Wide departed the White House on May 24, after briefing American Express representatives.

The reinstatement of five of the seven Travel Office employees. Within a week of their firing, five of the seven dismissed employees (all but the Director and Deputy Director) were reinstated and placed on administrative leave with pay, pending the outcome of the Justice Department's investigation.[130] In August, the five each received a letter from the Justice Department informing them that they were neither targets nor subjects of the pending criminal investigation.[131] The White House then sought to place the employees in other comparable jobs in the Executive Branch.[132]

Penny Sample leaves the White House. Penny Sample ended her volunteer service on June 2, 1993, contemporaneously with a report that her company had received a $1,400 commission for arranging the first White House press charter flight. Sample ordered the commission returned after the *Washington Post* asked her about it. Sample claimed that she was unaware of the commission and explained that the Air Advantage office in New Mexico had mistakenly deducted the commission from the payment to Midwest Express.[133] At the time she left, Sample had competitively bid press charters for three trips. Sample was initially replaced by a GSA employee who was detailed to the White House to make the press charter arrangements.[134] Later, employees from other Federal agencies were detailed to assist in making travel arrangements for the White House staff and press corps.[135]

The reprimands. At the July 2, 1993 White House announcement of the results of the White House Management Review, McLarty and Panetta said that four White House staffers had been reprimanded for their role in the Travel Office matter: David Watkins, Catherine Cornelius, Jeff Eller, and William Kennedy. No one was fired.[136] Questions were later raised whether, in fact, any of the four White House officials received a reprimand.[137]

At the July 2 briefing, McLarty said, "I have issued reprimands to David Watkins, William Kennedy, Jeff Eller, and Catherine Cornelius." Panetta added, "We've had serious discussions with each of the people involved as to the mistakes that were made. We also made it clear that we would make public the fact that these reprimands have been made with regards to each of these individuals."[138] White House Communications Director Mark Gearan later said that the four had received reprimands "both personally and publicly."[139]

In congressional testimony in March 1994, Panetta clarified that the reprimands were not given in writing, but were done orally by Panetta and McLarty.[140] McLarty further clarified to GAO that "[t]he reprimands were not documented in their personnel files, but the reprimands are clearly on their 'records.'"[141]

However, GAO notes of interviews of three of the four reprimanded officials contradict Panetta and McLarty. **Cornelius** admitted she was reprimanded, but denied she was reprimanded in person; she learned she was reprimanded from watching McLarty and Panetta's press conference. **Eller** also said his reprimand consisted solely of McLarty's public announcement on July 2.[142] **Kennedy**, too, said his only reprimand was McLarty's public announcement of the reprimand.[143] GAO did not discuss these discrepancies in its report; a GAO official later explained that GAO was not "doing an investigation of reprimands."[144]

Reading the transcript of the July 2 press conference, the most charitable construction is that McLarty and Panetta did not tell it straight at the press conference and that Panetta's 1994 testimony requires an amendment. The truth appears to be that the only reprimand received by any of the four White House officials was the **(incorrect)** public statement that they **had been** reprimanded. All McLarty or Panetta needed to have said on July 2 was something to the effect that, "By this announcement, we are hereby publicly reprimanding these officials." Why they said and testified differently is not apparent.

David Watkins was fired one year later after a highly-publicized report of his use of Marine One, a military helicopter, for a round of golf.[145]

The Indictment, Prosecution, and Acquittal of Billy Dale

On December 7, 1994, Billy Dale, the former Director of the Travel Office, was indicted by a Federal grand jury on two counts, one count of embezzlement and one count of conversion.[146] The indictment charged that, between 1988 and 1991, Dale deposited into his own personal bank account 55 checks from various media firms totaling $54,188.[147] The monies were travel reimbursements and related payments that should have been deposited in a separate Press Travel Fund account at a different bank. The indictment also charged that Dale diverted $14,000 of Press Travel Fund account monies from the Travel Office's petty cash fund to his own use.

Dale pleaded not guilty at a December 15 hearing before Judge Harold Greene.[148] Through his attorney, Dale contended that he substituted his own money for office checks he deposited in his own account, and that he could prove this if his missing records were found and the expense records could otherwise be obtained:

> Mr. Tabackman said Mr. Dale did deposit some checks made out in his name in a personal account. But for every dollar he deposited in his personal account, he said, Mr. Dale withdrew an equal amount from a kitty of cash he kept at his home.
>
> Mr. Tabackman said Mr. Dale, who often had up to $3,000 in his house at any one time, would bring the money to the travel office and he and his staff would use it for petty cash expenses such as tips for bus drivers and bribes demanded by foreign travel officials. . . .
>
> Mr. Tabackman said Mr. Dale recorded every cashed check and equal cash transfer from his house to the travel office's petty-cash account in a ledger kept in a credenza in his office. That ledger has never been found, and Mr. Dale's associates charge that Miss Cornelius or another Clinton administration official destroyed it in order to sink Mr. Dale.[149]

This would be Dale's defense on the facts. While at first blush it appeared improbable, Dale's former associates reportedly would back his account.[150] And Vince Foster, in a journal composed several days after Dale's dismissal (but not released until July 1995), did not foreclose the possibility of a "plausible" or "reasonable" explanation for Dale's practice of writing checks to "cash."[151] Foster's journal also appears to confirm that Cornelius removed Travel Office documents and did not return them, although it is unclear whether those documents included Dale's ledger and whether Foster's account (that the documents were never returned) is accurate.[152]

Dale's attorney added that there was nothing illegal about Dale's commingling personal funds with press reimbursements, and that the Travel Office's account was not subject to any Federal guidelines. In addition, the defense intended to show that the review conducted by Peat Marwick and the White House decision to fire Dale and the others were politically motivated.

However, the defense was precluded from probing either the removal of the ledger or the motivation behind Dale's dismissal. Soon after Dale's indictment, Dale's attorney requested court approval to issue subpoenas to the White House, World Wide Travel Services, Incorporated, and Air Advantage. The subpoena to the White House, directed to White House Counsel Mikva, asked for all documents taken from Dale's office before he was fired May 19, 1993, as well as records of several officials, including the First Lady, Foster, Kennedy, Watkins, and Cornelius.[153] In July 1995, Dale's attorney supplemented his request with a public written statement (accompanied by a sealed statement) alleging the existence of "evidence of White House obstruction of justice."[154] In August 1995, Dale's attorney renewed his discovery request, explaining the relevance of the discovery requested to the theory of the defense:

> . . . It is anticipated that the defendant would testify . . . that he maintained a ledger that kept track of the deposits into his account and the corresponding expenditures of his personal funds for the benefit of the Travel Office. Such a document, if it were available to the defendant, would, it may safely be said, provide powerful documentary corroboration of the defendant's oral testimony.
>
> The defendant would further testify that he placed that ledger in an envelope along with 10 years' worth of other Travel Office records, notably, petty cash records. Others would testify to seeing an envelope that matches the description of the one the defendant says he used in the Travel Office prior to the dismissal of the defendant and his colleagues. The defendant has also proffered the sworn affidavit of a credible and disinterested witness that he was handed a matching envelope on the day that the Travel Office officials were dismissed. Such testimony would further corroborate the existence of the missing documents;
>
> . . . the existence of the documents, and the fact that Mr. Dale carefully recorded the expenditures, impacts directly on the likelihood that a jury will either credit or reject the defendant's testimony that he did not convert the funds of others to his own use.
>
> . . . [D]efendant must be allowed to adduce evidence that others had the motive and opportunity to remove documents from the Travel Office, and that there is evidence corroborating the claim that they did so.[155]

District Judge Gladys Kessler, a Clinton appointee,[156] denied the defendant's discovery requests, ruling that Dale had not met his burden of establishing "a tenable relationship between the materials sought and the preparation for the defense."[157] The theory of the defense, according to the court, "raises tangential and collateral issues which simply do not bear on the central issue in this case—namely, his innocence or guilt. Second, he has provided no factual basis which would justify his request for documents and records from the White House as well as other entities such as the FBI and the Whitewater Independent Counsel."[158]

The court emphasized that Dale's innocence or guilt would turn on events that occurred before the Clinton Administration, and added:

The purported removal and/or destruction of exculpatory evidence is not—and will not become—the central issue in this rather straightforward embezzlement case. Moreover, to the extent that the Defendant wishes to corroborate his story about the existence of the two sets of ledgers, he is perfectly free to call any or all of his co-workers who may have personal knowledge of their existence and use.[159]

The trial court's ruling significantly hurt Dale's defense. Had Dale been convicted, Judge Kessler's decision refusing this line of inquiry would have provided ample ground for a reversal on appeal.[160]

The trial, originally set for September 11, 1995, began on October 26, 1995, and lasted for three weeks. The gist of the prosecution's case was that Dale could not have afforded his family's expenditures without the money he allegedly embezzled or converted.[161] Billy Dale took the stand in his own defense, explaining his "disastrous decision" to commingle media travel funds in his personal account, and to use funds resulting from inadvertent overcharging the media to grease the skids to reduce the hassles and delays involved in the travel of the White House press corps, especially overseas.[162] Dale's defense was bolstered by a number of character witnesses, including some media personalities, as well as by the testimony of a fraud expert who concluded that Dale could have afforded his expenditures on his salary and other income and gifts apart from any Travel Office funds.[163]

Ultimately, the prosecution failed to convince the jury that Dale converted any of the Travel Office funds to his or his family's personal use. The defense, while hampered by Judge Kessler's pre-trial ruling, did manage to get before the jury the fact that Dale's ledger was missing, and that others such as Cornelius and Patsy Thomasson had unrestricted access to the Travel Office and the documents therein.[164] The defense was bolstered by the testimony of an FBI agent who observed that the Travel Office was not secure following the wholesale dismissal of the Travel Office staff on May 19, noting that several persons with visitor's passes were inside the office. The agent, Dennis Sculimbrene, passed his concern to a career White House Records Office official, Lee Johnson. Johnson expressed his own concerns in a memorandum to John Podesta, who was responsible for conducting the White House Management Review.[165]

On November 16, 1995, it took the jury only a little over two hours to return a verdict of not guilty.[166] On the day of Dale's acquittal, Chairman Clinger suggested that he would continue his Committee's investigation of the Travel Office affair, and add the Dale prosecution as part of its investigation.[167] The Committee would ask the Justice Department to provide documents on the handling of the investigation and prosecution.[168]

The one missing piece of the Justice Department puzzle is whether its investigation of Harry Thomason and Catherine Cornelius was ever closed. The last press report, in December 1994, suggested that the investigation was still pending.[169] Little is known of this investigation; presumably, the Justice Department is examining whether either of them violated the conflict-of-interest law, 18 U.S.C. 208, and perhaps whether Cornelius destroyed Government records.

Currently, the White House Travel Office consists of eight people (including four from American Express), one more than the number who were working in the Office in May 1993.[170]

Analysis

The White House had Authority to Dismiss the Travel Office Employees, But Misled the Public as to What Prompted the Review of Their Conduct and Their Subsequent Dismissal

Even though the Travel Office employees were not considered political appointees, as White House Office employees they served at the pleasure of the President. Thus, the White House had ample authority to dismiss the employees at will, without giving any reason. In retrospect, of course, the White House probably wishes it had done just that. The White House press corps would have complained about any change in personnel or policy that resulted in inconveniences or increased costs, but such complaints would have faded over time once the new employees and procedures began functioning smoothly.

However, it was one thing to replace the Travel Office with a competitively selected outside travel agency for White House staff travel and similarly chosen air carriers for press charters. It was quite another thing, given the quasi-career status of the Travel Office employees, to replace them both in the White House and outside of the White House—without competitive bidding—with Arkansans who worked on or with the Clinton-Gore campaign and who were friends (and former colleagues) of the White House decisionmakers. Perhaps some in the White House realized this would not smell good, and thus looked for a reason that would focus on an immediate need to get rid of the current Travel Office staff. They believed they found such a reason in reports of financial misconduct. Although these "reports" began as rumors that were, in fact, initiated and then fanned by these very same White House officials, the allegations eventually matured into a Peat Marwick review and the initiation of an FBI criminal investigation (although not in that order).

Thus, the employees were not dismissed at will, but for cause, and publicly to boot. Each of the employees was scarred by White House statements on May 19 and thereafter that their financial mismanagement and misconduct, found by a Peat Marwick review and warranting a criminal investigation, were the primary reasons for their dismissal.

The White House Management Review, to its credit, found that tarnishing the reputation of five of the seven employees was improper. This judgment was based both on the inappropriate disclosure of the FBI investigation, as well as the fact that none of the five exercised financial authority in the Travel Office and thus should not have been linked to the allegations of misconduct.[171]

Moreover, as the White House Management Review determined:

[T]he abrupt manner of dismissal of the Travel Office employees was unnecessary and insensitive. . . . All of the employees should have had an opportunity to hear the reasons for their termination, especially the allegations of wrongdoing, and should have been afforded an opportunity to respond.[172]

Again, because the Travel Office employees served at the pleasure of the President, this recommended process was not required by law. Thus, the White House deserves some credit for committing prospectively to observe elementary notions of due process before removing employees for cause.

Why were the Travel Office employees let go? Several reasons were offered at various times in internal White House deliberations and public White House statements:

(1) Downsizing of White House staff, as part of President's pledge to reduce White House staff by 25%;

(2) Misconduct found as part of the National Performance Review (Vice President Gore's reinventing government team);

(3) Misconduct found by the Peat Marwick review; and

(4) The FBI's determination that sufficient evidence existed to warrant the initiation of a criminal investigation.

The most likely reason was one that was never publicly acknowledged: the Travel Office employees were tarred by their previous work in Republican Administrations and were simply in the way of several persons who saw the Travel Office as their reward, if not entitlement, for their previous work for the Clinton-Gore campaign.[173]

The strongest single piece of evidence to support such a conclusion is that the decision to fire the Travel Office employees was most likely made by David Watkins on May 13, before the Peat Marwick team began work, much less issued its (draft) report on May 17.[174] Cornelius and Harry Thomason may have wanted to get rid of the Travel Office staff days, weeks or months earlier, but neither of course had the authority to fire. Watkins did.

Watkins did not personally conduct any review of the Travel Office, nor did he discuss problems identified by Cornelius with Billy Dale or any other Travel Office employee. The information before Watkins at the time he made his decision to fire the Travel Office staff was supplied by Catherine Cornelius, Harry Thomason, and Darnell Martens. Each of these individuals had a personal, if not financial stake, in replacing the Tavel Office employees. Peat Marwick had not arrived on the scene, and the FBI had not made any independent conclusion **confirming** any of the rumors and allegations made by these three persons.[175]

Watkins may have taken comfort in learning on May 13 of the FBI's preliminary determination that the information furnished by Cornelius suggested misconduct warranting a criminal investigation. But the FBI did **not** conduct any investigation to verify or check the strength of Cornelius's charges. Rather, Cornelius persuaded the FBI based on the records she furnished—and not on any other records furnished by the Travel Office employees. At that time, the FBI investigators would have had no basis to discount the possibility that exculpatory documents existed in the Travel Office. Moreover, the FBI agents were not told of Cornelius's personal interest in replacing the Travel Office staff, and thus were not sufficiently wary of her pitch. Recall that the FBI initially believed earlier on May 13 that the evidence presented by William Kennedy was insufficient, notwithstanding the FBI's awareness (courtesy of Kennedy) of the high-level White House interest in the matter. It was only when Cornelius personally met with FBI agents, presented some Travel Office records, and provided her thoughts, that the FBI changed its mind.

Once Watkins brought in the Counsel's office and the FBI, Watkins needed to apprise McLarty and the First Lady of what he was going to do. Foster first counseled Watkins to not "take any action" until the Peat Marwick team conducted its review, but it is unclear what Foster meant—and what Watkins thought he meant—by the word "action." "Action" could refer either to the decision to fire or the announcement of the firing.

On May 14, the First Lady gave her complete support to Watkins for moving to get "our people" in the Travel Office, having engaged in several discussions over the previous two days with Harry Thomason, Foster, ad McLarty. But in written answers to questions from GAO, the White House stated:

> Mrs. Clinton does not know the origin of the decision to remove the White House Travel Office employees. She believes that the decision to terminate the employees would have been made by Mr. Watkins with the approval of Mr. McLary.
>
> Mrs. Clinton was aware that Mr. Watkins was undertaking a review of the situation in the Travel Office, but she had no role in the decision to terminate the employees.
>
> Mrs. Clinton did not direct that any action be taken by anyone with regard to the Travel Office, other than expressing an interest in receiving information about the review.[176]

The categorical nature of these answers is hard to square with the recollection of other White House officials, as found by GAO and the House Minority Study.

Watkins informed McLarty on May 17 of his decision to dismiss the Travel Office employees, thus giving McLarty an opportunity to stop Watkins, but the decision to fire was clearly Watkins' and it had already been made.

Downsizing the White House staff was the hook used by Cornelius initially to get Watkins' attention focused on a complete change of the Travel Office that would replace seven employees with two or three, Cornelius and Cerda among them. In return, when Watkins dispatched Cornelius to the Travel Office in April, he asked her to come up with a "reorganization" of the Travel Office that would achieve a 25% cut. And the First Lady reportedly had urged Watkins on May 14 to link the dismissal of the Travel Office staff with the 25% reduction target.[177] Even the President, in the days after the firings, defended the decision to dismiss the entire Travel Office by referring to his commitment to cut White House staff by 25% and save money.[178]

However, given Cornelius's desire from the outset to take over the Travel Office operations, Thomason's and Martens' allegations of misconduct, and a failure to competitively bid charter operations, the downsizing rationale was just a pretext. Watkins said he mentioned his commitment to the 25% reduction when he informed the Travel Office employees that they were being fired, but this was a non-sequitur. In his talk with the employees and later, Watkins based his firings on the Peat Marwick findings.[179] According to Ann Devroy, "The White House has denied it fired the seven in an effort to reach its goal of reducing its staff by 25 percent by Oct. 1."[180]

The review of the Travel Office was neither conducted by nor prompted by the National Performance Review (NPR), contrary to many White House statements. In his May 17 memorandum to McLarty, Watkins put the ongoing Peat Marwick review in the context of the NPR, as stated by the White House. When she announced the firings on May 19, Dee Dee Myers twice noted that the findings of misconduct and mismanagement stemmed from the NPR. Myers, again on May 20 and 24, and Stephanopoulos, on May 21, echoed this assertion. The White House Management Review accepted this explanation, although it also conceded (as had Myers on May 21) that the allegations made by Cornelius and Thomason were "contributing factors."

The White House's reliance on the NPR prompted some hostile questions from the press at the July 2 press briefing. John Podesta, who participated in the White House Management Review, put forth the following explanation:

> At the time the decision was made to have Peat Marwick go in, **a decision was also made to send in the performance review team to look overall at the management of the Travel Office**. That happened on Thursday, the 13th of May. The group that went in — O'Connor and company, had been going through office by office. The travel office employees were told that was a part of the regular review process, and that Peat Marwick was there because the financial management that they had was unique.
>
> That effort was conducted over the weekend within the context of that review. People were informed it was part of the review. Talking points were prepared by Watkins' shop in the context of that. The firings were carried out in the context of that overall sort of review. **I think the better judgement [sic] probably would have been not to have brought the National Performance Review into the picture**. We considered that. Todd [Stern] and I were given a pretty free range, I think as you can see, to make specific criticisms of people and conduct. And I think we ultimately concluded, after writing it one way and writing another way, that **there was enough linkage to this review process that it was fair**.[181]

Podesta thus stated that the NPR team was both **separate** from the Peat Marwick team and **in the same "context."** GAO interviewed two members of the NPR team identified by Watkins, Brian Foucart, and Jennifer O'Connor. Foucart told GAO that he "never saw any [NPR] reports regarding the travel office. He had not [sic] involvement with NPR, but thought that Ms. O'Connor did. He had no idea what Mr. Watkins was referring to when he said that NPR was reviewing the White House travel office."[182] O'Connor told GAO that she was the head of the NPR team for the Executive Office of the President. The Minority Study found that O'Connor:

> told the GAO interviewers that **her work did not include the Travel Office** and that the Travel Office was not singled out for staff reductions as part of the 25% White House staff cut. She also told GAO that her review of the Travel Office consisted of her and Foucart doing a one-hour interview with Billy Dale on May 15, 1993 and submitting a two page summary to Patsy Thomasson and David Watkins later that same day. She described her presence during the Peat Marwick review as that of an observer.[183]

Thus, GAO found that "[a] representative of the Vice President's office informed us that, while the review of the Travel Office was consistent with the objectives of the NPR, **it was not conducted under the auspices of the NPR**."[184]

The President's Explanations

On May 19 and in the days immediately following, the President was frequently asked about the Travel Office matter. Repeatedly, what the President said did not comport with the facts as they are known now. It is not known what the White House staff—many of whom, including the First Lady, were players in the controversy—had told him before the firings or thereafter, leaving open the real possibility that the President was misinformed. But this was not a time for the President to wing it. Moreover, his own statements over the week were internally inconsistent.

On May 19, some time after Dee Dee Myers' press briefing, the President stated:

> All I know about it is that I was told the people who were in charge of administering in the White House found serious problems there and thought there was no alternative. I'll have to refer to them for any other questions. **That is literally all I know about it. I know nothing else about it.**[185]

On May 21, he shifted emphasis, explaining that the Travel Office employees were removed primarily to help achieve his 25% cut in White House staff, and only secondarily because of the findings of misconduct. Defending the firings, he explained that the decision "was made based on striving to end inefficiency and mis-management[,]" pointing to the "review audit" by Peat Marwick (which was not really an audit). "And we're going to save the taxpayers money and save the press money, something I heard mentioned at the last press dinner."[186]

On May 25, the President said, "**All I knew was there was a plan to cut the size of the office, save tax dollars, save the press money**." He explained that he had asked McLarty to look into the matter and make a full report. Until then, "I simply can't tell you that I know something I don't. **I literally don't know anything other than what I've told you. . . .**" He was asked whether he thought contacting the FBI was inappropriate. Clinton said he did not have an opinion yet, and would not respond until McLarty's report. However, he volunteered that:

> [T]here's nothing funny going on here. **We really were just trying to save money for everybody. That was the only thing I was ever asked about personally**. And I don't believe that anybody else had any other motives that I know about. . . .[187]

At this point, after three days of critical press reports, the President clearly should have known about the reports that Cornelius, Thomason and Martens (not to mention Watkins and Eller) were not exactly disinterested parties. Moreover, the President was altering the scope of his own knowledge of the matter.

On May 26, President Clinton again tried to get reporters to focus on the White House's intent to save the press money. But this time he added that he had "repeatedly" and "everywhere" heard the press complain of "being gouged":

> I keep hoping I'll read that somewhere in these accounts. I think that ought to be accounted for. I was—**the press complained to me repeatedly about being gouged by the White House Travel Office. I kept hearing it everywhere.** So we put it out on a competitive bid and saved you 25 percent.[188]

What the President described on May 21 as an account he was given at a press dinner became on May 26 just one of a plethora of press complaints. Yet, the President did not acknowledge that he knew of any complaints from Thomason, Martens, and Cornelius.

On May 27, in response to a question of why the FBI was brought in, he said:

> We found out that there were seven people working in the Travel Office, primarily to book travel for the press, and that the press was complaining that the cost was too high. So there were all these recommendations made to change it.[189] But **nothing was done until an accounting firm came in** and reviewed the operation and found serious management questions in terms of unaccounted-for funds and things like that. So then the person in charge of that made the decision to replace them.
>
> ... [T]he FBI was called in to look at the auditor's report, not to accuse any of these people of doing anything criminal but because there were sufficient questions raised that there had to be a review of it. And the FBI sounds like a huge deal to you, but when you're President, you can't call the local police or the local prosecutor; that's who you call.
>
> ... But the report in the auditor's findings made us believe that someone at least ought to look into this and clear the air. And that's all we were trying to do.
>
> ... Let's not obscure what happened. We were trying to do the people's work with less money.[190]

The President should have observed his previously self-imposed injunction to refrain from substantive comment until the White House Management Review was released, because he obviously got it completely wrong. The FBI was brought in **before** Peat Marwick was contacted. And the FBI must have the criminal culpability of someone in mind to conclude that a factual predicate exists for a criminal investigation. The *Washington Post* began a stinging editorial the next day with "President Clinton played word games with both the point and the truth in discussing the affair of the White House travel office yesterday."[191] The *Post* focused on the May 21 White House meeting to revise an FBI press statement, which was not even alluded to by the President.

Later on May 27, Connie Chung of CBS asked the President whether he would concede that a mistake was made concerning the Travel Office. The President admitted that it was not "handled as well as it should have been. And I said so." He also said, "I take responsibility for any mistakes made in the White House, and mistakes were made in the way that was handled—absolutely." But in this answer the President told Chung, "I challenge you to tell the American people that I think we have a right to run an office with three people instead of the seven at taxpayers' expense[.]"[192]

Did any White House Officials Violate any Ethical Standards?

As White House employees, Cornelius, Eller, Kennedy, Watkins, and others were subject to the conflict-of-interest statute and the standards of conduct for Executive Branch employees.[193] None of these officials, save Cornelius, appears to have had any financial interest in the Travel Office matter; that is, none appears to have been in a position to benefit financially from the replacement of the Travel Office employees. Thus, for these officials there is no issue under the conflict-of-interest statute.

Cornelius, in contrast, possibly stood to gain financially if her White House salary would be increased upon assuming the reins of the Travel Office. The White House Management Review, because it did not analyze the conduct of Cornelius or anyone else specifically under the ethics statutes and regulations, avoided a discussion of whether the "personal stake" Cornelius had was also a "financial stake." If she did stand to benefit financially, all other elements of section 208 appear to be present here. Cornelius (1) participated personally and substantially (2) in a particular matter in which, (3) to her knowledge, (4) she had a financial interest. The dismissal of the Travel Office staff was likely to have a "direct and predictable effect" on Cornelius's White House salary, because she was likely to be installed, per her pre-Inaugural plan, as head of the White House Travel Office.

Yet, there is considerable debate about whether section 208 covers an Executive Branch employee's interest in one's job and salary. In September 1993, in another context, the Justice Department's Office of Legal Counsel concluded that the statute was intended to cover only "outside" financial interests, and thus an employee would not be prohibited from participating in matters affecting her compensation.[194] An interim regulation, published in August 1995 by the Office of Government Ethics (OGE)(with the Justice Department's concurrence), does not go as far, but appears to exempt Cornelius's conduct from section 208.[195]

In that interim rule, OGE assumed section 208's application and then exempted, under authority of section 208(d)(2), certain otherwise disqualifying financial interests arising from Federal employment. The regulation provides:

> An employee may participate in any particular matter, whether of general applicability or involving specific parties, where the disqualifying financial interest arises from Federal Government salary or benefits . . ., except an employee may not:
> (a) Make determinations that individually or specially affect his own Government salary and benefits[.][196]

OGE issued this interim rule for reasons of statutory interpretation and for practical reasons (to exempt routine requests for promotion, requests for travel reimbursement, participation in Senior Executive Service pools, as well as everyday conduct that is designed to earn or receive a promotion, bonus, or award). Its immediate application is for the many Executive Branch employees who currently may be participating in government downsizing efforts whereby their own job may be eliminated or privatized.

In the preamble, OGE made clear that "determinations" mean actions of approval or disapproval; the term does not extend to recommendations or requests.[197] Because Cornelius was not the **decisionmaker** to either conduct an investigation of the Travel Office, hire an outside auditor, fire the Travel Office employees, or restructure the Travel Office, her conduct in **urging** one or more of these things would be exempt from section 208 under this rule.

Thus, Cornelius may no longer have any exposure under section 208. The only other potential basis for the Justice Department's (still pending) investigation of her is whether she stole or destroyed government documents (which Billy Dale alleged, the Justice Department prosecutor denied, and the court never resolved) or whether she somehow stood to benefit financially from the dismissal of the Travel Office employees other than through a promotion or salary increase. However, no financial link existing in 1993 between Cornelius and World Wide Travel, TRM, or Air Advantage has been disclosed or alleged. Destruction of documents, knowing of their relevance to a pending investigation could potentially constitute obstruction of justice under 18 U.S.C. 1503 or 1505.

Apart from section 208's criminal restrictions, all White House employees are subject to the standards of conduct, which contain several general principles that apply to this matter:

• Employees shall not use public office for private gain.

• Employees shall act impartially and not give preferential treatment to any private organization or individual.

• Employees shall endeavor to avoid any actions creating the appearance that they are violating the law or the ethical standards set forth in this part. Whether particular circumstances create an appearance that the law or these standards have been violated shall be determined from the perspective of a reasonable person with knowledge of the relevant facts.[198]

Where an employee believes that a reasonable person with knowledge of the facts might question the employee's impartiality with regard to a matter, the employee should not participate in that matter unless he first consults with an agency ethics official and obtains the okay to participate.[199] Neither the White House Management Review nor the GAO discussed this regulation, nor did either note whether any White House official sought the advice of the Counsel's office about the propriety of their participation or actions.[200]

The White House Management Review concluded that Cornelius had a "personal stake" in the Travel Office matter, for she had been pushing herself as the one to replace the Travel Office Director since before the Inauguration. As such, Cornelius's objectivity could reasonably be questioned, and Watkins should not have assigned her in the first place to go to the Travel Office and snoop around.[201]

Jeff Eller's objectivity could also be reasonably questioned, because of his personal relationship with Cornelius. It was Eller who reportedly came into the White House with the impression that there may have been corruption in the Travel Office. The White House Management Review found that Eller's "actions with regard to the Travel Office were also influenced by his personal concern for Cornelius."[202]

David Watkins knew World Wide Travel and Penny Sample from the Clinton-Gore campaign; Watkins knew World Wide owner Betta Carney since Watkins' advertising agency used World Wide in the 1970s. The White House Management Review called them "long-time acquaintance[s]." Thus, Watkins' impartiality also could be reasonably called into question.

Both World Wide Travel and Penny Sample (Air Advantage) were brought into the White House on a no-bid basis. Given their previous association with White House officials in the Clinton-Gore campaign, it was improper for the White House (Watkins, Cornelius) to bring in these persons and entities without first engaging in competitive bidding. In any event, it was improper for these decisions to be made by officials with a personal friendship with one or more of the bidding entities. The White House Management Review criticized the White House (i.e., Watkins) for "demonstrating an insensitivity to the appearance of favoritism" in hiring World Wide and bringing in Penny Sample under these circumstances.[203]

Thus, at a minimum, actions by each of these three individuals gave the **appearance** of using public office for private gain or providing preferential treatment, in violation of basic ethical principles contained in the standards of conduct. It is also fair to conclude that Watkins and Cornelius **in fact** used their White House position for the private gain of World Wide and Air Advantage and gave them preferential treatment.

Did Harry Thomason or Darnell Martens Violate any Ethical Standard?

The key legal question is whether Thomason or Martens was a "special Government employee" as that term is defined in 18 U.S.C. 202(a). A special Government employee is subject to the conflict-of-interest statute and the standards of conduct governing conflicts and appearances of partiality and impropriety, to the same extent as full-time regular employees.

Elsewhere in this study,[204] I have analyzed the concept of the special Government employee. Special Government employees are individuals who exercise Federal functions on a basis other than regular and permanent, for a period not to exceed 130 days within any 365-day period, whether or not they are paid a salary or other compensation.

The criteria generally used to determine whether a person is a special Government employee are whether the person : (1) has sworn or signed an oath of office; (2) is paid a salary or expenses; (3) enjoys agency office space; (4) serves as a spokesperson for the agency; (5) is subject to the supervision of a Federal agency; and (6) serves in a consulting or advisory capacity to the United States.[205] Not all of the criteria need be satisfied, however. For example, whether a person is paid a salary is not determinative, because the words of section 202(a) expressly provide that special Government employees may be retained without compensation. And the oath of office should be seen as only a formality, or otherwise the statute could be easily avoided simply by not executing the oath.

Harry Thomason satisfied at least two of these criteria, and perhaps a third. He was given office space in the East Wing, and he was serving the President and perhaps other White House officials in a consulting and advisory capacity. Indeed, he was not simply a roving adviser, like Paul Begala for instance, but was given (or assumed) at least one specific responsibility—giving advice on the staging of White House events.[206] He also was expected to give broader advice on improving communications.[207] Although the White House Management Review criticized the White House for failing adequately to supervise Thomason, this criticism actually supports the notion that Thomason was regarded as someone **subject to** supervision within the White House. Thomason was also given a temporary White House pass, not just a daily pass such as the one given to visitors.[208] As GAO notes, Thomason's pass:

convey[ed] the appearance of influence and authority without the accountability that would be provided if such nongovernmental employees were
guided by and informed about the activities they were expected to carry out
or avoid.[209]

Informal consultants in the White House have historically posed difficult ethical as well as management problems. The White House Management Review acknowledged this, recommending that the Chief of Staff, with assistance from the
White House Counsel, issue appropriate rules for consultants' access to the White
House, which would provide for approval by the Chief of Staff and clearance from
the Counsel's Office "with respect to ethical matters."[210]

As a legal matter, both the Justice Department[211] and OGE have grappled with
this question, and have employed a functional test to determine whether an informal
consultant or adviser is a "special Government employee."[212] These opinions focus
on whether the consultant is engaged in setting up or chairing meetings in which he
provides advice or coordinates the White House's activities in a particular area, under the direction or supervision of the President.

On what little is revealed by the White House Management Review, the GAO
Report, and press reports, Thomason appears to have functioned as a White House
employee in every respect other than title and pay. The White House Management
Review did not discuss whether Thomason (or Martens) was a special Government
employee.[213] GAO concluded that "the available facts did not support a conclusion
that they were special government employees[.]"[214] But GAO's conclusion is based
primarily on the absence of a formal appointment, and secondarily on the lack of
factual support for the notion that Thomason was considered by other White House
officials as an employee. GAO used the caselaw developed in determining who is an
employee for purposes of Title 5, and concluded that to be a special Government
employee for purposes of Title 18, one must have received an appointment to a position or have "entered into a mutual understanding that an employment relationship
exists."[215] But this is too narrow a definition of the term "special Government employee" under the ethics laws.

GAO noted that it was not permitted to interview Thomason, at the Justice Department's request, but GAO did not realize what was implicit in this request. Why
would the Justice Department have Thomason under investigation unless Justice
believed he arguably was subject to section 208?

Assuming Thomason was a special Government employee, did he violate section 208? Thomason clearly participated in this "particular matter," "personally and
substantially." Not only did he forward reports of misconduct to the President, the
First Lady, David Watkins, Catherine Cornelius, and perhaps others in the White
House, Thomason sat in on deliberations of what official actions should be taken to
investigate these allegations and with respect to the Travel Office employees. The
Travel Office matter was a "particular matter" in that it was a personnel, contractual,
and investigatory matter involving a small number of identifiable persons and entities, including TRM, Air Advantage, and World Wide Travel. The key interpretative
questions are whether Thomason had a financial interest in a change in Travel Office
personnel and policy and whether these changes would have a "direct and predictable effect" on that interest.

The White House Management Review stated that Thomason's assertions that his actions were not motivated by financial gain "are not contradicted in the record." But the White House and Thomason were criticized nonetheless:

> Thomason should have avoided continued involvement in a matter in which his business partner and his friends in the charter business stood to benefit and in which there was an appearance of financial conflict of interest. But lax procedures allowed his continued participation in the process.
> ... No one objected when he began looking into the affairs of the Travel Office, which clearly extended beyond what he was originally asked to do.[216]

Thomason, as a partner in TRM, had a financial interest in any matter in which TRM had a financial interest. Thomason and Martens were business partners in TRM, not some company uninterested in White House press corps travel. The facts support the conclusion that Martens was interested in replacing Dale as the broker for press charters or as an additional broker, in part to steer charter business to TRM's clients such as Air Advantage. It strains credulity to believe that TRM did not stand to gain financially, either directly or through maintenance of good will, if Thomason and Martens could replace the White House Travel Office and open up the press charter business to entities such as Air Advantage.[217]

The other element in the conflict-of-interest analysis is whether the outcome of the Travel Office matter was likely to have a "direct and predictable effect" on Thomason's interest.[218] "Direct" means that there is "a close causal link between any decision or action to be taken in the matter and any expected effect of the matter on [Thomason's] financial interest[.]" "Predictable" means that there is a "real, as opposed to a speculative possibility that the matter will affect the financial interest. It is not necessary, however, that the magnitude of the gain or loss be known, and the dollar amount of the gain or loss is immaterial."[219]

Thomason's wife defended her husband against allegations of a conflict of interest by explaining that it would "ludicrous" for someone as wealthy as Harry Thomason to say:

> Ooh, I'm going to like take my six-figure salary a week and fly off to Washington and see if I can't get those seven little guys out of that travel office in the White House. It's sort of the equivalent of taking over a lemonade stand.[220]

But, as noted in the standards of conduct, the question is not whether the gain would only amount to a lemonade stand, it is whether there was a real possibility the Travel Office outcome would directly benefit TRM financially. The answer to this question is probably yes.

Even if the elements of section 208 are satisfied, there still remains a reservoir of prosecutorial discretion whether to prosecute Thomason. Because it is unlikely that the White House Counsel's office informed Thomason that he was subject to the ethics laws, Justice would probably not charge Thomason with a violation of section 208.

Assuming Thomason is found not to have violated section 208, as a special Government employee he was still subject to the standards of conduct. Under section 502(a), Thomason had a covered relationship with his business partner Martens and with their business TRM, and thus should not have participated in any White House deliberation in which Martens or TRM was interested without first seeking the advice and approval from the Counsel's office, which Thomason did not do. Thomason might be forgiven for failing to use the section 502 process, if no one in the White House informed him of this provision and that he was subject to it, but common sense should have prompted Thomason to check with the Counsel's office in any event to avoid the appearance of using his quasi-public office for private gain or giving preferential treatment. If Thomason was a special Government employee, he violated these ethical principles, too.

Darnell Martens did not seek a White House pass until May 12. He did so then probably in anticipation of assuming some role, formal or informal, in the new Travel Office. He also participated in at least one White House meeting before the May 19 firings. On May 19 Martens, for at least a moment, assumed the mantle of a White House official, calling Penny Sample to invite her, on behalf of the White House, to come to work as a volunteer and work on arranging press charters.[221] Martens, however, unlike Thomason, did not have any White House responsibilities. In addition to the Travel Office matter, Martens was also a frequent correspondent with and visitor to the White House from January through May 1993 in connection with his proposal for a consulting contract with GSA to study the fleet of civilian government aircraft. But Martens clearly pushed this proposal as an outsider. (Indeed, he considered Thomason as the insider.) It is therefore unlikely that Martens would be considered a special Government employee subject to section 208 or the standards of conduct.

The White House and the FBI

Perhaps the greatest level of media criticism of the White House related to the appearance, if not the reality, that the White House pressured the FBI in one or more respects; some even criticized the decision to contact the FBI in the first place.[222] Before analyzing these charges, it is helpful to recount briefly the several contacts the White House had with the FBI.[223]

(1) **The initial contact.** On May 12, William Kennedy called Jim Bourke, an FBI official with whom Kennedy worked regularly, and asked for assistance, but gave Bourke little to go on. He told Bourke "that an unspecified office in the White House was not 'running properly' and asked him to find out 'who to talk to' at the FBI about it."[224]

(2) **The request for expedition.** On May 13, when Bourke called Kennedy to find out more information to help the FBI to determine the appropriate Bureau component to consider the matter, Kennedy (having been dunned by Vince Foster) pressed Bourke for an FBI contact within fifteen minutes, or else Kennedy might turn to the IRS for help.

(3) **The FBI's request for more information.** On May 13, an FBI agent whom Bourke enlisted, Howard Apple, spoke with Kennedy in an effort to find out more information. Kennedy said only that it was a "very sensitive" matter involving theft or fraud, although not involving Federal funds. Kennedy resisted Apple's suggestion of using the local FBI office, telling Apple that "the matter was 'directed at the highest levels' in the White House."[225]

(4) **The initial FBI visit.** On May 13, Apple and another FBI agent (Foran) briefly met with Kennedy. Kennedy was still debating whether the FBI or IRS was the proper investigative agency. To this point, Kennedy revealed that the allegations concerned the Travel Office ad came from an "unnamed Travel Office employee."

Kennedy noted the high level White House interest in the matter and urged prompt consideration. Apple told Kennedy "he could not rule out criminal wrongdoing but the information provided warranted further follow-up before that determination could be made."[226] The agents concluded that another FBI unit was more appropriate.

(5) **The second FBI visit.** On May 13, two FBI agents (Wade and Carl) from a different FBI component met with Kennedy, with Foster joining the meeting. The agents initially informed Kennedy that the allegations were "insufficient" to warrant a criminal investigation, but changed their mind after Kennedy had them meet with Cornelius.[227]

(6) **The request to postpone the investigation.** After the FBI agents' meeting with Cornelius, Foster informed the FBI that Peat Marwick had been retained to conduct a review of the Travel Office and prevailed upon the FBI to await the results of that review before commencing an investigation. Foster also told the FBI agents he did not want the FBI present during Peat Marwick's review.228

(7) **Kennedy's status reports on the Peat Marwick review & the third FBI visit.** On May 14, Kennedy twice called the FBI to pass on developments in the Peat Marwick review. On Saturday, May 15, two FBI agents came over to the White House at Kennedy's request to receive a updated status report on the Peat Marwick review.

(8) **The White House's disclosure of the FBI investigation.** On May 19, Dee Dee Myers separately disclosed to two reporters that an FBI investigation had been initiated or was imminent and likely. There does not appear to have been any coordination or contact with the FBI before this disclosure.

(9) **The fourth FBI visit.** On May 21, the White House summoned the FBI's top public relations official, John Collingwood, to a meeting to discuss how to handle press inquiries. Collingwood was asked twice to revise an FBI press response, and did so. Collingwood faxed a revised press response to the White House. The White House then released the FBI response, treating it as a press release, without advance notice or clearance with the FBI.

The initial contact made by Kennedy on May 12 was not improper.[29] Kennedy, with information of possible corruption or mismanagement in the White House, simply asked the FBI for assistance. Although there is no Inspector General (IG) for the White House or Executive Office of the President, Kennedy could have asked for the services of an IG from an Executive Department to look into the matter, but he need not have done so.

The nature of the assistance Kennedy requested was not revealed in either the White House Management Review or the GAO Report. The Minority Study, however, relying on GAOs interview of Jim Bourke, sheds some light on this conversation. The Minority Study conclude that Kennedy "request[ed] assistance to conduct an internal audit to find support for the allegations levied against the Travel Office staff."[230] Bourke told GAO:

> Kennedy called me as a friend—someone who he could talk to. I felt Kennedy was seeking help to conduct an internal investigation. Not in my wildest thoughts did I think about a criminal investigation when Kennedy called.[21]

Of course, Kennedy kept Bourke in the dark about the allegations, even about the particular office in the White House where the alleged problems were.[232]

Merely asking for assistance did not contravene any existing guidance. The Clinton White House, like the White House under Presidents Carter, Reagan, and Bush, provided strictly that all communications about **pending** Justice Department investigations should be made only by the White House Counsel's office and only to the person or the office of the Attorney General or Deputy Attorney General. There was no current guidance, however, as to contacts made in order to request an investigation in the first place. The reason for any policy restricting White House contact with the FBI is to avoid both the fact and appearance of politicization of law enforcement, which had occurred on a grand scale in the Nixon White House.

The Bush White House, in which I served, construed this policy generally to extend also to referrals of information suggesting a crime and requests for an investigation. It is easy to see that politics could play a role in the decision to initiate an investigation, with similarly undesirable consequences. Thus, referrals about possible violations of criminal law by current and former White House employees, as well as by non-government persons, were sent to the Deputy Attorney General's office, which would then determine how to proceed.

Kennedy's initial call to the FBI appears to have been of a different variety. Kennedy was calling his FBI contact to ask for help, not to make a referral or even apparently, at this point, to request a criminal investigation. Although it would have been preferable for Kennedy to contact the Deputy Attorney General's office instead, Kennedy did not exert any pressure on Bourke in this conversation. If Kennedy should be faulted for this conversation, it should be because he was not forthcoming with Bourke.

When Kennedy and Bourke spoke the next day, however, Kennedy's **request for expedition** began to cross over the line between the proper and the improper, from a request for assistance to a demand for a timely response. Kennedy's request for a fifteen-minute turnaround is not an unusual request coming from a mid-level White House staffer to a Federal agency official, especially given a high-level White House push. These sorts of calls were commonplace in the Bush Administration—I made my share of them—and they undoubtedly are commonplace in the Clinton Administration. There is a significant difference, however, between asking a Federal agency for information, or even demanding an action or decision from the agency consistent with the President's policy program, and demanding expedition from a law enforcement agency with respect to a pending or putative investigation.

It was also unusual, and improper, to issue a thinly veiled threat that the FBI's failure to respond within fifteen minutes might prompt the White House to go to the IRS for help. Even if Kennedy did not intend this reference to the IRS as a threat, it should have been apparent to him that it was likely be perceived as one by the FBI. (On the other hand, Kennedy, in the White House for only a few months at this point, may not have known of the sense of competition between the FBI and IRS workforce over the conduct of investigations in which both have jurisdiction.)

The initial FBI visit on May 13 came about because Kennedy told Apple that the did not want to discuss the matter over the phone. Kennedy told Apple that he wanted someone from Bureau headquarters "to come over for a meeting as soon as possible."[233] In this meeting, which the FBI agents described as brief, Kennedy referred to the possible request to the IRS. Kennedy also made unmistakably clear the strong, high-level White House interest in the matter. At this point, it appears that Kennedy began pushing the FBI to conduct an investigation.

Kennedy continued this push during **the second FBI visit** later that day. Wade explained to Kennedy that the FBI could not conduct an audit unless it was part of a criminal investigation, for which an evidentiary predicate must exist.[234] But Kennedy (and Foster) failed to convince Wade and Carl that such a predicate existed on what the agents had been told or shown, so Catherine Cornelius was brought in, with documents, to persuade the FBI of the gravity and credibility of the allegations. The Bureau's change of mind during one sitting on May 13 suggests the agents felt pressured to decide that an investigation was warranted and to make such a conclusion while at the White House, without further discussions within the FBI or with the Justice Department.[235] At this point, the White House was clearly leaning on the FBI.

The White House Management Review found "inappropriate" Kennedy's comments "conveying urgency and high levels of White House interest" because they "risk[ed] creating the perception that the FBI is being improperly pressured."[236] It also concluded that the reference to the IRS was improper, because it "could have been interpreted as an ultimatum, even if that was not intended."[237] Kennedy denied linking the IRS with the failure of the FBI to respond appropriately, although two FBI agents told the GAO that Kennedy made it clear that "[u]nless the FBI cooperated quickly, he would go to the IRS."[238]

The request to postpone the investigation. On May 13, Foster informed the FBI that Peat Marwick had been asked to conduct a review of the Travel Office to begin the next day.[239] Thus, the FBI was not informed of Peat Marwick's review until after the FBI agents had concluded that a criminal investigation was warranted. In any event, at this stage, the White House should have deferred completely to the FBI's wishes with respect to the conduct and timing of its investigation. Assuming the *bona fides* of the FBI's conclusion that a criminal investigation was warranted, the criminal investigation clearly should have taken precedence over any audit or outside investigation of the same mater, and the White House officials from that point on should have played no role in the conduct of the matter. According to the FBI Agents, Foster and Kennedy apparently began pulling back, expressing reluctance to accuse any Travel Office employee of criminal misconduct, and desirous of an audit to verify Cornelius's allegations.[240] Foster's (successful) effort to dissuade the FBI from commencing an investigation until after the conclusion of the Peat Marwick review was improper. Even more astonishing is that the White House rebuffed an FBI request to participate or at least directly observe the Peat Marwick review! The FBI was apparently (and rightly) concerned about the integrity of the documentary evidence during the Peat Marwick review.[241] That the FBI acceded to these White House requests suggests that **either the FBI succumbed to what it perceived as White House pressure, or the FBI did not really believe the predicate for a criminal investigation had been satisfied** (notwithstanding what the FBI told the White House on the afternoon of May 13), and the Peat Marwick review could possibly provide he missing predicate.[242]

Although the White House deserves strong criticism for the way in which it directed the conduct of a criminal investigation of White House employees, the FBI should also be criticized for allowing itself to be subordinated to the White House on such matters.[243]

The GAO Report noted that "none of the FBI officials reported that they felt pressure or took inappropriate action" because of Kennedy's comments,[244] but this denial is to be expected from FBI agents with no incentive to admit they gave in to pressure or took "inappropriate action." Unfortunately, it does not comport with what the FBI actually did under the circumstances, which was to comply with each and every request of the Whit House, bend over backward to find a predicate for a criminal investigation, and to do so in the space of an afternoon. This is not to say that the FBI could not have concluded eventually that a criminal investigation was warranted. But any criminal investigator would have to admit that a decision to initiate a criminal investigation should not be made in one afternoon, after talking with only one person, without an independent look at the evidence, especially when others with no personal knowledge of the facts are pressing for an immediate determination, all the while noting that the matter is being overseen (if not directed) by high-level White House officials. **That** is pressure.

The analysis above examined the several contacts between the White House and FBI without reference to the context of the personal interest of those who made allegations of Travel Office misconduct: Cornelius, Thomason, and Martens.245 The analysis assumed that Kennedy and Foster did not know of the personal, if not financial, stake the three had in the matter.[246] Indeed, Kennedy did not inform the FBI of Cornelius's background and immediate job interests before he introduced her to the FBI as the person who knew most about the alleged misconduct. However, given their common background in Arkansas and the Presidential campaign, and the involvement of Watkins and the First Lady, it is hard to believe that neither Kennedy nor Foster knew that in pushing for a criminal investigation they were doing the bidding of an interested Cornelius, Thomason, and Martens. If, in fact, Kennedy or Foster knew of these personal interests, it was incumbent on them to apprise the FBI accordingly.[247] Their failure to do so would warrant additional criticism.

Dee Dee Myers' **disclosure of the FBI investigation** to reporters on May 19 was improper because the White House had not obtained approval from the FBI to disclose the investigation. The Justice Department, not the White House, should determine if and when the public should be informed about the initiation of a criminal investigaton.[248] Myers may have hedged a bit with one or both reporters, but the clear import of her discussion was that the Travel Office employees were, or would soon be, under criminal investigation. The White House Management Review criticized Myers as well as other White House officials (Eller, Watkins) for allowing this to happen.[249]

Myers may have avoided a reprimand because the responsibility to ensure that the FBI investigation would not be disclosed rested primarily with the drafters of the talking points (i.e., Watkins). It is not clear that Myers appreciated the problem with disclosing the existence of a criminal investigation, especially given the substantial participation of the White House Counsel's office in the White House deliberations. Myers should have assured herself, however, that the Counsel's office had signed off on the talking points.[250] It is not known what representations Watkins made when he delivered the talking points to Myers early May 19, but Watkins gave Myers talking points before obtaining clearance from the Counsel's office.

The FBI attempted to put some cold water on Myers' disclosure by releasing a statement later on May 19 that simply said the result of the Peat Marwick review would be referred to the FBI. Myers, for her part, dug a deeper hole during the May 19 afternoon press briefing by twice denying the existence of a pending criminal investigation after her acknowledgment of one to two reporters earlier in the day. Thus, in addition to the inappropriateness of disclosing the existence of an FBI investigation, Myers was not candid with the press.[251]

White House pressure on the FBI reached a second apex on May 21, during **the FBI's third visit**. When John Collingwood of the FBI came to the White House to hammer out press guidance about the criminal investigation, he was faced with a senior group of White House officials. Just as it was improper for the White House to involve itself in the conduct or timing of an FBI investigation, it was improper for the White House to involve itself in the FBI's characterization of its investigation. It is one thing for the White House, for example, to work out with the FBI its public statements on matters involving the President's program or policies, or on matters in which the President has an obvious official interest. The World Trade Center and Oklahoma City bombings are two cases in point. It is quite another thing, however, for the White House essentially to dictate what the FBI will say about its investigation of a part of the White House. To make matters worse, the White House, not the FBI, released a copy of the FBI press response, and did so without obtaining approval from the FBI.

The White House Management Review concluded that the circumstances of Collingwood's meeting at the White House "conveyed the appearance that the White House was leaning on the Bureau to tailor its statement to the White House's advantage."[252] I fact, this was not just an appearance; this was exactly what the White House was doing. The Whit House Management Review notes the absence of any evidence "that the White House tried to push the FBI to say anything inaccurate or inappropriate."[253] Even assuming this is so, it was still improper for the White House to push for inclusion, omission, or amendment, given the fact that the press guidance was **FBI** press guidance about an **FBI investigation** relating to possible misconduct **within the White House**. The obvious inference one can draw from these revisions is that their purpose was to support the White House's decision summarily to dismiss the entire Travel Office staff.[254]

In sum, what began (perhaps) on May 12 as a modest and innocent request for assistance in determining how best to look into allegations of misconduct, quickly degenerated into several egregious instances of the White House's involvement in the timing, conduct, and explanation of an FBI investigation. In the summary of its findings, the White House Management Review faulted Whit House officials for "not being sufficiently vigilant in guarding against even the appearance of pressure on the FBI."[255] The body of the report is a bit stronger, labeling certain conduct "improper" or "inappropriate." But the Review's criticism is always tethered to **appearances**. The GAO Report also does not go beyond criticism of the White House for creating bad appearances. To the contrary, the misconduct of White House officials in dealing with the FBI was far more than just a series of improper appearances to the public. Vis-a-vis the FBI, the White House interfered with several aspects of a criminal investigation.[256] That conduct was improper, whether or not the public was later made aware of it.

Did the FBI or Justice Department Bungle the Evidence?

The Minority Study found that the Justice Department did not exercise any control over the Travel Office records until June 10, 1993,[257] at which time the records were placed in the White House Counsel's Office, "under lock and key."[258] The Minority Study faulted the FBI because there is a substantial question whether the integrity of the documents was sufficiently safeguarded from May 13, when Cornelius first presented documentary evidence to FBI agents, until June 10. Further, the Minority Study questioned whether all of the documents Cornelius took from the Travel Office **before May 13** (and did not return because the file was located) were accounted for and now in the FBI's possession or custody. The GAO Report did not discuss the records issue at all, even though the Minority Study's findings are based primarily on notes of GAO interviews.[259]

From the Minority Study's account of the GAO interviews, it is not clear whether Cornelius or other White House officials with a potential stake in the investigation had access to at least some of the White House ravel Records between May 19 and June 10. This uncertainty stems from (1) the unknown fate of the documents Cornelius removed from the Travel Office before May 13; (2) the access to the documents during the Peat Marwick review (May 14-21) by four subordinates of David Watkins; (3) the fact that not all Travel Office records were placed in a locked file at any time; and (4) the uncertainty of who had access to the locked files.

In 1995, it was reported that Patsy Thomasson was seen in the Travel Office early on the morning of May 17 or 18, and the suggestion was made that Thomasson, in addition to Cornelius, may have removed Travel Office documents before the May 19 firings.[260]

Cornelius said she gave the Travel Office documents which she had taken home with her to Kennedy on May 12. The known chain of custody stops there.[261]

Patsy Thomasson told GAO in writing that, "[b]etween May 19, 1993 and the time the records wee taken into custody of the FBI and the Office of Records Management, the documents were secured in a separate room with access limited to the Secret Service, the Director of White House Personnel Security [D. Craig Livingstone] and the Acting Director of the White House Administrative Office [Brian Foucart].[262] However, Foucart told GAO that only the "bulk" of the Travel Office records were kept in the locked file room. Other Travel Office records were stored elsewhere and, therefore, presumably open to Cornelius, Sample, World Wide, and American Express during this time. Foucart said he removed "the checkbook, cash, journal and black notebooks on May 19 and gave them to the FBI on June 10."[263] Thus, there were some Travel Office records that were completely unprotected and available to Cornelius, among others, for a significant period of time.

The locks to the Travel Office were changed on or about May 19, 1993.[264] Apparently there was a lock on the office door and a lock on the door to the file room within the office. According to Foucart, Cornelius had a key to the office, but not the file room; World Wide and Penny Sample did not have either key. Livingstone and perhaps Foucart had the only keys to the file room, and, from May 19, he did not provide access to Cornelius, Sample, or World Wide.

The Minority Study's criticism appears largely justified, especially given the findings in the White House Management Review of several White House officials' personal stake in the matter, and the FBI's failure to take additional steps to safeguard the documents from access by those White House officials. One consequence of the Justice Department's failure to ensure the integrity of the documents was to play into the theory of Billy Dale's defense that exculpatory evidence was destroyed. At Dale's trial, an FBI agent testified that he and a White House Records Office official were both concerned that the Travel Office was not adequately secured after the firings on May 19. The defense was able to get before the jury the fact that Cornelius, Thomasson and others had free access to the Travel Office. Because of its poor handling of the Travel Office documents after May 13, 1993, the Government was unable to refute that argument.

Conclusions

The Conduct of White House Officials

White House officials engaged in many missteps and improper activities during the Travel Office matter. By way of summary, several officials (Cornelius, Watkins, Eler) with a personal and some with a financial stake in the matter inappropriately participated in a decision to fire the Travel Office employees. They also participated in contemporaneous efforts to manipulate the process to justify the firings by referring to reports and findings of misconduct as the predicate for a Federal criminal investigation. Another person with a financial stake in the Travel Office, Harry Thomason, should have been regarded as a special Government employee subject to the same ethics standards for regular White House officials. Their participation did not just present a problem of appearances; it also constituted violations of the standards of conduct in that they used their public office for private gain and gave preferential treatment to their Arkansan friends and former business or campaign associates.

White House officials clearly influenced the FBI's decision to initiate a criminal investigation. It strains credulity to believe that the FBI would have decided that a criminal investigation was warranted in the absence of the persistence of White House officials. Although it was not improper for the White House to seek the assistance of the FBI in the first place (assuming the improper motives of Thomason, Martens, and Cornelius were not known to Foster and Kennedy), the White House clearly overstepped in how it presented the need to come to a quick decision. Worse was the White House's rewriting and then release of an FBI press statement. Even worse was Foster's insistence that the FBI investigation, for which the White House initially pushed so vigorously, should take a back seat to the Peat Marwick review and that the FBI was not welcome to observe the Peat Marwick review.

The White House's public statements on May 19, 1993 and thereafter were lacking in candor. The White House appeared to have reached agreement internally on how to explain the firings, but that explanation—or more accurately, those explanations—did not comport with the facts. Even the President misspoke on more than one occasion, although it is not clear whether he did so intentionally, negligently, or simply that he was given bad information from a compromised staff.[265]

The White House Management Review

As internal reviews go, the White House Management Review should be credited with a somewhat candid assessment of the misconduct of Watkins, Cornelius, Eler, and Kennedy. In some respects, the White House Management Review was harder on White House officials vis-a-vis their discussions with FBI officials than was the 1994 OPR review. However, the White House Management Review's assessment was faulty in several significant respects. First, the Management Review did not analyze the conduct of White House officials under the specific ethics standards; indeed, it is not apparent that the White House Counsel's office (other than Foster and Kennedy) participated in the review. Second, the Management Review failed to appreciate that several persons (namely, Cornelius, Thomason, and Martens) not only had a personal stake but a financial stake in the matter. Third, the Management Review failed to acknowledge that White House officials engaged in improper conduct, not simply that they were insufficiently attentive to appearances of impropriety. Most notable in this respect was the Management Review's failure to appreciate the egregiousness of Foster's request to the FBI to desist from any action while the Peat Marwick review was conducted.

Another significant failing of the Management Review was in downplaying, if not ignoring, the substantial participation of the First Lady in monitoring developments and essentially providing the go-ahead (if not the direct order) to conduct a pretextual internal investigation and subsequently fire the Travel Office staff. The Management Review also ignored the responsibility of Vince Foster for much of the conduct of William Kennedy, for which Kennedy, not Foster, was criticized.[266] Kennedy, although deserving of a reprimand based on his conversations and meeting with the FBI post-May 12, was clearly following the direction of Vince Foster. Kennedy's initial call to the FBI on May 12th and his expressions of urgency came from Foster. Indeed, it was Foster, not Kennedy, who prevailed on the FBI to postpone its investigation. Both Foster and Bernard Nussbaum believed that Kennedy was made to shoulder a disproportionate share of the blame in the Travel Office matter.[267]

The White House did reprimand four White House officials, but the reprimands consisted only in the (incorrect) public statement at the July 2 press conference that they each had been reprimanded. The opprobrium that resulted from being criticized by name in the White House Management Review and at a White House press conference should not be underestimated. Yet, Foster and Stephanopoulos at a minimum (and perhaps Myers) should also have been given reprimands for their role in the Travel Office matter.

The FBI's Role

The FBI deserves a measure of criticism for allowing it to be put in a position where in a single afternoon it concluded (1) there is not sufficient evidence to warrant a criminal investigation; (2) there is sufficient evidence to warrant a criminal investigation; (3) the criminal investigation can wait for the conduct of a Peat Marwick review. Even if the FBI agents truly believe they were not pressured into changing their assessment of the facts, the FBI did act precipitously in finding that a sufficient criminal predicate existed based solely on the allegations of Cornelius and the documents she presented to them.

Once the FBI agreed with the White House that there was sufficient evidence to conduct a criminal investigation—assuming that conclusion was made in good faith and was correct—the FBI should not have allowed the Peat Marwick review to take place. If, as it appears, the FBI did not resist Foster's request that it postpone its investigation because the FBI was not really convinced that predication for a criminal investigation existed, it was imperative for the Bureau to inform the White House immediately that its determination reached on the afternoon of May 13 was incorrect, or at least, premature. Foster apparently would have been receptive to the Bureau's (second) change of heart, because he was the one pushing for the Peat Marwick review to be conducted first. Instead, the FBI proceeded later on May 13 and May 14 to obtain within the FBI and the Justice Department's Criminal Division the necessary approvals to conduct a criminal investigation. As a direct consequence, the White House (namely, Watkins) relied on the FBI's determination (soft, premature, conditional, or otherwise) to act with greater assurance that its summary dismissal of the Travel Office employees would be lauded publicly, or at a minimum, hold up to public scrutiny.

Moreover, the FBI did little to safeguard the integrity of the Travel Office documents during the Peat Marwick review (from which it was shut out) and thereafter.

The GAO Report

The GAO Report provided more information than did the White House Management review to support the criticism of White House officials. But its analysis of the conduct of White House officials suffered from the similar failure of seeing ethical problems only in terms of appearances or as an already-fixed problem of management and supervision. In one respect—the analysis of the applicability of the conflict-of-interest statute to Harry Thomason—GAO's analysis was inadequate. And as the Minority Study revealed, GAO hose to omit many clarifying (as well as damning) details of what occurred, again with he effect of shielding the First Lady and others from criticism.

The Billy Dale Prosecution

Justice Department guidelines provide that, "both as a matter of fundamental fairness and in the interest of the efficient administration of justice, no prosecution should be initiated against any person unless the government believes that the person probably will be found guilty by an unbiased trier of fact."[268] There is a serious question whether the indictment and prosecution of Dale was consistent with this policy. The Justice Department should have been wary of the "evidence" against Dale, because it was initially provided by a person with an interest in taking over the Travel Office functions. Moreover, the failure to secure Travel Office documents from May 13, 1993—not only May 19—raised a very real risk of the destruction of probative, and exculpatory evidence, given the interest of several White House officials with unrestrained access to the Travel Office post-May 13 in a conviction to justify the White House's firing of the Travel Office employees. Nor was there any witness to Dale's misconduct from the media or from his co-workers. It seemed that all Justice had to go on was the uncontested fact that Dale commingled Travel Office (non-government) funds with his own funds, and unaccounted for cash.

The evidence the prosecution wound up introducing was nothing more than a highly intrusive examination of the Dale family finances in support of a theory that Dale needed to embezzle and convert to pay the bills and to maintain his family's style of living. In the end, however, the prosecution did not prove that Dale converted any of the Travel Office funds for his personal use.

Both the conduct of the trial and the quickness of the jury's verdict of acquittal demonstrated that the Justice Department had a weak case at beginning and end. Why, then, did it seek an indictment and prosecute? Was there any encouragement from the White House to political appointees at Justice, who thereupon impressed the importance of the case upon career prosecutors? Did the FBI have an interest in a conviction to justify its about-face and precipitous conclusion on May 13 that the evidence was sufficient to commence an investigation? Did the Office of Public Integrity have a similar interest in justifying its May 14 concurrence with the FBI's determination? Or did career prosecutors conduct the investigation and prosecution without interference or involvement of any political appointee? Of course, an acquittal, even a quick one, does not necessarily mean that bringing the case was improper. But in the case of Billy Dale, there is much, much more, to suggest that no case should ever have been brought. These questions deserve examination by Congress.

Chapter Six

The
President's Use
of
Informal Advisers

President Clinton's reliance on the advice and counsel of advisers and consultants who are not Federal employees is perhaps without precedent. The manner in which these advisers have functioned in the White House, as much as the scope and extent of their involvement in official government decisionmaking, renders them largely indistinguishable from senior White House staff. Because they are not considered to be Federal employees, they are not subject to the conflict-of-interest laws or required by law to submit a financial disclosure report. And yet the presence of these advisers raises a host of ethical concerns because the advisers have jobs, interests, clients and affiliations outside of government.

The White House was very slow to acknowledge the potential for ethical problems and address the issue. It took a major scandal (the Travel Office firings) and a minor one (the inordinate delays in processing White House passes and conducting security checks), the dogged persistence of Representative Frank Wolf, and several published, detailed reports of the advisers' prominence inside the White House, before the Clinton Administration took steps to address the problem. To their credit, at the outset, the four main political consultants took some measures on their own initiative. The steps the White House eventually took were partly constructive and helpful, partly symbolic, and in the end, highly inadequate.

The meaning of the term "special Government employee" (SGE) remains elusive, yet whether an adviser is subject to certain criminal laws turns on this meaning. Perhaps a comprehensive examination of a President's use of informal advisers is timely. Some legislative or administrative clarification of the term—to make it clear that the test should be a functional one—could improve things, but would not eliminate the potential for abuse. At a minimum, Presidents must show greater sensitivity to the potential for conflicts of interest and preferential treatment. Informal advisers who are regularly called upon for general advice (as opposed to presenting the views of their client or business) should be required to disclose their financial interests and outside affiliations—without regard to whether they hold a White House pass—and a recusal or declaration policy should be instituted systematically.

Future Presidents should exercise more discipline in their reliance on, and use of, informal advisers than President Clinton has shown to date.

President Clinton, like every other President, has relied on advice regularly provided by persons who are not themselves government employees. President Clinton has relied upon the advice of Democratic National Committee (DNC) officials, former Clinton campaign officials, former Arkansas Government officials, former Executive Branch officials, and friends.

There is nothing unusual or wrong about the President or White House seeking advice from persons outside of government. Indeed, Presidents should be encouraged to develop and maintain contacts with persons outside of the Government, who can be called upon from time to time to provide impartial or disinterested advice, special expertise, or simply a perspective different from those found within government. Moreover, as *de facto* head of his political party, the President must be able to meet freely and regularly with party officials.

As private citizens, these advisers and consultants have jobs, professions, clients, financial interests, and other affiliations that could give rise to a potential conflict, or appearance of a conflict if they were Federal employees. However, so long as these informal advisers do not exercise any government function, or direct or supervise any Federal employee, they remain outside of the Government and are not subject to the laws and standards of ethical conduct.

Where an informal adviser performs certain functions that ordinarily would be performed by a Federal employee, the adviser risks being considered a "special Government employee."[1] An SGE is not necessarily required to sever any outside interest or affiliation, but is subject to conflict-of-interest restrictions, which prohibit the adviser from providing advice on, or otherwise participating in, any particular matter in which he has a financial interest.[2] In order to remedy an identified conflict or potential conflict, SGEs must either rid themselves of the conflicting interest or association, or recuse themselves from the matter which gives rise to the conflict.

Also, most SGEs are required by law to file a confidential financial disclosure report within thirty days of assuming their duties.[3] These reports are intended to assist agency ethics officials in identifying potential conflicts of interest.

Some of President Clinton's informal advisers have undertaken duties and responsibilities that should render them special Government employees.

Even if advisers avoid engaging in conduct that would make them an SGE, their financial interests and outside affiliations nonetheless carry the potential for ethics concerns. The President seeks outside advice from persons whose opinions and judgment he respects and trusts; he may well be unaware of an adviser's outside interests and affiliations, unless apprised by the adviser. The advisers, however, cannot easily be separated from their financial interests and outside affiliations. Because the informal adviser is given access to the White House not ordinarily provided to persons outside of government, the suspicion can arise that the adviser may be acting on behalf of a client or in furtherance of a financial or fiduciary interest, in addition to, or instead of, providing advice based on the adviser's general experience, expertise, or political perspective. This suspicion leads to the conclusion that the person or entity on whose behalf the adviser is acting is being given special access and preferential treatment. Special access and preferential treatment run afoul of a cardinal principle of government ethics: that "[e]mployees shall act impartially and not give preferential treatment to any private organization or individual."[4]

Without a financial disclosure report or other form of disclosure, the White House may be ignorant of the adviser's financial interests and affiliations that could color (or be seen to color) any advice offered, unless the adviser brings the interest to the White House's attention or until the media reveals the interest in a less-than-flattering light. Therefore, the White House is, for the most part, unable to identify potential conflicts. The public, of course, is even more in the dark.

A related ethics concern focuses on the **advisers**, as opposed to the Government officials. Advisers who are granted special entree into the White House by virtue of their affiliation with the President (through former government service, political campaigns, or business enterprises), and who use that special access to promote the interests of a client, are subject to criticism for trading on their former ties. This situation is virtually indistinguishable from the revolving door phenomenon to which the post-employment restrictions in statute[5] and executive order are addressed. Candidate Clinton decried the influence that former high-level Federal officials exerted over government, and pledged "stop the revolving door."[6] President Clinton signed Executive Order 12,834, "Ethics Commitments by Executive Branch Appointees,"[7] which subjects high-level Clinton Administration appointees to a general five-year cooling-off period. The concern over the revolving door is that recently departed Federal officials have inordinate influence over government decisionmaking by virtue of the associations they developed and the information they obtained while in government. Yet, this same concern is present when the President grants a meeting to a former campaign official or a former Arkansas official such as Betsey Wright.

Moreover, informal advisers who participate in White House policy and strategy meetings are likely to be privy to nonpublic information that may be of interest and use to an adviser's outside clients. This gives such outside interests a window on White House deliberations not open to all.

The Extensive and Pervasive Access and Influence of Outside Advisers to President Clinton

Every President has relied to varying degrees on the advice of persons outside of the Government. And every President has maintained a regular line of communication with his party's Chairman and other key party officials. This is normal and healthy for the Presidency, so long as the outsiders remain outside of the Government and do not assume the role of a Federal official or otherwise perform Federal functions. In the Clinton White House, informal advisers appear to have played a critical role in virtually every significant White House action since President Clinton took office.

The **scope and extent** of the advisers' role in the Clinton White House may well be unprecedented. What may also be unprecedented is the **manner** in which these non-government persons have provided their advice and counsel to the President: at the White House, in large meetings, participating in official deliberations and decisionmaking on an equal footing with other senior White House staff. They have been given official tasks; they have been put in charge of certain projects; they have had access in the White House and to the President on a par with other senior White House staff; and there has been little effort to maintain a divide—either physical or analytical—between official White House staff and the unofficial White House advisers.

The best evidence in support of these conclusions comes from two books about the first two years of the Clinton Administration: Bob Woodward's *Agenda*, published in May 1994, and Elizabeth Drew's *On The Edge,* published in November 1994, both by Simon & Schuster.[8] Two magazine articles, however, which preceded publication of these books, were the first to highlight the pervasive influence of the group of informal advisers and the ethics concerns presented by such influence.[9]

The list of non-government players who were featured in these books, magazine articles, and other reports looks a lot like the Clinton-Gore campaign staff, minus George Stephanopoulos, Dee Dee Myers, Bruce Lindsey and Mickey Kantor, all of whom formally joined the Administration. The list includes:

- James Carville (consultant, Carville & Begala, former campaign manager)
- Paul Begala (consultant, Carville & Begala, former campaign adviser)
- Mandy Grunwald (Grunwald, Eskew & Donilon, former campaign media consultant)
- Stanley Greenberg (pollster and former campaign pollster)
- Vernon Jordan (head of the President-elect's Transition Team)
- David Wilhelm (DNC Chairman)
- Tony Coelho (New York investment banker, political adviser)
- Betsey Wright (Chief of Staff to Governor Clinton, now a lobbyist with the Wexler Group)
- Harry Thomason and Linda Bloodworth Thomason (Hollywood producers, assisted campaign)
- Susan Thomases (lawyer with Willkie Farr & Gallagher in New York)
- Harold Ickes (New York lawyer, now Deputy White House Chief of Staff)

In November 1993, *Business Week* surveyed the "enormous clout" within the White House possessed by four former campaign aides: James Carville, Paul Begala, Stanley Greenberg, and Mandy Grunwald. Each held a White House pass; each "earn[ed] far more as consultants to the Democratic National Committee" than they would have earned as White House officials:

This arrangement permits them to act as troubleshooters while working for other candidates, corporations, even foreign political parties. Never before have so many key political advisers plied their trade as free-lancers—freed from the restrictive conflict-of-interest rules that govern Administration appointees.

. . . [Clinton] constantly enlists the inside-outsiders in his "permanent campaign." The four helped direct the fight for the President's economic plan, mopped up after early stumbles over Cabinet appointments, and provide brilliant image counseling for Hillary Rodham Clinton. More recently, they developed the marketing strategy for health reform[.][10]

Business Week noted that **Paul Begala** "spends hours at the White House polishing Clinton speeches. He also travels with the President to major events." **James Carville** was earning money on the lecture circuit, receiving honoraria from corporate entities. Although Carville denied "peddling access," members of the National Restaurant Association, at a speech Carville gave to the Association, were not shy in approaching him, requesting his assistance in dissuading the Administration from moving to limit the deductibility of business meals.[11]

Stanley Greenberg told *Business Week*, "I organized my DNC contract so I can spend all my time working for [Clinton]." At the time, Greenberg was "meet[ing] White House aides nearly every day and giv[ing] Clinton a weekly briefing[.]" **Mandy Grunwald**'s roles were perhaps more commingled than most. Grunwald handled media for the DNC's program in support of the President's health care reform initiative, and media for USA-NAFTA, a coalition of businesses in support of NAFTA. Both of these projects reportedly involved several multimillion dollars in fees.[12]

In March 1994, *U.S. News & World Report* concluded that:

Key functions of the White House are, in effect, contracted out to friends and allies of Bill and Hillary outside government. Nongovernment advisers and trouble-shooters such as political consultants James Carville, Paul Begala, Mandy Grunwald and pollster Stanley Greenberg operate in a twilight zone not subject to the legal requirements that apply to full-time federal employees and that are meant to disclose their financial interests and protect the public from potential abuses of power.[13]

U.S. News & World Report reported that the firm of Carville & Begala received $300,000 per year from the DNC. Grunwald's firm was on a $15,000 a month retainer with the DNC. Greenberg's firm received $1.7 million in 1993 alone for its services, which were provided to a number of Democrats in addition to the President.[14]

The role of other informal advisers was also the subject of news reports. *U.S. News* found that **Betsey Wright**, whom both Governor and President Clinton enlisted on more than one occasion to clip a budding scandal, "lobbied both Bill and Hillary Clinton on behalf of clients[,]" including the American Dietetic Association relating to health care reform. Wright also asked President Clinton directly for assistance on behalf of another client, although the President ultimately did not rule in favor of the client. Wright said:

I will always bend over backward never to abuse my relationship with the president. I only help with existing clients. I think there is an assumption that I am a rainmaker because of my association with Bill. That is not the case.[15]

Whether or not Betsey Wright gained new clients because of her ties to the President, "[m]ost lobbyists . . . can only dream of the kind of access she enjoys[.]"[16] At the same time Wright has been promoting her clients' interests with the President and others in the White House, she has served as informal adviser to the President, and as noted above, has functioned as the President's major outside trouble-shooter.[17]

U.S. News & World Report also mentioned **Susan Thomases'** special influence with the First Lady, noting some of her New York law firm's corporate clients.[18] For a time Thomases held a blue White House pass, giving her unfettered access through the White House complex. In the summer of 1993 there was speculation that she would take a leave of absence from her law firm to manage the President's schedule, akin to the position she held in the Clinton-Gore campaign.[19] But reportedly no agreement was reached "because of concerns about potential conflicts of interest with her clients." Moreover, Thomases reportedly "surrendered her pass after McLarty raised questions about her corporate clients."[20] This shows some recognition of the fact that her stint at the White House would have made her an SGE (if not a regular employee), and subjected her to the conflict-of-interest laws. Yet, it was also reported that the Chief of Staff informed the White House staff that "Thomases will [continue to] advise from afar."[21]

Harold Ickes' dual role as an informal White House adviser and as lobbyist on behalf of the Government of Puerto Rico was reported at length in a September 1993 article in the *Wall Street Journal*.[22] Ickes held a blue White House pass (permitting unrestricted access throughout the White House complex), provided informal advice to the White House at the same time as he lobbied members of Congress on behalf of Puerto Rico, and arranged two meetings between the Governor of Puerto Rico and White House staff (one with the First Lady and the other with White House aide Marcia Hale). Ickes' pass was reportedly revoked after he agreed to represent Puerto Rico to lobby to preserve corporate tax breaks contrary to the position of the Clinton Administration.[23]

On January 3, 1994, Ickes joined the White House staff as Deputy Chief of Staff.

Bob Woodward focused primarily on the efforts of the Clinton White House to pass an economic plan in 1993, whereas Elizabeth Drew examined the entire scope of the Clinton White House for its first eighteen plus months. In *Agenda*, Woodward gave Begala, Carville, Greenberg, and Grunwald as prominent a place in the White House as any other White House official other than the President and perhaps First Lady. Woodward considered Begala, more than any of the other consultants, to be a part of the Administration. Woodward noted that Begala's White House service began almost immediately after the Inauguration:

Clinton and Hillary asked Begala to come work full time at the White House. To avoid any conflict with his ongoing political consulting business, Begala decided to work without pay. He reported to work Monday, February 1.[24]

This invitation followed a meeting of the President's economic team, held at Camp David, January 30-31, 1993, after which the First Lady reportedly tasked Begala and Grunwald to write "the communications plan." "Take notes, she said, get others involved, and get back with a plan for telling the story [of the President's economic program]."[25] Begala and Grunwald, working with Greenberg and Carville, sent a memorandum addressed only to the First Lady at Camp David, on January 31.[26]

In *On The Edge*, Elizabeth Drew provided a similar account of the Administration's first few weeks:

> The campaign aides who were to be outside political consultants—an arrangement that would be made formal later—weren't much in evidence during Clinton's first couple of weeks in office, except for Begala, who was helping on the economic program. Carville was in and out of the White House. In the course of the Camp David retreat, Clinton told Begala, Greenberg, and Grunwald that he wanted them to be more involved. . . . "The President wanted a more strategically driven administration," Greenberg commented later. Within two weeks, the consultants were attending regular White House meetings, where they discussed with top aides the President's schedules and speeches, and White House announcements.[27]

Begala became a regular at the White House, and was given a blue White House pass.[28] He attended meetings of the National Economic Council (NEC),[29] and was a frequent participant in other economic meetings in the White House with the President, White House officials, and members of the Cabinet.[30]

Begala also worked on several Presidential speeches.[31] Presidents have often delegated the drafting of particular speeches, usually political ones, to persons outside the White House. But Begala's regular input on speeches was not materially different than what the Office of Speechwriting was being paid to do.[32]

Begala's business partner James Carville, like Begala, was a regular visitor to the White House during this time. *U.S. News & World Report* concluded in its March 1994 article that Carville visited the White House about once a week, and talked with Stephanopoulos daily. He also received a blue pass, and was invited to meetings of the NEC. But Carville purposefully attempted to limit his visits to, and presence, in the White House:

> [Carville] didn't want to become a member of the administration, even a temporary or unpaid one like Begala. Besides, he was getting fat speaking fees on the lecture circuit as the Democrats' Svengali and the man who made Clinton.[33]

Agenda revealed five memoranda sent jointly from the four consultants to the President or First Lady in the President's first year in office.[34] These four consultants were often viewed as a group, even though their opinions varied, sometimes greatly.

Drew found that in mid-April, with the Clinton Administration "in crisis" because President Clinton was not seen by the public as a "new" Democrat, the President **increased** his reliance on his outside advisers:

> And so the consultants became still more engaged in the President's decision making. But a poll-driven, consultant-ridden Presidency carried risks. Leadership could be preempted by the consensus of the moment. There might not be any leadership at all.[35]

Drew concluded that the consultants' role was "without precedent":

> Previous Presidents had pollsters and other outside political advisers, but
> never before had a group of political consultants played such an integral
> part in a Presidency. Clinton's consultants were omnipresent, involved in
> everything from personnel to policymaking to the President's schedule.[36]

She noted that, as of April 1993, the consultants attended a weekly meeting with the
President on his "political situation," and also attended "the daily five o'clock staff
meeting."[37] Later, when the White House organized a "War Room" in the Old Executive Office Building to handle the upcoming budget reconciliation fight, the consultants participated "on a regular basis. Begala was there every day, and Greenberg
and Grunwald came to the regular 6:45 p.m. meetings. (Carville came and went, as
usual.)"[38]

Drew explained that the consultants' role posed "problems of governance," in
that they "contributed to the clogging" of the information flow to the President, "sometimes muffled the President's instincts," were unaccountable (except to the President), and, in the eyes of White House officials, the consultants "didn't understand
or accept the realities of governing[.]"[39] Both Woodward and Drew told of the concern some White House officials voiced over the amount of responsibility the President vested in these consultants:

> Howard Paster was in a slow burn as he listened to Greenberg. He
> hated these meetings. It was outrageous that the outside consultants were
> providing the president with major policy option papers in confidential
> memos that Paster often never saw or saw only too late. If lobbyists with
> business clients had this kind of relationship with the president, it would
> be a giant scandal. The consultants had clients, some businesses, some
> politicians like Senator Moynihan, who paid big fees for their work. Paster
> wasn't sure the political consultants were that different from other outside
> businesses. He resented their influence and was sure they presented Clin-
> ton with a potentially serious liability. Valuable inside information and
> conflicts abounded.[40]

> For Panetta and some of the others, the meeting was highly unusual
> for the Clinton White House: Clinton had actually delegated a
> major responsibility of his presidency to other people.[41]

A White House aide told Drew that the "consultants second-guessing everything" was a "universal frustration in the White House:

> The consultants probably have more time in the White House than any
> consultants ever. It gets to everybody—even George, who is the closest to
> them, thick with them." Another White House official said, "There's general
> frustration with the consultants coming in and at the last minute blowing things
> up. People here say, 'Fine. Take these hours, take this salary.'"[42]

Harry Thomason's role as adviser was more formal than any of the informal
consultants, although narrower and of lesser importance. Thomason was given a spe-

cific responsibility—to advise the President and others on the staging of Presidential events—a function normally performed by a regular White House official. Thomason's role was also more short-lived, because he got caught in the Travel Office controversy in May 1993. By July 1993, Thomason had quit the White House and assumed a low profile. Until the Travel Office blow-up, Thomason was not only given a blue pass, but he was also given an office and a phone in the East Wing.[43]

Former Representative **Tony Coelho** also has played a prominent role as informal adviser to President Clinton. Coelho's prominence in the White House and his reemergence as a political figure were ironic, given that Coelho left Congress in 1989 under a dark ethical cloud. At the time Coelho began advising the President regularly, Coelho was President of Wertheim Schroeder Investment Services, Inc., a subsidiary of Wertheim Schroeder & Company. Wertheim Schroeder is an investment banking firm which manages money for pension funds, corporations and individuals.[44] How regular were Coelho's contacts?

> [H]e is on the telephone with someone there almost daily, and, even though he is based in New York, participates in White House meetings two or three times a month or sometimes even more frequently.[45]

Coelho reportedly began serving as an informal adviser to President Clinton following the 1992 election. The *New York Times* reported that Coelho attended "several high-level strategy meetings a month."[46] For months during 1993, Coelho met with McLarty almost every Friday. A year later, Harold Ickes, now Deputy Chief of Staff, told the *Journal* he spoke with Coelho on a weekly basis. The *Journal* reported that:

> members of [Coelho's] network both inside and outside the White House say his fingerprints have shown up on many of Mr. Clinton's tactics and strategies over the past several months, ranging from matters of scheduling to questions of policy.

Coelho's current role was not believed to raise any ethical flags at the time, because Coelho's firm reportedly did not engage in any lobbying or government relations work, and Coelho was seen as an adviser without a personal agenda.[47]

In early 1994, Coelho was asked to succeed Mac McLarty as Chief of Staff. Leon Panetta, who became Chief of Staff instead, subsequently offered Coelho the Chairmanship of the DNC, an offer which Coelho also turned down.[48] Panetta persisted. Coelho told the *New Republic*:

> I was told by several people at the White House that there was a feeling that if they could just get me involved a little bit, I wouldn't be able to give it up, and I would get more and more involved until I came on full time. But I told them I won't give up my work at the bank. I like it too much. And I won't give up my corporate boards. I like 'em too much!
>
> . . . When Leon [Panetta] got in there, he pleaded with me to come on board[.] And I turned him down. So Leon and several others pleaded with me to then . . . advise.[49]

In August 1994, the President chose Coelho to give political advice and represent the President's political interests in the 1994 midterm elections. Formally, Coelho accepted an unpaid position with the Democratic National Committee.[50] After the
election, when the Republicans had won a majority in both Houses of Congress,
Coelho's advice and presence were still welcome at the White House. "'I still go to
the White House most Thursdays and Fridays,' he says. 'I go to the senior staff
meetings. I answer any questions they might have.'"[51]

"I like to have fifteen balls in the air at once," he says. "The White
House. My work at the bank. My corporate boards. This bank doesn't lobby. It doesn't get involved in politics. So it's really just a question of time
management." Coelho is sitting pretty: as an "unpaid, temporary volunteer," he has authority but no responsibility. He's not technically culpable
for anything. "I was only there for what, seventy days?" he says.[52]

Coelho scoffed at the notion that his informal role raised ethics concerns:

Now I happen to believe—and I feel very strongly about this—that
what we do is we discourage volunteers. We discourage people who are
successful in other walks of life from helping out. The Naders of this world
want to say there are conflicts. And I just think they're crazy. I think they
are so, so wrong.[53]

But the *New Republic* article ended with a vignette describing how Coelho was
pivotal in bringing Starbucks coffee and products to the White House—and the CEO
of Starbucks to the White House for a meeting with the President—after Coelho's
business partner mused that it would be great if the White House drank Starbucks.
Starbucks, or at least the company's CEO, was a client of Coelho's firm.[54]

The most recent informal adviser to President Clinton to be noticed by the media is **Dick Morris**, a longtime campaign and political consultant, mostly to Republican candidates, although Morris advised Clinton back in the 1970's. Morris was
first identified by Ann Devroy of the *Washington Post* as "part of a shadow Clinton
strategic communications team, proposing whole speeches or pieces of speeches,
offering ideas for messages and then helping write them."[55] Morris was not being
called upon simply to give Clinton political advice. One official told the *Post* that
Morris has "turned into a general adviser of sorts[;]" Morris was said to speak with
the President weekly, sometimes several times a week.

Would Morris (and others) signal "a return to government-by-political consultant?" White House press secretary Mike McCurry answered that Morris would not.
He pointed to the process, overseen by Panetta, through which Morris's ideas, speech
edits, and comments must go. Others were not so confident.[56]

Indeed, reports of Morris's White House presence, activities, and influence proliferated into the summer of 1995. In June, Ann Devroy wrote:

Morris has become, in the views of several administration officials and
outside Democrats, a hidden hand in policy formulation and public performance in the Clinton White House[.]

... Morris now attends a regular Thursday evening White House meeting with Clinton, Vice President Gore, Chief of Staff Leon E. Panetta and the two deputy chiefs of staff, Harold Ickes and Erskine Bowles, where his ideas for the upcoming week or month are discussed with the president...

A senior official said yesterday Morris's proposals for speeches and speech language go through the normal White House process and that language and ideas are rejected or accepted, in the same manner as those of any other official.[57]

The *Wall Street Journal* reported that "Morris talks to Clinton several times a day, making a shamble of staff chief Panetta's effort to run things through him. After loud Panetta objections, some efforts are made to rein Morris in."[58]

By July 1995, Morris was seen working out of a White House office, and attending "regular 90-minute 'message' meetings at the Old Executive Office Building conference room to plot and plan with senior aides[.] ... Panetta chairs the meetings, we hear, and Morris 'guides' them. He is being what Panetta calls 'integrated' into the White House operation."[59]

By August, Ann Devroy described Morris as "a fixture in the White House," and also "on the campaign payroll at $15,000 per month[.]"[60] Throughout the fall of 1995, Devoy continued to showcase Morris's extraordinary influence with the President. [61]

Problems Encountered with Outside Advisers

In the beginning, the Clinton White House did not demonstrate any sensitivity to ethics concerns in its use of informal advisers. As a consequence, the White House ran the risk that one or more informal advisers would be involved in a conflict of interest in violation of law. Even if no law was broken, the Administration was and is susceptible to criticism that it has given preferential treatment to private interests whom the informal advisers represent by allowing them special access or influence. The Clinton Administration also faced criticism for freely providing passes to these advisers, without completion of a full field FBI background check required of other White House pass holders.[62]

The Travel Office Firings

The problem first surfaced in May 1993 when the White House announced the firing of the White House Travel Office staff.[63] It was revealed that Harry Thomason, a friend of the Clintons who had worked on the Inaugural and then moved into the East Wing of the White House to assist on public events, had played an instrumental role in the firings. Thomason was one-third owner of an aviation consulting business that had done work for the Clinton-Gore campaign, and Thomason helped get his business partner Darnell Martens' complaints about the White House Travel Office heard in the White House. Thomason subsequently participated in meetings with senior White House officials in which the fate of the Travel Office employees was deliberated; Thomason urged their summary dismissal. Notwithstanding Thomason's office in the White House, his possession of a White House pass allowing him access throughout the complex, and his substantial participation in White House internal deliberations, the White House did not consider him a Federal employee, either regular or special.[64]

The White House Management Review, issued on July 2, 1993, acknowledged that its supervision of Thomason was inadequate, and recommended the adoption of policies to control access to the White House by non-government employees. By the time the White House issued this Management Review, Congress had passed a provision directing GAO to investigate the Travel Office matter. GAO's review, which was not completed until May 1994, also looked into the role of Harry Thomason and Darnell Martens. GAO concluded that there was not enough facts to conclude that either person was an SGE, a question the White House Management Review did not even discuss. But GAO did make modest findings that by his possession of a White House pass and his conduct, Thomason gave the appearance of official authority and that his business relationship with Martens created an appearance of a conflict of interest.

Representative Wolf Questions the White House in a Series of Letters

After the release of the White House Management Review, Representative Frank Wolf wrote to the White House requesting information on whether non-government employees had White House passes and what security clearance procedures were used for these persons.[65] Chief of Staff McLarty responded that the security procedures in the White House were the same as in previous administrations. McLarty acknowledged that, "A limited number of non-government persons **who, for the most part, have rendered regular services to the Administration**, also have White House passes."[66] McLarty, however, declined to provide a list of these persons, which he called "confidential." McLarty added that, as a result of the White House Management Review, "there may be some modification of our pass policy with respect to non-government persons."[67]

In September 1993, in response to the White House Management Review's recommendation, the White House adopted a new policy on White House passes for non-government persons.[68] Under the policy, White House permanent passes are issued only to Federal employees (including special Government employees and full-time volunteers); the President's family; and "individuals employed or retained by the Democratic National Committee whose duties require regular consultation with the President and his staff." Exceptions to this policy could be granted only by the Chief of Staff, only after a review by the Counsel's office, and only upon a showing of exceptional circumstances. The Counsel's office would work with these persons to ensure that they avoid potential conflicts of interest.[69]

Wolf wrote the Chief of Staff again in September 1993, concerned about the "[s]erious ethical and conflict of interest problems" that are posed by the White House's use of informal advisers:

> [A]t least some of the non-government persons known to have White House passes are highly paid lawyers, consultants and lobbyists who are not subject to any kind of oversight or disclosure requirements that are routine for regular White House employees.[70]

Wolf asked for the names of the non-government persons referred to in McLarty's letter who provide "regular services" to the White House. He also asked a host of questions about whether they were required to comply with financial disclosure and security clearance requirements, whether they were given office space, and who paid for their salary (i.e., the DNC, labor unions, lobbying firms). In addition to Harry Thomason, Wolf noted the advisory role that Susan Thomases was expected to perform in the near future and complained about the access Harold Ickes had in the White House (at the time, a lawyer in private practice), given his role as a lobbyist on one or more matters of interest to the White House. Wolf also questioned the many temporary passes given to regular White House employees pending security clearance.[71]

A few weeks later, having received no response from the White House, Wolf wrote McLarty for the third time.[72] Wolf focused on two things: (1) The potential for conflicts of interest, because of the "unprecedented number" of political consultants and other non-government persons who hold passes, "while they represent foreign interests and work on campaigns that sometimes have interests quite contrary to those of the President (for example, opposition to Nafta)[;]" and (2) the delay in completing security clearances for White House employees and others who hold White House passes. Wolf asked why so many White House employees still held temporary passes, nine months into the Administration, and what were the reasons for this delay. Wolf argued that Associate Counsel William Kennedy, who was in charge of clearances for the Counsel's office, should be replaced.[73] Wolf concluded this situation posed "a potential threat to the Secret Service's ability to perform its statutory function of implementation of an access control system and assistance in providing independent judgment regarding suitability of individuals who serve as staff members at the White House."[74] Wolf also wrote letters to the FBI and Secret Service complaining about the delays in the clearance and pass process.[75]

This time, McLarty responded with only a brief, conclusory letter.[76] McLarty reiterated that the list of passholders was confidential, insisted that security clearances were "being handled in a timely manner," noted that the White House had "recently tightened procedures for the issuance of passes" to non-government persons, and defended the legality of the White House's acceptance of volunteer services from non-government persons whose salary is paid by others.[77]

In its response to Wolf, the FBI noted that the timeframes for FBI background checks established by agreement between the FBI and White House during the Bush Administration (forty-five days for first-time access; ninety days for five-year update) had been met by the FBI during the Clinton and Bush Administrations.[78] The FBI also acknowledged conducting background investigations for "certain, but not all, individuals who have required or received access to the White House but are non-government employees; e.g., C&P telephone service/repair persons." The FBI performed these investigations only at the request of the White House, so it was unaware of the number or identity of non-government persons with access to the White House on whom the FBI has not conducted a background check.[79]

More information relevant to Wolf's inquiries was contained in the November 1993 *Business Week* article on the four political consultants. The consultants explained the steps they took, on their own initiative, to avoid conflicts and the appearance of impropriety:

> Group members dismiss the notion that Clinton needs them 'round the clock. But they fret about possible conflicts. To insulate themselves, the quartet made a pact: No corporate lobbying and no deals with foreign

governments. "We asked for information from the White House and DNC counsel about laws that governed us," says Grunwald. "We found out there were very few. So we decided to make our own rules." The Clintonites see no problem with self-policing. Says [David] Wilhelm, "They come to me when there are questions. These are folks with good judgment.[80]

In December 1993, Wolf wrote McLarty for the fourth time, reiterating many of the questions he posed in October, which McLarty had not answered. Wolf also asked for a status report on the White House Management Review's findings and recommendations concerning access by outsiders.[81]

Two more months elapsed, with no response from the White House to Wolf's letters. On February 24, 1994, Wolf wrote the President directly, urging the White House to respond to his questions, made more critical, in Wolf's view, in light of public reports that CIA official Aldrich Ames had been a Soviet agent.[82] That same day, McLarty finally responded to Wolf, but did not answer a single question from Wolf's letters. To understand the non-responsive nature of McLarty's letter, the body of it is reprinted in full:

> Thank you for writing and for your continued concern regarding White House passes and security. I apologize for the delay in responding to your inquiries.
>
> As I have previously stated, to our knowledge, security clearances are being handled both in a timely manner and in accordance with the procedures of previous Administrations and the requirements of the law. Please be advised that the receipt of backgrounds from the Federal Bureau of Investigation is but one step in a multistep process of issuing permanent White House passes.
>
> Moreover, I continue to share the concern you state about the importance of dealing with conflicts of interest, and this Administration is constantly striving to see that the White House meets the highest standards of ethics.
>
> Again, thank you for your letter.[83]

The Controversy Over Passes and Security Clearances Ripens Into a Story of Gross Mismanagement

At this point, the back-and-forths between Representative Wolf and the White House spilled into the press. Columnists Tony Snow,[84] Gloria Borger,[85] and the editorial page of the *Wall Street Journal*[86] all took up Wolf's cause about the delays in performing clearances and issuing permanent passes. In March 1994, articles in the *Washington Post* and *Washington Times* revealed that hundreds of White House employees were still without a permanent pass, including one-third of the 125 senior White House staffers, and fifteen key aides. The bottleneck was identified as the Counsel's office.[87]

On March 17, the *Washington Post* reported that the White House had adopted new security clearance procedures after it determined that about one hundred out of 1,004 White House employees, including fifteen senior White House officials, had not completed the paperwork necessary to permit a full field FBI background investigation.[88] Current employees were directed to complete by the end of the week (March

18) all necessary paperwork (mainly, Form 86) to permit the FBI to conduct its full field investigation. Temporary passes would not be renewed upon expiration. New employees were required to complete all paperwork within forty-five to sixty days of coming on board, although a period of thirty days was later set. At this time the newly appointed White House Counsel, Lloyd Cutler, directed four informal advisers (Carville, Begala, Grunwald and Greenberg) to undergo "the routine FBI background check to retain free access."[89]

Representative Wolf finally got some answers to his questions after he wrote to Cutler in March 1994 complaining that he had received more information from the March 11 *Washington Post* article than from all the letters from the White House over the previous year.[90] Although most of the media focused on White House passes and security clearances, Wolf emphasized his equal concern over the potential for conflicts of interest, given that "individuals can work at the White House on a regular basis with no accountability or disclosure of outside activities[.]"[91]

Cutler first described the new policy on access to the White House, adopted in September 1993.[92] Cutler explained that political advisers to the President, who are "employed or retained" by the DNC, "are not properly characterized as employees."[93] However, since at least the adoption of the new policy on access, these advisers "receive counseling regarding the limits of their roles as political advisers and potential areas of conflict of interest."[94]

Cutler noted the long-standing practice of the White House to use volunteers to handle phones and correspondence. These volunteers enter into an agreement with the White House designed to protect nonpublic information and to avoid conflicts of interest. Cutler assured Wolf that other volunteers who "undertake substantive or policy-level work" are "subject to the conflict of interest laws applicable to persons serving without compensation[,]" and receive ethics counseling from the Counsel's office. Cutler declined, however, to answer any of Wolf's questions regarding any particular individual (such as Susan Thomases, Harry Thomason, or Harold Ickes).

Finally, Cutler assured Wolf that no one received a **permanent** pass until completion of the full field FBI background investigation, completion of ethics and security training, completion of a financial disclosure form, and undergoing IRS "and other" checks. But Cutler also noted that a person may be cleared for access to classified information with just a temporary pass, because access to this information is governed by different considerations.[95]

Soon thereafter, *U.S. News & World Report* ran its prominent article about the White House's use of outside advisers, entitled "Government off the books; A cadre of unappointed advisers roam the White House and cash in on their access."[96]

On March 22, 1994, Patsy Thomasson testified before a House Appropriations Subcommittee concerning the issuance of passes. Thomasson testified that all employees had submitted the necessary paperwork (save a few employees who had just begun their White House service), satisfying one of McLarty's directions. Second, all employees had passed a "preliminary background check," which is just a computer search for any criminal history and a review of any extant intelligence files. Third, Thomasson said the process to obtain a permanent White House pass, including the FBI's investigation, "now takes, on average, only four months."[97]

In an answer to a question submitted for the record, the White House explained the new process by which White House passes are provided to White House employees. Following an initial security interview conducted by the White House, a preliminary background check is performed and the employee is given a drug test. The employee is given thirty days to complete all paperwork to permit a full field FBI background investigation. Once the paperwork is complete, the employee may receive a temporary pass after going through a fingerprint check. The FBI reports to the White House the results of its full field investigation within ninety days of receipt of the paperwork. The White House Security Office and White House Counsel's office review the report, and then the Counsel's office sends the FBI file, with a recommendation, to the Secret Service for its determination of whether or not to issue a permanent pass.[98]

For persons who are not considered government employees, such as informal consultants, a similar process is involved, including completing Form 86 and passing the full field FBI background investigation. The White House reiterated its revised policy on access to non-government persons, which "restricts" White House passes to White House employees, members of the First Family, DNC officials, contractor personnel, and any other person who is given a pass under "exceptional circumstances," as determined by the Chief of Staff in consultation with the Counsel's office.[99] This policy would not automatically cause any of the informal advisers who held passes to give them up, because nearly all of them could qualify as an individual "employed or retained" by the DNC (Carville, Begala, Grunwald and Greenberg) and others could be granted a pass if the Chief of Staff found "exceptional circumstances," whatever that term means.

Associate Counsel William Kennedy was stripped of his responsibility to review FBI reports of background checks after it was disclosed that Kennedy had failed to pay (until early 1994) taxes on wages paid to a nanny for calendar year 1991 and was delinquent in paying these taxes in the first three quarters of 1992. When Kennedy eventually paid the 1992 taxes, the name used on the check was his wife's maiden name, which some perceived as an effort to disguise his role in the failure to pay taxes at a time when the nanny problem resulted in the non-selection of two persons as Attorney General (Zoe Baird and Kimba Wood). At the same time, it was reported that Kennedy was the single official most responsible for the main backlog in the clearance process, failing to forward "scores" or "hundreds" of completed FBI reports to the Secret Service.[100] McLarty and Thomasson, for instance, did not receive a permanent pass until sometime in March 1994, and Kennedy himself did not get a permanent pass until December 1993. The responsibility over the clearance process was given to Beth Nolan, another Associate Counsel with responsibility over other ethics matters.

Patsy Thomasson testified before the Senate Appropriations Subcommittee on March 25. She acknowledged for the first time that the Secret Service had recommended that several persons not receive a White House pass because of derogatory information, and that the White House had accepted the Service's recommendations and not retained the employees.[101]

Also that week, Representatives Wolf and Clinger asked GAO to investigate the handling of White House passes, and fourteen Republican Senators asked newly appointed White House Counsel Cutler to explain why so many senior White House aides still did not hold permanent passes.[102]

Wolf's Efforts to Pass Legislation to Address Ethics and Security Concerns

On May 18, 1994, Wolf sought an amendment to the Fiscal Year 1995 Treasury, Postal Appropriations bill in the House Treasury, Postal Service, General Government Appropriations Subcommittee to prohibit the use of any funds to issue a temporary or permanent White House pass to any "advisor or political consultant who is not a Federal officer or employee" unless the person has been the subject of a full field FBI background investigation and has filed the public financial disclosure report (SF-278) required by law to be filed by high-level Executive Branch officials. Wolf pointed out that requiring an FBI background investigation addressed only part of the problem posed by the influence of informal advisers. In Wolf's view, the White House had not taken any meaningful step to avoid the situation where an informal adviser participates in White House deliberations on a particular matter involving, or likely to have an effect on, an adviser's company or firm or the firm's clients. He also doubted the efficacy of the ethics briefings promised by Lloyd Cutler. Therefore, Wolf argued that the consultants ought publicly to disclose their clients and sources of outside income.[103] The amendment failed on a party-line vote.[104]

After the votes in committee, a *Washington Post* editorial called on the President to require his informal advisers to "disclose their outside clients and forbear from certain conduct in the clients' behalf."[105] Although it praised Wolf for raising the problem, the *Post* noted the underinclusive nature of the proposed amendment: an informal adviser without a pass could have just as much access and influence as one with a pass. "[W]hat's needed in this murky area is less a law than a policy. It ought to emanate from the president, and apply at least to his principal and paid advisers whether they have to call ahead to get into the White House or not."

Bob Woodward's book *Agenda* was released about this time, revealing a greater role for the informal advisers in the making of President Clinton's economic policy than previously reported.[106]

Representative Wolf next sought to amend the appropriations bill on the House floor,[107] but Democrats defeated Republican efforts in the House Rules Committee to permit a vote on the amendment.[108] Democrats noted that Republicans had failed to insist on any disclosure of the interests of informal advisers to Presidents Reagan and Bush. On June 9, the day Wolf attempted to amend the rule on the floor so that he could offer his amendment, the White House took steps to obviate any such legislative direction. Chief of Staff McLarty issued a "Directive" (announced by the press office on June 10) requiring some financial disclosure of non-government persons who are political consultants and who hold a White House pass:[109]

> Effective July 1, 1994, all holders of temporary or permanent White House passes who are political advisers or political consultants but are not government employees or special government employees shall file initial and annual statements reporting 1) clients providing more than $5,000 of compensation to the reporter or the reporter's business affiliation for services provided directly by the reporter during the reporting period, and 2) that information required from a special government employee by the Executive Branch Personnel Confidential Financial Disclosure Report (SF-450).

The initial financial reports required by the June 9 policy were due on July 15, 1994, for current passholders, covering only the first six months of 1994. Those applying for a pass in the future are required to file a report by the date the pass is issued. Passholders are also required to file annual reports on May 15, covering the previous calendar year. All reports are publicly available.

When the appropriations bill finally came to the House floor, only an amendment offered by Representative Steny Hoyer and relating only to the timeliness of security clearances passed, by voice vote. The amendment required White House employees—not consultants—to complete all necessary paperwork within thirty days and to obtain a White House pass within six months, or else be placed on leave without pay status (unless exempted by the President).[110] Although the amendment probably was offered to show that Democrats were not simply doing the White House's bidding, the amendment accomplished little, if anything, beyond what the White House had already pledged to do.

The Four Main Informal Advisers Declare Their Financial Interests

The four consultants who would soon be required to file financial reports—James Carville, Paul Begala, Mandy Grunwald and Stanley Greenberg, indeed the only ones covered by the directive[111]—wrote an op-ed article published in the *Washington Post* on June 10.[112] The consultants argued that informal advisers to Presidents Reagan and Bush may have lobbied for special interests and foreign governments, but they did not do so:

> We do not lobby. We do not represent foreign governments. We do not represent outside interests before the government.
>
> Nor are we government employees. None of us has a phone or a desk or an office or a staff at the White House. None of us receives a dime from the American taxpayer. None of us has the power or authority to make or enforce government decisions. We stick to political consulting.
>
> . . . And while it is true that it is common in our industry [campaign consultants] to both run campaigns and lobby elected officials, we do not do so; nor have we done so; nor will we do so. We've drawn a bright line, and we have held strictly to it.

The consultants also listed every client they have had since the inauguration, noting that they "have long since also disclosed the names of all our clients to the White House counsel." Nearly all of the clients listed were political candidates or political organizations. Carville & Begala listed the New Democracy Party of Greece, Greenberg listed Nelson Mandela (*qua* candidate) and the Israel Policy Forum, and Grunwald listed USA NAFTA, the National Women's Political Caucus and the Rockefeller Foundation.

The *Washington Post* responded in an editorial the same day. First, it took issue with the consultants' effort to minimize their influence. "Our own view is that they understate to the point of distortion their own roles inside the White House, as well as understate somewhat their various connections with the outside world."[113] *Agenda* would confirm, even buttress, the *Post*'s view. The *Post* commended the consultants' disclosure, but noted that the absence of any commercial entity on their lists does not mean that there is no potential for a conflict or impropriety. Political interests are just as likely to have an interest in White House and Executive Branch actions, albeit not the usual sort of financial interest.

Additionally, it is not sufficient for a consultant with outside interests simply to refrain from lobbying the White House or Federal agency on behalf of a client. The conflict-of-interest law provides that Federal employees should not **participate** in any particular matter in which they have a financial interest. The purpose of financial disclosure is to ensure that employees and consultants avoid such participation, not simply that they avoid lobbying on behalf of their clients.

Financial reports were filed by Carville, Begala, Grunwald and Greenberg by July 15, as directed.[114] The reports listed the consultants' clients, assets and income (including honoraria), liabilities, positions, and agreements and arrangements. No amounts were required, similar to the confidential financial disclosure report (SF-450) required of most SGEs. The reports were sufficient to enable the White House Counsel's office to advise the consultants—as if they were SGEs—on how to avoid potential conflicts of interest. They were not, however, sufficient to enable one to tell "if the four populists are getting rich having helped elect a president."[115]

Wolf Is Not Satisfied; Additional Questions Arise

Soon thereafter, Representative Wolf wrote Leon Panetta, newly installed Chief of Staff, complaining that the disclosure required by the McLarty directive was inadequate. Wolf noted that the information required of the consultants was much less than what Panetta and other senior White House officials are required to provide.[116] Wolf added that the reports did not have "any legal consequence," meaning perhaps that false reporting would not be a basis for criminal prosecution.

Wolf wrote Panetta twice more in September 1994, based on reports that Carville and Grunwald were involved in the upcoming Brazilian Presidential election,[117] and a *New York Times* profile of Tony Coelho's access to the White House, timely given the President's selection of Coelho to advise him on the November 1994 elections.[118] Wolf repeated his argument that the financial disclosure required of consultants was insufficient, and also asked for an explanation of Carville's and Grunwald's role in the Brazilian election. Wolf argued that Coelho should be required to file a public financial disclosure report under the McLarty directive, given his significant presence and influence in the White House.

Newly appointed White House Counsel Abner Mikva responded to Wolf's letters pertaining to Carville's and Grunwald's involvement in the Brazilian election. Judge Mikva wrote that Carville was not required to list his Brazilian client on his report because he did not receive $5,000 during the reporting period (January-June 1994). The $5,000 threshold is the same threshold used in public financial disclosure reports (SF-278). Mikva assured Wolf that if Carville were to receive fees in excess of $5,000 during the next reporting period, he would be required to report these fees and the client on his next report. Mikva also noted that Grunwald was not required to report any of her firm's clients unless she herself derived fees of $5,000 or more.[119]

Representative Wolf wrote Mikva the next day, complaining that he had failed to explain whether or not Carville was involved in the election and when that involvement began, as Wolf had previously asked. He also repeated his request that Coelho be required to provide a financial disclosure report.[120]

Judge Mikva's response to this letter did not refer at all to Wolf's questions about Carville.[121] As for Coelho, Mikva noted that Coelho's activities as an "unpaid adviser to the Democratic National Committee" were:

> limited to briefing the President and his aides regarding political issues and attending meetings on political strategy. He has no responsibility for, or input into, policy matters.[122]

Coelho's role was "much more limited—both in time and in duration" than the four advisers who filed reports. Coelho did not hold a White House pass. In any event, Mikva added, Coelho had filed a confidential financial disclosure report (SF-450) in connection with his appointment to the President's Committee on Employment of People with Disabilities, so that the Counsel's office was aware of potential conflicts.[123]

In both letters, Judge Mikva emphasized that the consultants were not government employees, yet were providing financial disclosure comparable to what SGEs are required to file.

When reports of the influence of Dick Morris surfaced in May 1995 and for months thereafter, no one in Congress or in the media appeared to take note of the potential ethics issues. It is not known whether Morris received an ethics briefing when he began advising the President regularly, but the White House did not consider him an SGE or require him to fill out an SF 450 (confidential financial disclosure report). The White House initially explained, in a *USA Today* story which called this an "ethics loophole," that Morris was not covered by the White House policy on informal advisers because he was not given a White House pass![124] The White House indicated that it would look into the question in the broader context of the structure of the re-election campaign.[125] But on the day the *USA Today* article was published, Mike McCurry stated that Morris:

> should be subject to ethics and disclosure requirements of some nature and they need to be defined. [Mr. Morris] has no trouble with that. He's willing to comply with whatever rules we establish that seem to be the right rules.[126]

Analysis

Are These Informal Advisers Special Government Employees?

The term "special Government employee"(SGE) was first defined by statute in 1962, as part of the recodification of the conflict-of-interest laws. Section 202(a), which defined the concept of an SGE, was made effective in 1963. The concept originated with President Kennedy's desire to ensure that advisers and consultants to the Federal Government would be subject to the same conflict-of-interest standards to which regular Federal employees are subject, while not being subject to the full panoply of ethics standards.[127] Previously, the ethics laws had been construed equally to apply to regular government employees and consultants who performed temporary or intermittent services to the Government. Because SGEs serve the public interest, they were made subject to the conflict-of-interest restriction of section 208 to the same extent as a regular employee. Because of the part-time, temporary, or intermittent nature of their service, however, the other ethics laws were applied to them in a more limited way.[128]

Also important was the distinction the new law implicitly drew between an SGE and a person who is not **any** type of Federal employee. Following the enactment of section 202(a), President Kennedy issued a memorandum dated May 2, 1963, entitled, "Preventing Conflicts of Interest on the Part of Special Government Employees." In it, Kennedy drew an important distinction between an **SGE** and a **representative**:

> It is occasionally necessary to distinguish between consultants and advisers who are special Government employees and persons who are invited to appear at a department or agency in a representative capacity to speak for firms or an industry, or for labor or agriculture, or for any other recognizable group of persons, including on occasion the public at large. **A consultant or adviser whose advice is obtained** by a department or agency from time to time **because of his individual qualifications and who serves in an independent capacity is an officer or employee of the Government**. On the other hand, **one who is requested to appear** before a Government department or agency **to present the views of a non-governmental organization or group which it represents, or for which he is in a position to speak, does not act as a servant of the Government and is not its officer or employee. He is therefore not subject to the conflict of interest laws[.]**[129]

Since that 1963 guidance, additional criteria have been used to determine whether someone is an SGE, as opposed to someone who is not any type of Federal employee: whether the person (1) has sworn or signed an oath of office, (2) is paid a salary or expenses, (3) enjoys agency office space, (4) serves as a spokesperson for the agency, (5) is subject to the supervision of a Federal agency, and (6) serves in a consulting or advisory capacity to the United States.[130]

Most of the practical questions concerning SGEs have involved participants in advisory committees and part-time government commissions.[131] Other interpretative issues have arisen in the context of informal advisers and outside consultants.

In 1977, the Office of Legal Counsel (OLC) was asked to determine whether a particular individual's frequent informal consultations with the President made him a "special Government employee." OLC determined that, as a general rule, even frequent consultations did not make an informal adviser an SGE, "just as Mrs. Carter would not be regarded as a special Government employee solely on the ground that she may discuss governmental matters with the President on a daily basis."[132]

However, OLC determined that because the individual in question had gone beyond the role of informal adviser, he had become an SGE and should be formally appointed and duly sworn:

> Mr. A, however, seems to have departed from his usual role of an informal adviser to the President in connection with his recent work on a current social issue. **Mr. A has called and chaired a number of meetings that were attended by employees of various agencies, in relation to this work, and he has assumed considerable responsibility for coordinating the Administration's activities in that particular area. Mr. A is quite clearly engaging in a governmental function when he performs these duties, and he presumably is working under the direction or supervision of the**

President. For this reason, Mr. A should be designated as a special Government employee for purposes of this work, assuming that a good faith estimate can be made that he will perform official duties relating to that work for no more than 130 out of the next 365 consecutive days. If he is expected to perform these services for more than 130 days, he should be regarded as a regular employee. In either case, he should be formally appointed and take an oath of office.[133]

In its first extended discussion of the concept of an SGE, the Office of Government Ethics also considered the status of informal advisers:

3. *Individuals Outside the Government Who Advise an Official Informally*
      A Federal official may occasionally receive unsolicited, informal advice from an outside individual or group of individuals regarding a particular matter or issue of policy that is within his official responsibility. . . . An incident of this sort sometimes prompts the inquiry whether the outsiders have become SGE's of the agency. In general, the answer is that they have not, for they are not possessed of appointments as employees **nor do they perform a Federal function.**
      However, as so often happens in considering the applicability of the conflict-of-interest laws, a generality is insufficient here and a *caveat* is in order. **An official should not hold informal meetings more or less regularly with a nonfederal individual . . . for the purpose of obtaining information or advice for the conduct of his office. If he does so, he may invite the argument that willy-nilly he has brought them within the range of 18 U.S.C. 202-209.**[134]

The White House has consistently stated that President Clinton's informal advisers are not Federal employees, even SGEs. What is probably the White House's fullest explanation is in the form of an answer, submitted for the record, to a question Representative Wolf posed to Patsy Thomasson at a House Appropriations Subcommittee hearing in March 1994:

Mr. Carville is not a special government employee. He is a political adviser to the President and his staff. Not every person who provides advice to the President and his staff is considered to be a federal employee. [After reciting the definition of an special Government employee in section 202(a), the White House continued:]
      The term "employee" itself is not defined by the conflict of interest statutes (or elsewhere in title 18). For this reason, the definition of employee found in title 5 of the United States code is frequently the starting point for analyzing whether the conflict of interest laws apply to a particular person. Title 5 offers three criteria by which employment status is judged: (1) appointment to federal office; (2) performance of a federal function under authority of law; and (3) supervision by a federal officer or employee. See 5 U.S.C. §2104, 2105.[135]

That was the entire White House explanation. The White House did not explain whether all three criteria need be met, just one or two of the three, or whether there is a balancing of factors. The White House did not explain whether Carville (and the others) satisfied none of the criteria, or whether he only satisfied one or two. And the White House did not explain what analysis if any, is performed after the "starting point."

The considerations used in determining whether someone is an SGE are similar to, **but not the same as**, the criteria in the definition of "officer" and "employee" in the Federal personnel statutes relied upon by the White House, 5 U.S.C. 2104 and 2105:

An "officer" means "an individual who is—
(1) required by law to be appointed in the civil service . . . ;
(2) engaged in the performance of a Federal function under authority of law or an Executive act; and
(3) subject to the supervision of [the President or Federal officer], while engaged in the performance of the duties of his office. . . .[136]

An "employee" means "an individual who is—
(1) appointed in the civil service . . .;
(2) engaged in the performance of a Federal function under authority of law or an Executive act; and
(3) subject to the supervision of [the President or Federal officer] while engaged in the performance of the duties of his position....[137]

Because the White House did not consider any of these informal advisers as a Federal employee, it did not "appoint" them to engage in a Federal function "under authority of law or an Executive act." But a formal appointment is not necessary to subject an informal adviser to the conflict-of-interest laws. In its 1977 opinion on whether informal advisers to the President are SGEs, OLC examined the criteria in the definitions of "officer" and "employee" in 5 U.S.C. 2104 and 2105. OLC stated that:

variants of these same three factors have, in fact, been utilized in one context or another under the conflict-of-interest laws.

For example, the first criterion under the civil service test—that the person be appointed in the civil service—is **analogous** to the definition of the term "special Government employee" for the purposes of the conflict-of interest laws: an officer or employee "who is retained, designated, appointed, or employed" to perform duties . . . . The quoted phrase connotes a formal relationship between the individual and the Government. . . . In the usual case, this formal relationship is based on an identifiable act of appointment. . . . **However, an identifiable act of appointment may not be absolutely essential for an individual to regarded as an officer or employee in an a particular case . . . perhaps where there was a firm mutual understanding that a relatively formal relationship existed.**[138]

Thus, OLC recognized that the definitions in the personnel statutes were not determinative of the applicability of the conflict-of-interest laws.[139] There are several additional reasons why sections 2104 and 2105, even if "starting points," do not resolve this question.

First, both sections 2104 and 2105 begin with the phrase, "For the purposes of this title" (Title 5), so that laws do not expressly define the words "officer" and "employee" for purposes of Title 18.[140]

Second, Title 5 concerns the U.S. Government civil service. But most employees of the White House Office are hired under authority of Title 3.[141] The distinction between Title 5 employees and Title 3 employees is significant. Under 3 U.S.C. 105(a)(1), the President enjoys broad discretion to "appoint and fix the pay of employees in the White House office without regard to any other provision of law regulating the employment or compensation of persons in Government service." In the early weeks of the Clinton Administration, the White House provided retroactive salary payments to many White House staffers, covering work done before their appointment papers were signed. The Justice Department determined that the President could legally authorize retroactive pay to certain White House Office employees in view of the President's broad discretion under 3 U.S.C. 105(a)(1).[142] GAO, asked to review the propriety of such retroactive appointments and other pay adjustments, noted that the law was not as flexible for Title 5 employees.[143] The Justice Department opinion confirms that employee status in the White House can arise from the nature of the work actually performed, regardless of the formal execution of appointment papers. If White House Office staff can receive pay for work done before a formal appointment is executed, surely the formal appointment requirements in sections 2104 and 2105 have little, if any, bearing on whether someone working in the White House Office is, in fact, a Federal employee.

Third, exempting a person performing a Federal function from the ethics laws merely for lack of a formal appointment would exalt form over substance and create a gap in coverage. The White House, or any other agency, would be able to exempt an unpaid adviser from coverage of the ethics laws simply by declining to execute the proper paperwork.

Fourth, the definition of an SGE in 18 U.S.C. 202(a) is broader than the definitions in sections 2104 and 2105. In the latter statutes, the second criterion requires an "appointment." Section 202(a), however, includes all those who are "retained, designated, appointed or employed" to perform government duties.[144]

The four political consultants, in their op-ed article, provided a more persuasive (and also more succinct) defense of their non-employee status than did the White House:

> Nor are we government employees. None of us has a phone or a desk or an office or a staff at the White House. None of us receives a dime from the American taxpayer. None of us has the power to make or enforce government decisions.[145]

While these factors are relevant to consider, they ignore the central factor that should be used to determine whether an informal adviser is an SGE: **is the adviser in fact performing a Federal function under the President's (or Chief of Staff's)**

supervision? Providing advice to the President is not inherently a Federal function, because the President receives advice from persons both inside and (clearly) outside of government. But an adviser who provides advice regularly, in official White House meetings, with other White House staff present, and which is often indistinguishable from the advice provided by the White House staff, most likely is performing a Federal function and serving as a *de facto* member of the White House staff.

The badges of government employment status—pay, title, paperwork, office, pass, and phone—are just that, indicia. They are concomitants of the exercise of a Federal function. The fundamental question remains whether the adviser is performing a Federal function. So the frequency of meetings, the nature of the meetings, and the manner in which the advice is solicited, given, and debated are all relevant. From what has been reported about the role of President Clinton's informal advisers, the better view would be that, at least Paul Begala was an SGE, and perhaps Mandy Grunwald, Stanley Greenberg and James Carville. Harry Thomason also should have been considered an SGE. Betsey Wright, Vernon Jordan, Harold Ickes, and Susan Thomases probably have not functioned as SGEs. Tony Coelho's role, first in 1993, then during the 1994 campaign, and now, is not as well known as the role played by the four political consultants and given such prominence in *Agenda* and *On The Edge*. From what has been reported of Dick Morris's advisory role, he certainly should be considered an SGE.

Having concluded that some of the President's advisers should have been considered SGEs does not mean that any engaged in conduct that would present a criminal conflict of interest under section 208. Aside from Harry Thomason's conduct in the Travel Office scandal, no such charge has been alleged, much less proven. Even if a particular conflict situation were identified, the failure of the White House to inform the advisers of their potential exposure to the criminal laws would make any prosecution highly unlikely.

Section 208 is not the only relevant ethics standard. The standards of conduct provide that employees shall not use public office for private gain, nor shall employees give preferential treatment to any person or entity. Even if the advisers are technically not subject to these standards either, the public's faith in the integrity of Government suffers if informal advisers are perceived as having special access without the accountability that accompanies a regular Executive Branch employee. Thus, other measures should be taken to avoid ethics concerns, even if not required by law.

The Steps Taken By the Four Main Informal Advisers

Apparently voluntarily, and without prompting, Begala, Carville, Greenberg, and Grunwald committed at the outset of the Administration to not engage in any lobbying or representational activity before the Federal Government on behalf of outside interests, as well as to refrain from representing foreign governments in connection with any matter. The pledge to refrain from making any communication or appearance before the Federal Government on behalf of any of their outside interests is a very effective measure to counter the notion that the advisers are trading on their close relationship with and access to the President.

While the Clinton White House consultants portrayed their self-restraint as an improvement over the role played by advisers to Presidents Reagan and Bush, the no-lobbying policy is in fact similar to the pledge made by senior Bush-Quayle cam-

paign officials during the 1992 campaign, and the pledge made by several professional spouses of cabinet and senior White House officials during the Bush Administration. Further, refraining from lobbying activity does not mean that the adviser is
refraining from giving advice to outside interests behind the scenes. These consultants did not pledge to not use information (public or deliberative) gathered in the
course of their participation in White House deliberations in discussions within their
business or with clients. Clearly, the degree of their access and influence in the White
House made each of these informal advisers, as well as the others, such as Betsey
Wright and Tony Coelho, very attractive to current and prospective clients interested
in matters pending with the White House, Executive Branch, or in Congress. So,
these advisers were (and are) still in a position to benefit outside interests and thus
receive personal financial gain.

Moreover, the consultants did not pledge to recuse themselves from any White
House meeting or discussion involving or having a direct and predictable effect on
their financial interests or clients, which the law would have required them to do
were they considered SGEs.

The Steps Taken By The White House

The White House took several steps, all of them in response to criticism from
the media and Congress, to address the ethics and security concerns posed by the
President's heavy reliance on outside advice.

First, in September 1993, the White House announced a new policy limiting
access to the White House. This step was in satisfaction of a recommendation of the
White House Management Review.

Second, around this same time, the White House Counsel's office gave one or
more **ethics briefings** to the political consultants. This also was a result of the Management Review.

Third, in March 1994, the four political consultants were directed to submit the
necessary paperwork to undergo the **full field FBI background investigation**. This
action was taken in response to media and congressional criticism.

Fourth, in June 1994, also in response to media and congressional criticism, the
four political consultants were required to file **financial disclosure** statements initially, and on an annual basis.

All of these steps, while they were reactive and late in coming, were nonetheless
steps in the right direction. On closer examination, however, they are far from adequate.

The **access** policy in fact only limits the number of persons able to obtain "blue"
White House passes. As the White House's experience with Dick Morris shows, this
policy does not limit any outside adviser's access to the White House, provided an
appointment is made beforehand with a member of the White House staff. A visitor's
pass is provided to persons who have an appointment with a White House staff member and who have previously furnished to that staff member their name, birth date
and social security number. Other than the cachet a White House pass signifies, the
pass only reduces the time and hassle involved in entry, to and exit from, the White
House complex. Without a blue pass, an adviser could be limited somewhat in the
amount of roaming around they can do once in the White House complex. But there
is little, if any, supervision of a visitor, once admitted, in the Old Executive Office
Building, and the West Wing offices all are in a tightly confined area. The access
policy also expressly permits White House passes to be issued to persons "retained"

by the DNC "whose duties require regular consultation with the President and his staff." This term would include Begala, Carville, Grunwald, Greenberg, Coelho, and now Morris (who is reportedly on the DNC payroll). Further, the access policy permits the Chief of Staff to provide a White House pass to other non-government persons upon a showing of exceptional circumstances. Thus, the access policy is more a symbolic limitation than a real one.

Requiring the four political consultants to undergo a **full field FBI background investigation** made sense, because of their regular presence in the White House. Whether other informal advisers should undergo a background investigation is uncertain. Clearly, if any adviser is privy to classified information, some background investigation must be conducted. Also, if any informal adviser is retained as an SGE, such as a speechwriter or a major participant in a war room type of project, an FBI background check would be in order. Finally, the full field investigation is also necessary if any of the advisers are given a White House pass.

The White House's initiation of **ethics briefings** for informal advisers was a positive step and should be institutionalized for all informal advisers on whom the President and White House staff depends, not just the four political consultants who received ethics briefings in the fall of 1993. Of course, the ethics briefings must go beyond a statement that the advisers are not subject to the ethics laws, even if such a statement is correct. First, the advisers should be told what actions and conduct they must refrain from to avoid becoming an SGE (and that the status of an SGE triggers the criminal conflict-of-interest provisions). For instance, an adviser cannot chair or schedule a White House meeting, or supervise the work of White House staff, or participate in any official decisionmaking chain.

Second, the advisers should be told that so long as they are being called upon as individuals, and not as representatives of special or specified interests, the advisers will be treated as if they are subject to the conflict-of-interest laws. Thus, they should be told they must not participate in any deliberations involving a particular matter in which they, their business or their clients have a financial interest. If there are any doubts about whether the matter to be discussed is "particular" or whether the matter would have a "direct and predictable effect" on their financial interest, the question should be forwarded to the Counsel's office **before** the discussion begins. Even for broad policy matters that the Counsel's office determines are not "particular matters," White House officials should be aware of financial interests or affiliations of the adviser that could be significantly affected by the outcome of the matter.

Third, the advisers should be counseled not to use the fruits of their White House access for the benefit of their clients by sharing nonpublic and predecisional information gathered while at the White House. Apparently, the White House has so advised the political consultants.[146]

If the White House does not wish to subject their informal advisers to the rigors of recusal, at a minimum the President and senior White House staff should be aware of the advisers' financial interests, so that any advice given by an adviser can be put in the proper context.

Either way, the advisers must be required to disclose their financial interests to the White House. The White House's decision to require the four political consultants to file a **financial disclosure** report was a good start. But under the policy, no financial disclosure is required of informal advisers who do not hold, or seek to hold, a White House pass. This is a considerable loophole, because an informal adviser does not need anything other than a visitor's pass to enter the White House. If Carville and others surrendered their blue White House passes, as reported, they are no longer required to file an annual report. It is unknown whether any annual report was filed in May 1995 by an informal adviser pursuant to this policy. And Dick Morris was not required to submit a report until the *USA Today* reported Morris' non-filing as an "ethics loophole."

The financial disclosure directive also is confined to "political advisers or political consultants." Thus, informal advisers without a formal relationship with the DNC, such as Vernon Jordan, Betsey Wright, and Susan Thomases, do not appear to be covered—yet another loophole in the directive.

The amount of information required to be disclosed—essentially what most special Government employees would be required to disclose on an SF-450, plus clients who have provided more than $5,000 compensation during the reporting period—appears adequate. The major difference between what senior White House staff must report and what the informal advisers would be required to report is the value of each of the assets and the amount of income derived from each asset. Without this information, as noted by the media, one cannot determine if any of the advisers is getting rich off of their association with the President, or if any adviser is being paid by a third party primarily, if not exclusively, to advise the White House. The argument for requiring informal advisers to report the information required of senior White House staff, the SF-278, is that they are functionally equivalent to senior White House staff. All Commissioned Officers on the White House Office staff (all Assistants, Deputy Assistants, and Special Assistants to the President) must file an SF-278. The staff members who file a SF-450 are lower-ranking aides. Given the role Begala and the other advisers have played and the role Dick Morris plays currently, the information required on an SF-278 would be more appropriate. However, the information contained on an SF-450 is sufficient to guard against conflicts of interest.

Thus, on balance, there is not much to be gained by requiring additional information. What is important is that all regular informal advisers file a report, whether or not they hold a White House pass, and whether or not they are labeled as a political consultant.

The other major difference between an SF-278 and an SF-450 is that the former is public and the latter is confidential. It is reasonable to make the financial reports of informal advisers publicly available, so long as they are functioning on a par with senior White House staff. Given an adviser's general lack of accountability, it would be appropriate to make all informal advisers' reports publicly available, as an extra check on potential abuse of the consultant relationship.

So the financial disclosure policy appears largely as a one-time response to media and congressional criticism, rather than an institutionalized policy to guard against conflicts of interest.

Recommendations and Conclusions

The concept of an SGE needs to be reexamined in light of the increasing reliance of Presidents on the advice and counsel of persons not formally employed by the Government. Currently, the line between an SGE subject to the criminal conflict-of-interest laws, and a non-government person not subject to any ethics standards, is not at all bright. A continuum exists, from the one-time visit with the President, to he periodic one-on-one visits by the President's pollster, to the regular participation in White House meetings, to the adviser with a White House pass, office and phone. Harry Thomason and Paul Begala were far enough along the continuum to be considered SGEs, although the White House did not so conclude. Dick Morris should be regarded as one now. With the others, it is not at all clear whether the law covered them.

The use of the definition of "officer" and "employee" in the personnel statutes, 5 U.S.C. 2104 and 2105, is neither correct nor very helpful. Yet, any attempt to clarify the definition of SGE to take into account the status of regular informal advisers may suffer from over- or under-inclusiveness. Codification of the functional tests used by Justice and OGE would be helpful, if only to dispel the notion that the absence of a formal appointment or paperwork is dispositive. But codification of the functional test does not obviate the exercise of judgment and discretion within the White House.

In any event, ethics concerns do arise with advisers without regard to whether they are technically SGEs. Thus, the two most meaningful steps to take are:

(1) require financial disclosure reports, initially and annually, of all informal White House advisers other than obvious representatives (e.g., the head of the AFL-CIO, the President of the National Organization for Women), making those reports publicly available; and

(2) treat the regular informal advisers as if they were subject to the conflict-of-interest laws, by requiring their recusal, or at least a declaration of their interests, affiliations, and clients (in essence, treating them as a representative of their interests for that purpose).

Ultimately, Presidents must exercise more discipline in their use of informal advisers. Structures and processes can be put in place to keep the informal advisers from policymaking deliberations and other official decisionmaking. The White House under Leon Panetta has apparently put a structure in place to ensure that the Chief of Staff is able to supervise the role and activities of the informal advisers, but Dick Morris's prominent place in the White House demonstrates the limits of any structure. Advisers can be kept from other White House staff, and can meet only with the President and a handful of senior aides present in the Oval Office, but no structure is going to keep anyone whose advice the President wants to hear from providing the President with that advice.

Further, no distinction between official and political advice is likely to work, anyway; in the White House, most actions are seen and packaged in a political light, even if they are taken on the merits.[147] It is disingenuous for the four political consultants to state that they "stick to political consulting," if by that statement they mean to suggest they do not get involved with official government policy. *Agenda* and *On The Edge* completely refute that explanation away.

Similarly, Dick Morris may be called a political adviser, but he clearly has been identified as involved centrally in official White House policy deliberations. Of the President's speeches and policy pronouncements in which Dick Morris has been identified as playing an instrumental role, some (if not most) have been characterized (properly) as official acts.

Part Three

The White House Struggles
with the Past

Chapter Seven

Whitewater in Washington

Whitewater and Madison: A Washington Chronology

The following is an account of the Washington developments in the so-called Whitewater matter, from the time reports first surfaced of a Resolution Trust Corporation (RTC) investigation of Madison Guaranty Savings & Loan (Madison), involving Whitewater Development Corporation (Whitewater), a company half-owned by the Clintons. These developments are discussed in the order in which they were reported or revealed.

This is not a complete chronology, however, for as this book went to press—three years into the Clinton Administration—additional material facts were being revealed on a regular basis, in Senate hearings and by the media. Senate hearings were expected to continue through February 1996, and the independent counsel investigation conducted by Ken Starr was expected to continue well into 1996 and perhaps beyond. As this chapter will demonstrate, the initial account of an event, a meeting, or a conversation often changed as additional facts and testimony came to light, months, even years, later.

The following chapter is an attempt to analyze the Washington aspects of the Whitewater controversy, based on this ever-developing, ever-changing tableau.

Initial Reports of the RTC's Criminal Referrals

Beginning in October 1993, reports surfaced that Madison Guaranty Savings & Loan, a defunct S&L owned by Arkansas businessman James B. McDougal, and Whitewater Development Corporation, a real estate venture half-owned by the Clintons and James McDougal and his wife Susan, were under investigation by the RTC and the United States Attorney in Little Rock. Within a matter of days, a number of news reports on the investigations and the underlying facts on the Clintons' investments and associations appeared.

The initial news report in the *Washington Post* revealed that in early October 1993 the RTC referred a series of allegations to the U.S. Attorney in Little Rock with a request to open up a criminal investigation of Madison.[1] The allegation given the most attention at the time was that Madison used depositors' funds improperly to contribute to Governor Clinton's 1986 gubernatorial campaign. The RTC referrals also reportedly included unspecified allegations involving real estate transactions of Whitewater Development, which maintained an account at Madison. The *Post* noted that "[t]here was protracted debate within the RTC about whether Madison transactions involving the Clintons should be included" in the referral, ostensibly because the investigation relates primarily to Madison officials' (i.e., Jim McDougal's) handling of the S&L funds.

Two days later, the *Post* expanded on the probe of Whitewater, noting that the RTC was questioning Whitewater's purchase in 1986 of rural property owned by the International Paper Company. The RTC requested that the U.S. Attorney open "a broad probe into whether Madison's depositor funds were improperly used to benefit local politicians," including whether funds were used to help retire Governor Clinton's 1984 gubernatorial campaign debt.[2] The *Post* also reported an allegation made by David Hale, former President of Capital Management Services, that in 1986 Governor Clinton and James McDougal pressured Hale to approve a $300,000 Small Business Administration (SBA) -backed loan to Susan McDougal, who arguably did not properly qualify for the loan.[3] A portion of this loan allegedly was used by Whitewater to purchase land from International Paper. Hale went public with this allegation while under indictment on fraud charges involving Capital Management. Before his indictment in September 1993, Hale offered to cooperate with the Government by sharing information about alleged misconduct by Arkansas political figures, but was rebuffed by Paula Casey, the U.S. Attorney in Little Rock who had been recently appointed by President Clinton.

The RTC also reportedly asked the U.S. Attorney to investigate current Arkansas Governor Jim Guy Tucker's business dealings with Madison.[4]

Other reports focused on the propriety of the Rose Law Firm's representation of Madison and, subsequently, the Federal Government in an action against Madison's former outside accounting firm.[5] Mrs. Clinton, Webster Hubbell, Vince Foster, and William Kennedy all were partners in the Rose Law Firm during this time.

On November 9, 1993, the Justice Department designated a special three-person prosecutorial team from Main Justice to handle the investigations following the recusal of Paula Casey.[6] Associate Attorney General Webster Hubbell also recused himself from the investigations because of his prior work for Madison as a Rose Law Firm partner, his close friendship with the Clintons, and his father-in-law's dealings with Madison. Hubbell was reported to have recused himself in October or November 1993, although it was unclear precisely when he did so.[7] Representative Jim Leach called for the House Banking Committee, of which Leach was Ranking Member, to hold hearings on Madison.[8] Leach also wrote letters to several Federal banking agencies, and to the President's personal attorney, seeking documents and information on Madison.

Whitewater Files Reported Removed From Foster's Office

In November and December 1993, news reports quieted down. The lull ended with the December 20, 1993, report by Jerry Seper of the *Washington Times* that records relating to Whitewater were found in Vince Foster's office after his death on July 20, 1993, removed by White House officials, and sent to the attorney representing Foster's family, James Hamilton.[9] Later that day, the White House confirmed the removal of certain Whitewater records on **July 22** from Foster's office, but stated that files on the Clintons' investments, including Whitewater, were sent by the White House Counsel to the Clintons' personal attorney and not the attorney for Foster's family.[10]

Foster had continued to serve as the Clintons' personal attorney after he became Deputy Counsel to the President in January 1993. In December 1992, before the inauguration, Foster handled the sale of the Clintons' one-half interest in Whitewater to McDougal. While serving in the White House, "Foster had prepared delinquent tax returns for Whitewater that were sent to McDougal in June for transmittal to the IRS."[11] Foster also worked on establishing a blind trust for the Clintons' assets.[12]

The White House Considers Whether to Release the Whitewater Files

Initially, the White House declined to release the Whitewater documents found in Foster's office or describe their contents. Press Secretary Dee Dee Myers said, "Being forthcoming, who I think the president and first lady have been, doesn't mean that you have to turn over every single file."[13] Another unnamed White House official said the Clintons were "entitled to the same privileges as other citizens when it comes to their personal records."[14]

On December 22, 1993, the President pledged his cooperation with the criminal investigations:

> [The file] related to work [Foster] had done before he came to work at the White House on our behalf. . . . There was never any indication that anyone wanted to see it. Obviously if anybody wants to—feels that there's some relevance to any ongoing investigation, we'll do what we can to cooperate.[15]

But the President added, "I have no reason to believe at this time that anybody thinks there's anything in there relevant to any ongoing matter."[16]

White House officials quickly qualified the President's pledge to cooperate, noting that he reserved the right to withhold any document he considered protected by the attorney-client privilege.[17] And the First Lady told reporters:

> I am bewildered that a losing investment . . . is still a topic of inquiry. . . . I think we've done what we should have done and don't feel the need to do any more than we've done.[18]

Also on December 22, Representative Leach wrote Attorney General Reno, requesting the appointment of a special counsel to take over the Justice Department's investigation of Madison and Whitewater. Senators Bob Dole and Alfonse D'Amato called for a Senate Banking Committee hearing.[19] Senate Banking Committee Chairman Don Riegle said the next day that he would not go forward with hearings "in the midst of an active investigation."[20]

The Attorney General told reporters that she would not appoint a special counsel because, without a statutory independent counsel, such a person would not be truly independent. She said that her selection of a special counsel:

> has almost more political implications than letting career prosecutors who have worked for several administrations and who have real experience in federal prosecution conduct it in the right way.[21]

> If I appoint a special prosecutor, it's still my prosecutor, and there will still be questions about that person's independence. . . . If I'm going to be responsible for the outcome of an investigation, then I want to make sure that it's done the right way.[22]

On December 23, the President directed his personal attorney, David Kendall, to give "all documents" relating to Whitewater to the Justice Department. White House aide Mark Gearan stated, "The president has voluntarily decided to release these documents for whatever relevance they may have to any Department of Justice law enforcement inquiries."[23] Gearan added that Justice had not requested the documents.[24] At the same time, however, the White House stated that the documents would **not** be turned over to the media, or to Leach, who had requested the documents in a letter to David Kendall.[25]

Two weeks later, however, it was revealed that on December 23, the same day the President had "voluntarily decided" to provide Justice with the Whitewater files, Kendall—with the knowledge of the White House Counsel's office and at the direction of the President—had discussed the Whitewater files with the Justice Department and had sought a subpoena of those documents for the purpose of shielding them from public view.[26] A subpoena was served on Kendall the next day, December 24. The documents were required to be provided by January 18, 1994.[27]

On January 2, 1994, George Stephanopoulos and Jeff Eller separately asserted that the Whitewater files had been turned over to Justice. In fact, no document had been turned over. On January 3, Dee Dee Myers acknowledged that the documents had not yet been provided, and would not be for "a couple weeks." Noting the volume of documents, Myers stated: "And **we** just want to make sure that it's catalogued, it's complete, and **we** will hand it over to the Justice Department."[28] These tasks were performed by the Clintons' personal attorney, although Kendall would coordinate the "processing" of them with the White House Counsel.[29]

Bruce Lindsey said that Kendall sought the subpoena "to assure the integrity of the documents and the privacy of the process as provided for by federal law."[30] Another account reported that the subpoena was the White House's idea: "'The staff discussions of this,' said one official, 'were that we should ask for a subpoena because then it becomes a crime to leak them and maybe that would keep them from being leaked.'"[31] Dee Dee Myers said, "It protects the confidentiality of the process."[32]

The White House also confirmed a report that when Kendall called the Justice Department to request a subpoena, Kendall was informed that a subpoena had already been drafted. Kendall then proceeded to seek an expansion of the subpoena's scope.[33] Lindsey added that the President had directed Kendall to negotiate with Justice. Lindsey reiterated that the Clintons "see no reason to publicly release" the documents, because of their private nature.[34]

Recall that Mark Gearan asserted on the morning of December 23 that the Justice Department had not requested the documents. After Kendall's December 23 discussions with Justice were revealed on January 5, Gearan explained that at the time he made the statement on the 23rd, "neither the president nor I" nor other senior officials were aware of the draft subpoena.[35]

Even before the disclosure of the subpoena, Senate Minority Leader Dole and House Minority Whip Newt Gingrich joined Leach's call for the appointment of a special counsel.[36]

The *Washington Post* also reported that the White House had put together a damage control team, under the direction of Harold Ickes, newly appointed Deputy Chief of Staff (as of January 4), and had begun daily strategy meetings.[37] The team consisted of Lindsey, David Gergen, Stephanopoulos, Gearan, and two outside advisers, Paul Begala and James Carville. The *Post* later reported that the damage control team was contemplating a strategy that would entail "selective public release of documents turned over to the Justice Department[.]"[38] Although White House officials had previously resisted public disclosure, relying heavily on the grand jury subpoena, the *Post* reported that "administration officials said the Clintons are not prohibited from releasing their own records."[39]

A Special Counsel is Appointed

The chorus for the appointment of a special counsel to conduct the Whitewater and Madison investigation grew almost daily from the close of December 1993 into the new year. First, several newspapers joined the Republicans' call for the appointment of a special counsel.[40] For several days, the Attorney General and the White House both resisted the suggestion. Attorney General Reno gave a little ground on January 6, when she (and her aides) indicated she would likely request the appointment of an independent counsel if the independent counsel law were reenacted.[41] But the Attorney General was careful to note that she would have to review the language of such a law before committing to seek an independent counsel.[42] Next, several Democratic Senators, starting with Senator Patrick Moynihan on January 9, urged the President to agree to an appointment of a special counsel.[43] This seemed to change the President's mind, and he let the Attorney General know on January 12 of his desire that a special counsel be appointed. Stephanopoulos stated:

> There have been no credible allegations of wrongdoing by the Clintons in this matter, and the president has full confidence in the ability of the Justice Department to independently and properly investigate this matter.
>
> Nevertheless, the president has decided to ask the attorney general to resolve the issues surrounding the controversy through a special counsel in order to ensure the public a full and fair accounting of this matter.[44]

On January 20, 1994, Attorney General Reno appointed as Special Counsel Robert Fiske, a Republican, New York lawyer, and a former United States Attorney. Fiske said that the Attorney General allowed him to craft his own charter. "I have been told time and time again by the top officials of the Justice Department, including the attorney general, that there are no limits on what I can do."[45] Fiske's charter was issued as a Department of Justice (DoJ) regulation. The basic substantive grant of authority provides the "Independent Counsel: in re Madison Guaranty Savings & Loan Association" with jurisdiction to investigate:

> whether any individuals or entities have committed a violation of any federal criminal or civil law relating in any way to President William Jefferson Clinton's or Mrs. Hillary Rodham Clinton's relationships with: (1) Madison Guaranty Savings & Loan Association; (2) Whitewater Development Corporation; or (3) Capital Management Services.[46]

In addition, Fiske was given authority to investigate other allegations or evidence of a violation of Federal criminal or civil law by any person or entity that is developed during Fiske's investigation and "connected with or arising out of that investigation[,]" as well as to investigate any false statement or obstruction of justice, or recalcitrant witness, in connection with his investigation.[47] Fiske added that his investigation would look into Vince Foster's death to determine whether it was in any way related to the Whitewater or Madison matters.[48]

The DoJ regulation concerning the general powers of special counsel provides that a special counsel, such as Fiske, may be removed by the Attorney General "for good cause."[49] But the Attorney General said, "I expect him to report to the American people, and I do not expect to monitor him."[50] Fiske said he expected that both the President and the First Lady would be asked to provide testimony under oath.[51]

Fiske set up an office in Little Rock and one in Washington. Within a couple or weeks, he obtained a court order to impanel a special grand jury in Arkansas to hear testimony limited to his investigation.[52]

Notwithstanding the appointment of a special counsel, Senator Dole and House Minority Leader Bob Michel called for the establishment of a select congressional committee to conduct hearings. A select committee was necessary, Michel said, because the two Banking Committee Chairmen, Senator Riegle and Representative Henry Gonzalez, had refused to hold hearings.[53] Fiske was cool to the idea, saying on the day his appointment was announced, "I think the history of these situations is that it is difficult to conduct this kind of investigation at the same time a congressional investigation is going on."[54] Democrats and the White House resisted this call, as well, expressing concerns that a parallel congressional investigation could interfere with Fiske's investigation.[55]

Republicans soon withdrew their push for a select committee, faced with the opposition of the Democratic leadership, but continued to seek oversight hearings by both Banking Committees.[56] Speaker Thomas Foley, however, declined to direct any committee to hold hearings, stating that "[t]here is no evidence of any credible nature pertaining to any misconduct by the president or first lady."[57] Republicans focused on House and Senate Banking Committee rules that provide for oversight hearings of the RTC once every six months; the Senate Banking Committee had not held an RTC oversight hearing since March 1993.[58] Banking Committee Chairmen Riegle and Gonzalez soon relented, promising oversight hearings later in February, yet, at the same time, continuing to oppose any inquiry into Madison and Whitewater that would overlap with the Special Counsel's investigation.[59]

At the Senate Banking Committee confirmation hearing of Ricki Tigert to chair the Federal Deposit Insurance Corporation (FDIC), held on February 1, 1994, Republicans pressed Tigert to recuse herself from participating in the FDIC's investigation of Madison, because of her personal friendship with the Clintons. Tigert declined to do so, pledging only to be sensitive to potential conflicts and to seek the advice of ethics officials.[60] When Republicans threatened to put a hold on her nomination, Tigert agreed to recuse herself from participating in any matter "concerning President or Mrs. Clinton in their personal capacities."[61] Tigert's recusal satisfied Senator D'Amato, but not Senator Lauch Faircloth, who asked Tigert to expand her recusal to include matters concerning Webster Hubbell, Vince Foster, and others, and to include matters in which the Clintons were involved in their "official capacities."[62] Tigert did not reply to this letter, and was approved by the Senate Banking Committee on February 10 over the lone opposition of Faircloth.[63]

On February 9, the *Washington Times* reported that, according to an employee of the Rose Law Firm, Whitewater-related documents (otherwise unidentified) in possession of the firm had been shredded recently.[64] The Special Counsel's office promptly determined to investigate the shredding allegation, as the Rose Law Firm issued a categorical denial.[65]

Around this time the RTC initiated a separate review to determine whether Madison should have been closed before 1989 and whether any person may be sued to recover the millions of Federal funds lost when Madison folded.[66] The first report of the RTC's review quietly mentioned that the agency had hired the firm of Pillsbury, Madison & Sutro to assist it. This retention would soon set off a firestorm of controversy (initially within the White House), because of former U.S. Attorney Jay Stephens' involvement in this matter as a partner of the Pillsbury firm.

The FDIC Issues Reports Finding No Conflicts-of-Interest Involving the Rose Law Firm

After Madison's failure in 1989, the Rose Law Firm, in a letter to the FDIC signed by Vince Foster, sought to represent the agency in a suit against Frost & Co., Madison's former accounting firm, which the FDIC alleged contributed to Madison's failure and to the Government's losses. The letter, using the present tense, asserted that the firm "does not represent any savings and loan association in state or federal regulatory matters." No mention was made of the firm's previous representation of Madison. The Rose Law Firm won the job, and Hubbell served as lead attorney. The FDIC sought $10 million in compensatory damages and another $10 million in punitive damages. The Rose Law Firm settled the suit for $1 million, much less than the amount of Frost's liability coverage, and received $400,000 in legal fees and expenses from this amount.

Two allegations of a conflict of interest were made involving the Rose Law Firm's representation of the FDIC. First, the firm (Hillary Clinton and others) had represented Madison several years earlier, asserting Madison's solvency before Arkansas State regulators and seeking approval to raise capital by issuing preferred stock, in part based on a 1984 audit by Frost; the firm, however, did not inform the FDIC of this prior representation. Second, Hubbell's father-in-law, Seth Ward, was in litigation with the Government over loans and commissions he earned as an executive of Madison, and records of Ward's loans would be used as evidence against Frost. After conducting a review of these allegations, the FDIC in February 1994 ruled that there was "no basis to determine that either of the alleged instances involved a conflict of interest."[67]

Although at the time of the Rose Law Firm's representation, attorneys within the FDIC raised questions about the propriety of retaining the firm given Hubbell's relationship with Ward,[68] the FDIC ruled that no conflict-of-interest standards existed in 1989 that required Hubbell to disclose potential conflicts. The FDIC acknowledged that, in part because of inadequate standards, "documentation regarding the retention of the firm is more limited that would be ideally hoped for." Further, although FDIC employees were not informed of the Rose Law Firm's prior work for Madison,[69] the FDIC determined that even had it known of the earlier representation, it would not have precluded the FDIC's retention of the firm. The FDIC stated that there was no indication that the Rose Law Firm "did anything more with respect to the audit . . . than take it at face value in its representation in 1985. As a consequence, the firm's representation in 1985 was not 'directly adverse' to its representation . . . in 1989."

Also in February, the FDIC determined that Mrs. Clinton did not violate any conflict-of-interest laws when she represented the Federal Savings and Loan Insurance Corporation (FSLIC) on a $3.3 million claim of the defunct First American S&L against Lasater & Company, which was settled in 1987 for $200,000. Lasater & Company is owned by Dan Lasater, a friend of the Clintons, political contributor to Governor Clinton's campaigns, and onetime employer of the President's half-brother. With Governor Clinton's assistance, Lasater & Company won a lucrative contract with the Arkansas State Government to handle a state bond issue for a new police radio system.[70] The FDIC ruled that Mrs. Clinton's involvement in the matter was too insubstantial to support the allegation that she influenced the decision to settle the claim, although she had signed an amended complaint that reduced the Government's claim to $1.3 million.[71]

The February 24 Hearing Before the Senate Banking Committee

Republicans seized on the FDIC's conflicts rulings during a Senate Banking Committee oversight hearing on February 24, 1994. Senators D'Amato and Faircloth obtained a pledge from the Acting Chairman of the FDIC to refer the reports to the agency's IG for a review.[72] D'Amato referred also to a February 8 report prepared by the **RTC** that came to a somewhat different conclusion than the **FDIC** on the question of the propriety of the Rose Law Firm's representation of the FDIC against Frost. The RTC staff report, which had been sent to the RTC's General Counsel for review, determined that the Rose Law Firm failed to disclose the potential conflict of interest resulting from the firm's prior representation of Madison. The Acting FDIC Chairman explained that the RTC regulations at the time were stricter than the FDIC regulations, which were concerned only with actual conflicts of interest, not with appearances of a conflict. D'Amato criticized the RTC's review, too, because it did not interview any current or former employee of the Rose Law Firm (i.e., Mrs. Clinton and Hubbell). Deputy Treasury Secretary Roger Altman, in his capacity as acting head of the RTC, also agreed to refer the RTC's review to the RTC's IG.

Of eventually much greater import was Roger Altman's testimony at the February 24 hearing. Altman, asked what contacts he had had with the White House relating to the Madison investigation, disclosed that he had offered and given a "heads up" briefing to White House officials earlier that month on the imminent expiration of the statute of limitations for civil claims against Madison's officers, directors, and lawyers.[73] In the meeting, held at the White House on February 2, Altman explained to White House Counsel Bernard Nussbaum, Harold Ickes, and Margaret (Maggie) Williams (the First Lady's Chief of Staff) that the RTC had to determine the merits of potential claims and either file those claims it found meritorious by February 28, 1994, or obtain a waiver of the deadline from the putative defendants to the claim.[74] (Soon after that meeting, Congress extended the statute of limitations for the class of such suits until the end of 1995.)

Altman and White House officials defended the meeting, explaining that Altman provided Nussbaum and others only with "the legal and procedural framework in which the RTC was working[,]" and informed them only of information Altman had provided to Members of Congress who had inquired about how the RTC would handle the Madison case. Altman added that he told the White House that he had instructed the RTC to handle Madison on an "exactly identical" basis as that which the RTC used on other cases.[75]

The next day, however, Altman conceded that he used "bad judgment" by offering the briefing,[76] and decided to recuse himself from participating any further in the Madison matter, in order to avoid any appearance of impropriety.[77] Altman also announced that, as expected, he would end his interim term as acting head of the RTC on March 30. Altman reportedly had asked both Treasury and RTC ethics officials if he "should recuse himself from Madison issues, and was told he wasn't legally obligated to do so[.]"[78]

Both the *Washington Post* and the *New York Times* castigated Altman and the White House for the briefing. The *Post* calmly stated that Altman's "heads up" was inappropriate because Altman is the head of an agency intended to be independent of political influence or direction and that the Clintons are Altman's "friends and who are also potential defendants in RTC civil suits." The *Post* also faulted the White House officials who agreed to such a briefing, because the "Whitewater probe is a personal matter for the Clintons and does not involve the presidency. . . . White House staff, absent a showing of an official link to the White House, should keep their hands off the probe."[79] The *New York Times* was much less kind, calling the "boneheaded conclave"

> improper on its face. It could never have taken place in a White House that had even a rudimentary respect for the common-sense rules on conflict of interest. The Clinton team has taken the nation back to the sham ethics of the early Reagan Administration.[80]

The *Times* called on Senator Riegle to "step up" his oversight activities and Speaker Foley and Majority Leader George Mitchell "to try to educate this White House about the normal protocols of governance. Explaining what Representative Leach meant when he said 'arm's length' would be a start."[81]

Republicans eventually found their voice on this meeting, too. On March 1, Leach asked OGE to determine the ethical propriety of the meeting, and called upon Altman to resign immediately from his general supervision of the RTC, concluding that Altman had "compromised" the RTC's independence. Senators Dole and D'Amato urged another Banking Committee hearing be held to take testimony under oath from the participants of the meeting; D'Amato called Altman's account a "fairy tale version." He said that "[n]o one who has ever taken Ethics 101 would have attended that meeting."[82] D'Amato also took issue with Altman's statement that he had provided similar briefings to the Hill, because at the time of Altman's White House briefing, D'Amato had yet to receive any information from RTC in response to his request.[83]

In a March 3 column, Al Hunt was the first to call for Nussbaum's dismissal, blaming him for allowing the Altman "heads up" briefing to take place, as well as other unspecified problems.[84] While arguing that Whitewater was not Watergate, Hunt criticized the Clinton White House, including the First Lady, for a "Whitewater paranoia" that led to mishandling of the growing scandal.

Additional Contacts Between Treasury and White House Officials are Revealed

The March 3, 1994 *Washington Post* reported that, months before Altman's "heads up" briefing, Treasury officials twice had briefed White House officials on the status of the RTC's investigation of Madison.[85] The initial *Post* report noted that the meetings occurred "just after" the RTC had sent a series of criminal referrals to the Justice Department, but in fact, the first of these meetings, held on September 29, 1993, occurred **before** the referral document was sent to Justice (on October 8).[86]

At the September 29 meeting, Jean Hanson visited Nussbaum to inform him that criminal referrals involving Madison had been prepared by the RTC for the Justice Department's consideration. Hanson told Nussbaum that the Clintons were named in RTC referral documents, not as targets, but as "potential beneficiaries" of misconduct. At the time, the RTC was without a General Counsel, so Hanson was said to be heavily involved in the oversight of RTC legal issues.[87]

A White House official said the next day that Nussbaum "had done nothing with the information except to share it with Bruce Lindsey[.]" (This just triggered the question as to what Lindsey did with the information.) Dee Dee Myers said that Nussbaum had the impression that the referral to Justice was a "fait accompli."[88]

The second meeting at the White House, held on October 14, 1993 in Nussbaum's office, was called by Treasury ostensibly to discuss how to respond to media questions on Madison and Whitewater. Present from Treasury were Hanson, Chief of Staff Josh Steiner, and Press Secretary Jack Devore. Lindsey and Gearan attended with Nussbaum. Lindsey said the meeting did not discuss the substance of the investigation.

A third additional contact, in late October or early November 1993, was Lisa Caputo's return of a phone call from an unidentified RTC employee, who informed Caputo, the First Lady's Press Secretary, of press inquiries involving Whitewater and Madison. Caputo said "she did not take action or brief anyone because of the call." White House officials "dismissed [the contact] as inconsequential."[89]

Hanson received the information about the RTC referrals and the naming of the Clintons from Bill Roelle, Senior Vice President of the RTC. The RTC has a strict policy against disclosing the contents of a criminal referral to those who are named in them. The *Washington Post* noted that "Treasury officials said [Altman] was unaware of the earlier White House meetings." This would turn out to be a critical question, because Altman had testified on February 24 that he knew of only one meeting between Treasury and White House officials relating to Madison and White-water.

The Administration Attempts Some Damage Control

Both the President and Treasury Secretary Lloyd Bentsen moved quickly to distance themselves from these briefings. The President said, "nearly as I can determine, nobody has done anything wrong or attempted to improperly influence any government action."[90] But he also said, "I think it would have been better if the meetings and conversations had not occurred."[91] The President directed Chief of Staff McLarty to issue a memorandum requiring any contact from an executive or independent agency relating to Madison or Whitewater to be referred to Deputy White House Counsel Joel Klein, bypassing Nussbaum, for a determination of whether to refer the contact to the Clintons' personal attorney, and no contact on these matters should be made by any White House official to an executive or independent agency without clearance by Klein.[92] Nussbaum was reported prepared to resign.

Secretary Bentsen asked OGE to review the ethical propriety of the Treasury-White House meetings. He asserted that "I did not attend any of these meetings, nor was I informed of any of these meetings."[93] Leach also asked OGE to review these additional contacts.[94] Forty-three Republican Senators signed a letter pledging to hold up the nomination of Ricki Tigert to head the FDIC unless the Democrats agreed to hold hearings on these meetings.[95]

The White House was excoriated again in editorials. The *Washington Post* commented, "[i]t's a bad sign when the president has to order his own staff to refrain from engaging in the sort of conduct most first-year law students would immediately recognize as improper."[96] The *Washington Times*, arguing that the meetings were improper not simply for the appearance of impropriety, called for a congressional investigation.[97] And the *New York Times* called on Fiske to subpoena records and depose all participants in the meetings, and urged the dismissal of Nussbaum and Hanson. The editorial criticized the President's response as "tepid," concluding that:

> his Administration is easily the most reckless in interfering with the integrity of Federal investigative agencies since that of Richard Nixon. . . .
>
> All this paints a picture of a White House dedicated to shortcutting justice if that is what it takes to shield the financial affairs of Mr. Clinton, his wife and their friends from scrutiny.[98]

The Administration's efforts at damage control, although they were taken quickly, were immediately blunted by a *New York Times* report that the special grand jury in Little Rock had received testimony that some of Vince Foster's files at the Rose Law Firm had been shredded.[99] The employee did not notice any reference to Whitewater, however, and the firm denied that any Foster files had been destroyed. But the *Times* also reported that twice in the summer of 1992, a Rose Law Firm employee picked up documents from Mrs. Clinton at the Governor's Mansion for shredding at the law firm, and several times after the November election a courier picked up documents from Mrs. Clinton's office at the firm for disposal.[100]

Fiske also acted quickly, causing subpoenas to be issued on March 4 to six White House officials (Nussbaum, Ickes, Williams, Caputo, Lindsey, and Gearan) and four Treasury officials (Altman, Steiner, Hanson, and DeVore), requesting their appearance before a grand jury on March 10.[101] A subpoena was also issued for any documents relating to contacts between Treasury or RTC and White House officials on Madison or Whitewater. In three memoranda issued by Deputy Counsel Klein, the White House also took steps to protect documents, including those on computer, from destruction or revision. At the same time, it was reported that Nussbaum had offered to resign.

White House Counsel Nussbaum Resigns

Nussbaum announced his resignation on March 5, although it would not be effective until April 5, to give time to find a successor.[102] The *Washington Post* prophetically reported that White House officials were looking for a "Lloyd Cutler type" to replace Nussbaum.[103] In his letter of resignation to the President, Nussbaum maintained the propriety of his conduct:

> As I know you know, from the day I became Counsel, my sole objective was to serve you as well and as effectively as I could, consistent with the rules of law, standards of ethics, and the highest traditions of the Bar. At all times I have conducted the Office of White House Counsel and performed the duties of Counsel to the President in an absolutely legal and ethical manner. Unfortunately, as a result of controversy generated by those who do not understand, nor wish to understand the role and obligations of a lawyer, even one acting as White House Counsel, I now believe I can best serve you by returning to private life.[104]

The *Washington Post* responded to Nussbaum's letter, offering "another possibility" why Nussbaum was leaving: "Mr. Nussbaum not only failed to keep his principal client out of trouble; he also generated much of the controversy and troubles himself."[105] The *New York Times* wrote:

> Robert Fiske has stepped into the Whitewater mess with precisely the authority and integrity that the White House, particularly in the person of Bernard Nussbaum, has so conspicuously failed to exhibit over the last few months.[106]

While praising Fiske and damning Nussbaum, the *New York Times* urged Congress to "think twice" before conducting a parallel investigation into the Treasury-White House meetings.

Both the *Washington Times* and the *Wall Street Journal* criticized the Administration more broadly. "Whatever criminal proceedings will come out of Mr. Fiske's efforts, at the very least, we should have an administration scrubbed of the conceit that ethics laws apply only to their enemies."[107] The *Journal* noted that the "ethical blind spots go beyond Mr. Nussbaum," and included Altman and Hanson. And the *Journal* took issue with Nussbaum's view of his job:

> A White House counsel has to make hard calls, but he is still paid by the

taxpayers, which means he has a broader duty to the public trust. Just ask John Dean.[108]

The President Mounts a Defense, but Whitewater Reports Continue

On March 7, 1994, the President answered questions on Whitewater, fiercely defending the First Lady's conduct and his Administration's ethics, and outlining the remedial actions he had taken in the past few days.[109] He also attacked Republicans for "partisan clamor and careless use of language and careless use of the facts[.]" He denied any analogy between Whitewater and Watergate other than the "hysteria that [the Republicans] can gin up around it."[110]

But the President also admitted receiving advance notice of the RTC referrals:

> Sometime in October, I was—I became aware of—I don't know when, but sometime in October, I became aware of the RTC finding with regard to the question—the referral, I think it's called, on the question of whether my campaign benefited improperly from checks which allegedly came from the S&L, and I knew about that. That was—I don't remember when I knew about it or who told me about it, but it was just sort of presented as a fact, a decision that had been made by the Government. And I didn't think much about it at the time. It was just something that I absorbed. It was told to me just as something that the Government had decided to do. Otherwise, I was not aware of any of these things.[111]

Also on that day, Fiske wrote to both Banking Committee Chairmen, asking them to postpone hearings on Whitewater and Madison because he believed hearings "would pose a severe risk to the integrity of our investigation."[112] Fiske was concerned not only with the possible grant of congressional immunity, but with the risk of premature disclosure of information that could allow witnesses to alter their testimony and with the potential for improper disclosure of the contents of the RTC criminal referrals. Senator Riegle agreed to Fiske's request; Representative Gonzalez did so effectively. Although the House Banking Committee hearing scheduled for March 24 would be held, according to Gonzalez it would not include testimony from any of the subpoenaed witnesses.

On March 8, Whitewater-related developments occurred on four fronts. The President selected Lloyd Cutler, former White House Counsel to President Carter, to serve as the President's White House Counsel, for an interim period not expected to exceed 130 days.[113] Cutler was designated a "special Government employee (SGE)," allowing him to retain his name partnership at the law firm of Wilmer, Cutler & Pickering and to receive outside earned income during this time. Cutler accepted the position without salary, and indicated he would handle only "one or two cases" in private practice, neither of which would involve the Federal Government.

At the same time, the White House acknowledged that there were additional contacts between Treasury and White House officials other than the three meetings previously revealed.[114] These contacts came to light as a result of file searches conducted over the previous two days at the White House and Treasury Department. The President said that, "based on what we know now, . . . any contacts were incidental and were follow-up conversations which had nothing to do with the substance of the RTC investigation."[115]

The President also pledged openness and cooperation, denying any wrongdoing as well as the existence of a "bunker mentality" in the White House. He repeated his statement of the day before, when he acknowledged being informed of the RTC referral "sometime in October," but denied taking any action on the basis of that information. The President recalled that it was probably Bruce Lindsey who told him of the RTC referral:

> I didn't discuss it or ask anybody to do anything or take any action. That never occurred to me. It was just something that I was being given as a matter of information.[116]

Also on March 8, Representative Leach released a list of forty Administration officials whose testimony he would seek at the House Banking Committee hearing scheduled for March 24.[117] Several of these persons were also under subpoena to appear before the grand jury.

Finally, the Rose Law Firm employee who previously said he had shredded documents from the files of Vince Foster said that he was directed to shred the records after Fiske had been appointed and had indicated publicly that his investigation would cover the Foster death insofar as it related to Whitewater or Madison.[118] A Rose Law Firm official continued to deny that any of Foster's files were destroyed.

The immediate issue for the White House and Congress was whether Congress should go forward with hearings, or refrain from conducting any hearing in deference to the Special Counsel's criminal investigation. The theory that a congressional hearing would interfere with the criminal investigation depended largely on the possibility that Congress might grant immunity to persons under investigation. But the Republicans made it clear that no immunity should be given. Another concern, that potential witnesses would be allowed to tailor their testimony, could be resolved fairly easily by allowing—as Republicans said they would do—the Special Counsel to obtain statements from potential witnesses before any testified before Congress.[119] The last legitimate concern—that sensitive investigatory information would be disclosed—was largely within the Special Counsel's discretion. The real basis for the Democratic opposition to the hearings was, in reality, not much different from the basis for the Republican push for hearings: the hearings were expected to embarrass or reflect poorly on the Clintons and the Clinton Administration.[120]

After meeting with the Special Counsel, Senate Republicans agreed to delay hearings until the Special Counsel completed his investigation of whether the White House improperly interfered with the investigation of Madison.[121]

On March 10, three White House aides—Williams, Gearan, and Caputo—testified before the grand jury, and the White House turned over about a thousand pages of documents in response to the grand jury subpoena.[122]

On March 11, Leach wrote to Fiske, expressing concern that RTC employees in the agency's Kansas City office "are being gagged and possibly coerced by the Washington R.T.C. office."[123] Leach did not specify his concerns publicly, but reportedly did so in a separate, confidential letter to Fiske.

On March 12, *Time* and *Newsweek* published separate interviews with the First Lady.[124] Although she discussed the Clintons' Whitewater investment, reporters were not allowed to ask any question under the jurisdiction of the Special Counsel.

On March 13, Lloyd Cutler properly stated that questions about the Clintons' involvement in Madison and Whitewater should be directed to David Kendall, their private lawyer, because Madison and Whitewater are private matters.[125] Yet, in the very same interview, Cutler ventured two opinions on the facts. First, he predicted the Clintons' exoneration: "At least as far as even a breath of criminal activity by either the president and the first lady, it will turn out to be nothing at all."[126] Second, he stated:

> From everything I have heard, it seems to be clear that no effort was made by any White House people to indicate to the Treasury people what they ought to do, and, indeed, the Treasury and the R.T.C. did not change their position.[127]

On March 14, Hubbell announced his resignation as Associate Attorney General amid an internal investigation by the Rose Law Firm into his billing practices. At a fundraiser, the President said the Republican Party was "committed to a politics of personal destruction," adding, "I never did them the way they are doing us in Washington, D.C. It is wrong and it is not good for the United States of America."[128]

At a March 16 House Appropriations Subcommittee hearing on the budget for the Office of Government Ethics, OGE Director Potts said that, at the request of the Special Counsel, OGE had agreed to postpone its review of the contacts between White House and Treasury officials that was requested by Secretary Bentsen, until such time as the Special Counsel completed his investigation of the contacts.[129]

On March 17, as Nussbaum and Ickes appeared before the grand jury, it was reported that George Stephanopoulos had also received a grand jury subpoena, making him the eleventh Administration official to be subpoenaed over the White House-Treasury contacts.[130]

Congressional Hearings are Planned

Representatives Lee Hamilton and Paul McHale on March 15 became the first Democrats to suggest that hearings be held on Whitewater.[131] But House Banking Committee Chairman Gonzalez, facing a March 24 oversight hearing on the RTC, resisted. First, he wrote the RTC and the Office of Thrift Supervision, which had previously received a request for documents from Ranking Member Leach. Gonzalez assured the agencies that they need not provide Leach with any documents.[132] Second, Gonzalez informed potential witnesses at the March 24 oversight hearing that questions about Madison Guaranty would not be pertinent.[133] Third, Gonzalez rebuffed Leach's offer to postpone the hearing a couple of weeks to allow the Special Counsel to complete his own investigation of the White House-Treasury contacts.[134]

On March 17, the Senate approved 98-0 a resolution that was widely seen as a commitment to hold hearings on the Madison and Whitewater affair, but was actually an agreement merely to negotiate an "appropriate timetable, procedures and forum" for such hearings.[135] The resolution cited Congress's authority under Article I of the Constitution to hold oversight hearings and directed Senate leaders to determine the nature and timing of appropriate hearings. The resolution further specified that no witness called to testify would be granted immunity and that the hearings should be structured to avoid interfering with the Special Counsel's investigation.

On March 20, with his trial only eight days off, David Hale agreed to plead guilty to one count of conspiracy and one count of wire fraud in connection with Capital Management Services, although further details were not then available. Hale agreed to cooperate with the Special Counsel's investigation.[136] In return, the Government would not pursue four other counts, and Hale would avoid any jail time.

On March 21, *Time* picked up on the February 19 Associated Press story that the RTC had retained the law firm of Pillsbury, Madison & Sutro to investigate civil claims arising out of Madison's failure.[137] RTC regularly hires outside law firms to assist it, but what made this story newsworthy was that Jay Stephens was one of the Pillsbury attorneys who was expected to work on the case. Stephens, a longtime Republican official, had previously served as the U.S. Attorney for the District of Columbia until his abrupt removal in March 1993 as part of the nationwide removal of all U.S. Attorneys who were political appointees (nearly all of them). Stephens did not go quietly, writing an op-ed piece critical of the President's decision, in part because of Stephens' pending criminal investigation of House Ways and Means Chairman Dan Rostenkowski. Within one week, the RTC's retention of Stephens would return to the news, this time the front pages.

Also on March 21, Chairman Gonzalez appeared to relent in the calls for hearings into Whitewater, extolling the virtues of a public hearing: "The good people who have been smeared have the right to clear their names, and the country deserves the chance to expose the Republican witch hunt for what it is."[138] At the same time, however, Gonzalez canceled the March 24 RTC oversight hearing, suggesting instead the creation of a select committee.[139]

The very next day, the House voted 408-15 to hold hearings on Madison and Whitewater, in a resolution identical in language to the one passed by the Senate the previous week.[140] Speaker Foley noted, however, that the resolution did not guarantee hearings; hearings would be held only if an agreement were reached.

Also on March 22, the Senate Banking Committee released a March 21 letter from Altman disclosing additional discussions with the White House he had relating to Madison and Whitewater and details concerning such discussions.[141] It was the third such letter from Altman to Riegle following Altman's February 24 testimony before the Committee, and was sent the day before Altman's grand jury appearance. Altman recalled discussing with White House officials, among them Nussbaum, McLarty, and Ickes, whether Altman should recuse himself from the Madison investigation. The issue of recusal was brought up on February 2, at the same White House meeting held to discuss the running of the statute of limitations for civil claims, and discussed briefly again on February 23, the evening before Altman's testimony before the Committee.

Altman downplayed the significance of these contacts, adhering to his previous testimony that he had only one "substantive" contact with the White House (the February 2 meeting). He added that no one at the White House had asked him to not recuse himself. Yet, the *Washington Post* reported that the White House resisted Altman's inclination to recuse. In particular, Nussbaum was reported to have "expressed doubt that Altman needed to recuse himself and concern about who would oversee the case if Altman, a political appointee serving as acting head of the Resolution Trust Corp., did step down[.]"[142]

Leach's Charges

On March 24, Leach went to the House floor to deliver a speech in which he made a number of accusations of misconduct by Madison, Whitewater, and the Clinton Administration. Referring to the contacts between White House and Treasury officials, Leach stated:

> Perhaps laws have not been broken, but seldom have the public and private ethics of professionals in the White House and executive departments and branch agencies been so thoroughly devalued.[143]

Leach concluded that:

> ... Whitewater may have begun as a legitimate real estate venture but it came to be used to skim, directly or indirectly, federally insured deposits from an S&L and a Small Business Investment Corporation. When each failed, the U.S. taxpayer became obligated to pick up the tab[.][144]
>
> On the landscape of political scandals Whitewater may be a bump, but it speaks mountains about me-generation public ethics as well as single party control of certain States and the U.S. Congress.[145]

Leach specifically accused the Administration of attempting to interfere improperly in the development of the RTC's investigation. Based apparently on the story provided by Jean Lewis and other Kansas City RTC investigators, Leach pointed out that the first meeting between Treasury and White House officials (September 29, 1993) occurred just a few days after the Kansas City office had forwarded the criminal referrals to Washington:

> ... Within a few weeks, in an unprecedented change of procedure, Washington demanded to review all Madison referrals. Within a few months, a senior Kansas City criminal investigator [Lewis] was removed from the case. Within a few more months, officials from RTC Washington visited Kansas City to pass on the determined message that senior RTC officials in Washington wanted it understood that they wished to claim Whitewater was not responsible for any losses at Madison.[146]

Leach disclosed notes taken by Lewis of a conversation she had with April Breslaw from RTC headquarters on February 2, 1994:

> April stated that "the people at the top" keep getting asked about Whitewater[.] She said eventually "this group" is going to have to make a statement about whether or not Whitewater caused a loss to Madison .... April stated very clearly that [Jack] Ryan and [Ellen] Kulka, the "head people," would like to be able to say that Whitewater did not cause a loss to Madison, but the problem is that so far no one has been able to say that to them. She felt like they wanted to be able to provide an "honest answer," but that

there were certain answers that they would be "happier about, because it would get them off the hook."[147]

Lewis told Breslaw she could not make such a statement, and in fact believed that Whitewater did cause a loss to Madison.

Breslaw called Lewis's account of their conversation a "complete fabrication." "I categorically deny the accusation that I said that anybody from Washington wanted any particular outcome on any issue."[148] Breslaw reportedly thought that Lewis "exaggerat[ed] the situation to mask a poor investigation she conducted into the matter."[149] Leach responded by revealing that a tape surreptitiously made by Lewis of her conversation with Breslaw, which Leach had heard, supported Lewis's account.[150] Jack Ryan, RTC's Deputy CEO, and Ellen Kulka, RTC's General Counsel, both denied in a letter to Leach making any statement to Breslaw that Lewis (or Breslaw) attributed to them. They also stated that no pressure has been brought to bear on their exercise of their RTC responsibilities by any one in the White House or Treasury Department.[151]

Referring to the Treasury-White House contacts and what had allegedly occurred within the RTC, Leach concluded that "[t]he independence of the U.S. Government's regulatory system has been flagrantly violated in an effort to protect a single American citizen."[152]

The President's News Conference on Whitewater

That evening, March 24, 1994, the President held a news conference, at which the majority of questions related to Madison and Whitewater. He opened by asserting his total cooperation with the investigation being conducted by the Special Counsel, adding somewhat disingenuously, "whose appointment I supported."[153] He also said he would support congressional hearings, "at an appropriate time that does not interfere with Mr. Fiske's responsibilities. . . . Cooperation, disclosure, and doing the people's business are the order of the day."[154]

The President was asked to respond to Leach's allegations. He tried to deflect the allegation of improper pressure on the Kansas City RTC office by pointing out (accurately) that Leach did not "even charge that any political appointee of our administration had any knowledge of this."[155] He twice referred to RTC officials as Republican appointees, although this was clearly incorrect.[156]

The President also attempted to explain his and his wife's involvement in Whitewater, strongly defending his wife's conduct and ethics, but also revising downward by $20,000 the previously stated amount of money ($70,000) the Clintons claimed they lost on the investment.[157] The President presented a somewhat convoluted explanation as to how he came to realize the amount of loss was different than previously stated. His explanation raised as many questions as it answered that evening.[158]

The President also defended the White House's general ethics performance, comparing it favorably to previous administrations. He even claimed credit for his Administration's attempt to admit mistakes. Concerning the contacts between Treasury and White House officials, the President agreed that it would have been better had the contacts not occurred:

Yes, I think it would have been. Do we have people here who wouldn't do anything wrong but perhaps weren't sensitive enough to how something could look in retrospect by people who are used to having problems in a Presidency or used to having people not telling the truth? I think that we weren't as sensitive as we should have been. And I've said before, it would have been better if that hadn't occurred.[159]

Later in the press conference, he reflected on what he perceived to be a different ethics standard, "not of right and wrong, that doesn't change, but of what may appear to be right or wrong." He added that:

> because of the experiences of the last several decades, of which I was not part in this city, I think there is a level of suspicion here that is greater than that which I have been used to in the past[.][160]

Objecting to the RTC's Retention of Jay Stephens

On March 26, the *Washington Post* reported that in two conversations with Treasury officials, two White House officials, George Stephanopoulos and Harold Ickes, expressed their displeasure upon learning of the RTC's hiring of Jay Stephens and Pillsbury, Madison & Sutro to pursue civil claims involving Madison, and that one or both of them asked Treasury officials whether anything could be done to remove Stephens from the matter.[161] This story was also prominently reported by *Time* and *Newsweek*, which noted that these conversations were under investigation by Special Counsel Fiske to determine whether any White House official attempted improperly to influence the RTC's investigation.[162]

Ickes and Stephanopoulos had called Altman on February 25 to express their displeasure that Altman announced his decision to recuse without alerting the White House in advance,[163] as well as to protest the hiring of Stephens as an "outrageous choice." They also asked Altman (now recused) whether the decision to hire Stephens was final or whether it could be changed. Altman responded flatly that he would not be party to getting rid of Stephens, and told Josh Steiner, Treasury Secretary Bentsen's Chief of Staff, of the call. Stephanopoulos reportedly also called Steiner, although it is unclear whether this call followed or preceded the White House conversation with Altman. Stephanopoulos asked Steiner whether "anything could be done about it," but Steiner said nothing could be done. The White House denied that either Ickes or Stephanopoulos asked that the RTC's decision be changed. The denial, however, came in the form of a lack of recollection rather than a categorical denial. Stephanopoulos said he only "blew off steam over the unfairness of that decision. . . . Once I got the facts from Josh, that ended the matter as far as I was concerned."[164] However, both Altman and Steiner understood the calls as looking for a way to get rid of Stephens, and *Time* reported that "top RTC officials . . . briefly considered removing the lawyer."[165]

The next day, it was revealed that Steiner kept a diary, detailing his several contacts with the White House relating to Madison and Whitewater, including his conversation with Stephanopoulos concerning the hiring of Stephens.[166] The diary reportedly revealed yet another White House contact (this one, from Staff Secretary John Podesta) with Steiner on the same subject. Lloyd Cutler called "perfectly natural" the "surprise" of White House officials over the retention of Stephens. Although he added that it "would have been better had these conversations not occurred," he said "[a]t the same time, these conversations should not be blown out of proportion."

Nonetheless, McLarty directed Cutler to conduct an internal review of these conversations.[167]

While D'Amato suggested the possibility that Stephanopoulos may have obstructed justice, Leach suggested that what was probably a mistake was also probably not criminal and should not be overstated.[168]

On March 28 based on documents released by Leach, Representative Spencer Bachus asked the Special Counsel to investigate reports that Madison financial records, initially discovered by RTC investigators in March 1992, could not be located as of May 1993. The suspicion was raised that Madison documents had been discarded or destroyed by Madison's successor institution, Central Bank & Trust, which was headed until April 1993 by a political fundraiser for the President. The supporter, Leonard Dunn, denied shredding or dumping any records.[169]

In April 1994, Senator Dole continued to argue for a select committee, and threatened to slow down the business of the Senate if the Democratic leadership refused to schedule hearings soon.[170] In the middle of April, Senate Republicans put a hold on the nomination of Ricki Tigert, preventing a vote on the Senate floor, pending the scheduling of a congressional hearing on Whitewater.[171]

Also in April, the President was asked after a speech to the American Society of Newspaper Editors to grade the performance of the media in covering the Whitewater affair. The President used the chance to criticize those who called for the appointment of a Special Counsel, with the implicit promise that "everyone could forget about it, and let the special counsel do his job, and I could go on and be President." Clinton said he went along with this, and surrendered his records, even though the criteria for the appointment of an **independent** counsel were not met and he had not been accused of any misconduct in connection with his Presidency or his Presidential campaign. He asserted that he has been "as candid and forthright as possible[;]" he has "done everything I know to do[;]" and he would continue to cooperate with the Special Counsel and the press. But the press should not expect him to have total recall of events that occurred years ago.[172]

Later in April, the First Lady held a press conference to answer questions about Whitewater and her own commodities trades. Although she was described as "contrite," "conciliatory," and the event as "unusual" and "extraordinary," the First Lady volunteered little in the way of new information concerning their Whitewater investment or the Administration's handling of the matter. She denied any knowledge of any shredding or destruction of Whitewater documents, or any personal knowledge of Treasury-White House contacts concerning Madison; she insisted that she and her husband were passive investors in Whitewater, ignorant of the transactions with Madison and of alleged Madison contributions to Governor Clinton's 1986 reelection campaign.[173]

On May 16, Lloyd Cutler stated that Fiske had given the White House the permission to review Treasury Department documents relating to the contacts between Treasury and White House officials.[174] Cutler said the White House needed to review the documents to prepare for upcoming congressional hearings. Fiske had previously objected to White House access to these documents, fearing that it would interfere with his investigation of the contacts, but now that all involved White House officials had gone before the grand jury, this fear was substantially reduced. What Fiske did not concern himself with, however, was the remaining risk of coordinated statements before Congress. Cutler said that White House and Treasury officials worked out procedures to ensure that no documents relating to the substance of the Madison and Whitewater investigation would be provided to the White House, but only documents relating to the meetings and other contacts. News reports at the time did not note that, among the Treasury documents Cutler would review before the hearings, would be unredacted depositions of Treasury **and RTC** officials conducted by the IG relating to their meetings and other conversations with White House officials.[175]

Senate and House Finally Schedule Limited Hearings

In late May 1994, Senate and House Republicans pressed again for hearings, threatening various floor actions if hearings were not scheduled soon.[176] After Fiske told Democratic leaders that, "barring some development," he would finish the first phase of his investigation (covering the death of Vince Foster and the Treasury-White House contacts) by the end of June, both Senate and House Democratic leaders pledged that (limited) hearings could be held by the end of July or early August.[177]

On June 14, after several days of debate on and off the Senate floor,[178] the Senate voted, 56-43, along strict party lines, to begin hearings no later than July 30, limited to three issues: (1) the investigation into Vince Foster's death; (2) White House handling of Foster's papers relating to the Clintons' financial matters; and (3) contacts between the Treasury Department and White House involving the RTC's investigation into Madison's failure.[179] However, the July 30 date was dependent on the completion of the Special Counsel's work on these three issues.

Republicans opposed the resolution because they wanted a broader avenue of inquiry. The following day, Republicans unsuccessfully sought a number of amendments to expand the subjects of the hearings to include: (1) Madison's failure; (2) RTC's efforts to recover funds lost because of Madison's failure; (3) the handling of the RTC criminal referrals to the Justice Department; and (4) Mrs. Clinton's commodities trades in the late 1970s and early 1980s.[180]

On June 15, House leaders agreed to hold hearings within thirty days of being informed by the Special Counsel that his investigation into the three matters noted above was complete.[181] Banking Committee Chairman Gonzalez wrote to the Speaker, objecting to the inclusion of the Foster case in the hearings.[182] Gonzalez argued that the Foster investigation lacks a "legitimate purpose, the Congress is ill-equipped to undertake the task, and any congressional review would inevitably be criticized rightfully as inexpert." Gonzalez added that "No congressional committee is in any way capable of acting as coroner or homicide investigator, even if there were some legislative purpose to be served in pursuing this case."[183]

On June 16, Republican Senators Trent Lott and William Cohen offered a compromise proposal that would expand the scope of the Senate-approved hearings to include the handling of the RTC criminal referrals and, possibly, the Justice Department subpoena for Whitewater documents, which was alleged to have been sought by the White House for the purpose of preventing public disclosure of the documents subpoenaed. Under this proposal, the hearings would remain limited to events that occurred since the President took office.[184]

As the Democratic leadership considered this offer, Democrats began to receive criticism. The *New York Times* stated plainly, "Senate Democrats are rushing toward a partisan cover-up of the Whitewater affair."[185] But the *Washington Post* disagreed:

"To denounce the present structure or the sequencing of hearings as a cover-up is wrong."[186] On June 21, 1994, the GOP proposal, to include any "illegal, improper, unauthorized or unethical activity" relating to Whitewater during the Clinton Presidency, was defeated on a straight party line vote, 54-44.[187]

In preparation for the hearings, the Senate Banking Committee sent letters to thirteen White House officials and thirteen other current or former Administration officials, requesting relevant documents by July 1.[188] The White House pledged its cooperation, but indicated that it would not make publicly available the documents it furnished to Congress.[189]

On the House side, Gonzalez scheduled hearings to begin on July 26, limited to two matters: (1) Treasury-White House contacts, and (2) the handling of Foster's papers after his death.[190] Leach objected to the limited scope of the hearing, which Gonzalez answered was consistent with the House leadership agreement.[191] Gonzalez invited Fiske to testify.

Special Counsel Fiske Issues a Limited Report

Fiske issued a statement on June 30, 1994, disposing of two issues: the cause of Vince Foster's death and the contacts between Treasury and White House officials relating to Madison.[192] The Special Counsel determined that:

> the evidence is insufficient to establish that anyone within the White House or the Department of the Treasury acted with the intent to corruptly influence an RTC investigation. Therefore, the evidence of the events surrounding the contacts between the White House and the Treasury Department does not justify the prosecution of anyone for a violation of [18 U.S.C.] 1505. We have also concluded that the evidence does not justify a criminal prosecution for violation of any other federal statute.[193]

Other than disclosing that his investigation uncovered more than **twenty** contacts between White House and Treasury officials, the Special Counsel declined to provide any details of the investigation, citing the restrictions on the disclosure of grand jury material in Rule 6(e) of the Federal Rules of Criminal Procedure. He added that his review did not look into the propriety of the meetings or whether anything unethical occurred at the meetings, noting that the OGE was expected to resume its probe into the meetings.[194]

Fiske predicted that he would complete his investigation into the handling of the Foster documents within two weeks, a prediction that would not come true.[195]

Cutler announced that his office would begin its own review of the contacts under applicable ethics standards.[196] OGE's review, it turned out, would focus only on the propriety of the conduct of **Treasury** officials.

On the same day that Fiske's report was announced, the President signed the law reauthorizing the independent counsel provisions of the Ethics in Government Act.[197] Attorney General Reno on July 1 asked the court of appeals to appoint an independent counsel under the newly authorized statute and recommended that the court appoint special counsel Robert Fiske as the independent counsel.[198]

The Focus Returns to the Upcoming Congressional Hearings

Fiske twice declined Gonzalez's invitation to testify, arguing that his "effectiveness" as independent counsel could be impaired if he were questioned "while the major part of my investigation is ongoing."[199] Moreover, Fiske told Congress on July 14 that he would not complete his investigation into the handling of the papers of Vince Foster by the time the hearings were scheduled to begin, expecting that it would be mid- to late August before he completed the Washington phase of the Whitewater investigation.[200] Thus, this issue was removed from the hearings' agenda, although Republicans insisted that a second round of hearings be held after Fiske completed the final portion of his Washington investigation.[201]

Cutler reached agreement with both Senate and House Banking Committees that access to White House documents would be safeguarded until the commencement of hearings. The Senate committee agreed to Cutler's request to treat the documents as if they were classified. Although the House committee balked at that request, both committees agreed to various provisions to limit access and guard against leaks.[202] Separately, Republicans voiced concern over the heavy redactions of the documents provided by the White House.[203]

Several Additional Disclosures Relating to White House-Treasury Contacts

In the days before the hearings, additional details were revealed concerning the contacts between the White House and Treasury Department, most of them emanating from informal interviews conducted by congressional staff in preparation for the hearings.[204] First, the *Washington Post* reported that Jean Hanson recalled that she was instructed by Roger Altman to brief the White House on the Madison investigation, contrary to Altman's testimony, and that Hanson gave several briefings to Altman and Secretary Bentsen, which appeared inconsistent with statements made previously by the Secretary.[205]

In particular, on September 30, 1993, Hanson sent Altman a memorandum stating:

> I have spoken with the Secretary and also with Bernie Nussbaum and Cliff Sloan.
> I have asked Bill Roelle to keep me informed. Is there anything else you think we should be doing?[206]

Second, in March 1993, Roelle, who was Vice President of the RTC at the time, briefed Altman about the initial set of RTC referrals to the Justice Department, which had been made in September 1992. Around this time, Altman faxed to Nussbaum's office copies of news articles on Whitewater that were written during 1992. These reports, if true, were inconsistent with Altman's previous testimony.[207]

Third, Cliff Sloan's notes of the September 29, 1993 meeting demonstrated that Hanson passed on to the White House substantive information about the nature of the referrals, contrary to statements White House officials had previously made about this meeting. Moreover, Bruce Lindsey's October 20, 1993 memorandum to the file showed that he received some information from RTC (most likely from Treasury officials or from White House lawyers), contrary to his previous claim that all his information was gathered from reporters.[208]

Fourth, a March 11, 1994 memorandum prepared by Eugene Ludwig, appointed by the President as Comptroller of the Currency, was released. In the memo, Ludwig disclosed a brief conversation with the President at the Renaissance Weekend event at the end of December 1993, which Ludwig described as "nonsubstantive":

The president asked me whether it would be permissible for me, as a lawyer knowledgeable about banking law, to provide advice and counsel on any of the legal/regulatory issues relative to the Whitewater matter. Beyond asking this questions, the only information I recollect that he imparted to me was that he had done nothing wrong and moreover had lost money in the transaction.[209]

That same day Ludwig asked Hanson and White House lawyers for advice on what to do. All told Ludwig—correctly—that it would be inappropriate for him to discuss these matters with either the President or First Lady. Although the Comptroller of the Currency has no jurisdiction over investigations of savings and loans, the Comptroller is one of three directors of the board that oversees the FDIC, which has a clear role concerning Madison's failure. Ludwig apparently told the President that he could not be of any help, but this may have taken place in the same conversation where Deputy White House Counsel Joel Klein, also at the event, told the President to curtail any contact with Ludwig on Whitewater or Madison.

It was not known why the President would raise the subject with Ludwig, although Ludwig had earlier that December sent the White House copies of Freedom of Information Act (FOIA) requests to the FDIC for Madison documents. Ludwig said that he had never discussed Whitewater or Madison with any FDIC official or fellow board member.

Lloyd Cutler, speaking for the President, said that Ludwig may have misunderstood the conversation, because the President maintained that he asked Ludwig only for the names of experts "in real estate transactions who could write about them for the public in a way the public could understand." Ludwig, however, disputed Cutler's account.

Ludwig did not curtail all contact with the White House, however. His March 11 memorandum notes that on January 19, 1994, he called Maggie Williams, and "offered my unsolicited view that the White House should promptly provide full public disclosure of all materials associated with Whitewater."[210] Ludwig also recommended that the White House set up a small damage-control staff because of the "great public visibility" of the Whitewater affair. "Otherwise, we did not exchange any information."[211]

Fifth, portions of the diary of Treasury Chief of Staff Josh Steiner revealed that the White House did not want Altman to recuse himself. Steiner wrote that Altman initially decided to recuse himself in late January or early February 1994 but declined to do so after he met with Nussbaum and others and the White House told him that recusal "was unacceptable." Thus, Altman did not recuse because of "intense pressure from the White House":

> They reacted very negatively to the recusal and RA backed down the next day. They were very concerned about him turning to RTC people they didn't know so RA did not formally commit himself to stepping down.[212]

The very next day, Steiner's lawyer said that Steiner never intended his diary to be a "complete and accurate recordation of historical events." Steiner reportedly had said this to congressional staff in an interview. In other words, Steiner was disavowing portions of his own diary![213]

Also that day, Altman gave a press conference, defending his February 24 testimony as "wholly accurate," discrediting the accuracy of Steiner's diary, and insisting that he did not recall asking Hanson to brief the White House in September 1993:

> I never had any discussions on the substance of the case, on the facts of the case, on the merits of the case, on the outlook for the case, with the president or the first lady or anyone else.[214]

That day, the President and Secretary Bentsen issued a statement supporting Altman.[215]

Sixth, a January 4, 1994 entry from a "scrapbook" kept by Altman implicated the White House and perhaps the First Lady in seeking to cabin the jurisdiction of the Special Counsel:

> Maggie [Williams] told me that HRC was "paralyzed" by it. If we don't solve this "within the next two days" you don't have to worry about her schedule on health care. . . . Maggie's strong inference was that the White House was trying to negotiate the scope of an independent counsel with Reno and having enormous difficulty. HRC "doesn't want [the counsel] poking into 20 years of public life in Arkansas.[216]

On the eve of the hearings, Cutler conceded on CBS's "Face the Nation" that White House officials made "some regrettable errors in judgment," while insisting that "there was no violation of any ethical legal standard."[217] Indeed, he defended as "perfectly appropriate" the giving of a "heads up" to the White House if a high-level Government official is "even tangentially involved," so "the White House will be able to deal with the inevitable press queries." He also said that a "heads up" can allow the President to avoid an innocuous contact that might later prove, or been seen as, improper or embarrassing.

House Banking Committee Hearings Begin

On July 26, House Banking Committee hearings began. Gonzalez insisted that questioning be limited to five minutes per member, alternating between parties, and prohibited any direct questioning by staff. He also arranged for witnesses to be grouped by agency. Leach objected to these provisions, as did others, to no avail.[218]

The first day's witness was Lloyd Cutler. Cutler asserted that his own investigation of the many contacts between Treasury and White House officials uncovered no violation of ethical standards. The *Washington Post* summarized the bases for Cutler's finding: Cutler found that no member of the White House staff involved in the contacts had any "financial or family relationships with the Clintons that would call their impartiality into question; none sought private gain for themselves or anyone else; and none used non-public information to further any private interests."[219]

Cutler's criticism of White House officials was modest:

> [W]hile the various Treasury-White House contacts violated no ethical standard, in my judgment it would have been better if some of these contacts had never occurred, and if fewer White House staff members had participated. . . . I found that there were too many people having too many discussions about too many sensitive matters, matters which were properly

the province of the Office of the White House Counsel. The contacts, in my view, were not sufficiently channelled between White House counsel and Treasury counsel and there were too many conversations in which no counsel participated. In retrospect, I believe we did not meet as high a performance standard as we should have set for ourselves.[220]

Cutler's own investigation consisted of interviews of White House staff, Altman, Steiner, Hanson's attorney, and a review of the work product of the Treasury Department's IG, which included depositions of Treasury and RTC officials. Neither the White House nor Cutler issued any seperate report on his investigation. Cutler's testimony served as his report on his investigation.

Cutler's main **defense** of the contacts was his assertion of the propriety of giving "heads up" to the President and his staff. His main **criticism** was one of process, criticizing the many contacts made without the approval of or notice to the White House Counsel's office.

Cutler advanced two justifications for the "heads up": preparing the President to respond to press inquiries and enabling the President better to perform his job:

> It was, obviously, important and appropriate for the Treasury to inform the White House about the leaks and resulting press queries so that the White House could prepare itself and brief the Treasury to answer the questions being raised by the press concerning President and Mrs. Clinton's investment in Whitewater and their knowledge as to the campaign contributions raised by Mr. McDougal.[221]

> There is nothing wrong with such advance warning, Cutler said, "when your superior is the president of the United States, who has to deal with press queries and carry on his job. He needs to know when either important people in his administration or he himself is, are or may be under some form of criminal or other investigation. That doesn't mean he should interfere with the investigation, but he needs to know to perform his job.[222]

But Leach disagreed, saying that because the RTC referrals involved the Clintons personally, there was a huge difference in how the information should have been handled:

> No American . . . including the President of the United States, is entitled to insider information on the development of criminal referrals that relate to that individual.[223]

Cutler disclosed that Ickes briefed the President and First Lady about the February 2 meeting with Treasury officials, including Altman's decision (at the time) not to recuse himself. Cutler said that neither Clinton recalled this discussion.[224]

Cutler acknowledged that Nussbaum had urged Altman to not recuse. He found that Nussbaum should have encouraged Altman to go with his initial decision to recuse, regardless of whether Nussbaum was correct that Altman had no legal or ethical duty to recuse. Nussbaum's view was that in the absence of a duty to recuse, a Government official had a duty to serve.[225]

Cutler also disclosed a brief "dinner-table conversation" initiated by Nussbaum with Webster Hubbell, concerning the appointment of an independent counsel. "Hubbell cut off the discussion quickly, reminding Nussbaum he was recused."[226]

Cutler was asked whether the President or anyone else in the White House gave Governor Tucker a "heads up" that Tucker also was under investigation by the RTC. Cutler said that the President was not told that Tucker's name was included in the referrals; therefore, he could not have told Tucker of this when they met in the Oval Office on October 6, 1993. But Cutler did not resolve this question, because other White House officials knowledgeable about the referrals may have spoken with Tucker, and because the President and Tucker met again in Seattle a month later, on November 18, where they attended the Asia Pacific Economic Cooperation Conference.

In fact, Cutler was forced to revise his remarks the next day, after being confronted with notes taken by Associate Counsel Cliff Sloan after Hanson briefed Nussbaum and Sloan on September 29.[227] The notes show that Hanson, passing on information she had received from Bill Roelle, described the nine referrals, noting that they included allegations against Tucker. Although the notes also show that Sloan was aware of queries being made by the *Washington Post*, the first *Post* story did not run until October 31, and at the time, the *Post* was not aware of the information contained in Sloan's notes. So Hanson must have relayed these details to Nussbaum and Sloan. Sloan then briefed Lindsey the same day of the Hanson briefing, September 29. (On October 7, 1993, Sloan provided Lindsey with additional information he had subsequently received from Hanson over the phone.) Cutler testified that it was Lindsey who eventually informed the President that the Clintons were named in the RTC referrals, but adhered to his view that the President was not aware of these referrals at all until October 7, the day after Tucker met with the President at the White House.

After one day's break, the House Banking Committee resumed hearings on July 28, when ten current White House officials and former White House Counsel Nussbaum testified.[228] Nussbaum denied exerting any pressure on Altman not to recuse. But Nussbaum conceded that he advised Altman that he had a "sworn duty to serve" where there was no legal or ethical basis to recuse. A public official should not avoid "his responsibilities simply because they are difficult or inconvenient or because officials find it personally or politically expedient to step aside."[229]

Nussbaum, as well as the other White House aides, all relied on the need to apprise the President of matters that are likely to break in the press and require the President's response. Nussbaum noted that two of his lawyers looked into the propriety of receiving the information from Treasury, and determined that it was proper, "because we were receiving it for an official purpose, to answer press inquiries." Stephanopoulos even justified his call to Steiner, in which he complained about the RTC's retention of Jay Stephens, on the basis of "anticipated" press inquiries. But it was clear that the Treasury briefings provided a great deal of information in addition to what the press knew at the time.[230]

Nussbaum did not remember any mention of the RTC referrals before September 29, 1993. In particular, he did not recall receiving the faxed news articles from Altman in March 1993, even though a copy of the fax was located in Nussbaum's files.[231]

Maggie Williams testified that she did not recall saying the words attributed to her in Altman's notes (that the First Lady was "paralyzed" by the Whitewater controversy).

None of the ten White House officials conceded any wrongdoing. All denied doing anything to interfere with the RTC or Justice Department investigation. Bruce Lindsey provided some answers concerning his briefing of the President. Lindsey acknowledged learning of the referrals from Sloan on September 29, but said he did not know that Tucker was included in the referrals until October 7. Lindsey also revealed learning on October 4 or 5 of additional information from James Lyons, the Denver attorney who had authored a report on Whitewater in 1992 for the Clinton-Gore campaign. But Lindsey denied passing any information about Tucker to the President or Tucker.[232] The President's agenda for this meeting with Tucker, not surprisingly, included no reference to Whitewater or Madison.[233]

On Friday, July 29, the Senate Banking Committee began its Whitewater hearings. The first day was devoted to opening statements, which were largely focused on Roger Altman, whom Republicans called on to resign, and on hearing from witnesses concerning the death of Vince Foster. The Government witnesses from the FBI and Park Police all agreed with Special Counsel Fiske that Foster committed suicide, and no Senator, Republican or Democrat, challenged that conclusion.[234]

The key new allegation made against Altman was taken from a deposition Harold Ickes gave the Senate about the February 2, 1994 meeting. Ickes recalled that Altman told the White House that it was:

> unlikely that the [Madison] investigation could be completed and a recommendation made by the [RTC] general counsel prior to the expiration of the statute of limitations.[235]

This fact, Republicans pointed out, was non-public information about the substance of the case. Had the RTC sought an agreement from the Clintons to extend the limitations period, Senator D'Amato said, the Clintons could "safely reject" such an offer, relying on this inside information. In statements, Altman and the White House denied these allegations; their turn to testify would come the following week.

At the end of the week, it was reported that Secretary Bentsen had provided White House Counsel Cutler with the transcripts of depositions of about twenty Treasury officials in advance of the House hearings.[236] The depositions were taken by the Treasury Department's Acting IG as part of the ethics review the Secretary ordered in February when the contacts were first disclosed. Cutler requested this information to prepare himself for his testimony. The Acting IG acceded to Cutler's request, provided that the transcripts would be used only by Cutler **and his staff**. Secretary Bentsen's spokesman noted that Cutler was not at the White House at the time of the contacts and was not a subject of the inquiry. Yet, two of Cutler's staff—Cliff Sloan and Neil Eggleston—were at the White House at the time of the contacts and were among the ten White House officials called to testify before the House Banking Committee because of their personal involvement. It was uncertain whether Culter had shared any of this information with others in the White House Counsel's office.

OGE's Report is Released by Secretary Bentsen

Finally, on a Sunday, Secretary Bentsen held a news conference at which he released a "Report to the Secretary of Treasury" from the Office of Government Ethics, which was actually a letter to the Secretary dated July 30 (Saturday).[237] The Report was an ethics review of the many Treasury-White House contacts, but OGE's review was unusual, and its findings limited and qualified. OGE's attempt to explain these limitations at the front of its letter was largely unsuccessful, as the OGE report was immediately heralded by the White House, the Treasury Department, and congressional Democrats for the conclusion of an independent ethics office that **no White House** or Treasury official violated any ethical standard of conduct.[238]

Although OGE did not find that any **Treasury official** violated any standard of conduct, it qualified this conclusion in several important respects. First, OGE did not examine the propriety of the conduct of White House staff. Second, OGE did not examine the truthfulness of any statements made by Treasury officials before Congress (i.e., Roger Altman's February 24 testimony), nor did it attempt to resolve patent discrepancies in the accounts of Treasury officials (i.e., Altman-Hanson, Bentsen-Altman, Roelle-Altman, Roelle-Hanson). The Treasury depositions did reveal, however, that the Secretary was more informed than he had acknowledged, and that Altman had indeed tasked Hanson to brief the White House. Third, OGE based its knowledge of the facts on the report prepared by the Treasury Department IG (assisted by the RTC IG), which was not completed until the day before, Friday July 29. (Certain depositions were given to OGE as they were finished, however.) Fourth, its actual conclusion with respect to Treasury officials was quite narrow: "we believe that **you might reasonably conclude** that the conduct detailed in the report . . . did not violate the Standards of Ethical Conduct for Employees of the Executive Branch. However, many of the contacts detailed in the report are troubling."[239]

OGE criticized some Treasury officials for misunderstanding the roles of RTC and Treasury officials and the standards that govern disclosure of nonpublic information:

> [I]t appeared that there were some misconceptions on the part of Treasury employees that may have contributed to the fact that those contacts occurred. Treasury employees who performed both Treasury and RTC functions seemed to have failed to appreciate which roles they were performing and, thus, which agency's policies and regulations applied. In addition, based on our reading of the testimony, there appears also to have been a misperception that the standard at 5 C.F.R. § 2635.703 regarding the use of nonpublic information was the only provision that needed to be taken into account in deciding whether information should be conveyed, And, finally, there appears to have been a misunderstanding of the function of recusal.[240]

Most significant were the two premises on which OGE's conclusion that no standard of conduct had been violated was based. Both are questionable. First:

> Matters that would be of only personal significance for other executive branch officials may take on official significance when the President of the United States is involved. . . . **[W]e are not in a position to question the validity of the assumption apparently made by those who participated in the contacts . . . that dealing with press inquiries regarding the President's and First Lady's personal lives . . . is a proper White House function. . . .** Whether it is an appropriate activity for Treasury officials to assist the White House in carrying out its functions in fielding questions about the personal interests of the First Family **would seem to be a management issue**.[241]

The second premise was that the **only** purpose of Treasury officials in contacting the White House was to assist the White House in responding to press inquiries. OGE specifically found no intention of any Treasury official to advance another person's private gain.

The Second Week of Congressional Hearings

On Monday, August 1, 1994, the second week of Whitewater hearings began in the Senate Banking Committee. The first day's witnesses were Jean Hanson, Treasury's General Counsel, Bill Roelle, former Vice President of the RTC, Ellen Kulka, RTC General Counsel, and Jack Ryan, Acting CEO of the RTC.[242] Hanson, whose testimony lasted seven hours, stuck with her recollection that Altman had asked her to brief the White House, while attempting to downplay discrepancies in recollections. Hanson relied on the press inquiry rationale, but it was pointed out that as of September 29, 1993, there had been no press leak regarding Madison or Whitewater.

Hanson was criticized for failing to take steps to correct the record after Altman's February 24 appearance. Hanson was present at the hearing and knew Altman's answer was incomplete or misleading at the time, but did not move promptly to provide the complete information. She said she had intended to do so, but neglected to because of other circumstances. Hanson was also criticized by Kulka, who testified that she had rejected Hanson's request that a briefing also be given to the Clintons' personal attorney. (It was revealed in November 1995 that the Clintons' personal attorney may have received a similar briefing from White House attorneys on November 5, 1993.) Hanson also testified that Nussbaum had complained about Kulka, because he knew her previously to be "tough-minded," and twice asked Hanson why Kulka was hired, even stating that he should have been consulted in the hiring decision! Hanson also testified that either Altman or Steiner asked her to examine the retention agreement of Jay Stephens' law firm to see if it was vulnerable to being terminated.

Roelle testified that he told Hanson not to discuss RTC's criminal referrals with anyone except Altman. Hanson did not recall being told this. Other RTC officials similarly "implored their bosses to keep the information confidential."[243]

The next day featured Altman, apologetic for not being "as forthcoming as I should have been," but not at all contrite, and Steiner, distancing himself from his diary entries, as predicted. Altman testified for ten hours, until 2 a.m. To support the truthfulness of his February 24 testimony that he had only one "substantive contact" with the White House on Madison and Whitewater, Altman relied on the adjective "substantive," ruling out even the discussion of whether he should recuse himself. But Altman also blamed Hanson for failing at the time to apprise him of the other Treasury-White House meetings of which she, but not he, knew. Of course, Hanson asserted that Altman knew of the September 29 meeting, because he had asked Hanson to brief the White House. Altman did not remember doing so, however. Altman also did not recall any discussion with Roelle in March 1993 concerning Madison.[244]

Steiner's backtracking from his diary was given little credence by the Committee.[245] Some Senators found his "disingenuous" testimony to be "a metaphor for what's wrong with the Clinton team."[246]

On Wednesday, August 3, hearings were held in both the House and Senate.[247] The Senate Banking Committee heard from Secretary Bentsen, who stuck to his story that he essentially was out of the loop, and conceded that Altman and Hanson had made some "errors in judgment."[248] He seemed to side with Altman over the question of whether Hanson was directed by Altman to brief the White House. (Hanson and Roelle testified that Hanson was.) Also, several White House officials testified, including Neil Eggleston and Joel Klein, both of the Counsel's office. Both of them buttressed earlier testimony that Altman's February 24 testimony about the February 2 meeting with the White House was recognized by the White House at the time as incomplete, and, if not corrected, misleading, because Altman omitted the recusal discussion. Klein explained that Nussbaum's problem with Kulka stemmed from private litigation in which Kulka and Nussbaum represented adversaries. Nussbaum had described her, based on that experience, as "unreasonable" and "unfair."

On the House side, Altman, Hanson, and other Treasury officials testified. What was most significant at the House hearing was the charge made by Leach that there were efforts, albeit unsuccessful, by Treasury or RTC officials to derail the RTC referrals to Justice.[249] Leach revealed that one day after Hanson's September 29 briefing of Nussbaum and Sloan, the RTC ordered an unusual headquarters review of the referrals, thus delaying their transmittal to Justice. RTC lawyers in Washington put together a legal analysis objecting to some of the recommendations, and Hanson appeared to have been involved somewhat in preparation of this analysis, although she did not recall being involved.

The President answered a few questions about Whitewater at a press conference on August 3. He expressed his continuing confidence in Altman, saying "he has now answered all the questions that the Senate could possibly have about an incident that involved no violation of the law and no violation of ethics."[250] Clinton also conceded that he was upset with Altman's decision to recuse, although he explained that the only reason he was upset was "I did not want to see him stampeded into it, if it wasn't the right thing to do. I just wanted the decision to be made on the merits."[251]

On Thursday, August 4, White House officials Bruce Lindsey, George Stephanopoulos, John Podesta, Harold Ickes, Mac McLarty, and Maggie Williams testified before the Senate.[252] Stephanopoulos and Ickes either denied or testified they did not recall any critical allegation made of them by other witnesses. Ickes testified that he believed that Altman provided nonpublic information about the RTC referrals during the February 2 meeting. Podesta said that he had discussed Altman's February 24 testimony directly with Altman, but left the matter of correcting the record up to the Deputy Secretary. Williams denied statements attributed to her by Altman, but otherwise confirmed that she was involved in the briefing and even suggested to Altman that he not recuse.

Nussbaum also testified before the Senate panel, adhering to his view that Altman should not have recused.[253] Indeed, Nussbaum testified that Altman's sole basis to recuse was that "he didn't want to take the heat." Nussbaum called Altman's recusal "totally unprincipled." Senator Riegle took strong issue with Nussbaum's testimony, telling Nussbaum he should not have injected himself into Altman's decision.

On Friday, August 5, the Senate Banking Committee concluded its hearings with the testimony of Lloyd Cutler. Cutler repeated his finding that no White House official had violated any standard of conduct and asserted that OGE had informally concurred with his conclusion. The House Banking Committee heard from several RTC officials, including April Breslaw of RTC headquarters.[254] Breslaw testified that she did not recall telling Jean Lewis that RTC headquarters officials would like to be able to say that Whitewater did not contribute to Madison's losses, even though Breslaw's statement to this effect was on tape. Breslaw virtually accused Lewis and others in the RTC Kansas City office of attempting to set her up during her February 2 visit, encouraging her to drink alcohol during lunch and to engage in casual conversation, as well as not informing her that their conversation was being recorded. Lewis declined to testify, objecting through her attorney to the limits on the scope of the hearings.[255]

When the hearings ended on Friday, thirty-five witnesses had appeared during the seven days of testimony (six in the Senate; five in the House). The House heard forty-three hours and the Senate seventy-one hours of testimony.[256] Commenters were not kind to the Clinton Administration in summing up the hearings. According to Michael Wines, "[T]he hearings left an ugly impression of integrity running a poor second to political expedience."[257] The *New York Times* was harsher, criticizing the Administration's witnesses as "tireless in their legalistic evasions and prickly self-justifications."[258] Nussbaum, Cutler, Altman, and Hanson were singled out for their "appalling disingenuousness," which "reduced even the more thoughtful Democrats to hand-twisting disbelief." The Administration was accused of tainting the investigative process, even if nothing illegal or unethical occurred. "That simply means the participants were careful and the nation lucky—this time." Moreover, the *Times* connected Whitewater with the Travel Office scandal, stating that "Clinton loyalists think they can poke and snoop anywhere in defending the President's political interests."[259]

Special Counsel Fiske is Replaced by Independent Counsel Ken Starr

The biggest story on the last day of Whitewater hearings was the surprise appointment of Ken Starr to serve as independent counsel, replacing Robert Fiske, whom Janet Reno nominated for the position. The court of appeals stated:

> It is not our intent to impugn the integrity of the Attorney General's nominee but rather to reflect the intent of the Act that the actor be protected against perceptions of conflict.
>
> As Fiske was appointed by the incumbent administration, the court therefore deems it in the best interest of the appearance of independence contemplated by the Act that a person not affiliated with the incumbent administration be appointed.[260]

Initially, Starr said he would "build on" Fiske's investigation, but vowed to make an independent judgment on the matters involved in the investigation.[261] It was unclear, however, whether Starr would reopen the two aspects of the investigation Fiske had completed: the cause of the death of Vince Foster and the Treasury-White House contacts.

What went largely unnoticed was that Starr's charter as independent counsel was narrower that Fiske's as Special Counsel. Fiske was given authority to investigate and prosecute both criminal and civil violations of Federal law in connection with Madison and Whitewater; Starr's charter was limited to criminal violations.[262] Should Starr want such authority, he would need to ask the Attorney General to appoint him as Special Counsel for that purpose, because the independent counsel law does not provide for jurisdiction over civil offenses.

Altman and Hanson Resign in Fallout From Congressional Hearings

On August 10, 1994, all eight Senate Banking Committee Republicans wrote Secretary Bentsen, urging him to dismiss Altman, Hanson, and Steiner, stating that "[t]hese officials have brought dishonor on your office[,]" and "have irretrievably lost the confidence of this committee."[263] Senators Riegle and Sarbanes communicated their views to the Administration privately, in a meeting with Lloyd Cutler on August 5 and in other subsequent conversations with the Secretary and the White House. As a result, reports surfaced that Altman and Hanson were likely to go.[264]

On August 17, Altman resigned.[265] Altman's resignation, however, was not effective until a new Deputy Secretary was confirmed. The next day, Hanson resigned.[266]

RTC Places Jean Lewis and Two Other Kansas City RTC Employees On Administrative Leave

On August 15, 1994, the RTC placed Jean Lewis, Richard Iorio, (Lewis's supervisor) and Les Ausen (Iorio's supervisor), all from the RTC's Kansas City office, on administrative leave for two weeks pending an internal investigation of allegations that the three violated RTC policies and procedures.[267] None was provided notice of the reason why they were placed on administrative leave, and no other explanation was given, prompting Senate and House Republicans to charge the Administration with attempting to punish the Kansas City office for its zealous investigation of Madison, or to intimidate the office from further actions perceived to be injurious to the Clintons.

Speculation over the basis for the administrative actions initially centered on the surreptitious taping by Lewis of her conversation with April Breslaw during Breslaw's February 2 visit to the Kansas City office.[268] Jack Ryan of the RTC wrote to Representative Peter King that paid administrative leave was ordered to allow for fact-finding "free from possible obstructive influences[,]" presumably, destruction of documents. He emphasized that "[t]his is not a punitive action." He did not reveal any additional information, so as to protect all employees. Ryan's stated concern over leaks of nonpublic information on the Madison investigation, which Gonzalez had recommended the RTC investigate, also suggested that the three were accused of leaking Madison and Whitewater information to reporters or perhaps to Leach. The *Washington Times* editorialized that:

> Of all the convoluted Whitewater machinations so far, the action taken against the Kansas City Three is the lowest, most petty and contemptible. It also highlights the fact that Whitewater is no longer a question of decades-old corruption in backwater Arkansas; it involves issues of abuse of power that reach the upper ranks of both the administration and Capitol Hill.[269]

On August 24, Riegle and D'Amato wrote Ryan seeking a detailed explanation of the RTC's administrative action, and whether it was coordinated with the White House or Treasury. Iorio's attorney, Joseph Bococh, also wrote a letter to Ryan, requesting that he reassign the administrative investigation of Iorio, Lewis, and Ausen from the Office of Human Resource Management to the IG to ensure the independence of the RTC's investigation. Bococh also asserted that Iorio was told as early as February 18, 1994 that "certain key RTC managers would take a 'dim view' of his office's investigation of Madison Guaranty."[270]

On August 29, Lewis, Iorio, and Ausen returned to their offices, at the end of their two weeks' leave.[271] The RTC investigation was transferred to the IG, but still no further information was revealed concerning the substance of the internal probe.

Independent Counsel Starr requested all RTC records of the administrative leave in a grand jury subpoena issued in mid-September, in an effort to ensure that no action be taken to obstruct the independent counsel's or the RTC's investigations.[272]

There has been no further report on the IG's investigation of Lewis and the others.

Representative Clinger and the other Republican Members of the House Government Operations Committee sent letters to the RTC and OTS requesting documents concerning Madison and Whitewater that had been previously denied Leach. Clinger invoked 5 U.S.C. 2954, which requires Executive agencies to provide "information" at the request of any seven members of the House Government Operations Committee (or five members of the Senate Government Affairs Committee).[273]

Senate Banking Committee Republicans wrote Starr on September 27, asking him to reopen the investigation into the Treasury-White House contacts in light of the testimony given at the July-August hearings, which the Senators believe may have been purposefully misleading in several respects.[274] After meeting with Starr later in the month, Riegle and D'Amato agreed to postpone further Whitewater hearings, which would look into the search of Foster's office, pending the completion of the investigative work by the independent counsel.[275]

Nomination of Ricki Tigert Held Up; Eventually Confirmed

D'Amato held up the nomination of Ricki Tigert to be Chairman of the FDIC for months until Whitewater hearings were held. Once the hearings, albeit limited ones, were held, D'Amato (joined by Senator Faircloth) continued his hold, arguing more generally that the FDIC should not be run by a friend of the Clintons. Tigert's recusal commitment no longer was deemed sufficient.[276] Democrats eventually blocked a filibuster, however, and Tigert was confirmed on October 4, 1994.[277]

On November 1, 1994, Senator Christopher Bond asked Riegle to reopen Senate Banking Committee hearings to look into whether Lloyd Cutler improperly received confidential information from the Treasury Department before the beginning of congressional hearings.[278] In particular, Bond charged that Cutler was given unredacted depositions of RTC attorneys and a discussion of the legal analysis prepared by the RTC, which allegedly contained specific information about the RTC criminal referrals. Before the hearings began in July, it was reported that Fiske had not objected to Bentsen sharing the depositions with Cutler. But it was not apparent then that some of the depositions were of RTC employees knowledgeable about the Madison investigation, instead of just the Treasury and White House officials involved in the Treasury-White House contacts. Moreover, the RTC's Inspector General's office was "surprised" that unredacted RTC depositions were sent to the White House Counsel. Cutler responded that he did not believe that there was much information that was not already publicly known in the documents he reviewed; he specifically denied receiving the RTC legal analysis.

A New Republican Majority in the House and Senate Makes Further Whitewater Hearings More Likely

The Republican takeover of the Congress, resulting from the November 1994 midterm elections, suggested that when the 104th Congress convened in January 1995, D'Amato and Leach would respectively chair the Senate and House Banking Committees. Both indicated after the elections that they would hold hearings, but the timing and scope of such hearings was not decided.[279]

Independent Counsel Starr Obtains Two Guilty Pleas

On December 5, 1994, **Robert Palmer**, an outside appraiser for Madison Guaranty in the 1980s, pled guilty to one felony count of conspiring to provide false appraisals for Madison, used to support loans Madison made, including one to Jim Guy Tucker.[280] Palmer's misconduct was not directly connected to the Clintons, but Palmer agreed to cooperate with the Independent Counsel. Palmer was sentenced in June 1995 to three years' probation, including one year's home detention, and was praised by Starr for his cooperation with his investigation.[281]

The day after Palmer pled guilty, **Webster Hubbell**, who resigned as Associate Attorney General in March amid an investigation into his billing practices at the Rose Law Firm, pled guilty to two felony counts of mail fraud and tax evasion in connection with the theft or conversion of at least $394,000 from the Rose Law Firm and the firm's clients, including the FDIC, from 1989 to 1992.[282] Hubbell's misconduct did not involve either of the Clintons. As part of the plea agreement, Hubbell agreed to cooperate with the independent counsel's investigation. In the days preceding and following Hubbell's plea, it was widely speculated that Hubbell could shed light on both the Arkansas and Washington aspects of the investigation.[283] In particular, Hubbell might know about U.S. Attorney Paula Casey's involvement in the RTC referrals before her recusal, as well as communications between the White House and Justice Department relating to Madison and Whitewater. What Hubbell knew, and whether he would provide incriminating information about either the President or First Lady, were, of course, unknown.[284]

In June 1995, Hubbell was sentenced to twenty-one months in prison, and ordered to make restitution of $135,000 of the $482,410 the prosecution and defense agreed Hubbell stole or converted from 1989 to 1992.[285] Hubbell was not fined. Nothing was said at sentencing or included in the papers filed with the court concerning what assistance, if any, Hubbell had provided to the independent counsel.[286]

Congressional Hearings are Delayed

In December 1994, D'Amato said he would subpoena United States Attorney Paula Casey to testify at Senate Banking Committee hearings, which he hinted could start in late January or February 1995.[287] But after meeting with Starr on December 13, D'Amato postponed hearings indefinitely, to avoid interfering with Starr's investigation.[288] D'Amato expressed satisfaction with the progress and results of Starr's investigation, and Starr reportedly assured D'Amato that the testimony of White House and Treasury officials at House and Senate hearings would be included in the investigation. While D'Amato asserted Congress's "independent authority," he said it would be "exercised in such a manner to assure that we will not unduly impede [or] make more difficult [Starr's] work in terms of getting the facts under his charge." This suggested that D'Amato would wait only for the independent counsel to obtain documents and conduct interviews and depositions, rather than wait for the conclusion of the investigation. Indeed, D'Amato indicated that hearings would begin later in 1995 and continue through early 1996.

Leach hoped for a "comprehensive wrap-up hearing" by the House Banking Committee by late spring or early summer 1995, but promised that he would move "very cautiously and very carefully[.]"[289] Leach would not meet with Starr until Leach assumed the Chairmanship of the Committee in January.

Senate Banking Committee Report on the Hearings is Released

On the last day of the 103d Congress, the Senate Banking Committee issued a lengthy report on the hearings held in the summer of 1994.[290] In nearly 250 pages, the Majority (Democratic) report documented numerous instances of incomplete or conflicting testimony by Administration witnesses, although it did not provide any new facts. The Majority Report found no evidence that the many contacts between Treasury and White House officials violated any ethics standard. Put another way, no ethics standard "clearly prohibited" these contacts. Otherwise, the Majority Report reached no conclusions as to the propriety of the contacts or the truthfulness of the testimony. The Majority Report recommended that the President issue an executive order "reinforcing that executive branch witnesses testifying before Congress should be fully candid and forthcoming and that they must testify truthfully, accurately and completely." The Report also recommended that the appearance of impartiality be given more weight in the decision whether to recuse oneself, and that the standards governing the confidentiality of criminal investigations be tightened.[291]

The fifty-six-page Minority (Republican) Report was harsher, concluding that Roger Altman lied, both in February and August hearings, and that White House officials had improperly attempted to manipulate the RTC's investigation and improperly received confidential information about the investigation. New White House Counsel Abner Mikva issued a statement, echoing the Administration and Democratic refrain that no ethics law or standard was violated by White House officials in their contacts with Treasury officials.

Senate and House Hearings are Scheduled in the 104th Congress

Over the next several months, the Senate and House Banking Committees began preparations for a second round of hearings. In early January, the Senate Committee requested documents from the RTC, FDIC, and OTS; the House Banking Committee sought documents from the RTC and OTS.[292] The Senate Committee's investigation and hearings would focus, in particular, on the role Paula Casey and Webster Hubbell may have played in the Justice Department's handling of the first RTC criminal referral, which were sent to Casey's predecessor, Charles Banks, in September 1992, as well as the second set of nine referrals, which were sent to Justice in October 1993.[293] In February, D'Amato looked for Senate hearings to start in May.[294]

Also in February, the White House established a team of four or more lawyers within the White House Counsel's office to defend the Administration before Congress and to assist in cooperating, as necessary, with requests from the independent counsel. In addition, the White House would appoint a spokesman devoted solely to Whitewater.[295]

Leach's request for documents from RTC and other agencies raised concerns with the independent counsel's office, which objected, in particular, to Leach's request for correspondence between the independent counsel's office and the Federal banking agencies.[296] House Banking Committee Democrats also objected to Leach's document requests on the grounds that they would likely reveal matters before the grand jury.[297] Leach explained that his committee was not examining the independent counsel's office, and he did not intend to interfere with Starr's investigation in any way. The documents Leach sought were not grand jury-sensitive because they existed prior to and independent of the grand jury. The ongoing nature of Starr's investigation, however, led Leach in March to refrain indefinitely from scheduling any Whitewater hearings.

On May 17, 1995, the Senate approved a resolution, 96 to 3, calling for a series of Whitewater hearings over a period of nine months, and addressing the following Washington subjects: the search of Vince Foster's office after his death; the propriety of Lloyd Cutler's review of RTC depositions and the preparation of White House witnesses before the July-August 1994 hearings; the inconsistent testimony given at the hearings; and any matter relating to possible interference with the RTC or Justice Department investigations and any cover-up of such interference.[298] The hearings would also delve into several Arkansas matters, such as the 1990 Clinton gubernatorial campaign practices and the "operation, solvency and regulation"—by both Federal and State banking agencies—of Madison, Whitewater and Capital Management Services.[299]

The first hearing, concerning the search of Foster's office, was scheduled to begin on July 18, 1995;[300] "every reasonable effort" would be made to complete hearings by February 1, 1996.[301] The special committee, named the Special Committee on Whitewater Development Corporation and Related Matters, was comprised of the Senators on the Banking Committee and one Senator of each party from the Judiciary Committee.[302] The resolution pledged the Senate to conduct hearings in a manner that would be unlikely to interfere with the independent counsel's investigation.

Leach set House Banking Committee hearings to begin August 7, 1995.[303] The House hearings would focus on the Arkansas phase of Whitewater, namely whether Whitewater contributed to Madison's losses and default.

Starr's Investigation Continues

In April 1995, the independent counsel and his staff interviewed the President and First Lady separately and under oath for about two hours. Also present were the Clintons' personal attorney and the White House Counsel.[304] The topics discussed were not revealed, although speculation centered, among other things, on the search of Vince Foster's office after his death and the handling of his papers relating to Whitewater.

Over the next few months, Starr obtained several indictments and convictions relating to the Arkansas phase of his investigation. In only one case did it appear that either of the Clintons was even indirectly involved with the facts—the prosecution of Neil Ainley—and even this matter did not relate to Madison or Whitewater. The value of these prosecutions, like the prosecution of Webster Hubbell, was seen largely in the cooperation the defendants agreed to or were expected to provide to the independent counsel's investigation. Only time would tell, however, whether any of these persons would materially assist the independent counsel in answering questions related directly to Madison and Whitewater. The prosecutions also seemed to confirm a widely held suspicion that there was a generous supply of business and government corruption in Arkansas during the 1980s.

On March 1, **Neil Ainley** was indicted on five felony counts. These included failure to report cash withdrawals to the IRS, making false entries in bank records and false statements to the Federal Government, and conspiracy, in connection with cash withdrawals the Clinton gubernatorial campaign made in 1990 from the Bank of Perry County, Arkansas, of which Ainley was President at the time.[305] Bruce Lindsey, who served as the campaign's treasurer, personally made the withdrawals.

Also in March, **Chris Wade**, a realtor who managed the Clintons' Whitewater property in the 1980s, pled guilty to two felony counts relating to Wade's personal bankruptcy in 1989.[306] Wade's misconduct was not related in any way to the Whitewater Development or the Clintons, but Wade agreed to assist the independent counsel's investigation, which assistance Starr said had already begun.

Soon after his indictment, Ainley entered a plea of not guilty,[307] although he eventually agreed to plead guilty in May. Ainley pled guilty to two misdemeanor counts of failing properly to notify the IRS of two cash withdrawals for the Clinton campaign totaling $52,000.[308] In exchange for the dropping of the five felony counts, Ainley reportedly agreed to testify that Lindsey directed Ainley to split up the payments into $7,500 amounts, thereby concealing the size of the withdrawal from Federal regulators.[309] These reports led to intense speculation that Lindsey would be indicted as a coconspirator, despite his denials of misconduct. Indeed, Lindsey received a letter in February 1995 from the independent counsel informing him that he was a target of the criminal investigation.[310] Lindsey, through his attorney, explained that he asked that payments be divided into smaller amounts to avoid bad publicity in the waning days of the campaign;[311] he denied directing Ainley not to inform the IRS of the withdrawal, and noted that the withdrawal was subsequently reported to Arkansas campaign officials.[312]

Starr issued a brief, cryptic statement late on May 19: "[C]ontrary to all speculation, this office will take no action with respect to initiating the prosecution of any individual on or before May 25, 1995. The investigation is, however, proceeding on all matters."[313] The speculation to which Starr referred was that, because the five-year statute of limitations on criminal conduct in connection with the May 25, 1990 cash withdrawals would expire in less than one week, Lindsey would be indicted by that time. Starr's statement did not completely foreclose prosecution of Lindsey, however, because other illegal cash withdrawals were made just before the November 1990 election.[314] Yet, it was widely assumed that Lindsey was off the hook, in part because the strongest case against Lindsey appeared to relate to the May 1990 withdrawals, and no indictment was issued as of the end of November 1995.

In June 1995, Arkansas Governor **Jim Guy Tucker**, **William Marks, Sr.**, a business associate of Tucker's, and **John Haley**, Tucker's lawyer, were indicted on a total of three felony counts in connection with Tucker's investments in cable television.[315] Tucker was charged with making false statements to Capital Management Services to obtain an SBA-backed $300,000 loan. The loan was not used in Arkansas for cable construction, as stated, but as partial collateral for a $8.5 million loan from other banks to purchase a cable television interest with a cable system in Florida. Tucker, Marks, and Haley were alleged to have conspired to defraud the IRS of $4 million in taxes due on the later sale of the Florida cable system in that they falsely claimed bankruptcy and falsely understated the value of the interest in bankruptcy proceedings. If convicted, Tucker could be removed from office, in addition to serving prison time.

Again, the facts alleged in the indictment did not relate directly to the Clintons, Madison, or Whitewater. The common thread was the role of David Hale's Capital Management Services, which also provided loans to Madison and other McDougal-owned companies.

At his arraignment on June 22, Tucker pled not guilty, attacked Starr's investigation as a "witch hunt," and attacked Starr personally as a "very thin-skinned man" who he alleged was using the Whitewater investigation as "his ticket" for an appointment to the Supreme Court.[316] Moreover, he said, "Mr. Starr has the reality of a conflict of interest in that most of his private clients will benefit from my removal from office."[317] Tucker did not elaborate, however. A trial was scheduled to begin August 30, but was subsequently postponed.

The day after Tucker's indictment, **Stephen Smith**, once a close assistant to Bill Clinton, before and during his terms as Governor, pled guilty to one misdemeanor count of conspiracy to misapply a $65,000 loan he obtained from Capital Management Services.[318] The plea agreement stated that, in 1986, Smith and James McDougal submitted a false loan application to Capital, indicating the loan would be used for his political consulting firm when, in fact, it was used to pay off a loan made by Worthen National Bank to King's River Land Company, a real estate investment firm owned by Smith, McDougal and Tucker.

The Clintons' personal attorney, David Kendall, and newly designated White House Whitewater spokesman Mark Fabiani correctly noted that the prosecution of Smith did not involve the Clintons or relate to Whitewater Development. Fabiani, however, went further, castigating Starr's investigation as "wildly off its original track and . . . now in uncharted territory, but it's territory that does not involve the Clintons."[319] Unlike Hubbell, Smith's friendship with the President was portrayed as somewhat estranged, and thus Smith could be more likely to assist Starr's investigation.

Larry Kuca, a real estate broker and business partner of Jim McDougal, pled guilty on July 13 to one count of conspiracy to misapply $143,000 in loan funds received from Capital Management Services.[320] Kuca falsely stated that he sought the funds for his brokerage firm. In fact, the funds were used to buy land on Campobello Island in New Brunswick, Canada, a business venture with McDougal that the RTC believes contributed to Madison Guaranty's failure. On October 11, Kuca was sentenced to two years' probation, eighty hours of community service, and ordered to provide $65,862 in restitution to the SBA. Kuca agreed to testify for the prosecution against Jim and Susan McDougal.[321]

On July 22, Starr conducted separate interviews of the President and First Lady at the White House.[322] White House Counsel Mikva, Associate Counsel Jane Sherburne, and the Clintons' private attorney David Kendall all were present for the interviews; it was the second time in three months that the Clintons had answered Starr's questions.

Congressional Hearings Resume

On July 18, the special Senate Committee began hearings; the House Banking Committee hearings began on August 7. Over a four-week period, the special Senate Committee heard thirteen days of testimony, focusing almost exclusively on the White

House's conduct following the death of Vince Foster. The House Banking Committee heard four days of testimony, concentrating on the RTC's investigation of Madison, but also looking into what occurred in Arkansas during the 1980s.

A week before the start of the Senate hearings, in an obvious effort to get its story out before the hearings, the White House released to the media documents found in Foster's office and other records concerning Foster's death, such as pager records and Secret Service reports on the access to Foster's office.[323] Some reports referred to the Foster office documents as **the** Whitewater "file," but there was, of course, no way that reporters could verify that the records they were shown constituted the entirety of the Whitewater records in Foster's office, or whether any record had been tampered with. Indeed, two days later, the White House released additional records dealing with Whitewater tax returns that were maintained in other files.[324]

Senator D'Amato complained that the White House's "selective" release was intended to "undermine the Senate's investigation."[325] No one brought up the point that among the documents the White House showed reporters in July 1995 were some (if not all) of the very documents the White House said in December 1993 and January 1994 it could **not** turn over because they had been subpoenaed by the grand jury! Fabiani defended the release of the documents in advance of the hearing with the remarkable statement:

> There is every reason for us to explain what we know about the events surrounding Vincent Foster's tragic death.[326]

Left unexplained was why these documents were not released in December 1993, rather than waiting until July 1995. D'Amato also noted that what the White House made available to reporters was "not even close" to the entirety of the documents sent to the Senate.[327] Fabiani replied that the initial group of records shown reporters was not intended to be every Whitewater document found in Foster's office.[328]

Special Counsel Fiske had found no evidence that the Whitewater controversy bore on Foster's decision to commit suicide. *Newsweek,* given access to "the Whitewater file" (but unaware that other Whitewater documents existed), conducted its own review and came to the same conclusion.[329] Yet, in a document subsequently released by the White House—which Fiske should have reviewed—Foster noted that the Whitewater tax matter was a "can of worms you shouldn't open."[330]

Following the delivery of opening statements by the Committee members, Webster Hubbell was the sole witness on the first day of the hearings.[331] Hubbell disclosed that he, Foster, and others at the Rose Law Firm compiled information on Madison and Whitewater for the 1992 campaign's possible use and that he provided the documents the firm generated to Betsey Wright with the campaign. The documents were returned to him at some point, following the November election, and Hubbell retained the documents at his home in Little Rock. He took them with him to Washington, and did not turn them over to David Kendall, the Clintons' personal attorney, until November 1993, following the first public reports of the (second) RTC referral to Justice.

Hubbell also acknowledged that Mrs. Clinton had, in fact, assisted in bringing Madison Guaranty legal business to the Rose Law Firm in 1985. During the 1992 campaign, Hubbell and others denied Mrs. Clinton's involvement, explaining that a junior associate brought the client into the firm.

Concerning Foster's death, the primary focus of this round of Senate hearings, Hubbell denied an allegation made by Park Police investigator Cheryl Braun that he kept her from talking with Foster family members on the night of his death. He also noted that he told Nussbaum on July 21 that "he ought to think about staying out of th[e investigation]," suggesting that it was better handled outside of the White House. Hubbell added that he later found out from Deputy Attorney General Philip Heymann that, contrary to his suggestion, Nussbaum had "put on his aggressive litigation hat."

Hubbell returned for a second day of testimony, in which he made no major revelations.[332] He repeated his unease with Nussbaum's actions following Foster's death, but said he was not personally involved in making the arrangements for the office search. He noted that the Park Police expressed its frustrations with the White House to Phil Heymann at Justice through Tom Collier, the Chief of Staff of the Interior Department (the Park Police is part of Interior.)

At the hearing, Republicans also objected to the limited disclosure by the Clintons' personal attorney of Whitewater documents originally located in Foster's office. Some documents were withheld and others redacted, pursuant to an ostensible (and also dubious) claim of executive privilege as well as a claim (also questionable) of attorney-client privilege. D'Amato threatened a subpoena; Kendall responded that he would reconsider.

On July 20, three Park Police officials testified about the several obstacles placed in their investigative path by White House officials, although, in response to questioning, they indicated that they did not believe that these obstacles affected the result of their investigation (that Foster committed suicide). However, the senior Park Police witness, Major Robert Hines, testified that he thought the investigation was "incomplete."[333] Sgt. Cheryl Braun said that about 11 p.m. the evening of Foster's death she requested David Watkins to seal the office, which Watkins agreed to do. Hines said that he spoke with Deputy Chief of Staff Bill Burton to the same effect. Neither Braun nor Hines was told that several White House officials had already entered Foster's office that evening. Moreover, the office was not sealed until the following morning. The officials also objected to Nussbaum's decision not to allow them personally to conduct the search of Foster's papers or office. Hines said that had the Park Police personally conducted the search, the torn-up handwritten note discovered on July 26 would have been discovered initially.

On July 25, the fourth day of Senate hearings, David Watkins, Patsy Thomasson, Mark Gearan, and Sylvia Mathews testified.[334] On the night of Foster's death, Watkins, who was at the Foster residence, paged Thomasson at a restaurant and asked her to go to the White House to look for a suicide note in Foster's office. Watkins did not know at the time that Thomasson lacked a security clearance, but he did not regard a security clearance as a prerequisite for searching Foster's office for a note. Watkins also did not inform the Park Police investigators at Foster's residence that he had asked Thomasson to go to Foster's office.

Thomasson testified that when she went to Foster's office, Nussbaum was already there. Four about ten minutes, she looked in drawers and on the desk, but found no note, and left with Nussbaum without taking anything with her. She also added that neither Nussbaum nor maggie Williams took anything out of the office.

Watkins did not remember being asked to seal the office, contrary to Braun's testimony. Mark Gearan recalled a discussion with Bill Burton concerning the need to lock Foster's office; Sylvia Mathews overheard Burton discussing the same with Nussbaum. Both assumed that the office was secured, when it was not.

Chairman D'Amato rejected a request made by Senator Faircloth that the First Lady be called as a witness. "It would have to be very, very, very strong evidence and facts that have been established very, very clearly" before D'Amato would agree to call her. There would have to be "clear and convincing fact and reason that necessitate the First Lady's appearance." Also, the Committee announced that, after having reviewed the unredacted Foster documents by the Committee's counsel, it was satisfied that no relevant material had been redacted.

The fifth day of Senate hearings featured the conflicting testimony of Maggie Williams and Secret Service Officer Henry O'Neill.[335] Williams testified that she took nothing from Foster's office the night of his death (indeed, she testified that "I did not look at, inspect, or remove documents," unlike Thomasson and Nussbaum, who did look at documents). O'Neill, however, observed her leaving the Counsel's office suite with two handfuls of folders, and going to her office down the hall, where she had to brace the documents against the wall to allow her to open her office. O'Neill said that he locked the Counsel's office suite at 11:41 that evening and went down the elevator with Williams.

Williams also explained that on July 22 she received from Nussbaum the Whitewater documents found in Foster's office during the search conducted that day, with directions to give them to the Clintons' personal attorney. Williams said she locked them in the Executive Residence because she was too tired to wait for a messenger from the law firm. (The documents remained in the Residence for several days before being sent to the Clintons' attorney.) Williams' testimony conflicted with the account of Tom Castleton, a White House aide who stated in a deposition that Williams told him the files were going to the Residence for the President's and First Lady's review.

Michael Spafford, a lawyer for the Foster family, FBI agent Scott Salter, and Justice Department attorney Roger Adams testified on the sixth day of Senate hearings.[336] All three were present during the search of Foster's office on July 22. Adams testified that when he arrived at the White House that day, Nussbaum backed out of the agreement reached with Justice the previous day that would have permitted the Justice attorneys (Adams and David Margolis) to look at the documents. Adams said that Justice was required to conduct the search to determine the motive or reason for Foster's death, including the possibility of blackmail or some other crime. Adams said that he and Margolis argued with Nussbaum and that Margolis told Nussbaum, "If this is the way the search is going, I might as well go back to my office and you can mail me the results of the investigation."

Salter, who also observed the search, testified that Nussbaum removed papers from Foster's briefcase, then declared the briefcase empty. Salter also said he was rebuked by Cliff Sloan, an Associate Counsel, who accused Salter of trying to get a peek at the documents when Salter stood up off the sofa.

Spafford testified that shortly after the Justice and Park Police investigators had left the White House Counsel's office, he overheard Sloan, Foster briefcase in hand, tell Nussbaum that he saw scraps of paper at the bottom of Foster's briefcase. "Mr. Nussbaum said something to the effect that we will get to that later." This account appeared to contradict Sloan's July 30, 1993, interview with the FBI, in which he said he "did not notice if there were any other items remaining in the briefcase."

The seventh day of Senate hearings was held on August 1. Testifying were Linda Tripp and Deborah Gorham, who were executive assistants in the Counsel's office in the West Wing, and Park Police officials Charles Hume and Peter Markland.[337] Gorham testified that she had prepared an index of the Clintons' personal and financial files that were maintained in Foster's office and placed it in a drawer in Foster's office, but the index was gone when she looked through Foster's drawers on July 22—two days after Foster's death—at Nussbaum's request. An index was later located on a computer, but Gorham was not certain that it was the same list that she had prepared. Gorham also complained that on July 26 or 27, Nussbaum demanded several times that Gorham tell him whether she had seen anything in Foster's briefcase. Gorham had previously told Tripp that the briefcase was empty except from some "little yellow sticky notes." Nussbaum's questioning of Gorham was contemporaneous with Neuwirth's discovery of the scraps of paper on July 26, and transfer of the torn-up note to the Justice Department on the 27.

E-mail messages between Tripp and Gorham, whose desks were only a few feet apart, revealed the assistants' view that Nussbaum and others had not conducted a thorough search of Foster's office, including Foster's burn (trash) bag and the briefcase.

Markland testified that he did not believe Nussbaum's account of the belated discovery of the note, and told Nussbaum that it would have been "impossible for him to have missed the note" during the July 22 search. Hume, who was seated across the room from Nussbaum during the search, testified that he also would have discovered the torn-up note had he conducted the search.

Philip Heymann, Deputy Attorney General at the time of Foster's death, testified on the eighth day of Senate hearings.[338] Heymann described the informal understanding reached with Nussbaum on July 21: Justice attorneys would look at the top page of each set of files and decide whether any were potentially relevant; Nussbaum would be permitted to reserve any files on grounds of privilege for a later resolution of their handling. When told the next day by Margolis of Nussbaum's change in the procedure, Heymann called Nussbaum, "loud, very angry, about the fact that I thought this was a terrible mistake." Heymann threatened to call Adams and Margolis back to Justice, but Nussbaum asked him not to do this. He promised Heymann he would get back to him that afternoon, but never did. The search ensued, under Nussbaum's protocols. Heymann called Nussbaum from home that night, telling Nussbaum that he "misused us." Heymann also asked Nussbaum whether he was hiding anything, to which Nussbaum replied, "No, Phil, I promise you, we're not hiding something." When Heymann learned of the discovery of the torn-up note, however, he asked the FBI to investigate why the discovery took so long.

Heymann acknowledged that the White House's reluctance to grant open access to its documents was understandable, but also said:

I thought that for the White House counsel's office to make these decisions largely by itself, as it did, was simply not an acceptable way of addressing them. A player with significant stakes in the matter cannot also be referee.

On August 3, 1995, the ninth day of Senate hearings, Cliff Sloan and Stephen Neuwirth of the Counsel's office testified.[339] Sloan denied Spafford's testimony that

Sloan had noticed yellow pieces of paper in Foster's briefcase following the July 22 search. Sloan and Neuwirth testified also that they did not believe that Nussbaum had reached an agreement with Justice on July 21 concerning the search.

Neuwirth described discovering the torn-up note on July 26 when pieces fell from the briefcase as he tipped it in an attempt to place it in a box that was being sent to Foster's widow. Neuwirth said he told Nussbaum that law enforcement officials should be notified immediately about the note, but Nussbaum decided to inform Lisa Foster and the President first. (Justice was not told of the note for twenty-seven hours.) Neuwirth also confirmed the understanding he got from a discussion with Nussbaum that both the First Lady and Susan Thomases were concerned "about anyone having unfettered access to Foster's office," but he did not know if those views had any affect on Nussbaum's position vis-a-vis the Justice Department.[340] He added that some of Foster's records might be subject to a claim of executive privilege.

Carolyn Huber and Tom Castleton also testified, concerning Maggie Williams' delivery of the Whitewater files from Foster's office to the Executive Residence on July 22. Castleton testified that he assisted Williams in taking a box of files, which he understood at the time had originated in Foster's office, from the West Wing (either from Foster's office or Williams' office) to the Residence. Williams told Castleton on the way to the Residence that the records were being delivered there to be reviewed by the First Lady. Huber was in the Residence to receive the box and place it in the locked closet where other Clinton financial records were kept. She said Williams told her the First Lady had asked that the files be sent to the Residence.

On August 7, 1995, the House Banking Committee commenced hearings on Whitewater, as the special Senate Committee continued with its tenth day of testimony.[341] The Senate Committee heard from four White House officials at the time, David Gergen, Mac McLarty, Bill Burton, and Jack Quinn. Quinn, who subsequently became Clinton's fourth White House Counsel, defended Nussbaum's screening of the files in Foster's office. Quinn said Nussbaum's duty to protect privileged government records was "not subject to compromise, I don't believe, for the sake of appearances or simply to expedite an investigation or to amount to good politics or good public relations."

Burton testified that he called McLarty at Nussbaum's request to tell him of the discovery of the torn-up note. McLarty explained that he decided to wait to tell the President of the discovery of the note "until we had a plan of action." McLarty, who was travelling with the President at the time, did not inform him until the next day. Burton also testified that Nussbaum brought the First Lady into Nussbaum's office to show her the torn-up note. She, however, left the office without reading the note (Nussbaum had begun reading portions of it to her), stating that privilege decisions and notifying the Foster family were matters for others to decide.

The House Banking Committee hearing was taken up largely by opening statements of the Members. House hearings were expected to focus primarily on the Arkansas part of Whitewater and Madison, but also would look into whether the Administration interfered with the RTC's investigation or the Justice Department's handling of the RTC referrals. Chairman Leach released voluminous documents compiled from Arkansas and by Federal banking institutions about Madison and Whitewater, and delivered a lengthy account of the Whitewater affair. Leach also strongly criticized the White House for its handling of the Whitewater matter, stating:

From a public perspective, Whitewater is a case model in how not to handle scandal. At every step in the road the White House and Congressional leadership moved in lock-step to avoid full disclosure and a hearing on the failure of Madison Guaranty and its ties to Whitewater.

Susan Thomases and Bruce Lindsey testified on the eleventh day of Senate hearings.[342] Thomases testified that the First Lady never mentioned Foster's documents or his office in the several conversations they had following Foster's death. Thomases denied playing the role of intermediary or any other role with respect to the Foster papers. She did acknowledge that in a call to Nussbaum just a few hours before the search on July 22, Nussbaum described his plan for handling Foster's papers to "protect all of the President's papers. I said, 'Sounds good to me.'" She insisted that she had "no particular role or interest in the process." She called Nussbaum simply, "to find out how he was feeling and how he was doing." Her call to Nussbaum was one of seventeen calls she made to the White House in the forty-three hours after Foster's death. Thomases' testimony thus conflicted with Nussbaum's deposition and Neuwirth's testimony.

The House hearings featured the testimony of Jean Lewis, the RTC investigator from Kansas City who developed the two sets of referrals on Madison Guaranty, and Lewis's two Kansas City supervisors, Richard Iorio and Lee Ausen.[343] Lewis testified that she believed that government officials made a "concerted effort to obstruct, hamper and manipulate" the results of her investigation. In particular, Lewis cited the legal review of the referral conducted by the RTC headquarters professional liability section, which she said "manipulated standard procedures and provided the Treasury Department the opportunity to review and selectively disseminate sensitive criminal referral information." Lewis also complained about the tortuous path the Justice Department followed in reviewing the two sets of referrals. She also recounted that she was removed from the Madison case on November 9, 1993, after the second set of referrals went public, and that she, Iorio, and Ausen all suffered personally and professionally as a result of an administrative suspension, the basis for which remained (and remains) unknown. Democrats on the Committee countered Lewis's views on the merits of the investigation with documents revealing that an FBI official, a Justice Department lawyer, and Charles Banks (the Little Rock U.S. Attorney before Paula Casey) each doubted the sufficiency of the evidence Lewis had assembled. (However, most, if not all, of the doubts expressed about the strength of the case Lewis assembled pertained to the first RTC referral, not the second set of nine referrals.) Democrats accused Lewis of partisanship and lacking the impartiality of an investigator. They also criticized Lewis for her surreptitious tape-recording of her conversation with April Breslaw during Breslaw's February 2, 1994 visit to the Kansas City office.

On the third day of House Banking Committee hearings, the tape Lewis made of her conversation with Breslaw was played, and Lewis testified for the second day.[344] These portions of the conversation have been cited by Lewis and Republicans in particular as evidence of pressure from RTC headquarters (italics in original):

BRESLAW: I think, if they can say it honestly, the head people, Jack Ryan and Ellen Kulka, would like to be able to say that Whitewater did not cause a loss to Madison. . . .

BRESLAW: They're looking for what they can say, and I do believe they want to say something honest, but I don't believe at all, and I don't want to suggest at all, that they want us to move to certain conclusions. I really don't get that feeling.

But there are answers they would be happier about, you know, because it would get them, you know, off the hook, you know, and that would be it about Whitewater. So that is why we keep getting asked the same things.

LEWIS: . . . As far as what would make them happier with a response, they would like to come back, I am sure, with a politically correct response, but the bottom line it seems to me is I don't know what they are going to be able to do, and I am not going to do anything to facilitate that.

BRESLAW: No, no, no. And I agree with that.

Bernard Nussbaum was the next witness before the special Senate Committee, testifying on August 9-10, the twelfth and thirteenth day of Senate testimony.[345] Nussbaum said that no files were removed from Foster's office on the night of his death and that he was certain that every document in Foster's office has been preserved to this date; he denied the existence of any agreement with Justice concerning the July 22 search of Foster's office, and even insisted that he accommodated the interests of law enforcement officials during the search; he added that neither the President nor First Lady played any role in determining the scope or manner of the search. Nussbaum maintained that he had a duty to screen the files in Foster's office because of privilege concerns. Nussbaum did not remember hearing Heymann's strong protest concerning the search, made from Heymann's home that night, to the effect that Nussbaum was making "a terrible mistake," nor did he recall agreeing to call Heymann back after Heymann first lodged a protest that afternoon.

Nussbaum said that Thomases initiated a discussion of the Foster files when she called him on the morning of July 22, Thomases testified that Nussbaum introduced the subject. Nussbaum also said he assumed Thomases was echoing the First Lady's concerns, even though she did not invoke the First Lady's name. Nussbaum also contradicted the testimony of Maggie Williams: Williams said that Nussbaum told her to give the Foster papers to the Clintons' personal attorney; Nussbaum testified that he told her to check with the Clintons about what to do with the documents. Nussbaum also said that he entered Foster's office on the night of his death, independently looking for a suicide note, and happened upon Patsy Thomasson and Maggie Williams. Thomasson testified that Nussbaum was there when she arrived.

Following Nussbaum as the last witness before the special Senate Committee was David Margolis, the senior career Justice Department attorney who was involved in the discussions relating to the search on July 21 and observed the search on July 22.[346] Margolis testified that he believed an agreement with Nussbaum had been "finalized" when Margolis was at to the White House on July 21. On July 22, when Nussbaum informed him there was "a change in plans," he told Nussbaum he was making "a big mistake, but it's your mistake," in not going through with the agreement. Margolis recounted how Nussbaum generically described the documents, which made it difficult to determine relevance. Nussbaum objected even to the request of law enforcement officials to review a news clipping in Foster's file, saying it "would be an invasion of the President's deliberative process." When Margolis told Nussbaum that, "If this were IBM, I would have a subpoena" issued, Nussbaum retorted, "If this were IBM, a smart lawyer would have removed the documents before the subpoena ever got here."

Margolis added that had he been assigned to look for a suicide note and failed to discover the torn-up note, "I would have gone to the Attorney General and submitted my resignation. I would have been humiliated." He concluded that he could not be certain that the integrity of the Foster note was not tampered with.

On this last day of Senate hearings, D'Amato indicated the Committee would pursue phone records of calls to or from Williams, Thomases, and others from July 20-22 and 26, 1993. He also pledged to obtain access to the White House computer that could contain the index to the Clintons' files prepared by Foster's assistant Deborah Gorham.

On the fourth and final day of House testimony, the Banking Committee heard from April Breslaw, Webster Hubbell, and the Inspectors General for the RTC and FDIC, John Adair and Jim Renick, respectively.[347] The hearing focused on the failures of the Rose Law Firm (namely, Hubbell) fully to disclose to the RTC and FDIC previous work the firm (namely, Mrs. Clinton) did for Madison and related entities and individuals. The FDIC and RTC Inspectors General presented the results of separate investigations they had conducted responsive to requests from Congress.[348] The RTC concluded that had the Rose Law Firm made full disclosure of actual or potential conflicts, the RTC might not have chosen the firm in six of the sixteen matters the firm eventually handled for the RTC. (The firm had conflicts in two other matters involving the RTC in which the firm represented another party.) In particular, the firm did not disclose its extensive representation of Madison in 1985 (including some work by Mrs. Clinton) in the indirect acquisition of the Castle Grande property, which acquisition violated Federal regulations and resulted in large losses to the S&L. The FDIC IG investigation also found "conflicting relationships" among the firm, Hubbell, and Hubbell's father-in-law, Seth Ward, who was in litigation with Madison. Documents released by the Committee showed a much greater involvement of Mrs. Clinton in the firm's representation of Madison. But neither IG testified that she had engaged in any improper conduct.

Breslaw denied the clear implication of her February 2, 1994 conversation with Jean Lewis that she was "carrying a message to Ms. Lewis" from RTC headquarters officials. Further, she denied that she or any other RTC official improperly interfered with the RTC investigation of Madison:

> The people at the RTC who have actively participated in the Madison investigation are nonpolitical professionals, like myself. We have never had any interest in anything other than an honest investigation.

Hubbell was asked about reports that he and U.S. Attorney Paula Casey spoke over the phone six times between September and November 1993. Hubbell answered that he did not remember speaking with Casey on any subject before January 1994.

Hubbell was also asked whether he learned of the first RTC referral, or a parallel SBA referral to Justice concerning Capital Management Services, in the spring of 1993, months before he had previously claimed he first learned of the Madison referral. Hubbell could not place the precise time when he learned of either referral, except that he insisted that he was not aware of the Madison referral until October 1993, based in part on a September 23 article in the *Arkansas Democrat-Gazette*. In any event, Hubbell denied taking any steps or contacting the White House regarding either referrals.

At the conclusion of the House hearings, Chairman Leach was uncertain whether he would hold additional hearings.[349] The special Senate Committee, however, planned to continue hearings over the next several months.

Starr Obtains Indictment of Tucker and the McDougals

On August 17, 1995, James McDougal, Susan McDougal, and Governor Jim Guy Tucker were indicted on twenty-one counts of fraud, conspiracy and false statements in connection with several loans from Madison Guaranty and Capital Management Services.[350] The indictment focused on eight loans from Madison or Capital totalling over $3.13 million, which were not used for their stated purposes but "to benefit [the defendants'] joint business ventures or to reward those who would or did assist them." One of these "false and fraudulent" loans is the $300,000 loan in 1986 from Capital to Susan McDougal's company Master Marketing, which David Hale alleged Governor Clinton pressured him to make. A portion of the loan to Master Marketing was diverted to Whitewater and used to purchase land from International Paper. Starr announced that the indictment "does not charge criminal wrongdoing" by the Clintons, and the Clintons were not mentioned in the indictment.[351]

All three defendants pled not guilty.[352] Trial was originally set for October 10, but a week before trial, the judge agreed to the defendants' request to delay the trial, rescheduling it for January 16, 1996.[353]

The indictments appeared to cover much of the substance of the first RTC referral compiled by the Kansas City office in 1992, and indicate that Starr finds Hale's story credible, at least to a point. What Starr's next step would be was impossible to predict. In mid- August, the independent counsel was granted a six-month extension of the Little Rock grand jury, until March 23, 1996.[354] The Clintons' personal attorney commented that "Whitewater is steadily evaporating."[355] Furthermore, it was readily apparent that neither Tucker nor either of the McDougals would cooperate with the independent counsel and implicate the Clintons in any misconduct.

On September 5, U.S. District Judge Henry Woods dismissed one of the two counts in the June indictment of Tucker and two others.[356] Woods held first that he had jurisdiction to review the scope of the independent counsel's jurisdiction; Starr, supported by Attorney General Reno, argued that his jurisdiction was not subject to review by the district court. He next held that the count alleging that Tucker falsified a loan application to Capital Management Services "bears no relation whatsoever" to Starr's charter, because the authority to investigate Capital was limited to matters involving the Clintons or the McDougals. Starr, again supported by the Attorney General, argued plainly that the count was covered by the section of his charter that authorizes him to "investigate other allegations or evidence or violation of any federal criminal law . . . by any person or entity developed during the independent counsel's investigation . . . and connected to and arising out of that investigation."

While Woods' ruling was seen as questionable from a legal standpoint,[357] his impartiality was also called into question.[358] In particular, Woods, a Carter appointee long active in Democratic politics, is a friend of the Clintons. He once appointed Mrs. Clinton as a special counsel on a case, wanted her to run for Governor at some point, and was an overnight guest at the White House on the night of the 1994 elections.[359] In 1993, Woods wrote to Vince Foster, asking Foster to "take up . . . with Hillary" whether Woods should talk to a reporter doing a profile on the First Lady.[360]

Starr appealed the dismissal to the Eighth Circuit, seeking expedited review. In his brief on appeal, Starr stated that on remand to the district court, the court of appeals should direct that Judge Woods be recused and the case assigned to another judge.[361]

Tucker and the McDougals were not successful, however, in their attempt to argue that the August indictment of them was also improper because it was out of the independent counsel's charter. On November 15, 1995, U.S. District Judge George Howard, Jr., denied the defendants' motion to dismiss, holding that the allegations of the indictment were within the scope of the independent counsel's jurisdiction.[362]

Senate Prepares For Another Round of Hearings; Issues Subpoenas For Documents

Aware that the special Senate Committee was contemplating further hearings on Whitewater and Madison to begin looking into matters that occurred in Arkansas under the jurisdiction of the independent counsel, Starr asked the Committee on September 27 to delay further hearings for an unspecified time.[363] Starr said that testimony about Madison, Whitewater, and Capital could involve witnesses he expected to testify at the January 1996 trial of Tucker and the McDougals. He argued that the independent counsel's "preparation for trial" would be "significantly impede[d]" and feared "the disclosure of certain nonpublic information that is the focus of ongoing criminal investigations." The Committee declined to postpone hearings. In an October 2 letter to Starr, Senators D'Amato and Sarbanes expressed concern that agreeing to any delay would not allow the Committee to finish its work by February 1, 1996, as specified in the Senate resolution. The Senators pledged to be sensitive to Starr's concerns.

Over the next several weeks, the Committee wrestled with the White House and others over documents, some of which were originally requested on June 2, 1995, and others on August 25, following the last round of hearings. Of interest to the Committee were records (including e-mail messages) of or concerning the following:

• phone calls to and from the White House made immediately after the death of Vince Foster

• phone calls allegedly made by Paula Casey and Webster Hubbell in 1993

• the interviews of the Clintons conducted by independent counsel Fiske and Starr

• contacts between the White House and the RTC

• contacts between the Administration and the RTC

• the handling of the RTC referrals by the Treasury and Justice Departments

• contacts between the White House Counsel's office and any witness at July-August 1994 House and Senate committee hearings

• Whitewater activities, investments, or tax liabilities [364]

The White House flagged its reluctance to turn over records created in preparation for the independent counsel or congressional investigations, as well as notes of the interviews with the President and First Lady.[365] Mark Fabiani said that D'Amato was "seeking the last refuge for a political witch hunter—complaining about technicalities and procedures."[366]

On October 26, the Committee unanimously voted to issue forty-nine subpoenas, nine for phone records and forty for other documents.[367] Among the recipients of the subpoenas were the White House, Treasury Department, Webster Hubbell, Paula Casey, Bruce Lindsey, Betsey Wright, Patsy Thomasson, Dan Lasater, Jim Blair, and accountants for Whitewater Development Corporation. Phone records were sought of calls made by April Breslaw, Jim Lyons, William Kennedy as well as some of the others listed earlier.

The Special Senate Committee Resumes Hearings

The Committee indicated that it would recall Susan Thomases and Maggie Williams to testify concerning the conversations they had with the First Lady and others following Foster's death. The Committee believed that phone records from July 21 and 22, 1993, released by the White House, cast doubt on the truthfulness and completeness of their previous testimony.[368] The calls were considered significant because they were made between 5 p.m. on July 21, when Justice officials believe they reached an agreement with Nussbaum on the protocol to search Foster's office, and 10 a.m. on July 22, when Nussbaum changed the procedure over the Justice Department's objection. Recall that both Thomases and Williams denied indicating to Nussbaum any views about the scope or manner of the search, including any held by the First Lady. But Nussbaum's assistant Steve Neuwirth recalled Nussbaum indicating to him that Thomases and the First Lady did not want "unfettered access" to Foster's office. Of course, the fact that these phone calls were made does not establish what was said on them, a point the White House was quick to add. On the other hand, Neuwirth's recollection could not be ignored.[369]

Jean Lewis, who resigned from the RTC in September,[370] responded on October 27 to a document request she received from the special Senate Committee.[371] Among the documents she turned over were copies of the two sets of referrals, her other files on Madison, copies of her home phone records for 1993, and a copy of the February 2, 1994 tape-recorded conversation with April Breslaw. Lewis was expected to testify the week of November 13.

Williams and Thomases (but not Neuwirth) returned to testify before the special Senate Committee on November 2.[372] Questioned about the many phone calls they were a party to from July 20-27, involving conversations with each other and with the First Lady and Nussbaum, neither Williams nor Thomases provided any new information about the substance of these calls. Thomases continued to maintain that her calls to the White House during this time consisted merely of her reaching out to White House staffers who were stricken with grief over Foster's death. Williams essentially did not recall making many of these calls or what was said on the calls she did remember making. Republicans suspected that both participated in discussions concerning the late night visit to Foster's office on July 20, the procedure for the search of Foster's office on July 22, and the discovery of the torn-up note on July 26. D'Amato, joined by three other Republicans, concluded that their testimony was "not credible, not responsive, very distressing and disingenuous." He contemplated asking the independent counsel to review Thomases' testimony for a possible charge of perjury. Faircloth renewed his call for the First Lady to testify, but D'Amato reserved judgment, saying that it was up to her to decide whether to shed any light on what happened following Foster's death.

The special Senate Committee turned next to a review of the internal Executive Branch investigations of the Treasury-White House contacts: (1) the investigative report of the Treasury Department Inspector General (in which the RTC Office of Inspector General participated); (2) the Office of Government Ethics analysis of the propriety of the actions of Treasury officials, contained in a July 30, 1994 report to Secretary Bentsen; and (3) Lloyd Cutler's analysis of the actions of White House officials, contained in his testimony to the House and Senate Banking Committees in July and August 1994. Republicans sought to show that the White House and political appointees at Treasury attempted to exercise some control over the Treasury's investigation that was intended to be independent, and would examine whether confidential information was improperly passed to White House or Treasury officials who were to be called as witnesses before the House and Senate in 1994 concerning the Treasury-White House contacts.

Former Treasury Secretary Bentsen led off testimony on the first of three days of hearings, followed by the RTC Inspector General James Adair and other RTC IG officials, Patricia Black, Steven Switzer, and Clark Blight.[373] The testimony concerned the regular communications between Francine Kerner, an attorney in the Treasury General Counsel's office who was assigned to the Treasury Inspector General's office for this investigation, and other attorneys in the General Counsel's office. In particular, a July 28, 1994 e-mail message from Ken Schmalzbach in the General Counsel's office to Ed Knight, Bentsen's Executive Secretary, recounted Kerner's call to Schmalzbach alerting him to a major dispute about whether to release transcripts of RTC witness interviews, publicly or to Congress, redacted or unredacted. Secretary Bentsen testified that he was unaware of Kerner's communications with the General Counsel's office. (Kerner would testify later in the week that she communicated with Schmalzbach so that he could keep the Secretary's office informed, because it would have been inappropriate to involve General Counsel Jean Hanson, an official whose conduct was under review in the investigation.)

Testimony also centered on the decision to provide White House Counsel Lloyd Cutler with the unredacted interview transcripts over the objection of RTC officials. Secretary Bentsen testified that he specifically authorized this, acceding to a request from Cutler, who asked to review the transcripts for the investigation of the contacts that Cutler was conducting. Bentsen may have agreed to Cutler's request without first seeking the views of the Treasury IG's office, although the former Secretary did not recall this specifically. He testified he saw nothing wrong with giving the transcripts to Cutler, emphasizing that only Cutler was to review them and only for that purpose. Cutler assured the Secretary that the transcripts would not be provided to any White House official expected to be called as witnesses before the Senate hearings.

All four RTC officials testified that they were surprised and disappointed when they learned of the Secretary's decision. Patricia Black said, "I was astonished, and I was angry. . . . This was an investigation of Treasury's improper leaks of RTC information to the White House and they had done it again!"[374] RTC officials also testified that their investigation was hastily conducted, against their wishes, so that the report could be completed before the start of the Senate hearings. (Recall that OGE's report was released by Secretary Bentsen on Sunday, July 31, 1994, midway through the summer hearings, and three days before the Secretary's testimony in the Senate.

Treasury officials testified on the next day.[375] The bulk of the testimony centered on the actions of Francine Kerner and the dispute inside of Treasury over the release of the interview transcripts. Kerner testified that she would not dispute the recollection of Schmalzbach that Kerner initially forwarded the transcripts to him in mid-July, and then asked for them back, before forwarding them to him again with a cover memorandum on July 23. Kerner defended her actions by reference to her role of liaison with the Secretary's office, via Schmalzbach, but also testified that her liaison function was not limited to contacts with him. Kerner did not believe her actions were inconsistent with the written direction that no information on the substance of the investigation was to be passed on to the General Counsel's office, disputing that the information she relayed dealt with the "substance" of the investigation.

James Cottos, Assistant Treasury Inspector General for Investigations, testified that he objected to the changes Kerner wanted to make to the draft Treasury IG report,[376] believing that she was "slanting the facts or attempting to slant the facts." Cottos also objected to Kerner's meetings with counsel for Josh Steiner and lawyers for two or three other witnesses, because Kerner would flag the topics of the interviews in advance and agree to limitations on the questions that would be asked.

Five other Treasury officials testified: Ed Knight, Ken Schmalzbach, Stephen McHale, Robert McNamera, Jr., and David Dougherty, all attorneys in the General Counsel's office (save Knight). In July 1994, the Treasury General Counsel's office had compiled written summaries of the IG interview transcripts, which apparently were provided to the White House before the scheduled appearance of White House officials before Congress. None of them, however, recalled how the White House obtained these summaries. Apparently the only summary shared with any White House witness was a summary of the interview transcript of RTC press official Steve Katsanos, which was given to the lawyer for the First Lady's Press Secretary Lisa Caputo. However, a White House Counsel's office memorandum apparently stated that it was Dougherty who provided the transcripts and summaries to the White House. Dougherty allegedly also told the White House that the restrictions on the use of the unredacted transcripts did not apply to the use of the Treasury summaries. Dougherty did not recall making these statements to the White House.

The content of Schmalzbach's July 28, 1994, e-mail message was again examined. Kerner apparently had left in the middle of a long meeting with RTC and Treasury IG officials to alert Schmalzbach by phone that Patricia Black had said that RTC General Counsel Ellen Kulka objected so strongly to the release of the unredacted transcripts to Congress, as well as to the public, that if they were released Kulka would testify before Congress that the internal investigation had been "under the sway of the Secretary." Schmalzbach strongly disagreed with Kulka's view, believed that Kulka's boss, Jack Ryan, could dissuade her from this course of action, and that perhaps someone in the Secretary's office could contact Ryan for this purpose. There was also a difference of opinion whether any information in the transcripts needed to be redacted, because some believed the information about the Madison investigation had been publicly reported. However, the transcripts eventually provided Congress were redacted, apparently because the RTC had not confirmed the accuracy of these news reports.

The last witnesses at the hearing on November 8, OGE Director Stephen Potts and Deputy General Counsel Jane Ley, testified too late in the day for any public report of their testimony. But it was recounted at the hearing the following day that OGE officials had testified (and had later sent the Committee a letter of clarification), disputing Lloyd Cutler's 1994 Senate testimony that OGE had "informally concurred" in his conclusion that no White House official violated any standard of ethical conduct in the contacts made with Treasury officials. Recall that the OGE report expressly limited its analysis and findings to the conduct of Treasury officials, and cautioned against applying its analysis to the conduct of White House officials. OGE officials did, however, informally concur with Cutler's view that no standards of conduct were violated by White House officials in discussions they had with Treasury officials about whether Roger Altman should recuse himself. OGE also reviewed Cutler's testimony in draft, and apparently did not object to any statement made therein. But Cutler and other White House officials went beyond the letter of his prepared testimony before the House and Senate Banking Committees.

At the November 9 hearing, Cutler conceded he "may have transgressed" and "may have gone too far" in relying on OGE's report and views informally expressed by Jane Ley and another OGE official. But he added that OGE made no objection to his testimony before the House on July 26, 1994 or the Senate on August 5, 1994.

Jane Sherburne, White House Special Counsel, denied that the White House Counsel's office had misused the interview transcripts it received from Bentsen:

> We did not use them in any way in connection with any witness-preparation efforts. We did not show the transcripts to any witness, any witness' lawyer, or anyone else. . . . In short, we scrupulously complied with Treasury's restrictions on the use of the IG transcripts.[377]

Cutler, however, testified that he used the transcripts to inform himself in conducting interviews of White House officials where there might be a conflict in testimony. "All we did is go back and say there may be some conflicting testimony. Are you sure of what you said?" Cutler also briefed the private lawyers of White House witnesses two days before the hearings began, including previewing what the witnesses would say.[377] Cutler explained he saw nothing improper in this briefing, nor did he believe it was inappropriate for him to both investigate White House officials and defend their actions.[379]

Scheduled to testify on November 14 before the special Senate Committee were Bruce Lindsey, William Kennedy, and Neil Eggleston. All three officials at one time worked in the White House Counsel's office, although Lindsey held a different position in 1993. According to a report on the eve of these hearings, in the fall of 1993 Bernard Nussbaum asked Eggleston to find out about the SBA's investigation of David Hale and Capital Management Services.[380] In the spring of 1993 the SBA had referred its investigation of Hale and Capital to the Justice Department for possible criminal investigation. Separately, the SBA prepared a report for House Small Business Committee Chairman John LaFalce. Eggleston asked for and obtained a copy of the SBA's report to Congress from the SBA General Counsel's Office on November 16 or 17, 1993. The General Counsel received clearance from the SBA's ethics official that it was appropriate to share this information with the White House. The SBA report apparently contained "confidential" information, although the privileged nature of the documents shared with the Small Business Committee and White House was not known.

When the SBA informed the Justice Department attorney of this transmission, Justice asked the SBA to retrieve the documents and any copies and notes made by the White House. Eggleston initially declined to return the document, asserting a right to monitor legislative action. Subsequently, however, on November 21, 1993, he agreed to do so, after the Justice lawyer called the FBI and Deputy Attorney General Heymann intervened. [381] Eggleston was expected to be asked what if anything he did with the document and information contained therein.

The next pre-hearing "revelation" was from the unredacted July 11, 1994 transcript of the deposition of Jean Hanson, taken as part of the Treasury IG's investigation of the White House-Treasury contacts.[382] In the deposition, Hanson recounted her September 27, 1993 conversation with Bill Roelle on the RTC's Madison referral, in which the Clintons were named as "potential beneficiaries," two days before she briefed the White House Counsel:

> He told me . . . . the language of that referral could lead to the conclusion that if additional work were done, that is further investigative work, the President and Mrs. Clinton might possibly be more than just witnesses.

This portion of the transcript was not shared with the Senate Banking Committee in 1994. Hanson had testified to this effect on August 1, 1994 before the Committee, but no news report mentioned this portion of her testimony at the time. (Thus, this transcript was initially thought by the *Washington Times* to break new ground, an error the *Times* later conceded.)[383]

The relevant portion of Hanson's public testimony:

> [Bill Roelle] told me that the President and Mrs. Clinton were included in the referrals solely as possible witnesses. He told me that there had been a referral the prior year and in which the language relating to President and Mrs. Clinton could be read in such a way that it could be inferred that if additional investigatory work was done, they might be something more than potential witnesses, but that in these referrals, these nine referrals, the President and First Lady's names included solely as possible witnesses.

The following day, it was reported that Glion Curtis, General Counsel of the RTC, when deposed on July 8, 1994 as part of the Treasury IG investigation, told investigators that in early October 1993 he shared the RTC headquarters legal analysis of second Madison referral with Hanson and Curtis' assistant John Bowman.[384] "I showed them the copy that I had, and they made a copy from that." Curtis' deposition was apparently not made available to the Senate Banking Committee in 1994, and Curtis was not called as a witness. The OGE report of the Treasury-White House contacts includes an October 7 call from Hanson to Cliff Sloan, in which Hanson reportedly advised Sloan further about press inquiries.

Because of the shutdown of the Federal Government that began on midnight November 13, Chairman D'Amato decided to postpone hearings until November 28.

Senate Hearings Resume After Government Shutdown

Senate hearings resumed on November 28, 1995, with the testimony of Bruce Lindsey and Neil Eggleston from the White House Counsel's office, former SBA Administrator Erskine Bowles (currently Deputy White House Chief of Staff), and four other SBA officials: Wayne Foren, formerly a Special Assistant, Charles Shepperson, Deputy Associate Administrator, John Spotilla, General Counsel, and Martin Tecker, Deputy General Counsel.[385] Bruce Lindsey declined to reveal what was discussed at a previously undisclosed November 5, 1993 meeting among White House and private attorneys at which he was present. He also would not reveal who else attended the meeting. On advice of White House Special Counsel Jane Sherburne and the Clintons' private attorneys, Lindsey cited the attorney-client privilege.

Remarkably, Lindsey also testified that he could not decipher some of his handwritten notes of a September 20, 1993 phone call to James Blair, the Little Rock attorney for Tyson Foods who was instrumental in Mrs. Clinton's earning profits from commodities trades in the 1970s. Lindsey called Blair after giving Jeff Gerth of the *New York Times* a lengthy interview about David Hale's allegations. Blair had discussed the Hale investigation with Jim McDougal's lawyer Sam Heuer, because both Blair and Heuer were concerned what Hale might say against McDougal and whether McDougal might face a later indictment. The notes mention a discussion between Heuer and an Assistant United States Attorney in Little Rock, Brent Bumpers, and refer to another Assistant in the office, Fletcher Jackson. The notes include this sentence: "Blair heard that $300,000 had been deposited in McD's account—jumped pretty high." Recall that Hale's central allegation is that Governor Clinton pressured him to make a $300,000 loan to a company owned by McDougal's wife, a portion of which eventually wound up in Whitewater's account. (Hale was indicted the next day.) Chairman D'Amato concluded that Lindsey obtained inside information about the U.S. Attorney's investigation of David Hale, and that Lindsey's inability to explain his notes was "preposterous."

The major development at the November 28 hearing, however, concerned White House communications with the SBA in 1993. Up to this point, all of the focus on White House communications with law enforcement agencies concerning Madison and Whitewater had been directed to the Treasury Department and the independent banking agencies such as the RTC, FDIC, and OTS. Wayne Foren testified that on May 5, 1993, then-SBA Administrator Erskine Bowles briefed McLarty on the SBA's investigation of Capital Management Services, and told Foren of his meeting with McLarty. (Shepperson recalled being told at the time by Foren of Bowles' meeting with McLarty.) Bowles received the information about Hale's company from Foren, who had briefed Bowles in preparation for his Senate confirmation hearing. Foren told Bowles that he intended to refer Capital Management Services to the SBA's IG for investigation, and that Bowles concurred. (Foren left the SBA after an unspecified dispute with Bowles.) Bowles, however, did not recall receiving any information about Hale or his company and did not recall giving any information to McLarty.

Foren testified that he began to investigate Hale as early as February 1993. Foren said that Hale told him, "This is the way we do business in Arkansas," and said that "he had influence with . . . Jim Guy Tucker and the President of the United States." Foren added that Fletcher Jackson of the Little Rock U.S. Attorney's office sent him a draft indictment of Hale in August 1993, a copy of which Foran forwarded to Bowles.

The hearing also confirmed the *Associated Press* report earlier in November that in November 1993, John Spotilla, a political appointee, sent an SBA file on Capital Management Services to Eggleston, at Eggleston's request. As recounted previously, the Justice Department, once informed of this, objected and demanded that Eggleston return the documents without retaining any copies. Neil Eggleston testified that he did not share with any one else at the White House the information he received from the SBA.

Charles Shepperson testified that an SBA official (Mitchell Stanley) received a call from George Stephanopoulos sometime in early 1993, before the President Clinton took office, in which Stephanopoulos praised the Small Business Investment Corporation (SBIC) program in the State of Arkansas, and asked specifically about Foren's management of the SBIC program. At the time, Capital Management Services was the only SBIC firm in the State. The White House responded that Stephanopoulos denied making this call.

On November 29, Jean Lewis and Richard Iorio testified.[386] The principal story the emerged from the hearing was the attempt by minority counsel Richard Ben-Veniste to impugn Lewis's integrity and impartiality by revealing portions of a personal letter Lewis had typed on an office computer, but which Lewis deleted and had not provided the Committee. Apparently, the Committee was able to resurrect the letter from the disk Lewis provided the Committee. In the letter, Lewis referred to President Clinton as a "lying bastard" in reference to the Gennifer Flowers episode. When asked about this, Lewis accused Ben-Veniste of a "real cheap shot." Lewis conceded that she was a conservative Republican, but insisted she held herself to a higher standard with respect to the Madison investigation to ensure her impartiality. The Democrats were interested in showing that Lewis might want to affect the 1992 election by pushing the RTC referral on Justice in the fall of 1992 and perhaps causing an "October surprise." Iorio, who was Lewis's supervisor, said that he did not think Lewis's investigation was affected by her personal views.

On December 4, Lewis filed a complaint against Senator Paul Sarbanes and Ben-Veniste with the Senate Ethics Committee, alleging that the disclosure violated her Fourth Amendment rights, Federal law, and Senate rules.[387] Sarbanes defended the letter's use largely because it was prepared on a government computer at the office. Most, if not all, commenters decried Ben-Veniste's use of Lewis's deleted personal letter, and most thought it backfired on the Senate Democrats, and perhaps caused some damage to the President.[388]

April Breslaw testified on November 30. Breslaw testified that she believed that Webster Hubbell misled her by failing to inform her of previous work the Rose Law

Firm had done on the Castle Grande Development, in which both Madison Financial (Madison Guaranty's real estate company) and Hubbell's father-in-law Seth Ward were involved. Breslaw said that had she been given complete information, the FDIC would not have retained the Rose Law Firm in 1989 to pursue claims against Madison's accounting firm.[389] When asked about Lewis's tape-recording of their February 2, 1994 conversation in Lewis's Kansas City office, Breslaw testified that she was not sure the voice on the tape was hers. D'Amato called her statement "unacceptable."[390]

Also on November 30, the Senate Committee sent a letter to the White House asking the First Lady to respond under oath to four questions concerning an unidentified ten-minute phone call the First Lady made from Arkansas at 10:41 p.m. Central time on the night of Foster's death.[391] This call would have been made shortly after Nussbaum, Williams, and Patsy Thomasson left Foster's office after unsuccessfully looking for a suicide note.

Also on this day, David Kendall wrote to the Committee, explaining that, contrary to the previous testimony of Maggie Williams, Williams was present when Bob Barnett, the Clintons' personal attorney before Kendall, came to the Residence on July 27, 1993 and reviewed the Clintons' Whitewater files taken from Foster's office. Barnett said he did not recall seeing Mrs. Clinton or Susan Thomases that day. Williams testified that she just briefly met with Barnett and unlocked the file closet and that he spent most of the time with the First Lady, although the White House said that Mrs. Clinton likewise does not recall meeting with Barnett that day. The letter stated, "Mr. Barnett conducted a cursory review of the files in the box to determine their nature. He returned to the box all materials that he reviewed and taped it up." White House logs show that Susan Thomases and Diane Blair, a friend of the Clintons, were in the Residence at the same time that Williams and Barnett, entering and leaving the Residence within moments of each other. The Committee thereupon decided to interview Barnett and recall Williams to testify again.

Over the next few days, the special Senate Committee heard testimony from various current and former Government officials, mostly from the Justice Department's Criminal Division, the Little Rock United States Attorney's office, and the FBI's Little Rock field office. On December 1, 1995, Paula Casey, the U.S. Attorney in Little Rock, David Hale's attorney Randy Coleman, Fletcher Jackson, an Assistant in the U.S. Attorney's office, and Webster Hubbell testified. On December 5, former Associate White House William Kennedy, former U.S. Attorney Charles Banks, and several FBI officials from the Little Rock office testified. On December 6, Jack Keeney, Deputy Assistant Attorney General, Gerald McDowell, head of the Criminal Division's Fraud Secton, Joseph Gangloff, head of the Criminal Division's Public Integrity section, and DOJ lawyer Allan Carver testified.

Hubbell was asked about the extent of work Mrs. Clinton did as a partner with the Rose Law Firm for Madison, including Madison Financial's interest in purchasing land for the Castle Grande project. (David Kendall on November 30 said that her total billings in 1986 were $6,000, and that her work on the Castle Grande project was limited to a "few narrow" questions of state law.) Republicans attempted to show that the RTC records of the hours for which Mrs. Clinton billed Madison were greater than previously acknowledged. Hubbell insisted that Mrs. Clinton's role in the matter was small, and suggested that the Committee get the actual records from the Rose Law Firm, rather than relying on RTC records. Rose Law Firm records in possession of the Committee showed that Mrs. Clinton's billings for Madison were greater than any other attorney at the Rose Law Firm except one junior associate. Other firm records may no longer be in existence, however. One firm partner said there were no billing records for the years 1983-86.[392]

Like Lindsey, Kennedy also refused to testify about the November 5, 1993 meeting when he appeared on December 5, although he did acknowledge the identity of the persons who attended the meeting: Nussbaum, Lindsey, Kennedy, Eggleston from the White House, and private attorneys David Kendall, James Lyons, and Steven Engstrom. He declined on the ground of attorney-client privilege, apparently under instructions from both the White House and David Kendall, the Clintons' personal attorney.[393] The Committee sought notes Kennedy took of the meeting, which were said to be in the possession of the White House. It was not initially clear whether the privilege the White House was asserting (as opposed to Kendall) was the attorney-client privilege, or the executive privilege, or whether the White House regarded the two as essentially the same for purposes of the President. In any event, whether the claim is executive privilege or the attorney-client privilege, the privilege must formally be asserted by the President or the client, respectively, not by his attorney. And there was no indication that President Clinton or the Clintons yet had made such an assertion. Lawyers from the Committee, the White House, and the Clintons were reported to meet later on December 5 to attempt to reach an agreement. The lawyers continued to discuss the matter on December 6 and 7, but no agreement was reached.[394]

Fletcher Jackson testified on December 1 that he developed the case against Hale and informed Casey when she came on board in August 1993 how the case could develop.[395] "From Hale, the path would lead to Mr. McDougal—from there one path would lead to Mr. Tucker, another path would lead to Whitewater and the Clintons." Coleman, Hale's attorney, testified that he informed Casey of Hale's value as a witness against Tucker, McDougal, and the Clintons, and offered to plead guilty to a misdemeanor. Casey declined Coleman's offer of cooperation and misdemeanor plea. Casey testified that neither Hale nor Coleman "...ever provided specific information about any person or wrongdoing." Michael Johnson supported Casey's decision not to make a deal with Hale unless and until Hale was personally questioned. They also insisted adamantly that Hale plead to a felony. Casey also denied talking about the substance of the Hale prosecution with anyone in the Clinton Administration.

Coleman said he contacted William Kennedy in mid-August 1993, telling Kennedy that they had clients with mutual interests in a Federal investigation under way in Little Rock. Kennedy asked Coleman what he wanted, and Coleman replied that he did not want anything but was only trying to determine "everyone's position" on the matter. Kennedy replied that he would have to check with his "clients." Kennedy brought the call to Nussbaum's attention. Kennedy called Coleman two days later and asked Coleman whether Hale would allege any "face-to-face meeting." Coleman replied in the affirmative. Kennedy told Coleman he might or might not call him back, and never did. Coleman acknowledged in his testimony that he contacted Kennedy in the hope that White House contacts with Justice would taint the Department's prosecution of his client.

Hubbell testified that around this time (late August or early September 1993) Kennedy called him to ask him whether Hubbell knew of any connection among

Hale, McDougal, and Madison Guaranty. Hubbell said he told Kennedy he did not know of any at the time, but said he later drew a connection when he read of Hale's allegations in the September 23 *Arkansas Democrat-Gazette*.

In addition to speaking with Bruce Lindsey on September 20, on or before that date, Jeff Gerth also called the Justice Department. Gerth called to discuss with Irv Nathan Gerth's interviews of Hale and his knowledge of the U.S. Attorney's investigation. Nathan, an Associate Deputy Attorney General, informed Jack Keeney, the senior Deputy of the Criminal Division, Gerald McDowell, Chief of the Fraud Section, and Joe Gangloff, Chief of the Public Integrity Section, of this call, without identifying Gerth. At some point on September 20, the U.S. Attorney's office faxed to Main Justice a copy of a letter from Coleman to Casey outlining Hale's offer of cooperation and Coleman's request that Casey recuse herself. Keeney separately called Casey and her first assistant Michael Johnson, a career Justice official, and engaged in a detailed discussion about Hale's allegation and offer. Keeney strongly advised Casey to recuse herself.[396] Casey considered Keeney's suggestion, but eventually declined (without informing Keeney), relying on Johnson's advice. Johnson did not believe an anonymous call (Gerth's) was a sufficient basis to recuse, and Casey did not believe Coleman's preview of what evidence Hale could provide on Arkansas political figures offer was sufficiently specific. Casey and Keeney discussed Coleman's dissatisfaction with the U.S. Attorney's office, and Keeney told Casey to inform Coleman that he and Hale could make an appeal to the Justice Department in Washington if he no longer wanted to negotiate with Casey. But Casey did not inform Coleman or Hale of this avenue, in writing or otherwise. Casey said she believed Hale through Coleman was attempting to manipulate the U.S. Attorney's office. Hale was indicted the very next day. (The indictment was unsealed on September 23)

Three days after the September 21 indictment, Casey met with the prosecution team, including the FBI agents. She told the team that she would recuse herself from the Hale prosecution after all, but that she did not want it to seem as if she was capitulating to Hale's allegations, so she would not announce her recusal publicly at the time. Yet, Casey thereafter met with Coleman regarding a proffer from Hale, and in October declined the first RTC referral. Casey also never informed the Justice Department of her apparent decision on September 24 to recuse.

Casey was in Washington on November 3 on other Department business when she met with Heymann, probably Keeney (though he did not recall attending), and other Criminal Division officials. The meeting was called a couple of days after the publication of the October 31 page one story in the *Washington Post* on the second set of (nine) RTC referrals. At the November 3 meeting, the Justice officials, including Heymann, suggested that Casey recuse herself immediately. Casey was initially inclined to agree to do so, but took umbrage at the tone of the meeting and said that she would consider their suggestion. Casey formally recused herself on November 5, which was publicly announced on November 9, in a letter to Main Justice asking that her office be removed from the case.

Also interesting was the account of what occurred with the first RTC referral, because it informed the judgment of Michael Johnson, the Assistant U.S. Attorney who initially advised Casey against recusing herself. Jean Lewis was under the impression that U.S. Attorney Charles Banks, Casey's predecessor, transferred the RTC referral to Main Justice in the fall of 1992. In fact, all Banks did was notify Main

Justice of his office's September 2 receipt of the referral. However, Banks did not inform Main Justice until October 6, at which time his office sent a copy of the referral to Washington. An FBI teletype dated October 9, 1992 to the FBI office in Little Rock directed the agents not to conduct any "overt" investigation at that time, meaning no witness interviews and no grand jury subpoenas. All the FBI agents were permitted to do was a preliminary review of the documents referenced in the referral. The FBI teletype otherwise told the Little Rock office to treat this case as it would any other. The FBI teletype resulted from an October 8 meeting at the Justice Department, at which time the decision was made.

One week later, Banks told the Little Rock FBI office in an October 16 letter that he would not do anything on the RTC referral until after November 3, 1992, the date of the presidential election. However, he did not tell Main Justice of this decision. Banks said that he believed that in the fall of 1992 Jean Lewis was applying pressure to move the case forward, and Banks did not want to be seen responding to any pressure on such a sensitive investigation. The local FBI office thereupon decided that it also would not conduct any investigation until the U.S. Attorney's office began work on the case.

Banks, however, did not take any action on the RTC referral from November 3, 1992 through apparently the end of January 1993. On January 27, 1993, Banks sent the first referral to Main Justice, asking for its views on whether it warranted prosecution. Banks wrote that he had a political conflict, because his office had lost an earlier prosecution of McDougal. Banks, a Bush Administration appointee, also informed Main Justice that he would leave on March 1, 1993. Banks believed that there was no basis to investigate any of the witnesses (Tucker and the Clintons), but that the McDougals should be interviewed as part of a limited preliminary investigation. Doug Frazier, who at the time was working in the Deputy Attorney General's office, referred the Banks letter and the first RTC referral to Jack Keeney of the Criminal Division.

On February 23, 1993, a Criminal Division trial attorney (Mark McDougal, no relation to the Jim McDougal) authored a memorandum concluding that the first RTC referral (a single allegation) did not warrant prosecution. In a memorandum dated March 19, 1993, Keeney informed Frazier that Banks (who had already left the Government) had no basis to recuse himself from the investigation. Keeney's memorandum and the February 23, 1993 memorandum were sent together to the U.S. Attorney's office months before Casey arrived. These memoranda, plus the lack of specificity in Coleman's offers, formed the basis upon which Michael Johnson initially advised Casey that there was an insufficient basis for her to recuse. Johnson and Casey may have initially thought that Justice did not believe Casey should recuse herself, but Casey's situation was different than Banks' in at least three respects. Casey had ties to the Clintons and was a Clinton appointee; her husband had been appointed to a civil service position by Governor Clinton and now worked for Governor Tucker; and Hale's allegations had now been made, however nonspecific.

Democrats downplayed Casey's refusal to inform Coleman of his avenue to Main Justice, because Coleman spoke with Webster Hubbell in July 1993 and September 1993 on a completely unrelated matter involving the Antitrust Division. Democrats concluded that Coleman knew how to reach the appropriate levels at the Justice Department if he wanted to do so, but he chose not to.

At the December 5 hearing, Steven Irons of the FBI's Little Rock office testified that an SBA lawyer informed him of a White House effort to get the SBA to "throw water" on Hale's allegations. Irons wrote a memorandum dated October 1, 1993, which stated, in pertinent part:

> [The SBA lawyer] advised she had spoken to SBA in Washington . . . and understood officials from the White House had urged SBA to make such a characterization due to the mention of White-water Development in some news accounts and White House desire to avoid any inference criminal activity could have occurred in relation to Whitewater Development and Hale's company.[397]

Irons also testified that, according to an Assistant United States Attorney in Little Rock, one of Hale's attorneys, Richard Mays, went to Washington on August 20, 1993 to "meet with unknown officials to attempt to have the investigation quashed." In an interview with the Committee, Mays denied meeting with any Federal officials.

Senate Committee Subpoenas Documents About November 5, 1993 Meeting for which the Clintons Assert Attorney-Client Privilege

On December 7, the White House responded to the Committee's request for information about the unidentified call Mrs. Clinton made on the night of Foster's death. The White House informed the Committee in a letter that the phone call went to an auxiliary White House number assigned to Administration officials on the road. The call was routed to the Chief of Staff's office, where it was answered by Bill Burton, McLarty's Deputy.[398] On December 8, the First Lady submitted a two-page affidavit to the Committee in response to the four questions it asked of her concerning the unidentified call she made on the night of Foster's death.[399] Mrs. Clinton said that she did not recall whom she called that night, other than the President, but that it "made sense" to her that she also called Maggie Williams, Susan Thomases, Harry Thomason, and Carolyn Huber. She specifically did not recall calling the switchboard number that was since identified as the number she called, but that it would not be unusual for her to be calling the White House.

Also on December 8, the special Senate Committee voted on party lines, 10-8, to subpoena the notes taken by William Kennedy at the November 5, 1993 meeting and a White House memorandum written about the meeting afterward.[400] The subpoena was returnable by 5 p.m. December 12. It was reported that the independent counsel had made a similar request for the documents, and was similarly rebuffed. David Kendall explained in a statement reported by the *Washington Post* that the November 5 meeting was "plainly privileged." (Bruce Lindsey, however, at the time was serving as Director of Presidential Personnel, not as a lawyer in the White House Counsel's office.) He said all of the participants were attorneys or "agents" for the Clintons:

> Its purpose was to brief new personal counsel concerning information and issues and to discuss the appropriate division of labor between personal counsel and White House counsel and to enable all counsel to provide legal advice and services.

According to the *New York Times,* the Clintons personally decided to assert the attorney-client privilege and direct Lindsey and Kennedy not to answer questions about the meeting.

Refusal to comply with the subpoena was expected to move the dispute to court. The Committee could vote to enforce the subpoena, or the Clintons could move to quash the subpoena. The Senate could also seek to hold Kennedy in contempt of Congress, but no report noted this possibility.[401]

The Committee also subpoenaed Bill Burton and Sylvia Mathews back for testimony on December 13 to answer questions relating to the unidentified call made by Mrs. Clinton on the night of Foster's death, although the subpoenas would be withdrawn in favor of their agreement to appear voluntarily. Susan Thomases was also subpoenaed to testify on December 14. This would be her third appearance before the special Senate Committee. The subpoena was issued after the Thomases' law firm informed the Committee earlier in the week of recently discovered records of additional phone calls Thomases made following Foster's death.

The flurry of new information, denials, failures to remember, and the first formal claim of privilege prompted the *New York Times* and *Washington Post* to issue uncharacteristically tough editorials. The *Times* concluded, if the Clintons have done nothing wrong:

> then why not come forward with a complete story? Without that story, what we are left with is a portrait that grows cloudier by the day of an Administration that always dodges full disclosure.[402]

The *Washington Post* concluded (italics in original):

> Has the White House, through these twists, managed to throw suspicion over matters of little consequence, or *is* something serious being covered up? The question is everywhere these days, in large part because of all the improbable and implausible responses that have been made to inquiries so far. If the White House can clear them up, it surely should. Congress and the independent counsel are clearly not going to let things stand as they are now.[403]

Chapter Eight

Whitewater
and
Madison:
Analysis

This analysis of the "Washington" aspect of the Whitewater matter covers:

• **The Disposition of the Whitewater files** (the search of Vince Foster's office and the response to media and Justice Department requests for Whitewater documents);

• **Separating the personal from the official** (Foster's personal work for the Clintons, the White House's role in responding to media inquiries concerning the Clintons in their personal capacity, and White House contacts with Treasury Department Officials); and

• **Alleged interference with the Madison investigation** (by RTC headquarters, Treasury, White House, Webster Hubbell, Paula Casey, and others).

For the most part, this chapter covers the actions taken by Clinton Administration officials and others since the beginning of the Administration. It does not examine the allegations made against various members of the Rose Law Firm, including Mrs. Clinton, or the conduct at issue in the so-called "Arkansas phase" of the independent counsel's investigation.[1]

The analysis in this chapter is not intended as a final accounting of the Whitewater matter. As this book goes to print, many questions remain; numerous conflicts in testimony are unresolved, some of which may never be resolved satisfactorily. Further congressional hearings and, ultimately, the report of the independent counsel are necessary before final conclusions may be reached as to the legality and propriety of the conduct of administration officials. At this point, however, the extensive public record does allow for several preliminary conclusions.

Disposition of the Whitewater Files

This subject includes the searches of Vince Foster's office after his death in July 1993, the disposition of the Whitewater files found in his office, and the response of the White House to the requests to make public the Clintons' Whitewater files.

The Foster Office Search—Factual Background

In the late afternoon of July 20, 1993, Vince Foster's body was found near a cannon in Fort Marcy Park in Virginia, dead from a gunshot wound to his head, an apparent suicide. Foster, Deputy White House Counsel, was a longtime, close friend of the Clintons. An investigation was initiated by the United States Park Police, because Fort Marcy Park is under the jurisdiction of the Park Police.[2]

As Park Police investigators went to Foster's home the night of his death to speak with Foster's wife, David Watkins, who was present at the Foster residence, called Patsy Thomasson and asked her to go to Foster's West Wing office and look for a suicide note. But he did not inform the Park Police of this request. The Park Police asked Watkins to seal Foster's office pending a search of the office (Watkins does not recall being asked to do this), and other White House officials understood that the office would be secured that evening. But the office was not sealed until around 11 a.m. the following day.

Thomasson joined Bernard Nussbaum and Maggie Williams in Foster's office around 10:45 p.m. on the evening of Foster's death. Each, apparently, arrived at the office separately. (Williams went to the White House soon after receiving a call from the First Lady, who was in Little Rock at the time.) All testified that they left the office without taking any documents after their brief search for a note proved unsuccessful. A Secret Service officer, however, testified that he saw Williams leave the Counsel's office and go to her office down the hall carrying file folders.

Although the reports concerning the roles of the Park Police and Justice Department at the time were confusing,[3] both Park Police and Justice officials were present during the search of Foster's office. However, the search was not conducted on July 21. On July 21, Park Police investigators attempted to conduct a search, but after arriving at Foster's office, they "waited outside the door until 6 p.m., barred by Secret Service agents, then finally gave up."[4]

While the Park Police officials were cooling their heels, the Justice Department and Nussbaum were negotiating a procedure for the search; Justice officials left the White House that afternoon, believing they had reached an agreement with Nussbaum whereby they would see the first page of each document to determine its potential relevancy, but that they would not automatically be entitled to any document because of privilege concerns. Nussbaum, however, denied reaching any firm understanding with Justice on July 21.

On July 22, before Justice and Park Police officials came over to the West Wing to participate in the search of Foster's office, Nussbaum received a call from Susan

Thomases, who had recently spoken with the First Lady and Maggie Williams. Nussbaum recalled that Thomases expressed the concern of some "people" that investigators not be given "unfettered access" to Foster's office. Nussbaum presumed Thomases was referring to the First Lady; Thomases denied expressing this view to Nussbaum; Steve Neuwirth, a White House lawyer, testified that Nussbaum told him that the First Lady objected to an unfettered search.

That afternoon, Nussbaum changed the arrangements for the search, insisting that he conduct the search with the investigators observing at some distance. Nussbaum would separate Foster's files into three categories: (1) official White House records, which would remain in the Counsel's office and be transferred to other attorneys; (2) Foster's personal papers, which would go to Foster's attorney; and (3) the Clintons' personal papers, which would go to the Clintons (or their private attorney). Nussbaum would identify any records of potential relevance to Foster's death or his state of mind.

Justice officials balked at Nussbaum's change in plans, and protested to Deputy Attorney General Phil Heymann. Heymann remonstrated with Nussbaum, and, according to Heymann, Nussbaum agreed to consult with unspecified others and get back to Heymann. He never did. The search was conducted that afternoon, frustrating both Justice attorneys and Park Police investigators. Secret Service and FBI investigators apparently were also present. That night, Heymann called Nussbaum to protest the way in which Nussbaum conducted the search, asking Nussbaum whether he was hiding anything. Heymann testified that Nussbaum denied that he hiding anything; Nussbaum does not recall being asked the question.

Nussbaum gave the Whitewater files discovered in Foster's office to Maggie Williams, who took them to the Executive Residence.[5] The Clintons' personal attorney at that time, Robert Barnett, picked them up five days later. Nussbaum testified that he gave the file to Williams and asked her to check with the Clintons to determine what to do with the files. Williams recalled Nussbaum asking her to give the file directly to the Clintons' private attorney, but she was tired and would not wait for a messenger from the law firm to pick them up. She took them to the Residence, after checking with the First Lady. The files were placed in a locked closet with other Clinton financial and personal records. Tom Castleton, who assisted Williams in taking the files to the Residence, recalled that Williams told him the files were being sent to the Residence for the First Lady's review. Williams denied saying this, and the Clintons' current personal attorney, David Kendall, stated that neither the President nor First Lady "examined or reviewed the documents[,] which were preserved and safeguarded until Bob Barnett could pick them up after the Foster funeral."[6]

On July 26, 1993, a handwritten note, torn into twenty-seven pieces, was found in Foster's briefcase by Steve Neuwirth, although Nussbaum had searched and emptied the briefcase in front of investigators during the July 22 office search. The investigators present during the search all testified that they would have discovered the note had they personally conducted the search; some also expressed doubts that the note was in the briefcase at the time of the search. But Michael Spafford, a Foster family lawyer, testified that he overheard Cliff Sloan mention to Nussbaum, immediately following the July 22 search, that he noticed scraps of paper at the bottom of the briefcase. Spafford said that Nussbaum told Sloan he would get to it later; Sloan denied having this conversation or noticing anything in the briefcase on July 22.

The torn-up note consisted of a series of eleven statements, several devoted to defending the actions of White House officials, including Foster's own conduct, and several alleging misconduct by others, such as the press, the FBI, the Republican Party, and even the White House Ushers Office.[7] The White House did not report the existence of the note to the Park Police for twenty-seven hours, after waiting to notify the President, Mrs. Foster, and the First Lady, and then discussing what to do with the note with the Attorney General.[8] Soon thereafter, the Justice Department disclosed that the FBI would interview White House officials on the handling of the note.[9]

On July 28, Park Police investigators visited the office of James Hamilton, Foster's attorney, to view a diary kept by Foster. The investigators were not permitted to copy or take notes. They concluded that the diary "shed no light on Foster's state of mind in the days prior to his death and did not pursue the matter further."[10]

On August 10, 1993, the Park Police closed its investigation, finding that Foster committed suicide. The same day the Justice Department announced two additional, separate inquiries related to Foster's death. First, the Public Integrity Section of the Criminal Division would examine the note's statements about the White House Travel Office, as part of its pending investigation of former Travel Office Director Billy Dale. Second, the Office of Professional Responsibility would investigate the note's assertion that the FBI "lied in their report [on the Travel Office] to the AG[.]"[11]

The visit of White House officials to Foster's office the night of his death to look for a suicide note was revealed soon after Foster's death. But the presence of Whitewater files in Foster's office, and the suspicion that White House officials removed documents from his office were not revealed until December 18, 1993.[12] The confirmation that Whitewater files were found in Foster's office prompted the Justice Department to review the White House's handling of these files.[13] It also prompted media requests for the documents. Dee Dee Myers initially rebuffed these requests, but as pressure mounted for their public release, they were given instead to the Justice Department, in January 1994. This transfer was in response to a subpoena served on December 24, 1993.

Nussbaum initially insisted that his staff sit in on Justice Department (OPR) interviews of the White House staff, but Justice officials objected. Nussbaum ultimately relented after discussing the matter with Heymann.[14]

The resulting furor over the belated confirmation of the July 20 visit to Foster's office, the discovery that some Whitewater documents were among those found in Foster's office, and the heavy hand of the White House Counsel in the Park Police investigation contributed to the call for the appointment of a special counsel to investigate the Clintons' financial dealings. When on January 20, 1994, Attorney General Reno appointed Robert Fiske as Special Counsel, Fiske said publicly that the Foster death would be included in his investigation to the extent it was related to the Clintons' financial dealings.[15] It became apparent later that Fiske intended also to review the Park Police's conclusion of suicide and whether White House officials had obstructed justice or otherwise improperly impeded the Park Police's investigation into the handling of Foster's documents following his death.[16]

On June 30, 1994, Fiske issued his report on the Foster death, concluding that Foster committed suicide. Fiske also found no evidence that "matters relating to Whitewater, Madison Guaranty or [Capital Management Services] played any role in his death."[17] However, Fiske noted that the third part of his office's investigation into Foster's death—relating to the search(es) of Foster's office and the handling of the documents found therein—was not yet completed. Fiske stated that the investigation "is in its final stages and should be completed shortly."[18] But Fiske later acknowledged that it would be delayed beyond the scheduled House and Senate hearings that summer.[19]

In July 1994, the Senate Banking Committee conducted a limited hearing into Foster's death, although the Committee, at Fiske's request, refrained from addressing the search of Foster's office and the handling of the Whitewater files. Republicans insisted that a second round of hearings would be needed following the conclusion of the remaining part of the Special Counsel's Washington investigation.

In August 1994, the court of appeals replaced Special Counsel Fiske with independent counsel Ken Starr. Starr gave no clear indication in the early days following his appointment whether he would revisit Fiske's conclusions relating to the Foster death, but it eventually became apparent that Starr would essentially conduct a *de novo* independent investigation. As of early November 1995, Starr's investigation into Foster's death and subsequent White House conduct remains pending.

The special Senate Committee, established in May 1995, held thirteen days of hearings in July-August 1995 focusing almost exclusively on the conduct of the White House following Foster's death. The analysis which follows is based largely on the testimony adduced at these hearings.

The Foster Office Search—Analysis

The July 20, 1993 Visit to Foster's Office. White House officials should not have entered Foster's office the night of his death without at least notifying the Park Police, since the Park Police had expressed an interest in searching the office and sealing it pending the search. Watkins knew of the Park Police's desires (although he testified he did not recall), yet he tasked Patsy Thomasson to go into Foster's office to look for a note. It is not clear whether Thomasson, Bernard Nussbaum or Maggie Williams knew of the Park Police's request that the office be sealed at the time they went through Foster's office, but others in the White House were aware of this that night. If these three officials were not aware of the Park Police's investigative interests, and **if**, as they have testified, they did not remove any documents (Williams' testimony has been rebutted by a Secret Service agent), then they committed no wrongdoings. It is natural for friends and colleagues of someone who is suspected of committing suicide to look for a note. Still, the presence of Williams **and** Thomasson **and** Nussbaum suggests another motive in looking for a note other than to discern Foster's reason for taking his life. The most warranted criticism of the White House concerning the July 20 visit is its failure to disclose this visit until it was reported five months later, suggesting that the officials did not want their visit revealed.

The Procedure Employed for the July 22 Search. On July 21, the Justice Department reached an agreement with Nussbaum on a procedure to search Foster's office. And because the agreement was quite favorable to the White House's legitimate interests, Nussbaum should have held to it. Nussbaum explained that he did not accept it because it "reflected an inappropriately cynical view of the White House."

He said that White House lawyers did not need a "watchdog."[20]

There is evidence that Nussbaum's change of mind was also prompted by what he understood from a conversation with Susan Thomases as the First Lady's wish that investigators not get "unfettered access" to Foster's office. It is curious why the First Lady would not speak with Nussbaum directly on this subject. She was not in Washington, but neither was Thomases. It would have been natural for the First Lady to be wary of opening up her financial files, and not surprising if she did get her views on the subject to Nussbaum, in some manner. But, like the Travel Office matter, her role was kept in the shadows, allowing the critics to assume something sinister.

Given the privileged nature of many of Foster's documents, it was proper for Nussbaum to attend to those privileges. All official White House documents are privileged to some extent, because the Freedom of Information Act does not apply to the White House Office. Many documents are protected by the deliberative process privilege: some by a form of that privilege called "executive privilege," with respect to advice to and communications between the President and his staff. Still other documents may be classified for reasons of national security. Finally, documents that are not official government documents, like the Whitewater files, may be subject to the attorney-client privilege. Nussbaum was certainly within his office to ensure that the **governmental** privileges would not be lost.[21]

But Nussbaum was not shielding documents from the media, or the public, or even from Congress. **White House Counsel Nussbaum was shielding documents from investigators of Executive Branch agencies.** Governmental privileges are not lost or waived by sharing documents with law enforcement agencies, especially if the documents remain physically in the White House.[22] In defending his actions two years later, Nussbaum wrote that he feared waiving this privilege.[23] However his fear was not well-founded. The media could not obtain these documents had they been reviewed by the Park Police or Justice Department. In any event, Nussbaum could have sufficiently protected the privileged nature of the documents by conducting the search pursuant to the understanding reached with Justice the day before.

Essentially, **Nussbaum** conducted the search of Foster's office, and the investigators were at his mercy in terms of what they saw of the documents or knew of their contents. It is true, as Nussbaum pointed out, that on many occasions documents that are produced pursuant to a congressional or litigation request are screened by the attorney representing the person or agency with ownership or custody of the documents. But this was an investigation into a death of a high-ranking official. The investigators were, for the most part, criminal investigators. And as of July 22, 1993, Foster's death should have been treated as a potential homicide; in fact, the Justice Department lawyers had not ruled out foul play as of July 22. In such circumstances, a search of an office by law enforcement is often done, without any screen of the documents by their owner, custodian, or attorney.[24]

The Whitewater documents in Foster's office were not government records. As such, no governmental privilege attached to them. The documents may have been protected by the attorney-client privilege, although this is far from certain, given Foster's dual role in the White House, as well as the content of the files. By allowing a government official (Foster) to be privy to the documents, the Clintons may have waived the privilege.[25] In any event, Nussbaum was not the person to assert or protect that privilege. Nussbaum should have called for the Clintons' personal attorney to participate in the search; he should have realized from the start that Foster's office would contain some personal records of the Clintons, given the internal notoriety of Foster's personal work for the Clintons. Park Police and Justice investigators could have dealt with the Clintons' personal attorney separately, as Justice officials eventually did months later.

Transferring the Clintons' Whitewater File to the Clintons or Their Attorney. Nussbaum was likely correct in determining that Foster's Whitewater file was the property of the Clintons. At this point, the documents could have been sent to the Clintons' personal attorney or to the Clintons. There was no outstanding law enforcement request for the Whitewater documents as of July 1993. Either destination would likely have been proper. If the documents were the Clintons' property, it was entirely appropriate for the Clintons to review them, at their discretion.

The handling of the Clintons' Whitewater file was controversial mainly because of (1) conflicting statements and testimony as to where the documents would go and whether they would be reviewed by the Clintons; (2) the belated discovery that Foster's office contained the Clinton's personal Whitewater files; and (3) the even more belated admission that the documents remained in the Residence for several days before being picked up by the Clintons' personal attorney.

The July 26 Discovery and Subsequent Handling of the Torn-Up Hand Written Note. The official White House account of the discovery of the note (the testimony of Neuwirth, Nussbaum, and Sloan) is suspect, because of the testimony of Michael Spafford, Linda Tripp, Deborah Gorham, and nearly all other observers of the July 22 search. The torn-up note should have been discovered then; Spafford testified that, in fact, it may have been discovered immediately thereafter. The mystery surrounding its discovery, as well as the inordinate delay in providing the note to investigators, fuels suspicion that the note was tampered with. In October 1995, three handwriting experts announced that the note was a forgery.[26]

Assuming the note was not forged or tampered with, its eventual transmission to law enforcement authorities was proper but also belated. There was no urgency to the investigation that would have demanded the immediate notification of the Park Police or Justice Department. The reasons for a delay—notifying Mrs. Foster and the President—are legitimate, but should not have required twenty-seven hours to satisfy. The delay suggests that the White House contemplated not turning over the note, but there was no testimony to this effect.

The White House's Response to the Requests for Whitewater Documents

The White House initially rebuffed media requests for the Clintons' Whitewater files found in Foster's office. The documents were eventually turned over to the Justice Department, pursuant to a subpoena. Once the subpoena was issued, the Clintons were for the most part considered off the hook. Most observers in the media and some Republicans accepted uncritically the explanation that the subpoena operated to keep the Whitewater documents from public view, but did criticize the discussions between the Clintons' attorney, David Kendall, and the Justice Department. They were wrong on both counts. Lawyers, on the other hand, for the most part found nothing improper or unusual in David Kendall's discussions with Justice or his request for a subpoena.[27]

Because the Clintons' involvement in Whitewater and Madison does not relate to the actions of the President or the First Lady in their Federal roles, it was correct to use David Kendall, instead of White House lawyers, to handle the requests for the Clintons' Whitewater documents. Moreover, as of December 1993, the Whitewater files physically were not in the White House (unless they were kept in the Executive Residence). Many press reports refer—incorrectly as far as is known—to the White House as the (or at least an) active player in discussions with the Justice Department concerning the documents.[28] The White House, alas, contributed to this misperception: senior White House aides repeatedly answered reporters' questions as if the matters involved official government documents. It was also revealed that the White House staff debated internally about what should be the President's response to the call for documents. If any White House official did engage in discussions with the Justice Department over the documents, this would have an improper participation in an ongoing criminal investigation. Even public statements made by White House officials about the documents should have been avoided, because such statements could be seen as indirect but not-so-subtle White House directions to Justice Department political appointees.

Kendall's Request not to Share Documents with the Office of Professional Responsibility. David Kendall called Justice to discuss (1) turning over documents, and, upon learning from Justice that a subpoena was being drafted for the documents, (2) the scope of the subpoena. This was appropriate conduct for a defense attorney. Defense counsel often may assist a prosecutor in describing the universe of documents, their volume, and organization. It is also proper for defense counsel to inform the prosecutor of privileges or privacy interests the client may possess. However, the Justice Department's conduct is open to question. Generally, Justice Department attorneys are precluded from acknowledging the existence of a grand jury, even if reports of one have surfaced in the press. Moreover, the Justice Department's exclusive concern is the expeditious collection of all relevant evidence; Justice should not "negotiate" a subpoena with defense counsel, if in doing so it sacrifices this objective.

Kendall's peculiar request that the documents not be shared with OPR was characterized as "unusual" and "extraordinary."[29] Under certain circumstances, Rule 6(e) of the Federal Rules of Criminal Procedure permits the disclosure of grand jury materials to other government attorneys conducting a criminal investigation or to other government attorneys.[30] Possibly Kendall wanted OPR to obtain a court order to gain access, which order would presumably subject OPR to an obligation of secrecy.[31] But, as subsequently explained , Rule 6(e) does not even cover the Whitewater files.

In any event, what is not known, and what piques curiosity, is not the legal basis for Kendall's request, but the reason for the request in first place. OPR generally has no jurisdiction over non-Justice Department personnel such as the Clintons.[32] OPR would have jurisdiction over allegations against Webster Hubbell, but there is no indication that OPR conducted an investigation of Hubbell, who recused himself in October or November 1993 from any involvement in the Madison and Whitewater matters. The only known pending OPR investigation concerned the White House Travel Office matter (a review of the FBI-White House contacts and an analysis of

Vince Foster's assertion that the FBI "lied" in its report to Attorney General Reno). OPR was also reported to have "begun questioning about the White House's cooperation with the Park Police and FBI during the investigation of Foster's death[,]" including questioning Park Police investigators about a diary kept by Foster, removed from Foster's office and given to James Hamilton, for any light it might shed on OPR's Travel Office inquiry.[33]

What possible explanations are there for Kendall's request that the documents not be shared with OPR? Kendall may have known about the existence of the OPR inquiry based on press reports, but the nature of the OPR investigation known to the public at the time was limited to the White House Travel Office matter. There was no indication on December 23, 1993, that OPR was looking into Foster's death per se or Whitewater. It was previously reported that the "Justice Department" was investigating both the Travel Office matter and Foster's death (although the latter investigation appeared to amount only to supervision of a Park Police investigation). One possible explanation is that the President or First Lady asked Kendall to keep the documents away from the Foster suicide investigation. Another possible explanation is that Kendall feared that disclosure of the documents to OPR might lead to a leak of some information to the public. Another is that he was doing the bidding for Hubbell. But this question remains a matter of speculation.

Grand Jury Secrecy Rules Did Not Prevent Public Release of the Whitewater Files. Contrary to what was widely reported, neither the grand jury subpoena nor the transmission of the Whitewater documents to the Justice Department prevented them from being released to the public. Criticism of the President for not releasing the Whitewater files largely subsided when the President agreed to turn over the documents to the Justice Department and a subpoena was served soon thereafter. The media accepted the explanation that the subpoena prevented the public from obtaining the Whitewater documents.[34] But this explanation is not true; no law stood in the way of a public release of the Clintons' Whitewater documents.

Rule 6(e) requires the secrecy of "matters occurring before the grand jury."[35] Wrongful disclosure may be punished as a contempt of court.[36] But Rule 6(e) did not preclude the Clintons or their attorney from releasing to the public the very same documents turned over to the Justice Department pursuant to the subpoena. First, Rule 6(e) imposes an obligation of secrecy only on:

> [a] grand juror, an interpreter, a stenographer, an operator of a recording device, a typist who transcribes recorded testimony, and an attorney for the government[.] . . . No obligation of secrecy may be imposed on any person except in accordance with this rule.[37]

This is why one frequently sees grand jury witnesses (or their attorneys) walking directly out of the grand jury room, facing a group of reporters, and describing their testimony. Rule 6(e) does not reach them.

Second, Rule 6(e) prohibits the disclosure of "proceedings." A grand jury proceeding commonly includes grand jury minutes, testimony before the grand jury, witness statements made to prosecutors in contemplation of a witness's appearance before the grand jury, and documents **created by or for** the grand jury. However,

documents that were created outside and independent of the grand jury do not automatically become subject to Rule 6(e) when they are subpoenaed by the grand jury.
Neither the fact that the documents were obtained pursuant to a grand jury subpoena
nor the fact that they were submitted to the grand jury is conclusive; "[r]ather, an
agency must establish a nexus between the release of that information and 'revelation of a protected aspect of the grand jury's investigation.'" For documents extrinsic
to the grand jury, this nexus must be apparent from the document itself and "the
government cannot immunize [it] by publicizing the link."[38]

Here, the entirety of Whitewater documents were created outside the grand jury
—indeed, all the documents were created before the grand jury was convened—and
were created and maintained for other purposes. Assume that one of the documents
subpoenaed is promotional literature for the Whitewater real estate development. If a
request for that document is made to an agency or person other than the Justice
Department prosecutor, the document is not subject to Rule 6(e). Thus, if the Clintons desired to turn over their Whitewater files to the public, they could have done
so. **Indeed, the Clintons and White House did provide at least some of these
documents to Congress and to the media, on a selective basis, two years later.**[39]

Of course, if no copy was made of the documents delivered to the Justice Department in response to the subpoena, there would no longer be any documents physically in the possession of the Clintons, and thus there would be nothing to release to
the public. No such explanation was offered, of course. No competent defense attorney ever turns over documents to the Government without first making a copy of the
set for his and his clients' own use. The failure to do so would be negligent unless the
clients expressly directed that no copies be made.

**The Freedom of Information Act (FOIA) Did Not Require the Release of
the Documents.** On the other hand, there were also incorrect statements made about
whether the documents were subject to required disclosure under FOIA. It is correct
that documents that are part of a pending criminal investigation, as well as documents subject to Rule 6(e), are exempt from required disclosure under 5 U.S.C.
552(b)(7) and (b)(3), respectively. However, even if these exemption did not apply,
FOIA may not be relied upon to obtain public disclosure of these documents.

First, the Whitewater documents initially sought were the Clintons' personal
records;[40] they were not "agency records" as that term is used in FOIA. A document
in the possession of a Government agency is an "agency record" if it is (1) either
created or obtained by an agency and (2) under agency control at the time of the
FOIA request.[41] These documents were not created by the White House, nor were
they obtained by the White House. These documents existed before Bill Clinton
became President, and were brought to the White House by the Clintons, by Vince
Foster, or by other aides who had previously served Governor Clinton. These documents did not exist for any Federal Government purpose or use. The mere fact of the
documents' original placement in Foster's West Wing office, without any indication
that the documents were used or held for governmental purposes, does not make the
documents "agency records." Second, the documents that were removed from Foster's office by Bernard Nussbaum were delivered separately to attorneys for the Clintons via the Residence and to Foster's widow. At the time of the FOIA request, they
were apparently no longer in the custody of the Government. Third, the White House

Office, and specifically the Office of the White House Counsel, is not subject to FOIA.[42]

The Public Interest Outweighs the Clintons' Privacy Interest. It is natural, even for a public official, to resist public disclosure of personal financial and business records. As a legal matter and as a matter of public policy, public officials generally should not be required to sacrifice the privacy of their personal life or waive any privileges. However, the sphere of privacy accorded Presidents by the media is severely circumscribed. Moreover, the Whitewater documents concern business transactions (and perhaps Arkansas Government actions) in which there is less of a personal privacy interest and in which there is a clear countervailing public interest in their disclosure. Where documents are sought in connection with allegations of official wrongdoing, an official's privacy interest may be subordinated to the public interest in determining the truth of the allegations.

Once a criminal investigation is underway, there is also a natural inclination of prosecutors (shared by those under investigation) to resist public disclosure of documents that are relevant to the investigation, to avoid compromising the investigation, to avoid prejudice to those who are subjects of the investigation, and to avoid a parallel trial in the press. But the prosecutor's interests must also be weighed against the public's interest in full and timely accounting of what happened.

Thus, the Clintons should have publicly disclosed their Whitewater files in December 1993 or soon thereafter.

The Delay in Responding to the Subpoena. The Clintons were criticized for the time it took to deliver the documents to the Justice Department once they were subpoenaed. Some criticism was justified. The Clintons were not helped by George Stephanopoulos's glib assertion on television on January 2, 1994 that all the records had been turned over when, in fact, none had been. This misstatement likely resulted from a failure of communication between Stephanopoulos and others in the White House who, according to reports, knew that the documents would not be turned over for several days, ostensibly to permit their culling and cataloging.

A subpoena generally allows the recipient a few days to find, assemble, and deliver documents, and this subpoena most likely did so. Many of us who have served in the Executive Branch, and have participated in responding to numerous congressional committee requests for documents, know that a response often cannot be made in a day or two. Also, it is standard practice for recipients of subpoenas (actually, their lawyers) to make a copy of the files and perhaps even to organize them for the benefit of both the requester and the recipient. This takes some time. Moreover, the subpoena was served on December 24. Even in the White House, or at Williams & Connolly, some leeway ought to be accorded because of the holiday season.

On the other hand, it is hard to imagine that the Clintons (or their attorney) had not previously collected all relevant Whitewater documents wherever found, given the intense media interest in those documents well before the subpoena was served. And there is no indication that the amount of documents subject to the subpoena was voluminous, as is often the case in responding to a congressional committee request. Indeed, when the White House (or Kendall) made available to reporters what it labeled as "the Whitewater file" on the eve of congressional hearings in July 1995, the documents totaled fewer than one hundred pages! It is not even clear that the White

House had any responsive documents in its possession or otherwise played any role in responding to the subpoena.

The White House's Failure to Separate the Personal from the Official

The Clinton White House has repeatedly demonstrated its failure to observe the fundamental distinction between matters of interest to the Government and matters that are personal to the Clintons. At the margins, the distinction between what is official and what is personal may not be clear, but the distinction is critical nonetheless. Although senior White House officials are not paid an hourly wage and are not on a leave system, there is no official purpose for these officials to involve themselves in matters that do not relate to government policies, programs, or decisions. Further, there are occasions when the interests of the presidency may diverge from the personal interests of the President, requiring Federal officials, such as the White House Counsel, to give allegiance to the President only in his official capacity. Most of the time the White House staff has shown little regard for this distinction; White House officials have played various roles in assisting the President and First Lady in their personal affairs.

The two most celebrated examples come from the White House Counsel's office, Bernard Nussbaum and Vince Foster. Nussbaum probably lost his job because, after vigorously asserting the Clintons' personal interests during the search of Vince Foster's office, he continued to attend to their personal interests relating to Whitewater. Foster was criticized after his death for having continued to serve, formally or informally, as the Clintons' personal attorney while also serving as Deputy Counsel to the President.

But the problem with the White House has been endemic. In 1993 and early 1994 Bruce Lindsey served as the White House official to respond to specific questions reporters posed about the Clintons' financial affairs and about alleged extramarital conduct by Governor Clinton. And the problem has not been confined to responding to media requests. White House officials proactively sought information about the Madison and David Hale investigations and even attempted to affect the conduct (questioning the hiring of Jay Stephens) and supervision (resisting the recusal of Roger Altman) of the Madison investigation.

Later, when a Special Counsel was appointed and Congress contemplated hearings, damage control teams were set up, with John Podesta and then Mark Fabiani serving as spokesmen. At this point, some White House involvement was necessary to respond to requests for official White House documents and the testimony of White House officials. But there would have been no White House documents and no information to elicit from White House staff had the White House not brought the Whitewater affair into the White House in the first place by its insistence on handling media inquiries relating to Whitewater.

Vince Foster's Personal Work for the Clintons

The first illustration of the perils involved in failing to keep personal and official matters separate is the personal work Vince Foster did for the Clintons in the White House. In addition to being a colleague of Mrs. Clinton at the Rose Law Firm in Little Rock, Foster had been a close friend of the Clintons for many years. While at the firm and during the transition, Foster assisted the Clintons in various personal business matters. When he joined the White House as Deputy White House Counsel, Foster continued to serve the Clintons as a personal attorney-adviser. Although it is unclear whether Foster had entered into or continued a formal attorney-client relationship with the Clintons, an attorney-client relationship can be established by the conduct and expectations of the parties, and it is apparent that the Clintons regarded Foster as both their official and personal counsel.

This undefined but close personal and professional relationship was carried into the White House. Foster was a key adviser to the First Lady and the Health Care Task Force she chaired, and he played a substantial role in the investigation of the White House Travel Office and the firing of the Travel Office employees.[43]

Foster also continued to handle some personal legal matters for the Clintons in the White House, including assisting the Clintons prepare their 1993 personal tax return (covering 1992) and assisting the Clintons' accounting firm in completing the delinquent corporate tax returns for the Whitewater Development Corporation for the years 1990-92.[44] Foster also helped the President complete his public financial disclosure report, which was filed on May 14, 1993, and assisted in the creation of the Clintons' blind trust, which was executed by the Clintons on July 4 of that year.[45] Foster kept in his West Wing office certain personal financial and business records of the Clintons, including a file or files relating to Whitewater.

Foster has been criticized posthumously for providing personal legal advice and services for the Clintons while also serving as Deputy White House Counsel. Some have alleged that Foster's personal work for the Clintons was a crime, or at least a violation of the ethics rules. Others point to the potential for a conflict between Foster's role as an attorney for the President and First Lady his role as an attorney for the Clintons personally.

It is a legitimate part of the job of an agency ethics official to assist an employee in completing a financial disclosure report and to counsel the employee on whether to establish a blind trust. However, the blind trust instrument should actually be drawn up by an employee's accountant, attorney, or the trustee, not by a Government employee. Moreover, the work Foster did for the Clintons concerning their personal tax liability and the delinquent Whitewater corporate tax returns was personal to the Clintons and lacked any official nexus. The most the White House should involve itself with concerning the President's taxes is to release the completed returns to the public through the Press Office, as was done in the Bush White House. The tax advice and services must be provided personally. In working on the Clintons' taxes, Foster was not engaged in official work.

The potential criminal offense is conversion.[46] The prohibition against converting a "thing of value of the United States" to one's personal use has been held to cover the misuse of Federal grant funds by a Federal contractor to pay for personal services provided to the contractor by an assistant.[47] Thus, a "thing of value" may consist of an employee's services.

However, the complete phrase used in the statute is "thing of value of the United States." The question therefore is whether all of Foster's work in the White House was "a thing of value of the United States." The ethics standards provide guidance in resolving this question.

As a commissioned officer appointed by the President and employed in the White House Office, Foster was not considered an "employee" subject to the Federal leave system. He did not punch a time clock, was not required to obtain approval to take off an hour or day from work, and did not accrue annual leave. Federal employees subject to a leave system are obligated to "use official time in an honest effort to perform official duties." But an official like Foster, not under a leave system, is obligated only "to expend an honest effort and a reasonable proportion of his time in the performance of official duties."[48] There is no suggestion that Foster devoted a **disproportionate** amount of time to the Clintons' personal matters, at least in the sense that he was unable to discharge his official responsibilities. Thus, so long as Foster spent a reasonable part of his work day on official matters, other work he did on the side did not consist of government services. Thus, it was not a crime for Foster to perform personal work for the Clintons.

The standards of conduct also prohibit an employee from "encourag[ing], direct[ing], coerc[ing], or request[ing] a subordinate to use official time to perform" personal services.[49] Apart from the question of whether Foster's personal work for the Clintons constituted "official time," this standard is directed to the supervising official (Clinton), not the subordinate (Foster), and the President is not considered an employee subject to this standard.[50] Thus, this ethics standard was not violated either.

Foster's use of paper and word processors could be considered misuse of Government property in violation of the standards of conduct,[51] but any violation most likely would be considered *de minimis*, something employees do from time to time.

The conflict question is more serious, as illustrated by the tax services Foster provided the Clintons. At some point, the United States Government might have a claim against the Clintons with regard to their tax liability. Foster, as an officer of the United States, could not have represented the Clintons before the IRS.[52] Yet, Foster could also have been on the hook for advice he provided the Clintons. Performing personal services for the President, as a general matter, may not always pose a problem, but the analysis is different if the personal services concern a matter before the United State Government.

Another problem with simultaneously serving as private counsel to the Clintons and Government counsel to the President (and First Lady) arises over the extent to which the communications between the President (or Mrs. Clinton) and Vince Foster were privileged. Communications between the President and members of his staff are subject to a claim of executive privilege. Communications between the Clintons and their personal attorney are subject to a claim of attorney-client privilege. The scope of each privilege, and whether it provides a legal or political shield from a subpoena issued by an independent counsel or Congressional committee, are unclear. But the attorney-client privilege may be waived if the otherwise privileged communication is disclosed to third parties, namely, United States Government officials.

Foster's dual role posed a risk to the Clintons with respect to the privileged nature of their communications, but that risk was not magnified until after his death. Indeed, the major dispute over privilege to this point is whether a November 5, 1993, meeting among the President's White House lawyers and the Clintons' personal attorneys is protected by the attorney-client privilege. Whether the claim of privilege is respected by Congress or the courts will depend, at least in part, on the fact that White House attorneys were present at the meeting.

In the end, Foster's personal work for the Clintons did not violate any law. However, in doing so, Foster went beyond his official duties, and he was responsible for bringing Whitewater documents into the White House Office (as opposed to the Executive Residence) that would prove to be a sustaining headache for the White House after his death.

Concerned that, following Foster's death, others in the White House were providing personal legal advice to the Clintons, Representative Frank Wolf wrote the White House asking whether any White House official had provided personal legal assistance to the President or the First Lady. Bernard Nussbaum responded in the negative:

> [T]he President and Mrs. Clinton are represented personally by a private attorney. No public funds are being used to compensate that attorney. Furthermore, no White House staff members are acting as lawyers for the President and the First Lady where there is no official nexus."[53]

In a White House written response to a question for the record following the March 22, 1994 congressional testimony of Patsy Thomasson, the White House repeated Nussbaum's statement and added, "In addition, to our knowledge, no government personnel outside the White House are providing or have provided legal counsel to the President or First Lady on matters relating to Whitewater or Madison Guaranty."[54]

These carefully written statements, taken together, allow for the conclusion that Vince Foster and perhaps others **did** provide legal counsel to the President or First Lady on matters relating to Whitewater or Madison before February 10, 1994. Moreover, the Nussbaum response just begs the question of whether there was an "official nexus" in advising the President on how to respond to media inquiries on Whitewater and Madison or other personal matters.

Lloyd Cutler, who in replacing Nussbaum made a major point of insisting that he would represent President Clinton in his official capacity, not his personal capacity, refused to criticize Foster for continuing to work on the Clintons' Whitewater tax returns while he served in the White House.[55]

Responding to Inquiries About the Clintons' Whitewater Investment and Madison Guaranty

When questions arose during the 1992 campaign concerning the Clintons' investment in Whitewater and their relationship to the McDougals and Madison Guaranty, it was natural for the campaign to prepare the candidate to respond. Campaign officials enlisted the Rose Law Firm to assemble documents and James Lyons, a Denver attorney and friend of Clintons and Foster, conducted a quick analysis that purported to put the controversy to rest. Although Foster was working on Whitewater tax returns in the first months in the White House, and knew of the Clintons' exposure to liability to the IRS as well as to further public criticism, it appears that no one else in the White House was engaged in any matter relating to Whitewater.

After Foster died on July 20, 1993, the Whitewater files found in his office on July 22 and determined to be the Clintons' personal property were properly sent to the Clintons in the Executive Residence and eventually given to the Clintons' personal attorney. At this point, Whitewater was neither a matter of public concern nor (apparently) a concern within the White House.

That changed in September 1993, when word came to the White House, via

Treasury Department political appointees, that the RTC had prepared a set of referrals to the Justice Department in which the Clintons were named as potential beneficiaries of alleged illegal conduct. Also in September 1993, David Hale's allegation that Governor Clinton pressured him to make a loan to a company owned by fellow-Whitewater owner Susan McDougal surfaced in the Arkansas media. (There are indications that the White House knew of Hale's difficulties—and perhaps his allegations—earlier through communications from the SBA or Hale's attorney.) This was the critical juncture for the White House; should the White House: get involved in preparing for and answering media inquiries concerning the Clintons' personal investment decisions made years before he became President, or should the matter be handled by the Clintons' personal attorney and accountant? There is no indication that anyone in the White House even flagged the issue, much less urged that these matters be handled privately. Instead, Clinton White House officials, many of whom had endured the brief Whitewater controversy during the campaign, naturally assumed that they would get involved in order to defend and protect the Clintons. This was an enormous mistake, revealing the political rather than the institutional mode of White House conduct.[56]

Once the Clintons retained a personal attorney to handle their business affairs (Robert Barnett then David Kendall), all questions directed to the White House from the media relating to Whitewater or Madison Guaranty (as well as questions about the trooper allegations), should have been referred to their private attorney. This would have allowed the President and the White House to devote their full attention to official government matters, and would have avoided the steady tide of conflicting, uninformed, and disingenuous statements from the White House staff on these matters. It also could have kept the White House staff from engaging in various information-gathering activities with Treasury Department and Small Business Administration officials.

In its analysis of the White House-Treasury contacts relating to the RTC's investigation of Madison Guaranty, OGE declined to find fault with Jean Hanson's alerting the White House to the RTC referral in which the Clintons were mentioned. (OGE did not examine the propriety of the conduct of White House officials.) The following passage has been relied upon as support for the White House's decision to involve itself in media inquiries relating to Madison and Whitewater:

> The question of whether Ms. Hanson's disclosure served an official interest raises a unique issue about the nature of the Office of the President. Matters that would be of only personal significance for other executive branch officials may take on official significance when the President of the United States is involved. White House staff has long been used in addressing press inquiries regarding essentially personal matters involving the President and First Lady. Since appropriated funds have been spent for these purposes from administration to administration without any legal objection of which we are aware, **we are not in a position to question the validity of the assumption apparently made by those who participated in the contacts . . . that dealing with press inquiries regarding the President's and First Lady's personal lives, including any involvement they may have had with Madison, is a proper White House function. . . .**[57]

This passage is a far cry from an imprimatur of the White House's actions; OGE was reluctant to make the call between what is official and what is not, and understandably so. But this should not excuse the White House Counsel from making such a call both at the time (Nussbaum) or later (Cutler). It cannot be right that everything of interest to the media concerning the President and First Lady warrants the participation of the White House. Where an inquiry does not relate to the President *qua* President or the First Lady in her official capacity, the most that the White House Press Office should do is to facilitate a response by directing the questioner to the President, the President's attorney, or promising to find out the information from the President or his attorney and relay that information back to the questioner. This does not justify the involvement of others outside the Press Office, engaging either as *de facto* spokesmen (i.e, Bruce Lindsey) or worse, as information-gathers or fact-finders.

Of course, there is no harm in the White House Press Office responding to inquiries concerning the President's birthday, the Clintons' anniversary, or even the President's vacation plans. The public has a natural, innocuous interest in such aspects of the President's and First Family's personal life. Within reason, the Press Office can accommodate this human interest dimension, assuming the President has no objection. But in these personal matters, there is no countervailing Federal interest. In the Whitewater matter, by contrast, White House officials injected themselves into a Federal law enforcement investigation pending with a Federal agency, indeed, an agency—the RTC—with an intended greater degree of independence from the White House than the Cabinet departments. Where a personal matter involving the President also is a matter of official interest to the Federal Government, the standards of conduct come into play:

> Each employee has a responsibility to the United States Government and its citizens to place loyalty to the Constitution, laws and ethical principles about private gain.[58]

Why is it prudent for White House officials to stay away from most personal matters involving the President and First Lady? First, these officials often will lack personal knowledge of what occurred, and thus are not accountable for what they say. Second, getting involved in these matters suggests there is a official purpose or interest in the matter. Third, White House involvement in a matter tends to make it something of greater interest to the media. The White House's insistence on responding to Whitewater questions from the outset illustrates these three points.

Most White House officials have no personal knowledge about what occurred relating to Madison and Whitewater, and thus they were put in a difficult position, risking misstatements and inaccuracies, when called upon to answer Whitewater questions. Even the Clintons' Arkansas friends, such as Mac McLarty, Bruce Lindsey, and Patsy Thomasson, could not be completely aware of the Clintons' financial investments. But even assuming that the Clintons could and did inform the White House staff of their opinions, their recollection of the facts, and supplied them with their Whitewater documents, it would not be appropriate for White House staff to engage in major activities regarding the matter, because they did not concern Bill Clinton as President or Hillary Rodham Clinton as First Lady. Moreover, the involvement of White House staff in information-gathering and "heads ups" served to bring the

Whitewater controversy into the West Wing. Without any White House staff involvement, there would be no White House documents of interest to Congress or the independent counsel and no information to elicit from White House staff.

Marlin Fitzwater, who served as Press Secretary to Presidents Reagan and Bush, contrasted the Clinton White House's response to Whitewater—"Whitewater has been so destructive of the Clinton presidency because the White House sticks to it like flypaper"— to his strategy in 1987 not to respond to or get involved with anything relating to Iran-Contra, because it was a matter under investigation. "My policy would be: This matter is being investigated by three outside bodies and not by the White House. We will leave all answers to them."[59]

There is some evidence that the White House gradually realized its error, as David Kendall (concerning Whitewater and Mrs. Clinton's commodity trades) and Bob Bennett (concerning the Paula Jones lawsuit) assumed the proper role of responding to media inquiries. Media squeamishness may be the reason why the Paula Jones allegations did not stick to the White House, but one major reason why the damage resulting from the stories on Mrs. Clinton's commodity trades was limited is that the controversy was confined to the Clintons, and to a period of time antedating the Presidency. By contrast, the White House made Whitewater a White House scandal, directly leading to present allegations of perjury and obstruction of justice.

Lloyd Cutler, who replaced Bernard Nussbaum as White House Counsel on a temporary basis in March 1994, accepted the job on two conditions: that he would serve no more than 130 days and that he would function as Counsel to the President *qua* President (not as his personal attorney). Cutler stressed that he would serve as counsel to "the president in office" and to "the presidency," leaving to Mr. Clinton's private counsel the task of advising on matters occurring before Clinton was inaugurated:[60]

> When it comes to the President's private affairs, particularly private affairs that occurred before he took office, those should be handled by his own personal private counsel and, in my view, not by the White House Counsel.[61]

Nussbaum's perceived failure to observe such a distinction was cited as a major reason why Nussbaum should have been, and was replaced. Yet, soon after his appointment, Cutler appeared on network television programs and defended the Clintons on the merits, despite his pledge to stay out of their private matters.[62]

Observing the distinction between matters personal and official does not mean that it was improper for the White House to assemble a damage control team made up of a combination of White House officials and outside advisers, once the Whitewater affair included questions concerning the propriety of conduct of White House officials in their ostensible official capacity and external investigations by the Special (and subsequently, independent) Counsel and Congress got underway. At this point, White House officials were potential grand jury and congressional witnesses (if not targets or subjects), and the White House had generated documents of potential relevance to these investigations. The White House had to charge one its own to coordinate responses to grand jury subpoenas and other requests for information and testimony. Even so, in commenting on the various indictments and guilty pleas obtained by the independent counsel in 1995 (which Mark Fabiani regularly has done), the White House's damage control team has ventured beyond a properly limited purpose. Once again, in attempting to convince the media the Arkansas prosecutions have no relevance to the Clintons, the White House continues to attract attention to itself, thus hindering its objective.

The Contacts Between Treasury Officials and the White House

The Administration received a great deal of criticism for several contacts between Treasury officials and members of the White House staff concerning various aspects of the RTC's investigation of Madison. After the initial crescendo of stories in March 1994 about three White House meetings (additional discussions between Treasury officials and senior White House staff were revealed later that month), Special Counsel Fiske immediately subpoenaed each official present at these meetings as well as others who were privy to the substance of what was discussed; Republicans in the House and Senate called for these officials to appear before Congress to reveal what was discussed; and Bernard Nussbaum resigned.

Fiske's immediate concern was whether White House or Treasury officials had obstructed justice by interfering in the RTC's investigation of Madison. Fiske issued a report in June 1994 concluding that "the evidence is insufficient to establish that anyone within the White House or the Department of the Treasury acted with the intent to corruptly influence an RTC investigation."[63] Fiske declined to provide any details of the investigation, citing the restrictions on the disclosure of grand jury material. He added that his review did not look into the propriety of the meetings or whether anything unethical occurred at the meetings, noting that this determination was up to OGE.

One month later, OGE issued a report on its examination of the Treasury-White House contacts under the standards of conduct, concluding that no ethics standards were violated by current Treasury officials. Although OGE did not find that any Treasury official violated any standard, its conclusion was phrased quite narrowly: "we believe that **you [Secretary Bentsen] might reasonably conclude** that the conduct detailed in the report . . . did not violate the Standards of Ethical Conduct for Employees of the Executive Branch. However, many of the contacts detailed in the report are troubling."[64]

OGE's conclusion, qualified as it was, was based on two premises, both of which are questionable. First, OGE deferred to the White House's view that "dealing with press inquiries regarding the President's and First Lady's personal lives" (regarding alleged misconduct antedating the Presidency) is a proper White House function.[65] The second premise was that the **only** purpose of Treasury officials in contacting the White House was to assist the White House in responding to press inquiries. OGE specifically found no intention of any Treasury official to advance another person's private gain. The same cannot be said of White House officials, however.

This study accepts the Fiske judgment, based on the present record, that no White House official intended to obstruct justice in the contacts with Treasury in the fall of 1993 and winter of 1994. However, OGE's reasoning should not be applied in evaluating the conduct of **White House officials** under the **standards of conduct**, because it is inappropriate to apply OGE's premises to the conduct of White House officials.[66] First, there is, for White House staff, a proper dichotomy between what is official and what is personal, and White House officials failed to observe it. Second, it is clear that there was more than one purpose behind the activities of White House officials in obtaining information about the RTC's referrals.

The issue is not simply whether it was an appropriate official function for Dee Dee Myers to respond to a question put to her by the White House Press Corps at the daily briefing. The conduct White House officials engaged in here involved gathering nonpublic information of certain particulars of a Federal law enforcement investigation and alerting the President and First Lady (and apparently their attorneys), whose private investments and personal conduct are at issue in the investigation, of these particulars. In my view, it was improper for White House officials to engage in these activities.

The three ethics standards most pertinent to the Treasury-White House contacts are:

An employee shall not use his public office for . . . the private gain of friends, relatives, or persons with whom the employee is affiliated in a nongovernmental capacity[.][67]

An employee shall not . . . allow the improper use of nonpublic information to further his own private interest or that of another, whether through advice or recommendation, or knowing unauthorized disclosure.[68]

Employees shall endeavor to avoid any actions creating the appearance that they are violating the law or the ethical standards[.][69]

The second quoted standard is more relevant to the conduct of Treasury officials, because they were in a better position to know that disclosure to the White House of some of the nonpublic information about the RTC referrals was unauthorized and improper. The issue for White House officials is whether obtaining nonpublic information from Treasury, about matters of personal interest to the Clintons, in order to relay that information to the Clintons (and others), constitutes using public office for private gain. It would seem it does, thus violating a standard of conduct. Moreover, the Treasury-White House contacts surely created the appearance of improper interference with a law enforcement investigation for no official purpose.

White House officials disagreed, of course. Nussbaum, as well as all other White House aides who participated in the contacts with Treasury officials, all asserted an official interest in apprising the President of matters that are likely to break in the press and require the President's response, regardless of whether those matters concern the President in his official or personal capacity. Nussbaum noted that two of his lawyers looked into the propriety of receiving the information from Treasury, and determined that it was proper, "because we were receiving it for an official purpose, to answer press inquiries." The press query, or "heads up" defense, soon became all-encompassing. George Stephanopoulos, who called Treasury officials to complain about the RTC's hiring of Jay Stephens, justified his actions on the basis of "anticipated" press inquiries![70] But, as will be shown, the Treasury contacts provided information beyond what would have been necessary to discharge an obligation to respond to a media inquiry.

Lloyd Cutler, appointed to replace Nussbaum, was promoted by the White House (and Cutler himself) as one who understood the distinction between matters personal and matters official. Yet he defended the Treasury-White House contacts on the same "heads up" rationale:

> It was, obviously, important and appropriate for the Treasury to inform the White House about the leaks and resulting press queries so that the White House could prepare itself and brief the Treasury to answer the questions being raised by the press concerning President and Mrs. Clinton's investment in Whitewater and their knowledge as to the campaign contributions raised by Mr. McDougal.[71]

> There is nothing wrong with such advance warning, Cutler said, "when your superior is the president of the United States, who has to deal with press queries and carry on his job. He needs to know when either important people in his administration or he himself is, are or may be under some form of criminal or other investigation. That doesn't mean he should interfere with the investigation, **but he needs to know to perform his job.**"[72]

On the contrary, it is far from clear how inside information on the RTC's referral would assist the President in "performing his job." If the inside information relates to a Cabinet official or other Presidential appointee, it would be reasonable to alert the President generally that one of his appointees is under investigation and may be implicated in criminal or ethical misconduct. But when the investigation personally concerns a public official, including the President, there is a huge difference in how the information should be handled. As Representative Leach stated succinctly:

> No American . . . including the President of the United States, is entitled to insider information on the development of criminal referrals that relate to that individual.[73]

The only criticism of the contacts White House Counsel Cutler voiced was this statement made to the House Banking Committee in 1994:

> [W]hile the various Treasury-White House contacts violated no ethical standard, in my judgment it would have been better if some of these contacts had never occurred, and if fewer White House staff members had participated. . . . I found that there were too many people having too many discussions about too many sensitive matters, matters which were **properly the province of the Office of the White House Counsel**. The contacts, in my view, **were not sufficiently channelled** between White House counsel and Treasury counsel and there were too many conversations in which no counsel participated. In retrospect, I believe we did not meet as high a performance standard as we should have set for ourselves.[74]

On first read, Cutler appears to object to the quantity of the contacts (employing three "too many's"), but, on closer examination, Cutler's criticism appears narrower: he objected only to the fact that persons outside of the White House Counsel's office were involved. Does this mean that Cutler found nothing objectionable about Ber-

nard Nussbaum's role in these meetings? If so, appointing Lloyd Cutler as Nussbaum's replacement did not represent anything like the sea change portrayed by the
media. And if the entire "heads up" rationale is based on the need to respond to
media inquiries, what is wrong with the involvement of other White House officials
from the Press and Communications offices (or even the Chief of Staff's office)?

Cutler, however, may also have hinted that the frequency of contacts, concerning "sensitive" matters (read: as in personal or confidential), gave the appearance of
improper interference with a law enforcement investigation of an independent agency. This suggestion just begs the question whether White House officials were pursuing
interests beyond preparing the President and First Lady to respond to the press.

Analyzed under the standards of conduct are the three White House meetings
involving Treasury officials and the several contacts made by the White House to
Treasury concerning the RTC's retention of the outside law firm of Jay Stephens.

September 28, 1993: Hanson Briefs the White House On the Second Set of RTC Criminal Referrals

Jean Hanson visited Bernard Nussbaum, with the knowledge (and probably at
the direction) of Roger Altman, to inform the White House that criminal referrals
against Madison had been prepared by the RTC for the Justice Department's consideration. Hanson told Nussbaum that the Clintons were named in the RTC referral
document, not as targets, but as "potential beneficiaries" of misconduct. In giving
Nussbaum this briefing, Hanson divulged confidential information that RTC employees are forbidden to disclose, even to other Government agencies such as the
White House.[75] For this reason, this meeting was called "the most ill-advised contact" and a "spectacular instance of bad political judgment."[76]

Hanson explained that she provided this briefing to prepare the White House to
respond to press inquiries. But this explanation is questionable; no press report on
the Madison referrals surfaced for weeks after this briefing. The White House (properly read: the Clintons) would have plenty of time to respond to a question when it
was presented to them. More important, Nussbaum did not bring Dee Dee Myers or
Stephanopoulos in to prepare them for a media question. The nonpublic information
was delivered to Bruce Lindsey, who informed the President in early October, around
the time the President met in the White House with Arkansas Governor Tucker, who
was also implicated in the referral.

OGE assumed for the purposes of its analysis that "there was a private advantage that could have been gained by the President [and First Lady] through knowledge of the referral." But it found that Secretary Bentsen could conclude that Hanson's sole purpose was "to enable the White House to perform its press function"
because "[t]here is nothing in the [Treasury IG's investigative] report that would
indicate that she had any reason to believe the information would be given to the
President's private counsel or to others who may have been mentioned in the referral."[77] OGE should not have had to look at the Treasury IG's **report** but to **human
nature** to resolve this question. Did anything or anyone give Hanson the impression
that Nussbaum would **not** relay the nonpublic information she provided him (and
other information, including some substance about the referrals, which she provided
to Cliff Sloan over the phone over the next few days) to the Clintons, and that the
Clintons would sit on the information and not discuss it with others, including Gov-

ernor Tucker, too? What little is known about the path of this nonpublic information confirms that it did not stop with Nussbaum or with the White House Press Office (if it ever got there). Anyone should have realized that this would happen.

Indeed, it is highly likely that at a November 5, 1993 meeting, where White House attorneys "passed the torch" to the Clintons' personal attorneys, nonpublic information was also passed. (What actually transpired during this two and one-half hour meeting was the subject of a dubious claim of attorney-client privilege by the Clintons at the time this book went to press.)

White House Counsel Nussbaum used his official White House position to cause inside information on a law enforcement investigation touching on the Clintons in their personal capacity to be conveyed to others in the White House, who subsequently informed the Clintons and, most likely, the Clintons' personal attorneys. Possessing information concerning a law enforcement matter before the information is public is potentially valuable. It allows one time to prepare a public response. But it also risks prejudice to the investigation if the person uses this information to contact other potential witnesses or defendants, or takes some other action to destroy or alter evidence. Where the person is someone with the authority of the presidency, possession of nonpublic law enforcement information is potentially explosive, because the President (in theory) can command the machinery of the Federal Government, including pieces of the machinery operating in his case. The President insisted that he believed the referral to the Justice Department was a *fait accompli* at the time he learned of it, but at the time of Hanson's first briefing, the referral was still ten days away, and was being held up pending a legal review in RTC headquarters.

OGE recognized that "having a public purpose for a disclosure does not preclude an employee from also having as a purpose the furtherance of a private interest."[78] OGE absolved Hanson on the record before it of having a dual purpose, but Nussbaum and other White House officials, whose conduct was not evaluated by OGE, would not fare as well. Their purpose in receiving and relaying this information was as much to alert and assist the Clintons as it was to prepare the President to respond to a future public inquiry. This became evident following the disclosure, in November 1995, of the November 5, 1993 meeting between White House and private attorneys.

October 14, 1993: Treasury Officials Meet with White House Officials to Discuss How to Handle Media Inquiries

This meeting was called by Treasury (Altman or Jack DeVore, Treasury's Press Secretary) to discuss how the White House and Treasury should respond to media questions on the Madison investigation that had been posed by Susan Schmidt of the *Washington Post*, Jeff Gerth of the *New York Times,* and the *Associated Press*; again, at this point, no story on the RTC referral had been published. Altman was accompanied by Hanson, DeVore, and Josh Steiner. The meeting was held in Nussbaum's office; Lindsey, Gearan, Sloan, and Neil Eggleston also attended. Some nonpublic information about the RTC referral was discussed at this meeting.[79]

The White House Counsel's office should have stated at the outset of this meeting:

The purpose of this meeting is to discuss how to respond to questions about an RTC investigation that apparently may touch on the Clintons in their

personal capacity but that is not otherwise relevant to the Presidency or the
White House. The RTC should conduct its investigation without involvement of or advance knowledge by the White House. If the White House
receives a press inquiry about an RTC investigation, we will refer the question to RTC. Questions addressed to the Clintons will be referred to their
private attorney.

The White House officials did not say this, of course. They received the nonpublic information from Treasury. What they did with this information is not yet
completely known, but, again, the November 5, 1993 meeting suggests that they did
not sit on it.

February 2, 1994 — Altman & Hanson Brief the White House on the Statute of Limitations on RTC Civil Claims Involving Madison, and Altman's Possible Recusal is Discussed

Altman disclosed this meeting in a February 24 hearing before the Senate Banking Committee, before the two meetings held in 1993 were revealed. Altman acknowledged that he had briefed the White House on the RTC's procedures in the
event civil claims are pursued as a result of the failure of Madison. Present at the
meeting were Nussbaum, Harold Ickes, Maggie Williams, and an unnamed assistant.
Altman was accompanied by Hanson.

Altman testified that he initiated the meeting to provide a "heads up" to the
White House on how the RTC might proceed. At the time, the RTC faced a statute of
limitations deadline of February 28 (which was subsequently extended by Congress)
on claims against individuals associated with Madison. "It was solely to be sure that
[Nussbaum] understood the legal and procedural framework[.]"[80] OGE also assumed,
based on the record before it and the Treasury ethics official's advance written clearance of the meeting (based on same assumption), that no nonpublic information was
discussed at this meeting. But the fact that the RTC would conclude its internal analysis of the potential civil claims before the expiration of the statute of limitations[81]
and the positions of Jack Ryan and Ellen Kulka do not appear to have been publicly
disclosed outside of this meeting.[82] OGE also accepted the Treasury assertion that its
briefing of the White House was similar to briefings it had provided Congress and the
media, when, in fact, this assertion was later disputed.

Whether or not any sensitive law enforcement information was discussed, the
White House had no business meeting with Altman to discuss a matter that con-
cerned the President and First Lady in their personal capacity. As the *Washington
Post* editorialized:

If, however, it was wrong for appearances sake for Mr. Altman to
offer a briefing, it was inappropriate for the same reason for [the White
House officials] to accept the invitation. The Whitewater probe is a personal matter for the Clintons and does not involve the presidency. . . .
White House staff, absent a showing of an official link to the White House,
should keep their hands off the probe.[83]

The RTC's investigation of Madison did not relate to the President in his official capacity or pose questions of legitimate interest to the President as Chief Executive. The presence of the First Lady's Chief of Staff in this meeting confirms the suspicion that the meeting was held for the Clintons in their personal capacity.

It was later revealed that at the end of the February 2, 1994 meeting, the participants discussed whether Altman should recuse himself from the Madison investigation. OGE saw nothing wrong under the standards of conduct with **Altman** consulting others whether or not to recuse. But among the persons Altman consulted were White House officials, at least two of whom, Nussbaum and Williams, approached the issue from the perspective of the Clintons' personal interests.

The recusal standard to which Altman was subject concerns circumstances other than financial conflicts of interest. It was promulgated in 1992 as a part of the comprehensive standards of conduct, but it reflects the long-standing requirement that Federal employees "avoid even an appearance of loss of impartiality."[84] Section 502(a) provides in pertinent part that, where an employee knows that "a person with whom he has a covered relationship is or represents a party to" a particular matter involving specific parties, "and where the employee determines that the circumstances would cause a reasonable person with knowledge of the relevant facts to question his impartiality in the matter, the employee should not participate in the matter unless he has informed the agency designee of the appearance problem and received authorization from the agency designee[.]"

An employee has a "covered relationship" with, *inter alia*, "[a]ny person for whom the employee has, within the last year, served as an officer, director, trustee, general partner, agent, attorney, consultant, contractor, or employee[.]"[85]

An agency designee who determines that "a reasonable person with knowledge of the relevant facts would be likely to question the employee's impartiality in the matter" may authorize the employee to participate in the matter only upon a determination that "the interest of the Government in the employee's participation outweighs the concern that a reasonable person may question the integrity of the agency's programs and operations." Otherwise, the employee is disqualified from participating in the matter.[86]

Among the factors to be considered are: (1) the nature of the relationship; (2) the effect that resolution of the matter would have on the financial interests of the person; (3) the nature and importance of the employee's role in the matter; (4) the sensitivity of the matter; and (5) the difficulty of reassigning the matter to another employee.[87]

Even if it is determined that the standard governing appearances of impropriety does not address a precise set of circumstances, the standard provides that "[a]n employee who is concerned that circumstances other than those specifically described in this section would raise a question regarding his impartiality should use the process described in this section to determine whether he should or should not participate in a particular matter."[88]

Altman recused himself on February 25, 1994, one day after he disclosed the February 2 White House meeting to the Senate Banking Committee.[89] Altman had considered recusing himself earlier that month after Ricki Tigert agreed to execute a recusal pledge in order to win confirmation as Chairman of the FDIC. It was reported that Altman "had previously asked the government ethics office and both the Treasury and RTC ethics officers if he should recuse himself from Madison issues, and was told he was not legally obligated to do so[.]"[90]

Yet, Altman was leaning in favor of recusal until he broached the subject at the February 2 meeting at the White House, when Nussbaum and perhaps others advised him that he need not and should not recuse. Altman also engaged in subsequent conversations with McLarty and Ickes.[91] The White House initially insisted that it had no discussions with Altman concerning whether he should recuse. And Altman, in a March 21, 1994 letter to the Senate Banking Committee, asserted that "No one at the White House ever asked me not to recuse myself."[92] Yet, this statement was, at best, disingenuous. The *Washington Post* reported Altman "encountered White House resistance to that step," namely from Nussbaum at the February 2 meeting. Nussbaum "questioned whether Altman should step aside absent a specific need to do so."[93]

On February 3, 1994, Leach wrote Altman, urging him to recuse from matters involving Madison and the Clintons. Leach stated that it was "ethically questionable for a political appointee of the Department of Treasury to make decisions for an independent federal agency when the President may be implicated in enforcement and civil actions."[94] D'Amato also called for Altman's recusal.

When Altman announced that he would recuse himself,[95] it came as a surprise to the White House, because it had been previously told that Altman would not recuse (thanks in no small part to the White House efforts at persuasion). The decision to recuse was made one day after the February 24 hearing and was most likely prompted by the furor that resulted from his testimony of the February 2 meeting at the White House (which testimony, by the way, did not reveal the discussion of recusal that took place at the end of the meeting).

Altman did not have a "covered relationship" with the Clintons, but his close friendship with the Clintons alone should have resulted in his recusal at the outset. The standards of conduct leave a lot of room for discretion, and OGE found that the decision whether to recuse was entirely up to Altman, in consulting with the agency ethics official.[96] But agency ethics officials should have been more sensitive to the nature of Altman's relationship with the President and First Lady. At the very least, when Altman sought clearance to brief White House officials, agency ethics officials perhaps should have understood that the possibility Altman would use his official position to provide information of use to the Clintons in their personal capacity posed an appearance problem. (It appears that Treasury ethics officials may not have been fully aware that nonpublic information would be provided or discussed at the meeting.)

Moreover, Altman himself was concerned enough about appearance problems to contemplate recusal despite being informed that he was under no legal obligation to do so. His mistake was involving the White House in his deliberations over whether to recuse, as well as meeting with the White House to discuss procedural aspects about the investigation, given the White House officials' attention to the personal interests of the President and First Lady.

What was most objectionable, however, was White House Counsel Nussbaum's resistance to Altman's inclination to recuse. Nussbaum was concerned about who would fill in for Altman in supervising the RTC in general and the Madison case in particular. Nussbaum even expressed his concern about RTC lawyer Ellen Kulka, based on his experience in private practice. In discussing this with Altman and others, Nussbaum clearly went well beyond his official role as White House Counsel, and attempted to inject himself into the conduct or supervision of the investigation for the benefit of the Clintons in their personal capacity.[97]

February 25, 1994—A Telephone Call Placed by George Stephanopoulos and Harold Ickes to Altman, and a Call From Stephanopoulos to Josh Steiner[98]

The order of the calls is uncertain. In one call, Stephanopoulos and Ickes called Altman, upon learning of Altman's decision to recuse himself from participating in the RTC's Madison investigation. It is not known what precisely was said in this conversation, but the subjects of Altman's recusal and the RTC's hiring of Jay Stephens and his law firm to conduct the RTC's civil investigation of Madison were reportedly discussed.

Concerning Altman's decision to recuse, Stephanopoulos explained that he "suggested as a courtesy that [Altman] write a letter to the President explaining his decision. I don't remember anything else about the conversation."[99] Others suggested that the White House staffers expressed their displeasure either with Altman's decision to recuse or with Altman's failure to alert the White House, or both.[100] However, there is no suggestion that either White House official attempted in this conversation to get Altman to reconsider his decision.

The other subject of the conversation—the hiring of Stephens—received greater attention. On February 24, the day before, the RTC had formally retained the law firm of Pillsbury, Madison and Sutro, of which Jay Stephens is a partner, to handle the RTC's investigation of any civil claims arising out of Madison's failure.[101] This could include whether to file a claim against the Rose Law Firm.[102] Stephens served in the Reagan and Bush Administrations in several capacities in the Justice Department and the White House, and served as U.S. Attorney for the District of Columbia until being removed in March 1993 as part of the Clinton Administration's decision to remove all U.S. Attorneys who were political appointees. At the time, Stephens publicly complained that his departure would adversely affect his office's criminal investigation of House Ways and Means Committee Chairman Dan Rostenkowski.

The RTC's decision to hire the Pillsbury law firm was made by a committee of RTC officials and approved by Ellen Kulka, the newly appointed General Counsel of RTC.[103] Apparently, the Pillsbury law firm was selected in part because of the firm's previous work for the RTC and in part because of Jay Stephens.[104] Anticipating criticism from Congress and from the media, at the conclusion of the investigation, that the RTC was insufficiently aggressive, the RTC attempted to preempt any such criticism by hiring an experienced Republican prosecutor with a reputation for being tough. One Federal official stated:

> They were trying to find the safest firm they could get and avoid the appearance of somebody who was at all sympathetic to the White House. They bent over backwards to pick someone beyond reproach.[105]

What was exchanged between the White House officials and Altman in this call is heavily controverted. Stephanopoulos did not remember the subject coming up in the call. (He did raise the subject in a separate call to Steiner). Altman's account, according to others, is that one of the White House officials asked, "What about Jay Stephens? Can anything be done about it, or are we stuck with this?"[106] This account states that Altman abruptly ended the conversation, refusing to entertain the notion of firing Stephens.

In his separate call to Steiner, Stephanopoulos explained that he "asked how Jay

Stephens had come to be retained by the RTC. I was puzzled and blew off steam over the unfairness of that decision because Jay Stephens had accused the President of acting improperly" in removing Stephens as U.S. Attorney while Stephens was presiding over the investigation of Rostenkowski. "Once I got the facts from Josh, that ended the matter, as far as I was concerned."[107] *Time* reported that:

> ... others describe the conversation differently. ... They say Stephanopoulos began with the classic "this conversation never happened" line and proceeded to ask Steiner, "How can we get rid of Stephens?" After further contacts between Steiner and Stephanopoulos, the conclusion reportedly was that Stephens could not be removed easily, so the subject was finally dropped.[108]

Stephanopoulos said that the President did not ask him to initiate this discussion. McLarty stated that Stephanopoulos and Ickes "have no recollection of asking anyone to change the RTC's decision to retain Mr. Stephens and his law firm[.] There is no suggestion that any action was taken."[109]

Cutler acknowledged that these calls were not permitted under the newly issued White House policy on contacts with regulatory agencies. "It would have been better had these conversations not occurred. ... I am confident that such conversations will not be repeated." He emphasized, however, that it was "perfectly natural that White House officials would be surprised" at Stephens' appointment" and that "these conversations should not be blown out of proportion."[110]

A Treasury spokesman stated on March 26, 1994, that "No action was taken either by Mr. Altman or Mr. Steiner as a result of the calls. No one tried to influence the negotiations one bit."[111] Altman himself said, "As far as I'm concerned, neither George nor Harold did anything wrong, ... based on my understanding of the conversation at the time."[112]

Most media reports of these conversations were highly critical, but other reports were mixed.[113] D'Amato suggested that any effort to remove Stephens could constitute an obstruction of justice, but Leach said it was "premature to draw any conclusions."[114] Some analysts concluded that because the interest in removing Stephens (assuming there was such an interest) did not go beyond these two phone calls—in other words, no one at Treasury took any action to remove Stephens— nothing improper occurred. But something probably did happen as a result of these calls: Hanson testified that either Altman or Steiner asked her to examine whether the RTC's retention of Stephens was vulnerable to being terminated. Observers who saw in these calls nothing more than what Stephanopoulos called "letting off steam" concluded that no criticism was deserved.[115] Others, including some House Democrats, argued that the **hiring** of Stephens was improper, considering Stephens' "grudge" against the President.[116]

This study accepts the conclusion that no action was taken to remove Stephens from the Madison case and that neither Altman nor Steiner relayed the White House officials' concern over the hiring of Stephens directly to any RTC official participating in the investigation. Thus, there was no actual interference with or impeding of the investigation: in other words, there was no actual obstruction of justice. Recall that Special Counsel Fiske determined (emphasis added) only that no one "acted with the **intent to corruptly influence** an RTC investigation." Although it appears that Stephanopoulos and Ickes were interested in Stephens' removal—inquiring as to whether the decision was "final"—it is not established that they expressly requested his removal to Steiner or Altman. But concluding that no White House official obstructed justice—or even intended to do so—does not answer the question whether these conversations were ethical or appropriate. For three reasons, they were not.

First, Altman had already recused himself by the time of the call from Stephanopoulos and Ickes. They knew that, because they called Altman to castigate him for doing so without giving advance notice to the White House. So, it was improper for the White House officials thereafter to engage Altman in any conversation about the handling of the investigation.[117] Altman properly cut short the discussion perhaps for this very reason. If these White House officials wished to protest Stephens' hiring (or even to obtain information about whether he had been formally retained), they could have contacted someone at the Department who was not recused from the matter.

Second, the calls violated White House policy on contacts with regulatory officials. Under the White House policy on contacts with regulatory agencies extant at the time of the calls, these calls were improper; they were also improper under the revised White House policy instituted in the aftermath following the disclosure of White House meetings with Treasury officials. Under these policies, any communication relating to a pending investigation conducted by a regulatory agency is presumptively improper and must be cleared in advance by the White House Counsel's office.

Third, White House officials took action in their official capacity for the benefit of the Clintons in their personal capacity. As noted previously, White House officials had no official business in discussing the Madison case with Treasury officials in the first place. Stephanopoulos and Ickes, of course, had no formal responsibility for overseeing the RTC; they did not call Treasury officials about the Madison case in furtherance of any official government policy; the calls were made for Clintons' personal benefit, regardless of whether the President or First Lady knew of their actions, not for the benefit of President Clinton *qua* President. In doing so, Stephanopoulos and Ickes were using their public office for private gain, a violation of the ethics standards.

Interference with the Madison Investigation

Various allegations have been made that White House or administration officials engaged in improper activities concerning the RTC's investigation of Madison Guaranty, the subsequent handling of the RTC's referrals by the RTC headquarters, Treasury Department, and the Department of Justice, the internal investigation of the Treasury-White House contacts, and the Administration's preparation for Congressional hearings.

• Jean Lewis has alleged that **RTC headquarters officials** attempted to hinder the Kansas City office's investigation of Madison in at least four ways: (a) RTC headquarters mandated a legal review of the referrals by the Professional Liability Section before sending it to Justice; (b) Lewis was removed from further work on the case on November 9, 1993; (c) April Breslaw's February 2, 1994 visit, in which Breslaw suggested that headquarters officials would be happier if the investigation concluded that Whitewater did not cause a loss to Madison; and (d) in August 1994 Lewis and her two Kansas City supervisors were suspended for several days and were locked out of their office without prior notice, pending an unspecified investigation into their conduct.

• Lewis and others allege that **Treasury officials**, by improperly disclosing information about the referrals to the White House in meetings and phone calls in September and October 1993, may have prejudiced the investigation. President Clinton or other **White House officials** are suspected of discussing the referrals with Governor Tucker on more than one occasion in the fall of 1993, and White House lawyers are believed to have passed nonpublic information about the referrals to the Clintons' personal attorneys at a November 5, 1993 meeting.

• **United States Attorney Paula Casey**'s participation in both sets of RTC referrals and in the investigation and prosecution of David Hale, before her recusal in November 1993, is alleged to have been improper based on her previous association with the Clintons.

• There are suspicions that **Webster Hubbell** may have participated in the Justice Department's deliberations concerning the RTC referrals, before and after his recusal in autumn 1993, based in part on a series of phone calls allegedly made between Hubbell and Casey during this time.

• There are allegations that **White House officials** attempted to affect the Madison investigations by (1) dissuading Altman from recusing himself; (2) seeking the removal of Jay Stephens; (3) and appointing Paula Casey and Ricki Tigert, a friend of the Clintons, to Federal positions.

• There are allegations that **Treasury** and **White House officials** compromised, or attempted to compromise, the independence of the Treasury IG's investigation of the Treasury-White House contacts.

• There are allegations that Whitewater documents maintained at the Governor's Mansion, the Rose Law Firm and perhaps other locations were shredded in an effort to keep them from investigators or from the public view.

On the present record, it is impossible to evaluate the merits of most of these allegations. It appears that a complete answer to whether anyone in the Clinton White House or Administration improperly interfered with the Madison investigation must await further congressional hearings or the report of the independent counsel. What follows is an analysis of what was in the public record through the beginning of December 1995.

Alleged Interference by RTC Headquarters
Lewis testified before the House Banking Committee in August 1995 that Administration officials made a "concerted effort to obstruct, hamper and manipulate" the results of her investigation. Although Lewis pointed to a number of circumstances in support of her allegation, for the most part she lacked personal knowledge of which officials may have acted improperly. To confirm her allegations would require documents or the testimony of others. Lewis's allegations were directed primarily

against RTC headquarters and Treasury Department officials, although she also alleged that the Justice Department improperly delayed consideration of the first RTC referral sent to U.S. Attorney Charles Banks in September 1992. As might be expected, the RTC headquarters witnesses contested Lewis's allegations, at both the 1994 and 1995 hearings, as did the witnesses from the Little Rock U.S. Attorney's office and FBI field office, at the 1995 Senate hearings. Thus, it is difficult to resolve these allegations on the present record.

Lewis may be correct that subjecting the second set of referrals to a legal review by the RTC's Professional Liability Section was unprecedented and contrary to procedure. It is also suspicious that the legal review was ordered on September 30, 1993, one day after Hanson alerted Nussbaum to the referrals. However, there has been no showing that the extra layer of review materially affected the substance of the referral,[118] or that the delay in referring the case to Justice (a little more than one week) prejudiced the investigation in any way. It is generally appropriate for the headquarters of an agency to give a harder look to an enforcement case that is likely to receive a great deal of notoriety because of its subject matter or the identity of the persons under investigation. Such cases are given greater scrutiny in the media and by Congress, and an agency has a legitimate interest in ensuring that its case is solid on the facts and law before going public with it. Even where the case is to be forwarded to the Justice Department for its consideration, an agency has a legitimate interest in ensuring that its conclusions are sound and its work product is given respect by Justice.

It is not clear why RTC headquarters decided to remove Lewis from further work on the case in November 1993, after the existence of the second set of referrals was publicly reported. One suspects that headquarters may have believed Lewis was too zealous an investigator; perhaps the Justice Department complained to the RTC about the several dunning calls Lewis (justifiably) made in 1992 and 1993 to find out the status of the first referral. Charles Banks said that he believes Lewis attempted to pressure his office to move forward with the first referral. RTC headquarters perhaps was interested in muzzling Lewis while the Justice Department considered the second set of referrals (at this time, Justice had assigned a special team to handle the matter, Paula Casey having recused). But this is all speculation at this point. Because Lewis's referrals had been, in fact, forwarded to Justice, and her supporting documents would be available upon request, it is not clear how removing Lewis would have interfered with the investigation.

April Breslaw's February 2, 1994 visit appears to be an awkward attempt to see if Lewis would object, publicly or to congressional Republicans, if the RTC were to report that the Madison investigation did not implicate the Clinton's Whitewater investment. Breslaw found out, of course, that Lewis would not sit quietly and agree to such a conclusion, at least without a further investigation by Justice or the Special Counsel. At the time, the RTC was in the process of retaining an outside law firm to assist it in prosecuting civil claims; in light of Ellen Kulka's decision to hire Jay Stephens, Breslaw's conversation with Lewis appears curious. Bear in mind, too, that the criminal referrals concerning Madison were under the jurisdiction of the Special Counsel by this time. So, it is not clear how Breslaw or any RTC headquarters official thought they could affect the investigation by talking with Lewis.

Finally, Lewis and her two supervisors were given administrative suspensions in August 1994 and kicked out of their office while the RTC conducted an unspecified investigation into their compliance with RTC policies and procedures. Speculation focused on Lewis's surreptitious recording of her conversation with Breslaw. The suspensions smack either of retaliation for Lewis's insistence on cooperating with House Republicans, or an attempt to discredit Lewis by uncovering some (unrelated) misconduct. Either way, the suspensions would be improper; but either way, the criminal investigation would not likely be affected. Discovering some evidence of misconduct could have damaged Lewis's credibility before Congress, but two events intervened: the suspension caught the eye of Congress and the independent counsel, and thus any improper discipline would itself be investigated, and Lewis declined to testify until well after the suspension was lifted. Lewis testified before the House Banking Committee in August 1995, but neither she, her colleagues, nor anyone could or would shed light on her suspension. At this point the public and Lewis are still in the dark as to the basis for the suspension as well as the resolution of the RTC's internal investigation. It appears that answers would be provided, if at all, only in the independent counsel's report.

Lewis eventually resigned from the RTC in September 1995. Her testimony before the special Senate Committee in November 1995 apparently did not add any material facts relevant to her allegations.

Alleged Interference by Treasury Officials

There is no evidence that has come to light that establishes that any Treasury official interfered with the RTC's deliberative process or the referral to Justice. Jean Hanson apparently was privy to and participated in the RTC headquarters legal review of the second set of referrals (she did not recall this), but there has been no showing that she affected or intended to affect the investigation in any material respect. Lewis's allegation concerning Treasury focuses on Treasury's eagerness to share nonpublic information, including the RTC headquarters legal analysis, with the White House.

Although nonpublic information about the Madison investigation was shared with the Clintons, and possibly with Jim Guy Tucker, it is uncertain whether the Clintons, Tucker, or anyone else took any action on the basis of this information to hinder or compromise the investigation. The risk was there, but the Clintons and the White House have denied it. (Disclosure of William Kennedy's notes of a November 5, 1993 meeting of White House and private attorneys would likely confirm that nonpublic information was provided to the Clintons' personal attorneys.)

Alleged Improper Participation of Paula Casey

Casey, the U.S. Attorney for the Eastern District of Arkansas, was nominated by President Clinton on August 6, 1993, and began service on August 15, pursuant to a court appointment.[119] She was confirmed on September 21. Casey was accused of attempting to protect the Clintons and Tucker from exposure. Jean Lewis also complained that the Justice Department sat on the first set of RTC referrals, sent to Casey's predecessor Charles Banks in the fall of 1992.

Lewis's allegation that Banks did not move with dispatch on the RTC's first referral is true. Banks received the RTC referral on September 2, 1992, but did not alert Main Justice (by phone call from Mac Dotson, his first assistant) to the referral until October 6, 1992, at which time his office also faxed a copy of the referral to Main Justice. (That same day, the Little Rock FBI office similarly notified FBI head-quarters of the referral.) The cover note from Dotson attached to the fax reportedly advised that, based on the facts developed by the RTC, further investigation was warranted. The Clintons reportedly were named in the referral as potential witnesses.[120]

At a meeting at Main Justice on October 8, attended by Criminal Division and FBI officials, the decision was made to treat this investigation as any other, as the FBI October 9 teletype to its Little Rock field office stated. Apparently on his own, Banks elected not to do anything on the case until after the election. Banks had lost a previous fraud prosecution of Jim McDougal, and did not want to be accused of conducting another prosecution of McDougal for partisan political purposes. Banks' caution was understandable, but he should not have waited five weeks before notify-ing Main Justice of the referral in the first place, and should have informed Main Justice that he would not take any action on the matter before the election, which Banks apparently did not do. (Banks told the Little Rock FBI of this on October 16) Had Banks done so, Main Justice may well have agreed with him, at least until after the election.

But Banks was not justified in apparently taking no action on the referral from November 3, 1992 to January 27, 1993, when he attempted to divorce himself from the matter entirely. And the first referral was returned to the U.S. Attorney's office in March 1993, yet it was not disposed of until Casey declined prosecution in October 1993. Lewis's frustration with the pace of the Department's consideration of the first referral is understandable, but there is no indication other than this delay that the Department's (Banks' and Main Justice's) **torpor** was the result of any desire to protect the President or Mrs. Clinton. Whether the **declination** of the first referral was proper is another question.

Casey's impartiality was questioned because she did some volunteer work in Mr. Clinton's gubernatorial campaigns, was one of his students at the University of Arkansas Law School, and served as a legislative aide to Senator Dale Bumpers. Additionally, Governor Clinton appointed Casey's husband, Gil Glover, to a State position.[121] Glover reportedly kept the same position in the Tucker Administration (it is not a political appointment).[122] Casey's impartiality was questioned also because of her belated recusal and her handling of the negotiations with David Hale's attor-ney. Casey testified before the special Senate Committee for the first time in Decem-ber 1995.

Following media reports about the investigations, Casey and her staff recused themselves[123] "because of their familiarity with some of the parties and the need to ensure that there be no misperceptions about the impartiality of the investigation[.]"[124] Simultaneously, the Justice Department named a new team of prosecutors to conduct the investigation, to be headed by Donald B. Mackay, a former U.S. Attorney for the Northern District of Illinois.[125] Casey, however, refused to recuse when asked to do so by a senior Justice Department official in September 1993, and eventually recused herself only after she had participated in at least two significant decisions in the investigations.

On October 8, 1993, the RTC referred to Casey's office nine allegations relating to Madison Guaranty, in which the Clintons were mentioned as "potential beneficiaries" of illegal conduct. This was the second time the RTC had asked Justice to investigate Madison. The first referral, which had been sent to Main Justice in January 1993, was returned to the U.S. Attorney's office in March.

Apparently no action was taken on the first referral for months. Although Lewis repeatedly asked the Justice Department for a status report during this time, Lewis was not even informed that the referral had been returned to the U.S. Attorney's office.

During this time, the U.S. Attorney's office also was investigating loans made by Capital Management Services, Incorporated., a Small Business Investment Corporation run by David Hale. It is not known whether the U.S. Attorney's office was aware of a 1986 loan of $300,000 made to Master Marketing, a company owned by Susan McDougal, partner with her husband and the Clintons in the Whitewater investment.[126] This is the loan that David Hale has said Governor Clinton and Jim McDougal pressured him to make. Hale's attorney, Randy Coleman, wrote Casey on September 15, seeking to enter plea negotiations and alleging that the U.S. Attorney's office's "reluctance" to discuss a potential plea resulted from "the potential political sensitivity and fallout regarding the information which Mr. Hale could provide to your office[.]"[127] Coleman wrote that Hale's information would provide "substantial assistance in investigating the banking and borrowing practices of some individuals in the elite political circles in the State of Arkansas, past and present." But it is not known whether Coleman noted Hale's allegation against Clinton in his pre-indictment discussions with the U.S. Attorney's office. Coleman specifically asked Casey to recuse herself and "to bring in an independent prosecutorial staff, who are not so involved with the history of the personalities and circumstances of this case[.]"[128]

Around the same time, Main Justice was informed of Hale's allegation from New York Times reporter Jeff Gerth. The U.S. Attorney's office faxed to Main Justice Coleman's September 15 letter to Casey. This resulted in two phone calls between Main Justice and the U.S. Attorney's office. On September 20, Jack Keeney, the senior Deputy Assistant Attorney General for the Criminal Division, strongly urged Casey to recuse herself. Casey, backed by her first Assistant, declined to do so, although she apparently did not inform Main Justice of her decision. "Casey said she saw no reason to step aside and that Hale's allegations lacked 'specifics.'"[129] The exchange of correspondence between Coleman and Casey ended with Casey's September 21 letter in which she stated that Coleman had repeatedly failed to provide specific information to support the general assertion of the significance of Hale's information.[130] Casey reportedly pledged to recuse herself on September 24, in a meeting with the Hale prosecution team, but said she would not announce it then in order to avoid the appearance that she was caving to Coleman's demands. Yet Casey did not recuse herself on September 24. On September 28, Hale was indicted on charges unrelated to Madison and Whitewater.

Then came the second set of RTC referrals, on October 8, 1993. The Washington Post reported that:

> On Oct. 27, with the stack of new criminal referrals sitting on her desk, Casey responded to six months of RTC inquiries about the fate of the first referral, then a year old. She told the RTC that she "concurred" with the Justice Department's decision to forgo an investigation due to "insufficient information."[131]

It is unclear whether Casey had reviewed the information and materials contained in the RTC's second set of referrals before declining to investigate the first referral, although it is difficult to believe that she was unaware of the later referrals. Casey's participation, in declining the first referral and in conducting discussions with Hale's attorney, was personal and substantial. Notwithstanding Casey's characterization that she "concurred" in a Criminal Division decision, the decision whether to go forward with the case clearly rested with her.

Under the standard of conduct governing personal and business relationships,[132] Casey did not have a "covered relationship" with the Clintons or with Madison directly. However, Casey did have a "covered relationship" with Governor Tucker, because of her husband's job with the State of Arkansas, not withstanding the civil service nature of his position. Tucker was implicated in both the Madison and Capital Services investigations, as the two indictments of him would subsequently confirm.[133] A reasonable person with knowledge of these facts would have questioned Casey's impartiality in any investigation involving the Clintons and Governor Tucker, whether as "potential beneficiaries" or even "potential witnesses." Casey was informed of the recusal of Charles Banks, the previous U.S. Attorney, who was a Bush Administration appointee. Although Casey was informed that Main Justice did not believe that Banks should have recused himself, the case for Casey's recusal was much stronger than the case for Banks' recusal. Casey's situation was different from Banks' in at least three respects. Casey had ties to the Clintons and was a Clinton appointee; her husband served in the Tucker Administration, having been appointed by Governor Clinton; and Hale's allegations had been made, alleging misconduct by high-level Arkansas officials for the first time. Casey should have recused herself from the Madison and Capital Management Services investigations from the start. When Hale's attorney suggested Hale's knowledge of misconduct by high-level Arkansas officials, Casey at least was put on inquiry notice that should have resulted in her immediate recusal.[134] When Jack Keeney suggested that Casey recuse herself, there should have been no doubt about whether she should do so. Her continued participation in the case was improper. It is not known whether the Justice Department ethics office was alerted to this apparent conflict, but under the standards of conduct in effect at the time, it should have been. If Keeney's advice to Casey had been the advice of the Justice ethics official, or if Keeney's advice was the product of consultation with the ethics official, under the standards of conduct, Casey would have been prohibited from further participation in the particular matter.

There is also the allegation that Casey was in regular communication with Webster Hubbell between September 29 (the day Hanson briefed Nussbaum on the second RTC referral) and November 9, the day her recusal was announced.[135] Six calls were reportedly made between the two during this six-week period. However, Casey has denied making or receiving any such calls, and Hubbell did not recall speaking with Casey during this time.[136]

Alleged Improper Participation by Webster Hubbell

Associate Attorney General Hubbell formally recused himself from any participation in the Justice Department investigations of Whitewater and Madison Guaranty on November 3, 1993.[137] The *Washington Post* reported that same day that Hubbell stated that he had "recused himself **several weeks ago** from the case when he read about it in an Arkansas newspaper."[138] Hubbell's formal recusal followed the September 23 story in the *Arkansas Democrat-Gazette* relating to the Justice Department's investigation and Hale's allegations.

Hubbell's recusal was proper. Hubbell had a "covered relationship" with the Rose Law Firm, but did not have a "covered relationship" with either Madison (more than one year had elapsed since he represented Madison) or the First Lady (Hubbell did not serve in any capacity **for** her, but served **with** her). Yet, Hubbell's previous representation of Madison, his law partnership association with Mrs. Clinton, and his close friendship with the Clintons compelled Hubbell to take himself out of all matters involving these persons and entities. This illustrates the narrowness of the term "covered relationship" in the standards of conduct. As noted earlier, however, the standards require recusal to be considered in any situation where a reasonable question regarding an employee's impartiality could be raised, even where a "covered relationship" does not exist. Hubbell's recusal is clearly supported by employing the factors provided in the regulation.

Was Hubbell's recusal timely? First, there is the report of the phone calls between Hubbell and Casey between September 29 and November 9, 1993, some of them reportedly made after Hubbell had recused himself.[139] Again, Hubbell does not recall speaking with Casey before January 1994, and Casey has denied engaging in these conversations.

Second, as early as the spring of 1993, when Hubbell was serving as the Justice Department liaison to the White House, Hubbell was reportedly aware of two Federal investigations involving Madison or Capital Management Services: the first RTC referral to Justice, which was returned to the U.S. Attorney's office from Main Justice in March 1993, and a May 20, 1993, criminal referral from the Small Business Administration to Justice relating to Capital.[140]

In testimony to the House Banking Committee, Hubbell denied knowing of the first RTC referral until much later, when he vaguely recalled seeing a memorandum cross his desk mentioning the Madison investigation. He could not place the date of this memorandum, however, but testified later that he was not aware of the first RTC referral until October 1993. Concerning the SBA referral, an SBA official testified that he briefed the head of the SBA at the time, Erskine Bowles, about the referral in May 1993; Bowles thereafter briefed White House Chief of Staff McLarty. Thus, McLarty could be expected to relay to the President, and perhaps to Hubbell, any information Bowles gave him.[141] Hubbell recalled seeing a letter from a Member of Congress on the SBA referral at some point—he did not recall when—but Hubbell denied contacting the White House or taking any action after learning of either matter.

When Hubbell testified before the Senate in December 1995, he noted receiving a call from William Kennedy at the White House, in late August or mid-September. Kennedy asked Hubbell whether he knew of any connection between Hale, McDougal, and Madison. Hubbell said he did not draw any such connection until the September 23 *Arkansas-Democrat* article.

Thus, allegations or suspicions that Hubbell took part in any discussion of these matters before his recusal or violated his recusal by engaging in such discussions after he has recused have not been proven.

Alleged Interference by the White House
Three of the allegations of White House interference have been previously dis-

cussed: attempts made by White House officials, most notably Nussbaum, to persuade Altman not to recuse; efforts by Stephanopoulos and perhaps others to remove Jay Stephens from handling the civil investigation of Madison; and suspicions that the Clintons and Tucker may have been tipped off about nonpublic information relating to the referrals.

In the end, Altman did recuse, and it does not appear that his supervision of the RTC up to that time affected the Madison case in any way. The White House protests of Stephens' hiring did not stop with Steiner and Altman, however. Hanson testified that she was asked by either Altman or Steiner whether the appointment of Stephens could be terminated.[142] However, Stephens was not removed from the investigation. Indeed, a report prepared by Stephens' law firm in the spring of 1995 has been cited by the White House as support for its defense against Republican charges![143] Concerning whether the Madison investigations were prejudiced by the disclosure of nonpublic information to the Clintons and perhaps Tucker, there has been no proof that anything was done with this information to hamper the probe, although the record is by no means complete.

The special Senate Committee hearings heard testimony suggesting that the White House was very interested in the SBA's investigation of Capital Management services and David Hale. Accepting Neil Eggleston's testimony that he did not share with anyone else any of the confidential information he received from SBA about its investigation, the most damaging allegation was made on December 5 by Steven Irons, of the FBI's Little Rock office. Irons testified that an SBA lawyer told him of a White House effort to enlist the SBA in discrediting Hale. The allegation is hearsay, of course, but must be pursued vigorously by the Senate Committee. If true, White House contacts with SBA officials could prove to be a even greater scandal than what resulted in 1994 from the disclosure of the contacts with the Treasury Department.

Further investigation is also required to look into another portion of Irons' testimony, that one of Hale's attorneys went to Washington on August 20, 1993 to meet with unidentified officials to attempt to quash the investigation of Hale. It would not be improper for the Government to meet with Hale's attorney to hear his argument. But the question is whether this meeting took place with government officials, such as White House officials, who were not part of the investigatory or prosecution team. Hale's attorney, Richard Mays, denied meeting with any Federal official, but the matter should not be resolved until various Federal officials are queried about this allegation.

The other allegations concern the President's appointment of Paula Casey to serve as U.S. Attorney and his appointment of Ricki Tigert as Chairman of the Federal Deposit Insurance Corporation. Casey was nominated on August 6, 1993. It is unclear whether President Clinton knew or had reason to know that any investigation potentially reaching his investments or conduct was pending in that office, although there is an allegation that Hubbell knew of the first set of RTC referrals as early as March 1993, and that Hubbell and McLarty knew of a criminal referral from SBA relating to David Hale's company as of May 1993. If Hubbell or McLarty passed this information to the President, it could serve as motivation for him to appoint someone whom he knew and trusted. Even without any such knowledge, actual or constructive, the President could be expected to appoint someone whom he knew and trusted to oversee criminal investigations that could touch on his tenure as Governor.

The President's appointment of Tigert is less controversial, although some Republican Senators were concerned about the appointment, because of her friendship with the Clintons. At the time of her nomination, Tigert had known the Clintons for eight years; they were considered good friends. *Time*, in writing on the 1993 Renaissance Weekend attended by the Clintons, described "Hillary's Favorite Activity: Hanging out with friends, including FDIC nominee Ricki Tigert[.]"[144] The *Washington Post* subsequently reported that "Democratic sources said she had met them fewer than a dozen times over a period of several years."[145]

At her confirmation hearing on February 1, 1994, Tigert stressed that she would be "extremely sensitive to potential conflicts or interest or any appearance of conflicts of interest," and would consult with FDIC ethics officials and the OGE on any such matter. But even after repeated questioning by Senators Faircloth and D'Amato, Tigert declined to commit to recuse herself from particular matters involving Madison. Tigert noted that both FDIC and OGE lawyers told her that "no actual conflict of interest is involved, given the casual nature of my friendship with the Clintons."[146] However, after Republicans threatened to put a hold on her nomination, Tigert agreed to recuse herself from participating in any matter "concerning President or Mrs. Clinton in their personal capacities[,]" in order to avoid "even the appearance of any conflict of interest." She was approved by the Senate Banking Committee on February 10, 1994, over the lone opposition of Faircloth.[147]

D'Amato then held up Tigert's nomination for months until Whitewater hearings were held. After hearings were scheduled, however, D'Amato and Faircloth continued the hold, arguing more generally that the FDIC should not be run by a friend of the Clintons. Tigert's recusal commitment was considered insufficient. Democrats eventually blocked a filibuster, however, and Tigert was confirmed on October 4, 1994.

It was proper for Tigert to recuse herself, notwithstanding the apparent opinion of agency ethics officials that she need not do so.[148] Even if Tigert believed her friendship with the Clintons was "casual," the impression left by reports of the Renaissance Weekend they spent together was otherwise.[149] Subsequent to Tigert's confirmation, there has been no report that she has failed to observe her recusal.

Alleged Improper White House or Treasury Conduct Relating to the Internal Reviews of the White House-Treasury Contacts

Senate Republicans questioned the integrity of the Treasury IG's investigative report on the Treasury-White House contacts, which served as the basis for OGE's analysis of these contacts, because of the role Francine Kerner, a Treasury General Counsel's office attorney assigned to the IG's office, played in that investigation. Kerner's role was criticized because she was a subordinate of General Counsel Jean Hanson, one of the officials whose conduct was under investigation, because Kerner communicated regularly about the IG investigation with the General Counsel's office and with the Office of the Secretary, and because she limited the scope of some of the interviews over the objections of the Treasury investigators. Other questions were raised over Secretary Bentsen's agreeing to White House Counsel Cutler's request for access to the unredacted interview transcripts, over the RTC's objections.

Kerner appears to have failed to follow the spirit (if not the letter) of written instructions that the IG investigation was to be conducted completely independent of the General Counsel's office. Also, Cutler's use of the transcripts in preparing White

House witnesses, even if he did not share the actual transcripts with them, did allow White House witnesses to iron out potential discrepancies in recollections before the hearing. At this juncture, however, it does not appear that either the underlying RTC investigation of Madison Guaranty or the Treasury IG investigation of the Treasury-White House contacts was compromised in any significant way.

Neither the Treasury investigation nor the OGE review took testimony from or examined the conduct of White House officials, notwithstanding the implication left by Cutler's 1994 testimony and other contemporaneous statements by White House officials. More than a year later, Cutler acknowledged that OGE had not "informally concurred" in his broad conclusion that no White House official violated any standard of ethical conduct.

Alleged Destruction of Whitewater Documents

Various reports surfaced in 1994 that Whitewater and Madison Guaranty documents maintained at the Governor's Mansion in Little Rock and at the Rose Law Firm were destroyed during and after the 1992 campaign and as late as January-February 1995, following the appointment of Robert Fiske as Special Counsel. Jeff Gerth's article in the *New York Times* during the 1992 campaign put the Clintons, Foster, Hubbell, and others on notice that the documents relating to Whitewater and Madison might be sought in connection with an official civil or criminal investigation. It was also suspected that Whitewater documents maintained in Vince Foster's office were destroyed or tampered with, following Foster's death. Any person who destroyed or tampered with a document after an investigation was commenced, or perhaps even in anticipation of a request or subpoena from the RTC, the United States Attorney, or Special Counsel Fiske, could be subject to prosecution for obstruction of justice.[150] All of these allegations have been denied, but they have not been resolved. That is the responsibility of the independent counsel.

Conclusions

As of this writing, the full story of the White House's response to Vince Foster's death and the Madison and Whitewater investigations is not known. Further Senate hearings may shed additional light on what happened, and months (if not years) from now, the independent counsel's report may also provide additional information or perspective. But it is most likely that the public will never know for certain the answers to many of the large questions involving Whitewater in Washington. It will be up to the public to weigh the conflicting testimony, the plethora of "I don't recalls" from White House officials versus the mostly solid recollections of career investigators, agents, and attorneys, and come to a judgment. But a few conclusions can be made.

First, White House officials engaged in many activities in furtherance of the Clintons' personal interests. By failing to observe the basic distinction between what is personal and what is official, White House officials violated the standards of conduct. They used their public office for the Clintons' personal benefit; they allowed the use of nonpublic information for unauthorized purposes; and, overall, they gave the appearance of attempting to interfere in law enforcement investigations in order to attend to the personal interests of the Clintons.

Second, the White House consistently failed to level with the media, the Congress, and the public as to what happened in Washington and why. The testimony of White House and Treasury officials, in both 1994 and 1995 hearings, constitute clear evidence of malfeasance on this score. The Whitewater documents initially were withheld from the public on a dubious legal basis; even their release two years later was piecemeal, raising further questions. The White House was not forthright with the public as to the July 20, 1993, search of Foster's office, the discovery of White-water files in Foster's office, the transmission of the Whitewater files to the Execu-tive Residence, and the transmission of the files to Justice. Altman was not forthright with Congress about his meetings and conversations with the White House. Testimo-ny of Treasury and White House officials concerning conversations between and among them often conflicted; memories regularly failed at opportune moments. The White House assumed a damage control posture from the very beginning (perhaps as early as Foster's death, if not the 1992 campaign), keeping the public from a full and timely accounting of the Clintons' conduct concerning Whitewater and Madison, as well as the White House's conduct with respect to the investigations.

Perhaps the sharpest critique of the testimony of White House and Treasury officials at the 1994 hearings came in the form of a recommendation in the January 1995 (Democratic) Majority Report of the Senate Banking Committee, that Presi-dent Clinton issue an executive order "reinforcing that executive branch witnesses testifying before Congress should be fully candid and forthcoming and that they must testify truthfully, accurately, and completely." The full story of the White House-SBA contacts concerning the SBA's investigation of David Hale and Capital Man-agement Services has also not been told. But serious allegations have also been made of White House attempts to interfere with, or obtain nonpublic information about, this investigation.

Third, administration officials, in the White House, the Treasury, and Justice Departments, and RTC headquarters, acted in many ways that **appear** as attempts to affect the conduct of the RTC's and Justice Department's investigation of Madison. These included attempting to dissuade Altman from recusing himself; protesting the hiring of Jay Stephens and asking whether the decision was final; relaying nonpublic information about the investigation to persons whose conduct is at issue in that in-vestigation; declining the RTC's first referral and refusing to negotiate with David Hale (decisions taken by U.S. Attorney Paula Casey); removing Jean Lewis from the investigation; visiting the Kansas City office (by April Breslaw) to express head-quarters' views about the more palatable outcome of the investigation; and suspend-ing Lewis and her supervisors for several days pending an investigation into their conduct. Any one of these might be discounted as minor or innocuous. When all these are considered together, however, there is, at a minimum, a clear appearance that the Administration attempted to ensure that the Madison investigation did the least amount of political (as well as legal) damage to the Clintons—and that it did so in violation of the standards of conduct.

An administration that, according to officials of its own party, must be reminded to tell the truth, has a serious credibility problem.

Of course, all these efforts thus far have produced exactly the opposite of the White House's intentions. The White House, more than any other person or entity, has succeeded in transforming Whitewater from an arcane and stale Arkansas finan-cial and real estate scandal into a present-day Washington scandal, felling the political careers of four Presidential appointees (Altman, Hanson, Nussbaum, Hubbell), keeping regular occupancy of page one of the national press, subjecting the White House staff to legal bills and adverse publicity unprecedented since Watergate, and failing utterly to dissipate the ethical cloud over the Clintons.

From what is now known, the criminal investigation conducted by the independent counsel and the civil investigation pending with the RTC do not appear to have been prejudiced or otherwise affected by these efforts. But it is important to point out two things: (1) we do not yet know (and may never know) the true extent of the Administration's actions that may have affected the investigation of Madison and Whitewater, and whether they did, in fact, hinder the investigation; and (2) the **ethics** of the Administration may be justly criticized, and unambiguously, on the basis that what the public has seen in the reports and testimony to date is a concerted effort by White House and Administration officials to protect the Clintons by using their Federal positions and by failing to level with the public, the Congress, and official investigators in doing so.

Chapter Nine

The President's Response to the Arkansas Trooper Allegations

Reports that the President offered Federal employment to one or more Arkansas troopers in an effort to save himself considerable embarrassment present the most serious single allegation against the President. This is because the allegation directly links the President, while President, with the commission of a Federal crime, and because there is sufficient testimonial evidence to warrant a criminal investigation. The issue went away following the President's denial and a sort-of-denial from one of the troopers. However, the issue would have been resolved more satisfactorily by a Justice Department (or independent) investigation. The Attorney General should be asked why no such investigation was initiated, and whether Justice would respond differently if the same allegation were made against a mid-level Federal official.

Allegations of the President's Discussions with the Troopers

In December 1993, several reports surfaced in which Arkansas State troopers who had served on Governor Clinton's security detail recounted a series of alleged personal and official indiscretions by the Governor, most of them of a sexual nature.[1]

In his article on the trooper allegations in the *American Spectator*, David Brock wrote of the effort of "Clinton and his surrogates" to attempt to "thwart publication of the [troopers' allegations]." After describing several phone conversations "Buddy" Young had with three troopers (Roger Perry, Larry Patterson, and Danny Ferguson),[2] Brock also described conversations the President had with Ferguson, based on Perry's account. Because of the seriousness of this allegation, Brock's passage is repeated in full:

> Perry said that Ferguson told him that Clinton called him personally while he was on duty at the Arkansas governor's mansion on at least two occasions after our first interview. During the initial call, according to Perry, **Clinton let it be known that he was willing to offer favors in return for the troopers' refusal to cooperate further. Clinton told Ferguson to tell Roger Perry that "Roger can have whatever he wants [not to talk]."** In another call to Ferguson, Clinton asked what precisely Perry and Patterson were saying, Perry said. "If you tell me what stories Roger and Larry are telling, I can go in the back door and handle it and clean it up," Clinton allegedly said. Perry said that Ferguson told him that in the course of the conversations **Clinton offered Ferguson a federal job—either as the U.S. marshal in Little Rock or as a regional FEMA director—explicitly in exchange for his help in thwarting publication of any stories.** This could be a violation by Clinton of a criminal statute barring the solicitation of money or anything of value (in this case, information) in consideration for the promise of federal employment. Ferguson said, "I'm not going to confirm anything Roger is saying I said, "I've talked to a lawyer and I'm not denying it. No comment." (The White House did not return calls for this story.)[3]

On December 21, 1993, the day after the Brock story came out, the *Los Angeles Times* featured a lengthy front page article in which the troopers' allegations were detailed as a result of an independent investigation by two *Los Angeles Times* reporters.[4] The article's second sentence stated: "Two of the troopers say that Clinton, as President, sought to discourage them from speaking out by offering them federal jobs."[5] In all material respects, the *Los Angeles Times* article and the Brock article are consistent.[6] Again, because of the seriousness of this allegation, the relevant portions of the *Los Angeles Times* article are repeated in full:

> Young said he met personally with Clinton in Washington and provided a report to the President on his conversations with the three troopers. . . .
> He also said he gave Clinton the name of one of the troopers involved who had told Young he was backing away from any deal to speak out.[7]
> Clinton telephoned that trooper [Ferguson], according to the White House.
> Perry said the trooper described to him several telephone calls from the President. The trooper who received the calls confirmed the accuracy of what Perry said about the substance of the calls. However, he refused to allow his name to be used in this story because he said he fears retaliation.
> Perry's following description is vehemently denied by the White House.
> According to Perry, Clinton reportedly asked the trooper what Perry and others were telling the press and how far along their plans were. Perry said the trooper told him that Clinton vowed to come in the back door and shut it down when told that Perry and others were planning to go public.

> Perry said that Clinton, according to the trooper, said that he could offer an unspecified federal job to Perry and one of two jobs to the trooper, saying that a job like Young's was open and so was a U.S. marshal's job.

White House aide Lindsey said "in the past few months, the President has had conversations about the fact that false stories were being spread about him as part of an orchestrated campaign to discredit him. There was nothing improper or inappropriate about any of these conversations," Lindsey said, adding that "any suggestion that the President offered anyone a job in return for silence is a lie."

In an interview, Lindsey said the President specifically recalled a telephone conversation with one of the troopers. "My understanding is that the President did not offer [him] a job," Lindsey said.

When asked if the President also had offered another job to Perry and another trooper, Lindsey said, "No, my understanding is not."[8]

Responses to the *American Spectator* and *Los Angeles Times* Stories

The immediate media response confirmed the seriousness of this allegation, as well as the media's general displeasure in reporting it. While nearly all observers recognized that the troopers' accounts suggested a Federal crime, every effort was made to discount these allegations. The *Washington Post* acknowledged that the allegation "could be a criminal offense if true. . . . **We hope it didn't happen.** . . . Th[e troopers] claim [Clinton] has since broken both the law and his word. But their case so far is suspect and short of convincing."[9]

The White House also recognized the gravity of the charge, taking immediate action to respond to the allegations. The *Washington Post* on December 23 reported:

> White House aide Bruce Lindsey said that earlier this week he had contacted Steven Engstrom, a Little Rock lawyer who is a friend of his, to see whether Ferguson had an attorney and would release a statement denying Perry's account. Engstrom spoke with Batton [Robert Batton, Ferguson's attorney] on his behalf, Lindsey said.
>
> "All I was trying to do was to lock down the one issue that everybody said gave this story any current substance, which was the job offer," Lindsey said yesterday.[10]

Simultaneously, Betsey Wright, Governor Clinton's Chief of Staff and a close friend of the Clintons, travelled to Little Rock to get Ferguson to recant. Wright said that "she took those actions as a private citizen and at her expense. She said she was in contact with the White House but was not sent by the Administration."[11] Wright met with Ferguson, showed him an advance copy of the *American Spectator*, suggested (according to an anonymous source) that the allegation "could get the man impeached," and urged Ferguson to hold a press conference, or failing that, asked him to execute an affidavit that Engstrom would prepare.

Ferguson, however, approached by both Lindsey (through Engstrom and Batton) and Betsey Wright,[12] refused to sign an affidavit. Instead, an "affidavit" was signed by Ferguson's attorney Robert Batton. This critical distinction was lost by most reporters and analysts.[13] "Batton said Ferguson agreed to provide a limited affidavit on the issue of the job offer because of the criminal implications. 'That needed to be addressed and cleared up and that is what the affidavit was for,' Batton said."[14]

The pertinent text of the document is below:

> My client does not wish to converse with any member of the media and, therefore, has authorized me to say on his behalf that **President Clinton never offered or indicated a willingness to offer any trooper a job in exchange for silence or help in shaping their stories.**
>
> In a phone conversation in early September, Danny Ferguson inquired whether the President received a memo from Rogers [sic] Perry requesting a position on one of the President's Councils on Drugs. The President was unaware of any such request. The President said he would try to track down Perry's request and asked Danny Ferguson to get in touch with Roger Perry to see what his memorandum said and to get back in touch with the President. No further discussions took place.
>
> Neither my client nor I will make any further statement.[15]

An affidavit is a document furnished on the basis of the personal knowledge of the affiant. It is highly unusual for an attorney to execute an affidavit on behalf of his client, and even more unusual to execute an affidavit simply to state what the client told the attorney. Batton's personal knowledge begins and ends with what Ferguson told him; Batton has no basis to know the truthfulness of what Ferguson said.

Furthermore, the affidavit does not recite that it was sworn or made under oath, which would absolve Batton of any liability for a false statement.[16] Note also that the denial in the affidavit is broader than Ferguson's personal knowledge, because Ferguson cannot speak for the other troopers.

Lindsey said that a White House search for Perry's memorandum, after the story broke on December 19, came up empty. "Asked why the president would express interest in helping secure a job for a man he believed to be spreading scandalous stories about him, a senior administration official said Clinton probably wanted to find out the reason for Perry's unhappiness. 'Why wouldn't you want to see the memo? the official said."[17]

Despite its many inadequacies, which were largely ignored by the media, the Batton affidavit (mistaken as Ferguson's affidavit), coupled with White House denials, appeared to put the matter to rest.[18] Yet, contrary to Batton's affidavit, Ferguson did make another statement. In a subsequent interview of Ferguson by the *Los Angeles Times* reporters who broke the initial story, Ferguson put additional distance between him and Batton's statement. According to the *Los Angeles Times*:

> In a subsequent interview Wednesday night, however, Ferguson confirmed his earlier statement to the *Times* that **Clinton had discussed a possible federal job for trooper Perry during a conversation with Ferguson in which, Ferguson said, the President was trying to find out what public disclosures Perry planned to make.** (. . . Ferguson also was a source in respect to the alleged job offers, but his identity was withheld, at his request, until he decided to release the affidavit Wednesday.)

Asked if Clinton expressly said that jobs would be offered if the troopers remained silent, Ferguson said, "He didn't say those words."

Perry had told the *Times* that he considered the timing of Clinton's interest a clear signal that he could be considered for a federal job "if I kept quiet."

Ferguson, in a taped interview last week, said that Clinton also had asked him if he was interested in one or two federal jobs—either as a regional head of the Federal Emergency Management Agency or as a U.S. marshal. Clinton did not connect the jobs to a specific request for silence, Ferguson said.

After his attorney issued the affidavit, Ferguson agreed to talk to the *Times* in an attempt to clear up apparent contradictions between the affidavit and what Ferguson previously had told the newspaper in interviews. **He confirmed that Clinton had discussed jobs during the calls and that the jobs had come up after Ferguson told Clinton that the troopers were unhappy with the President.**

In the affidavit, Ferguson was quoted as saying that he told Clinton about Perry's interest in an appointment to the President's council on drugs. The President told Ferguson to get more information from Perry and to "get back in touch with the President," according to the affidavit.

Perry previously has told the *Times* that Ferguson relayed Clinton's inquiry to him while the troopers were playing golf. Perry said that he thought it was an inducement for silence.

In a previous interview, Ferguson had confirmed Perry's interpretation. He said, "I have no problem with what Roger said."

In the Washington interview Wednesday, Clinton firmly denied the allegation by some of the troopers that he had offered a job or jobs in return for their silence about sexual misconduct.

"The allegations on abuse of the state or the federal positions I have—it's not true," Clinton said. "That absolutely did not happen."[19]

The troopers' credibility was called into question on December 24 with the publication of a story alleging that Perry and Patterson had participated in a 1990 insurance fraud scheme arising out of an auto accident.[20]

"By week's end," the *Los Angeles Times* reporters concluded, "the job offer issue remained clouded."[21] And, by week's end—only one week after the allegation surfaced—the issue became dormant.[22] For the most part, only the *Washington Times*, in editorials[23] and in an occasional op-ed column,[24] kept the issue afloat.[25]

Criminal Laws Potentially Implicated

Federal criminal law prohibits the payment or receipt of any money or anything of value in consideration of the use of influence or promise of support in obtaining a Federal appointment. Section 211 of Title 18 is directed to "whoever solicits or receives . . . any money or thing of value, in consideration of the promise of support or use of influence in obtaining for any person any appointive office or place under the United States[.]"[26] This statute would cover the President if he solicited or received any thing of value in consideration of assisting a trooper, or promising to assist the trooper, in obtaining a Federal position. A violation of section 211 is a felony, punishable by a fine of not more than $1000 and imprisonment of not more than one year.

A Federal official's offer of a government job to a person in exchange for something of value also suggests a violation of the illegal gratuities statute, 18 U.S.C. 201. The illegal gratuities statute covers a public official who, "directly or indirectly demands, seeks, receives, accepts, or agrees to receive or accept anything of value personally for or because of any official act performed or to be performed by such official[.]"[27] This provision carries a maximum punishment of two years imprisonment, plus fines.[28] Although this provision may technically cover the jobs-for-something allegation, the allegation is more directly addressed by section 211.

What Was Refuted and What Was Not

Piecing together (a) Ferguson's statements (including Batton's affidavit), (b) Perry's account of Ferguson's calls with the President, (c) Young's statements, and (d) the responses of the President and Bruce Lindsey, the following facts are unrefuted:

After the President learned that some members of his former Arkansas security detail were talking to reporters, the President discussed this matter with Buddy Young. Subsequently, Young contacted the troopers in an effort to discourage the troopers from going public. The President also called one of the troopers, Danny Ferguson, and in the course of inquiring into what the troopers were telling reporters and why they were talking, the President and Ferguson discussed the prospect of Federal employment for at least one of the troopers.

The only factual issue that is controverted is critical: whether the President promised, offered, or suggested a Federal job for one or more troopers **in return for** something of value. Section 211 explicitly covers "any money or thing of value." That "thing of value" could constitute (1) silence; (2) a change in the troopers' story; (3) refusal to cooperate further with reporters; (4) assistance in preventing publication of any stories; or (5), information on what the other troopers were saying. Proving an oral offer of a *quid pro quo* is often elusive, however.

What weight should be accorded the evidence? Perry's statement is hearsay, and thus is entitled to lesser consideration than Ferguson's own statements. Ferguson's initial statement to the *Los Angeles Times* and Batton's affidavit are inconsistent; Ferguson's subsequent statements to the *Los Angeles Times* do not completely reconcile the two, and do not conclusively rule out the offer of some kind of *quid pro quo*. Batton's affidavit and Bruce Lindsey's statements are also entitled to lesser consideration because they are simply reports of the statements of others. The affidavit also suffers somewhat from its specificity and narrowness. The White House pressure (including Wright) on Ferguson to issue a recanting statement, and Ferguson's unwillingness to execute an affidavit himself, also undercut the force of the affidavit. By contrast, the President's own denials, even if expected and self-serving, are entitled to some weight.

Thus, we are left with one or more conversations between the President and Ferguson in which both the nature of the troopers' allegations and the prospect of Federal employment for the troopers were discussed. Imagine if the same allegation—that an official had offered assistance in obtaining a Federal job in exchange for silence—surfaced against a mid-ranking Federal official, instead of the President. Would the allegation simply die out on its own, after the official denied it, or would the matter be investigated further? Unless the source of the allegation were inherently incredible, the allegation would be referred to the Justice Department, and an investigation would ensue, in which both witnesses and subjects would be put under oath.

This is what should have been done in response to the initial reports that the President had offered Federal jobs to troopers. The FBI could have interviewed Ferguson and Perry, with their testimony taken under oath. Then, if their sworn testimony suggested a *quid pro quo* between the President and one or more trooper, the Bureau could have interviewed the President (and Lindsey, Wright, and Young) to elicit a direct and specific response to the allegations.

Why Did This Story Die?

Initially, there was widespread aversion to reporting on the troopers' allegations, because the allegations concerned Governor, not President, Clinton, or because they dealt with Bill Clinton's personal life, or because they tended to support an unflattering image of the President that may hinder his ability to get things done.[29] Although the media, for the most part, did not relish covering the troopers' allegations, the job offer issue clearly presented a legitimate issue for the media to pursue. Yet, instead of calls for an investigation, the issue went away, to the obvious relief of the White House (and to the apparent relief of the mainstream media and the Congress). Why did this happen? Should the issue have gone away? There are several possible explanations.

First: The allegations themselves are incredible, because the troopers have been discredited, because they were in it for money, because of the story alleging their participation in a fraud scheme, or because they told their story to the *American Spectator*.[30] None of these explanations is sufficient. The troopers may have thought that they would reap some financial reward for coming forward, but apparently they have not done so, and the reporters who broke the story do not believe it affected their credibility. The allegations of fraud were refuted, but even if true, did not necessarily mean that the troopers were lying about what they witnessed on the job. And the troopers were talking to CNN and the *Los Angeles Times* at the same time they were talking with David Brock.[31]

Even assuming that trooper Perry's credibility is questionable, it is Ferguson who had the conversations with the President and confirmed Perry's account on this particular issue to the *Los Angeles Times*. Ferguson's credibility was not attacked—he did not allow his name to be used in either story—although his account of his discussions with the President wavered.

Second: The affidavit is conclusive or should be treated as such. This is clearly the reason some in the media relied on to justify their lack of attention to the story,[32] yet it does not hold up to scrutiny. The affidavit was not signed by Ferguson, but by Ferguson's lawyer Batton, and it is not based on Batton's personal knowledge. The denial contained in the affidavit is narrow and specific, and does not foreclose the possibility that a violation of law occurred. And Ferguson may well have been concerned about his own legal exposure.[33] In any event, Ferguson's later interview with the *Los Angeles Times* undercuts whatever force Batton's affidavit was intended to have.[34]

Third: It's a "He said-He said" dispute that is incapable of proof. Yet, this type of dispute—involving one person's word against another's, with no other eyewitnesses—is not unusual (e.g., Clarence Thomas-Anita Hill, Lorena Bobbitt-John Wayne Bobbitt). Even if a prosecutor would be justified, as a matter of discretion, in declining prosecution because the direct statements are in equipoise, that would not be a proper reason to decline even to investigate.

Fourth: The White House's account is believed to be the truth: The President "was merely contacting old friends to determine why scurrilous untruths were being leaked about him"[35] and that the subject of a Federal job came up only as an explanation for a trooper's ill will towards the President. But even if both of the above statements are accurate, a Federal crime still could have been committed if the promise of a job was linked with what the troopers would say.

Fifth: Out of respect for the **presidency**, the President's denial should be given credit where there is no contrary evidence other than the person making the allegation. This is a plausible explanation for the media's lack of interest, although no one said so. It is similar to the notion that Justice Thomas's denials should have been accepted absent any evidence to support Professor Hill's allegations. However, the media and many Democrats in Congress were not so ready to accept President Bush's denials that he had participated in an "October Surprise," and insisted on holding wasteful hearings.

Sixth: Also out of respect for the presidency, even if the allegation were true, there is great reluctance to pursue any allegation of a sexual or personal nature that may implicate the President in a criminal act and thereby jeopardize the presidency, without a stronger nexus between the allegation and the conduct of his office. There certainly is some nexus here, because Mr. Clinton made these phone calls as President; but according to this explanation, the underlying events that led to these calls derived from his conduct as Governor. This explanation is also a plausible reason why the story was not pursued more vigorously.

Seventh: The media was reluctant to focus on the job offer issue because of the sexual context in which it was presented.[36] Yet, this is not a satisfactory explanation, because the job offer issue is clearly separable from the underlying stories of sexual indiscretions. Indeed, the *Los Angeles Times* justified its story based almost entirely on Governor Clinton's alleged misuse of State employees and resources, and later on the White House's efforts to kill the story.

Eighth: Those who support the President and who want him to succeed do not want to concern themselves with matters that may weaken his political standing and thus make it more difficult to achieve his initiatives. This theory would explain the media's general acceptance of the Batton affidavit as Ferguson's affidavit as well as explain the media's general snap judgment that the troopers' themselves were not credible. This theory, however, covers only those Clinton Administration well-wishers in the media. The issue died down across-the-board, even among reporters and news organizations that did not exhibit the same reluctance to explore Whitewater allegations.

Ninth: After the allegation and the denials, there was nothing else to report. Unlike other scandals, which unfold gradually over time, the jobs-for-something allegation consisted of a few phone calls, with only a handful of players, who all spoke out publicly about what did or did not occur. This may explain why no additional story was filed after the first week, but it does not explain why there was a paucity of editorials and op-eds discussing the allegation and calling for an investigation.

These explanations satisfactorily account for the many reasons why the jobs-for-something allegation, **as a news story**, died so quickly and completely. But as **justifications** for why there was no call from any of the so-called public interest groups or ethics gadflies for an investigation of this allegation, they are less than satisfactory. A Justice Department investigation, or one conducted by a special or independent counsel, should have been conducted. Not conducting an investigation suggests that the President (or perhaps just this President) enjoys a *de facto* immunity from investigation of certain criminal offenses, either because of the nature of the presidency, or the nature of the offense, or both. The scope of such immunity, of course, is unclear to say the least. In all events, it is not too late to conduct such an investigation, and the Attorney General should do so, or explain why not. Congress should also look into why, apparently, there was no Justice Department inquiry when the story broke, and whether Justice would respond any differently if the same allegations were made against a Federal official other than the President.

Post Script: Did the President Learn any Lesson?

Months later, President Clinton again briefly found himself in some hot water for allegedly offering a Federal position in exchange for something of value. As the 1994 mid-term election neared, it looked like control of the Senate could turn on the outcome of the Virginia Senate race, where Senator Charles Robb and Oliver North were running neck-and-neck. On October 18, President Clinton met with former Virginia Governor Doug Wilder, in an effort to persuade Wilder to endorse Robb.[37] When the *Washington Times* reported that in the same meeting with Wilder, President Clinton had "discussed the prospect of Mr. Wilder accepting a 'roving ambassadorship' in Africa,"[38] the inference arose that the President had offered a Federal position in return for Wilder's support of Robb. Oliver North immediately wrote the Attorney General, requesting an investigation, although stopping short of accusing the President of violating the law.[39]

If the allegation were true, the President would have violated not only 18 U.S.C. 211, but also 18 U.S.C. 600, another criminal provision that makes it a crime to offer a Federal position in consideration of a promise of political support or endorsement.[40]

White House aides, aware of the seriousness of the charge, quickly moved to deny that any *quid pro quo* was discussed. Indeed, the White House denied that any question of a position for Wilder in the Clinton Administration came up. Dee Dee Myers said, "Ambassadorships were not discussed. No jobs were asked or offered."[41] A day later, President Clinton personally denied the allegation, too, yet his denial was notably narrow:

> [T]here was absolutely no discussion along the lines you mentioned of an ambassadorship to an African country **in return for** his endorsement of Senator Robb; that just did not happen. I would not do that, I would never be part of that, and that did not happen. The Vice President spoke to it today; I will tell you again, that did not happen. It did not happen.[42]

Wilder also denied the allegation.[43]

With no participant in or witness to the meeting coming forward to support the allegation, there was nothing left but speculation, and the story died.[44]

Nearly a year later, after the President agreed to make an appearance at a fundraiser to help retire Wilder's campaign debts, the White House again was again forced to deny that the President had promised Wilder anything in the October 1994 meeting.[45] Even had the President promised Wilder at the time to help him retire his debts, no law would have been implicated because no official action would have been involved.

Chapter Ten

The Establishment
of a
Legal Defense Fund

The President's decision to create a legal defense fund to defray his legal expenses was reasonable, given the alternatives. But his decision to retain attorneys who charge in excess of $400 an hour contributed significantly to the amount of money the fund would need to raise. The President may legally accept contributions from any individual, although he may not solicit contributions. The Presidential Legal Expense Trust contains several salutary provisions that reduce, but do not eliminate, the appearance that donors are contributing to further a personal or financial interest in a matter before the Government. The $1000 limit on individual yearly contributions is reasonable.

The initial decision to receive contributions from lobbyists, since reversed, was inconsistent with the President's rhetoric on the pernicious influence of lobbyists, and to this extent it was rightly criticized. The Clintons could reduce criticism further by rejecting contributions from persons seeking action from, or doing business with, the Government, regardless of whether they fit the narrower definition of a lobbyist.

The terms of the Trust allow the trustees to solicit contributions. The trustees subsequently decided, however, after belatedly consulting with the Office of Government Ethics (OGE), that neither the Clintons nor the trustees would engage in solicitation, in order to avoid the regulatory proscription against solicitation by the President. Contributions resulting from any solicitation by the trustees between the date the Trust was created and the belated discovery that standards of conduct prohibit solicitation must be returned. The White House Counsel's failure to obtain a written, detailed opinion from OGE before the Trust was established created problems that should have been avoided.

In May 1994, soon after President Clinton was sued by Paula Corbin Jones for alleged sexual misconduct that occurred in 1991,[1] the White House Counsel's office began looking into whether a legal defense fund could be set up to help the Clintons with their substantial legal bills.[2] David Kendall of Williams & Connolly, whom the Clintons retained to represent them on Madison, Whitewater, and other financial dealings that occurred before Bill Clinton became President, reportedly bills clients at $300-$400 per hour.[3] Robert Bennett of Skadden, Arps, Slate, Meagher & Flom, who was retained primarily to defend Clinton against the Jones suit, reportedly bills at $400-475 per hour.[4] Thus, the Clintons' legal fees were estimated to amount to hundreds of thousands of dollars, each month, perhaps accumulating to two million dollars per year.[5] This amount would substantially exceed the Clintons' net worth and income.[6]

There was no indication that either law firm representing the Clintons would provide a discount from their normal billing rates, or provide an extended payment plan, to account for the Clintons' limited financial resources.[7] A discount or extension from either law firm could give the appearance of currying favor from the Administration, given the interests of clients of Williams & Connolly and Skadden, Arps in matters before the Federal Government.[8] Therefore, the White House considered a legal defense fund.[9]

Because the President is not subject to the general gift restrictions that apply to Executive Branch employees,[10] he may legally accept contributions toward his legal expenses from any person or entity, in any amount, although he is required to report any contribution over $250 on his annual financial disclosure form.[11] Nonetheless, there would still be ethics considerations. The President would be open to criticism for taking contributions from persons and entities regulated by the Government, who may have a matter of interest pending with the White House or before the Administration, or who may be interested in an appointment to or position in the Administration or on the Federal bench.[12]

In light of these concerns, it was initially thought that the legal defense fund should be set up to keep the identity of donors from the President. Contributions would go from the donor to the legal defense fund to the law firm, with no involvement or knowledge by the Clintons. Under this system, an OGE official indicated that the donors' individual identities would not have to be disclosed on the President's financial disclosure form.[13] To ensure that others who work for or know the President do not inform the President or the White House of the names of contributors, the fund would need an independent trustee and staff. The clear disadvantage of this option is that, even with these protections, nothing would prohibit a contributor from personally informing the President or others of his contribution.

More effective ways to reduce the appearance problem would be to limit the size of contributions, prohibit contributions from certain persons or entities, and require public disclosure of the names of donors.[14] The greater the size of a contribution, the more likely the appearance of an attempt to curry favor or gain access. Disclosure both discourages giving by persons whose contribution would be criticized as well as informs the public of the persons who are contributing. This allows the public to judge the propriety of the contribution and any subsequent official actions. Also, appearance problems could be reduced if donations were prohibited from certain classes of persons or entities, such as all corporate and union interests, any person with a particular matter pending with the White House, or any Federal employee. Such restrictions would require an elaborate screening system and the involvement of the Clintons or White House ethics officials to perform the screen.

The Terms of the Legal Defense Fund

On June 28, 1994, Reverend Theodore M. Hesburgh and Nicholas de B. Katzenbach announced the creation of a legal defense fund for the Clintons, called the Presidential Legal Expense Trust.[15] The Trust is a grantor trust, created by the President and Mrs. Clinton. Hesburgh (President Emeritus of the University of Notre Dame) and Katzenbach (former Attorney General) were named Co-Chairmen of the Trust. The Trust is run day-to-day by Executive Director Michael H. Cardozo (who served as Deputy Counsel to President Carter) and managed by a nine-member Board of Trustees.[16] The Trust is administered entirely outside the Government and (except in two particulars) free from any involvement of or supervision by the Clintons and the White House.

In a press release issued the day the Trust was created, the Co-Chairmen stated:

> No previous president has had to face the enormous personal legal expenses confronting President Clinton, because of current legal proceedings based on events that allegedly occurred well before he took office. These expenses will be many times his total compensation as President. Whatever the merits or motivations of these proceedings, we believe it is in the public interest to assist the President in meeting a financial burden that could otherwise distract him from performing his public responsibilities.

Contributions to the Trust would be used to defray the "personal legal fees and related expenses" incurred by the Clintons since January 20, 1993.[17] Contributions would not be used to pay any settlement or judgment against the Clintons.[18] Nor would contributions be used to pay for legal expenses incurred by other White House officials.[19]

Contributions are limited to $1000 per individual per year and accepted only from individuals who are not employees of the Federal Government.[20] Contributions from corporations, unions, political action committees, and other entities are prohibited. All contributors must supply their name and address; those who contribute over $200 must furnish their occupation and name of employer, consistent with the requirements for contributions over $200 to candidates for Federal office.[21] A list of contributors is to be publicly disclosed every six months, by name, address, amount, and, for contributors over $200, by employer.[22]

Any individual (other than Federal employees) may contribute, including those persons who are doing business with the Government and those who may have an interest in a particular matter pending in the White House or Executive Branch, including lobbyists. Recognizing that some contributions from such individuals could pose an appearance problem, the Clintons are provided with a list of contributors every four months to enable them to reject contributions from persons whose contribution might be considered inappropriate. The Clintons are given thirty days to disclaim any contribution.[23]

The Trust indenture grants the trustees broad authority to engage in various types of solicitation, such as direct mail and advertising, and to employ consultants and other professionals to engage in the fund-raising At the time the Trust was created, the particulars had not been decided, other than that the President and First Lady would not themselves solicit. The trustees reportedly ruled out holding a single fund-raising event, concerned about whether such an event would injure the dignity of the presidency.[25] Subsequently, the Executive Director of the Trust explained that the trustees also would not engage in soliciting funds for the Trust.[26]

The Trust provides that money collected from contributions may be invested only in a savings account, Treasury bills, or in mutual funds investing exclusively in money-market funds.[27] If there is any money remaining in the Trust corpus after all of the Clintons' legal expenses are paid, the Trust provides that the money will be given to the Clintons, or their successors.[28] In a letter to the trustees dated June 28, 1994, the Clintons stated their intention "to donate any such surplus to one or more non-profit institutions of the United States Government, without claiming any incidental income tax deductions for ourselves or our estates."

The Trust also provides that the trustees, who serve without pay (they may be reimbursed for expenses),[29] may be removed by the Clintons without condition.[30]

Analysis of the Presidential Legal Expense Trust

President Clinton, facing the prospect of enormous legal bills that would eclipse his income, was presented with several alternatives, none of them very attractive. The Clintons obviously did not consider shouldering the responsibility alone, and going heavily into debt for a number of years. They should not be faulted for seeking to avoid that situation. Accepting free or discounted legal services, however, also was not an attractive option. This is because it would create an impression that the President was beholden to, or at least would be more solicitous of, the interests of his law firm and its clients, unless the lawyer or firm providing the discount had no business before the Federal Government. The President understandably hired competent counsel from within the Washington legal establishment, because the nature of the required legal representation. It was likely, then, that any lawyers he retained would have other clients with interests in matters pending before the Executive Branch.

A legal defense fund, too, was not without risks, in that instead of being beholden to one law firm and its clients, the President could be seen as being beholden to many of the maximum contributors to his fund. He would be receiving something of value from third persons whether the law firm or individual contributors.

On balance, the Clintons opted for a legal defense fund, because a legal defense fund spreads the amount of individual gifts among multiple contributors, and because other provisions could be included to reduce appearance concerns. The Clintons' choice was reasonable.

The need for a legal defense fund for the Clintons was generally accepted by the media, if not by the public;[31] initially, criticism by Members of Congress was notice-ably absent. For the most part, the Clintons' choice of lawyers who bill clients at $400 hour or more also was not challenged,[32] although competent counsel could have been found at half these rates.

The limitations on who may contribute are welcome, and go a long way to pre-vent an appearance problem. However, these provisions did not satisfy those who believe that any legal defense fund presents problems. For example, prohibiting cor-porations, unions, and political action committees from contributing to the Presi-dent's fund does not prevent senior officials and executives of such organizations from contributing personally. Paul Gigot wondered "how many donors . . . will in fact be making . . . quid-pro-quo calculations."[33] Professor Larry Sabato believes that contributions inevitably create political debts, even if they are not made initially with a particular governmental act or favor in mind.[34]

Public disclosure of contributions also is likely to discourage contributions from persons who have business with or are seeking action from the White House or Exec-utive Branch. Yet the disclosure provided by the terms of the Trust is deficient in one respect. The public reporting is too infrequent—only once every six months. Disclo-sure operates best when it is timely and regular, allowing the public to scrutinize the government official's contemporaneous actions.[35]

The strongest criticisms of the Trust were directed to the $1000 limit, the failure to prohibit contributions by lobbyists, the Trust's legality under Federal law, and the tax consequences to the Clintons. These issues will be discussed in turn.

The $1000 Limit On Individual Contributions

The $1000 limit was criticized as too high. Charles Lewis of the Center for Public Integrity remarked:

> There are not many little old ladies in Ohio who can cough up $1,000 for Bill's defense[.]
> [T]he less money there is, the less potential influence-buying there is. If you're going to these lengths to try to keep the president above the fray, so to speak, then you ought to do it the right way and the right way is $500 or even less.[36]

The White House's initial consideration of a $500 limit may have focussed more attention on the eventual selection of a $1000 limit.[37]

Obviously, there is no clear or consistently applied line between an amount of money that does not give rise to an appearance of impropriety and one that does. The gift standards for Executive Branch employees permit an employee to accept a gift of $20 or less, even from a person who has a matter pending before the employee.[38] The financial disclosure law requires Federal officials to report all gifts from any individ-ual aggregating to $250 or more, excluding any gift of $100 or less.[39] Presumably, this reflected a (recent) congressional judgment that gifts below $250 did not pose an ethics issue. (On the other hand, in 1995, the House of Representatives passed a measure prohibiting Members and staff from receiving nearly all gifts, regardless of amount.) Even Charles Lewis was not entirely uncomfortable with a $500 limit.

The $1000 limit was chosen primarily because it is the maximum amount an individual may contribute to a candidate for Federal office under Federal election law. It was thus thought that contributions of this amount would not be seen as improper attempts to affect government policy or decisions. The limit is also substantially lower than the contribution limits provided for legal defense funds for Members of Congress: House Members may receive contributions up to $5000; Senators may receive contributions up to $10,000 per year.[40]

For these reasons, the $1000 limit is not inappropriate.

Lobbyists May Contribute

The Trust's initial failure to prohibit contributions from lobbyists generated a considerable and somewhat justifiable amount of criticism.[41] The President was skewered largely because of the inconsistency between campaigning in 1992 against the pernicious influence of lobbyists and accepting in 1994 $1000 contributions from lobbyists to help defray his personal legal expenses. A *New York Times* editorial was particularly critical:

> [T]he decision to allow lobbyists and people who do business with the Government illustrates again the Clintons' uncanny ability to make a mess of a bad situation. . . . [Contributions from lobbyists] are intended to buy favor with a President who has shown himself all too willing to put his favor up for bids. . . . [T]he Clintons once again have chosen dollars over the principles of ethical government.[42]

The *New York Times* linked accepting contributions from lobbyists with what they regarded was the President's lack of will and clout to push for campaign finance reform, especially a ban on political action committees and curbs on soft money.[43]

Again, the Trust was defended by reference to the House and Senate rules at the time. Those permitted contributions from not only lobbyists, but also from corporations, unions, and PACs. The White House also explained that a restriction on contributions from lobbyists would be difficult to implement.[44] The trouble with the first defense is that the Senate earlier in 1994 passed a provision that would prohibit lobbyists (and registered foreign agents) from contributing to a Senator's legal defense fund, although the bill did not become law. (The House version would have required only that such contributions be disclosed.) The Trust's Executive Director responded weakly that if the Senate provision became law, the Trust would no longer accept contributions from lobbyists.[45]

The trouble with the second argument is that certain lobbyists are currently required by law to be registered, and the Clinton Administration has pushed lobbying reform legislation that, of course, contains a definition of lobbying. It is inconsistent to promote legislation that presumes the concept of lobbying and the identity of a lobbyist can be understood and applied, while, at the same time, complaining of the difficulty in screening contributions to the legal defense fund from lobbyists.

Although the screen held out the promise that the Clintons would turn away contributions from persons with business before or seeking action from the Executive Branch—a broader class of persons than "lobbyists"—the White House did not respond to the criticism of accepting contributions from lobbyists by emphasizing that the Clintons would use the screen to reject contributions to avoid an appearance of impropriety. Perhaps this is because the vast majority of contributions from lobby-ists were expected to pass through the screen. Commentators noted that the Trust did not exclude contributions from lobbyists, probably because that would deprive the Trust of a lucrative source of contributions.[46]

The disconnect between the President's rhetoric against the influence of lobby-ists and the terms of his legal defense fund was brought into focus by Senator Bob Dole following the State of the Union address in January 1995. In the speech, the President again pushed for lobbying reform, but went an extra step to plead with lawmakers voluntarily to "just say no" to gifts from lobbyists. The next morning, Dole labeled the President's remark a "cheap shot." Within hours, the Trust's Co-Chairman issued a statement that, henceforth, the Trust would not accept contribu-tions from registered lobbyists. The decision was made by the President and the First Lady, after Dole's complaint.[47]

It was determined that the new policy would take effect prospectively, and that contributions previously received from registered lobbyists would not be returned. Also, the new policy covers only "registered" lobbyists, not others who are directly seeking official action from the Government. (Under the lobbying disclosure bill enacted in 1995, the definition of "lobbyist" is expanded significantly.) Moreover, the screen for lobbyists may not be fail-safe, because only those contributions over $200 are required to state their occupation.[48]

The Legality of the Trust

The legality of the Trust was immediately challenged on several fronts, although initially only by the *Washington Times*.[49] Subsequently, the House Republican lead-ership wrote the Attorney General asking her to answer thirteen questions concern-ing the legality of the Trust.[50] Two House Republicans also wrote OGE a detailed, four-page letter asking several legal questions.[51]

A lawsuit charging that the Trust was an illegal Federal advisory committee was filed in August 1994 in U.S. District Court by Judicial Watch, Inc.[52] The advisory committee count was patently frivolous. Contrary to the complaint's unsupported assertions, the Trust is assuredly not an advisory committee under the Federal Advi-sory Committee Act because it was not established, and it will not be utilized, "to obtain advice or recommendations for the President."[53] Upon the Trust's motion to dismiss, District Judge Royce Lamberth dismissed the suit in February 1995, finding that whatever advice the Trust provides the President, it provides such advice to him in his personal, not official, capacity.[54]

Finally, on March 7, 1995, the Landmark Legal Foundation wrote the Attorney General, requesting the appointment of an independent counsel, alleging that Presi-dent Clinton's establishment of the legal defense fund constituted illegal solicitation. Deputy Assistant Attorney General Jack Keeney responded in April, rejecting the request on the ground that the letter did not meet the conditions for the appointment of an independent counsel.[55]

The legal issues fall into three categories: First, can the President **accept** contri-butions from any individual consistent with statutory and regulatory gift restrictions? Second, is fund-raising for the Trust, conducted outside of the President's control, **"solicitation"** from which the President is prohibited under the gift restrictions? Third, do contributions to the Trust amount to a **supplementation of salary** prohibited by 18 U.S.C. 209?

In addition, the failure of the White House Counsel's office or the Trust to obtain a written legal opinion from either Justice or OGE before the Trust was established deserves criticism.[56] The White House Counsel's office discussed the legal issues only informally with OGE before the Trust was created. Following the creation of the Trust, and the subsequent publication of articles critical of the Trust, the Trust's Executive Director met with OGE on July 11, 1994 to discuss the legal and ethical issues further. As a result, OGE provided a written opinion that the Trust is lawful,[57] but only after the Trust's Executive Director pledged in writing that neither the Clintons nor the Trustees would engage in solicitation.[58]

The Bush White House Counsel's office consulted OGE frequently on many matters involving the application of the ethics standards. While most of these consultations were informal, over the phone, a novel and sensitive issue such as the legal defense fund would have led us to seek an advance written opinion from OGE. The Clinton White House or Trust should also have done so before the trust fund was established.

The gift restrictions. The Federal gift statute, enacted as part of the Ethics Reform Act of 1989, provides in pertinent part:

> No . . . officer or employee of the executive . . . branch shall solicit or accept anything of value from a person —
> (1) seeking official action from, doing business with, or (in the case of executive branch officers and employees) conducting activities regulated by, the individual's employing entity; or
> (2) whose interests may be substantially affected by the performance or nonperformance of the individual's official duties.[59]

The term "officer or employee" includes the President and Vice President.[60]

Under the statute, OGE is authorized to provide "for such reasonable exceptions as may be appropriate." Also, an officer or employee of the Executive Branch may accept gifts "pursuant to rules and regulations established by [OGE]."[61] Thus, Congress gave OGE sufficient statutory authority to exempt the President from these gift restrictions.

Under the standards of conduct for Executive Branch employees, issued by OGE in 1992, there are two gift sections, one concerning gifts from outside sources and the other concerning gifts between Federal employees. The President and Vice President are exempt from the basic restriction on accepting gifts from outside sources:

> Because of considerations relating to the conduct of their offices, including those of protocol and etiquette, the President or the Vice President may accept any gift on his own behalf or on behalf of any family member, provided that such acceptance does not violate [secs.] 2635.202(c)(1) or (2), 18 U.S.C. 201(b) of 201(c)(3), or the Constitution of the United States.[62]

Some have argued that this exemption does not apply because a contribution to the President's legal defense fund is not the kind of gift contemplated by OGE when it crafted the exemption, in that it is not similar to a gift from a foreign head of state or other visiting dignitary.[63] But the regulatory exemption is not limited by the explanatory phrase, "including [considerations] of protocol and etiquette." These considerations are illustrative, not restrictive.[64]

In a similar vein, contributions for the President's personal legal expenses do not relate to the conduct of the President's office, or else any gift to the President would be so related. But the exemption does not mean that only gifts that relate to the conduct of the presidency are covered by the exemption. Such a construction would significantly narrow the exemption. Instead, that introductory phrase is shorthand for the realities of gift-giving to a President: OGE granted the President a complete exemption because of the nature of the presidency.

OGE explained the basis for the exemption in the preamble to the proposed rule:

> The ceremonial and other public duties of the President and Vice President make it impractical to subject them to standards that require an analysis of every gift offered. They are required to file an SF 278 public financial disclosure statement listing gifts . . . . In the case of an elected official of the stature of the President or Vice President whose personal conduct is closely scrutinized by the public and the press, this requirement for public disclosure provides sufficient restraint on their acceptance of gifts. . . . OGE anticipates that, as their predecessors have done in the past, the President and Vice President and their successors will establish their own discretionary standards for acceptance of gifts.[65]

Presidents receive thousands of unsolicited gifts each year from persons and entities, most of whom have never met the President or visited the White House.[66] The motives for these gifts, when not revealed by an accompanying message, are unknown, but they are presumed to be varied, including the donor's expression or demonstration of support for the President. Of course, these thousands of gifts are tangible; they are not gifts of money. And most of these gifts are ultimately not accepted by the President personally, but accepted on behalf of the United States. Some of the gifts retained (and therefore accepted) by the President are of intrinsic value (e.g., a sweatshirt, tennis racket, or salad bowl). However, though different in form, most contributions to a President's legal defense fund are likely to be prompted by motives similar to the ones behind tangible gifts.

Moreover, the President is ultimately responsible for all matters handled by the White House and Executive Branch. For the President, many if not most, of the thousands of donors could be viewed as a "prohibited source" because they are regulated by or do business with one or more agencies of the Executive Branch.[67] For the same reason that the President is exempt from the conflict-of-interest statute, 18 U.S.C. 208, he is exempt from the basic gift restriction. The requirement to report any gift over $250 on his financial disclosure form and the visibility of the President operate as checks on the President's discretion whether to accept a certain gift. As an elected official, the President is subject to political remedies for accepting gifts that pose an appearance of impropriety.

As elected officials, Members of Congress also enjoy exemptions from some ethics statutes, although they were included in the statutory gift restriction with the President and Vice President (with a similar grant of authority to the House and Senate to craft reasonable exceptions).[68] Also, as noted above, the Senate in 1995 imposed on Senators (as well as Senate staff) gift restrictions similar to those imposed on Executive Branch employees (other than the President and Vice President).

Still, the President's position as titular and ceremonial head of the United States Government, as well as the fishbowl environment of the White House, continue to distinguish the President from Members of Congress.

These realities of gift-giving to the President led OGE to permit the President to continue receiving gifts without restriction.[69] There is no qualification in the exemption as to the type, nature, or amount of the gift, or the identity of the donor in the exemption. Therefore, the President may legally accept even gifts of money.[70]

Critics have also suggested that, apart from the standards of conduct issued by OGE, the President is also governed by separate gift restrictions contained in the standards of conduct for the Executive Office of the President (EOP), 3 CFR Part 100,[71] which provide no express exemption for the President. (Indeed, the definitions of "employee" and "agency"[72] appear broad enough to include the President.) However, unbeknownst to these critics, the Justice Department years ago opined that the President is not subject to the EOP standards. In 1974, the Office of Legal Counsel concluded that these regulations "were not intended to and do not bind the President or Vice President."[73] Thus, previous White House Counsel's offices, including in the Bush Administration, treated the President as exempt from the EOP gift standards because it was understood that he was not covered by Executive Order 11,222 (as well as its successor, Executive Order 12,674). This was OGE's understanding as well when in the preamble to the proposed rule it discussed whether to exempt the President from the gift restrictions:

> The President and Vice President are not subject to the Standards of Ethical Conduct for Government Officers and Employees imposed by Executive Order 12674. . . . However, 5 U.S.C. 7353, added by the Ethics Reform Act, adopted a broad definition that, **for the first time**, results in the gift prohibitions being made applicable to individuals holding elected positions in all three branches of Government, including the President and Vice President.[74]

In any event, the EOP standards of conduct no longer have the force of law, having been superseded when the uniform Executive Branch-wide standards of conduct became effective on February 3, 1993. OGE explained the supersession in the preamble to the proposed and final rules.[75] However, as of the date the Trust was created, the Executive Office of the President had still not undertaken the housekeeping matter of formally repealing Part 100, thereby creating some confusion as to whether the President is subject to two sets of gift standards.

The citation of authority for 3 CFR Part 100 lists Executive Order 11,222 (issued by President Johnson on May 8, 1965) and 5 CFR Part 735, the model ethics standards issued initially by the Civil Service Commission (and subsequently, by the Office of Personnel Management).[76] When President Bush, in 1989 in Executive Order 12,674, revoked Executive Order 11,222,[77] thereby revoking the underlying authority for the EOP and other agency standards of conduct, he provided that "any regulations issued under Executive Order 11222 . . . shall remain in effect until properly amended, modified, or revoked pursuant to the authority conferred by this order or any regulations promulgated under this order."[78] In that Order, the President charged OGE with promulgating regulations "that establish a single, comprehensive, and clear set of executive-branch standards of conduct that shall be objective, reasonable, and enforceable."[79] So, when OGE's standards of conduct final rule, issued under this authority, became effective in February 1993, agency regulations issued under 5 CFR Part 735, including 3 CFR Part 100, were revoked, "pursuant to the authority conferred by this order[.]" OGE did not revoke agency standards; revocation was accomplished by the executive order. Perhaps OGE should have provided for revocation in the final rule itself, although doing so would not have made a difference as a matter of law.

Solicitation. OGE's regulatory exemption of the President from the restriction on gifts from outside sources is qualified, however, in two areas: bribery and solicitation.[80]

The President, like other Executive Branch officials and employees, may not:

> (1) Accept a gift in return for being influenced in the performance of an official act; [or]
> (2) Solicit or coerce the offering of a gift[.][81]

The second, and most serious, prong of legal attack on the legal expense fund is that it permits presidential solicitation prohibited by the standards of conduct. The Trust authorizes the trustees to "solicit donations to the trust from the general public[.]"[82] Some argue that the Trust permits the President personally to solicit contributions. Others argue that any solicitation by the trustees or others on behalf of the Trust amounts to solicitation by the President.[83]

"Solicitation" is not defined or explained in the section on gifts from outside sources. In the section on gifts between employees, however, "solicit" is defined as "to request contributions by personal communication or by general announcement."[84] A "personal communication" presumes a direct communication, in writing, over the phone, or in person, between the donee and the donor(s). Yet this definition is not much help, because the term "general announcement" is not defined. Of course, a "general announcement" could be a flier posted on a bulletin board or an advertisement that is run in the newspaper. The key question is whether there is solicitation if the announcement is not made by the official, but by others at the official's request or simply on the official's behalf.

By the ordinary use of the term, the President is not engaging in solicitation simply by creating a legal defense fund.[85] OGE agrees. Nor does the President or First Lady play any role in fund-raising. If the President were to sign a fund-raising appeal, or to make phone calls seeking contributions, he would, of course, be engaging in solicitation in violation of the regulation. But the Executive Director has confirmed that he will not do so.[86]

The difficulty arose because the Trust expressly provides that the **trustees** may solicit funds.[87] Although the trustees had not determined the ways in which funds would be solicited at the time the Trust was created, direct mail and personal solicitation by the trustees was contemplated. Some personal solicitation likely occurred contemporaneously with the creation of the Trust.[88]

Note that the general gift restriction, from which the President is exempt, prohibits Executive Branch employees from soliciting a gift, "directly or indirectly," from a prohibited source.[89] The President, of course, is subject to the restriction against solicitation, but that provision reads, "an employee shall not . . . [s]olicit or coerce the offering of a gift."[90] It is unclear whether the "directly or indirectly" language should be read into this provision. OGE apparently thinks so, although a straight textual analysis does not provide a sure answer.

"Indirect solicitation" is defined to "include" gifts given not to the employee, but to third persons with the employee's knowledge and acquiescence in the case of relatives, or by designation or on the recommendation of the employee in the case of any other person.[91] Although neither situation applies here, and "indirectly" is not otherwise defined or explained, it is likely that this definition was not meant to exclude the more common notion of indirect solicitation that occurs when an employee requests another person to solicit funds on the employee's behalf. This is the situation presented here: Because the Clintons are the Trust's Grantors, they have given the trustees authority to solicit funds on their behalf in the Trust indenture; it is as if the Clintons directed the trustees to solicit funds. Solicitation by the trustees under this authority most likely would constitute "indirect" solicitation. On the other hand, if the Trust had been set up independently of the Clintons, the trustees probably would have been permitted to solicit funds.

Apparently, OGE provided this advice to the Trust's Executive Director, because soon after the Executive Director's meeting with OGE in July 1994, the Executive Director pledged that, notwithstanding the language in the Trust indenture, the trustees would (henceforth) not engage in solicitation. "While third parties may solicit contributions that may be accepted by the Trust, these third parties will not be employed by or act as agents of the trustees."[92] OGE found no problem with these third party solicitations:

> Solicitation must involve some request. We do not see the manner in which you have outlined the trust's proposed activities as involving requests. Further, your desire to see that individuals who may voluntarily wish to solicit funds from the trust do not, through their actions or written materials, imply that the trust or the President is the solicitor or has authorized the solicitation is understandable. A review of those materials or a discussion with those individuals for that purpose is not an authorization of their solicitation.[93]

Under OGE's reading of the solicitation provision, the President would be engaged in solicitation, albeit indirectly, if (1) the trustees were personally to solicit, (2) the President were to authorize others to solicit, or (3) the trustees were to employ or authorize others to solicit.[94] The Trust's Executive Director indicated that the Trust would steer clear of solicitation. The Trust, therefore, must rely on the initial general publicity about the legal defense fund, and word-of-mouth among others, to generate contributions.[95] The Trust's fund-raising capabilities are reduced significantly.[96]

What OGE did not discuss, prompting criticism from Republicans in the House and some in the media, was the legality of the Trust's conduct from June 28, 1994, the date the Trust was established, until July 20, 1994, the date the Trust's Executive Director pledged that the Trust would not engage in solicitation (or July 11, the date the Executive Director may have been informed by OGE that the Trust could not solicit). It is highly likely that some trustees, acting individually if not in concert, began to solicit contributions from the inception of the Trust.[97] Under the standards of conduct, any check received as a result of improper solicitation must be returned.[98]

According to the first report of contributions, half of the contributions were made in the first month following establishment of the Trust, and two-thirds were made in the first two months.[99]

Supplementation of salary. Finally, critics suggested that contributions to the Trust might run afoul of 18 U.S.C. 209, as an illegal supplementation of the President's salary, on the strength of a 1985 OGE informal advisory letter.[100] Section 209 prohibits Federal employees from receiving "any salary, or any contribution to or supplementation of salary, as compensation for [the employee's] services[,]" from any source other than the United States Government.[101] OGE was asked to consider the legality of setting up a legal defense fund for a Federal employee who was involved in a grievance with his agency. OGE explained that the critical factor under section 209 is whether the payment is "compensation for services as an employee of the United States."[102]

Although the facts before OGE did not permit it to conclude that section 209 would not be implicated, the facts involving the Clintons' Legal Expense Trust do permit that conclusion. Both the Paula Corbin Jones lawsuit and the Whitewater matter do not relate to Bill Clinton as President, but concern matters that allegedly occurred while he was Governor of Arkansas. Contributions to the Trust may be motivated by a desire to protect a President from financial difficulties, but should not, because of that motivation, be seen as "compensation for his work as President." Moreover, there is little if any risk that contributions to the Trust would contravene the purpose of section 209, "that no Government official of employee serve two masters to the prejudice of his unbiased devotion to the interests of the United States."[103]

Tax consequences. The initial analysis of the tax consequences provided by the Counsel for the Trust was disputed. The legal question is whether contributions to the Trust are taxable income to the Clintons, or only interest on the corpus of Trust income, as asserted by the Trust's Counsel? The Trust stated that contributions would be considered gifts and, therefore, not taxable, although the Trust did not obtain a written ruling to this effect from the IRS or a written opinion from the firm of Sullivan & Cromwell, which prepared the Trust documents.[104]

Soon thereafter, Lee Sheppard, a New York tax attorney, wrote a lengthy article for the July 4, 1994 issue of *Tax Notes*, in which she questioned this conclusion.[105] For a contribution to qualify as a gift, the contribution must be made with "detached and disinterested generosity."[106] Sheppard canvassed several IRS Revenue Rulings and judicial decisions that make such a finding, at a minimum, problematic. Where public officials are concerned, the issues are whether the contribution helped the official carry out his government duties and whether the donor had sufficient donative intent both factual determinations. Suffice it for present purposes to conclude that the issue of the Clintons' tax liability is uncertain.

Recommendations and Conclusions

The Trust is now operating under much tighter restrictions than when it was first created. Trustees may not solicit personally, and contributions by registered lobbyists are now prohibited. The Trust should not have to return the contributions previously received from lobbyists; the problem, in my view, has always been more one of hypocrisy than of serious concern that a $1000 contribution from a lobbyist would present an improper appearance. In a year's time, lobbyists and the entities they represent, may give much greater sums in soft money contributions and in the total contributions their PACs give to Democratic party candidates. An additional $1000 is not going to make a difference.

The key disincentive to improperly motivated contributions, whatever their amount, is public disclosure. This disincentive would be strengthened if contributions were reported monthly or quarterly, instead of bi-annually.

The $1000 limit is reasonable, because it is the same as the limit on individual contributions to candidates for Federal office, and because there is no other widely accepted figure.

A possible recommendation would be to return any contribution which was the product of solicitation, from June 28 to July 11, 1994 or later, and thus was inconsistent with the gift standards. However, it would be impossible to determine which contributions were the product of improper solicitation without someone coming forward to admit to this. The Trust could offer the return of any contribution the donor of which believes resulted from solicitation from a trustee or a Trust employee. But it is highly unlikely that any donor would come forward to ask for a refund. This recommendation is not really practical, but the Trust should ask OGE whether any remedial action needs to be taken.

There is no need for legislation in this area. Not every President is sufficiently well-off to handle the substantial legal expenses that may beset him while in office. Presidents, like other politicians and citizens, should be permitted to set up a fund to receive help in paying legal bills. But a politician should not assume that just because a legal defense fund will help pay the bills, the politician may hire the highest priced legal talent. In the future, a President or other political figure should seek out competent counsel at more affordable rates.

Part Four

Allegations Against Members
of the Clinton Cabinet

Chapter Eleven

Allegations Against Secretary of Agriculture Mike Espy

Secretary Mike Espy violated ethics standards when he accepted gifts from Tyson Foods and Quaker Oats, companies regulated by the Agriculture Department. Secretary Espy also received gifts from his friend Richard Douglas, which, if they were paid by Douglas's company Sun-Diamond Growers, also violated the gift restrictions. Espy also did not comply with procedures in requesting approval to accept lodging and transportation from Tyson during an official trip. Approval would not likely have been given had the Secretary requested it. He may have also violated a criminal provision of the Federal Meat Inspection Act, although it is not certain that the law applied to him. On the evidence that is known, it does not appear that Secretary Espy violated the general illegal gratuities statute, but this conclusion must await the outcome of an independent counsel investigation, which is reviewing the Secretary's conduct in terms of these criminal laws.

In addition, Secretary Espy violated the standards of conduct in using a government car for personal purposes and traveling frequently to his hometown on ostensible official business, repeating the sins of many a former Presidential appointee.

Secretary Espy's conduct demonstrated his gross insensitivity to ethics standards and, with respect to at least Tyson Foods and Sun-Diamond, raise the question whether he gave preferential treatment to these companies, as illustrated by several Department actions favorable to the poultry industry and to Sun-Diamond. Conclusions may fairly be reached only following a complete investigation, but Espy's actions clearly gave the appearance of preferential treatment.

Secretary Espy's resignation (or firing) was appropriate under the circumstances. However, the subsequent White House report on the Secretary's conduct was weak, and its attempts to explain his problems by reference to his previous congressional service were inadequate. Given the pending criminal investigation, Secretary Espy was right to recuse himself from any matter involving meat and poultry inspection for the remainder of his tenure, although that recusal should have extended to all particular matters involving Tyson Foods or Sun-Diamond.

Background

On October 3, 1994, Secretary Mike Espy announced his resignation, effective at the end of the year. Espy's decision was made after consultation with, and most likely at the direction of, the White House. It followed the September 9 appointment of an independent counsel to examine whether Espy violated any criminal laws, and a steady stream of news reports detailing apparent ethical lapses.

Media Reports of Improper Conduct

Reports that Secretary Espy had improperly accepted gifts from companies regulated by the Department of Agriculture, primarily Tyson Foods, and that the Department gave preferential treatment to the poultry industry, surfaced as early as March 1994.[1] In June, it was revealed that the Inspector General of the Agriculture Department had conducted an investigation and forwarded a report to the Justice Department.[2]

Request for and Appointment of an Independent Counsel

On August 8, 1994, the Attorney General applied to the special division of the U.S. Court of Appeals for the District of Columbia for the appointment of an independent counsel to investigate allegations that Secretary Espy had improperly accepted gifts from Tyson Foods and other entities regulated by the Agriculture Department and that these gifts affected the Department's regulation of the poultry industry.[3] The Attorney General informed the court of the results of a preliminary investigation conducted by the Justice Department, based on the April 1994 referral from the Inspector General.[4]

Tyson Foods is the largest poultry producer in the country, controlling about 23% of the domestic chicken market.[5] Tyson Foods' President, Don Tyson, is a long-time friend of the President, and a contributor to his campaigns.[6] In the late 1970s, Tyson Foods' counsel, James Blair, assisted Mrs. Clinton realize profits from trading in commodities futures. Tyson, Tyson Foods' executives, and its political action committee (TyPAC) also contributed to the House campaigns of Mike Espy and his brother Henry.[7]

According to the Attorney General's application, Secretary Espy "accepted gifts from Tyson Foods in the course of two separate trips, one to Arkansas in May 1993 and one in Texas in January 1994. In total, the gifts amount to at least several hundred dollars in value." The Attorney General added that the Secretary allegedly accepted other gifts from "organizations and individuals with business pending before the Department of Agriculture[,]" yet noted that "[n]o evidence has been developed during the investigation that Secretary Espy accepted the gifts as a reward for, or in expectation of, his performance of official acts."

The Attorney General stated that under the independent counsel law, Justice must seek the appointment of an independent counsel "unless there is clear and convincing evidence that the person lacked such a state of mind." She therefore concluded, "There are reasonable grounds to believe that further investigation is warranted." The Attorney General's request covers potential violations of the Federal Meat Inspection Act of 1907, the general illegal gratuities statute, as well as allegations of false statements and obstruction of justice.[8]

Secretary Espy's lawyer, Reid Weingarten, issued a statement: "Secretary Espy has never misused his office in any way. There has been no misconduct in this case at all." Weingarten asserted that "All of Secretary Espy's official and personal travel and entertainment expenses have been properly accounted for and reimbursed."[9]

The day the Attorney General's application to the court was announced, White House Counsel Lloyd Cutler stated that the White House would ask the Office of Government Ethics (OGE) to conduct a review of whether Secretary Espy violated any (non-criminal) Federal standards of conduct by accepting gifts from persons or companies regulated by the Department.[10] No request was ever made, however.[11] Instead, the White House Counsel's office conducted its own review. The following day, in response to the Espy controversy, the White House tightened its travel policy for Cabinet officials and other political appointees.[12]

On September 9, the court of appeals granted the Attorney General's application and appointed Donald C. Smaltz as independent counsel. Smaltz's charter is as broad as that sought by the Attorney General. The independent counsel was charged to investigate whether Secretary Espy:

> committed a violation of any federal law . . . relating in any way to the acceptance of gifts by him from organizations or individuals with business pending before the Department of Agriculture.[13]

The investigation includes whether Secretary Espy's former Chief of Staff, Ronald Blackley, improperly directed Agriculture officials to halt work on improved poultry inspection standards and procedures. Smaltz was permitted to look into other alleged violations of Federal law that arise from the investigation, such as false statements or obstruction of justice. He also was authorized to investigate "other allegations or evidence of violations of any federal criminal law . . . by any organizations or individuals developed during the Independent Counsel's investigation . . . and connected with or arising out of that investigation."[14]

Espy's Resignation Amid Additional Reports of Improper Conduct and the Issuance of a White House Report

More stories critical of Secretary Espy's conduct appeared in September 1994. The Secretary's relationship with Sun-Diamond Growers, another major entity regulated by the Department, was called into question.[15] He disclosed his travel records in response to several Freedom of Information Act requests, revealing frequent official visits to Jackson, Mississippi, his hometown and near where his two children live. The records showed that on these trips the Secretary's official schedule often was thin compared with personal or political events he attended, and that he often left for Mississippi on a Thursday or Friday and returned to Washington at the start of the new week.[16] Following this report, Secretary Espy assigned an ethics lawyer in his Department to review his schedule and travel plans in advance to avoid future problems.[17] Then it was revealed that in 1993 he had used a Government-leased Jeep in Mississippi for some personal purposes.[18]

Secretary Espy began reimbursing the Government and private entities in the middle of September,[19] but whatever credit he might have received was blunted by the independent counsel's subsequent statement that reimbursement is not a defense to a violation of criminal law.[20] The independent counsel, at the time on the job only a couple of weeks, further opined that Secretary Espy is covered by the Meat Inspection Act, a critical and not-so-straightforward legal issue.[21] On top of these stories, Espy's former Chief of Staff, Ron Blackley, was the subject of articles critical of his conduct both as Espy's legislative aide and as his Chief of Staff.[22]

The drumbeat for Secretary Espy's departure began on September 21.[23] The White House Counsel's review of the Secretary's conduct was nearing completion when he met with White House Chief of Staff Leon Panetta and White House Counsel Abner Mikva on Friday, September 30 and again on Monday, October 3. The Secretary announced his resignation on that day, amid the backdrop of another report that his girlfriend Patricia Dempsey had received a $1,200 scholarship from a foundation run by Tyson Foods.[24]

The White House Counsel's report, in the form of a memorandum from Judge Mikva to the President, was dated and released October 11, 1994.[25] The Report concluded:

> In light of Secretary Espy's reimbursement of the costs of questionable transactions, his announced intention to resign at the end of this year, his recusal, and the institution of additional measures for reviewing his travel, we do not believe any further action should be taken at this time.[26]

Although the Report recited the applicable standards of conduct, with one exception it contained no findings or conclusions as to whether any of the standards were violated.[27] The President also had asked whether any actions should be taken to ensure that other Members of the Cabinet avoid Espy's mistakes. The White House Counsel stated only that his office would contact agency ethics officials to ensure that all Presidential appointees have received the required ethics training this year, and that any issues raised during this training be identified and resolved.[28]

The Broad (and Broadening) Scope of the Independent Counsel's Investigation and Efforts to Curtail It

As of this writing, the independent counsel's criminal investigation is proceeding, having been expanded substantially since its inception. The expansive scope of the inquiry, covering not just the Meat Inspection Act and illegal gratuities statute, but also nearly all the reported allegations against Secretary Espy, was first revealed by a review of document requests made by the independent counsel in October 1994.[29] Subpoenas were served on the White House, the Agriculture Department, the EOP Group (Dempsey's employer), and many other entities.[30]

In November 1994, the *Los Angeles Times* featured a lengthy story reporting a series of questionable activities during the 1992 presidential campaign by a political action committee in which Espy was involved.[31] The *Los Angeles Times* reported that many senior civil servants in the Department of Agriculture were solicited—some of them at the office—to contribute to the Clinton campaign through the Farmers & Ranchers '92 PAC. "Implicit in the invitation, some of the Civil Service employees now say, was the suggestion that their careers would benefit if they helped elect a Democratic President."[32] Espy and Grant Buntrock, who after the election was appointed by the President to head the Agricultural Stabilization and Conservation Service (ASCS), were involved with the PAC's activities. The *Los Angeles Times* reported that many of the ASCS employees who contributed to the PAC during the 1992 campaign received promotions or better job assignments in 1993. While Espy, Buntrock, and other Department officials insisted that nothing illegal or improper occurred, the *Los Angeles Times* reported that a whistleblower complaint had been filed with the Office of Special Counsel. A month after the *Los Angeles Times* article, the *Washington Times* reported that the independent counsel was examining these allegations as part of his investigation of Espy.[33] There was also a hint that congressional hearings might be held to look into these allegations.[34]

In October 1995, the *Los Angeles Times* reported that the House Agriculture Committee had agreed to postpone a scheduled hearing on this matter at the request of a senior Justice Department official who told the committee that the Justice Department—not the independent counsel—intended to present the matter to a grand jury as early as November seeking indictments.[35] The article did not discuss how this matter came to be handled by Justice rather than Smaltz, especially since Secretary Espy remains a covered official under the independent counsel statute until January 1, 1996, one year after leaving the Government.[36] It may be because Secretary Espy is not considered a target or subject of this investigation.

The *Los Angeles Times* reported that thirty-eight high-ranking Agriculture career employees contributed to the PAC in 1992, in amounts between $50 and $500, many of which were sent to the PAC through Buntrock; twenty-one of these employees have been promoted or given "more appealing temporary or permanent assignments" in the Clinton Administration. Two employees told the *Los Angeles Times* that they were solicited in their office, and one said he made his contribution to a fellow employee in the office:

> The other said that the senior colleague who approached him about donating to the PAC made it clear shortly before the 1992 election that he was talking "with people inside and outside the government about the movement of personnel in both career and appointed positions in preparation for the next Democratic administration.

Investigators reportedly told one solicited employee that "They could say, without doubt, that federal laws have been broken." Soliciting fellow Federal employees is a crime,[37] as are the following: soliciting or receiving political contributions in a Federal building; promising a benefit, including employment or a promotion, in exchange for a political contribution; and threatening to deny an employment opportunity upon refusal to contribute.[38]

In December 1994, the scope of the independent counsel's investigation was revealed to encompass Tyson Foods and Tyson employees, beyond the publicly known allegations involving Tyson and Espy.[39] Later that month, the independent counsel confirmed to *Time* that his office was examining allegations made by a former pilot for Tyson Foods, Joseph Henrickson, that (mostly during the 1980s) he transported envelopes full of $100 bills from the company to Little Rock, where he said the money was intended for Governor Clinton.[40]

Henrickson's credibility was instantly questioned: he had been fired by the company, and no corroborating witness (at the time) appeared to exist. However, Smaltz went so far as to comment positively on Henrickson's credibility ("Based upon the way his story unfolded, it has the ring of truth to it."),[41] prompting angry protests from an attorney for Tyson Foods, the President's personal attorney, and even the White House Counsel.[42] Smaltz was criticized, not only for his public statements on the investigation, but also (by Tyson's attorney) for allegedly exceeding the scope of his authority.[43]

In a letter to Smaltz, Judge Mikva complained of Smaltz's public comments. "This type of conduct goes directly against what I understand to be the proper behavior of a federal prosecutor. . . . I had thought that federal prosecutors presented their evidence to grand juries . . . not through comments to the press."[44] Judge Mikva's **official** interest in writing this letter was not apparent, although no report questioned Mikva's involvement in the investigation.

The authority Smaltz received from the court of appeals includes authority to investigate "other allegations or evidence of violation of any federal criminal law . . . by any organization or individual developed during the [independent counsel's investigation] and connected with or arising out of that investigation."[45]

The Henrickson allegations suggested that Smaltz's investigation of Secretary Espy could, at some point, reach the President. Smaltz said that he would limit his inquiry to the alleged "gratuity giver," not the alleged "gratuity receiver."[46] However, such a distinction is abnormal for criminal investigators and may well be prove impossible to draw.

As 1995 began, a Tyson official was seen visiting Senators and Representatives to complain about the independent counsel's investigation. Some thought the visits inappropriate; others, such as Representative Dickey, sympathized with Tyson's protests.[47] On February 10, Dickey and four others introduced H.R. 892, a bill to tighten controls on independent counsel. The bill would confine the scope of an independent counsel's investigation to the alleged violations in the Attorney General's request and other matters "directly related" to such criminal violations, such as perjury and obstruction of justice. It would require the independent counsel to comply with Justice Department policies at all times, not merely when to do so would be inconsistent with the purposes of the independent counsel law.[48] It also would provide that no funds could be expended by an independent counsel after two years, except as specifically appropriated by Congress for an additional period; would require an independent counsel to apply to the court for reappointment after two years; and would allow a subject of the investigation to petition the court to terminate the investigation after two years.[49]

Representatives Dickey and Jimmy Quillen also wrote the Attorney General requesting that she direct Smaltz to terminate his investigation of Tyson to the extent it did not directly relate to Secretary Espy. No action was reportedly taken on this request.[50]

In March 1995, it was reported that a Tyson Foods Vice President had sued Joseph Henrickson in Arkansas State court for defamation, asserting that he could be identified as the person who allegedly made the cash payments to Governor Clinton. In a letter to the State court judge, the independent counsel's office saw this lawsuit as a possible attempt to intimidate witnesses, or at a minimum, to obtain information from Henrickson about the independent counsel's investigation.[51]

In all likelihood, the torrent of criticism directed at the independent counsel prompted him to seek from the Attorney General an expansion or at least a clarification of his authority. The independent counsel law provides that the court of appeals may expand the independent counsel's jurisdiction only upon the request of the Attorney General.[52] An independent counsel who "discovers or receives information about possible violations of criminal law by persons . . . , which are not covered by the prosecutorial jurisdiction of the independent counsel, **may** submit such information to the Attorney General."[53] The Attorney General, according "great weight" to the independent counsel's recommendation, must conduct a preliminary investigation within thirty days. If the Attorney General determines that "there are no reasonable grounds to believe that further investigation is warranted," the Attorney General notifies the Special Division of the court of appeals and that is the end of it.[54] Otherwise, the court of appeals "shall expand" the independent counsel's jurisdiction accordingly.[55]

Smaltz's request to the Attorney General may also have been an effort to bolster his defense of motions to quash subpoenas, reportedly filed under seal in February 1995 by lawyers representing Tyson Foods and a former Tyson pilot.[56] Presumably, the motions to quash were predicated on the asserted lack of connection between the independent counsel's charter (i.e., the allegations against Espy) and the nature of the information requested from Tyson and current and former Tyson employees. Without an imprimatur from the Attorney General and court of appeals on the far-ranging nature of the independent counsel's investigation, the subpoenas might be quashed.

On March 27, *Legal Times* reported that the Attorney General rejected Smaltz's request.[57] No additional information was available at the time about the nature of Smaltz's request or the basis for Reno's denial. Months later, one report noted that Smaltz sought to clarify that he "had jurisdiction to probe Tyson's relationship with other government officials to determine whether the company had engaged in a pattern of gratuity-giving that was similar to the Espy case." The Attorney General determined that the independent counsel's charter did not cover Tyson's relationships with other officials.[58]

The Attorney General's ruling raised the question of whether the independent counsel could pursue allegations involving the conduct of Commerce Department officials, as reported in June 1995 by the *Associated Press*. According to the *Associated Press*, the independent counsel was scrutinizing two decisions made by the

Commerce Department overruling actions taken by the Pacific Fisheries Management Council relating to the commercial fishing of Pacific whiting.[59] In 1993, the Council proposed a formula giving factory trawlers, including two owned by Tyson Foods, 26% of the year's catch; Commerce changed the formula to give Tyson and other trawler owners up to 70% of the catch. In 1994, the Council determined that trawlers should pay twenty times as much for permits as do smaller boats, because of the greater capacity that the 200-foot trawler has over the 40-foot boats. Again, the Commerce Department overruled the Council, reducing the factor from twenty to twelve. Reportedly, these decisions greatly benefited Tyson Foods. The focus of the independent counsel reportedly was on whether Commerce officials, including Secretary Brown and Deputy Secretary Barram, met with Tyson executives on these issues and whether the decisions were based on factors other than the merits.[60]

On June 12, 1995, Thomas Green, Don Tyson's lawyer, wrote an eight-page letter to Attorney General Reno, requesting that she fire Smaltz.[61] In asserting that the independent counsel had "persisted in conducting a lawless investigation," Green noted that Smaltz was examining contractual disputes between Tyson and contract growers over the quality of feed and the weighing of birds as well as whether Tyson Foods had "procured 'prostitutes,' male or female, for entertainment of corporate guests." Green concluded, "I believe that Mr. Smaltz's indefatigable contempt for the constitutional limitations on his investigation present the rare case in which removal is appropriate."[62] Under the independent counsel law, the Attorney General may remove an independent counsel only for reasons of "good cause, physical or mental disability . . . or any other condition that substantially impairs the performance of such independent counsel's duties."[63]

On July 1, 1995, the *Washington Post* reported that Judge John Garrett Penn of the U.S. District Court for the District of Columbia, to whom ten motions to quash were referred, had recently issued several orders under seal significantly limiting the scope of some of the subpoenas.[64] One subpoena was reportedly quashed in its entirety; others were limited, and several motions remained pending as of the beginning of July. Judge Penn ruled that some of the information sought in the subpoenas was beyond the independent counsel's jurisdiction; some of the requests were overbroad; and some of the information sought was deemed irrelevant.[65]

Specifically, a request for the phone records of Sun-Diamond Growers and its lobbyist Richard Douglas over the past eight years was limited to cover only those records pertaining to Secretary Espy and Patricia Dempsey. Douglas is senior Vice President for Corporate Affairs for Sun-Diamond Growers, and an old college friend of Espy's. A subpoena to the daughter of a man whose business relationship with Don Tyson soured and fell apart years ago—the subpoena sought the father's 1988 memoirs!—was quashed in its entirety. Two other subpoenas, to Tyson counsel James Blair and former Tyson pilot Haskell Blake, were limited, although both were required to testify.[66]

Guilty Plea by James Lake Involving Fund-raising for Mike Espy's Brother Henry

On October 23, 1995, the independent counsel filed a three-count criminal information (one felony count of wire fraud and two misdemeanor counts of election law violations) charging James Lake, a prominent Republican lobbyist, with engineering $5000 in illegal campaign contributions to help retire the debt of Henry

Espy, who lost a special election to Congress in 1993.[67] Lake pled guilty the next day, admitting to a scheme whereby he and three colleagues at Robinson, Lake, Lerer & Montgomery, whom he solicited, each gave a $1000 check to the Henry Espy for Congress Committee through Richard Douglas, with the understanding that they would be reimbursed by Sun-Diamond.[68] Lake was allegedly approached by Douglas, who asked Lake to help by raising $5000, which Sun-Diamond would reimburse. Sun-Diamond wrote a $5000 check to the parent company of Lake's firm, ostensibly for reimbursement of expenses the firm incurred at a charity dinner, and the parent company then wrote a check to Lake for $5000. Lake reimbursed the three employees and kept the remaining $2000.[69] Corporations are prohibited from contributing to Federal elections; individuals may not contribute more than $1000.

Lake's prosecution triggered considerable speculation that the independent counsel was attempting to get Lake to implicate Richard Douglas and Sun-Diamond in illegal conduct, and thereafter to get Douglas or Sun-Diamond to implicate Mike Espy. Douglas's attorney said that Douglas's fund-raising activities for Henry Espy were legal; Sun-Diamond denied knowing about the scheme; and Mike Espy's attorney said the case had nothing at all to do with the former Secretary.[70]

Additional Allegations That Espy Received Improper Gifts from Douglas and Sun-Diamond Surface

Lake's prosecution returned the spotlight to the independent counsel's investigation, which was reported to be examining thousands of dollars in gifts to Secretary Espy and Dempsey from Sun-Diamond, as well as what official actions the Secretary may have taken that were favorable toward Sun-Diamond. The fund-raising investigation was also reported to focus on whether Douglas's efforts on behalf of Henry Espy were requested by Mike Espy; lawyers for both Secretary Espy and Douglas denied this.[71] At the time, Secretary Espy was prohibited by the Hatch Act from personally soliciting campaign contributions from anyone, as well as from requesting any person regulated by the agency to engage in any political activity.[72] And the illegal gratuities statute prohibited Espy from asking Douglas for anything of value in exchange for taking any official action.

Reports that Secretary Espy received $14,000-$25,000 in gifts from Douglas and Sun-Diamond were labeled "grossly inflated" by Espy's attorney.[73] Indeed, these totals appear to include expenses of Douglas, Espy's companion Dempsey, and perhaps others. Nonetheless, the Secretary was alleged to have received the following: a set of luggage ($2,500), a crystal bowl, tickets, and related expenses to two days at the U.S. Open tennis tournament ($9,000, covering Espy, Douglas, and two female companions), other meals (including a dinner in Los Angeles where Douglas introduced Espy to Karyn Parsons, an actress) and New York Knicks basketball tickets (which were given to Douglas by Greg Anthony of the Knicks). The first question is, who paid for these items? Did Douglas pay personally, or was he reimbursed by Sun-Diamond? In the case of the U.S. Open tickets, Secretary Espy reimbursed Douglas for the face value of the tickets, apparently not realizing that Douglas bought scalped tickets at a premium; Douglas was later reimbursed by Sun-Diamond. Douglas's attorney explained that these reimbursements were simply payment of Douglas's expenses while he was in Washington. At other times, Douglas paid out of his own pocket. Again, Douglas's gifts were defended by Espy's and Douglas's attorneys as justified based on their close and long-standing friendship. The independent counsel was reported to focus on several actions taken by Secretary Espy that were favorable toward Sun-Diamond's interests.

Smaltz was also reported to be examining the relationship between Espy, Tony Coelho, and the Monsanto Company, which retained Coelho to assist it in obtaining approval of bovine somatotropin, a chemical Monsanto manufactured to get cows to give more milk.[74] Approval of the chemical was hung up in Congress, not the Agriculture Department, but Monsanto is probably a "prohibited source," from whom Secretary Espy could not accept gifts. Coelho helped Henry Espy retire his campaign debts, but no link between Mike Espy and Coelho was specifically alleged.

These reports of the independent counsel investigation prompted another round of criticism of Smaltz and his staff, this time including their conduct in questioning witnesses.[75] Additional motions to quash subpoenas, including a subpoena issued to Tyson's Washington lobbyist Jack Williams, were reported pending with the district court as of November 1995.

The Gift Allegations

(1) On May 15, 1993, Secretary Espy addressed the Arkansas Poultry Federation at the Tyson Foods Management Center in Russellville, Arkansas. According to the Federation's President, the Secretary flew to Russellville from Oxford, Mississippi, where he had given a speech at the University of Mississippi. Espy flew to Arkansas aboard a University aircraft. Patricia Dempsey, who is not a Federal employee, and Senator David Pryor and his family flew to Arkansas on a Tyson-owned corporate jet leased by the Poultry Federation. Espy and Dempsey stayed overnight at the Management Center and returned to Washington on May 16 on board the Tyson jet.[76] Although "Tyson officials said they had always planned to fly the Secretary back to Washington[,]"[77] the Secretary explained that he used the corporate aircraft "because he was ordered back to the capital at the request of the White House to attend a meeting."[78]

Because Secretary Espy's trip was for an official purpose, the Agriculture Department later reimbursed Tyson Foods for his lodging and return transportation (at a cost of a first-class ticket).[79] Later, Dempsey reimbursed Tyson for lodging and airfare.[80]

(2) In the spring of 1993, "realizing that a trip to Chicago coincided with a [June 18] Chicago Bulls playoff game, Secretary Espy told an aide to call Quaker Oats, based in Chicago, to get him a ticket."[81] Espy received one of the season tickets held by William D. Smithburg, the CEO of Quaker Oats. Richard Douglas also received a ticket at Espy's request. A Quaker Oats spokesman said that an Espy staff member made the request by phone to Smithburg's office, but Smithburg did not personally take the call.[82] The ticket was valued at $45. Secretary Espy reimbursed Smithburg for his ticket and Douglas's ticket only after the investigation of the Secretary began.[83]

(3) In the fall of 1993, Patricia Dempsey received a $1200 scholarship from the Tyson Foundation to pursue educational opportunities at the University of Maryland.[84] Secretary Espy knew of the scholarship offer in advance, and reportedly suggested to Dempsey that she decline the scholarship, because of the potential appearance problem.[85] Before the scholarship was disclosed to the White House in late September 1994, Dempsey, at the Secretary's urging, reimbursed the Tyson Foundation

for the whole amount.[86] Espy's attorney explained: "Secretary Espy did not seek, encourage nor approve of this scholarship. Patricia Dempsey is a mature, independent woman who has her own life and has her own relationship with the Tysons."[87]

(4) In November 1993, Secretary Espy was given a party for his 40th birthday at the Sequoia restaurant in Washington, D.C. The party was co-hosted by Richard Douglas. Douglas said he was the only lobbyist on the guest list, and that he and other friends covered the entire cost of the party. He added that the Agriculture Department's ethics office cleared the party based on the Secretary's preexisting friendship with Douglas.[88] Douglas reportedly introduced Espy to various agricultural interests, but was "careful not to lobby his friend." The party of 150 included many Department employees; reportedly the Inspector General (IG) was looking into whether any Department employees "were pressured to contribute to cover its cost."[89]

(5) On January 16, 1994, Espy and Dempsey attended a Dallas Cowboys-New York Giants playoff game in Dallas, sitting in the Tyson Foods skybox as the guest of Don Tyson. Secretary Espy had traveled to Lubbock, Texas, for a meeting with a regional Agriculture official. According to the Secretary, when Dempsey learned of his trip, she contacted Tyson and requested tickets to the game. Espy later reimbursed Tyson Foods $64 for his ticket, but not Dempsey's. Later, at Secretary Espy's request, Dempsey reimbursed Tyson for her football ticket and for the limousine service they received while in Dallas.[90] Espy paid for his own lodging that night.[91]

(6) During an official trip to Atlanta in January 1994, Secretary Espy attended the Super Bowl with tickets provided by the Fernbank Museum of Natural History.[92] The Government paid $849 for the Secretary's transportation, two nights' lodging, and related expenses. Espy's trip was questioned because he characterized it as an official trip, and because he was given four tickets to the Super Bowl.[93] The Super Bowl event was considered official because Smokey the Bear, the mascot of the U.S. Forest Service, an agency of the Agriculture Department, was given a tribute in two halftime videos honoring the mascot's fiftieth anniversary. The Fernbank Museum assembled a Smokey the Bear display at the game under a subcontract with the Forest Service to build a Smokey the Bear exhibit.[94] The museum purchased the tickets after learning that Secretary Espy intended to attend the game.[95]

No other Smokey the Bear activities, other than the Secretary's attendance at the game, were reported.[96] Secretary Espy also attended at least one official meeting that weekend, a ninety-minute "working lunch" at the headquarters of Oglethorpe Corporation, although that meeting was scheduled after Espy's trip to the Super Bowl was set.[97]

Secretary Espy reported the gift of tickets on his 1994 financial disclosure report, which apparently was filed on June 30 (over a month late), but he reported only a gift of $350, which represented only the face value of his ticket and one other, when, in fact, he was given four tickets. In September 1994, Secretary Espy reimbursed the Fernbank Museum for the face value of all four tickets, $700.[98]

(7) On several occasions Secretary Espy attended New York Knicks basketball games with Richard Douglas, courtesy of Knicks guard and Douglas's friend Greg Anthony.[99]

(8) The Secretary attended the 1993 U.S. Open tennis tournament with Douglas and two companions, as Douglas's guest. He reportedly reimbursed Douglas for the face value of his tickets.

(9) Espy also was Douglas's guest at several dinners, and received other gifts, including a set of luggage and a crystal bowl, from Douglas or Sun-Diamond.

Analysis of the Gifts Under the Standards of Conduct.

A Federal official may not solicit or accept a gift from a "prohibited source" or "given because of the employee's official position," subject to some exceptions.[100] Tyson Foods, Quaker Oats, and Sun-Diamond are all prohibited sources[101] because they conduct activities regulated by the Department of Agriculture. A gift is considered to be given because of the employee's official position "if it . . . would not have been solicited, offered, or given had the employee not held his position as a Federal employee."[102] Secretary Espy's acceptance of the football ticket from Tyson plainly violated both gift restrictions.[103]

The remedy for a violation of the gift restrictions is to pay the donor the market value of the gift, which the Secretary subsequently did.[104] The standards provide that "an employee who, on his own initiative, promptly [pays the donor market value] will not be deemed to have improperly accepted an unsolicited gift."[105] The timing and circumstances of Secretary Espy's reimbursement to Tyson of the $64 cost of the ticket are not known. However, Espy's attorney's silence on the timing of reimbursement suggests strongly that the reimbursement was not "prompt."[106]

Secretary Espy also violated the standards of conduct in soliciting and accepting basketball tickets from Quaker Oats. In fact, three separate standards were violated. First, Quaker Oats is a prohibited source, from whom the Secretary was not permitted to receive any gift in excess of $20. Second, Espy was prohibited from accepting a gift given because of his official position. It is clear that Espy obtained the ticket by virtue of his position as Secretary. Third, Espy was prohibited from soliciting a gift, which is what he reportedly did. Although the Secretary's assistant made the phone call to Quaker Oats, the assistant made the call at Espy's request and direction. Because Espy failed to reimburse Quaker's CEO for the price of the ticket until over a year later, he cannot take advantage of the amnesty provision in the standards of conduct.

Secretary Espy's receipt of Super Bowl tickets from the Fernbank Museum of Natural History also violated the standards of conduct. The Museum is a prohibited source, because it is under a subcontract with the Department's Forest Service.[107] Espy's reimbursement was not timely. It also appears that the Super Bowl tickets were given to the Secretary because of his official position in violation of the standards of conduct.[108] It is doubtful that Espy needed a ticket in order to participate in his official capacity (recall that he did not perform any official activity at the Super Bowl other than attend it), but if he did, the Department should have paid for the ticket, or accepted the gift under its gift acceptance authority. Secretary Espy's reporting this gift on his financial disclosure report suggests that he considered tickets as a personal gift.[109]

The birthday party for Secretary Espy hosted by his friend Richard Douglas did not violate the gift restrictions if the money for the event came from Douglas and other friends personally (as reported) and not Sun-Diamond Growers, Douglas's employer. If so, Department ethics officials properly could have concluded that the motive for the gift is Douglas's close friendship with Espy.[110] The gift rules provide that "[a]n employee may accept a gift given under circumstances which make it clear that the gift is motivated by a family or personal relationship rather than the position of the employee."[111] Other gifts from Douglas to Espy (and Dempsey), such as the set of luggage, the crystal bowl, tickets to the Knicks games, and U.S. Open tournament, if also made by Douglas personally (not reimbursed by Sun-Diamond) and on the basis of their friendship, would also be proper.

The gifts of transportation and lodging bestowed on Secretary Espy by Tyson Foods in connection with his May 1993 speech to the Arkansas Poultry Federation stand on a different setting, because the expenses the Secretary incurred and Tyson assumed on the May 1993 trip were incurred in connection with an official speech. Thus, the transportation and related expenses assumed by Tyson Foods were not Espy's personal expenses but those of the Department. Ordinarily the Government pays for its employees' travel and related expenses. Non-Federal sources may pay for an employee's official travel and related expenses only in limited circumstances authorized by statute. The only statute that may apply here is 31 U.S.C. 1353, which authorizes **the Government** to accept payment of travel, subsistence, and related expenses from any non-Federal source, under conditions and procedures specified in a rule promulgated by the General Services Administration (GSA).[112]

The GSA rule requires the employee to obtain advance approval of payment from a non-Federal source,[113] which apparently was not done in this instance. In determining whether to approve the payment of travel expenses, the agency ethics official is required to conduct a conflict-of-interest analysis.[114] It is highly unlikely that, had they been asked, Agriculture officials would have approved of Tyson's payment of the Secretary's lodging expenses and the provision of corporate air travel, given the very appearance concerns that surfaced. The GSA rule provides that an official who accepts payment (including payment in kind) in violation of the procedures may be required to "repay for deposit to the general fund of the Treasury, an amount equal to the amount of the payment so accepted[,]" for which the official is not entitled to reimbursement.[115] Travel on a corporate aircraft is valued at the first-class rate that would have been charged by a common carrier for the trip.[116] Reportedly, the Department reimbursed Tyson for the price of a first-class ticket. Under the GSA rule, Secretary Espy should have been required to reimburse the Department for this amount.

The Tyson Foundation scholarship to Espy's friend, Patricia Dempsey, did not violate the gift standards. The scholarship would be considered an "indirect" gift from Tyson to Espy, and thus prohibited,[117] if the scholarship was given "on the basis of designation, recommendation, or other specification by [Espy]."[118] Also, if Tyson informed Espy of the scholarship offer in advance and he did not object, this could suggest that the Secretary allowed the use of his public office for private gain.[119] Apparently, however, Espy suggested to Dempsey that she decline the offer.[120]

The report of the scholarship certainly concerned the White House and played prominently in news stories about the Secretary's resignation. Despite the Secretary's claim that Dempsey knew Don Tyson independently,[121] and his account that he attempted to dissuade Dempsey from accepting the scholarship, the White House appears to have presumed that the Secretary could have prevented Dempsey from accepting the scholarship if he seriously wanted to do so.[122] Yet, if the scholarship was truly out of his control, he should not be faulted for the bad appearance that the scholarship posed. But consider that the scholarship was awarded to Dempsey in the fall of 1993, before any story emerged about Espy and Tyson Foods. Given Espy's relationship with Dempsey, and Tyson's relationship with Espy and the Department, it was inevitable that the scholarship would create an appearance that Secretary Espy was violating one or more ethical standards (public office for private gain, preferential treatment, acceptance of gifts from prohibited source),[123] an appearance that would be difficult to dispel notwithstanding the facts. While criticism of Secretary Espy over the scholarship alone should be muted, the scholarship assumes a larger role when considered with the other gifts and benefits bestowed on Espy and Dempsey by Tyson Foods.[124]

The other gifts to Dempsey[125] stand on the same footing. Because Dempsey and Espy are neither married nor otherwise related, gifts to Dempsey are not attributable to him, unless he directed or recommended that the gift be given to her. Whether he did so in any case is not known on what has been disclosed to date.[126]

Analysis of the Gifts Under Criminal Statutes

Most reports of the allegations that Secretary Espy improperly accepted gifts focus on a provision of the Federal Meat Inspection Act (FMIA or Act), enacted in 1907; this is the central criminal statute which resulted in the appointment of an independent counsel. The Meat Inspection Act is the strictest statute that could apply to the Secretary's improper acceptance of gifts. The only acknowledged gift that clearly is at issue under this statute is the ticket to the Cowboys-Giants game in January 1994, but other gifts may be at issue depending on the statute's reach.[127]

In all the reports that include the allegation that Secretary Espy may have violated the Meat Inspection Act, there is no discussion of the problematic wording of the statute or the paucity of court decisions interpreting the law. Section 12 of the Meat Inspection Act reads, in pertinent part:

> [A]ny inspector . . . or other officer or employee of the United States authorized to perform any of the duties prescribed by this subchapter who shall accept any money, gift, or other thing of value from any person, firm, or corporation, or officers, agents, or employees thereof, given with intent to influence his official action, or who shall receive or accept from any person, firm, or corporation engaged in commerce any gift, money, or other thing of value, given with any purpose or intent whatsoever, shall be deemed guilty of a felony and shall, upon conviction thereof, be summarily discharged from office and shall be punished by a fine not less than $1000 nor more than $10,000 and by imprisonment not less than one year nor more than three years.[128]

For purposes of analysis, this provision should be divided in two: (1) Agriculture officials may not accept any thing of value from **any person, given with intent to influence an official act**; and (2) Agriculture officials may not accept any thing of value from **any person engaged in commerce, given with any purpose of intent whatsoever**. The latter, broader prohibition applies here, because Tyson Foods is engaged in commerce. Thus, it is not necessary to establish that Tyson intended to influence Secretary Espy in the performance of his duties.[129] On the other hand, the courts have required that the gift be "in connection with or arising out of the performance of [the employee's] official duties."[130] Don Tyson and Tyson Foods' PAC contributed to Mike Espy's congressional campaigns, and therefore had a relationship with the Secretary that antedated his Cabinet position. But it would be difficult for Espy to claim that Tyson's generosity was unrelated to his position as Secretary of Agriculture.

The Attorney General stated in her application that the statute covers "the acceptance of non-trivial gifts of entertainment, transportation, lodging and meals by a Department of Agriculture official who has responsibilities under the Meat Inspection Act from an entity that is subject to regulation by the Department of Agriculture[.]"[131]

But whether a court would accept the Attorney General's broad construction of the statute is uncertain, because it is not clear that the statute applies to the Secretary. First, it is unclear whether Secretary Espy was designated as an inspector.[132] Second, although the law covers officials other than inspectors who are "authorized to perform any of the duties prescribed by this subchapter," the words "this subchapter" refer to meat inspection, not poultry inspection. There is no reported decision applying the law to Agriculture employees other than a line inspector (albeit there are only a few reported decisions). Secretary Espy claimed that he was not briefed by Agriculture officials on the existence of this criminal provision, and was not aware of its existence until the IG's investigation began.[133]

The Meat Inspection Act is included in the Department's standards of conduct, 7 CFR 0.735-24(a)(60), but is not prominently featured. The restriction is the **60th** provision listed in a "Miscellaneous statutory provisions" section. Subsection 0.735-24(a) states:

Each employee has a positive duty to acquaint himself or herself with each statute that relates to his or her ethical and other conduct as an employee[.]

Paragraph (60) states in its entirety:

The prohibition against the acceptance by an employee of money or other things of value given with intent to influence a decision in connection with the performance of duties under the Federal Meat Inspection Act, or when received from a person or firm engaged in commerce given for any purpose whatever (21 U.S.C. 622)[.]

This summary of the statute suggests that the Department believes the law's application is not limited to inspectors, but applies to "employees."

A September 1, 1993 memorandum to all employees of the Food Safety and Inspection Service (FSIS) gives prominent treatment to the provision, emphasizing that it is more restrictive than the Government-wide standards issued by OGE: "You should particularly note that FMIA prohibits inspection personnel from accepting anything of value from the industry we regulate." The use of the term "inspection personnel" instead of "Department employees" suggests that the Department believes the statute is limited to inspectors and their supervisors and managers in the Food Safety and Inspection Service. On the other hand, the term may have been used because the audience for the memorandum was FSIS personnel. It is not known whether this memorandum was provided the Secretary or, for that matter, whether he was put on notice of the terms of the Act in any written or oral ethics briefing he may have received upon joining the Department.

If Secretary Espy, in fact, was not briefed about this law, it would suggest either that Agriculture ethics officials believe that the statute does not apply to the Secretary, or they fell down on the job of keeping him apprised of the legal restrictions to which he would be subject.

Secretary Espy's lawyer, Reid Weingarten, said that he will argue the statute's inapplicability to the Secretary, on several grounds.[134] His defense would go something like this: The statute is addressed to inspectors, and those who are authorized to perform the duties of the Meat Inspection Act, not all Agriculture employees. The law addressed an obvious problem: line inspectors who perform their responsibilities in a company's facilities in close proximity to company officials are naturally vulnerable to develop a less-than-arm's-length relationship with company officials. Any gift to such inspector could affect his impartiality and perhaps lead him to overlook a problem discovered on the line, or to treat it less seriously than would be warranted. And this all would occur outside of the public's view. The Secretary, by contrast, is not generally in a position to affect an individual inspection. The Secretary does have broad responsibilities over inspection regulations and policies, but the actions he takes, unlike line inspections, are subject to public comment and criticism; some are also subject to judicial review. The public aura around the Secretary's actions provides a check against abuse that is absent in the case of line inspectors. In any event, if Congress wanted to cover all Agriculture officials in the chain of command, all the way up to the Secretary, it would have written the statute differently.[135]

A simple parsing of the words of the statute, however, includes the Secretary. The statute applies to "any inspector, deputy inspector, chief inspector, or **other officer or employee of the United States authorized to perform any of the duties prescribed by this subchapter[.]**"[136] "[T]his subchapter" means the entire Federal Meat Inspection Act, because in the original language of the prohibition, section 12 of the Act, the words "this act" are used instead of "this subchapter." Many statutory responsibilities in the Act are bestowed using the phrase, "the Secretary shall cause to be made, by inspectors appointed for that purpose, an examination and inspection of . . ." or similar language. Yet the Act also bestows many other responsibilities on the Secretary that are not to be performed by inspectors, such as authority to issues rules and regulations, and to grant exemptions.[137] Thus, the Secretary performs duties "prescribed by this subchapter."

Assuming the Secretary is not exempt from the statute, Espy would next argue that the gift must come from an entity regulated by the Act, not by just the Department as the Attorney General apparently believes. Espy would argue that, because section 622 is located in the meat inspection chapter of title 21 of the United States Code, and there is no similar provision in the poultry and poultry products inspection chapter, the bribery and gift prohibitions in 21 U.S.C. 622 do not apply to gifts from poultry companies not regulated by the meat inspection provisions. None of the few reported cases under this statute appears to have involved poultry inspection. Meat and poultry inspection authority is grounded in two different statutes, and inspection regulations are, for the most part, kept separate in the Code of Federal Regulations. However, based on the September 1993 memorandum to all FSIS employees, the understanding of the FSIS seems to be that the statute applies to all Agriculture employees authorized to perform inspections and other inspection-related duties, whether of meat or poultry. Also, Tyson Foods may, in fact, produce meat subject to meat inspection regulation.

Even if gifts from poultry companies are covered by the statute, Espy would argue that the statute is limited to entities subject to the Department's inspection functions. This argument has some force: the Act, by its terms, does not apply to all Agriculture employees, regardless of their responsibilities; Agriculture employees engaged in other non-inspection responsibilities are subject only to the government-wide gift and gratuity statutes and regulations. Further, this provision was enacted for the clear purpose of ensuring the integrity of inspections. Because neither Quaker Oats nor Sun-Diamond Growers is engaged in the production of meat or poultry, the gift of a basketball ticket from the CEO of Quaker Oats and any gift from Sun-Diamond does not implicate the Meat Inspection Act. This would leave only gifts from Tyson Foods as potential violations of the Meat Inspection Act.

Secretary Espy would not be able to argue that the football ticket was of insignificant value, however, in light of a case in which the Department fired an inspector for accepting a bottle of whiskey from an official of the plant he inspected.[138]

Secretary Espy could also argue that his reimbursement of Tyson for the cost of his ticket eliminates the gift. But this would be so only if his payment was contemporaneous with the event, or if Tyson understood from the Secretary at the time of the game that he would be paying for the ticket at some future point. Reimbursement that takes place a significant time after a gift is made and was not contemplated at the time does not change the gift's character. Although Secretary Espy's attorney has repeatedly defended his client by saying that he reimbursed Tyson for the cost of the ticket, it was not disclosed when the Secretary did so, suggesting that Espy did not reimburse Tyson until after the investigation began.

Recall that the independent counsel has already stated that the Meat Inspection Act covers Espy and that reimbursement is not a defense to prosecution.[139]

Even if Secretary Espy were not subject to the Meat Inspection Act, the gift must also be reviewed under the illegal gratuities statute, which makes it a crime for any Federal official to accept a gift in return for the performance of any official act.[140] There has been no suggestion that the Secretary accepted the basketball tickets from Quaker Oats in return for the performance of an official act. Indeed, Espy —through an assistant—solicited the ticket. There have been no reports of actions Secretary Espy took or failed to take favorably affecting or resulting in benefit to Quaker Oats. However, gifts Secretary Espy received from Tyson Foods and Sun-Diamond Growers implicate the illegal gratuities statute because of actions the Secretary or his Department took that were considered favorable to these companies.

Attorney General Reno's application for an appointment of an independent counsel refers to the illegal gratuities statute, although she noted that "No evidence has been developed during the investigation that Secretary Espy accepted the gifts as a reward for, or in expectation of, his performance of official acts."[141] This appears to be the primary focus of the independent counsel's investigation. Whether Secretary Espy provided preferential treatment in favor of Tyson or Sun-Diamond, discussed below, is relevant to this issue.

The Preferential Treatment Allegations

Tyson Foods and the Poultry Industry

In March 1994, the *Wall Street Journal* reported a series of Agriculture actions or decisions affecting Tyson Foods and the poultry industry that the paper headlined as "gentle treatment."[142] Secretary Espy acknowledged that he met with Tyson officials "all the time," but explained that he often met with consumer and labor groups, too, and denied giving any preferential treatment to Tyson.[143]

Don Tyson, Chairman of Tyson Foods, also denied that Tyson has received preferential treatment from the Clinton Administration: "Neither I personally, nor Tyson Foods Inc., has in any way asked for, or received, special or preferential treatment from any [sic] Clinton administration."[144]

The ethics question raised by Secretary Espy's treatment of the poultry industry is whether he accorded the poultry industry or Tyson Foods preferential treatment. The standards of conduct contain three general principles that are relevant to the allegations against the Secretary:

Employees shall not use public office for private gain.[145]

Employees shall act impartially and not give preferential treatment to any private organization or individual.[146]

Employees shall endeavor to avoid any actions creating the appearance that they are violating the law or the ethical standards set forth in this part. Whether particular circumstances create an appearance that the law or these standards have been violated shall be determined from the perspective of a reasonable person with knowledge or the relevant facts.[147]

The impartiality principle is further amplified in sections 502 and 702 of the standards of conduct. Section 702 provides:

An employee shall not use his office for his own private gain . . . or for the private gain of friends, relatives, or persons with whom the employee is affiliated in a nongovernmental capacity[.][148]

The section provides further:

To ensure that the performance of his official duties does not give rise to an appearance of use of public office for private gain or of giving preferential treatment, an employee whose duties would affect the financial interests of a friend, relative or person with whom he is affiliated in a nongovernmental capacity shall comply with any applicable requirements of [5 CFR] 2635.502.[149]

Section 502 governs personal and business relationships that could give rise to a conflict of interest, notwithstanding the absence of a direct financial interest. The regulation covers persons and entities with whom an employee has a "covered relationship," such as a family member, a close personal friend, business partner, or spouse's employer. Espy is not related, affiliated, or connected to Tyson or Tyson Foods, although he may be considered be a friend of the Tysons, and therefore covered by the standards of conduct. In any event, the standard provides that:

> An employee who is concerned that circumstances other than those specifically described in this section would raise a question regarding his impartiality should use the process descried in this section to determine whether he should or should not participate in a particular matter.[150]

Section 502 requires an official who believes his impartiality may reasonably be questioned to seek the advice and approval of an agency ethics official before participating in the particular matter that causes the concern. Notwithstanding the presence of an appearance concern, the ethics official considers several factors in determining whether to authorize the official to participate in the matter. At a minimum, Secretary Espy should have sought the advice of Agriculture ethics officials in determining whether to participate in particular matters involving Tyson Foods.[151]

Section 502 governs whether the Secretary should have **prospectively** recused himself from particular matters involving Tyson Foods in order to avoid the risk of appearing to favor Tyson. The issue remains whether Secretary Espy gave preferential treatment to Tyson Foods or whether his conduct, official or personal, gave the appearance of providing preferential treatment. If so, he violated the general ethical principles and section 702 noted above. Employees are charged to "respect and adhere to the principles of ethical conduct[,]" as well as the implementing standards in Part 2635.[152]

Whether Secretary Espy had a "covered relationship" with Tyson or Tyson Foods is debatable, but from all appearances, the relationship was cozy. Consider the following: Tyson and Tyson Foods' PAC donated to Mike Espy's congressional campaigns, and they donated to Henry Espy's 1993 congressional campaign during Mike Espy's tenure in the Cabinet. Tyson is a longtime campaign contributor and supporter of Bill Clinton. Tyson Foods is the largest poultry producer in the United States; therefore, of the companies regulated by the Department of Agriculture, Tyson has a relatively high profile. Because of Tyson Foods' prominence in the industry, Tyson executives and lobbyists are given regular access to top Agriculture political appointees, including Secretary Espy, to discuss matters of mutual interest.

Given all this, from the start Secretary Espy should have kept an arm's-length distance from Tyson and Tyson Foods, in both personal and official matters. Concerning the personal, the Secretary should have avoided any social contact where he might have been seen as a recipient of Tyson's generosity or hospitality, even if he, in fact, received no gift or benefit. In such close-knit circumstances, the perception will always arise that deals are being struck, favors are being requested, or, at the least, that Espy and Tyson are developing a personal friendship that could impair the Secretary's objectivity. Even assuming Espy paid Tyson fair market value for the Cowboys ticket, Espy should have avoided sitting in Tyson's skybox (just as Assistant Secretary Patricia Jensen also should have avoided sitting in Tyson's skybox at a basketball game). For the same reason, Espy should not have accepted return transportation to Washington aboard a Tyson corporate jet, even if the trip was official and the Government (eventually) paid Tyson for the transportation. The Secretary's conduct on the road has clearly given the appearance of favoring Tyson, thereby fueling suspicion that actions he took as Secretary that were seen as favorable to the poultry industry were affected by his relationship with Tyson. Thus, in accepting these gifts and engaging in these public social engagements, Espy violated the general appearance standard in creating the appearance that he has given preferential treatment to Tyson Foods.

Whether Secretary Espy, in fact, gave preferential treatment to Tyson Foods is difficult to determine conclusively on the evidence available. In one area (poultry inspection system), the Department's conduct appears irregular; in the others, favoritism cannot be ruled out, largely because of the gifts the Secretary received. The examples the *Wall Street Journal* and others used of favorable treatment of the poultry industry are discussed in turn.[153]

Fecal contamination. The most serious allegation that Espy's Department gave preferential treatment to Tyson Foods and the poultry industry is the Department's so-called "zero-tolerance" fecal-matter policy. The policy was announced in early March 1993 in the wake of a January 1993 outbreak of food-poisoning in the western U.S. from ground beef served at a Jack-In-The-Box restaurant that was tainted with E. coli bacteria, resulting in several deaths and hundreds of illnesses.[154] At the time, Agriculture's zero-tolerance policy did not extend to poultry, even though "salmonella, campylobacter and other bacteria cause millions of food-poisoning cases and thousands of deaths annually, as compared with 20,000 cases of E. coli poisoning, only some of which are fatal."[155]

The *Wall Street Journal* reported that career officials in the Department were also working at the time on a similar zero-tolerance policy for poultry. Poultry interests soon learned that the Department was working on a tougher poultry inspection policy that could cost millions of dollars annually to the industry in increased compliance costs. They sought and obtained meetings with Department officials to learn the details of the draft proposal and to express their concerns.[156] On March 8, 1993, poultry representatives met with Food Safety and Inspection Service (FSIS) officials to receive a briefing on the draft proposal.[157] On March 11, poultry representatives met again with FSIS officials, offering a compromise proposal that FSIS officials believed was inadequate.

A few hours after the March 11 meeting ended, Jack Williams, a Tyson lobbyist, met with Secretary Espy. The Tyson lobbyist said he never discussed the zero-tolerance policy with the Secretary, but Secretary Espy "acknowledged conferring with Mr. Williams on poultry issues, including zero tolerance."[158] An internal FSIS staff memorandum to the file states, "According to Kim Schnoor [Espy's domestic counselor] and Ron Blackley [then Chief of Staff], the poultry industry went directly to Secretary Espy to discuss their concerns[.]" The result? FSIS officials told the *Wall Street Journal* in 1994 that:

> they were told by Mr. Espy's office to drop the proposal and that an Espy aide ordered them to turn over all evidence of their work, including information in computers. They also say the department's food-safety spokesman was ousted after telling a reporter that zero-tolerance soon would be extended to poultry. The department says the spokesman was removed for unrelated reasons.[159]

Wilson S. Horne, a career official who at the time was Deputy Administrator of Inspection Operations for FSIS, "said Mr. Espy's aides demanded and received all computer records on his department's efforts to craft new standards."[160] "The message was very, very loud and clear that we were to stop the process."[161] Horne gave the following account of a meeting with Ronald Blackley and other Department officials who were working on the poultry policy:[162]

Horne . . . recalled that in the middle of the discussion about beef, "suddenly the subject changed to poultry."

Mr. Horne and other participants in the meeting said that Mr. Blackley had been surprised to learn that the department's staff was indeed working on a way to overhaul poultry inspections.

"He was not very pleased," Mr. Horne said. "He asked how far we were on this. We said it was in the computer, for final editing. He said to take it out of the computer. To us it was a clear indicator that we shouldn't go ahead. It was very clear.

"We were a little shell-shocked," Mr. Horne said, "wondering if we had all heard what we thought we'd heard. We put a stop to all the poultry activity."

. . . Other department officials have confirmed his account[.] They said that the computer files had been destroyed as ordered, but that inspection officials had kept paper copies.[163]

On April 2, Russell Cross, then FSIS Administrator, wrote a memorandum to Kim Schnoor:

You and Ron requested that Food Safety and Inspection Service take no further action on a policy for zero fecal tolerance until you had time to review this background information.[164]

Cross reportedly requested permission to lift the moratorium on the draft zero-tolerance policy.[165]

In an April 23, 1993, memorandum that did not surface publicly until it was reported by the *Wall Street Journal* in January 1995, Schnoor responded to Cross.[166] Stating that Espy "would like the agency to continue its efforts," Schnoor acceded to Cross's request and stated that FSIS should develop a proposal "similar to the policy announced by the secretary for red meat[.]" Schnoor added, "However, the work should remain confidential until [Espy] is further briefed . . . ."[167]

FSIS officials told the *Wall Street Journal* that they never received the April 23 memorandum, a copy of which apparently surfaced in response to an independent counsel subpoena to Schnoor in October 1994. Cross, the addressee, and others in his office said they never saw the memorandum before October 1994; the memorandum was apparently "improperly headed and routed," according to FSIS employees, who spoke with the *Wall Street Journal*:

To the staff, that go-ahead comes now as stunning news. Throughout the summer of 1993 and into the fall, officials say, the staff had implored

Mr. Espy's office for permission to resume work on a zero-tolerance standard for chicken and other fowl.

"The memorandum was the very thing we were begging to get," says one official.[168]

These officials said they did not get a green light until after Secretary Espy returned from a trip to Asia in October 1993. For the trip, FSIS officials prepared a briefing book on the zero tolerance policy in an effort to get the Secretary to give them the go-ahead. If Schnoor's memorandum had been received by FSIS officials, this effort of course would not have been necessary.[169]

After the publication of the initial *Wall Street Journal* article in March 1994, a Department spokeswoman denied that the Secretary stopped the proposal.[170] Indeed, a Department spokesman subsequently explained that Blackley's request for records was simply a means to assert some measure of control over a Department that previously was too close to the poultry industry![171] Blackley was quoted as terming Horne's account "absolutely false. . . . I've never told him or anyone else to stop work on any poultry initiative."[172]

On March 9, 1994, one week before the *Wall Street Journal* article appeared, the Secretary announced that the Department would propose a "Poultry Enhancement Program" for public comment, but in doing so, announced only the broad outlines of the program.[173] Consumer groups were left to speculate, and they instantly criticized the announcement as "weak," "tentative," and "phony." Current Agriculture regulations date from the late 1970s; they allow washing away the fecal matter instead of trimming the contaminated parts.[174] Those who were briefed on the details of the policy said that it emphasized washing off the fecal matter, as opposed to trimming the badly contaminated flesh, wings, or legs.[175]

In June 1994, Secretary Espy wrote an article asserting that the Department's zero-tolerance policy on fecal matter would be strictly enforced against meat **and** poultry producers, characterizing the March announcement as "an outline of a zero-tolerance policy for poultry."[176]

In a proposed rule published on July 13, 1994, the Department formally proposed a zero-tolerance policy for fecal contamination of poultry.[177] The proposal would provide that no visible fecal contamination may remain on poultry carcasses entering the cold-water bath called the "chiller"; any finding of fecal contamination would require the reprocessing of the contaminated carcass and reinspection; and every bird must be subject to a bacteria-cleansing rinse ("antimicrobial treatments or interventions") before it is placed in the "chiller."[178]

Although the Department heralded this proposal as a major improvement in poultry inspection, others criticized the Department's emphasis on visual inspection versus a microbial sampling process. Indeed, in the preamble to the Department's proposed rule, the Department acknowledged that salmonella and campylobacter, the two main "[p]athogens of concern" in poultry, "cannot be detected by sight, smell, or taste."[179] The Department indicated that a microbial sampling proposal would be announced later in 1994.[180] Carol Tucker Foreman, a former Agriculture official now with the Safe Food Coalition, said "I can't find anything in this that is likely to offend the poultry industry." Tom Devine of the Government Accountability Project said the proposal is "another example of the poultry industry receiving preferential treatment. If these rules are adopted, Don Tyson will have hit the jackpot."[181] Rodney Leonard, who was Administrator of the Food and Inspection Service in the Johnson Administration, said "The proposed regulations give the chicken industry everything they want."[182]

Following the appointment of an independent counsel, Secretary Espy announced proposed legislation to provide for microbial testing of meat and poultry.[183] The Secretary's announcement was praised by some, like Foreman, who had previously criticized the Department's efforts. Espy labeled as cynics others who suggested that his actions were designed to counter the impression that he was soft on the poultry industry.[184]

After Secretary Espy announced his intention to resign, the Department announced that it would not move toward a final rule on the July 1994 proposal, but would instead propose different rules for inspection later in the year.[185] One month after Secretary Espy left, at the end of January 1995, FSIS issued a proposed rule containing a tougher inspection policy—for both meat and poultry—incorporating mandatory microbial testing.[186] The proposal would "require at least one antimicrobial treatment during the slaughter process prior to chilling the carcass; . . . mandate daily microbial testing in slaughter establishments to determine whether targets [for pathogen reduction] are being met or remedial measures are necessary; and . . . require that all meat and poultry establishments develop, adopt and implement a system of preventive controls . . ., known as HACCP (Hazard Analysis and Critical Control Points).[187]

The independent counsel is looking into the allegation that the Department's fecal contamination policy with respect to poultry was improperly affected by Espy's relationship with Tyson Foods.[188] On the basis of what has been reported, what conclusions may be drawn?

The reported statements of former FSIS officials clearly indicate their impression that one or more of Espy's chief aides, at the Secretary's direction or with his knowledge, attempted to stop FSIS from proposing a zero tolerance inspection protocol for poultry that would parallel the system for beef. There may be a reasoned basis for treating beef and poultry differently, but the timing and nature of the actions the Secretary's office took in the spring of 1993 appear to have resulted directly from lobbying efforts by the poultry industry.[189] It is not unusual for an agency's political appointees to disagree with a staff proposal or recommendation generated by the agency's career officials. It is unusual, however, for political appointees to direct that a proposal—one in the final editing stages—be dropped, sight unseen. Moreover, it is highly unusual for the political appointees to direct that all records of the proposal be sent to the Secretary's office and that the computer records or the proposal be deleted. And the circumstances surrounding the April 23, 1993 green light memorandum that apparently was never received further muddy the water. The actions taken by Espy's Chief of Staff do not appear to have been based on the merits of the proposal, because the FSIS had not previously briefed the Secretary's office on the proposal. Instead, the Chief of Staff's order followed one or more contacts from poultry lobbyists to the Secretary's office seeking to delay or derail the proposal.

After the media spotlight was shown on this episode, Secretary Espy embarked on a very public campaign to improve poultry inspection, featured by the publication in July 1994 of a proposal that may well have been similar to the one nixed by his

Chief of Staff the previous year, and proposing legislation in September 1994 to require microbial testing. Nonetheless, the proposed rule was immediately criticized as inadequate; some observers said that Tyson would find nothing objectionable in the proposal. The timing of the Secretary's announcement of proposed legislation, which did seem to please his food safety critics, was suspect, coming in the midst of a series of allegations against the Secretary and so late in the Session that it did not fare any realistic chance of enactment in the 103d Congress. A tougher proposal was eventually issued after Espy's departure.

A final analysis of this allegation must await the report of the independent counsel.

Surprise slaughterhouse inspections. After the outbreak of E. coli poisoning in January 1993, Agriculture inspectors conducted ninety unannounced inspections of cattle slaughterhouses; thirty were closed temporarily. Although some turkey processing plants were also inspected in 1993, the *Wall Street Journal* reported that no unannounced inspections of chicken slaughterhouses were conducted. Given the relatively greater frequency of poultry contamination, the failure to conduct surprise inspections of poultry plants smacked of selective enforcement and favoritism toward Tyson Foods, which has sixty-six plants. A Department spokeswoman denied the charge, saying that fourteen Tyson plants received unannounced inspections in 1993.[190]

The surprise inspection blitz of cattle slaughterhouses immediately following the outbreak of E. coli poisoning is understandable. The Department responded to an immediate and very public health hazard. But the Department certainly knows that the public health is jeopardized more by contaminated poultry than beef, even if the public is generally unaware of this fact. Why were no chicken plants paid surprise visits at the same time? Although favoritism cannot be ruled out, the Department reported that it conducted surprise inspections of some Tyson Foods plants in 1993. Further, Deputy Secretary Richard Rominger testified that over two hundred poultry or meat and poultry plants had received unannounced inspections through June 1, 1994 (when these inspections began was not disclosed). On the basis of the *Wall Street Journal* allegation alone, there is insufficient facts to conclude that the Department provided preferential treatment to Tyson Foods by refraining from conducting surprise inspections of its poultry plants in 1993.

Fresh label laws.[191] Under the Poultry Products Inspection Act, labels used on poultry products must be submitted to the Department of Agriculture for review and approval. The Department has consistently approved use of the label "fresh" for chicken that has been frozen during transportation from the poultry plants in the Southeast United States to distant locations around the country. Chicken is frozen to prevent spoilage and bacterial growth. The Department, by regulation, requires only poultry frozen below zero degrees Fahrenheit to be labeled "frozen," but does not have a regulation that defines "fresh." Instead, the Department's policy has evolved through the label approval process. In 1988, the Department issued Policy Memo No. 022B, which provided, in pertinent part:

The word "fresh" may not be used in conjunction with the product name of: . . .
(3) Any poultry, poultry part, or any edible portion thereof that has been

frozen or previously frozen **to 26 degrees Fahrenheit or below** (at its center or core location).[192]

After "much deliberation on the issue," including complaints from the National Broiler Council and others,[193] the Department six months later issued a superseding memo, Policy Memo No. 022C, that provided:

> The word "fresh" may not be used in conjunction with the product name of: . . .
> (3) Any poultry, poultry part, or any edible portion thereof that has been frozen or previously frozen **at or below zero degrees Fahrenheit**.[194]

The Department explained:

> This decision is predicated on the belief that it is not practical, under existing marketing strategies and distribution patterns, to define "fresh" in terms of internal temperature beyond the scope of the current regulations, nor is it practical to define consumer expectations for poultry products labeled as "fresh." The consumer is the best judge of preference in chilling temperatures for unprocessed poultry products labeled as "fresh," and therefore the marketplace is best suited for making this type of decision.[195]

This was not the Department's finest hour. How can the consumer be the judge if he is unaware that the poultry was frozen in transit to the market? What the Department referred to as "not practical under marketing strategies and distribution patterns" meant simply that Southeastern poultry producers, such as Tyson Foods, would be hurt competitively if they were required to label their poultry "frozen" or some term other than "fresh." Consumers naturally would prefer "fresh" over "frozen," and expect a price differential to reflect that preference. Further, there is evidence that refreezing poultry, on the mistaken assumption that the poultry is being frozen for the first time, may risk bacterial growth.[196] In any event, these Policy Memos were issued in the waning days of the Reagan Administration. What is their relevance to Secretary Espy?

In 1993, California enacted the California Fresh Poultry Consumer Protection Act,[197] which provided that for poultry to be labeled "fresh" it may not, prior to sale, be refrigerated below 26 degrees. Although the goal of consumer protection was featured in the title of the legislation, the clear effect of the law (if not its purpose) was to improve California producers' competitive position vis-a-vis out-of-state producers such as Tyson Foods.[198] The National Broiler Council, the Arkansas Poultry Federation, and the American Meat Institute filed suit in Federal district court, arguing that the California law was preempted by Federal law. In April 1994, the district court ruled that the statute was preempted; in December, the court of appeals affirmed.[199] The Agriculture Department, represented by the Justice Department, filed an *amicus curiae* brief in support of the preemption argument at both levels. The Department took no position on the merits of the California law, however. The inference from the *Wall Street Journal* article was that Espy's Department took Tyson's side in a dispute, at Tyson's or the National Broiler Council's request, and that the

Department took the unusual step of intervening in private litigation. Neither inference is fair.

The National Broiler Council did approach the Department to seek its participation in the case, but the State of California also met with the Department to urge it to stay out. Apparently, the Department determined that it would keep out of the case, until the district court specifically requested the views of the United States. Under these circumstances, the Secretary had little choice but to comply with the court's request. Further, even in the absence of a court request, it would have been entirely appropriate for the Department to participate in the case, because of the nature of the issue: whether a Federal law under the Department's jurisdiction pre-empts State law.

The challenge to the California law was successful because the Federal Meat Inspection Act provides that a State shall not impose a labeling requirement that is "in addition to or different than" Federal labeling requirements.[200] Under this standard, the courts' rulings are unremarkable.

In February 1994, after the lawsuit was filed, Secretary Espy announced that he had directed FSIS to "reexamine its policy for use of the term 'fresh' on poultry product labels":

> I want to make sure consumers get the information and safety protections they have the right to expect whenever they buy raw poultry products. . . Because my top priority is to increase the safety of meat and poultry products, we must also make sure that any policy change does not open the door to problems like the growth of bacteria that could cause foodborne illnesses.[201]

At the June 1994 House hearing, Deputy Secretary Rominger testified that a new policy statement was likely to be issued sometime in the fall. Rominger pledged that the Department would hold public hearings and would review the work of a scientific advisory committee. Congressional critics of the Department's current "fresh" label policy at the hearing argued that the Department's position is plainly untenable, amounting to "fraud" and "deception."[202] An inference that reasonably may be drawn is that the Department's hesitancy to amend the policy—as well as the Department's insistence that there is a safety issue here[203]—was the result of the influence of the poultry giants represented by the National Broiler Council, including Tyson Foods. But it may well be that the poultry industry's influence over the Department on this issue is not materially different than the influence brought to bear on the Reagan Administration to kill Policy Memo No. 022B before its implementation.

Two weeks after Secretary Espy left the Department, FSIS proposed regulations to prohibit poultry from being labeled "fresh" if it has been frozen or chilled below 26 degrees.[204] In the preamble to the proposed rule, FSIS stated that Policy Memo No. 022C "has considerable potential to mislead consumers" and concluded that product safety is not an issue with raw poultry maintained at or below 40 degrees.[205] Recall that this proposal is substantially the same as what was contained in the short-lived Policy Memo No. 022B. The Department also proposed that poultry chilled between 0 and 26 degrees would have to be labeled "previously frozen," although it sought comment on various alternative descriptions.[206] Predictably, Tyson Foods and the National Broiler Council immediately issued statements criticizing the proposal.[207]

In August 1995, the Department issued its final rule regarding the labeling of poultry.[208] The rule, responding to over 26,000 comments, was essentially adverse to the interests of Tyson Foods, the National Broiler Council, and the Arkansas Poultry Federation. Under the rule, effective one year hence, poultry cannot be labeled "fresh" unless it has never been chilled below 26 degrees. Poultry refrigerated between zero and 26 degrees will be labeled "hard chilled." "Frozen" or "previously frozen" will be used for poultry frozen below zero degrees. The Arkansas poultry interests successfully avoided the word "frozen," as contained in the proposed rule, but the label "hard chilled" was seen as a clear advantage to California poultry producers and other producers of poultry that do not transport poultry over long distances.

In sum, the Department's participation in litigation challenging California's fresh label law does not appear to have resulted from improper pressure from Tyson or the National Broiler Council, or from a desire to take sides on behalf of Southeastern poultry producers. It does appear that the Department's historic reluctance to issue a fresh label policy where "fresh" means "fresh" was motivated more from a desire not to hurt the big poultry producers like Tyson, rather than from a public health objective. But, in this respect, Secretary Espy's Department appeared little different from the Department under the two previous Republican Administrations. In any event, Secretary Espy publicly began the process to reverse the Department's policy, and did so even before allegations of favoritism toward the poultry industry surfaced.

Puerto Rico Labeling Rule. *Newsweek* reported Secretary Espy's efforts on behalf of domestic poultry producers in a dispute with the Commonwealth of Puerto Rico in early 1993. After Puerto Rico adopted a rule requiring poultry products to display a label identifying the distributor, local Puerto Rican inspectors were "refusing to let mainland chicken in."[209] "[W]ithin days" Secretary Espy was able to persuade Governor Pedro Rossello to suspend the rule and release the detained poultry. A spokesman for the Governor explained later that the Secretary had broached the subject with Rossello at an event held in Washington. Two days later the chicken was released from detention:

> Secretary Espy said, "We have a problem in Puerto Rico," something like that, and then said, "We are going to send you a letter on that" and that was it.[210]

Tyson Foods explained that the National Broiler Council, not Tyson, handled the issue for the industry, and an Espy assistant remembered a contact from a producer other than Tyson. A Tyson spokesman said later that "No one at Tyson ever talked to Espy or anyone else at the USDA on this matter" and that Espy's actions were consistent with what previous Secretaries had done.[211] Still, *Newsweek* noted, Tyson "had the most at stake[,]" and Tyson Foods' PAC gave a $2000 donation to Henry Espy's House campaign three weeks after the Secretary's discussion with Rossello.[212]

Secretary Espy's conversation with Governor Rossello, which was taken in his first week as Secretary,[213] appears to be a reasonable action for a Cabinet member to take on behalf of a general industry subject to the Department's regulation, even if Tyson Foods had the most to gain or lose from the dispute with Puerto Rico. Further, Tyson Foods and the Department deny that the company contacted the Secretary or his office seeking assistance, although the National Broiler Council, of which Tyson

Foods is a member, did so. The Secretary's conduct is noteworthy here only in conjunction with other actions he and the Department took that have been beneficial to the poultry industry in general and Tyson Foods in particular.

In December 1994, it was reported that the independent counsel would look into the matter as part of his investigation.[214]

Sun-Diamond Growers. Secretary Espy is alleged to have favored Sun-Diamond Growers in several instances, largely because of his close friendship with Richard Douglas, Sun-Diamond's chief lobbyist.[215] Douglas and Espy attended Howard University together, and have remained close friends for over twenty years.[216] When Mike Espy was in Congress, Douglas and Sun-Diamond PACs provided more than $7,500 in campaign contributions and $8000 in honoraria.[217] One report noted that "Some agency insiders say Sun-Diamond's influence at the Agriculture Department surpasses even that of the Tyson family[.]"[218]

Under the standards of conduct governing personal and business relationships, 5 CFR 2635.502, Secretary Espy did not have a "covered relationship" with Douglas, despite being close personal friends. Nonetheless, under the residual provision, Espy should have sought the advice of Agriculture ethics officials before participating in any particular matter involving Sun-Diamond, because his close friendship with Douglas, and Douglas's senior position with a company regulated by the Department, raised a legitimate question regarding the Secretary's impartiality.[219] Douglas denied lobbying the Secretary, yet Espy acknowledged to the *Los Angeles Times* that "Douglas lobbied him formally at least three times on issues crucial to Sun-Diamond."[220] Even accepting Douglas's denial (over Espy's acknowledgment) that he discussed Sun-Diamond issues with Espy, under the standards of conduct the Secretary should have sought internal ethics advice before participating in official actions affecting Sun-Diamond.

The allegations of preferential treatment on behalf of Sun-Diamond are not as fully developed as the Tyson Foods allegations, and are based almost entirely on news reports. At this point, it is difficult to reach any conclusion whether Secretary Espy in fact gave favorable treatment to Sun-Diamond. The allegations are as follows:

Market Promotion Programs. Espy's Department reportedly took action to "protect a controversial federal program that funds overseas promotion of U.S. agricultural products—including those of Sun-Diamond."[221] Sun-Diamond co-ops reportedly have, "over the last decade," "benefited from more than $35 million in federal spending" from the Marketing Promotion Program ($1.5 million during Secretary Espy's tenure). But three Sun-Diamond affiliates were reportedly ineligible to receive additional Federal market promotion funds because of their size. In 1994, the Acting Administrator of the Department's Foreign Agricultural Service asked the Small Business Administration (SBA) to broaden its definition of a "business concern" in a way that would render the affiliates eligible for additional funding. It is not known whether Secretary Espy was personally involved in this matter or, if so, whether Douglas requested his involvement. Soon after the Secretary resigned, SBA rejected the Department's request.[222]

Methyl bromide. Methyl bromide is an "ozone-depleting chemical used by growers and exporters, including Sun-Diamond, to fumigate fruits, nuts and other produce."[223] Secretary Espy asked the EPA to phase out the pesticide as a fumigant, instead of banning it outright, to permit the development of alternatives, "although some already exist." Espy acknowledged that his request of EPA to postpone its ban on the use of methyl bromide until 2001 came after being lobbied by Douglas and Sun-Diamond.[224] EPA granted the delay.

It was subsequently reported that Secretary Espy initially asked EPA to exclude methyl bromide from the list of Class 1 ozone-depleting chemicals, but that EPA denied the request.[225]

School Lunches. Douglas's "longtime female companion," Patricia Kearney, received a $24,000 contract from the Department to provide consulting services on "rules improving the nutritional content of school lunches." Kearney previously served as chief of staff to Secretary Clayton Yeutter in the Bush Administration. Ellen Haas, Assistant Secretary for Food and Consumer Services, explained that Secretary Espy played no role in the retention of Kearney.[226] Even if he had, Kearney appears sufficiently qualified to have obtained the consulting contract without Douglas's help. Thus, this allegation appears to lack merit.

EOP Group, Inc. and Oglethorpe Power Corp. Patricia Dempsey is employed by a consulting firm named the EOP Group, Incorporated, as a "seminar planner and staff associate."[227] She was hired after Espy was appointed Secretary. Espy's attorney stated that, "As a precautionary measure, [Dempsey] was excluded at all times from contact with clients or issues at the EOP Group pertaining to the Agriculture Department."[228] During his tenure as Secretary, Espy met with EOP Group officials on several occasions, the most noteworthy of which was a "working lunch" at the headquarters of Oglethorpe Corporation in Atlanta during the 1994 Super Bowl weekend.

Oglethorpe hired the EOP Group in an attempt to get a meeting with Secretary Espy concerning its proposal to settle the remaining balance of an outstanding Rural Electrification Administration (REA) guaranteed $3 billion loan from the Federal Financing Bank of the Treasury Department.[229] In exchange for the Government's waiver of $286 million in penalties, Oglethorpe proposed to pay the remaining balance of the loan earlier than due, "pay $125 million in other fees[,] and not to seek future loans." REA, an agency of the Agriculture Department, had favored this proposal since the Bush Administration;[230] Oglethorpe was at the time reported to be REA's "largest customer." In August 1993, Secretary Espy wrote Treasury Secretary Bentsen recommending the proposal. Bentsen rejected it on January 7, 1994. A week later, Oglethorpe retained the EOP group to get the Government to reconsider.

Michael O'Bannon, an EOP partner who is a friend of Espy,[231] alerted Oglethorpe to the Secretary's plan to attend the Super Bowl, and arranged the luncheon meeting the day before the game. O'Bannon also arranged for another meeting between Oglethorpe and Secretary Espy at the Agriculture Department in the spring of 1994. Ultimately, Secretary Bentsen did not reverse his decision. O'Bannon stated that Oglethorpe officials did not know that the EOP Group had employed Dempsey.

The White House Counsel's Report found that these facts mitigated "any possible appearance issues of preferential treatment[.]"[232] Given Oglethorpe's prominence in REA's loan guarantee portfolio, Secretary Espy may well have met with Oglethorpe officials without the intervention of the EOP Group, but that is not clear. In any event, the Secretary should have sought the advice of agency ethics officials under the standards of conduct before meeting on official Department business with EOP Group officials.

The White House Counsel's Report did not consider two other reported instances where O'Bannon and the EOP Group represented clients before the Secretary.[233] The EOP Group, representing the National Agricultural Chemicals Association, "helped arrange" Secretary Espy's speech before the Association at the Greenbrier resort in September 1993. Also, O'Bannon and Association officials met with the Secretary in June 1994 "to discuss alleged violations of patents that protect U.S. producers of agricultural chemicals."

Frequency of Official Visits to Secretary Espy's Home State

The public release of Secretary Espy's official travel records, in response to FOIA requests, revealed that Espy traveled frequently to Jackson, Mississippi, his hometown and near where his two children live. Given Mississippi's prominence in agriculture, occasional, even regular, visits to the State would not seem unusual. But a review of the Secretary's travels shows that he visited his hometown disproportionately, giving rise to the inference that his motive in traveling there was sometimes for other than official purposes.

Secretary Espy took eighteen official trips to Mississippi—more than one a month—from January 21, 1993 to July 3, 1994. The several trips reviewed in a lengthy article in the *Washington Post* confirm the inference. "Many of the Mississippi trips are scheduled around weekends, with Espy reporting himself on duty although his schedule reflects minimal work":[234]

> On one trip, Espy spoke about agricultural careers at his children's school. . . . Espy answered questions for about 30 minutes, the only event on his schedule before departing for Washington at noon.
>   . . . On Thursday, May 26, . . . Espy took a late afternoon flight to Jackson. His schedule shows a 9 a.m. meeting with [a local Department official] the next morning, but nothing for the rest of the day.
>   On Saturday, Espy gave a commencement address at a Mississippi college, then returned to Jackson and made brief remarks at a reception honoring a local minister. His schedule shows no activities Sunday and Monday, except a meeting with [a farmer]. He returned to Washington Tuesday, billing the government $1,572 for air fare, hotel and rental car.
>   On one August 1993 trip to Mississippi that apparently cost the government $170 in meals and lodging, Espy's official business amounted to a Friday afternoon meeting with [a local FmHA official] and a 10-hour "Mike Espy Day" celebration in Greenwood.[235]

Secretary Espy's attorney explained that Espy traveled frequently to Jackson because he received a lot of invitations to speak there and because his minor two children live there.[236] Others suspected that he harbored ambitions to run for statewide office in the future. Secretary Espy acknowledged:

> In reviewing these notebooks it has become clear to me that I may have been inattentive to the appearance of impropriety. I regret that deeply, and have taken full responsibility to correct those perceptions.[237]

Espy stated that henceforth his travel schedule and speaking appearances would be reviewed in advance by Department ethics officials.[238]

Secretary Espy reimbursed the Government $193 for expenses incurred in a trip to Jackson in early 1993. Initially, the Secretary was listed as "on duty," but in fact he did not conduct any official business that weekend. From the *Washington Post* account alone, it is likely that several other trips should be recharacterized. The White House Counsel's Report, after noting Espy's reimbursement for one trip, added that "[i]f further reimbursements are necessary, they should be assessed as they become known or at the conclusion of the Independent Counsel investigation."[239]

Using an official event as a pretext for travel for predominantly personal or political purposes amounts to using public office for private gain, a violation of the standards of conduct.[240] At a minimum, the frequency of the Secretary's trips to Mississippi, and the nature of his official activities on some of these trips, give rise to an appearance that he used his public office for his private gain, also a violation of the standards.[241] Frequently traveling on official business to one's hometown is a bad habit picked up by many a high-level Government official in recent times. As explained elsewhere in this study, no administration in recent memory has been immune from stories of the abuse of official travel privileges.

Secretary Espy's Use of a Government Vehicle

Given the frequency of Secretary Espy's visits to Jackson, Mississippi, the Department decided to lease a Jeep Cherokee in Jackson for the use of the Secretary and other Department officials.[242] The Jeep Cherokee was the same vehicle the Clerk of the U.S. House of Representatives had leased for Espy's use as a congressman. The Government's lease covered the period from early 1993 to September 1993 (variously reported as six, seven, or eight months). Secretary Espy bought the vehicle in September or October 1993. Reports in September 1994 that the Secretary had used the government vehicle for his personal use, namely to take his children places, prompted him to repay the Government the full cost of the lease payments in 1993, around $6,200.

Secretary Espy's use of the jeep for personal travel was clearly forbidden by statute and regulation:

> Funds available to a Federal agency . . . may be expended by the Federal agency for the maintenance, operation, or repair of any passenger carrier only to the extent that such carrier is used to provide transportation for official purposes.[243]

"Willful" use of a passenger motor vehicle for other than official purposes requires the suspension of the employee for at least one month, and could result in the employee's removal from service.[244] Willful misuse is shown either by the employee's knowledge that his use was unofficial or his reckless disregard of whether the use was unofficial.[245]

The standards of conduct provide that: "An employee has a duty to protect and conserve Government property and shall not use such property, or allow its use, for other than authorized purposes."[246]

It was also reported that Secretary Espy's use of a Ford Explorer assigned to the Department's IG was under investigation by the independent counsel. Because Secretary Espy had portal-to-portal privileges as a member of the Cabinet (Government-chauffeured transportation between home and work), it is not clear why he needed to use the IG's official car. Espy used the car for about nine months beginning in July 1993, until the IG's office "retrieved the car" for its official use.[247] Although his use of an IG's car appeared highly irregular, there was no report that Secretary Espy used the car for other than official purposes.

Conclusions

Secretary Espy Committed Multiple Violations of the Standards of Ethical Conduct.

Secretary Espy's conduct in accepting gifts from Tyson Foods, associating with Tyson Foods, and soliciting a gift from Quaker Oats was patently unethical, and violated the standards of conduct for Executive Branch employees. If Secretary Espy was covered by the gift provisions of the Meat Inspection Act, which is not certain, he most likely violated the Act. The Meat Inspection Act provisions may be arcane, but the principle that a Secretary should not accept gifts or special favors from a company he regulates is not.

The value of the gifts may be small, but the nature of them demonstrate Secretary Espy's gross insensitivity to the appearance that he was partial to the poultry industry in general, and Tyson Foods in particular, as well as his inattention to the standards of conduct. On what is publicly known, there is no proof that Secretary Espy took any action as a result of any gift, or that any gift from Tyson was a reward for action taken, and thus no *quid pro quo* for which prosecution under the illegal gratuities statute would be called for.

Secretary Espy's use of a government car for other than official purposes also violated the standards of conduct, as well as a separate provision of Federal law. Lower-ranking Federal employees have received suspensions for similar conduct. His frequent travels to Jackson, Mississippi, for minor official purposes gave the strong appearance that he used his public office for his personal benefit, in violation of the standards of conduct.

A final verdict on whether Secretary Espy improperly accepted gifts from Sun-Diamond Growers, and whether he gave preferential treatment to Tyson Foods, Sun-Diamond, or the EOP Group, must await the independent counsel's investigation and report. On the reports to date, it can safely be concluded that Secretary Espy was insensitive to appearances of preferential treatment, and that he failed to use the process provided in the standards of conduct to resolve such appearance issues.

The White House's Responses Were Inconsistent and Questionable

Even without knowing whether Secretary Espy in fact gave preferential treatment to Tyson Foods, Sun-Diamond Growers, or the EOP Group, the Secretary's misconduct was serious. By the time Espy announced his resignation on October 3, 1994, the consensus view among media commentators was he should resign. Up until then, the Secretary had steadfastly defended himself, providing several explanations: his missteps were technical; they were caused by his inattention to detail; he had reimbursed entities for the gifts and benefits, and had made the Government whole for any alleged misuse of government property; the allegations of favoritism were false, spread by embittered employees; there would have been no controversy had Tyson Foods not been located in the President's home state; and the job he was doing as Secretary should trump any minor ethical transgressions.[248] The White House, too, defended the Secretary up to the end, along the lines of "innocent until proven guilty."

Columnists and editorial writers, however, had long turned against Secretary Espy. In August 1994, Richard Cohen wrote:

> Either Mike Espy's a fool or he thinks we are. The former is not likely, the latter just plain insulting—but nothing else accounts for [Espy's] insistence that he did nothing wrong in accepting favors from a humongous chicken producer with business before Espy's own department.[249]

Cohen added:

> The minimum Espy could do is own up to poor judgment and say he's sorry. But he has not—and that is at least as troubling as any possible technical violation of federal law. . . . His transgressions are blatant.

The *Washington Post* wrote, "As examples of public ethics, they are outrageous." It called Secretary Espy's failure to understand the nature of his conduct "astounding."[250] While stating that the allegations against Secretary Espy were "[o]n their face, . . . trivial[,]" the *New York Times* commented, "In this day and age, [Espy's close association with Tyson Foods] is colossally stupid behavior."[251] Tony Snow had a different take; he wrote that Secretary Espy's "unseemly transactions [with businesses regulated by the Department] expose not only venality but desperation."[252]

Given the number and nature of Secretary Espy's violations of the standards of conduct, the widespread impression that he played favorites with friends, and the cloud of a pending criminal investigation that did not look like it would dissipate any time soon, his resignation was appropriate.

There are conflicting accounts whether the Secretary was forced to resign, asked to resign, or simply did so on his own. The President's prepared statement and contemporaneous background statements of White House officials appear to confirm that Espy was told that he must resign. Departures of Cabinet members under an ethical cloud often are portrayed as voluntary, made for "personal reasons," with little or no acknowledgment of the public controversy encircling the official. When there is a hint of candor, it is usually to the effect that the official resigned for the sake of appearances, not because the official is contrite, much less admits any culpability. In truth, most such resignations are forced and are directly related to the reality and extent of ethical misconduct. It is a measure of how large has been the traditional dissonance between resignation statements and reality that the President's prepared statement, released on the day Espy announced his resignation, was seen as offering only tepid support to the Secretary.[253] Yet the most critical portion of the President's statement was not really that critical:

> Although Secretary Espy has said he has done nothing wrong, I am troubled by the appearance of some of these incidents and believe his decision to leave is appropriate.[254]

The President should have publicly stated that he had asked for Secretary Espy's resignation (assuming he or the White House did), or at least issued a reprimand. Once again, the President was unwilling to acknowledge any violation of the standards of conduct by a member of his Administration, criticizing only the improper appearances. True, a high-level official's resignation amid ethics allegations is widely regarded as sufficient damage to one's reputation, so that publicly firing Espy or issuing a reprimand could be seen as overkill, or at least redundant. In Secretary Espy's case, however, the President should have struck a clearer blow for the ethics of his Administration by decrying Espy's conduct, not just lamenting appearances. A reprimand containing findings that Secretary Espy violated the standards of conduct, could have been written and delivered in a manner that would not interfere with or prejudice the ongoing independent counsel investigation. Instead, much of whatever force the President's mildly critical statement on October 3 had was lost on October 11, with the release of the noncommittal White House Counsel's Report.

It was also right to have insisted that Secretary Espy recuse himself from participating in meat and poultry inspection matters for the remainder of his tenure. However, the White House should have insisted on a broader recusal, to cover all particular matters involving at least Tyson Foods, and perhaps Sun-Diamond Growers and the EOP Group.

The White House Counsel's Report, released October 11, and statements later made by White House Counsel Mikva, deserve criticism. The White House Report contained no finding that Secretary Espy violated any standard of conduct, including even the appearance standard! After a lengthy statement of the applicable standards, the report simply noted Espy's (and Dempsey's) reimbursements, and concluded that in light of the Secretary's resignation, recusal, and reimbursements, no further action was warranted.[255] If the White House believed it should not make any finding while the criminal investigation is pending, it should have said so. That it did not rely on the pendency of the criminal investigation suggests that the White House Counsel's Report was abbreviated significantly, after the Secretary agreed to resign, to remove the adverse findings and soften the blow. While such a compromise or accommodation would have been understandable, it should not have been made. The White House missed the chance to highlight its intolerance of ethical misbehavior.[256]

Further, Judge Mikva, interviewed on the "MacNeil/Lehrer Newshour," downplayed the seriousness of Secretary Espy's conduct, explaining that conduct, in part, by reference to the Secretary's difficult adjustment from lax congressional ethics standards to the high standards imposed by President Clinton.[257] Other commenters noted Espy's previous service in the House in an effort to understand how someone like Mike Espy could have committed such egregious ethical missteps.[258] This is not an adequate explanation, however.

At the time, ethics standards, especially gift restrictions, were not nearly as strict for Members of Congress as they are for Executive Branch officials. But this disparity should have come as no surprise to a former Congressman such as Secretary Espy, because of the highly publicized, and successful, effort to enact tighter congressional standards. In 1995, both Houses of Congress passed significantly tighter gift standards for Senators, Representatives, and congressional staff. However, Congress remains free of other ethics restrictions, such as 18 U.S.C. 208. Moreover, Secretary Espy knew he was no longer in the House and that he would be subject to different, tougher standards in the Executive Branch, for it is inconceivable that he was not given adequate ethics briefings at the time he joined the Cabinet. Even if Secretary Espy was correct in asserting that he never received notice of the gift provisions of the Meat Inspection Act, the very same conduct is clearly proscribed by the standards of conduct on which he was briefed (the only difference is the sanction).

Also, Secretary Espy presumably was aware of the troubles that beset Bush Administration officials, most notably Chief of Staff John Sununu, for abuse of travel privileges. Significantly, many other former Members of Congress have come into the Executive Branch and complied with the more rigorous ethics standards without difficulty. In the Bush Administration alone, Jack Kemp, Lynn Martin, Ed Madigan (a Secretary of Agriculture) and Manuel Lujan all entered the Bush Cabinet from the House of Representatives.

Ironically, it was another former Member of Congress, Leon Panetta, who best expressed why the White House determined that Secretary Espy had to go. In an interview with Juan Williams, asked whether the Administration made an example of Espy because of the President's poor standing in the polls or Panetta's need to assert authority as new Chief of Staff, Panetta responded:

> I have to tell you I think we would have called this one the same regardless of where the president stood [in the polls].
> I think it was pretty clear that we were looking at some fairly clear breaches with regard to ethics rules and it had reached the point where we had to take action. . . If you begin to ignore or excuse that kind of behavior it sends a terrible signal to others. It becomes acceptable. All of us, particularly myself, and the president, recognized that Mike was an outstanding secretary of agriculture . . . and yet what was clear was that . . . with the information we had received, that ultimately it would impact not only on our standard of ethics but ultimately on his ability to do his job.[259]

Secretary Espy, however, was largely unrepentant, blaming his forced departure on "this newspaper perception of wrongdoing" and:

> It's all perception and perception is reality—they take that to heart at the White House. They want me to explain it but it didn't matter. . . . It's Tyson and it's Arkansas all mixed up and I'm out of a job although I've done a good job.[260]

Judge Mikva also was incorrect to explain Secretary Espy's difficulties by reference to the standards of the Clinton Administration. In fact, the standards of conduct that apply to all Executive Branch employees, including Secretary Espy, were promulgated by OGE during the Bush Administration. The Clinton Administration has not tightened or changed these standards; the only change in ethics standards in the Clinton Administration relates to the revolving door, which apply only after an official leaves the Government. Moreover, the basic ethics principles Secretary Espy violated were not invented in the Bush Administration, but have existed in Executive Branch standards for decades.

Recommendations

1. Clarify the ethics standards with respect to an official's "significant other" or very close friend.

The gift standards do not currently proscribe a gift to the very close friend of an Executive Branch employee where that gift would be prohibited if made to the employee, unless it were made on the basis of the employee's "designation, recommendation, or other specification[.]"[261] This is so even if the gift to the friend were made because of the friend's relationship with the employee, because of the employee's official position, and with the employee's knowledge and acquiescence. Such gifts would be impermissible if made to the employee's parent, sibling, spouse, child or dependent relative, but not to the employee's "significant other."[262]

The regulation's failure to cover "significant others" may reflect the reality that employees do not have the same degree of control over whether gifts are offered to or accepted by persons outside of the family. The facts of the scholarship award from the Tyson Foundation, which Patricia Dempsey accepted despite Espy's contrary plea, appear to confirm that reality. Yet it is clear that gifts made to a Federal official's *intime* are likely to raise a similar, if not the same, appearance concern that the donor is seeking some official action from the employee. The facts of Tyson-provided travel and tickets for Espy and Dempsey certainly confirm this reality. In the latter situation, the employee does have some control over whether the gift is made. The ethics standards should be clarified to address this situation, perhaps to direct the employee to consider such gifts to one's companion to be gifts made to the employee, or to require the employee to seek the advice of ethics officials before such gifts are accepted. The standards would not hold an employee responsible for gifts given to a significant other without the employee's knowledge, or where the employee could show that he had no control over the giving or acceptance of the gift.

2. Repeal the gift provisions of the Meat Inspection Act.

Conduct prohibited by the Meat Inspection Act is also prohibited by the standards of conduct and the illegal gratuities statute. Conduct that would make out a *prima facie* violation of a Title 18 offense need not be separately proscribed by a special statute that applies only to one agency's workforce (indeed, only a portion of its workforce). In this respect, these provisions of the Meat Inspection Act are superfluous.

Conduct that would not satisfy the elements of the bribery or illegal gratuities provisions in 18 U.S.C. 201 is not sufficiently serious to warrant criminal prosecution. Bribes and illegal gratuities deserve criminal sanction because of the *quid pro quo* nature of these offenses. Where no *quid pro quo* is shown, the venality barometer is lowered, and the prosecutive appeal diminishes. Moreover, keeping the Meat Inspection Act on the books risks inconsistency in the Executive Branch's treatment of ethics transgressions. A major purpose behind President Bush's push for a "single, comprehensive and clear" set of ethical standards for Executive Branch employees, which OGE promulgated in 1992,[263] was the desire to eliminate the varying and inconsistent interpretation, application, and enforcement of ethics standards among similarly-situated Executive Branch employees. As the Espy matter shows, misconduct by an Agriculture Department official may trigger a criminal investigation (under the Meat Inspection Act) and result in a prison term, whereas the same misconduct by an official of another agency may result only in discipline, ranging from reprimand to removal. There does not appear any legitimate reason why the punishment of Federal officials for the same or similar conduct should depend, even in part, on the agency where they work. The prospects of removal from office and injury to one's reputation, plus proportional punishment for those who violate the standards of conduct, provide sufficient incentive to the Federal officials to comply with the standards.

3. Travel home at government expense, even for ostensibly official purposes, should be openly discouraged.

The Clinton Administration and succeeding administrations should strongly admonish Cabinet officials and other Presidential appointees to refrain from official travel to hometowns or the towns in which relatives live, except where there is a clear and substantive official purpose in the travel, and where the timing of the official visit does not coincide with previously scheduled personal activities or events. An ethics official should review any travel plan going to such destinations in advance, to ensure that the official purpose is *bona fide* and predominates over any personal or political purpose.

4. An independent counsel's jurisdiction should be circumscribed, by statute or charter, to cover only those offenses committed by the covered official or others in connection with the covered official's conduct.

One reason why independent counsel investigations, including the investigation of Secretary Espy, take so long is their jurisdiction is broad and without clear limitation. This permits an independent counsel to stray from the original charge, in hopes of uncovering more serious offenses or just in hopes of "turning" a non-covered person to offer evidence against the covered government official. From all reports, Donald Smaltz's investigation clearly has gone well beyond an inquiry into whether **Secretary Espy** violated the law. Whether or not the independent counsel's charter reasonably can be read to extend to offenses by others, even if those offenses bear no factual relation to Espy, the law or practice ought to be changed in the future to avoid such a prospect. A legislative provision such as H.R. 892, proposed in the 103d Congress, is one way of dealing with the problem. The Attorney General could just as easily ensure a circumscribed investigation by expressly defining the limits of the investigation in the charter proposed to the court of appeals. Indeed, it appears that Attorney General Reno attempted to do just that (in part) in her request for the appointment of an independent counsel to investigate Secretary Ron Brown and Nolanda Hill.

Case in Point:

Allegations Against Ronald Blackley

The most serious allegation that Secretary Espy provided preferential treatment to Tyson Foods and the poultry industry is that his Chief of Staff, Ronald Blackley, directed Department officials to terminate work on proposed poultry inspection regulations, delete the document from the Department's computer files, and send all records of the proposal to the Secretary's office. Blackley has denied taking these actions. Blackley is obviously a central player in this allegation. But this is not the only matter involving Blackley that is under official investigation.

Blackley is reportedly also under investigation by the IG into whether he provided favors for Mississippi farming interests, for whom he had served as a paid consultant before coming to the Agriculture Department, while he was on Espy's congressional staff.[1] Blackley confirmed that during the time he was a part-time staff member in Representative Espy's district office, he served as a paid consultant to farmers who enlisted his assistance in obtaining support payments from the Department.[2] Blackley asserted that he terminated his consulting business when he became an Executive Branch official, although the investigation is looking into whether he received any compensation while employed by the Department.

The IG investigation apparently focuses on five of Blackley's former clients whose requests for higher crop subsidies or disaster payments received favorable treatment from the Department in the early months of the Clinton Administration. During the Bush Administration, Blackley unsuccessfully represented them in appeals to the local, state and national boards of the Agricultural Stabilization and Conservation Service (ASCS). After Blackley became Chief of Staff, these cases were reopened and the decisions reversed. The IG is investigating whether Blackley participated in the Department's review and change of position. Several Department officials told the *Washington Post* that "it was virtually unheard of to have five cases in a small geographic area reviewed by the administrator."[3] The *Wall Street Journal* asserted that these cases "were reviewed at Mr. Blackley's request—and reversed by the acting ASCS administrator, Mr. Weber."[4]

The *Wall Street Journal* reported that the investigation also is looking into Blackley's involvement with Huber Farm Management, Incorporated, a Swiss-owned company now called American Agricultural Service, Incorporated, which oversees tenant farmers for foreign landowners. The *Wall Street Journal* explained that the $50,000-an-entity limit on subsidies could be avoided by creating different corporate and partnership structures, called "Mississippi Christmas trees," and that Blackley may have advised Huber on how to get around the limit. But it is not clear whether this would constitute a violation of law, either by the entities or Blackley.[5]

In February 1994, before Espy and Blackley were beset with adverse publicity over their closeness to Tyson Foods and the poultry industry, the Secretary reassigned Blackley, putting him in charge of a task force to collect delinquent loans issued by the Farmers' Home Administration (FHA).[6] If it was a move to defuse ethical concerns, it failed. Mississippi ranks second in delinquent FHA loans, and many of the borrowers live in Espy's former district. Blackley's participation in the task force is being looked at to see if he participated in the review of any particular loan to a former client.

If Blackley participated in any official way on behalf of a former client, such participation could have violated the standards of conduct in two particulars: using public office for private gain, and giving preferential treatment.[7] Further, if Blackley had served as a consultant or partner of a business within the last year, he had a "covered relationship" with that business, and therefore should have sought advice on whether he could participate in any particular matter involving the business.[8] Unless and until Blackley received authorization from an agency ethics official, Blackley would have been required to recuse himself. In all likelihood, given Blackley's former business relationship with these entities, approval would not have been given.[9]

To date, the IG's investigation apparently has not been completed. It is not clear whether the allegations against Blackley that appear to be independent of the allegations against Secretary Espy are part of the independent counsel's investigation.[10]

Chapter Twelve

Allegations Against Secretary of Commerce Ron Brown

Secretary Ron Brown was initially the subject of an allegation that he received or discussed receiving money from a Vietnamese businessman or the Vietnamese Government as a bribe to get Brown to push for the lifting of the U.S. trade embargo against Vietnam. Brown's innocence was eventually established by the Justice Department, which closed the investigation for lack of credible evidence. However, Secretary Brown exercised bad judgment in meeting with the businessman twice after being chosen to be Secretary—and apparently after knowing something of the businessman's interest. Moreover, the Secretary exhibited belated and inadequate candor with the public regarding whether the meetings even occurred.

Looking into the Vietnam allegation led to a series of questions about a Washington, D.C. town house Brown and his son purchased for Lillian Madsen, a friend of Brown who was present at two of the three meetings between Brown and the Vietnamese businessman. The full story about the financing of the town house has yet to be told. But based on what is now known, the town house arrangement is suspicious in at least two particulars. First, the terms of the deed of trust originally stated that the Browns would use the property as a second home and did not permit them to rent it out. Second, Madsen provided the down payment (from a loan arranged by a Brazilian business friend of Brown) and "contributed to" the mortgage payments. Her name is not on the deed, and the Secretary did not report the down payment as a gift or loan on either of his first two financial reports. On his third report, filed after the appointment of an independent counsel (in part to examine the town house arrangement), Secretary Brown reported that he held the property "pursuant to option agreement with L. Madsen," with no further elaboration. The town house arrangement should be investigated fully for compliance with false statement, real estate, banking, and tax laws, in addition to the truthfulness of the Secretary 's financial disclosure reports.

Secretary Brown's third ethical cloud is the darkest. When he was confirmed, the Secretary took a number of steps to rid himself of potential conflicts of interest, but he held on to several holdings in closely held companies, some of which, upon closer examination, are affiliated in varying degrees. The sloppiness of the Secretary's financial reports, and a *Washington Post* story suggesting that his single largest asset, in First International Communications Corporation, was connected somehow to Corridor Broadcasting, led to many questions about Brown's finances and his continued business ties. The link is important because of the Secretary's role in communications policy, and because Corridor's default led to a significant loss to the taxpayer. Secretary Brown denied any interest in Corridor and for nearly a year kept Representative Clinger in the dark about First International and several of his other holdings. When Clinger's staff uncovered evidence that First International and Corridor were linked financially, that Secretary Brown may have filed materially false financial disclosure reports, and that Brown may have participated as Secretary in matters involving his financial interests and partners, investigations were initiated at the FDIC and Justice Department at the request of Clinger and other congressional Republicans. Representative Clinger raised enough serious and substantial questions of legality that the Attorney General's eventual request for the appointment of an independent counsel was inevitable, although her decision not to refer certain allegations is questionable.

The outcome of the independent counsel's investigation, which includes the allegations concerning the town house, is difficult to predict, although a lengthy investigation is likely, given the complexity of Brown's financial interests and relationship with Nolanda Hill, his partner in First International and the head of Corridor.

Vietnam

In August 1993, an allegation first surfaced that Ron Brown had met with a Vietnamese businessman and received or discussed receiving $700,000 for assistance in lifting the U.S. trade embargo against Vietnam. The allegation was made by Ly Thanh Binh (Binh Ly), an associate of Nguyen Van Hao (Hao), the former Vietnamese government official with whom Brown met, (according to Binh Ly).[1] Binh Ly alleged that Brown "sought an exclusive contract, with the approval of the Vietnam government, to help [Hao's business] win clients in this country, seek projects in Vietnam, and lift the embargo."[2] Binh Ly had informed the FBI of Hao's involvement with Brown back in February and, after interviewing Binh Ly, the FBI initiated a criminal investigation of the allegation. The existence of a grand jury was first reported in August.

Binh Ly took his allegation also to the *Miami Herald*. The *Herald* asked for a response from Brown, and a Commerce Department spokesman initially stated that the Secretary denied that he even knew Hao. Later, when reports of Binh Ly's allegation surfaced in the press in August, the Commerce Department issued a statement that Secretary Brown never "had any business, financial or professional relationship with any Vietnamese individual, organization or group, or any person claiming to represent Vietnamese government or business interests."[3]

However, in September 1993, Secretary Brown's attorney, Reid Weingarten, acknowledged that Brown had met with Hao on three occasions within the past year.[4] According to Weingarten, the first meeting took place after the November 1992 election, but before Brown was named by the President-elect. Brown met with Hao in a Florida restaurant at the request of Marc Ashton. Ashton has been a friend of Brown since they met in Florida when Brown, a law partner with the firm Patton, Boggs & Blow, represented the Government of Haiti. Ashton apparently was an investment adviser to Baby Doc Duvalier at the time.[5] Ashton and Hao were "interested in becoming go-betweens with U.S. business executives seeking trade with Vietnam if relations between the two countries were reestablished." Ashton had been seeking a meeting with Brown since before the election. Ashton and Hao asked Brown to consider representing them and providing investment contacts. "There was no discussion of money." Brown was "noncommittal, saying he was not sure what his plans were."[6]

The second meeting between Brown, Hao, and Ashton took place on December 15, 1992, three days after the President-elect announced his selection of Brown. The meeting was held in the town house of Lillian Madsen, Ashton's sister-in-law and described as "Brown's friend."[7] Weingarten said that Brown "yielded to the importunities of a friend," referring to Ashton. Hao and Ashton had returned from a trip to Vietnam. Weingarten stated that the Secretary-designate refused to accept a letter, proffered by Hao as coming from a Vietnamese official, "explaining he could not represent them because he would be going into government."[8]

In February, after Brown was sworn in as Secretary, Hao, Ashton, and Brown had lunch in Washington. Afterward, the Secretary gave the two a brief tour of the Commerce Department and his office. According to Weingarten, "No business was discussed on that occasion."[9]

Soon after Secretary Brown's acknowledgment of these meetings, he appeared before a subcommittee of the House Committee on Foreign Affairs on another matter. Secretary Brown refused to answer questions from Representatives Dana Rohrabacher and Dan Burton on the merits of the allegations, citing the pending criminal investigation. But he did proclaim his innocence. Separately, Rohrabacher and Burton urged the Attorney General to appoint a special counsel.[10] Subsequently, the Republican House Minority Leader and Whip also called for a special prosecutor, "saying Mr. Brown was 'entitled to something better than prolonged trial by press account.'"[11]

Secretary Brown was interviewed by a Justice Department Public Integrity official and two FBI agents on October 11, 1993.[12] Hao testified before the grand jury in late 1993; Binh Ly, however, Brown's sole accuser, was not brought before the grand jury until January 4, 1994.[13]

On February 2, 1994, the Justice Department informed Brown's attorney in writing that the investigation was being closed. Among the excerpts of the letter, signed by Joe Gangloff, the Acting Chief of the Public Integrity Section of the Justice Department's Criminal Division, are the following: "We have completed a thorough investigation and have concluded that the evidence does not substantiate the allegation that Mr. Brown entered into any such agreement."[14] Nor did the evidence substantiate the charge that Secretary Brown "improperly agreed to use his influence as Secretary of Commerce to liberalize the trade policy of the United States toward Vietnam."[15] Therefore, "no further investigation is warranted. Accordingly, we are closing the investigation. We appreciate Secretary Brown's cooperation with the investigation."[16]

Hao's attorney released a statement supporting the Justice Department's decision; Binh Ly, however, was quoted as saying "wrongdoing is taking place and is being suppressed by the administration."[17]

One report noted that the Federal grand jury "found no evidence to support" Binh Ly's allegation.[18] Another concluded that the grand jury "found no wrongdoing[.]"[19] Notwithstanding these press reports, it is not clear that the grand jury issued a "no true bill," an uncommon step, or whether the prosecutor simply pulled the matter from the grand jury and decided to close the investigation as a matter of prosecutorial discretion.

Either way, the Justice Department's conclusion in entitled to respect, for several reasons. The Justice Department's Public Integrity Section, particularly Gangloff, has a solid reputation for approaching sensitive ethics matters aggressively yet fairly. There is no reason to doubt the thoroughness of its investigation.

Moreover, the Justice Department's decision did not surprise. From the outset, most observers did not believe the allegations against the Secretary, even after his lack of candor was revealed. While it was within character for a private citizen and high-powered lobbyist to have agreed to the first meeting,[20] a person reputed to be of high intelligence and savvy would not have engaged in conduct so palpably unseemly (if not illegal) after being chosen to head the Commerce Department. Also, Binh Ly's credibility suffered because his testimony was hearsay; he was not present at any of the meetings at which the alleged discussions took place, and Hao, from whom Binh Ly had received his information, did not confirm Binh Ly's account. Indeed, Hao claimed that Binh Ly was attempting to retaliate for Hao's firing of him.

Still, the language in the Justice Department's letter to Secretary Brown's attorney suggests that its investigation was limited to Brown's conduct as Commerce Secretary. If so, this may be because any discussion Brown may have had before he became Secretary—even if such a discussion occurred after the President-elect had announced his intention to nominate Brown—would not have implicated Federal law.

So, although Secretary Brown rightfully claimed exoneration from any criminal responsibility, he deserves criticism in two respects. First, the Secretary exhibited a lack of candor in acknowledging the meetings with Hao.[21] His initial denial was issued by a press officer. Accepting the explanation that Brown and the press officer may have miscommunicated with each other,[22] it was still incumbent on the Secretary to give his press officer a complete and accurate account. It is hard to believe that Brown would not recall someone with whom he met on **three** occasions within a three-month period within the past year, when all the meetings were small and private. Moreover, Secretary Brown should have quickly corrected the misimpression left with the media following publication of the incorrect press statement. Not only did Secretary Brown belatedly correct the misimpression that he had never met with Hao, but even after acknowledging the three meetings, he continued to deny that he had met with Hao for business reasons.[23] Whatever the characterization of the last meeting, the primary purpose of the first two meetings, from Hao's and Ashton's perspective, was to discuss business.

Second, Secretary Brown displayed poor judgment in meeting with Hao after their initial meeting, once after being informed by the President-elect he was to be nominated to be Commerce Secretary, and once after being sworn in as Secretary. Even accepting the Secretary's account that he declined to engage in discussions about trade with Vietnam in these latter two meetings, once his Federal position was offered, Brown should have cut off meetings with Hao, knowing the reason why Hao and Ashton wished to meet with him.

Further, given candidate Clinton's rhetoric on lobbyists and his campaign statements that he opposed the lifting of the trade embargo, Brown should have been more sensitive to the negative appearance that inevitably resulted when these meetings were acknowledged.[24]

In addition, it does not appear that the Secretary ever formally recused himself from participating in discussions over whether to lift the trade embargo, as it would have been prudent to do during the pendency of the criminal investigation.[25] A formal recusal would have been effected by a written document by which the Secretary took himself out of Vietnam policy deliberations to avoid a conflict or appearance problem. When the President slightly relaxed the ban in September 1993, allowing U.S. companies to bid on projects financed by the World Bank and International Monetary Fund, Secretary Brown said "he had not taken part in Clinton administration deliberations over lifting the embargo on Vietnam because other commitments took precedence."[26] This suggests that the Secretary's failure to participate in that decision was not (at least at the time) related to a perceived need to do so in order to avoid an appearance of a conflict of interest.

On October 8, 1993, Representative Bill Clinger wrote Brown, asking the Secretary for copies of any document that would indicate whether he had recused himself "from all matters pertaining to Vietnam." Brown never responded.[27] On October 27, 1993, seventeen Members of Congress wrote the President, urging him to "demand Secretary Brown's prompt recusal."[28] White House Counsel Bernard Nussbaum responded that "to avoid even the appearance of impropriety, Secretary Brown has not participated in decisions relating to Viet Nam."[29] This response did not satisfy House Republicans, who wrote the White House Counsel asking when Secretary Brown recused himself, whether the recusal was "formal" (i.e., in writing), whether the Secretary would continue to recuse himself prospectively, and whether any Commerce Department ethics officer considered whether the Secretary should formally recuse himself.[30] The White House Counsel never responded to this letter.

A written recusal is not required. All that 18 U.S.C 208 requires is that the official not participate in the particular matter in which he has a financial interest.[31] Similarly, all that the standards of conduct require in a situation where it has been determined that an official should not participate in a particular matter to avoid an appearance of impropriety is that the official not participate in the matter.[32] However, a written recusal is easily drafted, and for high-level officials, such as members of the Cabinet, it is always prudent. It offers protection from public criticism, provides assurance that the problem was timely noted and dealt with, and serves as notice to subordinates to ensure that the matter is not brought before the official in any manner. Secretary Brown's apparent failure to execute a written recusal warrants criticism for precisely these reasons.

Although the ethical standard governing appearances of impropriety unrelated to a financial interest, 5 CFR 2635.502, does not address these precise circumstances, the Secretary would have been well-advised to recuse himself. This would have avoided any suggestion that Brown's judgment with regard to lifting the trade embargo was affected by his meetings or by the criminal investigation.[33]

The Washington Town House

On November 28, 1992, Ron Brown and his son Michael Brown signed a purchase contract for a town house at 4303 Westover Place NW, in the District of Columbia.[34] The purchase closed on January 29, 1993, when the Browns signed a deed of trust.[35] The purchase price was $360,000. The 30-year adjustable rate mortgage of $252,000 provided for a fixed rate of 7.875% for the first five years.

Secretary Brown did not report his interest in the town house on his first financial disclosure report, which he filed as a nominee on January 1, 1993; he was confirmed on January 20th. On his first annual report filed May 15, 1994, covering calendar year 1993, Secretary Brown reported his purchase of this property on Schedule B (with a January 29th purchase date) and the asset on Schedule A as "Investment property located in Wash., D.C." He reported rental income in 1993, between $5,000 and $15,000.

Lillian Madsen, self-described "close personal friend" of Brown, lives in the town house.[36] Madsen, an artist, is a sister-in-law of Marc Ashton, who was responsible for getting together Brown and Vietnamese businessman Nguyen Van Hao.[37] When reports of Brown's meetings with Hao surfaced, the town house was mentioned because the second meeting, on December 15, 1992, was reportedly held in a town house, with Madsen present (she reportedly was also present at one of the other two meetings).[38]

The *Washington Post* reported that the Browns bought the property **for** Madsen.[39] "Madsen lives in a Northwest Washington town house that Brown and his son purchased for her early this year. Brown's attorney has said Brown helped Madsen buy the house because she and her family are longtime friends and she contributes to the mortgage payments."[40]

Although the *Washington Times* reported that the FBI and the grand jury were looking into the "personal and business" ties between Brown and Madsen, including the purchase of the town house,[41] it is not clear from the Justice Department's declination letter whether the town house was examined, or even what legal issues the town house was thought to raise.

Months later, it was reported that not only was Madsen "contributing" to the mortgage payments, but also that she had paid some or all of the down payment.[42] Indeed, a few months later, the *Washington Post* reported that "Brown said Madsen pays rent that covers the mortgage and put up the $108,000 down payment."[43] It thus is unclear whether (1) the Browns bought the property **for** Madsen, as was initially claimed, (2) Madsen and the Browns bought the property together, albeit with Madsen's participation undisclosed, (3) Madsen (secretly) bought the property for the Browns, or (4) Madsen (secretly) bought the property for herself, or (5) some other arrangement exists between Madsen and the Browns.

If, as reported, Madsen provided the entire down payment and pays rent "that covers the mortgage," it is not clear what money, if any, the Browns have provided to date. That Madsen's significant financial role appears to have been entirely behind the scenes (vis-a-vis the lender) suggests that there is a reason why the Browns have fronted for Madsen. According to the *Washington Post*, "Brown has said he purchased the house as [a] favor to Madsen because she was separated from her husband and her financial affairs were tied up in the faltering Haitian court system."[44] There are other possible and related reasons: Perhaps it was feared that Madsen would not qualify for the loan or could not obtain as favorable terms.[45] Or, perhaps Madsen or the Browns did not want Madsen's husband to acquire dower rights to the property under D.C. law.[46] Or perhaps the Browns' names were used to allow them to take a tax deduction for the depreciation of the property.

The down payment also raises questions. *U.S. News* reported that Jose Amaro Pinto Ramos, a Brazilian businessman with ties to Brazilian President Cardoso, arranged for a "substantial loan" from a French bank to Madsen in "late 1992 or early 1993."[47] Ramos did not personally provide funds, but declined to answer whether he had guaranteed the loan. Ramos described himself as a "longtime friend" of Madsen and also counts Ron Brown as a friend. In private practice, Brown reportedly represented some of Ramos's business clients.

According to Ramos, Madsen approached him for help with the financing of the town house, yet Ramos claims he did not know that Brown would own the town house. Although the size of the loan was not disclosed, it could be as much as the total down payment, $108,000, or greater.[48]

Ramos's business "puts together financial packages for transportation and energy construction projects." In June 1994, with Secretary Brown in Brazil on a trade mission, Ramos hosted a dinner for the Secretary at his home in Sao Paulo, with fifteen business and political leaders as guests. Ramos stated that the Secretary has not assisted his business in any way.[49]

According to the *Washington Post*:

> House investigators [presumably staff of the House Government Reform and Oversight Committee] . . . have obtained drafts of agreements between Brown and Madsen indicating she was to lend him the down payment money and expected to be repaid if the property is sold.
>
> Brown's attorney has said the agreements were never signed and the drafts do not reflect the way the transaction was ultimately handled, but Brown has never explained how the house purchase was set up.[50]

U.S. News also reported that the Justice Department, as part of its review of the Vietnam allegations in 1993, reviewed the "town house financing." But the nature of Justice's review is not clear. Ramos apparently was interviewed by Justice about whether he knew Hao's lawyer, Robert Wunker. Wunker, whose sister works for Ramos, asked Ramos in late 1992 or early 1993 "if he had a client interested in buying rice from Vietnam or Thailand." Ramos expressed no interest in the matter. Secretary Brown's lawyer said that Justice "'fully explored' Ramos's ties to Brown and found no improprieties[.]"[51] However, this account does not satisfy. *U.S. News* noted Justice's interest only in regard to whether Ramos was involved with the Vietnam allegations.

The town house raises five issues. First, was Secretary Brown required to report the town house on his first financial disclosure report he filed as a nominee, or to report Madsen's down payment on any of his reports? Second, did Brown violate the terms of the deed of trust in allowing Madsen to occupy the property and contribute to the mortgage payments, or improperly fail to disclose Madsen's multifaceted role? Third, was Brown given preferential treatment on the loan based on false information? Fourth, was Ramos's loan to Madsen improper? Fifth, did Brown improperly omit information about his liabilities on his loan application?

Financial Disclosure[52]

Secretary Brown was not required to report the town house as an asset on his initial report. First, the Browns' contract to purchase real estate, executed in 1992, was not an "interest in property" under the financial disclosure regulations. "Real estate" interests are required to be reported,[53] but there is no definition of real estate in the regulations and there is no specific mention of contracts to purchase property in the regulation's nonexhaustive list of property interests. Under principles of realty law, a purchaser of realty does not have an interest in the property until settlement. That event occurred on January 29, 1993, after the Secretary submitted his initial financial disclosure report.

Brown may have been entitled to occupy the property before settlement under a presettlement agreement, because Brown's second meeting with Hao reportedly took place on December 15, 1992 in this town house. His occupancy of the property at that time, however, would have constituted a rental, not ownership interest in the property.[54]

Second, the deed of purchase the Browns signed on November 28, 1992 is not a liability that was required to be reported. The regulations require the reporting of "the filer's liabilities over $10,000 owed to any creditor at any time during the reporting period[.]"[55] "Liability" is not defined, but the Browns did not incur any liability for the property until they signed the deed of trust on January 29, 1993.

Whether Madsen's contribution of most or all of the down payment was required to be reported is uncertain. Did Madsen provide money for the down payment directly to Ron Brown, or to Michael Brown, or to PaineWebber? Was it a loan or a gift? If she gave the money to PaineWebber, the lender might have inquired as to Madsen's status as a co-owner or renter or lender. If, instead, she gave money to Brown with no expectation of reimbursement, it would be considered a gift to him. Neither financial disclosure report lists such a gift. If Madsen gave Brown money for the down payment of the property in 1992, the Secretary's reporting obligation depends on whether the payment was a gift or loan. If it was a gift, there was no duty to report, because as a nominee, he was not required to report gifts received before entering public service.[56] If the gift was made in 1993, however, the Secretary was required to report this payment as a gift on Schedule B of his May 1994 report, which he did not do.[57]

If, on the other hand, the money was given as a loan, whether in 1992 or 1993, Brown would have been required to report the loan as a liability on Schedule C of both his nominee and annual reports, which he did not do.

On Secretary Brown's second annual financial disclosure report covering calendar year 1994, belatedly filed in August 1995, Brown reported the town house differently than his previous two reports. The Secretary reported that he held the real estate "pursuant to option agreement with L. Madsen." This report, without more information, raises additional questions, and answers none. What is the nature of this option agreement? When was it reached? Who has the option? Presumably, Madsen has the option to buy, based on Brown's reporting of his receipt of rental income in "Amounts to be paid pursuant to option agreement." Was the lending institution informed of this agreement?

The Second Home and 1-4 Family Riders
A more troublesome issue is the "Second Home Rider" the Browns signed as an amendment to the deed of trust on the same day, January 29, 1993. In that rider, the Browns agreed that:

> Borrower shall occupy, and shall only use, the Property as Borrower's second home. Borrower shall keep the Property available for Borrower's exclusive use and enjoyment at all times, and shall not subject the Property to any timesharing or other shared ownership arrangement or to any rental pool or agreement that requires Borrower either to rent the Property or give a management firm or any other person any control over the occupancy or use of the Property.

The Second Home Rider also provided that:

> Borrower shall also be in default if Borrower, during the loan application process, gave materially false or inaccurate information or statements to Lender (or failed to provide Lender with any material information) in connection with the loan evidenced by the Note, including, but not limited to, representations concerning Borrower's occupancy and use of the Property as a second home.

Lillian Madsen, not the Browns, lives in the town house and pays rent that covers the mortgage payments. These facts suggest that the Browns were in default of their mortgage for allowing Madsen to occupy the property. A possible defense to this charge is reading the Second Home Rider narrowly, to prohibit only a rental whereby the Borrower is **required** under a rental agreement to give occupancy of the property to another. Whether there is such an agreement between the Browns and Madsen is unknown, although the Secretary now reports that he and Madsen are parties to some sort of option agreement with respect to the property. The Browns can no longer argue that Madsen occupies the property, not under any rental agreement, but at the sufferance of the Browns, given Ron Brown's most recent financial disclosure report. Moreover, the primary focus of the Second Home Rider is on the use and occupancy of the property, and whether there is shared ownership, rather than just the legal right to occupancy.[58]

Another possible explanation would acknowledge that the use of the Second Home Rider was a mistake, but to blame the mistake on a failure to read the settlement documents carefully. Under this hypothesis, the Second Home Rider was naturally included in the package of documents because it was known that the Browns already had a primary home, and the Browns did not know what they were signing when they initialed the Rider. But this explanation also requires the lender to have been ignorant of the Browns' intent that the property was being bought for and would be occupied by Madsen.

A default would allow, but not require, the lender to call the mortgage. Because the loan application documents are not public, it is not known whether the Browns disclosed their planned use of the property during the loan application process.[59] It may be that the Browns informed the lender that Madsen would be living in the town house and helping out with the mortgage payments. If they did, the default of the Second Home Rider would not seem to be serious. If they did, however, it would not have made sense for the lender to provide a Second Home Rider in the first place. If the Browns knowingly provided false information during the loan application process, however, and the loan is Federally insured, Brown may have violated one or more false statement statutes, 18 U.S.C. 1001, 1010, and 1014.[60]

There is also a question whether Madsen's name should be on the title, as full or part-owner, given that she apparently has provided all of the down payment for the property, and reportedly holds a certain option interest in the property, which she may have held at the time of the loan application was submitted. If Madsen's financial participation was not disclosed in the lending process, that omission may also give rise to a violation of Federal law.

Whether or not Federal law is involved, the business dealings of a Cabinet official, at least those that are contemporaneous with the official's tenure, are legitimate matters of public interest. Here, the interest is greater because of Madsen's presence in Brown's meetings with Hao, and Ramos's help in arranging a loan for the down payment. These facts certainly raise questions that deserve a fuller response from the Secretary than he has given. As for the lender, PaineWebber should also be asked to explain what it did with the information that Brown may have been in default of the mortgage.

Perhaps because of questions in the press about the Second Home Rider,[61] it was removed from the deed of trust documents sometime in 1993, and replaced with a "1-4 Family Rider."[62] A copy of the Family Rider obtained from the D.C. Recorder of Deeds shows a date of November 8, 1993 at the bottom. Yet the front page of the Rider, which bears the initials of the Browns, recites that it was "made this **29th** day of **January 1993**[.]"[63] The Family Rider thus appears to be backdated. Why this was done is not known. Perhaps it was believed that the switch from a Second Home Rider to 1-4 Family Rider is a ministerial correction of an innocent mistake, and so there is nothing wrong with reflecting the original date of the deed of trust. Perhaps it was intended to deflect attention from a charge of potential misconduct by Ron Brown. Whatever the reason for the change of riders, there does not appear to be any justification for backdating the 1-4 Family Rider. Nonetheless, because the Second Home Rider was reported in the media, because the entire history of the deed and its concomitant riders is likely to be available on microfilm at the Recorder of Deeds, and because the dating of the rider may not have been done by the Browns, the backdating by itself probably does not constitute an actionable false statement.

The Family Rider allows the Browns to rent out the property,[64] which, according to the Secretary's attorney, was their original intent. The Family Rider also freed the Browns from a requirement in the deed of trust to occupy the property as their principal residence within sixty days of the execution of the deed of trust and thereafter continuously for a year, unless otherwise agreed by the lender.[65]

Preferential Treatment

Why would Brown knowingly execute the Second Home Rider on January 29, 1993, when he knew that Madsen would be living in the town house from the start?[66] Did the Secretary, because of his prominent position, obtain a benefit from the lender for himself, or for Madsen, to which he or she otherwise would not have been entitled?

With a down payment on the town house of around 30% of the purchase price, the Browns obtained an adjustable interest rate, fixed at 7.875% for the first five years. Generally speaking, a higher interest rate accompanies property with a Second Home Rider than an owner-occupied property (on the assumption that if the borrower gets into financial trouble, the borrower is more likely to protect his primary residence). Also, an even higher interest rate generally applies to property with a 1-4 Family Rider (on the assumption that homes, first or second, are closer to the borrower's heart than investment property). In the abstract, this could suggest that the Second Home Rider was deliberately used to obtain a more favorable rate of interest than would have been obtained if a 1-4 Family Rider was used. However, in the context of this case, where the down payment was sizeable, the interest rate differential, if any, would be small. Also, when the lender replaced the Second Home Rider with the 1-4 Family Rider, it made no adjustment to the interest rate.

Ramos's Loan to Madsen for the Down Payment

Even if we accept Ramos's account that he arranged for the loan to Madsen without knowing it was for a town house owned by Brown (also assuming that the Browns do in fact own the property), it is difficult to accept that Brown was unaware that Madsen's ability to cover or contribute to the down payment was due to the good offices of Ramos. If the Secretary was aware of Ramos's involvement, he should have avoided taking any action that would appear to give preferential treatment to Ramos or his business. Other than the Sao Paulo dinner party in June 1994, nothing has been reported to suggest that Ramos received any preferential treatment or special benefit, but the dinner party alone raises the question of what was discussed.

Possible Omissions on the Browns' Loan Application (or Brown's Financial Disclosure Reports)

In March 1995, Senator Charles Grassley, Chairman of the Subcommittee on Administrative Oversight and the Courts of the Senate Judiciary Committee, asked Secretary Brown, to clear up several discrepancies identified in comparing the Browns' loan application with Secretary Brown's two financial disclosure reports. In particular, three promissory notes reported on his financial disclosure reports were not listed on the loan application, and two liabilities listed on the loan application (to National Bank of Washington and First American Bank) were not reported on his financial disclosure reports.[67]

Secretary Brown declined to answer any questions about his loan application, expressing his displeasure "that you are in possession of personal financial records of mine associated with a confidential banking transaction which was totally unrelated to my government service."[68] But he did insist that he "did not mislead the mortgage company to its detriment in any fashion, or put any financial institution at risk by information that I provided." The Secretary further asserted that his financial reports were accurate as to his liabilities:

> I have discovered that the loan officer for my mortgage inserted these entries on the uniform residential loan application form, not based on information that I supplied, but rather based on a subsequently obtained, erroneous credit report.

Answers to the numerous questions about the town house that remain must await independent counsel's investigation and report.

Secretary Brown's Financial Interests

A lingering, troubling issue concerning Secretary Brown's compliance with conflict-of interest laws and financial disclosure requirements relates primarily to his various communications interests. Eventually, questions about the legality and propriety of Brown's holdings, affiliations, and activities led to the appointment of an independent counsel.

Secretary Brown's Financial Interests and Former Positions Relating to the Communications Sector

According to Secretary Brown's initial financial disclosure report and his disqualification statement of January 29, 1993, Brown held the following assets and positions relating to communications at the time of his nomination:

(1) **Kellee Communications, Inc**. Brown described Kellee Communications as a company that received a contract to install phones at Los Angeles International Airport. Brown held an equity interest of between $15,000 and $50,000, and received fees for serving on Kellee's Board of Directors. Upon confirmation, Brown resigned his position as director. He also pledged subsequently to divest himself of his equity interest, and agreed to disqualify himself for one year (presumably, after the date of divestiture) from participating "in any matter likely to have a specific and differential effect on" Kellee.

Brown's divestiture of his interest in Kellee was confirmed in a March 2, 1994 letter from Barbara S. Fredericks, Assistant General Counsel, Department of Commerce, to Representative Clinger. Yet, there is no mention of Kellee Communications on Schedule A (Income and Assets) or B (Transactions) of Secretary Brown's annual financial report dated May 15, 1994, suggesting that a reporting error was made, and leaving the public uncertain whether Brown continued to hold an interest in Kellee. Also, without knowing when the asset was disposed of, the end point of the Secretary's one-year recusal period could not be determined.

(2) **Albimar Communications, Inc**. Albimar is a holding company that, at the time and until recently, owned WKYS-FM, its only asset.[69] Secretary Brown's wife is employed by Albimar. Upon confirmation, Brown resigned from Albimar's Board of Directors. The extent of Brown's financial interest in Albimar at the time, howev-

er, could not be ascertained from his nominee report. On Schedule A, the Secretary listed his financial interest in Albimar on one line, suggesting that his only interest in Albimar is his wife's salary. However, the "valuation of asset" box is checked, between $50,000 and $100,000, which is inappropriate for a listing of spousal salary (salary is not an asset). This suggested that Ron Brown also has an ownership interest, but the Secretary failed to check any income box (including the "none" box), which he is required to do for each of his assets, thereby suggesting that the valuation of asset box was intended to refer to his wife's salary.[70] Ms. Fredericks informed Representative Clinger in her March 1994 letter that the Secretary has an equity interest in Albimar, which, according to her, was disclosed on his financial report. A similar ambiguity appears on Schedule A of the Secretary's May 1994 and August 1995 annual reports, although the "none" box is checked for "amount of income," suggesting his separate equity interest.

FCC records show that Brown owns 10% of Albimar and is one of four "principal" partners of Albimar.[71] Secretary Brown thus failed to report his partnership position on Schedule D of all three of his reports, as well as adequately report his equity interest on Schedule A of his first report.

Albimar originally bought WKYS from NBC in 1988 for $42.5 million. In so doing, NBC took advantage of the law favoring minority ownership and saved about $15 million in Federal income taxes. Albimar's partners reportedly put up less than $1 million to buy WKYS. They borrowed $10 million from NBC and the rest from banks. The loan from NBC was never paid off, and indeed was written off around the time Albimar sold WKYS to Radio One for $34 million earlier this year. NBC stated that Albimar would have likely filed for bankruptcy if the loan had not been forgiven.[72]

Because Secretary Brown's wife's salary is imputed to him, this interest alone required the Secretary to recuse himself, as he did, from participating "in any matter likely to have a direct and predictable effect on" Albimar, "including an effect on those interests as a member of an industry sector[.]"

(3) **Harmon International**. Harmon is described as a "wholly owned equipment leasing company which leases to Channel 50 in Washington, DC." According to his May 1994 financial disclosure report, Brown was President of Harmon International until January 1993. Brown's position was incorrectly omitted from his nominee report. According to a tax report filed with the State of Delaware, where Harmon is incorporated, as of February 1993 Harmon's officers were Michael Brown (Ron Brown's son), who is President and Secretary, and Nolanda Hill, who is Assistant Secretary. Ron Brown's interest in the company was valued at between $15,000 and $50,000. Secretary Brown indicated that he would recuse himself from participating "in any matter likely to have a direct and predictable effect on" Harmon, until such time as he received a waiver from the President.

Secretary Brown requested a waiver in a memorandum to the President on April 20, 1993, noting that his interest in Harmon was less than 1% of his net worth. A waiver was necessary because:

given the broad range of responsibilities of the Secretary of Commerce in telecommunications matters through the National Telecommunications and Information Administration (NTIA) and the International Trade Administration (ITA), such as matters concerning high definition television (HDTV) and international trade negotiations concerning telecommunications equipment, this interest might inhibit me from carrying out a broad range of . policy and regulatory responsibilities.

The waiver was granted by the President (although not until August 8, 1993), consistent with the statutory basis that Brown's interest in Harmon was not so substantial as to be likely to affect the integrity of the service the Government might expect from Brown as Secretary of Commerce.[73] As requested, the waiver was limited to "broad policy matters or matters of general applicability that rise to a level of particular matters even though they may affect this company as part of an industry sector or class." The waiver did not extend to particular matters in which Harmon is a party or which to Brown's knowledge would have a "unique effect" on the company.

Secretary Brown did not report Harmon International on either Schedule A (Assets and Income) or Schedule B (Transactions) on his May 1994 annual report, suggesting that Brown incorrectly omitted one or more references to Harmon. Even if he no longer held any interest in Harmon, he was required to report the sale of his interest if the amount of the transaction was over $1000.

(4) **First International Communications Corp.** On his nominee report, Brown described First International as a "company that provides international and domestic consulting and investment services." Brown's interest in the company was valued at between $500,000 and $1,000,000, constituting his single largest asset, although he reported no receiving income in 1992 from the asset.[74] Brown and Nolanda Hill were the firm's two partners, although the Secretary failed to disclose his partnership position on either of his first two reports. Instead, Brown reported on his nominee report that he had served as a Director for the company since 1990, although he failed to list a director position on his May 1994 report. It was eventually revealed that Brown never served as a director of First International.[75] Thus, he made three additional reporting mistakes.

Secretary Brown agreed to recuse himself from participating "in any matter likely to have a direct and predictable effect on" First International. On his May 1994 report covering calendar year 1993, Secretary Brown reported that he sold his interest in First International on December 15, 1993, for an amount between $250,000 and $500,000.[76] He reported no income from the company during 1993, or, as a result of the sale, on Schedule A. Finally, on Schedule A of his report covering calendar year 1994, which he filed in August 1995, subsequent to the appointment of an independent counsel, Brown reported receiving, **in 1994**, between $100,000 and $1 million in capital gains from "debt forgiveness and payment of debt pursuant to 12/93 stock redemption." On this report, Brown described First International as "100% owned by Nolanda Hill."

The unusual circumstances of Secretary Brown's divestment of his interest in First International would become the greatest ethics controversy of his tenure as Secretary.

At the time of Brown's entry into the Government, however, the steps he took or pledged to take to avoid potential conflicts regarding these communications interests appeared at first blush to have been sufficient. The Secretary resigned three positions (Albimar, Kellee, Harmon), pledged to recuse himself with respect to the interests he retained in Albimar, Kellee, Harmon, and First International, later obtained a waiver with respect to Harmon and pledged to dispose of his interest in Kellee. Later, Brown also disposed of his interests in Harmon and Kellee, although by undisclosed means.

Yet, the sloppiness of the Secretary's financial reports[77] and further information revealed outside of the financial reporting process raised questions as to the completeness of Brown's reporting as well as whether he had taken sufficient steps to avoid a conflict of interest.

Media and Congressional Interest in Brown's Communications Holdings, 1993-94

In November 1993, Jerry Wright of the *Washington Post* reported a close link between First International Communications and Corridor Broadcasting Company.[78] As will be recalled, until December 15, 1993, Brown was a co-owner of First International with Nolanda Hill, a Washington executive who owns Corridor Broadcasting Company, which, at the time, operated WFTY-TV, Channel 50. (As of the start of 1993, Hill also served as one of two officers of Harmon International, which leased equipment to Channel 50.) First International and Corridor Broadcasting shared the same address, and appeared closely related. The *Washington Post* reported that the name on the office door and the office directory was Corridor, not First International, and that First International did not have a listed phone number. Yet a phone call the *Washington Post* placed to Corridor's number was answered, "First International."[79] Dun & Bradstreet even listed First International Communications, Incorporated, as the "tradename" for Corridor Broadcasting, Incorporated.[80] These facts suggest that the companies are alter egos of each other.

The apparently close relationship between First International and Corridor Broadcasting is significant in several respects. One is whether Secretary Brown would have obtained a waiver with respect to his interest in Harmon, which was based on the insubstantiality of his interest. It appears that Brown may have had a substantial interest in Channel 50, by virtue of his ownership of First International, if First International and Corridor were considered the same entity. Given the magnitude of Brown's ownership interest in First International, it is unlikely that he would have received a waiver for that interest. Moreover, the propriety of the Secretary's waiver with respect to telecommunications issues is called into question. The waiver request contains no mention of First International or Corridor Broadcasting. Had Brown disclosed Harmon's relationship with Corridor Broadcasting and Corridor's relationship with First International, it is less likely that a waiver based on insubstantiality would have been granted. A predicate for the granting of a waiver under 18 U.S.C. 208(b)(1) is that the requesting official "make full disclosure of the financial interest" for which a waiver is being sought.[81] It is not known whether additional information was provided to the White House in connection with the waiver request, but the written waiver request by itself does not constitute full disclosure.

Further, Corridor was reported in late 1993 to be in danger of losing its license from the Federal Communications Commission (FCC) as a result of a default in early 1993 on a $26 million loan from Sunbelt Savings and Loan. Yet, despite Corridor's precarious financial status, Corridor gave $63,825 in soft money contributions to the Democratic Party in 1991 and 1992, while Ron Brown was head of the Democratic National Committee.[82] The outstanding loan was taken over by the FDIC following Sunbelt's failure, which cost the taxpayers more than $2 billion. The FDIC sold the loan to private investors John and Barbara Foster for $3.1 million, who foreclosed on the note and sought FCC permission to take over Channel 50's license. The Fosters' corporation, Jasas Corporation, acquired Channel 50 on October 15, 1993, and received its license on November 30, 1993.[83] Thus, Corridor's default cost taxpayers more than $23 million, plus interest.[84]

Secretary Brown's attorney said that, "Any effort to link Secretary Brown to that matter would be a grossly unfair attempt at guilt by association."[85] In an effort to end criticism of his business associations with Hill, Brown sold his interest in First International, as noted above, reportedly in December 1993, although this fact was not revealed until the filing of his annual financial disclosure report in May 1994. Further revelations regarding Brown's dealings with Hill would not come to light until over a year after the initial *Washington Post* story.

In February 1994, Representative Clinger asked the Secretary to answer questions concerning his current holdings and business relationships in the "information and telecommunications sector."[86] These questions concerned Brown's interest in Harmon and First International, and his association with Nolanda Hill and Corridor Broadcasting. Clinger noted Secretary Brown's responsibility for the NTIA and International Trade Administration (ITA), two components of the Commerce Department, and his position as the Co-Chairman of the United States Advisory Council on the National Information Infrastructure. Clinger emphasized that he was "not alleging that a conflict of interest, or even the appearance of such, currently exists[,]" but that the Secretary's initial financial disclosure report did not provide sufficient information to make such a determination.

In a March 2, 1994 letter, Barbara Fredericks responded on behalf of the Secretary. Fredericks briefly recited the Secretary's financial interests in Harmon, First International, Albimar, and Kellee, and stated flatly that "the Secretary does not have nor has he ever had a financial interest in Corridor Communication."[87] She declined to respond to any questions regarding persons other than Brown, and noted that the Secretary's next financial disclosure report, due May 15, "will undoubtedly answer many of the questions which you raise." She said that the Secretary "prefers to take the time to collect all relevant financial information and provide it in as complete a form as possible and in the manner prescribed by law, rather than in a piecemeal fashion."[88] Clinger wrote the Secretary that Fredericks' letter was not responsive, asking Brown for a complete response to his original letter by April 1.[89]

This time Clinger's letter was answered by Fredrick's superior, General Counsel Ginger Lew. Lew enclosed Secretary Brown's May 1994 annual report, certified by her as fully complying with reporting and conflict-of-interest requirements.[90] She added, "This filing answers questions raised in your letter of March 23, 1994."

The May 1994 report disclosed Brown's sale of his interest in First International, a transaction reported with a few more details in the *Washington Post* in June.[91] Brown reported that he sold his interest for between $250,000 and $500,000, although he reported no capital gains income from the sale on Schedule A. This was curious, given that Brown reportedly did not invest any funds in First International. The *Post* stated that Brown's shares were "repurchased by the company," according to aides to the Secretary. At the time, Secretary Brown declined to discuss his relationship with Hill, or First International's business.[92]

Representative Clinger's staff then met with the Commerce Department's legal staff on June 28 in an effort to obtain answers to Clinger's many questions. Following that meeting, Clinger wrote the Secretary, posing those questions directly to Brown which Commerce ethics officials had said were outside the scope of the financial disclosure review process.[93] Soon thereafter, Lew responded to Lisa Kaufman of Clinger's staff, stating in pertinent part:

> None of the remaining questions you have raised concern information which the Secretary is required to provide as part of the financial disclosure process. Congress dictated, in the Ethics in Government Act and the Ethics Reform Act, what information is needed from public officials to determine potential conflicts of interest. . . . It is reasonable and appropriate for Federal officials, including the Secretary, to refrain from providing such additional information, particularly when the requested information concerns the activities and personal financial holdings of private citizens. A decision not to respond to such requests is in keeping with the spirit and intent of the financial disclosure system and the legitimate expectation of privacy by non-Government officials.[94]

Secretary Brown responded to Clinger in a similar fashion on September 7, 1994. The Secretary noted that Commerce ethics officials had assured him that his financial disclosure reports were "complete and disclose no potential conflict of interest." He implicitly declined to answer other questions that in his view went "well beyond the scope of financial disclosure requirements."[95] He added that, save his interest in Albimar, he no longer held interests in any of the communications entities about which Clinger had sought information.

Still not satisfied with these responses, Clinger wrote to the Department's Inspector General (IG) and to the Office of Government Ethics (OGE) on October 5, 1994. In his letter to the IG, Clinger requested an investigation to determine whether Brown's holdings during his service as Secretary posed any conflict of interest.[96] In his letter to OGE, Clinger requested that OGE "order action to correct deficiencies" in the Commerce Department's ethics programs, based on the ethics officials' alleged "failure to obtain the necessary information to satisfactorily review and analyze" Secretary Brown's financial holdings before certifying his financial reports.[97]

Clearly frustrated with his inability to get his questions answered, Clinger went to the floor of the House on October 7 to criticize the Secretary and the Department for their failure to respond to his inquiries.[98] Clinger cited Brown's continuing financial interest in Boston Bank of Commerce and his previous interest in First International as posing potential conflicts and raising questions that went unanswered despite several written requests of the Secretary and the Department. Clinger expressed concern over the unexplained omission of two holdings listed on the Secretary's nominee report, the apparent link between First International and Corridor Broadcasting, notwithstanding the statements by the Department to the contrary, and Brown's association with Nolanda Hill, who is an officer of Corridor, First International, and Harmon. Clinger indicated that he would ask for hearings in the next Congress.

The IG, the Office of Government Ethics, and Secretary Brown Respond

The IG responded to Clinger on December 21, stating that the information provided by Clinger was insufficient by itself to open up any conflict-of-interest investigation. The IG added that his office would not take any action until OGE completed its review of the Secretary's financial disclosure reports, at which time his office would decide whether there is any suggestion of a conflict of interest or "other violations warranting further investigation." [99]

A week after the IG's response, and three months after Clinger's letter, OGE responded.[100] OGE concluded that "Commerce's review and certification of Secretary Brown's SF 278s and the steps undertaken to help the Secretary avoid conflicts were appropriate and sufficient."[101] OGE confirmed that Brown's reports contained several incorrect statements and omissions, but stated that, according to Commerce ethics officials, the "inaccuracies were apparently the result of . . . oversight[s] by the Secretary or his private counsel."[102] OGE found these reporting errors harmless, in view of the Secretary's recusal commitment.

Responding to the disappearance, on Secretary Brown's annual report, of his holdings in Kellee and Harmon, OGE noted that these interests were divested in a way that was not required to be reported. OGE implied that these two holdings were disposed of by gift. After noting that ethics officials have discretion to (and are "encouraged to") ask the official to annotate a report to contain additional information needed to clarify an entry, OGE stated that such additional information is not public unless the employee consents or the information is deemed necessary to explain an entry. In a truly remarkable overstatement, OGE concluded:

> In the full context of this guidance, we believe that Commerce's ethics officials correctly decided not to annotate the annual SF 278 or to ask the Secretary to amend it with information about divestiture of his equity interests in Kellee and Harmon.[103]

If OGE intends the words of this sentence as they are written, it means that OGE would have faulted a decision by Commerce ethics officials merely to ask the Secretary to amend the report. This is nonsense. When substantial assets reported on one year's financial report disappear from the subsequent report, without a trace, questions undoubtedly arise as to the completeness of the official's disclosure, perhaps giving rise to suspicion that there is something to hide. Given Secretary Brown's high-level position and Representative Clinger's interest, it would have well-behooved the Secretary or Commerce ethics officials to add a simple annotation that these two interests were disposed of in a manner that does not require their reporting. (Of course, it would have been even more preferable for Brown to explain how the assets were disposed of.) That would not have satisfied Clinger's curiosity—indeed, it would have piqued it—but without **any** explanation of what happened to Harmon and Kellee, the Secretary invited suspicion, not just curiosity. If OGE did not want to fault the Commerce ethics office, it could have concluded that it was not an abuse of discretion not to ask the Secretary to provide additional information. To call "correct," as did OGE, the failure even to ask Brown if he would consent to an annotation, especially in the context described above, is flat wrong.

Another statement in OGE's letter seems odd. OGE praised Brown for taking what it called the "more extreme step of divestiture."[104] Potential conflicts are remedied through recusal, waiver, or divestiture. Calling divestiture, a standard way to resolve a conflict, "extreme" is an exaggeration. But calling divestiture "more extreme" means that one or both of these other remedies are just plain "extreme," which is just plain wrong. There is nothing "extreme" about recusal or waiver. The tone of OGE's letter seems excessively protective of the Commerce ethics office, if not the Secretary.[105]

Secretary Brown followed OGE's letter with a letter of his own to Representative Clinger. The Secretary recited the many steps he took upon confirmation to fully disclose his holdings, to recuse himself and to dispose of several interests, even though some of these steps were not required.[106] He also explained that First International's business did not pose a conflict with his official responsibilities during the period he retained an interest. As OGE did in its letter to Clinger, Secretary Brown explained with a greater degree of specificity what First International did. A memorandum submitted to Commerce ethics officials by Brown's private counsel **in December 1992** noted activities pursuing investments in Eastern Europe, such as residential and commercial real estate, RF Transmissions leasing, and residential realty in Texas. In early 1993, First International's business was "limited to participation in business ventures involved in selling Eastern European poster art and porcelain, product development in Hispanic markets in the United States, and commercial paper transactions."[107] About this time First International also shed "Communications" from its title.

Secretary Brown then stated that he divested his interest in First International in December 1993, "[a]lthough no conflict existed," because of "unwarranted and unfair press inquiries concerning a private company in which I have had no involvement in either its management or operations since becoming Secretary of Commerce, other than my fully disclosed equity interest." What is noteworthy is that Brown explained that he divested his interest at Hill's request not on his own.[108]

Additional Allegations of Unethical or Improper Conduct are Reported, 1995

In January 1995, just over a week after the Secretary's letter to Clinger, the *Washington Post* reported that Nolanda Hill, Brown's business partner in First International, had assumed responsibility to pay some of Brown's personal debts as a manner of buying out his interest in First International.[109] Hill's attorney confirmed that this arrangement was part of the December 15, 1993 transaction whereby Brown divested himself of his interest. The *Washington Post* reported that Hill paid $190,000 **in 1994** to pay off Brown's creditors on mortgages on two vacation properties, lines of credit at two banks, and even some of Reid Weingarten's legal bills.

Weingarten explained that Hill's payments were based on First International's "ongoing activities and potential[.]" George Terwilliger, Hill's attorney, said, "Any suggestion that this was anything less than an arm's length, market value transaction would be unfair to both of them[.]"[110]

Yet if this transaction was so unremarkable, why were the payments laundered twice, once from First International to other companies owned or managed by Hill, including Jasas Corporation (the company that bought Channel 50 through an FDIC foreclosure proceeding), and once from these companies to Harry Barnett, Hill's Boston lawyer?

The tortuous trail of just one of these payments shows why Secretary Brown's finances look so suspicious. As a senior Jasas official, Nolanda Hill caused a $72,000 check to be written to the Polish American Trade and Services Association (PATSA), a Virginia company co-owned by First International (!) and Kristina Stachowiak, a Polish national. Two days later, PATSA wrote a $71,500 check to Barnett. The money was apparently used "immediately to repay some of Mr. Brown's debts."[111]

Hill's attorney said as far as he knew, Jasas was not responsible for paying Brown's debts, and Jasas owners John and Barbara Foster said they knew nothing of the payments. Although Hill was a Jasas management official, she was not an officer (according to FCC reports) and presumably would not have had authority to cause a check of this magnitude to be issued without the knowledge of either of the Fosters.[112]

Moreover, Secretary Brown's May 1994 financial disclosure report should have reported, but did not report, First International's (or Nolanda Hill's) obligation to Brown as an asset (accounts or funds receivable) on Schedule A, if this obligation arose in December 1993 as asserted. Recall that Secretary Brown also did not report any income from the sale of First International on Schedule A, even though he never put any money into the company.

The *Washington Post* article raised many more questions than it answered, but the Secretary, responding to questions about the *Post* story on his debts and the contemporaneous *U.S. News and World Report* story on his town house, stated, "[A] careful reading of the stories would clearly demonstrate that they are much ado about nothing."[113] When asked about the accuracy of the stories, he answered, "There is nothing wrong with whatever has been purported to be the truth in the stories that I've read. . . . I haven't read anything in the stories that is troubling, if that's what you mean."[114]

These two stories prompted renewed interest on Capitol Hill. Senator Larry Pressler wrote the Secretary requesting a "detailed response" to the financial dealings described in the press. Senator Lauch Faircloth asked the FDIC to explain its efforts to collect the millions of dollars lost when Corridor Broadcasting defaulted on its loan from Sunbelt, noting reports that Nolanda Hill made several substantial expenditures while Corridor was in default.[115]

FDIC Chairman Ricki Tigert Helfer promptly responded the next day to Faircloth. She wrote that the "FDIC's legal rights of recovery with regard to the loan were no greater than those of the original lender." An attached case summary continued:

> Corridor Broadcasting was liable as the borrower on the loan; other security on the loan was the stock of Corridor Broadcasting and the stock of all the subsidiaries of Corridor. . . . The borrower and its subsidiaries had no other assets than the TV stations [Corridor also owned Channel 27, WHLL in Worcester, Mass.] and their FCC licenses. There were no personal guarantors of the debt. Since Ms. Nolanda Hill was not personally liable for the loan, the FDIC had no ability to pursue any recovery against her or any other individual. The only available sources of recovery on the debt were the TV stations and their licenses.[116]

Senator Faircloth returned to the FDIC, asking for an investigation of whether Corridor's assets were "drained fraudulently or recklessly, while the loan was in default, by Ms. Hill, to benefit her personally, or other entities which she controlled or was affiliated with." He asked whether FDIC would have any remedies to recover these assets, and for a referral to Justice if fraudulent activity is suggested.[117]

On January 23, 1995, Representative Clinger, now Chairman of the House Committee on Government Reform and Oversight, wrote letters to the Secretary and FDIC Chairman Helfer. His letter to the Secretary accused him of failing to report income received in 1993 from "First International Communications Limited Partnership," an entity ostensibly different from First International Communications Corporation (from which the Secretary also reported receiving no income in 1993). Further, Clinger determined that the "primary source of income" for First International Communications, Inc. was a promissory note payable by Corridor Broadcasting! Because this financial link "seems contrary to" Secretary Brown's previous representation that there was no business relationship between Corridor and First International, Clinger asked for a complete explanation regarding the promissory note and how it became a source of revenue for First International.[118]

In Clinger's letter to the FDIC, he joined Faircloth's request and noted the following information obtained by his staff. Hill and Corridor had "extensive business dealings" with John Foster, majority owner of Jasas, before the FDIC's sale of the Sunbelt loan to Jasas. Hill also may have held an interest in Jasas after the loan was sold to Jasas, in that Jasas provided a portion of the money Hill used to purchase (or "redeem") Brown's interest in First International. Finally, Clinger stated that several thousand shares of Corridor stock were not included in the foreclosure sale, even though the stock had been pledged as security on the loan. Clinger concluded that the information suggested that Hill's relationship with Foster was "not appropriately distanced to meet the FDIC regulations governing this transaction" and that Foster "may have acted to protect" collateralized Corridor stock for Hill's benefit.

Brown's (and Hill's) defenders were caught off guard. Before Clinger's letters, Secretary Brown's press secretary said, "First International had absolutely nothing, nothing, nothing to do with Corridor Broadcasting." After Clinger's letters, Commerce ethics official Barbara Fredericks acknowledged that she did not know of the promissory note:

> Ms. Fredericks said that she had tried in the past to learn from Mr. Brown and his associates whether there was any link between First International and Corridor Broadcasting, but that nobody ever told her about the note.[119]

In 1992 and 1993, after defaulting on its FDIC loan, Corridor reportedly continued making interest payments of about $12,000 per month on the $875,000 note to First International.[120] This was apparently the only "significant source of income" to First International.[121] Another loan to Corridor, from Sandia Federal Savings Association for around $20 million, was written off by the Resolution Trust Corporation (RTC) as a complete loss in 1993. Hill's attorney explained that First International's note had priority over the FDIC and RTC loans. Secretary Brown's attorney maintained that the Secretary was unaware of any financial link between First International and Corridor.

On January 23, 1995, fourteen Republican Senators wrote the Attorney General about the financial transactions of First International and Corridor Broadcasting.[122] They stated, "There is evidence that in this financial relationship [Brown] may have filed inaccurate financial disclosure statements or engaged in tax avoidance. . . .

Given this information, we are inquiring as to what steps, if any, you are planning to take to determine if Mr. Brown has fully complied with the law in these circumstances." But, they did not request appointment of an independent counsel.[123]

The next day, the Justice Department agreed to review the allegations in the Senators' letter, and FDIC Chairman Hefler directed the FDIC's IG to conduct an investigation into Corridor's default. The Justice review would be conducted by the Public Integrity Section, but would not be done under the time constraints of the independent counsel law. Helfer asked for a report in sixty days. Secretary Brown wrote letters to Senator Pressler and Representative Clinger, defending his conduct and denying any impropriety.[124] Brown reiterated that he never had any interest in Corridor Broadcasting, and stated that he was not aware of the promissory note. He added that, as Secretary, he has not "acted in a matter in which Corridor is a party and no such matter was ever presented to me. Therefore, there could have been no conflict of interest with regard to Corridor."[125] He concluded that the remedial steps he took upon confirmation and afterward to avoid conflicts "have had the practical impact of assuring that I have avoided conflicts or appearances of conflict," citing OGE's December 29, 1994 letter.

As discussed above, however, OGE's letter did not discuss many of the allegations that surfaced for the first time in January 1995. Moreover, the conflict-of-interest statute extends to all particular matters having a direct and predictable effect on Corridor, regardless of whether Corridor is a "party" to such matter.

On January 26th, Clinger made public copies of three $45,000 checks to Ron Brown, dated April, July, and October 1993, from First International Communications Limited Partnership.[126] Two of the checks bear the notation, "Partnership Distribution."[127] Clinger wrote Secretary Brown a strongly worded letter expressing his displeasure at the Secretary's alleged unresponsiveness.[128] Clinger alleged that Secretary Brown failed to report these checks as income on his May 1994 financial disclosure report. According to the Secretary's attorney, the $135,000 paid by October 1993 was part of the proceeds of the **December 15, 1993** sale of Brown's interest in First International Communications Corporation![129] While Clinger directed his staff to continue its investigation, he said that it was too premature to hold or schedule hearings, or to request the appointment of an independent counsel, saying that he was not yet prepared to hold hearings and did not want to interfere with the House's top priority, consideration of the Contract With America.[130]

The next set of stories focused on a $78,000 loan to Brown from KNOW, Incorporated, which was forgiven as part of the proceeds from the sale of Brown's interest in First International.[131] The Secretary reported a promissory note to KNOW, Incorporated as a liability on both his financial disclosure reports.[132] This loan was originally received for $87,000 in 1989 from the National Bank of Washington. Brown put up his stock in Albimar as collateral. The loan was taken over by the FDIC after National Bank's failure in 1990. The FDIC then sold the loan to Finleasco, a Connecticut satellite equipment leasing company, under unusual circumstances. Finleasco President Val Boelcskevy said that Nolanda Hill's former husband, Billy Hill, Jr., Boelcskevy's friend and lawyer, suggested that he buy Brown's loan as an investment. Finleasco did just that, in August 1990, buying the loan from the FDIC for $72,032.89. It was the only time Finleasco has ever bought an FDIC loan. FDIC rules require the borrower to agree to the transfer of the loan, but FDIC files apparently do not reveal whether Brown assented.[133]

A year later, Finleasco traded the loan to Hill with $82,000 in cash to settle a $150,000 debt to a trust fund "controlled by Hill."[134] The loan then was transferred from the trust fund to KNOW, Incorporated. The remaining balance on the loan of $78,000 was eventually forgiven by KNOW as part of First International's payments to Brown.[135] FDIC regulations prohibit borrowers in default, such as Hill, or anyone else acting on behalf of such borrower, from buying FDIC loans.[136] The FDIC stated that it would look into the loan to see if it should be included in the scope of the IG's investigation.

Summing up the picture as it emerged at the end of January 1995: Secretary Brown reported that he sold his interest in First International, Inc., on December 15, 1993, **yet all the consideration he received for the sale was exchanged before and after December 15.** Brown received (1) $135,000 in three checks from First International Limited Partnership in 1993, months before December 15; (2) forgiveness of a $78,000 loan from KNOW, Incorporated, a company controlled by Nolanda Hill in January 1994; and (3) payment in June, July, and August 1994 of $190,000 by other companies, such as Jasas Corp., owned or controlled in some way by Hill, covering other of Brown's personal debts. Brown received a benefit of at least $400,000, on an investment into which he said he put no money, but which he valued to be over $500,000 (his single largest asset) on his first financial report. The *Washington Post* summarized the "heart of the inquiry," according to Republicans:

> How did Brown reap more than $400,000 from the sale of his stake in a company that never had any successful business ventures, in which he says he invested no money, and that he had nothing to do with operating?[137]

At the beginning of February 1995, Secretary Brown faced calls for his resignation from twenty-two House Republicans (notably not including Representative Clinger), who wrote to the President that the ethical cloud over the Secretary was harming the Administration and had eroded "the public's confidence" in the Secretary.[138] Yet the media was ambivalent. News stories sometimes would receive front page treatment, and other times they were buried in the business section. Indeed, the editorial pages of the *Washington Post* and *New York Times* remained silent throughout, while regularly writing about Speaker Gingrich's book deal and GOPAC.

The pace of negative stories continued with a lengthy, page one report in the *Los Angeles Times* concerning Brown's holding in Kellee Communications.[139] It will be recalled that until confirmation, Brown was on Kellee's Board of Directors. Brown also held an ownership interest in Kellee between $15,000 and $50,000. In his January 1993 disqualification statement, Secretary Brown pledged to divest his interest in Kellee and recuse himself from matters specially and differentially affecting Kellee for one additional year. Because the Secretary did not list Kellee on his May 1994 financial report, either as an asset or as a transaction, it was not clear what, if anything, he did with his holding. OGE's response to Clinger in December 1994 hinted that Brown disposed of his interest in Kellee by gift. The *Times* confirmed that Brown disposed of his stock by a gift to his son, but details of Brown's divestment remained unclear.[140]

The *Times* explained that most of Kellee's income came from its participation in a joint venture with AT&T to install pay phones at Los Angeles International Airport

(LAX), at a time when Secretary Brown was successfully promoting AT&T abroad (and requesting the President's assistance in also promoting AT&T) to obtain a $4 billion contract to install a phone system in Saudi Arabia. (Kellee's business is limited to the U.S.) The *Times* mentioned a few other matters in which Secretary Brown participated for the benefit of AT&T. AT&T reportedly approached Kellee in 1989 in an effort to win the LAX contract, because participation of minority firms was an important factor in the award of municipal contracts. In attempting to get the contact, James Kelly, a part-owner of Kellee, "punctuated his conversations with references to Brown" and other well-known minorities on Kellee's Board. Brown had purchased a modest stake in Kellee five days before the joint venture applied for the LAX contact. The AT&T joint venture at LAX, and subsequent joint ventures at other airports, significantly increased Kellee's revenues, from $200,000 in 1987 to $2.4 million in 1992.[141]

Secretary Brown's first financial disclosure report reported Kellee's contract to install phones at LAX; it did not, however, disclose that this contract was part of a joint venture with AT&T. And because Brown's financial report did not reveal any interest in or connection with AT&T, the Secretary did not recuse himself from AT&T, much less matters involving the telecommunications industry. Although a senior OGE official, Deputy Director Donald Campbell, said that the Secretary should have revealed this link to Commerce ethics officials, Commerce ethics official Fredericks disagreed.[142]

Secretary Brown was not required to report Kellee's financial deal with AT&T on his financial report. Also, Fredericks is correct that the standards of conduct are not clear on whether an employee is considered to have a financial interest in a company solely by its participation in a joint venture with a company in which the employee holds stock. The list of interests that are imputed to an official as if the official held them outright does not include entities doing business with companies in which the official holds stock.[143] A closer question would arise if Kellee were, in fact, a subsidiary of AT&T.

However, there is a clear appearance problem here. Brown's interest was given to his son, not quite an arm's length transaction, even if his adult son's interests are not imputed to the Secretary under 18 U.S.C. 208. His pledge to recuse himself from matters involving Kellee for a year after divestiture was a recognition of this appearance. It is likely that Brown knew of Kellee's business with AT&T at LAX and perhaps other airports. If he also knew, as he should have known, that Kellee's dramatic increase in revenue was primarily the result of its partnership with AT&T, Secretary Brown should have availed himself of the process provided in section 502 of the standards of conduct and sought advice from ethics officials as to whether he should participate in the AT&T matters. Section 502, dealing with personal and business relationships, does not expressly cover this situation, and in any event does not require recusal. But, as noted in other contexts in this study, it contains a residual provision designed to assist officials in situations just like this.

The general principle of appearances in the standards of conduct provides that employees "shall endeavor to avoid any actions creating the appearance that they are violating the law or the ethical standards[.]"[144] In addition to the general conflict-of-interest provision, the ethical standard potentially implicated by these facts is section 702, which prohibits an employee from using his public office for the private gain of relatives, among others.

Once again, a story about Secretary Brown's finances involved neither a clear conflict of interest under the laws and regulations, nor a clear failure to report. And once again, the Secretary's attorney denigrated the story, this time calling "silly" the notion that Brown's "efforts on behalf of AT&T were influenced in any way" by his son's holdings in Kellee.[145] But as the *Los Angeles Times* put it, "by refusing to answer questions about his affairs and by insisting on secrecy and limited disclosure, Brown has added fuel to the controversy." Representative Clinger, in fact, had asked the Secretary back in February 1994 for information about Kellee, which information was never furnished. In Secretary Brown's case, what was not known about his financial interests exacerbated the appearance caused by what was known.

Soon after the Kellee story appeared, attention shifted back to Nolanda Hill. It was reported that Hill had written the Secretary's office in May 1993, on First International letterhead, describing efforts to arrange a meeting between Commerce officials and Jasas owner John Foster while all were in Russia.[146] Commerce officials said no meeting was ever arranged and that Secretary Brown has not done anything to assist Foster. The addressee of the memorandum, an executive assistant to Brown, did not recall seeing it. Clearly, even if Brown held no interest in Jasas and had no other affiliation with Foster, it would have been contrary to the Secretary's recusal, if not a violation of section 208, for him to have taken any action on Hill's memorandum.

The Justice Department, FDIC and RTC Conduct Investigations

On February 6, 1995, the Justice Department responded to the January 23 letter from fourteen Republican Senators, informing them that Justice would begin a review under the independent counsel statute to determine whether to conduct a preliminary investigation.[147] The Justice Department letter was not clear whether the review would be limited to allegations contained in the news articles referred to in the Senators' letter, or would also include other and subsequent stories.[148]

On February 8, Senate Banking Committee Chairman Alfonse D'Amato sent document requests to the FDIC and RTC concerning Nolanda Hill, Sunbelt Savings, Corridor, First International (both Communications Corporation and Partnership), Jasas, National Bank of Washington, and KNOW, Incorporated.[149]

With both the Executive (Justice Department, FDIC, RTC) and Legislative (House Government Reform and Oversight, and Senate Banking Committees) Branches now scrutinizing Brown's conduct, it looked as if another battle over parallel proceedings might be waged. The *Wall Street Journal* weighed in first, arguing against the appointment of an independent counsel, who would "dig through this mess until the turn of the century." Instead:

We'd prefer Congressional hearings sometime after the GOP completes work on its Contract With America. A full airing would let the public judge what the facts mean. Let's clear up this matter before the next election.[150]

Well within the thirty days provided by the independent counsel law, Attorney General Reno determined on February 15, 1995, to conduct a preliminary investigation into whether an independent counsel should be appointed, and so notified the court of appeals.[151] The *New York Times* reported that the preliminary investigation would look into whether Brown violated "tax or financial disclosure laws and whether he was paid money by people seeking to influence the Commerce Department."[152] Under the law, the Attorney General had ninety days, or until May 17, 1995, to determine whether to request the appointment of an independent counsel.

Around this time, the *New York Times* and *Washington Post* published their first editorial concerning Ron Brown's financial reports and activities. The *New York Times* criticized Secretary Brown and the Commerce Department for giving Representative Clinger "inaccurate, incomplete and misleading answers[,]" and noted the various questions that require further investigation, criticizing the Secretary's response to date to these questions. The *New York Times* urged the President to "mak[e] an independent, public judgment about Mr. Brown's dealings. This, after all, is the Administration that came to town promising that it would not tolerate smelly deals."[153] The *Washington Post* followed a few days later with a mild editorial. Noting the contention of Brown's attorney that the Justice Department will conclude that the Secretary did not violate any law, the *Post* wrote sympathetically, "It will be terrible news if the investigation concludes otherwise." Viewing the ethical cloud over Brown with "dismay," the *Post* nonetheless wondered "how much of this has Mr. Brown brought on himself?" The *Post* limited its criticism of the Secretary to his failure to have provided "a fully documented public record to back up [Brown's] assertion" of his innocence.[154]

In the wake of the Justice Department inquiry, the President proclaimed his continued support of the Secretary:

> He's the best Commerce Secretary we've ever had. And he's gotten more results. That ought to be the test. He's a good Commerce Secretary. The questions that have been raised about what happened before he became Commerce Secretary are being looked into in an appropriate fashion. And meanwhile, he's on the job, and I'm supporting him in that.
>
> No Commerce Secretary has ever done more than he has to create jobs for Americans and to support the interest of American business. And that is the test. And he should go forward and do his job. That's what I want him to do.[155]

Once again, the President discounted the significance of reports of misconduct by pointing out that they allegedly occurred before the start of his Administration. This dichotomy between public and private corruption, which has also been an important part of the President's public defense against allegations relating to Whitewater, the reported misuse of State troopers, and Paula Jones, may have some merit. But with respect to the allegations against Ron Brown, the President's account does not comport with the facts. The allegations against the Secretary focus on financial disclosure reports the Secretary was required to file because of his government position. The allegations include the deal, reportedly made in 1993, to sell his interest in First International. The allegations include reports of Nolanda Hill's access to the Clinton White House, and her effort to get Ron Brown's Commerce Department to arrange a meeting with Jasas owner John Foster.

If the President defended the Secretary by relying on the presumption of innocence, he did so only indirectly, by noting the pendency of "appropriate" investigations. However, what the President clearly implied—that a public official's contributions, performance, and worth to the Government may trump serious unethical conduct by that official—is very troubling as a general principle. Although it may fit into the President's own effort to mitigate the damage caused by the pending Whitewater probe, it is dramatically at odds with the principle that government officials, in order both to function effectively and to maintain the trust and confidence of the public, should remain free of ethical scandal, whether from conduct on the job or from activities before joining the Government that are disclosed post-confirmation.

Ron Brown also defended himself publicly, telling a House Appropriations Subcommittee, "I am absolutely confident that in the outcome, there has been no improper activity, impropriety on my part."[156]

On February 27, 1995, Chairman Clinger requested the appointment of an independent counsel in a letter to Attorney General Reno.[157] Clinger attached a nineteen-page appendix of the allegations against the Secretary, and the factual basis for each of the allegations, which fell into five categories: (1) violations of financial disclosure reporting requirements; (2) illegal supplementation of salary;[158] (3) potential conflicts of interest; (4) misinformation to Congress; and (5) refusing to respond to Congress. Clinger complained to the Attorney General that "for over a year, in response to direct questions posed to the Secretary, I have received inaccurate, incomplete, and misleading responses, or no response at all." Clinger pledged to supply the Justice Department with copies of all relevant documents in the Committee's possession supporting the allegations. Clinger also indicated that he would continue the Committee's investigation, but would not hold hearings at the present time.

Outside of the letter, Clinger told reporters that the Secretary's financial dealings are "very, very complex and diverse," involving "an incredibly complicated series of transactions and undertakings." Citing the need for "a variety of investigative specialists," he said that an independent counsel would be better equipped than a congressional committee. But Clinger added that if the Attorney General declined to request an independent counsel, he would hold hearings.[159] Senator Faircloth said that "hearings are inevitable," adding that the appointment of an independent counsel "will not affect the Senate's decision on hearings one way or the other." The Secretary's lawyer labeled Clinger's letter "a partisan effort to prematurely influence Justice's investigation. . . . We're in the midst of one of those Washington media frenzies and Secretary Brown is on the receiving end."[160]

It was reported in March 1995 that both the FDIC and RTC were conducting investigations in connection with three loans made by now-defunct savings and loans to Corridor and other Nolanda Hill-owned companies.[161] The FDIC received $3 million on a $26 million loan to Corridor from Sunbelt Savings and Loan; the RTC wrote off as a total loss about $20 million in loans from Sandia Federal Savings Association of Albuquerque and from Bluebonnet Savings & Loan. The civil investigations would look into whether Hill illegally diverted money from Corridor: in particular, whether Hill "violated loan agreements that required Corridor's debts held by the government to be paid ahead of other creditors and defrauded lenders by using money lent to Corridor for other purposes."[162] Both probes are aimed at holding Hill personally liable for the debts of Corridor and affiliated companies, because the companies are without any assets.

The protracted, complicated, and ever-evolving nature of the controversy surrounding Secretary Brown's financial interests and his financial dealings was the focus of several lengthy profile features on Ron Brown and Nolanda Hill in February and March 1995. The articles served to provide some context in which to understand and evaluate the business relationship between Brown and Hill, and others.[163]

Additional Allegations of Unethical or Improper Conduct are Reported
While the Justice Department was conducting its preliminary investigation, more reports surfaced in the period of February to April 1995 that raised additional questions about Brown's business dealings, especially with Nolanda Hill. Some raised questions of propriety and legality. Others simply provided accounts of how Brown was able to use his talents, positions, and contacts to gain business and income.

First, the *Washington Post* and *Business Week* reported on efforts Brown and Hill made in the early 1990s, before Brown became Secretary, to buy oil from the governments of Angola and Saudi Arabia, and to engage in other business ventures in Europe, including a plan to convert surplus wine into fuel that would be eligible for Federal subsidies.[164] The Angolan oil venture and the other ventures were unsuccessful. In contrast with other stories, no violation of law was alleged.[165] The story reinforced the close working relationship between Hill and Brown,[166] in particular by showing Brown's personal involvement in First International's business, and it shed light into Brown's use of his Chairmanship of the Democratic National Committee to advance his personal financial interests.[167] The only apparent link to the Commerce Department was that the Secretary later appointed the two Hill & Knowlton lobbyists who helped arrange the meeting in Angola to positions at the Department.[168]

Second, *U.S. News and World Report* reported that Clinger's investigation also covered payments Corridor Broadcasting made to Brown's daughter, Tracey, and his daughter-in-law, Tamara.[169] The article also reported that Corridor sent James Hackney a $15,000 check on January 19, 1993, two days before he joined Secretary Brown's staff as a counselor. It was unclear whether the payment was a loan or compensation for services, or both, but Hackney did not report the money on his financial disclosure report. Hackney's attorney, John Payton, said the money went to Hackney's investment firm, in order to assist Corridor in refinancing a loan. "Within days, their agreement fell through. Payton says the funds were returned to Corridor—but not until late 1994."

Third, the *New York Times* reported the Democratic National Committee's payment of $75,000 to Columbia Productions, a company owned by Nolanda Hill, for a video tribute to Ron Brown's chairmanship of the DNC shown during the 1992 Democratic Convention.[170] Corridor produced the video, although Columbia, not Corridor, received payment. The video shows Ron Brown walking down the street in front of his law office (across the street from First International/Corridor) with Ken White, Vice President of Corridor. A Commerce Department spokeswoman said that Brown had no role in the selection of Columbia, although the DNC spokesman did not know. DNC rules at the time required contracts to be awarded to the most qualified firms, but did not prohibit a contract award to business partners of DNC officials.

Fourth, the *Washington Post* examined Brown's role in Capital/PEBSCO, a company he founded in 1984 in partnership with the Ohio-based Public Employees Benefit Services Corp. (PEBSCO), for which Brown had and was continuing to provide consulting services.[171] Capital/PEBSCO ran the District of Columbia's deferred compensation program under a contract with the City. Again, the story noted that "[t]here is no indication of anything improper in Brown's relationship with PEBSCO and the District." Prompted by questions from Republican Senators at his confirmation hearing, Brown agreed to sell his interest in Capital/PEBSCO. On his first financial disclosure report, Secretary Brown reported receiving in 1992 between $50,000 and $100,000 in income from Capital/PEBSCO and another estimated $40,000 from PEBSCO in "brokerage fees" concerning other cities' programs. Capital/ PEBSCO's 1992 commissions, which were made on investments chosen by District employees, amounted to $978,000. This was a $500,000 reduction from the amount of commissions the firm received in 1991. When Capital/PEBSCO won renewal of its contract with the District of Columbia (amid charges of political favoritism), it agreed to cap commissions at $978,000.

Fifth, the *Los Angeles Times* reported in April 1995 that on both of Secretary Brown's first two financial disclosure reports, he:

> has effectively concealed his personal investment in a trouble-plagued, low-income apartment complex that is part of the rental empire of a Los Angeles businessman whom federal officials consider a notorious slumlord.[172]

Secretary Brown reported the investment as "Potomac Housing Fund Ltd. Partnership - 881 Alma Real Dr., Suite 212, Pacific Palisades 90272[;] Residential Property located in Maryland (Potomac MD)[.]" The *Los Angeles Times* reported that the property, known as Belle Haven Apartments, is actually located in Landover, Maryland, in Prince George's County, on the other side of Washington, D.C. and "one of the area's poorer communities." Potomac, in Montgomery County, is among the nation's most affluent communities.

Secretary Brown is a limited partner. According to his Commerce Department press secretary, Brown is only a "passive investor" and "has no knowledge of [Belle Haven's] whereabouts." "As a limited partner, Secretary Brown does not now nor has he ever had any management or operating responsibilities." But as an investor, he would have been provided documents at the time of his investment in 1983 describing the property.

Brown's investment was made primarily to obtain tax write-offs under a Federal law that permitted investors to deduct the full amount of losses or depreciation from taxable income, even if the deduction exceeded the entire investment. Stephen D. Moses, the organizer of the investment, estimated that Brown obtained about $175,000 in deductions (over a ten-year period) from his 3% investment of $71,000.[172] Secretary Brown's lawyer explained to the *Times* that it was "'a typical 1980s investment'" in which a small investment promised a high rate of return. 'Everybody was doing it[.]'"

While Brown and other investors were benefiting financially, the apartment complex was in disrepair and run down; several units were found unfit for human habitation. The Los Angeles businessman is A. Brent Rozet, who was associated with Moses and whose firm bought the property's management company some years after Brown's initial investment. Both Moses and Rozet were large contributors to the DNC while Ron Brown was Chairman.

Rozet blamed the general partner, Wayne Bowie, for the property's dilapidated condition. Belle Haven owed more than $5 million to the Maryland Housing Fund from an original $6.2 million loan to buy and refurbish the development; payments stopped in 1992. In June 1995, Governor Parris Glendening said that the State would foreclose on the loan, because the State was "unable to determine a way for the owner to meet his obligations."[174] Upon foreclosure, Brown and other limited partners would be required to repay to the IRS some of the money deducted for depreciation, although they would not be liable for the loan.

For the *Times*, the significance of the misrepresentation of the property's location is that Secretary Brown was "no doubt spared . . . embarrassing questions during his confirmation hearings." The Secretary explained to the *Washington Post* that "the location was inadvertently listed as Potomac rather than Landover, Md., since the name of the fund is the Potomac Housing Fund."[175] But was the mistake inadvertent?

The Secretary's defenders pointed out that the K-1 tax reports Brown has received each year do not specify Belle Haven's location. On the other hand, the two businessmen who were in charge of the investment told the *Los Angeles Times* that Brown was told of its location. It also turns out that Patton, Boggs & Blow, Brown's law firm at the time, defended Rozet from efforts by HUD to block Rozet from acquiring additional low-income residential units, but Rozet denied that Brown personally was involved in representing him. Rozet settled with HUD, agreeing not to acquire any more HUD-subsidized low-income housing until August 1995 and to sell extant properties. Belle Haven was financed with assistance from the State of Maryland, not HUD.

The three angles pursued by the *Los Angeles Times* were: the Secretary's errors on his financial disclosure report; Brown's profiting off of a slum housing project;[176] and Brown's association, through this investment and his former position as head of the DNC, with a businessman who has been criticized for abuses by HUD Secretary Cisneros as well as by senior HUD officials in the Bush Administration.

Secretary Brown was required to report and "briefly describe" his investments in property.[177] For limited partnership and other ownership interests in real property, the name of the entity and the general location of the property must be listed to guard against possible conflicts. But how specific the description of the property's location need be is not provided in the regulations. For example, had Secretary Brown reported the property as located in the Maryland suburbs of Washington, D.C., it is likely that his report would have been found adequate, although a conscientious ethics official for an agency with regulatory or financial assistance responsibilities with respect to such properties would have inquired further and probably would have amended the report to describe the specific location.

Regardless of whether he was required to describe Belle Haven's specific location under the financial disclosure regulations, the secretary was under an obligation to report truthfully and accurately any information that he did report. Willful false statements on a financial disclosure report, whether or not the information was required to be reported, may be prosecuted as a felony under 18 U.S.C. 1001. Later in the week, it was reported that the Justice Department would include the reports of Brown's misrepresentation of the property's location as part of its preliminary investigation.[178]

On May 1, 1995, Senator Faircloth wrote letters to Maryland Governor Parris Glendening and Prince George's County Executive Wayne Curry, requesting all records relating to the management, financing, ownership, maintenance and inspections of the Belle Haven property.[179] Faircloth noted that his Subcommittee on the Department of Housing and Urban Development Oversight Structure would look into whether:

> investors [should] be receiving tax benefits if they maintain a property that is unfit for human habitation and is repeatedly cited for housing code violations? Furthermore, what is the liability for investors that borrow state funds and then default?[180]

Governor Glendening responded the nextmonth, acknowledging that upon foreclosure, limited partners such as Brown would be liable for repayment of taxes.[181]

Attorney General Requests the Appointment of an Independent Counsel

On May 16, 1995, Attorney General Reno requested the appointment of an independent counsel to investigate whether Brown committed any violation of Federal criminal law:

> (i) in connection with his acceptance of things of value from Nolanda Hill and/ or First International, inc. (First International); (ii) in connection with the financial disclosure reports he filed; or (iii) in connection with his application for a mortgage to finance the purchase of a townhouse in January 1993.[182]

The Attorney General also requested the independent counsel's charter to include an investigation of possible violations of Federal criminal law by Nolanda Hill or her companies. This was because the issues involving Brown and First International are "inextricably intertwined with questions about more than one of the entities that Hill formed, owned, or managed[.]"[183]

The Justice Department's preliminary investigation confirmed that Brown invested no money in First International, and that he received things of value worth nearly $500,000 while Secretary of Commerce. The Attorney General also stated that Brown sold his interest back to First International in December 1993, although this date is highly suspect. Allegations challenging the valuation of First International and linking the payments to Brown's official position could not be resolved, given the "number of witnesses [who] have declined to cooperate fully" and the limitations on the type of investigation Justice can conduct under the independent counsel law.[184]

The Justice Department's investigation also confirmed that Secretary Brown made errors of commission and omission on his financial disclosure reports. The Attorney General noted that "there is evidence tending to suggest" an absence of criminal intent, but that evidence was not "clear and convincing."[185]

The investigation also turned up evidence that Brown may have "signed an inaccurate application" for the mortgage on the town house, which, if material to the lender's decision regarding the mortgage, could violate 18 U.S.C. 1014 (The Attorney General did not refer to the other potentially applicable false statement provisions, 18 U.S.C. 1001,1010).

The Attorney General, however, did not refer other allegations included in Clinger's referral, all of them suggesting a potential violation of 18 U.S.C. 208, because there was "no factual basis to support" these allegations.[186] She found that Secretary Brown "was not personally or substantially involved" in the decision to invite the

Chairman and CEO of Digital, a company in which one of Brown's Boston Bank of Commerce partners held an interest, to a Commerce Department trade mission. Regarding Kellee Communications' joint venture with AT&T, she found that Secretary Brown's assisting AT&T obtain a contract from Saudi Arabia was not connected to Kellee's "enhanced business" either directly or indirectly. Finally, the Attorney General found that Secretary Brown "had no involvement in or influence over" invitations Nolanda Hill received to attend two White House functions. This last finding was less than satisfactory, given that the Attorney General did not provide any additional information how Hill could have been included among the other CEO's at one of these events if not for her relationship with Brown.

Clinger expressed concern that the Attorney General "has fenced-off" the conflict-of-interest allegations.[187] He urged her to accede to a request to expand the independent counsel's authority if the independent counsel uncovers evidence substantiating these allegations during his review. If not, Clinger promised hearings "at the appropriate time."

Would Secretary Brown be asked to resign? Not by the President, who promptly issued a statement of unequivocal support. He said that Brown's success as Secretary "is unparalleled."

> As I have noted in the past, the legal standard for [the appointment of an independent counsel] is low. I am confidant at the conclusion of the process, the independent counsel will find no wrongdoing by Secretary Brown. In the interim, I value his continued service on behalf of this country.[188]

Nonetheless, the White House was put in somewhat of an uncomfortable posture, given previous White House statements that the appointment of an independent counsel would not result in the resignation of Cabinet member so long as the alleged misconduct antedated the official's service in the Clinton Administration.[189] This was the distinction made between the respective fates of Secretaries Espy and Cisneros. The problem for the White House, of course, was that the allegations against Secretary Brown very much related to his tenure at Commerce. The payments from First International were made after Brown became Secretary, and Brown filed his financial disclosure reports in connection with his Cabinet position.[190] So the White House conceded that, in the words of the *Washington Post*, "there is no consistent principle about whether officials should continue in their jobs while being investigated[.]" White House Press Secretary Mike McCurry said that the President instead decided these matters case-by-case, explaining, "[t]here are different facts, different issues involved."[191]

The *New York Times,* however, called on the President to "ease [Brown] back into the private sector[,]" opining that the Secretary "has become an eyesore in an Administration that once endorsed high ethical standards." The *Times* offered a different test:

> Presidents have a right and sometimes a clear responsibility to dump cabinet members so tangled in their personal problems that they can no longer function effectively.[192]

Secretary Brown predicted his eventual complete exoneration, asserting:

I have never engaged in any official act to further my personal financial interests, there have been no conflicts of interest, and I have complied in good faith with my financial disclosure obligations.[193]

One commenter lamented the appointment of an independent counsel, because the nature of a criminal investigation would make less likely a full public accounting of Brown's questionable business relationships. And because of its inevitable length, the independent counsel's investigation would "shield Brown from the immediate political consequences of his actions.[194]

On July 6, 1995, the court of appeals appointed Daniel S. Pearson, a Miami lawyer, Democrat, former Federal prosecutor and state appellate judge, to serve as independent counsel.[195] With a July 1995 appointment, and given the complexity of the matter, it is unlikely that Pearson will complete his investigation before the 1996 election.

Conclusions

What is clear from the reports that surfaced in the past year and one half is that an independent counsel was warranted to determine whether Secretary Brown (1) made any actionable false statements on his financial disclosure reports in violation of 18 U.S.C. 1001; (2) took any actions as Secretary to benefit his current business partner Nolanda Hill or her partners in violation of 18 U.S.C. 208; (3) improperly accepted or received things of value from Hill or First International in violation of 18 U.S.C. 201 or 209; and (4) committed any violation of Federal criminal law in obtaining financing for and buying the town house in Washington for Lillian Madsen. Attorney General Reno's decision to close the investigation into the conflict-of-interest allegations appears dubious, but it is difficult to attack without knowing the facts and depth of the Justice Department's preliminary investigation.

Congressional hearings held the promise of exposing the shady business relationships Brown had with Hill and Hill had with others, as well as resolving whether Secretary Brown misused his office. However, the terms of the independent counsel law required the appointment of an independent counsel.

The FDIC and RTC investigations into Nolanda Hill's business dealings are also proper, but may appropriately be subsumed within the independent counsel's investigation. If so, Attorney General Reno should also give Pearson authority to investigate violations of civil law. Given Pearson's charter, the investigation of Hill can and should move forward regardless of evidence of Secretary Brown's involvement. If the FDIC and RTC are permitted to proceed, their reports prepared by these agencies should be available to the public.

Secretary Brown is entitled to the presumption that he is innocent of any criminal law violations. To date, the allegations that he has compromised his job in giving preferential treatment to his business associates are few in number and peripheral to his stewardship of Commerce. (As of this moment they are arguably not even within the independent counsel's jurisdiction.) But neither qualification mitigates the gravity of the misconduct that has been alleged. Further, Secretary Brown deserves a great deal of criticism for his stubborn refusal to cooperate with the House Government Reform and Oversight Committee and other congressional requesters who, for over a year, sought information and explanations from the Secretary and the Commerce Department. And the allegations that Secretary Brown has, to date, failed to refute, or even answer, paint at best a very unflattering portrait of his business relationships when he entered public service.

A lesson for agency ethics officials to be drawn from this episode is that the financial disclosure reports of the agency's highest ranking officials must be scrutinized with the greatest care to ensure that they are complete, accurate, and sufficiently descriptive and unambigious.

Chapter Thirteen

Allegations Against Housing and Urban Development Secretary Henry Cisneros

The Justice Department's findings that Henry Cisneros lied to the FBI during its background investigation of the Secretary-designate were serious enough to warrant the appointment of an independent counsel, as the Attorney General concluded. The Justice Department's preliminary investigation determined that Cisneros misrepresented to the FBI the amount of money he had been providing to his former girlfriend Linda Medlar, significantly understating the maximum individual amount and total annual amount of these payments. The possibility that Cisneros conspired with Medlar to conceal information about the payments from the FBI is also a legitimate avenue of inquiry for an independent counsel. It remains to be determined whether these false statements were "material" to the President's decision to appoint Cisneros or to the Senate's vote to confirm him. Because the Attorney General could not rule out the possibility that these statements could have had a bearing on the Secretary's appointment, this is an issue that must be resolved by an independent counsel.

Another related, and potentially more serious, allegation concerned the Secretary's relationship with businessman Morris Jaffe, who also made one or more payments to Medlar at Cisneros's request; namely, whether Secretary Cisneros provided any official benefit or favor as a quid pro quo for Jaffe's financial and other assistance to Medlar. The Attorney General found no evidence to support this allegation, and thus appropriately did not include it in her request for an appointment of an independent counsel.

While the Attorney General was rightfully criticized for taking too long to conduct a preliminary investigation, she did not deserve the criticism she received for deciding to request an independent counsel. Although there is no reason to believe that the Public Integrity Section could not have conducted a fair and objective investigation, that is not the standard for determining whether to request the appointment of an independent counsel. The proper object of criticism should be the independent counsel law itself.

The Nature of the Allegations

On July 29, 1994, Linda Medlar sued Henry Cisneros in Texas state court for $256,000 in support she alleged Cisneros promised her when their three-year affair ended in 1990. Secretary Cisneros acknowledged that he had made monthly payments to Medlar until he became HUD Secretary in January 1993, and thereafter provided some additional money to her in 1993. He explained that when they broke off their affair, he agreed to make these payments in order to provide assistance to Medlar and her teenage daughter. Medlar alleged that Secretary Cisneros promised to provide $4,000 per month until 1999, when Medlar's daughter would finish college. Medlar's suit seeks the additional money the Secretary would provide her were he to make $4,000 monthly payments through 1999. Secretary Cisneros stated that he stopped making payments when he could no longer afford them, given his modest Federal salary.[1] In his answer to Medlar's suit, he argued that he was not contractually obligated to her.[2] After the court refused to dismiss the case,[3] Medlar and Cisneros agreed in May 1995 to a settlement. Secretary Cisneros agreed to pay Medlar $49,000; Medlar agreed to dismiss her suit and to make no further claims against him. Medlar and Secretary Cisneros also mutually agreed in the future to not discuss their relationship publicly.[4]

Initially, this story appeared to be only a mild embarrassment to the Secretary and to the Administration. Cisneros's affair with Medlar was publicly disclosed in 1988, although his payments to Medlar had not been previously revealed. The best proof that Cisneros had successfully weathered the controversy over the affair was his nomination and confirmation to the Cabinet. Moreover, Secretary Cisneros said he told Clinton transition officials of these payments when he was interviewed for the HUD position.[5]

But on September 12, 1994, the television show "Inside Edition" ran a lengthy interview with Medlar, in which she revealed that she had tape-recorded hours of telephone calls with Cisneros in 1992 and 1993.[6] The content of the tapes revealed further embarrassing details of the affair, but Medlar also alleged that Cisneros had misled the FBI and President Clinton about the payments. Medlar produced a tape suggesting that Cisneros told the FBI that he had made about $60,000 in payments, when, according to Medlar, he had provided $150,000 up to that point. Secretary Cisneros explained: "I was forthright and described the fact that I had provided assistance[.] . . . And while there may be some disagreement on the precise amount, [that's because] I kept no records. I was speaking from memory."[7]

Thus, the Medlar tapes widened the news angle from simply one of public embarrassment to also a serious matter of ethics and potential criminality. Several allegations were derived from the Medlar tapes and published in news reports in September 1994.[8]

Did Secretary-Designate Cisneros Mislead the FBI?

The central allegation is that Cisneros lied to the FBI during its background investigation of him. Cisneros is heard on the tape of a January 15, 1993 conversation telling Medlar that the FBI had determined from discussions with his accountant that he had made $60,000 in payments to Medlar. Cisneros told Medlar that this was "virtually the truth, because they figured it out." A fuller account of this conversation follows (italics in original):

LM: What was the problem? Everything should be fine now.
HC: It all - you don't want to hear this -
LM: It all revolves around -
HC: The FBI questions about you and the money.
LM: To Mary Alice [his wife]
HC: Correct.
LM: And what did she say to them?
HC: She play[ed] along like she knew — and uh because she knew that if she didn't it would be blackmail.
LM: Blackmail.
HC: Their main concern about the money was that there was illegality involved - that you were - would be threatening me with something and that's why I was giving you the money - so that - and the main thing would be disclosure to spouse - also -I guess - just generally - so, um, you know - she understood that - and had to acknowledge that she knew - so that it wouldn't have been as an illegal thing.
LM: Did they have any amounts?
HC: I don't know what they - but they talked to 65 people and most of 'em about this, so they picked up bits and pieces . . .
HC (later): And they asked everybody . . . and they finally figured out the discrepancy between what comes in and what goes to other *expenditures and they did have that figure.*
LM: And what did they ask you?
HC: They didn't ever talk to me - well, I guess they talked to me amounts and I gave them the same fact situation that I had given them before - so it was real delicate.
LM: Is that basically why it didn't come up in the hearing?
HC: No - let me tell you something - it's in the report.
LM: Uh huh.
HC: The FBI report is - like- 40 pages.
LM: Yeh.
HC: In the FBI report is a full discussion of our situation and also the money- and it estimates $60,000 - because that's the discrepancy - see they had FBI agents here in San Antonio - they had agents in Washington - when I talked to you last week and you were so angry with me - I thought I was dead - I mean I thought it was over - and it wasn't what you would do - it was what the FBI was already getting - I went - I had a private meeting

with the lawyers in Washington - where they worked me over with every
possible follow-up prosecutorial question.
LM: And so, what did you tell 'em?
HC: I told 'm - you know - I told 'em - I - well - finally what it boils down
to is the truth - the fact of the matter is I have helped you - all along -
because I wanted you to have what you needed - not because - as I've told you
many, many, many, many times, because I was afraid of what you would do.
LM: But how much do they think you've given? What do they think
you've given?
HC: Well, they don't know - I mean the FBI thinks - I mean the FBI has
virtually the truth because they just figured it out - so it's in the report -
now on Monday afternoon - my thing [confirmation hearing] is Tuesday -
on Monday evening I get a call from the Clinton ethics people, to tell me
they have just been through the FBI report and that as far as they have
read it - at that moment they've read about half of it - there's nothing in
there that hasn't been known or I haven't been forthright about or hasn't
been public or that can't be faced - now the FBI report is supposed to go to
the Senate on Thursday afternoon but they're still working on it Monday . . . .

When confronted by accounts of these tapes, Secretary Cisneros explained to
the *Washington Post* that "'it is my understanding now' that the $60,000 represented
'an annual sum' over the three years. The numbers 'came from my accountant, and
questions that they asked of him,' Cisneros said."[9] Subsequent to the "Inside Edition" broadcast, Medlar conceded that she does not know what, in fact, Cisneros told
the FBI.[10] Again, it is extremely difficult to tell from reading the transcripts what the
Secretary-designate told the FBI, as opposed to what he told transition officials, or
what his wife told the FBI. What can be gleaned from these transcripts is that Cisneros knew the FBI did not have complete or accurate information, and yet he was
content to keep the FBI from getting the full story.

Even though Medlar alleged that Cisneros had lied to the FBI, which, if true,
could amount to a false statement under 18 U.S.C. 1001, the *Washington Post* initially refrained from pursing this allegation. Howard Kurtz explained why:

> But the tapes do not appear to support Medlar's main charge on "In-
> side Edition:" that Cisneros misled the FBI during a background check
> about the amount of money he paid her from 1990 to 1993. . . .
>
> The *Post's* Gugliotta said he didn't write a story about the tapes be-
> cause "I don't see any indication he willingly or consciously misled the
> FBI. The FBI's primary concern was whether he had paid hush money. It
> was never characterized by either Henry or Linda as hush money."[11]

Secretary Cisneros's Relationship with Morris Jaffe

Newsweek pursued a different angle. In a taped conversation, Medlar accused
Cisneros, while Mayor of San Antonio, of accepting $10,000 in cash from Morris
Jaffe, described as a "wealthy oil and real-estate entrepreneur."[12] the Secretary de-
nied receiving any such payment.[13]

In a November 22, 1992 conversation, Medlar and Cisneros discussed the potential problems Cisneros would face were he to run for the Senate seat vacated by

Lloyd Bentsen or accept a position in the Clinton Cabinet (italics in original):

LM: Okay? I'm just saying don't think that everything is just dead and buried because it's not. I mean there is a disaster and it's not me sitting there waiting to happen and if you don't know that - I can't believe that you don't know that - that the scrutiny that you will come under - and you go ahead and do it - the scrutiny that you will come under will be about you, about your past, about your financial dealings, your dealings about being a politician, i.e, Morris Jaffe.
HC: There's no problem there.
LM: There's no problem there. Henry, you took cash from him.
HC: No.
LM: You did to.
HC: No.
LM: I'm sorry, Henry, but you did.
HC: I'm sorry.
LM: Henry, you gave me the cash.
HC: Not from my campaigns. It may have been from some cause something
LM: No, for your campaigns.
HC: Bonds [or] something.
LM: You would go over there and you would have to sit in his office and you would bring an envelope back with $10,000 in it. Now you can try to tell me that's not true but I'm sorry Henry I was there. Now, I don't know that anybody else knows about that except Shipley and whoever Shipley's told because I never told anybody. Shipley told me when I first worked for you that you accepted cash to pay off your credit card bills.
HC: Absolutely not.
LM: That's what Shipley said.
HC: You think that's true?
LM: How many people has Shipley told?
HC: I don't have any idea but there is no truth to that I never ever ever have used public money for private purposes ever.

Later, in a December 15, 1992 conversation, Medlar asked Cisneros, "do they know anything about your dealings with Jaffe?" He responded, "There is no dealings with Jaffe" and "There is—there's—there's nothing there." But Medlar persisted (italics in original):

LM: Henry, when you went over to Jaffe's and came back with $10,000 in cash - that one was never reported by him and never reported by us.

Cisneros answered that he did not recall this, and asked whether Medlar was suggesting he improperly used the money for personal purposes (italics in original):

LM: No, I, I, honey, I'm not suggesting anything like that, I'm saying it is a problem.

HC: I don't think so.
LM: Because quite frankly it was never reported.

Cisneros told Medlar he did not want to talk anymore about the subject, wondering, "What if you tape record me or something?"

Secretary Cisneros did acknowledge that in 1993, while HUD Secretary, he asked Jaffe for help in finding a job for Medlar. Medlar said that she received a $5000 check from Jaffe, with the notation "loan," soon after the Secretary's appeal to Jaffe. However, Secretary Cisneros denied asking Jaffe to give money to Medlar. A transcript of a December 1993 call reveals that Medlar had recently received a check from Jaffe and the Secretary's surprise when Medlar informed him. Jaffe's office confirmed that he provided "checks" to Medlar, intending them as loans. Secretary Cisneros claimed that Jaffe, despite his extensive real estate holdings, has had no business with HUD and asserted that his request to Jaffe was not improper. He later said, "There has never been any favor-related, public thing I could do for him."[14] Yet transcripts of conversations with Medlar reveal that the Secretary was concerned about the appearance of asking Jaffe for help.[15]

On September 22, the *New York Times* ran an extensive piece on the Medlar tapes. Although it charitably volunteered at the start of the article that "[t]he tapes . . . show no evidence of wrongdoing,"[16] the *Times* detailed several additional areas of ethical concern:

Were the Payments Hush Money?

Secretary Cisneros said no, the payments were made simply to assist Medlar; it could not be hush money if there was nothing to hush. Webster Hubbell, who interviewed Cisneros during the transition, stated that the transition team accepted his explanation.[17] Yet, the transcripts reveal at least Medlar's view—and Cisneros's worries—that there was plenty of information about Cisneros's past that Medlar could potentially reveal, giving Cisneros a strong incentive to continue making payments to keep Medlar satisfied. In one conversation, Cisneros himself worried that his payments, if revealed, would be seen as "hush money."[18]

Did Secretary Cisneros Mislead the Public?

Following the filing of Medlar's suit in 1994, Cisneros stated , "I have not provided any assistance since assuming office in January of 1993." This statement was false. Secretary Cisneros later acknowledged making payments in February, March, and June of 1993, totaling $55,000.[19] Secretary Cisneros made conflicting public statements regarding whether he had terminated the payments.

His attempt to finesse the question did not persuade:

> But Mr. Cisneros said in the interview that those payments had been part of a final agreement reached with Ms. Medlar before he entered the Government, and he did not consider them 1993 assistance. He said his statement, which refers vaguely to help over "the forthcoming year," was hastily drafted and should have been more precise.[20]

It is unclear why the Secretary did not acknowledge his 1993 payments in some interviews, since he did so in an interview with the *Washington Post*. As early as July

1994, soon after Medlar filed suit, the Secretary told the *Washington Post* that he had "continued to give Medlar money 'out of my savings' for an additional year[.]"[21]

Did Secretary-Desinate Cisneros Mislead or Attempt to Mislead the Senate Concerning the Payments?

The suggestion comes primarily from a transcript of a December 24, 1992 conversation, in which Cisneros tells Medlar what he would say if asked about the payments (italics in original):

> *LM: Henry, you're going to be going through confirmation where they're going to be asking you questions.*
> *HC: The subject probably is not even going to come up.*
> *LM: And what if it does?*
> *HC: If it does I'll tell them what we agreed and the only person in the world who can sink me at that point - and I mean serious - I'm talking contempt of Congress, jail, is you - but it didn't - I mean I don't know what purpose that would serve - I intend to do it right.*[22]

Secretary Cisneros argued that this statement was taken out of context, and, in any event, does not state that **he** would mislead the Senate.[23] It is difficult, if not impossible, precisely and accurately to determine from the transcripts the terms of this "agreement" between Medlar and Cisneros.

Secretary Cisneros was not asked about the payments at his confirmation hearing. The FBI report, which most likely contained either a verbatim or summary account of Cisneros's statements to the FBI concerning his payments to Medlar, was made available by the White House to the Chairman and Ranking Member (not staff) on the Banking Committee.[24] However, it appears from the Medlar tapes that the FBI report was not provided to Chairman Riegle until after the confirmation hearing.

The substance of conversations Secretary-designate Cisneros may have had with individual Senators is not known, other than his account to Medlar of a conversation he had with Senator Riegle following the January 1993 confirmation hearing. Following the hearing, Cisneros called Riegle concerning a personnel selection. According to a transcript of a January 15, 1993 conversation with Medlar, this is that Cisneros recalled of his conversation with Riegle concerning the payments (italics in original):

> *HC: . . . [A]nd he said, I'm glad you're showing that kind of candor with me, because I want to talk about something sensitive with you, too, and then we got into the payments question, from the FBI report.*
> *LM: Um hum.*
> *HC: And he said, look, I need your explanation, and I need it, he said, I may send you some questions in writing, because, obviously if it comes up again in the future, someone may ask whether the FBI knew it, and they did, and then they may ask, well if the FBI knew it, why didn't the Senate Committee pursue it, and I want to be able to say that I did.*
> *LM: And so what did you tell him?*
> *HC: I told him . . . uh . . . I didn't . . . he didn't get into the numbers or anything like that. . . . now the only question standing at this moment is*

*whether D'Amato is going to, uh, want it, he's the only person who has
access to it. . . .*
LM: I wouldn't think he would.
*HC: Well, he is saying he doesn't give a s——. I mean, he said that to me in
those words, you know?*[25]

Later in that same conversation, Medlar again asked Cisneros to tell her what he
told Riegle (italics in original):

HC: I told him that, why I did it.
LM: And that's all that was said about it?
*HC: Uh huh, the FBI report makes clear it was not "hush" money, the FBI
report, itself, in the paragraph that deals with the issue, says it was not
"hush" money.*
LM: What does it say it was?
*HC: Assistance . . . understandable under the circumstances . . . your move
to Lubbock . . . so forth.*
LM: But he doesn't know any dollar amount?
HC: It's in the . . . it's in the . . . there are speculations in the report.
LM: $60,000 in assistance?
*HC: That's what it says. It says, you know, it doesn't actually, you know,
estimate the 60, but it says that's the amount that it could be, judging from
the way our accounting is . . .*
LM: And so what did the Clinton people say when they read that?
*HC: They haven't . . . I mean . . . they said it was not a problem, because
it's characterized as assistance. . . .*[26]

This transcript shows that Cisneros knew that Riegle was in possession of inaccurate information in the FBI report. Riegle must have read portions of the report to
Cisneros over the phone. Yet Cisneros did not inform Riegle of the falsity of that
information. Riegle may not have asked Cisneros directly about the amount of payments, but he may well have done so had he known that the payments were much
larger than what was contained in the report. This transcript therefore supports a
finding that Secretary-designate Cisneros knowingly misled the Senate.

Was Secretary-Designate Cisneros Truthful With Transition Officials?

Subsequently the *New York Times* added another area of concern, whether Cisneros misled the transition officials who interviewed him before he was nominated.
A transcript of a December 12, 1992 conversation quotes Cisneros telling Medlar
that he told Webster Hubbell that his payments came to "$10,000 to $15,000 over a
year[,]"[27] when yearly payments actually amounted to between $42,000 and $60,000.
Secretary Cisneros said that any discrepancy was inadvertent; he added that he did
not keep track of his payments to Medlar.

Cisneros provided Medlar with a more extended account of his meeting with
Hubbell (immaterial portions have been omitted, italics in original):

LM: What were the obvious questions?

HC: No, I mean the obvious question of the subject matter was you, honestly - um - the big problem - let me just be direct - the big problem is future payments - the big problem is -

LM: Why did you say anything to him?

HC: No, I didn't - I'm telling you - I'm telling you the question would be well the problem is if - in his words - the problem would be if you had to be support[ed] at particular points - and I did do that I changed it from - that changed it but I, I clearly gave the impression we are not talking about an absolute monthly . . .

HC (after an interruption): Um, so the question becomes if you have help[ed] periodically then why won't you be having to help periodically in the future?

LM (after broken-off conversation): What did he say when he left?

HC: Well, he said he was more comfortable than what he thought which was (tape skipped)

LM: He doesn't know anything about the monthly and he thinks that

HC: That you have needs that revolve around the start of school or the Christmas season or a summer camp or things like that that you need (tape skipped)

HC (later): I feel like I'm not going to be nominated and I have to figure out how to let people down.

LM: Why do you feel you are not going to be nominated since you think he was more comfortable?

HC: Cause I think Clinton has problems will have problems with the (tape skipped)

LM: You're not going to tell him about the monthly or the house or anything like that, right?

HC: But I mean they were worried about things like would the tellers at the bank who've seen you make the deposit be (tape skipped)

LM: Did you tell him about that?

HC: Well I mean he asked me how it was made.

LM: Henry, you are so dumb I could just brain you for that.

HC: Well, what do you expect me to do? You want me to tell lies?

LM: No, but I don't - I mean - all you should have said was directly....

LM (later): Well when are they supposed to let you know?

HC: He's probably going to talk to Clinton tomorrow but tomorrow Clinton is resigning the governorship so that may be difficult but Sunday at the latest. (tape skipped)

LM: They only know parts of it, right?

HC: Yeh.

LM: And they don't know about the rest, right, and he felt that - he felt better when he left.

HC: Yeh, much better.

LM: Is that what he said — then why do you have a bad feeling?

HC: Because I think that he is going to tell Clinton and Clinton's going -

well how come (tape skipped)
LM: How does he know that?
HC: Because he asked me - that's easy to check.
LM: Henry, couldn't you just say - couldn't you say
HC: I said your family helps and Stan helps you some and that you worked occasionally - special projects and things - I mean I had to say that because they wanted to know the total amount of what I had done in increments - I told them, well, it came to $10,000 - $15,000 over a year - you know - that's not enough to live on (tape skipped)
HC: Trying to get down to exactly, you know, how it's going to be explained - you know.
HC: (later): He couldn't make the call - he says it's Bill Clinton's decision - but he wanted to look me in the eye and get the facts about it - he's (tape skipped)
LM: Just laid it out as every once in a while, right?
HC: Umum - when special needs arise - and that it was - the largest sum I have ever given you was $2500.00 and that a total (tape skipped)
LM (later): Think you'll hear for a couple of days?
HC: Probably mid-week next week - I would say actually after the economic summit - uh, the key problem I think he could live with everything including the business about the future if the future could be timed so that at confirmation time I would say that there was nothing ahead.
LM: I've always said that.
HC: At confirmation time I could honestly look these people in the face and say there is not intent to provide payment in the future. (tape skipped)

A fair reading of these passages—as flawed as these transcripts are—is that Cisneros kept from transition officials (and therefore from the President-elect) the facts that (1) he had been and was continuing to provide Medlar with monthly payments; (2) that the amount of his monthly payments regularly was larger than $2500 and, thus, the yearly amount was much greater than $10,000-$15,000; and (3) that he had made a commitment to Medlar to support her in the future. Although the Secretary-designate discussed the question of future payments with Hubbell, it is not at all clear that he told Hubbell the straight story.

The Justice Department Begins a Review of the Allegations, the President Supports Secretary Cisneros, and a Senator Shows Interest

On September 22, 1994, it was revealed that the Justice Department had begun an initial review of the tapes to determine whether to conduct a preliminary inquiry that could ultimately lead to a request for the appointment of an independent counsel under the Ethics in Government Act.[28] The review would center on whether Secretary-designate Cisneros made any false statements to Federal officials during the background checks, and include an interview of Medlar. The *Washington Post* reported that any issue arising out of Justice's review of the tapes would also be looked into.[29]

Secretary Cisneros responded to these reports at a news conference on September 28, 1994, asserting that he expected to be vindicated:

The review that is under way will determine in the final analysis that I was forthright at every step. I have no fear that any new information is there that hasn't been borne out.

The decision makers had in their possession, from myself and other sources, all of the information that these tapes and a review of the facts later will bear out.[30]

On October 5, the *Washington Times* reported that Justice Department sources indicated the Secretary's resignation "could come this week."[31] But later that week, the President came to the Secretary's defense:

We knew what the facts were at the time and the legal counsel or the people—excuse me—who were handling it for me reviewed it, decided that there was nothing illegal or inappropriate about what was done by Secretary Cisneros, something that was fully known by his family. And no, I don't think it undermines his effectiveness. I mean, what he did in his past he's dealt with, and he's been pretty forthright. He's been, in fact, I think painfully forthright. And I think he has been an extraordinarily gifted HUD Secretary. . . . He is doing the job that I hired him to do for the American people. And as long as he is doing that job at a high level, I think he ought to be permitted to continue to do it.[32]

On October 11, Senator Faircloth asked the FBI for a copy of the FBI's background investigation file, asserting that any person who would lie to the FBI "has no place serving in high office."[33] This request was reportedly declined, pending the criminal investigation.[34]

It was reported on October 15 that the Justice Department had begun a preliminary investigation of the allegations against Secretary Cisneros to determine whether to seek the appointment of an independent counsel.[35] The Ethics in Government Act requires the initiation of a preliminary investigation if the Department determines that there is a specific allegation from a credible source that a Federal crime has been committed by a covered official, in this case, a Member of the Cabinet.[36] Although the precise scope of the investigation was not disclosed, the Secretary's lawyer said in a statement that "The focus of the investigation appears to be the details of the timing and amounts of the assistance" Cisneros provided Medlar.[37] This statement suggested that Cisneros may have indicated to the FBI that he had stopped (or intended by a certain date to stop) making payments, when, in fact, he continued to make payments through July 1993.

The Justice Department's decision to conduct a preliminary investigation prompted the *Washington Times*, rather prematurely, to call upon the Secretary to resign. Without concluding whether the allegations that Cisneros lied to the FBI were true, the *Washington Times* wrote that Secretary Cisneros should step down because he was "proving an embarrassment" to the Administration.[38]

In a televised interview with Jim Lehrer, White House Counsel Mikva attempted to downplay the matter by stating that Secretary Cisneros had made "full disclo-

sure. . . . Again, **all of this was known to the public**, to his constituency in San
Antonio, and to the administration when he was appointed, so I would hope it's not
a disqualification."[39] This statement is not accurate. Cisneros had not previously publicly disclosed the payments to Medlar.[40] Indeed, the Secretary's current problems
stem from Medlar's suit concerning the payments, and the release of tapes of their
conversations. Further, Judge Mikva could not have known whether Cisneros gave a
complete and accurate account of the payments to transition officials.

In the aftermath of the November 1994 elections, Senator Faircloth, who was in
line to be chairman of the Senate Banking subcommittee with oversight jurisdiction
of HUD, indicated through his staff that he intended to hold hearings on the matter in
the next Congress.[41]

In January 1995, at the end of the ninety days provided in the statute to determine whether to seek the appointment of an independent counsel or terminate the
matter,[42] Justice sought and obtained a sixty-day extension to make a decision.[43] As
permitted by law, Justice was given an additional sixty days, or until the middle of
March, to make a decision.[44] At the same time, Senator Faircloth stated his intent to
hold hearings, regardless of what the Attorney General decided.[45]

Although there were reports that the request for more time reflected a desire by
senior Justice officials for a more thorough investigation of one or more matters,[46]
the *Washington Times* justifiably criticized the Attorney General for the time the
Department was taking to investigate the charges, which the *Washington Times* called
"neither deep nor complicated." Based on what was publicly known of the allegations at the time, only a handful of witness interviews were needed and only a modest
amount of documents would need to be digested to determine whether to seek an
independent counsel.[47]

The Request for and Appointment of an Independent Counsel

On March 13, 1995, the Attorney General requested the appointment of an independent counsel.[48] The Justice Department determined that Secretary-designate
Cisneros misled the FBI in two respects relating to the payments of Medlar. First,
Cisneros told the FBI that no payment to Medlar was more than $2,500, when, in
fact, many of the payments were well over that amount.[49] Indeed, one payment, "substantially larger than $2,500," was made just before Cisneros's interview with the
FBI at which he said he had not made any payment over $2,500. Second, Cisneros
falsely told the FBI that the total annual payments to Medlar never amounted to more
than $10,000, when in fact Medlar received between $42,000 and $60,000 annually
from 1990 to 1993.

However, the request did not include or reference an allegation that Secretary-
designate Cisneros lied to the FBI about whether and when he had stopped making
payments. Possibly, the Justice Department accepted the Secretary's defense that he
meant only to convey to the FBI that he had decided to terminate the payments, not
that the payments had actually been terminated.[50]

A false statement to the Government may be a felony under 18 U.S.C. 1001 if
the statement is considered "material." Applied to the allegations against Secretary
Cisneros, the issue of materiality concerns whether the President or Senate might
have taken different actions had Cisneros told the truth. The Attorney General found
that Cisneros's false statements "were potentially a factor in three separate but related inquiries:" the vetting by transition officials, the FBI background check, and the

Senate confirmation process.[51] On this question, it was widely reported that there was a difference of opinion within the Justice Department. Some Criminal Division lawyers were prepared to conclude that Cisneros's false statements were not material, that they "could be viewed more leniently as off-the-cuff remarks that had only a marginal bearing on his appointment."[52] However, Attorney General Reno correctly determined that, under the independent counsel law, she had no choice:

> Although not all false statements are material as a matter of law, the materiality of Secretary Cisneros's false statements to the FBI is a close and difficult factual and legal issue that must be resolved by an Independent Counsel.[53]

The Attorney General also asked the court to include in the independent counsel's charter whether Cisneros and Medlar conspired to conceal the truth from the FBI, an allegation, like the others, derived from the Medlar's tapes of conversations with the Secretary, and which, if true, could violate the criminal conspiracy statute, 18 U.S.C. 371.

Notably, however, the Attorney General's request was rather narrow. The Attorney General found no evidence that Secretary Cisneros engaged in any improper activity with respect to Morris Jaffe and Jaffe's payment(s) to Medlar. While the Department found that Secretary Cisneros had asked Jaffe to help find Medlar a job or provide other assistance, and that Jaffe had made one $5000 payment and an additional $11,000 to Medlar, the Department found no nexus to any action taken by the HUD Secretary:

> [W]e have found no evidence that the money provided by the businessman had any connection to "any official act" that had been or might have been taken in the future by Cisneros as Secretary of HUD. Indeed, a review of the public records concerning the businessman's financial holdings has not disclosed even a hypothetical potential for Secretary Cisneros to take action as the head of HUD which would affect the businessman.[54]

The Attorney General also found no evidence that Secretary Cisneros failed to pay taxes in connection with the payments.[55]

Secretary Cisneros held a press conference that day to proclaim his innocence and to announce that he would not resign:

> . . . I am confident the independent counsel will conclude that I did not engage in any criminal wrongdoing. I regret any mistakes that I have made, but affirm once again that I have at no point violated the public's trust.

Secretary Cisneros apparently had offered to resign in a conversation with the President, but "[t]he President said that would not be necessary and that they should stick together."[56] So, he chose to "stay and fight." The President issued a statement, praising Secretary Cisneros's service as "outstanding" and calling him "a man of integrity and character":

> Secretary Cisneros is a good man and an effective public servant. He says he regrets any mistakes he has made. So do I. But that does not outweigh the excellent work he has been doing and will do as Secretary of Housing and Urban Development. I look forward to his continued valuable service.[57]

Senator Faircloth again threatened to hold a hearing, but this time said he would wait to discuss the matter with the independent counsel to ensure that the congressional probe would not interfere with the independent counsel's investigation.[58] Representative Chris Shays, the Chairman of the House Banking subcommittee with jurisdiction over HUD, said he would await the outcome of the independent counsel's investigation before deciding whether to hold hearings.[59]

On May 24, 1995, over two months after the Attorney General's request, the court of appeals appointed as independent counsel David M. Barrett, a Washington lawyer, Republican, and former special counsel to the House Ethics Committee.[60] Barrett said, "A special counsel is different from a special prosecutor because I will be acutely aware of matters which are exculpatory as well as those that would be incriminating."[61] The court of appeals included in Barrett's charter any matter related to the Secretary-designate's interviews with the FBI, including false statements, obstruction of justice, and conspiracy.

Analysis and Conclusions

Secretary Cisneros's False Statements Were Serious

The Department's finding that Secretary-designate Cisneros made false statements to the FBI is significant, contrary to what others argued in the wake of the Attorney General's decision. Al Hunt complained that the independent counsel law was triggered because Cisneros did not tell the FBI the "exact" amount of his payments to Medlar.[62] Paul Gigot wrote that Secretary Cisneros "must face a personal prosecutor for telling a small lie about a private matter. (He told the FBI about the payments to his former girlfriend, but lied about how much.)"[63] According to David Broder, Cisneros "underestimated the amounts of the payments." Broder concluded that the call for an independent counsel "converts a very narrow—almost irrelevant—legal question into a political controversy of truly large dimensions."[64] A consensus was quickly forming that Secretary Cisneros was guilty only of an understatement or, better, an underestimate.

What these analysts overlook is the Justice Department's implicit conclusion that Secretary-designate Cisneros's misstatements were not inadvertent, as he originally claimed, but were deliberate. A necessary element of an 18 U.S.C. 1001 offense is that the person knew the falsity of the statement at the time it was made. However, the only legal question identified by the Attorney General in her request is whether the false statements were material. In other words, the Department must have concluded that Cisneros intentionally misrepresented the facts to the FBI. The Medlar transcripts strongly support this conclusion.

Further, these analysts omit any reference to the allegation that Cisneros and Medlar may have conspired to keep the FBI (and the White House and the Senate) from knowing the extent and continuing nature of the payments. This allegation is supported by one reading of the Medlar tapes[65] and by Medlar's illness excuse for avoiding an FBI interview during the background check.[66]

On the other hand, Stuart Taylor, a respected commentator, while acknowledging that Secretary Cisneros's lies were "pretty petty," applauded the Attorney General's's decision because:

in the circumstances of this case, criminal prosecution may be the **only** way to vindicate the principle that high-level officials should not be allowed to commit crimes with total impunity.[67]

What exactly motivated Secretary-designate Cisneros to lie to the FBI has not yet been determined. Did Cisneros want to avoid further embarrassment that would more likely result from disclosure of $60,000 in annual payments rather than $10,000?[68] Probably. Did Secretary Cisneros believe that he would more likely get through the White House and Senate screening process without the additional undue controversy? Yes, certainly. Note that he is heard on tape worrying to Medlar that the President "will have problems" with nominating him because of the payments. The tapes reveal that Cisneros expressed serious concerns that his payments to Medlar—and perhaps other disclosures about his past—would torpedo his appointment.[69] He worried whether the payments would be seen as hush money, and he worried that continuing to make payments would be a problem.

Or was it something else, more or less sinister?[70]

Not all false statements prosecutable under 18 U.S.C. 1001 should be prosecuted. But the clearance process performs a critical screening role for an administration, and, to a lesser extent, for the Senate. The process is only as strong and effective as the completeness and accuracy of the information provided to the FBI and White House. The irony should not be lost that some of those who blame the incompetence of the White House vetting process for many of the Clinton Administration's appointments blunders are also the ones who effectively denigrate the importance of the same vetting process by refusing to acknowledge the strong public interest in ensuring candor to the FBI.

An Independent Counsel is Appropriate

The Attorney General correctly determined to request the appointment of an independent counsel. This is not to say that the Public Integrity Section of the Criminal Division could not be trusted to determine the matter—in my experience, it could—but only that the independent counsel law takes most prosecutorial discretion away from the Justice Department and reposes it in an independent counsel. (Nevertheless, the Justice Department should not have taken so long to come this conclusion.) Paul Gigot accurately identified the culprits as the independent counsel law and the politics of ethics that spawned the law (as well as its resuscitation), and not the Attorney General's prosecutorial zeal or a lack of political nerve.[71]

The weekend after the Attorney General's decision, the debate over the wisdom of the independent counsel law was again revived, as it always seemed to be following the call for an independent counsel to look into allegations against a Clinton Administration official. This time, former White House Counsel Lloyd Cutler and current private counsel to the President Robert Bennett both criticized what the independent counsel law has wrought.[72]

Should Secretary Cisneros Have Resigned?

Whether the Secretary should have resigned following the request for an independent counsel depends in large part on the ethics standards and expectations set by the President for his administration. Given that the President did not seem bothered by the Attorney General's conclusions that Secretary Cisneros had deliberately lied to the FBI, it is hard to fault the Secretary for not resigning. Note that the President did not even issue a reprimand; instead, he offered the Secretary support, sympathy (perhaps empathy) and even a defense.[73]

The President's embrace of Secretary Cisneros is not surprising, even if it does grate against the President's own rhetoric about his administration's high ethical pose. Stuart Taylor wrote of the many parallels between the former personal travails of the President and the Secretary, showing similarities between the Gennifer Flowers and Linda Medlar episodes. Taylor, seeing a larger lesson in both the Secretary's conduct and the President's passive response to that conduct, offered his theory why the President did not ask the Secretary to step aside:

> But these [other theories] cannot alone explain what is, after all, a historic first in the annals of political lying: a president who seems genuinely eager to "stick together" with an appointee who has just been exposed as a liar by the attorney general and may be on his way to prison.
>
> No, the principal reason why Cisneros is still standing tall as a symbol of Clintonite ethical standards is that the emperor has no clothes, and can ill afford to acknowledge the ethical nakedness of some of his courtiers.[74]

Keeping Secretary Cisneros at HUD to see the Department through a fundamental reorganization as well as through the difficult budget process in the 104th Congress may have been very important to the President. Of course, the converse argument is that the ability of the Secretary to get his message across may be hampered by the ethical cloud over him. The investigation could also distract Secretary Cisneros from the attention he must devote to his Cabinet position. Yet, the quiet nature of the independent counsel's investigation to date and virtual absence of adverse publicity since the independent counsel's appointment suggest that the Secretary is not distracted or hampered in the conduct of his office. This would more likely be a problem if the allegations of misconduct concerned Secretary Cisneros's actions at HUD.

A public official is entitled to the constitutional presumption of "innocent until proven guilty" in a court of law (even though the presumption is less well-suited for the field of politics). More particularly, the appointment of an independent counsel is not the equivalent of an indictment, although it is so perceived by many. Yet, in this case, the presumption has been eroded significantly by the Attorney General's findings. The Department has already found that Secretary Cisneros lied to the FBI and has implicitly determined that these false statements were made knowingly. The question of materiality, which goes to whether Secretary Cisneros can and should be prosecuted, remains, but clearly some damage to the Secretary's standing has already been done.

In August 1995, Secretary Cisneros announced that he would leave the Administration at the end of this term, regardless of whether President Clinton were reelected.[75] Thus, Secretary Cisneros will likely leave office before the independent counsel determines whether to seek an indictment.[76] Secretary Cisneros cited family reasons and the financial sacrifice involved in public service, which he said "has been more costly than I thought, in every respect[,]" an apparent reference to the controversy over the disclosure of payments to Medlar and the ensuing criminal investigation.[77]

What is the Likely Outcome of an Independent Counsel Investigation?

First, it is unlikely that Secretary Cisneros will be able to escape from the conclusions the Attorney General reached, that Secretary Cisneros misled the FBI on two particulars relating to payments made to Medlar. The tapes and the testimony of the FBI agents will be nearly impossible to rebut. Yet, Secretary Cisneros may well continue to maintain that these false statements were just "mistakes" and were not intentional misrepresentations. It is unlikely he can otherwise come up with an explanation of why he intentionally lied that is both credible **and** also mitigating.

Second, the central question to determine is whether any one (or more than one, in combination) of these false statements could have affected the President's decision to appoint Cisneros or the Senate's vote to confirm him. The courts have repeatedly held that a false statement will be found to be material if it tended to influence **or was capable of influencing** a government decision or other action.[78] However, the amount of weight to be accorded the views of the persons to whom the false statements were directed is not clear. Secretary Cisneros is not likely to be charged if the question of materiality depends on the testimony of the President, White House officials, transition officials, and Senators.

It is a virtual certainty that transition officials, White House officials, and, most importantly, the President all will tell the independent counsel that Secretary Cisneros would have been nominated even had he told the complete truth concerning the size of individual payments and the total amount of payments. Indeed, the President, through his press secretary, has already weighed in on this question: "Nothing contained in the attorney general's statement today would have changed the president's determination to nominate Henry Cisneros."[79]

The unequivocal and immediate nature of the President's public statement sent a clear (and questionable) signal to would-be witnesses from the transition and the White House.

The President's statements aside, it should be noted that had Secretary Cisneros kept the fact of his payments to Medlar from transition and White House officials (as opposed to the amount or timing of the payments), the case against him would be much stronger. But he disclosed to the FBI and the transition the most damning single fact: that he had been making regular payments to Medlar. The other facts, while certainly magnifying the potential scandal,[80] might not have led these officials to pull the nomination. And, given the President's own alleged past indiscretions, it might even have seemed inconsistent to keep Cisneros from the Clinton Cabinet because of a single extramarital affair, even if the payments added a twist. (On the other hand, such statements might have led the White House not to nominate Cisneros for fear of raising issues on which the President may have been vulnerable.)

Whether Cisneros's false statements materially misled the Senate is a more difficult question, but ultimately is likely to be resolved in favor of the Secretary. First, the independent counsel must determine what information about the payments to Medlar was included in the materials the Senators reviewed.[81] Second, those Senators who reviewed the FBI summary report must be interviewed as to whether they would have handled the nomination differently had the truth been disclosed.

In 1993, the Senate was controlled by the Democrats. It is unlikely, although not impossible, that a Democratic Senator would testify to the effect that Cisneros's nomination would not have been reported out of committee, or that he would not have been confirmed, had the full truth about the payments been told. Indeed, the day after the announcement of the Attorney General's request for the appointment of an independent counsel, it was reported that Senators Riegle and D'Amato previously had written letters to Secretary Cisneros's lawyer that Cisneros would have been confirmed even had he told the full truth with respect to the payments.[82] Senator D'Amato, in a December 8, 1994 letter, wrote:

> The specific amount of the payment made by Secretary Cisneros to the person in question would not have changed my judgment concerning Secretary Cisneros' qualifications for confirmation.

Senator Riegle wrote in a December 14, 1994 letter:

> Any specific amounts . . . were not relevant to my judgment as to his fitness to serve—or to my support of his nomination.

A potential wildcard is the conspiracy angle. Did Cisneros and Medlar conspire to keep the truth from the FBI? Note that the FBI did not interview Medlar during the background check. Apparently, Medlar was not interviewed because she said she was too ill.[83] Her excuse may be explored in connection with whether Cisneros and Medlar engaged in a conspiracy to conceal information from the FBI. The transcripts of the tapes, while highly relevant to this question, are flawed and inconclusive. Medlar's testimony is therefore critical on this question, but it may be unlikely that she would admit to engaging in a criminal conspiracy, even if promised immunity from prosecution.

Chapter Fourteen

Allegations Against Secretary of Transportation Frederico Pena

The Southern California Rapid Transit District Pension Board awarded a contract to Secretary Frederico Pena's former management firm just days after the Secretary was sworn. Together with the Secretary's subsequent approval of more than a billion dollars in funding to the District, these actions raised legitimate questions of propriety. The Justice Department, after a quick investigation, determined there was no specific and credible evidence of a violation of Federal criminal law. On the facts that are known, the Justice Department's decision was correct. Further, Secretary Pena did not violate any ethical standard, nor did he violate the terms of his recusal commitment.

However, the Secretary's one-year recusal from participating in matters involving his former company is plainly insufficient. Because Pena Investment Advisors (PIA) retained the Pena name, remains under contract with a DoT grantee, and apparently continues to emphasize Pena's former association with the firm as a selling point, the Secretary's recusal commitment should be extended to cover his entire tenure at DoT. Moreover, the Secretary should not participate in any further decision regarding funding for Southern California's Metropolitan Transit Authority without obtaining advance approval from the DoT ethics office.

Secretary Pena appropriately recused himself at the outset from participating in any particular matter involving the new Denver airport. As Mayor of Denver, Pena promoted the need for, and championed the development of, a new facility to replace Stapleton Airport. After many delays, Denver International Airport opened in February 1995.

Yet, the Secretary is still not in the clear concerning the new Denver airport. Investigations by the Securities and Exchange Commission, FBI, DoT Inspector General, Denver City Attorney, and Congress are all currently underway concerning cost overruns, delays, alleged bid-rigging, other alleged corruption in connection with contract awards, and diversion of airport revenue for non-airport purposes. Pena's conduct (as Mayor, not as Secretary) is at issue in some of these investigations, but it cannot be determined at this point whether he is at serious risk. One of the matters under investigation could adversely affect Commerce Secretary Ron Brown, who in private practice allegedly received funds from airport revenue to lobby on behalf of the City of Denver on matters unrelated to the airport. An allegation by a former DoT investigator that he was fired in retaliation for uncovering and revealing diversion of airport revenue for unrelated lobbying activities, if true, also could tar Secretary Pena, even if he had no role in the firing, as well as the Department's Inspector General (IG).

The Southern California Transit System Contract

In February 1995, the Justice Department began a review under the independent counsel provisions of the Ethics in Government Act, of what role, if any, Frederico Pena played in the February 1993 award to PIA, the Secretary's former company, of a contract to manage $5 million for the Southern California Rapid Transit District pension fund.[1] The review stemmed from a February 15, 1995 referral from the Inspector General of the Department of Transportation. The IG became involved after the *Los Angeles Times* published an article about the contract on February 10.[2]

Under the independent counsel statute, Justice had thirty days to determine whether to conduct a preliminary investigation (which it must do if it finds a specific and credible allegation that a Federal crime was committed) into whether an independent counsel should be requested.[3] On March 16, 1995, the Justice Department issued the following statement closing the matter without conducting a preliminary investigation: "The Criminal Division has found no specific and credible evidence of any violation of federal criminal law. Accordingly, the matter has been closed."[4] As usual in the case of a declination by the Justice Department, no further explanation was provided.

Secretary Pena and the President both issued statements expressing their pleasure at the outcome. Secretary Pena read the Justice Department's declination broadly, concluding, "I am pleased, but not surprised, that the Justice Department has found no evidence of wrongdoing in this matter."[5]

This statement is not accurate, however; Justice did not make such a broad conclusion. Justice reviewed the allegations under the provisions of criminal law, not the standards of ethical conduct to which Secretary Pena is also subject.[6] Thus, this chapter will consider the allegations against the Secretary under both the criminal law and the standards of conduct. The following factual account is taken from David Willman's February 10, 1995 *Los Angeles Times* article, which broke the story and which is still the most complete account.

The Efforts by Pena's Firm to Obtain the Contract

PIA was incorporated in December 1991. Until PIA obtained the pension fund management contract in February 1993, PIA's only institutional client was US West, a Colorado-based Baby Bell company. PIA first sought a contract from the Southern California Rapid Transit District in the middle of 1992. Pena was personally and directly involved in seeking this business; he spoke with at least two local officials during this time. However, PIA was not selected.

In late December 1992, PIA made another attempt to get a piece of the District's pension fund management business. In meetings with pension fund officials, PIA officials played on Pena's name, which would be retained despite his imminent resignation and divestiture. It is not clear whether any of these meetings occurred after the President's December 24, 1992 announcement of Pena as his choice for Transportation Secretary. Even before December 24, however, Pena was a player for the new Administration-in-waiting, serving as the head of the transition's Transportation Team, although it was not expected that he would be selected as Transportation Secretary. It is not known whether Pena participated in any of PIA's December efforts, although no one alleged his involvement during this time.

PIA Obtains the Contract

PIA was awarded the contract on February 8, 1993, just nineteen days after the Secretary was sworn in.[7] The contract was awarded by the Southern California Rapid Transit District's Pension Board, without engaging in competitive bidding.[8] The Board is composed of four management and three union representatives.

The contract was to manage $5 million for the pension fund.[9] The contract was expected to generate for PIA at least $37,500 in fees each year. Of perhaps greater benefit to PIA, this was PIA's first contract with a government agency. PIA joined ten other, larger, and more experienced management firms previously engaged to manage the fund. It appears that PIA was chosen at least in part because of its minority ownership, and in part because of its prior association with the new Secretary. PIA officials asserted, of course, that it won the contract on the merits. However, several persons who spoke on the record to the *Los Angeles Times* said that PIA might not have been chosen had Pena not been Transportation Secretary.[10]

Melvin Marquardt, the investment manager of the fund at the time, said, "I thought we were being pressured to make a decision that I didn't approve of[.] . . . I was more or less annoyed."

Marquardt's superior, Thomas Rubin, the Transit District's treasurer-controller, said, "We saw there was a connection to someone who was going to have a major role in the new Administration[.] . . . We figured it couldn't hurt." Rubin agreed with Marquardt's assessment that PIA officials "were capitalizing on [Pena's] nomination as secretary of transportation[.]"

Pena's Actions as Secretary

Upon confirmation, Secretary Pena severed all financial ties to his former firm, and agreed, in a January 5, 1993 letter to the Office of Government Ethics (OGE), to recuse himself for one year from participating "in any particular matter having a direct and predictable effect" on PIA.

In his two plus years as Secretary, Pena has approved about $1.9 billion in funding to the Metropolitan Transit Authority (MTA), the successor to the Southern California Rapid Transit District, for the construction of a subway in Los Angeles. Reportedly the Secretary's first approval was in May 1993.

Secretary Pena asserted, "There is no relationship between any of the decisions that this department has made, or I have made, as secretary, and the firm." Further, Secretary Pena claimed he had "very little" control over the subway funding, and no control over the amount of funding, which was set by Congress. He did have some control over the funds, however, because in 1994 he suspended funding for several weeks pending MTA's commitment and plans to improve management of the subway project.

Some of these Federal funds may have been used to fund the administration of the pension fund, including the contract awarded to PIA. However, the link between the MTA's subway construction funds and MTA's pension fund management contract was not established, only assumed, by reporters covering this story.

Analysis

Pena Was Not Involved in the Matter Pre-Award, as Secretary or Secretary-Designate
The facts suggest that the District's pension fund management contract may well have been awarded to PIA because of Pena's selection as Transportation Secretary. This may raise a question under California or Federal pension law, which generally requires contracting decisions to be taken in the best interests of the pensioners.[11] But even a finding that pension law was violated would not implicate Secretary Pena or the Clinton Administration, absent some evidence of the Secretary's involvement.

As for Secretary Pena's exposure, the facts suggest that he personally played no role in PIA's selection, either as Secretary or Secretary-designate. At least, no one came forward alleging any such role, either after December 24, 1992 and before confirmation, or after confirmation. And the quick decision by the Attorney General to close the investigation seems to confirm the absence of any incriminating fact of the Secretary's involvement.

One would expect Pena at least to have been kept abreast of PIA's continuing efforts to land the contract in December 1992 and January 1993, as well as its eventual success in February. Yet, a Department spokesman said the Secretary did not know of these efforts.[12] Secretary Pena's ignorance of PIA's efforts turns out to be critical to the determination of whether he should have recused himself from the outset from participating in the funding decisions for the Los Angeles subway.

On the Facts That Are Known, Pena's Participation in the Decisions to Provide Funding to MTA Did Not Violate the Conflict-of-Interest Statute
The ethics question is whether Pena improperly participated as Secretary in decisions awarding billions in funds to the Metropolitan Transit Authority, with whom PIA has a management contract. Pena apparently severed all financial ties to PIA before becoming Secretary.[13] Thus, 18 U.S.C. 208, the criminal conflict-of-interest statute, is not implicated. The Justice Department's declination may well have been predicated on this fact alone.

On the Facts That Are Known, Secretary Pena Was Not Required to Recuse Himself From Decisions to Fund the Los Angeles Subway

Secretary Pena also recused himself for one year from participating in any particular matter having a direct and predictable effect on PIA, and committed to do so to OGE and the Senate. The Secretary's recusal is consistent with the long-standing advice the White House Counsel's office and agency ethics officials have given to prospective presidential appointees. In essence, a reverse revolving door restriction, or cooling-off period, is imposed to guard against the appearance that the official is providing preferential treatment to a former employer in violation of ethics principles and standards.[14] In some cases, involving a prior employment or affiliation that is highly visible or that goes back many years, a recusal of longer duration—perhaps for the official's entire tenure—is recommended.

The standards of conduct, effective February 3, 1993, do not require recusal in so many words. Instead, the standards establish a process whereby potential nonfinancial conflicts or appearance concerns should be raised with agency ethics officials and resolved before the official participates in the matter giving rise to the concern. Under section 502, PIA was a "covered person," because, within the previous year, Pena had served as an officer of the company.[15] Under that section, Secretary Pena may not participate in any particular matter where he knows PIA is a party to that matter or where he determines that the circumstances would lead a reasonable person with knowledge of the facts to question his impartiality in the matter, unless he informs the agency ethics official of this appearance problem and receives authorization to participate.[16] The agency ethics official thereupon evaluates a number of factors to determine whether the interest of the Government in the Secretary's participation outweighs appearance concerns.[17]

Elsewhere in this study, the narrowness of section 502 is criticized. Secretary Pena's involvement in approving funding for the Los Angeles subway clearly raised a question of appearances, given that his former firm was under contract with the local government entity that is the recipient of the Federal funding. Yet, PIA technically was not a "party" to the grants. And Secretary Pena may argue that he did not know his former firm was a possible beneficiary of the Federal funding, the release of which he approved. Section 502 contains a residual provision to address appearance issues that do not fit squarely within the terms of the section's appearance trigger. "A person who is concerned that circumstances other than those specifically described in this section would raise a question regarding his impartiality should use the process described in this section to determine whether he should or should not participate in a particular matter."[18] Thus, assuming Secretary Pena was aware PIA was under contract with MTA, he should have used this process before participating in the funding decisions.

There is no indication that Secretary Pena asked for or received advice under section 502 or the terms of his recusal commitment before participating in the decisions relating to funding for MTA's subway construction project. Had the Secretary obtained approval to do so from DoT ethics officials, his office surely would have noted this to the media. The lack of review by the DoT ethics office suggests that no connection between PIA and the Los Angeles subway funding was made. Even if the ethics office did not, Secretary Pena should have made such a connection, unless, of course, he truly was kept in the dark about his former firm's success in finally land-ing a management contract with the pension fund. Without any additional facts, Secretary Pena's statement (through a spokesman) that he was unaware of PIA's renewed push for a contract should be accepted. Furthermore, it is far from clear that Secretary Pena's funding decisions would likely have a "direct and predictable effect" on PIA. So, even if the Secretary knew of PIA's contract to manage the pension fund, he may not have violated his recusal commitment.

Thus, on the facts that are known, Secretary Pena did not violate any law or ethical standard in connection with decisions regarding the funding provided MTA for the construction of the Los Angeles subway. He would have been better served if, following the Justice Department's closure of the investigation, the White House or DoT ethics office would have announced such a finding.[19]

Secretary Pena's Recusal Should Remain in Place Throughout His Tenure in Office and He Should Not Participate in Any Decision Regarding Funding of MTA Without Advance Approval From the DoT Ethics Official.

The Secretary's one-year recusal commitment is plainly insufficient, given PIA's retention of Pena's name in its title, and PIA's apparent proclivity to emphasize his former association with the company as a selling point.[20] Further, the Secretary was not merely associated with PIA, he founded it and has not ruled out returning to the firm after his service as Secretary. Under these circumstances, Secretary Pena's recusal from matters having a direct and predicable effect on PIA should be permanent.

Moreover, now that Secretary Pena knows of PIA's contract with MTA's Pension Board, and of the controversy that surrounded that contract, he should not participate in future MTA funding decisions without advance approval from the DoT ethics office. In particular, the DoT ethics office should determine if the funds going to MTA may result in some benefit to PIA.

The Denver International Airport Issues[21]

In March 1995, the *Los Angeles Times* reported that the Transportation Department's Inspector General was looking into whether millions of dollars in revenue from Stapleton Airport in Denver were illegally diverted to pay for certain legal expenses and lobbying activities unrelated to the airport or the development of the new Denver International Airport (DIA). Payments to the Washington law firm of Patton, Boggs & Blow are among the payments under review by the IG.[22]

This appears to be only one of a number of allegations of misconduct relating to the development and construction of the new DIA currently under investigation.[23] In addition to the IG's investigation, the **SEC** is conducting a formal investigation into whether purchasers of airport bonds were misled by Denver City and Adams County officials because the likelihood or risk of construction delays was not acknowledged. Delays at some point could have led to a default of bonds sold to finance the airport. SEC attorneys have interviewed Secretary Pena on this matter.

The airport bonds are also part of a nationwide SEC investigation into whether securities firms improperly obtained bond business in exchange for political contributions.[24] **Two private lawsuits,** filed by bond buyers, allege that local officials (Pena was not named) defrauded them by withholding information about construction delays. And the **Denver District Attorney,** the **FBI, and United States Attorney for the District of Colorado** are conducting investigations into potential fraudulent testing, contracting, and construction practices at the new airport. The Federal grand jury probe is focused on components of DIA, such as the runways, that were paid for with Federal funds. The local District Attorney's office is concentrating on airport buildings.[25] The FBI is also investigating the City's award of airport concession contracts to minority-run businesses, examining whether minorities improperly fronted for white-owned companies and whether contracts were steered to political supporters, but this investigation apparently does not cover Pena's tenure as mayor.[26]

There is some confusion whether the IG's diversion of airport revenue investigation was referred to the Justice Department. Indeed, when the Justice Department closed its investigation of the Los Angeles transit pension fund contract, some reports stated that Justice had also closed its investigation of the divresion matter.[27] But this is not correct. The Justice Department's statement refered to a "matter," as did Secretary Pena's statement issued that day. The Los Angeles transit contract and the Denver Airport issue are not related in any way, and thus the use of the singular "matter" indicated that Justice had not disposed of the Denver Airport allegations.

It also appears that in connection with the new Denver Airport, the Aviation Subcommittee of the House Committee on Transportation and Infrastructure, may be looking into PIA's contract with USWest to manage $10 million in USWest's pension fund, PIA's first and largest client. USWest obtained a $24 million contract to install a fiber optics wiring system in the new airport. USWest reportedly contributed $200,000 to Pena's campaigns for Mayor of Denver, and an additional $400,000 to the airport.[28]

Airports receiving airport development funds from the Federal Government are required to provide a written assurance that "revenues generated by a public airport will be expended for the capital or operating costs of :

(A) the airport;
(B) the local airport system; or
(C) other local facilities owned or operated by the airport owner or operator and directly and substantially related to the air transportation of passengers or property.[29]

The remedy for a violation of this grant assurance is to recoup the improperly spent funds from the airport or to withhold additional funds for the airport as an offset.

In 1991-1992, the City of Denver paid $240,000 to Patton, Boggs & Blow for a variety of lobbying activities performed by the firm, notably by Ron Brown, who at the time was a partner of the firm and also Chairman of the Democratic National Committee. The City's contract with Patton, Boggs & Blow apparently was not restricted to lobbying on behalf of the airport, and provided for lobbying "under the directive of the mayor."[30] Pena was Mayor of Denver from 1983 to 1991.

Secretary Pena spoke openly about the probe, acknowledging that Ron Brown handled several matters for the City of Denver, including some that were unrelated to the airport.[31] At a May 11, 1995 hearing of the House Aviation Subcommittee, Secretary Pena testified that Ron Brown was the lawyer responsible for securing Patton, Boggs & Blow's lobbying contract with the City, although the Secretary said Brown did not devote much time to airport-related lobbying.[32]

The legal question turns on whether the funds used by the City to pay Patton, Boggs & Blow came from airport revenue, which the *Los Angeles Times* reported was confirmed by City records provided to the IG.[33] If the lobbying contract was paid for entirely out of airport revenue, then the City of Denver violated its grant assurance to the extent Patton, Boggs & Blow devoted time to matters unrelated to Stapleton or DIA.

Denver's current City Attorney blasted the Inspector General's investigation as an "outrageous abuse of federal resources," asserting that all payments for lobbying activities were related to the airport. And at the May 1995 House hearing, both Secretary Pena and Cynthia Rich, FAA Associate Administrator for Airports, denied that the City had improperly diverted airport revenue.[34] But other local officials were not so sure. The City's practice was to pay for lobbying activities from a number of accounts, on a rotating basis. Thus, lobbying unrelated to the airport may have been paid from airport revenue, and lobbying related to the airport may have been paid from a non-airport revenue account. George Doughty, Director of Aviation for the City of Denver from 1984 to 1992, observed that Patton, Boggs & Blow did not perform much work for the airport, compared with other lobbying work performed for the City. He added that a different Washington firm handled the bulk of airport-related lobbying.[35]

In March 1995, a Department spokesman said he believed the investigation was "not directed at Pena per se. This is really an issue for bean counters."[36] If, as is likely, payment issues were not brought to the attention of the Mayor, Pena is not personally vulnerable to a finding that he violated the law. A Department spokesman said that Secretary Pena "was not specifically aware" how the City paid for lobbying services performed on its behalf. Yet, the Secretary testified in May 1995 that the City paid Patton, Boggs & Blow separately, depending on which department was the beneficiary of the lobbying, which suggests a certain degree of personal knowledge on his part.[37]

Whether or not Pena, as Mayor of Denver, was involved personally in the payments to Brown's law firm in 1991, Pena was responsible politically for all actions taken by his administration. The ethical cloud now over Secretary Brown could cast its shadow over Secretary Pena if the IG determines that an improper diversion of airport revenue occurred.

It seems logical that neither Brown nor Patton, Boggs & Blow would have been in a position to know or care about the particular City account out of which they were paid. To Brown and his firm, that would be an internal accounting matter for the City to determine. Thus, a finding of improper diversion also should not necessarily be held against Secretary Brown.

In August 1995, the diversion investigation took a twist. A former investigator in the DoT IG's office, John Deans, who had been investigating the diversion allegations, charged that he was fired because he uncovered evidence of diversion of hundreds of thousands of dollars of airport revenue for use on lobbying related to "crime programs, bridges, viaducts, and housing programs. The lobbying efforts represented 'everything but the airport.'"[38] Deans filed a claim with the Merit Systems Protection Board to get his job back, and sought representation by the Special Counsel under the Whistleblower Protection Act. Deans said that after he disclosed his findings within the IG's office, he was taken off the case, transferred from Denver to San Francisco, and prevented from discussing the matter with the U.S. Attorney. He was fired on June 19, 1995, effective June 24.

Deans' allegation of retaliation is more serious than his apparent findings of diversion, because it charges misconduct within the Department of Transportation, and, specifically, the IG's office.[39] At the start of the Clinton Administration, Pena, General Counsel Stephen Kaplan, and Chief of Staff Ann Bormolini all properly recused themselves from participating in any particular matter involving DIA. Bormolini was Pena's Chief of Staff in Denver; Kaplan was Denver City Attorney.[40] Thus, assuming these three honored their recusal commitments faithfully, Deans' allegation of retaliation must be directed at persons other than Secretary Pena and his Denver associates. Still, any finding of retaliation would injure the Secretary somewhat. And Dean's statements about diversion also are troubling for Secretary Pena, although it is not clear whether the diversion found by Deans, did so under Mayor Pena's watch.

Answers to whether improper diversion occurred and whether Mayor Pena was involved in any way must await the outcome of the investigations. Likewise, the truth of Deans' claim of retaliation cannot be evaluated on what is publicly known. So Secretary Pena and the Department remain under an ethics cloud until the investigations are concluded.

Part Five

Other Ethics Issues

Chapter Fifteen

Post-Employment Restrictions

The time has come to return some rationality to the set of post-employment restrictions governing the conduct of former Federal employees. The main Federal criminal statute, 18 U.S.C 207, is over-inclusive, excessive, and unduly complicated. The "revolving door" is not as large a problem as portrayed by politicians. While the revolving door is certainly capable of abuse, evidence is slight to show that abuse is serious or widespread. Moreover, the revolving door can foster a higher caliber of talent in government and can assist private interests in making responsible and constructive requests of government. In recent years these benefits have been ignored in the face of anti-government and anti-special interest rhetoric emanating from politicians of both parties and all political persuasions. But those who have examined the purposes and effects of the current set of post-employment restrictions in greater depth and without a political charge are coming around to the view that the law is in need of substantial reform.

President Clinton's executive order falls far short of the rhetoric he employed against the revolving door in the campaign and during the transition; it is replete with loopholes and qualifications. The President deserves criticism for unrealistically raising public expectations that he would "stop" the revolving door, as well as for discouraging many talented persons from serving in his Administration. In the short run, the President could revise the executive order to close its loopholes, but the better reform would be to rescind the executive order outright and push for a reform of the criminal statute. The President, of course, is unlikely to take these actions, but the next president should take them soon upon assuming office.

Congress, like the President, is moving in the wrong direction. Congress is seriously considering an even tighter post-employment restrictions regime, featuring provisions lacking a rational basis.

In recent years, politicians, public interest groups, and the media have increasingly criticized the practice of former high-level government officials who engage in lobbying and other representation on behalf of private interests in matters before the Federal Government. This practice is commonly referred to as "the revolving door:" Federal officials go out the door as they leave government for the private sector and come back through the door when they contact or meet with government officials on behalf of their new private client. The revolving door threatens to compromise the Government's decisionmaking processes through the misuse of nonpublic information, the improper degree of access and influence former officials have with their former agency, or the preferential treatment current employees provide future or prospective employers.[1]

A Brief History of Post-Employment Restrictions

Federal law has long restricted all former Executive Branch employees from representing private clients before any Executive Branch agency or any court with respect to a particular matter involving specific parties in which they were involved while in government.[2] In 1978, Congress significantly expanded the scope of post-employment restrictions by prohibiting certain former high-level Executive Branch officials for one year from making any appearance before their former agency on behalf of any person and from contacting their former agency or any of its employees regarding any particular matter in which the agency has a direct and substantial interest. This so-called "cooling-off" restriction applied regardless of whether the former official had participated in the matter while in government or even whether the matter was pending during the employee's government tenure.[3]

The 1978 law also prohibited former Executive Branch employees from rendering advice or assistance behind the scenes concerning any particular matter involving specific parties in which either the employee participated personally and substantially or that was under the employee's supervision. In a rare example of Congress pulling back in this area, one year later (1979) Congress "clarified" that the prohibition against the giving of advice or assistance applied only to advice or assistance provided in connection with an actual physical appearance before the Government and only in connection with a particular matter in which the employee participated personally and substantially while in government.[4] Congress became concerned about this post-employment restriction after hearing from several top Carter Administration officials about the ill effects on the Federal workforce.[5]

In the 1980s, highly publicized reports of revolving door abuse by recently departed officials of the Reagan Administration prompted Congress to push for even tougher post-employment restrictions. Initially, Congress focused on the departure of numerous Department of Defense (DoD) officials for lucrative jobs in the DoD procurement community.[6] In 1986, Congress enacted a complicated provision generally prohibiting certain former DoD officials who had exercised substantial responsibility over a particular major DoD procurement from receiving compensation for two years from the contractor for that procurement.[7]

In the next Congress, efforts were made to pass additional restrictions on current and former government procurement officials, not limited to DoD personnel, as part of a set of Federal procurement reforms. These efforts did not pick up steam until reports of major procurement scandals in the Defense Department surfaced in June 1988. The Justice Department's investigation of these scandals, called "Operation Ill Wind," eventually resulted in numerous convictions of DoD employees and contractor personnel for several different procurements. Allegations generally concerned the illegal disclosure of source selection sensitive information and the illegal exercise of influence by DoD employees for the benefit of contractors, who had offered DoD employees bribes, gratuities, and promises of future employment.

Congress responded to the "Ill Wind" scandals by passing the Office of Federal Procurement Policy Act Amendments of 1988, which included a new post-employment provision.[8] Under this "procurement integrity" provision, for two years from the last date of an official's personal and substantial participation in a particular procurement, the former official is prohibited from participating in any manner in any negotiations leading to the award or modification of that contract, or from participating personally and substantially in the performance of that contract.[9]

Other highly publicized revolving door abuses by former Reagan Administration officials prompted proposals for additional, tougher post-employment restrictions.[10] In the waning days of the 100th Congress, a bill imposing several new post-employment restrictions and containing significant amendments to current restrictions passed both Houses. The Post-Employment Restrictions Act of 1988, H.R. 5043, included broader cooling-off periods for top-level Executive Branch officials, imposed special one-year restrictions regarding the representation of foreign entities and work on trade negotiations, and included a cooling-off period for former Members of Congress and certain high-level congressional staff. The bill also would have limited the application of all post-employment restrictions to acts done for compensation.

On the recommendations of the Justice Department, the Office of Government Ethics (OGE), and other agencies, President Reagan pocket-vetoed the bill on November 23, 1988. The President called the bill "flawed, excessive, and discriminatory."[11] He was most concerned that the bill "would discourage from Government service America's best talent because of the unfair burdens it would impose."[12] In particular, he criticized the bill for weakening post-employment restrictions by adding a compensation element; for perpetuating the unequal treatment of Executive and Legislative Branch personnel; and for proscribing certain conduct "unrelated to genuine ethical concerns."[13] Nonetheless, President Reagan urged President-elect Bush and the incoming 101st Congress to enact a post-employment restrictions bill that would satisfy the Administration's concerns.[14]

Neither the Bush Administration nor the Congress let much time pass before moving to enact post-employment restrictions. The President's Commission on Federal Ethics Law Reform was set up in January 1989,[15] and issued its report in March, containing a series of recommendations, including some changes in the post-employment restrictions laws.[16] The House established a bipartisan task force, which issued a report in the fall of 1989, containing a similar set of recommendations.[17] In the Ethics Reform Act of 1989, enacted in November 1989, Congress tightened the post-employment restrictions governing Executive Branch officials and enacted for the first time post-employment restrictions covering Members of Congress and certain congressional staff.[18] Many of these restrictions were taken from the bill President Reagan had refused to sign the previous year, although the compensation requirement was dropped.[19] These new restrictions apply to officials who leave the Government on or after January 1, 1991.[20]

Political sentiment against the revolving door did not ebb with this legislation. Instead, seen as part and parcel of the inordinate influence special interests exert over Congress and the Executive Branch, the revolving door was constantly under attack, and had few defenders. Anti-revolving door rhetoric reached a crescendo in the 1992 presidential campaign, when Republican Pat Buchanan, Democratic Party nominee Bill Clinton, and independent H. Ross Perot all criticized President Bush because several high-level Bush campaign officials and advisers had been retained by corporate interests and foreign governments to represent and counsel them on matters before the Federal Government.[21]

Soon after the election, President-elect Clinton began to translate his campaign rhetoric into administration policy, issuing an executive order on his first day in office that imposed a set of tougher post-employment restrictions on senior officials of his Administration. Also, bills were introduced in the initial days of the 103d Congress that would have codified the President's new restrictions and imposed even tighter and broader restrictions. Although none of these bills was enacted, even tougher post-employment restrictions were introduced in the 104th Congress. This chapter examines the new post-employment restrictions imposed by President Clinton and the post-employment legislation proposed in the 103d and 104th Congresses. This examination concludes that the President's executive order and the legislative proposals that would place ever greater restrictions on the revolving door are, for the most part, bad public policy.

From Campaign Rhetoric to Government Policy

President Clinton came into office with a pledge to improve markedly the ethics in the Executive Branch by "stopping the revolving door." The Clinton/Gore campaign's treatise, *Putting People First*, in a section calling for a "Revolution In Government," linked the revolving door with the pernicious influence of lobbying on behalf of special interests:

> We must take away power from the entrenched bureaucracies and special interests that dominate Washington. . . .
>
> It's long past time to clean up Washington. The last twelve years were nothing less than an extended hunting season for high-priced lobbyists and Washington influence peddlers. . . .
>
> During the 1980s . . . [h]igh-level executive branch employees traded in their government jobs for the chance to make millions lobbying their former bosses. Experts estimate that nearly one of every two senior Amer-

ican trade officials has signed on to work for nations they once faced across the negotiating table. This betrayal of democracy must stop.

To break the stalemate in Washington, we have to attack the problem at its source: entrenched power and money. We must cut the bureaucracy, limit special interests, stop the revolving door, and cut off the unrestricted flow of campaign funds. The privilege of public service ought to be enough of a perk for people in government.[22]

During the transition, President-elect Clinton revealed a new set of post-employment restrictions to which his senior political appointees would be required to commit.[23] These restrictions were included in the first executive order of the Clinton Administration, signed on the day of inauguration.[24] This new set of restrictions was promised at the time to be President Clinton's first step on ethics reform.[25]

The President's executive order does not directly improve or change any standard of conduct governing Executive Branch employees in the performance of their duties. The order relates only to the revolving door between government and the private sector, governing conduct of former employees. Yet, even as late as March 1994, at his initial news conference to answer questions on Whitewater, the President continued to cite his executive order for his assertion that his Administration is subject to the highest ethical standards of any administration:

> But since you raised the issue, let me also ask you to report to the American people that we have and we have enforced higher standards against ethical conflicts than any previous administration. When people leave the White House, they can't lobby the White House. If they're in certain positions, they can't lobby the White House for a long time. If they're in certain positions now, they can never lobby on behalf of a foreign government.[26]

Contrary to the President's statement, post-employment restrictions do not directly relate to "ethical conflicts."[27] In any event, the Administration had not yet had a meaningful opportunity to "enforce" its tougher revolving door restrictions, because only a handful of officials subject to these new restrictions had left the Government.

Executive Order 12834
Executive Order 12834 contains three basic provisions:

(1) senior appointees may not lobby their former agency for **five years** (senior appointees in the Executive Office of the President (EOP) also may not lobby for five years any agency with respect to which they had personal and substantial responsibility);

(2) senior appointees may not **for life** engage in any activity on behalf of a foreign government or foreign political party that would require their registration as a foreign agent; and

(3) trade negotiators may not aid or advise foreign entities, including for-

eign corporations, with intent to influence a decision of the United States Government for **five years**.[28]

These post-employment restrictions apply to all full-time non-career presidential, vice-presidential, and agency-head appointees whose rate of basic pay is not less than an Executive Level V salary ($108,200 per year for 1993, 1994, and 1995), except that the trade negotiator restriction applies to political appointees regardless of salary.[29]

Under current Federal criminal law, "senior" officials are subject to a cooling-off period that prohibits them for one year after their departure from government from communicating with or making an appearance before any employee of their former agency regarding any official matter.[30] For "very senior" officials,[31] the one-year cooling-off period also prohibits communications to or appearances before all presidential appointees throughout the Executive Branch who are paid a salary under the Executive Schedule.[32] Former senior and very senior officials are prohibited for one year from representing **or advising** foreign governments and foreign political parties with respect to a matter before a department or agency of the United States (excluding Congress, but including other Legislative Branch agencies, such as GAO).[33] And all former employees are prohibited for one year from representing **or advising** anyone with respect to a trade or treaty negotiation in which they participated personally and substantially in their last year in government service, on the basis of privileged information obtained while in government.[34]

Government procurement officials are also subject to a two-year ban under the Procurement Integrity provision in section 27 of the Office of Federal Procurement Policy Act, codified at 41 U.S.C. 423(f). For two years from the last date of personal and substantial participation in the conduct of a particular contract, former procurement officials are prohibited from knowingly participating in any manner (advice as well as representation) in any negotiations leading to the award or modification of the contract, or from knowingly participating personally and substantially in the performance of that contract.

Therefore, the President's executive order essentially lengthened the basic cooling-off period from one to five years, broadened the scope of the ban for senior EOP officials to include all agencies with respect to which they had substantial responsibility, and set a lifetime ban on serving as a registered foreign agent.

The executive order's trade negotiator cooling-off period, however, bears little resemblance to the statutory prohibition: it is both broader and narrower than subsection 207(b). The executive order applies only to noncareer trade negotiators;[35] subsection 207(b) applies to all employees who participated in a trade or treaty negotiation, regardless of salary or career status. The executive order provides a five-year cooling-off period, instead of the one-year provision (and one-year lookback provision) in the statute. The executive order prevents former trade negotiators only from representing or advising any foreign entity, including private corporations, but with intent to influence any matter before the U.S. Government, regardless of the nature of the matter. By contrast, the statute is limited to activities with respect to the same trade or treaty negotiation in which the former official participated while in government, but it does not turn on the identity of the client.

The executive order contains a waiver provision, but waivers may be granted only by the President.[36]

The executive order is enforced by an "ethics pledge" each senior appointee must sign as a condition of appointment. The pledge is deemed a contract between the appointee and the Government; government employment is the consideration.[37] Violations of any of the commitments contained in the ethics pledge may result in debarment proceedings within the affected agency (upon notice and hearing, with judicial review), or in civil proceedings in which the Attorney General may seek declaratory and injunctive relief (including a temporary restraining order). Also, a constructive trust may be established for the benefit of the United States to recover any money or thing of value received by or payable to the former appointee arising out of the breach of the ethics pledge.[38]

For the most part, the President's post-employment restrictions initially received praise. The praise began with Warren Christopher's announcement of the planned restrictions from Little Rock during the transition. Christopher proclaimed that these reforms would "stop the revolving door[.]" He added, "These rules seek to change the climate in Washington, and usher in a new era of public service[.] . . . These pledges go well beyond existing ethics rules, and are designed to signal a clear break with existing practice."[39] While Christopher may be forgiven some rhetorical hyper- bole, his first claim—that the restrictions would "stop" the revolving door—was simply false. Fred Wertheimer of Common Cause displayed somewhat more modest enthusiasm. He said the restrictions "represent a real breakthrough in the effort to deal with the revolving-door problem."[40] Legislators and interest groups pushing for even further statutory post-employment restrictions cited the President's executive order in support of their proposals.

Does Executive Order 12834 Close the Revolving Door?

From the start, President Clinton's executive order was recognized largely for its symbolic value. Upon closer examination, the executive order was criticized for its narrow reach and its many loopholes.[41]

The restrictions initially were intended to cover about one-third of the expected 3,500 political appointees in the Clinton Administration, including about 100 White House officials.[42] It later turned out that only ten to twenty White House officials are covered.[43]

The general five-year cooling-off period in Executive Order 12834, although longer than current law, is not nearly as strict as it may seem at first read. Like 18 U.S.C. 207, President Clinton's executive order does not prohibit former appointees in any way from lobbying or contacting Members of Congress or congressional staff. Also, like the criminal statute, the general "no contact" ban in Executive Order 12834 covers only communications to and appearances before the Government; it does not generally reach the giving of advice behind the scenes.[44]

Moreover, the definition of "lobbying" in the executive order is subject to a number of exceptions based on the subject-matter of the representation or the identi- ty of the client. "Lobbying" does not include representing state or local governments, representing educational, scientific, or charitable institutions with respect to a grant, contract, or similar benefit, or representing any person before a court or with regard to a law enforcement investigation or proceeding.[45] The first two exceptions are gen- erally reflected in section 207;[46] however, the third exception—what is essentially an exemption for lawyers—is not reflected in Federal law.

The executive order's lifetime ban on serving as a foreign agent applies only to representing foreign governments and political parties, not foreign business entities. Although this same limitation appears in section 207, those who see evil in the representation of anyone and anything foreign deemed this a major loophole.[47]

Even with these exceptions and exemptions, the President's post-employment restrictions are, for the most part, tougher than the restrictions in section 207. But as tight as they may be, they were not designed to stop, shut, close, or lock the revolving door, only to slow it down a little. And any lingering notion the public may have had that the President's executive order would curtail the practice of "cashing in" was eliminated in November 1993, when two senior White House officials resigned to take lucrative positions in the private sector after less than a year's service in the White House.

Howard Paster, Assistant to the President for Legislative Affairs, left the White House to rejoin Hill & Knowlton, a large public relations and lobbying firm. Roy Neel, Deputy Chief of Staff and former Chief of Staff to Vice President Gore, left the White House to serve as President of the United States Telephone Association.[48] Neel worked on telecommunications issues when he served as Vice President Gore's Chief of Staff. When he worked for Senator Gore, he was said to have been the Senator's "principal adviser on communications issues."[49] Both former officials were expected to receive a salary in the high six-figures.

Paster and Neel, as well as other White House officials, stressed that they would strictly observe the requirements of the executive order, and not personally engage in "lobbying," as that term is defined—**and circumscribed**—in the executive order.[50] No one contended otherwise.[51] Instead, their transition to lucrative positions in the private sector—companies that regularly engage in lobbying—vividly illustrated the executive order's modest scope.[52]

Pamela Gilbert, of Public Citizen's Congress Watch, said, "This Administration has made a very big deal about stopping business as usual, and this is exactly business as usual." Charles Lewis, of the Center for Public Integrity, said, "They can attempt to finesse it all they want, but two of the most important figures in the Clinton White House have gone into the lobbying community, and that's the bottom line."[53]

Administration officials, caught on the ethics defensive, began to sound countervailing considerations. Press Secretary Dee Dee Myers said, "You can't expect that people in Government will never have another job."[54] Roy Neel explained, "Common sense dictates that these laws are not about . . . eliminating the ability of someone to simply come into the private sector and to build on an experience they had in government[.] . . . The public interest is not well served by having no one from the private sector go into government or having no one from government go out to the private sector."[55] Even the President spoke sincerely yet cogently: "I don't think we should discourage people from moving in and out of government. . . . I don't think we should have a permanent government class and a permanent private sector . . . across the divide from each other."[56]

These countervailing considerations were known—even voiced—at the time the new restrictions were revealed in December 1992 during the transition. At a lower decibel level than **candidate** and **President-elect** Clinton's rhetoric about the "betrayal of democracy" and lobbyists' "stranglehold" on government, it was clear that the Clinton **Administration** never really intended to "stop" the revolving door, as Christopher had proclaimed at the time. In particular, the exceptions to the definition of "lobbying" reflected a policy judgment that some revolving door activity is not at all bad.[57] More generally, Christopher acknowledged that "we of course have sought to balance the need for reform with the desire to attract the very best people into government."[58]

Revolving Door Proposals in the 103d Congress

From the other end of Pennsylvania Avenue, Congress continued to consider additional post-employment restrictions. Senator Dennis DeConcini introduced S. 79, which would have codified in part the restrictions in Executive Order 12834, lengthened the time period of the current restrictions in section 207, and broadened the coverage of the foreign entity restriction.[59] Senator David Boren and four others introduced S. 420, which also would have gone well beyond current law and the executive order.[60]

At a March 5, 1993 hearing before the Subcommittee on Oversight and Government Management of the Senate Committee on Governmental Affairs to discuss both bills, Senators Boren, DeConcini, and John McCain each linked the revolving door with the erosion of the public's trust in the Federal Government.[61]

In early 1994, Senators Boren and McCain offered the "Post-Employment Reform Act of 1994," as an amendment to S. 1935, a bill to ban Senators' acceptance of certain gifts.[62] The amendment, scaled back significantly from S. 420, would have extended the one-year cooling-off periods for "senior" and "very senior" officials in subsections 207(c) and (d) to two years, the one-year trade and treaty negotiation cooling-off period in subsection 207(b) to ten years, and the one-year foreign entity cooling-off period in subsection 207(f) to two years. It would have broadened the definition of "foreign entity" to include corporations and other entities incorporated or having their principal place of business outside the United States. S. 1935, as amended by the post-employment language, passed the Senate in May 1994.

On the House side, the House-passed bill on lobbying disclosure, which included a gift ban, did not contain a post-employment restrictions provision. The House and Senate went to conference on the lobbying disclosure bills that passed each House, so that the Senate's post-employment restrictions provision was not on the table at conference.[63] Thus, no comprehensive post-employment restrictions bill was enacted by the 103d Congress.[64]

Revolving Door Proposals in the 104th Congress

Congressional zeal for stronger post-employment restrictions did not wane in the new, Republican-controlled Congress. On the contrary, legislation to restrain the revolving door got a boost by its association with other "good government" reforms of the political and governmental process, such as lobbying disclosure, gift rules, and campaign finance reform. What was actually proposed was far more draconian than even President Clinton's executive order. If enacted, these proposals would go a long way toward stopping the revolving door. Of course, they would also significantly harm the Government's ability to attract talented people, far more than may be discouraged currently by law or executive order.

On January 4, 1995, the first week of the new Congress, Senators McCain and Russ Feingold introduced S. 129, a post-employment restrictions bill similar to the proposals McCain made in the previous Congress.

In May, Representatives Richard Zimmer and Marty Meehan introduced H.R. 1576, the Revolving Door Act of 1995. This bill would signal a major expansion of post-employment restrictions. Zimmer's press release touted that this bill would "stop" the revolving door. The bill would:

• Extend the one-year foreign entity ban to life, and broaden the definition of foreign entity to include a foreign national;[65]

• Broaden the "senior" and "very senior" cooling-off periods in current subsections 207(c) and (d) to cover Executive Branch officials with salaries of $70,000 or more, as well as the President (who is not covered under current law); as broadened, the one-year cooling-off period with respect to communications to or appearances before one's former agency would be extended to five years (with a five-year lookback provision), and the one year super cooling-off period with respect to communications to or appearances before all Presidential appointees with salaries set by the Executive Schedule would be extended to ban contact with **any** Executive Branch employee of any agency and of any rank, for two years.

• Prohibit Executive Branch officials with salaries of $70,000 or more (including the President and Vice President) for two years from making any communication to or appearance before any Member or congressional employee seeking official action on any matter. This would be the first inter-branch post-employment restriction.

• Prohibit certain former senior Legislative and Executive Branch officials from "hold[ing] a supervisory position over any person who is likely to make a communication or appearance" to Congress or the Executive Branch.[66] This would be the first generally applicable post-employment restriction containing an employment ban and, because of its attenuated nexus to the prevention of corruption, would be of dubious constitutionality.[67]

Similar restrictions would apply to former Members of Congress and senior congressional staff.

Under Zimmer's bill, a former Executive Branch official who earned a $70,000 salary (a senior career official, GS-15, or a mid-level political appointee) would be precluded from (1) seeking official action on behalf of any other person from anyone in the Executive or Legislative Branch for two years, (2) seeking official action on behalf of any other person from anyone in the official's former agency (or agencies over the past five years) for five years; and (3) representing or advising any foreign person or entity for life with regard to any matter before the United States. The exceptions to the restrictions proposed in the bill would not significantly soften its harshness.

No action had been taken on either S. 129 or H.R. 1576 by the end of November 1995. However, more particularized post-employment restrictions tucked inside of other bills (lobbying disclosure and procurement reform) fared better.

On July 25, 1995, the Senate passed the Lobbying Disclosure Act of 1995, 98-0, which includes yet another post-employment restriction concerning trade and treaty negotiations.[68] Section 21 contains both a post-employment restriction and a "limitation on appointments" provision. Section 21(a), amending section 207(f), simply would extend to life the current three-year ban on representing or advising foreign entities that was imposed in 1992, only on the U.S. Trade Representative, and would also subject the Deputy U.S. Trade Representative to this restriction. Section 21(b) would amend 19 U.S.C. 2171(b) and prohibit any person who has ever directly represented or advised a foreign entity in any trade negotiation or trade dispute from being appointed as U.S. Trade Representative or Deputy U.S. Trade Representative. This latter provision would apparently be the first instance in the United States Code of prohibiting the appointment of someone because of prior representational activity. This section was added as an amendment to the lobbying disclosure bill, by Senators Dole, McCain, and Mitch McConnell, all Republicans.[69]

Senate Majority Leader Dole's statement on the floor in favor of this provision was brief and unpersuasive:

> The real problem here is one of appearance—the appearance of a re-volving door between government service and private-sector enrichment. This appearance problem becomes all the more acute when former high Government officials work on behalf of foreign interests.
>
> Service as a high Government official is a privilege, not a right. This amendment may discourage some individuals from accepting the U.S.T.R. job, but in my view, this is a small price to pay when the confidence of the American people is at stake.[70]

Dole went even further in his floor statement, lamenting the fact that the lobby-ing bill was not also amended to codify President Clinton's executive order![71]

On November 29, 1995, the House passed without change the Senate lobbying disclosure bill, 421 to 0, including the post-employment and limitation on appoint-ment provisions (thereby obviating a conference between the two Houses). President Clinton said that he would sign the legislation.[72]

Encouraged by the success in passing lobbying disclosure reforms, several Members of Congress (led by Representative Barney Frank) indicated that they would introduce a bill early in the next Session combining further post-employment restric-tions with other related reforms.[73]

The only action going in the other direction is procurement reform legislation sponsored by Bill Clinger, Chairman of the House Government Reform and Over-sight Committee, and several others.[74] Introduced in May 1995, Clinger's bill would repeal outright the procurement integrity restriction (41 U.S.C. 423 (f)), the two-year employment ban (10 U.S.C. 2397b), and the currently suspended criminal selling statute (18 U.S.C. 281). Both the Bush and Clinton Administrations pushed for these reforms. In introducing this bill, Clinger said:

> The accumulation over time of several layers of tailored post-employment restrictions has complicated efforts to provide guidance and advice to those who must abide by the rules, and has frustrated Federal agencies in attract-ing the highest quality talent from industry and academia.

H.R. 1670 was reported out of committee in July 1995 and passed the House without a single "no" vote on September 14, 1995.[75] However, as of the end of No-vember 1995, no similar provision had been introduced in the Senate. By contrast, a

Senate bill entitled the Department of Defense Acquisition Management Reform Act of 1995, S. 646, contains an amendment, not a repeal, of the procurement integrity post-employment restrictions provision. Section 161 (c) of the Senate bill would replace both the two-year procurement integrity provision (41 U.S.C. 324(f)) and the two-year employment ban (10 U.S.C. 2397b) with a one-year employment ban applying only to contracts or claims of $500,000 or more. No action had been taken on this bill as of the end of November 1995.

Another potential legislative vehicle to achieve procurement integrity reform in the First Session of the 104th Congress was the National Defense Authorization Act for Fiscal Year 1996. Representative Clinger inserted the procurement integrity provisions of H.R. 1670 into the House-passed bill, H.R. 1530, including the repeal of the post-employment restrictions provision (section 831(b)) and the employment ban. The Senate-passed bill, S. 1026, did not contain a similar provision. As of the end of November 1995, the authorization legislation was mired in conference, with uncertain prospects for enactment.

Striking the Right Balance

The most basic post-employment restriction is intended to prevent a former employee from switching sides in a particular matter. A cooling-off period is a special type of post-employment restriction, because it restricts a former employee's conduct without regard to whether the employee was involved in the matter while in the Government or even whether the matter was pending during the employee's government tenure, and because it covers all matters, regardless of their scope or specificity. A cooling-off period is designed to protect the government's decisionmaking processes from being improperly skewed, either by former officials on the outside or current officials on the inside, as well as to avoid the public perception that the Government's processes are tainted.[76] Cooling-off periods are intended primarily to reduce what is perceived as the disproportionate access and influence former officials possess by virtue of the connections they made while in government. Secondarily, they are intended to limit the opportunity of Federal officials to take official action for prospective financial gain as well as discourage persons from working for the Government who might be inclined to use public office for future private gain.[77]

Post-employment restrictions must be crafted in recognition of their effect on the ability of government to attract the best-qualified persons from outside of government to serve in senior policy positions.[78] Moreover, the revolving door has several inherent benefits. In the wake of the enactment of the first cooling-off period, Justice Department attorney Ed Kneedler spoke eloquently about how the revolving door benefits government, the public, and the individuals:

> Turnover at all levels also serves to infuse fresh blood into what is increasingly criticized as an overgrown, unresponsive bureaucracy. It allows government policies to be established with the advice of those who have in the past felt the effects of those policies of who have special insights into the sector of society to which government action is directed.
>
> . . . [T]he free movement out of government enhances the government's ability to recruit people to come in because it assures them that they will not substantially injure their future career prospects and life choices by accepting an appointment.

... Persons who have held a position in an agency are often in the best position to point out errors or abuses by that agency after they have left. They can educate the public, their advocates and clients about the agency's work. Because of their expertise, they are often more effective advocates on behalf of those whom they serve in the private sector. This expertise can frequently increase the efficiency of the government's response to private sector concerns as well.[79]

In 1989, the President's Commission on Federal Ethics Law Reform warned that post-employment restrictions:

> must tread a narrow line, because the so-called "revolving door" has many healthy attributes. In particular, the flow of individuals between private life and occasional government service is a source of invigoration to both sectors, and provides a valuable exchange of information about the workings of government which improves the understanding of each sector about the other. Our system of government in a sense mandates a substantial amount of "revolving door" activity every four or eight years.[80]

Following the 1989 amendments to section 207 and the issuance of President Clinton's executive order, the American Bar Association Committee on Government Standards (ABA Committee) issued a report on Government ethics that also recognized the limits of government regulation of the revolving door.[81] While "commend[ing] the ethical sensitivity of recent Executive and Legislative proposals that would give greater weight to the public interest in preventing abuse of former government position[,]" the ABA Committee "urge[d] caution lest the zeal of regulatory reform produce an over-correction . . . ."[82]

> For reasons of both political principle and pragmatic necessity, our country prizes the ability to draw on the skills of citizens who have been, and will return to be, private-sector managers, physical and social scientists, technical experts, and medical and legal professionals. Truly effective regulation in this area will forestall the exploitation of public office without so cabining post-employment activities that noncareer government service becomes undesirable to these people. Moreover, it will take into account the tacit but fundamental premise of citizen government: Most who serve are honorable persons who would disdain any intentional abuse of power or position.[83]

Finding the right balance between these competing considerations is not easy. The current landscape of post-employment restrictions is, at best, uneven. Some legislators and public interest groups view current law as inadequate, riddled with loopholes. Other advocates of even tougher restrictions on the revolving door wish to see established and maintained a permanent, separate, and adversarial relationship between the public and private sectors. These advocates believe that the public interest is not served by the regular exchange between the regulators and the regulated. This view, to the extent it is reflected in law, encourages into government service only professors and public interest group members; corporate officials, on the other hand, are discouraged.

Having repeatedly linked revolving door lobbyists with the corruption of our democratic processes, legislators, and other political figures have shown little regard for the adverse effects current and proposed post-employment restrictions may cause. Indeed, in the immediate wake of the departure of Howard Paster and Roy Neel, President Clinton's executive order was severely criticized as too weak. The executive order, for example, goes too far in at least three respects. But the better view is that the scheme of post-employment restrictions is excessive and in need of some relaxation and greater rationality.

First, there is no ethics basis for a ban on serving as a registered foreign agent. This restriction is nothing more than a political response to the xenophobic rhetoric of the sort that emanated from Ross Perot and Pat Buchanan during the 1992 Presidential campaign.[84] Moreover, there is no rational basis for a lifetime ban on serving as a foreign agent. Conceding that the choice of any time limit is arbitrary does not mean that the choice of a lifetime ban is rational. A lifetime ban on switching sides on a particular matter involving specific parties, reflected in 18 U.S.C. 207(a)(1), makes sense, but even this ban, in practice, is not likely to last more than a few years.[85] A lifetime ban on representing certain clients, however, is not a cooling-off period. It is a freeze: a permanent penalty for prior public service that is not imposed on any other government employee.

Second, the five-year trade negotiator provision is considerably overbroad. Under the executive order, a former Department of Agriculture official whose only involvement with a trade negotiation concerned wheat exports to Russia would be prohibited for five years from advising Swiss Air on how to seek certain route authority from the U.S. Department of Transportation. This hypothetical presents no potential for concern over improper access or influence. In addition, the trade negotiator provision—like the foreign entity provisions—suffers from the bias against persons and things foreign, without any ethics nexus.

Third, even if one year is considered to be too short of a basic cooling-off period, a five-year period is too long. For any Clinton Administration official who does not depart until the end of this four-year term, the cooling-off period will extend into the term of another President, perhaps of a different party. The five-year period also is far more likely to deter talented people from coming into government than the one-year periods in section 207.

There are now some signs of recognition that post-employment restrictions regulation has gone too far. First, there have been occasional reports that the executive order's five-year cooling-off period has, in fact, discouraged applicants for certain Administration positions.[86] Indeed, one year into the Clinton Administration, three senior officials—then-Treasury Secretary Lloyd Bentsen, then-OMB Director Leon Panetta, and White House Deputy Chief of Staff (and former head of Presidential Personnel) Phil Lader—all publicly acknowledged that the executive order's restrictions seem to have discouraged a number of persons from applying for certain posts.[87] Panetta suggested that "[i]t probably isn't a bad idea to begin to take another look to make sure that it isn't inhibiting us from getting the most talented people back into government. Somehow there's got to be a better way to do this and protect the public interest."[88]

Second, at the March 1993 Senate hearing, several persons, including Gary Davis, the General Counsel of the Office of Government Ethics (OGE), testified in opposition to the legislative proposals under consideration.[89] Davis urged that Congress give the new post-employment restrictions imposed by the Ethics Reform Act of 1989 and Executive Order 12834 "the necessary time to operate, rather than legislating and adding to the already complex array of post-employment restrictions."[90] In prepared testimony, Davis stated OGE's opposition in even stronger terms:

> In our view, this legislation goes beyond that which the government has a legitimate need to control, and thus threatens good government by posing unnecessary impediments to recruitment and retention of the most qualified individuals.[91]

Alexander Trowbridge, representing the Council for Excellence in Government, expressed his organization's concern that the bills would hinder the Government's ability to attract the best qualified persons for government positions and would discourage the healthy mobility between public and private sectors.[92] In a written submission, the Senior Executives Association also criticized the bills, disputing their premise that current law is inadequate, and asserting that the bills would compromise the speech, associational, and contract rights of former government employees.[93]

The American Civil Liberties Union (ACLU) expressed its view that the bills would not pass constitutional muster, and added that "there is no demonstrable record of actual misconduct that is not adequately covered by current law."[94] Although Professor Eskridge believed that the bills were "generally" constitutional, he identified several constitutionally "problematic" provisions. Further, he opposed the differential treatment accorded foreign nationals, and expressed his view that post-employment restrictions were better enforced civilly, rather than through the criminal code.[95]

In the end, the draconian bills did not emerge from the 103d Congress, but similar provisions remain pending in the 104th..

Third, the report of the ABA Committee on Government Standards made three recommendations that would require changes in section 207 and Executive Order 12834; two of them would generally curtail the reach and length of the cooling-off periods currently provided by statute and executive order.[96] Although the ABA Committee would lengthen the one-year cooling-off periods in subsections 207(c)-(e), it would shorten the five-year period in the executive order. The ABA Committee would also abolish special cooling-off provisions that turn on the identity of the client or the type of issue (e.g., foreign entity and trade negotiator bans, the procurement integrity restrictions, and the exception for representation of state and local governments).

Concerning the length of cooling-off periods, the ABA Committee stated that "a restriction that affects a substantial range of post-employment behavior should be counterbalanced by [having a] relatively short term:"[97]

> [W]e are convinced that the five-year period chosen by Executive Order 12,834 is considerably too long. . . . The risk that the abusive power of personal influence and contacts will survive not only the passage of time but also the vicissitudes of politics is too insignificant to justify such sub-

stantial curtailment of citizens' professional lives after they leave government.[98]

The ABA Committee noted that client-specific provisions (e.g., foreign entities, state and local governments) "cannot be justified on ethical grounds. . . . Whatever conception of the public interest motivates such rules, these rules have nothing to do with ethics policy." The ABA Committee criticized the premise of subject-specific provisions (e.g., procurement integrity, trade negotiations), that certain subject-matter areas are more prone to abuse. Instead of a "political response to particular scandals or crises," such rules should be instituted "only when careful study demonstrates the presence of unique ethical concerns."[99]

Finally, in September 1995, the President's third White House Counsel, Abner Mikva, criticized the current regime of post-employment restrictions in a speech to the Annual Conference of the Office of Government Ethics held in Williamsburg, Virginia. In an answer to a question from the audience, Judge Mikva stated, "I think we have racheted the bar too high in that respect." He added that "we are losing good people," and extolled the benefits to government and the private sector resulting from the public sector-private sector exchange of top officials. Speaking specifically about the President's executive order, Mikva said, "I am very unhappy about the pledge that President Clinton exacted from people before they came to work for the White House . . . ."

While his criticism was limited to the provision of the executive order relating to representation and assistance to foreign entities, which he said was "wrong," the context of Mikva's remarks suggests that he would favor a repeal of the whole executive order. Referring to the executive order, Mikva said he believes it has hurt recruiting and retention of persons.[100]

Recommendations

President Clinton's campaign against the revolving door reached its apogee on January 20, 1993, the day he signed Executive Order 12834. Beginning that very day, the executive order came under criticism for its many exceptions and exemptions. With the departure at the end of 1993 of Howard Paster and Roy Neel, the bloom appeared to be very much off the rose.

The fundamental problem with the executive order, however, is not its limited application or its differential treatment of subject matters and clients, although there is plenty of both. Rather, the fault lies in the President's initial failure to grasp that every racheting of post-employment restrictions is not without a real public policy cost. At the end of the first year of the Clinton Administration, with many high-level administration posts still vacant, several senior administration officials publicly voiced concern about the effect of the executive order on the recruitment for senior positions. Put in a defensive posture by the departures of Paster and Neel, the President eventually began to recognize the public policy benefits derived from the movement of people "in and out of government[,]"[101] although he stopped short of acknowledging that his executive order was costing his administration highly qualified persons. And at the end of his brief tenure as White House Counsel, Judge Mikva also voiced the conclusion that the President's executive order had cost the Administration some good people.

The Executive Order Should Be Repealed, or at a Minimum, Changed Significantly

In several respects, the executive order is simply excessive. In other respects, like current section 207, it is discriminatory or without an ethics foundation. It is, of course, too much to expect the President to revise his executive order, much less to repeal it, even after (one of) his White House Counsel criticized it. Under frequently criticism for his administration's perceived ethical missteps, the President has been understandably reluctant to take any action that will be seen as a loosening of ethics standards for his administration—and, unfortunately, any relaxation of revolving door restrictions would be so perceived. But the next President should repeal the executive order outright, soon upon assuming office, or at least make appropriate revisions in several areas.[102]

First, the five-year cooling-off periods should be reduced, perhaps to two, for the reasons cited in the ABA report. Second, the foreign entity and trade negotiator provisions should be repealed as excessive and discriminatory against foreign governments. Third, the lawyers' exemption should be repealed. If the justification for this exemption is that the proceedings in which the lawyer would provide representation would be public, should there not also be an exemption for any kind of representation that is made publicly?

Judging by the enactment of additional post-employment restrictions in 1995, it does not appear that the current Congress is in the mood to pull back and rationalize its scheme of post-employment restrictions (aside from procurement integrity restrictions whose fate remains uncertain). That also is unfortunate, because there is a broad-based coalition that supports a rational rewriting of the post-employment laws: OGE,[103] the ABA Committee on Government Standards, the Council for Excellence In Government, the Senior Executives Association, the Government employee unions, and the American Civil Liberties Union.

Section 207 Should Be Revised

First, at least for lawyers, extend the lifetime ban on representing a client on the same particular matter involving specific parties in which the former employee was personally and substantially involved to include advice given behind the scenes. Many bar rules now proscribe this activity; the ABA Committee on Government Standards recommends this reform. This would further reduce the risk of misuse of nonpublic information. And it should not be onerous, given its limited applicability to the same particular matter involving specific parties in which the former official participated personally and substantially while in government.

Second, repeal the foreign entity cooling-off period, including the special provision relating to the U.S. Trade Representative and by virtue of the 1995 lobbying disclosure legislation, the Deputy Trade Representative. As amended, the three-year ban is now a lifetime ban. As the ABA Committee and others have recognized, these restrictions have nothing to do with ethics. The law's hostility to foreign governments is fundamentally inconsistent with the free trade thrust beyond NAFTA and GATT, and overlooks that the counseling of foreign governments by former U.S. Government officials may result in fewer international disputes, fewer misunderstandings of U.S. law or of the U.S. Government's position, as well as a legitimate check on the sometimes overzealous or discriminatory Government actions vis-a-vis foreign governments.

Third, repeal the exceptions for representation of state and local governments, and charitable, educational, and religious institutions, consistent with the recommendations of the ABA Committee. There is no reason these interests deserve a special exemption; they, too, stand to gain or lose financially from actions of the Executive Branch.[104] The procurement integrity provision imposes an enormous administrative burden that is not worth the marginal, if any, benefit of having a special post-employment restriction governing procurements.

Fourth, the trade or treaty negotiation cooling-off period and procurement integrity post-employment restrictions are sufficiently similar to the switching sides provisions in subsection 207(a) that they can and should be repealed. The trade or treaty negotiation restriction prohibits only advice and representation provided on the basis of privileged information.

Fifth, as discussed in the next section, the cooling-off periods in subsections 207 (c), (d), and (e) should be revised to permit communications and appearances engaged in solely for political purposes, along the lines of legislation proposed by President Bush in 1991, and pending in the 104th Congress.

Ultimately, abuses of the revolving door can best be prevented by those who are in government, who take to heart the ethics principle that employees "shall not give preferential treatment to any private organization or individual."[105] Agency officials should exercise caution in any meetings or conversations with recently departed high-level officials, providing only so much information that would be warranted in response to any other person making the same request, and taking only those actions that would be warranted on the merits. Only in this way can an agency reduce the risk of getting into trouble because of a former official's eagerness to satisfy a client.[106]

Case in Point:

George Stephanopoulos and the Cooling-Off Period

George Stephanopoulos appears to have violated the criminal post-employment restriction provision to which he was subject after leaving Capitol Hill in the fall of 1991, when he met with House leaders in the summer of 1992 on behalf of candidate Bill Clinton. There is a legitimate question whether Stephanopoulos was covered by the law because of the unusual nature of his compensation, but the better statutory analysis is that he was covered by the law. If he was exempt, the law contains a potentially large loophole that should be closed, because Stephanopoulos was precisely the sort of senior Hill aide who should be subject to a cooling-off period. However, as a matter of policy, the law should not restrict purely political communications by recently departed high-level officials, made on behalf of political parties or candidates. Accordingly, Congress should amend the post-employment restrictions law along the lines proposed by the Bush Administration in 1991.

As a former assistant to House Majority Leader Richard Gephardt, George Stephanopoulos was subject to a one-year cooling-off period when he left Capitol Hill in the fall of 1991 to join the Clinton campaign. A new provision added by the Ethics Reform Act of 1989 extended post-employment restrictions for the first time to former Members of Congress and certain senior congressional staff.[1] Stephanopoulos served as Executive Floor Assistant to the House Majority Leader.

The cooling-off period prohibited Stephanopoulos, for one year after he left the Hill, from making any communication to or appearance before any House leader or leadership staff member in connection with any matter on which he was seeking official action on behalf of another person.[2] Unlike other post-employment restrictions that are limited to "particular matters involving a specific party or parties" in which the employee was previously involved, a cooling-off period prohibits a former official from seeking official action on any matter.[3]

From the latter part of 1991 through the 1992 election, Stephanopoulos served on Governor Clinton's paid campaign staff as deputy campaign manager and communications director. In that capacity, it is clear that he personally met with the House leadership on issues of legislation relevant to the campaign on at least one occasion; undoubtedly, he met or spoke with the leadership at other times. David Broder wrote of two meetings on July 2, 1992, within one year of Stephanopoulos's departure from the Hill: a morning meeting with "three dozen top House Democrats," and the weekly luncheon of Democratic Senators.[4] *National Review* asserted that Stephanopoulos "was frequently seen on Capitol Hill consulting with his former colleagues."[5] Stephanopoulos, therefore, made "a communication to or appearance before" a Member of the House leadership on behalf of another person[,]" namely, Governor Clinton. Also, it is plain that Stephanopoulos made these appearances "knowingly."

Stephanopoulos presented two defenses to reporters who asked him questions about these meetings. First, he asserted that he was exempt from the cooling-off period because his salary was below the threshold of coverage. Second, he denied that he sought official action from any Member in those meetings. While the first defense has some technical merit, Stephanopoulos' second defense is not persuasive.

Was Stephanopoulos Exempt from the Cooling-Off Period?

Stephanopoulos stated that he believes he was exempt from the cooling-off period because his salary was under the threshold set by the law. If Stephanopoulos is correct, it is not on the basis of the explanations he provided. Moreover, if Stephanopoulos is correct, there is a major loophole in the coverage provision of the post-employment restrictions law, which requires legislative correction.

The cooling-off period for the leadership staff covers only a former employee who "for at least 60 days, in the aggregate, during the one-year period before that former employee's service as such employee terminated, was paid a rate of basic pay equal to or greater than an amount which is 75 percent of the basic rate of pay payable for a Member of the House of Congress in which such employee was employed."[6] In 1991, the salary for a House Member was $125,100, so that the salary threshold for leadership staff such as Stephanopoulos was $93,825. Whether a staffer is subject to a cooling-off period thus would appear to be a simple matter that could be determined with mathematical certainty. In fact, the determination in Stephanopoulos's case is neither simple nor certain. Determining Stephanopoulos's "rate of basic pay" is difficult because he left the Hill before the end of the year, and because he was paid in uneven installments.

Stephanopoulos told Fred Barnes his salary was $90,000, below the threshold.[7] On the January 24, 1993, "This Week With David Brinkley" show, Stephanopoulos stated, "There's also a question of whether or not I was covered by the law because my salary level was actually too low to be covered by the law. . . . My salary was—under Congress—I think went from $88,000 to $92,000." Bob Woodward wrote that Stephanopoulos's salary on the Hill was $95,000.[8]

Barnes noted that Stephanopoulos received "$9,591 a month in at least two months in 1991, an annual pay rate of $105,000."[9] Stephanopoulos protested that the two-month figure used by Barnes was "illusory," noting that he was on both the Majority Leader's payroll and Representative Gephardt's personal office payroll, and that his salary in other months was "far less." Stephanopoulos is correct that his salary in some other months was less than $9,591, but not for the reason he offered.

The four House Clerk's Reports for the year 1991 show no payment to Stephanopoulos from Representative Gephardt's personal office payroll. For all of 1991, Stephanopoulos is listed in the House Clerk's Reports as exclusively on the Majority Leader's payroll.[10] What Stephanopoulos may have been thinking of is that his salary on the Majority Leader's payroll varied from month-to-month in 1991. The Clerk's Reports show that Stephanopoulos's salary alternated between $9,591 (for the position "Floor Assistant (statutory)") for one month and $5,777.83 (for the position "Floor Assistant") for the next month, and so on for nine months, from January to September 1991. It appears that Stephanopoulos's salary was arranged this way to provide him with more compensation than would have been possible had his salary come entirely out of the limited statutory allotment for the Majority Leader's office.[11] By alternating the source of Stephanopoulos's salary between the statutory allotment and a lump sum allocated to the leadership offices, Stephanopoulos and others with similar arrangements were able to receive a greater salary.

The statute refers to the rate of basic pay paid to the official "for at least 60 days, in the aggregate[.]" In the usual case, an official's rate of basic pay is set at the beginning of the year, based on a total salary amount, and the official monthly pay is the same. It also is not uncommon for a government official to receive a pay increase in the middle of a calendar year. In such a case, the higher salary rate is used for purposes of the cooling-off period if the official works at that higher salary for 60 days. Here, Stephanopoulos's salary went up and down throughout the year, never staying the same for two consecutive months. It is not known what total salary was intended for Stephanopoulos at the beginning of 1991 (most likely **some** set figure was intended); Stephanopoulos's varying recollection that his salary was $90,000 or $92,000 (or perhaps $95,000, *pace* Woodward) may be based on such a determination, but it is not clear that such a figure, if known, would be determinative. The statute uses the phrase "in the aggregate" and turns on the rate of basic pay the employee was in fact "paid." Most likely the statute did not contemplate Stephanopoulos's extraordinary compensation scheme. There are several possible constructions.

If a two consecutive month ("at least 60 days") period were used, Stephanopoulos's annualized rate is $92,212.98, just under the threshold of $93,875.[12] However, if a three consecutive month period were used ("**at least** 60 days, in the aggregate"), in the first and third quarters of 1991 Stephanopoulos received $24,959.83 ($9,591 in two months and $5,777.83 in the other month), which translates into an annual pay rate of $99,839.32, over the threshold.[13] If only the higher salaried months were considered (again, "at least 60 days, in the aggregate," but not consecutive), Stephanopoulos's salary would be annualized at $115,092, well over the threshold. And if the total salary received by Stephanopoulos in 1991 for less than ten full months ($73,570.05 for 9.43 months) were annualized over a full year, his rate of pay ($93,719.81) would fall under the threshold by less than $200.

Because the statute looks back to the previous year of the official's service, Stephanopoulos might also be covered by the cooling-off period if he was paid a rate of basic pay in the last two months of 1990, or in the last month of 1990 and the first month of 1991, in an amount equal to or great than 75% of the salary of a House member. Seventy-five percent of a House member's 1990 salary ($98,400) was $73,800. Stephanopoulos' combined pay for December 1990 and January 1991 ($4,686.50 and $9,591 = $14,277.50) is over the threshold, 76.65% of what a House Member's salary would have been during this two month period ($8,200 and $10,425 = $18,265).[14]

The better statutory construction of the phrase "for at least 60 days, in the ag-gregate, during the one-year period before that former employee's service as such employee terminated," does not incorporate a requirement that the period of "at least sixty days" be at least sixty **consecutive** days. The statute does not use the words, "for any consecutive period of at least 60 days." The only construction that gives meaning to each of the three phrases—"at least sixty days," "in the aggregate," and "during the 1-year period"—looks to whether, during the previous year, the employ-ee's rate of pay, for at least sixty days during that year, aggregated to 75% or more of a House Member's salary. Under this construction, Stephanopoulos was covered, because in five separate months in 1991 and one in 1990, his rate of pay clearly exceeded 75%. Even if a consecutive day period were required, his salary in Decem-ber 1990 and January 1991 exceeded the 75% threshold during that period.

This construction is also recommended as a matter of policy, because the cool-ing-off period was intended to cover senior House leadership staff. Considering the nature and scope of his responsibilities as the Majority Leader's Chief Floor Assis-tant, Stephanopoulos was precisely the type of leadership staff employee the law was intended to cover.[15] If the law did not cover Stephanopoulos, then the leadership staff provision contains a loophole by which the provision could be emasculated.

As a matter of criminal law, however, Stephanopoulos would receive the bene-fit of any ambiguity found to be in section 207's coverage provision, unless he had been informed that he was a covered official before or upon his departure from the Hill. But is the statute ambiguous on its face, or simply difficult to apply? Whether the statute applies to Stephanopoulos is difficult, not because the words in section 207's coverage provision are ambiguous, but because terms of his compensation were unusual. Whether a court would find the provision ambiguous **as applied** to Stephanopoulos, and thus fatal to a prosecution, is uncertain, but it is likely that this difficulty would dampen a prosecutor's enthusiasm to seek an indictment, especially if it could be established that Stephanopoulos was not informed of the law's cover-age. Ambiguities in the criminal law are generally construed in favor the defendant, under the judicially-recognized "rule of lenity," to comport with Due Process Clause of the Fifth Amendment.[16] But a defendant may not assert the vagueness of a law that has been authoritatively construed to apply to him.

Was Stephanopoulos informed, either in writing or orally, at any time in 1991 or upon his departure, that he was subject to a cooling-off period?[17]

Did Stephanopoulos Seek Official Action from a Member of Congress?

The cooling-off period would not have been violated by just any communica-tion to or appearance before a Member of Congress. The critical question is whether, in one or more meetings, Stephanopoulos sought any action from any Member of the House leadership or their staff in their official capacity, on behalf of the Clinton campaign or any other person.[18]

Stephanopoulos denied "lobbying" anyone in Congress while he was subject to the cooling-off period. He told Fred Barnes that "there was 'only an exchange of information' at meetings he attended with members of Congress[.]"[19] On "This Week with David Brinkley" he said, "I deny that I was lobbying. I often called for political information and giving political information from the campaign to the Hill, which is entirely proper. . . . I was just giving back information and that is proper." Stephan-opoulos's account, however, conflicts with David Broder's contemporaneous ac-count of the June 1992 meeting:

Clinton sent his pollster, media adviser and communications director to meetings Thursday with Senate Democrats and House leaders, soliciting political advice and asking for help in getting out his message. . . .

Stephanopoulos said they had a "terrific" reception and [Stanley] Greenberg said he found the members of Congress "much more upbeat" about Clinton's prospects than earlier.

One immediate outgrowth of the meetings, according to Rep. Vic Fazio (D-Calif.), the chairman of the Democratic Congressional Campaign Committee, is that lawmaker-delegates will meet with the Clinton high command each morning of the Democratic National Convention, which starts July 13, to work out "a coordinated message for the day."[20]

It seems unlikely that these meetings and phone conversations were confined simply to an exchange of information between the House leadership and the Clinton campaign (as Stephanopoulos contended), or even that the Clinton campaign sought only political, not official action, from the legislators (as a literal reading of the Broder article might suggest). It seems logical, if not probable, that a purpose of these meetings was also to discuss what the House leadership could do, *qua* legislators, to assist, or least not to harm candidate Clinton during the remainder of the 102d Congress.[21] Meetings between the Clinton campaign and the Democratic leadership would logically discuss what legislation should move, what legislation should not, whether hearings should be held on one or more matters, and even when Congress should adjourn in the fall.

Is this enough to establish Stephanopoulos's culpability (assuming the law applies to him)? No, because in matters involving potential violations of criminal law, it is not sufficient to surmise an essential element of the crime (here, whether Stephanopoulos was "seeking official action" is problematic) based on what is logical or probable from a particular situation. What exactly transpired in the July 2, 1992 meeting is not known. Also unknown is the nature or extent of other meetings or phone conversations in which Stephanopoulos may have conferred with the House leadership or leadership staff.

But certainly there is credible, sufficient information to warrant a criminal investigation.[22] Such an investigation would involve determining first, by obtaining pay and personnel records and questioning House ethics counsel and others, whether Stephanopoulos was ever informed, in writing or orally, that he was subject to a cooling-off period and that the cooling-off period prohibited him from seeking official action on behalf of a political candidate. Second, the investigation would entail obtaining testimony from those Members and staff who attended any meeting or engaged in any conversation with Stephanopoulos during the campaign.

Should This Conduct be Considered Criminal?

By now the reader may wonder what is so objectionable about Stephanopoulos returning to the Hill to carry candidate Clinton's message and to seek assistance from members of his own party. What, after all, is the purpose of the cooling-off period? It is to prevent recently-departed high-level officials from obtaining special access to government or exercising undue influence in furtherance of their own private interests, simply by virtue of the connections made during their previous government service. Even assuming that Stephanopoulos sought official action from House leaders on behalf of candidate Clinton, is there something inherently wrong about seeking official action on behalf of a candidate for public office?[23]

No, say some political observers, even some who believe Stephanopoulos violated the law. Michael Barone wrote that "a strong case can be made that one top Clinton staffer, George Stephanopoulos, has violated the current antilobbying law. Last summer, less than a year after leaving the House leadership staff, he met as a representative of the Clinton campaign with his former bosses, presumably to influence official actions—conduct forbidden by criminal law."[24] But Barone pardoned Stephanopoulos in the very next sentence:

> It must be added that no sensible prosecutor would bring such an indictment; prosecutorial discretion should avoid intrusion on the sensitive business of politics and government in the absence of obviously criminal behavior like burglary or vote fraud.[25]

National Review also noted that going to prison for such conduct would be "unreasonable."[26]

For precisely this reason, the Bush Administration attempted in 1991 to amend the law when the potential reach of the law came directly into play. In February 1991, Clayton Yeutter resigned as Secretary of Agriculture to become Chairman of the Republican National Committee. In a memorandum to Secretary Yeutter describing the scope of his post-employment restrictions, the White House Counsel's office concluded that Yeutter, for one year following his termination from Federal service, should not meet with Cabinet officials and certain officials of the Executive Office of the President (e.g., the Director of the Office of Management and Budget, the United States Trade Representative, and the Director of National Drug Control Policy), on any matter involving official Government policy.

Secretary Yeutter was covered by 18 U.S.C. 207(d), a new cooling-off period added by the Ethics Reform Act of 1989.[27] Sub-section 207(d) applies to former "very senior" officials, a definition that includes the Members of the Cabinet and certain Assistants to the President.[28] In addition to being subject to the one-year cooling-off period covering employees of the former official's agency,[29] the former official is also prohibited from seeking official action from any official whose salary is determined by the Executive Schedule under 5 U.S.C. 5312-5316.[30] Essentially, this latter category consists of all presidential appointees who are subject to Senate confirmation. Yeutter was not prevented from meeting with the President, Vice President, or White House Office staff, because they are not listed in sections 5312-5316. However, the problem would arise if Yeutter were invited to the White House to discuss one or more matters with the President or White House staff, and Richard Darman, Carla Hills, or Governor Martinez, or any Cabinet member were present, because these officials' salary was determined by 5 U.S.C. 5312. Yeutter, therefore, would be prohibited from seeking official action from them.

Yeutter could attend such meetings within the letter of the law, provided that the only potential actions under discussion were political.[31] But, of course, it was not practical to attempt to structure such meetings to avoid any discussion of official policy. With the President, as with other elected officials, the line between political and official action during a campaign often is not bright. In any event, there was concern that Yeutter's mere presence in the White House complex would likely be noticed by the sophisticated White House press corps and result in a story featuring a defensive White House, criticism from ethics watchdogs, and calls from Democrats for a criminal investigation, regardless of whether Yeutter scrupulously refrained from seeking official action.

Therefore, the strong advice the White House Counsel's office gave Yeutter and senior White House staff was simply to avoid such meetings.[32]

The advice the White House Counsel's office gave Secretary Yeutter did not sit well with him, or with RNC officials or senior White House staff. They did not understand how a law that was intended to restrict former high-level officials from personally trading on their position should apply to former officials whose sole purpose in meeting with senior political appointees would be political, not to further any private or financial interests. Further, with the 1992 presidential campaign just around the corner, White House officials anticipated additional departures from the White House and Cabinet to join the campaign effort. They foresaw substantial hindrances to the White House and the campaign if these officials were precluded from meeting with White House officials and attending certain Cabinet meetings.

Therefore, in January 1991, the White House Counsel's office began working with the Office of Government Ethics (OGE), the Justice Department, and the White House Office of Legislative Affairs to draft legislation that would amend the post-employment restriction to permit political communications. On July 26, 1991, the President transmitted to Congress a proposed bill called the "Post-Employment Restriction Technical Correction Act of 1991." The bill would have clarified that the one-year cooling-off period "was not intended to apply to appearances or communications made by former senior Government officials on behalf of candidates for office, election committees, and political party organizations."[33] President Bush stated that he did "not believe that the Congress intended the post-employment restrictions to sweep so broadly."[34]

The bill received bipartisan support in both Houses. It was considered a "good government" reform, and members of both parties saw a need for the amendment.[35] The Administration made no secret of its desire for this amendment; inside the Bush White House the bill was alternatively called the "Yeutter fix" or the "Mosbacher fix." But it was made clear to congressional staff that, without this amendment, senior Hill staff who left the congressional payroll to participate in Federal campaigns (not just the Presidential campaign) would also be restricted. On the Hill, the provision was also called the "Stephanopoulos fix."

In the House, the amendment was attached to a bill to amend the honoraria restrictions of the Ethics Reform Act of 1989, H.R. 3341. In introducing the bill, Representative Barney Frank stated:

> We in my judgment forgot to include in that set of [post-employment] exemptions the Democratic and Republican National Committee and appropriate political campaigns, so that if someone leaves the President's Cabinet and goes to work in the President's election campaign he or she will not be forbidden to talk to his or her colleagues.[36]

This provision passed the House on November 25, 1991.

The bill was also introduced in the Senate and approved by the Senate Government Affairs Committee, but was never submitted to a vote of the full Senate because of an impasse over the scope of the honoraria amendments. In November 1991, near the end of the First Session of the 102d Congress, the White House was told that the Senate leadership would move the bill if the President would support other, unrelated legislation. Senate Democrats, sensing the Administration's strong and immediate desire for this reform, attempted to leverage the Administration by holding it hostage. When the White House refused to agree to this offer from the Democratic leadership, the bill died.

Because Congress failed to amend the law, departing Executive and Legislative Branch officials (in particular, Clayton Yeutter, Robert Mosbacher, and Sam Skinner of the Bush Administration) were circumscribed in which political communications they could lawfully engage during the 1992 Presidential campaign. Fred Barnes wrote that "Republicans were scrupulous about avoiding the appearance of a violation."[37] From the reports of Stephanopoulos's activities, however, it does not appear that the Clinton campaign was similarly disadvantaged.

On May 15, 1995, Representative Barney Frank reintroduced an honoraria bill, H.R. 1639, which includes a provision exempting purely political communications from the cooling-off periods in section 207. As of the end of November 1995, no action had been taken on this bill.

Recommendations

Regardless of whether Stephanopoulos's activities are formally investigated, several steps should be taken immediately, as the 1996 campaign cycle has already begun. First, section 207 should be amended as originally proposed by the Bush Administration and passed by the House in 1991, and as proposed in H.R. 1639, explicitly to permit political communications that otherwise would be barred by the cooling-off periods. The Clinton Administration should endorse this legislative solution, or else it should begin a formal investigation of the allegations against Stephanopoulos (which would include a determination of whether Stephanopoulos was covered by the law).

Second, to ensure that the most senior congressional staff are covered, Congress should lower the salary threshold or make the coverage provision triggered by persons appointed to certain named or classified positions.[38]

Third, all Federal employees, including congressional staff, who are covered by a cooling-off period should be briefed in person on the scope of the no-contact ban upon the triggering of the law. Both Houses should ensure that all departing congressional staff are informed also in writing as to whether they are covered by section 207(e). If necessary, the ethics committee of each House should clarify how the salary of a staffer is determined for purposes of that section.

Chapter Sixteen

Preconfirmation Activities by Prospective Presidential Appointees

Several Clinton Administration appointees, acting as consultants before they were confirmed, exceeded their authority by taking part in policy or management decisions. Such breaches, while avoidable, are not unexpected for a new administration. Existing guidance, if properly followed, could have prevented some, but not all, of the mistakes. Clearer guidance should be disseminated throughout the Executive Branch, and tighter regulatory and management controls on the use of consultants by Federal agencies should be promulgated. Administrations should exercise greater self-restraint in placing prospective appointees in an agency, especially before their nomination.

The Nature of the Problem

In the Clinton Administration, like previous administrations, some presidential appointees[1] were brought into the agency for which they were designated before they were confirmed by the Senate and took the oath of office. Some who were brought in receive titles such as special assistant, adviser, or counselor; others were not given any special title or position other than consultant. Some were paid a consultant's wage; others were reimbursed only for travel and living expenses. Some were brought in after they were nominated, or after the President's intention to nominate was announced; others waited until their confirmation hearing was held. However, it is assumed in this study that most Clinton Administration nominees, like previous administrations, waited until confirmation before coming on board.

As this analysis will demonstrate, it was not clear to the Clinton Administration, as it should have been, that waiting until confirmation is the only safe choice for a nominee, the agency, and the Administration.

A prospective appointee arriving before confirmation may do so for a number of unobjectionable reasons: to receive advice on ethical restrictions to which the appointee will be subject; to receive assistance in completing financial disclosure reports for the Executive Branch and the appropriate Senate committee; and to receive overview briefings of the agency's duties and other briefings to prepare a nominee for the confirmation hearing.

Because a nominee generally can receive all this advice and assistance in just a couple of visits to the agency, there usually is another reason why a nominee is formerly retained as a consultant and given office space and a title before confirmation.[2] The reason is that the White House or agency head wants the prospective appointee immediately to begin participating in deliberations about agency policies and programs, either because of a existing policy void in the agency, or perhaps because of the special expertise or perspective the individual is expected to bring to the agency. An administration that wants to hit the ground running, or an agency in need of particular expertise to address time-sensitive priorities, sees the weeks and sometimes months that elapse between nomination and confirmation as a hindrance. This is when agencies and nominees begin to court trouble.

An agency has legal authority to hire prospective appointees as consultants under 5 U.S.C. 3109(b).[3] Until its sunset at the end of 1994, the *Federal Personnel Manual (FPM)* defined "consultant" as:

> a person who serves primarily as an adviser to an officer or instrumentality of the Government, as distinguished from an officer or employee who carries out the agencies' duties and responsibilities. A consultant provides views or opinions on problems or questions presented by the agency, but neither performs nor supervises performance of operating functions.[4]

The *FPM* was considered to be only **guidance** to Federal agencies. In the Technical and Miscellaneous Civil Service Amendments Act of 1992, Congress directed the Office of Personnel Management (OPM) to issue **regulations** concerning the "criteria governing the circumstances in which it is appropriate to employ an expert or consultant[.]"[5] Subsequently, as part of the Clinton Administration's "reinventing government" initiative, major portions of the *FPM* were eliminated, including, as of December 31, 1994, Chapter 304, which contained guidance on the use of consultants.

The guidance in the *FPM* relating to consultants was essentially included in the rule OPM issued in September 1995 to comply with the 1992 amendment to section 3109.[6] The final rule states:

> [S]ubject to the conditions of this part, an agency may appoint an individual awaiting final action on a Presidential appointment to an expert or consultant position.[7]

A consultant position is defined as:

> one that requires providing advice, views, opinions, alternatives, or rec-
> ommendations on a temporary and/or intermittent basis on issues, prob-
> lems, or questions presented by a Federal official.[8]

Under the rule, an agency may not appoint an expert or consultant:
(3) To perform managerial or supervisory work, . . . to make final decisions
on substantive policies, or to otherwise function in the agency chain of
command (e.g., to approve financial transactions, personnel actions, etc.).
(4) To do work performed by the agency's regular employees.[9]

The Senate, of course, dislikes the practice of nominees beginning work at an
agency prior to confirmation. The Senate's advice and consent responsibilities are
expressly grounded in the Constitution.[10] Coming on board before confirmation gives
the appearance of taking the Senate's consent for granted. *A fortiori*, the Senate likes
it even less when a person takes a consultant position in the agency before his nomination, because it gives the appearance of treating the Senate's advice as irrelevant.

In addition to the obvious affront to the Senate, this practice poses even greater
dangers for nominees. First, nominees are likely to face a more difficult confirmation
process, because they will be charged with knowledge of and responsibility for decisions made by the agency during their tenure as consultants. Their desire to begin
their formal appointment without a track record and without an extensive list of commitments to Congress is often dashed. Second, a person who settles into an agency
office and begins to participate in agency deliberations becomes a special Government employee (SGE), subject to nearly all of the ethics restrictions to which the
person would be subject upon being sworn in. Third, while consultants do not have
authority to make agency decisions, the line between giving advice and decisionmaking tends to blur as agency officials naturally tend to defer to the views of a
person who will shortly be their superior. An agency decision made by or approved
by one who has not yet been sworn in also may be challenged and overturned in court
for lack of authority.

Given these risks, an administration should be very reluctant to bring prospective appointees on board before confirmation. Moreover, once on board, prospective
appointees, as well as agency officials with whom they will be working, should receive clear advice on the standards of conduct restrictions that apply to SGEs and the
limits of a consultant's authority.

The Clinton Administration Encounters the Problem
The following four examples suggest that the Clinton Administration, if it has
learned these lessons at all, has done so the hard way. Three of the four examples
come from the Department of Defense (DoD).

On April 22, 1993, Senators Sam Nunn and Strom Thurmond, Chairman and
Ranking Member of the Committee on Armed Services, respectively, wrote Defense
Secretary Les Aspin expressing concern over reports regarding the actions of nomi-
nees and prospective nominees as Pentagon consultants.[11] The Senators noted that:

Our Committee traditionally has advised the Department that their activities with respect to the position for which they may be appointed should be limited to discussions necessary to familiarize nominees with their prospective duties. We have consistently asked the Department to ensure that any such nominees and prospective nominees act in accordance with three concerns . . . :

First, that such persons adhere to the applicable laws and regulations governing conflicts of interest, particularly with regard to private sector investments and employment.

Second, that authoritative guidance in the Department of Defense should come from the Department's civilian and military officials, not from consultants.

Third, that nominees and prospective nominees should assume no duties and take no actions that would appear to presume the outcome of the confirmation process.[12]

The Secretary was asked to describe which actions he might take pursuant to the Committee's concerns.[13]

Secretary Aspin responded, stating that he had previously issued written guidance on March 9 that addressed each of the Senators' concerns.[14] The March 9 memorandum told nominees that:

You may offer general advisory views on policy matters, but on a strictly informal basis. . . . You are not to sign any documents that give the appearance of having assumed official duties. . . . You are not to undertake to hire, transfer or terminate members of your potential future organization, or otherwise reorganize its management.[15]

In his letter, Secretary Aspin added that while consultant nominees:

may offer me informal advice as I make decisions as a duly confirmed Secretary of Defense, they are not to act in any way that suggests that they have the authority they would have only after they are confirmed by the Senate. In addition, each potential nominee received an extensive briefing from the Department's Office of Standards and Conduct to delineate the legal requirements concerning their tenure as consultants, prospective nominees and nominees. . . .

I gave this clear directive to all prospective nominees to insure that no one here in DoD would presume to any authority that can come only from the Senate's confirmation.[16]

As will be shown, three DoD consultants breached these guidelines while awaiting confirmation.

Ashton B. Carter

On April 13, 1993, the President announced his intent to nominate Ashton Carter to be Assistant Secretary of Defense for Nuclear Security and Counter-Proliferation, a position established by Secretary Aspin in a policy reorganization of the Pentagon intended to handle Defense policy issues in the aftermath of the Cold War.[17] Before then, Carter had been retained as a DoD consultant. He was formally nominated on April 29, 1993. At his confirmation hearing on May 25, Carter was asked whether he had "made any authoritative decisions or provided authoritative guidance" or had "assumed any duties or undertaken any actions that would appear to presume the outcome of the confirmation process." Carter responded in the negative to both questions.[18]

After the hearing, and just prior to the Committee's vote on the nomination, Senator Dirk Kempthorne provided the Committee with a copy of a May 17, 1993 memorandum signed by Carter, in which Carter requested the Defense Nuclear Agency to transfer funds that were designated to assist the dismantling of nuclear weapons in the former Soviet Union, in order to pay for contacts between U.S. and Russian military officials.[19] Subsequently, other internal DoD documents signed or initialed by Carter were obtained by the Committee.[20]

Carter's nomination was held up for a couple of weeks to allow the Committee to look into whether Carter had exceeded his authority as a consultant or misled the Committee at his confirmation hearing.[21] Between the May 25 hearing and June 11, the date the Committee approved the nomination, several meetings were held between members of the Armed Services Committee and DoD officials, including Carter, to discuss specific reports that Carter had engaged in conduct inconsistent with the guidelines for consultants and prospective appointees.

The Defense Department took several remedial actions during this time in response to concerns expressed by the Committee. First, Deputy Secretary William Perry told Chairman Nunn that "[w]e have received the good faith assurance of each nominee [other than Carter] that he or she has not given authoritative guidance or signed documents in an official capacity."[22]

Second, General Counsel Jamie Gorelick issued a May 29 memorandum to all prospective DoD Presidential appointees entitled, "Implementing Guidance for Activities Prior to Appointment."[23] The memorandum dealt with meetings (inside and outside the Pentagon),[24] speeches, use of stationery,[25] contacts with Congress, travel, internal decisionmaking,[26] documents,[27] and hiring.[28] The General Counsel's guidance tightly circumscribed the activities in which consultants could engage pending confirmation.

Third, Deputy Secretary Perry announced that:

> Henceforth, no potential appointee will become a consultant to the Department for the purpose of rendering advice pending appointment. Rather, the sole purpose for which unpaid consultant status will be granted is to permit the potential nominee to engage in activities in preparation for undertaking his or her position and/or in connection with the confirmation process (e.g., receiving briefings, reading background material and making courtesy calls).[29]

Fourth, Perry also directed the General Counsel "to review all documents signed by potential presidential appointees who are pending confirmation to determine whether any action of the Department has been effected through an inappropriate assumption of authority."[30] The General Counsel subsequently "found no action of the Department that is required to be reversed or ratified."[31]

Fifth, Ashton Carter informed Secretary Aspin that he was terminating his service as a consultant while his nomination was pending. Carter acknowledged that he exceeded his authority by signing the May 17 memorandum, calling it "a careless error, which I deeply regret." He ended his consultant services "[t]o avoid any potential for further problems of this sort."[32]

Ultimately, Carter's nomination was approved by the Committee.[33] After extensive debate on the Senate floor, Carter was subsequently confirmed on June 29, 1993.[34] Chairman Nunn blamed "this whole situation" on the Administration's slow pace in making nominations, and praised the Pentagon for its remedial steps that "go far beyond the requirements of law, as well as the requirements of custom."[35]

Graham Allison

On March 31, 1993, the President announced his intent to nominate Graham T. Allison, Jr. to be Assistant Secretary of Defense for Plans and Policy, another position created by Secretary Aspin. Like Carter, Allison was retained by the Defense Department as a consultant before even the intent to nominate him was announced.[36] Allison got into trouble for his actions in two official DoD matters that resulted in a benefit to Harvard University, from which he was on unpaid leave.

In April 1993, the Inspector General's (IG) office received allegations involving Allison and concerning the activities of Robert D. Blackwill, a Harvard University official serving as a DoD consultant under a contract with the RAND Corporation.[37] The Deputy IG issued a report dated June 22, 1993, determining that Allison in two instances violated standards of conduct in his dealings with Blackwill.[38]

In the first instance, the IG's Report found that Allison had asked Blackwill whether he would consider advising Allison on the upcoming Vancouver summit meeting between Presidents Clinton and Yeltsin. They identified the RAND contract as a vehicle by which Blackwill's services could be provided. Allison then contacted DoD and RAND officials to determine whether Blackwill's services could be obtained in this manner. The contract administrators for DoD and RAND were "reluctant" to cite Allison as the sponsoring official (a prerequisite for the tasking) because of his consultant status, so they designated another office as sponsor in a letter which requested the tasking of Blackwill. When that office learned that it had been designated the sponsor without its knowledge or approval, it objected, and a new letter was prepared using Allison's supervisorial office, the Office of the Under Secretary for Policy, as the sponsor.[39]

The Inspector General's Report concluded:

> Dr. Allison could properly have advised a government official having authority to request research support under the RAND contract that obtaining the services of Mr. Blackwill would be beneficial to DoD. However, it appears to us that his actions were directive rather than advisory in nature, and therefore, exceeded the limitations on his authority as a consultant.[40]

In the second instance, the IG's Report found that Allison, in an April 13, 1993 meeting with the Russian Defense Attache, had promoted the holding of a General Staff Academy Seminar proposed by Blackwill to be run by Harvard (and to be privately funded, not by DoD). The meeting was intended primarily to discuss Secretary Aspin's anticipated meeting with the Russian Defense Minister and some matters on the Russian-United States security agenda. At the meeting, Allison stated that the Secretary had endorsed Blackwill's project. The Report determined that Allison's continued affiliation with Harvard meant that he had a "covered relationship" with the university under the standards of conduct concerning personal and business relationships,[41] and that his actions in promoting Blackwill's proposal "would cause a reasonable person with knowledge of the relevant facts to question [Allison's] impartiality in the matter." Thus, Allison was required under the standards of conduct to inform an appropriate agency official of the appearance issue and to obtain prior authorization to participate in the matter, neither of which he had done.[42] The IG's Report concluded, "In the absence of an explicit grant of authority, Dr. Allison's actions did not comply with the new regulatory requirements."[43] The IG's Report did not speculate whether authorization to participate would have been given under the circumstances.

Significantly, the IG's Report found that Secretary Aspin had authorized Allison to represent DoD at the April 13 meeting. The IG's Report matter-of-factly informed the Secretary that "[t]his authorization superseded the prohibition set forth in your March 9, 1993, memorandum prohibiting consultant/nominees from attending meetings as the DoD representative."[44] Secretary Aspin deserved criticism for waiving the standards he had set just one month earlier, which otherwise would have precluded Allison from representing DoD at the meeting.

A *Washington Post* article on the then-unreleased IG's findings reported Allison's nomination to be "in jeopardy." A Pentagon spokesman stated:

> Dr. Allison overstepped his authority in one case and misunderstood the application of a new regulation in another, neither of which the secretary condones. . . . But the secretary believes that Dr. Allison's actions were taken in good faith and supports his nomination.[45]

The *Washington Post* reported, "[e]xasperated colleagues at the Pentagon said Allison had repeatedly been warned to avoid offending the Senate while awaiting confirmation. 'If he goes down, he brought it on himself.'"[46]

Allison's nomination was formally sent to the Senate on July 22, 1993. At his confirmation hearing on July 29, Allison was contrite. He admitted that he had made a mistake, wished he had been "more sensitive to the issue of appearances," and promised to not repeat the mistake:[47]

> It was not a willful mistake, and certainly not for any personal advantage. I was a new kid on this bureaucratic block struggling to try to support the Secretary as an advisor, in the uncomfortable position of being a consultant, mindful of the constitutional responsibilities of the Senate, seeking not to presume, or appear to presume, the outcome of the confirmation process, while simultaneously trying to serve the Secretary. Despite these extenuating circumstances, to explain is not to excuse.[48]

Allison was also asked about his initialed approval of Ashton Carter's signed memorandum of May 17 requesting a transfer of funds. He said this was a "dumb mistake." He explained that he initialed the memorandum, "without looking and thinking carefully about the document," at the request of a "lower level" staff person who said, "You're supposed to initial this."[49]

Allison, who appeared after the Ashton Carter controversy, testified that "with the benefit of hindsight" he could see how some of his actions could be seen as presuming the outcome of the confirmation process, although he did not intend to do so. Allison said that the guidelines initially issued by Secretary Aspin left a "zone of ambiguity" which "puts people in a very uncomfortable and difficult position." Since the tightening of the guidelines, Allison added, he had followed them "pristinely."[50]

Allison was confirmed on August 5, 1993.[51]

Morton Halperin

On March 31, 1993, the President announced his intent to nominate Morton H. Halperin to be Assistant Secretary of Defense for Democracy and Human Rights.[52] Like Carter's and Allison's position, Halperin's position was established by Secretary Aspin as part of his post-Cold War reorganization of the Pentagon. Like Carter and Allison, Halperin was retained as a consultant even before the President announced his intent to nominate Halperin.[53] Halperin was made a consultant to the Secretary and to the Undersecretary for Policy, Frank Wisner. Halperin was not formally nominated until August 6, 1993.

Unlike Carter and Allison, Halperin was never confirmed. One day after Halperin's November 19, 1993 hearing before the Senate Armed Services Committee, the Senate returned the nomination to the President without action.[54] Halperin's nomination ran into many obstacles; had the President resubmitted the nomination, Halperin would have faced one or more additional Committee hearings and the very real prospect of being defeated on the Senate floor, if not in committee. Among the several concerns of Senators were numerous reports that Halperin had engaged in conduct inconsistent with the limitations on the activities of consultants.[55] At the hearing, Halperin acknowledged making mistakes:[56]

> [D]uring the first months of the administration, I and my colleagues in the Office of Policy engaged in practices which we later learned were inappropriate. As my colleagues have done, I want to apologize to this committee for my actions.
>
> I can only assure you that they were done without any intention of presuming the Senate's right to confirm nominees. We were all eager to begin to do what the Secretary wanted us to do, and we failed and I failed to fully brief myself about this committee's legitimate expectations.
>
> Since May I have been scrupulous in following the expanded guidelines provided by the General Counsel of the Department. . . .
>
> Nothing I did during this period was intended in any way to express disrespect for the rights and expectations of this committee. I regret very much that my behavior in the early months did not live up to the standard that it should.[57]

Halperin denied "sign[ing] any memo, hiring anybody, or directing that anybody be hired." Yet, when he was confronted with a memorandum he had signed that, according to Senator Trent Lott, "looks like a very direct, clear personnel action," Halperin acknowledged the memorandum (although he did not recall it), and conceded it was inconsistent with the guidelines.[58]

Halperin conceded that he had served as the Pentagon's point of contact with the Justice Department on the issue of homosexuals in the military, and had written several memoranda to the Secretary on the subject. Halperin explained that he served only in a liaison capacity with the Justice Department, communicating the Secretary's views, and did so only by phone. He denied that he had directed any policy by written memoranda, but acknowledged that the form of his written advice was inconsistent with what he now understood was the appropriate role of a consultant.[59]

Halperin acknowledged that he had provided advice to the Secretary and others with respect to Somalia, but denied taking part in the decision not to send armor to U.S forces in Somalia. Halperin recognized that some of the advice was provided in a form inappropriate for a consultant.[60]

Halperin denied he had ordered a U.S. military commander to end a military exercise in Guatemala. Upon questioning he explained that he "telephoned General Joulwan only to obtain information, not to intrude in the chain of command."[61]

Halperin was asked about other matters where he may have exceeded his authority as consultant, but a discussion of those matters was reserved for a later, closed session.[62] The closed session was never held.[63]

George Frampton

An allegation was also made that George T. Frampton, Jr., nominee to be Assistant Secretary of the Interior for Fish and Wildlife, exceeded his authority as a consultant to the Department of Interior before confirmation. Although the Interior Department and the OPM found that Frampton did not engage in any improper activity, this matter illustrates the problems that ensue when prospective appointees are brought in as consultants before confirmation.

Frampton was retained as a consultant to the Secretary on March 3, 1993. He was formally nominated by the President on April 28. On May 18, after his confirmation hearing, Frampton signed a memorandum addressed to the members of the Steering Committee and the Implementation Team for the National Biological Survey (NBS). In this memorandum, Frampton stated:

I want to assign the following tasks and deadlines. I have tentatively scheduled the next meeting of the Steering Committee and Implementation Team for Monday . . . . Those designated should be prepared to give the following reports: . . . .

According to a May 26, 1993 press release of the "ad hoc Committee for Responsible Land Management Appointees," Frampton exceeded his authority as consultant in making these assignments. The ad hoc committee urged the Senate Committee on Energy and Natural Resources to ask for a General Accounting Office (GAO) review of Frampton's activities. The Chairman and Ranking Member of the Committee on Energy and Natural Resources wrote Secretary Bruce Babbitt the next day, asking that the Secretary review the allegations and provide an explanation to the Committee.[64]

On June 4, 1993, Secretary Babbitt responded, stating that "I am advised that there was no violation of applicable laws, regulations or ethical standards."[65] The

Secretary provided supporting opinions of the Department's Solicitor and Department ethics lawyers. These documents explained that Frampton had sent the May 18 memorandum at the specific request of Tom Collier, the Secretary's Chief of Staff, that the information Frampton requested would assist Collier in providing advice to the Secretary, and that because the NBS had not yet been formed, there were no "operating functions" of the NBS for Frampton to have performed.

Only the first explanation—that Frampton acted at the request of the Chief of Staff—deserves serious consideration.[66] In fact, this explanation served as the sole basis for the opinion of James B. King, Director of OPM, that Frampton did not exceed his authority as a consultant. King conceded that the May 18 memorandum:

> could give the appearance that [Frampton] was acting in a supervisory or managerial, rather than an advisory capacity, and thus, in contravention of OPM's guidance. In light of the Chief of Staff's letter to Minority Counsel Ellsworth, however, we cannot conclude that this was the case. While he neglected to so inform the addressees, Mr. Frampton's memo apparently only communicated a plan of action that he had recommended and the Chief of Staff had approved.[67]

This explanation is, however, not persuasive. First, it would have been easy for Frampton to have stated in the memorandum that he had been asked by the Secretary or Chief of Staff to make these assignments; it would have been easier still for the Chief of Staff to have signed the memorandum. Consultants are supposed to consult and advise, not direct or supervise. Even if, as claimed, Frampton acted at the specific direction of Collier, Frampton nevertheless engaged in directing Interior Department personnel to devote official time to produce information. On its face, the May 18 memorandum is inconsistent with the limited role of a consultant as specified in the OPM guidance.[68]

Senator Malcolm Wallop wrote Secretary Babbitt on June 9, questioning another memorandum, signed by Frampton on April 29, 1993, regarding the NBS.[69] Collier responded that he had requested Frampton "to arrange the meeting," referred to in the memorandum. Collier added that "It was not my intention to have [Frampton] in a position of making decisions or determining what instructions should be issued to the Fish and Wildlife staff. Obviously, it appears to you that we have come too close to the line with respect to this matter." Collier pledged to "stay far enough within the lines" to avoid similar questions in the future.[70]

After some debate on the floor of the Senate, Frampton was confirmed by voice vote on June 30, 1993.[71] Senator Bennett Johnston spoke in favor of confirmation, noting that the Interior Department ethics officials and OPM had concluded that Frampton had not "violated any applicable guideline or rule[.]"[72] Senator Wallop spoke against confirmation, on the basis that Frampton and other administration nominees had "crossed the line from advice to action." Wallop stated that nominees are properly brought into an agency "to learn about the position for which they seek Senate approval. I emphasize, learn not act. I submit that this administration appears not to understand or appreciate that important distinction." So Wallop opposed Frampton's confirmation to send "a strong message that the type of conduct by unconfirmed individuals, evidenced by Mr. Frampton's activities, is unacceptable to this Senator and to the Senate."[73]

How to Fix the Problem

It is clear from these four examples that this is a recurring problem throughout the Executive Branch, one that is most acute at the beginning of an administration. Part of the problem stems from inadequate guidance, from OPM to agencies and from agencies to prospective nominees. Part of the problem stems from inadequate attention to existing guidance, by agency managers and by prospective appointees.

The problem of **inadequate guidance** can be minimized by clearer, tighter standards, like the memorandum ultimately issued by General Counsel Gorelick after the Department's run-in with the Senate Committee on Armed Services. The General Counsel's memorandum covered virtually every activity a prospective appointee could be expected to perform or participate in, and drew clear lines of do's and don't's. OPM could have adopted these guidelines as part of the rulemaking to implement the 1992 amendments to 5 U.S.C. 3109, but did not do so. The President should direct OPM to amend the recent rulemaking to implement section 3109, in order to promote a uniform understanding throughout the Executive Branch. Legislation probably is not necessary.

The problem of **inadequate compliance** by prospective appointees with the limitations on their activities also would be eased somewhat if the guidance were clearer. It is obviously easier to comply with rules that are understood than ones that are ambiguous or subject to differing interpretations. Prospective appointees could also be required to certify that they have read and understood the guidance.

Compliance would also be improved if there were a penalty for noncompliance that operated as an effective deterrent. But the potential penalties are not very attractive. Terminating the consultant relationship as a result of a prospective nominee's breach of the guidelines, or denying the consultant compensation (which could be mandated by legislation or regulation), does not have much teeth, because the consultant relationship is short-lived, existing only as a way station before formal appointment following confirmation. The Senate could refuse to confirm. But this seems to be an excessive response absent egregious conduct by a prospective appointee, and, in any event, would be unlikely where the Senate and the White House are in the hands of the same party. Somewhat more promising is to take away an individual agency's authority to hire consultants, as a penalty for an agency's consistently poor compliance. But aside from the locking-the-barn-door-after-the-horses-are-gone nature of this remedy, it would also be subject to the political balance between the Senate and the White House.

Compliance would certainly improve if prospective appointees, before beginning work, were required to read the guidance and certify that they have done so.[74] A certification would be effective in increasing compliance, even without a penalty for exceeding a consultant's authority, although any risk of sanction would boost the incentive to comply.

Another legislative response would be to prohibit prospective appointees from performing government functions. This is the approach in a bill introduced in June 1993 by Senator Kempthorne.[75] This legislation would allow prospective appointees to function as consultants, so long as they did not perform "any function which is authorized or required by law to be performed by an officer of the United States[.]"[76] Essentially, this bill captures the essence of the OPM rule. However, many of the current problems result from insufficient guidance and this bill, in the absence of more detailed guidance as to what constitutes a prohibited function, would not be likely to promote compliance. Moreover, it is not clear what the penalty against either the consultant or the agency would be, if any, for violating this prohibition.

Yet another legislative response would be to make the unauthorized assumption of authority by a consultant a Federal crime. This solution, however, seems inappropriate for what is more a management problem than one involving the public's trust, and, in any event, seems unduly harsh for conduct not particularly egregious. Further, unless guidance to consultants were improved, a prospective appointee caught by such a criminal provision could argue that the provision does not provide fair notice of the conduct that is proscribed and thus is unconstitutionally vague.

The best option would be to prohibit agencies, across-the-board, from using appropriated funds to hire prospective appointees, or from retaining them as unpaid consultants, yet authorizing the expenditure of funds for travel and per diem to bring prospective appointees to Washington.[77] An agency official who violated this prohibition would be subject to punishment under the Anti-Deficiency Act.[78] This legislation would accept the proposition that the only legitimate reasons to hire prospective appointees is to pay expenses necessary for them to receive briefings and other assistance needed to prepare the nominees for their confirmation hearing. It would not necessarily deny an agency the benefit of a person's advice, because agencies, with some limitations, can enlist the views of persons outside of government on any matter. Similarly, this legislation would not completely restrain the activities of a prospective appointee who served as a consultant without pay or reimbursement. It would also not restrain a full-time employee who is under consideration for a presidential appointment from improperly assuming the authority of the position for which the employee is being considered.

Conclusion

The preferred option is legislation to prohibit agencies from hiring prospective appointees as consultants. In the absence of such restrictive legislation, guidance to prospective appointees should be improved, and such consultants should be required to certify that they have read and understand the guidance. These two administrative steps alone would go a long way to ensure that prospective appointees stay within their limited role. Expediting the nominating process would also help marginally, although expedition is unlikely at the start of any new administration.

Ultimately, however, an administration should show greater respect for the Senate's advice-and-consent responsibility by exercising more self-restraint in placing prospective appointees at agencies before confirmation, and especially before nomination.

Chapter Seventeen

The
Public Disclosure
of Bush
Political Appointees' Files

The disclosure to a reporter of contents of State Department White House Liaison Office files on Bush Administration political appointees was illegal under the Privacy Act as well as in violation of ethics standards. However, no evidence was uncovered that any Presidential appointee at the State Department or White House was involved in the retrieval, search, or disclosure. Secretary Christopher properly fired the two officials who participated in the retrieval and disclosure, and appropriately awaited the report from the Inspector General before doing so. No justification appears for the actions taken by the two mid-level political appointees, who undoubtedly were aware of the Passportgate investigation and of President-elect Clinton's well-publicized statement that a similar occurrence in his Administration would be dealt with by summary discharges. It is not known why the Justice Department declined to prosecute, but in light of the firings and concomitant public opprobrium, declination appears appropriate.

The Disclosure

In a brief passage in the *Washington Post* on September 1, 1993, Al Kamen reported that State Department officials had asked the Department's archives to retrieve the personnel files of 160 political appointees who served in the State Department during the Bush Administration.[1] Contents of the files of at least two former officials—Elizabeth Tamposi, Assistant Secretary for Consular Affairs, and Jennifer

Fitzgerald, Deputy Chief of Protocol—were given to the *Post*.[2] Joseph Tarver, Director of the State Department's White House Liaison Office and a former Clinton campaign worker, and Deputy Director Simon Kahn, also a Schedule C (noncareer) employee, were later identified as participating in the retrieval and search of the files.

The Requests for an Investigation

The next day, Senator Mitch McConnell asked the Attorney General to appoint a "Special Prosecutor" to conduct an investigation of the matter.[3] (The independent counsel law had lapsed the previous year, and had not yet been reenacted.) McConnell did not believe that the State Department "or any other entity" could guarantee either impartiality or expedition. Also, three House Republicans (Representatives Gilman, Clinger, and Hyde) asked the GAO to conduct an expedited investigation. On September 3, the State Department responded to McConnell's letter to the Attorney General, explaining that the matter was being referred to the Inspector General (IG) for investigation. The Department confirmed that "the files in question were those of the Department's White House Liaison Office which had been retrieved from storage by staff members of that office."[4]

The Justice Department did not respond until November 3, 1993, after McConnell had placed a hold on five nominations for diplomatic posts pending substantive response to his letter to the Attorney General and a follow-up letter to the Secretary of State. The Justice Department declined McConnell's invitation to appoint a special counsel, explaining that no "extraordinary circumstances are present" that would warrant such an appointment. In addition, the Justice Department revealed that its Criminal Division was currently investigating the matter, "in conjunction with" the IG's investigation.[5] That same day, Inspector General Sherman Funk informed the Senate that he expected to complete his investigation within the next few days, whereupon he would forward a report to the Justice Department.[6]

The IG forwarded a "prosecutive summary" of potential Privacy Act violations to the Justice Department on November 8, 1993. The IG's office interviewed sixty-two persons—some under oath—and reviewed telephone and other records.[7] On November 9, White House spokeswoman Dee Dee Myers said that no action would be taken until Justice finished its criminal investigation,[8] but after receiving a briefing from the IG, Secretary Christopher on November 10, fired Liaison Office Director Joseph Tarver and Mark Schulhof, an assistant to the Assistant Secretary for Public Affairs.[9] Although the State Department would not reveal the contents of what it had sent to the Justice Department, a State Department spokesman relayed the Secretary's conclusion that, based on a briefing the Secretary received from the IG, "there is absolutely no evidence at all indicating knowledge or involvement by senior managers of the department."[10]

On January 28, 1994, in a letter to Sherman Funk, the Justice Department declined to prosecute anyone involved in the improper retrieval and search.[11] Funk was reported to be "surprised[;]" a staffer in the IG's office added, "We are going to be raising hell."[12] The declination letter was not released to the public.

The Inspector General's Report

On the same day the Justice Department's declination was announced, the State Department released the findings of the IG's investigative report dated January 31,

1994.[13] Unless otherwise noted, the following account is derived from the IG's report.

In July 1993, Joseph Tarver directed his staff assistant to retrieve Bush Administration White House Liaison records from storage. On July 9, the staff assistant requested retrieval of the files so that they could be "reorganized, incorporated, and some possibly destroyed."[14] These records were separate from the Official Personnel Files, which were not obtained.[15] However, Liaison Office records "frequently contain copies of documents contained in the Office Personnel Files."[16] The records were delivered to the Liaison Office about July 13, 1993, four days before they were scheduled to be destroyed.[17]

Tarver explained that the decision to retrieve the documents was his alone, taken without direction or knowledge from any higher level political appointee or White House official. Why did Tarver want the records? He explained that his "primary purpose" was to help himself understand the functions and duties of the Liaison Office. This explanation was obviously insufficient, for Tarver offered two additional motives. Tarver said he wanted to identify all Bush Administration Schedule C's to determine whether any had burrowed into the Department by switching to career status.

Tarver also said he wanted to see if any records contained information relevant to the Clinton passport investigation conducted by an independent counsel, but this explanation was probably just pretextual. Five months earlier, Tarver had complied with the independent counsel's subpoena, and Kahn testified that Tarver did not ask him to look for records relevant to the passport investigation. Tarver also did not mention the subpoena to Kahn during their review of the Bush Liaison Office files. Further, Tarver did not notify the Legal Advisor's office (which would likely have been in charge of replying to the subpoena), either before or after the search of the Bush Liaison Office files. The IG found that no Department employee, other than Tarver, directed the retrieval of the records.[18]

On July 27, Tarver and the other two Liaison Office staff members reviewed the records "for storage and classification purposes."[19] They filled four burn bags' worth of records, but, in so doing, violated records disposal procedures and possibly the Federal Records Management statute.[20] Public Affairs assistant Schulhof dropped by the office while the review was ongoing and learned of the retrieval of the files and the review of the contents of the Fitzgerald and Tamposi files.

That very afternoon Schulhof talked with *Washington Post* reporter Kamen, informing him of the file search and the empty Fitzgerald file. He also gave Kamen Tarver's name as an additional source, but denied giving Kamen any information about Tamposi's file. Schulhof's boss, Assistant Secretary Thomas Donilon, was out of the office that day. Donilon told the IG that Schulhof was not authorized to speak to the press, and would not have received permission to speak with Kamen about the files had he asked.[21] Under Secretary of Management Richard Moose said that in June 1993, while Moose was awaiting confirmation as an unpaid consultant, he spoke with Tarver and asked to be kept informed about Liaison Office activities, yet Moose was not told of the retrieval and search until the *Washington Post* story appeared.[22]

Schulhof later told Tarver (who had since been detailed out of the building to a NAFTA working group) that Kamen wanted to speak with him about the Fitzgerald file, and Tarver subsequently spoke with Kamen twice. Tarver spoke to Kamen "off the record," explained the separate records system, confirmed that Fitzgerald's file was empty, discussed the Clinton passport subpoena, but denied telling Kamen anything about Tamposi's file. Schulhof also denied knowing anything about the contents of Tamposi's file or discussing the Tamposi file with Kamen. Tarver did admit, however, that he discussed with Kamen the same concerns about Tamposi's qualifications that were contained in Tamposi's file.[23] The IG report concluded: "it is highly unlikely that [information in Kamen's article] came from any other source."[24]

The Inspector General found:

> [A]s a result of Schulhof's initial contact with Kamen, in which he disclosed privacy protected information, Schulhof set in motion a series of events which resulted in publication of Kamen's column. Tarver aided and abetted this effort by accepting Schulhof's referral, by speaking with Kamen, and by confirming as well as probably releasing additional information which also was privacy protected. . . .[25]
>
> Tarver and Schulhof were the sole Department employees responsible for the unauthorized dissemination of privacy-protected information from these files outside of the Department. No evidence was found or developed which indicated that anyone else in the Department (outside of the WHLO) or anyone in the White House directed or knew in advance of the records retrieval, knew of the contents of the files before Kamen's disclosures, or were involved in the unauthorized dissemination of Department privacy-protected information.[26]

Although the IG found that other Department employees "may be responsible for acts of omission or commission in the conduct of their duties[,]" there was no evidence tying them to criminal misconduct.[27]

Further Congressional Interest

After learning of the Justice Department declination, Senators McConnell and John Kerry wrote the Secretary of State on February 2, inquiring whether any presidential appointee was aware of or participated in the search and disclosure of the contents of the files, or discussed the activity with the White House or the Democratic National Committee.[28] On February 4, three months after he had completed his investigation, the IG received sworn testimony from Under Secretary Moose and Assistant Secretary Donilon. Funk's supplemental investigation appeared to be in direct response to the Senators' February 2 letter.[29]

On February 7, Secretary Christopher responded to Senators Kerry and McConnell:

> The Inspector General has concluded that the evidence he developed throughout his entire investigation reflects that neither Under Secretary Moose, Assistant Secretary Donilon, nor any other Departmental Presidential appointee was aware of the intent to search or disclose the contents of the Bush Administration political appointee files, participated in or ordered any such activity, or discussed or coordinated the search of disclosure with anyone in the White House or at the Democratic National Committee.[30]

Senator McConnell was not satisfied by this response, which likely prompted a Republican effort to seek a sense-of-the-Senate resolution calling on the State Department to release the IG's full investigative report, which at that point, only the White House had seen. The effort failed, 55-39, on February 10.[31]

The GAO Reports

In July 1994, GAO issued two reports concerning the protection of personnel files of political appointees. One was a report on GAO's investigation of the file retrieval incident at the State Department.[32] The other was a review of the adequacy of the controls over personnel records of political appointees of several selected agencies, including State.[33] Both reports were responses to the September 1993 congressional requests.

In its review of agency controls, GAO found that weaknesses in the State Department's management and control of records "enabled the Clinton Administration's political appointees in State's White House Liaison Office to retrieve the White House liaison files on Bush political appointees."[34] GAO also found similar weaknesses at other agencies whose controls GAO reviewed. Weaknesses included a failure to identify a system of records (a prerequisite for Privacy Act protection) and a failure to prepare disposition schedules. GAO recommended that the Archivist issue to all Federal agencies a standard disposition schedule for White House liaison records to provide generally for destruction of such records at the close of the each administration. GAO also recommended that the Office of Management and Budget (OMB) ensure that agencies identify White House liaison political appointee records as a system of records under the Privacy Act. The State Department, in particular, was encouraged to clarify its system of records description to make sure White House liaison and presidential appointment records would be protected, and to amend its manuals to specify the time when Official Personnel Folders should be retired.[35]

Analysis

The Retrieval

The IG found that the retrieval of Bush Administration Liaison Office files, "standing alone," did not violate any standards or policies. The IG concluded that the Liaison Office probably retrieved the records to discover any Bush Administration holdovers who might have quietly burrowed into the Department bureaucracy, a purpose the IG found, correctly, to be legitimate.[36]

The stated purpose of familiarizing the new Liaison Office staff with the Office's functions was probably just camouflage. The files were not requested until months after the beginning of the Administration, and information on the workings of the Liaison Office easily could have been obtained by other means.

If the motive of these Democratic appointees was to see if there was any negative information on their predecessors, which is also likely,[37] the retrieval surely would have been improper, although not specifically proscribed by existing standards.[38] Such misconduct could still form the basis for discipline, even if no ethics standard was implicated.

The Disclosure

Regardless of the motive for the retrieval of the files, proper or improper, there could be no legitimate motive in disclosing their contents to the *Washington Post*. The purpose of disclosure was most likely to provide some negative information, or at least a smidgen of gossip, about two Bush Administration officials.[39]

The Privacy Act prohibits the disclosure of records, such as White House Liaison Office files, that are contained in an approved Privacy Act system of records, without the written consent of the person whom the records concern.[40] Although there are exceptions that allow disclosure under certain circumstances, none applies here. Willful disclosure of records protected by the Privacy Act, knowing that disclosure is prohibited, is a crime.[41]

Ethics standards also are relevant. The IG cited the prohibition against disclosing official information which has not been made available to the general public "[f]or the purpose of furthering a private interest."[42] He also cited the admonition to avoid taking any action that adversely affects the public's confidence in the integrity of the Government,[43] or any conduct that is prejudicial to the Government.[44]

It is clear that both Tarver and Schulhof violated the Privacy Act and the misuse-of-information standard in disclosing contents of the files to Kamen. What's more, they clearly knew or should have known that their actions were improper. Given the recent notoriety surrounding efforts of the Bush Administration State Department to locate files on Bill Clinton's passport during the 1992 election (so-called Passportgate), which resulted in the highly publicized dismissal of Betty Tamposi and the appointment of an independent counsel, Tarver's and Schulhof's conduct was also just plain stupid. Clinton Administration appointees, at all levels, were put on notice that such conduct, if uncovered, would result in severe embarrassment to the Administration as well as their summary dismissal.

Indeed, President-elect Clinton, responding to a question at a news conference held soon after the election, indicated that he would not tolerate any similar abuse in his Administration:

> Well, I'm glad Ms. Tamposi had to leave her job six weeks early. I thought that was an appropriate thing to do. I don't know that I know enough to give you a final judgment. Let me just say this. If I catch anybody using the State Department like that when I'm President, you won't have to wait until after the election to see them gone. I don't want to talk about what happened in the past. I just want you to know that the State Department of this country is not going to be fooling with Bill Clinton's politics, and if I catch anybody doing it, I will fire them the next day. There won't be—it won't have to have an inquiry, or rigamarole, or anything else because that is—it is too important to me that the rest of the world see us as having a coherent and, as much as possible, nonpolitical foreign policy. . . . [45]

The Dismissal of Tarver and Schulhof

Secretary Christopher fired Tarver and Schulhof immediately following the conclusion of the IG's investigation; he did not await the outcome of the criminal investigation, nor should he have. A Justice Department investigation or prosecution was not necessary to establish any essential fact. Dismissal was obviously called for. But the White House received some criticism, somewhat tongue-in-cheek, for not taking more precipitous action. Here, again, the President's rhetoric was thrown back at him.[46] Dee Dee Myers explained that the President-elect "certainly didn't ever suggest we would take away their right to due process."[47] On the contrary, that is precisely what the President-elect said on November 12, 1992.

Indeed, it appears that the Clinton Administration proceeded at a more deliberate pace in 1993 than did the Bush Administration in 1992. Elizabeth Tamposi was fired on November 10, 1992, the day it was reported (incorrectly) that Tamposi had also directed the search of Ross Perot's passport files. (In fact, the independent counsel found, Tamposi acted solely to secure these files from tampering or disclosure.[48]) Tamposi was fired at the insistence of President Bush, who was incensed by the report of the Perot file search. The Bush Administration dismissed Tamposi **before** Sherman Funk's report was completed; Funk announced his report and findings on November 18. In the case of the Clinton Administration search and disclosure, Tarver and Schulhof were not fired until **after** Funk's investigation was completed. Even measured as the time between the initial press report and the date of firing, there was little difference. The initial Clinton passport story ran in the October 12, 1992 *Newsweek*, (available on October 5, 1992);[49] the initial Bush appointees' files story ran in the *Washington Post* on October 1, 1993. Tamposi and Tarver, and Schulhof were all dismissed on November 10, exactly one year apart.

The Conduct of the Investigations

For the most part, the IG investigation appears to have been conducted thoroughly, fairly, and without undue delay. Although Republicans in Congress expressed dissatisfaction with the IG's investigation, this may have been based, in part, on the IG's initial reluctance to grant congressional access to the complete IG Report. The IG did conduct a supplemental investigation, involving interviews under oath of Donilon and Moose. Given the previously expressed clear interest of the congressional requesters in possible involvement of these officials, they should have been interviewed as part of the initial investigation.[50]

The IG's reluctance to share the details of his investigation pending the Justice Department investigation was understandable, even appropriate, viewed in isolation. Public statements or release of witness statements could compromise a subsequent criminal investigation. But the same IG did not exhibit a similar reluctance at the apparent conclusion of his Passportgate investigation, when he held a press conference and distributed copies of his investigative report to the media.[51] Was there a double standard? One difference is that at the time of Sherman Funk's press conference on Passportgate (November 18, 1992), it appeared as if no referral to the Justice Department under the Privacy Act would be made.[52] His report was not even styled as a report of investigation, but, instead, was called a "special inquiry." Although Funk reported that the Privacy Act was violated in the release to *Newsweek* of the fact of the search of Bill Clinton's passport file (and the suspicion that it had been tampered with), this violation was not referred to Justice. No referral was made either because a violation of the Privacy Act is a misdemeanor, or because it was not apparent who violated the Privacy Act. Independent counsel diGenova similarly failed to determine who violated the Privacy Act by leaking to *Newsweek*.

Funk did make a referral to the Justice Department, on November 16, 1992, although this referral was not made public until after Funk's press conference and release of his report.[53] And this referral was based solely on evidence that Janet Mullins, Assistant to the President for Political Affairs, had lied to the IG's office during its investigation, an element that was apparently not present with respect to the IG's investigation of the disclosure of the Bush appointees' files.

It took the Justice Department about two months to conduct an investigation and to decline to prosecute. This is to be contrasted favorably with the protracted independent counsel investigation of Passportgate, which began in late 1992 and was not formally concluded until the November 30, 1995 release of the independent counsel's report. But the independent counsel's investigation of Passportgate was considerably more involved than the Justice Department's investigation of Tarver and Schulhof.[54] Because the public cannot be privy to Justice's investigation of Tarver and Schulhof, the adequacy of the investigation cannot be gauged. Instead, what criticism there was of Justice focused on the declination.

Was Declination Appropriate?

Michael Mitchell, a State Department political appointee in the Bush Administration, complained that the decision to decline prosecution, "represents a new standard in which Democrats have lifted themselves above the law, and it holds dangerous consequences that move far beyond this file-search crime."[55] Mitchell argued that the decision "gutted" the Privacy Act and sent a signal that IG recommendations are "worthless. . . . By letting violators get off scot-free, Justice has turned the Privacy Act into the legal equivalent of the Maginot Line."[56]

However, it appears the decision to decline prosecution made sense, even given a clear violation of the Privacy Act. First, the offense is a just a misdemeanor.[57] There were no aggravating circumstances, such as a cover-up or obstruction of justice. Most likely, the Justice Department did not believe the differing recollections of the State Department officials during the IG investigation suggested obstruction or perjury, or it would have pursued prosecution. Second, the subjects of the investigation, although political appointees, were middle-level officials, a GS-15 and a GS-11.[58] Third, and most important, their dismissal following the IG investigation was public and ignominious. They did not "get off scot-free." No additional punishment seems warranted.

Should a Special Counsel Have Been Appointed?[59]

Several calls were made for an independent investigation of the Clinton political appointees,[60] at least pointing out the apparent double standard vis-a-vis Passportgate. But it was appropriate for the Justice Department to conduct the investigation itself. There were major differences between Passportgate and the disclosure of the Bush State Department White House Liaison Office files. The IG uncovered no evidence of White House or presidential appointee involvement in the disclosure of the Liaison Office files, and the basis for the criminal investigation was primarily the Privacy Act. Attorney General Barr requested the appointment of an independent counsel to look into the Clinton passport search because the preliminary investigation uncovered possible evidence of a felony by a senior White House official, a covered official under the independent counsel law.[61]

Should Congressional Hearings Be Held in the 104th Congress?

Considering the thoroughness of the IG's investigation and the GAO reports, congressional hearings are unlikely to uncover any new and significant facts. Hearings have the potential to inform the public of what occurred, yet the passage of time and the lack of involvement by any senior administration official reduce significantly the public and media interest in such hearings. The misconduct is likely an isolated case, although a similar situation could develop given the GAO's findings of the inadequate controls over political appointee files throughout the Executive Branch. Congress should instead request the GAO to follow-up its report with another study in 1996, to ensure that its recommendations have been followed.

Questions about the Clinton Administration's handling of this matter include whether the IG's investigation was adequate, the appropriateness of the Justice Department's declination, and the refusal to appoint a special counsel to conduct the investigation. A congressional hearing is not likely to shed much additional light on any of these issues.

Conclusion

Was the misconduct by the two State Department officials serious? Yes, of course. From the prospective of the Bush officials whose files were raked over, it makes no difference that only junior politicos leaked contents to the *Washington Post*. The damage was done nonetheless. The *Washington Post* called it "no trivial matter, and it is no less offensive than when Mr. Clinton himself was on the receiving end of such abuse."[62] In some respects, what these State Department officials did was just as bad as, if not worse than, what the Bush Administration State Department political appointees were found to have done in Passportgate. The Bush Administration State Department officials, although of higher rank (two Assistant Secretaries of State), were responding to several FOIA requests filed by the media and a separate request from a Congressman. The motive of the Bush Administration officials in expediting the search and disclosing it to the media may have been improperly political, but the apparent motives of the Clinton Administration officials in retrieving, searching, and disclosing the Bush appointees' files were just as base.

The prompt firing of the culpable officials, and the strong public opprobrium attached to their actions, were both appropriate and sufficient, obviating a criminal prosecution. A congressional hearing at this point would not be likely to generate much public interest, nor would it result in uncovering new facts or recommendations for changes in the law.

Chapter Eighteen

Travel

In the first two-plus years of the Clinton Administration, there were as many reports of abuse of government aircraft and official travel funds as there were in the Bush Administration, despite President Clinton's initial efforts to reduce the abuse of government perks. This is one area where President Clinton marginally tightened a standard of conduct (governing the use of government aircraft), although the ethics standards (governing the use of government property) were not changed. Promulgating standards is one thing; compliance with them is another. The use of a Marine helicopter to attend a golf outing by the White House Office Director of Administration was the most notorious example of the continuing misuse of government aircraft by senior administration officials. Further, several members of his Cabinet and agency heads made a disproportionate number of official trips to their hometowns; the official event often appeared simply as a pretext to justify the expenditure of official travel funds.

Current ethics standards and OMB rules are sufficient to address the recurring problem of misuse of government aircraft, but only if these standards are strictly enforced by the White House, backed up with the promise of discipline and the threat of dismissal. However, current ethics standards are not sufficiently explicit to discourage the use official travel funds for personal or political purposes, so the President should issue such an appropriate directive, holding his agency heads personally accountable for their own conduct and the conduct of their political appointees.

Abuse of travel privileges, including the use of government aircraft, continues to plague administrations. The most notable Bush Administration figure to be seen abusing travel privileges was Chief of Staff John Sununu, whose frequent travels on military aircraft (pursuant to a policy that arguably required the Chief of Staff to travel on military aircraft), especially trips to visit his dentist or to a ski resort, ultimately contributed to his resignation. The Clinton Administration, despite initial efforts by the President to avoid another Sununu controversy, has experienced a comparable number of embarrassing stories, although they have not attracted nearly the same amount of media attention as did the travels of Governor Sununu. The extent of such abuse is unknown, but the likelihood is that the stories recounted here are simply representative of improper conduct that is committed throughout the Executive Branch.

Although the problem is sometimes seen not as a matter of government ethics, but rather as a question of the proper use of government property and appropriated funds, abuse of travel privileges does implicate several ethics provisions in the standards of conduct for Executive Branch employees. These include two of the general principles of ethical conduct:

Employees shall not use public office for private gain.

Employees shall protect and conserve Federal property and shall not use it for other than authorized activities.[1]

Similarly, a separate standard of conduct provides:

An employee has a duty to protect and conserve Government property and shall not use such property, or allow its use, for other than authorized purposes.[2]

Another general principle exhorts Federal employees to "avoid any actions creating the appearance that they are violating the law or the ethical standards set forth in [the standards of conduct]."[3]

These are the standards used by the Office of Government Ethics in evaluating the review of Governor Sununu's use of military aircraft conducted by the White House Counsel's office.[4]

Use of Government Aircraft

As part of his campaign against perks and misuse of Government resources, President Clinton issued a memorandum dated February 10, 1993, strictly limiting use of government aircraft by Executive Branch officials.[5] However, the President did not write on a clean slate. The Bush Administration had issued two policies on the use of government aircraft; the effect of this President's memorandum was to further restrict who could use government aircraft and under what circumstances.

The Bush Administration's policy on the use of government aircraft was instituted in two steps. First, on May 9, 1991, President Bush directed that any use of military aircraft by the Chief of Staff or National Security Adviser (the only two White House officials previously authorized to use military aircraft other than the President and Vice President) required approval in advance, in writing, by the White House Counsel's office, pursuant to specific written criteria.[6] This policy was established following the Counsel's office's review of the Chief of Staff's use of military aircraft,[7] which was directed by President Bush after the *Washington Post* published in April 1991 an account of the more than sixty trips Governor Sununu took on military aircraft over a two-year period.[8]

Second, on May 22, 1992, the Office of Management and Budget issued a revised OMB Circular A-126, entitled "Improving the Management and Use of Government Aircraft."[9] Stung by the notoriety of Governor Sununu's use of military aircraft and other reports that high-level officials regularly used more-expensive government aircraft rather than commercial,[10] the Bush Administration revised OMB Circular A-126 in order:

> to restrict the operation of government aircraft to defined official purposes; restrict travel on such aircraft; require special review of such travel on government aircraft by senior officials or non-Federal travelers . . .; and codify policies for reimbursement for the use of government aircraft.[11]

As revised, OMB Circular A-126 provided that "Agencies shall operate government aircraft only for official purposes. Official purposes include the operation of government aircraft for (i) mission requirements, and (ii) other official travel":[12]

> Official travel that is not also required use travel or to meet mission requirements shall be authorized only when:

> (i) no commercial airline or aircraft (including charter) service is reasonably available (i.e., able to meet the traveler's departure and/or arrival requirements within a 24-hour period, unless the traveler demonstrates that extraordinary circumstances require a shorter period) to fulfill effectively the agency requirement; or

> (ii) the actual cost of using a government aircraft is not more than the cost of using commercial airline or aircraft (including charter) service.[13]

OMB Circular A-126 also provided for special approval requirements (e.g., trip-by-trip for non-required use or mission requirements travel by senior officials) and required each agency to report semiannually to the General Services Administration (GSA) all use of government aircraft by senior officials and all non-Federal travelers.[14]

President Clinton's February 1993 memorandum provided that only the Secretaries of State and Defense, the Attorney General, and the Directors of the Federal Bureau of Investigation and Central Intelligence may use government aircraft for nongovernmental purposes, only upon reimbursement at "full coach fare," and only upon White House authorization that a security threat exists or "when continuous 24-hour secure communication is required." In OMB Circular A-126, their travel is considered "required use" travel. The major difference from the Bush policy is that express White House authorization is required on a trip-by-trip basis.[15]

For all other senior officials,[16] the President prohibited the use of government aircraft for "[u]ses other than those that constitute the discharge of an agency's official responsibilities[.]"[17] And he restricted using government aircraft further:

> When travel is necessary for governmental purposes, Government aircraft shall not be used if commercial airline or aircraft (including charter) service is reasonably available, i.e., able to meet the traveler's departure and/or arrival requirements within a 24-hour period, unless highly unusual circumstances present a clear and present danger, an emergency exists, use of Government aircraft is more cost-effective than commercial air, or other compelling operational considerations make commercial transportation unacceptable. Such authorization must be in accordance with [OMB Circular A-126].[18]

Thus, the President severely restricted the number of officials who could use government aircraft for personal travel, and it appears that he prohibited senior officials from using government aircraft, even if consistent with the criteria above, unless the travel would also meet mission requirements. In other words, presidential appointees and White House staff could not use government aircraft to give speeches or attend conferences, meetings, or site visits.

But old habits die hard, especially among the military services and civilian agencies with their own fleet of aircraft, such as NASA, DoT, and FAA. Despite OMB Circular A-126 and the President's February 1993 policy statement, there have been regular reports of high-level officials' inappropriate use of government aircraft in the Clinton Administration.

A few weeks after the February 1993 memorandum, Deputy Defense Secretary John Deutsch travelled on board an Air Force jet to Brussels for an annual NATO meeting. Use of government aircraft for this trip was authorized by the White House Counsel's office, but the basis for the approval was unclear. According to a DoD spokesman, Deutsch would have lost a day or more if he flew commercial. In fact, as the *Washington Post* pointed out, Deutsch would have lost only a half day.19

Defense Secretary Les Aspin's trip to Europe in May 1993 on a military plane created a bigger stir, because, while over in Europe on official business, he "spent four of the last seven days vacationing with a female friend at a five-star hotel in Venice. In the meantime, his jet sat on the tarmac and thirty-one members of his traveling party cooled their heels in Italy at taxpayer expense."[20] The Government covered the food and lodging expenses of the DoD traveling party during this time. The Secretary was authorized to use military aircraft to go to Europe, and his use of military aircraft was consistent with A-126 and the President's policy. The problem concerned the duration of the trip. Even the DoD Secretary needs a vacation now and then, but his decision to vacation in Europe with his extensive entourage in tow resulted in an unwarranted expenditure of government resources.

Another Pentagon official's travels raised ethics questions. On September 9, 1994, General Joseph Ashy, newly-appointed head of the U.S. Space Command, traveled from Naples, Italy, nonstop to Colorado on an Air Force C-141 with the crew, his Air Force valet, and his cat.[21] Otherwise, the plane with a capacity for 200 passengers was empty, even though requests from other military personnel for seats on the flight were turned down. The plane refueled in midair twice. The C-141 was flown empty to Naples from New Jersey for the sole purpose of picking up Ashy, although Ashy claimed he asked to use any available government aircraft. Ashy considered, but rejected, returning on board a commercial aircraft the next day because it might not have given him enough time to take an official training course "on procedures for alerting the president in event of an air attack." But the assertion that commercial travel was unavailable is suspect, given that one or more of Ashy's plans in Italy and the United States could have easily been adjusted to facilitate commercial travel. Ashy's trip cost $116,232, compared to a commercial fare of $650. In Colorado for a day, Ashy then flew with his wife on a military aircraft to Washington, D.C. for a promotion ceremony.

Newsweek columnist David Hackworth initially pursued the story, complaining to Senator Charles Grassley when he encountered a series of misstatements from Air Force officials from whom he sought explanations for Ashy's travel. Grassley, in turn, asked the Pentagon's Inspector General (IG) to review the circumstances of Ashy's travel.

The IG's report, released in June 1995, criticized not only Ashy's return trip from Italy, but eleven other flights (of only fifteen flights reviewed) by generals or admirals where cheaper commercial flights were available, but not taken.[22] Adding to the cost, in every case but one the military aircraft was used solely to transport a Pentagon official. The IG concluded that Ashy's trip did not violate DoD rules, but the decision to use a military aircraft "reflects a culture that apparently lacks adequate cost consciousness in providing service to senior officials."[23] Ashy's trip certainly conflicted with President Clinton's policy memorandum, fairly construed, and could be seen as inconsistent with A-126.

Moreover, the IG found that Ashy's trip two days later to Washington, D.C. was necessary only because Ashy returned home to Colorado from Italy instead of travelling straight to Washington. (The ceremony could also have been held in Colorado.) The report called this trip a "waste of funds" and recommended that Ashy be required to reimburse the Government for Ashy's and his wife's travel, which he did by writing a $5,020 check.

Finally, the IG confirmed Hackworth's complaints about the Air Force's account of Ashy's travel:

> The Air Force was inept in its response to media inquiries about the flight. The presentation of a series of incorrect facts, careless communications and lack of central direction . . . defined the Air Force performance. . . . The Air Force did not comply with its policy objectives regarding the quick and candid release of unfavorable information.[24]

The Air Force responded to the IG findings by revising its policy in May 1995.[25] However, it is difficult to see how continual policy revisions were expected to accomplish anything; OMB Circular A-126 and President Clinton's February 10 memorandum should suffice, if they were strictly and faithfully followed. The only way to deter this conduct may be to impose stricter discipline for violations of these policies.

Civilian agencies with aircraft fleets also came under scrutiny and criticism. In the Reagan and Bush Administrations, use of the Federal Aviation Administration's (FAA) extensive fleet of aircraft by the Secretary of Transportation and Administrator of the FAA was given regular scrutiny by GAO and others. In the first year of the Clinton Administration, an audit performed by NASA's IG found that travel by NASA officials on NASA aircraft in Fiscal Year 1993 (covering the last four months of the Bush Administration) cost $5.9 million more than the cost of travelling on commercial flights.[26]

The misuse of government aircraft was not limited to fixed-wing aircraft. Rotorcraft (helicopters), too, were often used where less expensive ground transportation would have sufficed. The *Washington Post* found that in 1993 Pentagon generals and admirals took 238 helicopter trips between Andrews Air Force Base and the Pentagon, costing about $1,000 to $3,000 per trip, instead of taking a cab (a 14-mile drive), which costs about $22.[27] The *Washington Post* noted that the Pentagon's helicopter pool is "a convenience available to almost no one else in government save the president." The Air Force defended the trips on three grounds: some trips involved the transport of classified information; some were necessary to keep military pilots currently qualified; and schedules were often too tight to use ground transportation. The *Washington Post*, however, concluded that helicopter travel is used because it is readily available, and simply more convenient. It is hard to understand how many of these trips could be squared with OMB Circular A-126 and the President's February 10, 1993 policy.[28]

More celebrated than any of these stories was a single use of a military helicopter by David Watkins, Assistant to the President for Management and Administration. On May 24, 1994, just three weeks after the page one *Washington Post* report on the abuse of military helicopters by Pentagon officials, Watkins and Alphonso Maldon, the politically appointed Director of the White House Military Office, took a military helicopter for an afternoon golf outing at Holly Hills Country Club in Ijamsville, Maryland, an hour's drive from the White House. The helicopter costs about $2,400 per hour to operate; it made two round trips in transporting Watkins. The ignominy of the trip was starkly illustrated by a page-one picture of Watkins carrying his golf bag from a golf cart to the waiting "United States of America" helicopter; an Air Force officer stands at attention by the steps, saluting one of Watkins' golf partners.[29] It was not Watkins' first brush with an ethics scandal; he was knee deep in the mishandling of the Travel Office firings.[30] The President wasted no time in asking for Watkins' resignation, announcing that the Government would be reimbursed for the cost of the trip.[31] The White House said that Maldon was reprimanded, removed from his position, and would be reassigned.[32]

The White House suffered further embarrassment from the episode because the White House Press Office initially defended the trip on the basis of a statement prepared by the White House Military Office that turned out to be just a cover story. The Military Office attempted to justify the trip as a "'training mission' to familiarize the crew with the layout of the course" in anticipation of a presidential visit. The round of golf was played "in order to familiarize themselves with all aspects of the course, especially those aspects related to actual time of play and associated impact of security plans."[33] But neither Watkins nor Maldon was responsible or qualified to conduct security or advance for a presidential visit, and the White House had no plans for any such presidential visit there.

The day after the golfing trip was revealed, the White House (after initial denials) acknowledged that a second helicopter made the trip, too, as usually occurs with all trips of Marine One. Watkins resigned but was unrepentant, and did not agree to reimburse the full cost of the helicopter trip, which amounted to $13,129.66, although Watkins' net worth was estimated in excess of one million dollars. So Acting Director of Administration Phil Lader solicited contributions from senior White House aides, securing pledges from thirteen officials, including David Gergen, George Stephanopoulos, and Lloyd Cutler. While these contributions could be seen as an effort to fulfill the President's commitment that full reimbursement would be made, and Lader so portrayed the effort, Mark Gearan said the contributions were intended "as a gesture of friendship to Mr. Watkins and Mr. Maldon."[34]

The next week, on May 31, Watkins decided to make full reimbursement, to relieve White House officials of any financial burden.[35] Also that day, the White House Chief of Staff issued by memorandum a new policy regarding the use of military aircraft (not just helicopters) by White House staff and Cabinet officials for "White House Support Missions," requiring trip-by-trip approval by the Chief of Staff or his Deputy (or White House Counsel or his Deputy, in the case of a request involving the Chief of Staff as passenger). Approval previously rested with the Director of White House Administration, Watkins' position until his dismissal.

So, in 1994 the Clinton White House put in place what essentially was the same review and approval process the Bush White House issued three years earlier in response to the publicity of Governor Sununu's travels, the only difference being the official designated to review and approve the use of aircraft.[36]

Also on May 31, the White House released a list of twelve trips on board military helicopters taken by White House and Cabinet officials other than the President and Vice President; only the golf outing was identified as an improper use. Representative Roscoe Bartlett was not satisfied with this response, however, because it did not report intermediate stops, return flights, or the use of second helicopters, and because it included only "sanitized" passenger lists, instead of the manifests he requested.[37] Bartlett unsuccessfully sought to amend the Treasury, Postal Appropriations bill for Fiscal Year 1995 on the House floor, by reducing the funds for the White House office by the cost of Watkins' trip, a move Bartlett acknowledged was symbolic.[38] Eventually, he asked GAO to conduct a review.

The GAO report was not issued until a year later.[39] The skimpy report found that White House and Cabinet officials took fourteen trips without the President or Vice President between January 21, 1993 and May 24, 1994, the date of the golf outing. It also found no written procedures for requesting the use of helicopters or criteria governing their use, and thus the report contained no finding that any of the trips was proper or improper.[40] However, GAO failed to note that OMB Circular A-126 and the President's February 10, 1993 memorandum expressly prohibited the use of a government helicopter (1) for personal travel, or (2) when less expensive ground transportation was available (subject to some limited exceptions). Thus, the GAO report was clearly inadequate.

Use of Official Travel Funds for Other than Official Purposes

There is no law, rule, or policy that prohibits a Federal official from using government funds to take a trip to one's hometown, provided the trip is made to attend one or more official events. Nor is there any provision discouraging the frequency of official trips taken to one's hometown. Partly because there is no such law or policy, many Federal officials have for years made a disproportionate number of official trips to their hometowns or to other locations where personal events are also scheduled. Of course, it would be improper to arrange for an official event in one's hometown or other location solely to permit the official to use government funds to attend a personal event (like a child's wedding, birthday, or graduation) or simply to go home. This would be using public office for private gain, in violation of a cardinal principle of ethics. But rare is the government official who will concede that an official trip was scheduled to get the Government to cover the travel expenses in order to attend a personal matter.

Yet, this is exactly what the public sees when it is reported that a certain Federal official travelled a disproportionate amount of time to his hometown, primarily on weekends, with only a light schedule of official events. These officials are contributing to the distrust and disgust in which many Americans hold public officials, for it appears that these officials are using taxpayer funds to underwrite personal or political travel. In other words, they are using public office for private gain, and using government property for other than official purposes.

This is not a new problem. Several Bush Administration officials made frequent official trips to their hometown, with itineraries thin on official events and thick with time with family and friends. Chief of Staff Sununu traveled on military aircraft regularly to New England for speaking engagements that allowed him to spend time with family, friends, and former colleagues, as well as to visit his dentist (for which he reimbursed the Government at a coach fare rate). While Director of the Peace Corps, Paul Coverdell made twenty-six of his first forty-five official visits (covering an eighteen-month period) to his home state of Georgia, where his wife and home were.[41] "The vast majority of his trips to Georgia have required him to leave Washington Thursday evening or Friday and leave Atlanta Monday."[42] Coverdell was accused of traveling frequently to Georgia to prepare for a Senate race. (Coverdell indeed ran and won a Senate seat in 1992.) Coverdell said he travelled frequently to Georgia to increase the participation of Southerners and minorities in the Peace Corps, and because he received many invitations to speak there. Coverdell saw part of the Peace Corps' mission as educating Americans about the world, so that Coverdell needed to travel frequently throughout the United States.

One of the reasons President Clinton dismissed FBI Director Sessions in July 1993 was a finding by the outgoing Bush Administration Attorney General that Sessions engaged in "a pattern of abuse of travel . . . resulting in the use of government funds for clearly personal travel on a number of occasions."[43] Attorney General Bill Barr informed Judge Sessions that:

> you and your wife used the FBI plane to make personal trips and then sought to characterize these trips as "official" to avoid reimbursing the government. For example, you have made a number of extended trips on the FBI plane to San Francisco to visit your daughter during holiday seasons. You appear to have charged this all to the government because after you planned the trips you arranged isolated functions of trivial, if any, value to the government, such as a breakfast meeting with a handful of local

businessmen. The conclusion is inescapable that these functions were arranged for the sole purpose of allowing you to avoid paying for these personal trips.[44]

Judge Sessions responded, through his attorneys:

There is no question that when the director has visited family members in various cities, he has scheduled significant FBI business at the same time. The director is confident that business has not been viewed as "trivial" by the FBI field officials or others with whom he had dealt on these occasions. . . . FBI counsel reviews each of the director's trips, and the director has treated each trip as personal or business pursuant to FBI legal counsel's determination.[45]

Given the tremendous notoriety of the travels of both Sununu and Sessions, Clinton Administration appointees should have assiduously avoided this travel trap. On the contrary, the Clinton Administration's record appears no better, or perhaps even worse. During his first eighteen months as Agriculture Secretary, Mike Espy took eighteen official trips to his hometown of Jackson, Mississippi. And while in Mississippi, Secretary Espy used a jeep leased by the Government for personal travel.[46] No one doubts the presence of agricultural interests in the State of Mississippi, but many of the Secretary's trips were transparently personal. Yet they were paid for by the Government, because Espy attended one or more official events. One weekend trip consisted of just one "official" event: a thirty-minute talk to his children's school about pursuing a career with the Department of Agriculture.

Secretary of Veterans Affairs Jesse Brown traveled to his hometown of Chicago on official business twenty times in his first twenty months, amounting to 40% of all his official travel during this time. As the *Los Angeles Times* reported, "[m]any of the visits included weekends or involved lengthy stays with light public schedules."[47] The VA defended Secretary Brown's proclivity to visit Chicago because he is frequently invited there and because VA "has a tremendous presence there [a regional office and four VA hospitals]." But the Secretary did not visit as frequently other locations, such as Florida, with even a greater VA "presence." Secretary Brown said that all of his trips to Chicago were official, and added that he did not charge the Government for lodging, because he always stays with his mother while there.[48] But the *Los Angeles Times* noted that "no official events were listed on Brown's schedule for 35 of the weekdays he was in his hometown[.]" Secretary Brown even counted as an official visit a five-day stay in Chicago in 1994 where the "only public activity listed . . . was an address at the eighth-grade graduation ceremonies at St. Dorothy's School. Brown's nephew was among the graduates."[49]

Kathy Jurado, Secretary Brown's Assistant Secretary for Public and Intergovernmental Affairs, shared his propensity for official visits home. Jurado, who is from Tampa, Florida, made eleven official visits to Florida (seven to Tampa) out of twenty-five official trips in sixteen months at the VA. To her credit, Jurado traveled home nine times at her own expense. But as *Washington Post* columnist Al Kamen noted sardonically in reporting on her travels, "[t]he first trip she made in her new job, in November 1993, forced her to return to Tampa over Thanksgiving."[50]

The Administrator of the General Services Administration (GSA) also came under fire for his travels.[51] Roger Johnson took five of his first nine official trips to the Los Angeles area, where his wife and home are. Generally, Johnson conducted official business in southern California on Fridays and Mondays. He also visited his other home in Utah on two weekends during official trips. Johnson protested that "I have not ever contrived or structured trips to go through Orange County." But he acknowledged, "Did I take every opportunity to get home? I certainly did."[52] Facing a *Wall Street Journal* report on his travels, Johnson took the preemptive steps of asking GSA's Inspector General (IG) to review his travel and reimbursing the Government for the portion of the per diem expenses he received while in Laguna Beach and Utah attributable to personal time. At the time, however, Johnson did not reimburse the Government for any air fare.

Johnson thereafter provided an additional reimbursement after a review conducted by GSA's Chief Financial Officer, who concluded that Johnson did not violate any Federal travel rules.[53] Johnson also reimbursed the Government for thirty-nine overnight pieces of mail and 184 long distance phone calls that were determined to be personal. The Inspector General's report, released April 20, 1994, found in addition that Johnson improperly used his government credit card on a few occasions when he received the government air fare rate for personal trips. But the IG exonerated Johnson of the charge that he conducted personal travel at government expense, and concluded that his misuse of government resources was due to his "unfamiliarity with official travel rules and regulations."[54]

Johnson was unable to avoid getting into further trouble. First, he and his Chief of Staff improperly accepted an upgrade to first class on an official trip to Chicago; they quickly reimbursed United Airlines when informed that accepting the upgrades could violate ethics rules (United has a contract with GSA, and the upgrade was probably given because of Johnson's official position).[55] Then, it was reported in October 1994 that the IG had initiated a second investigation of Johnson, this time looking into reports that Johnson used GSA employees for personal errands and other business, such as writing memoranda to Johnson's personal business consultants, going to Johnson's house to wait for furniture deliveries and repairmen, and taking his Mercedes to the car wash.[56] Johnson's tin ethics ear was explained by reference to mistakes made during his transition from thirty-five years as a corporate executive in the private sector. GSA called these mistakes "inadvertent actions," most of which occurred during Johnson's first months on the job. "As Mr. Johnson became aware of any actions which were inappropriate, he took full responsibility for the infractions and ensured that similar actions did not occur."[57] Johnson said:

> I know what's ethical and what's not. . . . I've had to live that way all my life. It's just [that there are] very different rules here [with] some of the technical stuff that goes on, and I guess for good reason. . . . I know I didn't understand [every technical guideline]. I wasn't naive, but I didn't understand it. [But] I do now.[58]

These stories are only the reported abuses of travel privileges. Undoubtedly, a comprehensive investigation of the travel of Cabinet and sub-Cabinet officials would reveal other abuses.

Conclusions and Recommendations

Use of Government Aircraft

OMB Circular A-126, as tightened by President Clinton's February 1993 policy memorandum, does not need any further tightening. If it were conscientiously followed throughout the Executive Branch, misuse of government aircraft would be held to a minimum. However, it appears that the Circular is not consistently observed by the Pentagon, and perhaps other agencies. What is needed is not another rule or policy statement, but stricter enforcement of the current rules. The White House should focus attention on this issue, holding Cabinet officials personally accountable for their agency officials' travels as well as their own. The President should make it clear that any abuse of the terms of the OMB Circular will not be tolerated and could result in dismissal.

If the Pentagon continues to believe that its frequent use of military helicopters to fly across town to Andrews Air Force base is warranted under OMB Circular A-126, which is dubious, the White House could simply prohibit such use of military helicopters for anyone other than the Secretary and Deputy Secretary of Defense.

Use of Government Funds to Make Official Trips to One's Hometown

Travel home at government expense, even to attend a bona fide official event, should be discouraged by the President. The President should issue a memorandum directing all political appointees from engaging in official travel to one's hometown or a town in which relatives live or personal events are scheduled, except where there is a clear and substantial official purpose for the travel, and where the official visit has not been scheduled to coincide with a previously scheduled personal activity or event. All official trips home, or to destinations where a personal or political event is also planned, should be reviewed by an agency ethics official in advance, to ensure that the official purpose is bona fide and predominates over any personal or political purpose.

The President should inform his appointees that he will not tolerate any report of disproportionate travel to one's hometown, or any other official trip that serves to cover a personal or political purpose behind the travel. As a check on this policy, agency heads should report to the White House, once every six months, all official trips taken by political appointees to destinations involving any personal or political event or purpose, such as visiting friends or relatives at home.

This recommendation may seem the height of Presidential micromanagement of the conduct of his appointees and display a lack of trust in their judgment. But history proves that such micromanagement is necessary and such distrust is well-founded. Abuse of travel perks and privileges, when revealed, strikes a chord of resentment and anger in most Americans, because the message it sends of an official using public office for private gain is so clear and confirms a stereotype of political appointees abusing their office.

Appendix One:

Recommendations

Section 207 and the Revolving Door Statutes Should be Significantly Revised

First, at least for lawyers, extend the lifetime ban on representing a client on the same particular matter involving specific parties, in which the former employee was personally and substantially involved, to include advice given behind the scenes. Many bar rules now proscribe this activity, and the ABA Committee on Government Standards recommends this reform. This would further reduce the risk of misuse of nonpublic information.

Second, repeal the foreign entity cooling-off period, including the special provision relating to the U.S. Trade Representative and, by virtue of the lobbying disclosure legislation enacted in 1995, his Deputy. As amended, the three-year ban is now a **lifetime ban**. As the ABA Committee and others have recognized, these restrictions have nothing to do with ethics. The law's hostility to foreign governments is fundamentally inconsistent with the free trade thrust beyond NAFTA and GATT, and overlooks that the counseling of foreign governments by former U.S. Government officials may result in fewer international disputes, fewer misunderstandings of U.S. law or of the U.S. Government's position, as well as a legitimate check on the sometimes overzealous or discriminatory government actions vis-a-vis foreign governments.

Third, repeal the exceptions for representation of state and local governments, and charitable, educational, and religious institutions, consistent with the recommendations of the ABA Committee. There is no reason these interests deserve a special exemption; they, too, stand to gain or lose financially from actions of the Executive Branch.[1]

Fourth, the trade or treaty negotiation cooling-off period and procurement integrity post-employment restrictions are sufficiently similar to the switching sides provisions in subsection 207(a) that they can and should be repealed. The trade or treaty negotiation restriction prohibits only advice and representation provided on the basis of privileged information. The procurement integrity provision imposes an enormous administrative burden that is not worth the marginal, if any, benefit of having a special post-employment restriction concerning government acquisitions.

Fifth, the cooling-off periods in subsections 207(c), (d), and (e) should be revised to permit communications and appearances engaged in solely for political purposes, similar to legislation proposed by President Bush in 1991 and pending in the 104th Congress.

Sixth, to ensure that the most senior congressional staff are covered, Congress should lower the salary threshold or make the coverage provision applicable to persons appointed to certain named or classified positions.[2] Both Houses should ensure that all departing congressional staff are informed in writing as to whether they are covered by section 207(e). If necessary, the ethics committee of each House should clarify how the salary of a staffer is determined for purposes of that section.

Apply the Conflict-Of-Interest Statute to Broad Legislative Proposals in Certain Circumstances

OGE's current interpretation of the term "particular matter," which provides that comprehensive legislation should be examined only as an indivisible whole, weakens section 208, exempting some conduct that fits the classic notion of a conflict of interest. OGE recently proposed to codify its conclusion that health care legislative reform in which the First Lady participated was not a "particular matter" in an example used in a proposed rule. The proposal would also create an untenable distinction between legislation and rulemaking. The Justice Department must have concurred in OGE's interpretation of this criminal provision, so it is unlikely that either OGE or Justice will change its view in the final rule. Thus, Congress must act to overrule OGE's interpretation or direct OGE and the Justice Department to revisit the matter.

Clarify the Applicability of Conflict-of-Interest and Other Laws to the President's Spouse

Under current Federal law, the legal status of the First Lady is unclear. Until the First Lady was given formal and defined responsibilities over Federal policy—responsibilities both important and different from those traditionally exercised by the First Lady—it may not have been necessary to determine the First Lady's status. But it certainly is possible, if not likely, that future Presidents will consider giving their spouse similar responsibilities. Congress should clarify the legal status of the President's spouse for purposes of section 208, the Federal Advisory Committee Act, and the anti-nepotism law.

Should the President's spouse be given the same exemption from the conflict-of-interest laws that the President, Vice President, and Members of Congress enjoy? In my view, the reasons for the exemption for these elected officials do not justify extending the exemption to include the President's spouse. There are two bases for the exemption.

First, the President has authority over the entire Executive Branch; indeed, he has a constitutional duty to ensure that the laws are faithfully executed. His decision-making and policymaking authority covers virtually all of what Americans and American businesses do. Almost any financial interest could pose a conflict; recusal would not be practical or fair to the President. In essence, this argument is akin to the Rule of Necessity, which under common law permitted judges to decide cases that could affect them personally because all judges could be similarly affected. The same argument can be made in support of the exemptions for Members of Congress.

A President's spouse is not given any authority as a result of the President's election. It is up to each President whether to delegate any authority or assign any responsibility to his or her spouse. Even the pillow talk that inevitably goes on regularly between President and spouse need not concern every subject under the sun. Thus, the President's spouse does not need an exemption.

Second, as an elected official under the most intense public scrutiny, the President is held accountable to the public for any conflicts of interest, real or apparent. This accountability discourages Presidents from holding any interests or outside affiliations that would give rise to an appearance of impropriety. (Members of Congress, on the other hand, have not historically been held accountable to the electorate to the same degree.) The President's spouse, by contrast, is not similarly accountable to the electorate. Because a spouse's financial interests must be disclosed in the President's financial disclosure report, the public is guaranteed to be informed of her interests. However, the public is not likely to know all of the spouse's official activities without the visibility of a formal delegation, such as President Clinton's delegation of health care reform to his wife. Moreover, the electorate is not necessarily going to hold the President accountable for a spousal ethical lapse.

Legislation should provide that the President's spouse shall not be considered an employee of the Government simply by virtue of the informal advice she may directly provide the President from time-to-time, nor by her supervision of her immediate staff (assuming the staff is limited to the traditional ceremonial functions of the First Lady). However, she should be regarded as a Federal official as to any other supervisorial or line responsibility she is given, as well as to her participation in the White House or government deliberative process. (As a Federal employee, the President's spouse would clearly be entitled to seek a conflict-of-interest waiver under section 208(b)(1).)

The Federal Advisory Committee Act should be amended to conform to the holding of the D.C. Circuit Court in *Association of American Physicians and Surgeons*. A group consisting entirely of full-time Federal officials and the President's spouse should not be considered an advisory committee under FACA.

It is not a satisfactory answer to whether the anti-nepotism law has been violated to say that there is no legal sanction for its violation.[3] Presidents are charged with upholding and complying with all Federal laws, not simply the ones with criminal or civil penalties attached, and the President is subject to the anti-nepotism law. The public policy against nepotism seems less urgent in the White House Office, where it is normal practice for the President to hire persons on the basis of long-standing friendships and other loyalties.[4] Moreover, the President's spouse does not receive a separate salary, so there is no concern that the President is putting his family members on the Federal payroll. Thus, the President should be free to appoint his spouse to a White House Office position.

Clarify the Definition of a "Special Government Employee" (SGE)

The concept of a special Government employee needs to be reexamined in light of the increasing reliance of Presidents on the advice and counsel of persons not formally employed by the Government. Using the definition of "officer" and "employee" in the personnel statutes, 5 U.S.C. 2104 and 2105, is neither correct nor very helpful. Yet, any attempt to clarify the definition of special government employee to account for the status of regular informal advisers may suffer from over- or under-inclusiveness. Codification of the functional tests used by Justice and OGE would be helpful, if only to dispel the notion that the absence of a formal appointment or paperwork is dispositive. But codification of the functional test does not obviate the exercise of judgment and discretion within the White House.

Repeal Statutory Ethics Laws That Duplicate or Go Beyond the General Ethics Rule, Such as the Gift Provisions of the Meat Inspection Act

Conduct prohibited by the Meat Inspection Act is also prohibited by the standards of conduct and the illegal gratuities statute. Conduct that would be a *prima facie* violation of a Title 18 offense need not be separately proscribed by a special statute that applies only to one agency's workforce (indeed, only a part of its workforce). In this respect, these provisions of the Meat Inspection Act are superfluous.

Conduct that does not satisfy the elements of the bribery or illegal gratuities provisions in 18 U.S.C. 201 is not sufficiently serious to warrant criminal prosecution. Bribes and illegal gratuities deserve criminal sanction because of the *quid pro quo* nature of these offenses. Where no *quid pro quo* is shown, the venality barometer is lowered, and the prosecutive appeal diminishes. Moreover, keeping the Meat Inspection Act on the books risks inconsistency in the Executive Branch's treatment of ethics transgressions. A major purpose behind President Bush's push for a "single, comprehensive and clear" set of ethical standards, including gift standards, was the desire to eliminate the varying and inconsistent interpretation, application, and enforcement of ethics standards among similarly-situated Executive Branch employees. As the Espy matter shows, misconduct by an Agriculture Department official may trigger a criminal investigation (under the Meat Inspection Act) and result in a prison term, whereas the same misconduct by an official of another agency may result only in administrative discipline, ranging from reprimand to removal. There does not appear to be any legitimate reason why the punishment of Federal officials for the same or similar conduct should depend, even in part, on the agency where they work. The prospects of removal from office and injury to one's reputation, plus proportional punishment for those who violate the standards of conduct, provide sufficient incentive to the Federal officials to comply with the standards.

Repeal the Independent Counsel Law; at a Minimum, an Independent Counsel's Jurisdiction Should be Circumscribed, by Statute or Charter, to Cover Only Those Offenses Committed by the Covered Official or Others in Connection With the Covered Official's Conduct

The objections to the independent counsel law, other than constitutional ones regrettably rejected by the Supreme Court,[5] are many, and are well-known.[6]

An independent counsel, with no limit on money, staff, or time, functions as no other prosecutor does. Because of the perceived political climate surrounding the allegations, an independent counsel is expected to investigate until every possible criminal violation is uncovered or refuted. As a consequence, independent counsel investigations seem interminable; it is not unusual for an independent counsel investigation to take three or more years.[7] Independent counsels are not accountable to the principles of Federal prosecution and the policies of the Justice Department to the same extent as Justice Department attorneys. They are not strictly required to observe Justice Department policies, but must do so "except to the extent that to do so would be inconsistent with the purposes of this chapter."[8]

An independent counsel investigation, because of its protracted nature, and because Congress often refrains from conducting a hearing out of deference to the wishes of a prosecutor, also works to deny Congress and the public an opportunity for a timely report on serious ethics allegations. Congress may have a legitimate legislative interest in correcting whatever alleged abuse led to the appointment of an independent counsel. And the public, at some point, deserves an accounting of certain matters, to permit its informed exercise of the franchise.

Finally, the appointment of an independent counsel is treated by the media and the public as tantamount to an indictment, when in fact it only begins a formal investigation. And the Attorney General has only limited tools to conduct a preliminary investigation, and limited discretion to terminate an investigation without seeking the appointment of an independent counsel. Thus, independent counsels are sometimes appointed in circumstances where the Justice Department would decline to prosecute anyone. Moreover, targets and subjects of independent counsel investigations are assumed guilty of some malfeasance, subject only to the independent counsel's decision (months or years later) not to prosecute, a decision that is not likely to provide sufficient exoneration to the official.

The independent counsel law is cited by many as contributing significantly to the politicization of ethics, as well as the criminalization of public policy disputes.[9]

On the other side of the debate is only one argument: The Justice Department, headed by presidential appointees, cannot be trusted to investigate fellow Presidential appointees.[10] Watergate is always cited as the example, yet there was no independent counsel law at the time. The Watergate prosecutions were handled by a Special Counsel appointed by the Attorney General. Indeed, President Nixon's decision to fire Archibald Cox backfired on the President, resulting in the appointment of an equally independent prosecutor, Leon Jaworski, and significantly greater political and public opposition. Similarly, during the period 1992-1994 when the independent counsel law had lapsed, Attorneys General Barr and Reno used their extant authority to appoint persons from outside the Department to conduct a few investigations free from the supervision of the Department's political appointees. In minor cases, there is no reason why career prosecutors in the Public Integrity Section of the Criminal

Division, subject to the supervision of a career Deputy in the Criminal Division, could not adequately and fairly review a matter and earn the public's respect. This is what was done with allegations that Ron Brown illegally accepted money from a Vietnamese businessman.

In higher profile cases, such as the Madison and Whitewater matters, or in matters involving high-level Justice Department officials, a person may be appointed from outside the Department, who would assemble a staff of career investigators and prosecutors.

President Clinton, who pushed vigorously for the resuscitation of the law as a candidate and (not so vigorously) as President, has probably come to rue the existence of the law, as he has seen himself and several of his appointees come under an independent counsel's scrutiny.[11] His second and third White House Counsels, Lloyd Cutler and Judge Mikva, as well as his personal attorney Robert Bennett, all have commented this year about the abuses the independent law has caused.[12] President Clinton may be hamstrung politically from recommending the law's repeal, considering his initial support of the law and his current involvement in an independent counsel investigation. But the next President should do so.[13]

As noted above, one reason independent counsel investigations take so long is their broad jurisdiction and lack of clear limitations. This permits an independent counsel to stray from the original charge, in hopes of uncovering more serious offenses, or just in hopes of turning a non-covered person to offer evidence against the covered government official. Donald Smaltz's investigation clearly has gone well beyond an inquiry into whether Secretary Espy violated the law. Whether or not Smaltz's charter reasonably can be read to extend to offenses by others, where those offenses bear no factual relation to Espy, the law or practice ought to be changed in the future to avoid such a prospect. A legislative provision such as proposed in H.R. 892 is one way of dealing with the problem. The Attorney General could just as easily ensure a circumscribed investigation by expressly defining the limits of the investigation in the charter proposed to the court of appeals. Indeed, it appears that Attorney General Reno attempted to do just that (in part) in her request for an independent counsel to investigate Secretary Brown and Nolanda Hill.

Some critics of the independent counsel law believe some of its abuses could be curbed by raising the threshold for the appointment of an independent counsel.[14] The better approach is to repeal the statute outright, and return to the Attorney General the authority—and the accountability—to determine whether to use career prosecutors or appoint an out side counsel.

If the law were repealed, Congress should consider requiring the filing of a public report by the Justice Department or Attorney General-appointed Special Counsel in any case involving a public official. This would ensure a public accounting of what happened, which will often be more important than whether someone is indicted. Also, Congress could require OGE to conduct an ethics investigation of a high-level administration official where the Justice Department has declined to prosecute. OGE has limited investigative authority, and generally defers to each agency. Congress may need to push OGE into a more active role, in the absence of an independent counsel law, by authorizing it to conduct such investigations.

Restrict the Placement of Prospective Appointees in the Government Prior to Confirmation

If, as is likely, future administrations continue to bring on board a prospective appointees before they are confirmed, actions must be taken to reduce the problems of inadequate guidance to these appointees and inadequate compliance by them. The problem of **inadequate guidance** can be minimized by clearer, tighter standards, like the memorandum ultimately issued by Jamie Gorelick after the Defense Department's run-in with the Senate Committee on Armed Services. Gorelick's memorandum covered virtually every activity a prospective appointee could be expected to perform or participate in, and drew clear lines of do's and don't's. OPM could have adopted these guidelines as part of the rulemaking to implement the 1992 amendments to 5 U.S.C. 3109, but did not do so. The President should direct OPM to amend the recent rulemaking to implement section 3109, in order to promote a uniform understanding throughout the Executive Branch. Legislation probably is not necessary.

The problem of **inadequate compliance** by prospective appointees with the limitations on their activities also would be eased somewhat if the guidance were clearer. It is obviously easier to comply with rules that are understood than with ones that are ambiguous or subject to differing interpretations. Prospective appointees could also be required to certify that they have read and understand the guidance.[15] A certification would be effective in increasing compliance, even without a penalty for exceeding a consultant's authority, although any risk of sanction would boost the incentive to comply.

The preferred option is legislation to prohibit agencies, across-the-board, from using appropriated funds to hire prospective appointees, or from retaining them as unpaid consultants, yet authorizing the expenditure of funds for travel and per diem to bring prospective appointees to Washington.[16] An agency official who violated this prohibition would be subject to punishment under the Anti-Deficiency Act.[17] This legislation would accept the proposition that the only legitimate reasons to hire prospective appointees is to pay expenses necessary for them to receive briefings and other assistance needed to prepare them for their confirmation hearing. It would not necessarily deny an agency the benefit of a person's advice, because agencies, with some limitations, can enlist the views of persons outside of government on any matter. This legislation, however, would not completely restrain the activities of a prospective appointee who served as a consultant without pay or reimbursement. It would also not restrain a full-time employee who is under consideration for a Presidential appointment from improperly assuming the authority of the position for which the official is being considered.

RECOMMENDATIONS FOR WHITE HOUSE ACTION

Rescind the Executive Order on the Revolving Door

President Clinton's revolving door executive order should be rescinded in its entirety. At a minimum, the foreign entity ban and the special trade negotiator restrictions should be repealed.

Restrict the Use of Prospective Presidential Appointees Before Their Confirmation

In the absence of restrictive legislation, guidance to prospective appointees should be improved, and they should be required to certify that they have read and understand the guidance. These two administrative steps alone would go a long way to ensure that prospective appointees stay within their limited role of a consultant.

Further, an administration should show greater respect for the Senate's advice and consent responsibilities by exhibiting restraint in placing prospective appointees in agencies. Expediting the nominating process would also help marginally, although expedition is unlikely at the start of any new administration.

Place Tighter Controls on the Use of Informal Consultants

Ethics concerns arise with advisers without regard to whether they are technically special Government employees. Thus, the two most meaningful steps for the White House to take are:

(1) require public disclosure of the financial interests and outside affiliations held by all regular informal White House advisers other than obvious representatives (e.g., the head of the AFL-CIO, the President of the National Organization for Women), initially and on an annual basis, without regard to whether they hold a White House pass; and

(2) treat regular informal advisers as if they were subject to the conflict-of-interest laws by requiring their recusal, or at least a declaration of their interests, affiliations, and clients (in essence, treating them as a representative of their interests for that purpose).

Ultimately, it is up to future Presidents to exercise more discipline in their reliance on and use of informal advisers. Structures and processes can be put in place to keep the informal advisers from policymaking deliberations and other official decisionmaking. But no structure is going to keep anyone whose advice the President wants to hear from providing the President with that advice.

Travel Home at Government Expense, Even for Ostensible Official Purposes, Should be Openly Discouraged

The Administration should strongly admonish Cabinet officials and other presidential appointees to refrain from official travel to hometowns or a town in which a relative lives, or a personal event is scheduled, except where there is a clear and substantial official purpose for the travel, and where the timing of the official visit has not been scheduled to coincide with a previously scheduled personal activity or event. An ethics official should review in advance any travel plan going to such destinations, to ensure that the official purpose is *bona fide* and predominates over any personal or political purpose.

The First Lady Should Remedy Her Conflict of Interest and Avoid Future Conflicts by Selling Her Interest in Valuepartners

The President or the First Lady should obtain permission from OGE to communicate with the trustee of the blind trust for the sole purpose of instructing the trustee to sell the First Lady's partnership interest. After obtaining permission, the trustee should promptly sell the interest.

RECOMMENDATIONS FOR THE OFFICE OF GOVERNMENT ETHICS

Revise the Interpretation of "Particular Matter" in Connection with Legislative Matters

OGE and the Justice Department can obviate legislative correction or direction by reconsidering the opinion that comprehensive legislative proposals cannot be considered a "particular matter."

Clarify the Ethics Standards with Respect to an Official's "Significant Other" or Very Close Friend

The gift standards do not currently proscribe a gift to the very close friend of an Executive Branch employee where that gift would be prohibited if made to the employee, unless it were made on the basis of the employee's "designation, recommendation, or other specification[.]"[18] This is so even if the gift to the friend were made because of the friend's relationship with the employee, because of the employee's official position, and with the employee's knowledge and acquiescence. Such gifts would be impermissible if made to the employee's parent, sibling, spouse, child or dependent relative, but not to the employee's significant other.[19]

The regulation's failure to cover "significant others" may reflect the reality that employees do not have the same degree of control over whether gifts are offered to or accepted by persons outside of the family. The facts of the scholarship award from the Tyson Foundation, which Patricia Dempsey accepted despite Secretary Espy's contrary plea, appear to confirm that reality. Yet, it is clear that gifts made to a Federal official's *intime* are likely to raise a similar, if not the same, appearance concern that the donor is seeking some official action from the employee. The facts of Tyson-provided travel and tickets for Espy and Dempsey certainly confirm this reality. In the latter situation, the employee does have some control over whether the gift is made. The ethics standards should be clarified to address this situation, perhaps to direct the employee to consider such gifts to one's companion to be gifts made to the employee, or to require the employee to seek the advice of ethics officials before such gifts are accepted. The standards would not hold an employee responsible for gifts given to a significant other without the employee's knowledge, or where the employee could show that he had no control over the giving or acceptance of the gift.

Expand the Reach of Section 502, Governing Non-Financial Conflicts

Section 502 of the standards of conduct provides a useful process to guard against appearances of impropriety that do not become a financial conflict.[20] However, that process applies only in connection with particular matters involving specific parties, yet appearance concerns surface just as regularly with particular matters that do not involve specific parties. The process also is triggered by certain covered relationships, such as relatives and former business partners, even though an appearance concern may arise in situations not involving one of the covered relationships. Although section 502 contains a residual provision, this provision is often overlooked. Moreover, whereas an agency ethics official may directly raise with an employee appearance concerns that come independently to the ethics official's attention, and may make the initial determination (in lieu of the employee) that an appearance concern exists, that provision covers only appearance concerns contemplated by the section (i.e., covered relationships in the context of particular matters involving specific parties). OGE should consider amending section 502 to broaden its reach to particular matters, and expressly to allow ethics officials (in lieu of the employee) to determine that an appearance concern exists. OGE should encourage agency ethics officials to emphasize the applicability of the section 502 process to all matters giving rise to appearance concerns.

RECOMMENDATIONS FOR CONGRESS

Conducting Oversight Generally
The frequency of congressional oversight of Executive Branch ethics has fluctuated dramatically over the last few years, matching the changing electoral landscape in 1992 and 1994. From 1981 to 1992, Congress did not hesitate to hold hearings to air allegations and reports of unethical conduct by Reagan and Bush Administration officials. Following the Presidential election in 1992, however, Congress lost its appetite for oversight of alleged ethical missteps by the White House and Executive Branch. And this was certainly not due to the lack of ethics controversies. In the 103d Congress, no committee hearings were held relating to any of the following subjects involving the ethics of the Clinton Administration:

- the Health Care Task Force
- the First Lady's financial interests in health care firms
- the White House Travel Office firings
- the Clintons' Legal Defense Fund
- the President's and White House's response to the trooper allegations
- the retrieval and disclosure of Bush Administration personnel files by State Department political appointees
- the access and influence of informal advisers to the President
- Ron Brown's business relationships[21]

What little the public learned about these matters came from media disclosures and from Republicans in Congress. Republicans, who as members of the minority party could not assume the authority of a committee, were similarly dependent on the media to pick up their complaints and questions. In a few cases, Republicans requested a GAO investigation, but the GAO reports were not an adequate substitute for a committee investigation or hearing.

Congress did hold hearings on Whitewater and Madison, but only reluctantly, and only after reports of misconduct proliferated and the tide of editorial opinion turned solidly in favor of congressional oversight. In an effort to prevent questions about Whitewater and Madison, the Banking Committees failed for months to hold

Resolution Trust Corporation (RTC) oversight hearings as required by rule. The House Banking Committee hearings eventually held were a farce. Both the Senate and House hearings were very limited in scope, in deference to the pending independent counsel investigation.

With the change in control following the 1994 elections, the Republican Congress only gradually stepped up the pace of oversight hearings and investigations. Hearings were held on Whitewater and the Travel Office, with more to follow on these two subjects. Other oversight hearings on matters other than ethics have also been held, such as the Energy Department's contracts with an outside firm to analyze the news coverage of the Secretary and the Department.

A neutral observer of the last few years would conclude that oversight has been used primarily as a partisan weapon: wielded when Congress and the Presidency are held by different parties, kept in check when they are held by the same party. Some of the most vocal opponents of politicization of ethics during the 1980s have not been heard decrying the Republican efforts in 1995 to showcase the Administration's ethical mistakes. Similarly, it took a Democratic President and a Republican Congress before many Democrats would join this lament. In fact, it is naive to ask for an ethics oversight truce between the parties, because it will not happen. What should be demanded instead is a consistent exercise of oversight no matter which party controls Congress and the White House, and oversight that is as fair as it is thorough.

Without congressional oversight of Executive Branch ethics, an administration is likely to escape accountability for any ethical misconduct and lapses in integrity. The ethics watchdogs and police that are internal to the Executive Branch—agency ethics officials, the Office of Government Ethics, Inspectors General, and the Justice Department—often act outside of public view. The degree of their independence varies greatly, and they exercise great control over the scope and thoroughness of any particular investigation, without much of a check from outside. And it is not sufficient to rely on the media to perform an oversight role that is a legitimate exercise of congressional authority.

There remains the problem of adequate congressional oversight when, as in 1993-94, the Presidency and the Congress are controlled by the same party. Representative Clinger has proposed that during such times the minority be given the same subpoena power as the majority party. This proposal deserves consideration, but the remedy for the failure of Congress to conduct oversight of Executive Branch malfeasance should be largely political. In other words, the minority can protest, and appeal to the media and ultimately the voters, if a situation like the House Banking Committee's Whitewater hearings under Chairman Henry Gonzalez recurs. The minority party does have some authority to demand that an Executive agency provide information upon request, although this law does not require in so many words an agency to turn over all records, including privileged documents.[22]

How oversight is conducted is important. First, reports and allegations of ethical misconduct involving an Executive Branch official generally should be addressed initially to the appropriate Executive Branch component for a suitable investigation or response, before a committee embarks on its own investigation or holds a hearing. An agency should be allowed a reasonable opportunity to account for the behavior of its officials and to take or recommend corrective action.

Second, letters alleging misconduct or inquiring about the ethics of certain officials or actions should ordinarily not be released to the press until received by the agency or official charged with misconduct, plus a reasonable time for the agency or official to prepare a response. This reduces the likelihood that allegations that are capable of refutation or explanation are reported widely, unjustly tarring an official's reputation.

Third, committee rules of procedure should be changed to facilitate truth-gathering and to discourage grandstanding, posturing, or obfuscation. For instance, the five-minute rule (a member from the majority party has five minutes to ask questions and then a member from the minority has five minutes, and so on) makes it nearly impossible to pursue a complex or involved line of questioning.

The Special Problem of Parallel Proceedings

The value of timely and thorough oversight must often compete with a parallel criminal investigation, whether conducted by the Justice Department, the FBI, an independent counsel, or other agency. Prosecutors and investigators often request Congress to hold its hearings or investigation in abeyance pending the outcome of a criminal investigation, or at least to structure the congressional inquiry to make sure that it will not compromise the investigation and potential prosecution. Congressional investigators respond that there is a greater public interest in a timely public accounting of the matter.

Congress undoubtedly has authority to hold hearings while a criminal investigation is pending. But the value of such hearings may be diminished significantly if the main witnesses refuse to testify asserting their right against self-incrimination, and if the Executive Branch agency is limited in what it discloses because of the highly privileged nature of a criminal law enforcement investigation (whether or not a grand jury has been convened). So it is in the interest of Congress to work something out with the prosecutor or investigative agency.

Because the problem of parallel proceedings frequently arises in a highly charged political environment, politics plays a major role in resolving these competing claims. Nonetheless, some neutral guidelines can be agreed upon by both parties in Congress and the Justice Department. Among the factors to be considered are:

(1) Is there a public policy interest in the matter that is broader than the interest in investigation and prosecution of possible crimes? (e.g,, Iran-Contra, Whitewater, yes; Henry Cisneros, no)

(2) Is there a need to provide ongoing, contemporaneous oversight of a Federal program or function, to consider a legislative remedy? Will the length of the criminal investigation frustrate a timely legislative correction?

(3) Is the criminal investigation, because of its narrow scope or nonpublic nature, not likely to achieve a full accounting of the matter (i.e., **what happened**, rather than was a law violated, or was a crime committed for which prosecution is warranted)? An independent counsel is required to file a report with the Special Court, which is normally made public. The Justice Department, however, if it declines to prosecute, rarely provides any additional comment or explanation. (This could be changed by statute.)

(4) Can the risk of injury to a criminal probe be reduced by (a) refraining from granting immunity; (b) allowing prosecutors to freeze witness testimony before congressional hearings; and (c) allowing all testimony be taken before any hearing, to prevent witnesses to anticipate questioning? Prosecutors should refrain from asserting Rule 6(e) privilege with respect to preexisting documents. For example, the Whitewater hearings were delayed, and then limited, to handle only those issues for which the special counsel had completed his investigation.

Republicans and Democrats should meet with Justice Department officials to work out guidelines on how best to assert and protect both interests in parallel proceedings, and attempt to execute an appropriate memorandum of understanding.

Appendix Two

Widely Attended Gatherings, the White House, and the Media

The following is an account of the White House's first clear brush with the ethics rules, concerning whether White House and Cabinet officials could accept invitations to widely attended dinners sponsored by a media organization if the invitation came from someone other than the sponsor of the event. It is an amusing illustration of how quickly and openly the White House—solicitous of the media as well as of the White House Staff's desire to attend such dinners—agreed to push OGE to relax the ethics rules, contemporaneously with the President's promising of his Administration's compliance with the highest standards of conduct. It also serves to illustrate the lack of sensitivity the new White House had to ethics concerns, and foreshadowed in part the problems in which President Clinton's first White House Counsel would eventually become embroiled.

It has long been the position of the Office of Government Ethics (OGE) that news organizations and reporters are considered "prohibited sources," that is, persons who seek official action from the employees of a Federal agency.[1] Under the standards of conduct promulgated by the Bush Administration, although not effective until February 3, 1993, Federal employees may not accept a gift over $20 from a news organization unless the gift is free attendance at all or part of a "widely attended gathering," attendance is considered to be in the agency's interest, and the gift is made by the sponsor of the event.[2] The widely attended gathering exception to the gift rules was previously contained in many agency ethics rules, and was recognized as an appropriate exception many years ago. The standards of conduct merely added an express provision that, to avoid any appearance of impropriety, the invitation and gift should be made by the sponsor of the event. In other words, "CBS News" could buy a table at the annual White House Correspondents Dinner, and the White House Correspondents Association could invite White House and Cabinet officials to sit at the table, but the invitation could not come from CBS nor could CBS dictate who would sit at its table.[3]

This is the policy we followed in 1991-92 when I served in the White House Counsel's office. The media and some White House officials did not like it very much, and it probably is the case that our policy was regularly ignored by White House officials who accepted such invitations without clearing them with our office.[4] Like many in the media who did not see any appearance problem, some in the Bush White House did not treat an invitation from the *Washington Post* or Capital Cities/ABC as they would an invite from Archer Daniels Midland or IBM.

When the media were apprised in early 1993 of the new OGE rules and their application to media dinners, a chorus of protest was directed to the White House. Some steadfastly asserted, wrongly, that news organizations could not be a "prohibited source;" others simply misunderstood the OGE rule.[5] The rule does not prevent White House and Cabinet officials from attending such dinners, receptions, or other widely attended events; all that is required is that invitations come from the sponsor of the event, whether it is the White House Correspondents Association, the Gridiron Dinner, or the *New York Times*. Simply put, a news organization cannot buy a seat next to a named official. Many in the media did not welcome this policy.

As columnist Al Kamen described it :

> The papers howled that this would not work. They were paying good money and scrambling to get key power brokers to dine at their tables—not to spend the night with know-nothing flunkies picked by the dinner committees.[6]

The media quickly won a reprieve. The White House, barely in office one month, agreed to waive application of the ethics rule to widely attended media dinners. White House Counsel Bernard Nussbaum, in a March 9, 1993 memorandum to agency ethics officials, declared that "the White House will hold the application of this rule in abeyance for six months[.]." Nussbaum based this action on the desire to "foster a positive relationship between executive branch officials and the press," the "newness of the rule and the fact that planning for these events occurred prior to the implementation of the rule[.]" In the technical words of OGE, the White House "declared a six-month suspension of application to press dinners of that portion of § 2635.204(g)(2) that limits acceptance of invitations to widely attended gatherings to those issued by the sponsor of the event."[7]

It was then, and remains, unclear what legal authority the White House relied on to "hold in abeyance" (Nussbaum's words) or "suspend" (OGE's word) application

of a rule promulgated by OGE, and to do so by memorandum as opposed to an amendment of the rule. Nussbaum did not cite any authority in his memorandum (nor did he say he was acting on behalf of the President). OGE's authority to promulgate gift standards stems **both** from Executive Order 12674 and 5 U.S.C. 7353, a provision added by the Ethics Reform Act of 1989.[8] The Ethics Reform Act delegated rulemaking authority directly to OGE, so that Nussbaum probably would not be justified relying on whatever residual authority the President has under Executive Order 12674. Perhaps the White House Counsel thought he would get around this question by simply suspending "administrative enforcement" of the rule, which the President, as official superior and manager of the entire Executive Branch workforce, could probably do.[9]

The media continued to wear down the White House on this issue, meeting with senior White House officials in October 1993 to request a change in the rules; the White House agreed to review the matter further.[10] On December 21, 1993, in a memorandum from Bernard Nussbaum to all agency heads, the White House "asked" agency heads "to suspend, until August 1, 1994, or until such time as OGE responds to our petition for a rule change, whichever is later, administrative enforcement of the rule[.]" Note how the White House Counsel shied away from directing a suspension of the rule or even directing agency heads not to enforce it, suggesting the March 9, 1993 memorandum was *ultra vires*.

The memorandum referred to a petition for a rule change, which the White House simultaneously submitted to OGE. In the memorandum to agency heads, Nussbaum explained the basis for the White House's request for a rule change:

> Our ethics regulations should recognize and preserve the special role of the press in our democratic system. The press is unlike other non-federal individuals, organizations and entities. When performing their official function, members of the press do not seek to do business with, nor do they seek official action from, the government officials about whom they are reporting. . . . The press, in effect, functions on behalf of the greater public good. In recognition of the special nature of the press' role, and specifically of its relationship to government officials, we believe that it is therefore not appropriate to treat news associations and organizations (and their respective members and employees) the same as all other non-federal actors, including lobbyists.

In the preamble to a proposed rule on the subject, OGE took on the White House Counsel's memorandum and had no trouble thoroughly refuting it:

> More often than not, however, those who report about the actions of Government officials or about Government programs do interview, or seek to interview, those who are the subject of their reporting or who have official knowledge about the subject. When that occurs they and the press organizations they represent often are seeking official information from Government officials and are seeking to occupy their official time. They are "prohibited sources" within the meaning of 5 CFR 2635.203(d)(1) to the same extent as are others who seek official action from the employees of a Fed-

eral agency." How successful they are in obtaining that official information impacts upon their work product and redounds to their benefit or detriment and, ultimately, to the benefit or detriment of the news organizations they serve. Members of the press and press organizations have interests that may be substantially affected by the performance or nonperformance of the official duties of the Government officials of who they seek information and, thus, also meet the definition of prohibited sources in 5 CFR 2635.203(d)(4). . . . We agree with the White House view that reporting by the press often serves the public good. Whether the product or service is a new cancer medication approved by the Food and Drug Administration or a blockbuster documentary on World War I funded, in part, by a grant from the National Endowment for the Humanities, the same can be said of the products or services of many others who are prohibited sources.[11]

Norman Ornstein was even more direct:

> Reporters and editors start months in advance to grab top Cabinet officers, Senators, and other bigwigs, both in a macho effort to top their rivals and show their prestige and clout to pressies and policymakers alike —while also impressing their out-of-town bosses. This is not just for show, however. It is for getting phone calls returned, and to get a leg up on booking busy, in-demand policy stars for talk shows. And it's undeniable that such access has a financial payoff.[12]

Ornstein also noted that there were several policy matters, such as network syndication of programming, before the Executive Branch in which media organizations could have a substantial interest. In this respect, there really is no difference between Time Warner and Archer Daniels Midland.

However, OGE agreed with the White House that its current rule "may be unnecessarily restrictive[.]" Accordingly, it proposed to permit the acceptance of invitations to widely attended events by persons other than the sponsor "where more than 100 will be in attendance and where the gift of free attendance has a market value of $250 or less."[13] The 100-person limit was designed to limit the exception to "events which, by their large, more public nature are unlikely to prompt questions regarding the appropriateness of their characterization as widely attended." The $250 ceiling was chosen because Congress provided that gifts under $250 need not be reported on a Federal official's financial disclosure report; thus, the $250 ceiling "comports with legislative consensus that gifts below that amount are of a value that need not be subjected to public scrutiny." Together, these provisions minimize the risk that the exception would be abused by providing "lavish entertainment" for government officials.[14]

So, the gift standards will eventually be amended to take care of this inconvenience to the press and high-level Executive Branch officials, however flimsy the justification for a change.

Appendix Three

Financial Disclosure, the Confirmation Process, and Secretary of the Navy John Dalton

On April 21, 1993, President Clinton announced his intention to nominate John H. Dalton as Secretary of the Navy.[1] The White House biographical statement released to the media at the time noted Dalton's previous government service as Chairman of the Federal Home Loan Bank Board (Bank Board) in the Carter Administration, and his most recent position as an executive with the Arkansas firm of Stephens, Incorporated.[2] Dalton was formally nominated in July 1993. The Senate Armed Service Committee held a hearing on his nomination on July 13, 1993; a portion of the hearing was held in executive (closed) session, to discuss certain matters that were included in the FBI background report. Dalton was confirmed easily.

A year later, Jeff Gerth of the *New York Times* reported Dalton's role in a failed savings and loan, a role that was not publicly acknowledged by the White House or Armed Services Committee at the time of Dalton's nomination.[3] From 1984 to 1988, with Dalton serving as the head of Seguin Savings Association, Seguin tripled its holdings to $145 million, a growth rate that reportedly violated Federal rules. Seguin was seized by the Bank Board on December 29, 1988, and later sold to investors at a loss to taxpayers of $100 million. The Federal Deposit Insurance Corporation (FDIC), which was prepared to file a civil suit against Dalton and four other Seguin officials for various claims, including "gross negligence" and violations of State and Federal laws, settled with Dalton and the others in January 1993 by receiving $3.8 million from Seguin's insurance company.

After leaving Seguin, Dalton was hired by Centex Corporation, the largest homebuilder in the country, which was interested in purchasing failed S&Ls from the Federal Home Loan Bank Board. Centex asked Dalton to arrange a meeting with Bank Board officials, for which Dalton would be paid a finder's fee of $750,000. Centex eventually bought four S&Ls from the Bank Board for $26 million. On the day it seized Seguin, the Bank Board also nixed the finder's fee. George Barclay, Dallas Bank Board President, said "it was inappropriate for Government money to be going to an individual whose own institution was being put through a receivership that very day. Dalton, however, sued to collect the finder's fee. He dismissed his suit on April 20, 1993, only a day before the President announced his intent to nominated Dalton.

Dalton also was liable on a loan he personally obtained to purchase a condominium, which was subsequently lost through foreclosure.[4] On February 2, 1994, the Resolution Trust Corporation (RTC) sent Dalton a notice for liability of $27,000 on the loan. Dalton settled this claim in July 1994 by paying the Government $17,783.

Dalton informed the White House of his role in Seguin (apparently on an internal form called a Personal Disclosure Statement, or PDS), and the FBI background report reportedly noted Seguin's failure and Dalton's settlement with the FDIC. The closed hearing of the Senate Armed Services Committee also discussed Seguin's failure with Dalton, but did not disclose this matter to the full Senate, which voted to confirm Dalton without knowledge of his S&L troubles. Moreover, on the Committee questionnaire requesting Dalton to list "all jobs held" within the last ten years, Dalton did not list his positions with Seguin. He did list his positions with Seguin's holding company, Freedom Capital, but Seguin was not identified as a holding of Freedom Capital. Thus, **nothing about Dalton's relationship with a failed S&L was put on the public record**. In particular, the White House biographical statement accompanying the announcement of the intent to nominate Dalton did not mention Dalton's position with Seguin.

Dalton's first public financial disclosure statement filed as a nominee in July 1993 did not report his liability on the condominium loan.[5] Dalton initially explained that he was unaware of this liability until he received a second notice from the RTC (apparently he did not receive the first notice), at which time he promptly settled the claim. He later explained that he delayed payment of the loan because he believed he would repurchase the mortgage.[6]

The White House did not explain its omission of Dalton's Seguin role from its public statements about his nomination. Armed Service Committee Chairman Sam Nunn explained that a closed session was held in order to discuss matters include in the confidential FBI report. It wa• also pointed out that the parties to the $3.8 million settlement had agreed not to "initiate" the release "to the media" of any information about the settlement. Senator Nunn's explanation was unpersuasive, of course, because Seguin's failure, Dalton's role in Seguin, and the Centex finder's fee all could have easily been discussed at the public hearing without reference to the FBI report. All these matters were publicly available from the banking agencies or the courts. Indeed, the FDIC Communications Director explained that the FDIC is forbidden by law from entering into any confidential settlements. He said that this settlement clause applied only to the lawyers representing the parties, obligating them only not to "initiate" the release of information.[7]

Both the *Washington Post* and *New York Times* called for a public explanation from the White House and from the Committee, but apparently none was ever provided.[8]

In sum, **Secretary Dalton** omitted a debt from his financial disclosure statement (a willful failure to report would be a violation of 18 U.S.C. 1001); and omitted his positions with Seguin on his Senate questionnaire. Listing his position with Seguin's holding company was insufficient disclosure. The **White House** knew about but omitted any mention of Dalton's S&L position in statements concerning his nomination and appointment. While one can certainly appreciate the fact that the White House did not wish to feature or highlight Dalton's S&L ties, the White House's omission of his S&L position from its biographical statement made the statement misleading. The **Armed Services Committee** held a closed session to discuss the S&L matter, and did not inform the full Senate about this before the Dalton was confirmed. Senator Warner, the Committee's Ranking Member, later conceded that it was a mistake to have conducted the discussion of Dalton's S&L conduct in executive session. Thus, Dalton and the White House avoided public controversy over the nomination, which could have spelled difficulty for Dalton before the full Senate as well as embarrassed the Clinton Administration by linking it with the S&L scandals of the 1980s.

The financial and background disclosure requirements have been widely criticized as excessive and intrusive. It is true that several of the requirements are unrelated to a person's fitness for a given Federal appointment. In the case of Navy Secretary-designate John Dalton, however, the financial and background disclosure requirements made sense. Yet, even had Dalton fully disclosed his liability on his public financial disclosure form and his S&L position on his Senate questionnaire, Dalton, the White House, and the Armed Services Committee would have similarly avoided public controversy over Dalton's S&L role without additional disclosures by the White House or Committee that were not required by law. When Dalton's S&L ties were later reported, a year after his confirmation, there was a brief period of criticism from the national media, and calls for an explanation. But within a week, the story had died, and Dalton and the White House appear to have escaped any further criticism.

This vignette remains a good example of the White House's less than candid approach to disclosures concerning its appointees, even though Secretary Dalton received less criticism than Secretary Ron Brown did for similar inadequate disclosures and the White House virtually escaped any accountability for its conduct.

NOTES

Chapter One

[1]Exec. Order 12834; 29 *Weekly Compilation of Presidential Documents* 77 (Jan. 20, 1993).

[2]See 29 *Weekly Compilation of Presidential Documents,* 167-69 ("Memorandum on Fiscal Responsibility," (Feb. 10, 1993)(executive dining facilities and conferences); "Memorandum on Restriction of Government Aircraft," (Feb. 10, 1993); "Memorandum on Use of Government Vehicles," (Feb. 10, 1993).

[3]The comprehensive standards of conduct issued by the Office of Government Ethics (OGE) were first effective in February 1993, but they were issued during the Bush Administration. President Clinton's tough revolving door rules, which he imposed by exacting pledges from his appointees as a condition of their appointment, do not take effect until an official has left the Government. His restrictions on perks simply continued the campaign against perks begun in the Bush Administration.

[4]30 *Weekly Compilation of Presidential Documents,* 631 (Mar. 24, 1994)(emphasis added). At the time the President made these remarks, there had been little opportunity to "enforce" his executive order, because only a few officials subject to the executive order had left the Government. Moreover, the President's answer was a non-sequitur, because when asked about the many allegations of unethical conduct by White House officials while in office, he relied on standards that apply only after an official leaves the Administration. And the revolving door restrictions he put in place do not relate to "ethical conflicts" as that term is generally understood.

[5]31 *Weekly Compilation of Presidential Documents,* 353 (Mar. 3, 1995). The example the President provided, however, dealt with random drug testing standards for White House employees, which he compared to Congress's own standards, not the standards of previous administrations.

[6]These factors are well-covered in Suzanne Garment's 1991 book *Scandal: The Culture of Mistrust in American Politics* (Times Books). From the President Clinton's defenders come explanations of a green administration unprepared, as was Vince Foster, for the sport of scandal-mongering. Bob Bennett, President Clinton's lawyer, in defending Bernard Nussbaum, referred to "the scandal machine in which the combined currents of law enforcement, politics and the press create a Bermuda Triangle through which only the most sophisticated legal sailors in the ways of Washington can navigate." Birnbaum, "Despite Clinton's Vow To Reform the Capital, It's Business as Usual," *Wall Street Journal,* A1 (Mar. 7, 1994).

White House Press Secretary Mike McCurry said the current political climate is less tolerant of ethical missteps. "[T]he level of scrutiny has changed so dramatically[.] We're now calling 'sleaze' and 'corruption' matters so insignificant they would have gone unreported in earlier years. . . . The threshold of scandal has been lowered." Kurtz, "The Big Sleazy," *Washington Post,* C1, C2 (Mar. 26, 1995). McCurry also explained, "What happened? I think it is a sign of our times that people can kick up a cloud of dust, allegations can swirl and they get a great deal of attention by those on the Hill and those of you who follow these matters." J. Broder, "Administration Ethics: What Went Wrong?," *Los Angeles Times,* A18 (Feb. 25, 1995).

Others blame the media for fanning the flames:

A sad episode in American political history is being played out here. So many Clinton friends set out for Washington with dreams of hope and glory, and so many have been destroyed. The invective, the name-calling, the juvenile spit balls hurled at the White House add insult to injury. Some of us have lost our manners and have forgotten that the presidency has already cost Bill and Hillary Clinton plenty. We may not owe them our political allegiance or our votes, but for the moment a little sympathy wouldn't hurt.

Cohen, "A Little Sympathy," *Washington Post,* A27 (Dec. 13, 1994).

[7]Stengel & Beckwith, "Morality Among the Supply-Siders," *Time,* 18 (May 25, 1987). This number is most likely doubly inflated, because (1) it includes allegations of mismanagement, policy errors, and legal misjudgments, many of which should not be considered a matter of ethics, and (2) it includes any allegation, no matter if it later proved baseless.

[8]B. Ginsberg & M. Shefter, *Politics By Other Means,* 1-37 (Basic Books, 1990).

[9]Ibid., 26.

[10]The index of 261 articles was compiled by the House Subcommittee on Civil Service. The Subcommittee noted that "[t]he allegations have not been further investigated by the Subcommittee." Also, the Subcommittee inaccurately stated that the articles concerned Reagan officials "who have been the subject of charges of unethical conduct." In fact, many of the articles bore no relation to ethics. Two examples will suffice:

89. Jo Ann Gasper, Deputy Assistant Secretary, Department of Health and Human Services, reportedly directed that all Planned Parenthood birth-control clinics be denied federal Family Planning funds, an action which appeared to violate the intent of Congress. Ms. Gasper was reprimanded and her order rescinded. (*WP* 2/4/87)

237. Lawrence A. Uzzell, Special Assistant to the Under Secretary, Depart. of Education, advocated that every federal program for elementary and secondary education—including aid to the handicapped—be abolished. Mr. Uzzell resigned. (*WP* 4/19/85)

[11]From the draft introduction, set for DNC Chairman Ron Brown's signature:

Since Bush took office, the Bush team has set a torrid pace of ethical impropriety that actually exceeds the unethical prowess of the eight-year Reagan presidency.

All told, there are at least 100 cases of ethical missteps: enough violations, in fact, to require additional space in the Republican Hall of Shame.

Included among the "missteps" and "violations" were the following:

• David Bates and Dean Burch (not a Federal employee) both allegedly lied when they provided an alibi for President Bush against charges that he participated in an "October surprise" in 1980 to delay the release of the hostages held by Iran. (11-12) The DNC noted that .35 inches of rain fell in Washington on the day that both said they played tennis with George Bush!

• Teresa Gorman, a Special Assistant to President Bush in the Office of Policy Development, and in charge of a White House task force on wetlands, was cited for instructing EPA Administrator Bill Reilly not to criticize a House wetlands bill. (22)

• Constance Newman, Director of the Office of Personnel Management, was criticized for revising the security clearance form for Federal employees (SF-86), offering a "frightening indictment of the Bush Administration's views on the Privacy Act and activities protected under the First Amendment." (30)

• Joy Silverman, a prominent Republican donor who was nominated to be Ambassador to Barbados, but whose nomination was later withdrawn by President Bush, was criticized for her alleged lack of qualifications. (36)

[12]The independent counsel law was enacted in 1978, and lapsed during a two-year period in 1992-94 spanning the end of the Bush Administration and the beginning of the Clinton Administration.

[13]Secretary Brown was also previously investigated by the Justice Department in 1993-94 and exonerated of allegations that he accepted money from a Vietnamese businessman in exchange for taking or promising to take official action.

[14]Stengel & Beckwith, "Morality Among the Supply-Siders," *Time*, 18 (May 25, 1987).

[15]As shown in the subsequent chapters of this book, the Clinton Administration has featured officials, both those who have "fallen" and those who are (at this time) standing, in each of the latter three categories. Secretary Ron Brown and GSA head Roger Johnson would be considered Public-Service Privateers. The loyalty the White House Arkansans (and a few others such as Roger Altman and Josh Steiner) have shown the Clintons has been remarkable, even though it has cost several of them dearly; and Secretaries Ron Brown and Henry Cisneros as well as the President himself, all have been plagued by actions taken before entering service, although at this point none has been "undone" by his past.

The first category involves considerations broader than ethics, including legitimate policy views that are not affected by financial or personal interests. And it is a category skewed against those generally supportive of deregulation. So it is not surprising that Clinton appointees have not appeared as "Foxes in the Chicken Coop."

[16]5 CFR 2635.101(b)(7), (8), (14).

[17]This of course is not a final judgment; several matters remain pending, such as Whitewater, Travel Office, and the investigations of Secretaries Ron Brown and Mike Espy. Moreover, there is still a year left in the Clinton Administration; during this year the Administration must navigate the ethically tricky waters of an election year.

[18]Jeffrey Birnbaum wrote in March 1994 that "the kind of cronyism that drew controversy to the White House under Presidents Carter and Reagan is cropping up again." He explained that the downside of the heavy reliance the President places on Arkansas loyalists in the White House is that "many of the loyalists seems to have a blind spot for the public interest." Birnbaum, "Despite Clinton's Vow To Reform the Capital, It's Business as Usual," *Wall Street Journal*, A1 (Mar. 7, 1994).

[19]The White House, in Ira Magaziner's infamous March 3, 1993 declaration, did pay lip service to ethics standards. But the working group in fact functioned largely free of ethics restraints.

[20]This vignette is recounted in Appendix Two.

[21]This cavalier attitude toward ethics standards was foreshadowed even before the President took office. Congressional Democrats, well aware in 1991 that the post-employment restrictions law restricted the activities of former senior Federal officials (including former Members and Hill staff) who left government to work on a presidential campaign, refused to amend the law. While several departing Republican appointees chafed under the post-employments restrictions in 1991-92, George Stephanopoulos—and perhaps others—was not so troubled.

[22]See, for example, Cohen, "Her Own Worst Enemy," *Washington Post*, A21 (Mar. 10, 1994)("If any-

one has threatened the Clintons' 'political agenda,' it is the Clintons themselves. For some reasons—arrogance, a sense of victimization, the need to hide something—they have refused to look the public in the eye and give candid responses to certain questions."); Blumenthal, "The Education of a President," *The New Yorker*, 31 (Jan. 24, 1994)("The Clintons' assertion of innocence [relating to Whitewater] unleashed the logic of scandal: their stubborn insistence on privacy had the inevitable effect of intensifying the clamor.").

[23]E.J. Dionne, writing about the White House's response to Whitewater allegations, asked:

If the Clintons have nothing to hide, why do they seem to be hiding things?... [If there's nothing in fact to Whitewater], then the Clintons' problem lies not with Whitewater itself, but in a White House permeated by a hatred of the press, a resentment of disclosure and an attitude of permanent embattlement.

Dionne, "Whitewater: Who Made This Monster?," *Washington Post*, A17 (Mar. 22, 1994)("Most Americans want to talk about [things other than Whitewater.] But to change the subject, the Clintons need to stop seeing legitimate questions as invasions of privacy. They and their lieutenants need to overcome the 'us' against 'them' syndrome, which could do them a lot more damage than Whitewater.").

[24]"[T]he shared assumption of those who populate the Clinton White House seems to be that because they all view themselves as 'good people,' the public shouldn't question their motives. Some critics see this as a kind of baby-boomer arrogance that has made Clinton officials too quickly dismissive of ethics questions." Birnbaum, "Despite Clinton's Vow To Reform the Capital, It's Business as Usual," *Wall Street Journal*, A1, A9 (Mar. 7, 1994).

[25]According to Jeffrey Birnbaum, White House Counsel Bernard Nussbaum repeatedly violated "[a] basic rule of political damage control in Washington[:] err on the side of candor, especially where documents are concerned." Ibid.

[26]Three journalists, writing at different points of the Clinton Presidency, offered complementary descriptions of the President's credibility problem:

This president salts his remarks with so many inventions, half-truths, and self-serving exaggerations that reporters who cover him often have to choose between truth-squadding every speech or ignoring his fibs... There are many ways politicians butcher the truth. They fib about personal indiscretions, dissemble about broken campaign promises, and grossly exaggerate their accomplishments. There are deceptions in staff-written speeches, simple slips of the tongue, falsities based on historical ignorance, Reaganesque flights of fancy, and, finally, . . . willful shadings of the truth for partisan advantage...Bill Clinton has tried them all[.]

C. Cannon, "Bill Clinton's Pathetic Lies," *Weekly Standard*, 25, 26 (Oct. 2, 1995).

The President's essential character flaw isn't dishonesty so much as a-honesty. It isn't that Clinton means to say things that are not true, or that he cannot make true, but that everything is true for him when he says it, because he says it. Clinton means what he says when he says it, but tomorrow he will mean what he says when he says the opposite. He is the existential President, living with absolute sincerity in the passing moment.

Kelly, "The President's Past," *New York Times Magazine*, 20, 45 (July 31, 1994).

It doesn't matter whether the issues are large or small, public or intensely private, Mr. Clinton often chooses to skate along the slippery edges of truth... Bill Clinton has a major credibility problem. He seems to approach the truth the way a sculptor approaches marble, or a lump of clay—as a medium to be molded and shaped to achieve a particular end.

Herbert, "The Truth Sculptor," *New York Times*, A21 (Jan. 12, 1994).

[27]Marcus, "The White House Isn't Telling Us the Truth," *Washington Post*, C9 (Aug. 21, 1994).

[28]Schmidt, "Republicans Accuse Clinton Aides of Misconduct in WHitewater Report," *Washington Post*, A12 (Jan. 4, 1995)

[29]See, for example, Birnbaum, "Despite Clinton's Vow To Reform the Capital, It's Business as Usual," *Wall Street Journal*, A1 (Mar. 7, 1994)("Mr. Clinton and his Arkansas crew come from a much more freewheeling and forgiving environment.").

[30]30 *Weekly Compilation of Presidential Documents,* 432 (Mar. 4, 1994)(emphasis added). A few days later, the President remarked:

They have been, on the whole, blatantly partisan, and it's obvious that they want to do something that I don't think the American people ought to let them get away with, which is to deter this Administration and the entire Federal Government from meeting its responsibilities to the people.

Ibid., 450 (Mar. 7, 1994).

[31]31 *Weekly Compilation of Presidential Documents,* 354 (Mar. 3, 1995). The President acknowledged that both Roger Altman and Mike Espy resigned amid charges that they had abused their position, but he said that Altman had been found to have violated "no law and no rules of ethics" and downplayed Espy's misconduct as involving a small amount of money, all of which Espy had reimbursed. Ibid., 353.

[32]Ibid., 353.

[33]This study did not examine: Mrs. Clinton's response to allegations concerning her commodities trades in the 1970s; President Clinton's response to allegations of his complicity in illegal drug activity at the airport in Mena, Arkansas; and the President's response to Paula Jones's allegations of sexual harassment.

[34]"Statement on Washington, D.C. Investigation," 4 (June 30, 1994).

[35]Report to the Secretary of the Treasury, from the Office of Government Ethics, 3 (July 31, 1994) (hereafter, *OGE Report*) (emphasis added).

[36]Ibid., 8. Indeed, it added that "[w]hether it is an appropriate activity for Treasury officials to assist the White House in carrying out its functions in fielding questions about the personal interests of the First Family would seem to be a management issue."

[37]OGE's report to Bentsen stated plainly, "[O]ur analysis is not intended to cover, **nor should it in any way reflect upon**, the actions of individuals who are employed by the White House." *OGE Report*, 2 (emphasis added).

[38]Brock, "Living With The Clintons," *American Spectator*, 18, 22 (Jan. 1994).

[39]Rempel & Frantz, "Troopers Say Clinton Sought Silence on Personal Affairs," *Los Angeles Times*, A1 (Dec. 21, 1993).

[40]At one time it appeared that the independent counsel was also looking into allegations that a PAC co-chaired by then-Representative Espy importuned career Agriculture Department officials during the 1992 campaign to contribute to the Clinton-Gore campaign, with the understanding that such support would inure to their career benefit if they won. Subsequently, it was reported that the Justice Department (as opposed to the independent counsel) may seek indictments. Miller, "Charges Planned in PAC Probe at Agriculture," *Los Angeles Times*, A1 (Oct. 11, 1995). This suggests that Secretary Espy is not a target of this investigation, because otherwise it would be a matter that is within the provisions of the independent counsel law. Secretary Espy previously denied any connection between PAC contributions and USDA personnel actions.

[41]Williams, "Out to Pasture," *Washington Post*, C2 (Oct. 16, 1994)(emphasis added).

[42]Thomas & Gugliotta, "Special Counsel Sought To Investigate Cisneros," *Washington Post*, A1 (Mar. 15, 1995).

[43]31 *Weekly Compilation of Presidential Documents*, 276 (Feb. 18, 1995); Pear, "Clinton Backs Secretary of Commerce As 'the Best'," *New York Times*, sec. 1, 30 (Feb. 19, 1995).

[44]31 *Weekly Compilation of Presidential Documents*, 846 (May 17, 1995).

[45]Harris, "Special Counsel To Probe Brown," *Washington Post*, A1, A10 (May 18, 1995).

[46]Whether PIA should have been allowed to keep "Pena" in its name is open to question. In the Bush Administration, the White House Counsel's office told presidential appointees who were named partners at law, consulting, or public relations firms to ask that their name be removed from the title of the firm unless the firm had no dealings with the Federal Government.

[47]Transcript of November 12, 1992 news conference at Old State House, Little Rock, Arkansas (prepared by Federal Information Service Corporation) (ellipses added).

[48]"What About That Files Search?" *Washington Post*, C6 (Nov. 7, 1993).

[49]5 CFR 304.103(b), 60 *Federal Register*, 45647 (Sept. 1, 1995).

[50]5 CFR 2635.101(b)(7),(9). These principles are also found in Executive Order 12674, as amended, which served as the basis for the OGE standards of conduct.

[51]5 CFR 2635.704(a). "Authorized purposes" are "those purposes authorized in accordance with law or regulation." 5 CFR 2635.704(b)(2).

[52]"Memorandum on Restriction of Government Aircraft," 29 *Weekly Compilation of Presidential Documents*, 168 (Feb. 10, 1993). The other actions taken by the President on February 10 were a "Memorandum on Use of Government Vehicles," Ibid., 169, and a "Memorandum on Fiscal Responsibility," Ibid., 167 (concerning executive dining facilities and conferences).

[53]29 *Weekly Compilation of Presidential Documents*, 168. This language is identical to the definition of mission requirements travel in OMB Circular A-126.

[54]Lancaster, "Defense Brass Flying High—But Not Far," *Washington Post*, A1 (May 1, 1994).

[55]However, seven weeks later, Maldon was reportedly still on the job. The White House explained that it was difficult to find a successor, that Maldon was doing a good job, and that Maldon traveled with Watkins for the golf outing at Watkins' request, so that he should not be punished "for simply following orders." Jehl, "White House Delays Rebuke In Copter Case," *New York Times*, A12 (July 17, 1994).

[56]Watkins resigned but was unrepentant, and did not agree to reimburse the full cost, which amounted to $13,129.66, notwithstanding that Watkins' net worth was estimated in excess of one million dollars. So Acting Director of Administration Phil Lader solicited contributions from senior White House aides. While these contributions could be seen as an effort to fulfill the President's commitment that full reimbursement would be made, and Lader so portrayed the effort, Mark Gearan said the contributions were intended "as a gesture of friendship to Mr. Watkins and Mr. Maldon. Marcus, "Aides Offer To Pay for Golf Flight," *Washington Post*, A1, A13 (May 28, 1994). The next week, Watkins decided to make full reimbursement, to relieve any financial burden to White House officials.

[57]The Bush Administration policy required the approval of the White House Counsel's office. When considered with President Clinton's February 1993 policy memorandum, however, use of military aircraft was more tightly circumscribed.

[58]Memorandum from William P. Barr to William Sessions, "OPR Report on Alleged Misconduct," 4 (Jan. 15, 1993). The Bush Administration presented the new Clinton Administration with the responsibility to consider the findings of the Justice Department's Office of Professional Responsibility, which were contained in a 161-page report dated January 12, 1993. President Clinton did not ask Judge Sessions to leave until six months later, and when Sessions refused to resign, the President fired him. Isikoff & Marcus, "Clinton Fires Sessions as FBI Director," *Washington Post*, A1 (July 20, 1993).

[59]Miller & Morris, "VA Chief Logs Frequent Trips to Hometown," *Los Angeles Times*, A1 (Feb. 12, 1995).

[60]Ibid., A13.

[61]Kamen, "Travel Agency," *Washington Post*, A17 (Mar. 15, 1995).

[62]Birnbaum, "GSA's Johnson Asks for Review Of Travel Items," *Wall Street Journal*, A2 (Mar. 14, 1994).

[63]"GSA Report Says Official Improperly Used Resources," *Wall Street Journal*, A4 (Apr. 26, 1994); Pierce, "GSA chief repays government for travel, phone calls," *Washington Times*, A7 (June 8, 1994).

[64]Pierce, "GSA chief under fire in second probe in a year," *Washington Times*, A6 (Oct. 6, 1994); Associated Press, "G.S.A. Chief Undergoing Inquiry," *New York Times*, A27 (Oct. 6, 1994).

Chapter Two

[1]See, for example, S. Garment, *Scandal: The Culture of Mistrust in American Politics* (Times Books, 1992); L. Sabato, *Feeding Frenzy*, (Free Press, 1991); B. Ginsberg & M. Shefter, *Politics By Other Means* (Basic Books, 1990). Mikva, "From Politics to Paranoia," *Washington Post*, C2 (Nov. 26, 1995).

[2]Compare Executive Order 12674, § 101 (Apr. 12, 1989), with Executive Order 11222, §101, 201(a), (c)(1-6)(May 8, 1965).

[3]57 *Federal Register* 35006 (Aug. 7, 1992), codified 5 CFR Part 2635.

[4]Johnson's executive order was self-executing, although it charged the Civil Service Commission with issuing regulations to implement the order's gift standards (which contemplated exceptions) and with issuing other appropriate regulations to implement the other provisions of the order. The Civil Service Commission's ethics rules were codified 5 CFR Part 735. Agencies republished these regulations and were authorized by the executive order to supplement them with rules of "special applicability to the particular functions and activities of [each] agency." By contrast, Bush's executive order, which repealed Johnson's, was not self-executing (except for the limitations on outside earned income contained in § 102); instead, it charged OGE with issuing a single set of standards for the entire Executive Branch (§ 201).

[5]Hoffman, "Bush Pledges Staff 'Code of Conduct,'" *Washington Post*, A4 (July 27, 1988).

[6]Ibid.

[7]Executive Order 12668 (Jan. 25, 1989).

[8]*To Serve With Honor*, Report of the President's Commission on Federal Ethics Law Reform (Mar. 9, 1989).

[9]Executive Order 12674 (Apr. 12, 1989).

[10]*Putting People First: A Strategy for Change*, 23-25 (1992). A paragraph entitled "Stopping the Revolving Door" previewed the contents of what would be Executive Order 12834. Ibid., 26.

[11]Transcript of Nov. 12, 1992 news conference at Old State House, Little Rock, Arkansas (Prepared by Federal Information Services Corporation). He also promised to push for lobbying and campaign finance reform.

[12]It was also reported by the Associated Press that President-elect Clinton pledged "the strictest code of ethics in history for his administration[.]" Ball, "Clinton cracks whip on ethics," *San Diego Union*, A1 (Nov. 13, 1992)(not a quote), but this language does not appear on the written transcript of his news conference. Some in the media also attribute to the President-elect a similar but different pledge that his administration would be the most ethical in history. The author could not confirm that Bill Clinton made either statement during the campaign or transition; however, President Clinton has not distanced himself from such statements when they have been attributed to him.

[13]Marcus, "Clinton Unveils Ethics Code for Transition," *Washington Post*, A14 (Nov. 14, 1992); Friedman, "The Transition: The President-Elect; Clinton Issues Ethics Policies for Transition Team," *New York Times*, 1 (Nov. 14, 1992). The post-transition restrictions did not apply to current Federal employees.

In 1988, President-elect Bush had imposed the first set of ethics restrictions on transition workers. President-elect Clinton's transition rules were patterned largely after the Bush rules, although Clinton added the six-month post-transition restriction and also forbad Transition Board members, because of their broad responsibilities, from lobbying any Federal agency during the transition. Concerns about misuse of transition positions by private sector personnel were not as acute during the Bush transition, because many transition workers, including top-level transition staff, were at the time Executive Branch officials and did not have potentially conflicting outside clients or interests.

[14]Executive Order 12834; 29 *Weekly Compilation of Presidential Documents* 77 (Jan. 20, 1993).

[15]See 29 *Weekly Compilation of Presidential Documents* 167-69 ("Memorandum on Fiscal Responsibility," (Feb. 10, 1993)(executive dining facilities and conferences); "Memorandum on Restriction of Government Aircraft," (Feb. 10, 1993); "Memorandum on Use of Government Vehicles," (Feb. 10, 1993)).

[16]The comprehensive standards of conduct issued by OGE were first effective in February 1993, but they were issued during the Bush Administration. President Clinton's tough revolving door rules, which he imposed by exacting pledges from his appointees as a condition of their appointment, do not take effect until an official has left the Government. His restrictions on perks simply continued the campaign against perks begun in the Bush Administration.

[17]30 *Weekly Compilation of Presidential Documents* 631 (Mar. 24, 1994)(emphasis added). At the time the President made these remarks, there had been little opportunity to "enforce" his executive order, because only a few officials subject to the executive order had left government. Moreover, the President's answer was a non-sequitur, because when asked about the many allegations of unethical conduct by White House officials **while in office**, he relied on standards that apply only **after** an official leaves the Administration. The revolving door restrictions put in place do not relate to "ethical conflicts" as that term is generally understood.

[18]31 *Weekly Compilation of Presidential Documents* 353 (Mar. 3, 1995)(emphasis added). The example President Clinton provided, however, dealt with **random drug testing** standards for White House employees, and which President Clinton compared to **Congress's** own standards, not the standards of previous administrations!

[19]1060, § 20; 141 *Cong. Rec.* H13749 (daily ed. Nov. 29, 1995).

[20]"Special Message to the Congress on Conflict-of-Interest Legislation and on Problems of Ethics in Government," 1961 *Public Papers* 326 (Apr. 27, 1961)(emphasis added).

[21]Executive Order 10939 (May 5, 1961)(emphasis added).

[22]Executive Order 11222, § 201(c)(emphasis added). Section 203, relating to financial conflicts, provided in part that "[e]mployees may not . . . have direct or indirect financial interests that conflict substantially, or **appear to conflict substantially**, with their responsibilities and duties as Federal employees[.]" (Emphasis added.)

[23]Executive Order 12674, § 101(n)(emphasis added).

[24]5 CFR 2635.101(b)(14).

[25]57 Federal Registry 35008 (preamble to the final rule); Ibid. ("[T]he requirement to judge appearances from the perspective of a reasonable person with knowledge of the relevant facts will insulate employees from unreasonable application of the appearance principle.")

[26]5 CFR 2635.502.

[27]5 CFR 2635.502(c), (d).

[28]5 CFR 2635.502(b)(1)(defines "covered relationship").

[29]5 CFR 2635.502(a)(2). This residual provision is often overlooked.

[30]Thompson, "Paradoxes of Government Ethics," 52 *Public Administration Review*, 254, 257 (May/June 1992)("The only reliable way that citizens can judge whether improper actions took place is by looking at the circumstances under which officials act.").

[31]Ibid.

[32]Ibid., 255-56.

[33]For a provocative discussion of perils of the appearance principle, see Morgan, "The Appearance of Propriety: Ethics Reform and the Blifil Paradoxes," 44 *Stanford Law Review* 593, 610-11 (1992)(Blifil is taken from a character in the Henry Fielding novel, *Tom Jones*):

> Grand Blifil has two intertwined consequences. The first, and most obvious, is that when we require professionals and public officials to maintain proper appearances, proper appearances are primarily what we get. . . . The second consequence of Grand Blifil is that even the best intentioned professionals and public servants become involved in efforts to conceal the truth from the public. When these people attempt to create the proper appearances upon which we so fervently insist, they almost inevitably conceal unsightly facts that, if left in plain view, would destroy the overall image of propriety.

[34]By "good" I do not mean saintly; "good" is used as shorthand for competence, skill, expertise and sound judgment.

[35]5 CFR 2635.204(a); 57 Fed. Reg. 35015-16 (Aug. 7, 1992)(preamble to final rule).

[36]Generally, Members of Congress are not held accountable for these allegations when they prove baseless or wrong. On one occasion, however, OGE dressed down a subcommittee chairman for overreach-

ing. In 1991-92, Henry Waxman, Chairman of the House Subcommittee on Health and the Environment, charged Alan Hubbard, Chairman of Vice President Quayle's Council on Competitiveness, with multiple violations of section 208 and the Government with improperly granting Hubbard a waiver under section 208(b)(1). Waxman asked OGE to answer several questions about Hubbard's conduct and the actions taken by the Vice President's Counsel and the White House Counsel's Office (namely the author). In a strong response, OGE Director Stephen Potts wrote:

> Before an individual's reputation is sullied by accusations of criminal conduct, great care should be exercised to ascertain the pertinent facts and apply them to the applicable statute with an understanding of the letter and spirit of the law. Unfortunately, these time honored principles have been violated in Mr. Hubbard's case.

Letter to Honorable Henry A. Waxman, at 7 (Feb. 4, 1992).

[37]The gift standards, for instance, consume six pages in the *Federal Register*, 57 Fed. Reg. 35044-51, yet the basic prohibitions take up just a couple of paragraphs.

[38]5 CFR 2635.101(b)(8).

[39]There is also some indication that it is not being used internally when it should be. This problem is discussed more extensively in the Appendix One.

Chapter Three

[1]29 *Weekly Compilation of Presidential Documents*, 96 (Feb. 1, 1993).

[2]See Kurtz, "White House Dispatches Trauma Team on Health," *Washington Post*, A8 (Sept. 20, 1993)(describing background briefings given to reporters by the First Lady, where she was to be described as a "senior administration official"); Shalit, "Bitter Pills," *The New Republic*, 19 (Dec. 13, 1993)(describing the First Lady's September 28, 1993 appearance before Congress).

[3]See, for example, E. Drew, *On The Edge*, 22-23 (Simon & Schuster, 1994):

> There were also long discussions in Little Rock among the Clintons, their friends, and their advisers about what, actually, Mrs. Clinton's role was to be, and though it was never announced, she was basically put in charge of domestic policy for the Administration. Economic policy excluded, she would oversee the agencies (Health and Human Services) and issues (children, welfare) she was interested in.
>
> The title Domestic Policy Adviser was seriously considered, but it was decided that Mrs. Clinton would essentially have the role without the title—it would be less threatening.

[4]See, for example, B. Woodward, *The Agenda* 109-11, 120-24, 244-256 (Simon & Schuster, 1994); Drew, *On The Edge, passim*.

[5]The President is required to report the assets and income of his spouse, as those interests are imputed to him under 18 United States Code (U.S.C.) 208(a). See 5 CFR 2634.309.

[6]The name of the fund is variously spelled as "Value Partners," "ValuePartners," and "Valuepartners."

[7]The reporting period for an official filing as an incumbent is the previous calendar year for income, and December 31 of the previous year for assets. President Clinton properly filed as an incumbent in May 1993 because he had previously filed public financial disclosure reports in 1992 as a Presidential candidate. Had he filed as a "new entrant," he would have been required to file a report within thirty days of assuming office, and the reporting period would have extended to the date of filing. See 5 CFR 2634.201(a) (incumbents), (b)(1) (new entrants), (b) (2) (ii) (exception to new entrant filing requirement).

[8]The President's financial disclosure form values the asset at between $50,000 and $100,000.

[9]Her income could have been dividends, interest, or capital gains.

[10]Valuepartners' holdings since President Clinton's inauguration were not required to be disclosed in **this** report. Thus, the nature and amount of Valuepartners' health care holdings from January 1, 1993 until May 14, 1993 (the date the report was filed) could not be determined from this report. That some of Valuepartners' health care-related interests were sold—and that stock in additional health care companies was purchased—during this time was confirmed by the President's calendar year 1993 financial disclosure report filed May 16, 1994. See text at notes 19-20, *infra*.

[11]Columbia Hospital's name has since been changed to Columbia Healthcare.

[12] Gordon, "Mrs. Clinton Is Investor in Fund With Health Care Stocks," *Associated Press* (May 20, 1993).

[13]Ibid. Gordon stated that as of December 31, 1992, Valuepartners "had invested $1.2 million in stocks of ten health care companies." In fact, Valuepartners had interests in thirteen health care-relate companies; the market value of Valuepartners holdings in these companies was over $1.7 million in common stock and an additional $226,000 in short positions.

[14]Ibid.

[15]Lalli, "How Blind Is Your Trust?" *Money*, 5 (July 1993).

[16]Ibid.

[17]Ibid.

[18]The trust agreement was executed by the Clintons on July 4, 1993. Representatives of Boston Harbor Trust Company (the trustee) and Essex Investment Management Company, Inc. (the investment manager), "accepted" the trust by signing the agreement on July 23.

[19]There is no report of Valuepartners on Schedule A, assets and income. Instead, all of the First Lady's holdings that were placed in the blind trust (including Valuepartners) are reported in a single entry, "OGE certified blind trust," with no further description. President Clinton was not required to report the **assets** of Valuepartners on Schedule A because by the end of the reporting period, December 31, 1993, the First Lady's interest in Valuepartners had been placed in the blind trust, and the Clintons are prohibited from knowing the current asset portfolio of Valuepartners. However, the President **was** required to report on Schedule A any **income** over $200 that the First Lady received from Valuepartners before creation of the blind trust. The report discloses that during 1993 she received between $15,000 and $50,000 in unspecified income from all her blind trust holdings combined. Because in 1992 she received over $5,000 in income from the Valuepartners investment alone, it is hard to believe that she did not receive more than $200 of dividends, interest, or capital gains income from Valuepartners in the six-plus months of 1993 before the creation of the blind trust. This suggests either that her Valuepartners pre-trust income was incorrectly omitted, or that such income was incorrectly included in the income figure for the combined blind trust holdings and should have been separately listed.

[20]The report does not distinguish between common stock and short positions. All transactions are valued at between $1,000 and $15,000. A footnote states that "Mrs. Clinton was [sic] a limited partner in Value Partners I, and as such, at the time of the transactions, she had no knowledge of, control over, or input into the transactions."

[21]Vital Signs and Synergen do not show up on the December 31, 1992 portfolio listing, suggesting that an error was made on either the 1993 or 1994 report.

[22]Assuming that each sale of stock in a particular company disposed of Valuepartners' entire holdings in that company, Valuepartners would have disposed of interests in seven health care related companies in early 1993. However, even with this assumption, Valuepartners maintained interests in at least six health care related companies, and **acquired** interests in an additional eight health care companies during this time.

[23]18 U.S.C. 208(a). Section 208(a) provides in pertinent part:

[W]hoever, being an officer or employee of the executive branch of the United States Government . . . including a special Government employee, participates personally and substantially as a Government officer or employee, through decision, approval, disapproval, recommendation, the rendering of advice, investigation, or otherwise, in a judicial or other proceeding, application, request for ruling or other determination, contract, claim, controversy, charge, accusation, arrest or other particular matter, in which, to his knowledge, he, his spouse, minor child, general partner, organization in which he is serving as officer, director, trustee, general partner or employee . . ., has a financial interest—

Shall be subject to the penalties set forth in section 216 of this title.

The statutory prohibition is also contained in the standards of conduct governing Executive Branch employees, 5 CFR 2635.402(a). The purpose of section 208 is reflected also in several principles of ethical conduct listed in section 101 of Executive Order 12674, as amended:

(b) Employees shall not hold financial interests that conflict with the conscientious performance of duty.

(g) Employees shall not use public office for private gain.

[24]18 U.S.C. 216.

[25]Gordon, "Mrs. Clinton Is Investor in Fund With Health Care Stocks," *Associated Press* (May 20, 1993); Lalli, "How Blind Is Your Trust?" *Money*, 5 (July 1993). Charles Smith, Executive Director of the Center for Public Integrity, told *Money* that Mrs. Clinton's interest, although "tenuous," posed "an appearance of a conflict:"

Simply put, Hillary's investment in a fund trading health stocks fails "the red-face test—you know, do you want to see this on the front page of some newspaper?" What's more, the Clintons should have known better. "If you are going to be involved with policy, especially something as explosive as health policy," he says, "you've got to put yourself beyond the pale entirely. . . . We live in an age where there is very little trust of government, and this doesn't help things."

[26]Safire, "Weighing on Foster's Mind," *New York Times*, A17 (Aug. 16, 1993).

[27]Tony Snow also wrote on this subject. Snow, "Side Benefits of Rx Rhetoric," *Washington Times*, A16 (Nov. 18, 1993); Snow, "Standards shift for Hillary?" *Washington Times*, A16 (Nov. 22, 1993).

[28]5 U.S.C. App. FACA § 10(a)(1).

[29]5 U.S.C. App. FACA § 3(2)(iii).

[30]In the court of appeals, the Justice Department first asserted that the First Lady was either an officer or an employee, later asserted that she was a "Federal officer," and at argument declined to specify which. *Association of American Physicians and Surgeons, Inc. v. Clinton*, 997 F.2d 878, 917 (D.C. Cir. 1993)(Buckley, concurring in the judgment).

[31]*Association of Amer. Phys. and Surgeons, Inc. v. Clinton*, 813 F. Supp. 82, 87 (D.D.C. 1993).

[32]Ibid. Judge Lamberth therefore ordered the Task Force meetings to be open to the public, except when it met to formulate advice or recommendations to the President. In this latter capacity, he ruled that FACA's application to the Task Force was an unconstitutional encroachment on the President's authority to receive advice for the purpose of proposing legislation. 813 F. Supp., 89-90.

[33]*Association of Amer. Phys. and Surgeons, Inc. v. Clinton*, 997 F.2d 878 (D.C. Cir. 1993). The appeal was argued on April 30, 1993; the decision was issued on June 22.

[34]997 F.2d 910-11.

[35]997 F.2d 911 & n.10. Judge Buckley disagreed with the majority's reasoning but concurred in the judgment. He would have held that Mrs. Clinton is not a "full-time officer or employee" under FACA, but also would have held that application of FACA's public disclosure provisions to the Task Force was unconstitutional. 997 F.2d 920-25.

The court also considered whether the First Lady's status as an officer or employee violates the *Anti-Nepotism Act*, 5 U.S.C. 3110. That law, enacted in 1967 in response to President Kennedy's appointment of his brother as Attorney General, prohibits any "public official" (which includes the President) from appointing or employing any relative (which includes a spouse) in a position in "an Executive agency[.]" 5 U.S.C. 3110(b). The court concluded that Congress did not intend the term "Executive agency", 5 U.S.C. 3110(a)(1)(A), to include the White House, relying on previous decisions relating to different statutes. 997 F.2d 905. In any event, the court added, the *Anti-Nepotism Act* may bar appointment only to paid positions. 997 F.2d at 905. The *Anti-Nepotism Act* is a civil statute, with no penalties other than loss of pay. 5 U.S.C. 3110(c)("An individual appointed [or] employed . . . in violation of this section is not entitled to pay . . . .). The law does not contain a provision requiring the removal of a person appointed or employed in violation of the law. Judge Buckley, on the other hand, found that the *Anti-Nepotism Act* was probably intended to cover the White House. 997 F.2d 920-21.

The *Anti-Nepotism Act* was enacted as part of the *Postal Revenue and Federal Salary Act* of 1967, Pub. L. No. 90-206. A review of the legislative history sheds no light on whether the provision was intended to cover positions in the White House office. See 1967 *U.S. Cong. & Admin. News* 2258, 2284-85 (90th Cong., 1st. Sess.). This is an issue that should be clarified by Congress.

[36]Letter to Honorable Bernard Nussbaum (Jan. 26, 1994); Letter to Honorable Stephen D. Potts (Jan. 26, 1994). See Snow, "Gleam of a Clinton stockgate in GOP eyes," *Washington Times*, A18 (Jan. 31, 1994). The three Representatives also wrote the Chairman of the Securities and Exchange Commission. Letter to The Honorable Arthur Levitt, Jr. (Jan. 26, 1994). Harlan, "SEC Asked to Seek Data on Fund Used By Hillary Clinton," *Wall Street Journal*, A4 (Feb. 1, 1994). They asked the SEC whether "the actions of the Clintons constitute possible violations of the antifraud provisions of the federal securities laws and the prohibitions against market manipulation and insider trading." The letter sought various information about the partnership, including records of transactions. Chairman Levitt provided only some public record information in response, explaining that Commission policy precluded commenting on whether any matter was under investigation. Letter to Honorable Christopher Cox (Feb. 9, 1994).

[37]Letter to Honorable Stephen D. Potts, 2 (Jan. 26, 1994).

[38]Letter to Honorable Robert L. Livingston, Honorable George W. Gekas, and Honorable Christopher Cox (Feb. 11, 1994).

[39]Ibid.

[40]Ibid.

[41]Letter to Honorable Christopher Cox (Feb. 10, 1994).

[42]OGE also pointed out that section 208 is not part of the *Ethics in Government Act*.

[43]Letter to Honorable Stephen D. Potts (Mar. 9, 1994). Additional letters were sent to OGE on March 17, 1994 (from Representatives Livingston, Gekas and Cox) and March 28 (from Representative Cox). See Harlan, "Probe of Mrs. Clinton's Stockholdings Is Sought by 81 GOP House Members," *Wall Street Journal*, A20 (Mar. 10, 1994).

[44]Ibid.

[45]Letter to Honorable George W. Gekas (May 3, 1994).

[46]Ibid., 2. OGE declined to conduct an "investigation," explaining that its investigative authority is limited to administrative restrictions, not criminal statutes. Under section 402(f)(5) of the *Ethics in Government Act*, OGE is precluded from making any finding that a provision of Title 18 "has been or is being violated." If OGE were to come upon sufficient information to warrant a criminal investigation, it would refer the matter to the Justice Department. Ibid., 1-2.

[47]Ibid., 10.

[48]Ibid., 4.

[49]In its letter to House Republicans, OGE left the door open on the status of the First Lady: That is not to say the spouse of a President could never be an officer or employee of the executive branch; we recognize that Mrs. Clinton has been given a very public role with the Task Force. But is it far from settled that by virtue of that role she is therefore an officer or employee of the executive branch for purposes of the conflicts statutes. Letter to Honorable George W. Gekas, 3 (May 3, 1994).

[50]Safire, "Weighing on Foster's Mind, *New York Times*, A17 (Aug. 16, 1993)(quoting statement of Bernard Nussbaum). Interestingly, the White House Counsel chose not to make this assertion in his response to the letter from the three House Republicans. The only reference to this issue in Nussbaum's response was in his conclusion that "the First Lady's involvement as chair of the Health Care Task Force and her limited partnership interest in Value Partners—were fully consistent with the federal ethics laws (**even assuming their applicability in this context**) and did not constitute a conflict of interest as defined in those laws." Letter to Honorable Robert L. Livingston, Honorable George W. Gekas, Honorable Christopher Cox, 2 (Feb. 11, 1994)(emphasis added).

[51] Memorandum to Kenneth Lazarus, Associate Counsel to the President, from Assistant Attorney General Scalia, Office of Legal Counsel (Dec. 19, 1974); Letter to Senator Howard Cannon from Acting Attorney General Silberman (Sept. 20, 1974); Memorandum for Richard T. Buress, Office of President, from Deputy Attorney General Silberman (Aug. 28, 1974). In 1983, the Office of Government Ethics agreed. OGE Informal Advisory Letter 83 X 16 (Oct. 20, 1983).

[52]Memorandum for Richard A. Hauser, Deputy Counsel to the President, from Ralph W. Tarr, Acting Assistant Attorney General (Feb. 27, 1985)(unpublished). It is this Reagan Administration opinion—and only this opinion—on which the Clinton Administration's White House Counsel apparently relied in responding to Safire.

The White House Counsel conceded that it did not ask OLC to render an opinion concerning Mrs. Clinton's status. Safire, "Weighing on Foster's Mind," *New York Times,* A17 (Aug. 16, 1993). Safire summed up, "The non-coverage of this most governmentally energetic First Lady was not sanctioned by Congress, not approved by the courts, not even reviewed by Justice."

[53]OLC recommended that both the First Lady and President avoid taking any official government action with regard to the fund.

[54]The White House also apparently has asserted that the President's exemption must include his wife, because her assets are commingled with the President's. Snow, "Gleam of a Clinton stockgate in GOP eyes," *Washington Times*, A18 (Jan. 31, 1994). This is a rather remarkable claim. First, the asset in question is clearly identified on the President's financial disclosure report as the First Lady's. Second, only if the Clintons are viewed by virtue of their marriage as one person—a notion that this Administration would likely reject in every other context as antiquated—would this commingling argument have merit. That First Lady's financial interests are imputed to the President for purposes of his financial disclosure obligations does not mean these interests are no longer considered hers for purposes of conflict-of-interest standards.

[55]18 U.S.C. 202(a). Initially, a "government official" argued that because First Lady was not on the Federal payroll, she was not covered by the ethics laws. Gordon, "Mrs. Clinton Is Investor in Fund With Health Care Stocks," *Associated Press* (May 20, 1993). This is plainly wrong under the express terms of section 202(a).

[56]See Memorandum to the Heads of Executive Departments and Agencies (Feb. 9, 1962), cited in OGE Informal Advisory Letter 82 X 22 (July 9, 1982), 328-332. The definition of "special Government employee" (SGE) was added to the U.S. Code in 1962 when the ethics laws were recodified. See S. Rep. 2213, 80th Cong., 2d Sess., reprinted in 1962 *U.S. Code Cong. & Admin. News* 3854-58.

[57]18 U.S.C. 208(a).

[58]SGEs are distinguished from "representatives" and "independent contractors," neither of whom are considered "employees" for purposes of conflict-of-interest laws. A "representative" generally serves on a government committee, board, or task force, and is expected to present the views of a private interest, such as a corporation, labor union, or trade association, rather than the public interest. They are expected to be "interested"; that is, to bring to the table their own financial and other interests. Obviously, it would not make sense to subject such persons to the conflict-of-interest standards. See OGE Informal Advisory Letter 82 X 22 (July 9, 1982). Independent contractors are expected to perform a task for the Government, but are not subject to the supervision of a Federal employee.

[59]OGE Informal Advisory Letter 81 X 8 (Feb. 23, 1981), citing B. Manning, *Federal Conflict of Interest Law* 26-30 (1964).

[60]"Hillary said she still wanted an office in the West Wing of the White House, the business and policy hub where the president's Oval Office was located." B. Woodward, *The Agenda* 104 (1994).

[61] See Kurtz, "White House Dispatches Trauma Team on Health," *Washington Post,* A8 (Sept. 20, 1993)(describing background briefings given to reporters by Mrs. Clinton, where the First Lady was to be described as a "senior administration official").

[62] ". . . Clinton called together his staff and key cabinet members in the Roosevelt Room after lunch to announce that his wife was going to head the task force. She was to be treated like anyone else, Clinton said, and be challenged and questioned like any other member of the cabinet." B. Woodward, *The Agenda,* 104 (1994).

[63] The second criterion—pay—is not determinative, because section 202(a) expressly provides that SGEs may be retained without compensation. The first criterion—oath of office—is a formality the absence of which also should not be deemed determinative. The third criterion—supervision by a Federal agency—is relevant to the concept of independent contractors, who, largely because they operate without direct government supervision, are not deemed employees of the United States. In any event, the First Lady performs under the President's supervision.

[64] 5 U.S.C. 2104(a).

[65] 5 U.S.C. 2105(a).

[66] In creating the Health Care Task Force, the President was engaged in an Executive act. After the Task Force terminated, the First Lady continued to be engaged in the performance of Federal functions under an implicit delegation from the President.

[67] In *Association of Amer. Phys. and Surgeons,* the court of appeals determined that the definitions of "officer" and "employee" in 5 U.S.C. 2104 and 2105 do not apply to FACA, which is placed in the U.S. Code in the **appendix** to Title 5. 997 F.2d at 904. Judge Buckley disagreed. He concluded that sections 2104 and 2105 should apply to FACA. 997 F.2d at 917-19. He also considered other definitions, concluding that First Lady could not be considered an "employee" because she is not paid. However, Judge Buckley ignored the definition of "special Government employee" in 18 U.S.C. 202(a), which expressly includes persons who do not receive compensation. He also determined that the First Lady could not be considered an "officer," because she has not taken an oath of office and because First Ladies do not occupy an office with duties. 997 F.2d, 919-20. However, even assuming that the Office of First Lady, with a staff of Federal employees, does not qualify, First Lady's position as Chairman of the Task Force is most certainly an office with duties, in the ordinary sense of those words.

[68] See 3 U.S.C. 105.

[69] Memorandum for Bernard Nussbaum, Counsel to the President, from Daniel L. Koffsky, Acting Assistant Attorney General, Office of Legal Counsel (July 10, 1993).

[70] United States General Accounting Office, *Personnel Practices: Retroactive Appointments and Pay Adjustments in the Executive Office of the President* (Washington, DC: U.S. Government Printing Office, Sept. 1993) 11, 16.

[71] 2 Op.O.L.C. 20 (Feb. 24, 1977).

[72] Ibid., 20-21 (emphasis and ellipses added; footnote omitted).

[73] Ibid., 22. In *Association of Amer. Phys. and Surgeons,* the Justice Department argued before the court of appeals that "the traditional, if informal, status and 'duties' of the President's wife as 'First Lady' gives her *de facto* officer or employee status." The court answered:

We are not confident that this traditional perception of the President's wife, as a virtual extension of her husband, is widely held today. As this very case suggests, it may not even be a fair portrayal of Mrs. Clinton, who certainly is performing more openly than is typical of a First Lady. 997 F.2d, 904.

[74] Ibid., 23 (emphasis added). A White House official argued that this OLC opinion was superseded by the *1978 Ethics in Government Act.* Novak, "Conflict Complications," *Washington Post,* A27 (Feb. 3, 1994). But how so? The Act did not expressly exempt the First Lady, or change the definition of "special Government employee." In any event, an OGE informal advisory letter containing the same conclusion was written after the *Ethics in Government Act* was enacted.

[75] OGE Informal Advisory Letter 82 X 22 (July 9, 1982). That letter also discussed the criteria in 5 U.S.C. 2104 and 2105. The OGE informal opinion quoted the same passage from Professor Manning's book that was relied upon in the 1977 OLC opinion. Ibid., 336-37.

[76] Memorandum for Richard A. Hauser from Ralph Tarr (Feb. 27, 1985) (unpublished), 3 (footnote omitted). Ironically, this advice is contained in the very same OLC opinion on which White House Counsel Nussbaum relied for his legal conclusion that the First Lady is **not** subject to the conflict-of-interest laws!

[77] These key words, as they appear in section 208:

[W]hoever, being an officer or employee of the executive branch of the United States Government . . . . including a special Government employee, **participates personally and substantially** as a Government officer or employee, through decision, approval, disapproval, recommendation, the rendering of advice, investigation, or otherwise, in a judicial or other proceeding, application, request for ruling or

other determination, contract, claim, controversy, charge, accusation, arrest or other **particular matter, in which, to his knowledge, he,** his spouse, minor child, general partner, organization in which he is serving as officer, director, trustee, general partner or employee . . ., **has a financial interest**—
Shall be subject to the penalties set forth in section 216 of this title.
18 U.S.C. 208(a)(emphasis added).
The White House also argued that no one believes First Lady's statements and actions on health care reform are motivated by her financial interest. Columnists who have covered this issue agree. See Safire, "Weighing on Foster's Mind," *New York Times*, A17 (Aug. 16, 1993)("Reasonable ethicists will grant that Mrs. Clinton's health-related holdings are, as Nussbaum writes, 'clearly insubstantial, because they are both a small amount of money and an insignificant part of the Clintons' total assets.' Nobody suggests she was out to make a buck on short sales of medical stocks."); Snow, "Standards shift for Hillary?" *Washington Times*, A16 (Nov. 22, 1993)("And no one seriously believes she has tried to get rich off the market because her reformist flame burns pure."); Borger, "Double standards in Clintonland," *U.S. News & World Report*, 58 (Mar. 14, 1994)("No one says the first lady was out to make a killing."). Lack of motive, however, is simply not a defense to a charge that the law has been violated.

[78]5 CFR 2635.402(b)(4). In its letter to House Republicans, OGE did not discuss this term separately. Instead, OGE considered together "personal and substantial" participation in a "particular matter." Letter to George W. Gekas, at 2 (May 3, 1994).

[79]See Farina, "Keeping Faith: Government Ethics & Government Ethics Regulation," 45 *Administrative Law Review,* 287, 300 (1993)(Report of ABA Committee on Government Standards) (hereafter, *ABA Report*) ("Whether, and to what extent, [section] 208 currently reaches official action other than matters involving a small number of identified parties remains unclear. (The principal interpretive issue concerns the statutory phrase 'particular matter.')").

[80]Bernard Nussbaum stated, "We believe that, under relevant statutory and regulatory provisions, the First Lady's activities did not constitute participation in a 'particular matter'[.]" Letter to Honorable Robert L. Livingston, Honorable George W. Gekas, Honorable Christopher Cox (Feb. 11, 1994). Nussbaum did not provide any basis for this conclusion.

[81]Letter to George W. Gekas, 4-5 (May 3, 1994).

[82]5 CFR 2635.402(b)(3). This definition reflects the opinion of OLC, which assisted in the drafting of this and other definitions.

[83]Letter to George W. Gekas, 4 (May 3, 1994) (emphasis in original). OGE added, "We do not believe that additional information could establish this element in this context and therefore section 208 is not implicated." Ibid., 4-5.

[84]It was also a mistake to confine its analysis to the Administration's health care plan. A number of competing legislative proposals were introduced, some of which were not as comprehensive in scope; undoubtedly, the First Lady's involvement in the health care debate extended to these proposals, as well.

[85]H.R. 3600, Title II [New Benefits], Subtitle A [Medicare Outpatient Prescription Drug Benefit], §§ 2001, et seq.

[86]60 *Federal Register*, 47208 (Sept. 11, 1995).

[87]Ibid., 47210 (emphasis added).

[88]Ibid., 47225 (emphasis added).

[89]93 OGE 1, 2 (Jan. 7, 1983), published in *The Informal Advisory Letters and Formal Opinions of the United States Office of Government Ethics*, 861. See also *United States* v. *Gorman*, 807 F.2d 1299, 1303 (6th Cir. 1986)("A financial interest exists on the part of a party to a Section 208 action where there is a real possibility of gain or loss as a result of developments in or resolution of a matter. Gain or loss need not be probable for the prohibition against official action to apply. All that is required is that there be a real, as opposed to a speculative, possibility of benefit or detriment."); 60 *Federal Register*, 47209 (Sept. 11, 1995)(preamble to proposed rule).

OGE's letter to House Republicans states, "The ownership of stock cannot be equated to the term financial interest as that term is used in section 208. Financial interest as used in section 208 is not an ownership concept; it is a result." Letter to George W. Gekas, at 5 (May 3, 1994).

[90]OGE Informal Advisory Letter 87 X 6, at 713 (Apr. 1, 1987).

[91]Therefore, White House aide Ricki Seidman's defense that the nature of the First Lady's investment does not create the potential for a conflict of interest is incorrect. See Gordon, "Mrs. Clinton Is Investor in Fund With Health Care Stocks," *Associated Press* (May 20, 1993).

[92]Letter to Honorable Robert L. Livingston, Honorable George W. Gekas, Honorable Christopher Cox (Feb. 11, 1994).

[93]5 CFR 2635.402(a).

[94]5 CFR 2635.402(b)(1)(i) and (ii).

[95]Letter to Honorable Robert L. Livingston, Honorable George W. Gekas, Honorable Christopher Cox, 2 (Feb. 11, 1994).

[96]Safire, "Weighing on Foster's Mind," *New York Times*, A17 (Aug. 16, 1993).

[97]Snow, "Gleam of a Clinton stockgate in GOP eyes," *Washington Times*, A18 (Jan. 31, 1994); see also, Snow, "Side benefits of Rx rhetoric?," *Washington Times*, A16 (Nov. 18, 1993).

[98]Novak, "Conflict Complications," *Washington Times*, A27 (Feb. 3, 1994). Novak concluded that "about one-fifth of the stocks were in a 'short' position[.]" See also Greenberg, "The other rapids . . . a ripple too far?" *Washington Times*, A21 (Mar. 21, 1994)("The congressmen charge that Mrs. Clinton's attacks on the pharmaceutical firms slam-dunked their stock prices. True."); Shalit, "Bitter Pills," *The New Republic*, at 20 (Dec. 13, 1993)("The administration's criticism of drug prices is already having a financial effect. . . . In a year and a half, the [pharmaceutical] industry has lost almost half of its equity[.] . . . If the prospect of health care reform is denting big drug companies' stock, it's wreaking havoc on small biotechnology companies.").

[99]Pirrong, "Political Rhetoric and Stock Price Volatility: A Case Study," Catalyst Institute (Nov. 1993). Pirrong noted that "drug stocks fell over 27% from January 1, 1993 through September 9, 1993[.] . . . The under performance of drug stocks is almost certainly attributable to announcements concerning the Clinton health care program." Ibid., 18. Pirrong's industry portfolio consisted of twenty-three pharmaceutical stocks. During this period in 1993, he found that investors lost nearly $62 billion, except those persons who held short positions during this time. Ibid., 5. Pirrong pointed to two specific periods where drug stocks were most dramatically affected by pronouncements by the Clinton Administration: February 16-22, 1993, when the Administration coupled criticism of the pharmaceutical industry with hints at price controls; and August 16-September 2, 1993, when the President appeared to back off price controls. Ibid., 7.

The empirical demonstration of the effects the Clinton Administration's health care proposal and pronouncements had on the pharmaceutical industry also highlights the weakness of OGE's narrow interpretation of "particular matter." If Valuepartners had held significant short positions in Bristol-Myers Squibb or Merck & Co. in 1993, for instance, OGE's refusal to look at health care reform except as an indivisible whole, for purposes of identifying conflicts of interest, would not be taken seriously. Professor Pirrong had no difficulty in concentrating his study on those portions of the Administration's health care reform package and those Administration pronouncements that specifically concerned the pharmaceutical industry. In identifying potential conflicts of interest, it is often better to view the matter from the perspective of the regulated, rather than the regulator; often the former will constitute a "discrete and identifiable class of persons."

[100]Letter to George W. Gekas, at 7-8 (May 3, 1994). The manager of Valuepartners, William Smith, told the *Wall Street Journal* that Valuepartners "didn't hold any pharmaceutical stocks at the time of Mrs. Clinton's speeches" on health care. Smith added that, during the first quarter of 1993, Valuepartners "was 'long'—or betting that prices would rise—in the stocks of two health-maintenance organizations[.]" "Manager of Hedge Fund Disputes GOP Statements," *Wall Street Journal*, A14 (Mar. 11, 1994).

[101]The Pirrong study refers only to speeches by the President and other pronouncements by the "administration;" it makes no mention of any speech by the First Lady.

[102]Letter to Honorable Robert L. Livingston, Honorable George W. Gekas, Honorable Christopher Cox (Feb. 11, 1994). Subsequently, President Clinton's May 1994 financial disclosure report states: "Mrs. Clinton was a limited partner in Value Partners I, and as such, at the time of the transactions, she had no knowledge of, control over, or input into the transactions." This statement says nothing about the First Lady's knowledge of Valuepartners' portfolio at other times.

[103]Ibid.

[104]Greenberg, "The other rapids . . . a ripple too far?," *Washington Times*, A21 (Mar. 21, 1994).

[105]Further, the claim that the First Lady has not "sought to profit from any transactions involving health-related stocks" is peculiar. Surely, any reasonable investor seeks to make a profit off an investment. The very nature of a passive investor is to leave the decisions on specific transactions to the investment manager. But, of course, in doing so the passive investor remains desirous of a profitable outcome, however achieved.

[106]Letter to George W. Gekas, 9 (May 3, 1994).

[107]Greenberg, "The other rapids . . . a ripple too far?" *Washington Times*, A21 (Mar. 21, 1994).

[108]Cox, "What did Mrs. Clinton invest and when did she do it?" *Washington Times*, A19 (Mar. 24, 1994); Snow, "The other rapids . . . a ripple too far?" *Washington Times*, A21 (Mar. 21, 1994).

[109]The First Lady also would also have had no assurance that Valuepartners had not subsequently acquired other health care-related stocks. The December 31, 1992 Valuepartners report, which was attached to President Clinton's SF-278 filed in May 1993, no longer showed these two pharmaceutical stocks, but it did show short positions in four other health care related stocks. See text at note 10, *supra*.

[110]Obviously, recusal from participating in health care matters was not a viable option here.

[111]Such a waiver would be available to the public, upon request. 18 U.S.C. 208(d)(1).

[112]Some members of the press have already accepted that conclusion. See Safire, "Weighing on Foster's Mind," *New York Times*, A17 (Aug. 16, 1993) ("Reasonable ethicists will grant that Mrs. Clinton's health-related holdings are, as Nussbaum writes, 'clearly insubstantial, because they are both a small amount of money and an insignificant part of the Clintons' total assets.' Nobody suggests she was out to make a buck on short sales of medical stocks."); Snow, "Standards shift for Hillary?" *Washington Times*, A16 (Nov. 22,

1993)("And no one seriously believes she has tried to get rich off the market because her reformist flame burns pure.")

[113]And if a sale would otherwise result in capital gains income, the First Lady could defer the tax consequences of divestiture by obtaining from OGE a certificate of divestiture and by investing the proceeds of the sale in a suitable excepted investment fund. See 5 CFR 2634 Subpart J, implementing section 502 of the *Ethics Reform Act of 1989* (codified in 26 U.S.C. 1043). This might require OGE to find that, for purposes of the certificate of divestiture, the First Lady is a Federal employee.

[114]5 CFR 2634.403(b)(9)(i), (ii)(D). This regulation implements section 102(f)(3)(C)(vi) of the *Ethics in Government Act of 1978*, as amended. This provision does not exactly fit this situation, because it addresses a real or apparent conflict "due to duties subsequently assumed by the filer"—subsequent to the creation of the blind trust—and the First Lady assumed health care responsibilities in January 1993, before the creation of the blind trust. However, the policy reflected in this provision would seem to have no less force with respect to a real or apparent conflict posed by duties that were assumed **before** the creation of the blind trust. In both cases, the communication to the trustee is intended solely to remedy a real or apparent conflict of interest. Thus, a letter instructing the trustee of the Clintons' blind trust to sell the First Lady's Valuepartners interest should receive OGE's approval. In 1989, Secretary of State James Baker sold his Chemical Bank stock, notwithstanding the fact that he had placed the stock in a blind trust eight years earlier. See 117, *infra*.

[115]For the most part the Clintons avoided criticism over this delay. There were a couple of exceptions, however: Lalli, "How Blind Is Your Trust?" *Money*, 5 (July 1993)("The President and the First Lady are working on it, a press aide told *Money*. That's not good enough. The damage to the public trust has already been done."); Borger, "Double standards in Clintonland," *U.S. News & World Report*, 58 (Mar. 14, 1994)("[T]he issue is that the potential conflict should have been handled sooner.").

Some of this delay is likely attributable to Vince Foster, who was initially in charge of drafting a blind trust and securing its approval by OGE. Safire, "Weighing on Foster's Mind," *New York Times*, A17 (Aug. 16, 1993). Some of the delay, at least from some point in May 1993, may be attributable to OGE, which must approve a qualified blind trust. See Gordon, "Mrs. Clinton Is Investor in Fund With Health Care Stocks," *Associated Press* (May 20, 1993)(stating that, according to Beth Nolan, an Associate Counsel to the President, "the Clintons' attorneys have submitted documents to the Office of Government Ethics with a view to setting up the blind trusts."). These papers could have and should have been sent to OGE much earlier. The extent of the Clintons' interests could have been discerned from the financial disclosure report Bill Clinton filed as a candidate for the presidency in May 1992. Second, more current information about the Clintons' assets could have been readily available in December 1992 and January 1993 from the fund's management company.

[116]Perhaps this is not recognized by the White House Counsel's office, either. Note the use of the past tense in Bernard Nussbaum's letter to Congress:

The First Lady, as a limited partner in Value Partners, never **had** any input, control, communication, review or oversight with respect to any investments made by Value Partners. The First Lady's investments **amounted** to less than one percent of the entire fund. In July 1993, the First Lady's interest in Value Partners was placed in the Clintons' blind trust.

Letter to Honorable Robert L. Livingston, Honorable George W. Gekas, Honorable Christopher Cox (Feb. 11, 1994) (emphasis added). Similarly, the President's calendar year 1993 financial disclosure report, filed May 16, 1994, contains the following statement (emphasis added): "Mrs. Clinton **was** a limited partner in Value Partners I[.]"

At least one observer understands the inefficacy of the Clintons' blind trust. Chu, "What Did the Clintons Know & When Did They Know It?," *Commentary*, 21, 24 (March 1994).

[117]5 CFR 2634.401(a)(ii). This provision implements section 102(f)(4)(A) of the *Ethics in Government Act*, as amended, 5 U.S.C. App. 6. This has been the law since the enactment of the *Ethics in Government Act of 1978*. See also OGE Informal Advisory Letter 86 X 12, at 657 (Sept. 8, 1986)("Before the Act, all holdings of a blind trust were often considered "blind" upon establishment of the trust, even though it was obvious that the trust almost certainly still contained the same assets that were placed in it the government official for at least some period of time.").

By contrast, if the Clintons' blind trust were a "qualified diversified trust," as opposed to a "qualified blind trust," the trust holdings would not be considered financial interests for purposes of the conflict of interest laws. 5 CFR 2634.401(a)(1)(iii); section 102(f)(4)(B) of the *Ethics in Government Act*, as amended, 5 U.S.C. App. 6. But to be certified as a "qualified diversified trust," the trust assets must "comprise a widely diversified portfolio of readily marketable securities, and [must] not initially include the securities of any entities having substantial activities in the same area as the government official's primary area of responsibility." Ibid. A portfolio is considered "widely diversified" if the value of the securities in any one industrial, economic or geographic, sector is no more than 20% of the total and the value of the securities of any single issuer is no more than 5% of the total. 5 CFR 2634.404(b)(2). The Clintons' trust is a qualified blind trust, not a qualified diversified trust.

[118]In 1989, criticism of Secretary of State James Baker's ownership of Chemical Bank stock compelled him to sell his interest in Chemical Bank and all publicly traded companies, notwithstanding the fact that this stock had been placed in a blind trust in January 1981 when he became Chief of Staff to President Reagan. (The Secretary of State was expected to participate in policy discussions concerning Third World debt, and Chemical Bank was a major lender to Third World countries.) The blind trust provided Baker with no protection from either the law or criticism. See Pincus, "Which Ethical Rules for Baker?", *Washington Post*, A25 (Mar. 23, 1989); Shenon, "Experts Disagree if Baker's Stocks Posed Conflict With Treasury Post," *New York Times*, B12 (Feb. 16, 1989); Friedman, "Baker Selling His Stocks to Avoid Any Conflict in State Dept. Role," *New York Times*, A1 (Feb. 15, 1989). As an illustration of what she concluded were "Double standards in Clintonland," *U.S. News & World Report*, 58 (Mar. 14, 1994), Gloria Borger compared the virtually non-existent coverage of the First Lady's situation with "the front-page stink" resulting from stories about Baker's investment. "[Baker's] investment was in a blind trust, but all the heat forced Baker to immediately—and appropriately—sell his stock."

[119]Soon after the creation of the Health Care Task Force, Representative Clinger informed the White House that he intended to introduce a bill to make the spouses of the President and Vice President "full-time employees" for purposes of FACA. Letter to President William J. Clinton (Feb. 1, 1993). The White House Counsel responded that legislation was unnecessary. Letter to Honorable William F. Clinger (Feb. 5, 1993)("We believe . . . that the existing statute already provides for such a result.").

[120]U.S. Constitution, art. II, sec. 3.

[121]See *ABA Report, supra* note 79, at 301(emphasis in original) ("[F]ew, (if any) types of financial interests are reliably "conflicts proof" for [elected] officials. At the same time, the remedial alternative to divestment—recusal—is peculiarly inappropriate for them. In some instances (as with the President), recusal would leave literally no other person who could perform the required official functions.").

[122]See *ABA Report, supra* note 79, at 302 ("[B]oth the political environment and the high public profile of most Presidential (and Vice Presidential) actions reduce the risk that narrowly self-serving decisions will go unchallenged.).

[123]As a Federal employee, the President's spouse would clearly be entitled to seek a conflict-of-interest waiver under 18 U.S.C. 208(b)(1).

[124]In *Association of Amer. Phys. and Surgeons*, the D.C. Circuit relied in part on the lack of any sanction in the anti-nepotism law (other than forfeit of salary), for its interpretation that the law "may well bar appointment only to paid positions in government." 997 F.2d at 905.

[125]Cf. *Association of Amer. Phys. and Surgeons*, 997 F.2d at 905 (doubting that Congress intended to include White House or Executive Office of the President in the statute's definition of "agency").

[126]OGE may reconsider its interpretation of this term in the context of its ongoing rulemaking concerning exemptions from section 208. See 60 Fed. Reg. 47208 (Sept. 11, 1995). Comments were due by November 13, 1995, and a final rule is not expected until sometime in 1996..

Chapter Four

[1]29 *Weekly Compilation of Presidential Documents* 96 (Feb. 1, 1993).

[2]The members were: Secretaries of Treasury, Defense, Commerce, Labor, Health & Human Services, and Veterans Affairs; Director of OMB; Assistant to the President for Domestic Policy; Assistant to the President for Economic Policy; Chair of the Council of Economic Advisers; and Senior Advisor to the President for Policy Development.

[3]The plan was shown informally to Congress in September 1993. Priest & Weisskopf, "Health Care Reform: The Collapse of a Quest," *Washington Post,* A6 (Oct. 11, 1994).

[4]Letter from William F. Clinger, Jr. to Honorable William J. Clinton (Feb. 1, 1993). Clinger at the time was Ranking Member of the House Committee on Government Operations, which had oversight jurisdiction over the administration of FACA.

[5]See 5 U.S.C. App. FACA § 2 (findings and purpose).

[6]5 U.S.C. App. FACA § 3.

[7]5 U.S.C. App. FACA § 10(a)(1). Clinger also asked GAO to look into whether the Task Force could conduct business in private. Priest, "GOP Congressman Questions Hillary Clinton's Closed-Door Meetings," *Washington Post*, A5 (Feb. 10, 1993). According to a House Government Operations Committee staff person, no formal GAO consideration of this question was pursued once the issue was joined in court.

[8]FACA §§ 10(a) (open meetings); (c) minutes. Meetings may be closed for reasons consistent with the Sunshine Act, but closure requires a written Presidential decision containing findings. FACA § 10(d). A Federal employee must chair or attend each meeting. FACA § 10(e).

[9]FACA § 10(b). FACA § 11 requires meeting transcripts to be publicly available.

[10]FACA § 10(a)(2).

[11]FACA does not define "timely notice." GSA regulations do. 41 CFR 101-6.1015(b).

[12]FACA § 9(c).

[13]Letter from Bernard W. Nussbaum to Honorable William F. Clinger, Jr. Feb. 5, 1993). Nussbaum therefore told Clinger that legislation making the First Lady a "full-time officer or employee" for purposes of FACA, which Clinger had offered to introduce, was unnecessary. Nussbaum also denied that the Task Force had held any meeting up to that point.

The White House Counsel provided the same response to three associations with an interest in health care reform, who subsequently filed suit.

[14]*Association of Amer. Phys. & Surgeons, Inc, et al.* v. *Hillary Rodham Clinton, et al.*, Civil Action No. 93-399 (D.D.C.)(hereafter, *AAPS*).

[15]5 U.S.C. App. FACA § 3(2)(iii).

[16]The Justice Department further argued that if FACA were applied to the Task Force, it would uncon-stitutionally interfere with the President's authority to make legislative recommendations to Congress and therefore violate separation of powers principles. York, "Justice Department Calls Open-Meeting Law In-valid," *Washington Post*, A8 (Mar. 4, 1993).

[17]The working group was organized into general subject matter areas, called "cluster groups," each of which was further organized into several "sub-groups."

[18]Answer to Second Amended Complaint, ¶18 (May 4, 1994).

[19]Declaration of Ira Magaziner, ¶5, 2-3 (Mar. 3, 1993). Later, however, the Justice Department ac-knowledged that the working group was established not merely to gather information but also to "develop alternatives for health care reform." Answer to Second Amended Complaint 21 (May 4, 1994).

[20]Ibid., ¶¶11, 4.

[21]Ibid., ¶¶11, 12, 4-5.

[22]Ibid., ¶13, 6.

[23]Ibid. The distinction he drew between "members" and consultants was that the latter would not exercise any supervisorial or decision making functions.

[24]Ibid., ¶31, 13.

[25]*AAPS*, 813 F. Supp. 82, 87 (D.D.C. 1993). Judge Lamberth held that Mrs. Clinton did not fit the definition of either "officer" or "employee" used in 5 U.S.C. 2104 and 2105, respectively. In addition, Judge Lamberth stated that there was "no evidence or other indicia of employment[,]" such as the oath of office or a Standard Form 50.

[26]813 F. Supp. 89-90.

[27]813 F. Supp. 89 11.

[28]The charter estimated the cost of the Task Force to be below $100,000 and explained that—halfway through the 100 days—the Task Force still had not met. However, this does not mean that during this time there were no White House meetings on health care in which some or most of the Task Force members were present. See E. Drew, *On the Edge*, 191 (Simon & Schuster, 1994)(describing one such meeting "during Clinton's first week in office[.]").

The below $100,000 figure proved to be a gross underestimate. In November 1995, the General Ac-counting Office (GAO) determined that Total Federal Government spending on the Task Force was at least $13.8 million. Letter to Honorable Paul Coverdell, et al. from J. William Gadsby, re: Health Care Task Force (Nov. 9, 1995). That figure included about $434,000 in funds spent on the *AAPS* lawsuit, and $7,698,813 in costs developing a legislative proposal after the Task Force was formally terminated in May 1993. Counting only the Task Force's costs from its creation in January 1993 to its formal termination, the cost of the Task Force and working groups was $5,686,253. Each of these figures is subject to an increase of an undetermined amount to account for the cost of personnel at the Executive Office of the President, which includes the White Office and OMB. Inexplicably, the EOP did not provide personnel costs to GAO, as did other Federal agen-cies. Representative Clinger, now Chairman of the House Committee on Government Reform and Oversight, said in a press release that "[w] hat we have here is another example of the Clinton Administration not being forthcoming with the Congress or the American people about the entire scale, scope, and cost of their tax-payer-funded activities." Bedard, "Hillary's health care reform task force cost $13.8 million," *Washington Times*, A3 (Nov. 10, 1995); McAllister, GAO Price Tag on White House's Failed Health Care Initiative: Almost $14 million," *Washington Post*, A13 (Nov. 10, 1995). Clinger suggested that the FACA provision that requires an estimate of costs may need to be amended to require some verification of the estimate.

[29]Letter from Bernard W. Nussbaum to Dr. Jane Orient (Apr. 1, 1993), Exhibit K to Plaintiffs' Verified Second Amended and Substituted Complaint. The non-exempt Task Force documents consisted of thousands of letters on health reform received from members of the public in response to a White House solicitation. That month, the documents were available to the public in a reading room at the Department of Health and Human Services.

[30]Ibid.

[31] Second Declaration of Ira Magaziner, ¶4, 2 (June 18, 1993).

[32] The only public meeting the Task Force ever held was on March 29. Recall that Judge Lamberth's ruling permitted the Task Force to hold its policy deliberations in private.

[33] Second Declaration of Ira Magaziner, ¶ 9, 4 (June 18, 1993). Although Magaziner asserted that since May 30, 1993, "the Task Force has not conducted any business[,]" he noted that the President had consulted with his White House staff, "some of whom were members of the Task Force[.] The Task Force, however, has not been reconvened since the expiration of its charter, and no plans exist to reconvene the Task Force at any time." Ibid., ¶10, 4.

[34] The Justice Department filed an appeal on March 18; the three associations appealed on March 22. Several other groups, including the U.S. House of Representatives and the Reporters' Committee for the Freedom of the Press, filed amicus curiae briefs in support of the three associations.

[35] AAPS, 997 F.2d 898 (D.C. Cir. 1993).

[36] 997 F.2d 910-11. The court strongly suggested that if the Task Force were subject to FACA, the court would have held such an application of FACA to be unconstitutional.

[37] Judge James Buckley disagreed with the majority's reasoning but concurred in the judgment. He would have held that Mrs. Clinton is not a "full-time officer or employee" under FACA, addressed the constitutional question, and found application of FACA's public disclosure provisions to the Task Force unconstitutional. 997 F.2d at 920-25. For a criticism of the majority's approach (and also the approach of the Supreme Court in *Public Citizen* v. *United States Department of Justice*, 491 U.S. 440 (1989)), see J. Bybee, *Advising the President: Separation of Powers and the Federal Advisory Committee Act,* 104 Yale L.J. 51, 94-96 (1994).

[38] 997 F.2d 914.

[39] Ibid., 916.

[40] Bedard, "Health panel's ethics questioned," *Washington Times*, A1 (Oct. 1, 1993).

[41] Bedard, "Hillary's task force lacks records," *Washington Times*, A1 (Oct. 21, 1993).

[42] Letter from John Conyers, Jr. and William F. Clinger, Jr. to Honorable Bernard W. Nussbaum (Oct. 21, 1993). On June 15, 1993, plaintiffs had obtained an order from Judge Lamberth requiring the Government to preserve records of the Task Force and working group. Following the Justice Department's showing that procedures were in place to preserve records pursuant to the Presidential Records Act, Judge Lamberth rescinded his preservation order as no longer necessary. *AAPS*, Memorandum opinion and order (July 22, 1993).

[43] Letter from Bernard W. Nussbaum to Honorable John Conyers, Jr. and Honorable William F. Clinger, Jr. (Oct. 25, 1993).

[44] Representative Clinger wrote the White House Counsel again on November 9, asking the White House to prepare an inventory of all Task Force records and to make the inventory available to the House Committee on Government Operations. Letter from William F. Clinger, Jr. to Honorable Bernard W. Nussbaum (Nov. 9, 1993). According to Committee staff, the White House Counsel's office rebuffed this request, asserting that the Ranking Member lacked authority to require the production of the inventory.

[45] AAPS, 837 F. Supp. 454 (D.D.C. 1993). Bedard, "Judge demands health panel's papers from White House," *Washington Times*, A1 (Nov. 10, 1993); York, "Judge Assails Health Team On Data Curb," *Washington Post*, A25 (Nov. 10, 1993).

[46] 837 F. Supp. 457. Judge Lamberth also ordered the Government to pay the plaintiffs' costs and legal fees. Ibid., 458.

[47] 837 F. Supp. 456-57.

[48] Bedard, "Clintons seek to seal key papers," *Washington Times*, A1 (Nov. 29, 1993). Justice made public some Secret Service entry records, payroll records and travel vouchers. Placed under seal were about twenty pages of meeting agendas, which were protected because they were deliberative working group documents subject to privilege (assuming the inapplicability of FACA). These documents were later unsealed and released.

[49] Bedard, "White House promises health papers—a day late," *Washington Times*, A3 (Nov. 30, 1993).

[50] Plaintiffs' Memorandum of Points and Authorities In Support of Motion for Summary Judgment and Permanent Injunction (Mar. 23, 1994).

[51] Ibid., 22.

[52] Ibid., 183-211.

[53] Ibid., 217-227.

[54] Ibid., 212-216. Plaintiffs also charged that the First Lady violated conflict-of-interest restrictions by selecting Lois Quam to serve as a member of the working group. Quam is Vice President of United HealthCare Corp., a company included in Mrs. Clinton's Valuepartners I investment portfolio, which she placed in a blind trust in July 1993. Ibid., 216. See also Bedard, "Lies by panel, possible conflicts by Hillary emerge in health suit," *Washington Times*, A1 (Mar. 24, 1994).

[55]Defendants' Cross-Motion for Summary Judgment (May 4, 1994).

[56]As of the date of Magaziner's first declaration (March 3, 1993), the working group already consisted of 340 members.

[57]Third Declaration of Ira Magaziner (May 4, 1994).

[58]The memorandum also scheduled the first Task Force meeting for January 27, 1993. This meeting either was not held or was held as a working group, not Task Force meeting.

[59]Third Declaration of Ira Magaziner, ¶3, 2 (May 4, 1994).

[60]Ibid., ¶18, 8.

[61]Ibid., ¶6, 3.

[62]Ibid., ¶7, 3.

[63]Ibid., ¶8, 4.

[64]Ibid., ¶¶9, 12, 4-6.

[65]Ibid., ¶¶24, 25, 11-12. Although the working group may not have provided written or oral advice "as a group," the separate cluster groups and subgroups did provide such group papers and advice.

[66]Ibid., ¶27, 28, 12-13.

[67]Ibid., 2 n.1.

[68]See Bedard, "White House says Hillary task force suit is political move," *Washington Times*, A3 (May 6, 1994).

[69]Defendants' Memorandum in Opposition to Plaintiffs' Motion for Summary Judgment, 11-23.

[70]Ibid., 26-32. In addition, Justice explained that the White House SGEs were briefed on the ethics restrictions to which they were subject and were checked for possible conflicts.

[71]5 CFR 2634.905(a).

[72]Justice borrowed and adopted the conclusions the Office of Government Ethics made with respect to Mrs. Clinton's stock interests in the Valuepartners investment partnership, conclusions assailed in Chapter Three of this study.

[73]Order (July 26, 1994). See Bedard, "Hillary, aides face civil trial," *Washington Times*, A1 (July 26, 1994); Locy, "Health Advisers Ordered to Stand Trial," *Washington Post*, A6 (July 26, 1994); Pear, "Justice Dept. Defends Setup That Created Health Plan," *New York Times*, A16 (July 26, 1994); Bedard, "Health panel secret unveiled," *Washington Times*, A1 (July 27, 1994).

On July 27, Rep. Ernest Istook asked the Attorney General to appoint a Special Counsel to investigate whether Patsy Thomasson, Special Assistant to the President for Management and Administration, lied to a House Appropriations Subcommittee when she testified on the membership and cost of the Task Force and working groups. "White House official accused of lying," *Washington Times*, A6 (July 28, 1994). (In 1993, Thomasson estimated the cost of the Task Force and working groups to be around $325,000; in November 1995, GAO estimated that total costs would exceed $13.8 million, over $5 million of which was attributed to the Task Force from January-May 1993. See note 28 *supra*. Thomasson insisted that she never intended her estimate to cover the entire Executive Branch costs. Bedard, "Health care task force costs exposed," *Washington Times*, A1 (Mar. 11, 1995); Bedard, "Taxpayers may pay White House fine," *Washington Times,* A3 (Mar. 15, 1995).)

Attorney General Reno responded to Istook on December 2, 1994, concluding that prosecution was not warranted. Istook pursued the issue in a January 17, 1995 letter to the Attorney General, in which Istook also asked for a Special or Independent Counsel to investigate Ira Magaziner. Istook argued that the Justice Department's investigation of Thomasson was inadequate and that the Department had an internal conflict of interest. The Justice Department responded to Istook's second letter, rejecting his request, the same day it determined that it would not seek the appointment of an independent counsel for Ira Magaziner. Letter from Kent R. Markus to Honorable Ernest J. Istook, Jr. (Mar. 3, 1995). See text note 96, *infra*.

[74]*Associated Press*, "Suit over Hillary's panel might be settled," *Washington Times*, A3 (Aug. 5, 1994). In an August 4, 1994, order, Judge Lamberth directed the parties to keep their settlement discussions confidential. Judge Lamberth rescinded this order by order dated August 28, 1995.

[75]Pear, "White House Seeks Settlement of Health Suit," *New York Times*, A16 (Aug. 10, 1994).

[76]Locy, "Settlement of Health Task Force Suit Rejected," *Washington Post*, A17 (Sept. 16, 1994). Thereupon, the lawyers representing the Association moved to withdraw from the case. Although the basis for withdrawal was not revealed, it is reasonable to speculate that the lawyers had urged the Association to accept the settlement offer. The Association's Executive Director cited a "philosophic difference of opinion" between the lead lawyer, Kent Masterson Brown, and the Association. "Doctors won't settle suit over health panel," *Washington Times*, A4 (Aug. 16, 1994).

[77]Bedard, "Tales of shredding prompt probe of Hillary's task force," *Washington Times*, A4 (Sept. 1, 1994).

[78]*Associated Press*, "White House to Release Health Team Files," *New York Times*, A21 (Aug. 18, 1994) (emphasis added).

[79]Bedard, "Health plan papers released," *Washington Times*, A1 (Sept. 8, 1994).

[80]Bedard, "Lawyers for Hillary, doctors continue fight," *Washington Times*, A8 (Oct. 10, 1994).

[81]One of the documents released in September 1994 is dated September 1993 and stamped "working group." Bedard, "Magaziner ordered by judge to testify," *Washington Times*, A3 (Oct. 15, 1994).

[82]Bedard, "Judge skeptical of Hillary task force," *Washington Times*, A1 (Oct. 14, 1994). Before the hearing, the plaintiffs claimed that documents may have been destroyed after the suit was filed, or taken by working group members to their home and not returned. Bedard, "Tales of shredding prompt probe of Hillary's task force," *Washington Times*, A4 (Sept. 1, 1994). The Justice Department acknowledged at the hearing that four working group members had not yet responded to a White House request for any official documents they may have taken with them, and that the documents released in September were screened and redacted to delete non-responsive and privileged matters.

[83]Bedard, "Magaziner ordered by judge to testify," *Washington Times*, A3 (Oct. 15, 1994).

[84]The plaintiffs had earlier contested Magaziner's statement in his June 1993 declaration that the Task Force had disbanded on May 31, 1993. At the time, the Justice Department represented to the court that the working groups, too, were no longer in place.

[85]Seper, "Health panel removed records," *Washington Times*, A1 (Oct. 28, 1994). Justice did not provide this explanation earlier, when plaintiffs alleged post-May 31 activities.

[86]Locy, "Judge to Review Health Files Before Ruling on Access," *Washington Post*, A4 (Nov. 11, 1994). It was unclear whether all of the documents were generated after the official termination of the Task Force and working group, or included other documents generated during the life of the Task Force but withheld for other reasons.

According to a person who has reviewed the Task Force documents filed at the Archives, the withheld documents include not only documents dated after May 31, 1993, but also documents deemed by the Justice Department and White House Counsel's office to be privileged. Pages and other portions of documents were redacted for reasons of personal privacy and other privileges.

[87]*AAPS*, Memorandum and Order (Dec. 1, 1994). Pear, "Misconduct Found on Clinton Health Plan," *New York Times*, A22 (Dec. 2, 1994); Bedard, "No trial over health task force," *Washington Times*, A1 (Dec.2, 1994); Associated Press, "White House Misconduct Cited in Health Panel Secrecy Case," *Washington Post*, A2 (Dec. 2, 1994).

[88]Ibid., 5-6 (quoting *AAPS*, 997 F.2d at 915). Lamberth added that he would impose sanctions at a later date for the "defendants' misconduct during the course of this litigation[.]" Ibid.

[89]Locy, "Justice Dept. to Release Health Panel Documents," *Washington Post*, A6 (Dec. 3, 1994); Associated Press, "Administration pledges to release health care papers," *Washington Times*, A3 (Dec. 3, 1994).

[90]*AAPS*, Memorandum and Order (Dec. 21, 1994). Judge Lamberth stated that he was satisfied that the Justice Department had conducted a complete search for responsive documents. In fact, however, as of May 1995, a total of 289 boxes of documents were in the Archives, **with some boxes added as recently as March 1995**. According to a person who has reviewed these documents, many of the records are not organized; pages are missing from some documents, others appear to have been redacted, and a couple were partially shredded.

[91]The question of possible civil contempt of court was mooted by a dismissal of the case. *AAPS*, Memorandum and Order, 2.

[92]Ibid., 3.

[93]Judge Lamberth added that "defendants, and/or their counsel, may have engaged in sanctionable conduct . . . when they did not promptly correct [the March 3 declaration][.]" Ibid., 4. He scheduled a January 9, 1995 status conference to consider plaintiffs' request for sanctions, fees, and costs. Ibid., 6.

[94]Ibid., 6.

[95]Ibid. See also, Locy, "Judge Asks U.S. Attorney to Probe Magaziner Statement," *Washington Post*, A9 (Dec. 22, 1994); Scarborough, "Judge wants probe of Magaziner's words," *Washington Times*, A1 (Dec. 22, 1994); Pear, "Architect of Health Plan Could Face Charges," *New York Times*, B12 (Dec. 22, 1994).

After a White House lawyer publicly criticized Judge Lamberth for referring the matter to the U.S. Attorney without holding a hearing in district court ("We're going to fight back. That judge has put him under a cloud."), Judge Lamberth offered Magaziner an opportunity to have the matter heard in a contempt trial before the judge. Bedard, "Magaziner faces perjury probe over health-panel secrecy case," *Washington Times*, A1 (Jan. 18, 1995); Locy, "Health Advisor Declines Judge's Offer," *Washington Post*, A4 (Jan. 18, 1995). Magaziner rejected the offer, through his newly appointed private counsel, Charles F.C. Ruff, who served as U.S. Attorney for the District of Columbia in the Carter Administration. Magaziner may have been counseled that the standard of proof is much higher in a criminal proceeding for perjury or a false statement than in a civil contempt proceeding, that statements made in the district court could be used against him in a criminal investigation, and that a fresh look by the U.S. Attorney's office would be preferable to a review by the same judge who had labeled Magaziner's declaration "misleading, at best." See "Contempt and Ira

Magaziner," *Washington Times*, A20 (Jan. 19, 1995); "Ira's Story," *Wall Street Journal*, A12 (Jan. 20, 1995).

[96]Johnston, "Ruling on Top Health Care Aide Brings Worry for Administration," *New York Times*, A20 (Dec. 23, 1994).

[97]Letter from Henry J. Hyde, et al. to Honorable Janet Reno (Feb. 2, 1995); Bedard, "GOP presses Magaziner probe," *Washington Times*, A4 (Feb. 3, 1995). Earlier, the *Washington Times*, while no fan of the independent counsel statute, argued that Magaziner's case "would seem to be the perfect instance for the application of the statute[,]" given the Justice Department's role in defending Magaziner in the civil case. "Mr. Magaziner's comeuppance," *Washington Times*, A16 (Dec. 27, 1994).

[98]28 U.S.C. 591(c)(1). The independent counsel law provides that upon request of a majority of the majority party members of either Judiciary Committee, the Attorney General has thirty days to report to Congress on whether she has decided to initiate a preliminary investigation. 28 U.S.C. 592(g)(1),(2).

[99]Letter from Janet Reno to Honorable Henry J. Hyde (Mar. 3, 1995); Thomas & Locy, "Special Magaziner Counsel Rejected," *Washington Post*, A11 (Mar. 4, 1995); Associated Press, "Reno says no to Magaziner counsel," *Washington Times*, A2 (Mar. 4, 1995); Johnston, "Reno Rejects G.O.P. Request For Prosecutor," *New York Times*, sec. 1, 15 (Mar. 5, 1995).

[100]Letter to Honorable Royce C. Lamberth (Aug. 3, 1995) (*Jarrett letter*); Bedard, "U.S. won't prosecute health aide Magaziner," *Washington Times*, A1 (Aug. 4, 1995); Pear, "U.S. Decides Not to Prosecute Clinton Health Plan Architect," *New York Times*, A22 (Aug. 4, 1995); Locy, "Clinton Health Aide Won't Face Charges in Task Force Dispute," *Washington Post*, A3 (Aug. 4, 1995). The letter was actually signed by someone else, on behalf of Marshall Jarrett (initials appearing to be RJL). Jarrett's signature (albeit by someone else's hand) was likely an attempt to portray the decision as one made by career prosecutors rather than the politically appointed Holder. Given the significance of the letter, it is peculiar that Jarrett did not sign for himself.

[101]*Jarrett letter, supra* note 100, 2.

[102]Ibid.

[103]Ibid., 17 ("It appears that [Magaziner] relied upon the advice of White House attorneys, who assured him that the classifications within the declaration were legally appropriate and could be applied to the working group to ensure that all ethical requirements were met.")

[104]Locy, "Holder Blames White House Lawyers for Dispute Involving Magaziner," *Washington Post*, A4 (Aug. 5, 1995).

[105]Letter to the Honorable Janet Reno (Aug. 8, 1995); "Ira Beats The Rap," *Wall Street Journal*, A8 (Aug. 9, 1995). Barr, himself a former U.S. Attorney, may have used the phrase "government counsel" to include the conduct of White House lawyers in the OPR investigation. OPR generally lacks jurisdiction over the conduct of attorneys outside of the Justice Department, although any investigation of Justice Department lawyers would inevitably encompass much of the conduct of the White House Counsel's office.

[106]Bedard, "Judge 'troubled' by Hillary's defense in health care suit," *Washington Times*, A2 (Aug. 12, 1995).

[107]Letter to the Honorable Royce C. Lamberth, at 1 (Aug. 30, 1995).

[108]Ibid., 2.

[109]It means simply that the working group cannot avail itself of the fulltime employee exemption from the law.

[110]997 F.2d 915.

[111]Justice made much of the fact that the Task Force was situated as a buffer between the working group and the President, rendering the working group's work product "staff and support."

[112]Further, the D.C. Circuit did not accept Justice's arguments that the working group provided only staff support. It held that direct contact with the President was not required, and that the characterization of the working group as staff was belied by the fact that, because the Task Force was **not** an advisory committee, the working group became "the point of contact between the public and the government." 997 F.2d 912-913.

[113]997 F.2d 913 (rejecting Justice's consensus argument) ("[A] group is a FACA advisory committee when it is asked to render advice or recommendations, **as a group**, and not as a collection of individuals.") (emphasis added).

[114]Also, payroll records were not formally kept for any working group member or participant until March 6, 1993, after many had reported to work by February 8, 1993 and had worked 80 hours by February 20, 1993.

[115]That section provides:
[T]he term "special Government employee" shall mean an officer or employee of the executive . . . branch of the United States Government . . ., who is retained, designated, appointed, or employed to perform, with or without compensation, for not to exceed one hundred and thirty days during any period of three hundred and sixty-five consecutive days, temporary duties either on a full-time or intermittent basis[.]

[116]18 U.S.C. 208(a); 5 CFR 2635.402(a).

[117]See OGE Informal Advisory Letter 82 X 22 (July 9, 1982) (describing history of concepts of "representative" and "special Government employee" and application to several specific advisory committees).

[118]*Jarrett letter, supra* note 100, 11.

[119]Another line of defense was that circumstances changed after Magaziner executed his declaration.

[120]997 F.2d 915.

[121]5 CFR 2634.905(a). Defendants' Memorandum in Opposition to Plaintiffs' Motion for Summary Judgment, 27 (May 4, 1994).

[122]5 CFR 2634.905(a)(Example 1); 57 Fed. Reg. 11829 (Apr. 7, 1992).

[123]The plaintiffs alleged that three working group members were "officials [of] or consultants to large managed care entities that were the ultimate beneficiaries of their work[,]" noting the managed care scheme proposed in the Health Security Act. Plaintiffs' Memorandum of Points and Authorities in Support of Motion for Summary Judgment and Permanent Injunction, 213-214 (Mar. 23, 1994).

[124]Defendants' Memorandum in Opposition to Plaintiffs' Motion for Summary Judgment, 30-32 (May 4, 1994).

[125]See Chapter Three.

[126]Determining whether the effect on the financial interests of particular working group participants was direct and predictable would require a factual analysis of the nature of each participant's financial interests or outside affiliations and their role on the working group.

[127]Locy, "Holder Blames White House Lawyers for Dispute Involving Magaziner," *Washington Post*, A4 (Aug. 5, 1995).

[128]Jarrett took issue with both the D.C. Circuit and Judge Lamberth in finding that the Government never expressly asserted the position that the working group was exempt from FACA because it was composed solely of Federal employees. *Jarrett letter, supra* note 100, 6-8 and n.5. In the District Court, the Government relied on the all-employee defense with respect to the Task Force; with respect to the working group, it relied primarily on a previous FACA case involving a different test, *National Anti-Hunger Coalition v. Executive Committee*, 557 F. Supp. 524 (D.D.C.), *aff'd* 711 F.2d 1071 (D.C. Cir. 1983)(group performing "staff" role not directly "utilized" by President). On the other hand, the Government did not formally abandon the all-employee argument until May 1994, and even when it did so, it did not concede the legal point. Moreover, the peculiar (indeed, misleading) wording of Magaziner's declaration makes little sense if the Government did not intend to use it in defense of the lawsuit.

[129]Determining Magaziner's state of knowledge is impossible to do on the public record. One document suggests some awareness on Magaziner's part of the legal ramifications involved. Magaziner was urged in a February 2, 1993 memorandum that, "[t]o avoid ethical difficulties, the members of the cluster groups, and especially the heads of issue working groups, must be full government employees." Solomon, "Health care task force enriched big-money consultants", *Washington Times*, A3 (Feb. 21, 1995). This document was uncovered by the Associated Press well after the lawsuit was dismissed, and even after its publication, received little notice. The entire document, however, was not available to the author.

[130]*Jarrett letter, supra* note 100, 11-12.

[131]Ibid., 12-13 & n.9.

[132]Ibid., 14.

[133]Ibid.

[134]Ibid.

[135]Ibid., 15 (emphasis added). The use of the past tense "was" in this discovery response suggests that the term "membership" was not "operative" at the time it was purposefully used in the declaration!

Here as well, Jarrett refrained from accusing Government lawyers of bad faith, suggesting only that "government counsel seemingly did not focus on the apparent conflict between [the theory of the working group as an unstructured "horde"] and the position taken in Mr. Magaziner's previously filed declaration."

[136]Ibid., 16.

[137]Although the letter reporting the results of the U.S. Attorney's investigation was not signed by Holder, there was no indication that Holder did not participate or concur in the report's conclusions.

[138]This is the opinion of the *Wall Street Journal*. "Holder's Dilemma," *Wall Street Journal*, A18 (Mar. 7, 1995)("Mr. Magaziner's actions . . . deserve to be reviewed by someone who inspires more confidence that a Clinton political appointee. Perhaps the best solution would be for Mr. Holder to turn over the decision to prosecute Mr. Magaziner to a career civil servant at Justice.").

[139]Of course, even in disregard of FACA's requirements, it did not accomplish its mission on time.

[140]Indeed, the White House scoffed at even the idea of a conflict, relying on the dubious defense that health care reform (whatever its content or contours) is not a "particular matter."

[141]Fallows, "A Triumph of Misinformation," *Atlantic Monthly*, 26 (Jan. 1995).

[142]Fallows did not distinguish between the Task Force and the interdepartmental working group. Im-

plicitly, therefore, he rejected the narrow Magaziner and Justice Department definition of "member."

[143]Ibid., 29(ellipses in original).

[144]Fallows did not refer to the lawsuit.

[145]These meetings were legally closed to the public, given the D.C. Circuit's ruling that the Task Force, as opposed to the working group, was not an advisory committee under FACA.

[146]Locy, "Holder Blames White House Lawyers for Dispute Involving Magaziner," *Washington Post*, A4 (Aug. 5, 1995) (emphasis added).

Chapter Five

[1]Hereafter, *White House Management Review*.

[2]Pub. L. No. 103-50, 107 Stat. 241 (July 2, 1993).

[3]GAO, B-255157, *Travel Office Operations* (May 2, 1994)(hereafter *GAO Report*). The law required GAO to report its findings by September 30, 1993. On September 30, 1993, GAO informed Congress that its report would be delayed because of difficulties in reaching agreement with the White House and Justice Department on GAO's access to persons and documents. *GAO Report*, 14; Associated Press, "Delays Cited in GAO Probe Of Travel Office," *Washington Post*, A5 (Oct. 3, 1993).

[4]Letter to Honorable John Conyers, Jr. (Oct. 7, 1994) (hereafter *Minority Study*).

[5]The OPR report made available at the October 1995 hearing was a memorandum from Michael E. Shaheen, Jr. to Jo Ann Harris, re: Report of OPR's review of the conduct of the FBI in connection with the White House Travel Office matter (Mar. 18, 1994) (hereafter the *Shaheen report*). The report responded to a July 28, 1993 request from Deputy Attorney General Philip Heymann to examine the FBI's contacts with the White House Travel Office matter and an August 3, 1993 request from Heymann to look into Vince Foster's complaint, in a torn-up handwritten note found after his death, that "the FBI lied in their report to the AG." OPR assumed that Foster was referring to the FBI's June 1, 1993 internal management report to the Attorney General, which was provided to the White House for its use in conducting the White House Management Review.

Also, the *American Spectator* published two lengthy articles on the subject that are relied on in this chapter. Brock, "The Travelgate Cover-Up," *American Spectator*, 30 (June 1994)(hereafter *Brock*); York, "Have GAO Will Travel," *American Spectator*, 20 (Dec. 1994)(hereafter *York*). This chapter also relies on Elizabeth Drew's book on the first two years of the Clinton Administration, *On the Edge* (Simon & Schuster, 1994), which includes a chapter entitled "May Troubles" that discusses the Travel Office matter at length (174-83).

[6]The GAO report stated that the dismissals were effective June 5, 1993. *GAO Report*, *supra* note 3, 46. This probably includes the two weeks' severance pay the employees received. Devroy & Kamen, "Longtime Travel Staff Given Walking Papers," *Washington Post*, A1 (May 20, 1993).

[7]Some members of the media travel occasionally.

[8]See, for example, Devroy & Kamen, "Longtime Travel Staff Given Walking Papers," *Washington Post*, A1 (May 20, 1993); Murray, "Travel agency in loop," *Washington Times*, A1 (May 21, 1993); Devroy, "Staff Denies Clinton Ally Had Role in Firings," *Washington Post*, A7 (May 21, 1993); Devroy & Marcus, "Clinton Friend's Memo Sought Business," *Washington Post*, A1 (May 22, 1993); Turque & Miller, "Judgment Calls," *Newsweek*, 18 (May 31, 1993).

[9]See, for example, Devroy & Isikoff, "Clinton Staff Bypassed Reno to FBI," *Washington Post*, A1 (May 25, 1993); "With Friends Like These . . .," *Washington Post*, C6 (May 23, 1993); "The Missing Voice," *Washington Post*, A18 (May 26, 1993); "Travel Office (Cont'd)," *Washington Post*, A22 (May 28, 1993).

[10]Marcus & Devroy, "White House Backs Off on Firings of 5," *Washington Post*, A1 (May 26, 1993).

[11]Letter to Honorable William Sessions (May 24, 1993); Letter to Honorable William Sessions (June 7, 1993); Letter to Honorable William Sessions (June 11, 1993).

[12]Letter to Honorable William S. Sessions (June 7, 1993). The letter asked a series of detailed questions about the FBI's role. The FBI's answers to the Dole and Hatch letters are discussed, as appropriate, in this chapter's subsequent discussion and analysis of the facts. Much of the information provided by the FBI was included in the GAO Report issued in May 1994.

[13]139 *Cong. Rep.* S8433 (July 1, 1993) (Conference report).

[14]Devroy, "Clinton Friends Cited In Travel Staff Purge," *Washington Post*, A1 (July 3, 1993). The report was released at a press conference held on the Friday afternoon before the Fourth of July weekend.

[15]The Supplemental Appropriations Act of 1993, Pub. L. No. 103-50, 107 Stat. 241 (July 2, 1993).

[16]*White House Management Review*, *supra* note 1, 3.

[17]Ibid., 2-3.

[18]There is no indication that anyone from the White House Counsel's office—the office within the White House charged with handling ethics matters—participated in the White House Management Review. The staff work for McLarty and Panetta was done by John Podesta and Todd Stern, neither of whom was

from the Counsel's office.

[19]Ibid.

[20]Devroy, "Democrats Foil Effort for Hill Inquiry on Travel Firings," *Washington Post*, A16 (July 15, 1993).

[21]*GAO Report*, *supra* note 3, 6-7. See Rodriguez & Bedard, "No laws broken in travel office," *Washington Times*, A1 (May 3, 1994); Marcus, "Clinton Allies Criticized In Travel Office Firings," *Washington Post*, A21 (May 3, 1994); Labaton, "First Lady Urged Dismissals At Travel Office, Study Says," *New York Times*, B8 (May 3, 1994).

[22]Ibid.

[23]Ibid., 7-8.

[24]Ibid., 45-66.

[25]Ibid., 75.

[26]*Brock*, *supra* note 5, 30.

[27]Letter to Honorable John Conyers, Jr. (Oct. 7, 1994)(*Minority Study*); Associated Press, "House Republicans cite violations in travel office snafu," *Washington Times*, A4 (Oct. 8, 1994). The findings of the House Republicans' review were contained in several attachments to the letter.

[28]Ibid., 1.

[29]Ibid., 2-4. Soon thereafter, GAO's report was also criticized in York, "Have GAO Will Travel," *American Spectator*, 20 (Dec. 1994).

[30]Eisele, "House to probe Clinton travel office," *The Hill*, 1 (Nov. 16, 1994).

[31]Kellman, "Travelgate signs point to Hillary," *Washington Times*, A1 (Oct. 25, 1995); Schmidt & Locy, "Papers Detail Clinton Friend's Contract Push," *Washington Post*, A4 (Oct. 25, 1995); Associated Press, "Clinton and Hollywood Producer Met on Contract, a Memo Shows," *New York Times*, B6 (Oct. 25, 1995).

[32]Kellman, "Travelgate signs point to Hillary," *Washington Times*, A1, A13 (Oct. 25, 1995).

[33]Bedard, "Foster troubled by Travelgate firings," *Washington Times*, A1 (July 28, 1995).

[34]Schmidt, "White House Kept Foster's Travel Office Notebook From Investigators for a Year," *Washington Post*, A14 (Sept. 16, 1995).

[35]Locy, "Foster Journal Shows Worry About Travel Office," *Washington Post*, A8 (July 29, 1995).

[36]DeFrank, "Travelgate Redux," *The Weekly Standard*, 7 (Sept. 25, 1995).

[37]Schmidt, "White House Kept Foster's Travel Office Notebook From Investigators for a Year," *Washington Post*, A14 (Sept. 14, 1995).

[38]Schmidt, "Nussbaum Denies Withholding Foster Notebook From Investigators," *Washington Post*, A2 (Sept. 19, 1995); Bedard, "'Travelgate' investigator says Nussbaum hid Foster's diary," *Washington Times*, A3 (Sept. 19, 1995).

[39]Bedard, "Clinton may cite executive privilege," *Washington Times*, A1 (Sept. 8, 1995); Devroy, "Clinton May Assert Executive Privilege," *Washington Post*, A13 (Sept. 8, 1995); Mitchell, White House Refuses to Release Files in Travel Office Incident," *New York Times*, A19 (Sept. 8, 1995).

[40]Kellman, "'Uncooperative' Clinton friend may get a Travelgate subpoena," *Washington Times*, A1 (Dec. 4, 1995); Associated Press, "House Panel May Subpoena Thomason Documents," *Washington Post*, A14 (Dec. 4, 1995). The Committee first requested documents from Thomason in August 1995. The deadline was set in a December 1, 1995 letter to Thomason's attorney Robert Bennett, and responded to Bennett's November 15 letter to the Committee, objecting to the breadth of the document request and declining to participate in what he called a "political fishing expedition."

[41]Two weeks after the election, a World Wide Travel official told *Arkansas Business*, "World Wide is studying the possibilities of opening an office in Washington, D.C. to handle travel plans for Clinton's staff when he becomes president." World Wide reportedly received over $1 million from the campaign. It now handles travel for the Democratic National Committee. *Brock*, *supra* note 5, 31.

[42]*White House Management Review*, *supra* note 1, 4. Watkins knew World Wide Travel and its owner Betta Carney from his company's use of World Wide back in the mid-70's. *Brock*, *supra* note 5, 31.

[43]*White House Management Review*, *supra* note 1, Exhibit D. GAO found that the analyses Cornelius provided in the December 31 memorandum contained "significant errors." In particular, GAO found that Cornelius' descriptions of the benefits of her rebate proposal were "inaccurate," resulting in "estimates of costs and savings that were significantly misleading[.]" *GAO Report*, *supra* note 3, 50.

[44]*White House Management Review*, *supra* note 1, Exhibit E. The memorandum reveals that Cornelius and Watkins had previously engaged in discussions about the Travel Office, possibly before they began working in the White House.

[45]*White House Management Review*, *supra* note 1, Exhibit F. This document appears to have been a response to Watkins' request, made to another staffer earlier that month, for an organizational review of the Travel Office. *Minority Study*, *supra* note 4, Attachment A (GAO notes of interviews of Watkins and Cornelius). Cornelius told GAO that Watkins requested both the January and February memoranda. Watkins,

however, denied asking for any of the memoranda. *GAO Report, supra* note 3, 50 12.

Typed notes of the White House Management Review interview of Clarissa Cerda, at 5-6, released at the October 1995 House hearing, relate the following:

> On May 20, Cerda and CC [Cornelius] are paged by Patsy Thomasson (Cerda doesn't connect with Patsy but CC does). CC tells Cerda that Patsy called to make sure that they state (in any public comments) that David Watkins didn't read the Feb. 15 memorandum (the story is fairly hot in the press at this point). [author's note: handwritten words illegible] CC is led to believe that not telling that David read the memo is "part of the press strategy." (note: Cerda believes he read the memo).
>
> On May 21, Cerda is called into Dee Dee Myer's office. Outside her office, she recalls that she's approached by David Watkins who states, "you never saw me read the memo," and "you guy's did this on your own, right." Cerda responds to David saying he suggested they develop a counter-proposal to Moore's travel office memo. When David and Cerda meet with Dee Dee, David tells Dee Dee (falsely in Cerda's eyes) that Cerda can verify his story.

[46]An organizational chart showed World Wide Travel with one branch for White House travel and another for Democratic National Committee or political travel. *White House Management Review, supra* note 1, Exhibit F.

[47]Ibid.

[48]*White House Management Review, supra* note 1, 5.

[49]Thomason, Martens and Dan Richland each own one-third of the company; Martens is President.

[50]Drew, *On The Edge, supra* note 5, 178. It was elsewhere reported that Thomason's office was in the Old Executive Office Building. Turque & Miller, "Judgment Calls," *Newsweek,* 19 (May 31, 1993).

[51]Thomason received "a temporary pass for several months[.]" *GAO Report,* 56. From my experience in the White House, it is routine to receive a temporary White House pass until the complete background check is finished. Thomason applied for and was given a pass in March 1993. *Minority Study, supra* note 4, Attachment B, 3 (GAO notes of interview of Craig Livingstone). Thomason's pass privileges either expired or were rescinded in July 1993, following issuance of the White House Management Review. Romano, "We've Heard That," *Washington Post,* C3 (July 29, 1993)(noting that Thomason's "60-day" pass had expired with no effort by him to renew it).

The *Washington Times* reported that Thomason "was given office space and a secretary during the first month of the Clinton administration." Bedard, "GOP says Thomason may have broken law," *Washington Times,* A1 (July 9, 1993).

[52]*White House Management Review, supra* note 1, 6 (suggesting that Thomason began this work at the end of April 1993).

[53]*GAO Report, supra* note 3, 55. At the Justice Department's request, GAO did not interview Harry Thomason or Darnell Martens. Ibid., 51 16.

[54]*White House Management Review, supra* note 1, Exhibit G, 1. Martens' "confidential" memorandum is captioned, "White House Press Corps Report."

[55]Ibid. In an interview held after his acquittal, Billy Dale explained that he told Martens, "I've got the same contacts at the airlines that you do. Why do I need to call you to call them on my behalf?" Locy, "Acquitted Aide Blames Clinton For Difficulties," *Washington Post,* A3 Nov. 18, 1995).

[56]According to David Brock, Martens was "Sample's boyfriend." *Brock, supra* note 5, 32.

[57]This "research" was in part based on a discussion Martens had with Penny Sample. *White House Management Review, supra* note 1, 5.

[58]Ibid., 3. Martens alleged that UltrAir's predecessor, Airline of the Americas, attempted unsuccessfully to provide free charter operations to the press "in order to insure good press coverage of Bush campaign appearances." He also wrote that American Trans Air had rejected TRM's offer to do business with the Clinton campaign, informing Martens "point blank that they had a limited relationship with the White House and that limited business with Bush was better than no business with Clinton." Ibid., 2. The allegations against Airline of the Americas were denied by the carrier's former CEO, Charles Caudle, who sued Harry Thomason for defamation as a result of the Travel Office controversy. Bedard, "Clinton TV pal Thomason sued for libel in 'Travelgate'," *Washington Times,* A3 (Mar. 25, 1994). David Brock also found no support for Martens' allegations. *Brock, supra* note 5, 33.

[59]Martens' memorandum is confusing on this point. The memorandum refers to TRM as the entity seeking to compete for the press charter business, although TRM is simply a broker, not a carrier. Dale apparently viewed TRM as a potential threat to his job, and Martens failed to disabuse Dale of this fear. See *Brock, supra* note 5, 33 (suggesting that TRM was seeking to replace Dale's operation), and note 55 *supra.*

Both Martens and Thomason "strongly denied in interviews yesterday that they were seeking business for their own company, even though the memo is phrased repeatedly in those terms." Devroy & Marcus, "Clinton Friend's Memo Sought Business," *Washington Post,* A1 (May 22, 1993). Robert Bennett, who represents Martens and Thomason (and also Bill Clinton in the Paula Jones lawsuit), "said that despite the language in the memo, Martens was not interested in the press business but was concerned about competitive bidding." Locy, "For White House Travel Office, a Two-Year Trip of Trouble," *Washington Post*, A4 (Feb. 27, 1995). Similarly, a "correction" in the *New York Times* highlights a concerted effort to deny that Martens and Thomason were seeking personal financial gain. The original article read, "Thomason . . . owned an air charter company that wanted a share of the White House travel business." Johnston, "White House Travel Chief Expects to Face Embezzlement Charges," *New York Times*, A17 (Dec. 5, 1994). The "correction" appearing a few days later read: "Thomason owned one-third of an aviation consulting business that represented air charter companies and was interested in determining how such companies could bid on the White House travel business."

[60]*White House Management Review, supra* note 1, 5.

[61]Neither the White House Management Review nor the GAO Report identified the source. Martens was not interviewed by the GAO, at the Justice Department's request. David Brock wrote that as early as **December 1992**, Clinton aide Jeff Eller (and Cornelius's boyfriend) told reporters "that there were unspecified 'problems' in the travel office and that he would not be surprised if some people got fired." *Brock, supra* note 5, 31-32.

[62]*White House Management Review, supra* note 1, 5.

[63]GAO stated that Watkins asked Cornelius to consider how the Travel Office functions could be reorganized to help meet the direction to reduce White House staff by 25 percent *GAO Report, supra* note 3, 51. Elizabeth Drew concluded, "In retrospect, this appeared to be a setup." *On The Edge, supra* note 5, 177.

[64]A May 17 memorandum from David Watkins states that Cornelius "had been observing the Travel Office for 45 days," thus putting Cornelius' start around the third of April. *White House Management Review, supra* note 1, Exhibit H.

[65]*GAO Report, supra* note 3, 52 (based on interview of Watkins).

[66]The *White House Management Review supra* note1, 6, stated that Watkins believes that Thomason called him after Cornelius had begun work in the Travel Office. David Brock, however, placed the Thomason call "within a few days of" Thomason's late March conversation the President, and concluded that Watkins assigned Cornelius to the Travel Office "to substantiate rumors that she not only had an interest in fanning but had helped originate in the first place." *Brock, supra* note 5, 33-34.

[67]Cornelius "aroused the suspicion of the other employees when a duplicate of a check she tried to copy jammed in the copy machine and was subsequently discovered by the employees. The Assistant Director in the Office reacted by placing the financial files in a locked cabinet. This made it impossible for Cornelius to return a file of documents she had previously taken home." *White House Management Review, supra* note 1, 6. Of course, it was not "impossible" for Cornelius to return the documents, just impossible for her to do so without also acknowledging to her Travel Office colleagues her involvement in surreptitious activities.

[68]According to the *GAO Report, supra* note3, 53:

[S]he saw documents indicating that numerous checks written to cash were signed and endorsed by the Director and Deputy Director, invoices that seemed to be for trips for the Bush political campaign, large fluctuations in the cash balance at the local bank, and an apparent failure to reconcile estimated bills with the invoices for actual costs and services provided.

[69]Ibid.

[70]The following information comes from documents publicly revealed by the House Committee on Government Reform and Oversight at the October 24, 1995 hearing on the Travel Office firings. The hearing was reported in Kellman, "Travelgate signs point to Hillary," *Washington Times*, A1 (Oct. 25, 1995); Schmidt & Locy, "Papers Detail Clinton Friend's Contract Push," *Washington Post*, A4 (Oct. 25, 1995); and Associated Press, "Clinton and Hollywood Producer Met on Contract, a Memo Shows," *New York Times*, B6 (Oct. 25, 1995).

[71]Chronology prepared by House Government Reform and Oversight Committee staff (Oct. 24, 1995)(hereafter, *HGRO Chron.*), 7.

[72]Watkins believes this meeting was held on May 10. *Minority Study, supra* note 4, Attachment B, n.16.

[73]*White House Management Review, supra* note 1, 7.

[74]That day Martens, who had no other association with the White House, applied for a White House pass. *GAO Report, supra* note 3, 56. His application noted that he "would be reporting to 'Harry Thomason/ Darnell Martens'." Watkins told the Director of White House Security that Martens was helping Thomason, and Martens was issued a pass that is provided to volunteers. There was considerable confusion about what Martens was expected to do, and even whether he had obtained a pass. *Minority Study, supra* note 4, Attachment B, 3 (GAO notes of interview of Craig Livingstone). In fact, Martens received a pass that same day. *HGRO Chron. supra* note 71, 8.

[75]*HGRO Chron. supra* note 71, 9.

[76]Brock reports that Cornelius retrieved these documents from home on the 13th, to persuade the FBI

that grounds existed for a criminal investigation. *Brock, supra* note 5, 34.

[77]*GAO Report, supra* note 3, 53. In *On The Edge, supra* note 5, 177, Elizabeth Drew presents a slightly different chronology, one that involves Foster in the matter before his May 12 meeting with Watkins:

> After Martens was turned away by Dale, Thomason raised the question of the travel office with both the President and Mrs. Clinton. . . . According to White House staff members, after Thomason complained to Mrs. Clinton, she asked both McLarty and Vince Foster to look into the matter. On May 12, Watkins took the matter to Foster . . . .

Thomason's conversation with the First lady and her charge to McLarty and Foster are not mentioned in either the White House Management Review or the GAO Report.

[78]*White House Management Review, supra* note 1, 11.

[79]*GAO Report, supra* note3, 66.

[80]World Wide sent one agent on May 13 or 14 and several others on May 19, the day the Travel Office staff was fired. Cornelius told GAO that Watkins directed her to make the second call. *GAO Report, supra* note 3, 66-67.

[81]David Brock wrote that Foster asked Kennedy to contact the FBI. *Brock, supra* note 5, 34.

[82]*White House Management Review, supra* note 1, 7.

[83]*White House Management Review, supra* note 1, 8. See also, Isikoff & Devroy, "FBI Says White House Invoked IRS," *Washington Post*, A1 (June 11, 1993)(reporting on findings of "internal FBI summary" of the Travel Office matter)(also noting that IRS local office, based on news reports of allegations against UltrAir, began unannounced audit of the firm on May 21, prompting suspicion of White House influence). The White House Management Review concluded that "there is no evidence that the White House contacted the Internal Revenue Service in connection with either the Travel Office or any charter company engaged by the Travel Office." *White House Management Review, supra* note 1, 19. The *GAO Report, supra* note 3, 64-66, noted that the IRS Inspection Service and the Treasury Department's Inspector General also uncovered no evidence of any White House communication to the IRS. See also, Isikoff, "IRS Finds No White House Role in Audit of Air Charter Firm," *Washington Post*, A11 (June 17, 1993).

[84]Apple told GAO that Kennedy was "nebulous and cryptic," not even identifying the Travel Office as the locus of the problem. *GAO Report, supra* note 3, 59.

[85]Kennedy recalled that he indicated only that Foster and Watkins were "looking over his shoulder." *White House Management Review, supra* note 1, 8.

[86]*GAO Report, supra* note3, 60.

[87]Ibid.

[88]The next day, May 14, Joe Gangloff, the Acting Chief of the Justice Department's Public Integrity Section "agreed there was predication for an investigation." *GAO Report, supra* note 3, 61. In response to a question on this point from Senator Dole, the FBI stated: "The final determination that there was sufficient predication to initiate a criminal investigation was made by Mr. Gangloff after being briefed by SSA Carl." Letter to Honorable Bob Dole, at 4 (June 28, 1993).

[89]*White House Management Review, supra* note 1, 9.

[90]The *White House Management Review, supra* note 1, 9, reveals two conversations between Foster and the First Lady on May 13 relating to the Travel Office, both of them initiated by Mrs. Clinton's interest in the matter. Foster reportedly informed Mrs. Clinton of the developments with Peat Marwick and the FBI, and most likely asked for the First Lady's views on whether the FBI should be present during the Peat Marwick review.

[91]*White House Management Review, supra* note 1, 9.

[92]Cornelius had been called by a reporter on May 11 and asked if she is a cousin of the President. Cornelius told Eller about this call, and her suspicion that a Travel Office employee gave this fact to the reporter. Eller in December 1992 had told reporters "that there were unspecified 'problems' in the travel office and that he would not be surprised if some people got fired." *Brock, supra* note 5, 32.

[93]*Minority Study, supra* note 4, Attachment C, 4.

[94]"Mr. Eller said that **since the decision to fire them had been made**, he was advising that such a decision be carried out as soon as possible." *Minority Study, supra* note 4, Attachment C, 4 (GAO notes of interview of Jeff Eller)(emphasis added).

[95]*GAO Report, supra* note 3, 54. While the Peat Marwick review was ongoing, the Travel Office employees were told falsely that the Peat Marwick team was participating in a White House management review of the Travel Office, as part of Vice President Gore's National Performance Review (NPR). See *GAO Report, supra* note 3, 57, 26 ("[A] representative of the Vice President's office informed us that, while the review of the Travel Office was consistent with the objectives of the NPR, it was not conducted under the auspices of the NPR.").

[96]This document was released at the October 1995 House hearing.

[97]*GAO Report, supra* note 3, 53-54. Kennedy also received periodic briefings throughout the review, and passed on such information in two calls to FBI agent Wade on May 14, and in a meeting with FBI agents

Wade and Bowie held at the White House on Saturday, May 15, at Kennedy's request. Patsy Thomasson and Larry Herman of Peat Marwick were also present at this meeting. *Brock, supra* note 5, 36 (quoting from June 28, 1993, letter from FBI Director Sessions to Senator Dole, 6).

[98]*GAO Report, supra* note 3, 53-54. Mrs. Clinton acknowledged to GAO (in writing) only that Watkins had told her "his office was taking appropriate action."

[99]There is some question whether these White House staff assisted Peat Marwick or were present on their own. The *White House Management Review* stated, *supra* note 1, 9, that the Peat Marwick team was "accompanied by a team from Watkins' office, who had been routinely reviewing the management practices of various White House offices as part of an effort that would later be incorporated into the Vice President's National Performance Review." A Peat Marwick official told GAO that the White House did not participate in its review, and two White House staff members said they interviewed Billy Dale on May 15 only "in the event they needed to run the Office." *GAO Report, supra* note 3, 57. At a March 25, 1994 Senate hearing, however, Patsy Thomasson stated, "The process of review of the Travel Office was done by a group of staff from the White House as well as assisted by Peat Marwick for the financial side and for doing numbers." *Brock, supra* note 5, 36, 4.

[100]*White House Management Review, supra* note 1, 10. In fact, Watkins' decision was made much earlier, according to Jeff Eller as well as the head of the Peat Marwick review team, Larry Herman.

> This surprised him [Herman] because the normal course of events in this type of situation is that he would issue a report to the client before taking action. However, in this case the decision was made before the issue date.

Minority Study, supra note 4, Attachment C, 4 (GAO notes of interview of Larry Herman).

[101]*White House Management Review, supra* note 1, Exhibit H.

[102]The staff of the new Travel Section would consist of three employees, instead of seven: Cornelius, a financial specialist, and an administrative assistant who had worked on the Clinton campaign.

[103]*White House Management Review, supra* note 1, Exhibit H.

[104]Ibid.

[105]*White House Management Review, supra* note 1, Exhibit B, 1 (emphasis added).

[106]Two of the seven employees were out of town on the 19th, and learned of their dismissal from news reports. *GAO Report, supra* note 3, 46, 1. Neither the White House nor the GAO interviewed any of the Travel Office employees for their report.

[107]*Brock, supra* note 5, 30. Billy Dale had attempted to meet with Watkins on May 17 to announce his intention to resign, but Watkins put off the discussion for a later time. *White House Management Review, supra* note 1, 10.

[108]*Minority Study, supra* note 4, Attachment C, 4 (GAO notes of interview of David Watkins).

[109]*Minority Study, supra* note 4, Attachment C, 4 (GAO notes of interview of David Watkins); *GAO Report, supra* note 3, 46; *Brock, supra* note 5, 30.

[110]Ibid.

[111]York, "Travelgate Survivors," *American Spectator*, 22, 24 (Nov. 1995).

[112]*White House Management Review, supra* note 1, 11.

[113]Watkins said that he passed on the instructions from the Counsel's office to Jeff Eller, who would pass them on to Myers, but didn't reach Myers "in time." *White House Management Review, supra* note 1, 11. But Jeff Eller told GAO that two sets of talking points were prepared, one with a reference to the FBI and one without. "Mr. Watkins gave him the copy with the reference to the FBI investigation. Mr. Eller was not instructed by Mr. Watkins to let Ms. Myers know about a second version and Mr. Eller didn't even know that she had a copy of the earlier version (with reference to the FBI)." *Minority Study, supra* note 4, Attachment F, 2 (GAO notes of interview of Jeff Eller). The *White House Management Review, supra* note 1, 18, mentioned that Eller had prepared an earlier draft of the talking points, but that this draft also mentioned the FBI investigation.

[114]*Minority Study, supra* note 4, Attachment F, 2 (GAO notes of interview of Dee Dee Myers). The White House Management Review did not mention this contact.

[115]*White House Management Review, supra* note 1, 11. Elizabeth Drew, *On The Edge*, 75, incorrectly puts Myers' disclosure (she notes only one) **after** the briefing in which she announced the firing of the Travel Office staff.

[116]*Minority Study, supra* note 4, Attachment F, 3. Despite these public denials, the *Washington Post* on May 20 reported that "Dee Dee Myers said . . . the financial mismanagement . . . was serious enough to ask the FBI to investigate." Devroy & Kamen, "Longtime Travel Staff Given Walking Papers," *Washington Post*, A1 (May 20, 1993). This suggests either that one of the *Washington Post* reporters was the second reporter with whom Myers spoke before the press briefing, or that Myers contradicted herself in a later conversation with the *Washington Post*.

[117]Cornelius had called World Wide officials on the evening of May 18, asking them to meet with

Watkins the next morning.

[118]*GAO Report, supra* note 3, 61. The FBI's press release makes sense only with the knowledge that the White House had been telling reporters of the FBI's involvement. FBI Director Sessions, in a June 2, 1993, letter to Senator Dole, (page) 2, stated that the May 19 FBI press release was prepared "in response to the large number of press inquiries generated as a result of the announcement[,]" referring to the White House's disclosure that the FBI had been called into investigate. Sessions erroneously thought the White House disclosure occurred at the daily press briefing.

[119]Ibid., 62, 33.

[120]*White House Management Review, supra* note 1, 12.

[121]According to Bernard Nussbaum, the three White House Counsel's office participants in the meeting, which was called by Stephanopoulos and held in his office, did not know that Collingwood or any other FBI official would be present. Drew, *On The Edge*, 180.

[122]*White House Management Review, supra* note 1, 12

[123]*GAO Report, supra* note 3, 62 (brackets in original)(emphasis added).

[124]*GAO Report, supra* note 3, 62 (the language added in response to Dee Dee Myers' request is highlighted). In light of the White House Management Review and the GAO Report (based in part on an interview of Collingwood), FBI Director Sessions' statement that "Mr. Collingwood did not believe that anyone either asked or suggested that he change the response" is not credible. Letter to Honorable Bob Dole, 12 (June 28, 1993).

[125]At this briefing, Stephanopoulos also released the Peat Marwick report. Drew, *On The Edge*, 179-80.

[126]David Brock summarized that the FBI over three days wrote four versions of press guidance that "changed subtly to foster the misleading impression of a relationship between the audit and the investigation." *Brock, supra* note 5, 71. A few days later, President Clinton also conveyed this false impression, stating in an interview:

[T]he FBI was called in to look at the auditor's report, not to accuse any of these people of doing anything criminal but because there were sufficient questions raised that there had to be a review of it.

[T]he report in the auditor's findings made us believe that someone at least ought to look into this and clear the air. And that's all we were trying to do."

31 *Weekly Compilation of Presidential Documents* 961 (May 27, 1993).

[127]Devroy & Isikoff, "Clinton Staff Bypassed Reno to FBI," *Washington Post*, A1 (May 25, 1993).

[128]*GAO Report, supra* note 3, 67.

[129]*White House Management Review, supra* note 1, 13; *GAO Report, supra* note 3, 68-69 (American Express under contract as of May 1994; five-year contract was to be awarded by September 1994).

[130]Bedard, "White House to hire back 'Travelgate 5'," *Washington Times*, A1 (Aug. 5, 1993); Marcus & Devroy, "White House Backs Off on Firings of 5," *Washington Post*, A1 (May 26, 1993). George Stephanopoulos attempted, without success, to engage in some revisionism by arguing that the employees "had not really been fired but had been on administrative leave all along[.]"

[131]Ibid. Director Billy Dale and Deputy Director Gary Wright were reportedly still under investigation. Wright eventually retired. Dale was indicted, tried, and acquitted.

[132]Ibid. Marcus, "White House Seeks Jobs for Travel Aides," *Washington Post*, A16 (Aug. 6, 1993).

In October 1993, Congress passed an amendment to the DOT Fiscal Year 1994 appropriation bill to provide $150,000 to pay for legal fees incurred by the five Travel Office employees who were not considered subjects of the criminal investigation. Pub. L. No. 103-122, 107 Stat. 1198 (Oct. 27, 1993). See Devroy, "Cost of Clinton Travel Firings Still Growing," *Washington Post*, A21 (Oct. 7, 1993)(noting that the White House did not oppose the amendment). According to Senator Dole, each of the five employees, none of whom made over $60,000 a year, had incurred legal bills of $30,000 or more. Ibid.

[133]Devroy & Marcus, "Volunteer Travel Aide Got $1,400," *Washington Post*, A1 (June 2, 1993).

[134]*White House Management Review, supra* note 1, 13; *GAO Report, supra* note 3, 68, 71-72.

[135]Bedard, "White House to hire back 'Travelgate 5'," *Washington Times*, A1 (Aug. 5, 1993).

[136]David Broder criticized the fact that the President did not fire anyone. Broder, "Talk Is Not Enough," *Washington Post*, A21 (July 14, 1993).

[137]*Minority Study, supra* note 4, Attachment J; *York, supra* note 5, 20.

[138]*Minority Study, supra* note 4, Attachment J, 1 (transcript of White House press briefing). See also, Devroy, "Clinton Friends Cited in Travel Staff Purge," *Washington Post*, A1 (July 3, 1994) ("McLarty said he had reprimanded four White House aides who handled the situation, but none lost their jobs, ranks or pay.").

[139]Ibid.

[140]"The reprimands were given orally by Mr. McLarty and me." Hearings before Subcommittee on Treasury, Postal Service, and General Government Appropriations of House Committee on Appropriations

concerning appropriations for Fiscal Year 1995, 103rd Cong., 2d Sess. 772 (answer to question for the record)(Comm. Print 1994), quoted in *Minority Study*, *supra* note 4, Attachment J, 1-2; Ibid., 709 ("We did it orally and Mr. Kennedy was one of the ones we reprimanded at the time.")(testimony of Leon Panetta).

[141]*Minority Study*, *supra* note 4, Attachment J, 2. McLarty added that Panetta "met with each of the four individually about the reprimands."

[142]Eller did meet with McLarty to protest the criticism of his conduct.

[143]*Minority Study*, *supra* note 4, Attachment J, 2-3 (GAO notes of interviews of Catherine Cornelius, Jeff Eller, and William Kennedy, respectively).

[144]*York*, 25.

[145]Devroy & Marcus, "Golf Outing Sinks White House Aide," *Washington Post*, A1 (May 27, 1994). See Chapter Eighteen.

[146]Locy, "Travel Unit's Ousted Head Is Indicted," *Washington Post*, A1 (Dec. 8, 1994); Bedard, "Fired travel chief indicted," *Washington Times*, A3 (Dec. 8, 1994); Associated Press, "Jury Indicts Travel Aide For President," *New York Times*, B18 (Dec. 8, 1994).

[147]Fourteen of these checks are beyond the statute of limitations, and thus were not technically part of the indictment. Ibid., A6.

[148]Bedard, "Ousted travel director seeks Foster papers," *Washington Times*, A1 (Dec. 16, 1994).

[149]Bedard, "Ex-official faces Travelgate indictment," *Washington Times*, A1, A13 (Dec. 5, 1994).

[150]Bedard, "Colleagues blast Travelgate charges against ex-director," *Washington Times*, A9 (Dec. 9, 1994).

[151]Bedard, "Foster troubled by Travelgate firings," *Washington Times*, A1, A8 (July 28, 1995).

[152]Ibid. Locy, "Foster Journal Shows Worry About Travel Office," *Washington Post*, A8 (July 29, 1995).

[153]Bedard, "Ousted travel director seeks Foster papers," *Washington Times*, A1 (Dec. 16, 1994); Locy, "White House Travel Records Sought in Travel Office Case," *Washington Post*, A33 (Dec. 16, 1994).

[154]Bedard, "White House accused of Travelgate cover-up," *Washington Times*, A1 (July 29, 1995).

[155]*United States v. Billy R. Dale*, No. 94-469, Defendant's Supplemental Memorandum To The Court On The Issue Of Document Production, The Defense Theory And The Scheduling Of The Trial (Aug. 3, 1995).

[156]It was revealed during the trial that both of Judge Kessler's law clerks had served internships in the White House Counsel's office during the Clinton Administration. Although neither was apparently involved in the Travel Office matter, Clarissa Cerda was the official supervisor of one of the interns. "The clerk in the travel office case," *Washington Times*, A16 (Nov. 2, 1995); "Travelgate trials," *Washington Times*, A18 9Nov. 8, 1995).

[157]Citing *United States v. Poindexter*, 727 F. Supp. 1470, 1480 (D.D.C. 1989).

[158]*United States v. Billy R. Dale*, No. 94-469 (D.D.C.), Memorandum-Order, at 2-3 (Aug. 7, 1995).

[159]Ibid., 4. Labeling this case a "rather straightforward embezzlement case" suggested the district court's disinclination to believe Dale's defense, if not outright hostility to the defense's theory. The unique nature of the White House Travel Office operation alone made this case other than "straightforward."

[160]Locy, "Ex-Travel Office Chief Is Denied Records," *Washington Post*, A4 (Aug. 9, 1995)("major setback").

[161]Locy, "Jury Gets Differing Pictures of Travel Office Defendant," *Washington Post*, A4 (Oct. 31, 1995); Kellman, "Dale: Aim was to help media," *Washington Times*, A3 (Oct. 31, 1995); Locy, "Government Presses Travel Office Case," *Washington Post*, A4 (Nov. 5, 1995).

[162]Locy, "Ex-White House Travel Chief Testifies He didn't Steal Funds," *Washington Post*, A12 (Nov. 8, 1995); Bedard, "Dale denies charges he stole money from travel office," *Washington Times*, A4 (Nov. 8, 1995); Bedard, "Former White House travel aide blames Fitzwater for troubles," *Washington Times*, A7 (Nov. 9, 1995); Locy, "Ex-Travel Office Director Cites Networks' Pressure," *Washington Post*, A3 (Nov. 9, 1995); Bedard, Dale tells of 'disastrous system' he used for cash in travel office," *Washington Times*, A5 (Nov. 10, 1995); Locy, "Travel Office Chief's Deposits Traced to 1985," *Washington Post*, A5 (Nov. 10, 1995).

[163]Locy, "Journalists Defend Former Travel Office Director," *Washington Post*, A4 (Nov. 7, 1995); Bedard, "Travelgate judge asks for Clinton aide's notes," *Washington Times*, A1 (Nov. 7, 1995); Locy, "Fraud Expert Doubts Motive In Travel Case," *Washington Post*, A8 (Nov. 14, 1995); Bedard, "Accountant testifies Dale financially set," *Washington Times*, A3 (Nov. 14, 1995).

[164]Locy, "Travel Office Trial Enlivened By Outburst," *Washington Post*, A12 (Nov. 2, 1995);

[165]Bedard, "Dale jury told of travel file looting," *Washington Times*, A1 (Nov. 4, 1995); Locy, "FBI Agent Says Travel Office Unsecured on Day of Firings," *Washington Post*, A8 (Nov. 4, 1995).

[166]Locy, "Fired Travel Office Director Acquitted of Embezzlement," *Washington Post*, A1 (Nov. 17, 1995); Bedard, "Travelgated jury quickly finds Dale not guilty," *Washington Times*, A1 (Nov. 17, 1995); Johnston,

"Ousted White House Travel Chief Is Cleared of Embezzlement," *New York Times*, B11 (Nov. 17, 1995).

[167]Ibid.

[168]Dale would also make a provocative witness, considering a few comments he made after his acquittal. Bedard, "Dale scores FBI, Clinton for Travelgate," *Washington Times*, A1 (Nov. 18, 1995); Locy, "Acquitted Aide Blames Clinton For Difficulties," *Washington Post*, A3 (Nov. 18, 1995).

[169]Associated Press, "Jury Indicts Travel Aide For President," *New York Times*, B18 (Dec. 8, 1994)("Ms. Cornelius and Mr. Thomason remain under investigation but are not expected to be charged, according to a Justice Department official who spoke on condition of anonymity."). See also, Associated Press, "Travel Unit Probe Looks at Celebrity," *Washington Post*, A5 (Sept. 20, 1994)(reporting grand jury subpoena issued to White House for records relating to Thomason and Martens; Thomason's lawyer, Robert Bennett, said "that based on 'conversations with the Department of Justice,' he was sure that neither is a target.").

[170]Locy, "For White House Travel Office, a Two-Year Trip of Trouble," *Washington Post*, A4 (Feb. 27, 1995)

[171]*White House Management Review, supra* note 1, 15.

[172]Ibid.

[173]The *Minority Study, supra* note 4, Attachment D, provides an excellent account of this issue.

[174]*Minority Study, supra* note 4, Attachment C, 4 (GAO notes of interview of Jeff Eller)("It was a foregone conclusion that Mr. Watkins and Ms. Thomasson had decided to fire the employees during the May 13 meeting and that they were only asking [Eller] how the matter should be handled from a media standpoint."). It is unclear whether Watkins decided to fire the Travel Office employees before or after he learned that the FBI had been persuaded by Cornelius that there was a sufficient predicate of misconduct for a criminal investigation.

[175]*Minority Study, supra* note 4, Attachment C, 4 (GAO notes of interview of Larry Herman of Peat Marwick)("This surprised him because the normal course of events in this type of situation is that he would issue a report to the client taking action. However, in this case, a decision was made before the issue date [May 17].").

[176]The extent of the First Lady's involvement was not apparent at the time of the May 19 firings, and was downplayed considerably in the White House Management Review. Drew, *On The Edge*, 178. The GAO Report was seen as revealing a greater role for her in the matter, despite the limited information contained in the White House's written responses. Labaton, "First Lady Urged Dismissals At Travel Office, Study Says," *New York Times*, B8 (May 3, 1994) ("The [GAO] report . . . goes significantly beyond a White House review last July[.] The new account depicts Mrs. Clinton as playing a more active role in the dismissals after the White House accused the workers of mismanagement.").

But the *Minority Study, supra* note 4, Attachment K, 3-4, criticized GAO for accepting written responses prepared by the Counsel's office to questions posed to Mrs. Clinton. "[H]er responses yielded few conclusive answers, and actually raised additional questions in some instances. . . . Because GAO did not follow up on [] possible additional conversations involving the First Lady, . . . or [did not] inquire about any Travel Office discussions involving either the President or First Lady prior to May 12th, the agency was unable to determine the roles of either the President or the First Lady[.]"; See also *York*, 22.

[177]*GAO Report, supra* note 3, 53-54. See also text at note 96, *supra*. (First Lady told Watkins that "[w]e need our people in—we need the slots [.]"

[178]On May 27 Clinton said:

Every operation at the White House was reviewed, because I said I was going to cut the White House staff by 25 percent. . . . The bottom line is if we can run an office with three that they were taking seven to run, and we can save 25 percent off a trip because we have competitive bidding when they didn't competitive bidding, the press saves money and the taxpayers save money. That was my only objection.

31 *Weekly Compilation of Presidential Documents* 960-61 (May 27, 1993).

[179]This is from GAO's interview of Watkins; none of the Travel Office employees was interviewed at the request of the Justice Department, but they told the *American Spectator* that Watkins had referred to the Peat Marwick findings. See text at note 111 *supra*.

[180]Devroy, "Staff Denies Clinton Ally Had Role in Firings," *Washington Post*, A7 (May 21, 1993).

[181]*Minority Study, supra* note 4, Attachment D, 3-4 (transcript of White House press briefing, July 2, 1993)(emphasis added). GAO notes of a September 1993 interview of Dee Dee Myers do not help matters, either:

There was no "clear" or "objective" answer about whether the travel office investigation was part of the National Performance Review. Mr. Watkins believes that the travel office "came to his attention" through the performance review.

Ibid., 5 (GAO notes of interview of Dee Dee Myers). Given Cornelius's memoranda, Watkins' conversations with Thomason and Martens, and the "fact" that the NPR team began on May 14, it is preposterous to say that Watkins learned of the travel office problems through the NPR.

Patsy Thomasson and William Kennedy also told GAO that Peat Marwick's review was part of the NPR; Thomasson also said that the NPR team did a separate review. Ibid., 5.

[182]Ibid., 5 (GAO notes of interview of Brian Foucart).

[183]Ibid., 5-6 (emphasis added).

[184]*GAO Report, supra* note 3, 57 (emphasis added).

[185]31 *Weekly Compilation of Presidential Documents* 909 (May 19, 1993) (emphasis added).

[186]Ibid., 929 (May 21, 1993).

[187]Ibid., 947 (May 25, 1993) (emphasis added).

[188]Ibid., 956 (May 26, 1993) (emphasis added).

[189]Footnote added. Actually, the recommendations came only from Cornelius, Cerda, Martens and Thomason.

[190]31 *Weekly Compilation of Presidential Documents* 961 (May 27, 1993)(emphasis added).

[191]"Travel Office (Cont'd)," *Washington Post*, A22 (May 28, 1993).

[192]*Minority Study, supra* note 4, Attachment I, 2 (transcript of Office of White House Press Secretary).

[193]18 U.S.C. 208; 5 CFR Part 2635, effective February 3, 1993.

[194]Memorandum for Stephen D. Potts, re: Ethics Issues Related to the Federal Technology Transfer Act of 1986 (Sept. 13, 1993).

[195]60 Fed. Reg. 44706 (Aug. 28, 1995).

[196]5 CFR 2640.101.

[197]60 Fed. Reg. 44707.

[198]5 CFR 2635.101(b)(7),(8),(14).

[199]5 CFR 2635.502. That section involves non-financial conflicts or potential conflicts based on a "covered relationship," which technically does not appear to apply here. But paragraph 502(a)(2) contains a residual clause providing that employees who believe that circumstances other than those contained in the section could pose an appearance problem should use the consultation and review process set forth in section 502.

[200]The Counsel's office was brought in on May 12, but only to help determine what should be done about the Travel Office employees.

[201]*White House Management Review, supra* note 1, 20 ("[H]er role in the decision-making process after she became, in effect, an 'accuser' of the Travel Office employees . . . was inappropriate."). The *White House Management Review, supra* note 1, 21, also criticized Watkins for placing a biased, inexperienced Cornelius in the Travel Office to look for evidence of misconduct.

[202]Ibid. ("Eller's participation in the decision-making process and advocacy for a decision that was in Cornelius' interest were imprudent.").

[203]*White House Management Review, supra* note 1, 20. Much later, it was reported that the White House had used World Wide Travel to make travel arrangements for the Health Care Task Force working group participants (which consisted of hundreds of persons), up until the Travel Office controversy in late May 1993, even though the White House Travel Office had previously made arrangements for the travel of non-Government persons whose expenses would be covered by the Government. Bedard, "Health task force used 'Travelgate' firm," *Washington Times*, A1 (Oct. 6, 1994); Snow, "Not the last to succumb," *Washington Times*, A20 (Oct. 9, 1994). Apparently, Cornelius had written a memorandum giving World Wide authority to issue tickets when White House Travel Office employees were unavailable. Ibid., A20. The White House enlisted World Wide without engaging in competitive bidding. "Maybe we should just call it White-House-gate," *Washington Times*, A20 (Oct. 10, 1994).

[204]See Chapters Three (The First Lady's Conflict of Interest), 17-19, 22-25; Four (The Health Care Task Force), 28-31; and Six (The President's Use of Informal Advisers), *passim*.

[205]OGE Informal Advisory Letter 81 X 8 (Feb. 3, 1981), citing B. Manning, *Federal Conflict of Interest Law* 26-30 (1964).

[206]In the Bush White House, this responsibility was discharged by an Assistant to the President, Sig Rogich.

[207]*GAO Report, supra* note 3, 55. The *Minority Study, supra* note 4, Attachment B, 5 (GAO notes of interview of Rita Lewis), notes that Thomason "was asked [by the Political Affairs office] to provide advice on 'how to use the White House better as a physical plant.'" After several meetings, Thomason submitted a five-page report. Thomason also continued to work on winding down matters from the Inaugural for about a month after he got his pass. Ibid., 6 (GAO notes of interview of Craig Livingstone).

[208]Thomason was given a blue pass, because the *White House Management Review, supra* note 1, 21, states that Thomason was afforded "open passage throughout the White House complex."

[209]*GAO Report, supra* note 3, 56.

[210]*White House Management Review, supra* note 1, 28. The new White House policy on the issuance of passes to and access to the White House complex by nongovernment employees was adopted on September 16, 1993, although the text of the policy was not revealed until a March 18, 1994 letter from White House

Counsel Cutler to Representative Frank Wolf. The new policy is discussed in Chapter Five.

[211]2 Op.O.L.C. 20 (Feb. 24, 1977).

[212]OGE Informal Advisory Letter 82 X 22 (July 9, 1982).

[213]There are conflicting accounts whether the White House Counsel's office made any such determination. Two White House officials told GAO that the Counsel's office had refrained from making any such determination, either during Thomason's stint at the White House or subsequently. *Minority Study, supra* note 4, Attachment B, at 6-7 (GAO notes of interviews of Bernard Nussbaum and Neil Eggleston). But previously, the *Washington Post* had reported: "Asked if the White House examined this issue, a senior official there said the lawyer in charge of ethics, Beth Nolan, looked into it and concluded Thomason was not covered by the law." Kamen, "White House May Clamp Down on Passes," *Washington Post*, A19 (July 9, 1993). The official did not say when Nolan had made this determination, or whether she had been fully apprised of the nature and level of Thomason's participation in White House activities.

[214]*GAO Report, supra* note 3, 49.

[215]Ibid., 55.

[216]*White House Management Review, supra* note 1, 21. Thus, the White House Management Review criticized as "not a good practice" permitting Thomason to "work on problems outside the scope of his . . . assignment." This criticism was directed at the White House generally, not McLarty, Watkins or Thomasson, who might have been considered Thomason's supervisor.

[217]George Stephanopoulos, after talking with Thomason, said on May 20 that TRM did not stand to gain business from the Travel Office. But it appears that Thomason understood the question to be whether Thomason "had any financial interest in any company bidding on White House work," and answered "no" because TRM was not an air carrier, but a consulting firm. *White House Management Review, supra* note 1, 19.

The story put out by Martens and Thomason when Martens' memo was released to the press on May 21 was that "they were acting on behalf of charter companies they worked with, firms that complained the travel office long had shut them out of competition for the business of transporting the White House press corps on its travels with previous presidents." But as the *Washington Post* pointed out, assisting air charter companies was a part of TRM's business! Devroy & Marcus, "Clinton Friend's Memo Sought Business," *Washington Post*, A1 (May 22, 1993).

[218]5 CFR 2635.402(a).

[219]5 CFR 2635.402(b)(1)(i) and (ii).

[220]Drew, *On The Edge*, 183. Thomason told the *Washington Post* in the immediate wake of the Travel Office controversy:

I do find it surprising that a person who was as instrumental as I was in the Clinton campaign cannot pick up a phone in the White House and ask for information for people. . . If President Bush was in office, I would do the same thing if I had this access.

Devroy, "Travel Office Flap Cited as Evidence of Need for White House Staff Changes," *Washington Post*, A6 (May 27, 1993).

[221]*White House Management Review, supra* note 1, 11. See also, *Brock, supra* note 5, 79 ("On whose authority Martens made this rather spectacular offer of a White House job to his girlfriend is not known.").

[222]See, for example, "The Missing Voice," *Washington Post*, A18 (May 26, 1993); "Travel Office (Cont'd)," *Washington Post*, A22 (May 28, 1993); "The travel office controversy isn't over," *Washington Times*, F2 (July 12, 1993).

[223]This account comes from the *White House Management Review*, at 9, 12-13, 16-19, unless otherwise noted.

[224]*GAO Report, supra* note 3, 59.

[225]Ibid. The White House Management Review did not discuss this communication.

[226]*GAO Report, supra* note 3, 60.

[227]*GAO Report, supra* note 3, 60.

[228]*GAO Report, supra* note 3, 61; *Minority Study, supra* note 4, Attachment G, 2.

[229]The *White House Management Review, supra* note 1, 17, and the *GAO Report, supra* note 3, 59 and 63, agreed; GAO called it "reasonable."

[230]*Minority Study, supra* note 3, Attachment G, 1.

[231]Ibid. (GAO notes of interview of Jim Bourke).

[232]GAO found that Kennedy's "secrecy" in keeping pertinent information from Bourke (as well as in two subsequent conversations with the FBI) created "some confusion." *GAO Report, supra* note 3, 58.

[233]*Shaheen report, supra* note 5, 17. The OPR report was released by the House Government and Oversight Committee at its October 1995 hearing. An internal memorandum of this phone call stated that Kennedy was "adamant" that a headquarters Bureau agent visit him at the White House that morning. Ibid. 19, 23.

[234]*Minority Study, supra* note 4, Attachment G, 2 (GAO notes of interview of Tom Carl). *Shaheen report, supra* note, 29. Foran had told Kennedy the same thing during the first visit. Ibid., 23.

[235]The agents told OPR that they told the White House they would need to confer with FBI Headquar-

ters and Justice before "confirming" that sufficient predication existed. *Shaheen report, supra* note 5, 32. The agents, consistent with FBI policy, eventually did seek and obtain approval with the Department for the initiation of an investigation. The necessary approvals were obtained on May 14, before the White House used the FBI's conclusion in any public way.

[236]*GAO Report, supra* note 3, 58, agreed that Kennedy's remarks "created an inappropriate appearance of White House pressure on the FBI."

[237]*White House Management Review, supra* note 1, 17.

[238]*Minority Study, supra* note 4, Attachment G, 4 (GAO notes of interview of Jim Bourke; GAO notes of interview of Tom Carl). According to an FBI letter to Senator Dole, Bourke did not believe Kennedy was attempting to put pressure on him. "Rather, in the context of the conversation, Mr. Kennedy was expressing the need for guidance and assistance from some sources and Mr. Bourke understood the reference to IRS to mean that if the FBI decided it could not assist him, he would simply have to turn to another agency." Letter to Honorable Bob Dole (June 30, 1993)(emphasis in original). This is putting Kennedy's reference to the IRS in the most innocent light, which does not take into account that the reality that the IRS is not just another agency, it is the FBI's chief law enforcement rival.

[239]*Minority Study, supra* note 4, Attachment G, 2 (GAO notes of interview of Tom Carl). Foster told the FBI that the Peat Marwick review was part of the National Performance Review, which was not true.

[240]*Shaheen report, supra* note 5, 32-33.

[241]*Minority Study, supra* note 4, Attachment G, 3 (GAO notes of interview of Tom Carl). However, the FBI showed no regard for this concern for many days, because it did not seek to establish some control over the Travel Office records until June 10, and even then, the control provided insufficient protection against loss, destruction or tampering. Ibid., Attachment H.

[242]The *White House Management Review, supra* note 1, 18, did not criticize Kennedy or Foster for these requests. In fact, it appears the White House Management Review saw this conduct as ameliorative! The GAO Report does not even discuss this conversation. The *Minority Study*, on the other hand, found that Foster and Kennedy "did direct, and thereby interfere with, the FBI investigation[.]" Letter to Honorable John Conyers, Jr., 3. The discussion in the *Shaheen report* suggests that the FBI intentionally or by its passivity, allowed the White House to dictate whether and when the FBI would initiate a criminal investigation.

Also interesting is Kennedy's efforts to inform the FBI of information being developed in the course of the Peat Marwick review. The FBI, having been snubbed by Foster from participating in or even observing Peat Marwick's review, was given instead twice-filtered status reports.

[243]The *Minority Study, supra* note 4, Attachment G, 3 (GAO notes of interview of Tom Carl), adds that on May 19, when told of the decision to dismiss the Travel Office staff, the FBI expressed the desire that "in a perfect world" the White House employees should not be fired at that time (before the initiation of the FBI investigation), but that Kennedy said the decision had been made.

[244]*GAO Report, supra* note 3, 58. The *Shaheen report* came to the same conclusion. It also concluded that the FBI's actions in meeting with White House officials and determining the predicate for a criminal investigation were appropriate. *Shaheen report, supra* note 5, 93-98.

[245]The *Shaheen report* also did not refer to the personal interest of the only person who claimed some personal knowledge of misconduct by the Travel Office employees. When Cornelius met with Wade and Carl, she did not reveal that she was the President's cousin or that she was interested in running the Travel office herself. *Shaheen report, supra* note 5, 30-31.

[246]Kennedy so told GAO. *Minority Study, supra* note 4, Attachment G, 2.

[247]The FBI's knowledge of Cornelius's interest alone would have affected its view of her credibility. *Minority Study, supra* note 4, Attachment G, 2 (GAO notes of interview of Tom Carl).

[248]The White House Management Review stated that "[t]he FBI has a standing policy not to confirm or deny the existence of investigations." Ibid., 18. Of course, this policy is subject to exceptions. The point is, however, that the Justice Department, not the White House, should decide whether and when to reveal the existence of an investigation, and what to say about it.

[249]Ibid., 18.

[250]The *White House Management Review, supra* note 1, 18, faulted Myers for not double-checking the "propriety of making reference to a possible FBI investigation."

[251]*Minority Study, supra* note 4, Attachment F, 3-4. Myers may have in fact believed she said basically the same thing to the reporters and at the press briefing. She told one reporter that an investigation was **likely**, and she told the White House press corps that there was no investigation **at this time**. But the way in which she responded to questions indicates that she was attempting to backtrack during the press briefing after she had been told that the existence of the FBI investigation should not have been disclosed. The cat, however, was out of the bag, as the FBI knew that afternoon, and the readers of the *Washington Post* learned the next morning.

The *Minority Study, supra* note 4, Attachment E, pointed out that Dee Dee Myers denied to GAO that she ever had any contact with Darnell Martens, when in fact she had at least two contacts with him. Myers told GAO that she was "surprised" to be shown the February memorandum written by Martens in which he recounted his phone call with Myers and stated that she had told him (and Thomason) that she saw no reason why TRM could not compete for the air charter business. Although it is clear that Myers' statement to GAO was false, there is no apparent reason why Myers would lie about this, given her candor at a May 21 press briefing about her invitation to Martens to come to Washington to handle press inquiries after the firings. Most likely, Myers assumed the GAO question related to pre-May 19 contacts, and perhaps Myers had forgotten about Martens' February call to her.

[252]Ibid., 18-19. It also acknowledged that it was a mistake for the White House to "seek ... the FBI statement, which it subsequently released."

[253]Ibid., 19. Similarly, FBI Director Sessions noted that on May 21, apparently before Collingwood was summoned to the White House, the FBI in response to media inquiries "began confirming that criminal investigations are carefully governed by Attorney General guidelines and that the threshold for conducting a criminal investigation had been met, i.e., there was a basis for the FBI to conduct a criminal investigation." Letter to Honorable Bob Dole, 2 (June 2, 1993). Thus, if Judge Sessions' account is true, Collingwood agreed to revise his press response to state only that which he had previously confirmed to reporters.

[254]See "The Missing Voice," *Washington Post*, A18 (May 26, 1993)("It looks as if the FBI logo was being used by the White House as a political shield. . . . [T]he apparent muscling of the FBI to put a stronger gloss on the case (even as its director fights and is beholden to the White House to keep his job) was wrongest of all.").

[255]*White House Management Review, supra* note 1, 2.

[256]This is made clear by a review of GAO interviews of the FBI officials, which were brought to light in the Minority Study, and later publicized in the *American Spectator*.

[257]*Minority Study, supra* note 4, Attachment H, 1 (per a written response of Patsy Thomasson to GAO, "[t]he FBI and White House Office of Records Management began taking custody of the Travel Office records of June 10, 1993 and substantially completed the process on June 17, 1993.")

[258]*Minority Study, supra* note 4, Attachment H, 2 (GAO notes of interview of Joe Gangloff). FBI approval was required for any White House access to the documents.

[259]See also *York*, 21-22.

[260]Bedard, "New reports wide probe of Travelgate," *Washington Times*, A1 (May 17, 1995). Billy Dale's attorney argued that a senior unidentified White House official (other than Cornelius) took Travel Office documents from the office. Ibid., A12.

There was also some question whether any relevant Travel Office records were in Vince Foster's office and removed from that office following his death on July 20, 1993. GAO did not find any evidence to support the conclusion that Foster's office had any such records other than a letter to GAO some years ago complaining about the White House Travel Office during the Reagan Administration. *Minority Study, supra* note 4, Attachment H, 3 (notation of Nancy Kingsbury of GAO, appended to GAO notes of interview of Bernard Nussbaum). However, in July 1995, it was revealed that a notebook Foster maintained on the Travel Office matter was found in his briefcase during the July 22, 1993 search and kept in the White House Counsel's office. Thus, GAO was not privy to this document.

[261]Ibid., 1 (GAO notes of interview of Catherine Cornelius). Cornelius apparently used these documents on May 13, when she met with FBI agents.

[262]*Minority Study, supra* note 4, Attachment H 1-2.

[263]Ibid., 3 (GAO notes of interview of Brian Foucart).

[264]One report states that the locks were changed the weekend before May 19 (May 15-16). If so, and if Thomasson had access to the office on May 17 or 18, she must also have had a key to the office.

[265]Drew, *On The Edge*, 179 ("However valid the criticisms of the travel office were, the matter couldn't have been handled worse. The picture that was drawn was of cronyism and looseness with the truth."

[266]Drew, *On The Edge*, 183 ("The report was relatively tough, but it left some things, and some names, out."). Drew noted, 178, that Mrs. Clinton's "real interest in the matter" was not known at the time. Notwithstanding the White House Management Review's gentle treatment of the First Lady, she nevertheless complained that it was too hard on the White House. Thus, according to Drew, in December 1993 when McLarty pushed John Podesta, who had drafted much of the White House Management Review, for the position of Deputy Chief of Staff to replace the departing Roy Neel, "Mrs. Clinton's displeasure with Podesta's zeal in looking into the travel office affair came back to keep him from getting this slot." Ibid., 347.

[267]Drew, *On The Edge*, 183. At the time, Foster expressed general displeasure at the White House Management Review, and specifically took issue with the relative blame the Review (and the media) placed on Kennedy vis-a-vis himself. *Shaheen report, supra* note 5, 82-92.

[268]United States Department of Justice, *Principles of Federal Prosecution*, 6 (July 1980).

Chapter Six

¹"[T]he term 'special Government employee' shall mean an officer or employee of the executive . . . branch of the United States Government . . ., who is retained, designated, appointed, or employed to perform, with or without compensation, for not to exceed one hundred and thirty days during any period of three hundred and sixty-five consecutive days, temporary duties either on a full-time or intermittent basis[.]" 18 U.S.C. 202(a).

²18 U.S.C. 208(a); 5 CFR 2635.402(a).

³5 CFR 2634.904(b). Some SGEs, by virtue of their rate of pay or significant responsibilities, could be required to file a public financial disclosure report. See 5 CFR 2634.202.

⁴Executive Order 12,674 (as amended), sec. 101(h); 5 CFR 2635.101(b)(8).

⁵18 U.S.C. 207(c), (d), (f).

⁶*Putting People First: A Strategy for Change*, 23-25 (Times Books, 1992). A paragraph entitled "Stopping the Revolving Door" previewed the contents of what would be Executive Order 12,834. Ibid., 26.

⁷29 *Weekly Compilation of Presidential Documents* 77 (Jan. 20, 1993). Chapter Fifteen of this study contains a discussion of the revolving door laws and President Clinton's executive order.

⁸Hereafter cited as *Agenda* and *On The Edge*. These books do not tell the complete story of the pervasive access and influence of informal advisers to President Clinton, because both were published before Dick Morris became a regular fixture in the White House.

⁹Garland & Walczak, "It's The Money, Stupid," *Business Week*, 163 (Nov. 15, 1993)(*Business Week*); Walsh, Pound & Cohen, "Government off the books," *U.S. News & World Report*, 28 (Mar. 28, 1994).

¹⁰*Business Week supra* note 9.

¹¹An association spokeswoman said, "They hoped he would bring back a message to the President." The article did not say whether Carville did so.

¹²See also, Shepard, "Mandy? Mandy who? A consultant's yo-yo life," *Washington Times*, A9 (June 17, 1994)("When Mr. Clinton moved into the White House, Miss Grunwald moved out of Greer, Margolis & Mitchell and took the president's business with her.").

¹³*U.S. News & World Report*, *supra* note 9, 28.

¹⁴*U.S News & World Report*, *supra* note 9, 31-32. *Business Week* noted that Grunwald's firm, Grunwald, Eskew & Donilon, received $113,000 from the DNC in consulting fees covering only May and June 1993.

¹⁵Ibid., 30. It was separately reported that one phone call from Wright to the White House ensured that a meeting sought by the American Forest & Paper Products Association was arranged. Baquet, "Ex-Aide Is Now Lobbyist With White House Ties," *New York Times*, A1 (May 12, 1994).

¹⁶Baquet, "Ex-Aide Is Now Lobbyist With White House Ties," *New York Times*, A21 (May 12, 1994).

¹⁷See also Masters, "Clinton's Loose Cannon," *Washington Post*, C1, C4 (May 30, 1994)("Wright has demonstrated that she can tap straight into Bill or Hillary's office at least to get her clients a hearing, even if their wishes aren't always granted. The relationship 'has been a good thing for her, for us, for our clients,' says Anne Wexler.").

¹⁸*U.S. News and World Report*, *supra* note 9, 32 (Morgan Guaranty, Isuzu, Time Warner, Cellular Telecommunications Industry Association and Prudential Insurance). The article did not state that Thomases acted as lawyer for any of these clients, much less that she contacted Mrs. Clinton or anyone else at the White House on behalf of a client of the firm.

¹⁹Romano, "The Reliable Source," *Washington Post*, D3 (Sept. 21, 1993).

²⁰*Business Week, supra* note 9.

²¹Romano, "The Reliable Source," *Washington Post*, C3 (Sept. 24, 1993). So, Thomases was expected to engage in conduct that could have posed a conflict of interest were she housed within the White House on a regular basis! Thomases' extensive communications with White House officials in the hours and days immediately after Vince Foster's death July 20, 1993, which confirmed her close relationship with the White House, were not revealed until the 1995 Senate Whitewater hearings.

²²Birnbaum, "Ickes, Clinton Insider and Puerto Rico Advocate, Shows Not All Who Lobby Must Wait in the Hall," *Wall Street Journal,* A24 (Sept. 21, 1993).

²³*Business Week*, *supra* note 9, as corrected in Dec. 13, 1993 edition.

²⁴*Agenda*, 113. Of course, whether or not Begala received pay is not dispositive of whether he was (and is) subject to the conflict-of-interest laws as a special Government employee, nor is it relevant to whether a conflict of interest existed in fact, even if not in law.

²⁵*Agenda*, 111.

²⁶*Agenda*, 112.

²⁷*On The Edge*, 50. Ibid., 65 ("Soon Begala began working full time on the economic program— mainly the marketing of it.").

²⁸Snow, "Careless security slippage throughout Clinton village," *Washington Times*, A16 (Feb. 28,

1994).

[29]Judis, "Old Master," *The New Republic*, 21, 28 (Dec. 13, 1993)(noting Robert Rubin's invitation to both Begala and Carville to attend NEC meetings).

[30]The index of *Agenda*, 338, carries the following separate entry for "Begala, Paul: ... in White House meetings, 93-94, 131, 142, 144, 164-65, 178, 238-240, 259, 264-65, 311."

[31]*Agenda*, 138 (speech to Joint Session of Congress, February 17, 1993); 266 (speech to Congressional Democrats, July 20, 1993); 284 (speech to Nation from Oval Office, early August 1993; Begala and two other speechwriters worked on draft).

[32]In fact, Begala once confronted Presidential counselor David Gergen, who had provided the President directly with his own version of the beginning for a speech, informing Gergen that although he would work with him in the future, he would not trust him. *Agenda*, 284-85.

[33]*Agenda*, 119. *U.S. News & World Report*, *supra* note 9, 30, estimated that Carville had delivered seventy speeches in about fourteen months, getting upwards of $20,000 per appearance.

[34]*Agenda*, 171-72 (Apr. 20, 1993 (two memos)); 226-27 (June 1993, "Strategic Rethinking"); 242-43 (July 2, 1993); 315 (Aug. 11, 1993, "Journey"). Also, the January 31, 1993 memorandum from Begala and Grunwald included input from Carville and Greenberg.

[35]*On The Edge*, 123-24.

[36]Ibid., 124.

[37]Ibid., 125.

[38]Ibid., 260.

[39]*On The Edge*, 124. Drew added that the consultants believed that the White House staff played "too much of an 'inside' game, that they had been co-opted by Washington."

[40]*Agenda*, 247 (discussing July 3, 1993 meeting in White House solarium).

[41]*Agenda*, 257 (discussing same meeting).

[42]*On The Edge*, 347.

[43]A more complete discussion of Harry Thomason's role in the Travel Office firings is contained in Chapter Five.

[44]Engleberg, "Democrats' New Overseer Is Everybody's Mr. Inside," *New York Times*, A1 (Aug. 19, 1994). Coelho was reportedly in the process of selling his interest in the company. Romano, "The Reliable Source," *Washington Post*, B3 (May 31, 1995).

[45]Birnbaum, "Coelho, Returning to Capital as Outside Adviser To Clinton, Puts His Mark on White House Moves," *Wall Street Journal*, A18 (Mar. 29, 1994);

[46]Engleberg, "Democrats' New Overseer Is Everybody's Mr. Inside," *New York Times*, A16. The *Times* also noted that Coelho solicited contributions for the Clintons' Legal Expense Trust.

[47]The *Journal* noted the Coelho was not alone among outside consultants. The *Journal*, without any reference to Carville, Begala, and the other former campaign officials, mentioned **Jody Powell**, President Carter's Press Secretary; **Kirk O'Donnell**, former aide to Tip O'Neill, **Harry McPherson**, former Johnson adviser, and **Vernon Jordan**, senior partner of the Washington law firm, Akin, Gump, Strauss, Hauer & Feld.

[48]Shalit, "The Undertaker," *New Republic*, 17, 24 (Jan. 2, 1995).

[49]Ibid., 18 (ellipses in original).

[50]Engleberg, "Democrats' New Overseer Is Everybody's Mr. Inside," *New York Times*, A1 (Aug. 19, 1994)(calling him "chief strategist and spokesman").

[51]Shalit, "The Undertaker," *New Republic*, 18 (Jan. 2, 1995).

[52]Ibid., 25. The reference to seventy days may be to Coelho's time in the White House, or the time he spent advising the President on the 1994 election campaign, albeit much of the time in the White House.

[53]Ibid., 18.

[54]Ibid., 25 (quoting Dan Levitan):

"This . . . was all as a result of my calling up Tony and saying, you know, this would be helpful to us. It's vintage Coelho. It's a win for the president, because it's a way for him to meet companies like Starbucks who are doing things synonymous with what he's trying to accomplish. It's a win for Starbucks, because it gives it visibility in Washington. And obviously, it's a win for Wertheim. What does Tony get out of that except everyone's admiration?"

[55]Devroy, "Clinton Turns to Outsiders to Amplify Message," *Washington Post*, A8 (May 20, 1995). Devroy noted other members of this group of outside advisers: Frank Greer, Robert Squier, Jody Powell, Leslie Dach, Michael Berman, Ann Lewis, and Tony Coelho. Some of these persons were expected to formally join the re-election campaign staff.

[56]Ibid. Morris's assistance to President Clinton did not sit well with Republicans. Rothenberg, "President Clinton's Controversial GOP Consultant for '96," *Roll Call*, 20 (May 25, 1995)(reporting that Morris repeatedly assured some Republicans that he was not assisting the President; "But there is little doubt that Morris has been advising Clinton for months and has a role, regardless of whether it technically is informal,

in Clinton's re-election effort.").

[57]Devroy, "Republican Adviser Stages a Quiet White House 'Coup'," *Washington Post*, A1 (June 18, 1995). See also Safire, "Deficit Epiphany," *New York Times*, A13 (June 19, 1995); Mariness, "Clinton's Elusive Adviser," *Washington Post*, A1 (June 23, 1995)(explaining Morris's long ties to Bill Clinton, dating back to 1977); Kolbert, "The Stealth Strategist Refocusing Clinton," *New York Times*, 1 (July 1, 1995).

[58]"Washington Wire," *Wall Street Journal*, A1 (June 30, 1995); see also Mitchell, "Panetta's Sure Step in High-Wire Job," *New York Times*, B12 (Aug. 17, 1995)("Mr. Panetta and Mr. Morris have now reached a detente. With Mr. Clinton's blessings, the elusive consultant has been incorporated into the formal staff structure."). According to an account in the *New Republic*:

> Panetta went to Bill Clinton recently to insist that political strategist Dick Morris be brought into some kind of staff structure, instead of allowed to steer policy from afar. Clinton agreed, and Morris didn't fight it. To seal the deal, Panetta's people issued a memo announcing that meetings with Morris would be made through the chief of staff's office.

Cooper, "The Explanation," *New Republic*, 16 (Aug. 21 & 28, 1995).

[59]Kamen, "Morris and the Message," *Washington Post*, A25 (July 28, 1995).

[60]Devroy, "Clinton Reelection Machinery in Place—Already," *Washington Post*, A9 (Aug. 3, 1995).

[61]Devroy, "Opponents' issues Drive Clinton's Political Recovery," *Washington Post*, A1 (Oct.9, 1995). (Across the government and outside the White House, many officials now "routinely refer to Morris as the de facto chief of staff, more central to Clinton than the actual chief of staff, Leon E. Panetta."); Devroy, "Clinton' Shifts Show of Influence Of Consultant," *Washington Post*, A1 (Nov. 3, 1995) (crediting Morris in large part with the President's shift in policy and pronouncements).

[62]Indeed, as noted later, one year into the Administration, a number of senior White House officials still had not received clearance from the FBI background check, and thus were still using temporary passes.

[63]See Chapter Five of this study.

[64]Kamen, "White House May Clamp Down on Passes," *Washington Post*, A19 (July 9, 1993). It was later revealed that Darnell Martens also had requested a White House pass a few days before the firings were announced.

[65]Letter to Mr. Thomas McLarty III (July 29, 1993).

[66]Letter to Honorable Frank R. Wolf (Aug. 19, 1993)(emphasis added).

[67]Ibid.

[68]However this policy was not publicly announced at the time. In a letter from Chief of Staff McLarty on October 27, 1993, Rep. Wolf was told that a new policy had been adopted, but he was not told what the policy was until Lloyd Cutler's letter of March 18, 1994.

[69]Letter to Honorable Frank R. Wolf, 1-2 (Mar. 18, 1994).

[70]Letter to Mr. Thomas McLarty III (Sept. 22, 1993).

[71]Ibid., 2.

[72]Letter to Mr. Thomas McLarty III (Oct. 14, 1993).

[73]Ibid., 2.

[74]Ibid., 1-2.

[75]Letter to Mr. James Bourke (FBI)(Oct. 14, 1993); Letter to Mr. Guy P. Caputo (Secret Service)(Oct. 14, 1993).

[76]Letter to Honorable Frank R. Wolf (Oct. 27, 1993).

[77]McLarty referred to an Office of Legal Counsel opinion, issued during the Reagan Administration, that determined the White House has authority to accept the services of volunteers, who may be paid by outside sources. OLC concluded that since Congress did not set any minimum rate of pay for employees in the White House Office, the White House could retain persons without pay.

[78]Letter from John E. Collingwood to Honorable Frank R. Wolf (Nov. 17, 1993) 2.

[79]Ibid.

[80]Garland & Walczak, "It's The Money, Stupid," *Business Week*, 163 (Nov. 15, 1993).

[81]Letter to Mr. Thomas McLarty III (Dec. 21, 1993). Wolf also determined that the White House, not the FBI, was responsible for the delays in issuing permanent passes, and faulted the White House Counsel's office in particular. Wolf added his concern whether persons without permanent passes (that is, without a complete background investigation and clearance from the Counsel's office) were privy to classified information. Ibid., 2-3.

[82]Letter to Honorable William J. Clinton (Feb. 24, 1994).

[83]Letter to Honorable Frank R. Wolf (Feb. 24, 1994).

[84]Snow, "Careless security slippage throughout Clinton village," *Washington Times*, A16 (Feb. 28, 1994).

[85]Borger, "Double standards in Clintonland," *U.S. News & World Report*, 58 (Mar. 14, 1994)(released March 7).

[86]"Who Is Patsy Thomasson?" *Wall Street Journal*, A18 (Mar. 10, 1994).

[87]Devroy & Isikoff, "After Year, 15 White House Aides Have Yet to Receive Security Clearances,"

Washington Post, A10 (Mar. 11, 1994)("A significant number of White House workers have not received FBI benediction more than 13 months into this presidency."); Rodriguez, "White House lags badly on background checks," *Washington Times,* A1 (Mar. 12, 1994); Devroy, "100 on White House Staff Lack Clearance," *Washington Post,* A5 (Mar. 14, 1994).

[88]Devroy, "White House Tightens Security Procedures," *Washington Post,* A4 (Mar. 17, 1994); see also, Jehl, "Review Likely to Find Taxes Were Underpaid," *New York Times,* 1 (Mar. 19, 1994).

In the wake of the Aldrich Ames scandal, the Chairman and Ranking Member of the House Permanent Select Committee on Intelligence wrote CIA Director Woolsey on March 17, asking him what steps the CIA had taken to ensure that classified information is not disseminated to White House staff members lacking appropriate clearances. Letter to Honorable R. James Woolsey (Mar. 17, 1994), reprinted in *Wall Street Journal,* A14 (Mar. 24, 1994). The White House regularly receives classified papers, reports and briefings.

[89]Devroy, "Clinton Aide Pays Back Taxes," *Washington Post,* A1, A15 (Mar. 23, 1994). By "routine" Cutler meant the full field FBI background investigation.

[90]Letter to Mr. Lloyd Cutler (Mar. 14, 1994).

[91]Ibid., 2.

[92]Letter to Honorable Frank R. Wolf (Mar. 18, 1994); see text at notes 68-69, *supra.* Cutler stated that he was responding to Wolf's December 21, 1993 letter at McLarty's request.

[93]Although Cutler did not identify these persons, he probably had in mind: Wilhelm, Carville, Begala, Greenberg, Grunwald, and perhaps Coelho, among others.

[94]Ibid., 2. One can therefore infer that no such ethics counseling was performed until at least after the issuance of the new policy in September 1993.

[95]Ibid., 2-3.

[96]Walsh, Pound & Cohen, "Government off the books," *U.S. News & World Report,* 28 (Mar. 28, 1994)(released March 21, 1994); see text notes 13-21, *supra.*

[97]*Treasury, Postal Service, and General Government Appropriations For Fiscal Year 1995: Hearings before a Subcommittee of the Committee on Appropriations, House of Representatives,* 103d Cong., 2d Sess. 510 (1994) (hereafter, *Hearings*)(testimony of Patsy Thomasson).

[98]Ibid., 585.

[99]Ibid., 585-86; see also, Ibid., 548 (testimony of Patsy Thomasson) (referring to Begala, Carville, Greenberg and Grunwald).

[100]The first report is contained in Ingersoll, "Kennedy, Clinton's Ethics Gatekeeper, Hadn't Paid Taxes on Nanny's Wages," *Wall Street Journal,* A16 (Mar. 22, 1994). Additional facts were reported in Devroy, "Clinton Aide Pays Back Taxes," *Washington Post,* A1 (Mar. 23, 1994); Scarborough, "Passes stalled by White House aide," *Washington Times,* A1 (Mar. 23, 1994). White House officials said that Kennedy asked to be reassigned to other responsibilities and that the "action was taken at his request." Devroy, "Clinton Schedules Prime Time Forum As Surveys Register Whitewater's Toll," *Washington Post,* A16 (Mar. 24, 1994). But the reassignment was largely reported to be a disciplinary step, with Kennedy avoiding being fired because of sympathy for his personal situation (he was going through a divorce proceeding at the time). Murray & Scarborough, "Clinton demotes associate counsel," *Washington Times,* A1 (Mar. 24, 1994); Jehl, "White House Slaps Counsel for Failing To Pay 'Nanny Tax'," *New York Times,* A1 (Mar. 24, 1994)(concluding that Kennedy's reassignment resulted as much from his failure to process the clearance paperwork in a timely manner as his failure to pay timely taxes for his nanny.).

[101]Scarborough, "Secret Service rejected workers," *Washington Times,* A1 (Mar. 26, 1994).

[102]Ibid., A9.

[103]See Wolf, "The White House's Outside Insiders," *Washington Post,* A19 (May 23, 1994)(op-ed authored by Rep. Wolf); Pierce, "White House political consultants should reveal finances, Wolf insists," *Washington Times,* A6 (May 23, 1994); "Disclosure Deficit," *Wall Street Journal,* A10 (May 20, 1994).

[104]The May 18 vote before the Subcommittee was 6-3. The amendment also failed before the full Appropriations Committee on May 26. The proposed amendment differed only slightly, in that the financial disclosure report that would have been required was one "similar to" the public financial disclosure report.

[105]"Ins and Outs," *Washington Post,* A16 (May 31, 1994).

[106]See, for example, Thomas, "'This Thing Is A Turkey'," *Newsweek,* 24 (June 13, 1994)(released June 6); "Clinton's Shadow Staff," *Wall Street Journal,* A14 (June 9, 1994); see text notes 24-41, *supra.*

[107]See June 7, 1994 "Dear Colleague" letter.

[108]Associated Press, "GOP loses bid for data on aides," *Washington Times,* A6 (June 9, 1994).

[109]Marcus, "White House Orders Consultants to Disclose Finances," *Washington Post,* A9 (June 10, 1994)("There was no public announcement of the directive."); Taylor, "Clinton political consultants ordered to disclose finances," *Washington Times,* A3 (June 11, 1994).

[110]Barr, "House Approves Pay Raise Legislation," *Washington Post,* A23 (June 16, 1994).

[111]Marcus, "White House Orders Consultants to Disclose Finances," *Washington Post,* A9 (June 10,

1994).

[112]Begala, Carville, Greenberg and Grunwald, "'We Do Not Lobby'," *Washington Post*, A29 (June 10, 1994).

[113]"Ins and Outs (Cont'd)," *Washington Post*, A28 (June 10, 1994).

[114]Associated Press, "Clinton consultants reveal other ties," *Washington Times*, A10 (July 22, 1994).

[115]Kamen, "Advisers' Disclosure: No $," *Washington Post*, A21 (July 22, 1994).

[116]Letter to Honorable Leon E. Panetta (July 27, 1994)("[T]he consultants were not required to file any dollar ranges of their assets, list gifts and travel accommodations, or identify accounts on which they work indirectly as well as directly."). Wolf essentially argued that the consultants should have been required to report the information required by SF-278.

In the interim, Panetta said on the July 10, 1994 edition of Face the Nation that the outside consultants "ought not to just have free access in the White House to all people. They ought to operate through a group that deals with strategic planning, and nothing else." Devroy, "West Wing Redecorating a la Panetta," *Washington Post*, A15 (July 13, 1994).

[117]Letter to Honorable Leon E. Panetta (Sept. 8, 1994);—Cong. Rec. H9143-46 (daily ed. Sept. 13, 1994). In late August, the *Washington Times* reported that Carville had travelled to Brazil on several occasions, beginning in April 1994, to advise a candidate for the presidency of Brazil, Fernando Henrique Cardoso. Carville, however, did not list this candidate or his political party as a client on his financial disclosure report. McCaslin, "Inside the Beltway," *Washington Times*, A6 (Aug. 29, 1994); McCaslin, "Inside the Beltway," *Washington Times*, A7 (Sept. 15, 1994)(reporting that Brazilian papers confirmed Carville's activities on behalf of Cardoso); see also—140 Cong. Rec. H9145-46, (daily ed. Sept. 13, 1994) (reprinting translation of Brazilian article).

[118]Letter to Honorable Leon E. Panetta (Sept. 8, 1994). See Engleberg, "Democrats' New Overseer Is Everybody's Mr. Inside," *New York Times*, A1 (Aug. 19, 1994).

[119]Letter to Honorable Frank R. Wolf (Oct. 4, 1994).

[120]Letter to Honorable Abner J. Mikva (Oct. 5, 1994).

[121]*U.S. News & World Report* reported after Cardoso's election (in which the Clinton Administration was officially neutral) that Carville insisted he did not perform any services for Cardoso until after July 1, and that he provided advice through an American research firm. The article added that Grunwald's partner, not Grunwald, provided "strategic advice" to Cardoso. "Southern Strategy," *U.S. News & World Report*, 28 (Oct. 24, 1994).

[122]Letter to Honorable Frank R. Wolf (Oct. 14, 1994).

[123]Ibid., 2.

[124]Nichols, "New Clinton advisers use ethics loophole," *USA Today*, 64 (Nov.1, 1995) (Mike McCurry: "None of the outside political consultants are currently subject to those requirements because they only apply to hard pass holders.").

[125]Chief of Staff Panetta asked his deputy, Erskine Bowles, to work on this issue with the Counsel's Office. The *USA Today* article also included in the list of new advisers with "easy access" to the White House Robert Squier, Mark Penn, and Doug Shoen, but added that these three, in contrast to Morris, served the President in "more of a campaign capacity."

[126]"Quick Reaction, "*Washington Times*, A6 (Nov.2, 1995).

[127]See Memorandum to the Heads of Executive Departments and Agencies (Feb. 9, 1962), cited in OGE Informal Advisory Letter 82 X 22 (July 9, 1982), 328-332.

[128]Basically, SGEs are treated as regular employees for purposes of 18 U.S.C. 207 (post-employment restrictions) and 208 (conflicts-of-interest), but subject to lesser restrictions in 18 U.S.C. 203, 205, and 209. And, unlike some regular officers or employees, SGEs may engage in outside employment for compensation. For example, SGEs who are appointed by the President are not subject to the outside earned income ban imposed by Executive Order 12,674 (as amended).

[129]Quoted in OGE Informal Advisory Letter 82 X 22, 325 at 329-30 (July 9, 1982) (emphasis in OGE letter).

[130]OGE Informal Advisory Letter 81 X 8 (Feb. 23, 1981), citing B. Manning, Federal Conflict of Interest Law 26-30 (1964). The second criterion—pay—is not determinative, because section 202(a) expressly provides thatSGEs may be retained without compensation. The first criterion—oath of office—is a formality the absence of which also should not be deemed determinative. The third criterion—supervision by a Federal agency—is relevant mainly to the concept of independent contractors, who, largely because they operate without direct Government supervision, are not deemed employees of the United States.

[131]See Chapter Four of this study for a discussion of the particular problems involving participants in the Health Care Task Force working group.

[132]2 Op.O.L.C. 20 (Feb. 24, 1977).

[133]Ibid., 23 (emphasis added). A White House official argued that this OLC opinion was superseded by

the 1978 Ethics in Government Act. Novak, "Conflict Complications," *Washington Post*, A27 (Feb. 3, 1994). But how so? The Act did not change the definition of "special Government employee." In any event, the OGE informal advisory letter containing the same conclusion, discussed immediately below, was written **after** the Ethics in Government Act was enacted.

[134]OGE Informal Advisory Letter 82 X 22, 325, 336 (July 9, 1982)(emphasis added). That letter also discusses the criteria contained in 5 U.S.C. 2104 and 2105. Ibid., 332-35.

[135]*Hearings, supra* note 97, 549 (1994)(statement of Patsy Thomasson).

[136]5 U.S.C. 2104(a).

[137]5 U.S.C. 2105(a).

[138]2 Op.O.L.C. 20-21 (emphasis and ellipses added; footnotes omitted).

[139]Similarly, OGE's 1982 informal advisory letter considered sections 2104 and 2105 as "instructive" in interpreting the definition of an SGE in the context of advisory committees.

[140]Title 18 does not contain a definition of "officer" or "employee." In *Association of Amer. Phys. and Surgeons*, the court of appeals determined that the definitions of "officer" and "employee" in 5 U.S.C. 2104 and 2105 do not apply to Federal Advisory Committee Act, which is placed in the U.S. Code in the **appendix** to Title 5. 997 F.2d at 904. *A fortiori,* sections 2104 and 2105 should not apply to a different **title** of the U.S. Code.

[141]See 3 U.S.C. 105.

[142]Memorandum for Bernard Nussbaum, Counsel to the President, from Daniel L. Koffsky, Acting Assistant Attorney General, Office of Legal Counsel (July 10, 1993).

[143]"Personnel Practices: Retroactive Appointments and Pay Adjustments in the Executive Office of the President," General Accounting Office, 11, 16 (Sept. 1993).

[144]Perhaps this difference is why OLC concluded that the standards in the personnel statutes are only "analogous."

[145]Begala, Carville, Greenberg & Grunwald, "'We Do Not Lobby'," *Washington Post*, A29 (June 10, 1994).

[146]*Hearings, supra* note 97, 653 (answer to question submitted for the record)("These individuals have been briefed regarding various ethics issues, including not using their status as consultants to the White House to the advantage of their private clients.").

[147]On the other hand, when the Clinton-Gore re-election campaign committee is established, the Clinton White House must insist on certain demarcations between what is official and what is campaign-related at a minimum to comply with Federal Election Commission laws and regeulations. Blurring the distinctions is fraught with peril, aside from FEC laws, because of the danger that offices of government will be used for campaign purposes. Yet, campaign officials who meet with White House officials during the campaign to discuss Presidential actions should be required to disclose their financial interests and clients, as the senior Bush-Quayle officials were required to do in 1992.

Chapter Seven

[1]Schmidt, "U.S. Is Asked to Probe Failed Arkansas S&L," *Washington Post*, A1 (Oct. 31, 1993). This was not the first time the RTC had referred allegations against Madison to the Justice Department. It was later revealed that the first RTC referral to Justice was made in September 1992, addressed to Charles Banks, the U.S. Attorney at the time. Weiner, "Trail of Memos on Whitewater Inquiry," *New York Times*, sec. 1, 20 (Mar. 27, 1994).

[2]Isikoff & Schneider, "Clintons' Former Real Estate Firm Probed," *Washington Post*, A1, A7 (Nov. 2, 1993).

[3]Isikoff & Schneider, "Clintons' Former Real Estate Firm Probed," *Washington Post*, A1 (Nov. 2, 1993). Hale's allegation was first reported by the *Arkansas Democrat-Gazette.*

[4]Ibid. Schneider, "Gov. Tucker's Finances Become Probe Focus," *Washington Post*, A3 (Nov. 3, 1993).

[5]Schmidt, "Regulators Say They Were Unaware of Clinton Law Firm's S&L Ties," *Washington Post*, A4 (Nov. 3, 1993); Seper, "Probe of S&L chief touches on Hillary's legal fee," *Washington Times*, A1 (Nov. 5, 1993).

[6]Casey had previously declined David Hale's attorney's suggestion that she recuse herself. It was later revealed that Casey also rebuffed the Justice Department's suggestions made on September 20, 1993, that she recuse.

[7]Hubbell initially was reported to have recused himself "several weeks ago" (sometime in early to mid-October) after he read about the investigation in the Arkansas press. Schneider, "Gov. Tucker's Finances Become Probe Focus," *Washington Post*, A3 (Nov. 4, 1993). It was later determined that the *Arkansas Democrat-Gazette* ran a story on David Hale's allegations on September 23, 1993.

[8]Isikoff & Schmidt, "U.S. Steps Up Investigations In Arkansas," *Washington Post*, A1 (Nov. 10, 1993).

[9]Seper, "Clinton papers lifted after aide's suicide," *Washington Times*, A1 (Dec. 20, 1993). In the days before his death, Foster began discussions with Hamilton concerning possible representation of Foster or

others in the White House Counsel's office in connection with the investigation of the firing of the Travel Office employees. At some point, the Foster family formally retained Hamilton. Isikoff, "Foster Was Shopping for Private Lawyer, Probers Find," *Washington Post*, A20 (Aug. 15, 1993).

[10]Murray, "White House confirms search of Foster's office," *Washington Times*, A1 (Dec. 21, 1993). Files personal to Foster and his family were sent to Hamilton. See also, Isikoff, "Whitewater Files Were Found in Foster's Office, White House Confirms," *Washington Post*, A16 (Dec. 22, 1993). Records concerning official Government matters were disseminated within the White House Counsel's office.

[11]Isikoff, "Whitewater Files Were Found in Foster's Office, White House Confirms," *Washington Post*, A16 (Dec. 22, 1993).

[12]Drehle, "The Crumbling Of a Pillar In Washington," *Washington Post*, A1, A20 (Aug. 15, 1993).

[13]Seper, "White House keeps a lock on files from Foster's office," *Washington Times*, A1 (Dec. 22, 1993).

[14]Ibid.

[15]Schmidt, "Hill Seeks Probe of Land Deal," *Washington Post*, A1, A10 (Dec. 23, 1993)(not contained in *Weekly Compilation of Presidential Documents*). President Clinton's account conflicts with reports that Foster worked on Whitewater's tax returns **after** Clinton was sworn in.

[16]Ibid. Richter & Ostrow, "Clinton Vows Land Deal Cooperation, *Los Angeles Times*, A14 (Dec. 23, 1993).

[17]Seper, "Clinton puts limits on offer to help probe," *Washington Times*, A1, A13 (Dec. 23, 1993).

[18]Ibid.

[19]Schmidt, "Hill Seeks Probe of Land Deal," *Washington Post*, A1 (Dec. 23, 1993); see also, Leach, "A Special Counsel for Whitewater," *Washington Post,* A21 (Dec. 31, 1993).

[20]Richter & Ostrow, "Clinton Releases Land Deal Files to Investigators," *Los Angeles Times*, A1, A19 (Dec. 24, 1993).

[21]Ibid.

[22]Marcus & Isikoff, "Clinton Releases Files on Land Deal," *Washington Post*, A1, A6 (Dec. 24, 1993)(as discussed below, no files were released on December 23 or for days thereafter).

[23]Ibid.

[24]Ibid.; see also Richter & Ostrow, "Clinton Releases Land Deal Files to Investigators," *Los Angeles Times*, A1 (Dec. 24, 1993)(again, this headline is misleading; no files were released for some time after the President's pledge).

[25]Ibid.

[26]See Isikoff & Devroy, "Subpoena Issued For Clinton Files," *Washington Post*, A1, A4 (Jan. 6, 1994); Devroy & Schneider, "A Damage Control Mess," *Washington Post*, A1 (Jan. 7, 1994).

[27]Isikoff & Devroy, "Subpoena Issued For Clinton Files," *Washington Post*, A1 (Jan. 6, 1994). Why did the White House delay in disclosing the subpoena? "[T]he White House did not publicly disclose the subpoena until yesterday because, aides said, they did not consider it relevant." Id. Although the White House did not say at the time why the subpoena was revealed when it was, on that very same day, January 5, David Marston, a Republican lawyer, filed a FOIA request for the documents. Frisby, "Clinton Lawyer Secured U.S. Subpoena To Prevent Release of Whitewater Files," *Wall Street Journal*, A14 (Jan. 6, 1994). Another possible explanation was that the existence of the subpoena was not known outside of the White House Counsel's office until January 5: "Once more politically attuned White House aides learned of its existence Wednesday, this official and others said, Stephanopoulos sought immediate release of that fact." Devroy & Schneider, "A Damage Control Mess," *Washington Post*, A1, A4 (Jan. 7, 1994).

[28]Murray & Seper, "Clinton stalls on records, Leach charges," *Washington Times*, A1 (Jan. 4, 1994) (emphasis added).

[29]Ibid.

[30]Frisby, "Clinton Lawyer Secured U.S. Subpoena To Prevent Release of Whitewater Files," *Wall Street Journal*, A14 (Jan. 6, 1994).

[31]Isikoff & Devroy, "Subpoena Issued For Clinton Files," *Washington Post*, A1 (Jan. 6, 1994).

[32]Murray & Seper, "Clinton to send records to grand jury," *Washington Times*, A1, A15 (Jan. 6, 1994). *See also*, Rosenbaum, "Insisting on Privacy, Clinton Seems to Accept the Punishment It May Bring," *New York Times*, A19 (Jan. 7, 1994)("The [White House's] version of events is that they asked the Justice Department to subpoena [the] documents . . . so it would be less likely that the material would be disclosed publicly.").

[33]Isikoff & Devroy, "Subpoena Issued For Clinton Files," *Washington Post*, A4 (Jan. 6, 1994).

[34]Ibid. In a conversation with *Washington Post* reporters and editors on December 6, 1993, "Bruce Lindsey said that the White House did not want to release any Whitewater records to the news media because it would only raise more questions about the investment." Schneider & Babcock, "An Ever-Growing Paper Trail," *Washington Post*, A1, A9 (Jan. 8, 1994).

[35]Ibid. One White House official said that the President's personal and White House attorneys "thought [the subpoena] was a routine legally mechanical part of turning over the files. When we asked later why in

God's name they didn't tell us this subpoena thing was going on, they said, 'Why should we, it's just the routine thing in getting this done.'" Devroy & Schneider, "A Damage Control Mess," *Washington Post*, A1, A4 (Jan. 7, 1994).

[36]Dewar, "Independent Counsel Urged in Arkansas Probe," *Washington Post*, A5 (Jan. 3, 1994); Price, "GOP tells Reno to name counsel for Whitewater," *Washington Times*, A1 (Jan. 3, 1994).

[37]Devroy & Schneider, "A Damage Control Mess," *Washington Post*, A1, A4 (Jan. 7, 1994).

[38]Devroy, "New Whitewater Strategy May Entail Selective Release of Documents," *Washington Post*, A7 (Jan. 10, 1994).

[39]Ibid. This correct statement was largely lost among the many news reports, at the time and subsequently, which asserted the contrary.

[40]"Yes to an Independent Counsel," *Washington Post*, A18 (Jan. 5, 1994); "The president's mounting legal bills," *Washington Times*, A18 (Jan. 5, 1994)(also urged reenactment of independent counsel law); "Janet Reno's Shameful Delay," *New York Times*, A30 (Jan. 7, 1994); "Pass an Unaltered Counsel Law," *New York Times*, sec. 4, 20 (Jan. 9, 1994).

[41]At the time, the Senate had passed an independent counsel bill, and the House was set to consider a bill in the near future.

[42]Isikoff, "Reno: Counsel Possible," *Washington Post*, A1 (Jan. 7, 1994); Lewis, "Reno to Ask for Special Counsel In Clinton Land Deal, Aides Say," A1 (Jan. 7, 1994); Seper, "Dole sees conspiracy in probe of Whitewater affair," *Washington Times*, A14 (Jan. 7, 1994).

[43]Bedard, "White House shifts on probe," *Washington Times*, A1 (Jan. 10, 1994)(Moynihan); Isikoff & Devroy, "9 Democrats Join Call for Prosecutor," *Washington Post*, A1 (Jan. 12, 1994); Moss & Murray, "7 Democrats join the call for Whitewater counsel," *Washington Times*, A1 (Jan. 12, 1994).

[44]"White House, Dole give thoughts on Whitewater probe," *Washington Times*, A13 (Jan. 13, 1994); *see also*, Balz & Isikoff, "Clinton Yields to Calls For Land Deal Probe," *Washington Post*, A1 (Jan. 13, 1994); Birnbaum, "Clinton Seeks Special Counsel On Whitewater," *Wall Street Journal*, A1 (Jan. 13, 1994); Murray, "Clintons yield on Whitewater inquiry," *Washington Times*, A1 (Jan. 13, 1994).

[45]Isikoff, "Whitewater Special Counsel Promises 'Thorough' Probe," *Washington Post*, A1 (Jan. 21, 1994).

[46]28 CFR 603.1(a).

[47]28 CFR 603.1(b), (c).

[48]Johnston, "Counsel Granted A Broad Mandate in Clinton Inquiry," *New York Times*, A1 (Jan. 21, 1994).

[49]28 CFR 600.3(a)(1).

[50]Isikoff, "Whitewater Special Counsel Promises 'Thorough' Probe," *Washington Post*, A1 (Jan. 21, 1994).

[51]Seper, "Fiske says he wants Clintons to give testimony under oath," *Washington Times*, A1 (Jan. 21, 1994).

[52]Schmidt, "Whitewater Investigation Outlined," *Washington Post*, A1 (Feb. 17, 1994). Fiske told the court his investigation could take one and one-half years to complete.

[53]Moss, "Dole demands investigation by select congressional panel," *Washington Times*, A13 (Jan. 13, 1994).

[54]Davidson, "Fiske, in Probe of Whitewater, Plans To Take Testimony From the Clintons," *Wall Street Journal*, A16 (Jan. 21, 1994).

[55]See Lambro, "Congress keeping hands off Clinton," *Washington Times*, A1 (Jan. 15, 1994); Reuter, "Dole Calls for Whitewater Answers," *Washington Post*, A5 (Jan. 17, 1994)(Vice President Gore called the select committee idea "premature").

[56]Moss, "Call for Whitewater select panel put off; Michel still wants probes," *Washington Times*, A3 (Jan. 26, 1994).

[57]Moss, "Foley won't order Whitewater hearings," *Washington Times*, A1 (Jan. 27, 1994).

[58]Meanwhile, Jim Leach, the Ranking Member of the House Banking Committee, continued his investigation into Madison and Whitewater even in the absence of hearings. Seper, "Leach cites 'Milkenesque' scent in unfolding Whitewater inquiry," *Washington Times*, A1 (Feb. 1, 1994).

[59]Schmidt, "Hill Democrats Promise Hearings on Thrifts," *Washington Post*, A6 (Feb. 2, 1994); Rodriguez, "Gonzalez flip-flops on Whitewater hearings," *Washington Times*, A1 (Feb. 2, 1994).

Also, Rep. Lamar Smith asked House Judiciary Committee Chairman Jack Brooks to hold hearings, insofar as he doubted the Justice Department's willingness to prosecute wrongdoing. And Rep. Jan Meyers, Ranking Member on the House Committee on Small Business, introduced a resolution of inquiry calling on the President to answer questions about his knowledge and participation in the 1986 SBA-backed loan of $300,000 from Capital Management Services to Susan McDougal, $110,000 of which allegedly was diverted to the Whitewater account at Madison. Seper, "Lawmaker seeks Clinton's answers on Whitewater," *Wash-*

ington Times, A10 (Feb. 11, 1994).

[60]Reuters, "GOP senators grill FDIC nominee," *Washington Times*, A15 (Feb. 2, 1994).

[61]Knight, "FDIC Choice Pledges Whitewater Recusal," *Washington Post*, C1 (Feb. 9, 1994); Bedard, FDIC nominee told to widen Whitewater recusal," *Washington Times*, A8 (Feb. 10, 1994). Tigert noted that both FDIC and OGE lawyers had told her that "no actual conflict of interest is involved, given the casual nature of my friendship with the Clintons."

[62]Bedard, "FDIC nominee told to widen Whitewater recusal," *Washington Times*, A8 (Feb. 10, 1994).

[63]Brown, "Senate panel OKs FDIC nominee," *Washington Times*, A14 (Feb. 11, 1994). Two weeks later, Senators D'Amato and Faircloth put another hold on Tigert's nomination, pending the scheduling of hearings on Whitewater. Tigert was not confirmed until October 1994.

[64]Seper, "Rose firm shreds Whitewater records," *Washington Times*, A1 (Feb. 9, 1994).

[65]Seper, "Paper-shredding added to probe," *Washington Times*, A1 (Feb. 10, 1994); Schmidt, "Alleged Whitewater Shredding to Be Probed," *Washington Post*, A7 (Feb. 10, 1994).

[66]Associated Press, "Failed Arkansas thrift comes under scrutiny once more," *Washington Times*, A3 (Feb. 19, 1994).

[67]Bacon & Birnbaum, "FDIC Finds No Evidence of Violations In Rose Law Firm's Work With a Thrift," *Wall Street Journal*, A14 (Feb. 18, 1994); Seper, "Rose firm cleared for lack of evidence," *Washington Times*, A1 (Feb. 18, 1994); Schmidt, "FDIC Rules Out Rose Law firm Sanctions Over Potential Madison Case Conflict," *Washington Post*, A4 (Feb. 18, 1994).

[68]After these concerns were rebuffed by FDIC official April Breslaw at the time, Breslaw got Hubbell to write a letter to the FDIC stating that he had not represented Seth Ward with regard to his disputes with Madison.

[69]Hubbell claimed that he had "very generally" informed the FDIC of the prior work orally, but no FDIC employee remembered this or any other notice. See Safire, "Whitewater Cover-Up," *New York Times*, A21 (Mar. 3, 1994)("That Government attorney directly disputed Hubbell's story; so did his supervisor. Even the Rose partner working on the account differs from the Hubbell version. Yet the Clinton F.D.I.C. chose to believe the profoundly conflicted Hubbell.").

[70]Gaines & Marx, "The ethical snarl of Hillary Clinton and a troubled ally," *Chicago Tribune*, 1 (Feb. 3, 1994).

[71]Seper, "Conflicting reports extend Rose probe," *Washington Times*, A1 (Feb. 17, 1994). The FDIC found that Mrs. Clinton had only signed the amended complaint, billing FSLIC for only two hours of work. But later it turned out that Mrs. Clinton had signed three additional pleadings in the Lasater matter. Schneider, "Hillary Clinton's role in Lawsuit Appears Larger," *Washington Post*, A16 (Mar. 3, 1994). These FDIC rulings were greeted with skepticism by the *Wall Street Journal*, and were openly criticized by Republicans in Congress. Commenting on the FDIC's ruling involving the Rose Law Firm's representation of the FDIC in its suit against Frost, the *Journal* remarked:

Somehow it seems to us the interests of a conservator trying to clean up a mess are pretty much adverse to the interests of the folks responsible for making the mess. Indeed, who needs a legal opinion to explain what is clearly a conflict on its face?"

Arkansas Forbearance," *Wall Street Journal*, A20 (Feb. 22, 1994). Concerning the FDIC's exoneration of Hillary Clinton, the *Journal* noted, "While none of this looks like a hanging offense, Ed Meese would no doubt have been hanged if he'd done something comparable." "The FDIC Clears Another," *Wall Street Journal*, A20 (Feb. 23, 1994).

[72]Schmidt, "Agencies Accused of 'Whitewash' on Whitewater," *Washington Post*, A9 (Feb. 25, 1994); Karr, "RTC Suggests Mrs. Clinton's Law Firm Improperly Failed to Disclose S&L Link," *Wall Street Journal*, A2 (Feb. 25, 1994); Munroe, "GOP persuades regulators to reopen probe of Rose," *Washington Times*, A12 (Feb. 25, 1994).

[73]Schmidt, "Agencies Accused of 'Whitewash' on Whitewater," *Washington Post*, A9 (Feb. 25, 1994); Karr, "RTC Suggests Mrs. Clinton's Law Firm Improperly Failed to Disclose S&L Link," *Wall Street Journal*, A2 (Feb. 25, 1994)

[74]The Treasury Department's General Counsel, Jean Hanson, accompanied Altman to the meeting.

[75]Karr & Ingersoll, "RTC Chief Altman Recuses Himself From Matters of Failed Arkansas Thrift," *Wall Street Journal*, A16 (Feb. 28, 1994).

[76]"Whitewater Recusal," *Washington Post*, A16 (Feb. 28, 1994).

[77]Schmidt & Babcock, "Senior Official Steps Aside in Probe Of S&L Linked to Clintons' Venture," *Washington Post*, A7 (Feb. 26, 1994); Hedges, "Treasury deputy Altman quits Whitewater probe," *Washington Times*, A1 (Feb. 26, 1994); Karr & Ingersoll, "RTC Chief Altman Recuses Himself From Matters of Failed Arkansas Thrift," *Wall Street Journal*, A16 (Feb. 28, 1994).

[78]Karr & Ingersoll, "RTC Chief Altman Recuses Himself From Matters of Failed Arkansas Thrift," *Wall Street Journal*, A16 (Feb. 28, 1994).

[79]"Whitewater Recusal," *Washington Post*, A16 (Feb. 28, 1994).

[80]"Slovenly White House Ethics," *New York Times*, sec. 4, 14 (Feb. 27, 1994).

[81]Ibid.

[82]Bedard & Rodriguez, "Republicans want hearings on secret Madison briefing," *Washington Times*, A1 (Mar. 2, 1994); Babcock, "GOP Assails RTC Head's White House Visit," *Washington Post*, A11 (Mar. 2, 1994).

[83]D'Amato, "A Whitewater Whitewash," *Wall Street Journal*, A10 (Mar. 2, 1994).

[84]Hunt, "Whitewater: It's the Coverup More Than the Deal," *Wall Street Journal*, A17 (Mar. 3, 1994).

[85]Devroy & Schmidt, "Treasury Officials Told White House Status of S&L Probe," *Washington Post*, A1 (Mar. 3, 1994).

[86]Jehl, "Clinton Distances Himself From Inquiry Briefings," *New York Times*, A22 (Mar. 4, 1994).

[87]Devroy & Schmidt, "Treasury Officials Told White House Status of S&L Probe," *Washington Post*, at A18 (Mar. 3, 1994).

[88]Jehl, "Clinton Distances Himself From Inquiry Briefings," *New York Times*, A22 (Mar. 4, 1994).

[89]Ibid. The RTC official was subsequently identified as RTC press official Steve Katsanos.

[90]Birnbaum & Bacon, "Whitewater Is Starting to Have Diverse Impact; First Key Victim Could Be White House Counsel," *Wall Street Journal*, A10 (Mar. 4, 1994).

[91]Devroy & Marcus, "Clinton Faults Contacts With Officials on Probe," *Washington Post*, A1 (Mar. 4, 1994).

[92]Bedard, "GOP senators target nominee to get hearings," *Washington Times*, A1, A15 (Mar. 4, 1994).

[93]Jehl, "Clinton Distances Himself From Inquiry Briefings," *New York Times*, A22 (Mar. 4, 1994). Bentsen also directed his Inspector General to review the Treasury contacts with the White House.

[94]Bedard, "Nary a storm misses 'Dr. No'," *Washington Times*, A1, A15 (Mar. 4, 1994).

[95]Bedard, "GOP senators target nominee to get hearings," *Washington Times*, A1, A15 (Mar. 4, 1994).

[96]"Bad to Worse," *Washington Post*, A22 (Mar. 4, 1994).

[97]"It's not 'appearances,' Mr. President, it's conflict," *Washington Times*, A18 (Mar. 4, 1994).

[98]"White House Ethics Meltdown," *New York Times*, A26 (Mar. 4, 1994).

[99]Engelberg, "Grand Jury Is Reportedly Told Of Shredding at Little Rock Firm," *New York Times*, A1 (Mar. 4, 1994).

[100]Ibid., A22; see also Seper, "Rose staffers say Hillary ordered papers shredded," *Washington Times*, A1 (Mar. 7, 1994). The *New York Times* report pointed out that the shredding allegation was different from the shredding allegation contained in the February *Washington Times* story.

[101]Devroy & Marcus, "White House Counsel Ready to Quit," *Washington Post*, A1 (Mar. 5, 1994); Bedard, "Whitewater counsel subpoenas 6 in White House," *Washington Times*, A1 (Mar. 5, 1994).

[102]Marcus & Devroy, "Nussbaum Quits White House Post," *Washington Post*, A1 (Mar. 6, 1994); Seper, "Fiske turns up the heat; Nussbaum bows out," *Washington Times*, A1 (Mar. 6, 1994); Ifill, "Nussbaum Out as White House Counsel," *New York Times*, 1 (Mar. 6, 1994).

[103]Ibid., A1, A8.

[104]30 *Weekly Compilation of Presidential Documents* 443 (Mar. 5, 1994).

[105]"Mr. Nussbaum Goes—Not the Mess," *Washington Post*, C6 (Mar. 6, 1994).

[106]"Repairing the White House Mess," *New York Times*, p. 14 (Mar. 6, 1994).

[107]"His ex-attorney Bernie," *Washington Times*, A20 (Mar. 7, 1994).

[108]"C.O.B.'s," *Wall Street Journal*, A14 (Mar. 7, 1994).

[109]Marcus & Devroy, "Clinton: Whitewater, Watergate Not Alike," *Washington Post*, A1 (Mar. 8, 1994); Jehl, "Another Question Raised By Clinton On Land Dealings," *New York Times*, A1 (Mar. 8, 1994); Bedard, "Clinton jumps to defense of Hillary's ethics," *Washington Times*, A1 (Mar. 8, 1994); Frisby & Ingersoll, "Clinton Says He Was Told in Advance RTC Wanted Criminal Probe of Madison," *Wall Street Journal*, A3 (Mar. 8, 1994).

[110]30 *Weekly Compilation of Presidential Documents* 450 (Mar. 7, 1994).

[111]30 *Weekly Compilation of Presidential Documents* 447 (Mar. 7, 1994).

[112]Babcock & Cooper, "GOP, Special Counsel At Odds Over Hearings," *Washington Post*, A8 (Mar. 8, 1994); Seper, "Fiske says hearings would harm probe," *Washington Times*, A13 (Mar. 8, 1994).

[113]Marcus & Balz, "President Picks Capital Insider as Counsel," *Washington Post*, A1 (Mar. 8, 1994); Marcus & Dewar, "Call for Hearings Grows in Congress," *Washington Post*, A1 (Mar. 9, 1994); Murray, "Clinton picks man of stature to take Nussbaum's place," *Washington Times*, A8 (Mar. 9, 1994); Frisby & Thomas, "Clinton Names Cutler Counsel At White House," *Wall Street Journal*, A3 (Mar. 9, 1994); Ifill, "President Chooses A Special Counsel; Openness Is Vowed," *New York Times*, A1 (Mar., 9, 1994).

[114]Bedard, "White House discloses more talks with probers," *Washington Times*, A1 (Mar. 9, 1994); Devroy, "File Search Indicates Other S&L Contacts," *Washington Post*, A1, A6 (Mar. 9, 1994).

[115]30 *Weekly Compilation of Presidential Documents* 463 (Mar. 8, 1994).

[116]Ibid., 468.

[117]Seper, "Republicans seek to question 40," *Washington Times*, A1 (Mar. 9, 1994).

[118]Engelberg, "Rose Courier Now Says Shredding Took Place After Inquiry Was Set," *New York Times*, A1 (Mar. 9, 1994).

[119]Rodriguez, "GOP won't yield on hearings," *Washington Times*, A1 (Mar. 10, 1994); Dewar & Devroy, "Fiske, Hill Negotiate On Hearings," *Washington Post*, A1 (Mar. 10, 1994).

[120]Most commenters supported hearings, and assumed that the Special Counsel Fiske's concerns could and would be met. "Getting at the Core of Whitewater," *Washington Post*, A18 (Mar. 9, 1994); "How to Investigate Whitewater," *New York Times*, A14 (Mar. 9, 1994); "No immunity, just hearings on Whitewater," *Washington Times*, A18 (Mar. 9, 1994); "The Fiske Coverup," *Wall Street Journal*, A12 (Mar. 9, 1994); Kondracke, "Congress Can't Duck Hearings On Whitewater," *Roll Call*, 6 (Mar. 10, 1994); Krauthammer, "No Immunity, No Problem," *Washington Post*, A25 (Mar. 11, 1994).

[121]Rodriguez, "GOP won't yield on hearings," *Washington Times*, A1 (Mar. 10, 1994); Dewar & Devroy, "Fiske, Hill Negotiate On Hearings," *Washington Post*, A1 (Mar. 10, 1994).

[122]Frisby & Thomas, "Whitewater Investigator Brings 3 Aides From White House Before Grand Jury," *Wall Street Journal*, A14 (Mar. 11, 1994); Devroy & Babcock, "First Lady's Top Aides Testify," *Washington Post*, A1 (Mar. 11, 1994); Seper, "Clinton aides testify on briefings," *Washington Times*, A1 (Mar. 11, 1994). The documents, which were collected from 40 White House officials, demonstrated that additional White House officials were involved in or knew of the contacts between Treasury and White House. Jehl, "Wider Group Knew About S&L Talks In The White House," *New York Times*, A1 (Mar. 11, 1994).

[123]Schmidt, "Whitewater Investigators Complain of Pressure," *Washington Post*, A9 (Mar. 12, 1994)(also citing "agency sources" saying that Kansas City investigators "have complained privately that they felt pressured by agency lawyers to play down the involvement of [the Clintons] in their preparation of criminal referrals[.]"); Hedges, "Leach accuses White House of gagging regulators," *Washington Times*, A4 (Mar. 12, 1994)(Leach did not refer to the White House, however); Johnston, "Lawmaker Says Officials Were Gagged Over S&L," *New York Times*, 8 (Mar. 12, 1994).

[124]*Time*, 38 (Mar. 21, 1994), *Newsweek*, 35 (Mar. 21, 1994).

[125]Devroy, "Desire for Privacy Cited on Whitewater," *Washington Post*, A1, A7 (Mar. 14, 1994).

[126]Taylor, "Clintons' partner pleads for records," *Washington Times*, A1, A8 (Mar. 14, 1994).

[127]Rosenbaum, "Clinton Partner Denies One Allegation," *New York Times*, B6 (Mar. 14, 1994).

[128]Marcus, "Clinton Angrily Denounces Republicans," *Washington Post*, A1 (Mar. 15, 1994)(the President referred to matters in addition to Whitewater).

[129]"Rostenkowski joins call for Whitewater hearings," *Washington Times*, A1, A10 (Mar. 17, 1994).

[130]Rosenbaum, "Senior Adviser To Clinton Gets Jury Subpoena," *New York Times*, A21 (Mar. 18, 1994); Dewar & Devroy, "Senate Leaders Make Whitewater Hearings Deal," *Washington Post*, A1 (Mar. 18, 1994); Rodriguez, "Senate OKs Whitewater hearings," *Washington Times*, A1 (Mar. 18, 1994).

[131]Rodriguez & Seper, "Hamilton opts for hearings on Whitewater," *Washington Times*, A1 (Mar. 16, 1994); Dewar, "House Democrat Suggests Hearings to Clear Clinton," *Washington Post*, A2 (Mar. 16, 1994).

[132]Rosenbaum, "Senior Adviser To Clinton Gets Jury Subpoena," *New York Times*, A21 (Mar. 18, 1994). When RTC and OTS complied with Gonzalez's request and denied Leach access to the documents, Leach filed suit in Federal district court. The agencies based their denial on the conclusion that as an individual Member of Congress, Leach was not entitled to any information that would be protected from disclosure by the Privacy Act or exempt from required disclosure under the Freedom of Information Act. Seper, "Leach files own suit to get RTC records," *Washington Times*, A1 (May 12, 1994); Schmidt, "Leach Sues to Force Release of Whitewater Files," *Washington Post*, A8 (May 12, 1994); Simpson, "Leach Files Lawsuit Over Right to Files," *Roll Call*, 1 (May 12, 1994).

[133]Lambro, "Hill panel divided on S&L hearing," *Washington Times*, A1 (Mar. 20, 1994).

[134]Safire, "Leach Vs. Gonzalez," *New York Times*, A17 (Mar. 21, 1994)("Nothing is subtle about Gonzalez stonewalling: never in the history of the United States Congress has there been such a blatant effort by a committee chairman to protect the White House by strangling a needed investigation in its crib.").

[135]Dewar & Devroy, "Senate Leaders Make Whitewater Hearings Deal," *Washington Post*, A1 (Mar. 18, 1994); Rodriguez, "Senate OKs Whitewater hearings," *Washington Times*, A1 (Mar. 18, 1994).

[136]Seper, "Hale to detail Clinton's role in Whitewater," *Washington Post*, A1 (mar. 21, 1994); Gerth, "Whitewater Prosecutor Agrees on Plea," *New York Times*, B7 (Mar. 21, 1994); Schneider & Schmidt, "Clinton Accuser Agrees to Plea, Testify," *Washington Post*, A10 (Mar. 22, 1994).

[137]"Suddenly, an Old Nemesis," *Time*, p. 28 (Mar. 28, 1994).

[138]Schmidt & Cooper, "House Banking Chairman Calls For Hearings on Whitewater," *Washington Post*, A10 (Mar. 22, 1994).

[139]Wines, "Senior Democrats Back Full Hearing Into Whitewater," *New York Times*, A1 (Mar. 22, 1994); Harwood & Pollock, "Gonzalez Delays House Panel Hearing GOP Hoped to Use for Whitewater Probe," *Wall Street Journal*, A4 (Mar. 22, 1994); Rodriguez, "Gonzalez gives in, calls for hearings," *Wash-*

ington Times, A1 (Mar. 22, 1994).

[140]Moss, "House approves planning for Whitewater hearings," *Washington Times*, A1, A16 (Mar. 23, 1994); Ifill, "Prosecutor Says Loan Questions Will Get Review," *New York Times*, A18 (Mar. 23, 1994); Dewar & Cooper, "House, Senate Edge Toward Whitewater Hearings," *Washington Post*, A15 (Mar. 23, 1994); Bacon & Pollock, "Senate, House Move Closer to Hearings On Whitewater' Dates Are Still Vague," *Wall Street Journal*, A4 (Mar. 23, 1994).

[141]Marcus & Devroy, "Altman, White House Discussed Recusal,"*Washington Post*, A1 (Mar. 23, 1994); Ifill, "Prosecutor Says Loan Questions Will Get Review," *New York Times*, A18 (Mar. 23, 1994).

[142]Ibid., A1, A14.

[143]140 Cong. Rec. H2003 (Mar. 24, 1994 daily ed.)

[144]Ibid., H2004.

[145]Ibid., H2001.

[146]Ibid., H2002.

[147]Ibid., H2006.

[148]Rosenbaum, "Papers Raise Question on Clinton's Account of Deal," *New York Times*, A17 (Mar. 25, 1994).

[149]Ibid.

[150]Rosenbaum, "A Disputed Talk Is Reported Taped," *New York Times*, 6 (Mar. 26, 1994).

[151]Marcus, "Leach's Whitewater Assertions Contradicted," *Washington Post*, A9 (Mar. 31, 1994).

[152]140 Cong. Rec. H2004 (Mar. 24, 1994 daily ed.)

[153]30 *Weekly Compilation of Presidential Documents* 627 (Mar. 24, 1994).

[154]Ibid., 628.

[155]30 *Weekly Compilation of Presidential Documents* 629 (Mar. 24, 1994).

[156]Hedges, "RTC free of GOP appointees," *Washington Times*, A1 (Mar. 26, 1994); "Republicans and the RTC," *Washington Times*, A16 (Mar. 29, 1994).

[157]30 *Weekly Compilation of Presidential Documents* 628, 632-33 (Mar. 24, 1994).

[158]Babcock & Schneider, "Error Is Linked To Confusion Over '81 Loan," *Washington Post*, A19 (Mar. 25, 1994); Schneider & Crenshaw, "'Forgotten' Clinton Loan Generated Few Documents," *Washington Post*, A4 (Mar. 26, 1994). The next day the Clintons, through their private attorney, released tax records from 1977-79 and other financial information. These disclosures, although generally supporting the Clintons' claim that Whitewater was a losing investment, did not put the issue to rest. Gerth, "Clintons Release Tax Data Showing Land Deal Losses," *New York Times*, p. 1 (Mar. 26, 1994); Seper, "Clinton tax papers lack support for deductions," *Washington Times*, A1 (Mar. 26, 1994); Devroy & Babcock, "Tax Records Back Clinton Account," *Washington Post*, A1 (Mar. 26, 1994).

[159]Ibid., 631.

[160]Ibid., 634.

[161]Marcus, "RTC Lawyer Drew White House Ire,"*Washington Post*, A1 (Mar. 26, 1994).

[162]Church & Kramer, "Into the Line of Fire," *Time*, 22 (Apr. 4, 1994); Turque, et al., "In the Line of Fire," *Newsweek*, 20 (Apr. 4, 1194); Frisby, "Whitewater Counsel Asks Whether Aides of Clinton Targeted Foe in RTC Inquiry," *Wall Street Journal*, A14 (Mar. 28, 1994).

[163]According to *Time*, Ickes and Stephanopoulos were also upset that Altman had decided to recuse himself, contrary to the White House's consistently stated desire that Altman remain in charge. Ibid., 23.

[164]Marcus, "RTC Lawyer Drew White House Ire," *Washington Post*, A1, A5 (Mar. 26, 1994).

[165]Church & Kramer, "In the Line of Fire," *Time*, 22 (Apr. 4, 1994).

[166]Devroy, "Whitewater Investigator Is Studying Treasury Department Official's Diary," *Washington Post*, A8 (Mar. 27, 1994).

[167]Jehl, "White House Aide Becomes Subject Of New Inquiries," *New York Times*, 1, 1 (Mar. 27, 1994).

[168]Taylor, "D'Amato suspects obstruction by two Clinton aides," *Washington Times*, A1 (Mar. 28, 1994); Devroy, "Stephanopoulos Call Played Down," *Washington Post*, A1 (Mar. 28, 1994); Ifill, "Top Clinton Aide Gains Defender in Odd Quarter," *New York Times*, A12 (Mar. 28, 1994).

[169]Frisby & Ingersoll, "First Lady Turned $1,000 Investment Into a $98,000 Profit, Records Show," *Wall Street Journal*, A2, A11 (Mar. 30, 1994).

[170]Seper, "Dole threatens GOP will slow Senate," A1 (Apr. 9, 1994); Dewar, "Senate Leaders Disagree on Hearings," *Washington Post*, A4 (Apr. 13, 1994).

[171]"Justice Mitchell on Whitewater," *Wall Street Journal,* A18 (Apr. 12, 1994).

[172]30 *Weekly Compilation of Presidential Documents* 803 (Apr. 13, 1994); Devroy, "Before Newspaper Editors, Clinton Defends Handling of Whitewater," *Washington Post*, A8 (Apr. 14, 1994); Jehl, "Clinton Bristles at Skepticism Over Deals," *New York Times*, B10 (Apr. 14, 1994; Murray, "Some editors cheer Clinton's scolding," *Washington Times,* A1 (Apr. 14, 1994).

[173]Schmidt & Babcock, "First Lady's Explanations Yield Little Information," *Washington Post*, A11

(Apr. 23, 1994); Murray, "Hilary denies ethical lapses, regrets stalling," *Washington Times,* A1 (Apr. 23, 1994); Frisby, "Hillary Clinton Burnishes Image In Press Session," *Wall Street Journal,* A4 (Apr. 23, 1994); Duffy, "Open and Unflappable," *Time,* 65 (May 2, 1994); Dowd, "Contrition as Weapon," *New York Times,* A1 (Apr. 23, 1994).

[174]Devroy & Schmidt, "First Phase of Whitewater Investigation Is Near End, Fiske Tells White House," *Washington Post,* A10 (May 17, 1994); Associated Press, "Fiske OKs review of Treasury papers," *Washington Times,* A4 (May 17, 1994).

[175]Later, reports surfaced that the unredacted deposition transcripts given to the White House Counsel included some nonpublic information about the referrals and the RTC's investigation, notwithstanding this agreement with Treasury.

[176]Dewar, "Pressure for Whitewater Hearings Rises," *Washington Post,* A6 (May 21, 1994); Hallow & Seper, "GOP moves to force hearings," *Washington Times,* A1 (May 25, 1994); Seper, "GOP senators harden stand on Whitewater," *Washington Times,* A1 (May 26, 1994).

[177]Seper, "Parties see July start of hearings," *Washington Times,* A1 (May 27, 1994); Cooper & Dewar, "Phase 1 of Whitewater Probe Nears End," *Washington Post,* A4 (May 27, 1994).

[178]Dewar, "Senate Democrats, GOP Propose Divergent Whitewater Plans," *Washington Post,* A9 (June 10, 1994); Seper, "Whitewater obstruction charged," *Washington Times,* A1 (June 10, 1994).

[179]Rosenbaum, "Senate Will Hold Hearings on Whitewater," *New York Times,* A22 (June 15, 1994).

[180]Cooper & Dewar, "House Banking Committee to Hold Limited Whitewater Hearings," *Washington Post,* A11 (June 16, 1994); Seper, "Whitewater hearings agreed to in House," *Washington Times,* A1 (June 16, 1994). The Senate also defeated a Republican proposal to begin hearings by July 15.

[181]Ibid. Republicans unsuccessfully urged that hearings also be held by the House Government Operations and Judiciary Committees.

[182]Seper, "Gonzalez rejects panel probe into death of Foster," *Washington Times,* A3 (June 21, 1994).

[183]The *Washington Times* responded: "Ah, if only lawmakers would take Mr. Gonzalez' concern fully to heart: Were lack of expertise a limit on congressional activity, the Hill would be a most serene environment." "The Whitewater stonewall, cont'd.," *Washington Times,* A16 (June 21, 1994).

[184]Seper, "Dole pushed to limit Whitewater hearings," *Washington Times,* A4 (June 17, 1994); Dewar, "GOP Offers Concessions On Whitewater Inquiry," *Washington Post,* A10 (June 17, 1994).

[185]"Running for Cover on Whitewater," *New York Times,* A30 (June 17, 1994). See also "Don't Go Near the Whitewater," *Wall Street Journal,* A16 (June 16, 1994); "The Whitewater Stonewall, cont'd.," *Washington Times,* A16 (June 21, 1994).

[186]"Congress and Whitewater," *Washington Post,* C6 (June 19, 1994).

[187]Seper, "Broader hearings rejected again," *Washington Times,* A1 (June 22, 1994); Dewar, "Dole Warns Democrats on Whitewater," *Washington Post,* A5 (June 22, 1994).

[188]Wines, "Senate Panel Asks for Whitewater Files," *New York Times,* A12 (June 24, 1994); Murray, "Senate panel starts own probe into limited area of Whitewater," *Washington Times,* A5 (June 24, 1994). The Administration officials included officials from the Justice Department, Treasury Department, RTC, and United States Park Police.

[189]Schmidt, "White House Pledges to Cooperate With Hearings," *Washington Post,* A17 (June 24, 1994).

[190]Seper, "House panel invites Fiske to testify," *Washington Times,* A3 (June 28, 1994); Novak, "Hearings on Whitewater Are Scheduled For Late July by House Banking Chief," *Wall Street Journal,* A20 (June 28, 1994).

[191]Seper, "Leach criticizes narrowed hearings," *Washington Times,* A4 (June 30, 1994).

[192]Fiske's conclusion that Vince Foster committed suicide, and a discussion of his possible reason for doing so, were contained in a lengthy *Report of the Independent Counsel In Re Vincent W. Foster, Jr.,* (June 30, 1994). The issue involving the contacts was treated only briefly in a *Statement on Washington, D.C. Investigation,* signed by Robert Fiske on June 30, 1994.

[193]Statement 4.

[194]OGE was asked in February by Secretary Bentsen to look into the ethical propriety of these meetings, but OGE postponed its investigation at the Special Counsel's request.

[195]Schmidt & Devroy, "Fiske Won't Bring Charges Over High-Level Contacts," *Washington Post,* A1, A16 (July 1, 1994).

[196]Ibid., A16. At the end of the day, however, the White House Counsel's office would not issue any report.

[197]"Independent Counsel Law Reauthorized," *Washington Post,* A16 (July 1, 1994).

[198]Seper, "Reno seeks a change in Fiske's status," *Washington Times,* A1 (July 2, 1994).

[199]Garrett, "Fiske again refuses to testify in House before bank panel," *Washington Times,* A4 (July 13, 1994).

[200]Schmidt, "Whitewater Hearings Face New Obstacle," *Washington Post,* A12 (July 15, 1994). This

prediction, alas, also would not come true.

[201]Associated Press, "Fiske report's delay will limit hearings," *Washington Times*, A12 (July 15, 1994).

[202]Schmidt, "Congress to Shield Whitewater Papers," *Washington Post*, A5 (July 13, 1994).

[203]Seper & Garrett, "Deletions in papers concern panel," *Washington Times*, A4 (July 14, 1994).

[204]Upset that the confidentiality procedures agreed to with the White House were not failsafe, Riegle and D'Amato asked the Senate Ethics Committee to conduct a leak investigation. Seper, "Ethics probe sought to find leaks," *Washington Times*, A12 (July 20, 1994); Schmidt, "Probe of Whitewater Leaks Is Sought," *Washington Post*, A4 (July 20, 1994).

[205]Schmidt, "Treasury Deputy Knew of Whitewater Meetings, Senate Told," *Washington Post*, A7 (July 17, 1994).

[206]Labaton, "Aide Is Said to Contradict Bentsen in Whitewater Case," *New York Times*, p. 6 (July 23, 1994); Schmidt, "Altman Testimony Disputed," *Washington Post*, A1, A8 (July 24, 1994).

[207]Ibid., A1. Altman's lawyer said Altman had no recollection of Roelle's briefing.

[208]Schmidt, "Whitewater Files Detail Discussions," *Washington Post*, A1, A4 (July 23, 1994).

[209]Schmidt, "Comptroller Says Clinton Sought His Advice on Whitewater," *Washington Post*, A4 (July 19, 1994); Hitt, "Clinton Asked Help on Whitewater Case From U.S. Comptroller, Was Rebuffed," *Wall Street Journal*, A16 (July 19, 1994); Bradsher, "Clinton Asked Advice From Top Regulator," *New York Times*, A12 (July 19, 1994); Associated Press, "Clinton approached bank regulator," *Washington Times*, A18 (July 19, 1994).

[210]Associated Press, "Clinton approached bank regulator," *Washington Times*, A18 (July 19, 1994).

[211]Ibid.

[212]Labaton, "Diary Says White House Sought To Keep Ally on Whitewater Case," *New York Times*, A1, B7 (July 25, 1994).

[213]Labaton, "Treasury Official Is Disavowing Whitewater Details in His Diary," *New York Times*, A1 (July 26, 1994).

[214]Garrett & Seper, "GOP cites Whitewater leaks," *Washington Times*, A1, A15 (July 26, 1994); Marcus & Schmidt, "Altman: Testimony 'Wholly Accurate'," *Washington Post*, A1 (July 26, 1994); Pollock, "Treasury's Altman Defends Meetings With Officials on Whitewater Affair," *Wall Street Journal*, A18 (July 26, 1994).

[215]Ibid.

[216]Schmidt & Schneider, "On Whitewater, Questions Just Kept Growing," *Washington Post*, A1, A4 (July 26, 1994)(ellipsis and brackets supplied by *Post*).

[217]LaFraniere, "Cutler Faults Clinton Aides' Judgment," *Washington Post*, A1 (July 25, 1994); Calmes & Pollock, "As House Whitewater Hearings Open, Democrats Anxiously Watch the Volatile Man With the Gavel," *Wall Street Journal*, A16 (July 25, 1994).

[218]Garrett & Seper, "Partisan feud over hearings escalates," *Washington Times*, A11 (July 22, 1994); "Obstructionism at the Whitewater hearings," *Washington Times*, A20 (July 22, 1994); "Censorship, Gonzalez Style," *New York Times*, A22 (July 28, 1994).

Gonzalez also prohibited any questioning relating to Foster's death, saying that "no responsible person would dispute" Fiske's conclusion that Foster committed suicide. Associated Press, ""Gonzalez rejects any Foster probe," *Washington Times*, A6 (July 27, 1994).

[219]Schmidt, "Cutler Says Whitewater Contacts Were Ethical," *Washington Post*, A1, A18 (July 27, 1994).

[220]"Opening Statements," *Washington Post*, A18 (July 27, 1994).

[221]Associated Press, *Washington Times*, A6 (July 27, 1994)(quoting Cutler's testimony).

[222]Marcus, "Propriety of Alerting White House to Criminal Probe Debated," *Washington Post*, A16 (July 28, 1994).

[223]Ibid.

[224]Schmidt, "Cutler Says Whitewater Contacts Were Ethical," *Washington Post*, A1, A18 (July 27, 1994).

[225]Labaton, "Presidential Aide Called In Hearing Into Whitewater," *New York Times*, A1 (July 27, 1994).

[226]Ibid., A18; Associated Press, "Cutler mentions Hubbell," *Washington Times,* A6 (July 27, 1994).

[227]Schmidt, "Cutler Revises Date White House Learned of S&L Investigation Targets," *Washington Post*, A17 (July 28, 1994); Seper & Garrett, "Documents hint Clinton advised Tucker of probe," *Washington Times*, A1 (July 28, 1994).

[228]Schmidt & LaFraniere, "White House Aides Defend Their Conduct," *Washington Post*, A1 (July 29, 1994). The ten officials who testified were: Cliff Sloan, Neil Eggleston, Bruce Lindsey, George Stephanopoulos, Harold Ickes, Maggie Williams, Lisa Caputo, Mac McLarty, John Podesta and Mark Gearan.

[229]Lewis, "Ex-Aide Explains His Whitewater Role to House Panel," *New York Times*, A18 (July 29,

1994).

[230]Schmidt & LaFraniere, "White House Aides Defend Their Conduct," *Washington Post*, A1, A20 (July 29, 1994).

[231]Ibid.

[232]Garrett & Seper, "On Capitol Hill, a chorus of denials,"*Washington Times*, A1, A8 (July 29, 1994).

[233]Pollock & Calmes, "Republicans in Hearings on Whitewater Suggest Clinton Got Improper Warnings," *Wall Street Journal*, A12 (July 29, 1994).

[234]Seper, "GOP senators accuse Altman of lying to panel," *Washington Times*, A1 (July 30, 1994); Schneider, "Senate Banking Panel Turns to Foster Death," *Washington Post*, A7 (July 30, 1994); Labaton, "Senate G.O.P. Sees Altman as Its Focus In Whitewater Case," *New York Times*, A1 (July 30, 1994). Park Police witnesses did express their frustration that White House officials notably Nussbaum and also Webster Hubbell prevented them from following standard procedures, thus making their investigation more difficult.

[235]Schmidt, "Republicans Say Altman Gave White House 'Inside Information'," *Washington Post*, A1, A6 (July 30, 1994).

[236]Chandler, "Treasury Ethics Documents Forwarded to White House," *Washington Post*, A3 (July 31, 1994). It was also not known at the time that the Secretary personally approved providing Cutler with the documents. Only later was it revealed that among the depositions Cutler reviewed were depositions of RTC officials, and that Cutler was given access to the unredacted transcripts. The two Banking Committees, however, received access only to redacted deposition transcripts.

[237]Report to the Secretary of the Treasury, from the Office of Government Ethics (July 31, 1994)(July 30, 1994 letter from Stephen D. Potts to Honorable Lloyd Bentsen)(hereafter, *OGE Report*).

[238]Schmidt, "No Violations Of Ethics Cited At Treasury," *Washington Post*, A1 (Aug. 1, 1994); Labaton, "Whitewater Talks Troubling, Not Unethical, Agency Says," *New York Times*, A1 (Aug. 1, 1994).

OGE explained that the Secretary asked OGE by letter of March 3 to review the contacts under the standards of ethical conduct. But OGE did not conduct an investigation, nor did it participate in the Treasury Department Inspector General's investigation other than to provide general advice and assistance. Rather, it obtained the work product and deposition transcripts from that investigation, and eventually the Inspector General's "final report." "Our only purpose in this letter is to provide an analysis of the standards we believe are applicable for your consideration in whatever decisions you make." *OGE Report, supra* note 237, 1-2.

Also unusual is the Treasury IG's "final report." The report consisted of the deposition transcripts and reports of interviews, other records relating to the contacts, and a chronology of the contacts. The Inspector General's report does not contain any analysis, conclusions or recommendations. And recall that no White House report of Lloyd Cutler's investigation was ever done or released; Cutler's testimony was tantamount to the White House's investigative report. Thus, for all intents and purposes, **OGE's letter to Bentsen is the only Executive Branch report on the Treasury-White House contacts that specifically analyzed the contacts under ethics laws, regulations and policies**.

[239]*OGE Report, supra* note 237, 3 (emphasis added).

[240]Ibid.

[241]Ibid., 8 (emphasis added).

[242]LaFraniere & Schmidt, "Treasury Aide Is Grilled on Whitewater," *Washington Post*, A1 (Aug. 2, 1994); Labaton, "Treasury Lawyer Disputes Account Of Top Officials," *New York Times*, A1 (Aug. 2, 1994); Seper, "Treasury was warned, panel told," *Washington Times*, A1 (Aug. 2, 1994); Pollock, "Treasury Aide Says Whitewater Talks With White House Were Appropriate," *Wall Street Journal*, A16 (Aug. 2, 1994).

[243]Labaton, "Treasury Lawyer Disputes Account Of Top Officials," *New York Times*, A1 (Aug. 2, 1994).

[244]LaFraniere & Schneider, "Altman: No Intent To Mislead Congress," *Washington Post*, A1 (Aug. 3, 1994); Pollock & Calmes, "Altman Apologizes for Not Being 'Forthcoming' On Whitewater, Puts Some Blame on Hanson," *Wall Street Journal*, A12 (Aug. 3, 1994); Rosenbaum, "Senators Assail Treasury Deputy," *New York Times*, A1 (Aug. 3, 1994); Seper, "Altman offers his apologies to angry senators," *Washington Times*, A1 (Aug. 3, 1994).

[245]Associated Press, "Senate panel grills young aide on diary," *Washington Times*, A12 (Aug. 3, 1994).

[246]Dowd, "Bentsen Aide's Lessons, Penned in Diaries, Emerge Painfully in Public," *New York Times*, A16 (Aug. 3, 1994).

[247]Labaton, "Bentsen Denies Aides' Assertions Of Briefings on Whitewater Talks," *New York Times*, A1 (Aug. 4, 1994); Pollock & Calmes, "Bentsen Testifies That He Steered Clear Of Whitewater, Doesn't Defend Aides," *Wall Street Journal*, A16 (Aug. 4, 1994); Seper, "GOP sees effort to control Whitewater probe," *Washington Times*, A1 (Aug. 4, 1994); Schmidt & Marcus, "Altman Retains Clinton's 'Confidence'," *Washington Post*, A1 (Aug. 4, 1994).

[248]Secretary Bentsen said there was not one piece of paper "written to me" showing that Hanson or Altman briefed him on anything regarding Madison, and added that he did not recall any such discussion. This qualification was necessary in light of Hanson's September 30, 1993 memorandum **to Altman** noting that she had briefed the Secretary. Bentsen testified he did not "learn ... the extent of these meetings" until

March 3, 1994.

[249]Leach, "Candor Was the Casualty . . .," *Wall Street Journal*, A8 (Aug. 5, 1994).

[250]30 *Weekly Compilation of Presidential Documents* 1617 (Aug. 3, 1994).

[251]Ibid., 1620.

[252]Seper, "Senators focus on Hillary's probe link," *Washington Times*, A1 (Aug. 5, 1994); Rosenbaum, "Clinton Aide Offers Qualified Contradiction of Altman," *New York Times*, A16 (Aug. 5, 1994); Pollock & Calmes, "Clinton Aide Suggests Altman Provided Confidential RTC Data to White House," *Wall Street Journal*, A10 (Aug. 5, 1994).

[253]Schmidt & LaFraniere, "Senator Says Ex-Counsel Nussbaum 'Crossed the Line' in Whitewater," *Washington Post*, A8 (Aug. 5, 1994).

[254]Seper, "RTC lawyer doesn't remember taped comment," *Washington Times*, A1 (Aug. 6, 1994); Schneider & LaFraniere, "Bickering Continues as Hill Ends Whitewater Hearings' First Phase," *Washington Post*, A9 (Aug. 6, 1994); Cushman, "White House Counsel Criticizes Altman," *New York Times*, 8 (Aug. 6, 1994).

[255]Lewis's supervisor, Richard Iorio, who also met with Breslaw on February 2, did seek to testify, "but was told by a senior RTC official that his appearance was 'unnecessary.'" Adams, "April and Webb and Jean and Jack," *American Spectator*, 41, 46 (Oct. 1994).

[256]Wines, "Boredom Mixed With a Danger," *New York Times,* 1, 26 (Aug. 7, 1994).

[257]Ibid. See also, Duffy, "Culture Of Deception," *Time*, p. 15 (Aug. 15, 1994); Kosova, "True Lies," *New Republic*, 14 (Aug. 22 & 29, 1994)(Writing of the frequently invoked "I don't recall," Kosova said it was "essentially a Kevlar jacket against perjury.").

[258]"Whitewater's Wreckage, So Far," *New York Times*, 4, 16 (Aug. 7, 1994).

[259]Ibid. See also, "Whitewater after the hearings," *Washington Times*, A18 (Aug. 9, 1994)("The Clinton team can't tell a straight story. This much is the universal, incontrovertible conclusion of everyone who watched the hearings.").

[260]Labaton, "Judges Appoint New Prosecutor For Whitewater," *New York Times*, 1 (Aug. 6, 1994); Seper, "Judges name ex-Bush official to Fiske's job," *Washington Times*, A1 (Aug. 6, 1994); Schmidt, "Judges Replace Fiske as Whitewater Counsel," *Washington Post*, A1 (Aug. 6, 1994).

[261]Schmidt & Locy, "Starr Says He Plans to Build on Fiske's Whitewater Work," *Washington Post*, A4 (Aug. 11, 1994); Jehl, "Building on Whitewater Investigation," *New York Times*, B10 (Aug. 11, 1994); Seper, "Starr says he'll build on work by Fiske," *Washington Times*, A2 (Aug. 11, 1994).

[262]Apparently the only explanation of Starr's limited charter was provided by Profesor Gilbert Cranberg in "The Whitewater Gavotte," *New York Times*, A23 (Dec. 6, 1994).

[263]Chandler, "Republicans Urge Bentsen to Fire 3," *Washington Post*, D9 (Aug. 11, 1994).

[264]Marcus & Chandler, "Altman Is Poised to Leave Treasury Job, Sources Say," *Washington Post*, A1 (Aug. 13, 1994); Seper, "Hanson urged to resign," *Washington Times*, A1 (Aug. 14, 1994); Thomas, "Altman's Resignation Appears Likely In Face of Eroding Support in Congress," *Wall Street Journal*, A12 (Aug. 15, 1994); Roman, "White House weighing Altman's fate, Panetta says," *Washington Times*, A4 (Aug. 15, 1994).

[265]Marcus & Chandler, "Altman Quits As Deputy At Treasury," *Washington Post*, A1 (Aug. 18, 1994); Seper, "Altman quits, regrets 'errors of judgment'," *Washington Times*, A1 (Aug. 18, 1994); Bradsher, "Deputy Treasury Secretary Resigns," *New York Times*, B10 (Aug. 18, 1994); Novak & Thomas, "Altman Resigns His Post as No. 2 At the Treasury," *Wall Street Journal*, A14 (Aug. 18, 1994).

[266]Seper, "Hanson follows Altman in exit from Treasury Department," *Washington Times*, A1 (Aug. 19, 1994); Bradsher, "Treasury Department's Counsel Resigns," *New York Times*, A16 (Aug. 19, 1994); Chandler, "Bentsen Picks Top Treasury Aides, Moves to Mend Relations on Hill," *Washington Post*, C1 (Aug. 19, 1994); Novak, "Treasury Counsel Jean Hanson Resigns Amid Criticism of Whitewater Contacts," *Wall Street Journal*, A4 (Aug. 19, 1994).

[267]Seper, "GOP lawmakers suspect RTC cover-up," *Washington Times*, A1 (Aug. 17, 1994). Iorio and Ausen were summarily escorted out of their office; Lewis was in the hospital at the time for a bleeding ulcer.

[268]Seper, "Hanson follows Altman in exit from Treasury Department," *Washington Times*, A1, A22 (Aug. 19, 1994).

[269]"The RTC Witch Hunt," *Washington Times*, A18 (Aug. 23, 1994).

[270]Karr, "RTC Investigator Says Agency Officials Tried to Halt Madison Guaranty Probe," *Wall Street Journal*, A14 (Aug. 24, 1994); Seper, "New tale of RTC 'control'," *Washington Times*, A1 (Aug. 25, 1994). The "dim view" quote is taken from a Kansas City RTC inter office memorandum from Gary Davisdon to Richard Lorio released publicly in November 1995. "A 'Sensitive' Investigation," *Wall Street Journal*, A14, (Nov. 28, 1995).

> April felt I should know there are some RTC people in management positions that would take a "dim view" of me investigating Madison Guaranty. She also advised me that I should be very

careful of who I talk to and what I say, because of the people associated with Madison Guaranty.

[271]Seper, "Lewis, 2 other RTC probers back on job; inquiry pledged," *Washington Times*, A10 (Aug. 31, 1994); Associated Press, "S. & L. Bailout Agency Ends Suspension of 3," *New York Times*, A12 (Aug. 31, 1994)(repeating prior news reports that in addition to the taping, the investigation concerned "misuse of time sheets and compensatory time, use of the agency's equipment for personal reasons and questionable business trips.").

[272]Seper, "Starr to get RTC records," *Washington Times*, A3 (Sept. 24, 1994).

[273]Simpson, "House GOP Dusts Off an Obscure 1928 Law To Force Release of Whitewater Documents," *Roll Call*, p. 5 (Sept. 22, 1994); Seper, "New GOP attempt to get Madison files," *Washington Times*, A5 (Sept. 22, 1994). Leach's suit under FOIA was unsuccessful in the courts.

[274]Associated Press, GOP senators want more Whitewater," *Washington Times*, A4 (Sept. 28, 1994). On November 29, 1994, Senate Banking Committee Republicans again wrote Starr, requesting that he specifically examine the testimony of Stephanopoulos and Ickes for possible perjurious statements. Scarborough, "Republicans doubt Clinton aides' word," *Washington Times*, A14 (Nov. 30, 1994); Labaton, "Whitewater Counsel Nears Decision on Indictments," *New York Times*, A14 (Dec. 1, 1994).

[275]Associated Press, "Senators to delay hearings for Starr," *Washington Times*, A11 (Sept. 30, 1994).

[276]Associated Press, "Nominee to head FDIC remains hostage of Whitewater politics," *Washington Times*, A14 (Sept. 17, 1994); Karr, "Republicans Hold Up Tigert's FDIC Nomination Over Whether She Is a Friend of the Clintons," *Wall Street Journal*, A20 (Sept. 28, 1994).

[277]Glater, "Filibuster Over Tigert Is Blocked," *Washington Post*, C1 (Oct. 4, 1994)(the vote was 63-32); Associated Press, "Senate confirms new chief of FDIC," *Washington Times*, A5 (Oct. 5, 1994)(the vote was 90-7).

[278]Seper, Senator questions timing of contacts," *Washington Times*, A1 (Nov. 2, 1994); Schmidt, "Cutler Got Confidential Depositions In Whitewater Probe, Senator Says," *Washington Post*, A6 (Nov. 2, 1994).

[279]Seper, "New Whitewater hearings likely with broader scope," *Washington Times*, A1 (Nov. 10, 1994); Seper, "Leach vows 'careful' Whitewater probe," *Washington Times*, A1 (Nov. 12, 1994).

[280]Pollock, "Madison S&L Appraiser Pleads Guilty In Starr's First Whitewater Prosecution," *Wall Street Journal*, B10 (Dec. 6, 1994); Schmidt, "S&L Figure Pleads Guilty In Arkansas, *Washington Post*, A1 (Dec. 6, 1994); Seper, "Starr gets first Whitewater conviction," *Washington Times*, A1 (Dec. 6, 1994); Labaton, "Appraiser on Madison Loans in Plea Accord," *New York Times*, B9 (Dec. 6, 1994).

[281]Seper, "No jail for appraiser in Whitewater case," *Washington Times*, A2 (June 17, 1995).

[282]Schmidt, "Hubbell Pleads Guilty to Fraud Charges," *Washington Post*, A1 (Dec. 7, 1994); Seper, "Hubbell pleads guilty to fraud," *Washington Times*, A1 (Dec. 7, 1994); Labaton, "A Clinton Friend Admits Mail Fraud And Tax Evasion," *New York Times*, A1 (Dec. 7, 1994); Novak & Pollock, "Hubbell Pleads Guilty to Two Felony Counts, As New Round of Whitewater Inquiries Begin," *Wall Street Journal*, A16 (Dec. 7, 1994).

[283]Schmidt, "Hubbell's Plea Agreement May Yield Whitewater Clues," *Washington Post*, A1 (Dec. 3, 1994); Seper, "Hubbell may play key role in probe," *Washington Times*, A1 (Dec. 3, 1994); Safire, "And Then There Were Two," *New York Times*, A19 (Dec. 5, 1994).

[284]The *Wall Street Journal* "remain[ed] to be persuaded that his cooperation will be more than pro forma." "Who Was Webster Hubbell—II," *Wall Street Journal*, A18 (Dec. 8, 1994).

Starr obtained a delay of Hubbell's April 28, 1995 sentencing date until June 28, in order to continue efforts to obtain Hubbell's cooperation in the investigation, which efforts Starr described as incomplete. Seper, "Hubbell gets time to talk about role in Madison probe," *Washington Times*, A3 (Apr. 12, 1995).

[285]Lardner, "Hubbell Gets 21 Months For Fraud," *Washington Post*, A1 (June 29, 1995); Seper, "Hubbell handed 21-month jail term," *Washington Times*, A1 (June 29, 1995); Gerth, "Ex-Clinton Confidant Gets 21 Months," *New York Times*, B6 (June 29, 1995).

[286]One reporter concluded that Starr's rejection of Hubbell's request for a shorter sentence "was a sign that his cooperation with the authorities had yielded little new substantive information." Gerth, "Ex-Clinton Confidant Gets 21 Months," *New York Times*, B6 (June 29, 1995). Earlier, Sara Fritz reported that Hubbell "has told friends that he has no knowledge of any wrongdoing." Fritz, "Only Small Fry Snared So Far in Whitewater," *Los Angeles Times*, A1, A21 (Apr. 2, 1995). Similarly, the *Wall Street Journal*, A1 (May 12, 1995), reported that, "[t]o the disappointment of Whitewater prosecutors," Hubbell "shed ... little light on allegations that Clinton officials thwarted the [RTC investigation]."

[287]Price, "D'Amato to call on U.S. attorney to testify on Whitewater referrals," *Washington Times*, A1 (Dec. 4, 1994). In the summer of 1994, Fiske had objected to Casey's appearance before the House Banking Committee, fearing that it could interfere with his investigation.

[288]Seper, "D'Amato defers inquiry to Starr," *Washington Times*, A1 (Dec. 14, 1994); Schmidt, "D'Amato Delays Whitewater Hearings," *Washington Post*, A9 (Dec. 14, 1994); Labaton, "D'Amato Delays New Whitewater Hearings," *New York Times*, A19 (Dec. 14, 1994); Novak, "D'Amato to Delay Panel's Hearings Into Whitewater," *Wall Street Journal*, B4 (Dec. 14, 1994).

[289]Seper, "Leach's Whitewater pace will be cautious," *Washington Times*, A5 (Dec. 20, 1994).

[290]Schmidt, "Republicans Accuse Clinton Aides of Misconduct in Whitewater Report," *Washington Post*, A12 (Jan. 4, 1995); Seper, "GOP attacks Whitewater testimony," *Washington Times*, A1 (Jan. 4, 1995); Labaton, "Senate Reports on Whitewater Offer Glimpse of Partisan Battling Still in Store," *New York Times*, A14 (Jan. 4, 1995); Margasak & Solomon, "Draft of Senate Whitewater Report Details Conflicts in Testimony," *Washington Times*, A4 & *Washington Post*, A6 (Dec. 27, 1995)(original Associated Press story).

[291]Schmidt, "Republicans Accuse Clinton Aides of Misconduct in Whitewater Report," *Washington Post*, A12 (Jan. 4, 1995).

[292]Seper, "Two chairmen seek Whitewater papers," *Washington Times*, A4 (Jan. 5, 1995).

[293]Seper, "Hubbell probed anew on Madison," *Washington Times*, A1 (Jan. 11, 1995); Seper, "Did Hubbell block federal probe of S&L?" *Washington Times*, A1 (Feb. 27, 1995). In May 1995, Jerry Seper reported that congressional and independent counsel investigators were reviewing seven phone calls Hubbell made to Casey over a six-week period, between September 29 and November 9, 1993, some of which were allegedly made after Hubbell said he had recused himself. Seper, "Timing of calls by Hubbell examined," *Washington Times*, A1 (May 8, 1995). Casey recused herself on November 5, although it was not announced until November 9; Hubbell said on November 3, 1993 that he had recused himself "several weeks earlier."

[294]Seper, "D'Amato to start hearings in May," *Washington Times*, A2 (Feb. 4, 1995).

[295]Schmidt & Devroy, "White House Assembling Whitewater Legal Team," *Washington Post*, A7 (Feb. 8, 1995); Bedard, "'Nightmare scenario' rattles Democrats," *Washington Times*, A1 (May 5, 1995)(reporting that no spokesperson had yet been appointed).

[296]Hitt, "Whitewater's Chief Counsel Assails Leach," *Wall Street Journal*, A16 (Mar. 15, 1995); Seper, "Leach to meet Starr on Whitewater files," *Washington Times*, A3 (Mar. 16, 1995).

[297]Seper, "Leach delays hearings into Whitewater affair," *Washington Times*, A8 (Mar. 21, 1995).

[298]Schmidt, "Whitewater Hearings Approved, *Washington Post*, A1 (May 18, 1995); Seper, "Senate sets up special panel on Whitewater," *Washington Times*, A1 (May 18, 1995); Pollock, Senate to Hold Whitewater Hearings, Likely Running Into the '96 Campaign," *Wall Street Journal*, A4 (May 18, 1995); Labaton, "Senate Votes To Establish Inquiry Panel," *New York Times*, B14 (May 18, 1995); see also, Seper, "Probe of 'contacts' may be compromised," *Washington Times*, A1 (May 9, 1995); Seper, "D'Amato panel to hunt for lies from past Whitewater hearings," *Washington Times*, A3 (May 16, 1995); Seper, "What Clinton said to Tucker will get new Senate scrutiny," *Washington Times*, A4 (June 14, 1995); Seper, "Whitewater hearings to spotlight Nussbaum," *Washington Times*, A4 (June 16, 1995); Seper, "Whitewater depositions begin," *Washington Times*, A4 (June 20, 1995)(noting depositions taken of Park Police employees involved in investigation of Foster's death); Seper, "Whitewater panel to plumb possible leaks,"*Washington Times*, A4 (June 26, 1995).

[299]However, the hearings would not examine Mrs. Clinton's commodities trades, or Governor Clinton's campaigns before 1990.

[300]Seper, "Foster papers up first as Whitewater hearings open July 18," *Washington Times*, A6 (July 7, 1995).

[301]Sands, "D'Amato sets Whitewater hearings for early July," *Washington Times*, A15 (June 28, 1995).

[302]Phil Gramm, because of his candidacy for the Republican nomination to oppose the President in the 1996 elections, said he would not serve on the Special Committee. Kellman, "Gramm steps down from panel probing Clintons," *Washington Times*, A6 (May 31, 1995).

[303]Schmidt, "House Whitewater Hearings Planned," *Washington Post*, A8 (June 14, 1995).

[304]Schmidt & Devroy, "Clintons Questioned by Independent Counsel," *Washington Post*, A6 (Apr. 23, 1995); Labaton, "Clintons Give Testimony On Finances," *New York Times*, sec. 1, p. 25 (Apr. 23, 1995); Associated Press, "Whitewater prober questions president and first lady," *Washington Times*, A4 (Apr. 23, 1995).

[305]Schmidt, "Ex-Bank Official Indicted Over Clinton Election Cash," *Washington Post*, A1 (Mar. 1, 1995); Seper, "Indictment covers loans to Clinton campaign," *Washington Times*, A1 (Mar. 1, 1995); Labaton, "Arkansas Banker Is Indicted in Transactions Tied to Clinton's 1990 Campaign for Governor," *New York Times*, A12 (Mar. 1, 1995); Pollock, "Grand Jury Indicts Ex-Bank President In Whitewater Case," *Wall Street Journal*, B10 (Mar. 1, 1995).

[306]Engleberg, "Whitewater Salesman Pleads Guilty to Fraud," *New York Times*, A15 (Mar. 22, 1995); Schmidt, "Ex-Whitewater Property Manager Due in Court Today," *Washington Post*, A6 (Mar. 21, 1995); Seper, "Starr wins fourth Arkansas guilty plea," *Washington Times*, A3 (Mar. 22, 1995); Pollock, "Arkansas Who Sold Whitewater Lots For the Clintons Enters Guilty Pleas," *Wall Street Journal*, B6 (Mar. 22, 1995). On December 1, 1995, Wade was sentenced to fifteen months in prison, fined $3,000, and ordered three years of probation upon his release. Wade's attorney said he would appeal the sentence; Starr was satisfied. Associated Press, "Whitewater figure gets 15 month for guilty plea," *Washington Times*, A14 (Dec. 2, 1995).

[307]Seper, "Arkansas banker expected to deny guilt, point finger," *Washington Times*, A1 (Mar. 9, 1995);

"Arkansan Offers Plea in Case Linked to Clinton's '90 Campaign," *New York Times*, A20 (Mar. 10, 1995); Seper, "Ex-banker pleads not guilty to fraud," *Washington Times*, A6 (Mar. 10, 1995).

[308]Seper, "Plea gives Starr fifth conviction in Whitewater probe," *Washington Times*, A1 (May 3, 1995); Pollock, "Arkansas Banker Pleads Guilty in Case Over Withdrawals for Clinton Campaign," *Wall Street Journal*, B2 (May 3, 1995); Schmidt, "Independent Counsel Probes Whitewater From Bottom Up," *Washington Post*, A1, A16 (May 3, 1995).

[309]Labaton, "Top Clinton Aide Ordered Payments Hidden," *New York Times*, A20 (May 3, 1995); Seper, "Ex-banker expected to implicate Lindsey in Whitewater testimony," *Washington Times*, A1 (May 4, 1995); "Schmidt & Devroy, "Probe Moves Closer to Clinton," *Washington Post*, A1 (May 4, 1995). A Currency Transaction Report is required to be filed with the IRS for cash withdrawals of $10,000 or more.

[310]The existence of the target letter was not disclosed until May 1995. Devroy & Schmidt, "Lindsey Told Months Ago He Is Whitewater 'Target'," *Washington Post*, A1 (May, 5, 1995). Lindsey's lawyer said Lindsey told the President of the target letter within days. Pollock, "Clinton Aide Lindsey Is Target of Probe; Supporters Believe He Will Be Indicted," *Washington Post*, A14 (May 5, 1995).

[311]Also, Arkansas election law prohibits a campaign from spending more than $50 in cash in a single transaction.

[312]Schmidt & Devroy, "Key Adviser to Clinton Won't Make Moscow Trip," *Washington Post*, A5 (May 6, 1995); Associated Press, "Lindsey money move is explained," *Washington Times*, A7 (May 9, 1995).

[313]Schmidt, "Lindsey Avoids Key Charges," *Washington Post*, A1 (May 20, 1995); Labaton, "Clinton's Counsel, Lindsey, Will Not Face Indictment on Banking Charges," *New York Times*, p. 8 (May 20, 1995)(noting that Lindsey had not yet received a declination letter); Seper, "Facing deadline, Starr opts not to indict Lindsey next week," *Washington Times*, A4 (May 20, 1995); Pollock, "White House Aide Lindsey Gets Reprieve From Whitewater Independent Counsel," *Wall Street Journal*, A4 (May 22, 1995).

[314]On November 2, 1990, Ainley allegedly went into his bank's mailroom to remove a Currency Transaction Report that had been prepared by another bank employee for a Clinton campaign withdrawal over $10,000. If Lindsey directed Ainley to intercept this report, he would still be subject to prosecution until November 1995. Adams, "Starr Witnesses," *American Spectator*, 24, 25 (Aug. 1995).

[315]Seper, "Whitewater grand jury indicts Tucker," *Washington Times*, A1 (June 8, 1995); Schmidt, "Ark. Governor Indicted In Probe of Whitewater," *Washington Post*, A1 (June 8, 1995); Gerth, "Arkansas's Chief Accused of Fraud," *New York Times*, A1 (June 8, 1995); Pollock, "Arkansas Gov. Tucker Accused of Lying As Whitewater Probe Is Pushed in State," *Wall Street Journal*, B4 (June 8, 1995).

[316]Pressley, "Amid Friends, Tucker Is Arraigned," *Washington Post*, A6 (June 23, 1995); Smothers, "For Arkansas Democrats, The Times Turn Painful," *New York Times*, A22 (June 23, 1995).

[317]Seper, "Tucker pleads not guilty, attacks counsel's ethics," *Washington Times*, A4 (June 23, 1995).

[318]Schmidt, "Early Clinton Ally Pleads Guilty To Loan Conspiracy in Arkansas," *Washington Post*, A1 (June 9, 1995); Seper, "Ex-Clinton aide takes Whitewater plea deal," *Washington Times*, A1 (June 9, 1995); Gerth, "Former Clinton Aides Pleads Guilty to Misusing U.S.-Backed Loan," *New York Times*, A20 (June 9, 1995); Pollock, "Former Clinton Aide in Arkansas Pleads Guilty to Misusing U.S.-Sponsored Loan," *Wall Street Journal*, B9 (June 9, 1995).

[319]Schmidt, "Early Clinton Ally Pleads Guilty To Loan Conspiracy in Arkansas," *Washington Post*, A1, A16 (June 9, 1995).

[320]Seper, "Starr secures another plea deal," *Washington Times*, A13 (July 14, 1995); Pollock, "McDougal Partner Enters Plea Pact In Whitewater Case," *Wall Street Journal*, B4 (July 14, 1995).

[321]Associated Press, "Figure Who Falsely Secured Loan Is to Testify," *Washington Post*, A11 (Oct. 12, 1995).

[322]Associated Press, "Starr spends hours interviewing Clintons," *Washington Times*, A4 (July 23, 1995).

[323]Purdum, "White House Offers Documents to New Whitewater Hearings," *New York Times*, B8 (July 10, 1995); Schmidt, "Probe Into Handling of Foster Files May Highlight Some Discrepancies," *Washington Post*, A4 (July 10, 1995); Pollock, "Clinton Aides Vulnerable to GOP Attach Over Versions of Vincent Foster Case," *Wall Street Journal*, A16 (July 10, 1995).

[324]Schmidt & Babcock, "Foster Worried About Audit On Whitewater," *Washington Post*, A1 (July 14, 1995).

[325]Associated Press, "Foster's papers released," *Washington Times*, A10 (July 11, 1995).

[326]Ibid.

[327]Pollock, "McDougal Partner Enters Plea In Whitewater Case," *Wall Street Journal*, B4 (July 14, 1995).

[328]Schmidt & Babcock, "Foster Worried About Audit On Whitewater," *Washington Post*, at A9 (July 14, 1995).

[329]Isikoff, "The Night Foster Died," *Newsweek*, 20, 21 (July 17, 1995).

[330]Schmidt & Babcock, "Foster Worried About Audit On Whitewater," *Washington Post,* A1 (July 14,

1995); Safire, "Vincent Foster's 'Can of Worms'," *New York Times*, A13 (July 24, 1995).

[331]Seper, "Hubbell kept Whitewater files at home," *Washington Times*, A1 (July 19, 1995); Labaton, "Details Emerge On Whitewater As Panel Starts," *New York Times*, A1 (July 19, 1995); Schmidt & Kovaleski, "Partisan Tone Marks Hearing on Foster Death," *Washington Post*, A1 (July 19, 1995).

[332]Labaton, "G.O.P. Senators Demand All Files On Whitewater," *New York Times*, A1 (July 20, 1995); Seper, "Waco, Whitewater figures tell disturbing tales," *Washington Times*, A1 (July 20, 1995); Schmidt & Kovaleski, "Hubbell Says Nussbaum Kept Probers From Files," *Washington Post*, A1 (July 20, 1995).

[333]Seper, "Police not told of Foster office search," *Washington Times*, A1 (July 21, 1995); Kovaleski, "Hearing Focuses on Search of Foster's Office," *Washington Post*, A1 (July 21, 1995); Labaton, "White House Role Faulted In Inquiry on Aide's Suicide," *New York Times*, A1 (July 21, 1995).

[334]Seper, "Justice was wary of Foster probe," *Washington Times*, A1 (July 26, 1995); Babcock & Schmidt, "White House Aides Tell Of Foster Office Search," *Washington Post*, A14 (July 26, 1995); Labaton, "No Intention To Question First Lady," *New York Times*, A14 (July 26, 1995).

[335]Labaton, "2 Conflicting Accounts on Files From White House Aide's Office," *New York Times*, A1 (July 27, 1995); Schmidt & LaFraniere, "Senators Hear 2 Stories On Foster Office Search," *Washington Post*, A16 (July 27, 1995); Seper, "Hillary's top aide took Foster files, lawman testifies," *Washington Times*, A1 (July 27, 1995); Pollack, "Guard Tells Senate Whitewater Panel He Saw Files Taken From Foster's Office," *Wall Street Journal*, A12 (July 27, 1995).

[336]Seper, "Hearings yield new Foster note tale," *Washington Times*, A1 (July 28, 1995); Babcock & Schmidt, "Foster's Note Allegedly Ignored," *Washington Post*, A4 (July 28, 1995); Labaton, "Nussbaum Becomes Focus Of Whitewater Testimony," *New York Times*, A16 (July 28, 1995).

[337]Seper, "Clinton aide lied about Foster note, police officer says," *Washington Times*, A1 (Aug. 2, 1995); Labaton, "Clinton Papers' Index in Foster Office Vanished After Suicide, Aide Says," *New York Times*, A14 (Aug. 2, 1995); LaFraniere, "Nussbaum Acted Harshly, Foster Top Aide Tells Panel," *Washington Post*, A2 (Aug. 2, 1995).

[338]Labaton, "White House Hurt Inquiry on Suicide, Ex-Official Says," *New York Times*, A1 (Aug. 3, 1995); Seper, "No. 2 Justice official saw 'disaster' in Foster probe," *Washington Times*, A1 (Aug. 3, 1995); LaFraniere, "Ex-Justice Aide Recalls Fights on Foster Probe," *Washington Post*, A4 (Aug. 3, 1995).

[339]Seper, "Hillary got Foster files, panel told," *Washington Times*, A1 (Aug. 4, 1995); LaFraniere, "Two Witnesses Dispute Foster Search Testimony," *Washington Post*, A8 (Aug. 4, 1995); Labaton, "Whitewater Panel Focuses on Mrs. Clinton," *New York Times*, A22 (Aug. 4, 1995).

[340]See also, Schmidt, "Lawyer Says Hillary Clinton Urged Strict Limit," *Washington Post*, A1 (July 23, 1995)(reporting Neuwirth's deposition to the Senate).

[341]Merida, "Whitewater Hearings Begin on a Testy Note," *Washington Post*, A1 (Aug. 8, 1995); Schmidt, "Clintons Depicted As Active in Venture," *Washington Post*, A1 (Aug. 8, 1995); Seper, "'Rampant' fraud at Madison S&L helped Whitewater, prober found," *Washington Times*, A1 (Aug. 8, 1995); Gerth, "House Panel Opens A New Front In the Whitewater Investigations," *Washington Times*, A1 (Aug. 8, 1995).

[342]LaFraniere, "Friend's Testimony Contradicts President's Aide," *Washington Post*, A4 (Aug. 9, 1995); Kellman, "Clinton pal denies calling about papers," *Washington Times*, A1 (Aug. 9, 1995); Lewis, "Justice and Treasury Officials Hindered Whitewater Inquiry, Investigator Says," *New York Times*, A14 (Aug. 9, 1995).

[343]Seper, "Democrats fail to halt tale of Madison scam," *Washington Times*, A1 (Aug. 9, 1995); Merida & Schmidt, "Witness Says Probe Was Blocked," *Washington Post*, A1 (Aug. 9, 1995); Novak & Pollack, "RTC Investigator Claims U.S. Officials Sought to 'Obstruct' Probe of Whitewater," *Wall Street Journal*, B8 (Aug. 9, 1995).

[344]Merida, "Whitewater Tape Played," *Washington Post*, A1 (Aug. 10, 1995); Kellman, "RTC official on spot after panel hears prober pressured," *Washington Times*, A1 (Aug. 10, 1995).

[345]LaFraniere & Schmidt, "Nussbaum Defends His Handling of Search of Foster's Office," *Washington Post*, A14 (Aug. 10, 1995); Pollack & Novak, "Nussbaum Defends Actions Following Foster's Suicide," *Wall Street Journal*, B7 (Aug. 10, 1995); Labaton, "Nussbaum Appears Before Whitewater Panel and Defends Handling of Foster's Files," *New York Times*, B7 (Aug. 10, 1995); Seper, "Nussbaum rejects others' testimony," *Washington Times*, A1 (Aug. 10, 1995).

[346]Lewis, "Top Justice Official Testifies of Limits On Foster Inquiry," *New York Times*, A1 (Aug. 11, 1995); Seper, "Nussbaum contradicted again," *Washington Times*, A1 (Aug. 11, 1995); LaFraniere, "Justice Department Official Criticizes Nussbaum," *Washington Post*, A15 (Aug. 11, 1995).

[347]Schmidt, "Hearing Puts Focus on Rose Law Practice," *Washington Post*, A1 (Aug. 11, 1995); Kellman, "Hillary may have signed S&L as client," *Washington Times*, A10 (Aug. 11, 1995); "Rose Law Firm's conflicts detailed," *Washington Times*, A10 (Aug. 11, 1995)(excerpts from testimony).

[348]The reports were released a few days before the hearings. Schmidt, "FDIC, Rose Law firm Faulted By Agency Inspector General," *Washington Post*, A1 (Aug. 1, 1995); Labaton, "Regulators See Conflict at

Firm Tied to Clintons," *New York Times*, A11 (Aug. 1, 1995); Seper, "Rose Law Firm may be penalized," *Washington Times*, A6 (Aug. 1, 1995); Schmidt, "Report Reveals Rose Law Firm Role in Land Deal," *Washington Post*, A1 (Aug. 5, 1995); Seper & Bedard, "RTC critical of Hillary's former law firm," *Washington Times*, A1 (Aug. 5, 1995). At the time of their release, the White House released the written replies of the President and First Lady to the questions posed by the RTC. Engleberg, "Clintons, in Responses on Whitewater, Cite Role as 'Passive Investors'," *New York Times*, 8 (Aug. 5, 1995).

[349]Merida, "Republicans' Dive Into Whitewater Scores Some Points," *Washington Post*, A1, A6 (Aug. 14, 1995).

[350]Schmidt, "Whitewater Partners Face Fraud Charges," *Washington Post*, A1 (Aug. 18, 1995); Seper, "McDougals, Tucker indicted on fraud charges," *Washington Times*, A1 (Aug. 18, 1995); Labaton, "Fraud Charges Against Couple Tied to Clinton," *New York Times*, A1 (Aug. 18, 1995); Novak, "Arkansas Governor, Clintons' Partner In Whitewater Are Charged With Fraud," *Wall Street Journal*, A12 (Aug. 18, 1995). Nineteen counts named Jim McDougal, 11 Tucker and 8 Susan McDougal.

[351]However, the count relating to the $300,000 loan alleges that Hale, the McDougals, "and others known to the grand jury" arranged for the loan. Schmidt, "Whitewater Partners Face Fraud Charges," *Washington Post*, A1, A14 (Aug. 18, 1995).

[352]Tucker pled not guilty on August 28, Jim McDougal on August 29, and Susan McDougal on August 30. Seper, "Tucker pleads not guilty," *Washington Times*, A1 (Aug. 29, 1995); Labaton, "Governor of Arkansas Pleads Not Guilty to Fraud Charges," *New York Times*, A14 (Aug. 29, 1995); Labaton, "Not Guilty Plea in Whitewater," *New York Times*, A15 (Aug. 30, 1995); Seper, "Madison owner pleads not guilty," *Washington Times*, A1 (Aug. 30, 1995); Seper, "Susan McDougal pleads not guilty," *Washington Times*, A1 (Sept. 1, 1995).

[353]Seper, "Judge delays Tucker trial," *Washington Times*, A4 (Oct. 5, 1995).

[354]Schmidt, "Whitewater Partners Face Fraud Charges," *Washington Post*, A1 (Aug. 18, 1995).

[355]Thompson, "Caught in the Whitewater Quagmire," *Washington Post*, A1, A14 (Aug. 28, 1995).

[356]Seper, "Judge drops fraud charges against Tucker," *Washington Times*, A1 (Sept. 6, 1995); Schmidt, "1 Whitewater Indictment of Tucker Dismissed," *Washington Post*, A6 (Sept. 6, 1995).

[357]Murray, "Legal analysts say indictment of Tucker likely to be restored," *Washington Times*, A1 (Sept. 8, 1995).

[358]"Judge Woods to the rescue, " *Washington Times*, A18 (Sept. 6, 1995); "Henry Comes Through," *Wall Street Journal*, A14 (Sept. 7, 1995). Both papers had urged Woods to recuse himself back in June 1995, when the case was first assigned.

[359]Johnson, "Judge Henry Woods and the long arm of the law," *Washington Times*, A15 9Sept. 12, 1995); Morrison, "Arkansas Judge Runs the Clock on Whitewater," *Wall Street Journal*, A14 (Oct. 4, 1995).

[360]"Dear Vince, . . . Very Truly Yours, Henry,'" *Washington Times*, A18 (Oct. 10, 1995).

[361]Schmidt, "Citing Tie to Hillary Clinton, Starr Seeks Recusal of Judge," *Washington Post*, A11 (Oct. 12, 1995).

[362]Seper, "Federal judge leaves in place Whitewater case indictments," *Washington Times*, A3 (Nov. 16, 1995).

[363]Seper, "Whitewater hearings to push on,"*Washington Times*, A1 (Oct. 3, 1995).

[364]Seper, "Subpoenas coming, D'Amato warns," *Washington Times*, A1, A16 (Oct. 26, 1995)(excerpt of statement of Michael Chertoff, Special Counsel to the Committee). Also of concern to the Committee was a report that the Treasury Department's Office of Inspector General shredded a significant amount of documents relating to the IG's review of the White House-Treasury contacts. The matter was brought to the Committee's attention by an employee in the IG's office, who said she was told that only copies of documents were shredded.

[365]Seper, "D'Amato readying blanket subpoena," *Washington Times*, A1 (Oct. 25, 1995); Schmidt, "White House Faces Subpoena Over Whitewater," *Washington Post*, A1 (Oct. 26, 1995)

[366]Seper, "Subpoenas coming, D'Amato warns," *Washington Times*, A1, A16 (Oct. 26, 1995).

[367]Seper, "Whitewater subpoenas target Clintons, aides," *Washington Times*, A1 (Oct. 27, 1995); Schmidt, "Senate Whitewater Panel Votes 49 Subpoenas for White House, Others," *Washington Post*, A8 (Oct. 27, 1995); Labaton, "Senate Whitewater Panel Seeks More Documents From Clintons," *New York Times*, A28 (Oct. 27, 1995). Democrats on the Committee voted in favor the subpoenas after the Republicans agreed to reduce the scope of some of the subpoenas to not cover certain documents arguably protected by the attorney-client and attorney work product privileges (i.e., notes of interviews of the Clintons, records generated in preparation for the investigations).

[368]At 7:44 on the morning of the 22nd, Maggie Williams called the First Lady in Arkansas. The First lady then called Susan Thomases a little before 8. Thomases then paged Nussbaum at 8:01. Williams called the First Lady again shortly after noon.

[369]Labaton, "Telephone Records Lead to New Subpoenas in Whitewater Case," *New York Times*, A18

(Oct. 26, 1995); Seper, "Subpoenas coming, D'Amato warns," *Washington Times*, A1, A16 (Oct. 26, 1995); Schmidt, "Senate Whitewater Panel Votes 49 Subpoenas for White House, Others," *Washington Post*, A8 (Oct. 27, 1995).

[370]Seper, "RTC Whitewater prober quits," *Washington Times*, A1 (Sept. 19, 1995).

[371]Seper, "Former RTC official submits papers to Whitewater panel," *Washington Times*, A2 (Oct. 28, 1995).

[372]Seper, "Hillary's closest advisers lied on phone calls, senators fume," *Washington Times*, A1 (Nov. 3, 1995); Labaton, "Advisers to Mrs. Clinton Are Questioned Anew in Foster Case," *New York Times*, A26 (Nov. 3, 1995); Schmidt, "Republicans Doubt Testimony on Plans for Foster Office Search," *Washington Post*, A9 (Nov. 3, 1995).

[373]Seper, "Senators told of Madison tip-off," *Washington Times*, A1 (Nov. 8, 1995); Schmidt, "GOP: Treasury Officials Received Leaked Data," *Washington Post*, A12 (Nov. 8, 1995); Labaton, "Treasury Officials Accused of Undermining Review in Whitewater Case," *New York Times*, D24 (Nov. 8, 1995).

[374]This quote is a combination of the somewhat differing quotes from the *Washington Post* and *New York Times* stories. A hearing transcript was not available at the time of publication.

[375]Schmidt, "GOP Assails Lawyers at Treasury," *Washington Post*, A3 (Nov. 9, 1995); Seper, "Treasury witness denies improperly passing papers," *Washington Times*, A3 (Nov. 9, 1995).

[376]According to an OGE official, no draft of the OGE report was shown to Treasury or the White House.

[377]Seper, "Cutler says he 'may have transgressed,'"*Washington Times*, A8 (Nov. 10, 1995)(ellipses in *Times* article).

[378]Schmidt, "Cutler Concedes He Misstated Ethics Finding," *Washington Post*, A19 (Nov. 10, 1995).

[379]Labaton, "Ex-Official Spars With Whitewater Panel," *New York Times*, A25 (Nov. 10, 1995).

[380]Associated Press, "Lawyer had Whitewater documents," *Washington Times*, A4 (Nov. 13, 1995).

[381]Heymann initiated an internal review of what occurred, which resulted in a written FBI summary from which the Associated Press derived much of the information for its story.

[382]Seper, "White House knew of aim of RTC inquiry, "*Washington Times*, A1 (Nov. 14, 1995).

[383]"'More than potential witnesses'," *Washington Times*, A14 (Nov. 29, 1995).

[384]Seper, "RTC passed a legal analysis of Madison case to Treasury," *Washington Times*, A3 (Nov.15, 1995).

[385]Seper, "Whitewater panel resumes hearing on Madison probe," *Washington Times*, A7 (Nov. 28, 1995); Schmidt, "Aides Say SBA Shared Data On Clinton Foe," *Washington Post*, A1 (Nov. 29, 1995); Seper, "Clinton aide mum on Whitewater talk," *Washington Times*, A1 (Nov. 29, 1995); Labaton, "Whitewater Panel Explores Clinton Link to Arkansas Judge," *New York Times*, B10 (Nov. 29, 1995).

[386]Schmidt, "Whitewater Prober Accused Of Prejudice Against Clinton," *Washington Post*, A1 (Nov. 30, 1995); Seper, "Whitewater witness rushed to hospital," *Washington Times*, A1 (Nov. 20, 1995); Labaton, "Senate Hearing Touches on Clinton's Integrity," *New York Times*, B14 (Nov. 30, 1995).

[387]Seper, "Witness files ethics charges over airing of personal letter," *Washington Times*, A3 (Dec. 5, 1995); Schmidt, "Whitewater Witness Alleges Her Privacy Was Violated," *Washington Post*, A4 (Dec. 5, 1995); "The ransacking of Jean Lewis' computer files," *Washington Times*, A17 (Dec. 5, 1995)(text of letter from Mark Levin to Senate Ethics Committee).

[388]Gigot, "Senate Dems Play 'Gennifer' Card. Really." *Wall Street Journal*, A14 (Dec. 1, 1995); "The attack on Jean Lewis," *Washington Times*, A20 (Dec. 1, 1995); Cohen, "A Dead Letter Lives Again," *Washington Post*, A19 (Dec. 5, 1995); "Ethics and Jean Lewis," *Washington Times*, A20 (Dec. 6, 1995); "Sarbanes' Plumbers," *Wall Street Journal*, A20 (Dec. 6, 1995); "The White House Mess," *Washington Post*, A22 (Dec. 7, 1995).

[389]Labaton, "Republican Whitewater Inquiry To Focus on Role of Mrs. Clinton," *New York Times*, A30 (Dec. 1, 1995).

[390]Seper, "Panel sends Hillary queries about mystery call," *Washington Times*, A1, A22 (Dec. 1, 1995).

[391]Schmidt, "Senate Panel Examines Inconsistent Accounts Surrounding Foster File Review," *Washington Post*, A13 (Dec. 1, 1995); Simpson, "Senate's Whitewater Panel Is to Request Mrs. Clinton Submit Written Testimony," *Wall Street Journal*, A16 (Dec. 1, 1995).

[392]Seper, "Documents reveal Hillary's extensive work for Madison," *Washington Times*, A1 (Dec. 2, 1995); Labaton, "Senate Hearing Homes In On First Lady's Credibility," *New York Times*, 8 (Dec. 2, 1995).

[393]Seper, "Second Clinton aide claims privilege," *Washington Times*, A1 (Dec. 6, 1995); Schmidt, "White House Balks at Discussing 1993 Meeting Before Whitewater Panel," *Washington Post*, A7 (Dec. 6, 1995); Labaton, "Clinton Adviser Is Ordered Not to Answer Whitewater Queries," *New York Times*, A20 (Dec. 6, 1995).

[394]Labaton, "Subpoena Vote Looms Over Impasse on Whitewater Evidence," *New York Times*, A28 (Dec. 8, 1995);

[395]Schmidt, "Whitewater Witnesses Tell Panel Clinton Information Was Rebuffed," *Washington Post*,

A2 (Dec. 2, 1995).

[396]Seper, "Clinton aides told to talk or else," *Washington Times*, A1, A10 (Dec. 7, 1995).

[397]Schmidt, "White House Balks at Discussing 1993 Meeting Before Whitewater Panel," *Washington Post*, A7 (Dec. 6, 1995).

[398]Seper, "Hillary's mystery phone call apparently routed to McLarty," *Washington Times*, A1 (Dec. 8, 1995).

[399]Seper, "Hillary: 'I do not recall' call made to White House on the night Foster died," *Washington Times*, A4 (Dec. 9, 1995).

[400]Seper, "Whitewater panel votes for subpoena," *Washington Times*, A1 (Dec. 9, 1995); Schmidt, "Panel Votes Whitewater Subpoena," *Washington Post*, A1 (Dec. 9, 1995), Labaton, "Clinton Rebuffs A Senate Demand Over Whitewater," *New York Times*, p. 1 (Dec. 9, 1995). It was unclear from news reports whether the subpoena was limited to Kennedy's notes or also included the White House memorandum.

[401]In December 1982, the House of Representatives found EPA Administrator Anne Gorsuch in contempt of Congress for refusing to turn over enforcement-sensitive documents over which President Reagan had issued a formal claim of executive privilege. The Executive Branch filed suit seeking a declaratory judgment upholding the claim of executive privilege, but the suit was dismissed as nonjusticiable. *United States v. House of Representatives of the United States House,*—55 6F. Supp. 150——(D.D.C. 1983). The district court held that the proper judicial recourse in which to assert the privilege would be in a criminal contempt proceeding. The documents were eventually turned over. Subsequently, in August 1983, the U.S. Attorney quietly brought the contempt citation to the grand jury, which declined to indict, returning a "no true bill."

[402]"Whitewater Evasions, Cont.," *New York Times*, A22 (Dec. 6, 1995).

[403]"The White House Mess," *Washington Post*, A22 (Dec. 7, 1995) (emphasis in original). See also "The White House's privileges," *Washington Times*, A20 (Dec. 7, 1995).

Chapter Eight

[1]This study also does not include an analysis of whether Vince Foster committed suicide. Both the Park Police and Special Counsel Fiske determined that Foster took his own life, but independent counsel Starr reopened the matter and his investigation is continuing.

[2]The FBI is authorized to investigate the homicide of the President, Vice President and senior White House Officials, such as the Deputy Counsel to the President, which is a separate Federal felony, 18 U.S.C. 175 (a), (i). But the FBI apparently left the investigation to the Park Police because the death was assumed from the start to be a suicide. "Closing a Case," *Wall Street Journal*, A12 (Aug. 9, 1994). Justice Department Criminal Division lawyers, however, participated in the investigation and at the time of the search had not ruled out the possibility of foul play.

[3]Initially, the White House said that Justice would be the "point of contact" for the Park Police's investigation. Marcus & Devroy, Clintons Mystified By Aide's Death," *Washington Post*, A1, A6 (July 22, 1993). A Justice spokesman subsequently suggested that the Department would conduct an inquiry into the death, Devroy, "Clinton Finds No Explanation To Aide's Death," *Washington Post*, A4 (July 23, 1993), but later Justice spokesman Carl Stern said "[t]here is no investigation being conducted by the Justice Department[;]" the Department would only monitor the investigation by receiving periodic reports from the Park Police. "Self-Fulfilling Prophecy," *Wall Street Journal*, A14 (July 28, 1993). This statement was not accurate, in light of the involvement of senior Criminal Division officials in the search of Foster's office on July 22.

[4]LaFraniere & Marcus, "Nussbaum Staff Monitored Poster Probe Interviews," *Washington Post*, A4 (Feb. 5, 1994). A Park Police spokesman explained:

Our investigators went over to the White House the day after the suicide but didn't get into Vince's office[.] They sat and waited. We were informed that everything would be coordinated by the Justice Department. We were waiting for the Justice Department representative. He was in charge. He didn't show up until the second day.

Davidson, "Justice Official Objected to Involvement Of White House in Foster Investigation," *Wall Street Journal*, A16 (Feb. 7, 1994).

[5]This fact was not revealed by the White House until August 1994, nine months after the White House had said the Whitewater files had been delivered from Nussbaum to the Clintons' personal attorney. Marcus, "Whitewater File Was Kept At White House Residence," *Washington Post*, A4 (Aug. 2, 1994); Wines, "New Misstatements Admitted In Handling of Foster's Files," *New York Times*, A16 (Aug. 3, 1994).

[6]Ibid.

[7]Isikoff & Balz, "Foster Note Reveals Anguished Aide," *Washington Post*, A1 (Aug. 11, 1993). The text of the note in full:

I made mistakes from ignorance, inexperience and overwork

I did not knowingly violate any law or standard of conduct

No one in the White House, to my knowledge, violated any law or standard of conduct, including any action in the travel office. There was no intent to benefit any individual or specific group
The FBI lied in their report to the AG
The press is covering up the illegal benefits they received from the travel staff
The GOP has lied and misrepresented its knowledge and role and covered up a prior investigation
The Ushers Office plotted to have excessive costs incurred, taking advantage of Kaki and HRC
The public will never believe the innocence of the Clintons and their [loyal][legal] staff
The WSJ editors lie without consequence
I was not meant for the job or the spotlight of public life in Washington. Here ruining people is considered sport.

[8]Devroy & Isikoff, "Handling of Foster Case Is Defended," *Washington Post*, A1 (July 30, 1993). The text of the note was not made public until August 10, when a typed transcription was released by the Justice Department on the day the Park Police closed its investigation.

[9]"FBI Probes Handling of Foster Note," *Washington Post*, A11 (July 31, 1993).

[10]But the *Washington Post* reported that the Justice Department was seeking access to the diary in connection with Foster's Travel Office allegations, and added that an investigator "recalls seeing 'paperwork' related to [James] McDougal in the pile of documents inspected at Hamilton's office." Isikoff, "Probe Pursues White House Aide's Undisclosed Diary," *Washington Post*, A10 (Dec. 18, 1993).

[11]Isikoff & Balz, "Foster Note Reveals An Anguished Aide," *Washington Post*, A1 (Aug. 11, 1993). The Park Police report was not released to the public until July 1994, and even then, about 20 pages of material addressing the White House's involvement in and response to the Park Police investigation were redacted. The redactions were made at Special Counsel Fiske's request, because that portion of his investigation had not been completed. Johnston, "Prosecutor Seeking White House Files on Foster," *New York Times*, A18 (July 21, 1994).

[12]Seper, "Clinton papers lifted after aide's suicide," *Washington Times*, A1 (Dec. 18, 1993).

[13]Isikoff, "Whitewater Files Were Found in Foster's Office, White House Confirms," *Washington Post*, A16 (Dec. 22, 1993).

[14]LaFraniere & Marcus, "Nussbaum Staff Monitored Foster Probe Interviews," *Washington Post*, A4 (Feb. 5, 1994); "Davidson, "Justice Official Objected to Involvement Of White House in Foster Investigation," *Wall Street Journal*, A16 (Feb. 7, 1994).

[15]Isikoff, "Whitewater Special Counsel Promises 'Thorough' Probe," *Washington Post*, A1, A20 (Jan. 21, 1994); Johnston, "Claims Wide Writ In Clinton Inquiry," *New York Times*, A1 (Jan. 21, 1994).

[16]In May 1994, it was disclosed that Fiske had served subpoenas on the White House and White House officials seeking all documents that were in Foster's office at the time of his death, as well as other documents written by or concerning Foster. Murray, "Fiske subpoenas Foster documents from White House," *Washington Times*, A1 (May 6, 1994); Devroy, "Fiske Issues Broad Subpoena for White House Foster Files," *Washington Post*, A4 (May 6, 1994); Johnston, "Prosecutor Subpoenas All Files on Foster," *New York Times*, A19 (May 6, 1994); Birnbaum, "Fiske Subpoenas White House for Data On Foster With Focus on Nussbaum Role," *Wall Street Journal*, A16 (May 6, 1994).

[17]"Statement on Washington, D.C. Investigations," at 2 (June 30, 1994).

[18]Ibid., 1.

[19]Schmidt, "Whitewater Hearings Face New Obstacle," *Washington Post*, A12 (July 15, 1994); Associated Press, "Fiske report's delay will limit hearings," *Washington Times*, A12 (July 15, 1994); Garrett, "Hearings to exclude Foster office search," *Washington Times*, A1 (July 16, 1994).

[20]Nussbaum, "What I Did and Why I Did It," *New York Times,* A21 (Aug. 8, 1995).

[21]Nussbaum also asserted that official records in the Counsel's office were protected by the attorney-client privilege, but, with respect to the Government, this is really the same as the deliberative process, or executive privilege.

[22]Brickman, "Foster's Papers: What Executive Privilege?" *New York Times*, A19 (Aug. 2, 1995).

[23]Nussbaum, "What I Did and Why I Did It," *New York Times*, A21 (Aug. 8, 1995).

[24]Nussbaum apparently did not regard any of the papers as relevant to a law enforcement investigation. Ibid.

[25]Brickman, "Foster's Papers: What Executive Privilege?" *New York Times,* A19 (Aug. 2, 1995). Professor Stephen Gillers, in responding to Professor Brickman, stated, "The Clintons' files were theirs to reclaim, not because of attorney-client privilege but because the files were their property. . . . Returning the Clintons' own property to them was not obstruction of justice." Gillers, "White House Counsel Acted Within Law," *New York Times*, A18 (Aug. 10, 1995).

[26]Ruddy, "Experts Say Foster 'Suicide Note' Forged," *Pittsburgh Tribune-Review* (Oct. 25, 1995).

[27]Roman, "'A good strategy' by Clinton's lawyer," *Washington Times*, A1 (Jan. 7, 1994).

[28]A *Post* subheadline is typical: "White House Helped Shape Clinton Subpoena," A4 (Jan. 6, 1994).

[29]Devroy, "President's Lawyer Tried To Limit Justice Dept. Use of Whitewater Files," *Washington Post*, A9 (Jan. 8, 1994).

[30]Fed. R. Crim. Pro. 6(e)(3)(A).

[31]Ibid.

[32]28 CFR 0.39a.

[33]Isikoff, "Probe Pursues White House Aide's Undisclosed Diary," *Washington Post*, A10 (Dec. 18, 1993); Isikoff, "List Found With Foster Is Under Scrutiny," *Washington Post*, A9 (Jan. 13, 1994).

[34]*See,* for example, Fineman & Cohn, "Troubled WATERS," *Newsweek* 14,15 (Jan. 17, 1994)("Why? Because disclosing information from a subpoenaed document is a federal crime."); Schneider & Babcock, "An Ever-Growing Paper Trail," *Washington Post*, A1 (Jan. 8, 1994)("The release follows a Justice Department subpoena that the Clintons requested so the documents would be protected by grand jury secrecy rules."); Gigot, "What Did He Know, and When Did He Know It?" *Wall Street Journal*, A10 (Jan. 7, 1994)("By conspiring to have Justice issue a subpoena for the documents, the White House made sure nosy reporters can't obtain those documents under the Freedom of Information Act.").

[35]Fed. R. Crim. Pro. 6(e)(2).

[36]Ibid.

[37]Ibid.

[38]U.S. Department of Justice, *Freedom of Information Act Guide and Privacy Act Overview*, at 67 (Sept. 1992 edition), quoting *Washington Post Co. v. Department of Justice*, 863 F.2d 96, 100 (D.C. Cir. 1988).

[39]Further, as a matter of policy, Rule 6(e) is designed to protect grand jury deliberations, in order to protect persons who have not been formally charged of a crime from being implicated in a criminal investigation and therefore suspected of criminal activity. However, the text of the subpoena was released to the press. Thus, no harm of the sort contemplated by Rule 6(e) would result from the disclosure of the Whitewater files that were in the Clintons' custody or possession.

[40]Later, documents in the possession of the White House relating to White House-Treasury contacts and other matters were also sought. These later-created documents, by contrast, are Government records.

[41]5 U.S.C. 552(a); *Department of Justice v. Tax Analysts*, 494 U.S. 135, 144-45 (1989).

[42]*National Security Archive v. Archivist of the United States*, 909 F.2d 541 (D.C. Cir. 1990); see also, *Rushforth v. Council of Economic Advisors*, 762 F.2d 1038, 1042-43 (D.C. Cir. 1985); *Nixon v. Sampson*, 389 F. Supp. 107 (D.D.C. 1975).

[43]Von Drehle, "The Crumbling Of a Pillar In Washington," *Washington Post*, A1, A20 (Aug. 15, 1993).

[44]*Report of the Independent Counsel In Re Vincent W. Foster, Jr.* (hereafter, *Fiske Report)*, at 18, 20 (June 30, 1994).

[45]Ibid., 20. White House lawyers have traditionally exercised these latter responsibilities, although a President's personal attorney has also been involved.

[46]18 U.S.C. 641.

[47]*United States v. Croft*, 750 F.2d 1354, 1362 (7th Cir. 1984). The one precedent to the contrary, *Chappell v. United States*, 270 F.2d 274, 277 (9th Cir. 1959), which limited application of section 641 to tangible property, may no longer be good law. See *United States v. Schwartz*, 763 F.2d 1054, 1060 (9th Cir. 1985). Most of the reported cases involve whether section 641 applies to the unauthorized disclosure of government records or information, and hold that it does. See *United States v. Fowler*, 932 F.2d 306, 309 (4th Cir. 1991) (classified records)

[48]5 CFR 2635.705(a).

[49]5 CFR 2635.705(b).

[50]5 CFR 2635.102(h).

[51]5 CFR 2625.704.

[52]18 U.S.C. 205.

[53]Letter to Honorable Frank Wolf (Feb. 10, 1994).

[54]*Treasury, Postal Service, and General Government Appropriations for Fiscal Year 1995: Hearings Before the Subcomm. on the Treasury, Postal Service, and General Government Appropriations of the House Comm. on Appropriations*, 103d Cong., 2d Sess., 528, 601 (1994) (response of White House).

[55]Price, "Cutler envisions 'fully disclosed' Clinton tax data," *Washington Post*, A1, A12 (Mar. 20, 1994)("I would rather look forward. . . . I don't know what Vince Foster was doing in those early days, but I think it was just cleaning up a few details like the Whitewater tax returns[.]").

[56]Here are 3 examples of the White House's involvement in responding to press inquiries relating the Clintons' personal affairs, all relating to questions about the Clintons' tax liability: (1) After several reports were published that the Clintons would probably pay back taxes as a result of a review by the Clintons' personal attorney, "the White House subsequently issued a statement that seemed to back away from the

possibility of underpayment." Clift & Cohn, "Clinton's Bleak House," *Newsweek*, 20 (Mar. 28, 1994); (2) "Asked about it by TIME last month, presidential adviser Bruce Lindsey angrily brandished folders of documents (which he refused to show) that he insisted proved all the deductions they took related to Whitewater were legitimate." "Will They Pay," *Time*, 29 (Mar. 28, 1994); (3) "A senior White House official who discussed the status of Mr. Kendall's review said it was too soon to say for sure whether the Clintons overestimated their loss of underestimated their tax liability." Jehl, "Review Likely to Find Taxes Were Underpaid by Clintons," *New York Times*, 1 (Mar. 19, 1994).

[57]Report to the Secretary of the Treasury, from the Office of Government Ethics, at 8 (July 31, 1994)(July 30, 1994 letter from Stephen D. Potts to Honorable Lloyd Bentsen)(hereafter *OGE Report*)(emphasis added).

[58]5 CFR 2635.101(a).

[59]M. Fitzwater, *Call the Briefing!*, 84 (Times Books, 1995). The parallels are uncanny. Fitzwater wrote:
It took me only one day in the White House to realize that no one there knew the story of Iran-Contra, had any idea what had happened, or knew how to deal with the aftermath. All of the real participants had left or been fired. . . . Ibid., 83.

. . . It was a problem to solve in terms of providing documents to the investigators, and that was assigned to lawyers in the counsel's office who were not involved in policy matters. Thus the whole investigation was not threatening to the new staff in any personal way. Except for the President, none of us were involved. Ibid., 84.

[60]Murray, "Clinton picks man of stature to take Nussbaum's place," *Washington Times*, A8 (Mar. 9, 1994); Ifill, "President Chooses A Special Counsel; Openness Is Vowed," *New York Times*, A1, B7 (Mar. 9, 1994); Devroy, "Desire for Privacy Cited on Whitewater," *Washington Post*, A1, A7 (Mar. 14, 1994).

[61]30 *Weekly Compilation of Presidential Documents* 465 (Mar. 8, 1994).

[62]Taylor, "Clintons' partner pleads for records," *Washington Times*, A1, A8 (Mar. 14, 1994)(on "*Meet the Press*": "At least as far as even a breath of criminal activity by either the president and the first lady, it will turn out to be nothing at all[.]"); Price, "Cutler envisions 'fully disclosed' Clinton tax data," *Washington Times*, A1 (Mar. 20, 1994)(on "*Evans and Novak*": "I'm not going to say, obviously, what I'm going to advise [on whether the Clintons should release all remaining Whitewater tax records.]).

[63]*Statement on Washington, D.C. Investigation*, 4 (June 30, 1994).

[64]*OGE Report*, *supra* note 57, 3 (emphasis added).

[65]Indeed, it added that "[w]hether it is an appropriate activity for Treasury officials to assist the White House in carrying out its functions in fielding questions about the personal interests of the First Family would seem to be a management issue." Ibid., 8.

[66]OGE's report to Bentsen stated plainly, "[O]ur analysis is not intended to cover, **nor should it in any way reflect upon**, the actions of individuals who are employed by the White House." *OGE Report*, *supra* note 57, 2 (emphasis added).

[67]5 CFR 2635.702.

[68]5 CFR 2635.703(a).

[69]5 CFR 2635.101(b)(14).

[70]Schmidt & LaFraniere, "White House Aides Defend Their Conduct," *Washington Post*, A1, A20 (July 29, 1994).

[71]Associated Press, *Washington Times*, A6 (July 27, 1994)(quoting Cutler's testimony).

[72]Marcus, "Propriety of Alerting White House to Criminal Probe Debated," *Washington Post*, A16 (July 28, 1994) (emphasis added).

[73]Ibid.

[74]"Opening Statements," *Washington Post*, A18 (July 27, 1994) (emphasis added).

[75]*OGE Report*, *supra* note 57, 6, 8.

[76]Lacayo, "Shadow Of Doubt," *Time*, 28, 30 (Mar. 14, 1994).

[77]*OGE Report*, *supra* note 57, 8-10.

[78]Ibid., 10.

[79]*OGE Report*, *supra* note 57, 13-16.

[80]Schmidt, "Agencies Accused of 'Whitewash' on Whitewater," *Washington Post*, A9 (Feb. 25, 1994).

[81]Moreover, in a deposition to the Senate Banking Committee, Harold Ickes recalled that Altman told the White House that it was:
unlikely that the [Madison] investigation could be completed and a recommendation made by the [RTC] general counsel prior to the expiration of the statute of limitations.
Schmidt, "Republicans Say Altman Gave White House 'Inside Information'," *Washington Post*, A1, A6 (July 30, 1994).

[82]*OGE Report*, *supra* note 57, at 18-19.

[83]"Whitewater Recusal," *Washington Post*, A16 (Feb. 28, 1994).

[84]5 CFR Part 2635, Subpart E; 57 Fed. Reg. 35006, 35025 (Aug. 7, 1992).

[85]5 CFR 2635.502(b)(1)(iv).

[86]5 CFR 2635.502(c),(d)(listing factors for the agency designee to consider).

[87]5 CFR 2635.502(d)(1)-(5).

[88]5 CFR 2635.502(a)(2). OGE rejected the suggestion that the definition of "covered relationship" be expanded to include "close personal friends," because of its potential breadth. However, OGE noted that the residual clause in section 502(a)(2) "is intended to alert employees to the fact that the covered relationships described in [the regulation] are not the only relationships that can raise appearance issues and to encourage employees to use the process set forth in [the regulation] to address any circumstances that would raise a question regarding their impartiality." 57 Fed. Reg. 35,026 (Aug. 7, 1992).

[89]Altman did not, however, immediately remove himself from his role as Acting Director of the RTC. Altman ended his acting position at the end of March.

[90]Karr & Ingersoll, "RTC Chief Altman Recuses Himself From Matters of Failed Arkansas Thrift," *Wall Street Journal*, A16 (Feb. 28, 1994). It was not reported whether Altman sought and was given this advice before or after the February 2 meeting at the White House.

[91]Rodriguez, "Altman letter reveals 2nd Madison meeting," *Washington Times*, A1 (Mar. 19, 1994). The McLarty discussion and additional conversation with Ickes were disclosed in a March 21 letter from Altman to the Senate Banking Committee, and are recounted in OGE's analysis of the Treasury-White House contacts, *OGE Report, supra* note 57, 20-22.

[92]Ifill, "Prosecutor Says Loan Questions Will Get Review," *New York Times*, A18 (Mar. 23, 1994).

[93]Marcus & Devroy, "Altman, White House Discussed Recusal," *Washington Post*, A1 (Mar. 23, 1994). The *Post* cited sources that said McLarty and Ickes both told Altman to use his own judgment.

[94]Marcus & Devroy, "Altman, White House Discussed Recusal," *Washington Post*, A1, A14 (Mar. 23, 1994). Leach also asked Altman to terminate his general supervision of the RTC. Leach said it was "structurally unseemly for a political appointee of an Executive Branch department to make what are, in effect, law enforcement decisions for an independent federal agency as they may touch upon the President." "FOB Regulation," *Wall Street Journal*, A18 (Feb. 10, 1994).

[95]Hedges, "Treasury deputy Altman quits Whitewater probe," *Washington Times*, A1 (Feb. 26, 1994); Schmidt & Babcock, "Senior Official Steps Aside in Probe Of S&L Linked to Clintons' Venture," *Washington Post*, A7 (Feb. 26, 1994).

[96]*OGE Report, supra* note 57, 20.

[97]Nussbaum even spoke with Hanson about the prospect of transferring the RTC's Madison civil investigation to newly appointed Special Counsel Fiske. *OGE Report, supra* note 57, 21.

[98]OGE's analysis of the Treasury-White House contacts lists a phone call Steiner received from Podesta or Stern during the week of February 14-18, 1994, in which Steiner was asked "how the RTC had come to hire Mr. Stephens to handle the Madison case." Steiner returned the call later in the week to explain that "Stephens had been selected in accordance with normal procedures by a panel which reviews bids." *OGE Report, supra* note 57, 23-24. As noted previously, OGE's analysis examined the conduct only of Treasury officials.

[99]Church & Kramer, "In The Line Of Fire," *Time*, 21, 23 (Apr. 4, 1994).

[100]Frisby, "Whitewater Counsel Asks Whether Aides Of Clinton Targeted Foe in RTC Inquiry," *Wall Street Journal*, A14 (Mar. 28, 1994)(Stephanopoulos: "All I remember about the conversation with Mr. Altman was that we asked Mr. Altman to explain his decision to recuse himself from all of the matter."); Barnes, "Knives Out," *New Republic*, 15 (Apr. 18, 1994)("Stephanopoulos and Ickes were incensed that Altman made the move without consulting or notifying them."); Marcus, "RTC Lawyer Drew White House Ire," *Washington Post*, A1, A5 (Mar. 26, 1994)("Ickes and Stephanopoulos were furious Altman had announced his recusal without telling White House officials."); Jehl, "White House Aide Becomes Subject Of New Inquiries," *New York Times*, sec. A, at 1 (Mar. 27, 1994)("Mr. Ickes angrily criticized [Altman] for failing to give the White House advance notice of his decision to recuse[.]"). The White House apparently learned of Altman's recusal from reporters. Ibid.

[101]Marcus, "RTC Lawyer Drew White House Ire," *Washington Post*, A1, A5 (Mar. 26, 1994). However, OGE's analysis suggests that the firm had been retained more than a week earlier.

[102]Devroy, "Stephanopoulos Call Played Down," *Washington Post*, A5 (Mar. 28, 1994).

[103]Kulka was appointed by Altman, in his capacity as Acting Director of the RTC.

[104]Cooper, et al., "The avenging angel Fiske," *U.S. News & World Report*, 22, 23 (Apr. 11, 1994).

[105]Labaton, "Republican Was Hired For Inquiry For a Reason," *New York Times*, 8 (Apr. 2, 1994). See also, Church & Kramer, "In The Line Of Fire," *Time*, 22 (Apr. 4, 1994)("The RTC, however, chose Stephens precisely because he could be trusted to carry out an investigation that would not back away from information potentially embarrassing to Clinton.").

[106]Ibid. See also, Marcus, "RTC Lawyer Drew White House Ire," *Washington Post*, A1, A5 (Mar. 26, 1994)(Either Ickes or Stephanopoulos "raised the subject of Stephens, asserting his hiring was an 'outra-

geous choice,' and asking, 'Can anything be done about it? Is it final?' according to sources familiar with the conversation."). Ickes "has no memory of such a question." Turque, et al., "In The Line Of Fire," *Newsweek*, 22, 24 (Apr. 4, 1994).

[107]Turque, et al., "In The Line Of Fire," *Newsweek*, 22-24 (Apr. 4, 1994). Stephanopoulos later added, in an interview with CNN on March 26, "Do I wish now that I hadn't gotten angry, that I hadn't blown off steam? Of course I do. . . . But I was just trying to get information." Devroy, "Whitewater Investigator Is Studying Treasury Department Official's Diary," *Washington Post*, A8 (Mar. 27, 1994).

[108]Ibid., 23. See also Marcus, "RTC Lawyer Drew White House Ire," *Washington Post*, A5 (Mar. 26, 1994)(Steiner was asked "whether that [Stephens's hiring] was final, whether anything could be done about it." Steiner responded that "there was nothing he could do.").

[109]Marcus, "RTC Lawyer Drew White House Ire," *Washington Post*, A5 (Mar. 26, 1994).

[110]Devroy, "Whitewater Investigator Is Studying Treasury Department Official's Diary," *Washington Post*, A8 (Mar. 27, 1994).

[111]Jehl, "White House Aide Becomes Subject Of New Inquiries," *New York Times*, sec. 1, 1, 20 (Mar. 27, 1994). Steiner appeared before the grand jury on March 31. Although he declined to discuss his testimony, it was reported that Steiner testified that "he did not believe he was being pressured to intervene" in the Madison investigation. Labaton, "Treasury Aide Denies Pressure To Intervene In S&L Case," *New York Times*, A21 (Apr. 1, 1994).

[112]Borger, "The White House: Time to get a grip," *U.S. News & World Report*, 26 (Apr. 11, 1994). But Fred Barnes reported, "Asked if they had pressured him to fire Stephens, Altman wouldn't answer." Barnes, "Knives Out," *New Republic*, 15 (Apr. 18, 1994).

[113]The April 4 cover of *Time* magazine was entitled, "Deep Water: How the President's men tried to hinder the Whitewater investigation." The opposite view was expressed by Al Hunt, who considered these two phone calls "[t]he most dramatic catalyst in conservative efforts to "hamstring executive prerogatives," which he concluded is "situational positioning [that] is dangerously shortsighted."

It would have been unthinkable for any White House aide not to complain about this appointment; imagine John Sununu or Ed Meese timidly accepting the appointment of a ferociously partisan liberal Democrat to investigate matters involving President Reagan or Bush.

Hunt, "In Praise of Presidential Prerogatives," *Wall Street Journal*, A15 (Apr. 7, 1994). Whether Sununu or Meese would have done what Stephanopoulos and Ickes did is not the issue (although had they done so, they surely would not have escaped heavy criticism). The question is whether these calls were an appropriate exercise of executive authority; they were not.

[114]Taylor, "D'Amato suspects obstruction by two Clinton aides," *Washington Times*, A1, A16 (Mar. 28, 1994); Ifill, "Top Clinton Aide Gains Defender in Odd Quarter," *New York Times*, A12 (Mar. 28, 1994).

[115]Kinsley, "Curious George," *New Republic*, 4 (Apr. 18, 1994); Hunt, "In Praise of Presidential Prerogatives," *Wall Street Journal*, A15 (Apr. 7, 1994).

[116]Langdon, "Hill Democrats anti Stephens, too," *Washington Times*, A4 (Apr. 4, 1994)(Representative Joseph Kennedy even called for an investigation into how Stephens was hired: "It reeks of Republican cronyism." [In fact, Stephens' firm was hired by a Clinton Administration appointee, acting on the recommendation of career RTC official.]). Gloria Borger suggested the hiring of Stephens "—once touted as a GOP Senate candidate and still a Clinton critic—represented a clear conflict of interest to his would-be employers. Any interest in removing him was legitimate." Borger, "The White House: Time to get a grip," *U.S. News & World Report*, 26 (Apr. 11, 1994).

[117]One source familiar with the call told *Time*: "It seems to have gone right from acknowledging the recusal to ignoring it, in that Altman was almost immediately asked to help think of a way to fire Stephens." Church & Kramer, "In The Line Of Fire," *Time*, 23 (Apr. 4, 1994).

[118]RTC lawyers did object to some of Lewis's recommendations, but it is unclear whether these recommendations were revised or omitted from the referral to Justice.

[119]Under 28 U.S.C. 546(d), the district court is authorized to appoint a person to serve as U.S. Attorney until the vacancy is filled. The Attorney General's authority to appoint a U.S. Attorney to fill a vacancy, without the advice and consent of the Senate, is limited to 120 days, 28 U.S.C.(a), (c).

[120]Schmidt & Isikoff, "Arkansas Probe Sensitive From Start," *Washington Post*, A1 A (Jan. 5, 1994) (Reporting date of Dotson's memorandum as October 7.)

[121]Seper, "Records missing in Ark. S&L case," *Washington Post*, A1 (Nov. 14, 1993).

[122]Church, "Search for the Missing Pieces," *Time*, 23 (Jan. 17, 1994).

[123]The *Washington Times* stated that Casey recused herself on November 9, a Tuesday. "Your guide to Whitewater," *Washington Times*, A9 (Jan. 14, 1994). But the *Washington Post* reported on November 10 that Casey "late last week" had informed Justice Department officials that she "was stepping aside." Isikoff & Schmidt, "U.S. Steps Up Investigations In Arkansas," *Washington Post*, A1 (Nov. 10, 1993). In fact, Casey recused herself on November 5, 1995.

[124]Isikoff & Schneider, "U.S. Steps Up Investigations in Arkansas," *Washington Post*, A1 (Nov. 10,

1993)(quoting Justice Department statement).

[125]Ibid.

[126]The indictment of Tucker and McDougals obtained by the independent counsel alleges that the loan was deposited in a Madison account and portions of the proceeds were transferred to Whitewater. At least one other loan went to Tucker, currently the employer of Casey's husband.

[127]"Bargaining in Little Rock," *Wall Street Journal*, A8 (Mar. 4, 1994). Coleman has said that he told Casey on September 7 that Hale would "wear a wire" to prove his allegations, but that Casey refused to discuss it. Seper, "Timing of calls by Hubbell examined," *Washington Times*, A1, A26 (May 8, 1995).

[128]Ibid. Isikoff & Schneider, "U.S. Steps Up Investigations In Arkansas," *Washington Post*, A1 (Nov. 10, 1993).

[129]Ibid.

[130]Ibid.

[131]Ibid. See also Seper, "Records missing in Ark. S&L case," *Washington Times*, A1 (Nov. 14, 1993)(referral was declined "because of a lack of evidence—specifically a dearth of documents detailing what moneys were funneled from, to and between the [Madison and Whitewater]"). Casey's office sent a memorandum to the Justice Department's Criminal Division explaining that the referral was being declined for "lack of specific evidence." Ibid.

[132]5 CFR 2635.502.

[133]Schneider & Isikoff, "Subpoena of Gov. Tucker Outlines Scope of Probe," *Washington Post*, A3 (Jan. 22, 1994)("Tucker had numerous business dealings with Madison, McDougal, and former Little Rock municipal judge David Hale[.]").

[134]"Poison, Then Recuse," *Wall Street Journal*, A8 (Mar. 4, 1994)(Casey "had no business in the middle of these negotiations. Mr. Hale and Mr. Coleman were being asked to deliver their evidence to a longtime associate and appointee of someone it purported to implicate."); Church, "Search for the Missing Pieces," *Time*, at 23 (Jan. 17, 1994)("She would have trouble claiming impartiality").

[135]Seper, "Timing of calls by Hubbell examined," *Washington Times*, A1 (May 8, 1995).

[136]Hubbell told the House Banking Committee, "I don't remember ever talking to Paula Casey until January of 1994. . . . I may have met Ms. Casey sometime prior to that at a social function, but I didn't know her. . . . I really don't remember ever calling Ms. Casey." It is possible that Hubbell spoke with someone else in Casey's office. Recall that when Casey recused herself on November 5, 1993, other unnamed persons in her office also recused themselves. It is also possible that one or more of Hubbell's assistants may have spoken with the U.S. Attorney's office. These possibilities have not been alleged, however.

[137]"How Officials Responded to Whitewater," *Washington Post*, A10 (Mar. 13, 1994). The *Washington Times* uses November 10 as the date.

[138]Schneider, "Gov. Tucker's Finances Become Probe Focus," *Washington Post*, A3 (Nov. 4, 1993).

[139]Seper, "Timing of calls by Hubbell examined," *Washington Times*, A1 39(May 8, 1995).

[140]Wilson, "In this White House, no one ever inhales," *Washington Times*, A20 (July 21, 1995)(the author, James C. Wilson, served as minority counsel for the Senate Banking Committee in 1994).

[141]There are also phone records showing frequent phone calls between Hubbell and the White House Counsel's office in March 1993, right around the time Altman was faxing, twice, a 1992 *New York Times* article by Jeff Gerth on Whitewater and Madison to Nussbaum. Again, the substance of these conversations has not been disclosed.

[142]It is unclear when Hanson received this request.

[143]At the conclusion of the August 1995 House hearings, Mark Fabiani said, referring to the report prepared by Stephens' firm, "The House hearing managed to ignore the definitive document on the Whitewater investment." Merida, "Republicans' Dive Into Whitewater Scores Some Points," *Washington Post*, A1, A6 (Aug. 14, 1995). The 143-page "preliminary" report, reportedly completed in April 1995, was not altogether favorable to the Clintons, however. Gerth & Engelberg, "Documents Show Clinton Enjoyed Far Vaster Protection From Whitewater Losses," *New York Times*, sec. 1, 18 (July 16, 1995).

[144]"Should Auld Connections Be Forgot . . . ," *Time*, 16 (Jan. 17, 1994).

[145]Knight, "FDIC Choice Pledges Whitewater Recusal," *Washington Post*, C1, C7 (Feb. 9, 1994).

[146]Knight, "FDIC Choice Pledges Whitewater Recusal," *Washington Post*, C1 (Feb. 9, 1994).

[147]Brown, "Senate panel OKs FDIC nominee," *Washington Times*, A14 (Feb. 11, 1994). Faircloth criticized her recusal as too narrow (he asked her to expand her recusal to include matters concerning Webster Hubbell, Vince Foster and others, and to include matters in which the Clintons were involved in their "official capacities."). Bedard, "FDIC nominee told to widen Whitewater recusal," *Washington Times*, A8 (Feb. 10, 1994).

[148]Tigert's friendship with the Clintons did not constitute a "covered relationship," but under the circumstances their friendship should have triggered an analysis of the factors in the recusal standard.

[149]Tigert need not have broadened her recusal, however, as Faircloth urged; the term "personal capacities" is sufficient to cover the Madison and Whitewater investigations and related matters.

[150]18 U.S.C. 1503 covers obstruction of justice in connection with grand jury proceedings; 18 U.S.C.

1505 covers obstructions in connection with congressional or Federal agency investigations. A key fact under either statue is whether a grand jury or agency proceeding was pending at the time of the destruction, and whether the defendant had notice of the investigation. The case law under section 1503 appears to require the existence of a subpoena, although this requirement may be satisfied by a Justice Department subpoena that was issued without direction from, or presentation to, the grand jury. The text of section 1505 provides two felony offenses: willful destruction or alteration of documents for the purpose of obstructing compliance with a administrative subpoena "duly and properly made;" and corrupt obstruction or attempt to corruptly obstruct or impede "the due and proper administration of the law under which any pending proceeding is had [.] The latter provision does not appear to require the existence of an administrative subpoena.

It is not known when the RTC began its investigation of Madison, and if and when it provided notice of the investigation to the McDougals or others, but its first referral to the Justice Department was made on September 2, 1992, well before the election, so that its investigation must have commenced months before. It is also not known when in 1993 the U.S. Attorney in Little Rock convened a grand jury for the first time to consider the allegations against David Hale.

Chapter Nine

[1]Brock, "Living With the Clintons," *American Spectator,* 18, 22 (Jan. 1994); Rempel & Frantz, Troopers Say Clinton Sought Silence on Personal Affairs, *Los Angeles Times*, A1 (Dec. 21, 1993). The *American Spectator* issue was released on December 20, but several news organizations received an advance copy on December 19. One of them, CNN, first reported the story, airing interviews of troopers Perry and Patterson on Sunday evening, December 19. E. Drew, *On The Edge*, 382 (Simon & Schuster, 1994). The next day the Associated Press reported the story of the CNN interviews. Associated Press, "Arkansas Police Allege Clinton Sexual Liaisons," *Washington Post*, A9 (Dec. 20, 1993).

[2]Ibid., 22. Raymond L. "Buddy" Young was appointed as the Regional Administrator of the Federal Emergency Management Agency (FEMA) for the Southwest Region. Young previously served as the chief of Governor Clinton's security detail. "[Young] told AP he tried to discourage the officers from making any part of the Clintons' private lives public because it violated the trust that has to exist between those who are protected and the security personnel who protect them." He denied "trying to intimidate either officer." Associated Press, "Arkansas Police Allege Clinton Sexual Liaisons," *Washington Post*, A9 (Dec. 20, 1993).

[3]Brock, "Living With the Clintons, *American Spectator*, 22 (Jan. 1994)(emphasis added).

[4]Rempel & Frantz, "Troopers Say Clinton Sought Silence on Personal Affairs," *Los Angeles Times*, A1 (Dec. 21, 1993). The headline flags the *Times'* judgment that this particular allegation was either the primary allegation justifying the newspaper's devotion of a significant amount of text to stories involving Bill Clinton's personal conduct before becoming President, the most serious allegation made by the troopers, or both.

[5]Ibid.

[6]This point is often overlooked by those who have criticized David Brock's reporting of the story as well as the *American Spectator* for publishing it. See, for example, J. Brummett, *Highwire*, 258 (Hyperion, 1994).

[7]Footnote added. Brock wrote that "Young denied having been in contact with the president or anyone in the White House on this subject." "Living With the Clintons," *American Spectator*, 22 (Jan. 1994). Yet according to the *Los Angeles Times*, Young made the calls after talking with the President. Young "said he made the calls after Clinton told him he had heard reports that his former bodyguards were talking to the press and possibly negotiating a deal for a tell-all book. . . . 'He [Clinton] heard several rumors about this and that,' said Young. 'Like they were going to get $100,000 for a book. So I primarily called Roger Perry to find out what was going on.' Rempel & Frantz, "Troopers Say Clinton Sought Silence on Personal Affairs," *Los Angeles Times*, A26 (Dec. 21, 1993).

[8]Ibid., 26 (emphasis added).

[9]"Once More Into the Muck," *Washington Post*, A20 (Dec. 22, 1993)(emphasis added). The next day three columnists came to the President's defense, sort of. McGrory, "It's a Blunderful Life," *Washington Post*, A3 (Dec. 23, 1993)("White House friends pointed out that the allegations, however sordid and undermining of the president's moral authority, do not relate to impeachable offenses. A new element—charges that Clinton called up one of the singing cops and offered him a job to keep him and the others quiet—is probably not provable, if true."); Cohen, ". . . So Who Cares?," *Washington Post*, A23 (Dec. 23, 1993).("But if in the process of guarding his alleged secrets, Clinton is found to have abused his office—pay off people with jobs to ensure their silence, for instance—his public conduct will become an issue. Up to now, that hasn't happened and so, unsure of what to make of the allegations, the American people have decided to make nothing at all of them. Clinton is no innocent, but neither, anymore, are we."); Kinsley, "The Spectator Story: Unbelievable," *Washington Post*, A23 (Dec. 23, 1993)("If Clinton tried to bribe a trooper to keep quiet, that's obviously very bad too. But I don't believe it, at least on the evidence offered.").

Similarly, Suzanne Garment wrote that "the trooper scandal is not exactly impeachment material. The charges about bribes and intimidation are important ones. But the President has denied them. It is hard to see how his accusers could prove the truth of their account; their credibility is already being challenged." Garment, "To the Public, This Just Isn't Important," *Los Angeles Times*, M1 (Dec. 26, 1993). Ben Wattenberg, however, was more cautious: "Two of the troopers claim Mr. Clinton promised a federal job to hush up the story. Will there be a federal investigation?" Wattenberg, "Sexgate and the sitting president," *Washington Times*, A16 (Dec. 23, 1993).

[10]Marcus & Schneider, President Denies Any Wrongdoing," *Washington Post*, A1, A10 (Dec. 23, 1993). Lindsey and others took several damage control measures, but no one apparently attempted to dissuade the President from making the calls in the first place. A book about President Clinton's first year faults the White House staff for lacking "the constant access and good sense to stop Clinton before he telephoned state troopers in Arkansas to talk even indirectly about jobs for some of their colleagues rumored to be going public with charges about his personal life[.]" J. Brummett, *Highwire*, 270.

[11]Rempel & Frantz, "Little Rock A Battleground of Credibility in Clinton Flap," *Los Angeles Times*, A1 (Dec. 26, 1993).

[12]Elizabeth Drew concluded that the affidavit was signed "[a]t Wright's urging, and with Lindsey's involvement[.]" *On The Edge*, 388. "Wright said she did not help draft the document but said Engstrom did confer with Ferguson's lawyer." Rempel & Frantz, "Little Rock A Battleground of Credibility in Clinton Flap," *Los Angeles Times*, A1, A24 (Dec. 26, 1993).

[13]Many misidentified Ferguson as the affiant. See, for example, E. Drew, *On The Edge*, 388.

[14]Marcus & Schneider, "President Denies Any Wrongdoing," *Washington Post*, A10 (Dec. 23, 1993). Yet, Ferguson did not furnish an affidavit, he only authorized Batton to issue a statement of what he told Batton.

[15]Affidavit of Robert Batton, *reprinted in* Roth, "Lawyers eye significance of affidavit in trooper case," *Arkansas Democrat-Gazette*, 1A, 8A (Dec. 30, 1993)(emphasis added).

[16]However, Steven Engstrom, who gave a copy of the affidavit to the *Arkansas Democrat-Gazette*, told the paper, "Just keep in mind that the affidavit is made under oath."

[17]Ibid. Marcus & Schneider, "President Denies Any Wrong Doing," *Washington Post*, A10, (Dec. 23, 1993).

[18]Sabato & Lichter, *When Should the Watchdogs Bark?* 39 (1994, Center for Media and Public Affairs)(hereafter, *Watchdogs*)("Yet the [allegation] faded quickly from print and air because of a further development [the affidavit of Ferguson's lawyer]"). The *Post* concluded that the affidavit "rebuts one of the most damaging allegations in the recent reports." Marcus & Schneider, "President Denies Any Wrongdoing," *Washington Post*, at A10 (Dec. 23, 1993). Charles Peters candidly remarked, "[M]ost of us were relieved. This had been the most troubling element in the stories of sexual scandal in The American Spectator and Los Angeles Times." "Whitewater, and Other Thin Ice," *New York Times* A21 (Jan. 12, 1994). Peters, however, also incorrectly described the affiant as Ferguson.

[19]Broder & Rempel, "Did Nothing Wrong, Clinton Says, but He Avoids Specifics," *Los Angeles Times*, A1, A16 (Dec. 23, 1993)(emphasis added).

[20]Wines, "Troopers Who Accuse the President Are Questioned on Their Own Pasts," *New York Times*, A18 (Dec. 24, 1993). The *Los Angeles Times*, which knew of the allegation at the time it ran its first story, concluded that the troopers had not committed any fraud:

> We looked into that carefully, and it wasn't insurance fraud at all. In fact, all it amounted to was that in order to get an insurance payment made [after an accident with a state car], one of them had to sue the insurance company of the other. It was the normal course of events in a case of this kind.

Watchdogs, supra note 18, 44 (quoting Roger Smith, editor of the *Times)*. Yet, others in the media eagerly seized upon this single report to discredit the entirety of the allegations made by the troopers, including troopers other than the two, Perry and Patterson, who were involved in the alleged fraud.

[21]Rempel & Frantz, "Little Rock a Battleground of Credibility in Clinton Flap," *Los Angeles Times*, A24 (Dec. 26, 1993).

[22]*Watchdogs, supra* note 18, 10 ("In essence, the entire story was dead within a single week.")

[23]In a lengthy editorial, the *Washington Times* summed up the Clintons', Lindsey's, Wright's response as "a denial that denies nothing. . . . Perhaps the White House has successfully shut down this round of the 'Clinton affairs'. But that's not because there was no credible allegations of wrongdoing to investigate." "State of the sex scandal, part 1", *Washington Times*, A22 (Jan. 10, 1994).

[24]For example, Charen, "Scandal," *Washington Times*, A17 (Dec. 27, 1993)("If he offered them jobs in exchange for silence or threatened them in any way, he has broken the law. It strains credulity to suppose, as the president's defenders insist, that a wounded president was calling merely to ask why the officers were spreading lies about him."); Grenier, "The statesman as sexual acrobat?" *Washington Times*, A19 (Dec. 27, 1993)("Mr. Clinton's efforts to cover up this Arkansas Sexgate, with the means he's alleged to have used to silence informants, are reminiscent of other great cover-ups. If the allegations are true, we're dealing here

with felonies."); Greenberg, "Awaiting the Clinton Follies finale," *Washington Times*, A15 (Jan. 3, 1994)("It wasn't the juicy stories that landed our ever-young president in trouble, but his discussing possible federal jobs with a state trooper. That's all it took to raise the question: When is a job offer only a job offer, and when is it a bribe to ensure silence? . . . [S]urely it is unusual even for an obsessive president to be recruiting federal marshals and regional-level administrators out the innocent blue. The call clearly had some connection with the breaking scandalette."). Also, Robert Novak suggested that the story would not go away unless the President refuted the job offer allegation. "Ineffective Damage Control," *Washington Post*, A17 (Dec. 27, 1993).

The weaknesses of Batton's affidavit were pointed out in a letter to the editor from an Arkansas attorney. Watson, "Trooper Affidavit Is a Farce," *Wall Street Journal*, A15 (Jan. 11, 1994).

[25]Months later, in May 1994, when the trooper allegations resurfaced in the context of Paula Corbin Jones's lawsuit against the President, there was no mention of the job offer issue. Following the November 1994 elections, the *Washington Times* called upon the newly elected Republican majority to conduct oversight hearings into a number of matters, including "Troopergate." "Time to remedy the oversights in oversight," *Washington Times*, A24 (Nov. 10, 1994).

[26]Section 211 is directed also to a person who solicits or receives any thing of value "in consideration of aiding a person to obtain employment under the United States . . . by referring his name to an executive department or agency of the United States[.]"

A companion statute, 18 U.S.C. 210, is directed to a person who "pays or offers or promises any money or thing of value" to obtain consideration of "appointive office." This statute would cover any trooper who provided something of value to the President in consideration of a Federal appointment.

[27]18 U.S.C. 201(c)(1)(B).

[28]The general bribery provision covers a public official who:

"directly or indirectly, corruptly demands, seeks, receives, accepts, or agrees to receive or accept anything of value personally . . . in return for (A) being influenced in the performance of any official act[.]"

18 U.S.C. 201(b)(2). This bribery provision carries a more serious sanction: maximum imprisonment of 15 years, fines, and disqualification from office. This statute does not neatly fit here, because the allegation is not that the President was "being influenced in the performance of any official act."

Other provisions in section 201 prohibit any person from promising anything of value with intent to influence a witness' testimony, section 201(b)(3), or as a reward for a witness' testimony, section 201(c)(2). Section 201(b)(3) covers any person who:

directly or indirectly, corruptly . . . offers, or promises anything of value to any person . . . with intent to influence the testimony under oath or affirmation of such first-mentioned person as a witness upon a trial, hearing or other proceeding, before any court, . . . or any agency . . . or officer authorized by the laws of the United States to hear evidence or take testimony, or with intent to influence such person to absent himself therefrom[.]

Section 201(c)(2) covers any person who:

directly or indirectly, gives, offers, or promises anything of value to any person, for or because of the testimony under oath or affirmation given or to be given by such person as a witness upon a trial, hearing or other proceeding, before any court . . . or any agency . . . or officer authorized by the laws of the United States to hear evidence or take testimony, or for or because of such person's absence therefrom.

These provisions also are inapposite. Even assuming that the President offered a Federal job in order to influence whether the troopers would talk to reporters and what they would say, at the time of his conversations with Ferguson there was no pending or reasonably imminent hearing, investigation or proceeding.

[29]Journalists' reluctance initially to cover the story and subsequently to pursue it is thoroughly discussed in a study on the "Media Coverage of the Clinton Scandals" entitled, "When Should the Watchdogs Bark?, conducted by Larry Sabato and Robert Lichter for the Center for Media and Public Affairs. *Watchdogs, supra* note 18. The authors interviewed many reporters and editors in an effort to determine the reasons for their reluctance. Among the findings:

Many journalists, socially liberal by nature, are relatively unconcerned about sexual transgressions. Reportage about such matters is frowned upon in their profession, and by much of the public, as sleaze mongering or at least déclassé. Ibid., 52

Another motive was journalists' revulsion at the tabloid and ideological sources pushing the stories to the fore. Ibid., 33

With journalists uneasy about sex stories to begin with, the fact that the stories involve the president seems to magnify their aversion to covering them. . . . [F]ew in the mainstream media would take comfort from diminishing the office of the presidency without a reason of constitutional proportions. Ibid., 35

The immediate response of many journalists to the troopers' allegations was that Bill Clinton's messy personal life while governor of Arkansas had no relevance to his presidency. Ibid., 37-38

[30]*Watchdogs, supra* note 18, 42-47.

[31]Drew, *On The Edge*, 388 ("That the troopers weren't without fault, and might have been elaborating at least some of their story and been in it for the money, didn't automatically make the gist of the story untrue.").

[32]*Watchdogs, supra* note 18, 37 ("But some news organizations, already uncomfortable with Troopergate, used Ferguson's supposed recantation to step away from the controversy—exactly [Betsey] Wright's intent.").

[33]Under 18 U.S.C. 210, the person who provides something of value in consideration of a Federal appointment is guilty of a felony.

[34]Drew, *On The Edge*, 388 (referring to Ferguson's post-affidavit interview with the *Times*, Drew wrote that Ferguson "essentially took it back[.] . . . Ferguson had told the *Los Angeles Times* that the President had discussed jobs for him and for Perry, the other trooper who went on the record, and he stuck with this even after the affidavit was issued."). *Watchdogs, supra* note 18, 39 ("Ferguson merely issued a statement through a lawyer that was *not* a sworn affidavit and that simply said Mr. Clinton has not *specifically* offered a federal position as a *quid pro quo* for silence. The original charge was still intact, but Ferguson's phantom affidavit seemed to dampen whatever enthusiasm the national press may have had for the federal jobs angle of Troopergate.")(emphasis in original).

[35]Ifill, "All Presidents Call Congress. Calling Troopers Is Different," *New York Times*, sec. 4, 3 (Dec. 26, 1993). Ifill suggests that the President's calls were consistent with his "devotion to detail."

[36]Bartley, "On Arkansas Sex, Not Inhaling, And Whitewater," *Wall Street Journal*, A12 (Jan. 6, 1994)("The damage from the troopers is contained by a natural, in this libertine age even touching, reluctance to traffic in sexual gossip.".

[37]Wilder previously had dropped his own independent bid for the Senate seat, but remained cool to Robb's candidacy, due to a long-running feud between the two Democrats.

[38]Kellman & Murray, "Clinton implores Wilder to help Robb, may offer him Africa post," *Washington Times*, A1 (Oct. 20, 1994). The article cited unnamed "Democratic sources."

[39]Kellman & Murray, "North calls for probe of president," *Washington Times,* A1 (Oct. 21, 1994).

[40]18 U.S.C. 600 provides, in pertinent part:

Whoever, directly or indirectly, promises any employment, position, . . . [or] appointment, . . . as consideration, favor, or reward for any political activity or for the support of or opposition to any candidate or any political party in connection with any general or special election . . . , shall be fined not more than $10,000 or imprisoned not more than one year, or both.

[41]Kellman & Murray, "North calls for probe of president," *Washington Times*, A1 (Oct. 21, 1994). Also, Harold Ickes said, "There were no jobs discussed or offered." Jenkins & O'Harrow, "Wilder, in Exchange for Endorsement, Asks Robb for Help Paying His Debt," *Washington Post*, D1, D2 (Oct. 21, 1994)("But other administration officials acknowledged that in light of North's charges, they had little choice but to deny discussing specific positions with Wilder.").

[42]30 *Weekly Compilation of Presidential Documents* 2103 (Oct. 21, 1994)(emphasis added).

[43]Jenkins & O'Harrow, "Wilder Endorses Longtime Rival Robb, Climaxing Weeks of High-Level Talks," *Washington Post*, B1, B4 (Oct. 22, 1994).

[44]This was not the first time a White House meeting with Wilder raised a question of legality. According to some reports, Vice President Gore offered Wilder a Federal appointment in exchange for Wilder's earlier withdrawal from the race and endorsement of Robb. In July, when Wilder was still a candidate, Vice President Gore met with him to urge him to withdraw for the good of the Party. Baker, "Wilder Rebuffs Gore Appeals To Leave Race, Support Robb," *Washington Post*, C1 (July 15, 1994). According to the *Washington Times*, Wilder was reported to have said after the meeting that the Vice President informed him that he would receive a Presidential appointment if he withdrew. Kellman & Murray, "Clinton implores Wilder to help Robb, may offer him Africa post," *Washington Times*, A1, A12 (Oct. 20, 1994); Kellman & Murray, "North calls for probe of president," *Washington Times*, A1 (Oct. 21, 1994). The Vice President himself at the time recounted that he asked for an endorsement of Robb and "left the door open" for an appointment for Wilder. Kellman, "Clinton denies offering Wilder post," *Washington Times*, A14 (Oct. 22, 1994). Thus, statements attributed to both Wilder and Vice President Gore support the notion that a deal was offered. If true, the Vice President would have run afoul of the law.

However, a contemporaneous *Washington Post* story contains denials from both Wilder and the Vice President's office:

Both Wilder and a Gore aide said there was no discussion of giving Wilder a position in the Clinton Administration, and Wilder said Gore carried no message to him from the President.

Some Democratic leaders hoped the Clinton Administration could find a position for Wilder — perhaps as an ambassador to an African nation — so that he would drop out of the divisive four-way race and improve Robb's chances for reelection.

"The vice president offered me no position," Wilder said. "There was no need for a *quid pro quo*."

Baker, "Wilder Rebuffs Gore Appeals To Leave Race, Support Robb," *Washington Post*, C1 (July 15, 1994).

[45]Baker, "Wilder to Get Clinton's Aid At Fund-Raiser," *Washington Post*, A13 (July 20, 1995)("It's no ambassadorship, and they still insist there was no deal . . . .").

Chapter Ten

[1]Isikoff, "President Named Defendant In Sexual Harassment Suit," *Washington Post*, A1 (May 7, 1994); Hedges, "Sexual harassment suit filed against president," *Washington Times*, A1 (May 7, 1994); Labaton, "Ex-Arkansas State Employee Files Suit Accusing Clinton of a Sexual Advance," *New York Times*, 9 (May 7, 1994).

[2]Bedard, "Whitewater, Jones suit may spur legal defense fund for Clintons," *Washington Times*, A1 (May 10, 1994); Devroy, "White House Ponders Legal Defense Fund," *Washington Post*, A1 (May 10, 1994); Johnston, "Clinton Aides Consider Fund To Pay His Private Legal Fees," *New York Times*, A20 (May 10, 1994).

[3]Johnston, "Clinton Aides Consider Fund To Pay His Private Legal Fees," *New York Times*, A20 (May 10, 1994)("$400-an-hour range"); Bedard, "Whitewater, Jones suit may spur legal defense fund for Clintons," *Washington Times*, A1 (May 10, 1994)($350 to $400); Devroy, "White House Ponders Legal Defense Fund," *Washington Post*, A1 (May 10, 1994)("at least $400 an hour"); Marcus, "Clintons Establish Fund To Meet Legal Expenses," *Washington Post*, A1 (June 29, 1994)("$300 to $400 an hour").

[4]Ibid. Johnston, ($475); Bedard, ($450); Marcus ($475). In addition, other Skadden, Arps lawyers who were expected to assist Bennett were reported to bill up to $200-$300 per hour. Bedard, A6.

[5]Jehl, "Clinton Planning To Solicit Money For His Legal Aid," *New York Times*, A1 (June 21, 1994)("could easily exceed $2 million"); Marcus, "Clintons Establish Fund To Meet Legal Expenses," *Washington Post*, A1 (June 29, 1994)("could run as high as $2 million annually"); Johnston, "Clintons Create Fund to Accept Gifts to Pay Their Rising Legal Costs," *New York Times*, A18 (June 29, 1994)("could amount to $1 million to $2 million"); Scarborough, "Clintons' legal fund creates ethical doubts," *Washington Times*, A4 ("expected to incur legal bills of $1 million to $2 million annually"). In February 1995, the Trust reported total legal bills for 1994 of over $1.2 million. Labaton, "$830,000 Debt for Clinton Legal Fund," *New York Times*, 8 (Feb. 4, 1995).

[6]With the resuscitation of the independent counsel law in 1994, President Clinton may be entitled to reimbursement for legal fees incurred in responding to the Whitewater-Madison investigations subsequent to the court appointment of Independent Counsel Kenneth Starr to investigate these matters. 28 U.S.C. 593(f)(1)(award authorized for "an individual who is the subject of" the independent counsel investigation but who is not indicted). This would not cover legal expenses incurred in defending the Paula Jones suit, however, regardless of when they were incurred.

[7]Any discount would constitute a gift under 5 CFR 2635.203(b) if a similar accommodation were not also provided other similarly situated clients. If a discount were made available to all Federal employees on the same basis (some Washington attorneys provide discounts to Federal employees), it would not constitute a "gift" under the standards of conduct. 5 CFR 2635.203(b)(4), (c)(2)(iii). A payment schedule that allowed the Clintons more time to repay than other clients would also probably constitute a gift. 5 CFR 2635.203(b)("gift" includes any "forbearance" having monetary value).

It was reported months later that Bennett offered to provide his legal services without charge but was told "by White House lawyers that Government ethics rules prohibited so large a gift to the President." Labaton, "$830,000 Debt for Clinton Legal Fund," *New York Times*, 8 (Feb. 4, 1995). This must be incorrect, for as pointed out below, the President is not subject to the gift restrictions in the standards of conduct. The amount of the gift is relevant only in terms of the President's reporting obligation (gifts over $250 from one source must be reported), and appearance questions which would be present regardless of the extent of the discount or free services provided.

[8]Klaidman, "Bennett Brings Clinton Firepower, Some Baggage," *Legal Times*, 1 (May 9, 1994); Devroy, "White House Ponders Legal Defense Fund," *Washington Post*, A1 (May 10, 1994). For some of the same reasons, the Justice Department's Office of Legal Counsel issued an opinion August 7, 1980, discouraging White House employees who incurred legal expenses in the Billy Carter investigation from accepting free or discounted legal services. OLC was also concerned that such benefits would be seen as bestowed on the White House officials because of their Government position.

Concern was expressed also over Robert Bennett's simultaneous representation of three other clients with ties to President Clinton: White House aides Harold Ickes and John Podesta, and Representative and former House Ways and Means Committee Chairman Dan Rostenkowski. Bennett's representation of the two White House officials would pose a problem only if Bennett were to provide advice or other assistance to David Kendall in relation to the Madison, Whitewater, and Vince Foster probes. There is no factual link between the Jones suit and the Clintons' financial dealings. Even were Bennett to assist Kendall, a conflict would emerge only if his clients' interests began to diverge. (A similar potential conflict exists by virtue of Bennett's representation of both Ickes and Podesta regarding allegations of impropriety in meetings between White House and Treasury officials relating to Madison. Neither official was linked to White House actions taken in the aftermath of Foster's death.)

The conflict scenario regarding Rostenkowski is far-fetched. To believe it, one must believe either that the Justice Department, acting alone or at the urging of the White House, would go easy on Rostenkowski to ensure Bennett's vigorous and zealous representation of the President, or that Justice, fearful of accusations that it would go soft on Rostenkowski because of Bennett's dual representation, would actually take a tougher approach to the prosecution. There is no reason to suspect Justice was affected either way because of Bennett's retention by the President. If there was an appearance problem with the President and Rostenkowski, it existed **before** Bill Clinton hired Bennett (for example, the removal of U.S. Attorney Jay Stephens in March 1993; the President's trip to Chicago to appear with Rostenkowski in the final days of Rostenkowski's tough primary campaign). The President's hiring of Bennett did not change or worsen appearances.

[9]President Clinton appears to be the first President to have established a legal defense fund while in office. Leftover funds from the 1972 Presidential campaign were used to pay for the legal expenses of certain Watergate defendants while President Nixon was still in office, and for some of Nixon's fees after he resigned, but apparently Nixon was not involved in setting up such a fund. Jehl, "Clinton Planning To Solicit Money For His Legal Aid," *New York Times*, A1, A15 (June 21, 1994). Other government officials who established a legal defense fund are National Security Council staffer Oliver North, Labor Secretary Ray Donovan, Senator Bob Packwood, Senator Kay Bailey Hutchinson, and Rostenkowski. Ibid. Devroy, "White House Ponders Legal Defense Fund," *Washington Post*, A1, A8 (May 10, 1994). On the other hand, Leonard Garment said that the idea of a legal defense fund for Attorney General Ed Meese was rejected. Bedard, "Whitewater, Jones suit may spur legal defense fund for Clintons," *Washington Times*, A1, A6 (May 10, 1994).

[10]5 CFR 2635.204(j); 2635.303(d). As discussed below, however, the President is subject to the restriction against solicitation.

[11]5 CFR 2634.304(a).

[12]Such persons and entities would be considered "prohibited sources" under 5 CFR 2635.203(d) from whom Executive Branch employees (other than the President and Vice President) generally may not accept gifts. 5 CFR 2635.202(a)(1).

[13]Johnston, "Clinton Aides Consider Fund To Pay His Private Legal Fees," *New York Times*, A20 (May 10, 1994)(statement of Deputy Director Donald E. Campbell).

[14]See "Mr. Clinton's Legal Bills," *Washington Post*, A20 (May 11, 1994).

[15]Press release dated June 28, 1994. The White House also announced the creation of the legal defense fund. Marcus, "Clintons Establish Fund To Meet Legal Expenses," *Washington Post*, A1 (June 29, 1994); Murray, "Clintons start a defense fund for Whitewater, sex cases," *Washington Times*, A4 (June 29, 1994); Johnston, "Clintons Create Fund to Accept Gifts to Pay Their Rising Legal Costs," *New York Times*, A18 (June 29, 1994).

[16]The trustees are Cardozo, Hesburgh, and Katzenbach, and John Brademas (former Congressman and President Emeritus of New York University), John Whitehead (former Deputy Secretary of State), Elliot Richardson (former Attorney General, Secretary of Defense, and Secretary of HEW); Michael Sovern (President Emeritus and law professor of Columbia University), Barbara Jordan (former Congresswoman and University of Texas Professor), and Ronald Olson (Los Angeles lawyer). M. Bernard Aidinoff of Sullivan & Cromwell was named Counsel to the Trust. Presidential Legal Expense Trust (Trust), 1; Press Release dated June 28, 1994; Johnston, "Clintons Create Fund to Accept Gifts to Pay Their Rising Legal Costs," *New York Times*, A18 (June 29, 1994).

[17]Trust, Article FIRST, 2.

[18]Murray, "Clintons start a defense fund for Whitewater, sex cases," *Washington Times*, A4 (June 29, 1994).

[19]Johnston, "Clintons Create Fund to Accept Gifts to Pay Their Legal Costs," *New York Times*, A18 (June 29, 1994).

[20]Trust, Article SECOND, 2-3. At the inception of the Trust the Clintons each contributed $1000. Trust, Annex A, 10.

[21]Press release dated June 28, 1994.

[22]Trust, Article SECOND, 3. The first report was not made public until February 3, 1995, over one

month late. Marcus, "Legal Fund Raises $608,000; Clintons Still Owe $981,000," *Washington Post*, A1 (Feb. 4, 1995).

[23]Trust, Article SECOND, 3; Johnston, "Clintons Create Fund to Accept Gifts to Pay Their Rising Legal Costs," *New York Times*, A18 (June 29, 1994); Murray, Clintons start a defense fund for Whitewater, sex cases," *Washington Times*, A4 (June 29, 1994).

[24]Trust, Article THIRD, 3-4.

[25]Murray, "Clintons start a defense fund for Whitewater, sex cases," *Washington Times*, A4 (June 29, 1994).

[26]The Executive Director of the Trust explained:

The Grantors [Clintons] have not and will not solicit contributions to the Trust. While the Trustees are authorized to exercised the powers enumerated in Article THIRD to manage the trust, the Trustees will not engage in the solicitation of donations to the Trust.

Letter from Michael H. Cardozo to Stephen D. Potts (July 20, 1994), 4.

[27]Trust, Article THIRD, 4.

[28]Trust, Article FIRST, 2.

[29]Trust, Article NINTH, 7-8.

[30]Trust, Article SEVENTH.

[31]"A new CNN-*USA Today*-Gallup poll found that 80 percent of those interviewed think the defense fund is inappropriate and that 92 percent would not donate." Murray, "Analyst: Clinton legal fund may be taxed," *Washington Times*, A4 (July 7, 1994).

[32]A rare exception was Mark Levin of the Landmark Legal Foundation. Levin, "The indefensible legal fund," *Washington Times*, A21 (July 15, 1994)("[Mr. Clinton] chose a super-expensive, big-firm, Washington lawyer whom he knew he could not afford on his 'modest' $200,000 a year, plus perks, salary. . . . Why, then, did they hire such expensive lawyers? If their cost estimates are true, the Clintons can cut their legal expenses by $500,000 to $1 million by simply hiring reasonably priced lawyers. This they refuse to do."). Following the public release of the Clintons' legal expenses in February, 1995, there was only a hint that the enormity of their expenses was due, at least in part, on their choice of "two of the nation's most expensive firms[.]" Labaton, "$830,000 Debt for Clinton Legal Fund," *New York Times*, 8 (Feb. 4, 1995).

[33]Gigot, "Why a President Shouldn't Have To Go Begging," *Wall Street Journal*, A12 (July 1, 1994).

[34]Rodriguez & Bendavid, "Clinton LDF Faces Delicate Fund-Raising Job," *Legal Times*, 1, 20 (July 4, 1994).

[35]See "Mr. Clinton's Defense Fund," *Washington Post*, A22 (June 29, 1994); Snow, "Presidential panhandling rules," *Washington Times*, A18 (Aug. 15, 1994).

[36]Marcus, "Clinton Defense Fund Limit May Go to $1000," *Washington Post*, A17 (June 24, 1994). The $1000 limit received milder criticism from the *Washington Post*, "Mr Clinton's Defense Fund," A22 (June 29, 1994), and Richard Cohen, "Clinton's Defense Fund," *Washington Post*, A25 (July 1, 1994).

[37]See Jehl, "Clinton Planning To Solicit Money For His Legal Aid," *New York Times*, A1 (June 21, 1994); Marcus, "Clinton Defense Fund Limit May Go to $1,000," *Washington Post*, A17 (June 24, 1994).

[38]5 CFR 2635.204(a).

[39]5 CFR 2634.304(a), (d). These amounts were increased in 1991 by Pub. L. No. 102-90. Previously, gifts aggregated over $100 were required to be reported, excluding individual gifts of $35.

[40]Johnston, "Clintons Create Fund to Accept Gifts to Pay Their Rising Legal Costs," *New York Times*, A18 (June 29, 1994). One commenter asserted that the limit did not exceed $1000 to "ensure that [donors] qualify for the gift tax exclusion." Sheppard, "The tax treatment of the Clintons' legal defense fund," *Washington Times*, A21 (July 8, 1994)(reprinted from *Tax Notes*). An undated Trust fact sheet entitled "Discussion of Income and Gift Tax Issues" states that the Trust "is structured in order for donors to the trust to make donations free of gift tax." Because the gift tax does not kick in unless a donor gives a donee more than $10,000 per year, it is unlikely that the **$1000** limit was selected for tax reasons.

[41]See, for example, "Mr. Clinton's Defense Fund," *Washington Post*, A22 (June 29, 1994); "The Tainted Defense Fund," *New York Times*, A22 (June 30, 1994).

[42]"The Tainted Defense Fund," *New York Times*, A22 (June 30, 1994).

[43]Ibid. See also Mears, "Lure of the political money culture," *Washington Times*, B1 (July 10, 1994); Devroy, "Political Business Mostly as Usual," *Washington Post*, A1 (July 31, 1994).

[44]Marcus, "Clintons Establish Fund To Meet Legal Expenses," *Washington Post*, A1, A14 (June 29, 1994).

[45]Marcus, "Clinton Legal Defense Fund Won't Bar Lobbyists' Gifts," *Washington Post*, A11 (June 30, 1994). In light of the Senate vote, Fred Wertheimer of Common Cause argued that "President Clinton and his legal defense fund should not be accepting contributions from lobbyists and foreign agents in the interim." Scarborough, "Clintons' legal fund creates ethical doubts," *Washington Times*, A4 (July 1, 1994).

In July 1995, the Senate internally adopted a set of gift rules, effective January 1, 1996, that prohibit lobbyists from contributing to a Senator's legal defense fund. Clymer, "Senate Votes 98-0 For Strict Limits On Lobbyist Gifts," *New York Times*, 1, 7 (July 29, 1995).

[46]This was basically confirmed by the Trust's Executive Director, who said, "[I]f we continue to impose even more restrictions it becomes very, very difficult to accomplish the missions for which the trust was created." Marcus, "Clinton Legal Defense Fund Won't Bar Lobbyists' Gifts," *Washington Post*, A11 (June 30, 1994).

[47]Marcus, "Clinton Legal Fund Bars Donations by Lobbyists," *Washington Post*, A1 (Jan. 26, 1995); Associated Press, "Clinton legal defense fund to refuse lobbyists' gifts," *Washington Times*, A10 (Jan. 26, 1995).

[48]Ibid.

[49]"Illegal defense fund?" *Washington Times*, A18 (June 29, 1994); "Illegal defense fund—Part Two," *Washington Times*, A18 (July 7, 1994).

[50]Letter from Reps. Michel, Gingrich and Armey, to Honorable Janet Reno (July 21, 1994), reprinted in *Washington Times*, A19 (July 26, 1994); LaFraniere, "GOP Leaders in House Ask Reno For Ruling on Clinton Legal Fund," *Washington Post*, A4 (July 23, 1994).

[51]Letter from Reps. Deborah Pryce and Chris Cox to Stephen D. Potts (August 3, 1994), reprinted in "A few questions for the Office of Government Ethics," *Washington Times*, A21 (Aug. 5, 1994)(footnotes omitted).

[52]*Judicial Watch, Inc. v. Hillary Rodham Clinton, et al.*, No. 94CV01688 (D.D.C. filed Aug. 4, 1994). See Bedard, "Clintons' legal fund challenged in court," *Washington Times*, A1 (Aug. 5, 1994). Judicial Watch describes itself as "a non-profit corporation . . . organized for the promotion and protection of justice and social welfare, including preventing abuses and violations of the public trust[.]" The FACA count included allegations that the President and others violated three criminal statutes (18 U.S.C. 201(c), 208 and 209) and various other ethics statutes and regulations. The lawsuit also requested relief under the Freedom of Information Act from OGE and the Trust.

[53]5 U.S.C. App. sec. 3(2).

[54]Locy, "Judge Dismisses Challenge To Clinton Defense Fund," *Washington Post*, A12 (Feb. 22, 1995). The court also upheld OGE's denial of Judicial Watch's FOIA request, finding that the requested records were properly exempt from required disclosure under the deliberative process privilege exemption, 5 U.S.C. 552(b)(5).

[55]Hedges, "Justice rejects Clinton fund probe," *Washington Times*, A3 (Apr. 18, 1995). Although it appears Justice did not explain the basis for its decision, presumably Justice concluded that the letter did not allege the commission of a felony, which is a necessary prerequisite for the appointment of an independent counsel.

[56]The Trust's Executive Director eventually asked OGE for advice whether any aspect of the Trust's activities raised legal issues. OGE replied that, based on the description of the Trust provided by the Executive Director, the "existence and proposed operation of this trust does not or will not violate" any law or standards of conduct. Letter from Stephen D. Potts to Michael H. Cardozo (July 22, 1994).

[57]Letter from Stephen D. Potts to Michael H. Cardozo (July 22, 1994).

[58]Letter from Michael H. Cardozo to Stephen D. Potts, 4 (July 20, 1994).

[59]5 U.S.C. 7353(a).

[60]5 U.S.C. 7353(b)(2).

[61]5 U.S.C. 7353(b)(1), (b)(2)(A).

[62]5 CFR 2635.204(j).

[63]Gigot, "Why a President Shouldn't Have To Go Begging," *Wall Street Journal*, A12 (July 1, 1994)("Christmas turkeys, Chinese vases and the like received from official visitors"); "Illegal defense fund?" *Washington Times*, A18 (June 29, 1994)("ceremonial African mask").

[64]Moreover, gifts from foreign governments and officials are governed by the Foreign Gifts and Decorations Act, 5 U.S.C. 7342, and expressly not subject to the gift restrictions in the standards of conduct. 5 CFR 2635.204(l)(2).

[65]56 Fed. Reg. 33783 (July 23, 1991).

[66]This observation is based on my personal experience in the White House Counsel's office during the Bush Administration, where I worked closely with the White House Gift Office.

[67]Under 5 CFR 2635.202(a), Executive Branch employees "shall not, directly or indirectly, solicit or accept a gift . . . [f]rom a prohibited source[.]" "Prohibited source" is defined as any person who:

(1) Is seeking official action by the employee's agency;

(2) Does business with or seeks to do business with the employee's agency;

(3) Conducts activities regulated by the employee's agency;

(4) Has interests that may be substantially affected by performance or nonperformance of the employee's official duties; or

(5) Is an organization a majority of whose members are described in paragraphs (d)(1) through

(4) of this section.

5 CFR 2635.203(d).

[68]5 U.S.C. 7353(a), (b). Members of Congress remain exempt from conflict-of-interest restrictions such as 18 U.S.C. 208.

[69]Before the enactment of section 7353, the President and Vice President were not subject to the gift restrictions applicable to Federal employees. See 56 Fed. Reg. at 33783 (1991)(preamble to proposed provision exempting the President and Vice President).

[70]The section concerning gifts between employees, which implements 5 U.S.C. 7351, is a bit more complicated. One provision prohibits employees from giving a gift to an official superior, 5 CFR 2635.302(a), but "official superior" is defined in the regulation to exclude the President and Vice President, 5 CFR 2635.303(d). The other provision prohibits an employee, including the President and Vice President, from "accepting a gift from an employee receiving less pay than himself unless: (1) The two employees are not in a subordinate-official superior relationship; and (2) There is a personal relationship between the two employees that would justify the gift." 5 CFR 2635.302(b). Because the President is not considered an "official superior," the President may accept contributions from Federal employees so long as the gift is motivated by a personal relationship.

An additional exception for "special, infrequent occasions" could allow the President to accept contributions from Federal employees, apart from any personal relationship they might have with him, if the contribution were considered "a gift appropriate to the occasion . . . in recognition of infrequently occurring occasions of personal significance such as marriage, illness, or the birth or adoption of a child[.]" 5 CFR 2635.304(b). This would require a conclusion that the financial difficulty in which the Clintons found themselves as a result of the Jones lawsuit is an "infrequent occasion of personal significance."

In any event, the Trustees determined to not accept any contribution from a Federal employee, of any Branch, to avoid any question of appearances.

[71]3 CFR Part 100.735-14.

[72]3 CFR 100-735-2(a), (c).

[73]Memorandum from Antonin Scalia, Assistant Attorney General, to Kenneth A. Lazarus, Associate Counsel to the President, 1 (Dec. 19, 1974). OLC concluded that because the word "officer" in Executive Order 11,222 was not intended to include the President, 3 CFR Part 100, the authority for which was derived from the executive order, also did not apply to the President. Ibid., 2-3.

[74]56 Fed. Reg. 33783 (1991)(emphasis added).

[75]In the preamble to the final rule, 57 Fed. Reg. 35006 (1992), OGE stated: "When effective in 180 days, part 2635 will supersede most of subparts A, B and C of 5 CFR part 735 and agency regulations thereunder[.]"

In the preamble to the proposed rule, 56 Fed. Reg. 33778 (1991), OGE provided a somewhat more expanded statement:

The Office of Government Ethics proposes to issue uniform standards of ethical conduct for officers and employees of the executive branch of the Federal Government . . . that will supersede most of subparts A, B and C of 5 CFR part 735 and agency regulations thereunder[.]

. . . Section 502(a) of Executive Order 12674 provides that, except insofar as irreconcilable with its provisions, regulations issued under the 1965 Executive order shall remain in effect until properly amended, modified, or revoked. Under this savings provision, individual agency regulations remain in effect until the uniform regulations, which are the subject of this notice, take effect.

[76]The Federal gift statute, 5 U.S.C. 7353, was not enacted until 1989, and thus is not authority for 3 CFR Part 100.

[77]Executive Order 12674 (as amended), sec. 501(a).

[78]Executive Order 12674 (as amended), sec. 502(a).

[79]Executive Order 12674 (as amended), sec. 201(a).

[80]A third qualification, that the President may not accept any gift in violation of the Constitution, relates to the emoluments provisions in Articles I and II. Article I, Sec. 9, Par. 8 provides:

[N]o person holding any Office of Profit or Trust under [the United States] shall, without the Consent of the Congress, accept any present, Emolument, Office, or Title, of any kind whatever, from any King, Prince, or foreign State.

(The Foreign Gift and Decorations Act, 5 U.S.C. 7342 provides authority to accept certain gifts from foreign governments.)

Article II, Sec. 1, Par. 7 provides:

The President shall, at stated Times, receive for his Services, a Compensation, which shall neither be increased nor diminished during the Period for which he shall have been elected, and he shall not receive within that Period any other Emolument from the United States, or any of them.

The legal defense fund does not implicate either provision.

[81]5 CFR 2635.202(c)(1),(2). The President's exemption from the gift restrictions also does not extend to the criminal bribery statutes, 18 U.S.C. 201(b), (c)(3).

[82]Trust, Article THIRD, 4.

[83]See, for example, "Illegal defense fund—Part Two," *Washington Times*, A18 (July 7, 1994)("The bottom line here is that the president, directly and indirectly, is soliciting gifts. He can't do that, and there is nothing in the law to suggest otherwise."); "The indefensible legal fund," *Washington Times*, A21 (July 15, 1994)("The sole purpose of the Clinton legal defense fund is to solicit up to $2 million in cash contributions. If this is not illegal, the prohibition [against solicitation] is meaningless."); Murray, "Clinton won't solicit for fund," *Washington Times*, A1 (July 28, 1994).

[84]5 CFR 2635.303(e).

[85]The President and Mrs. Clinton are the Trust's Grantors. Trust, 1.

[86]Letter from Michael H. Cardozo to Stephen D. Potts, 4 (July 20, 1994); LaFraniere, "GOP Leaders in House Ask Reno For Ruling on Clinton Legal Fund," *Washington Post*, A4 (July 23, 1994).

[87]Trust, Article THIRD, 4.

[88]This is suggested in the editorial, "The illegal defense fund's after-the-fact lawyering," *Washington Times*, A18 (Aug. 1, 1994).

[89]5 CFR 2635.202(a)(1). The statutory gift restriction does not include the phrase, however.

[90]5 CFR 2635.202(c)(2).

[91]5 CFR 2635.203(f)("A gift which is solicited or accepted indirectly includes a gift . . .); 57 Fed. Reg. 35105 (1992).

[92]Letter from Michael H. Cardozo to Stephen D. Potts, 4 (July 20, 1994).

[93]Letter from Stephen D. Potts to Michael H. Cardozo, 1-2 (July 22, 1994).

[94]This answers a question raised by the *Washington Times* whether the Trust would rely on "independent contractors" to solicit funds. "The illegal defense fund's after-the-fact lawyering," *Washington Times*, A18 (Aug. 1, 1994). Under OGE's construction of the solicitation provision as applied to the Clintons' Grantor Trust, persons may solicit contributions only if the solicitation is done without direction or authorization from the Clintons or the Trustees.

[95]OGE also found that the Trust's preparation and "provision" (apparently, dissemination upon request) of a "fact sheet" did not constitute solicitation. Letter from Stephen D. Potts to Michael H. Cardozo, 1 (July 22, 1994).

[96]Future publicity (albeit not all positive) about the Trust would be generated with each public report of contributions.

Because of the restrictions under which the Trust may operate, the Trust has reportedly continued to discuss with OGE other possible fundraising entities that would be sufficiently independent of the President. Additionally, supporters of President Clinton are considering setting up an independent organization to raise funds. Marcus, "Clintons' Legal Defense Fund Considers Independent Effort to Boost Collections," *Washington Post*, A22 (Dec. 18, 1994) (reporting that Trust had received more than $500,000 in six months). The *Post* quickly frowned on the idea of a "new, superseding trust that will be able to solicit contributions without violating the ethics laws [,]" calling it a "poor idea." "The President's Legal Bills." *Washington Post*, A22 (Dec. 18,1994. The *Post* apparently believes that the superseding trust would entail (or be seen as entailing) "[the} president's publicity asking for help," but this is not so. For a trust to be able to solicit lawfully, it must do so independent of the President, and thus it must be independently established and publicized.

[97]Some also argued that the White House had engaged in solicitation, in announcing the existence of the Trust and the address where contributions could be sent. Because such statements, without more, were not "requests," it is unlikely that they would be seen as "solicitations" within the meaning of the OGE standards. Nonetheless, the White House should not have participated in making statements about the Trust other than referring reporters to the Trust's Executive Director or spokesman.

[98]5 CFR 2635.205 (a) (1) provides that employees shall "[r] eturn any tangible item to the donor or pay the donor its market value.

[99]Marcus, "Legal Fund Raises $608,000; Clintons Still Owe $981,000." *Washington Post*, A1 (Feb. 4, 1995); Labaton, $830,000 Debt for Clinton Legal Fund, *New York Times*, 8 (Feb 4, 1995).

[100]OGE Informal Advisory Letter 85 X 19 (Dec. 12, 1985).

[101]18 U.S.C. 209 (a).

[102]OGE Informal Advisory Letter 85 X 19, 603 (Dec. 12, 1985). Elsewhere OGE stated, "All that the statue actually requires is that a Government employee receive outside compensation for his or her Government work [.]" Ibid., 604.

[103]Ibid., 603, quoting 33 Op. Att'y Gen. 272, 275 (1942).

[104]Murray, "Analyst: Clinton legal fund may be taxed," *Washington Times*, A4 (July 7, 1994); Johnston,

"Clintons Create Fund to Accept Gifts to Pay Their Rising Legal Costs," *New York Times*, A18 (June 29, 1994).
[105]The article was reprinted in full in the July 8, 1994 edition of the *Washington Times*, A21. See also "Illegal defense fund?," *Washington Times*, A18 June 29,1994); Levin, The indefensible legal fund," *Washington Times*, A21 (July 15, 1994).
[106]*Commissioner v. Duberstein*, 363 U.S. 278 (1960).

Chapter Eleven

[1]Ingersoll, "Tyson Foods, With a Friend in the White House, Gets Gentle Treatment From Agriculture Agency," *Wall Street Journal*, A18 (Mar. 17, 1994).
[2]Johnston, "Agriculture Secretary Is Questioned," *New York Times*, A12 (June 9, 1994); Schneider & Thomas, "Espy's ties To Food Firm Under Study," *Washington Post*, A4 (June 10, 1994); Seper, "Espy investigated for reported favors from Tyson Foods," *Washington Times*, A3 (June 10, 1994). The investigation was prompted by the March news stories.
[3]Thomas & Locy, "U.S. Seeks Probe Of Secretary Espy," *Washington Post*, A1 (Aug. 10, 1994); Johnston, "Agriculture Chief Faces New Inquiry On Business Gifts," *New York Times*, A1 (Aug. 10, 1994); Seper, "Reno asks for Espy probe by counsel," *Washington Times*, A1 (Aug. 10, 1994).
[4]Weeks before the Attorney General's application, at a time when there was no independent counsel law in effect, it was reported that the Department was close to determining that prosecution of Secretary Espy was not warranted. Apparently, the Department determined not to close the case on the eve of the law's resuscitation because of the possibility that a decision to spare Espy an independent counsel investigation would be seen as politically motivated. "Independent Counsel Law Reauthorized," *Washington Post*, A16 (July 1, 1994).
After the Inspector General's referral to Justice, a joint hearing on the Agriculture Department's inspection system for poultry was scheduled by two subcommittees of the House Committee on Government Operations (the Subcommittee on Human Resources and Intergovernmental Relations and the Subcommittee on Information, Justice, Transportation, and Agriculture), at which Secretary Espy and the Department's Inspector General, Charles Gillum, were invited to testify. Espy was not available for the hearing, and the Inspector General, with the concurrence of Justice, declined to appear because of the pendency of the criminal investigation. See Letter from Charles G. Gillum to Honorable Edolphus Towns (June 14, 1994); Letter from John C. Keeney to Honorable Edolphus Towns (June 15, 1994). Deputy Secretary Rominger and two other Department officials appeared at the June 16 hearing, but the Members refrained from any questions concerning the matters under investigation. Reuters, "USDA secretary hires lawyer for "gifts' defense," *Washington Times*, A4 (July 27, 1994).
[5]Isikoff & Hosenball, "The Chicken King Plays Hard-Boiled Politics," *Newsweek*, 33 (July 18, 1994). In the larger category of broiler meat, Tyson holds a 17.7% share of the market. McGraw, "The Birdman From Arkansas," *U.S. News & World Report*, 42, 43 (July 18, 1994). Tyson Foods produces twice as many chickens as the second-largest producer, ConAgra. In 1994 the company was projected to show $5.2 billion in sales and $200.1 million in profits. Frantz, "How Tyson Became the Chicken King, *New York Times*, sec. 3, 1, 6 (Aug. 28, 1994).
[6]Don Tyson, members of his family, and Tyson Foods executives contributed a total of $29,000 to Bill Clinton's presidential campaign. Frantz, "How Tyson Became the Chicken King," *New York Times*, sec. 3, 1, 6 (Aug. 28, 1994).
[7]Tyson and Tyson Foods executives contributed $6000 to help retire the campaign debt of Henry Espy. Ibid., 6.
[8]Seper, "Reno asks for Espy probe by counsel," *Washington Times*, A1 (Aug. 10, 1994). An allegation that documents were improperly shredded in the spring of 1993 during the internal debate over the Department's enforcement policy toward the poultry industry was reported to be a part of the Justice Department's preliminary investigation. Johnston, "Agriculture Secretary Is Questioned," *New York Times*, A12 (June 9, 1994); Schneider & Thomas, "Espy's Ties To Food Firm Under Study," *Washington Post*, A4 (June 10, 1994). It is unclear whether the reference to obstruction of justice relates to this shredding allegation, or even whether the alleged shredding was included in the appointment request.
[9]Johnston, "Agriculture Chief Faces New Inquiry On Business Gifts," *New York Times*, A1 (Aug. 10, 1994). However, a report in the *New York Times* asserts only that "some [of the gifts] have been repaid." Ibid. See also, Baquet & Johnston, "U.S. Expanding Scope in Review Of Gifts to Agriculture Secretary," *New York Times*, sec. 1, 1 (Aug. 7, 1994).
[10]LaFraniere, "White House to Request Espy Probe," *Washington Post*, A5 (Aug. 11, 1994).
[11]Interview with OGE official. An account of OGE's involvement in the White House Counsel's report on Espy ("The White House inquiry, undertaken by the Office of Government Ethics, quickly bogged down."),

Johnston, ""A Report on Espy's Ethics, but No Conclusions," *New York Times*, A18 (Oct. 12, 1994) is wrong. According to the OGE official, OGE did not undertake any inquiry at the request of or on behalf of the White House. Even if the White House had made such a request, OGE would have likely refrained from conducting any review until the criminal investigation was completed.

[12]Marcus & LaFraniere, "White House Bans Gifts, Free Travel for Appointees; Changes Tune on Espy," *Washington Post*, A14 (Aug. 12, 1994); Murray, "Clinton tells Cabinet to refuse free corporate rides, lodging," *Washington Times*, A4 (Aug. 12, 1994); Wines, "White House Opens Inquiry on Agriculture Chief," *New York Times*, A17 (Aug. 12, 1994). The new White House policy prohibits the acceptance of transportation on corporate aircraft and related travel benefits such as lodging from companies that do business with or are regulated by the official's agency, even if the company is to be reimbursed by the official or the Government. Current Executive Branch ethics standards do not prohibit **personal travel** on corporate aircraft or the receipt of related benefits so long as the company is (contemporaneously) paid fair market value for the transportation and related benefits, because in such a case there is no gift. 5 CFR 2635.203(b)(9). Current Executive Branch standards allow **the Government** to accept from outside sources the payment of travel expenses for **official travel**, including in-kind payments such as transportation on board corporate aircraft. 41 CFR Part 304-1. However, these standards also require a conflict-of-interest analysis, 41 CFR 304-1.5, which would have made even the Department's acceptance of travel benefits from Tyson Foods inappropriate. Thus, the new White House policy was more a symbolic gesture than a substantive change in policy.

Further, it is uncertain whether companies such as Tyson Foods may receive payment for the travel of Government officials without a certificate from the Federal Aviation Administration permitting it to conduct air transport operations for compensation and hire. The Federal Aviation Regulations provide a narrow exception where the travel is made for the benefit of the company, but such a finding would also prove embarrassing to the Government official.

[13]Thomas & Schneider, "Los Angeles Attorney Chosen To Head Investigation of Espy," *Washington Post*, A3 (Sept. 10, 1994).

[14]Ostrow & Weinstein, "Independent Counsel Appointed to Investigate Espy," *Los Angeles Times*, A14 (Sept. 10, 1994). The wide but not unlimited scope of the independent counsel's inquiry was later revealed when subpoenas were issued to the White House and other entities in October 1994, the scope of which was successfully challenged in several instances. See text at notes 29-75 *infra*.

[15]Miller & Fritz, "Espy-Douglas Ethics Probe a Cloud Over dual Successes," *Los Angeles Times*, A1 (Sept. 6, 1994); Ingersoll & Novak, "Espy's Problems May Be Rooted in a Failure To Realize That He's Not in Congress Anymore," *Wall Street Journal*, A12 (Sept. 16, 1994). Sun Diamond is "an umbrella group for five West Coast cooperatives that produce raisins, prunes, walnuts, hazelnuts and figs." Associated Press, "Senior Adviser to Espy Subpoenaed in Inquiry," *Washington Post*, A4 (Oct. 16, 1994). Sun Diamond has received millions of dollars in Federal subsidies. Baquet & Johnston, U.S. Expanding Scope in Review Of Gifts to Agriculture Secretary," *New York Times,* sec. 1, 1, 24 (Aug. 7, 1994).

[16]LaFraniere & Schmidt, "Espy Billed U.S. for Monthly Trips Home," *Washington Post*, A1 (Sept. 17, 1994); Johnston, "Espy Releases Documents on 135 Trips," p. 10 (Sept. 17, 1994); Novak & Ingersoll, "Espy Appoints Lawyer in Farm Agency To Review Schedule of His Activities," *Wall Street Journal*, A16 (Sept. 19, 1994).

[17]Ibid. Brosnan, "Ethics lawyer hired to be Espy's guide," *Washington Times*, A5 (Sept. 17, 1994)(from *Memphis Commercial Appeal*).

[18]Schmidt & LaFraniere, "Espy Reimburses USDA for Lease Payments on Jeep," *Washington Post*, A4 (Sept. 20, 1994); Ingersoll & Novak, "Secretary Espy Drove U.S.-Leased Auto For Personal Use, Violating Strict Rules," *Wall Street Journal*, A10 (Sept. 20, 1994).

[19]See, for example, LaFraniere, "Espy Repays Group, Museum," *Washington Post*, A12 (Sept. 21, 1994).

[20]Fritz, "Espy To Be Held to Higher Standard," *Los Angeles Times*, A10 (Sept. 26, 1994); Associated Press, "Independent counsel on Espy says reimbursing is no defense," *Washington Times*, A5 (Sept. 27, 1994).

[21]Ibid.

[22]Ingersoll, "Agriculture Department Aide's Intervention On Behalf of Some Farmers Is Being Investigated," *Wall Street Journal*, A16 (Sept. 12, 1994); Schmidt, "Choice of Top Aide Raised Questions From the Start," *Washington Post*, A16 (Sept. 28, 1994).

[23]Reuters, "Espy 'dead' as reports of improper conduct continue," *Washington Times*, A5 (Sept. 22, 1994).

[24]Devroy & Schmidt, "Agriculture Secretary Espy Resigns," *Washington Post*, A1 (Oct. 4, 1994); Johnston, "Agriculture Chief Quits As Scrutiny Of Conduct Grows," *New York Times*, A1 (Oct. 4, 1994).

[25]Memorandum from Abner J. Mikva to the President, re: Report on Secretary Espy (Oct. 11, 1994)(hereafter, *Mikva Report*). See also Marcus, "White House Report Mildly Critical of Espy," *Washington Post*, A7

(Oct. 12, 1994); Johnston, "A Report on Espy's Ethics, but No Conclusions," *New York Times*, A18 (Oct. 12, 1994).

[26]Ibid., 6. On October 6, Secretary Espy recused himself from participating in meat and poultry inspection matters for the remainder of his tenure. Ibid., 4.

[27]Ibid. Concerning an allegation that the Secretary may have provided preferential treatment to a company that employs Dempsey, the *Mikva Report* concluded that the circumstances "sufficiently mitigated any possible appearance issues of preferential treatment[.]" Ibid., 6.

[28]Ibid., 7.

[29]Associated Press, "Counsel expands probe of Espy conflict charges," *Washington Times*, A5 (Oct. 21, 1994); Reuters, ""White House to Turn Over Espy Documents," *New York Times*, B13 (Oct. 20, 1994).

[30]See also, Hedges, "Espy probers 'busy,' says man in charge," *Washington Times*, A3 (Nov. 5, 1994); Kovaleski, "Chicken Flap In Puerto Rico To Be Probed," *Washington Post*, A4 (Dec. 29, 1994); Behar, "On Fresh Ground," *Time*, 111 (Dec. 26, 1994/Jan. 2, 1995)(noting over 50 subpoenas had been served).

[31]Miller, "USDA Staffers Were Targets of '92 Clinton Fund Raising," *Los Angeles Times*, A1 (Nov. 19, 1994).

[32]Ibid.

[33]Hedges, "USDA donations to Clinton queried," *Washington Times*, A1 (Dec. 12, 1994)(Smaltz said, "We are considering this matter very carefully. . . . Yes, I believe it's in our jurisdiction.").

[34]*Wall Street Journal*, A1 (Feb. 10, 1995)(noting unspecified "plans" by Reps. Roberts and Clinger to hold hearings).

[35]Miller, "Charges Planned in PAC Probe at Agriculture," *Los Angeles Times*, A1 (Oct. 11, 1995). Jack Keeney, the senior Deputy Assistant Attorney General of the Criminal Division, reportedly spoke with Hill staffers on September 26.

[36]28 U.S.C. 591(b)(7).

[37]18 U.S.C. 602. Personal solicitation by a Federal employee is also a violation of the Hatch Act, 5 U.S.C. 7323. The Hatch Act, which is a civil statute, was liberalized in 1993, but the restriction on solicitation remains.

[38]18 U.S.C. 211, 600, 601, 606, 607, 610.

[39]Johnston, "Poultry Empire Under Scrutiny In Espy Inquiry," *New York Times*, p. 1 (Dec. 10, 1994); Thompson, "Independent Counsel Widens Agriculture Inquiry," *Washington Post*, A8 (Dec. 11, 1994); Novak, "Tyson's Ties To Government Under Scrutiny," *Wall Street Journal*, B4 (Dec. 12, 1994).

[40]Behar, "On Fresh Ground," *Time*, 111 (Dec. 26, 1994/Jan. 2, 1995); Kovaleski, "Ex-Employee Accuses Tyson Foods," *Washington Post*, A4 (Dec. 19, 1994).

[41]Ibid. See Hedges, "Payoff accusations studied," *Washington Times*, A5 (Dec. 20, 1994).

[42]Kovaleski, "Tyson's Attorney Labels Espy Probe a 'Witch Hunt,'" *Washington Post*, A8 (Dec. 23, 1994); Fritz, "Counsel's Reach in Espy Inquiry Raises Outcry," *Los Angeles Times*, A1 (Dec. 24, 1994). Tyson's general counsel complained that independent counsel was "hunting for something to politically punish Tyson Foods. The irony is that 90 percent of Tyson's executives are Republicans." Johnston, "Tyson Foods Fights to Keep Out of Espy Investigation," *New York Times*, 7 (Dec. 24, 1994).

[43]Smaltz said he responded to *Time* magazine only after it was apparent *Time* was in possession of a "confidential investigative document." Fritz, "Counsel's Reach in Espy Inquiry Raises Outcry," *Los Angeles Times*, A1 (Dec. 24, 1994). The *Washington Post* summarized Smaltz's expanded reach:

> Former Tyson employees say they've been questioned about whether Chairman Don Tyson sent cash payments to Clinton while he was Arkansas governor, the choking death of Tyson's brother in 1986, whether Tyson's son or any company executives ever used or trafficked in drugs, and whether firm representatives bribed Mexican officials. Several witnesses said they were asked few, if any, questions about Espy when called before a grand jury.

Kovaleski, "Widening of Espy Probe Is Criticized as Excessive," *Washington Post*, A1 (Feb. 9, 1995).

[44]Kovaleski, "Widening of Espy Probe Is Criticized as Excessive," *Washington Post*, A1, A10 (Feb. 9, 1995).

[45]Ibid., A10.

[46]Behar, "On Fresh Ground," *Time*, 111 (Dec. 26, 1994/Jan. 2, 1995).

[47]Hedges, "Lawmaker says Espy probe unfairly targets Tyson Foods, *Washington Times*, A4 (Jan. 26, 1995); Hedges, "Tyson official makes rounds on Hill to protest Espy probe," *Washington Times*, A3 (Feb. 9, 1995). Among those questioning the propriety of Tyson's Capitol Hill visits were the independent counsel's staff, Senator Faircloth's staff, and Public Citizen's Congress Watch.

[48]The current provision, 28 U.S.C. 594(f), was liberalized considerably when the independent counsel statute was reenacted in 1994.

[49]Under the bill, if the investigation were substantially complete, the court could turn the remainder over to the Justice Department; or it could terminate the investigation outright if continuation of the investigation were not in the public interest.

[50]Kovaleski, "Judge Limits Scope of Subpoenas in Espy Investigation," *Washington Post*, A1, A12 (July 1, 1995).

[51]Hedges, "Independent counsel fears Tyson intimidation in probe," *Washington Times*, A3 (Mar. 21, 1995).

[52]28 U.S.C. 593(c)(1).

[53]28 U.S.C. 593(c)(2)(A) (emphasis added). The use of the permissive "may" does not mean that an independent counsel need not obtain approval to expand his charter. The language of the section, considered as a whole, makes it clear that approval must be sought. "May" in this context means only that the independent counsel need not pursue an expanded inquiry. Nevertheless, the statutory language is unsatisfactory because it does not expressly allow the Justice Department to handle the new information rather than the independent counsel. The language could be read to suggest that the matter is to be dropped if it is not handled by the independent counsel. If the information does not relate to a covered official or directly to the subject matter of the independent counsel investigation, and if Justice's handling of this investigation would not pose a personal, financial, or political conflict of interest, the Department should be allowed to handle the matter itself.

[54]The independent counsel may not appeal the Attorney General's decision nor may he directly request expansion from the court of appeals. Likewise, the court of appeals lacks authority to expand the independent counsel's jurisdiction over the Attorney General's objection; it may only remand the matter back to the Attorney General to request further explanation. 28 U.S.C. 593(c)(2)(B), (d).

[55]28 U.S.C. 593(c)(2)(C).

[56]Ingersoll, "Tyson Foods Inc. Joins Effort to Quash Subpoena Issued in Espy Investigation," *Wall Street Journal*, A4 (Feb. 9, 1995).

[57]Klaidman, "Reno Reins In Espy Prosecutor," *Legal Times*, 1 (Mar. 27, 1995); Hedges, "Reno bars expansion of Espy-Tyson probe," *Washington Times*, A4 (Mar. 28, 1995); Reuter, "Reno Rejects Expansion of Espy Probe," *Washington Post*, A6 (Mar. 28, 1995).

[58]Kovaleski, "Judge Limits Subpoenas in Espy Probe," *Washington Post*, A1, A12 (July 1, 1995).

[59]Associated Press, "Commerce Department cut cost of Tyson fishing permits," *Washington Times*, A6 (June 30, 1995).

[60]Barram was seen visiting the Tyson Food corporate box at a February 1, 1994 University of Arkansas basketball game. Commerce and Tyson officials both denied discussing Pacific whiting issues at this game. The precise extent of Ron Brown's involvement in the decisions was not known, although a National Marine Fisheries Service official said that the Secretary's assistants "frequently contacted him with questions about the formula." Ibid.

[61]Klaidman, "Another Setback for Smaltz," *Legal Times*, 1, 18 (July 3, 1995); Associated Press, "Tyson Foods wants Smaltz's probe halted," *Washington Times*, A4 (July 2, 1995); Gray, "Judge Agrees to Restrict Inquiry Into Ex-Secretary of Agriculture," *New York Times*, sec. 1, 20 (July 2, 1995).

[62]Klaidman, "Another Setback for Smaltz," *Legal Times*, 18 (July 3, 1995).

[63]28 U.S.C. 596(a)(1). An independent counsel may seek judicial review of his removal by filing suit in the U.S. District Court for the District of Columbia. 28 U.S.C. 596(a)(3).

[64]Kovaleski, "Judge Limits Subpoenas in Espy Probe," *Washington Post*, A1 (July 1, 1995).

[65]Ibid. Because the motions and orders are under seal, the account in the text is based exclusively on news reports.

[66]Ibid. Klaidman, "Another Setback for Smaltz," 1, 20 (July 3, 1995); Hedges, "Judge kills subpoenas in Tyson-Espy inquiry," *Washington Times*, A3 (July 1, 1995)(reporting that 5 subpoenas had been "blocked").

[67]Simpson & Ingersoll, "GOP Lobbyist To Leave Firm Over Allegations," *Wall Street Journal*, A20 (Oct. 23, 1995); Devroy & Kovaleski, "GOP Lobbyist Admits Fraud In Fund-Raising," *Washington Post*, A1 (Oct. 24, 1995); Seper, "Lobbyist charged in campaign donation," *Washington Times*, A1 (Oct. 24, 1995); Johnston, "Inquiry Wins A Guilty Plea From Lobbyist," *New York Times*, A16 (Oct. 24, 1995); Ingersoll & Simpson, "Lake's Decision to Cooperate in Probe Pressures Longtime Espy Confidant," *Wall Street Journal*, A24 (Oct. 24, 1995).

[68]A fourth colleague declined Lake's solicitation. Lake was initially promised immunity, in exchange for his cooperation against Richard Douglas. Lake then revealed the scheme to the independent counsel's office. When that office informed Lake that his firm remained exposed to criminal charges, Lake pled guilty in exchange for an agreement to not charge the firm.

[69]One of these employees, Mark Helmke, resigned his position as communications director for the presidential campaign of Senator Richard Lugar after his participation in the scheme was revealed. Kovaleski, "Lugar Campaign Aide Resigns in Fallout From Espy Investigation," *Washington Post*, A6 (Oct. 26, 1995). Helmke acknowledged his "stupid mistake," but added that "I felt I had no choice but to do what Lake asked me to do," explaining that he was "caught in the cross-fire" of an internal political feud within Lake's firm.

[70]Smaltz was also reported to be investigating fundraising efforts on behalf of Henry Espy by Alvarez Ferouillet, a New Orleans attorney who helped secure a $75,000 loan after the election to cover Henry Espy's campaign debts.

[71] Simpson & Ingersoll, "Farm Lobbyist Said to Link Mike Espy To Fund-Raising Effort for His Brother," *Wall Street Journal*, A24 (Oct. 26, 1995).

[72] 5 U.S.C. 7323. For most of the Federal workforce, the Hatch Act was liberalized in 1993, but the exemption from the Hatch Act previously enjoyed by Cabinet members was eliminated. Thus, Secretary Espy was subject to the solicitation prohibitions.

[73] Simpson & Ingersoll, "Independent Counsel Investigating Gifts Allegedly Given Espy by Growers' Group," *Wall Street Journal*, A16 (Nov. 3, 1995); Kovaleski, "Sources Say Fruit Grower, Lobbyist Courted Espy," *Washington Post*, A12 (Nov. 8, 1995).

[74] Kovaleski, "Independent Counsel Turns Up the Heat, Controversy in Espy Case," *Washington Post*, A5 (Oct. 30, 1995).

[75] Ibid.

[76] Baquet & Johnson, "U.S. Expanding Scope in Review Of Gifts to Agriculture Secretary," *New York Times*, sec. 1, 24 (Aug. 7, 1994); Brosnan, "Ethics lawyer hired to be Espy's guide," *Washington Times*, A5 (Sept. 17, 1994)(from *Memphis Commercial Appeal*). While in Russellville, Espy attended a party given in honor of John Tyson, Don's son and President of Tyson Foods' Beef and Pork Division. Ingersoll & Novak, "Espy's Problem May Be Rooted in a Failure To Realize That He's Not in Congress Anymore," *Wall Street Journal*, A12 (Sept. 16, 1994).

[77] Ibid.

[78] Johnston, "Agriculture Secretary Is Questioned," *New York Times*, A12 (June 9, 1994).

[79] Seper, "Espy investigated for reported favors from Tyson Foods," *Washington Times*, A3 (June 10, 1994); Baquet & Johnson, "U.S. Expanding Scope of Investigation of Gifts to Agriculture Secretary," *New York Times*, sec. 1, 1, 24 (Aug. 7, 1994); Marcus & LaFraniere, "White House Bans Gifts, Free Travel for Appointees; Changes Tune on Espy," *Washington Post*, A14 (Aug. 12, 1994).

[80] *Mikva Report*, *supra* note 25, 5.

[81] Ibid.

[82] Thomas, "Espy Probe May Get Independent Counsel," *Washington Post*, A5 (Aug. 8, 1994).

[83] Baquet & Johnston, "U.S. Expanding Scope in Review of Gifts to Agriculture Secretary," *New York Times*, sec. 1, 1, 24 (Aug. 7, 1994)(reimbursement not provided, per Quaker Oats spokesman); *Mikva Report*, *supra* note 25, 5.

[84] Devroy & Schmidt, "Agriculture Secretary Espy Resigns, "*Washington Post*, A1 (Oct. 4, 1994).

[85] The *Washington Post* reported that Espy and his lawyer initially denied that Espy was aware of the scholarship when it was made, but later acknowledged that Espy knew of it before it was awarded. Devroy & Schmidt, "Agriculture Secretary Espy Resigns, "*Washington Post*, A1 (Oct. 4, 1994).

[86] Johnston, "Agriculture Chief Quits As Scrutiny Of Conduct Grows," *New York Times*, A1, A16 (Oct. 4, 1994).

[87] Seper, "Espy will quit to fight charges," *Washington Times*, A1, A17 (Oct. 4, 1994). Dempsey's relationship with the Tysons was not explained.

[88] Miller & Fritz, "Espy-Douglas Ethics Probe a Cloud Over dual Successes," *Los Angeles Times*, A1 (Sept. 6, 1994). Douglas and other friends must have paid personally for the gift to be approved under the friendship exception.

[89] Baquet & Johnston, "U.S. Expanding Scope in Review Of Gifts to Agriculture Secretary," *New York Times*, sec. 1, 1 24 (Aug. 7, 1994). Douglas also helped organized a dinner in March 1994 to assist Henry Espy in retiring the $75,000 debt left from his unsuccessful 1993 House campaign. The Secretary reportedly did not attend. Engelberg, "Democrats' New Overseer Is Everybody's Mr. Inside," *New York Times*, A1, A16 (Aug. 19, 1994).

On a mid-1993 official trip to Greece where the Secretary spoke to the International Nut Council, Douglas, Espy, Dempsey, and Espy aide (and former Sun-Diamond official) Kim Schnoor dined together. Douglas paid for Dempsey's dinner, but not Espy's or Schnoor's. Miller & Fritz, "Espy-Douglas Probe a Cloud Over Dual Successes," *Los Angeles Times*, A1 (Sept. 6, 1994).

[90] *Mikva Report*, *supra* note 25, 5. The amount of Dempsey's reimbursement was not stated.

[91] Baquet & Johnston, "U.S. Expanding Scope in Review of Gifts to Agriculture Secretary," *New York Times*, Sec. 1, 1, 24 (Aug. 7, 1994); Brosnan, "Ethics lawyer hired to be Espy's guide," *Washington Times*, A5 (Sept. 17, 1994)(from *Memphis Commercial Appeal*).

[92] Before the facts of Espy's trip to Atlanta were reported in detail, the *New York Times* mistakenly reported that a Tyson Foods official said that Espy reimbursed Tyson for the Super Bowl tickets. Baquet & Johnston, "U.S. Expanding Scope in Review Of Gifts to Agriculture Secretary," *New York Times*, sec. 1, 1, 24 (Aug. 7, 1994).

[93] Associated Press, "Super Bowl: Official Business?" *Washington Post*, A9 (Aug. 25, 1994); Associated Press, "Smokey got Espy hot ticket to game," *Washington Times*, A4 (Aug. 25, 1994); Associated Press, "Agriculture Chief Was Given Tickets To '94 Super Bowl," *New York Times*, A13 (Aug. 25, 1994).

[94] Ingersoll & Novak, "Espy's Problems May Be Rooted in a Failure To Realize That He's Not in

Congress Anymore," *Wall Street Journal*, A12 (Sept. 16, 1994). These reports thus dispute the previous *New York Times* report that Espy reimbursed Tyson Foods for the Super Bowl tickets.

[95]Ibid. Atlanta Falcons owner Rankin M. Smith, Sr., a trustee of the Museum, invited Espy to promote Smokey the Bear at the Super Bowl. LaFraniere, "Espy Repays Group, Museum," *Washington Post*, A12 (Sept. 21, 1994).

[96]A planned pre-game interview with Secretary Espy was canceled.

[97]Ibid. Oglethorpe Power Corporation has $3 billion of debt guaranteed by the Rural Electrification Administration, an agency within the Department.

[98]*Mikva Report, supra* note 25, at 5; LaFraniere, Espy Repays Group, Museum," *Washington Post*, A12 (Sept. 21, 1994). Espy reportedly gave away three of the tickets.

Secretary Espy also reportedly accepted tickets to the 1994 Academy Awards ceremony in Los Angeles, although the circumstances of this gift, including the identity of the donor, were not made clear. Seper, "Espy investigated for reported favors from Tyson Foods," *Washington Times*, A3 (June 10, 1994).

Also, in September 1993, Secretary Espy gave an official speech at a conference at the Greenbrier resort in White Sulphur Springs, West Virginia. His lodging was picked up by the American Crop Protection Association, although Espy's lawyer explained that the Secretary never intended for the organization to pay his expenses. Espy repaid the Association $450, and, because it was an official event, sought reimbursement from the Department. LaFraniere, "Espy Repays, Group, Museum," *Washington Post*, A12 (Sept. 21, 1994).

[99]Miller & Fritz, "Espy-Douglas Probe a Cloud Over Dual Successes," *Los Angeles Times*, A1 (Sept. 6, 1994).

[100]5 U.S.C. 7353; 5 CFR 2635.202(a)(1). For example, an employee may accept a gift with a value of $20 or less, 5 CFR 2635.204(a), and may accept a gift from a prohibited source if the gift is clearly motivated by a personal friendship, 5 CFR 2635.204(b).

[101]"*Prohibited source* means any person who:

(1) Is seeking official action by the employee's agency;

(2) Does business or seeks to do business with the employee's agency;

(3) Conducts activities regulated by the employee's agency;

(4) Has interests that may be substantially affected by performance or nonperformance of the employee's official duties; or

(5) Is an organization a majority of whose members are described in paragraphs (d)(1) through (4) of this section. 5 CFR 2635.203(d).

[102]5 CFR 2635.203(e).

[103]Also, Espy may have indirectly solicited the tickets, in that reportedly Patricia Dempsey, Espy's travelling companion, asked Tyson for tickets for both of them. Such solicitation of a gift from a prohibited source is a separate violation of the standards of conduct. 5 CFR 2635.202(a); 2635.202(c)(2).

[104]5 CFR 2635.205(a)(1).

[105]5 CFR 2635.205(c).

[106]Also, it is likely that the White House Counsel's Report would have noted the timing of the Secretary's reimbursement had it been prompt and unprompted.

[107]5 CFR 2635.203(d)(2).

[108]5 CFR 2635.202(a)(2). The Associated Press reports that the gift was "exempt from the ban" are thus incorrect. See "Super Bowl: Official Business," *Washington Post*, A9 (Aug. 25, 1994); "Agriculture Chief Was Given Tickets To '94 Super Bowl," *New York Times*, A13 (Aug. 25, 1994).

[109]There was some question whether Espy improperly under-reported the gift of tickets. Espy need not report the ticket to his companion or any child who is not a dependent. 5 CFR 2634.309(a)(2). Also, even though Espy is required to report the fair market value of gifts, 5 CFR 2634.304(e), which was the price the museum paid for the tickets, the reporting requirements also contain a note mandating the use of the face value of tickets. The OGE standards most likely did not anticipate the gift of a scalped ticket, or one sold at a premium. Thus, any mistake in reporting is negligible.

[110]Employees of the Agriculture Department, however, would not have been permitted to contribute to the event, and the Secretary would not have been permitted to accept such contributions, because these contributions would have constituted a gift to a superior in violation of statute and regulation. 5 U.S.C. 7351 prohibits both the giving and the receipt of such gifts. 5 CFR 2635.302(a) prohibits the giving and soliciting of such a gift. It is unclear whether any person other than Douglas contributed to the cost of the event.

The ethics standards would be violated even in the absence of any pressure exerted on employees to give. Of course, any pressure exerted by a superior on a subordinate to contribute to the party would be a violation of the ethics standards, too. 5 CFR 2635.302(c). The standard is clear: "[A]n employee may not . . . [d]irectly or indirectly, give a gift or make a donation toward a gift for an official superior."

5 CFR 2635.302(a)(1). This language tracks the statute: "An employee may not . . . make a donation as a gift or give a gift to an official superior[.]" 5 U.S.C. 7351(a)(2).

Subordinate employees may contribute to gifts for superior officials only in certain limited circumstances. A cash donation for the Secretary's birthday party is not one of them. Items other than cash with a value of less than $10 are permitted, 5 CFR 2635.304(a)(1), as well as gifts "appropriate to the occasion . . . in recognition of infrequently occurring occasions of personal significance such as marriage, illness, or the birth of adoption of a child," 5 CFR 2635.304(b)(1). A birthday is not such an occasion because it is recurring.

[111]5 CFR 2635.204(b).

[112]41 CFR Part 304-1.

[113]41 CFR 304-1.4(a)("An agency may accept payment for employee . . . travel from a non-Federal source when a general authorization to accept payment . . . is issued in advance of the travel[.]").

[114]41 CFR 304-1.4(a)(3); section 304-1.5(a) sets forth the conflict-of-interest analysis:

Payment from a non-Federal source shall not be accepted if the authorized agency official determines that acceptance under the circumstances would cause a reasonable person with knowledge of all the facts relevant to a particular case to question the integrity of agency programs or operations. In making this determination, an authorized agency official shall be guided by all relevant consideration, including, but not limited to:

(1) The identity of the non-Federal source;

(2) The purpose of the meeting or similar function;

(3) The identity of other expected participants;

(4) The nature and sensitivity of any matter pending at the agency affecting the interests of the non-Federal source;

(5) The significance of the employee's role in any such matter; and

(6) The monetary value and character of the travel benefits offered by the non-Federal source.

[115]41 CFR 304-1.8(b).

[116]41 CFR 304-1.9(a)(4)(i).

[117]5 CFR 2635.202(a)(1).

[118]5 CFR 2635.203(f)(2).

[119]5 CFR 2635.702(a) provides in pertinent part, "An employee shall not . . . permit the use of his Government position or title . . . in a manner that is intended to . . . induce another person . . . to provide any benefit . . . to friends, relatives, or persons with whom the employee is affiliated in a nongovernmental capacity."

[120]A gift is also accepted "indirectly" if it is given "with the employee's knowledge and acquiescence to his parent, sibling, spouse, child, or dependent relative because of that person's relationship to the employee[.]" 5 CFR 2635.203(f)(1). Note that close friends or "significant others" are not included, so this provision does not apply here.

[121]Williams, "Out to Pasture," *Washington Post*, C2 (Oct. 16, 1994).

[122]Ibid. Espy told the *Washington Post*'s Juan Williams, "I could have been more adamant about it but we have no blood relationship and she knew Don Tyson, on her own." Insisting that she decline the award would have been "a bit condescending to womanhood, treating her like an appendage."

[123]5 CFR 2635.101(b)(14) (apperance principle).

[124]Without additional facts regarding the Academy Awards ceremony, there is no basis to evaluate the propriety of the gift of tickets to this event.

[125]The gifts are: lodging and corporate air travel from Tyson in May 1993; the football ticket and ground transportation from Tyson in January 1994; a mid-1993 dinner in Greece, picked up by Richard Douglas (or Sun-Diamond) and other gifts Dempsey received from Douglas or Sun-Diamond when attending events with Espy.

[126]The White House Counsel's Report inexplicably did not discuss the circumstances of these gifts. Dempsey's reimbursements were too tardy to qualify for the amnesty provision.

[127]Apparently, a Tyson Foods gift to Patricia Jensen, Assistant Secretary for Inspections, also implicated the Meat Inspection Act. The Department's Inspector General found that Jensen violated Department rules when she sat in Tyson's private skybox during a basketball game. Baquet & Johnston, "U.S. Expanding Scope in Review Of Gifts to Agriculture Secretary," *New York Times*, sec. 1, 1 24 (Aug. 7, 1994). The matter was referred to Justice, which "determined that prosecution of Ms. Jensen is not warranted under the circumstances of this case." LaFraniere, "White House to Request Espy Probe," *Washington Post*, A5 (Aug. 11, 1994)(quoting from Justice Department declination letter). Jensen told the *Post* that she contemporaneously reimbursed $13 to Jack Williams, a Tyson lobbyist. Jensen also flew first class back to Washington, apparently unaware at the time that her upgrade was courtesy of a frequent flyer upgrade provided by Williams. Jensen said she checked with an ethics official upon her return, who said that nothing needed to be done, but that she gave Williams a check for $84 when she later found out that Williams had arranged for the first class transportation. Even though Jensen paid for her ticket to the game, simply being seen in the private box of Tyson Foods conveyed a less-than-arm's-length distance between the regulator and the regulated. Especially

given the nature of her official responsibilities, Jensen should have avoided giving the appearance of a special relationship with Tyson Foods. Considered with the allegations against Espy, Jensen's conduct contributed to the appearance that the entire Department hierarchy under Secretary Espy had a cozy relationship with Tyson Foods.

[128]21 U.S.C. 622.

[129]In any event, conduct proscribed by the first and narrower provision is also proscribed by the bribery and illegal gratuities provisions of 18 U.S.C. 201.

[130]*United States v. Seuss*, 474 F.2d 385 (1st Cir.), *cert. denied*, 412 U.S. 928 (1973); *United States v. Mullins*, 583 F.2d 134 (5th Cir. 1978). This judicial gloss was deemed necessary to avoid a challenge that the law was unconstitutionally vague.

[131]Fritz, "Espy To Be Held to Higher Standard," *Los Angeles Times*, A10 (Sept. 26, 1994). The Attorney General acknowledged a 1976 Memorandum of Understanding (MOU) between the Justice and Agriculture Departments that excepted from the statute trivial gifts and gifts motivated by personal relationship.

[132]High-level officials in agencies are sometimes given the designation of rank-and-file employees to allow them to participate in inspections, visits, and other actions, without challenge from outside the agency.

[133]Brosnan, "Independent counsel to probe ties to Tyson, Espy predicts," *Washington Times*, A4 (Aug. 9, 1994)(from *Memphis Commercial Appeal*).

[134]Fritz, "Espy To Be Held to Higher Standard," *Los Angeles Times*, A10 (Sept. 26, 1994).

[135]The problem with this construction is that it leaves civil servants subject to a stricter gift standard and stricter penalties than high-level Department officials.

[136]21 U.S.C. 622 (emphasis added).

[137]See, for example, 21 U.S.C. 621, 623.

[138]*Jones v. United States*, 617 F.2d 233 (Ct. Cl. 1980). In *Jones*, the Court of Claims upheld the Department's removal of the inspector on this charge alone. It was also reported that the law has been enforced so strictly that inspectors have faced suspension for accepting a free car windshield wash. Schneider & Thomas, "Espy's Ties To Food Firm Under Study," *Washington Post*, A4 (June 10, 1994)(quoting Elaine Dodge of the Government Accountability Project).

[139]See text notes 20-21, *supra*.

[140]18 U.S.C. 201(c)(1)(B) provides:

Whoever — . . . being a public official, . . . directly or indirectly demands, seeks, receives, accepts or agrees to receive or accept anything of value personally for or because of any official act performed or to be performed by such official . . . shall be fined under this title or imprisoned for not more than two years, or both.

The general bribery statute, 18 U.S.C. 201(b)(2), in pertinent part prohibits public officials from accepting "anything of value personally . . . in return for . . . being influenced in the performance of any official act[.]" The penalties for bribery are more serious: imprisonment for not more than 15 years, a fine up to three times the amount of the thing of value, and disqualification from office.

[141]Thomas & Locy, "U.S. Seeks Probe Of Secretary Espy," *Washington Post*, A1, A6 (Aug. 10, 1994). *A fortiori*, no evidence was developed to make out an allegation of bribery.

[142]Ingersoll, "Tyson Foods, With a Friend in the White House, Gets Gentle Treatment from Agriculture Agency," *Wall Street Journal*, A18 (Mar. 17, 1994).

[143]Ibid. It was also reported that Tyson and Tyson Foods officials had contributed $4,000, and the Tyson political action committee (PAC) $2000, to the unsuccessful 1993 congressional campaign of Mike Espy's brother Henry. Ibid. Tyson's PAC had previously contributed to Espy's campaigns when the Secretary was in Congress. Schneider & Thomas, "Espy's Ties To Food Firm Under Study," *Washington Post*, A4 (June 10, 1994).

[144]"Truth and Fiction About Tyson Foods," *Wall Street Journal*, A13 (Apr. 22, 1994)(letter to the editor).

[145]5 CFR 2635.101(b)(7).

[146]5 CFR 2635.101(b)(8).

[147]5 CFR 2635.101(b)(14).

[148]5 CFR 2635.702.

[149]5 CFR 2635.702(d).

[150]5 CFR 2635.502(a)(2).

[151]As noted earlier, Secretary Espy recused himself on October 6, 1994 from participating in meat and poultry inspection matters. However, this recusal does not appear to have covered all particular matters in which Tyson Foods may have been involved or interested.

[152]5 CFR 2635.101(a). 5 CFR 2635.101(b) provides that: "Where a situation is not covered by the standards set forth in this part, employees shall apply the principles set forth in this section in determining whether their conduct is proper."

[153]Documents later obtained by a House subcommittee confirmed a plethora of contacts between Tyson officials and lobbyists and Department officials during Espy's tenure, on a variety of subjects. Ingersoll & Novak, "Espy's Problems May Be Rooted in a Failure To Realize That He's Not in Congress Anymore," *Wall Street Journal*, A12 (Sept. 16, 1994).

[154]Sugarman & LaFraniere, "Espy's Problems Feed USDA Feud About Lax Regulation," *Washington Post*, A19 (Aug. 18, 1994).

[155]Ibid. Secretary Espy reported a Centers for Disease Control estimate that between 145 and 389 Americans die annually from E. coli. Deaths from all food-borne pathogens are estimated at more than 9,100 each year. Espy, "Administration Is Beefing Up Meat Safety Standards," *Roll Call*, 5 (June 23, 1994).

[156]Baquet & Johnston, "U.S. Expanding Scope in Review Of Gifts to Agriculture Secretary," *New York Times*, sec. 1, 1, 24 (Aug. 7, 1994)(reports March 1993 meeting between Department officials and National Broiler Council and poultry industry officials). *Newsweek* reported that among the "fresh list of eight contacts between Espy and Tyson" under review by the independent counsel is a February 1993 meeting between Espy and Tyson lobbyist Jack Williams, implying that the meeting related to the fecal contamination policy. "Tyson Tie?," *Newsweek*, 4 (Sept. 19, 1994).

[157]The March 8 and 11 meetings were first reported in detail months after the appointment of the independent counsel, in Ingersoll, ""Espy Inquiry Focuses on Mystery Memo to Learn If Coverup Occurred Over Industry Favoritism," *Wall Street Journal*, A16 (Jan. 16, 1995).

[158]Ibid. It is not clear whether Espy acknowledged speaking with Williams on March 11 on this subject.

[159]Ibid.

[160]Greene, "Critics find Espy soft on the poultry industry," *Washington Times*, A19 (Mar. 21, 1994).

[161]Ibid. (quoting Horne). *Newsweek* reported:

According to Wilson Horne, . . . an Espy aide "was definitely upset" by the work Horne had been doing on the new regulations. Horne said the aide ordered him to "stop the whole thing" and erase the draft from his computer. "It was unusual," Horne saIbid. Isikoff & Hosenball, "The Chicken King Plays Hard-Boiled Politics," *Newsweek*, 33, 36 (July 18, 1994).

[162]This meeting occurred in March 1993, perhaps soon after the March 11 meeting with poultry representatives and Espy's meeting with a Tyson lobbyist.

[163]Ibid.

[164]Associated Press, "Chicken firms rule roost in White House," *Washington Times*, A8 (Mar. 29, 1994). The memorandum reportedly also confirmed Blackley's request for the documents. Horne and Cross have since left the Department.

[165]Ingersoll, ""Espy Inquiry Focuses on Mystery Memo to Learn If Coverup Occurred Over Industry Favoritism," *Wall Street Journal*, A16 (Jan. 16, 1995).

[166]Ingersoll, ""Espy Inquiry Focuses on Mystery Memo to Learn If Coverup Occurred Over Industry Favoritism," *Wall Street Journal*, A16 (Jan. 16, 1995).

[167]Ibid.

[168]Ibid.

[169]The mysterious circumstances of the April 23 memorandum were brought to the attention of the independent counsel. See note 188 *infra*.

[170]Dishneau, "Espy says Tyson doesn't influence USDA policies," *Washington Times*, B12 (Mar. 18, 1994).

[171]Associated Press, "Chicken firms rule roost in White House," *Washington Times*, A8 (Mar. 29, 1994).

[172]Sugarman & LaFraniere, "Espy's Problems Feed USDA Feud About LAX Regulation," *Washington Post*, A19 (Aug. 18, 1994).

[173]Press release entitled, "Espy Announces Proposal To Improve Poultry Inspection Program," (Mar. 9, 1994).

[174]Associated Press, "Chicken firms rule roost in White House," *Washington Times*, A8 (Mar. 29, 1994).

[175]Ingersoll, "Tyson Foods, With a Friend in the White House, Gets Gentle Treatment From Agriculture Agency," *Wall Street Journal*, A18 (Mar. 17, 1994).

[176]Espy, "Administration Is Beefing Up Meat Safety Standards," *Roll Call*, 5 (June 23, 1994). Espy recounted the Department's efforts to improve the inspection and labeling system, connecting the words "meat and poultry" 12 times.

[177]59 *Federal Regulation* 35639 (July 13, 1994).

[178]59 *Federal Regulation* 35641-45. Sugarman, "USDA Tightens Poultry Inspection Standards," *Washington Post*, A10 (July 4, 1994). Comments on the proposal were due by October 11, 1994.

[179]59 *Federal Regulation* 35645.

[180]Burros, "U.S. Seeks Tighter Controls on Poultry," *New York Times*, A14 (July 7, 1994).

[181]Isikoff & Hosenball, "The Chicken King Plays Hard-Boiled Politics," *Newsweek*, 33, 36 (July 18, 1994).

[182]Sugarman & LaFraniere, "Espy's Problems Feed USDA Feud About Lax Regulation," *Washington Post*, A18 (Aug. 18, 1994).

[183]Sugarman, "Administration Moves To Tighten Inspections," *Washington Post*, A15 (Sept. 15, 1994). The proposed legislation was named the Pathogen Reduction Act, and was introduced as H.5055 and S.2453. No action was taken on these bills in the 103d Congress.

[184]McGinley, "Agriculture Agency Unveils System To Improve Food Testing for Bacteria," *Wall Street Journal*, B5 (Sept. 15, 1994).

[185]Burros, "Agriculture Dept. Scraps Poultry Bacteria Plan," *New York Times*, A20 (Oct. 27, 1994).

[186]60 *Federal Regulation* 6774 (Feb. 3, 1995).

[187]Ibid. Comments were due June 5, 1995.

[188]Associated Press, "Senior Adviser to Espy Subpoenaed in Inquiry," *Washington Post*, A4 (Oct. 16, 1994). As part of this inquiry, the independent counsel also is reportedly examining whether Kim Schnoor's April 23, 1993 memorandum was fabricated or backdated, which could lead to an obstruction of justice charge. Ingersoll, "Espy Inquiry Focuses on Mystery Memo to Learn If Coverup Occurred Over Industry Favoritism," *Wall Street Journal*, A16 (Jan. 16, 1995). Schnoor's attorney, after the *Journal* article appeared, denied that memorandum was fabricated, and said that he and Schnoor had met with the independent counsel's office the previous week and received assurances that Schnoor is "neither a target nor a subject of the investigation." Reuters, "Espy's aide denies she is probe target," *Washington Times*, A4 (Jan. 17, 1995).

[189]They do not appear to be prompted by any gifts or benefits bestowed by Tyson on Espy, however, because the first benefit Espy reportedly received from Tyson was in May 1993, one month after Espy's Chief of Staff reportedly directed a halt to the poultry inspection rulemaking.

[190]Dishneau, "Espy says Tyson doesn't influence USDA policies," *Washington Times*, B12 (Mar. 18, 1994). In the fall of 1993, Espy announced that the Department intended to conduct unannounced inspections of 1000 meat and poultry processing plants. Deputy Secretary Rominger testified at a House hearing on June 16, 1994, that as of June 1, 400 plants had received surprise inspections, 69% of which were performed at poultry only or combined meat and poultry plants.

[191]This account of the longstanding controversy comes largely from the June 16, 1994 House hearing, which was primarily devoted to this issue.

[192]Food Safety and Inspection Service, Policy Memo No. 022B (July 11, 1988)(emphasis added). The choice of 26 degrees was not explained in the memorandum, but has been elsewhere stated that this is the lowest temperature at which ice crystals do not form in the muscle tissue of poultry.

[193]See "The Chilly Chicken War," *Washington Post*, C6 (May 15, 1994).

[194]Food Safety and Inspection Service, Policy Memo No. 022C (Jan. 11, 1989)(emphasis added).

[195]Ibid.

[196]See "Home To Roost," *New Republic,* 8 (July 11, 1994).

[197]California Food and Agriculture Code, Section 26661 (Sept. 27, 1993).

[198]A rather embarrassing, revealing exception in the California law allowing local retailers to freeze poultry down to 5 degrees was eliminated in by amendment enacted in June 1994.

[199]*National Broiler Council v. Voss*, 851 F. Supp. 1461 (E.D. Cal. 1994); *aff'd in part and rev'd in part*, 44 F.3d 740 (9th Cir. 1994). The court of appeals reversed on the question of whether the labeling provision was severable from the rest of the statute; the appeals court ruled that the other California provisions are valid, including one that prohibits **advertising** as "fresh" any poultry that was previously chilled below 26 degrees. Concurring in the 9th Circuit's decision, 44 F. 3d at 749, Judge O'Scannlain summed up nicely both the Federal regulation and California's practical victory:

> I would note that Congress has given a federal bureaucrat the power to order that frozen chickens be labeled "fresh." We affirm this absurdity by holding, quite properly, that the California legislature is federally preempted from requiring that frozen chickens be labeled "frozen."
>
> Our opinion should not be viewed as a retreat from the battle scene of federalism, however. Rather, we "hold the field and, at the very least, render a little aid to the wounded." ... Indeed, the States are not without devices of their own to protect their citizens when Congress permits the federal bureaucracy to impose the absurd. California stores can still be required by state law to tell the truth in advertising and to display frozen chickens for what they are "frozen" — even though the labels on the chickens themselves are required by federal law to say "fresh."
>
> Lewis Carroll's Humpty Dumpty may well be speaking for the federal bureaucracy when he says "When I use a word, it means just what I choose it to mean—neither more nor less." Let us hope that Alice's world can be confined to the Wonderland within the Washington Beltway.

[200]21 U.S.C. 467(e).

[201]Press release, "USDA Seeks To Reevaluate Policy For Use Of 'Fresh' on Labels," (Feb. 10, 1994).

[202]In July 1994, H.R. 4839 was introduced to codify a policy that "fresh" could not be used with poultry that had at any time been chilled below 26 degrees. No action was taken on this bill in the 103d Congress.

[203]There is a safety issue if poultry is transported above a certain temperature, at which point spoilage and bacterial growth may occur. Experts differ on what that temperature is. But a change in the Department's fresh label policy would not require poultry producers to change their freezing process. Producers would change their process for economic or competitive reasons, because of the value of a "fresh" label, not for reasons of public health. The Department's deference to the economic arguments demonstrates the tension that exists within the Department between its public health regulatory responsibilities and its charge to promote agriculture. This conflict prompted the Vice President's National Performance Review to recommend that responsibilities over meat and poultry safety and inspection be removed from Agriculture and transferred to the Food and Drug Administration, a move that would require legislation.

Late in the Second Session of the 103d Congress, Congress enacted the Department of Agriculture Reorganization Act of 1994, Pub. L. No. 103-354, 108 Stat. 3178 (Oct. 13, 1994). The Act established a position of Undersecretary for Food Safety, and required food safety and inspection functions to be kept separate from marketing and promotional responsibilities within the Department.

[204]60 *Fed. Reg.* 3454 (Jan. 17, 1995).

[205]60 *Fed. Reg.* 3458.

[206]60 *Fed. Reg.* 3459.

[207]Burros, "Freeze Poultry but Don't Call It Fresh, U.S. Says," *New York Times*, A19 (Jan. 12, 1995). The National Broiler Council stated, "We maintain our position that fresh poultry cannot be defined at one precise and arbitrary temperature and that frozen is not the opposite of fresh." Sugarman, "Poultry Labeling Plan Could Chill Shippers," *Washington Post*, A25 (Jan. 12, 1995). A Tyson Foods spokesman said the proposed definition of "previously frozen" did not make sense because "frozen" is defined as chilled below zero degrees. "How could a product that has never been officially 'frozen' be called 'previously frozen?'" Ibid.

[208]60 *Fed. Reg.* 44396 (Aug. 25, 1995); Sugarman, "USDA Acts To Redefine 'Fresh' Birds," *Washington Post*, A1 (Aug 25, 1995).

[209]Isikoff & Hosenball, "The Chicken King Plays Hard-Boiled Politics," *Newsweek*, 33, 36 (July 18, 1994).

[210]Kovaleski, "Chicken Flap In Puerto Rico To Be Probed," *Washington Post*, A4 (Dec. 29, 1994)(statement of Alberto E. Goachet). Goachet said a "technical" letter discussing the implementation of import regulations followed.

[211]Ibid. (quoting Archie Schaeffer III).

[212]Ibid.

[213]Behar, "On Fresh Ground," *Time*, 111 (Dec. 26, 1994/Jan. 2, 1995).

[214]Kovaleski, "Chicken Flap In Puerto Rico To Be Probed," *Washington Post*, A4 (Dec. 29, 1994). A member of the Puerto Rico House of Representatives, Severo Colberg Toro, wrote Attorney General Reno in August 1994, asking for an investigation. The letter was forwarded to the independent counsel, who wrote in November 1994 that his office would look into the allegations. Ibid.

[215]Also, Kim Schnoor, Espy's chief domestic policy adviser, previously provided lobbying services on behalf of Sun-Diamond. Associated Press, "Senior Adviser to Espy Subpoenaed in Inquiry," *Washington Post*, A4 (Oct. 16, 1994).

[216]Miller & Fritz, "Espy-Douglas Ethics Probe a Cloud Over Dual Successes," *Los Angeles Times*, A1 (Sept. 6, 1994).

[217]Ibid. Ingersoll & Novak, "Espy's Problems May Be Rooted in a Failure To Realize That He's Not in Congress Anymore," *Wall Street Journal*, A12 (Sept. 16, 1994).

[218]Ibid. Douglas denied talking with Espy or Schnoor about policy. He said that he has not "called Kim on an issue since she's been there; I don't need to." Ibid.

[219]5 CFR 2635.502 (a) (2).

[220]Miller & Fritz, "Espy-Douglas Ethics Probe a Cloud Over Dual Successes," *Los Angeles Times*, A1 (Sept. 6, 1994).

[221]Ibid. Ostrow & Weinstein, "Independent Counsel Appointed to Investigate Espy," *Los Angeles Times*, A14 (Sept. 10, 1994).

[222]Simpson & Ingersoll, "Independent Counsel Investigating Gifts Allegedly Given Espy by Growers' Group," *Wall Street Journal*, A16 (Nov. 3, 1995); Kovaleski, "Sources Say Fruit Grower, Lobbyist Courted Espy," *Washington Post*, A12 (Nov. 8, 1995).

[223]Ingersoll & Novak, "Espy's Problems May Be Rooted in a Failure To Realize That He's Not in Congress Anymore," *Wall Street Journal*, A12 (Sept. 16, 1994).

[224]If true, this would refute Douglas's claim that he did not approach Espy on any Sun-Diamond matter.

[225]Kovaleski, "Sources Say Fruit Grower, Lobbyist Courted Espy," *Washington Post*, A12 (Nov. 8, 1995). Harmonizing the two press reports, it appears that Secretary Espy was unsuccessful in excluding methyl bromide, but successful in obtaining a delay of the ban until 2001.

[226]Ibid.

[227]*Mikva Report, supra* note 25, 6. She has no ownership interest in the company.

[228]Most of the account of this episode is taken from Sharon LaFraniere's article, "Espy Met With Client of Firm That Hired His Girlfriend," *Washington Post*, A6 (Sept. 16, 1994).

[229]There is some dispute whether Oglethorpe unsuccessfully sought a meeting with Espy before it retained the EOP Group for this purpose.

[230]*Mikva Report, supra* note 25, 6.

[231]O'Bannon was said to be, with Douglas, "good friends of the Secretary [who] often socialize with him." The EOP Group also represents FMC Corp., an agricultural chemical producer. Novak & Ingersoll, "Espy Appoints Lawyer in Farm Agency To Review Schedule of His Activities," *Wall Street Journal*, A16 (Sept. 19, 1994).

[232]*Mikva Report, supra* note 25, 6.

[233]These are reported in LaFraniere, "Espy Repays Group, Museum," *Washington Post*, A12 (Sept. 21, 1994).

[234]LaFraniere & Schmidt, "Espy Billed U.S. for Monthly Trips Home," *Washington Post*, A1 (Sept. 17, 1994).

[235]Ibid.

[236]Ibid.

[237]Johnston, "Espy Releases Documents On 135 Trips," *New York Times*, 10 (Sept. 17, 1994).

[238]Brosnan, "Ethics lawyer hired to be Espy's guide," *Washington Times*, A5 (Sept. 17, 1994)(from *Memphis Commercial Appeal*).

[239]*Mikva Report, supra* note 25, 6.

[240]5 CFR 2635.702.

[241]5 CFR 2635.101(b)(14).

[242]Ingersoll & Novak, "Secretary Espy Drove U.S.-Leased Auto For Personal Use, Violating Strict Rules," *Wall Street Journal*, A10 (Sept. 20, 1994); Schmidt & LaFraniere, "Espy Reimburses USDA for Lease Payments," *Washington Post*, A4 (Sept. 20, 1994).

[243]31 U.S.C. 1344(a)(1). GSA's implementing regulation is found at 41 CFR 101-38.301.

[244]31 U.S.C. 1349.

[245]*Gotshall v. Department of Air Force*, 37 M.S.P.R. 27 (1988). In one case, an employee's use of a government car to transport her child from the airport to the office was found to be willful misuse. *Campbell v. Department of Health & Human Services*, 40 M.S.P.R. 525 (1989).

[246]5 CFR 2635.704(a). See also 5 CFR 2635.101(b)(9).

[247]Ingersoll & Novak, "Possible Misuse Of Second U.S. Car By Espy Is Probed," *Wall Street Journal*, B11 (Sept. 21, 1994).

[248]Brosnan, "Independent counsel to probe ties to Tyson, Espy predicts," *Washington Times*, A4 (Aug. 9, 1994)(from *Memphis Commercial Appeal*).

[249]Cohen, "Gift Seat In a Tyson Skybox," *Washington Post*, A31 (Aug. 11, 1994).

[250]"Mr. Espy's Chicken Feed," *Washington Post*, A30 (Aug. 11, 1994).

[251]"Tainted Gifts to Mr. Espy," *New York Times*, A22 (Aug. 11, 1994); see also, "Mr. Espy Resigns," *New York Times*, A20 (Oct. 4, 1994).

[252]Snow, "Not the last to succumb," *Washington Times*, A20 (Oct. 9, 1994).

[253]Johnston, "Agriculture Chief Quits As Scrutiny Of Conduct Grows," *New York Times*, A1 (Oct. 4, 1994).

[254]30 *Weekly Compilation of Presidential Documents* 1974 (Oct. 3, 1994).

[255]Two wire service reports noted that the White House Counsel's Report found that Espy had "run afoul" of ethics standards, Reuters, "White House to Turn Over Espy Documents," *New York Times*, B13 (Oct. 20, 1994); Associated Press, "White House asked for papers on Espy," *Washington Times*, A11 (Oct. 20, 1994). But this conclusion is only an inference. The cited quote comes from the "General Measures" section of the report:

> Members of the Cabinet should set an example for all federal employees. When they run afoul of the Standards of Conduct, however inadvertently, their actions reflect negatively on the President and the Executive Branch, and promote distrust of the government. *Mikva Report, supra* note 25, 7. This is fine as a general statement, but the report nowhere states that Secretary Espy violated any particular standard of conduct.

[256]The day after the release of the report, the headlines in the major papers told the story: Marcus, "White House Report Mildly Critical of Espy," *Washington Post*, A7 (Oct. 12, 1994); Johnston, "A Report on Espy's Ethics, but No Conclusions," *New York Times*, A18 (Oct. 12, 1994); Associated Press, "White House lets Espy off the hook, for now," *Washington Times*, A4 (Oct. 12, 1994). The *Washington Times* called Mikva's report "the latest in a long string of self-exculpatory examinations the White House has come up with

. . . designed to protect the White House from its ethical lapses." "Abner Mikva on ethics . . .", *Washington Times*, A18 (Oct. 17, 1994).

[257]Lehrer asked:

It was suggested when he got in there and had his problems, was it maybe he was operating under an ethical system that was okay in Congress and he got confronted with a new set of rules in the Executive Branch. Is that valid?

JUDGE MIKVA: Well, it is, it is a legitimate comment of the facts of life. This President has imposed a very high standard of ethical conduct. I have never seen as high a standard of conduct imposed in any unit of government that I've ever seen, whether it's Congress or the Judiciary, or even previous Executive branches that I was familiar with. And it's a high set of standards.

"Strictly Business," Transcripts of "MacNeil/Lehrer Newshour" (Oct. 13, 1994), 4-5.

[258]See, "The Espy Issue," *Washington Post*, A22 (Oct. 5, 1994)("Mr. Espy's problem is said to have been, in part, that he carried over to the executive branch the habits of a congressman. In fact, that's so."); "The Cozy Culture of Washington," *New York Times*, A20 (Aug. 25, 1994)("He seems to have been blinded by his six years in the House to the impropriety of sponging off those with a huge stake in his official decisions. After all, members of Congress do it all the time."); "Espy's World," *Wall Street Journal*, A16 (Oct. 5, 1994). A *Washington Post* profile written before Espy's resignation offered several explanations:

Depending on who one talks to, he is either a manager so busy he can't keep track of his affairs, a former congressman who forgot to shed his congressional habits, or a cavalier official who knew the rules but brushed aside aides who pointed out transgressions.

LaFraniere & Gugliotta, "The Promise and Puzzle of Mike Espy," *Washington Post*, A1, A16 (Sept. 28, 1994).

[259]Williams, "Out to Pasture," *Washington Post*, C2 (Oct. 16, 1994)(ellipses in original). Panetta's statements, as well as other reports in the Williams article, strongly indicate that Secretary Espy was told to resign. Compare with Judge Mikva's answer to Jim Lehrer's question:

. . . There have been stories that you were the one who pushed to get Leon Panetta . . . to get Sec. Espy to resign — is that true?

JUDGE MIKVA: No, that's not true. What I think Mr. Panetta tried to do and I tried to do, and more important, the President and the Secretary tried to do was to come to closure on this so that it wouldn't just keep dragging on to the Secretary's embarrassment and more important, to the Department's inability to perform its functions. And the Secretary, when all the facts were presented to him, decided that the thing for him to do was resign.

"Strictly Business," "MacNeil/Lehrer Newshour" (Oct. 13, 1994), at 4.

[260]Ibid (ellipses in original).

[261]5 CFR 2635.203(f)(2).

[262]5 CFR 2635.203(f)(1).

[263]Sec. 201(a), Executive Order 12,674, as amended (Apr. 12, 1989).

Case in Point

[1]Baquet & Johnston, "U.S. Expanding Scope in Review Of Gifts to Agriculture Secretary," *New York Times*, sec. 1, 1, 24 (Aug. 7, 1994). Blackley also ran into trouble during a previous stint as a Department employee. Blackley reportedly was asked to leave the Department in the 1980s when it was learned that he had received consulting fees from Mississippi farmers at the same time he was working on calculating Federal support payments for these farmers, a patent conflict of interest.

[2]Ibid. One farmer said he paid Blackley $3600 to provide advice and represent his interests over a four-year period ending in 1992. Another farmer said that he paid Blackley for advice on ASCS matters. Ingersoll, "Agriculture Department Aide's Intervention On Behalf of Some Farmers Is Being Investigated," *Wall Street Journal*, A16 (Sept. 12, 1994).

Blackley's moonlighting concerned Department officials. One Department official said, "We never knew what hat he was wearing or whether he was speaking for Congressman Espy or not[.]" Ibid. Officials "told Senate staff members they were never quite sure who Blackley was representing—Espy's constituents or Blackley's own clients." Schmidt, "Choice of Top Aide Raised Questions From the Start," *Washington Post*, A16 (Sept. 28, 1994). Of course, Blackley's clients were also Representative Espy's constituents. While wearing two hats in meetings with the Department would be a patent conflict of interest, it seems unlikely that Blackley would have worn only one hat in such meetings.

Blackley's confirmation that he received consulting fees conflicts with Secretary Espy's testimony at his confirmation hearing that Blackley assured him that he did not receive compensation from Delta farmers while he served on Espy's district staff. Ibid.

[3]Schmidt, "Choice of Top Aide Raised Questions From the Start," *Washington Post*, A16 (Sept. 28,

1994).

[4]Ingersoll, "Agriculture Department Aide's Intervention On Behalf of Some Farmers Is Being Investigated," *Wall Street Journal*, A16 (Sept. 12, 1994).

[5]Blackley reportedly was a partner with two Huber executives in BMF, Inc., a farm equipment leasing company. Ibid. See also, Schmidt, "Choice of Top Aide Raised Questions From the Start," *Washington Post*, A16 (Sept. 28, 1994)("Some foreign landowners have sought exotic ways around a 1989 ban on U.S. crop subsidies.").

[6]This was reported as a demotion, suggesting that at the time Espy knew of the scope of the Inspector General's investigation (of Espy, or Blackley, or both) before it was disclosed to the public.

[7]5 CFR 2635.101(b)(7),(8)(general principles). Note, however, that the section on using public office for private gain is limited to actions for the benefit of the employee, "friends, relatives, or persons with whom the employee *is* affiliated in a nongovernmental capacity." 5 CFR 2635.702(a). Thus, Blackley's former clients are not necessarily covered.

[8]5 CFR 2635.502(a); 2635.502(b)(1)(iv).

[9]See 5 CFR 2635.502(d)(listing factors to be considered in determining whether to authorize participation).

[10]In September 1994, Common Cause asked the Office of Government Ethics to investigate these allegations. Ingersoll & Novak, "Secretary Espy Drove U.S.-Leased Auto For Personal Use, Violating Strict Rules," *Wall Street Journal*, A10 (Sept. 20, 1994). OGE, explaining that it was not responsible for such investigations in the first instance, forwarded Common Cause's letter to the Inspector General.

Chapter Twelve

[1]Pound, Cohen & Robinson, "Vietnam contacts," *U.S. News & World Report* (Aug. 23, 1993).

[2]Seper, "Haitian woman key in probe of Brown," *Washington Times*, A1, A6 (Oct. 21, 1993).

[3]Davidson, "Brown Cleared Of Allegations On Trade Deal," *Wall Street Journal*, A16 (Feb. 3, 1994).

[4]Babcock, "Brown Now Says He Met With Businessman," *Washington Post*, A1 (Sept. 28, 1993).

[5]Hunt, "Ron Brown, His Own Worst Enemy," *Wall Street Journal*, A17 (Oct. 14, 1993).

[6]Babcock, "Brown Now Says He Met With Businessman," *Washington Post*, A12 (Sept. 28, 1993).

[7]If this town house is the same as the one the Brown and his son reportedly purchased for Madsen, this meeting took place before settlement.

[8]Ibid. "[Brown] 'flatly and respectfully declined' [Hao's] offer, Mr. Weingarten said." Murray, "Brown cleared of peddling easing of Vietnam sanctions," *Washington Times*, A3 (Feb. 2, 1994).

[9]Ibid.

[10]"Brown Predicts Exoneration, Clashes With GOP Lawmakers," *Washington Post*, A7 (Sept. 30, 1993).

[11]Seper, "Haitian woman key in probe of Brown," *Washington Times*, A1 (Oct. 21, 1993).

[12]Knight & Babcock, "Justice Dept. Investigators Question Brown on Vietnam Trade Allegations," *Washington Post*, A6 (Oct. 14, 1993).

[13]Cole, "Grand Jury Resumes Probe of Brown," *Washington Post*, F2 (Jan. 5, 1994).

[14]Davidson, "Brown Cleared Of Allegations On Trade Deal," *Wall Street Journal*, A16 (Feb. 3, 1994).

[15]Pound, "Case closed on Ron Brown," *U.S. News & World Report*, 21 (Feb. 14, 1994).

[16]Associated Press, "Brown 'pleased' by exoneration in Vietnam probe," *Washington Times*, A3 (Feb. 3, 1994).

[17]Davidson, "Brown Cleared Of Allegations On Trade Deal," *Wall Street Journal*, A16 (Feb. 3, 1994).

[18]Knight, "Justice Dept. Set to Clear Ron Brown," *Washington Post*, A1 (Feb. 2, 1994).

[19]Associated Press, "Brown 'pleased' by exoneration in Vietnam probe," *Washington Times*, A3 (Feb. 3, 1994).

[20]See Hunt, "Ron Brown, His Own Worst Enemy," *Wall Street Journal*, A17 (Oct. 14, 1993).

[21]Ibid. ("So why won't the story go away? First, because Ron Brown hasn't told the truth.")

[22]Novak, "Ron Brown's Town House," *Washington Post*, A19 (Oct. 4, 1993).

[23]Ibid.

[24]See Hunt, "Ron Brown, His Own Worst Enemy," *Wall Street Journal*, A17 (Oct. 14, 1993)("[E]mbittered friends say he's being savaged by the press. If instead this were about, say, Education Secretary Riley, they contend, the story would disappear. They're right. But Mr. Riley never would have consorted with the likes of Marc Ashton and Nguyen Van Hao.").

[25]The White House's awareness of the link between the criminal investigation of Brown and the Vietnam trade embargo decision is suggested by the timing of the President's announcement lifting the embargo—just a few days following word that the Justice Department was closing the investigation. Murray, "Brown cleared of peddling easing of Vietnam sanctions," *Washington Times*, A3 (Feb. 2, 1994). Also, fourteen Members of Congress had written the President on September 30, 1993, asking "that no further steps be taken to relax the trade embargo against Vietnam until the grand jury investigation of Secretary Brown is complete."

No response to this letter was ever received.

[26]Babcock, "Brown Now Says He Met With Businessman," *Washington Post*, A1, A12 (Sept. 28, 1993).

[27]Letter from William F. Clinger, Jr. to Honorable Ronald H. Brown, 2 (Oct. 8, 1993). The Associated Press reported that Robert J. Stein, Secretary Brown's Chief of Staff, obtained a waiver from the conflict-of-interest restrictions in November 1993 to allow him to work on "issues before the department concerning trade policy regarding Vietnam." "Brown aide gets waiver to work on Vietnam," *Washington Times*, A4 (Dec. 4, 1993). Stein asked for the waiver because of a small interest he held in a inactive consulting business that was established in 1991 to help U.S. companies compete for business in Vietnam if the embargo were lifted, and, according to a Commerce spokeswoman, because "'issues relating to Vietnam were obviously being raised in relation to the department' as a result of the Brown investigation." Ibid.

[28]Letter from Rod Grams, et al. to Honorable Bill Clinton, 2 (Oct. 27, 1993).

[29]Letter from Bernard W. Nussbaum to Honorable Dana Rohrabacher (Nov. 24, 1993).

[30]Letter from Hon. Dan Burton and Hon. Dana Rohrabacher to Mr. Bernard W. Nussbaum (Dec. 7, 1993).

[31]5 CFR 2635.402(c)(2), 2635.502(e)(2).

[32]5 CFR 2635.502(e)(2).

[33]See 5 CFR 2635.502(a)(2)("An employee who is concerned that circumstances other than those specifically described in this section would raise a question regarding his impartiality should use the process described in this section to determine whether he should or should not participate in a particular matter.").

[34]The November 28, 1992 date is the date noted by the realtor. The *Washington Times* reported that "records at the D.C. Recorder of Deeds" show that the purchase contact was signed on December 15, 1992. Seper, "Haitian woman key in probe of Brown," *Washington Times*, A1, A6 (Oct. 21, 1993).

[35]The Browns may have obtained permission to occupy the property before settlement under a presettlement occupancy agreement.

[36]Pound, Cohen & Robinson, "Vietnam contacts?," *U.S. News & World Report*, 27 (Aug. 23, 1993).

[37]Babcock, "Brown Now Says He Met With Businessman," *Washington Post*, A1 (Sept. 28, 1993). Madsen reportedly is not a United States citizen, but is from Martinique. Madsen's husband, from whom she is separated, is Haitian.

[38]Novak, "Ron Brown's Town House," *Washington Post*, A19 (Oct. 4, 1993). There is some question whether the December meeting was in this town house, or in a different one occupied by Madsen but not purchased by the Browns.

[39]The fact that the town house was purchased by Brown and his son for Madsen was first reported by Robert Novak. "Ron Brown's Town House," *Washington Post*, A19 (Oct. 4, 1993).

[40]Knight & Babcock, "Justice Dept. Investigators Question Brown on Vietnam Trade Allegations," *Washington Post*, A6 (Oct. 14, 1993).

[41]Seper, "Haitian woman key in probe of Brown," *Washington Times*, A1 (Oct. 21, 1993).

[42]Pound & Cohen, "It's what friends are for," *U.S. News & World Report*, 38 (Jan. 23, 1995).

[43]Knight, "GOP Senator Questions Commerce's Brown on Mortgage Loan Disclosure," *Washington Post*, A5 (Apr. 4, 1995).

[44]Ibid.

[45]Madsen's financial wealth is not known. Her ability to "contribute" to the mortgage payments is not probative; also, the loan or gift of part or all of the $108,000 down payment does not necessarily mean that Madsen is well-off, because the funds were provided from a bank through the good offices of a mutual friend. Plus, Madsen's employment status could have made it more difficult to qualify for a loan from a United States bank. Madsen's alienage, however, would not be a legitimate ground to disqualify her.

[46]Under D.C. law, if Madsen's name were on the title, Lillian Madsen could not dispose of her property interest without her husband's consent.

[47]Pound & Cohen, "It's what friends are for," *U.S. News & World Report*, 38 (Jan. 23, 1995).

[48]Ibid.

[49]Ibid. Another interesting connection reported by *U.S. News* is that Ramos is friends with James Carville, having met him at President Clinton's inaugural. Carville served as an adviser to Brazilian President Cardoso during his 1994 campaign.

[50]Knight, "GOP Senator Questions Commerce's Brown on Mortgage Loan Disclosure," *Washington Post*, A5 (Apr. 4, 1995).

[51]Ibid.

[52]A willful failure to report information required to be reported on a financial disclosure report may be prosecuted as a false statement. 18 U.S.C. 1001. In addition, under the Ethics in Government Act, a civil penalty of an amount not to exceed $10,000 may be sought for a willful or knowing failure to file information required to be reported. 5 U.S.C. App. 102 (App. 5). Administrative sanctions are also available. See 5 CFR 2634.701. Often, however, there is no evidence that the failure to report information was willful or knowing. In

such case, the remedy is simply to file an amended report containing the previously unreported information.

[53]5 CFR 2634.301(b)(1).

[54]Had Brown acquired an interest in property when he signed the purchase contract in 1992, he would not have been entitled to the "personal residence" exception. Excepted from the requirement to report real estate interests is a "personal residence of the filer," 5 CFR 2634.301(c)(3). But "personal residence" is defined as "any real property used exclusively as a private dwelling by the reporting individual or his spouse, which is not rented out during any portion of the reporting period." 5 CFR 2634.105(l). From the start, the town house has not been used exclusively by Brown, and Madsen's contributions toward the mortgage payments constitute rent. Brown properly reported this property on his annual report as "investment property."

[55]5 CFR 2634.305(a). There is an exception for "[a]ny mortgage secured by a personal residence of the filer or his spouse[,]" 5 CFR 2634.305(b)(2), but Brown cannot take advantage of this exception because the town house does not constitute his "personal residence."

[56]5 CFR 2634.308(b).

[57]Brown checked the "Rents and Royalties" column under "type of income" on Schedule A of his annual report.

[58]If Madsen were in reality part (or full) owner of the property, she should have been listed on the title. The failure to disclose Madsen's ownership could also lead to a default of the mortgage.

[59]As discussed *infra*, page 14, Senator Grassley has a copy of the loan application.

[60]Section 1010 provides that a knowing false statement made to obtain a HUD-insured loan or benefit is a felony punishable by a prison term of not more than two years. Section 1014 provides that a false statement knowingly made for the purpose of influencing an action of a Federal financial institution is also a felony, punishable by a prison term of not more than thirty years.

[61]Robert Novak's column on the town house appeared in October 1993.

[62]The last page of the deed of trust contains a series of boxes, each signifying a different type of rider that might be attached as part of the deed of trust. The Second Home Rider box is checked on the initial last page, but the 1-4 Family Rider box is not. The replaced last page shows the 1-4 Family Rider box checked, and the Second Home Rider box blank.

[63]Bold indicates words typed on an otherwise standard form document.

[64]The Family Rider is subtitled, "Assignment of Rents." Covenant H provides that in the event of borrower's default, rents are assigned to the lender. Thus, the ability to rent the property is implied.

[65]The standard language is in Uniform Covenant 6. Covenant F (Borrower's Occupancy) of the Family Rider deletes the first sentence of Uniform Covenant 6. The Second Home Rider also had superseded this particular residency requirement.

Although PaineWebber Mortgage Finance, Incorporated in listed as the lender on the deed of trust and the Family Rider, Secretary Brown's May 1994 financial disclosure statement reports that the mortgage holder is now First Federal Savings and Loan of Rochester. (The terms of the mortgage are reportedly the same.) Changing lenders is not unusual in the real estate business.

[66]This assumes that Brown executed the Second Home Rider knowing what it meant.

[67]Letter from Charles E. Grassley to Honorable Ronald H. Brown (Mar. 22, 1995); Knight, "GOP Senator Questions Commerce's Brown on Mortgage Loan Disclosure," *Washington Post*, A5 (Apr. 4, 1995).

[68]Letter from Ronald H. Brown to Honorable Charles E. Grassley (Apr. 4, 1995).

[69]In November 1994, it was reported that Albimar would sell WKYS-FM to Radio One, Inc for $34 million. Yorke, "Area Firm to Purchase WKYS-FM," *Washington Post*, D1, D7 (Nov. 1, 1994). The FCC approved the sale in early 1995. Knight, "NBC to Forgive Loan to Firm Owned by Brown, Others," *Washington Post*, C1, C2 (Feb. 25, 1995).

[70]Brown's January 29, 1993 disqualification statement does not indicate the nature of Brown's financial interest in Albimar.

[71]Yorke, "Area Firm to Purchase WKYS-FM," *Washington Post*, D1, D7 (Nov. 1, 1994); Knight, "NBC to Forgive Loan to Firm Owned by Brown, Others," *Washington Post*, C1 (Feb. 25, 1995).

[72]Knight, "NBC to Forgive Loan to Firm Owned by Brown, Others," *Washington Post*, C1 (Feb. 25, 1995). An NBC spokeswoman said NBC's attorneys were unaware of Brown's partnership and ownership interest.

[73]See 18 U.S.C. 208(b)(1).

[74]The *Post* initially reported that "there is no indication that he invested any money in the business." Knight, "Brown Keeps Holdings In First International," *Washington Post*, A8 (Nov. 28, 1993). Jerry Knight later reported that "Brown has said he invested no money in First International." Knight, "Ex-Partner Paid Some of Ron Brown's Debts," *Washington Post*, A1 (Jan. 14, 1995).

[75]Letter to Honorable William F. Clinger from Stephen D. Potts, 2 (Dec. 29, 1994). The Commerce Department General Counsel's office previously indicated that Brown's sole interest in First International was an equity interest.

[76]Yet, in Barbara Fredericks' *March 2, 1994* letter (emphasis added), she stated that "the Secretary's

sole financial interest in this entity is that he *owns* an equity interest."

[77]In addition to the reporting errors noted above, there were a couple of other, minor reporting mistakes made.

[78]Knight, "Despite Debt, TV Firm Gave To Democrats," *Washington Post*, A1 (Nov. 27, 1993); Knight, "Brown Keeps Holding In First International," *Washington Post*, A9 (Nov. 27, 1993).

[79]Knight, "Brown Keeps Holding In First International," *Washington Post*, A9 (Nov. 27, 1993).

[80]Letter from William F. Clinger, Jr. to Stephen D. Potts, 4 (Oct. 5, 1994). According to OGE, Dun & Bradstreet later issued a correction notice dated October 12, 1994, stating that this was in error. Letter from Stephen D. Potts to Honorable William F. Clinger, Jr., 7 (Dec. 29, 1994).

[81]See also 5 CFR 2635.402(d)(2)(i)(B)(full disclosure of "the nature and extent of the disqualifying financial interest" required).

[82]Knight, "Despite Debt, TV Firm Gave To Democrats," *Washington Post*, A1 (Nov. 27, 1993).

[83]Ownership report dated December 1, 1993 and filed with the Federal Communications Commission upon transfer of control or assignment of license.

[84]Knight, "Despite Debt, TV Firm Gave To Democrats," *Washington Post*, A1 (Nov. 27, 1993).

[85]Ibid. The *Washington Post*'s lengthy report was followed only by an editorial in the *Washington Times*. "Anyone for sleaze?" *Washington Times*, A16 (Dec. 1, 1993).

[86]Letter from William F. Clinger, Jr. to Honorable Ronald H. Brown (Feb. 10, 1994).

[87]Fredericks apparently was unaware at the time that the Secretary had disposed of his interest in First International. This suggests that Fredericks did not ask the Secretary or his personal attorney about the current status of his holdings (more than a year following the filing of his first financial disclosure report) and that the Secretary did not review Fredericks' letter before it was sent.

[88]Letter from Barbara S. Fredericks to Honorable William F. Clinger, Jr., 2 (Mar. 2, 1994).

[89]Letter from William F. Clinger, Jr. to Honorable Ronald H. Brown (Mar. 23, 1994).

[90]Letter from Ginger Lew to the Honorable William F. Clinger, Jr. (Jun. 1, 1994).

[91]Knight, "Commerce Secretary Sells Interest in D.C. Company," *Washington Post*, C11 (June 2, 1994).

[92]Ibid., C14. Only later, on his August 1995 financial disclosure report covering 1994, did Brown report this sale as a "stock redemption." On this report Brown also noted that he received capital gains income in 1994 as a result of this transaction.

[93]Letter from William F. Clinger, Jr. to Honorable Ronald H. Brown (July 20, 1994). Also, on July 11, 1994, Lisa Kaufman of Clinger's staff wrote Barbara Fredericks to memorialize their June 28 discussion and to outline the remaining questions, which were subsequently included in Clinger's July 20 letter to Brown.

[94]Letter from Ginger Lew to Ms. Lisa Odle Kaufman, 2 (July 27, 1994).

[95]Letter from Ronald H. Brown to Honorable William F. Clinger, Jr. (Sept. 7, 1994).

[96]Letter from William F. Clinger, Jr. to Frank DeGeorge (Oct. 5, 1994).

[97]Letter from William F. Clinger, Jr. to Stephen D. Potts (Oct. 5, 1994).

[98]140 Cong. Rec. H11415-18 (daily ed. Oct. 7, 1994).

[99]Letter from Francis D. DeGeorge to Honorable William F. Clinger, Jr. (Dec. 21, 1994).

[100]Letter from Stephen D. Potts to Honorable William F. Clinger, Jr. (Dec. 29, 1994).

[101]Ibid., 1.

[102]Ibid., 2-3.

[103]Ibid., 4.

[104]Ibid., 8.

[105]OGE added that it had requested Commerce officials to ensure that no potential conflicts exist because of Brown's promissory note to KNOW, Inc. The identity of KNOW was not known by Commerce ethics officials. According to one report, in 1991 KNOW changed its name to First International!

[106]Letter from Ronald H. Brown to Honorable William F. Clinger, Jr. (Jan. 3, 1995).

[107]Ibid., 2.

[108]Elsewhere it has been reported as a joint decision, Knight, "Commerce Secretary Sells Interest in D.C. Company," *Washington Post*, C11 (June 2, 1994)(statement of Commerce spokeswoman) or as Brown's alone, Knight, "Ex-Partner Paid Some of Ron Brown's Debts," *Washington Post*, A1 (Jan. 14, 1995).

[109]Knight, "Ex-Partner Paid Some of Ron Brown's Debts," *Washington Post*, A1, A8 (Jan. 14, 1995).

[110]Ibid., 8.

[111]This account comes from Bradsher, "Secretary's Debt Payments Are Scrutinized," *New York Times*, A17 (Feb. 8, 1995).

[112]Back in June 1994, when the *Post* first reported Brown's divestment, Barnett was said to not "know the source of the money Hill used to buy Brown's share of the firm." Knight, "Commerce Secretary Sells Interest in D.C. Company," *Washington Post*, C11, C14 (June 2, 1994). The next day, the *Post* printed a correction, stating, "Barnett said he was not aware of the specifics of Brown's sale of his interest in First International[.]" *Washington Post*, A2 (June 3, 1994).

JASAS owner John Foster said "he knew nothing about the payment of Brown's debts." Although the

Fosters had retained Hill to run the station during the pendency of the license transfer proceeding before the FCC, JASAS received its license in November 1993, yet Hill remained in a unspecified management role until she was fired in December 1994, "after a dispute with the [Fosters]." Knight, "Ex-Partner Paid Some of Ron Brown's Debts," *Washington Post*, A8 (Jan. 14, 1995).

Attorneys Barnett and Terwilliger both denied that any of the money used to pay Brown's debts came from any source other than Hill personally. Terwilliger specifically denied that any money from Corridor Broadcasting was used to pay off Brown's debts. Terwilliger's statement that Jasas was not responsible for Brown's debt, and Barbara Foster's denial were reported by Bradsher, "Secretary's Debt Payments Are Scrutinized," *New York Times*, A17 (Feb. 8, 1995).

[113]"Brown dismisses stories on finances," *Washington Times*, A5 (Jan. 17, 1995).

[114]Reuter, "Brown Dismisses Reports," *Washington Post*, D1 (Jan. 17, 1995).

[115]Knight, "Republicans Raise Questions About Brown's Finances," *Washington Post*, D9 (Jan. 19, 1995).

Also, on January 19, 1995, Judicial Watch filed suit in U.S. district court seeking documents relating to Secretary Brown's official travel missions abroad. Judicial Watch suspected that certain persons were selected to accompany the Secretary based on their contributions to the Democratic Party. Judicial Watch filed a FOIA request with the Commerce Department for the names of participants on Brown's missions, and other information. Its suspicion was raised when it was reported that Melinda Moss, who as director of the Office of Business Liaison is responsible for selecting a trip's participants, formerly served as a fund-raiser for the DNC while Ron Brown was its Chairman. A Commerce spokesman denied the allegation. Seper, "Watchdog group seeks records of Brown's travel," *Washington Times*, A3 (Jan. 20, 1995).

Commerce asked the court to postpone for four months the release of some 30,000 travel records, but U.S. District Judge Royce Lamberth denied the request and directed Commerce to decide within 24 hours whether to grant a waiver of the $13,000 in copying fees. Seper, "Judge backs disclosure of Brown's trips abroad," *Washington Times*, A4 (May 9, 1995); Locy, "Commerce Told to Act on Documents' Release," *Washington Post*, D3 (May 9, 1995). The documents were released on May 18, 1995, and were seen by some, including Rep. Clinger, as confirming that Secretary Brown and the Commerce Department favored Democratic Party contributors in selecting business leaders for foreign trade missions. Knight, "Records Said to Show Brown Took Party Patrons on Trips," *Washington Post*, D1 (May 20, 1995); Borders & Benes, "Travels with Ron Brown," *Washington Times*, A21 (May 19, 1995).

[116]Letter from Ricki Tigert Helfer to Honorable Lauch Faircloth (Jan. 19, 1995)(attachment). FDIC also noted that Jasas's bid of $3.01 million for the loan was selected because it was the only bid that conformed to the directions, and because it was valued at 95% of expected recovery. Ibid.

[117]Letter from Lauch Faircloth to Ms. Ricki Tigert Helfer (Jan. 20, 1995). Hill's attorney referred to Hill as a "political football in a contest between Brown and his political opponents." Knight, "Senator Seeks FDIC Probe of Former Brown Partner," *Washington Post*, C1 (Jan. 21, 1995). A Commerce spokeswoman labeled Faircloth's letter "a deliberate, well-orchestrated smear campaign without any substance." Bradsher, "Senate Republicans Seek an Investigation of the Commerce Secretary's Former Partner," *New York Times*, 10 (Jan. 21, 1995).

[118]Letter from William F. Clinger, Jr., to Honorable Ronald H. Brown (Jan. 23, 1995).

[119]Bradsher, "Commerce Secretary Is Accused of Profiting From Company That Defaulted on Federal Loan," *New York Times*, A16 (Jan. 24, 1995).

[120]Knight, "Commerce's Brown Challenged On Links to Broadcasting Firm," *Washington Post*, A1 (Jan. 24, 1995).

[121]Later it was reported that this note provided "the company's only income in 1993." Knight, "Investigators Focus on Brown's $400,000," *Washington Post*, A1, A6 (Jan. 30, 1995).

[122]Letter from Lauch Faircloth, et al. to Honorable Janet Reno (Jan. 23, 1995).

[123]Knight, "14 GOP Senators Seek Probe of Brown Deals," *Washington Post*, F1 (Jan. 25, 1995); Bradsher, "New Push by Senators on Commerce Secretary," *New York Times*, A15 (Jan. 25, 1995).

[124]Bradsher, "Justice Dept. and F.D.I.C. to Review Commerce Secretary's Dealings," *New York Times*, A16 (Jan. 26, 1995); Sniffen, "GOP senators target Brown," *Washington Times*, A4 (Jan. 26, 1995); Knight, "Brown's Ex-Partner Faces Probe," *Washington Post*, D10 (Jan. 26, 1995).

[125]Letter from Ronald H. Brown to Honorable William F. Clinger, Jr. (Jan. 25, 1995).

[126]Bradsher, "Commerce Secretary Is Accused Of Failing to Disclose Income," *New York Times*, A1 (Jan. 27, 1995).

[127]Seper, "Ron Brown failed to disclose $135,000 in partnership fees," *Washington Times*, A3 (Jan. 27, 1995).

[128]Letter from William F. Clinger to Honorable Ronald H. Brown (Jan. 26, 1995).

[129]These entities were described by Brown's lawyer and a Commerce spokesman as "alter egos" of each other, but provided no additional explanation. Knight, "Investigators Focus on Brown's $400,000,"

Washington Post, A1, A6 (Jan. 30, 1995).

[130]Bradsher, "Further Action in Commerce Secretary Inquiry to Be Delayed," *New York Times*, p. 7 (Jan. 28, 1995).

[131]The following account comes mainly from Knight & Walsh, "Brown's NBW Loan Examined," *Washington Post*, F1 (Feb. 1, 1995).

[132]His first report states the liability was incurred in 1988; his annual report corrected that to show that it was incurred in 1989.

[133]Bradsher, "Agency Starts Checking Sale Of a Key Debt," *New York Times*, B10 (Feb. 2, 1995).

[134]Nolanda Hill obtained the $150,000 debenture from Finleasco as part of her divorce settlement with Bill Hill.

[135]Apparently, in 1991 KNOW, Inc., changed its name to First International.

[136]Hill's attorney was not prepared to respond to this story, because he was not in possession of the relevant documents.

[137]Knight, "Investigators Focus on Brown's $400,000," *Washington Post*, A1 (Jan. 30, 1995).

[138]Hedges & Seper, "22 House Republicans prod Clinton to sack Ron Brown," *Washington Times*, A3 (Feb. 3, 1995). The letter also brought up the Vietnam allegations, stating that questions about the Secretary's truthfulness remained. In addition to Clinger, House Speaker Gingrich also did not sign the letter, telling reporters that he did not know enough to make a judgment, but that hearings would help develop the record. This was generously construed as a call from the Speaker for hearings on Ron Brown. Associated Press, "Gingrich wants hearings," *Washington Times*, A4 (Feb. 4, 1995).

[139]Fritz & Connell, "Commerce Secretary's ties to AT&T Partner Questioned," *Los Angeles Times*, A1 (Feb. 5, 1995).

[140]Other information indicates that Brown gave the stock to his children, not just his son. The *Los Angeles Times* reported that Brown informed Commerce ethics officials that he disposed of Kellee stock on June 15, 1993, outside of the 90-day period required for divestiture of potentially conflicting interests. That requirement, 5 CFR 2635.403(d), would apply only if Commerce had directed Brown to dispose of his Kellee holdings, something OGE's December 1994 letter suggests Commerce did not do. (The provision also includes an escape clause in cases of "unusual hardship.")

The *Los Angeles Times* noted that a Los Angeles International airport document dated January 12, 1994, based on written information furnished by James Kelly, a part owner in Kellee, states that Ron Brown held a 8.9% share. Kellee's September 1994 application for a contract at Atlanta's Hartsfield Airport disclosed that Ron Brown "had transferred **most** of his Kellee stock into the name of his adult son Michael[.]" (Emphasis added.) This suggests that Ron Brown retained (through at least September 1994) some of his interest in Kellee, contrary to representations made by Commerce and OGE.

[141]Ibid., A1, A16-17.

[142]Ibid.

[143]5 CFR 2635.402(b)(2).

[144]5 CFR 2635.101(b)(14).

[145]Knight, "Brown's Ties to Phone Firm Probed for Possible Conflicts," *Washington Post*, A7 (Feb. 6, 1995).

[146]Bradsher, "Secretary's Debt Payments Are Scrutinized," *New York Times*, A17 (Feb. 8, 1995).

[147]Letter from Sheila F. Anthony to Honorable Lauch Faircloth (Feb. 6, 1995).

[148]Brown's attorney responded, "I am confident that in discharging [its] responsibilities, the department will conclude that the senators' letter does not even allege any cognizable offense." Bradsher, "More Scrutiny for Commerce Secretary's Deals," *New York Times*, A19 (Feb. 9, 1995).

[149]Seper & Hedges, "Brown partner's loan records sought," *Washington Times*, A4 (Feb. 8, 1995).

[150]"What Is First International?—II," *Wall Street Journal*, A14 (Feb. 9, 1995).

[151]Knight & Thomas, "Justice Dept. Starts Probe of Brown," *Washington Post*, A1 (Feb. 17, 1995); Hedges & Seper, "Reno orders investigation of Brown," *Washington Times*, A3 (Feb. 17, 1995); Bradsher, "Justice Officials Start Preliminary Inquiry on Commerce Secretary," *New York Times*, A19 (Feb. 17, 1995); Cooper, "U.S. Launches Criminal Probe of Ron Brown," *Wall Street Journal*, A? (Feb. 17, 1995).

[152]Bradsher, "Justice Officials Start Preliminary Inquiry on Commerce Secretary," *New York Times*, A19 (Feb. 17, 1995)

[153]"End the Dodging on Ron Brown," *New York Times*, A26 (Feb. 16, 1995).

[154]"The Ron Brown Probe," *Washington Post*, A28 (Feb. 20, 1995). Columnist Tony Snow also criticized Brown for a year's worth of "stonewalling" with Clinger, and wrote that "People have gone to jail for withholding far less information than this from federal ethics cops." Snow urged that congressional hearings be held, and that Brown provide a public explanation. "[T]he sooner Ron Brown explains everything, the sooner he can get off the front page and back to the business of running the department." Snow, "Less than candid in the inquiry," *Washington Times*, A18 (Feb. 24, 1995).

The *Washington Times* also ran an editorial around this time, urging the Justice Department to conduct its investigation swiftly (as opposed to the time Justice took reviewing the allegations against HUD Secretary Cisneros), but avoiding any criticism of the Secretary. "Ron Brown and the Justice Department," *Washington Times*, A18 (Feb. 21, 1995).

[155]31 *Weekly Compilation of Presidential Documents* 276 (Feb. 18, 1995); Pear, "Clinton Backs Secretary of Commerce As 'the Best'," *New York Times*, sec. 1, 30 (Feb. 19, 1995).

[156]Bradsher, "Brown Expresses Confidence About Investigation," *New York Times*, A15 (Feb. 24, 1995).

[157]Letter from William F. Clinger, Jr. to Honorable Janet Reno (Feb. 27, 1995).

[158]This allegation, according to Clinger, is supported by the payments to Brown from First International (Partnership and Corporation) and the forgiveness of the promissory note to KNOW, Inc., all of which occurred while Brown was Secretary. To constitute an illegal supplementation of salary under 18 U.S.C. 209, Brown must have received these payments "as compensation for services as" Commerce Secretary, and not as proceeds from the sale of his interest in First International or payments for services rendered before joining Commerce. See *United States v. Raborn*, 575 F.2d 688, 691-92 (9th Cir. 1978), cited in OGE Informal Advisory Letter 91 X 21, at 78 (July 2, 1991)("the answer will depend largely upon the subjective intent of the parties and the inferences that can reasonably be drawn from the circumstances surrounding a proposed arrangement.").

[159]Earlier, Clinger said that calls for Brown's resignation were "premature." Larson, "House oversight panel interested in Brown's finances, travelgate," *Washington Times*, A6 (Feb. 17, 1995).

[160]Hedges & Seper, "Clinger says Brown evaded Congress, calls for counsel," *Washington Times*, A3 (Feb. 28, 1995); Knight, "Outside Counsel Sought in Brown Probe," *Washington Post*, A5 (Feb. 28, 1995).

[161]Knight, "FDIC, RTC Probing Loans to Firm Owned by Nolanda Hill," *Washington Post*, D1 (Mar. 4, 1995). Recall that in January, the FDIC Chairman directed an Inspector General investigation into the failure of Corridor Broadcasting.

Later in March, the *Washington Times* reported complaints of four FDIC investigators that the investigatory team was inappropriately headed by an auditor and suspicions of some within the FDIC that the investigation of Hill and Corridor may become "politicized." Seper & Hedges, "FDIC's probe of Brown called a face-saving sham," *Washington Times*, A1 (Mar. 23, 1995). (The FDIC investigation relates to Hill and Corridor, although their dealings with Brown are certainly relevant. Also, no one in the article was quoted as calling the investigation a "sham.") Soon thereafter, the FDIC Inspector General, in a letter to the FDIC Chairman, asserted that the team was appropriately staffed and equipped with full authority to issue subpoenas. However, he noted that "we do not anticipate an early completion of this investigation" (which began in January 1995) because of the scope and complexity of matter under review. Seper & Hedges, "FDIC inspector responds to Brown probe criticisms," *Washington Times*, A3 (Mar. 28, 1995).

[162]Ibid.

[163]Ron Brown: See Walsh, "Ron Brown, as Complex as His Finances," *Washington Post*, A1 (Feb. 26, 1995); Bradsher & Bernstein, "Web of Business Connections Haunts Commerce Secretary," *New York Times*, A1 (Feb. 28, 1995)("Investigations now under way . . . have so far drawn only modest public attention, involving as they do a blizzard of numbing details."); Nolanda Hill: See Fritz & Jackson, "Entrepreneur Plays Key Role in Brown's Financial Dealings," *Los Angeles Times*, A5 (Feb. 22, 1995); Bradsher, "Commerce Inquiry Focuses on a Brash Motivator," *New York Times*, sec. 1, 16 (Mar. 5, 1995); Walsh, "Dramatic Flair, Deal-Making Put Nolanda Hill in Spotlight," *Washington Post*, A1 (Mar. 27, 1995).

[164]Knight, "Ronald Brown, Partner Sought to Buy Angolan Oil," *Washington Post*, B1 (Feb. 17, 1995); Harbrecht & Dwyer, "What Did Ron Brown Know, And When Did He Know It?," *Business Week*, 88 (Feb. 27, 1995). First International also unsuccessfully sought to import "hand-painted china and art posters from Poland and wine from Hungary." Bradsher & Bernstein, "Web of Business Connections Haunts Commerce Secretary," *New York Times*, A1, A18 (Feb. 28, 1995).

[165]The attempt to purchase oil from Angola was described as "unusual" because Angola has long-term export contracts with major international oil companies. Others were suspicious of the deep discounts proposed in the deal. Brown's attorney said that Angola offered discounts to leading U.S. black-owned businesses "as a gesture of African solidarity."

[166]Hill sent Brown a memorandum dated April 29, 1992, about various "projects and/or entities in which you have a direct ownership interest." Hill urged Brown expeditiously to write Angolan Government authorities, as the "ball is in your court as far as I am concerned." Harbrecht & Dwyer, "What Did Ron Brown Know, And When Did He Know It?," *Business Week*, 89.

[167]Brown met the President of Angola on a trip to Africa in 1991 sponsored by the DNC.

[168]Lauri Fitz-Pegado was selected to head the U.S. Foreign and Commercial Service. Jill Schuker was appointed Director of Public Affairs. Fitz-Pegado's husband, Fernando Pegado, was formerly Assistant Manager of the London office of the Angolan state-owned oil monopoly, Sonangol. Pegado, Brown and Hill worked together on the Angolan oil project and one other involving an effort to buy Saudi light crude oil from

Aramco, the Saudi Arabian state-owned oil company.

[169]Pound, "Ron Brown, Under The Microscope," *U.S. News & World Report*, 17 (Feb. 27, 1995). Tracey Brown "was paid $12,000 in five checks issued on one day in August 1991" for allowing Corridor to use Tracey's law school residence in New York with a mailing address, answering machine and fax. Tamara Brown was on Corridor's payroll as a Vice President. Associated Press, "Brown daughter, aide got payments," *Washington Times*, A4 (Feb. 18, 1995)(reporting *U.S. News* article, but including additional information); Walsh, "Dramatic Flair, Deal-Making Put Nolanda Hill in Spotlight," *Washington Post*, A1, A8 (Mar. 27, 1995) (Tamara's position with Corridor).

[170]Bradsher, "Inquiry on Commerce Chief Focuses on Campaign Video," *New York Times*, p. 8 (Feb. 18, 1995). A DNC spokesman said the $75,000 also went to "consulting services," yet the DNC's filing with FEC described it as only "video production."

[171]Babcock, "Web of Contacts Gave Brown Lucrative Deal With District," *Washington Post*, F1 (Mar. 22, 1995). On his financial disclosure report, Secretary Brown reported this entity as "PEBSCO Mun. Emp. Securities Corp.-Columbus Ohio[;] This Company Administers Public Employee Deferred Compensation Plans, it manages no money, a wholly owned subsidiary of Nationwide Ins. Company." Brown also dated his involvement in Capital/PEBSCO from 1985.

[172]Fritz & Connell, "Secretary of Commerce Linked to Slum Housing," *Los Angeles Times*, A1 (Apr. 9, 1995). An earlier edition of the story was headlined, "Documents Obscure Commerce Secretary's Link to Slum Housing."

[173]Ibid., A19.

[174]Hedges, "Secretary Brown may owe PG housing-default debt," *Washington Times*, C6 (June 20, 1995)(quoting from letter to Senator Faircloth).

[175]Knight, "Brown Statement Errs on Investment Property Site," *Washington Post*, A9 (Apr. 13, 1995). The *Post* story ran four days after the *Los Angeles Times* report. The other local paper, the *Washington Times*, wrote a prominent profile on the property the day before, "This Ain't Potomac," *Washington Times*, C1, C5 (Apr. 12, 1995). Secretary Brown correctly reported the location of this investment on his calendar year 1994 report, which he filed on August 14, 1995.

[176]This was the focus of the Associated Press article, picked up in "Tax Breaks For Secretary Of Commerce Are Disclosed," *New York Times*, A16 (Apr. 11, 1995); "Slum apartments in PG gave Brown huge tax write-off," *Washington Times*, A3 (Apr. 10, 1995); and the editorial, "Secretary Brown's favorite loophole," *Washington Times*, A12 (Apr. 12, 1995).

[177]5 CFR 2634.301(a).

[178]*Washington Post*, F2 (Apr. 15, 1995).

[179]Seper, "Glendening, Curry queried in Senate probe of Brown," *Washington Times*, A4 (May 2, 1995).

[180]Letter to Honorable Parris N. Glendening, at 2 (May 1, 1995); Letter to Honorable Wayne K. Curry, 2 (May 1, 1995).

[181]Hedges, "Secretary Brown may owe PG housing-default debt," *Washington Times*, C6 (June 20, 1995). Glendening added that the unfit rental units comprise only 5% of the project, and that "those units were either damaged in a fire in 1994 or were basement-level apartments that have been troubled by flooding and sewer system malfunctions, hence the existence of waste in the apartments."

[182]*Application*, 1. The Application was released by the court of appeals on May 17. Harris, "Special Counsel To Probe Brown," *Washington Post*, A1 (May 18, 1995); Bradsher, "Special Prosecutor Is Sought For Commerce Chief Inquiry," *New York Times*, A1 (May 18, 1995); Novak, "Clinton Wants Brown to Stay in Office Despite Call for Independent Inquiry," *Wall Street Journal*, A18 (May 18, 1995); Seper, "Independent counsel sought for Brown probe," *Washington Times*, A1 (May 18, 1995).

[183]*Application*, 5.

[184]*Application*, 4.

[185]Ibid., 6-7.

[186]Ibid., 8-12.

[187]Press release, 2 (May 17, 1995).

[188]31 *Weekly Compilation of Presidential Documents* 846 (May 17, 1995).

[189]Indeed, on the eve of the public announcement of the Attorney General's request, the *Post* initially reported:

Administration officials said Clinton is prepared to follow the same standard with Brown that he and the White House counsel's office put in place when the rash of allegations against Cabinet members surface over the past year: If the charges relate to official duties, the Administration official should leave office while pursuing vindication. If the charge relates to behavior that occurred before the official took office and had nothing to do with official duties, the person can retain his post.

Devroy & Thomas, "Brown to Keep Cabinet Post if Counsel Is Named, Officials Say," *Washington*

Post, A10 (May 17, 1995).

[190]Of course, this distinction was also dubious with respect to Secretary Cisneros, because the set of allegations against the HUD Secretary related to statements made to Federal authorities in connection with his nomination and appointment.

[191]Harris, "Special Counsel To Probe Brown," *Washington Post*, A10 (May 18, 1995).

[192]"Mr. Clinton's Ron Brown Problem," *New York Times*, A30 (May 19, 1995). President Clinton would no doubt respond to this editorial by asserting that his view of the Secretary's effectiveness was not materially affected.

[193]Novak, "Clinton Wants Brown to Stay in Office Despite Call for Independent Inquiry," *Wall Street Journal*, A18 (May 18, 1995). Brown's attorney, Reid Weingarten, said the appointment was the result of a "cynical, partisan effort to take advantage of a badly flawed statute to create as much mischief as possible for Secretary Brown." Hedges, "Independent counsel sought for Brown probe," *Washington Times*, A1, A14 (May 18, 1995).

[194]York, "Ron Brown's Booty," *American Spectator*, 34, 38-39 (June 1995). York wrote that even an indictment of Secretary Brown "on those two very inside-the-Beltway crimes [false statements on financial disclosure reports and withholding information from Congress] would completely miss the moral dimension that is so clear in the Brown case: he hooked up with a slick operator throwing around millions in S&L money, and he took hundreds of thousands of dollars without doing anything to earn it."

[195]Johnston, "A Miami Lawyer Is Chosen to Investigate Commerce Secretary's Finances," *New York Times*, A14 (July 7, 1995); Knight, "Special Counsel Named to Investigate Brown," *Washington Post*, C3 (July 7, 1995); Novak, "Court Names a Miami Lawyer to Probe Commerce Secretary's Business Dealings," B8 (July 7, 1995); Seper, "Independent counsel to look into Brown's financial dealings," *Washington Times*, A3 (July 7, 1995).

Chapter Thirteen

[1] Gugliotta, "HUD Secretary Cisneros Sued For $256,000 by Former Lover," *Washington Post*, A2 (July 30, 1994).

[2] Associated Press, "Cisneros Seeks Dismissal of Suit," *Washington Post,* A4 (Aug. 23, 1994). A formal motion to dismiss was not filed until October. Hendricks, "Cisneros to seek dismissal of lawsuit," *Washington Times,* A9 (Oct. 19, 1994) (from *San Antonio Express-News*). According to Secretary Cisneros's attorney, even assuming that Cisneros and Medlar entered into a oral contract, under Texas law oral contracts for more than a year are unenforceable.

[3] On February 3, 1995, the Texas State District Court denied Secretary Cisneros's motion to dismiss. "Judge refuses to block suit against Cisneros," *Washington Times*, A2 (Feb. 5, 1995).

[4] Hedges, "Cisneros settles suit with ex-mistress," *Washington Times*, A4 (May 20, 1995); Gugliotta, "Cisneros to Pay $49,000 to Settle Suit by Former Mistress," *Washington Post*, A4 (May 20, 1995).

[5] Gugliotta, "HUD Secretary Cisneros Sued For $256,000 by Former Lover," *Washington Post*, A2 (July 30, 1994).

[6] Medlar sold two tapes and 140 pages of transcripts (covering about forty hours of communications) to "Inside Edition." Hosenball, "An Affair to Forget," *Newsweek*, 45 (Sept. 26, 1994). According to the application for the appointment of an independent counsel, the tapes cover nearly a four-year period.

[7] Jakle, "Cisneros says ex-lover's lawsuit was aimed at ruining his career," *Washington Times*, A5 (Sept. 13, 1994)(from *San Antonio Express-News*).

[8] Transcripts of phone conversations from November 22, 1992 through December 1993 were provided to the media, and were reviewed by the author. The transcripts were prepared by Medlar and Medlar's counsel, but their authenticity apparently has not been questioned by Secretary Cisneros or the media. Secretary Cisneros did argue that it would be unfair to use these tapes as proof of anything because Medlar tape-recorded these conversations without his knowledge or consent. Yet, the Secretary also relied on portions of the tapes that are arguably exculpatory or that show Medlar pressing him hard to concede misconduct. DeParle, "Housing Secretary Faces New Questions," *New York Times*, A18 (Sept. 22, 1994).

The quality of the transcripts is spotty; aside from mistakes of spelling and punctuation, critical portions of transcripts are often punctuated with references to "tape skipped." The incompleteness of the transcripts may well be the Secretary's best defense against their probative value.

[9] Gugliotta & Thomas, "Cisneros Under U.S. Scrutiny," *Washington Post*, A2 (Sept. 23, 1994).

[10] Frisby, "Cisneros Fights To Keep Post As HUD Leader," *Wall Street Journal*, A9 (Oct. 6, 1994).

[11] Kurtz, "From Bedroom To Newsroom," *Washington Post*, D1 (Sept. 17, 1994). The FBI's concern during the background check may have been limited to whether the payments were hush money, but it is a non-sequitur to conclude that an alleged false statement to the FBI respecting the payments is not newsworthy.

[12] Hosenball, "An Affair to Forget," *Newsweek*, 45 (Sept. 26, 1994). This edition hit the newsstands on

September 17.

[13] *Newsweek* neglected to note that Secretary Cisneros denied this allegation in the very same phone call with Medlar.

[14] Gugliotta & Thomas, "Cisneros Under U.S. Scrutiny," *Washington Post*, A2 (Sept. 23, 1994).

[15] From a transcript of an undated December 1993 conversation:

HC: *Okay, I'm going to be square with you okay and I don't even know if I'm being taped or not—Am I?*

LM: *No, you're not.*

HC: *All right, let me lay this out—first of all you complicate things immensely with me talking to Morris because I'm a federal official—if he makes a loan to me I have to disclose it, okay—in my disclosure forms—if he—and it can't be any other way—but then you're talking major federal stuff that can be pretty serious- and he knows that too because he just came through ?? stuff.*

[16] DeParle, "Housing Secretary Faces New Questions," *New York Times*, A18 (Sept. 22, 1994). The subheadline is entitled, "Ex-Girlfriend's Tapes Are Putting Cisneros in a Bad Ethical Light."

[17] Secretary Cisneros said that the transition team requested that he end the payments. ". . . I promised my wife it would end, I promised the transition it would end." Associated Press, "Justice Dept. mulls a probe of Cisneros," *Washington Times*, A6 (Sept. 23, 1994). Yet the Secretary told the *Washington Post* that he "told the transition team that he intended to make further payments to Medlar in 1993, after he took office." Gugliotta & Thomas, "Cisneros Under U.S. Scrutiny," *Washington Post*, A2 (Sept. 23, 1994).

[18] From the transcript of a December 12, 1992 conversation (portions are omitted):

LM: *I don't understand why this would cause a problem—I mean, Henry.*

HC: *Because it looks like a payoff.*

LM: *If you have never said anything about it.*

HC: *. . . [I]t would be much worse if everybody's teeth fell out of their mouth's when that came up at the Senate hearing because I was asked a direct question—it's a big deal in the sense it looks like hush money.*

LM: *Is that what they [transition officials] said?*

HC: *No, but I mean—that's what it sounds like.*

[19] Medlar initially said that she received her last payment in January 1994. Associated Press, "Justice Dept. mulls a probe of Cisneros," *Washington Times*, A6 (Sept. 23, 1994). But her attorney later provided bank records detailing the payments made following Cisneros's confirmation: $15,000 on Feb. 16, 1993; $15,000 on Feb. 24; $10,873.45 on Mar. 15; and $15,000 in July 1993 (A total of $55,873.45). Hendricks, "Cisneros sent funds after joining HUD," *Washington Times*, A4 (Oct. 8, 1994)(from *San Antonio Express-News*).

[20] DeParle, "Housing Secretary Faces New Questions," *New York Times*, A18 (Sept. 22, 1994).

[21] Gugliotta, "HUD Secretary Cisneros Sued For $256,000 by Former Lover," *Washington Post*, A2 (July 30, 1994).

[22] The word "sink" was initially transcribed (and later reported) as "upset." See Gugliotta & Thomas, "Cisneros Had Obtained Senators' Assurances About Issue of Payments," *Washington Post*, A13 (Mar. 17, 1995)("upset"). Later, after his confirmation hearing, Cisneros is asked by Medlar what he would have testified if the question about the amount of payments came up.

LM: *But, but what were you going to say if they'd said something about the amount?*

HC: *Well, I was gonna do my very best to, to, to answer the way we'd agreed, which is what, the position I'd taken all along.*

LM: *And it that what [your wife] thinks?*

HC: *Uh, she had her suspicions, she thinks it's been monthly, you know.*

LM: *Hmm.*

[23] Gugliotta & Thomas, "Cisneros Under U.S. Scrutiny," *Washington Post*, A2 (Sept. 23, 1994).

[24] Other Senators on the Committee, but not staff, are entitled to review the report upon request. The report, like all FBI background reports, is not publicly available.

[25] Ellipses in original. Expletive deleted.

[26] Ellipses in original.

[27] Johnston, "U.S. Begins Inquiry Into Payments by Cisneros," *New York Times*, A22 (Sept. 23, 1994).

[28] Johnston, "U.S. Begins Inquiry Into Payments by Cisneros," *New York Times*, A22 (Sept. 23, 1994); Gugliotta & Thomas, "Cisneros Under U.S. Scrutiny," *Washington Post*, A2 (Sept. 23, 1994).

[29] Gugliotta & Thomas, "Cisneros Under U.S. Scrutiny," *Washington Post*, A2 (Sept. 23, 1994).

[30] Associated Press, "Cisneros professes complete honesty," *Washington Times*, A4 (Sept. 29, 1994).

[31] Bedard, "Payments to his ex-mistress may force Cisneros to resign," *Washington Times*, A1 (Oct. 5, 1994). Bedard asserted flatly that Cisneros had misled the FBI and made false statements. Bedard also

reported that Cisneros had falsely told "investigators" that he had stopped making payments. Ibid., A22. This was repeated in a later article. Seper, "FBI's Cisneros report sought," *Washington Times*, A4 (Oct. 12, 1994). That this allegation was included in the Department's investigation was later confirmed by the Secretary's attorney, who suggested that Cisneros's statement regarding the timing of payments was also at issue.

[32] 30 *Weekly Compilation of Presidential Documents*, 1972 (Oct. 7, 1994).

[33] Seper, "FBI's Cisneros report sought," *Washington Times*, A4 (Oct. 12, 1994).

[34] Hedges, "Senate hearings expected in probe of HUD secretary," *Washington Times*, A16 (Nov. 23, 1994).

[35] Thomas & Marcus, "Justice Dept. to Investigate Cisneros," *Washington Post*, A7 (Oct. 15, 1994); Labaton, "Cisneros Investigation Moves Into New Phase," *New York Times*, 26 (Oct. 15, 1994); Associated Press, "Cisneros probe hits 2nd stage," *Washington Times*, A3 (Oct. 15, 1994).

[36] 28 U.S.C. 591.

[37] Ibid.

[38] "Secretary Cisneros' troubles," *Washington Times*, A16 (Oct. 18, 1994).

[39] "Strictly Business," Transcript of "MacNeil/Lehrer Newshour" (Oct. 13, 1994)(emphasis added) 5.

[40] Al Hunt made a similar mistake in belittling the allegations against Cisneros. Hunt, "Janet Reno Runs for Cover on Cisneros," *Wall Street Journal*, A23 (Mar. 16, 1995). Hunt wrote that Cisneros's affair "was out in the open, freely acknowledged and written about. . . ." In the next sentence, he criticized the Attorney General's decision to request an independent counsel solely because Cisneros "lied to the FBI about exactly how much money he paid his former mistress." This suggests to the unsuspecting reader that it was public knowledge that Cisneros was making payments to Medlar, when it was not. Also, the use of the word "exactly" tends to support Secretary Cisneros's initial claim that he provided the FBI with his best estimate about the amount of the payments, which turned out to be inaccurate. In fact, had the Attorney General concluded that Cisneros's statements were just inadvertent inaccuracies, she would have appropriately closed the investigation without requesting the appointment of an independent counsel.

[41] Hedges, "Senate hearings expected in probe of HUD secretary," *Washington Times*, A16 (Nov. 23, 1994).

[42] 28 U.S.C. 592(a)(1).

[43] Johnston, "Justice Dept. Extends Inquiry On Cisneros," *New York Times*, A21 (Jan. 13, 1995). The *Times* report inaccurately treated the matter as a Justice Department decision. Justice must make a request to the Special Division of the D.C. Circuit, which may grant the extension upon a showing of good cause. 28 U.S.C. 592(a)(3).

[44] Thomas & Gugliotta, "Judges Extend Probe Of HUD Chief Cisneros," *Washington Post*, A6 (Jan. 14, 1995).

[45] Hedges, "Faircloth to press for probe of Cisneros despite Reno," *Washington Times*, A5 (Jan. 13, 1995).

[46] Thomas & Gugliotta, "Judges Extend Probe Of HUD Chief Cisneros," *Washington Post*, A6 (Jan. 14, 1995).

[47] "Time for a decision in the Cisneros case," *Washington Times*, A20 (Jan. 16, 1995)(calling the delay "profoundly frustrating—not to say highly suspicious . . . .".

[48] "Application to the court pursuant to 28 U.S.C. 592(c)(1) for the appointment of an Independent Counsel," *In re Henry G. Cisneros* (Mar. 13, 1995) (hereafter, *Application*). See Johnston, "Concluding That Cisneros Lied, Reno Urges a Special Prosecutor," *New York Times*, A1 (Mar. 15, 1995); Thomas & Gugliotta, "Special Counsel Sought To Investigate Cisneros," *Washington Post*, A1 (Mar. 15, 1995); Seper, "Reno calls for probe of Cisneros," *Washington Times*, A1 (Mar. 15, 1995); Novak, "Reno Requests Counsel to Probe Cisneros Matter," *Wall Street Journal*, A4 (Mar. 15, 1995).

[49] This allegation had not surfaced earlier in the press, even though the $2500 figure is mentioned in a taped conversation and Medlar's lawsuit alleged the existence of an oral contract whereby Cisneros agreed to pay her $4000 a month.

[50] The tapes, while inconclusive as to what the Secretary told the FBI on this question, also do not support the Secretary's explanation.

[51] *Application, supra* note 48, 3.

[52] Johnston, "Concluding That Cisneros Lied, Reno Urges a Special Prosecutor," *New York Times*, B9 (Mar. 15, 1995).

[53] *Application, supra* note 48, 4.

[54] *Application, supra* note 48, 5. The Attorney General's statement, however, gives no indication that the Justice Department examined Medlar's insistent allegation that Jaffe provided Cisneros with large sums of cash while Cisneros was Mayor.

[55] The Attorney General decided not to include reports that Secretary Cisneros failed to file informational gift tax returns relating to the payments to Medlar. "[E]ven if his failure to do so was willful, such minor violations are not prosecuted criminally by the Department of Justice absent aggravating circumstances not present here." *Application, supra* note 48, 4. The revised independent counsel law allows the Attorney

General under these circumstances (prosecution would be inconsistent with Department policies) to conclude that no further investigation is warranted. 28 U.S.C. 592(c)(1)(B).

[56] Johnston, "Concluding That Cisneros Lied, Reno Urges a Special Prosecutor, *New York Times*, B9 (Mar. 15, 1995).

In December 1993, when allegations of Governor Clinton's sexual indiscretions were made by Arkansas State troopers who had served on the Governor's security detail, it was Secretary Cisneros who forcefully came to the President's defense when asked on NBC's "Meet the Press" whether the news media was inappropriately covering the personal lives of politicians. Secretary Cisneros replied in the affirmative, castigating the media for its "search and destroy, slash and burn" tactics." He complained, "What's the point of slashing up the president with three years to go in an administration when the American people voted for him knowing that he was not a perfect person? None of us is." Lee, "Cisneros Assails 'Search and Destroy' Coverage," *Washington Post*, A4 (Dec. 27, 1993).

[57] 31 *Weekly Compilation of Presidential Documents* 417 (Mar. 14, 1995). The White House Press Secretary explained, "The president indicated that he regrets mistakes that were made. . . . And I think it's also fair to say that not every mistake requires capital punishment." Harris & Gugliotta, "Cisneros Assets Said to Outweigh Liabilities," *Washington Post*, A7 (Mar. 15, 1995).

[58] Thomas & Gugliotta, "Special Counsel Sought To Investigate Cisneros", *Washington Post*, A13 (Mar. 15, 1995).

[59] Hedges, "Cisneros' troubles loom large as HUD's crunch time nears," *Washington Times*, A11 (Mar. 16, 1995).

[60] Hedges, "Lawyer active in GOP to head Cisneros probe," *Washington Times*, A1 (May 25, 1995); Johnston, "Lawyer Linked to 80's HUD Scandal Is Named to Investigate Housing Chief," *New York Times*, B10 (May 25, 1995).

[61] Locy & Gugilotta, "Court Appoints D.C. Lawyer as Special Counsel in Cisneros Case," *Washington Post*, A8 (May 25, 1995).

[62] Hunt, "Janet Reno Runs for Cover on Cisneros," *Wall Street Journal*, A23 (Mar. 16, 1995).

[63] Gigot, "Friendly Fire: 'Ethics Weapons Hits Cisneros," *Wall Street Journal*, A10 (Mar. 17, 1995).

[64] Broder, "If We Lose Cisneros," *Washington Post*, C7 (Mar. 19, 1995).

[65] Cisneros is heard first urging Medlar to talk to the FBI, but in later conversations he and Medlar discuss what each would say to transition officials, the FBI and the Senate, if asked about the payments. From the transcript of a January 4, 1993, conversation:

LM: *Well, when is the FBI going to come back to you - first of all.*
HC: *Probably Wednesday.*
LM: *Wednesday?*
HC: *I would think so.*
LM: *Do you think they will ask you anything on that?*
HC: *(silence)*
LM: *All right, you're going to tell them the same thing?*
HC: *What we spoke about before. (silence)*
LM: *All right - well, I need to know what they said.*

[66] Medlar was, in fact, temporarily unavailable because of some medical treatment, but the lengthy conversations she had with Cisneros during this time belie her illness excuse for not talking with the FBI at all over a two-week period. In at least one taped conversation (January 4, 1993), Medlar and Cisneros discussed whether she would be called, and if so, whether she would submit to an interview, and if so, what she would (and should) say.

[67] Taylor, "The Clinton-Cisneros Web of Deception," *Legal Times*, 23 (Mar. 27, 1995) (emphasis in original).

[68] The "most plausible explanation," according to Al Hunt, is that Cisneros "didn't want his wife to know the size and scope of the payments." Hunt, "Janet Reno Runs for Cover on Cisneros," *Wall Street Journal*, A23 (Mar. 16, 1995). But this is not really plausible. Why would his wife know what he told the FBI? FBI reports are neither publicly available nor privately available to the nominee or his spouse. Why, too, should one presume that the Secretary's wife did not know the truth about the payments? The tapes, while clearly suggesting that Cisneros kept certain matters from his wife, provides little support for Hunt's theory.

[69] Medlar clearly expressed to Cisneros her opinion that she could do him in were she to disclose certain matters from his past. Cisneros did not seem to take issue with that assessment, although he denied several of the allegations upon which she based her judgment of his vulnerability.

[70] A more sinister, although unsupported, allegation is that Cisneros withheld the true amount of the payments because the money may have come from a source other than his personal funds. Sobran, "Sleaze factor revisited," *Washington Times*, A17 (Mar. 21, 1995)(". . . $60,000 a year, which is so much money that you have to wonder where it came from. If he thought the true amount was worth concealing, it may be

significant. Did the money come out of his own pocket, or the taxpayers?"); Irvine & Goulden, "Media's softened lens on Cisneros," *Washington Times*, A19 (Mar. 26, 1995)("[W]e could offer another explanation that is just as plausible: Mr. Cisneros . . . lied because he did not care to tell the FBI where he found $200,000 to salve the hurt feelings of a discarded mistress.").

[71] Gigot, "Friendly Fire: 'Ethics' Weapon Hits Cisneros," *Wall Street Journal*, A10 (Mar. 17, 1995)("In most of the world, lying is a sin but not a crime. . . . Only in Washington can lying be a crime but not a sin.").

[72] Associated Press, "Clinton's lawyer lambastes independent counsel law," *Washington Times*, A4 (Mar. 20, 1995); "Converts' Zeal," *Wall Street Journal*, A20 (Mar. 20, 1995).

[73] Al Hunt favored ridicule and a reprimand, but not an independent counsel investigation. Hunt, "Janet Reno Runs for Cover on Cisneros," *Wall Street Journal*, A23 (Mar. 16, 1995).

[74] Taylor, "The Clinton-Cisneros Web of Deception," *Legal Times*, 23 (Mar. 27, 1995).

[75] Gonzalez, "HUD secretary to step down after '96," *Washington Times*, A5 (Aug. 15, 1995)(reprinted from *San Antonio Express-News*); Gugliotta, "Cisneros: One Term Is Enough," *Washington Post*, A17 (Aug. 16, 1995)(reporting brief HUD press statement following *Express-News* article).

[76] Stuart Taylor recommended that Secretary Cisneros resign in exchange for no prosecution, an eventuality that is not likely to come to pass.

[77] Remarkably, the news report of the Secretary's announcement, which was made to the editorial board of the *Express-News*, made no mention of the pendency of the independent counsel investigation.

[78] See, for example, *United States v. Hubbard*, 16 F.3d 694 (6th Cir. 1994), rev'd in part, 115 S. Ct. 1754 (1995); *United States v. Harrod*, 981 F.2d 1171 (10th Cir. 1992); *United States v. Brittain*, 931 F.2d 1413 (10th Cir. 1991).

[79] Thomas & Gugliotta, "Special Counsel Sought To Investigate Cisneros," *Washington Post*, A1 (Mar. 15, 1995).

[80] At that point (December 1992-January 1993), Cisneros did not foresee that Medlar would file a breach of contract suit against him, much less that she had taped embarrassing conversations with him and that she eventually would reveal these tapes and her story on "Inside Edition." Several times in his taped conversations with Medlar, Cisneros either asked Medlar if she was taping the conversation (she denied it) or expressed his fear that his phone was being tapped (which she discounted). On December 12, 1992, Cisneros is quoted as exclaiming, "Well, if this phone is tapped we're sunk anyway."

[81] The Attorney General's application does not make this clear, although Senator Faircloth's repeated requests for the "FBI file" suggests that he did not review the FBI summary of its interview of Cisneros relating to the payments. On the other hand, it appears from the Medlar tapes that then-Chairman Riegle read the FBI report on the payments, and that Ranking Member D'Amato was at least aware of what was in the report.

[82] Gugliotta & Thomas, "Cisneros Had Obtained Senators' Assurances About Issue of Payments," *Washington Post*, A13 (Mar. 17, 1995). According to this report, "the letters and the president's views were known to the Justice Department[.]" It was not clear how the President's views were made known to the Department.

[83] Johnson, "Concluding That Cisneros Lied, Reno Urges a Special Prosecutor," *New York Times*, B9 (Mar. 15, 1995).

Chapter Fourteen

[1] Willman & Ostrow, "Independent Counsel Weighed in Pena Case," *Los Angeles Times*, A8 (Mar. 1, 1995)(Wash. ed.); Hedges, "Pena's role in deal with L.A. subway probed by Justice," *Washington Times*, A1 (Mar. 2, 1995); Johnston, "Justice Dept. Initiates Review Regarding Transportation Chief," *New York Times*, B7 (Mar. 2, 1995); Associated Press, "U.S. Reviews Award of Contract to Pena's Former Company," *Washington Post*, C13 (Mar. 2, 1995).

[2] Willman, "Hiring of Pena's Ex-Firm in L.A. Raises Questions," *Los Angeles Times*, A1 (Feb. 10, 1995). Given the extremely short time between the *Los Angeles Times* article and the referral, it is doubtful that the Inspector General conducted any investigation of these reports; most likely, she simply forwarded to Justice the bare allegations contained in news reports.

[3] 28 U.S.C. 591(d)(1)(standard), (d)(2)(30 days).

[4] Thomas & Phillips, "Reno Closes Investigation of Pena's Business Deals," *Washington Post*, A13 (Mar. 17, 1995)(the headline is misleading; there was no Pena business deal involved); Hedges, "Reno rules evidence is lacking to investigate Pena, closes case," *Washington Times*, A3 (Mar. 17, 1995); Johnston, "Secretary of Transportation Will Not Face a Prosecutor," *New York Times*, A20 (Mar. 17, 1995); Barrett, "Justice Department Has Closed Inquiry Of Federico Pena," *Wall Street Journal*, B2 (Mar. 17, 1995).

[5] Ibid.

[6] Secretary Pena's statement is similar to the statement most public officials make after a criminal ethics investigation or prosecution has been dropped or ended in an acquittal. All claim "full" or "total" exoneration

or vindication. It must always be remembered, however, that conduct that is not found to be criminal may nonetheless be unethical under the standards of conduct.

[7]Secretary Pena was sworn in on January 23. President-elect Clinton had announced Pena's selection on December 24, 1992. During the transition, Pena led the group responsible for suggesting persons for political positions at DOT.

[8]The Southern California Rapid Transit District merged in 1993 with the Los Angeles County Transportation Commission to form the Metropolitan Transportation Authority (MTA).

[9]At the time the pension fund held about $500 million in assets.

[10]Further, one pension fund official noted that the pension fund was already being managed by several minority-owned firms.

[11]The MTA conducted an expeditious internal review, which ended in February 1995 "with no conclusion as to whether wrongdoing occurred." The MTA's Inspector General's review is ongoing. Willman & Ostrow, "Independent Counsel Weighed in Pena Case," *Los Angeles Times*, A4 (Mar. 1, 1995)(Wash. ed.)

[12]"Barnes, "Pena said to be target of probe," *Traffic World*, 4 (Mar. 6, 1995)("Pena saw no need to recuse himself from the routine approval of grant money to Los Angeles early in his tenure because he was unaware of his company's renewed interest in the subway project, Mintz said."). Contrast that statement with Secretary Pena's assertion to the *Los Angeles Times* that "his partners waged a 'continuous' effort in 1992 for the pension fund's business. 'I don't think it's a question of stopping and going' to exploit his new status, he said." Willman, "Hiring of Pena's Ex-Firm in L.A. Raise Questions," *Los Angeles Times*, A1 (Feb. 10, 1995).

[13]According to the *Los Angeles Times*, Pena divested himself of his interest "within the first two weeks of January, 1993," at a loss. The *Washington Post*, however, states only that "Pena **was selling** his interest in the firm he founded at the time the decision was made [February 8]." Phillips, "Calif. Transit District Chose Company Founded by Pena," *Washington Post*, A8 (Feb. 11, 1995)(emphasis added). A Pena spokesman said that Pena "fully divested himself of his financial interest in [PIA] in December, 1992." Willman and Ostrow, "Independent Counsel Weighed in Pena Case," *Los Angeles Times*, A4 (Mar. 1, 1995). The Secretary told the *Los Angeles Times* that the price he got for selling his interest was not affected by PIA's expected or hoped-for contract.

[14]See 5 CFR 2635.101(b)(8).

[15]5 CFR 2635.502(b)(1)(iv).

[16]5 CFR 2635.502(a).

[17]5 CFR 2635.502(d).

[18]5 CFR 2635.502(a)(2).

[19]Perhaps such a finding may be forthcoming. Or perhaps the White House determined to leave matters be, considering the media's general treatment of the Justice Department's decision as the final ethics word on the matter. Keep in mind, however, that MTA's Inspector General was also reported to be conducting a review of pre-award actions by local officials.

[20]Whether PIA should have been allowed to keep "Pena" in its name is open to question. In the Bush Administration, the White House Counsel's office told Presidential appointees who were name partners at law, consulting or public relations firms to ask that their name be removed from the title of the firm unless the firm had no dealings with the Federal Government.

[21]The author served as Chief Counsel of the Federal Aviation Administration from 1988-1990, during part of the time when DIA was being promoted, planned, and designed. To his recollection, the author has no personal knowledge of any of the matters reportedly under review by the Inspector General, including specifically City payments for lobbying activities.

[22]Willman, "Probe Of Airport Funds Puts Pena Under Scrutiny," *Los Angeles Times*, A1 (Mar. 12, 1995). *Aviation Daily*, a trade publication, reported this story in the fall of 1994.

[23]Years before the new DIA even opened, it was beset with controversy and subject to criticism. For example, Fumento, "Federico's Folly," *American Spectator*, 42 (Dec. 1993); Fumento, "Denver's castle in the air," *Washington Times*, A17 (Aug. 24, 1994). Initially set to open in 1993, DIA did not open until February 28, 1995.

[24]Heath, "Denver Airport's Turbulent Takeoff," *Washington Post*, E1, E4 (May 16, 1995).

[25]Associated Press, "Denver, federal prosecutors probe construction of $3.7 billion airport," *Washington Times*, A12 (Aug. 26, 1994).

[26]Heath, "Denver Airport's Turbulent Takeoff," *Washington Post*, E1, E4 (May 16, 1995).

[27]See Thomas & Phillips, "Reno Closes Investigation Of Pena's Business Deals," *Washington Post*, A13 (Mar. 17, 1995)("The department's criminal division had been investigating Pena's ties to the recently opened international airport in Denver. . . ."); Welch, "Justice drops investigation of Pena's business dealings," *Inside DOT & Transportation Week*, 3 (Mar. 24, 1995)("The Justice Department had been looking into several matters involving Pena . . . .").

[28]Hedges, "Pena's role in deal with L.A. subway probed by Justice," *Washington Times*, A3 (Mar. 2, 1995)($200,000); Fumento, "Federico's Folly," *American Spectator*, 46 (Dec. 1993)($400,000). Hedges later reported that the Justice Department had looked into the US West contract in connection with the Southern California Rapid Transit District contract. Hedges, "Reno rules evidence is lacking to investigate Pena, closes case," *Washington Times*, A3 (Mar. 17, 1995). However, there is no other indication that the US West contract was part of the Department's thirty-day review.

[29]49 U.S.C. 47107(b)(1).

[30]Willman, "Probe Of Airport Funds Puts Pena Under Scrutiny," *Los Angeles Times*, A1 (Mar. 12, 1995).

[31]Ibid.

[32]Barnes, "GAO gives panel new details on Denver Airport," *Traffic World*, 18, 20 (May 29, 1995).

[33]Willman, "Probe Of Airport Funds Puts Pena Under Scrutiny," *Los Angeles Times*, A1 (Mar. 12, 1995).

[34]Barnes, "GAO gives panel new details on Denver Airport," *Traffic World*, 20 (May 29, 1995).

[35]Willman, "Probe Of Airport Funds Puts Pena Under Scrutiny," *Los Angeles Times*, A1 (Mar. 12, 1995).

[36]Phillips, "Denver Airport Funding Under Investigation," *Washington Post*, A6 (Mar. 13, 1995).

[37]Barnes, "GAO gives panel new details on Denver Airport," *Traffic World*, 20 (May 29, 1995).

[38]"Former DOT Investigator Says He Found Revenue Diversion At Denver," *Aviation Daily*, 272 (Aug. 18, 1995)(quoting Deans).

[39]Notwithstanding the seriousness of Deans' allegations of diversion and retaliation, as of November 1995, they had not been reported by the national press, but only by the trade publication, *Aviation Daily*.

[40]Willman, "Probe of Airport Funds Puts Pena Under Scrutiny," *Los Angeles Times*, A1 (Mar. 12, 1995). Kaplan has since left the Department.

Chapter Fifteen

[1]The phrase "revolving door" is often used interchangeably with the pejorative expression "cashing in," whereby departing high-level officials leave their modest government salary after a short period (say, one or two years) for a significant salary increase in the private sector. The salary differential is typically seen as based on the experience and contacts the former official gained in government and the expectation that such recent experience will be of financial reward to the private sector employer. Indeed, much of the popular criticism directed at the revolving door stems from the public's resentment of cashing in. As a matter of semantics, however, this practice does not constitute a "revolving" door unless and until the former official uses his access and influence with his former agency on behalf of his private employer. Many who believe the post-employment restrictions are not tough enough wish to limit the opportunity to "cash in," regardless of whether government processes are at risk of being compromised.

The phrase "revolving door" is also sometimes used to describe the practice of returning to government service after some time spent in the private sector. However, returning to government service does not strictly pose an ethics issue, because once the person returns to the Executive Branch he is subject to the full panoply of ethics restrictions.

[2]The first post-employment restriction was enacted in 1872. The lifetime ban currently set forth in 18 U.S.C. 207(a)(1) was enacted in 1962 as 18 U. S.C. 207(a). Public Law Number (Pub. L. No.) 87-849, 76 Statute (Stat.) 1123 (1962). That law repealed two post-employment statutes, 18 U.S.C. 284 and 5 U.S.C. 99, that imposed two-year bans. Former section 284 prohibited former Federal employees for two years from "prosecut[ing] or act[ing] as counsel, attorney, or agent for prosecuting, any claims against the United States involving any subject matter directly connected with which such person was so employed or performed duty[.]" Pub. L. No. 80-772, 62 Stat. 698 (1948). Former 5 U.S.C. 99 prohibited a former employee for two years from "prosecuting a claim which was pending, during the period of his incumbency, either in that or in any other department[.]" S. Rep. 2213, 80th Cong., 2d Sess., reprinted in 1962 *U.S. Code Congress & Admin. News* 3854. Both statutes were faulted for their narrow application; section 99 was also criticized for its overbreadth, because it applied even if the former employee had been unaware of the claim while in government. Ibid.

[3]*Ethics in Government Act of 1978*, Pub. L. No. 95-521, 92 Stat. 1864 (1978)(codified as 18 U.S.C. 207(c)). A year earlier, a similar one-year cooling-off period for certain former Department of Energy employees was enacted as part of the *Department of Energy Organization Act*, codified at 42 U.S.C. 7215. This provision was modeled after the cooling-off period provision in draft legislation that eventually became the *Ethics in Government Act of 1978*, but covered a broader set of employees than the Executive Branch-wide provision in 18 U.S.C. 207(c). Not until 1993 was this special DoE provision repealed, so that DoE employees are now subject to the same post-employment restrictions as employees of other Executive agencies.

Section 3161 of the *National Defense Authorization Act* for Fiscal Year 1994, Pub. L. No. 103-160 (Nov. 30, 1993).

Retired military officers have also been long subject to post-employment restrictions. The criminal selling statute, 18 U.S.C. 281(a), prohibits retired military officers for two years from prosecuting any claim against the United States, or representing any person in the sale of anything to the U.S. Government through the department from which they retired. The civil selling statute, 37 U.S.C. 801(b), prohibited the payment of retired pay to any retired regular officer who, within three years after leaving the service, engages in selling supplies or war materials to an agency of DoD, the Coast Guard, the Public Health Service or the National Oceanic and Atmospheric Administration. In 1994, the civil selling statute was repealed and the criminal selling statute was suspended until 1997. Section 6001 of the *Federal Acquisition and Streamlining Act of 1994*, Pub. L. No. 103-355 (Oct. 13, 1994).

[4]Pub. L. 96-28, 93 Stat. 76 (June 22, 1979).

[5]H. Rep. 115, 96th Cong., 2d Sess., reprinted in 1979 *U.S. Code Cong. & Admin. News* 328.

[6]One example cited in the legislative history involved a Navy official who negotiated contract settlements with General Dynamics and then took a job with the company. 132 Cong. Rec. H10131 (Oct. 15, 1986)(statement of Rep. Bennett). It was noted, however, that the practice of DoD officials in leaving Government for private sector positions with DoD contractors was longstanding.

[7]Section 931 of the *National Defense Authorization Act for Fiscal Year 1987*, Pub. L. 99-500, 100 Stat. 1783-156 (Oct. 18, 1986)(codified at 10 U.S.C. 2397(b)). This provision was criticized for its narrowness of application (it covers only a small number of DoD officials); its onerousness (it is a ban on employment, not simply on representational activities); and its lack of necessity (in light of other post-employment restrictions).

[8]Pub. L. 100-679, sec. 27(e), 102 Stat. 4063 (Nov. 17, 1988)(codified 41 U.S.C. 423(f)).

[9]The procurement integrity restriction is broader than the general lifetime ban contained in section 207(a)(1) in only one respect: it prohibits for two years the rendering of behind-the-scenes advice and assistance on the particular procurement, not simply communications and appearances. The greater onus of the procurement integrity law is in the enormous administrative burden imposed by the certification requirements and the law's broad coverage provision, which makes any Executive Branch employee who uses a government credit card on official travel a "procurement official."

Although the "Ill Wind" investigations prompted the procurement integrity legislation, a subsequent review of the "Ill Wind" prosecutions revealed "no evidence that any of the individuals who have been indicted or have pleaded guilty would have violated the Act's post-employment restrictions." Prepared statement of Chester Paul Beach, Jr., Principal Deputy General Counsel, Department of the Navy, before the Subcommittee on Defense Industry and Technology of the Senate Committee on Armed Services (Mar. 21, 1990), at 15. Other procurement integrity provisions do address conduct prosecuted as part of the "Ill Wind" probe, but even this conduct was adequately prosecuted under extant statutes.

[10]Michael Deaver, former Chief of Staff to President Reagan, was investigated by an independent counsel in 1986 for allegedly violating post-employment restrictions after he left the White House in 1985 and set up a consulting firm. Deaver's high-profile case got the attention of Democrats in both the House and Senate, who initiated investigations and later requested the appointment of an independent counsel. See S. Garment, *Scandal: The Culture of Mistrust in American Politics* (Anchor Books, 1992 ed.), 107. Deaver was indicted in 1987 for perjury, based on statements made to Congress in the course of its investigations, not for a violation of the post-employment restrictions law. He was convicted in 1988.

Following an independent counsel investigation, former Reagan White House aide Lyn Nofziger was indicted in 1987 and convicted in 1988 of three counts of violating the one-year cooling-off period, 18 U.S.C. 207(c), by contacting the White House (1) on behalf of Welbuilt Electronic Die Corp. (Wedtech) to assist the company in obtaining an Army contract; (2) on behalf of National Marine Engineers Beneficial Association, AFL-CIO urging the use of civilian (read: union) crews on noncombat Navy vessels; and (3) on behalf of Fairchild Republic Corporation urging implementation of a Presidential directive to encourage the export sales of Fairchild's A-10 aircraft. Nofziger's conviction was reversed by the court of appeals, *United States v. Nofziger*, 878 F.2d 442 (D.C. Cir. 1989), which held that subsection 207(c) should be construed to require the government to allege and prove (which it had not done) that Nofziger had knowledge of each element of the offense, particularly that the White House had a direct and substantial interest in the particular matters he raised with them. The *Ethics Reform Act of 1989* changed section 207 significantly to cure the ambiguities and inconsistencies identified by the court.

[11]Memorandum of Disapproval, 24 *Weekly Compilation of Presidential Documents*, 1561 (Nov. 23, 1988).

[12]Ibid.

[13]Ibid., 1561-62.

[14]Ibid., 1563.

[15]Executive Order 12,668, 25 *Weekly Compilation of Presidential Documents.* 114 (Jan. 25, 1989).

Notes

[16]*To Serve With Honor: Report of the President's Commission on Federal Ethics Law Reform* (Mar. 1989)(hereafter, *To Serve With Honor*).

[17]*Report of the House Bipartisan Task Force on Ethics on H.R. 3660*, 101st Cong., 1st Sess. (Comm. Print 1989).

[18]*Ethics Reform Act of 1989*, Pub. L. No. 101-194, 103 Stat. 1716 (1989)(codified as amendments to 18 U.S.C. 207). The cooling-off restrictions were strengthened, in prohibiting former "senior" Executive Branch officials for one year from making any appearance before or communication to their former agency in connection with any matter on which the former employee seeks official action, 18 U.S.C. 207(c), and, for former "very senior" officials, by prohibiting them for one year from contacting to the same extent any one in their former agency and nearly all Presidential appointees throughout the Executive Branch, 18 U.S.C. 207(d).

[19]The Bush Administration's effort to repeal the procurement integrity provision failed, however.

[20]Former employees who left the Government before January 1, 1991, are subject to the previous version of section 207.

[21]For example, Duffy, "When Lobbyists Become Insiders," *Time*, 40 (Nov. 9, 1992). The criticism was off the mark, for two reasons. First, the Bush campaign officials and advisers identified as representing foreign and corporate clients (for example, James Lake, Charles Black) were not former Bush Administration officials. In other words, there was no revolving door. Second, the Bush campaign, working with the White House Counsel's office, set up a strict regime to prevent even the appearance that any government action was being taken because of or at the request of any Bush campaign official or adviser. These campaign officials agreed to refrain from contacting any Executive Branch official during the pendency of the campaign, and refrain from lobbying any person on issues involved in the campaign.

[22]*Putting People First: A Strategy for Change*, 23-25 (1992). A paragraph entitled "Stopping the Revolving Door" previewed the contents of what would be Executive Order 12834. Ibid., 26.

A staple of Mr. Clinton's rhetoric on the campaign stump was an attack on the inordinate influence lobbyists and special interests have on the Federal Government. For example, on February 22, 1992, he said: "We must discard the ethics of the 80's—the turn a quick buck, make it big and forget about your neighbor mentality." Woodlief, "Hopefuls pull out stops to garner votes in Maine," *Boston Herald*, 1 (Feb. 23, 1992). On July 20, 1992, he said, "We're going to break the stranglehold of the lobbyists on the American government and give it back to the people." UPI report of July 20, 1992. In a similar vein, candidate Clinton proclaimed on July 16, 1992, the night of his nomination, "He [President Bush] won't break the stranglehold the special interests have on our elections and the lobbyists have on our government, but I will."

[23]Kamen & Von Drehle, "Ethics Policy Toughened," *Washington Post*, A1 (Dec. 10, 1992); Ifill, "Clinton Team Issues 5-Year Lobby Ban," *New York Times*, D19 (Dec. 10, 1992).

[24]Executive Order 12,834, "Ethics Commitments by Executive Branch Appointees," 29 *Weekly Compilation of Presidential Documents* 77 (Jan. 20, 1993).

[25]The ethics reforms identified during the transition as subsequent steps were lobbying reform (disclosure of the identity of lobbyists, their clients, activities and expenditures) and campaign finance reform. Barr, "Clinton's Ethics Rules: Balance or Barrier?" *Washington Post*, A21 (Dec. 14, 1992). Neither of these reforms is addressed to Executive Branch employees.

In a series of memoranda to agency heads, President Clinton also cut back on the use of government aircraft, the use of portal-to-portal privileges (home-to-work chauffeured transportation), and the use of executive dining rooms and health clubs by high-level officials. 29 *Weekly Compilation of Presidential Documents,* 167-169 (Feb. 10, 1993). These actions were intended to reduce the perquisites available to high-level officials.

[26]30 *Weekly Compilation of Presidential Documents,* 631 (Mar. 24, 1994).

[27]President Clinton's non-sequitur was telling: when asked about the many allegations of unethical conduct by White House officials **while in office**, he retreated to standards that operate only **after** an official leaves the Administration.

[28]Executive Order 12,834, Sec. 1(a), (b); 29 *Weekly Compilation of Presidential Documents,* 77 (Jan. 20, 1993). The executive order employs the term "lobbying" although it defines the term to cover communications and appearances without regard to whether compensation is received. Executive Order 12,834, Sec. 2(c).

[29]Executive Order 12,834, Sec. 2(a), (b).

[30]18 U.S.C. 207(c).

[31]"Very senior" officials consist of the Vice President, the Members of the Cabinet, and Assistants to the President. 18 U.S.C. 207(d)(1).

[32]18 U.S.C. 207(d). This excludes United States Attorneys and most ambassadors, whose salary is provided under different authority.

[33]18 U.S.C. 207(f). A former U.S. Trade Representative is subject to a 3-year ban on representing or advising foreign entities. 18 U.S.C. 207(f)(2), added by Pub.L. No. 102-395, §609(a)(2), 106 Stat. 1873 (Oct. 6, 1992)(Fiscal Year 1993 Appropriations Act for Commerce, State and Justice).

[34]18 U.S.C. 207(b). The trade negotiation portion of the trade or treaty restriction may no longer have any effect, because the definition of "trade negotiation" requires a Presidential determination under section 1102 of the *Omnibus Trade & Competitiveness Act of 1988*. That section, codified at 19 U.S.C. 2902, authorizes such Presidential determinations only until June 1, 1993, or until April 16, 1994 with respect to the Uruguay Round. 19 U.S.C. 2902(a)(1)(A), (b), (c)(1), (e)(1).

[35]Executive Order 12,834, Sec. 2(b).

[36]Executive Order 12,834, Sec. 3.

[37]Executive Order 12,834, Sec. 1(a).

[38]Executive Order 12,834, Sec. 5.

[39]Kamen & Von Drehle, "Ethics Policy Toughened," *Washington Post*, A1 (Dec. 10, 1992).

[40]Ibid.

[41]Kaplan, "The Revolving Door Still Spins," *Washington Post*, C5 (Jan. 31, 1993).

[42]Kamen & Von Drehle, "Ethics Policy Toughened," *Washington Post*, A1 (Dec. 10, 1992)(700 appointees confirmed by the Senate, 100 EOP staffers and 300 other appointees in the Executive Branch with salaries in excess of $104,000).

[43]The small number of White House officials covered was credited to President Clinton's decision to reduce the salaries of top White House staff. Kamen, "Salary Cuts Crimp Clinton Ethics Rules," *Washington Post*, A13 (Feb. 22, 1993)(20 officials); *Hearing on S. 420, The Ethics in Government Reform Act of 1993, and S. 79, The Responsible Government Act of 1993*, 103d Cong., 1st Sess. (1993)(testimony of Sen. Boren)(10 officials).

[44]However, the five-year trade negotiator restriction and the lifetime foreign entity ban, like their statutory counterparts, 18 U.S.C. 207(b) and (f), also reach the giving of advice behind the scenes.

[45]Executive Order No. 12,834, Sec. 2(c). Administrative proceedings, however, including rulemakings, are covered.

[46]18 U.S.C. 207(j)(1),(2)(A)(representing state and local governments), (2)(B)(representing educational institutions, hospitals, and medical research organizations).

[47]Kaplan, "The Revolving Door Still Spins," *Washington Post*, C5 (Jan. 31, 1993).

[48]Devroy, "At White House, Revolving Door Redux," *Washington Post*, A1 (Dec. 8, 1993).

[49]Ibid.

[50]Associated Press, "Quitting aides test Clinton ethics code," *Washington Times*, A4 (Nov. 26, 1993).

[51]In a display of naivete, White House officials even stressed the departing officials' good moral character. Devroy, "At White House, Revolving Door Redux," *Washington Post*, A1, A8 (Dec. 8, 1993). However, to the media and public, Neel and Paster were taking lobbyist jobs, as the term is popularly used. See, for example, Frisby, "Two Lobbyists Spark Concern by Attending Democrats' Forum," *Wall Street Journal*, A12 (July 22, 1994)(Months after leaving the White House, Neel appeared on a DNC-sponsored panel with Administration officials to discuss telecommunications policy; Neel's attendance was cleared by White House Counsel's office); Andrews, "Phone-Bill Lobbyists Wear Out Welcome," *New York Times*, D1 (Mar. 20, 1995)("Roy M. Neel, President Clinton's deputy chief of staff in 1993, is now the top lobbyist for an association of local telephone companies.").

[52]See, for example, Jehl, "Job Plans of Clinton Aides Renew Debate on Lobbying," *New York Times*, A22 (Dec. 8, 1993)("The appearance that the revolving door that Mr. Clinton so vehemently criticized can still operate at near-full whirl has prompted a chorus of criticism from some of those who most enthusiastically applauded the new ethics standards."); "Roy Neel and the Clinton ethicists," *Washington Times*, A18 (Nov. 29, 1993)("'In time-honored tradition, Mr. Neel seems to be cashing in."); "Mr. Paster and Mr. Neel Step Out," *Washington Post*, A24 (Dec. 9, 1993)("[T]hese resignations follow months of sanctimony on the part of this president and this administration about how this time it wasn't going to happen."); "Mr. Clinton Spins the Lobby Door," *New York Times*, A30 (Dec. 9, 1993)("Instead of the promised end to business as usual, this Administration has come up with an income enhancement plan for well-connected Democrats. . . . If Mr. Clinton wants to institutionalize lobbying once removed, that's his business. But it's an insult to call it reform[.]").

[53]Jehl, "Job Plans of Clinton Aides Renew Debate on Lobbying," *New York Times*, A22 (Dec. 8, 1993).

[54]Ibid.

[55]Devroy, "At White House, Revolving Door Redux," *Washington Post*, A1, A8 (Dec. 8, 1993).

[56]Broder, "Clinton Defends Circumstances of Aides' Exit," *Washington Post*, A4 (Dec. 9, 1993).

[57]The *Washington Post* reported that "[s]ome noted that the exceptions to the rules appeared to reflect the president-elect's biases." Kamen & Von Drehle, "Ethics Policy Toughened; Top Appointees to Face 5-Year Lobbying Curb," *Washington Post*, A1 (Dec. 10, 1992). Another report stated that "there were also some loopholes that transition officials acknowledged they were unable to close." Ifill, "Clinton Team Issues 5-Year Lobby Ban," *New York Times*, D19 (Dec. 19, 1992). However, this was not a matter of the Administration's ability, but of its free will. The so-called "loopholes" in the executive order were choices

made by the President.

[58]Ifill, "Clinton Team Issues 5-Year Lobby Ban," *New York Times*, D19 (Dec. 10, 1992).

[59]Specifically, S. 79 would have: (1) lengthened all but one of the current one-and two-year restrictions (18 U.S.C. 207(a)(2), (b), (c), (d), (e)) to five years; (2) lengthened the current one-year foreign entity ban to life; and (3) imposed on all officials and employees of the Executive and Legislative Branches a two-year cooling-off period with respect to representing, aiding or advising any foreign entity with respect to a matter before the United States.

[60]Specifically, S. 420 would have broadened and lengthened the existing general one-year cooling-off periods in subsections 207(c)(former "senior" officials) and 207(d)(former "very senior" officials): (1) all Executive Office of the President (EOP) noncareer employees making over $70,000 would have been subject to a five-year ban on representing any other person before any agency with which they had substantial responsibility and a two-year ban with respect to representational activities before all other senior officials; (2) all Executive Branch noncareer officials making over $70,000 would have been subject to a five-year ban on representing any other person before their former agency; (3) all Executive and Legislative employees, regardless of salary, would have been subject to a one-year cooling-off period with respect to their former agency. (Under current law, the threshold for being covered by a cooling-off period—to which career officials are also subject—is over $100,000.) Similar restrictions would have covered Members of Congress and senior legislative staff. The one-year trade or treaty negotiation cooling-off period would have been made permanent for senior non-career Executive Branch officials. Senior Executive and Legislative Branch noncareer officials would also have been barred for life from representing for compensation any foreign entity, including foreign businesses and persons, and would have been barred for life from receiving any thing of value from a foreign government.

[61]Hearing on S. 420, *The Ethics in Government Reform Act of 1993,* and S. 79, *The Responsible Government Act of 1993,* 103d Cong., 1st Sess. (1993)(hereafter, *March 1993 hearing*). Senator Boren explained that "Public opinion polls indicate that Americans don't believe that there is a high standard of public service that there should be. They know people are trying to profit from the positions they have held in high public office." He predicted that his bill would be a "strong and effective step toward restoring the faith of the American people in all of us who work as government servants." Ibid., 8, 9. Senator McCain stated, "This revolving door has been a major factor in the public's losing faith and trust in its government." Ibid., 11. Senator DeConcini blamed "the revolving door syndrome" in part for eroding the public's confidence in government. Ibid., 13.

[62]This amendment effectively took the place of S. 79 and S. 420, neither of which was reported out of subcommittee.

[63]Separately, Representative John Conyers introduced H.R. 1593, the *Revolving Door Sunshine Act of 1993,* to require former Members of Congress and certain congressional staff, and certain former Executive Branch officials, to publicly report for five years all official contacts made to either Congress or the Executive Branch on behalf of private interests. The bill was intended to close gaps in the current requirements to disclose lobbying activities and to cover—through public disclosure—certain post-employment activities that are not prohibited by either 18 U.S.C. 207 or Executive Order 12834. H.R. Rep. No. 103-354, 103d Cong., 1st Sess. 4-5 (1993). In November 1993, the bill was reported favorably out of the House Committee on Government Operations, which Representative Conyers chaired, but was never acted upon by the full House.

[64]In section 6001 of the *Federal Acquisition Streamlining Act of 1994,* Pub. L. 103-355 (Oct. 13, 1994), 108 Stat. 3243, Congress repealed the civil selling statute, 37 U.S.C. 801(b), and suspended the criminal selling statute, 18 U.S.C. 281(a), through the end of 1996. The conference report noted that these actions were taken "in anticipation of a thorough review and reform of the procurement integrity statutes in the next Congress." H. Rept. 103-712 to S.1587, 140 Cong. Rec. H8879, at H8936 (daily ed. Aug. 21, 1994). Section 4301(c) of the law also created a "micro-purchase" exemption from the procurement integrity restrictions for contracts under $2500.

[65]The bill as drafted (§2(c)) does not appear to cover Executive Branch officials, although the press statement and section-by-section analysis show an intent to cover these officials.

[66]This provision as drafted appears to apply only to former Legislative Branch officials, although the accompanying materials show an intent to cover "ex-public officials who supervise lobbyists, even if they do not personally engage in lobbying." Press Release for Rep. Zimmer (May 3, 1995). The provision is ambiguously drafted, in any event. The way it is written, the duration of this employment ban is potentially for life.

[67]There is a two-year employment ban in 10 U.S.C. 2397b, prohibiting certain former DoD procurement officials from receiving any compensation from a contractor on a DoD procurement. H.R. 1735 is considerably broader.

[68]141 *Congressional Record* S10603 (daily ed., July 25, 1995).

[69]141 *Congressional Record* S10575 (daily ed., July 25, 1995). Another provision in the lobbying bill,

added by Senators Levin and McConnell, would amend the financial disclosure requirements in the Ethics in Government Act to require a filer to report income, assets, and liabilities in categories over $1,000,000. Currently, a filer with income, assets, or liabilities over $1,000,000 checks the box entitled "Over $1,000,000" for each such source of income, asset, or liability. Under section 20 of the bill, categories of income between $1 million and $5 million, and greater than $5 million would be added. For assets and liabilities, categories between $1 million and $5 million, $5 million and $25 million, between $25 million and $50 million, and greater than $50 million, would be added. This provision has absolutely no relation to government ethics. A source of income, an asset, or a liability in an amount of $1 million that does not pose a conflict of interest, potential conflict, or otherwise raise an ethics issue, would not under any circumstance do so were the amount increased 5, 25, 50 million dollars or more.

[70]141 *Congressional Record* S10597 (daily ed., July 25, 1995). Senator Dole did not explain why working for a foreign interest would exacerbate an appearance problem, much less why any appearance problem would arise in the first place.

[71]Ibid. ("While I was hopeful that we could have made a number of additional changes, including codifying President Clinton's executive order . . . .").

[72]141 Cong. Rec. H13738-13750 (Daily Rd.) Nov. 29, 1995. Dewar, "House Gives Final Approval to Lobbyist Disclosure Bill," *Washington Post*, A1 (Nov. 30, 1995); Clymer, "Congress Passes Bill to Disclose Lobbyists' Roles," *New York Times*, A1 (Nov 30, 1995). The day before, Representative Phil English proposed an amendment to provide that senior trade officials of the Commerce Department and Members of the International Trade Commission would be subject to the bill's lifetime ban on representing or advising foreign entities, in addition to the two officials, the United States Trade Representative and the Deputy Trade Representative, who were covered by the bill. The bill narrowly failed, 221 to 201. Dewar, Lobby Reform Bill Moves Toward Final House Vote," *Washington Post*, A14 (Nov. 29, 1995).

[73]Love, "Congress Approves First Overhaul of Lobbying Disclosure law Since '40s," *Roll Call*, 1,24 (Nov. 30, 1995).

[74]*Federal Acquisition Reform Act of 1995*, H.R. 1670, sec. 305.

[75]141 *Congressional Record* H 8936-7 (daily ed., Sept. 14, 1995). There was no discussion of the procurement integrity post-employment restrictions during floor debate on September 13 and 14.

[76]"Restrictions on the activities of former government employees are intended to ensure the integrity of the government's decision-making process, and thereby to protect the public interest." *To Serve With Honor*, *supra* note 16, 53.

[77]In testimony at the *March 1993 Senate Hearing*, Professor Eskridge identified three types of bias problems that warrant post-employment restrictions:

> The problem of access bias, that certain interests might have excessive access to existing government officials; incentive bias, the monetary incentives the revolving door might offer for officials to slant their current decisions; and apparent bias, or the loss of faith in government by the American people.

March 1993 Hearing, supra note 61, 42 (testimony of W. Eskridge). Access bias and incentive bias correspond to the two objectives listed in the text.

A third, frequently cited, reason for post-employment restrictions is to prevent former employees from using confidential or other non-public information obtained while in government on behalf of a private interest. See *To Serve with Honor, supra* note 16, 53; *March 1993 Hearing, supra* note 61, 1 (statement of Sen. Levin); ABA Committee on Government Standards, "Keeping Faith: Government Ethics & Government Ethics Regulation," 45 *Administrative Law Review* 287, 326-27 (summer 1993)(hereafter, *ABA report*). This is the basis for the lifetime ban and two-year official responsibility ban in 18 U.S.C. 207 (a)(1) and (a)(2). Although the trade or treaty negotiation cooling-off period in subsection 207(b) addresses this concern, other cooling-off periods (subsections 207(c), (d), and (f)) operate regardless of whether the former employee possesses non-public information.

See also "The 'Revolving Door'—Should It Be Stopped?, 32 *Administrative Law Review* 383, 397-98 (1980)(remarks of Edwin S. Kneedler).

[78]There also may be some constitutional limits to Congress's authority to proscribe actions of former Federal officials. See *March 1993 Hearing, supra* note 61, 133 (statement of William N. Eskridge, Jr.); 158 (statement of Robert S. Peck).

[79]"The 'Revolving Door'—Should It Be Stopped?," 32 *Administrative Law Review* 396-97 (remarks of Edwin S. Kneedler).

[80]*To Serve with Honor, supra* note 16, 53.

[81]*ABA report, supra* note 75.

[82]Ibid., 326-27.

[83]Ibid., 327.

[84]Of course, the executive order's foreign entity provision also was built on the statutory foreign entity cooling-off period, which has a similarly unfortunate pedigree.

[85]By their very nature, most particular matters involving specific parties (for example, claims, contracts, grants, subsidies, lawsuits) are concluded within a year or two.

[86]One story reported that Richard Metzger turned down the position of Director of the Federal Communication Commission's Common Carrier Bureau in order to avoid being subject to the executive order's cooling-off periods. Nonetheless, he was hired to another position at the FCC that allows him to participate in common carrier issues. The story indicated that the FCC Chairman was contemplating "recasting the position to avoid the rule." Skrzycki, "FCC Tests Five-Year Lobbying Ban In Finding Key Role for a Regulator," *Washington Post*, D5 (Mar. 1, 1994).

[87]Powell, "Clinton's ethics rules called obstacle to filling key posts," *Washington Times*, A4 (Feb. 28, 1994). Powell also quoted an unnamed "senior White House official" that "many dozens of strong potential candidates" have been discouraged from government service when faced with a myriad of restrictions and procedures, including the new post-employment restrictions. George Stephanopoulos replied that he did not think "the ethics guidelines per se" are discouraging prospective appointees, but rather the "extensive background checks and the highly partisan confirmation process that has had some effect."

[88]Ibid.

[89]Curran, "Bills to Shut 'Revolving Door' for Members And Aides Paid $70,000+ Face Tough Road," *Roll Call*, 16-17 (Mar. 8, 1993). On the other hand, Charles Lewis, of the Center for Public Integrity, testified of the "systemic abuse" by former trade officials and also former officials who had responsibility in the S&L and Superfund areas. *March 23 Hearing, supra* note 61, 30-33. Lewis pointed out that current law does not reach the role of party and campaign officials, who often have power and influence as great or greater than many senior administration officials. Lewis also criticized the exemptions in current law and in the President's executive order. He concluded that "the existing restrictions are practically irrelevant to the kinds of systemic abuse and influence peddling that we have found in our work." Ibid. Fred Wertheimer, President of Common Cause, testified generally in support of Senator Boren's bill, but recommended some modifications. Ibid., 33-41.

[90]*March 23 Hearing, supra* note 61, 22.

[91]Ibid., 92 (statement of G. Davis).

[92]Ibid., 26-30 (testimony of A. Trowbridge).

[93]Ibid., 206 (statement of J. Shaw). Also, AFGE and NTEU, two government employee unions, filed statements opposing the bills on similar grounds. Ibid., 193-198 (statement of R. Tobias); 199-205 (statement of J. Sturdivant).

[94]Ibid., 44, 46 (testimony of R. Peck).

[95]Ibid., 41 (testimony of W. Eskridge).

[96]The one ABA recommendation that would tighten current standards would extend the general lifetime ban in subsection 207(a) to reach advice and assistance provided behind the scenes. Currently, many local bar rules prohibit lawyers from providing assistance behind the scenes (as well as making communications and appearances) on behalf of a client concerning a particular matter involving specific parties in which the lawyer was personally involved while in government. The ABA Committee would not, however, expand the cooling-off periods in section 207 and the executive order to reach this conduct.

[97]*ABA Report, supra* note 75, 331.

[98]Ibid.

[99]Ibid., 333.

[100]In openly criticizing the President's executive order, Judge Mikva displayed a candor unusual for a senior White House official. One week later, however, Mikva announced his resignation as White House Counsel, see Devroy, "Mikva Will Step Down As White House Counsel," *Washington Post*, A29 (Sept. 21, 1995), which may account, in part, for his frank assessment.

[101]Broder, "Clinton Defends Circumstances of Aides' Exit," *Washington Post*, A4 (Dec. 9, 1993).

[102]Regrettably, Senator Dole, if elected President, would also be unlikely to repeal the executive order, considering the floor statement he made in support of it during the Senate's consideration of the lobbying disclosure bill.

[103]Although OGE testified that it would prefer that the recent amendments to the law, including the executive order, be given time to work, OGE's testimony suggests that the executive order goes too far.

[104]It may be appropriate, however, to exempt **elected** state and local officials from the cooling-off periods, because of the special responsibilities entrusted to these officials and their accountability to the electorate.

[105]Executive Order 12,674 (as amended), sec. 102(h); 5 CFR 2635.101(b)(8).

[106]See "Roy Neel and the Clinton ethicists," *Washington Times*, A18 (Nov. 29, 1993)("'Cashing in' wouldn't work if those still in government made a practice of shutting out those who dive through the revolving door. Because trying to control those who have left is largely fruitless, the ethical burden is heaviest on those still in government.").

Case In Point

[1]18 U.S.C. 207(e)(4)(B)(i). The coverage provision states: "(i) in the case of a former employee on the leadership staff of the House of Representatives, those persons are any Member of the leadership of the House of Representatives and any employee on the leadership staff of the House of Representatives[.]" The terms "employee on the leadership staff of the House of Representatives" and "Member of the leadership of the House of Representatives" are defined in 18 U.S.C. 207(e)(7)(H) and (L). The House Majority Leader is included in the latter definition.

[2]The text of sub-section 207(e)(4) provides:
(A) Any person who is an employee on the leadership staff of the House of Representatives . . . and who, within 1 year after the termination of that person's employment in such staff, knowingly makes, with the intent to influence, any communication to or appearance before any of the persons described in subparagraph (B), on behalf of any other person (except the United States) in connection with any matter on which such former employee seeks action by a Member, officer, or employee of either House of Congress, in his or her official capacity, shall be punished as provided in section 216 of this title.

[3]18 U.S.C. 216. Persons who violate the cooling-off period are subject to a maximum punishment of imprisonment for one year (five years if the violation is willful) and a $50,000 fine.

[4]Broder, "Democrat Starts Courting Congressional Supporters," *Washington Post*, A8 (July 4, 1992).

[5]Untitled editorial, *National Review*, 16 (Feb. 1, 1993).

[6]18 U.S.C. 207(e)(6)(A).

[7]Barnes, "The Importance of Being George," *New Republic*, 17, 20 (Sept. 6, 1993). Barnes incorrectly stated that the threshold was $92,000.

[8]B. Woodward, *The Agenda* 27 (1994)("His salary [from the campaign] would be $60,000 plus a housing allowance, a substantial cut from his current $95,000."). The way in which Woodward conducted his research suggests that the $95,000 figure came from Stephanopoulos himself. Ibid., 12.

[9]Actually, the annualized rate would be $115,092 (12 X $9591).

[10]Even if Stephanopoulos were correct that he had been paid from Gephardt's personal office, it would not make a difference. The statutory coverage provision refers to the "rate of basic pay," received "in the aggregate" and thus would include any salary received from whatever payroll or pay source. That phrase may have been intended to exclude bonuses and awards; construing it also to exclude Stephanopoulos's salary from Gephardt's congressional office payroll would provide an enormous loophole by which all leadership staff could escape from the cooling-off period.

[11]Stephanopoulos was one of several employees on the Majority Leader's staff payroll paid in this manner.

[12]This would have been Stephanopoulos's salary had he worked all of 1991 on the House payroll and received six months of salary at $9,591 per month and six months of salary at $5,777.83 per month.

[13]*Report of the Clerk of the House* (July 1 to Sept. 30, 1991), House Doc. No. 102-168; *Report of the Clerk of the House* (Jan. 1 to Mar. 31, 1991), House Doc. No. 102-87. According to the House Clerk's Report for the second quarter, Stephanopoulos received $21,146.66. *Report of the Clerk of the House* (April 1 to June 30, 1991), House Doc. No. 102-138. For the last quarter of 1991, in which Stephanopoulos worked only a short time before leaving to join the Clinton campaign, Stephanopoulos received $2,503.73. *Report of the Clerk of the House* (Oct. 1 to Dec. 31, 1991), House Doc. No. 102-194.

[14]Stephanopoulos' salary in 1990 alternated in the same manner it did in 1991. For November 1990 ("Floor Assistant (statutory)"), he was paid $7,808.50 ($93,702 annualized) and for December 1990 ("Floor Assistant") he was paid $4,686.50 ($56,238 annualized). Report of the Clerk of the House (Oct. 1 to Dec. 31, 1990), House Doc. No. 101-46.

[15]If Stephanopoulos did not hold the most senior position on the Majority Leader's staff, he was clearly among the two or three most senior.

[16]See, for example, *Bifulco v. United States*, 447 U.S. 381 (1980).

[17]It may be concluded that Stephanopoulos was not informed that he was exempt, because he certainly would have said so in his defense.

[18]If so, it would seem to follow that Stephanopoulos made the communication or appearance "with intent to influence," another necessary element of the offense.

[19]Barnes, "The Importance of Being George, *New Republic*, 20 (Sept. 6, 1993).

[20]Broder, "Democrat Starts Courting Congressional Supporters," *Washington Post,* A8 (July 4, 1992)..

[21]It is widely believed that the Democratic leadership throughout the latter part of 1991 and all of 1992 engaged in a concerted effort to stall or frustrate President Bush's domestic initiatives so as to confirm the Democrats' and Bill Clinton's argument that President Bush lacked a domestic program and was without much in the way of domestic accomplishments. It is equally plausible that Democrats sought to embarrass the President by passing legislation that the President was on the record opposing, thereby forcing his veto hand,

even though Democrats knew they did not have the votes to override a veto. Adam Clymer wrote that the Second Session of the 102d Congress distinguished itself from the usual Congress that is "far less worried about electing a President than about reelecting themselves:

One recent Congress did seem to be dedicated to affecting a Presidential election. In 1992, the Democrats went to great lengths to embarrass George Bush. They arranged vote after vote on extending emergency unemployment compensation. They stalled on a family leave bill until not long before Election Day. They put nice-sounding bills before him that they expected him to veto so they could attack him for that. The most spectacular was their campaign reform measure, which passed in the House only after Speaker Thomas S. Foley personally guaranteed reluctant Democrats that Mr. Bush would veto the bill.

Clymer, "In Congress, It's Nearly 1996," *New York Times*, sec. 4, 4 (June 25, 1995); see also, Krauss, "Democrats Scale Back Aims in Congress to Win at Polls," *New York Times*, A12 (Sept. 18, 1992).

[22]Stephanopoulos is probably covered by the resuscitated independent counsel law, either because he served as a national campaign official for the Clinton/Gore campaign or because of his senior White House position. 28 U.S.C. 591(b)(3), (6). (If Stephanopoulos is not covered, the independent counsel law's coverage provision is underinclusive.) Under the facts, the Attorney General likely would be required to conduct a preliminary investigation and subsequently apply for the appointment of an independent counsel.

[23]Seeking action from Congress is accorded some constitutional protection: the First Amendment provides that "Congress shall make no law respecting . . . the right of the people . . . to petition the Government for a redress of grievances." U.S. Const. amend. I. Seeking action from Congress as part of the political process would seem to deserve a greater measure of protection than seeking action for pecuniary reasons. A presidential nominee was not likely the special interest lobbyist Congress had in mind when it enacted the cooling-off period.

[24]Barone, "How to do the transition right," *U.S. News & World Report*, 50 (Nov. 23, 1992).

[25]Ibid. Barone noted the Stephanopoulos matter in an unsuccessful attempt to dissuade the Clinton Administration from its "impulse to make the system even purer by" extending from one to five years the cooling-off period for former high-level officials. Barone wrote that "The problem with this is becoming clear now that Democrats are taking over the whole government." Ibid.

[26]Untitled editorial, *National Review*, 16 (Feb. 1, 1993). The magazine wryly added that it would support a presidential pardon.

[27]A few months earlier, there had been some concern expressed over the extent to which the post-employment laws would restrict William Bennett, who was under consideration for Chairman of the Republican National Committee, and who would be subject to a new cooling-off period if he left after January 1, 1991. When Bennett withdrew his name from consideration in December 1990, it was reported that he did so in order to avoid any appearance of a conflict of interest that might result from his desire to earn speaking fees on behalf of corporate interests while serving as Chairman and meeting regularly with the White House. Devroy, "Bennett Shuns GOP Post," *Washington Post*, A1 (Dec. 14, 1990):

Mr. [Boyden] Gray warned him . . . that it appeared to be a potential problem because if he took a speaking fee from a group and then the Administration made a favorable decision regarding that group, or if Mr. Bennett talked about issues important to the group at the White House, he would be vulnerable to a conflict-of-interest charge.

Dowd, "Bennett Rejects Top G.O.P. Post, Adding to White House Disarray," *New York Times*, A1 (Dec. 14, 1990). But it was also reported that concerns were expressed that Bennett could run afoul of the cooling-off period by "lobbying the White House on behalf of the Republican Party[.]" McQueen, "Bennett Decides Not to Accept GOP Position," *Wall Street Journal*, A20 (Dec. 14, 1990).

[28]Those employed in a position in the Executive Office of the President at a rate of pay payable for Level II of the Executive Schedule, and those appointed by the President under 3 U.S.C. 105(a)(2)(A). 18 U.S.C. 207(d)(1)(B),(C).

[29]18 U.S.C. 207(d)(2)(A).

[30]18 U.S.C. 207(d)(2)(B).

[31]Because the law prohibits "appearances" as well as "communications," it would not suffice for Yeutter to remain silent during these meetings, if his presence were intended to influence official action.

[32]The same advice was given to Commerce Secretary Robert Mosbacher, upon his departure from the Administration to serve as campaign chairman of the President's re-election campaign. Mosbacher could meet with the President, Vice President, and White House Office staff, but not with Cabinet members or with Darman or Hills present.

This restriction again came into play when Secretary James Baker left the State Department to become Chief of Staff in August 1992. It was widely reported in the weeks before Baker joined the White House staff that he was also being considered for a senior position with the Bush campaign. One difficulty with such a move was that outside of the Administration Baker could not meet with the President to discuss government policy with Darman or any Cabinet member present. And for departing Chief of Staff Samuel K. Skinner and Clayton Yeutter (who had left his RNC post to serve in the White House as Assistant to the President for Domestic Policy), their "very senior" ban extended to the President and Vice President, as well as senior Presidential appointees, because Skinner's and Yeutter's former agency was the Executive Office of the President, of which the President and Vice President are specifically named as "officers." 18 U.S.C. 207(i)(A).

[33]Letter from George Bush to Congress, July 26, 1991. The exception for political communications would not have extended to former officials who also represent, as an attorney or agent or otherwise, any other person in the same matter.

[34]Ibid.

[35]Associated Press, "White House and Congress Seek to Revise Ethics Rule for Elections," *New York Times*, A15 (July 24, 1991); McAllister, "Bill Would Relax Rules On Honoraria," *Washington Post*, A23 (Sept. 13, 1991); Glasser, "Frank's Panel Restores Honoraria for Staffers," *Roll Call*, 1, 20 (Sept. 16, 1991).

[36]137, *Cong. Rec.,* H11268, 11269 (Nov. 25, 1991).

[37]Barnes, "The Importance of Being George," *New Republic*, 20 (Sept. 6, 1993).

[38]See 18 U.S.C. 207(c) and (d)(applying cooling-off period to certain White House officials by reference to their appointment under 3 U.S.C. 105 and 106).

Chapter Sixteen

[1]For purposes of this chapter, the terms "nominee" and "prospective appointee" are used interchangeably, unless otherwise noted.

[2]One reason why a prospective appointee is formerly retained as a consultant may be in order to receive reimbursement for travel and per diem expenses incurred in preparing for nomination and confirmation. But some agencies, such as DoD, reimburse nominees for expenses under "invitational travel orders," without retaining the nominee as a consultant. See *Nominations, infra* note 11, 1055.

[3]Section 3109 provides for the employment by contract of the "temporary (not in excess of 1 year) or intermittent services of experts or consultants[,]" when "authorized by an appropriation of other statute[.]" Congress routinely gives authority and funds to agencies to hire consultants.

[4]*Federal Personnel Manual (FPM)*, Chap. 304, Subchapter 1-2(1). This definition is taken from an opinion of the Comptroller General, 23 Comp. Gen. 497, 499 (1944). An agency management official must certify that the appointment is proper and "is of a purely advisory nature, and does not include the performance or supervision of operating functions." *FPM*, Chap. 304, Appendix A, "Internal Agency Controls On Employment."

Chapter 304 of the *FPM* quoted from guidance contained in OMB Circular A-120, that agencies are prohibited from using consulting services to perform work of a "policy/decisionmaking or managerial nature which is the direct responsibility of agency officials." OMB Circular A-120, Guidelines for the Use of Consulting Services (April 14, 1980), cited in *FPM*, Chap. 304, Subchapter 1-10(b)(2). OMB Circular A-120 was rescinded in November 1993, 59 Fed. Reg. 63593 (Dec. 2, 1993), after much of the guidance contained in the circular had been revised and incorporated into several OMB policy documents. One of those policy documents, Office of Federal Procurement Policy (OFPP) Policy Letter 93-1, expressly excludes services obtained through personnel appointments. 58 Fed. Reg. 63593 at 63596. Linda Williams, Deputy Associate Administrator of OFPP, explained in a phone conversation that guidance on consulting services obtained through personnel appointments is the province of OPM, not OMB.

[5]Pub. L. No. 102-378, section 2(8)(Oct. 2, 1992), codified at 5 U.S.C. 3109(d).

[6]60 Fed. Reg. 45647 (Sept. 1, 1995). The preamble to the proposed rule states that "[u]se of the authority for persons awaiting Presidential appointment is clarified." 59 Fed. Reg. 67232 (Dec. 29, 1994). None of the ten comments submitted discussed the issue of using section 3109 to appoint prospective Presidential appointees.

[7]5 CFR 304.103(b)(1). The phrase "awaiting final action" is not defined in the rule or explained in the preamble to either the proposed or final rule. According to an OPM official, this phrase encompasses prospective presidential appointees at all stages, including those individuals who have not yet been nominated and even those for whom an intention to nominate has not yet been announced.

[8]5 CFR 304.102(c). A "consultant" is defined as "a person who can provide reliable and pertinent advice generally drawn from a high degree of broad administrative, professional, or technical knowledge or experience." 5 CFR 304.102(b).

[9]5 CFR 304.103(b).

[10]*U.S. Constitution.* art. II, sec. 2, cl. 2 ("[The President] shall nominate, and by and with the Advice and Consent of the Senate, shall appoint . . . Officers of the United States . . . .").

[11]Letter from Sam Nunn and Strom Thurmond to Honorable Les Aspin (April 22, 1993), reprinted in *Nominations Before the Senate Armed Services Committee*, First Session, 103d Congress (1993)(hereafter,

Nominations), S. Hrg. 103-414, at 912-913. The letter followed several reports in the trade newsletter *Defense Daily* beginning in February that several nominees retained by DoD as consultants had assumed an active role in policymaking.

[12]Ibid.

[13]Ibid., 913.

[14]Letter from Les Aspin to Honorable Sam Nunn (April 29, 1993); *Nominations, supra* note 11, 914.

[15]*Nominations, supra* note 11, 915.

[16]*Nominations, supra* note 11, 914.

[17]Gellman, "Perry Moves to Erase Aspin's Marks Upon Pentagon Organization," *Washington Post*, A14 (Feb. 17, 1994).

[18]*Nominations, supra* note 11, 731-32.

[19]*Nominations, supra* note 11, 917. That document also contains the initials of Graham Allison on the line entitled, "Approved by Dr. Allison." At the time, Allison was also serving as a consultant awaiting nomination.

[20]For example., April 5, 1993 memorandum from Carter to Aspin ("As you requested, I attach a binder containing the essential information on the Cooperative Threat Reduction (CTR) Program. Tabs 8-10 are provided for your information only; **I have not yet approved them.**")(emphasis added); April 27, 1993 memorandum from Carter to Aspin ("Tomorrow's meeting has the purpose of giving your people . . . your reactions to **our plans to implement** the new Nunn-Lugar ("CTR") program.")(emphasis added).

In response to a set of written questions from Senator Robert Smith, Carter also acknowledged that on "rare occasions" he was the only person from DoD at interagency meetings at the White House and State Departments, although he asserted he did not voice any opinion at such meetings as the "Department's official representative." See 139 Cong. Rec. S8180-8185 (daily ed. June 29, 1993)(statement of Sen. Kempthorne); Gertz, "Pentagon nominee has acted officially," *Washington Times*, A4 (June 8, 1993).

[21]*Nominations, supra* note 11, 892-93 (opening statement of Sen. Nunn); Gertz, "Senators probe Pentagon pick's denial of assuming duties early," *Washington Times*, A4 (June 2, 1993).

[22]Letter from William J. Perry to The Honorable Sam Nunn (May 27, 1993).

[23]*Nominations, supra* note 11, 910-11.

[24]Ibid., 910 ("You should not meet with anyone outside the Department unless you are accompanied by a "responsible official" of the Department who can speak for the Department[.]").

[25]Ibid. ("Do not use Department stationery.").

[26]Ibid., 911 ("You should not make any decision for a component of a Department. . . .").

[27]Ibid. ("You may not originate an action, have official actions of the Department pass through you or approve or disapprove any actions of the Department. . . . In general, you are not to sign any documents in such a way as to give the appearance of having assumed official duties.").

[28]Ibid. ("You are not to undertake to hire, transfer or terminate members of your potential future organization or otherwise reorganize its management. . . .").

[29]Memorandum For Potential Appointees, "Procedures To Be Followed Pending Formal Appointment" (June 2, 1993), *Nominations, supra* note 11, 908-09.

[30]Ibid., 908. See also Gertz, "Pentagon appointees under probe," *Washington Times*, A4 (June 9, 1993).

[31]Letter from Jamie S. Gorelick to The Honorable Dick Kempthorne (June 17, 1993).

[32]Letter from Ashton B. Carter to Secretary of Defense Les Aspin (June 1, 1993).

[33]*Nominations, supra* note 11, at 907.

[34]139 Cong. Rec. S8215 (daily ed. June 29, 1993). Eighteen Republicans voted against the nomination.

[35]139 Cong. Rec. S8177 (daily ed. June 29, 1993)(statement of Sen. Nunn). Senator Edward Kennedy blamed the guidelines, which he called "unclear" and "murky." 139 Cong. Rec. S8190 (daily ed. June 29, 1993)("What this episode demonstrates is that prospective nominees were asked to carry out duties as consultants to the Secretary of Defense, without any clear lines between permitted and proscribed activity."). Senators Smith and Kempthorne urged their colleagues to vote against Carter to send a signal to this and future administrations to respect the advice-and-consent process. Senator Smith also asserted that Carter had repeatedly exceeded his authority as consultant. 139 Congressional Record S8209-8213 (daily ed. June 29, 1993)(separate statements of Sens. Kempthorne and Smith).

[36]Allison was retained as a consultant effective February 1, 1993.

[37]The existence of the Inspector General's investigation was reported by Al Kamen in "A Bump Along the Way Impedes Progress on Pentagon Confirmation," *Washington Post*, A19 (June 11, 1993).

[38]Memorandum for Secretary of Defense from Deputy Inspector General Derek J. Vander Schaaf (June 22, 1993)(hereafter, *Inspector General's Report*). See also Gellman, "Report Cites Breaches By Pentagon Nominee," *Washington Post*, A15 (July 8, 1993).

[39]This irregularity was discussed without comment in the *Inspector General's Report, supra* note 38, 2-3.

[40]Ibid., 3.

[41]5 CFR 2635.502(b)(1)(iv).

[42]5 CFR 2635.502(a). Although this standard was promulgated in 1992 as a part of the comprehensive standards of conduct for Executive Branch employees, it reflects the longstanding requirement that Federal employees "avoid even an appearance of loss of impartiality." 57 Fed. Reg. 35006, 35025 (Aug. 7, 1992).

[43]*Inspector General's Report, supra* note 38, 7-8.

[44]*Inspector General's Report, supra* note 38, 6.

[45] Gellman, "Report Cites Breaches By Pentagon Nominee," *Washington Post*, A15 (July 8, 1993)(quoting Vernon A. Guidry).

[46]Ibid.

[47]*Nominations, supra* note 11, 1050.

[48]*Nominations, supra* note 11, 1052 (prepared statement of Graham T. Allison).

[49]*Nominations, supra* note 11, 1054.

[50]*Nominations, supra* note 11, 1056.

[51]Upon William Perry's confirmation as Secretary of Defense in January 1994, Allison submitted his resignation. Perry accepted Allison's resignation and abolished Allison's position. It was reported at the time, however, that Perry asked Allison to continue to serve as a consultant, as a "day-a-week special adviser." Gellman, "Perry Moves to Erase Aspin's Mark Upon Pentagon Organization," *Washington Post*, A14 (Feb. 17, 1994).

[52]This position was later titled as Assistant Secretary for Democracy and Peacekeeping. At the time of the White House's March 1993 announcement, the Office of Democracy and Peacekeeping apparently had not been formally established. The Assistant Secretary position for which Halperin was named was one of several Assistant Secretary positions provided by Congress without any set responsibilities.

[53]Indeed, a few days before the inauguration of President Clinton, Secretary-designate Aspin asked Halperin for assistance in working on the policy towards homosexuals in the military. *Nomination of Dr. Morton H. Halperin to be Assistant Secretary of Defense for Democracy and Peacekeeping, Before the Senate Committee on Armed Services* (hereafter, *Halperin Nomination*), 103d Cong., 1st Sess. 64 (afternoon session)(Nov. 19, 1993)(statement of Morton H. Halperin).

[54]The White House quickly indicated that the President would resubmit Halperin's name when Congress began the Second Session of the 103d Congress in January 1994. But, following his nomination as Aspin's successor in December 1993, Bobby Ray Inman was reported to question the need for the position designed for Halperin by Aspin. Halperin wrote to the President in January 1994, two weeks before Inman's scheduled confirmation hearing, and asked that his name not be resubmitted. The President accepted Halperin's withdrawal "with real regret." Lippman, "Halperin Say No To Renomination For Defense Post," *Washington Post*, A17 (Jan. 11, 1994). Inman himself announced on January 18 that he had asked the President to withdraw his name from consideration as Secretary. Aspin's confirmed successor, William Perry, announced in February his intention to abolish the position of Assistant Secretary for Democracy and Peace Keeping. Gellman, "Perry Moves to Erase Aspin's Marks Upon Pentagon Organization," *Washington Post*, A14 (Feb. 17, 1994).

The Legal Affairs Council, a conservative legal policy group, issued a paper in December 1993, asking the Senate Armed Services Committee to investigate two incidents of "possible deceit" in Halperin's hearing testimony. That testimony was not under oath. One of the incidents concerned Halperin's call to a commander recommending the termination of a military exercise. Scarborough, "Group says Halperin was misleading," *Washington Times*, A4 (Dec. 30, 1993). After Halperin withdrew his name, the Legal Affairs Council called for the Attorney General to appoint a special counsel to investigate whether Halperin lied to Congress. "Halperin bows out," *Washington Times*, A18 (Jan. 12, 1994)(endorsing the Council's call for an investigation).

[55]Senator Kempthorne noted that the Committee had received forty-seven documents signed by Halperin, and over 100 memoranda signed, approved, initialed or concurred in by Halperin, in his capacity as consultant. *Halperin Nomination, supra* note 53, 32, 44 (aft. sess.) (statement of Sen. Kempthorne). Halperin responded that "many of them are consistent with the guidelines. Clearly some of them are not." Ibid., 44 (testimony of Morton H. Halperin).

[56]See Gertz, "Halperin concedes he acted improperly while a nominee," *Washington Times*, A1 (Nov. 20, 1993); "Morton Halperin explains himself," *Washington Times*, A16 (Nov. 24, 1993).

[57]*Halperin Nomination, supra* note 53, 27 (morn. sess.)(testimony of Morton H. Halperin).

[58]*Halperin Nomination, supra* note 53, 5 (aft. sess.)(testimony of Morton H. Halperin).

[59]Halperin explained that under the new DoD guidance, he was permitted to send advice to the Secretary in a memorandum, so long it did not proceed through the formal Departmental review and clearance process. *Halperin Nomination, supra* note 53, 45, 64-66 (aft. sess.)(testimony of Morton H. Halperin).

[60]*Halperin Nomination, supra* note 53, 60 (morn. sess.), 28, 67 (aft. sess.)(testimony of Morton H. Halperin).

[61]*Halperin Nomination, supra* note 53, 25 (morn. sess.)(testimony of Morton H. Halperin). In response to questioning from Senator Lott, Halperin explained:

I called him because I received a phone call from somebody in the State Department indicating that the killer of an American had just been allowed to walk out of a Guatemalan jail, and raising with me the fact that he had learned that there was an ongoing military exercise in Guatemala and that the State Department was considering proposing that the exercise be terminated in retaliation for that, and asking what my view might be on that.

I did not know about any such exercise. I called General Joulwan. I asked him about the exercise. He told me that it was ongoing, that it was going to be terminated soon, and that he was not planning to attend the closing ceremony because of what had just happened, and he thought that was an appropriate response. I told him that that sounded right to me, and that was the end of the conversation.

Ibid., 6 (aft. sess.). Later, in response to questioning from Senator William Cohen, Halperin said, "I did not express any view of my own on that[,]" referring to the State Department's recommendation to terminate the exercise. Ibid., 105 (aft. sess.).

[62]*Halperin Nomination, supra* note 53, 46 (aft. sess.)(remarks of Senator Kempthorne).

[63]Interview with Committee staff.

[64]Letter from J. Bennett Johnston and Malcolm Wallop to Honorable Bruce Babbitt (May 27, 1993).

[65]Letter from Bruce Babbitt to Senator Malcolm Wallop (June 4, 1993); 139 Congressional Record S8217-18 (daily ed. June 29, 1993).

[66]The question is not whether the information solicited by Frampton was needed for him to brief the Secretary; the question is whether the manner by which Frampton sought the information was inconsistent with the limited, advisory role of a consultant. Also, even though the NBS had not been formally created, and therefore there were no operating functions of the NBS, Frampton's memorandum was directed to Federal employees in their official capacity. Organizing the NBS is as much an operating function of the Department, for which there are supervisors and subordinates, as would be running the NBS. So, the Department's (and OPM's) only plausible explanation that remains is that Frampton sent the memorandum at the specific direction of the Chief of Staff.

[67]Letter from James. B. King to Senator Malcolm Wallop (June 7, 1993); 139 Cong. Rec. S8217 (daily ed. June 29, 1993). King asserted that "There are no Governmentwide regulations defining the appropriate uses of consultants." At the time, the use of consultants was governed only by OPM guidance reflecting opinions of the Comptroller General. A rule containing some of this guidance was issued in September 1995. See text at notes 6-9, *supra*.

[68]Senator Wallop disagreed with OPM's conclusion. 139 Cong. Rec. S8216 (daily ed. June 29, 1993)(statement of Sen. Wallop)("I find it incredible that the OPM guidelines on consultants can be rendered meaningless, merely if a consultant is directed to take a prohibited action by a departmental official such as the Secretary's Chief of Staff did in the case of Mr. Frampton.").

[69]Letter from Malcolm Wallop to The Honorable Bruce Babbitt (June 9, 1993); 139 Cong. Rec. S8217 (daily ed. June 29, 1993).

[70]Letter from Tom Collier to The Honorable Malcolm Wallop (June 14, 1993); 139 Cong. Rec. S8217 (daily ed. June 29, 1993). In the letter, Collier also explained that he had briefed each consultant in the beginning, and "discussed at length the need to avoid issuing directions to employees in their area, and the need to avoid being a decisionmaker. Instead, we looked to consultants to provide advice to the Secretary or to me according to specific requests from us." Both the April 29 and May 18 memorandum went beyond what was initially contemplated by the consultant relationship.

[71]Most of the debate concerned statements and positions previously taken by Frampton as President of the Wilderness Society.

[72]139 Cong. Rec. S8219 (daily ed. June 29, 1993)(statement of Sen. Johnston).

[73]139 Cong. Rec. S8216 (daily ed. June 29, 1993)(statement of Sen. Wallop). Senator Frank Murkowski also opposed Frampton's confirmation for this and other reasons. 139 Cong. Rec. S8293 (daily ed. June 30, 1993)(statement of Sen. Murkowski). Although Senator Smith also found that Frampton had exceeded his authority as consultant, he opposed Frampton's confirmation on other grounds. 139 Cong. Rec. S8216 (daily ed. June 29, 1993)(statement of Sen. Smith).

[74]Currently, consultants are required to sign an acknowledgment that they are covered by certain **ethical** standards. This certification is lacking in that the standards are not specified on the form or on an attachment, and the standards most likely do not include the limitations on permissable activities. To achieve the highest degree of compliance, the certification should be executed on the document containing the guidelines for consultants.

[75]S. 1147, the Presidential Nominee Reform Act. Senator Kempthorne attempted to attach this bill to the National Defense Authorization Act for Fiscal Year 1994, but was defeated in a party-line vote at commit-

tee mark-up. No action was taken on the bill by the Government Affairs Committee in the 103d Congress, to which the bill was referred upon its introduction. A similar bill may be reintroduced in the current Congress.

[76]S. 1147, Section 1(a)(2). The bill would not cover recess appointees, and would not apply "to any officer of the United States with respect to the functions of the office held by such officer at the time of nomination by the President for appointment to another office." Ibid., Section 1(c)(1), (3). The bill is arguably under-inclusive, because it would not operate until a prospective appointee is formally nominated. Prospective appointees are often brought into an agency before nomination (and even before the President has announced his intention to nominate).

[77]A variation on this proposal would lift the prohibition after a confirmation hearing were held, while still restricting the pre-confirmation activities of the prospective appointee.

[78]31 U.S.C. 1341(a). The threat of discipline would operate not against the consultant, but the disbursement official, who would have little control over the subsequent conduct of the consultant.

Chapter Seventeen

[1]Kamen, "Found! Jennifer Fitzgerald's Personnel File", *Washington Post*, A20 (Sept. 1, 1993).

[2]Ibid. Kamen reported that two files were maintained for each appointee: a "standard resume file" and a "working file." Kamen reported that Fitzgerald's working file, unlike others, was empty. He reported sources saying that Tamposi's "hefty" file "recorded concerns from very senior State Department types that she was not ready for an assistant secretaryship."

[3]Letter from Mitch McConnell to Honorable Janet Reno (Sept. 1, 1993). According to a letter from McConnell to the Secretary of State on September 2, McConnell held the letter to the Attorney General for a day with the hope that the State Department would provide an explanation in response to staff inquiries made following the publication of the *Washington Post* report.

[4]Letter from Wendy R. Sherman to Senator Mitch McConnell (Sept. 3, 1993). On September 9, 1993, Senators Dole and McConnell sent a letter to the Secretary of State, containing four questions. Other than responding that "the staff of the White House Liaison officer is still employed by the Department[,]" the State Department declined to respond to the other questions pending the conclusion of the Inspector General's investigation. Letter from Wendy R. Sherman to Senator Mitch McConnell (Sept. 10, 1993).

[5]Letter from Sheila F. Anthony to Senator McConnell (Nov. 3, 1993).

[6]Associated Press, "Senate Confirms Five Nominees After Accord," *Washington Post* (Nov. 4, 1993); "An inquiry (at last) on the file search," *Washington Times*, A22 (Nov. 5, 1993).

[7]Letter from Sherman M. Funk, Inspector General, to Senator Claiborne Pell (Nov. 3, 1993). See also Pincus, "Disclosure of Bush Files May Have Violated Law," *Washington Post*, A10 (Nov. 9, 1993).

[8]Hedges, "2 fired at State for searching files," *Washington Times*, A1 (Nov. 11, 1993).

[9]Ibid. Pincus, "2 State Dept. Political Aides Fired for Disclosing Personnel File Data," *Washington Post*, A10 (Nov. 11, 1993)(Pincus referred to the two fired employees as "lower-level" appointees. Tarver was a GS-15; Schulhof was a GS-11). Deputy Liaison Office Director Kahn was not disciplined or named as a subject in the referral to Justice. He left the Department on February 18, 1994. *GAO Records Retrieval Report, infra* note 32, 13.

[10]Pincus, "2 State Dept. Political Aides Fired for Disclosing Personnel File Data," *Washington Post*, A10 (Nov. 11, 1993).

[11]Hedges, "No charges against those who searched State Department files of Bush officials," *Washington Times*, A1 (Feb. 2, 1994).

[12]Ibid.

[13]*Report of Investigation: Privacy Act Violation*, OIG Case No. 93-173 (*IG Report*).

[14]*GAO Records Management Report, infra* note 33, 7. The assistant had contacted the Department's research branch on July 8, and obtained by fax from that office a storage manifest for the records. The IG report does not include the text of the staff assistant's July 9 request, which appears inconsistent with the later attempts to explain the purposes of the retrieval.

[15]The IG Report noted that the Liaison Office also attempted to get access to the Official Personnel Files of the Bush appointees, but was rebuffed by the Bureau of Personnel. *IG Report* 5, *supra* note 13, 5, Report Annex, 3. GAO found that Tarver was "repeatedly denied access to the official folders of [Bush] appointees because personnel officials felt that it was not appropriate and his name was not on the authorized user list." GAO further found that records of access to the personnel office contained several lengthy gaps in 1993, so Tarver's access to these records during this time could not be ruled out. *GAO Records Management Report, infra* note 33, 7-8.

[16]*IG Report, supra* note 13, 5.

[17]Neither the IG nor GAO could determine with certainty whether anyone in the Liaison Office was aware of the imminent date for destruction of the files.

[18]*IG Report, supra* note 13, 12, 15, 21. The other staff assistant, however, recalled that Tarver told her that the records needed to be reviewed to satisfy a subpoena. Ibid., 10.

[19]First, however, the Liaison Office had to get the files back from the Security Office. The Liaison Office received nine security violations for improper storage of classified documents contained in several of the retrieved boxes, after the boxes were found on the floor of the Liaison Office copy room on July 26. Liaison Office staff apparently were unaware that some of the records were classified.

[20]The IG Report cites 18 U.S.C. 2071, subsection (a) of which provides, in pertinent part, that "[w]hoever willfully and unlawfully . . . destroys . . . any document, . . . filed or deposited . . . in any public office, . . . shall be fined not more than $2,000 or imprisoned not more than three years, or both." Subsection (b) provides also for the removal and disqualification from Federal office of any person who willfully and unlawfully destroys any such document over which the person has custody. The IG called the destruction of Bush Administration Liaison Office records "potentially a technical violation." Most likely, the conduct of the Liaison Office officials was not willful in the sense that they were not aware of proper disposal procedures. There were conflicting recollections as to what advice had been sought and received on whether the records could be destroyed. *IG Report, supra* note 13, 7-9.

[21]However, the IG found that records of Schulhof's direct phone line revealed forty-five calls to Kamen's extension at the *Washington Post* in a five-month period ending September 1, 1993. Ibid., 19.

[22]Ibid., 25.

[23]Kamen declined to be interviewed by the IG.

[24]*IG Report, supra* note 13, 18.

[25]Ibid., 32.

[26]Ibid., iv. The full investigative report contains several areas where officials provided inconsistent recollections. Tarver and Schulhof declined to submit an affidavit to the IG, on advice of counsel. Ibid., 17, 19.

The finding that no high-level appointee was involved or knew of the search before it was disclosed in the *Washington Post* is supported by the account in the IG Report of several high-level State Department meetings held on the day the Kamen article appeared and the next day, when senior officials attempted, with mixed results, to get the facts from Tarver, Kahn, and Schulhof. Ibid., 21-25.

[27]In particular, during the pendency of the IG investigation, Tarver's successor, Awilda Marquez, told her secretary to throw away a telephone log containing records of incoming calls from July through September 1993, which log the IG report called "highly relevant and important." Marquez knew of the IG investigation at the time, but said she did not believe she was destroying any evidence. Moreover, when asked for telephone logs by the IG investigators, she failed to inform them that she had discarded the most recent log. Marquez explained simply that "she preferred a different system for taking telephone messages." Yet Marquez directed the destruction of only the most recent log, and left alone the previous ten logs in the office's file room. Ibid., 27. Marquez received an "official admonishment" for ordering the destruction of the log. *GAO Records Retrieval Report, infra* note 32, 2.

[28]The Senators did not have possession of the full IG report at this time.

[29]"2 State officials questioned anew in files-leak probe," *Washington Times,* A3 (Feb. 10, 1994).

[30]Letter from Secretary of State Warren Christopher to Senator Mitch McConnell (Feb. 7, 1994).

[31]"Republicans lose bid to open IG files, *Washington Times*, A6 (Feb. 11, 1994).

[32]B-257322, *Records Management: Retrieval of State Department's Political Appointee Files* (GAO, July 13, 1994) (*GAO Records Retrieval Report*).

[33]B-256931, *Records Management: Inadequate Controls Over Various Agencies' Political Appointee Files* (GAO, July 13, 1994) (*GAO Records Management Report*).

[34]Ibid., 3.

[35]Ibid., 14.

[36]*IG Report, supra* note *13,* 30, Report Annex, 5. The *Washington Times* likened this to the White House Travel Office matter, where there was "an effort to get information with which longtime workers can be forced out of their jobs, making room for Clinton cronies, campaign workers and second cousins[.]" The *Washington Times* concluded that if this was "what has been going on" at the State Department, then "[b]eyond doubt, this would be a far more serious abuse of power than the search of Mr. Clinton's passport file that Miss Tamposi is being investigated for." "The State Department files," *Washington Times*, E2 (Sept. 7, 1993). However, there is nothing wrong with finding out which former political appointees converted to career status just before a change in administration. If the conversion was legal, the new career civil servant may not be removed simply because of his prior status as a political appointee, and may challenge any adverse action that he believes is improperly motivated. Although an effort to get rid of civil servants because of political affiliation would amount to an abuse of power, acquiring knowledge of those employees whose performance should be watched closely is not.

[37]The IG report stated that two Liaison staff members said that Tamposi's file was reviewed out of curiosity rather than to comply with the subpoena. Ibid. Report Annex, 2. The *Washington Times* suspected

such a motive. "The State Department files," *Washington Times*, E2 (Sept. 7, 1993); "Hope for an independent 'Filesgate' inquiry," *Washington Times*, G2 (Sept. 9, 1993).

[38]Moreover, as GAO noted, the IG report did not consider that the Bush Liaison Office files were intentionally removed from the Liaison Office upon the change in administration, sent to the Records Center on January 21, 1993, and were slated for imminent destruction at the time of their retrieval. *GAO Retrieval Report, supra* note 32, 7-8.

[39]"Hope for an independent 'Filesgate' inquiry," *Washington Times*, G2 (Sept. 9, 1993)("There were no Freedom of Information Act requests in this case. It appears merely to have been a matter of a *quid pro quo* act of political revenge—actually, rather a cutesy one[.]"); "The Clinton passport files," *Washington Times*, A22 (Dec. 5,1994)("[N]o one could even begin to argue that the action was anything but payback of a particularly nasty sort.).

[40]5 U.S.C. 552a(b).

[41]5 U.S.C. 552a(i)(1). The offense is a misdemeanor, and carries with it a maximum fine of $5,000. Under 5 U.S.C. 552a(g), persons damaged by improper disclosure may sue for compensatory damages in Federal court.

[42]The IG cited the State Department's misuse of information provision, 22 CFR 10.735-208, although, at the time of the conduct giving rise to the investigation, that provision had been superseded by the comprehensive standards of conduct issued by the Office of Government Ethics, which were effective in February 1993. 57 Fed. Reg. 35006 (Aug. 7, 1992). Although the IG failed to refer to the applicable OGE standard, the analysis would be the same, given that the wording of the two provisions is essentially the same. Under the OGE standard, 5 CFR 2635.703(a), an employee shall not "allow the improper use of nonpublic information to further his own private interest or that of another, whether through advice or recommendation, or by knowing unauthorized disclosure."

[43]This principle was found in the State Department's standards of conduct, 22 CFR 10.735-201(a)(6), which also was superseded by the OGE standards in February 1993.The OGE standards do not contain a correlative principle. Thus, this provision no longer applied, and should not have been cited by the IG.

[44]Simultaneously with the effective date of the comprehensive OGE standards, OPM separately reissued verbatim the admonition against engaging in conduct prejudicial to the Government, 5 CFR 735.203(a). 57 Fed. Reg. 56434 (Nov. 30, 1992).

[45]Transcript of Nov. 12, 1992 news conference at Old State House, Little Rock, Arkansas (Prepared by Federal Information Services Corporation).

[46]"The State Department files," *Washington Times*, E2 (Sept. 7, 1993)("Well, it's the next day and then some, but no one has been fired yet. Bill Clinton is learning the hard way the dangers of making my-ethics-are-better-than-yours promises."); "What About That Files Search?" *Washington Post*, C6 (Nov. 7, 1993)("Well, here we are, two months after the launching of a probe . . . and the White House is giving the affair the silent treatment. Republicans aren't letting the Clinton administration get away with stonewalling, and they shouldn't.").

[47]Hedges, "2 fired at State for searching files," *Washington Times*, A6 (Nov. 11, 1993).

[48]*Final Report of the Independent Counsel in re: Janet G. Mullins*, vol. I, 239-241 (Nov. 30, 1995) (Hereafter, *diGenova Report*).

[49]Howard & Zeman, "And Now, Doctored Files," *Newsweek*, 6 (Oct. 12, 1992).

[50]Mitchell, "Justice denied, this time, in a case of file ransacking," *Washington Times*, A21 (Feb. 25, 1994).

[51]Hedges, "2 fired at State for searching files," *Washington Times*, A1, A6 (Nov. 11, 1993)(quoting Sen. McConnell, "Either he handled it wrong then or he is handling it wrong now.").

[52]The IG's report concluded that the Privacy Act had been violated, but the document did not include any referral. Office of Inspector General, *Special Inquiry Into The Search and Retrieval of William Clinton's Passport Files*, 35-36 (Nov. 18, 1992). Initially, on October 2, 1992, the IG referred to the Attorney General the allegation (which was more a suspicion) that Bill Clinton's file had been tampered with. The FBI announced on October 9, 1992, that there was no evidence of tampering. (On October 15, 1992, the IG initiated an investigation into the legality of the monitoring of phone calls by the State Department's Operations Center. Although the monitoring arguably suggested a violation of 18 U.S.C. 2511, Funk did not refer this matter to the Justice Department.) *diGenova Report, supra* note 48, vol.II, 3-4, 371.

[53]*diGenova report, supra* note 48, vol. II, 350 (August 4, 1995 statement of Sherman Funk, 5); see Pincus, "U.S. Broadens Inquiry Into Passport File Search," *Washington Post*, A1 (Nov. 29,1992).

[54]In December 1994, independent counsel Joseph E. diGenova stated, "we have completed our investigation and determined no charges will be brought against any person involved in the passport search matter." Pincus, "Charges Against Ex-Bush Officials In Clinton Passport Case Rejected." *Washington Post*, A10 (Dec.2, 1994); Hedges, "Passport-file probe comes up empty," *Washington Times*, A1 (Dec. 2, 1994); Johnston, "No Charges to be filed For Search of Clinton Files," *New York Times*, 11 (Dec.3, 1994). At the time of these reports the independent counsel had not yet completed his report, as required by law. Following the April 7,

1995 submission of the independent counsel's report to the court of appeals, the persons criticized in the report were given an opportunity to contest its contents or the public disclosure of those portions of the report, and to suggest amendments to the report. *diGenova Report, supra* note 48, vol.II. See 28 U.S.C. 594 (h).

[55]Mitchell, "Justice denied, this time, in a case of file ransacking," *Washington Times*, A21 (Feb. 25, 1994).

[56]Ibid.

[57]By contrast, Attorney General Bill Barr's request for the appointment of an independent counsel to investigate the Clinton passport search was based not on a misdemeanor violation of the Privacy Act, but on felony statutes concerning, for example, false statements, obstruction of justice, conspiracy and use of official position to interfere with a Federal election. *diGenova Report, supra* note 48, vol.II, 6-7. Isikoff & Pincus, "Bush Aide, Passport Case Linked," *Washington Post*, A1, A8 (Dec. 22, 1992).

[58]The lack of any connection to a presidential appointee or Clinton campaign official supports the Justice Department's decision early on not to appoint a special counsel.

[59]At the time, the independent counsel law had expired. It was not resuscitated until June 1994. In the interim period, the Justice Department was authorized under existing regulations to appoint a special counsel from outside the Department.

[60]"Hope for an independent 'Filesgate' inquiry", *Washington Times*, G2 (Sept. 9, 1993)(urging that the Passportgate independent counsel's jurisdiction be expanded to included these allegations); "Tilted Town," *Wall Street Journal*, A22 (Sept. 15, 1993)("[N]o such calls have gone out for Janet Reno to do the same for the overly eager Clintonites.").

[61]Independent counsel diGenova found, however, thaat not only was there no credible evidence that the official, Janet Mullins, made a false statement (or violated any other criminal law), but also that the evidence was so lacking that the allegation against Mullins should not have been referred to the Justice Department in the first place. *diGenova Report, supra* note 48, vol. I, 384-415.

[62]"What About That Files Search?" *Washington Post*, C6 (Nov. 7, 1993).

Chapter Eighteen

[1]5 CFR 2635.101(b)(7),(9). These principles are also found in Executive Order 12674, as amended, which served as the basis for the OGE standards of conduct.

[2]5 CFR 2635.704(a). "Authorized purposes" are "those purposes authorized in accordance with law or regulation." 5 CFR 2635.704(b)(2).

[3]5 CFR 2635.101(b)(14).

[4]OGE Analysis of Counsel to the President's May 9, 1991 Memorandum to the Chief of Staff Regarding the White House Review of His Travel on Military Aircraft, 4-5 (Mar. 23, 1992)(citing comparable standards in Executive Order 12674).

[5]"Memorandum on Restriction of Government Aircraft," 29 *Weekly Compilation of Presidential Documents* 168 (Feb. 10, 1993). The other actions taken by the President on February 10 were a "Memorandum on Use of Government Vehicles," Ibid., 169, and a "Memorandum on Fiscal Responsibility," Ibid., 167 (concerning executive dining facilities and conferences).

[6]White House Press Release, "Travel Policy," (May 9, 1991). Under the policy, military aircraft was authorized for **official travel** only "where security, communications or scheduling needs require the use of military aircraft." For **personal travel**, an "immediate and compelling need" was also required, such as "to attend to the serious illness of a close relative when security, communications or scheduling needs would prevent travel on commercial aircraft." Travel on military aircraft for **political purposes** was prohibited unless the official purpose of the trip was predominant or unless the President personally authorized the trip. Travel for **mixed purposes** was allowed on the same terms as official travel provided the Counsel's office determined in advance that the official purpose was the predominant reason for travel.

The policy did not apply to the Secretaries of State and Defense and Attorney General, "who, pursuant to longstanding policies, regularly use government aircraft for official and unofficial travel." The policy statement explained that use of government aircraft was necessary for communications and security reasons, and to prepare for exigencies.

[7]Memorandum for Governor Sununu, from C. Boyden Gray, "Results of our review of your travel on military aircraft" (May 9, 1991). The author of this study participated in the review conducted by the White House Counsel's office, as well as the drafting of the President's May 9, 1991 policy statement.

[8]Babcock & Devroy, "Sununu: Frequent Flier On Military Aircraft," *Washington Post*, A1 (Apr. 21, 1991).

[9]57 Fed. Reg. 22150 (May 26, 1992).

[10]In the wake of critical reports of the use of government aircraft by Governor Sununu and other Bush Administration officials, the General Accounting Office was requested to conduct two reviews. The reports are entitled: *Military Aircraft: Policies on Government Officials' Use of 89th Military Airlift Wing Aircraft*, B-

244084 (Apr. 9, 1992); *Military Aircraft: Travel by Selected Executive Branch Officials*, B-245638 (Apr. 7, 1992).

[11]The author also participated in the drafting of the revisions to the OMB Circular.

[12]Ibid., ¶7. "Mission requirements" do not include official travel to conferences, meetings or site visits. Ibid., ¶5(b). "*Official travel* means (i) travel to meet mission requirements, (ii) required use travel, and (iii) other travel for the conduct of agency business." Ibid., ¶5(c). "*Required use* means use of government aircraft for the travel of an Executive Agency officer or employee, where the use of the government aircraft is required because of *bona fide* communications or security needs of the agency or exceptional scheduling requirements." Ibid.,¶5(d).

[13]Ibid., ¶8(a).

[14]Ibid., ¶11, 10(c).

[15]For required use travel, OMB Circular A-126 required trip-by-trip approval by an official's deputy or senior legal official unless the President determined "that all travel, or travel in specified categories, by the agency head qualifies for required use travel." Ibid., ¶11(b). Thus, OMB Circular A-126 was consistent with President Bush's May 9, 1991 policy statement.

[16]Defined as Senate-confirmed Presidential appointees and White House staff.

[17]29 *Weekly Compilation of Presidential Documents* 168. This language is identical to the definition of "mission requirements" travel in OMB Circular A-126.

[18]Ibid.

[19]Lancaster, "Trip Tests White House "No-Fly' Policy," *Washington Post,* A17 (Apr. 21, 1993).

[20]Lancaster, "Aspin's Venice Respite Causes Costly Hold," *Washington Post,* A15 (June 1, 1993). Secretary Aspin's companion returned with him on board the military plane, flying "space available" and paying full coach fare.

[21]Harris, "Air Fare, Rome to Colorado: $120,000," *Washington Post,* A1 (Dec. 9, 1994); Hackworth, "Scandals: Was it worth $200,000 to fly one air force general home?," *Newsweek,* 28 (Dec. 19, 1994). Ashy paid $85 fare for the cat, consistent with Federal rules. The valet, Ashy's assistant Christa Hart, was misidentified on the manifest as Ashy's dependent.

[22]Priest, "Pentagon Faults Plane Trip for General, Cat," *Washington Post,* A16 (June 28, 1995); Associated Press, "Pentagon probing high-flying generals," *Washington Times,* A14 (June 28, 1995).

[23]Quoted in Priest, "Pentagon Faults Plane Trip for General, Cat," *Washington Post,* A16 (June 28, 1995).

[24]Priest, "Air Force Flew Loose With 'Facts,'" *Washington Post,* A21 (July 5, 1995), quoting Inspector General's Report (ellipses in *Washington Post* article). At the time of the article, no Air Force official had been disciplined for the travel or the improper responses to Hackworth.

[25]Ibid.

[26]Anderson & Binstein, "NASA's Fear of Commercial Flying," *Washington Post,* D28 (Dec. 19, 1994)(reporting that eighteen trips by NASA Administrator Dan Goldin in a 6-month period cost $514,000 more than had Goldin traveled on commercial airlines).

[27]Lancaster, "Defense Brass Flying High—But Not Far," *Washington Post,* A1 (May 1, 1994).

[28]The Pentagon told the *Washington Post* that its executive travel policy was "under review."

[29]Devroy & Marcus, "Golf Outing Sinks White House Aide," *Washington Post,* A1 (May 27, 1994). The picture first appeared in the *Frederick News-Post.*

[30]The *New York Times* said that Watkins would be remembered as the "Typhoid Mary of travel arrangements," and said that even Governor Sununu's travels to his dentist in Boston "pale[] beside the adventures of David Watkins[.]" "I'll Fly Away," *New York Times,* A26 (May 27, 1994).

[31]Birnbaum, "White House Aide Is Forced to Resign For Using U.S. Helicopter for Golf Trip," *Wall Street Journal,* A12 (May 27, 1994); Ifill, "Using Clinton's Helicopter Costs an Aide His Job," *New York Times,* A20 (May 27, 1994); Murray, "Clinton friend, aide quits after copter ride," *Washington Times,* A4 (May 27, 1994).

[32]However, seven weeks later, Maldon was reportedly still on the job. The White House explained that it was difficult to find a successor, that Maldon was doing a good job, and that Maldon traveled with Watkins for the golf outing at Watkins' request, so that he should not be punished "for simply following orders." Jehl, "White House Delays Rebuke In Copter Case," *New York Times,* A12 (July 17, 1994).

[33]Devroy & Marcus, "Golf Outing Sinks White House Aide," *Washington Post,* A1, A4 (May 27, 1994). The *Washington Post* responded:

Right, and we propose to familiarize ourselves with all aspects of every four-star restaurant in Paris in preparation for the president's D-Day visit, especially those aspects related to the actual time it takes to consume a meal and associated impact on security plans of consuming several bottles of Bordeaux.

"In the Rough," *Washington Post,* A28 (May 28, 1994).

[34]Marcus, "Aides Offer To Pay for Golf Flight," *Washington Post*, A1, A13 (May 28, 1994); Murray, "13 White House aides offer to help pay for chopper use," *Washington Times*, A3 (May 28, 1994); Ifill, "Clinton Aide Balks at Cost Of Contrition," *New York Times* 6 (May 28, 1994); Marcus, "Official's Golf Flight Cost \$13,129.66," *Washington Post*, A8 (May 29, 1994)(explaining the White House's eventual abandonment of the friendship rationale).

[35]Marcus, "Ex-White House Aide to Cover Golf Outing Tab," *Washington Post*, A4 (June 1, 1994); Jehl, "Clinton Aides Often Used Helicopters," *New York Times*, A17 (June 1, 1994); Associated Press, "Watkins agrees to pay for golf flight," *Washington Times*, A3 (June 1, 1994).

[36]The Bush Administration policy required the approval of the White House Counsel's office. When considered with his February 1993 policy memorandum, however, President Clinton more tightly circumscribed military aircraft use.

[37]Bartlett, "White House flights of fancy," *Washington Times*, A19 (June 13, 1994).

[38]Pierce, "GOP: White House taking us for a ride," *Washington Times*, A6 (June 16, 1994). Also, Representative Dan Burton unsuccessfully sought to amend the same bill by cutting \$5 million from the White House Office budget, to cover the estimated cost of the twenty-six government aircraft used to transport Federal officials, including the President, for a D-Day anniversary celebration in Europe. Associated Press, "Pentagon Paid the Freight for D-Day Fete," *Washington Post*, A3 (June 17, 1994).

It was also reported that the Navy billed the White House for \$562 worth of towels and bathrobes improperly removed by White House staff from the USS George Washington during their trip across the English Channel for the D-Day events in France. The White House Office of Scheduling and Advance asked those who traveled with the President on the USS George Washington to reimburse the Government for whatever they may have taken. Pending a response, head of the office Ricki Seidman wrote a personal check to cover the entire amount. Murray & McCaslin, "D-Day's dirty laundry," *Washington Times*, A1 (June 17, 1994); Marcus, "Not Exactly a Clean Getaway, *Washington Post*, A3 (June 17, 1994); Dowd, "Who Took the Towels? D-Day Turns to T-Day for Clinton Staff," *New York Times*, A18 (June 17, 1994).

[39]*White House: Staff Use of Helicopters*, B-261222 (July 14, 1995).

[40]Ibid., 2.

[41]Kamen, "Director's Domestic Trips Favor His Home Town," *Washington Post*, A5 (January 2, 1991).

[42]Ibid.

[43]Memorandum from William P. Barr to William Sessions, "OPR Report on Alleged Misconduct," at 4 (Jan. 15, 1993). The Bush Administration presented the new Clinton Administration with the responsibility to consider the findings of the Justice Department's Office of Professional Responsibility, which were contained in a 161-page report dated January 12, 1993. President Clinton did not ask Sessions to leave until six months later, and when Sessions refused to resign, the President fired him. Isikoff & Marcus, "Clinton Fires Sessions as FBI Director," *Washington Post*, A1 (July 20, 1993).

[44]Ibid., 3. Judge Sessions was also cited for a number of other ethics violations, including (1) Sessions "engaged in a sham arrangement for the clear purpose of improperly claiming an exemption from the obligation to pay income tax on your government-provided home-to-work transportation" (improperly claiming police vehicle exemption on the basis of carrying an unloaded gun in his trunk); (2) Sessions' wife accompanied him on FBI aircraft to 111 locations, reimbursing the Government for only one trip, even though she was not qualified to fly without reimbursement for most of these flights; (3) FBI cars were used to drive Mrs. Sessions for various personal purposes; (4) Sessions failed to account for frequent flyer travel mileage accrued on official travel; (5) Sessions "affirmatively blocked . . . the investigation into allegations that [he] received a 'sweetheart deal' from Riggs Bank on [his] home mortgage[;]" and (6) Sessions misused Government funds to construct a privacy fence at his home. Ibid., 1-4. Judge Sessions responded to each of these charges specifically, labelling the charges "wrong," "absurd," and "picayunish." LaFraniere, "Sessions Assails Bias in Ethics Charges," *Washington Post*, A1 (Jan. 24, 1993).

[45]LaFraniere, "Sessions Assails Bias in Ethics Charges," *Washington Post*, A1, A18 (Jan. 24, 1993).

[46]See Chapter Ten.

[47]Miller & Morris, "VA Chief Logs Frequent Trips to Hometown," *Los Angeles Times*, A1 (Feb. 12, 1995).

[48]See also, "Brown on Visits to Chicago," *Los Angeles Times* (Feb. 27, 1995)(letter to the editor).

[49]Ibid., A13.

[50]Kamen, "Travel Agency," *Washington Post*, A17 (Mar. 15, 1995).

[51]The story was first reported by Jeffrey Birnbaum in "GSA's Johnson Asks for Review Of Travel Items," *Wall Street Journal*, A2 (Mar. 14, 1994). See also, Barr, "GSA Head Plans to Repay Some Costs Of Business Trips to His Home Town," *Washington Post*, A17 (Mar. 15, 1994). There is a certain irony in Johnson's travails, since Johnson's agency GSA regulates the use of government vehicles and equipment.

[52]Ibid. The *Wall Street Journal* contrasted Johnson's travels with the travel of Julia Stasch, his Deputy Administrator. Stasch traveled frequently to Chicago, her home, but she paid for her twice-monthly trips

herself and did not claim any per diem expenses for the other five trips to Chicago which were deemed official in nature, only one of which occurred over a weekend.

[53]Birnbaum, "GSA Head Plans To Reimburse U.S. For Trip Expenses," *Wall Street Journal*, A9 (Mar. 21, 1994); Barr, "GSA Head Gets Bill for His Trips Home," *Washington Post*, A15 (Mar. 22, 1994).

[54]"GSA Report Says Official Improperly Used Resources," *Wall Street Journal*, A4 (Apr. 26, 1994); Pierce, "GSA chief repays government for travel, phone calls," *Washington Times*, A7 (June 8, 1994).

[55]Kamen, "A First-Class Bump," *Washington Post*, A25 (Aug. 12, 1994).

[56]Barr, "GSA Inspector General Probing Agency Chief," *Washington Post*, A21 (Oct. 5, 1994).

[57]Pierce, "GSA chief under fire in second probe in a year," *Washington Times*, A6 (Oct. 6, 1994); Associated Press, "G.S.A. Chief Undergoing Inquiry," *New York Times*, A27 (Oct. 6, 1994).

[58]Barr, "GSA Inspector General Probing Agency Chief," *Washington Post*, A21 (Oct. 5, 1994)(brackets and ellipses in original).

Appendix One

[1]It may be appropriate, however, to exempt **elected** state and local officials from the cooling-off periods, because of the special responsibilities entrusted to these officials and their accountability to the electorate.

[2]See 18 U.S.C. 207(c) and (d)(applying cooling-off period to certain White House officials by reference to their appointment under 3 U.S.C. 105 and 106).

[3]In *Association of American Physicians and Surgeons v. Clinton*, 997 F.2d 898, 905 (D.C. Cir. 1993), the D.C. Circuit relied in part on the lack of any sanction in the anti-nepotism law (other than forfeit of salary), for its interpretation that the law "may well bar appointment only to paid positions in government."

[4]Cf. *Association of Amer. Phy. and Surgeons*, 997 F.2d, 905 (doubting that Congress intended to include White House or Executive Office of the President in the statute's definition of "agency").

[5]*Morrison v. Olson*, 487 U.S. 654 (1988).

[6]See, for example, Terry Eastland, *Ethics, Politics and the Independent Counsel* (National Legal Center for the Public Interest, 1989). Among the more thoughtful articles that have appeared recently, several deserve mention: Lynch & Howard, "Special Prosecutors: What's the Point?," *Washington Post*, C7 (May 28, 1995); Richardson, "Special Counsels, Petty Cases," *New York Times*, A15 (June 5, 1995)(Richardson, a former Attorney General, recommends making the appointment of an independent counsel more difficult); Taylor, "Crawling All Over the Presidency," *Legal Times*, 25 (May 22, 1995); Mikva, "From Politics to paranoia," *Washington Post*, C2 (Nov. 26, 1995); diGenova, "Investigated to Death," *New York Times*, A25 (Dec. 5, 1995).

[7]See York, "Counselgate, Again," *Weekly Standard*, 10 (Oct. 23, 1995)(noting three investigations that have lasted three or more years); York, "Independent Counsel Keeps Going and Going and Going," *Wall Street Journal*, A14 (June 7, 1995).

[8]28 U.S.C. 594(f)(1).

[9]Lynch & Howard, "Special Prosecutors: What's the Point?," *Washington Post*, C7 (May 28, 1995)("[S]pecial prosecutors play into a pathology that thrives on an appetite for scandal and a distrust of our system of government.")

[10]See, for example, "Reviving the Independent Counsel," *New York Times*, A26 (June 24, 1994); "For Independent Counsels," *Washington Post*, A26 (June 24, 1994). Similar editorials have appeared regularly in the *Times* and *Post*.

Kenneth Starr, who is currently independent counsel for the Madison and Whitewater investigation, gave a speech to Duke Law School in May 1995, excerpted in "Independent Counsels—Accountable to Whom?," *Wall Street Journal*, A20 (May 17, 1995), in which he outlined the steps he has taken to "guard against arbitrary and capricious decisionmaking" and "to ensure accountability."

[11]Publicly, the President has criticized only the low legal threshold for the appointment of an independent counsel. 31 *Weekly Compilation of Presidential Documents*, 846 (May 17, 1995)(in reference to Ron Brown).

[12]Bedard, "Clinton aide would revisit counsel law," *Washington Times*, A5 (May 12, 1995)(Mikva remarks to ABA); "Converts' Zeal," *Wall Street Journal*, A20 (Mar. 21, 1995)(Cutler and Bennett remarks on ABC's "This Week with David Brinkley"); Associated Press, "Clinton's lawyer lambastes independent counsel law," *Washington Times*, A4 (Mar. 20, 1995)(Bennett); Mikva, "From Politics to paranoia," *Washington Post*, C2 (Nov. 26, 1995).

[13]Many Republicans in Congress who opposed the independent counsel law when they witnessed Democrats use it as a political bludgeon against the Reagan and Bush Administrations showed no similar qualms about the law in voting for its reauthorization in 1994. Their change of mind is more likely due to the fact that a Democratic administration would now be subject to the law's political havoc than due to a newfound concern that the Justice Department cannot be entrusted to handle these investigations fairly and vigorously. See Cannon, "The Vendetta Machine," *Weekly Standard*, 10 (Nov. 6, 1995).

[14]See, for example, diGenova, "Investigated to Death," *New York Times*, A25 (Dec. 5, 1995); Mikva, "From Politics to paranoia," *Washington Post*, C2 (Nov. 26, 1995)

[15]Currently, consultants are required to sign an acknowledgment that they are covered by certain **ethical** standards. This certification is lacking in that the standards are not specified on the form or on an attachment, and the standards most likely to do include the limitation on permitted activities. To achieve the highest degree of compliance, the certification should be executed on the document containing the guidelines for consultants.

[16]A variation on this proposal would release the prohibition after a confirmation hearing were held, while still restricting the pre-confirmation activities of the prospective appointee.

[17]31 U.S.C. 1341(a). The threat of discipline would operate not against the consultant but the disbursement official who would have little control over the subsequent conduct of the consultant.

[18]5 CFR 2635.203(f)(2).

[19]5 CFR 2635.203(f)(1). The standards on misuse of position provide that "[a]n employee shall not use or permit the use of his Government position or title or any authority associated with his public office in a manner that is intended to coerce or induce another person . . . to provide any benefit . . . to himself or to friends [or] relatives[.]" 5 CFR 2635.702(a). However, this standard would not cover a situation where no coercion or inducement is intended or caused.

[20]5CFR 2635.502.

[21]According to Chairman Bill Clinger of the House Committee on Government Reform and Oversight, the House Committee on Government Operations (the Committee's predecessor) held 40% fewer hearings in the first year of the Clinton Administration compared to the first year of the Bush Administration. Clinger, "A shortage of 'openness' from the administration," *Washington Times*, A19 (May 10, 1994).

[22]Indeed, the law requires an agency only to provide "information." 5 U.S.C. 2954 provides that an Executive agency "shall submit any information requested of it relating to any matter with the jurisdiction of the" House Committee on Government Reform and Oversight (upon request of seven members) or the Senate Committee on Government Affairs (five members).

Appendix Two

[1] 5 CFR 2635.203(d). See OGE Informal Advisory Letter 87 X 13, 744-45, 747 (Oct. 23, 1987).

[2] 5 CFR 2635.204(g).

[3] 5 CFR 2635.204(g)(5)("The cost of the employee's attendance will not be considered to be provided by the sponsor where a person other than the sponsor designates the employee to be invited and bears the cost of the employee's attendance through a contribution or other payment intended to facilitate that employee's attendance.").

[4] The gift rules for the Executive Office of the President, 3 CFR 100.735-14, which applied to the White House at the time, did not address this question. My recollection is that the White House Counsel's office began applying the requirement that the invitation to a widely attended gathering must come from the event's sponsor once we became aware of OGE's intention to include this provision in the comprehensive standards of conduct. The sponsor requirement was included in the proposed rule that was in circulation in early 1991, and published in July of that year. 56 Fed. Reg. 33778, 33797-98 (July 23, 1991).

OGE had not previously focused on the question of the propriety of accepting invitations to widely attended gatherings from persons other than the sponsor. However, the widely attended gathering exception recognized by OGE and adopted by several Federal agencies **assumed** that the sponsor of the event was the one providing the gift. See OGE Informal Advisory Letter 87 X 13, 751 (Oct. 23, 1987)(emphasis added):

The general standards we expressed to the FCC and others in the past . . . is that any exception to the basic restriction should include the following concepts: . . .

(2) **the sponsor of the event** should not be one individual or entity that is regulated by the agency, or one individual or entity that has some other business connection with an agency or is directly involved in a matter pending before the agency so that the timing or the reason for the event would create an appearance of impropriety[.]

Thus, non-sponsor provided invitations fell outside of the exception, and thus were not permitted. It is, therefore, technically incorrect to describe the OGE rule that was effective in 1993 as "new" as in a change from existing guidance.

[5] Roberts, "The End of the News Schmooze?," *Washington Post*, C1 (Feb. 3, 1993).

[6] Kamen, "Listening to the Howls of the Media," *Washington Post*, A17 (Jan. 19, 1994).

[7] 60 Fed. Reg. 31415 (June 15, 1995). See also, "Guess Who's Coming to Dinner—for Free," *Washington Post*, C3 (Mar. 10, 1993); Kurtz, "The Press Whines to Dine," *Washington Post*, C1 (Mar. 11, 1993).

[8] See 57 Fed. Reg. 35006 (Aug. 7, 1992)(preamble to final rule).

[9] This is the language Nussbaum used in his second memorandum on this subject, this one to agency heads, and discussed in the text.

[10] "Come to Dinner, Please," *Washington Post*, C3 (Oct. 13, 1993); Kamen, "Listening to the Howls of the Media," *Washington Post*, A17 (Jan. 19, 1994)(crediting David Gergen with pushing the White House Counsel's office to change the rule).

[11] 60 Fed. Reg., 31416.

[12] Ornstein, "Press Dines Out On Hypocrisy At Gridiron, Etc.," *Roll Call*, 6 (Apr. 1, 1993). See also Kurtz, "The Press Whines to Dine," *Washington Post*, C1, C9 (Mar. 11, 1993)(Michael Kinsley described the process of "brown-nosing" officials whom reporters cover as "ethically corrupt.")

[13] 60 Fed. Reg., 31416

[14] Ibid. Around ten comments were submitted in response to the notice. OGE expects to publish a final rule early in 1996.

Appendix Three

[1] 29 *Weekly Compilation of Presidential Documents*, 644 (Apr. 21, 1993).

[2] Dalton also served as a major fundraiser for Bill Clinton's Presidential campaign.

[3] Gerth, "Quiet Handling of a Nominee's S. & L. Tenure," *New York Times*, A1 (July 22, 1994).

[4] Gerth, "Navy Chief Settles Old Debt, $17,900, to Savings and Loan Bailout Agency," *New York Times*, 6 (July 23, 1994); Marcus & Knight, "Senate Panel Kept Dalton's S&L Links Private," *Washington Post*, A8 (July 23, 1994).

[5] Dalton was not required to report the $3.8 million settlement, which was made by Seguin's insurer in January 1993, because the claim never amounted to a liability.

[6] "A Tale of Two Nominees," *Wall Street Journal*, A10 (July 27, 1994).

[7] Lewis, "How much do we have a right to know about elected, appointed leaders?," *Houston Chronicle*, 5 (July 31, 1994) (statement of Alan J. Whitney).

[8] "Secretary Dalton's Secret, *Washington Post*, C6 (July 24, 1994); "Senate Secrecy and Secretary Dalton," *New York Times*, A20 (July 27, 1994)(calling for release of record of executive session).

Index

A

Air Advantage 147, 153, 155, 157, 166, 168
Allison, Graham 67, 477
Altman, Roger 18, 43, 47, 56, 221, 235, 240, 241, 248, 265, 287, 297
appearance of impropriety 20, 77, 79, 84, 96, 111, 113, 140, 194, 221, 223, 333, 334, 337, 372, 387, 506, 518

B

Barnett, Robert 47, 278, 291
Begala, Paul 22, 40, 184, 185, 198, 205, 209, 217
Bentsen, Lloyd 223, 421, 459
blind trust 93, 95, 96, 98, 110, 111, 114, 215, 288, 511
Breslaw, April 43, 305, 306, 315
Brown, Jesse 24, 71, 501
Brown, Ron 18, 25, 28, 30, 59, 60, 62, 64, 83, 87, 379, 383, 384, 388, 389, 390, 391, 392, 395, 397, 404, 408, 409, 410, 411, 438, 443, 509, 513, 523

C

Carter, Ashton 67, 475, 476, 478
Carville, James 22, 40, 217
Casey, Paula 23, 43, 214, 247, 248, 249, 258, 260, 262, 270, 276, 305, 306, 307, 312, 315
Cerda, Clarissa 36, 146
Cisneros, Henry 18, 25, 57, 58, 59, 87, 417, 418, 433, 515
Clinger, Bill 25, 140, 387, 456
Coelho, Tony 22, 184, 189, 199, 205, 206, 352
cooling-off period 30, 31, 63, 82, 183, 441, 448, 451, 452, 454, 455, 457, 459, 460, 462, 463, 464, 465, 466, 467, 468, 469, 470, 471, 504, 505
Cornelius, Catherine 21, 36
Corridor Broadcasting 25, 60
Cutler, Lloyd 49, 145, 195, 197, 224, 225, 227, 232, 233, 236, 237, 244-246, 249, 263-265, 290, 293, 296, 297, 345, 431, 499, 509

D

Dale, Billy 28, 38, 279
Dempsey, Patricia 54, 512
Douglas, Richard 54, 343, 350, 351, 352, 353, 354, 370

E

Eggleston, Neil 50, 145, 240, 243, 266, 267, 268, 312
EOP Group 55, 56, 347, 371, 372, 374, 376
Espy, Mike 18, 24, 54, 71, 343, 344, 350, 351, 352, 357, 361, 370, 372, 375, 376, 501
Executive Order 12834 28, 450, 452, 454, 460, 461

W

waiver 89, 221, 452
Watkins, David 18, 21, 36, 69, 143, 144, 146, 149, 154-156, 160, 162, 166, 168, 176, 253, 254, 277, 498
White House Management Review 21, 38, 39, 41, 140, 142-146, 151-155, 158, 159, 162, 164-169, 171, 173-175, 177-179, 192, 194, 206
Whitewater Development 22, 288
Williams, Maggie 44, 236, 240, 243, 254, 256, 259, 262, 269, 274, 277, 278, 280, 299
World Wide Travel 36, 146, 148, 150, 152-154, 157, 166, 168
Wright, Betsey 22, 42, 51, 52, 183-186, 205, 206, 208, 253, 262, 319

Statutes

18 U.S.C. 207 29, 452, 459, 469
18 U.S.C. 208 20, 57, 60, 93, 96, 98, 111, 112, 118, 123, 158, 337, 376, 397, 406, 416, 440

About the Author

Gregory S. Walden is counsel with the law firm of Mayer, Brown & Platt in Washington, D.C. He received a B.A. cum laude from Washington & Lee University in 1977 and a J.D. magna cum laude from the University of San Diego School of Law in 1980. After a clerkship with the U.S. Court of Appeals for the District of Columbia, where he clerked for Judge Robert Bork, Mr. Walden served in several positions in the Reagan and Bush Administrations. He was Special Assistant to the Assistant Attorney General for the Justice Department's Civil Division from 1983-86, and then served as an Associate Deputy Attorney General, 1986-88. He was Chief Counsel of the Federal Aviation Administration, 1988-90, before joining the White House as Associate Counsel to the President in December 1990. In the White House, Mr. Walden provided day-to-day ethics advice to the White House staff and participated in the clearance process for Presidential appointees to the Executive Branch. In January 1993, he received a recess appointment to the Interstate Commerce Commission from President Bush.

Mr. Walden resides in Alexandria, Virginia.

About Hudson Institute

Hudson Institute is a private, not-for-profit research organization founded in 1961 by the late Herman Kahn. Hudson analyzes and makes recommendations about public policy for business and government executives, as well as for the public at large. The institute does not advocate an express ideology or political position. However, more than thirty years of work on the most important issues of the day has forged a viewpoint that embodies skepticism about the conventional wisdom, optimism about solving problems, a commitment to free institutions and individual responsibility, an appreciation of the crucial role of technology in achieving progress, and an abiding respect for the importance of values, culture, and religion in human affairs.

Since 1984, Hudson has been headquartered in Indianapolis, Indiana. It also maintains offices in Washington, D.C.; Madison, Wisconsin; and Brussels, Belgium.